# Lecture Notes in Computer Science  16486

Founding Editors

Gerhard Goos
Juris Hartmanis

Editorial Board Members

Elisa Bertino, *Purdue University, West Lafayette, IN, USA*
Wen Gao, *Peking University, Beijing, China*
Bernhard Steffen, *TU Dortmund University, Dortmund, Germany*
Moti Yung, *Columbia University, New York, NY, USA*

The series Lecture Notes in Computer Science (LNCS), including its subseries Lecture Notes in Artificial Intelligence (LNAI) and Lecture Notes in Bioinformatics (LNBI), has established itself as a medium for the publication of new developments in computer science and information technology research, teaching, and education.

LNCS enjoys close cooperation with the computer science R & D community, the series counts many renowned academics among its volume editors and paper authors, and collaborates with prestigious societies. Its mission is to serve this international community by providing an invaluable service, mainly focused on the publication of conference and workshop proceedings and postproceedings. LNCS commenced publication in 1973.

Ricardo Campos · Adam Jatowt · Yanyan Lan ·
Mohammad Aliannejadi · Christine Bauer ·
Sean MacAvaney · Avishek Anand ·
Zhaochun Ren · Suzan Verberne · Nan Bai ·
Masoud Mansoury
Editors

# Advances in Information Retrieval

48th European Conference on Information Retrieval, ECIR 2026
Delft, The Netherlands, March 29 – April 2, 2026
Proceedings, Part IV

 Springer

*Editors*
Ricardo Campos (ID)
University of Beira Interior
Covilhã, Portugal

Yanyan Lan (ID)
Tsinghua University
Beijing, China

Christine Bauer (ID)
University of Salzburg
Salzburg, Austria

Avishek Anand (ID)
TU Delft
Delft, The Netherlands

Suzan Verberne (ID)
Leiden University
Leiden, The Netherlands

Masoud Mansoury (ID)
TU Delft
Delft, The Netherlands

Adam Jatowt (ID)
University of Innsbruck
Innsbruck, Austria

Mohammad Aliannejadi (ID)
University of Amsterdam
Amsterdam, The Netherlands

Sean MacAvaney (ID)
University of Glasgow
Glasgow, UK

Zhaochun Ren (ID)
Leiden University
Leiden, The Netherlands

Nan Bai (ID)
TU Delft
Delft, The Netherlands

ISSN 0302-9743    ISSN 1611-3349  (electronic)
Lecture Notes in Computer Science
ISBN 978-3-032-21320-4    ISBN 978-3-032-21321-1  (eBook)
https://doi.org/10.1007/978-3-032-21321-1

# Preface

The 48th European Conference on Information Retrieval (ECIR 2026) was held in Delft, The Netherlands, from 29 March to 2 April 2026, bringing together researchers and practitioners from Europe and around the world.

These proceedings contain the papers presented at ECIR 2026, including contributions from the main conference, findings, demonstrations, reproducibility, resource, and IR4Good tracks, as well as the doctoral consortium, workshops, tutorials, and other satellite events. The ECIR 2026 program showcased a broad spectrum of novel and impactful research, reflecting both the maturity of the information retrieval field and its rapid evolution in response to new methodological and societal challenges.

Alongside established ECIR tracks, the 2026 edition continued to support venues that encourage diversity in contribution types and research perspectives. The Findings track provided an outlet for solid and well-executed work that could not be accommodated in the main track. The IR4Good track highlighted research addressing societal challenges such as fairness, accountability, transparency, privacy, and sustainability in information retrieval systems, often at the intersection of computer science and the social sciences. This year, IR4Good was an integral part of the main conference program.

The ECIR 2026 program comprised papers across multiple tracks, reflecting the breadth and diversity of contemporary information retrieval research. From 530 submissions sent for review, the final program comprised 46 full papers, 10 findings papers, 9 reproducibility papers, 17 resource papers, 19 IR4Good papers, as well as 37 short papers, 13 demonstration papers, 14 doctoral consortium papers, 10 industry track papers, 16 invited CLEF papers, and 7 invited FDIA papers. In addition, one session in the program was devoted to papers published in the first two issues of the Information Retrieval Research Journal (IRRJ)[1]. This initiative reflects ECIR's ongoing effort to strengthen the connection between archival journal research and the conference community.

In the research tracks, submissions were peer-reviewed by at least three members of the international Program Committee to ensure that only work of high relevance and quality was included in the conference. The review process was double-blin. Acceptance decisions were informed by detailed reviewer discussions coordinated by Senior Program Committee members.

The accepted papers cover the state of the art in information retrieval and related areas, including user-centric IR, retrieval models and systems, learning and optimization methods, evaluation, recommender systems, retrieval-augmented generation, and emerging challenges at the intersection of IR, AI, and society. As in previous years, ECIR 2026 featured a strong presence of student-led work, alongside contributions from academia, research institutes, and industry.

In addition to the technical papers, the ECIR 2026 program included three keynote talks, seven tutorials, eleven workshops, a doctoral consortium, and an industry day. Keynote speakers included Katja Hofmann (Microsoft Research Cambridge) and

---

[1] https://irrj.org/.

Madeleine I. G. Daepp (Public Democracy America and Microsoft Research), as well as the Keith van Rijsbergen Award winner.

The tutorials covered a broad range of topics, including ranking models, conversational search with large language models and agents, reasoning for IR and IR for reasoning, practical in-memory inverted indexes, mechanistic interpretability, neural lexical search with learned sparse retrieval, uncertainty quantification for large language models, and economic perspectives on fairness in information retrieval.

The workshops brought together participants to discuss a diverse set of themes, including narrative extraction from texts (Text2Story 2026), Search Futures, geographic information extraction (GeoExT 2026), information access in uncertainty scenarios (INFUSE), information retrieval for accountability and integrity (IRAI), scholarly information access (SCOLIA 2026), credible information retrieval to reduce online misinformation (ROMCIR 2026), open web search (WOWS), late interaction and multi-vector retrieval (LIR), Conversational Search for Complex Information Needs, and Synthetic Data and Simulation Synergy for Information Retrieval, covering both foundational and emerging challenges in the field.

The success of ECIR 2026 would not have been possible without the dedication and effort of a large team of volunteers and reviewers. We wish to thank all reviewers and meta-reviewers for their careful evaluations and constructive feedback, which were essential in ensuring the high quality of the conference program. We are also grateful to the many chairs who contributed to the organisation of ECIR 2026, including the reproducibility track chairs Andrew Yates and Venktesh V.; the IR4Good track chairs Bhaskar Mitra and Maria Heuss; the resource track chairs Petra Galuščáková and Panagiotis Eustratiadis; the demonstration track chairs Yue Feng and Sandipan Sikdar; the industry day chairs Benjamin Piwowarski and Vinay Setty; the doctoral consortium chairs Aldo Lipani and Julian Urbano; the CLEF Labs chairs Julia Maria Struß and Sean MacAvaney; the workshop chairs Negar Arabzadeh and Franco Maria Nardini; the tutorial chairs Faegheh Hasibi and Manish Gupta; the Collab-a-thon chairs Maik Fröbe, Jan Heinrich Merker, and Harry Scells; the best paper awards committee chair Craig Macdonald; the sponsorship chairs Ujwal Gadiraju and Edgar Meij; the proceedings chairs Alisa Rieger and Johannes Kiesel; the local organisation chairs Masoud Mansoury and Nan Bai; and the publicity chairs Yifei Yuan and David Graus.

We would also like to thank all student volunteers, whose commitment and hard work were instrumental in ensuring a smooth, welcoming, and memorable experience for all participants and attendees. We further acknowledge the support of our sponsors and partners, whose contributions helped make the conference possible.

Finally, we thank all authors and participants for their contributions to ECIR 2026 and for continuing to make ECIR a vibrant, inclusive, and forward-looking forum for information retrieval research.

April 2026

Ricardo Campos
Adam Jatowt
Yanyan Lan
Mohammad Aliannejadi
Christine Bauer
Sean MacAvaney
Avishek Anand
Zhaochun Ren
Suzan Verberne
Nan Bai
Masoud Mansoury

# Organization

## General Chairs

Avishek Anand      Delft University of Technology, Netherlands
Zhaochun Ren      Leiden University, Netherlands
Suzan Verberne      Leiden University, Netherlands

## Program Chairs – Full Papers

Adam Jatowt      University of Innsbruck, Austria
Ricardo Campos      University of Beira Interior/INESC TEC, Portugal
Yanyan Lan      Tsinghua University, China

## Program Chairs – Short Papers

Sean MacAvaney      University of Glasgow, UK
Mohammad Aliannejadi      University of Amsterdam, Netherlands
Christine Bauer      University of Salzburg, Austria

## Reproducibility Chairs

Andrew Yates      Johns Hopkins University, USA
Venktesh V.      Delft University of Technology, Netherlands

## IR4Good Chairs

Bhaskar Mitra      Independent Researcher, Canada
Maria Heuss      University of Amsterdam, Netherlands

## Resource Track Chairs

Petra Galuščáková             University of Stavanger, Norway
Panagiotis Eustratiadis       University of Amsterdam, Netherlands

## Demo Chairs

Yue Feng                      University of Birmingham, UK
Sandipan Sikdar               Leibniz University Hannover, Germany

## Industry Day Chairs

Benjamin Piwowarski           CNRS, Sorbonne University, France
Vinay Setty                   University of Stavanger/Factiverse AS, Norway

## Doctoral Consortium Chairs

Aldo Lipani                   University College London, UK
Julian Urbano                 Delft University of Technology, Netherlands

## CLEF Labs Chairs

Julia Maria Struß             FH Potsdam, Germany
Sean MacAvaney                University of Glasgow, UK

## Workshop Chairs

Negar Arabzadeh               University of California, Berkeley, USA
Franco Maria Nardini          ISTI-CNR, Italy

## Tutorial Chairs

Faegheh Hasibi                Radboud University, Netherlands
Manish Gupta                  Microsoft Research, India

## Collab-a-thon Chairs

| | |
|---|---|
| Maik Fröbe | Friedrich-Schiller-Universität Jena, Germany |
| Jan Heinrich Merker | Friedrich-Schiller-Universität Jena, Germany |
| Harry Scells | University of Tübingen, Germany |

## Best Paper Awards Chair

| | |
|---|---|
| Craig Macdonald | University of Glasgow, UK |

## Sponsorship Chairs

| | |
|---|---|
| Ujwal Gadiraju | Delft University of Technology, Netherlands |
| Edgar Meij | Bloomberg, UK |

## Proceedings Chairs

| | |
|---|---|
| Alisa Rieger | GESIS - Leibniz Institute, Germany |
| Johannes Kiesel | GESIS - Leibniz Institute, Germany |

## Local Organization Chairs

| | |
|---|---|
| Masoud Mansoury | Delft University of Technology, Netherlands |
| Nan Bai | Delft University of Technology, Netherlands |

## Publicity Chairs

| | |
|---|---|
| Yifei Yuan | University of Copenhagen, Denmark |
| David Graus | University of Amsterdam, Netherlands |

## Senior Program Committee

| | |
|---|---|
| Qingyao Ai | Tsinghua University, China |
| Dyaa Albakour | Signal AI, UK |
| Mohammad Aliannejadi | University of Amsterdam, Netherlands |

| | |
|---|---|
| James Allan | University of Massachusetts Amherst, USA |
| Omar Alonso | Amazon, USA |
| Ioannis Arapakis | Telefónica Research, Spain |
| Jaime Arguello | University of North Carolina at Chapel Hill, USA |
| Leif Azzopardi | University of Strathclyde, UK |
| Ebrahim Bagheri | Ryerson University, Canada |
| Krisztian Balog | University of Stavanger & Google Research, Norway |
| Alejandro Bellogin | Universidad Autónoma de Madrid, Spain |
| Ludovico Boratto | University of Cagliari, Italy |
| Mohand Boughanem | IRIT University Paul Sabatier Toulouse, France |
| Jamie Callan | Carnegie Mellon University, USA |
| Ben Carterette | Spotify, USA |
| Charles Clarke | University of Waterloo, Canada |
| Fabio Crestani | Università della Svizzera Italiana, Switzerland |
| Yashar Deldjoo | Polytechnic University of Bari, Italy |
| Tommaso Di Noia | Politecnico di Bari, Italy |
| Laura Dietz | University of New Hampshire, USA |
| Zhicheng Dou | Renmin University of China, China |
| Carsten Eickhoff | University of Tübingen, Germany |
| Tamer Elsayed | Qatar University, Qatar |
| Liana Ermakova | Université de Bretagne Occidentale, France |
| Alessandro Fabris | University of Trieste, Italy |
| Guglielmo Faggioli | University of Padua, Italy |
| Hui Fang | University of Delaware, USA |
| Antonio Ferrara | Politecnico di Bari, Italy |
| Maurizio Ferrari Dacrema | Politecnico di Milano, Italy |
| Nicola Ferro | University of Padua, Italy |
| Ingo Frommholz | Modul University Vienna, Austria |
| Michael Färber | ScaDS.AI & TU Dresden, Germany |
| Eric Gaussier | LIG, Université Grenoble Alpes, France |
| Lorraine Goeuriot | Université Grenoble Alpes, CNRS, Grenoble INP, LIG, France |
| Julio Gonzalo | Universidad Nacional de Educación a Distancia, Spain |
| Marcos Gonçalves | Federal University of Minas Gerais, Brazil |
| Jiafeng Guo | Institute of Computing Technology, CAS, China |
| Ido Guy | Meta, Israel |
| Matthias Hagen | Friedrich-Schiller-Universität Jena, Germany |
| Martin Halvey | University of Strathclyde, UK |
| Allan Hanbury | TU Wien, Austria |
| Faegheh Hasibi | Radboud University, Netherlands |

| | |
|---|---|
| Claudia Hauff | Spotify, Netherlands |
| Ben He | University of Chinese Academy of Sciences, China |
| Jiyin He | Signal AI, UK |
| Jin Huang | University of Amsterdam & Delft University of Technology, Netherlands |
| Amir Ingber | Pinecone, Israel |
| Dietmar Jannach | University of Klagenfurt, Austria |
| Olivier Jeunen | Aampe, Belgium |
| Joemon Jose | University of Glasgow, UK |
| Jaap Kamps | University of Amsterdam, Netherlands |
| Jussi Karlgren | AMD Silo AI, Finland |
| Makoto P. Kato | University of Tsukuba, Japan |
| Gabriella Kazai | Amazon, USA |
| Johannes Kiesel | GESIS - Leibniz Institute for the Social Sciences, Germany |
| Manolis Koubarakis | National and Kapodistrian University of Athens, Greece |
| Christin Katharina Kreutz | TH Mittelhessen - University of Applied Sciences & Herder Institute for Historical Research on East Central Europe, Germany |
| Udo Kruschwitz | University of Regensburg, Germany |
| Oren Kurland | Technion, Israel |
| Dawn Lawrie | Johns Hopkins University, USA |
| Jochen L. Leidner | Coburg University of Applied Sciences, Germany/University of Sheffield, UK/KnowledgeSpaces, Germany |
| Dirk Lewandowski | HAW Hamburg, Germany |
| Elisabeth Lex | Graz University of Technology, Austria |
| Haiming Liu | University of Southampton, UK |
| Yiqun Liu | Tsinghua University, China |
| Domenico Lofù | Politecnico di Bari, Italy |
| Sean MacAvaney | University of Glasgow, UK |
| Craig Macdonald | University of Glasgow, UK |
| Joel Mackenzie | University of Queensland, Australia |
| Joao Magalhaes | Universidade NOVA de Lisboa, Portugal |
| Maria Maistro | University of Copenhagen, Denmark |
| Antonio Mallia | Pinecone, USA |
| Jiaxin Mao | Renmin University of China, China |
| Mirko Marras | University of Cagliari, Italy |
| Philipp Mayr | GESIS - Leibniz Institute for the Social Sciences, Germany |
| Graham McDonald | University of Glasgow, UK |

| | |
|---|---|
| Dana McKay | RMIT University, Australia |
| Ida Mele | IASI-CNR, Italy |
| Jose G. Moreno | University of Toulouse - IRIT, France |
| Yashar Moshfeghi | University of Strathclyde, UK |
| Josiane Mothe | University of Toulouse, France |
| Animesh Mukherjee | Indian Institute of Technology, Kharagpur, India |
| Cataldo Musto | University of Bari, Italy |
| Henning Müller | University of Applied Sciences and Arts of Western Switzerland, Switzerland |
| Marc Najork | Google, USA |
| Franco Maria Nardini | ISTI-CNR, Italy |
| Julia Neidhardt | TU Wien, Austria |
| Jian-Yun Nie | University of Montreal, Canada |
| Iadh Ounis | University of Glasgow, UK |
| Javier Parapar | University of A Coruña, Spain |
| Gabriella Pasi | University of Milano-Bicocca, Italy |
| Maria Soledad Pera | TU Delft, Netherlands |
| Raffaele Perego | ISTI-CNR, Italy |
| Aleksandr Petrov | University of Glasgow, UK |
| Marco Polignano | Università degli Studi di Bari Aldo Moro, Italy |
| Claudio Pomo | Politecnico di Bari, Italy |
| Kevin Roitero | University of Udine, Italy |
| Alan Said | University of Gothenburg, Sweden |
| Mark Sanderson | RMIT University, Australia |
| Eric Sanjuan | Laboratoire Informatique d'Avignon- Université d'Avignon, France |
| Rodrygo Santos | Federal University of Minas Gerais, Brazil |
| Philipp Schaer | TH Köln - University of Applied Sciences, Germany |
| Ralf Schenkel | Trier University, Germany |
| Gianmaria Silvello | University of Padua, Italy |
| Clemencia Siro | Centrum Wiskunde & Informatica, Netherlands |
| Annelien Smets | imec-SMIT, Vrije Universiteit Brussel, Belgium |
| Mark Smucker | University of Waterloo, Canada |
| Hussein Suleman | University of Cape Town, South Africa |
| Aixin Sun | Nanyang Technological University, Singapore |
| Nava Tintarev | University of Maastricht, Netherlands |
| Marko Tkalčič | University of Primorska, Slovenia |
| Nicola Tonellotto | University of Pisa, Italy |
| Salvatore Trani | ISTI-CNR, Italy |
| Julián Urbano | Delft University of Technology, Netherlands |
| Ryen White | Microsoft, USA |

| | |
|---|---|
| Eugene Yang | Johns Hopkins University, USA |
| Yifei Yuan | ETH Zurich, Switzerland |
| Hamed Zamani | University of Massachusetts Amherst, USA |
| Eva Zangerle | University of Innsbruck, Austria |
| Markus Zanker | Free University of Bozen-Bolzano, Italy and University of Klagenfurt, Austria |
| Min Zhang | Tsinghua University, China |
| Shuo Zhang | Bloomberg, Norway |
| Yi Zhang | University of California Santa Cruz, USA |
| Justin Zobel | University of Melbourne, Australia |
| Maarten de Rijke | University of Amsterdam, Netherlands |
| Arjen de Vries | Radboud University, Netherlands |

## Program Committee

| | |
|---|---|
| Soheil Abadifard | Kansas State University, USA |
| Zahra Abbasiantaeb | University of Amsterdam, Netherlands |
| Mustafa Abualsaud | Thomson Reuters Labs, Canada |
| Prabhat Agarwal | Pinterest, USA |
| Potito Aghilar | Polytechnic University of Bari, Italy |
| Mrinal Ahlawat | Google, USA |
| Dirk Ahlers | NTNU - Norwegian University of Science and Technology, Norway |
| Dyaa Albakour | Signal AI, UK |
| Marco Alessio | ISTI-CNR & University of Pisa, Italy |
| Mohammed Ali | University of Innsbruck, Austria |
| Mohammad Aliannejadi | University of Amsterdam, Netherlands |
| Ismail Sengor Altingovde | Middle East Technical University, Turkey |
| Evelin Amorim | INESC TEC, Portugal |
| Vito Walter Anelli | Politecnico di Bari, Italy |
| Tarique Anwar | RMIT University, Australia |
| Negar Arabzadeh | University of Waterloo, Canada |
| Hidir Aras | FIZ Karlsruhe, Germany |
| Morten Arngren | Anthill Agency, Denmark |
| Kushagr Arora | Bloomberg LP, USA |
| Matteo Attimonelli | Politecnico di Bari, Italy |
| Amit Awekar | Indian Institute of Technology, Guwahati, India |
| Hosein Azarbonyad | Elsevier, Netherlands |
| Abdelghani Azri | Hassan I University, Morocco |
| Ismail Badache | Aix-Marseille University, France |
| Ebrahim Bagheri | Ryerson University, Canada |

| | |
|---|---|
| Ting Bai | Beijing University of Posts and Telecommunications, China |
| Krisztian Balog | University of Stavanger & Google Research, Norway |
| Alberto Barrón-Cedeño | Università di Bologna, Italy |
| Mina Basirat | University of Central Florida, USA |
| Christine Bauer | University of Salzburg, Austria |
| Andrea Bellandi | Institute for Computational Linguistics, Italy |
| Alejandro Bellogin | Universidad Autónoma de Madrid, Spain |
| Patrice Bellot | Aix-Marseille Université - CNRS (LIS), France |
| Alessandro Benedetti | Sease, UK |
| Klaus Berberich | Saarbrücken University of Applied Sciences, Germany |
| Rafael Berlanga | Universitat Jaume I, Spain |
| Nolwenn Bernard | TH Köln, Germany |
| Pietro Bernardelle | University of Queensland, Australia |
| Filippo Betello | Sapienza University of Rome, Italy |
| Keping Bi | Institute of Computing Technology, Chinese Academy of Sciences, China |
| Veronika Bogina | Tel Aviv University, Israel |
| Marco Bombieri | University of Verona, Italy |
| Ludovico Boratto | University of Cagliari, Italy |
| Gloria Bordogna | National Research Council of Italy - CNR, Italy |
| Florian Boudin | Université de Nantes, France |
| Marco Braga | University of Milano-Bicocca, Italy |
| Martin Braschler | ZHAW Zurich University of Applied Sciences, Switzerland |
| David Brazier | Edinburgh Napier University, UK |
| Timo Breuer | TH Köln - University of Applied Sciences, Germany |
| Francesco Busolin | Università Ca Foscari, Italy |
| Luca Cagliero | Politecnico di Torino, Italy |
| Sylvie Calabretto | LIRIS-INSA Lyon, France |
| B. Barla Cambazoglu | Kayra & Mergen Corp., Panama |
| Jacopo Cecchetti | University of Pisa, Italy |
| Andreas Chari | University of Glasgow, UK |
| Shubham Chatterjee | Missouri University of Science and Technology, USA |
| Despoina Chatzakou | Information Technologies Institute, Centre for Research and Technology Hellas, Greece |
| Catherine Chavula | University of Strathclyde, UK |
| Tong Chen | University of Copenhagen, Denmark |

| | |
|---|---|
| Xuanang Chen | Institute of Software, Chinese Academy of Sciences, China |
| Gong Cheng | Nanjing University, China |
| Max Chevalier | IRIT, France |
| Adrian-Gabriel Chifu | Aix-Marseille Université, CNRS, LIS, France |
| Philipp Christmann | Max Planck Institute for Informatics, Saarland Informatics Campus, Germany |
| Michal Chudoba | University of Stavanger, Norway |
| Charles Clarke | University of Waterloo, Canada |
| Benjamin Clavié | Answer.AI, Japan |
| Fabio Crestani | Università della Svizzera Italiana, Switzerland |
| Luís Filipe Cunha | University of Minho, Portugal |
| Washington Cunha | Federal University of Minas Gerais, Brazil |
| Arthur Câmara | Zeta Alpha Vector, Netherlands |
| Preetam Prabhu Srikar Dammu | University of Washington, USA |
| Savvina Daniil | CWI, Netherlands |
| Sudeshna Das | IIT Kharagpur, India |
| Maxime Dassen | Universiteit van Amsterdam, Netherlands |
| Suchana Datta | University College Dublin, Ireland |
| Bhargav Dave | Dhirubhai Ambani Institute of Information and Communication Technology, India |
| Nilou Davoudi | University of British Columbia, Canada |
| Francesco Luigi De Faveri | University of Padua, Italy |
| Yashar Deldjoo | Polytechnic University of Bari, Italy |
| Yuhao Deng | Beijing Institute of Technology, China |
| Ervin Dervishaj | University of Copenhagen, Denmark |
| Emanuele Di Buccio | University of Padua, Italy |
| Angela Di Fazio | Politecnico di Bari, Italy |
| Giorgio Maria Di Nunzio | University of Padua, Italy |
| Stefan Dietze | GESIS - Leibniz Institute for the Social Sciences, Germany |
| Karlijn Dinnissen | Utrecht University, Netherlands |
| Michael Dinzinger | University of Passau, Germany |
| Taoufiq Dkaki | Intitut de Recherche en Informatique de Toulouse, France |
| Peter Dolog | Aalborg University, Denmark |
| Gregor Donabauer | University of Regensburg, Germany |
| Antoine Doucet | University of La Rochelle, France |
| Arnab Dutta | eBay GmbH, Germany |
| Sajad Ebrahimi | University of Guelph, Canada |
| Carsten Eickhoff | University of Tübingen, Germany |
| Alaa El-Ebshihy | TU Wien and Research Studio Austria, Austria |

Sohaila Eltanbouly | Qatar University, Qatar
Ro Encarnacion | University of Pennsylvania, USA
Ege Erdogan | Koç University, Turkey
Liana Ermakova | Université de Bretagne Occidentale, France
Panagiotis Eustratiadis | University of Amsterdam, Netherlands
Ralph Ewerth | University of Marburg and hessian.AI – Hessian Center for Artificial Intelligence, Germany
Guglielmo Faggioli | University of Padua, Italy
Fabrizio Falchi | ISTI-CNR, Italy
Kim Falk | DPG Media, Belgium
Jinyuan Fang | University of Glasgow, UK
Hossein Fani | University of Windsor, Canada
Diego Fernández Iglesias | University of A Coruña, Spain
Antonio Ferrara | Politecnico di Bari, Italy
Rafael Ferreira | Universidade Nova de Lisboa, Portugal
Thibault Formal | Naver Labs Europe, France
Sebastien Fournier | Université d'Aix-Marseille, CNRS, France
Ingo Frommholz | Modul University Vienna, Austria
Alexander Frummet | dab: Daten - Analysen & Beratung GmbH, Germany
Maik Fröbe | Friedrich-Schiller-Universität Jena, Germany
Cong Fu | Zhejiang University, China
Xiao Fu | University College London, UK
Luke Gallagher | Independent, Australia
Elena Garcia-Morato | Universidad Rey Juan Carlos, Spain
Alba García Seco de Herrera | Universidad Nacional de Educación a Distancia, Spain
Dario Garigliotti | University of Bergen, Norway
Eric Gaussier | Université Grenoble Alpes, France
Thomas Gerald | Université Paris Saclay, CNRS, SATT, LISN, France
Kripabandhu Ghosh | Indian Institute of Science Education and Research Kolkata, India
Shrestha Ghosh | University of Tübingen, Germany
Anastasia Giachanou | Utrecht University, Netherlands
Alessandro Giuliani | Department of Mathematics and Computer Science, University of Cagliari, Italy
Daniela Godoy | ISISTAN Research Institute (UNCPBA-CONICET), Argentina
Lorraine Goeuriot | Université Grenoble Alpes, CNRS, Grenoble INP, LIG, France
Johannes Goller | Zalando, Germany
Gabriela González Sáez | Université Grenoble Alpes, France

| | |
|---|---|
| Michael Granitzer | University of Passau, Germany |
| Hongchao Gu | University of Science and Technology of China, China |
| Francesco Guerra | Università di Modena e Reggio Emilia, Italy |
| Vincent Guigue | AgroParisTech, France |
| Adrien Guille | ERIC Lyon 2, EA 3083, Université de Lyon, France |
| Nuno Guimarães | CRACS - INESC TEC, Portugal |
| Lei Guo | Shandong Normal University, China |
| Dhruv Gupta | Norwegian University of Science and Technology, Norway |
| Fabian Haak | TH Köln, Germany |
| Ahmed Hamdi | Université de La Rochelle, L3i, France |
| Qiwei Han | Nova School of Business and Economics, Portugal |
| Allan Hanbury | TU Wien, Austria |
| Donna Harman | National Institute of Standards and Technology, USA, USA |
| Claudia Hauff | Spotify, Netherlands |
| Rima Hazra | IIT Kharagpur, India |
| Farinam Hemmatizadeh | Thompson Reuters, Canada |
| Gijs Hendriksen | Radboud University, Netherlands |
| Mariya Hendriksen | University of Amsterdam, Netherlands |
| Danula Hettiachchi | RMIT University, Australia |
| Frank Hopfgartner | Universität Koblenz, Germany |
| Anett Hoppe | TIB Leibniz Information Centre for Science and Technology; L3S Research Centre, Leibniz Universität Hannover, Germany |
| Sha Hu | Southwest University, China |
| Jimmy Huang | York University, Canada |
| Gilles Hubert | IRIT, France |
| Stéphane Huet | LIA - Université d'Avignon, France |
| Andreea Iana | University of Mannheim, Germany |
| Wiradee Imrattanatrai | Kyoto University, Japan |
| Oana Inel | University of Zurich, Switzerland |
| Bogdan Ionescu | Politehnica University of Bucharest, Romania |
| Ornella Irrera | University of Padua, Italy |
| Gabriel Iturra-Bocaz | University of Stavanger, Norway |
| Raghav Jain | IIT Patna, India |
| Anubhav Jangra | Columbia University, USA |
| Dietmar Jannach | University of Klagenfurt, Austria |
| Faizan Javed | Kaiser Permanente, USA |

| | |
|---|---|
| Richard A. A. Jonker | IEETA - Institute of Electronics and Informatics Engineering of Aveiro, University of Aveiro, Portugal |
| José L. Jorro-Aragoneses | Universidad Autónoma de Madrid, Spain |
| Dylan Ju | University of Amsterdam, Netherlands |
| Emil Kalbaliyev | University of Tartu, Estonia |
| Anup Kalia | IBM, USA |
| Tobias Kalmbach | L3S Research Center, Germany |
| Eleni Kamateri | International Hellenic University, Greece |
| Jaap Kamps | University of Amsterdam, Netherlands |
| Jingwei Kang | University of Amsterdam, Netherlands |
| Yashal Kanungo | Amazon, USA |
| Pinar Karagoz | Middle East Technical University, Turkey |
| Jasmin Kareem | TU Eindhoven, Netherlands |
| Sarvnaz Karimi | CSIRO, Australia |
| Venkata Satya Pradeep Karuturi | Instacart, USA |
| Kateryna Kasianenko | Queensland University of Technology, Australia |
| Mesut Kaya | IT University of Copenhagen, Denmark |
| Jüri Keller | TH Köln (University of Applied Sciences), Germany |
| Roman Kern | Graz University of Technology, Austria |
| Jalal Khalil | St. Cloud State University, USA |
| Maleq Khan | Texas A&M Univeristy-Kingsville, USA |
| Urja Khurana | TU Delft, Netherlands |
| Johannes Kiesel | GESIS - Leibniz Institute for the Social Sciences, Germany |
| Benjamin Kille | Norwegian University of Science and Technology, Norway |
| Tracy Holloway King | Adobe, USA |
| Anastasiia Klimashevskaia | University of Bergen, Norway |
| Norman Knyazev | Radboud University, Netherlands |
| Michal Kompan | Kempelen Institute of Intelligent Technologies, Slovakia |
| Anton Korikov | University of Toronto, Canada |
| Ivica Kostric | University of Stavanger, Norway |
| Dominik Kowald | Know-Center, Austria |
| Thorsten Krause | Radboud University, Netherlands |
| Christin Katharina Kreutz | TH Mittelhessen - University of Applied Sciences & Herder Institute for Historical Research on East Central Europe, Germany |
| Andreas Konstantin Kruff | TH Köln, Germany |
| Hrishikesh Kulkarni | Georgetown University, USA |
| Jayant Kumar | Adobe Inc., USA |

| | |
|---|---|
| Raghvendra Kumar | Indian Institute of Technology, Patna, India |
| Rohan Kumar | Carnegie Mellon University, USA |
| Wojciech Kusa | NASK National Research Institute, Poland |
| Susana Ladra | University of A Coruña, Spain |
| Monica Landoni | Università della Svizzera italiana, Switzerland |
| Dawn Lawrie | Johns Hopkins University, USA |
| Yibin Lei | University of Amsterdam, Netherlands |
| Francesco Lettich | Institute of Information Science and Technologies (ISTI), National Research Council (CNR), Pisa, Italy |
| Anchen Li | Aalto University, Finland |
| Dan Li | Elsevier, Netherlands |
| Hang Li | University of Queensland, Australia |
| Roger Zhe Li | Huawei Ireland Research Centre, Ireland |
| Yongkang Li | University of Amsterdam, Netherlands |
| Tao Lian | Taiyuan University of Technology, China |
| Robert Litschko | LMU Munich, Germany |
| Marina Litvak | Shamoon College of Engineering, Israel |
| Yuanna Liu | University of Amsterdam, Netherlands |
| Andreas Lommatzsch | TU Berlin, Germany |
| David Losada | University of Santiago de Compostela, Spain |
| Natalia Loukachevitch | Research Computing Center of Moscow State University, Russia |
| Bernd Ludwig | University Regensburg, Germany |
| Riccardo Lunardi | University of Udine, Italy |
| Simon Lupart | University of Amsterdam, Netherlands |
| Yougang Lyu | University of Amsterdam, Netherlands |
| Chuangtao Ma | Aalborg University, Denmark |
| Joel Mackenzie | University of Queensland, Australia |
| Maria Maistro | University of Copenhagen, Denmark |
| Daniele Malitesta | CentraleSupélec, Inria, Université Paris-Saclay, France |
| Tanwi Mallick | Argonne National Laboratory, USA |
| Francesca Maridina Malloci | University of Cagliari, Italy |
| Alberto Carlo Maria Mancino | Politecnico di Bari, Italy |
| Thomas Mandl | University of Hildesheim, Germany |
| Watheq Mansour | University of Queensland, Australia |
| Behrooz Mansouri | University of Southern Maine, USA |
| Masoud Mansoury | Delft University of Technology, Netherlands |
| Marcelo G. Manzato | University of São Paulo, Brazil |
| Stefano Marchesin | University of Padua, Italy |
| Mirko Marras | University of Cagliari, Italy |

Silvio Martinico — University of Pisa, Italy
Bruno Martins — IST and INESC-ID - Instituto Superior Técnico, University of Lisbon, Portugal
Luis Martínez — University of Jaén, Spain
Sérgio Matos — IEETA, Universidade de Aveiro, Portugal
James Mayfield — Johns Hopkins University, USA
Richard McCreadie — University of Glasgow, UK
Jack McKechnie — University of Glasgow, UK
Giacomo Medda — University of Cagliari, Italy
James Meese — RMIT University, Australia
Parth Mehta — Parmonic, India
Rachana Mehta — Pandit Deendayal Energy University, India
Kidist Amde Mekonnen — University of Amsterdam, Netherlands
Chuan Meng — University of Edinburgh, UK
Laura Menotti — University of Padua, Italy
Jan Heinrich Merker — Friedrich-Schiller-Universität Jena, Germany
Felice Antonio Merra — Cognism, Italy
Selina Meyer — University of Technology Nuremberg, Germany
Lien Michiels — University of Antwerp and imec-SMIT, Vrije Universiteit Brussel, Belgium
Mandar Mitra — Indian Statistical Institute, Kolkata, India
Fengran Mo — Université de Montréal, Canada
Alistair Moffat — University of Melbourne, Australia
Marta Moscati — Johannes Kepler University Linz, Austria
Josiane Mothe — Université de Toulouse, France
Jamshid Mozafari — University of Innsbruck, Austria
Tendai Mukande — Dublin City University, Ireland
Philippe Mulhem — LIG-CNRS, France
Cristina Ioana Muntean — ISTI CNR, Italy
Sheshera Mysore — University of Massachusetts Amherst, USA
Henning Müller — University of Applied Sciences and Arts of Western Switzerland, Switzerland
Peter Müllner — Know-Center, Austria
Ashwin Nagappa — Queensland University of Technology, Australia
Fedelucio Narducci — Politecnico di Bari, Italy
Fatemeh Nazary — Politecnico di Bari, Italy
Julia Neidhardt — TU Wien, Austria
Vera Neplenbroek — University of Amsterdam, Netherlands
Thong Nguyen — University of Amsterdam, Netherlands
Jian-Yun Nie — University of Montreal, Canada
Shuzi Niu — Institute of Software, Chinese Academy of Sciences, China

| | |
|---|---|
| Sérgio Nunes | INESC TEC and University of Porto, Portugal |
| Diana Nurbakova | National Institute of Applied Sciences of Lyon (INSA Lyon), France |
| Harrie Oosterhuis | Radboud University, Netherlands |
| Salvatore Orlando | Università Ca' Foscari Venezia, Italy |
| Iadh Ounis | University of Glasgow, UK |
| Mourad Oussalah | University of Oulu, Finland |
| Panagiotis Papadakos | FORTH-ICS and University of Ioannina, Greece |
| Vincenzo Paparella | Politecnico di Bari, Italy |
| Andrea Papenmeier | University of Twente, Netherlands |
| Monica Lestari Paramita | University of Sheffield, UK |
| Javier Parapar | University of A Coruña, Spain |
| Andrea Pasin | University of Padua, Italy |
| Arian Pasquali | University of Porto, Portugal |
| Pavel Pecina | Charles University, Czechia |
| Georgios Peikos | University of Milano-Bicocca, Italy |
| Gustavo Penha | Spotify, Netherlands |
| Sole Pera | TU Delft, Netherlands |
| Ladislav Peska | Charles University, Czechia |
| Roxana Petcu | University of Amsterdam, Netherlands |
| Marinella Petrocchi | IIT-CNR, Italy |
| Aleksandr Petrov | University of Glasgow, UK |
| Francesca Pezzuti | University of Pisa, Italy |
| Fabio Pinelli | IMT Lucca, Italy |
| Florina Piroi | TU Wien, & ZFDM, Austria |
| Bhawna Piryani | University of Innsbruck, Austria |
| Jakub Piskorski | Joint Research Centre of the European Commission, Italy |
| Gabrielle Poerwawinata | University of Amsterdam, Netherlands |
| Claudio Pomo | Politecnico di Bari, Italy |
| Martin Potthast | University of Kassel, hessian.AI, and ScaDS.AI, Germany |
| Antonio Purificato | Sapienza University of Rome, Italy |
| Erasmo Purificato | Joint Research Centre, European Commission, Italy |
| Prakash Reddy Putta | Instacart, USA |
| Anxo Pérez | University of A Coruña (UDC), Spain |
| Danrui Qi | Simon Fraser University, Canada |
| Vahid Rahimzadeh | University of Tehran, Iran |
| Fiana Raiber | Technion, Israel |
| Theresia Veronika Rampisela | University of Copenhagen, Denmark |
| Weixiong Rao | Tongji University, China |

| | |
|---|---|
| Mandeep Rathee | L3S, Germany |
| Yongli Ren | RMIT University, Australia |
| Anja Reusch | Technion - Israel Institute of Technology, Israel |
| Myrthe Reuver | Vrije Universiteit Amsterdam, Netherlands |
| Guido Rocchietti | Università di Pisa - ISTI-CNR, Italy |
| Adam Roegiest | Zuva, Canada |
| Luca Rossetto | Dublin City University, Ireland |
| Julien Rossi | Amsterdam Business School, Netherlands |
| Mehrdad Rostami | University of Oulu, Finland |
| Dwaipayan Roy | Indian Institute of Science Education and Research, Kolkata, India |
| Davide Rucci | ISTI-CNR, Pisa, Italy |
| Anna Ruggero | Sease Ltd, Italy |
| Cosimo Rulli | ISTI-CNR, Italy |
| Clara Rus | University of Amsterdam, Netherlands |
| Mahdis Saeedi | University of Windsor, Canada |
| Chandan Kumar Sah | Beihang University, China |
| Sourav Saha | Indian Statistical Institute, India |
| Harshita Sahijwani | Emory University, USA |
| Abbas Saleminezhad | Toronto Metropolitan University, Canada |
| Eric Sanjuan | Laboratoire Informatique d'Avignon- Université d'Avignon, France |
| Aécio Santos | New York University, USA |
| Javier Sanz-Cruzado | University of Glasgow, UK |
| Shawon Sarkar | University of Washington, USA |
| Ali Satvaty | University of Groningen, Netherlands |
| Harrisen Scells | University of Tübingen, Germany |
| Philipp Schaer | TH Köln - University of Applied Sciences, Germany |
| Ralf Schenkel | Trier University, Germany |
| Ferdinand Schlatt | Friedrich-Schiller-Universität Jena, Germany |
| Sebastian Schultheiß | Hamburg University of Applied Sciences - HAW Hamburg, Germany |
| Florence Sedes | I.R.I.T. Université Toulouse III Paul Sabatier, France |
| Riddhima Sejpal | Instacart, USA |
| David Semedo | Universidade NOVA de Lisboa, Portugal |
| Procheta Sen | University of Liverpool, UK |
| Vinay Setty | University of Stavanger, Norway |
| Faisal Shehzad | University of Klagenfurt, Austria |
| Gianmaria Silvello | University of Padua, Italy |
| Sneha Singhania | Max Planck Institute for Informatics, Germany |

| | |
|---|---|
| Mark Smucker | University of Waterloo, Canada |
| Paolo Sorino | Politecnico di Bari, Italy |
| Heydar Soudani | Radboud University, Netherlands |
| Hugo Sousa | INESC TEC, Portugal |
| Marc Spaniol | Université de Caen Normandie, France |
| Francesca Spezzano | Boise State University, USA |
| Giuseppe Spillo | University of Bari, Italy |
| Damiano Spina | RMIT University, Australia |
| Prithvishankar Srinivasan | SSN College of Engineering, India |
| Efstathios Stamatatos | University of the Aegean, Greece |
| Alain Starke | University of Amsterdam, Netherlands |
| Moritz Staudinger | TU Wien, Austria |
| Lynda Tamine | IRIT, France |
| Guanru Tan | Hunan Univeristy, China |
| Xing Tang | Shenzhen Technology University, China |
| Yubao Tang | University of Amsterdam, Netherlands |
| Junichi Tatemura | Google, USA |
| Leila Tavakoli | Services Australia, Australia |
| Carla Teixeira Lopes | University of Porto, Portugal |
| Ketan Thakkar | LinkedIn Corp, USA |
| Nandan Thakur | University of Waterloo, Canada |
| Fangzheng Tian | University of Glasgow, UK |
| Antonela Tommasel | ISISTAN Research Institute, CONICET-UNCPBA, Argentina |
| Nicola Tonellotto | University of Pisa, Italy |
| Salvatore Trani | ISTI-CNR, Italy |
| Giovanni Trappolini | Sapienza University of Rome, Italy |
| Christos Tryfonopoulos | University of the Peloponnese, Greece |
| Chun-Hua Tsai | University of Nebraska Omaha, USA |
| Theodora Tsikrika | Information Technologies Institute, CERTH, Greece |
| Yannis Tzitzikas | University of Crete and FORTH-ICS, Greece |
| Md Zia Ullah | Edinburgh Napier University, UK |
| Moshe Unger | Coller School of Management, Tel Aviv University, Israel |
| Robin Ungruh | Delft University of Technology, Netherlands |
| Apoorva Upadhyaya | Indian Institute of Technology, Patna, India |
| Kelsey Urgo | University of North Carolina at Chapel Hill, USA |
| Svitlana Vakulenko | Amazon Alexa AI, Spain |
| Marco Valentini | Poilitecnico di Bari, Italy |
| Christophe Van Gysel | Apple Inc., USA |
| Vojtěch Vančura | Czech Technical University, Czechia |

| | |
|---|---|
| Ali Vardasbi | University of Amsterdam, Netherlands |
| Alberto Veneri | Domyn, Italy |
| Rossano Venturini | Università di Pisa, Italy |
| Thanasis Vergoulis | IMSI, "Athena" RC, Greece |
| João Vinagre | Joint Research Centre - European Commission, Spain |
| Giorgio Vinciguerra | University of Pisa, Italy |
| Marco Viviani | Università degli Studi di Milano-Bicocca, Italy |
| Maria Vlachou | University of Copenhagen, Denmark |
| David Vos | University of Amsterdam, Netherlands |
| Sanne Vrijenhoek | Universiteit van Amsterdam, Netherlands |
| Stefanos Vrochidis | Information Technologies Institute, Greece |
| Jonas Wallat | L3S Research Center, Germany |
| Jiexin Wang | South China University of Technology, China |
| Xi Wang | University of Sheffield, UK |
| Xiao Wang | University of Glasgow, UK |
| Xiaxia Wang | University of Oxford, UK |
| Christa Womser-Hacker | University of Hildesheim, Germany |
| Wentao Wu | Microsoft Research, USA |
| Xin Xin | Shandong University, China |
| Takeshi Yamada | Kindai University, Japan |
| Takehiro Yamamoto | University of Hyogo, Japan |
| Diji Yang | University of California Santa Cruz, USA |
| Eugene Yang | Johns Hopkins University, USA |
| Kailai Yang | University of Manchester, UK |
| Andrew Yates | Johns Hopkins University, USA |
| Mert Yazan | Amsterdam University of Applied Sciences, Netherlands |
| Sudarshan Yerragunta | Indian Institute of Information Technology, Sri City, India |
| Hai-Tao Yu | University of Tsukuba, Japan |
| Ran Yu | GESIS - Leibniz Institute for the Social Sciences, Germany |
| Weijie Yu | University of International Business and Economics, China |
| Yi Yu | Kyoto University, Japan |
| Richard Zanibbi | Rochester Institute of Technology, USA |
| Fattane Zarrinkalam | University of Guelph, Canada |
| Oleg Zendel | RMIT University, Australia |
| Saber Zerhoudi | Universität Passau, Germany |
| Crystina Xinyu Zhang | University of Waterloo, Canada |
| Dake Zhang | University of Waterloo, Canada |

| | |
|---|---|
| Hengran Zhang | Institute of Computing Technology, Chinese Academy of Sciences, China |
| Min Zhang | Tsinghua University, China |
| Shuo Zhang | Bloomberg, UK |
| Weijia Zhang | Amazon, USA |
| Yang Zhang | Kyoto University, Japan |
| Yihong Zhang | Osaka University, Japan |
| Zhuowei Zhao | University of Melbourne, Australia |
| Yinghao Zhou | University of Birmingham, UK |
| Guangnan Zhu | Queensland University of Technology, Australia |
| Morteza Zihayat | Toronto Metropolitan University, Canada |
| Frans van der Sluis | University of Copehagen, Denmark |
| Weronika Łajewska | University of Stavanger, Norway |

# Contents

**Demo Papers**

**CLEF Overview Papers**

**Resource Papers**

# Tutorial Papers

# Practical, Efficient, In-Memory Inverted Indexes

Joel Mackenzie[1(✉)] [ID], Sean MacAvaney[2] [ID], Antonio Mallia[3] [ID],
and Michał Siedlaczek[4] [ID]

[1] The University of Queensland, St. Lucia, Australia
joel.mackenzie@uq.edu.au
[2] University of Glasgow, Glasgow, UK
[3] Seltz, San Francisco, USA
[4] MongoDB, New York, USA

**Abstract.** Inverted indexes are the backbone of most large-scale information retrieval systems. Although conceptually simple, high-performance inverted indexes require a deep understanding of low-level system optimizations, memory layouts, data compression techniques, and index traversal strategies. With the widespread adoption of in-memory search engines, the rise of learned sparse retrieval (LSR), and the increasing complexity of ranking pipelines, the design space for efficient indexing and retrieval systems has expanded significantly. This tutorial addresses a critical knowledge gap between textbook-style explanations and advanced techniques required for efficient and optimized retrieval. It aims to equip researchers and practitioners with a comprehensive understanding of how modern in-memory search systems are designed, built, and optimized for high-performance retrieval across large-scale document collections.

**Keywords:** Efficiency · Inverted Index · Query Processing · Compression

## 1 Motivation

Efficient indexing and retrieval remain foundational to information retrieval (IR) systems at all scales, from academic testbeds to large-scale commercial search engines. At the heart of these systems lies the inverted index, a decades-old data structure that continues to evolve in response to new retrieval paradigms and performance demands. While many students and early-career researchers are introduced to inverted indexes through textbooks or simplified implementations, the gap between these resources and the requirements of high-performance, in-memory search engines remains substantial. Furthermore, the complexity of these highly optimized solutions presents a significant barrier to entry for those interested in understanding and working in the efficiency space.

Recent advances in retrieval – particularly the rise of learned sparse retrieval (LSR) models [1,4,9,14,19,26,36], hybrid search pipelines [5,7,11,15],


R. Campos et al. (Eds.): ECIR 2026, LNCS 16486, pp. 3–10, 2026.
https://doi.org/10.1007/978-3-032-21321-1_1

and retrieval-augmented generation (RAG) applications [10] – have renewed interest in efficient sparse retrieval techniques that can be tightly integrated with modern machine learning and cascade ranking workflows. In particular, the use of traditional sparse indexes to serve model-generated representations has led to new challenges in indexing, scoring, and top-$k$ retrieval, motivating the development of specialized pruning strategies such as BM25-guided traversal [8,20,28], Block-max Pruning [25], and list decomposition [16] among many others.

Despite these developments, many researchers and practitioners face a steep learning curve when experimenting with efficient retrieval infrastructures, making it difficult to reproduce results, run scalable experiments, or explore new optimization techniques. To address this gap, this tutorial provides both theoretical foundations and practical guidance for building high-performance sparse retrieval systems. Using the open-source *Performant Indexes and Search for Academia* (PISA) engine [22] and its Python bindings via PyTerrier [13], we demonstrate how classical indexing techniques are implemented in practice and how they can be extended to emerging applications such as LSR and RAG.

The tutorial is particularly relevant to the ECIR community, where interest in efficient retrieval, reproducible experimentation, and integration with neural models has grown rapidly in recent years. By equipping attendees with both the conceptual background and the practical skills required to build and experiment with state-of-the-art sparse retrieval systems, this tutorial aims to lower the barrier to entry and foster new research directions at the intersection of classical IR and modern machine learning. The tutorial will also improve the visibility of ongoing work and open directions for inverted index-based search systems.

## 2   Objectives

We organize our tutorial around a set of Intended Learning Outcomes (ILOs) that attendees will be able to achieve by the end of the tutorial. These outcomes are designed to accommodate a broad audience – from those new to information retrieval, to more experienced researchers – by combining foundational theory with hands-on practical skills via the PISA engine. Furthermore, we aim to provide valuable content to both *end-users* (those who want to effectively apply inverted indexes in their research) and *tinkerers* (those who want to dig into the implementations and contribute to new research in this domain). The ILOs for the tutorial are described below.

**ILO1: Theoretical Understanding of Inverted Indexes.** Attendees will develop a solid understanding of how inverted indexes are structured and used in IR systems. They will learn how core components – such as posting lists, lexicons, and skip lists – are implemented and organized in memory, how they are compressed, and how these design choices impact retrieval scalability.

**ILO2: Fast Top-$k$ Retrieval with Dynamic Pruning.** Attendees will gain insight into *dynamic pruning-based* retrieval techniques (such as MaxScore [33] and BMW [3,6,21]) that accelerate top-$k$ search. They will understand the principles behind these algorithms, including any assumptions, sensitivities to different indexing or parameter choices, and the underlying trade-offs involved with different pruning strategies. Attendees will also gain insights into the current state-of-the-art methods for accelerating inverted index-based algorithms, including threshold estimation [17,24,27], advanced skipping or pruning methods [23,29,30,34], and anytime retrieval strategies [18].

**ILO3: Current Trends and Research Directions.** Attendees will understand how traditional inverted index-based retrieval fits into modern IR systems. They will learn how emerging methods – such as learned sparse retrieval – influence traversal strategies, including problems caused by learned sparse data distributions. Then, we will introduce ongoing research to remedy these issues including BM25-guided traversal, list decomposition, and *anytime* retrieval, as well as emerging methods tailored to sparse neural representations such as Block-Max Pruning (BMP) [25] and Seismic [2].

**ILO4: Building and Running Experiments with PISA.** Attendees will gain practical experience using the PISA engine to build indexes, run retrieval experiments, and evaluate performance. They'll learn how to apply different scoring functions and retrieval algorithms to analyze efficiency and effectiveness trade-offs. We plan to offer two levels of access; (1) the PyTerrier-PISA python bindings for users who wish to interact with PISA via the PyTerrier interface; and (2) directly via PISA's command line tool interface.

**ILO5: Integration of PISA in Modern Applications.** Attendees will be able to use PISA as a backend in applied research contexts, such as incorporating keyword search into retrieval-augmented generation (RAG) pipelines.

## 3   Relevance

This tutorial is designed for both newcomers to information retrieval and experienced researchers who want to better understand efficient retrieval methods. Although there has been a significant focus on semantic search methods over the last decade, lexical retrieval is still a core component of many search systems at various scales, and the efficient deployment of lexical search systems is a key requirement for the community. Our tutorial complements recent tutorials [31,35] and surveys [32] by focusing specifically on the efficient design and implementation of such retrieval systems, from traditional models and simple indexes to state-of-the-art techniques. To ensure relevance with modern IR trends and ongoing work, we specifically focus on how traditional inverted index methods can be integrated into modern applications, and dedicate a section of the tutorial to ongoing work and emerging trends.

## 4   Format and Schedule

The tutorial will be presented as a series of modules, interleaving the theoretical aspects with practical, hands-on activities. We also intend on providing a more advanced "post tutorial" extension task for those who wish to continue to develop their knowledge, but our main goal is to reduce the barrier to entry for attendees. To this end, no "pre-work" is required, and we expect to have both runnable notebooks available to support the python-oriented sections, as well as a Docker image with PISA pre-installed for the command line work. Thus, participants are only expected to have Docker installed and a functioning Python environment. This will facilitate rapid set-up, and these resources will be made available before the workshop with support available from the team prior to, during, and after the tutorial. Note that all timelines listed below are indicative, and are intended to have some level of flexibility to adapt to the audience needs or interests.

**Session 1: Indexing and Retrieval [75 min].** The first session will be focused on exploring the fundamentals of the inverted index. We will begin with a discussion on where the PISA family (including Python bindings) fits into the wider tool landscape, and compare it against other common tools that serve a similar purpose. We will then motivate the need for inverted indexes, followed by a series of brief, visual tutorials on in-memory indexing. These will include details on the representation of inverted indexes, and practical examples of indexing common IR collections. Next, we will move from indexing to retrieval, again using visual tutorials to outline how exhaustive retrieval operates over inverted indexes. Following this, we will move to efficient dynamic pruning algorithms (using the more simple WAND or MaxScore algorithms as exemplars). We will complete this session with a small empirical comparison of top-$k$ retrieval algorithms using PISA on the indexed collection. An indicative timeline is as follows:

- Introduction and motivation [5–10 minutes]
- Inverted indexing and retrieval fundamentals [20 min]
- Fast and compact in-memory index representations [20 min]
- From exhaustive to fast top-$k$ retrieval [20 min]

*Practical Aspects.* The first session will aim at familiarizing attendees with the notebook/Docker image, and to run some basic indexing and querying. We expect this part to rely on a small and freely available collection such as a subset of an open-source Wikipedia dump. We will start with building a basic index, and running simple conjunctive and disjunctive queries. Then, we will build additional structures required to support (fast) ranking, and explore exhaustive document-at-a-time top-$k$ retrieval. Finally, we will move to deploying dynamic pruning algorithms like WAND and MaxScore.

**Break [15 min].** Aligned with the conference coffee break.

**Session II: Learned Sparse Retrieval [60 min.]** The second session will focus on the challenges and opportunities of combining traditional inverted index structures with modern learned sparse retrieval (LSR) techniques. We begin with a high-level overview of LSR, covering their motivation, model architectures, and how they differ from statistical rankers like BM25. We then discuss how LSR changes the structure and usage patterns of inverted indexes – including new characteristics of posting lists, term distributions, and score distributions that arise from model-generated representations. Next, we explore how traditional indexing and retrieval algorithms can be adapted to efficiently support LSR, with a particular focus on pruning strategies that help mitigate long and noisy LSR postings. An indicative timeline is as follows:

- From Statistical to Learned Models [10 min]
- LSR: A trouble-maker for Inverted Indexes [20 min]
- Accelerating Inverted Indexes in the context of LSR [30 min]

*Practical Aspects.* This session will include a practical walk-through, showing how PISA can be used to index LSR-generated output (e.g., in JSON or CIFF [12]) format and how these indexes can be queried using the same high-performance retrieval infrastructure. These experiments will also demonstrate the slowdowns caused by LSR in practice. The session concludes with a demonstration of how PISA can be integrated into Python-based research pipelines via PyTerrier, enabling its use as a first-stage retriever in modern workflows, including hybrid retrieval and, if time permits, retrieval-augmented generation (RAG) systems.

**Session III: Alternatives and New Directions [30 min.]** Our final session will broaden the focus of the tutorial beyond document-ordered inverted indexes with the intent of providing useful pointers to alternative approaches being investigated by the efficiency community. We will also outline some open problems and ongoing work in the efficiency space.

## 5   Materials

Attendees will be provided with: (1) Slides covering theoretical content and code walk-throughs, including diagrams or animations to improve understanding; (2) Access to a Docker image for PISA, and notebooks (Jupyter or Colab) for the PyTerrier interface; (3) Sample datasets and prebuilt indexes for experimentation; and (4) Links to relevant publications, code repositories, and further readings.

We intend to provide some post-tutorial resources and guides for those attendees interested in learning or engaging further. For example, we plan to provide links to the PISA repository (and the PyTerrier counterpart), detailed documentation, the PISA Slack channel, and a guide on how to contribute further to the project. We will also provide a set of references to recent and ongoing work, and any further material we develop that was not covered during the tutorial.

## 6 Conclusion

Efficient indexing and retrieval remain central challenges in the design of high-performance information retrieval systems. This tutorial bridges the gap between foundational concepts and cutting-edge developments by offering both theoretical insights and hands-on experience with state-of-the-art tools. It focuses on in-memory inverted indexes and their role in both classical and modern retrieval pipelines—including learned sparse retrieval and retrieval-augmented generation. This tutorial is designed to support both newcomers to information retrieval and experienced researchers interested in efficiency-focused methods. By the end of the session, attendees will have a strong understanding of core indexing and retrieval techniques, along with practical experience that equips them to apply these approaches in their own research and experimental workflows.

**Disclosure of Interests.** The authors have no competing interests of any sort.

## References


1. Basnet, S., Gou, J., Mallia, A., Suel, T.: Deeperimpact: optimizing sparse learned index structures. In: Proceedings of ReNeuIR at SIGIR (2024)
2. Bruch, S., Nardini, F.M., Rulli, C., Venturini, R.: Efficient inverted indexes for approximate retrieval over learned sparse representations. In: Proceedings of SIGIR, pp. 152–162 (2024)
3. Ding, S., Suel, T.: Faster top-k document retrieval using block-max indexes. In: Proceedings of SIGIR, pp. 993–1002 (2011)
4. Formal, T., Piwowarski, B., Clinchant, S.: SPLADE: sparse lexical and expansion model for first stage ranking. In: Proceedings of SIGIR, pp. 2288–2292. ACM (2021)
5. Gao, L., Dai, Z., Callan, J.: COIL: revisit exact lexical match in information retrieval with contextualized inverted list. In: Proceedings of NAACL-HLT, pp. 3030–3042 (2021)
6. Grand, A., Muir, R., Ferenczi, J., Lin, J.: From MaxScore to Block-Max Wand: the story of how Lucene significantly improved query evaluation performance. In: Proceedings of ECIR, pp. 20–27 (2020)
7. Huang, K., et al.: ColBERT-Serve: efficient multi-stage memory-mapped scoring. In: Proceedings of ECIR, pp. 21–30 (2025)
8. Kulkarni, H., MacAvaney, S., Goharian, N., Frieder, O.: Lexically-accelerated dense retrieval. In: Proceedings of SIGIR, pp. 152–162 (2023)
9. Lassance, C., Clinchant, S.: An efficiency study for splade models. In: Proceedings of SIGIR, pp. 2220–2226 (2022)
10. Lewis, P.S.H., et al.: Retrieval-augmented generation for knowledge-intensive NLP tasks. In: Proceedings of NeurIPS (2020)

11. Lin, J., Ma, X., Lin, S., Yang, J., Pradeep, R., Nogueira, R.: Pyserini: a python toolkit for reproducible information retrieval research with sparse and dense representations. In: Proceedings of SIGIR, pp. 2356–2362 (2021)
12. Lin, J., et al.: Supporting interoperability between open-source search engines with the common index file format. In: Proceedings of SIGIR, pp. 2149–2152 (2020)
13. MacAvaney, S., Macdonald, C.: A python interface to pisa! In: Proceedings of SIGIR, pp. 3339–3344 (2022)
14. MacAvaney, S., Nardini, F.M., Perego, R., Tonellotto, N., Goharian, N., Frieder, O.: Expansion via prediction of importance with contextualization. In: Proceedings of SIGIR, pp. 1573–1576 (2020)
15. Macdonald, C., Tonellotto, N., MacAvaney, S., Ounis, I.: Pyterrier: declarative experimentation in python from BM25 to dense retrieval. In: Proceedings of CIKM, pp. 4526–4533 (2021)
16. Mackenzie, J., Mallia, A., Moffat, A., Petri, M.: Accelerating learned sparse indexes via term impact decomposition. In: Findings of the ACL: EMNLP 2022, pp. 2830–2842 (2022)
17. Mackenzie, J., Moffat, A.: Examining the additivity of top-k query processing innovations. In: Proceedings of CIKM, pp. 1085–1094 (2020)
18. Mackenzie, J., Petri, M., Moffat, A.: Anytime ranking on document-ordered indexes. ACM Trans. Inf. Syst. **40**(1), 1–32 (2021)
19. Mallia, A., Khattab, O., Suel, T., Tonellotto, N.: Learning passage impacts for inverted indexes. In: Proceedings of SIGIR, pp. 1723–1727 (2021)
20. Mallia, A., Mackenzie, J., Suel, T., Tonellotto, N.: Faster learned sparse retrieval with guided traversal. In: Proceedings of SIGIR, pp. 1901–1905 (2022)
21. Mallia, A., Ottaviano, G., Porciani, E., Tonellotto, N., Venturini, R.: Faster block-max WAND with variable-sized blocks. In: Proceedings of SIGIR, pp. 625–634 (2017)
22. Mallia, A., Siedlaczek, M., Mackenzie, J.M., Suel, T.: PISA: performant indexes and search for academia. In: Proceedings of OSIRRC at SIGIR, vol. 2409, pp. 50–56 (2019)
23. Mallia, A., Siedlaczek, M., Suel, T.: Fast disjunctive candidate generation using live block filtering. In: Proceedings of WSDM, pp. 671–679 (2021)
24. Mallia, A., Siedlaczek, M., Sun, M., Suel, T.: A comparison of top-$k$ threshold estimation techniques for disjunctive query processing. In: Proceedings of CIKM, pp. 2141–2144 (2020)
25. Mallia, A., Suel, T., Tonellotto, N.: Faster learned sparse retrieval with block-max pruning. In: Proceedings of SIGIR, pp. 2411–2415 (2024)
26. Nguyen, T., MacAvaney, S., Yates, A.: A unified framework for learned sparse retrieval. In: Proceedings of ECIR, vol. 13982, pp. 101–116 (2023)
27. Qiao, Y., Carlson, P., He, S., Yang, Y., Yang, T.: Threshold-driven pruning with segmented maximum term weights for approximate cluster-based sparse retrieval. In: Proceedings of EMNLP, pp. 19742–19757 (2024)
28. Qiao, Y., Yang, Y., Lin, H., Yang, T.: Optimizing guided traversal for fast learned sparse retrieval. In: Proceedings of WWW, pp. 3375–3385 (2023)
29. Siedlaczek, M., Mallia, A., Suel, T.: Using conjunctions for faster disjunctive top-k queries. In: Proceedings of WSDM, pp. 917–927 (2022)
30. Tolosa, G., Mallia, A.: Many are better than one: algorithm selection for faster top-k retrieval. Inf. Proc. Manag. **60**(4) (2023)
31. Tonellotto, N., Macdonald, C.: Efficient query processing infrastructures: a half-day tutorial at sigir 2018. In: Proceedings of SIGIR, pp. 1403–1406 (2018)

32. Tonellotto, N., Macdonald, C., Ounis, I.: Efficient query processing for scalable web search. Found. Trends Inf. Retr. **12**(4–5), 319–500 (2018)
33. Turtle, H.R., Flood, J.: Query evaluation: strategies and optimizations. Inf. Proc. Manag. **31**(6), 831–850 (1995)
34. Yafay, E., Altingovde, I.S.: Faster dynamic pruning via reordering of documents in inverted indexes. In: Proceedings of SIGIR, pp. 2001–2005 (2023)
35. Yates, A., Lassance, C., MacAvaney, S., Nguyen, T., Lei, Y.: Neural lexical search with learned sparse retrieval. In: Proceedings of SIGIR-AP, pp. 303–306 (2024)
36. Yu, P., Mallia, A., Petri, M.: Improved learned sparse retrieval with corpus-specific vocabularies. In: Proceedings of ECIR, pp. 181–194 (2024)

# Conversational Search: Foundations, Large Language Models, and Agents

Chuan Meng[1]([envelope]) [iD], Fengran Mo[2] [iD], Mohammad Aliannejadi[3] [iD],
Jeff Dalton[1] [iD], and Jian-Yun Nie[2] [iD]

[1] The University of Edinburgh, Edinburgh, UK
{chuan.meng,jeff.dalton}@ed.ac.uk
[2] Université de Montréal, Montréal, Canada
{fengran.mo,nie}@iro.umontreal.ca
[3] University of Amsterdam, Amsterdam, The Netherlands
m.aliannejadi@uva.nl

**Abstract.** Conversational search enables multi-turn interactions between users and systems to fulfill users' complex information needs. During this interaction, the system should understand the users' search intent within the conversational context and then return the relevant information through a flexible, dialogue-based interface. Large language models (LLMs) with capacities of instruction following, content generation, and reasoning, attract significant attention and advancements, providing new opportunities and challenges for building up conversational search systems. More recently, LLMs have begun to drive search systems towards agentic paradigms, acting as autonomous entities that can plan strategies, execute dynamic retrieval, and support a wide range of autonomous behaviours. This tutorial aims to connect fundamentals with recent agentic paradigms in conversational search. It is designed for students, researchers, and practitioners from both academia and industry. Participants will gain a comprehensive understanding of both the fundamental principles and the latest developments enabled by LLMs and agents, equipping them with the knowledge to contribute to the next generation of conversational search systems.

**Keywords:** Conversational search · Conversational agents · Conversational retrieval-augmented generation

## 1 Motivation, Scope and Relevance

Search engines are essential for modern society to fulfill users' information needs [39]. The initial ad-hoc search systems rely on keywords or short phrases as input queries, which cannot capture user search intent accurately with limited interactions [13, 30, 45]. The recently developed conversational search [21, 31, 43] enables multi-turn interactions between users and systems to meet users' complex information needs, supporting the flexibility of interactions. To further enhance interaction quality, conversational search systems are increasingly


R. Campos et al. (Eds.): ECIR 2026, LNCS 16486, pp. 11–18, 2026.
https://doi.org/10.1007/978-3-032-21321-1_2

adopting mixed-initiative strategies (e.g., clarification [5,22]), where both the user and the system can take the initiative at different points in a conversation [37].

**Motivation.** The advent of LLMs [8,25,47,49] has advanced the ability of systems to understand conversational context, reason over complex queries, and generate coherent, context-aware responses. Meanwhile, users have become more accustomed to multi-turn and natural interactions with AI systems. The growing integration of LLMs with search engines [15,17] enables conversational interfaces that flexibly handle diverse input forms (context-dependent queries, task-oriented instructions, or even multimodal signals) and deliver outputs in multiple formats, such as direct answers, ranked results, summaries, or clarification questions. This paradigm shift is transforming user information-seeking behaviour from single-turn retrieval to sustained conversational interaction.

Building on this momentum, LLMs are now driving search systems toward *agentic paradigms* [15,17,38,41], in which LLMs act as autonomous entities capable of reasoning, planning, executing retrieval, and reflecting on their own outputs dynamically. Recent research in conversational search explores various dimensions of this shift. E.g., recent work uses test-time scaling [48] to enhance the reasoning ability of conversational systems through computation-intensive inference. Other studies introduce agentic capabilities such as search-result reflection [23], and interleaving search and reasoning [20], where LLMs plan how to solve conversational queries, perform dynamic retrieval, and generate answers using retrieved evidence in an iterative way. This timely topic provides valuable insights for both researchers and practitioners by tracing the evolution from traditional reactive conversational search to autonomous, self-improving systems.

**Scope.** This tutorial covers the evolution of conversational search from its foundations to the emerging agentic frontiers. On the foundational side, it introduces basic concepts, core conversational search paradigms, mixed-initiative, and personalized conversational search. On the frontier side, it explores emerging topics driven by LLMs and agents, such as conversational search with LLM-based generation, test-time scaling, reflection, and interleaving of search and reasoning in conversations. We will conclude the tutorial with a discussion on future research directions, such as retrieving tools, user memory, or past system experience in conversations. This tutorial will help IR researchers and practitioners understand how conversational search is being reshaped by LLMs and agents, preparing them for the next generation of conversational systems.

**Differences from Previous Tutorials.** This tutorial builds on our SIGIR 2025 tutorial on conversational search [32], which bridged the gap between foundational techniques and LLM-based approaches in conversational search. However, the ECIR 2026 edition significantly broadens the scope to cover recent advances in agentic conversational search systems, including test-time scaling, reflection, and the interleaving of search and reasoning in conversations.

**Relevance to the IR Community.** The topics covered align with ECIR's focus on search and ranking, interactive IR, conversational search, and LLMs for IR.

## 2  Format, Length, and Outline

This tutorial is planned as a half-day, lecture-style event (3 h). The tutorial will be delivered entirely in person. It consists of two parts: fundamentals and emerging topics, delivered in two 90-min sessions with a break in between.

**Part I: Fundamentals (90 min)**

**Introduction to Conversational Search [10 min].** We will define conversational search, and highlight the key characteristics that distinguish it from traditional ad-hoc search. For example, user queries in conversational search are context-dependent user queries, i.e., they may contain omissions, co-references, or ambiguities [43], making it challenging for ad-hoc search methods to capture the underlying information need [37]. Also, we will provide an overview of widely used datasets in conversational search. Moreover, we will introduce evaluation metrics widely used in conversational search, such as traditional IR metrics and recent nugget-based evaluation [1].

**Fundamental Conversational Search Paradigms [30 min].** Recovering the underlying information need from conversational history is a key challenge in conversational search. To address it, two main approaches of methods have been developed:

- Query-rewriting-based retrieval methods: rewrite a context-dependent query into a self-contained query, which is then reused by an ad-hoc retriever [33, 40, 42].
- Conversational dense retrieval methods: train a query encoder to encode the current query within the conversational history into a contextualized query embedding [19, 35, 43].

**Mixed Initiative [25 min].** We will cover two core aspects of research on mixed-initiative interactions:

- What type of initiative to take: clarification [5, 7, 44], elicit user preferences, proactively provide background information and suggestions [26], and so on.
- When to take the initiative: clarification need prediction [5], system initiative prediction [22], and so on.

**Personalized Conversational Search [15 min].** Personalized conversational search systems aim to tailor the generated outputs according to their users' background and historical preferences. The additional challenge lies in dynamically incorporating users' profiles, preferences, or history into each turn [1,4,29,36]. We will introduce the recent advances in personalized conversational search.

**Part II: Emerging LLM & Agent Topics (90 min)**

**Conversational Search with LLM-Based Generation [25 min]** . LLMs have transformed conversational interfaces, changing how users access information and interact with systems. This section discusses the integration of conversational search and LLMs, which enables new information needs and interactive retrievalgeneration workflows [14,28]. We focus on two emerging directions:

- Conversational generation-augmented retrieval (GAR) [34]: GAR can enhance the search systems by generating pseudo data, producing fluent and consistent interaction, identifying the information value among the generation, and decomposing complex or instruction-based queries.
- Conversational retrieval-augmented generation (RAG): Similarly, the conversational RAG [9,16,27], which integrates conversational search results into the prompt that can contribute to improving truthfulness in the answer generation of LLMs by grounding answers in the retrieved documents, thus reducing hallucinations. It also helps increase information diversity.

**Test-Time Scaling for Conversational Search [10 min].** Test-time scaling is a promising approach for large language models (LLMs) that leverages additional test-time computation (e.g., longer reasoning chains) to improve performance, enabling LLMs to double-check their answers and often correct flawed reasoning steps. We will review recent studies in conversational search, e.g., [48] use reasoning to improve query rewriting.

**Search Result Reflection in Conversations [10 min].** We will discuss how to automatically evaluate ranking quality of conversational search systems. Recent studies have explored using LLMs to automatically generate relevance judgments for search results produced by these systems [2,3,24]. The resulting automatic evaluations can then be used to trigger the refinement of search results.

**Interleaving Search and Reasoning in Conversations [30 min]** . Our tutorial will mainly focus on the recently widely investigated agentic paradigm of interleaving search and reasoning [15,20,38], in which large language models (LLMs) perform planning, execute dynamic retrieval, and examine retrieved results in an autonomous and interactive manner. We will discuss two main approaches:

- Prompt-based methods. E.g., [17] prompts LLMs to use search engines.
- Reinforcement learning (RL)-based methods. E.g., [15,38] apply RL to train LLMs to use search engines dynamically during multi-step reasoning. [20] has also explored this paradigm in conversational scenarios.

**Summary and Discussion with the Audience [15 min].** We will summarize the key topics covered and outline promising future research directions.

## 3   Target Audience and Prerequisites

This tutorial targets a broad audience with varying familiarity with IR, LLMs, and conversational systems. For participants with prior IR knowledge, it offers an opportunity to extend their expertise toward LLM-integrated and agentic search. Attendees are expected to have a basic understanding of machine learning, deep learning, and core IR concepts such as indexing, relevance modeling, and evaluation metrics. The tutorial will remain self-contained, providing sufficient background to ensure accessibility to all participants.

## 4   Tutorial History

This tutorial is a continuation of the tutorial "Conversational Search: From Fundamentals to Frontiers in the LLM Era" presented at SIGIR 2025 [32],[1] which introduced recent advances in conversational search driven by LLMs. The previous tutorial attracted about 30 participants. This tutorial differs from the previous one in two main ways: First, we significantly expand the content to cover recent advances in agentic conversational search systems [41], such as reflection, and the interleaving of search and reasoning in conversations. Second, we have refined the proposal structure based on feedback from the previous presentation.

In addition, several tutorials on related topics have been presented in recent years, including (i) "Conversational Information Seeking: Theory and Application" at SIGIR 2022 [10], (ii) "Conversational Information Seeking: Theory and Evaluation" at CHIIR 2022 [6], (iii) "Interactive Information Retrieval: Models, Algorithms, and Evaluation" at SIGIR 2021 [46], and (iv) "Recent Advances in Conversational Information Retrieval" at SIGIR 2020 [12]. Unlike the earlier tutorials conducted before the emergence of LLMs, our tutorial focuses on bridging the fundamentals of conversational search with new research frontiers enabled by LLMs and agents.

Although some recent tutorials [11,18] have discussed the use of conversational agents in the LLM era, they primarily address general proactive dialogue systems (e.g., for task completion) rather than search-oriented systems.

---

[1] The website and slides are available at https://convsearch.github.io/.

## 5    Tutorial Materials

A comprehensive set of supporting materials will be disseminated in advance, including slides, references, and links to public code, demos, checkpoints and datasets. These resources will be hosted on a dedicated GitHub repository and website several weeks before the conference. Portions of the content are supported by a recent survey authored by the organizers [30].

**Acknowledgments.** This research was partially supported by the Engineering and Physical Sciences Research Council (EPSRC) grant EP/V025708/1.

**Disclosure of Interests.** The authors declare that they have no competing interests.

## References


1. Abbasiantaeb, Z., Lupart, S., Azzopardi, L., Dalton, J., Aliannejadi, M.: Conversational gold: evaluating personalized conversational search system using gold nuggets. SIGIR (2025)
2. Abbasiantaeb, Z., Meng, C., Azzopardi, L., Aliannejadi, M.: Can we use large language models to fill relevance judgment holes? (2024)
3. Abbasiantaeb, Z., Meng, C., Azzopardi, L., Aliannejadi, M.: Improving the reusability of conversational search test collections (2025)
4. Aliannejadi, M., Abbasiantaeb, Z., Chatterjee, S., Dalton, J., Azzopardi, L.: Trec ikat 2023: a test collection for evaluating conversational and interactive knowledge assistants. In: SIGIR, pp. 819–829 (2024)
5. Aliannejadi, M., Kiseleva, J., Chuklin, A., Dalton, J., Burtsev, M.: Building and evaluating open-domain dialogue corpora with clarifying questions. In: EMNLP, pp. 4473–4484 (2021)
6. Aliannejadi, M., Trippas, J.R.: Conversational information seeking: Theory and evaluation: Chiir 2022 half day tutorial. In: CHIIR (2022)
7. Aliannejadi, M., Zamani, H., Crestani, F., Croft, W.B.: Asking clarifying questions in open-domain information-seeking conversations. In: SIGIR, pp. 475–484 (2019)
8. Askari, A., Meng, C., Aliannejadi, M., Ren, Z., Kanoulas, E., Verberne, S.: Generative retrieval with few-shot indexing. In: ECIR (2026)
9. Cheng, Y., et al.: Coral: benchmarking multi-turn conversational retrieval-augmentation generation. In: NAACL (2024)
10. Dalton, J., et al.: Conversational information seeking: theory and application. In: SIGIR, pp. 3455–3458 (2022)
11. Deng, Y., Lei, W., Huang, M., Chua, T.S.: Rethinking conversational agents in the era of llms: proactivity, non-collaborativity, and beyond. In: SIGIR (2023)
12. Gao, J., Xiong, C., Bennett, P.: Recent advances in conversational information retrieval. In: SIGIR, pp. 2421–2424 (2020)
13. Gao, J., Xiong, C., Bennett, P., Craswell, N.: Neural approaches to conversational information retrieval. arXiv:2201.05176 (2022)
14. Gong, P., Li, J., Mao, J.: Cosearchagent: a lightweight collaborative search agent with large language models. In: SIGIR, pp. 2729–2733 (2024)
15. Jin, B., et al.: Search-r1: training LLMs to reason and leverage search engines with reinforcement learning. In: COLM (2025)

16. Katsis, Y., et al.: Mtrag: a multi-turn conversational benchmark for evaluating retrieval-augmented generation systems. arXiv:2501.03468 (2025)
17. Li, X., et al.: Search-o1: agentic search-enhanced large reasoning models. arXiv preprint arXiv:2501.05366 (2025)
18. Liao, L., Yang, G.H., Shah, C.: Proactive conversational agents in the post-chatgpt world. In: SIGIR, pp. 3452–3455 (2023)
19. Lin, S.C., Yang, J.H., Lin, J.: Contextualized query embeddings for conversational search. In: EMNLP, pp. 1004–1015 (2021)
20. Lupart, S., Aliannejadi, M., Kanoulas, E.: Chatr1: reinforcement learning for conversational reasoning and retrieval augmented question answering. arXiv preprint arXiv:2510.13312 (2025)
21. Mao, K., Dou, Z., Chen, H., Mo, F., Qian, H.: Large language models know your contextual search intent: a prompting framework for conversational search. In: EMNLP (2023)
22. Meng, C., Aliannejadi, M., de Rijke, M.: System initiative prediction for multi-turn conversational information seeking. In: CIKM (2023)
23. Meng, C., Arabzadeh, N., Askari, A., Aliannejadi, M., de Rijke, M.: Query performance prediction using relevance judgments generated by large language models. TOIS **43**(4), 1–35 (2025)
24. Meng, C., Faggioli, G., Aliannejadi, M., Ferro, N., Mothe, J.: QPP++ 2025: query performance prediction and its applications in the era of large language models. In: ECIR, pp. 319–325 (2025)
25. Meng, C., Liu, J., Aliannejadi, M., Mo, F., Dalton, J., de Rijke, M.: Re-rankers as relevance judges. arXiv preprint arXiv:2601.04455 (2026)
26. Meng, C., Tonolini, F., Mo, F., Aletras, N., Yilmaz, E., Kazai, G.: Bridging the gap: from ad-hoc to proactive search in conversations. In: SIGIR, pp. 64–74 (2025)
27. Mo, F., et al.: UniConv: unifying retrieval and response generation for large language models in conversations. In: ACL, pp. 6936–6949 (2025)
28. Mo, F., et al.: Leveraging historical information to boost retrieval-augmented generation in conversations. Inf. Process. Manag. **63**(2), 104449 (2026)
29. Mo, F., et al.: Towards adaptive personalized conversational information retrieval. In: CIKM (2025)
30. Mo, F., et al.: A survey of conversational search. TOIS **43**(6), 1–50 (2025)
31. Mo, F., Mao, K., Zhu, Y., Wu, Y., Huang, K., Nie, J.Y.: Convgqr: generative query reformulation for conversational search. In: ACL, p. 4998–5012 (2023)
32. Mo, F., Meng, C., Aliannejadi, M., Nie, J.Y.: Conversational search: from fundamentals to frontiers in the LLM era. In: SIGIR, pp. 4094–4097 (2025)
33. Mo, F., et al.: Learning to relate to previous turns in conversational search. In: SIGKDD (2023)
34. Mo, F., Yi, B., Mao, K., Qu, C., Huang, K., Nie, J.Y.: Convsdg: session data generation for conversational search. In: WWW (2024)
35. Mo, F., et al.: Convmix: a mixed-criteria data augmentation framework for conversational dense retrieval. arXiv preprint arXiv:2508.04001 (2025)
36. Mo, F., Zhao, L., Huang, K., Dong, Y., Huang, D., Nie, J.Y.: How to leverage personal textual knowledge for personalized conversational information retrieval. In: CIKM, pp. 3954–3958 (2024)
37. Radlinski, F., Craswell, N.: A theoretical framework for conversational search. In: CHIIR, pp. 117–126 (2017)
38. Song, H., et al.: R1-searcher: incentivizing the search capability in llms via reinforcement learning. arXiv preprint arXiv:2503.05592 (2025)

39. White, R.W., Shah, C.: Information Access in the Era of Generative AI. Springer, Heidelberg (2025)
40. Wu, Z., et al.: Conqrr: conversational query rewriting for retrieval with reinforcement learning. In: EMNLP, pp. 10000–10014 (2022)
41. Xi, Y., et al.: A survey of llm-based deep search agents: paradigm, optimization, evaluation, and challenges. arXiv preprint arXiv:2508.05668 (2025)
42. Yu, S., et al.: Few-shot generative conversational query rewriting. In: SIGIR, pp. 1933–1936 (2020)
43. Yu, S., Liu, Z., Xiong, C., Feng, T., Liu, Z.: Few-shot conversational dense retrieval. In: SIGIR, pp. 829–838 (2021)
44. Zamani, H., Dumais, S.T., Craswell, N., Bennett, P.N., Lueck, G.: Generating clarifying questions for information retrieval. In: WWW, pp. 418–428 (2020)
45. Zamani, H., Trippas, J.R., Dalton, J., Radlinski, F., et al.: Conversational information seeking. Found. Trends Inf. Retr. (2023)
46. Zhai, C.: Interactive information retrieval: models, algorithms, and evaluation. In: SIGIR, pp. 2444–2447 (2020)
47. Zhao, W.X., et al.: A survey of large language models, vol. 1, no. 2. arXiv preprint arXiv:2303.18223 (2023)
48. Zhu, C., Wang, S., Feng, R., Song, K., Qiu, X.: Convsearch-r1: enhancing query reformulation for conversational search with reasoning via reinforcement learning. arXiv preprint arXiv:2505.15776 (2025)
49. Zhu, Y., et al.: Large language models for information retrieval: a survey. arXiv:2308.07107 (2023)

# Economic Perspectives on Fairness in Information Retrieval

Chen Xu[2], Clara Rus[1(✉)], Yuanna Liu[1], Marleen de Jonge[1], Jun Xu[2], and Maarten de Rijke[1]

[1] University of Amsterdam, Amsterdam, The Netherlands
{c.a.rus,y.liu8,m.r.h.dejonge,m.derijke}@uva.nl
[2] Renmin University of China, Beijing, China
{xc_chen,junxu}@ruc.edu.cn

**Abstract.** Fairness-aware information retrieval (IR) systems have been receiving more attention. Numerous fairness metrics and algorithms have been proposed. The complexity of fairness and IR systems makes it challenging to provide a systematic summary of the progress that has been made. This complexity calls for a more structured framework to navigate future fairness-aware IR research directions. The field of economics has long explored fairness, offering a strong theoretical and empirical foundation. Its system-oriented perspective enables the integration of IR fairness into a broader framework that considers societal and intertemporal trade-offs. In this tutorial, we first highlight that IR systems can be understood as a specialized economic market. Then, we reorganize fairness algorithms into an economic framework, which consists of three key economic dimensions: macro vs. micro, demand vs. supply, and short-term vs. long-term. We effectively view most fairness categories in IR from an economic perspective. Finally, we illustrate how this economic framework can be applied to various real-world IR applications and point out the future directions inspired by such a framework. Different from other fairness-aware tutorials, our tutorial not only provides a new and clear perspective to re-frame fairness-aware IR but also inspires the use of economic tools to solve fairness problems in IR. We hope this tutorial provides a fresh, broad perspective on fairness in IR, highlighting open problems and future research directions.

**Keywords:** Fairness · Economics · Information Retrieval

## 1 Motivation and Scope

### 1.1 Background on Fairness in IR

Information retrieval (IR) systems are designed to help users efficiently access information. However, IR systems such as search engines or recommender systems also influence and shape users' thoughts according to the given information [31]. This requires that IR systems should not only focus on accuracy, but also give attention to broader beyond-accuracy objectives such as fairness [22],


R. Campos et al. (Eds.): ECIR 2026, LNCS 16486, pp. 19–26, 2026.
https://doi.org/10.1007/978-3-032-21321-1_3

bias mitigation [5], and novelty [17] to promote a healthier ecosystem. Among these factors, fairness is crucial for IR systems as it ensures that the system does not discriminate against certain user groups [32] and provides more support for the long tail of valuable creators or item categories [33]. Although numerous fairness-aware IR algorithms have been proposed, they are categorized into more than ten distinct levels [11,20,39], including group vs. individual fairness [3], user vs. item fairness [32,33], static vs. dynamic fairness [40], and short-term v.s. long-term fairness [37]. Moreover, the measures of fairness also vary, such as max-min fairness [33], gini index [7], and demographic parity [29]. This complexity in categorization stems from the diverse definitions of fairness itself [28] and the involvement of multiple stakeholders, with distinct goals (e.g., users, items, platforms, creators) in IR [1]. This complexity makes it challenging for the IR community to systematically summarize the existing work and identify clear future research directions.

## 1.2   An Economic Perspective on Fairness in IR

Inspired by the field of economics, we can use established economic theory to systematically summarize and tackle complex fairness challenges in IR. In this tutorial, we first demonstrate that IR systems can be mapped to roles in a specialized economic market: users as consumers, items/documents as suppliers, and the platform as a central node, similar to the role of governments [36]. Specifically, in this market, users seek high-quality items, providers strive for maximum exposure of their products, and the platform aims to maximize profits and user satisfaction by delivering personalized services to users. Meanwhile, resources are limited (with a finite number of ranking slots), and the market price resembles the estimated ranking scores [4]. Given their shared structure, it is natural to bridge fairness issues in economics with those in IR systems.

**Benefits of Using an Economic Perspective.** The field of economics has long studied fairness, primarily focusing on how to allocate limited resources to best satisfy humans' unlimited desires [18,27]. Due to the established body of literature, an economic perspective on fairness offers a stronger theoretical and empirical foundation, allowing for a more structured analysis of complex fairness challenges in IR. Furthermore, the field of economics is concerned with interactions of different stakeholders in a system and analyzes the implications thereof over varying time spans. This systems-oriented thinking allows IR fairness to be embedded within a broader framework of societal and intertemporal trade-offs. By building on these well-established economic principles, fairness research in IR can benefit from greater coherence and avoid the proliferation of narrowly scoped or disconnected approaches.

**IR Fairness Framework from an Economic Perspective.** In this tutorial, we will elaborate on the following three economic dimensions: scale (macro vs. micro), objects (demand vs. supply), and time (long-term vs. short-term) of economic modeling to re-organize fairness-aware IR algorithms and evaluation methods. This perspective not only provides a novel and structured approach to reframing fairness-aware IR but also underscores the potential of applying economic principles and methodologies, such as game theory [25] and taxation theory [36], to rethink and tackle fairness challenges in IR systems.

## 2  Learning Objectives

Grounded in economic theory, this tutorial seeks to introduce and summarize fairness-aware IR from an economic perspective. By leveraging the well-established economic literature on fairness, we will systematically categorize and analyze fairness-related data, algorithms, and evaluation methodologies in IR, providing a unique perspective that not only deepens understanding but also identifies key open research directions for future exploration. Furthermore, this tutorial aims to equip attendees with economic insights to better comprehend and tackle broader trustworthy IR challenges beyond fairness, such as novelty, diversity, and interpretability. By drawing parallels between IR systems and economic markets, we hope to provide a fresh perspective that enables participants to design more equitable and transparent IR systems.

## 3  Scope

The tutorial will cover basic notions of fairness proposed in the IR community, economic perspectives on (un)fairness mitigation and evaluation, and build bridges between the two, with a special focus on teaching participants about conceptual tools and resources from economics and their potential in IR. The tutorial will *not* cover the long histories of fairness in either field nor offer a comprehensive side-by-side comparison of the many notions of fairness proposed in either field.

## 4  Relevance

Given the increasing importance and urgency of developing fair and trustworthy IR systems, we believe this is the right time to present a tutorial that helps researchers and industry practitioners consolidate current advancements and explore future directions in fairness-aware IR systems, especially in the era of LLMs. Moreover, our tutorial offers a fresh, well-structured perspective on emerging fairness issues in IR, enabling participants to develop a deeper understanding of these challenges while gaining economic insights to address them effectively in future research. This tutorial is highly relevant to the core themes of ECIR, with a specific focus on Fairness, Accountability, Transparency, Ethics, and Explainability (FATE) in IR, poised to inspire advancements in other trustworthy associated web applications.

## 5   Format

The tutorial will be a mixture of lectures, interactive demonstrations based on the FairDiverse environment [34], and Q&A sessions.

## 6   Length

The tutorial is 3 h (half day).

## 7   Detailed Outline

The outline for this tutorial is as follows:

**00:00–00:20** Introduction
- Introduction of information retrieval systems.
- Introduction of fairness definition.
- Taxonomy for fairness in IR.
- Organization of the tutorial.

**00:20–00:50** An Economic View on Fairness in IR (Chen)
- Introduction of economics.
- Introduction of fairness in economics.
- Relating IR systems to the economic markets.
- Re-framing fairness in IR through economics.

- **00:50–01:00** Q&A

- **01:00–01:30** Economic-based Fairness Mitigation and Evaluation Strategies I
- Objective: demand vs. supply
    - Demand (user) fairness [19,21,29].
    - Supply (provider) fairness [6,33,35,36].
    - Economic tools: taxation [36].

**Break, with Q&A**

**01:30–02:00** Economic-based Fairness Mitigation and Evaluation Strategies II
- Scale: macro vs. micro
    - Micro (individual) fairness [30].
    - Macro (group or amortized) fairness [3,24,33,35].
    - Economic tools: game theory [2].

**02:00–02:30** Economic-based Fairness Mitigation and Evaluation Strategies III
- Time: long-term vs. short-term
    - Long-term or dynamic fairness [13,37].
    - Short-term or static fairness [26,33].
    - Economic tools: risk theory [14].

**02:30–02:50** Open Problems, Future Directions, and Conclusions
- Ignoring fairness problems in the IR markets.
- Benchmarks and evaluation.
- Conclusions.

**02:50–03:00** Q&A

## 8   Target Audience

This tutorial explores fairness in IR from an economic standpoint, making it valuable for researchers, practitioners, and students interested in fairness, bias, and trustworthiness in IR systems such as search and recommendation, as well as for those investigating the economic dimensions of IR. It assumes only a basic understanding of IR and fairness, with no prior knowledge of economics required. The tutorial introduces essential economic concepts, such as taxation and interest rates, through clear, intuitive examples to ensure accessibility and understanding. Our goal is for the audience to learn how to apply economic frameworks and tools to understand fairness issues, and to extend this perspective to broader challenges such as bias and misinformation.

## 9   Tutorial History

We presented an earlier version of the tutorial at SIGIR 2025, with more than 30 people attending. The tutorial slides and materials are provided on the website https://economic-fairness-ir.github.io/. Compared to this earlier version, the current tutorial has been updated to include the latest research on unfairness [15,16,38] presented at recent conferences such as SIGIR and KDD. We have also added more economic examples to clarify key concepts and algorithms.

## 10   Related Tutorials

For fairness-aware IR, several related tutorials have emerged, including **Recsys'19, SIGIR'19** [9], considering fairness mainly from user study and evaluation perspective, **Recsys'20** [12], proposing different strategies to mitigate and evaluate unfairness in IR, **SIGIR'21** [23], proposing a taxonomy on fairness-aware algorithms in recommender systems, **CIKM'22** [10], focusing on a fairness taxonomy for search systems from the machine learning perspective and **ECIR'25** [8] providing a concise roadmap to fairness in information retrieval. The key distinction of our tutorial is that we organize the body of knowledge on fairness in IR through the structured lens of economics. This unique perspective not only provides a more systematic way to understand fairness in IR but also introduces economic tools for designing fair IR systems.

## 11   Materials

**Slides and Bibliography.** The slides and a bibliography file will be released on the tutorial website https://economic-fairness-ir.github.io/.

**Related Benchmark.** We provide a benchmark that introduced fairness-aware IR algorithms, evaluation metrics, and datasets [34], available on https://github.com/XuChen0427/FairDiverse.

**Acknowledgments.** This work was funded by the National Natural Science Foundation of China (No. 62472426). This research was (partially) supported by the Dutch Research Council (NWO), under project numbers 024.004.022, NWA.1389.20.183, and KICH3.LTP.20.006, and the European Union's Horizon Europe program under grant agreements No. 101070212 (FINDHR) and No. 101201510 (UNITE). All content represents the opinion of the authors, which is not necessarily shared or endorsed by their respective employers and/or sponsors.

**Disclosure of Interests.** The authors have no competing interests to declare that are relevant to the content of this article.

# References


1. Abdollahpouri, H., et al.: Multistakeholder recommendation: survey and research directions. User Model. User-Adap. Inter. **30**(1), 127–158 (2020). https://doi.org/10.1007/s11257-019-09256-1
2. Ben-Porat, O., Tennenholtz, M.: A game-theoretic approach to recommendation systems with strategic content providers. Adv. Neural Inf. Process. Syst. **31** (2018)
3. Biega, A.J., Gummadi, K.P., Weikum, G.: Equity of attention: amortizing individual fairness in rankings. In: The 41st International ACM SIGIR Conference on Research & Development in Information Retrieval, pp. 405–414 (2018)
4. Calvano, E., Calzolari, G., Denicolo, V., et al.: Economics of recommender systems. In: Proceedings of the 18th ACM Conference on Recommender Systems, RecSys '24, pp. 1279–1280 (2024)
5. Dai, S., Xu, C., Xu, S., et al.: Bias and unfairness in information retrieval systems: new challenges in the LLM era. In: Proceedings of the 30th ACM SIGKDD Conference on Knowledge Discovery and Data Mining, pp. 6437–6447 (2024)
6. Do, V., Corbett-Davies, S., Atif, J., et al.: Two-sided fairness in rankings via lorenz dominance. Adv. Neural. Inf. Process. Syst. **34**, 8596–8608 (2021)
7. Do, V., Usunier, N.: Optimizing generalized gini indices for fairness in rankings. In: Proceedings of the 45th International ACM SIGIR Conference on Research and Development in Information Retrieval, pp. 737–747 (2022)
8. Ekstrand, M.D.: Fairness in information access conceptual foundations and new directions. In: Advances in Information Retrieval: 47th European Conference on Information Retrieval, Part V, pp. 262–265. Springer, Heidelberg (2025). https://doi.org/10.1007/978-3-031-88720-8_41
9. Ekstrand, M.D., Burke, R., Diaz, F.: Fairness and discrimination in retrieval and recommendation. In: Proceedings of the 42nd International ACM SIGIR Conference on Research and Development in Information Retrieval, pp. 1403–1404 (2019)
10. Fang, Y., Liu, H., Tao, Z., et al.: Fairness of machine learning in search engines. In: Proceedings of the 31st ACM International Conference on Information & Knowledge Management, pp. 5132–5135 (2022)
11. Fang, Y., Singh, A., Tao, Z., et al.: Fairness in search systems. Found. Trends Inf. Retr. **18**(3), 262–416 (2024)

12. Gao, R., Shah, C.: Counteracting bias and increasing fairness in search and recommender systems. In: Proceedings of the 14th ACM Conference on Recommender Systems, pp. 745–747 (2020)
13. Ge, Y., Liu, S., Gao, R., Xian, Y., Li, Y., Zhao, X., et al.: Towards long-term fairness in recommendation. In: Proceedings of the 14th ACM International Conference on Web Search and Data Mining, pp. 445–453 (2021)
14. Grandell, J.: Aspects of Risk Theory. Springer, Heidelberg (2012)
15. Guo, H., Sun, Z., Wang, D., et al.: Enhancing new-item fairness in dynamic recommender systems. In: Proceedings of the 48th International ACM SIGIR Conference on Research and Development in Information Retrieval, pp. 1707–1716 (2025)
16. Gupta, A., Henzinger, T.A., Kueffner, K., et al.: Monitoring robustness and individual fairness. In: Proceedings of the 31st ACM SIGKDD Conference on Knowledge Discovery and Data Mining, vol. 2, pp. 790–801 (2025)
17. Hurley, N., Zhang, M.: Novelty and diversity in top-n recommendation-analysis and evaluation. ACM Trans. Internet Technol. **10**(4), 1–30 (2011)
18. Hurwicz, L.: The design of mechanisms for resource allocation. Am. Econ. Rev. **63**(2), 1–30 (1973)
19. Li, Y., Chen, H., Fu, Z., et al.: User-oriented fairness in recommendation. In: Proceedings of the Web Conference, pp. 624–632 (2021)
20. Li, Y., et al.: Fairness in recommendation: foundations, methods, and applications. ACM Trans. Intell. Syst. Technol. **14**(5), 1–48 (2023)
21. Li, Y., Chen, H., Xu, S., Ge, Y., Zhang, Y.: Towards personalized fairness based on causal notion. In: Proceedings of the 44th International ACM SIGIR Conference on Research and Development in Information Retrieval, pp. 1054–1063 (2021)
22. Li, Y., Du, M., Song, R., Wang, X., Wang, Y.: A survey on fairness in large language models. arXiv preprint arXiv:2308.10149 (2023)
23. Li, Y., Ge, Y., Zhang, Y.: Tutorial on fairness of machine learning in recommender systems. In: Proceedings of the 44th International ACM SIGIR Conference on Research and Development in Information Retrieval, pp. 2654–2657 (2021)
24. Naghiaei, M., Rahmani, H.A., Deldjoo, Y.: Cpfair: personalized consumer and producer fairness re-ranking for recommender systems. arXiv preprint arXiv:2204.08085 (2022)
25. Owen, G.: Game Theory. Emerald Group Publishing (2013)
26. Patro, G.K., Biswas, A., Ganguly, N., et al.: FairRec: two-sided fairness for personalized recommendations in two-sided platforms. In: Proceedings of the Web Conference, pp. 1194–1204 (2020)
27. Ramsey, F.P.: A contribution to the theory of taxation. Econ. J. **37**(145), 47–61 (1927)
28. Rawls, J.: Justice as fairness. Phil. Rev. **67**(2), 164–194 (1958)
29. Rus, C., Yates, A., de Rijke, M.: A study of pre-processing fairness intervention methods for ranking people. In: European Conference on Information Retrieval, pp. 336–350. Springer, Heidelberg (2024). https://doi.org/10.1007/978-3-031-56066-8_26
30. Saito, Y., Joachims, T.: Fair ranking as fair division: impact-based individual fairness in ranking. In: Proceedings of the 28th ACM SIGKDD Conference on Knowledge Discovery and Data Mining, pp. 1514–1524 (2022)
31. Stray, J., Halevy, A., Assar, P., et al.: Building human values into recommender systems: an interdisciplinary synthesis. ACM Trans. Recommend. Syst. **2**(3), 1–57 (2024)

32. Wang, L., Joachims, T.: User fairness, item fairness, and diversity for rankings in two-sided markets. In: Proceedings of the 2021 ACM SIGIR International Conference on Theory of Information Retrieval, pp. 23–41 (2021)
33. Xu, C., Chen, S., Xu, J., et al.: P-MMF: provider max-min fairness re-ranking in recommender system. In: Proceedings of the ACM Web Conference 2023, pp. 3701–3711 (2023)
34. Xu, C., Deng, Z., Rus, C., et al.: FairDiverse: a comprehensive toolkit for fair and diverse information retrieval algorithms (2025)
35. Xu, C., Xu, J., Ding, Y., et al.: FairSync: ensuring amortized group exposure in distributed recommendation retrieval. In: Proceedings of the ACM Web Conference 2024, WWW '24, pp. 1092–1102 (2024)
36. Xu, C., Ye, X., Wang, W., et al.: A taxation perspective for fair re-ranking. In: Proceedings of the 47th International ACM SIGIR Conference on Research and Development in Information Retrieval, pp. 1494–1503 (2024)
37. Xu, C., Ye, X., Xu, J., et al.: LTP-MMF: towards long-term provider max-min fairness under recommendation feedback loops. arXiv preprint arXiv:2308.05902 (2023)
38. Xu, C., Zhao, J., Wang, W., et al.: Understanding accuracy-fairness trade-offs in re-ranking through elasticity in economics. In: Proceedings of the 48th International ACM SIGIR Conference on Research and Development in Information Retrieval, pp. 539–548 (2025)
39. Zehlike, M., Yang, K., Stoyanovich, J.: Fairness in ranking, part ii: learning-to-rank and recommender systems. ACM Comput. Surv. **55**(6), 1–41 (2022)
40. Zhu, Z., He, Y., Zhao, X., et al.: Popularity bias in dynamic recommendation. In: Proceedings of the 27th ACM SIGKDD Conference on Knowledge Discovery & Data Mining, pp. 2439–2449 (2021)

# Tutorial on Reasoning for IR & IR for Reasoning


Mohanna Hoveyda[1(✉)], Panagiotis Eustratiadis[2], Arjen P. de Vries[1], and Maarten de Rijke[2]

[1] Radboud University, Nijmegen, Netherlands
{mohanna.hoveyda,arjen.devries}@ru.nl
[2] University of Amsterdam, Amsterdam, Netherlands
{p.efstratiadis,m.derijke}@uva.nl



**Abstract.** Information retrieval has long focused on ranking documents by semantic relatedness. Yet many real-world information needs demand more: enforcement of logical constraints, multi-step inference, and synthesis of multiple pieces of evidence. Addressing these requirements is, at its core, a problem of *reasoning*. Across AI communities, researchers are developing diverse solutions for the problem of reasoning, from inference-time strategies and post-training of LLMs, to neuro-symbolic systems, Bayesian and probabilistic frameworks, geometric representations, and energy-based models. These efforts target the same problem: to move beyond pattern-matching systems toward structured, verifiable inference. However, they remain scattered across disciplines, making it difficult for IR researchers to identify the most relevant ideas and opportunities. To help navigate the fragmented landscape of research in reasoning, this tutorial first articulates a working definition of reasoning within the context of information retrieval and derives from it a unified analytical framework. The framework maps existing approaches along axes that reflect the core components of the definition. By providing a comprehensive overview of recent approaches and mapping current methods onto the defined axes, we expose their trade-offs and complementarities, highlight where IR can benefit from cross-disciplinary advances, and illustrate how retrieval process itself can play a central role in broader reasoning systems. The tutorial will equip participants with both a conceptual framework and practical guidance for enhancing reasoning-capable IR systems, while situating IR as a domain that both benefits and contributes to the broader development of reasoning methodologies.


## 1 Motivation

While dense and generative models excel at semantic matching across queries and documents, real-world information needs often demand reasoning: enforcing negation [32,43], exclusion [51], composing sets [27], and synthesizing (conflicting) evidence across various sources remain difficult for neural retrievers despite advances [12]. Recent IR benchmarks contain queries that expose clear empirical weaknesses of current retrieval systems [6,21,37].



R. Campos et al. (Eds.): ECIR 2026, LNCS 16486, pp. 27–34, 2026.
https://doi.org/10.1007/978-3-032-21321-1_4

In parallel, theoretical findings indicate that embedding-based retrieval methods, despite their empirical success, are subject to intrinsic representational limits, that may not be alleviated by pure scale of model and/or data size [42]. Large language models (LLMs), though often regarded as general-purpose reasoning systems and used as an alternative to transcend such limitations through generative reasoning, nonetheless exhibit persistent weaknesses in grounding and inference control, with outputs frequently lacking evidential support [20]. Considered together, these results suggest that information retrieval is reaching the limits of pattern-matching systems. In various subfields of AI, building models that can perform *reasoning* has once again attracted significant attention.

Inference-time strategies seek to elicit structured 'thinking' from LLMs, through chain-of-thought and iterative refinement [25,41,48]. Reinforcement learning (RL) has been explored as a mechanism to induce and regulate reasoning in LLMs, by defining reward signals over intermediate derivations, aligning model trajectories with human or automated preferences, and coupling language generation with structured search and planning procedures [19,30]. Neuro-symbolic approaches couple statistical generalization with formal inference [29]. Probabilistic and Bayesian frameworks cast reasoning as inference under uncertainty [31]. Some other line of work focuses on alternative representation spaces, using non-Euclidean embeddings to capture hierarchical structure [5] or compositional representations to model Boolean operations in queries [26]. Lastly, energy-based formulations interpret reasoning as iterative optimization in latent space [10]. These directions offer avenues with distinct strengths, but the approaches remain fragmented across disciplines. They highlight aspects of the reasoning problem, making it essential to connect them within a bigger picture of how representations, inference mechanisms, and learning signals interact.

IR both benefits from and contributes to this momentum. It provides a natural testbed where reasoning models must operate at scale, ground their steps in external evidence, and be judged by rigorous evaluation. The goal of this tutorial is to consolidate reasoning methodologies into a coherent framework for IR, and to show how IR can serve not only as a beneficiary but also as a useful ground for increasingly robust reasoning architectures.

## 2   Learning Objectives

The tutorial is designed to provide a conceptual overview of and practical guidance into reasoning for IR. Specifically, participants will be able to:

1. Identify the requirements of complex IR tasks, including negation, exclusion, set composition, temporal constraints, and multi-hop evidence synthesis, as well as an overview of applicable benchmarks.
2. Understand the main methodological families for reasoning: (i) *LLM-based (including inference-time strategies, and reinforcement learning approaches), (ii) neuro-symbolic integration, (iii) probabilistic frameworks, (iv) alternative representation spaces and optimization approaches.*

3. Compare methods along three axes: (i) *representational adequacy,* (ii) *mechanisms of inference and learning,* and (iii) *computational viability for IR.* They can consequently analyze trade-offs between approaches with respect to requirements of an IR system.
4. Apply the conceptual framework introduced in the tutorial to propose novel solutions for IR and recognize opportunities where IR can enhance the development of more general reasoning architectures.

## 3    Scope

The area to be covered is broad and touches on many sub-discipliens in IR and AI. Since the topics covered are broad and technically diverse, the tutorial will not aim for exhaustive coverage of each reasoning method and its use or potential in or with IR, but rather to provide participants with an overarching view of the challenges and the research possibilities. Slides and reference materials will be shared with participants so as to help them to continue to explore the area.

## 4    Relevance

Recent IR benchmarks expose clear weaknesses of current models in handling complex user queries. Meanwhile, advances in LLM-based and neuro-symbolic, and other alternative approaches to reasoning remain scattered across fields, limiting their practical uptake in IR. This tutorial unifies these developments within a coherent analytical framework, clarifying how reasoning can be defined, modeled, and evaluated in IR and and helping researchers identify transferable methods and understand their trade-offs.

## 5    Tutorial Format

The format is primarily lecture-style, organized in four main blocks (see the detailed outline below), but will include interactive polls and short Q&A slots after each block to encourage engagement.

## 6    Detailed Outline

We will teach a half-day (3 h) tutorial, aligned with the two breaks organized by the conference. The tutorial will be organized in four main blocks:

### 6.1    Introduction (15 Minutes)

Why reasoning is central to information retrieval; overview of tutorial's objectives, structure, and relevance to IR community.

## 6.2   Reasoning: Definition and Its Challenges in IR (30 Minutes)

(1) Definition of reasoning in IR.
(2) Empirical and theoretical challenges:
  (a) *Tasks and datasets:* NevIR [12,32,43]; ExcluIR [51]; QUEST [27]; BRIGHT [37]; BrowseComp-Plus [6]; complex retrieval tasks [21].
  (b) *Limits of current systems:* theoretical limits of embedding-based retrieval [42]; taxonomy for negation [32]; LLM hallucinations [20].


## 6.3   Methodological Families (90 Minutes)

(1) *LLM inference-time strategies and optimization for reasoning*: Approaches that elicit or refine reasoning at LLMs' decode/test time, including chain-of-thought prompting [41], IRCoT for multi-step questions [38], Self-Refine for iterative self-feedback and revision [25], test-time adaptation/active fine-tuning [18], and implicit chain-of-thought without explicit prompts [40]. Complementary results link these behaviors to procedural knowledge acquired during pretraining of LLMs [35].
(2) *LLMs + RL*: Reinforcement learning (RL) has been increasingly explored as a means to incentivize and enhance reasoning in LLMs. Building on instruction-following models trained with human feedback [30], recent systems such as *DeepSeek-R1* [2] and *Search-R1* [19] use structured rewards and interaction with search or planning environments to promote step-wise reasoning. In parallel, complementary analyses question whether such RL-based fine-tuning genuinely improves reasoning ability beyond the pre-trained model [50], and examine the limits of language-based policy optimization [34].
(3) *Neuro-symbolic approaches:* Early efforts to ground IR in non-classical logic [39] offered a rigorous theoretical foundation but faced scalability and practical limitations. Recent work on reasoning explores use of symbolic solvers, provers and logic engines alongside neural components to enhance the reliability of inference in reasoning-intensive tasks [29]. LINC use the LLM as a semantic parser from natural language to first-order logic, delegating deductive inference to external theorem provers [29]. Other approaches target reasoning under uncertainty by prompting LLMs to produce formal representations (e.g., code, probabilistic logic) that can be executed or queried [28], or by synthesizing task-specific probabilistic formulations on demand to support bayesian inference for open-world cognition [44,45].
(4) *Probabilistic and Bayesian Frameworks*: This line of research approaches reasoning by explicitly modeling uncertainty and integrating Bayesian inference to achieve a probabilistic reasoning system [13,17,33,49].
(5) *Alternative representation spaces and optimization approaches:* Several works enhance the representation space for queries and documents to support explicit set/logic operations and hierarchical structure, including: Box-Embeddings [7], Set-Compositional [22], , and hyperbolic representation

spaces [5,9,46,47]. Complementarily, some alternative approaches model reasoning as iterative inference in latent space via energy-based optimization [10,14].

### 6.4 Bridging Current Methodologies & Future Directions (45 Minutes)

We first introduce our comparative framework and then map the discussed methods regarding to the framework's axes;

(1) *Representational adequacy*; to what extent the representation space encodes logical structures, hierarchies and uncertainty about predicates across the various approaches,
(2) *Mechanisms of inference verification and learning*; how inference and updates are applied over the representation space,
(3) *Computational viability for IR*; to what extent each of the reasoning frameworks can be applied in a high-scale real-world IR setting.

We end with a roadmap of open problems and research directions for reasoning in IR and leveraging IR within broader reasoning models.

## 7   Target Audience

The tutorial is designed for a broad audience within and beyond the IR community, with a focus on three groups: (i) *Early-career IR researchers and PhD students* who wish to tackle complex information needs (e.g., negation, set-composition, and multi-hop), and who are seeking conceptual frameworks to guide new research directions. (ii) *Applied researchers and practitioners* in search, recommendation, or conversational systems who want to enhance the robustness of their products in edge cases where current semantic-matching approaches fail. (iii) *Researchers from related fields* (e.g., NLP, ML, knowledge representation) who are interested in how diverse reasoning methodologies can be applied to IR and, conversely, how IR can serve general reasoning models. We assume familiarity with modern IR models, but no prior expertise in formal logic or specialized representations/optimization approaches, remaining accessible to newcomers yet technically engaging for experts.

## 8   Tutorial History and Related Events

This tutorial is new and prepared exclusively for ECIR 2026. Relevant past events with a reasoning theme across various venues in IR, NLP, and AI include:

(1) EMNLP'20: Machine Reasoning: Technology, Dilemma and Future [11]
(2) ECIR'23: Neuro-Symbolic Approaches for Information Retrieval [8]
(3) ACL'23: Complex Reasoning in Natural Language [52]

(4) AAAI'23: Advances in Neuro-Symbolic Reasoning and Learning [36]
(5) KDD'23: Knowledge Graph Reasoning and Its Applications [24]

Alongside the enumerated tutorials, several existing surveys on reasoning in LLMs, RL, optimization-based formulations, geometric representations, and logic-based IR will inform the content of this tutorial [1,3,4,15,16,23]. In contrast to prior tutorials, we define reasoning specifically within the context of IR and organize recent methodological advances into a unified analytical framework which connects developments across representation, inference and learning, and computational viability, providing a clear structure for analyzing, comparing, and developing reasoning-capable information access systems.

## 9   Materials

A dedicated website will contain slides, references, as well as pointers to libraries and experimental environments that help participants of our tutorial examine the area further. See https://reasoning-for-ir.github.io.

**Acknowledgements.** This research was (partially) supported by the Dutch Research Council (NWO), under project numbers 024.004.022, NWA.1389.20.183, and KICH3.LTP.20.006, and the European Union under grant agreements No. 101070212 (FINDHR) and No. 101201510 (UNITE). All content represents the opinion of the authors, not necessarily shared or endorsed by their respective employers and/or sponsors.

**Disclosure of Interests.** The authors have no competing interests to declare that are relevant to the content of this article.

## References

1. Abdulahhad, K., Berrut, C., Chevallet, J., Pasi, G.: Modeling information retrieval by formal logic: a survey. ACM Comput. Surv. (2019)
2. AI, D.: Deepseek-R1 incentivizes reasoning in LLMs through reinforcement learning. Nature (2025)
3. Carbone, D.: Hitchhiker's guide on the relation of energy-based models with other generative models, sampling and statistical physics: a comprehensive review. TMLR (2025)
4. Casper, S., Davies, X., Shi, C., et al.: Open problems and fundamental limitations of reinforcement learning from human feedback. TMLR (2023)
5. Chen, W., Han, X., Lin, Y., et al.: Hyperbolic pre-trained language model. IEEE ACM Trans. Audio Speech Lang. Process (2024)
6. Chen, Z., Ma, X., Zhuang, S., et al.: Browsecomp-plus: a more fair and transparent evaluation benchmark of deep-research agent (2025). CoRR arxiv:2508.06600
7. Chheda, T., Goyal, P., Tran, T., et al.: Box embeddings: an open-source library for representation learning using geometric structures. In: EMNLP (2021)
8. Dietz, L., Bast, H., Chatterjee, S., et al.: Ecir 23 tutorial: neuro-symbolic approaches for information retrieval. In: ECIR (2023)

9. Dong, T., Jamnik, M., Liò, P.: Neural reasoning for sure through constructing explainable models. In: AAAI (2025)
10. Du, Y., Mao, J., Tenenbaum, J.B.: Learning iterative reasoning through energy diffusion. In: ICML (2024)
11. Duan, N., Tang, D., Zhou, M.: Machine reasoning: technology, dilemma and future. In: EMNLP (2020)
12. van den Elsen, C., Barkhof, F., Nijdam, T., et al.: Reproducing NevIR: negation in neural information retrieval. In: SIGIR 2025 (2025)
13. Feng, Y., Zhou, B., Lin, W., Roth, D.: BIRD: a trustworthy bayesian inference framework for large language models. In: ICLR (2025)
14. Gladstone, A., Nanduru, G., Islam, M.M., et al.: Energy-based transformers are scalable learners and thinkers (2025). CoRR arxiv:2507.02092
15. Hase, P., Hofweber, T., Zhou, X., Stengel-Eskin, E., Bansal, M.: Fundamental problems with model editing: how should rational belief revision work in LLMs? Trans. Mach. Learn. Res. (2024)
16. He, N., Madhu, H., Bui, N., et al.: Hyperbolic deep learning for foundation models: a survey. In: ACM SIGKDD (2025)
17. Hoffman, M.D., Phan, D., Dohan, D., Sothers: training chain-of-thought via latent-variable inference. In: NeurIPS (2023)
18. Hübotter, J., Bongni, S., Hakimi, I., Krause, A.: Efficiently learning at test-time: active fine-tuning of LLMs. In: Adaptive Foundation Models: Evolving AI for Personalized and Efficient Learning (2024)
19. Jin, B., Zeng, H., Yue, Z., et al.: Search-R1: training LLMs to reason and leverage search engines with reinforcement learning. In: COLM (2025)
20. Kalai, A.T., Nachum, O., Vempala, S.S., et al.: Why language models hallucinate (2025), CoRR arxiv:2509.04664
21. Killingback, J., Zamani, H.: Benchmarking information retrieval models on complex retrieval tasks (2025). CoRR arxiv:2509.07253
22. Krasakis, A.M., Yates, A., Kanoulas, E.: Constructing set-compositional and negated representations for first-stage ranking (2025). CoRR arxiv:2501.07679
23. Li, J., Fu, Y., Fan, L., et al.: Implicit reasoning in large language models: a comprehensive survey (2025). CoRR arxiv:2509.02350
24. Liu, L., Tong, H.: Knowledge graph reasoning and its applications. In: ACM SIGKDD (2023)
25. Madaan, A., Tandon, N., Gupta, P., et al.: Self-refine: iterative refinement with self-feedback. In: NeurIPS (2023)
26. Mai, Q., Gauch, S., Adams, D.: Setbert: enhancing retrieval performance for Boolean logic and set operation queries. In: NLPIR (2024)
27. Malaviya, C., Shaw, P., Chang, M.W., et al.: QUEST: a retrieval dataset of entity-seeking queries with implicit set operations. In: ACL (2023)
28. Nafar, A., Venable, K.B., Kordjamshidi, P.: Reasoning over uncertain text by generative large language models. In: AAAI (2025)
29. Olausson, T., Gu, A., Lipkin, B., et al.: Linc: a neurosymbolic approach for logical reasoning by combining language models with first-order logic provers. In: EMNLP (2023)
30. Ouyang, L., Wu, J., Jiang, X., et al.: Training language models to follow instructions with human feedback. In: NeurIPS (2022)
31. Paruchuri, A., Garrison, J., Liao, S., et al.: What are the odds? language models are capable of probabilistic reasoning. In: EMNLP (2024)
32. Petcu, R., Bhargav, S., de Rijke, M., et al.: A comprehensive taxonomy of negation for NLP and neural retrievers. In: EMNLP (2025)

33. Qiu, L., Sha, F., Allen, K.R., et al.: Bayesian teaching enables probabilistic reasoning in large language models (2025). CoRR arxiv:2503.17523
34. Ramamurthy, R., Ammanabrolu, P., Brantley, K., et al.: Is reinforcement learning (not) for natural language processing: benchmarks, baselines, and building blocks for natural language policy optimization. In: ICLR (2023)
35. Ruis, L., Mozes, M., Bae, J., et al.: Procedural knowledge in pretraining drives reasoning in large language models. In: ICLR (2025)
36. Shakarian, P., Simari, G.I., Baral, C., et al.: Advances in neuro-symbolic reasoning and learning: 2023 AAAI tutorial. In: AAAI (2023)
37. Su, H., Yen, H., Xia, M., et al.: BRIGHT: a realistic and challenging benchmark for reasoning-intensive retrieval. In: ICLR (2025)
38. Trivedi, H., Balasubramanian, N., Khot, T., et al.: Interleaving retrieval with chain-of-thought reasoning for knowledge-intensive multi-step questions. In: ACL (2023)
39. Van Rijsbergen, C.J.: A new theoretical framework for information retrieval. In: SIGIR Forum (1986)
40. Wang, X., Zhou, D.: Chain-of-thought reasoning without prompting. In: NeurIPS (2024)
41. Wei, J., Wang, X., Schuurmans, D., et al.: Chain-of-thought prompting elicits reasoning in large language models. In: NeurIPS (2022)
42. Weller, O., Boratko, M., Naim, I., Lee, J.: On the theoretical limitations of embedding-based retrieval (2025). CoRR arxiv:2508.21038
43. Weller, O., Lawrie, D.J., Durme, B.V.: Nevir: negation in neural information retrieval. In: EACL (2024)
44. Wong, L., Collins, K.M., Ying, L., et al.: Modeling open-world cognition as on-demand synthesis of probabilistic models (2025). CoRR arxiv:2507.12547
45. Wong, L., Grand, G., Lew, A.K., et al.: From word models to world models: translating from natural language to the probabilistic language of thought (2023). CoRR arxiv:2306.12672
46. Yang, M., Feng, A., Xiong, B., Liu, J., King, I., Ying, R.: Enhancing LLM complex reasoning capability through hyperbolic geometry. In: ICML 2024 Workshop on LLMs and Cognition (2024)
47. Yang, M., Feng, A., Xiong, B., Liu, J., King, I., Ying, R.: Hyperbolic fine-tuning for large language models (2024). CoRR arxiv:2410.04010
48. Yao, S., Yu, D., Zhao, J., et al.: Tree of thoughts: deliberate problem solving with large language models. In: NeurIPS (2023)
49. Yin, Z., Sun, Q., Guo, Q., et al.: Reasoning in flux: enhancing large language models reasoning through uncertainty-aware adaptive guidance. In: ACL (2024)
50. Yue, Y., Chen, Z., Lu, R., et al.: Does reinforcement learning really incentivize reasoning capacity in LLMs beyond the base model? In: AI for Math Workshop @ ICML 2025 (2025)
51. Zhang, W., Zhang, M., Wu, S., et al.: ExcluIR: exclusionary neural information retrieval. In: AAAI (2025)
52. Zhao, W., Geva, M., Lin, B.Y., et al.: Complex reasoning in natural language. In: ACL (2023)

# Neural Lexical Search with Learned Sparse Retrieval

Andrew Yates[1]($\boxtimes$), Carlos Lassance[2], Cosimo Rulli[3], Eugene Yang[1],
Sean MacAvaney[4], Siddharth A. K. Singh[5], Thong Nguyen[5], and Yibin Lei[5]

[1] Johns Hopkins University HLTCOE, Baltimore, MD, USA
`{andrew.yates,eugene.yang}@jhu.edu`
[2] Cohere, Grenoble, France
`carlos@cohere.com`
[3] ISTI-CNR, Pisa, Italy
`cosimo.rulli@isti.cnr.it`
[4] University of Glasgow, Glasgow, UK
`sean.macavaney@glasgow.ac.uk`
[5] University of Amsterdam, Amsterdam, The Netherlands
`{s.a.k.singh,t.nguyen2,y.lei}@uva.nl`


**Abstract.** Learned Sparse Retrieval (LSR) techniques use neural machinery to represent queries and documents as learned bags of words. In contrast with other neural retrieval techniques, such as generative retrieval and dense retrieval, LSR has been shown to be a remarkably robust, transferable, and efficient family of methods for retrieving high-quality search results. This half-day tutorial aims to provide an extensive overview of LSR, ranging from its fundamentals to the latest emerging techniques. By the end of the tutorial, attendees will be familiar with the important design decisions of an LSR model, know how to apply them to text and other modalities, and understand the latest techniques for retrieving with them efficiently. Website: https://lsr-tutorial.github.io.

**Keywords:** Learned Sparse Retrieval · First-stage Retrieval · Neural IR

## 1 Overview

Neural information retrieval approaches, which use deep learning to improve ranking based on the similarity of query and document content, have greatly improved search quality [32]. They have significantly facilitated the development of retrieval-augmented generation models [28,53], where performance is largely influenced by the effectiveness of retrieval [65]. These approaches can be divided into two categories: re-ranking methods that use a transformer to compare query and document text at query time and first-stage retrieval methods that produce document representations offline and store them in an index. Re-ranking methods use a pre-trained language model like BERT, T5, or ChatGPT to predict relevance scores at inference time, which is a slow but effective strategy [32,59]. First-stage retrieval methods produce query and document representations independently, so document representations can be pre-computed and only a query


R. Campos et al. (Eds.): ECIR 2026, LNCS 16486, pp. 35–43, 2026.
https://doi.org/10.1007/978-3-032-21321-1_5

representation needs to be computed at query time. While these methods are not as effective as re-ranking methods, they are substantially faster and often used to identify promising candidate documents to rerank in a later stage.

First-stage retrieval methods can be divided into generative ranking, dense retrieval, and learned sparse retrieval. *Generative retrieval* is an emerging approach in which document representations are stored in the transformer model itself, removing the need for a separate index but creating new efficiency and scalability challenges [30,51,60]. *Dense retrieval* methods, on the other hand, build dense, fixed-dimensional representations for each document, which are then indexed and retrieved over [25]. However, dense retrieval comes with several limitations. Retrieval does not scale without using approximation techniques like HNSW [38], dense representations can be costly in terms of storage [63], and the latent vector representations used are inherently challenging to interpret [24].

Learned Sparse Retrieval (LSR) techniques provide a solution to these problems by representing documents as sparse vectors, typically with dimensions that represent terms in a vocabulary, akin to traditional Bag-of-Words (BoW) models. However, unlike BoW models, LSR models learn representations' tokens [36] and weights [15] through training, allowing them to match semantically, as dense and generative retrieval models do. Moreover, their sparsity allows them to leverage efficient posting-list-based retrieval algorithms for fast, exact top-$k$ retrieval [26]. It has become clear that learned sparse retrieval is a competitive alternative to dense retrieval that comes with its own advantages, which motivates us to fill the gap by covering LSR in depth specifically. Furthermore, its integration into industry search products, such as OpenSearch and ElasticSearch, suggests that LSR has matured into a compelling family of neural retrieval models.

This tutorial covers LSR from its fundamentals to emerging topics for an intermediate audience. After the tutorial, attendees will understand the concepts behind learned sparse retrieval (LSR) and know how to apply it in practice. Specifically, attendees will learn to: (1) Compare LSR methods to other transformer-powered ranking methods; (2) Evaluate LSR methods using standard datasets and evaluation practices; (3) Describe the components of LSR methods, such as the choice of sparse encoders and sparse regularizers, and their associated design decisions; (4) Compare the impact of LSR methods' components in terms of effectiveness and efficiency; (5) Describe the design of state-of-the-art LSR methods; (6) Apply LSR to scenarios outside of monolingual text retrieval, such as multilingual and multimodal settings; (7) Describe how learned sparse representations can be stored in an inverted index for first-stage retrieval; (8) Describe strategies for improving the efficiency of retrieval from an inverted index; and (9) Understand hybrid approaches that further improve effectiveness by combining LSR methods with dense retrieval methods.

## 2   Topics and Schedule

### Part 1 (90 min) – Fundamentals

**Introduction to LSR [20 min].** To introduce LSR, we start with a definition of sparse retrieval. Sparse retrieval is characterized by representing queries and documents as a set of their terms (BoW) [56] and using probability-based methods [12,13] that score term matches independently from each other [55], with one famous example being BM25 [54]. The main advantage of this natural representation of documents is that it is effective at retrieving documents that have lexical matches to the query, which is a signal of relevance [57]. However, while lexical matching is a useful prior, it can be too restrictive, as it does not include synonyms, regionalisms and other different ways of expressing the same idea [22]. In an effort to fix this lexical mismatch, document and/or query expansion methods [14,19,50] have been proposed. Inspired by prior efforts to design both the scoring function and term expansion, LSR methods appeared as a way of learning scoring and expansion rather than defining heuristics (e.g., [21,36,66,70]).

**Datasets and Evaluation [10 min].** LSR approaches have most often been trained on the MSMARCO passage retrieval dataset [2], which consists of Web queries and passages. In-domain evaluation is typically with the MSMARCO query devset (small 6980 queries version) with the main metric being MRR@10 [62] or the TREC-DL tasks [10,11] that use the MSMARCO corpus. Out-of-domain, most experiments use the BEIR [61] benchmark, which is where LSR methods showcase their effectiveness, for example by greatly outperforming both BM25 and the dense retrieval methods of the time in [20].

**LSR Framework [25 min].** Learned sparse retrieval can be described as a framework [49] consisting of three primary components: a *sparse encoder*, a *sparse regularizer*, and a *supervision signal*. The sparse encoder projects raw queries and documents into the vocabulary space, generating lexical or bag-of-words representations. This encoder has two key properties: weighting and expansion. Weighting can either be learned or fixed [23,45] (e.g., BM25 and inference-free methods), while expansion can be learned, reused from existing methods, or omitted altogether. The *sparse regularizer* controls the sparsity of the lexical representation by approximating it through a differentiable weighted loss term. This component is crucial as it affects the size of the inverted index and the retrieval latency. Finally, the *supervision signal* refers to the techniques employed to train the LSR model, such as hard negative mining and distillation.

**Text LSR [25 min].** The previously introduced framework offers a foundation for analyzing various LSR methods from the literature. In the context of text retrieval, we will examine several prominent approaches, including SNRM [66], DeepImpact [39], EPIC [36], SPLADE [20,21], and UniCoil [31], through the unified lens of this framework. In this section, alongside discussing the differences between these methods, we will provide a quantitative analysis of how these distinctions impact the effectiveness and efficiency of LSR models.

**Initialization of LSR Methods [10 min].** For most of the previous work, LSR methods were initialized with encoder-only pretrained language models based on Masked Language Modeling (MLM) [21,36]. However, more recent LSR methods have shifted away from purely MLM-based models, using additional vocabulary [18,46], decoder-only auto-regressive models [27,52,67], or sparse-autoencoders [1]. We will discuss these different initialization choices.

### Part 2 (90 min) – Emerging Topics

**Multilingual LSR [20 min].** While common LSR methods like SPLADE are monolingual, other work has explored challenging multilingual settings in which the input text is not restricted to a single language [43,44,48]. In this setting, using a large multilingual vocabulary can substantially increase computational costs and introduce difficulties aligning representations across languages [43].

**Multimodal LSR [20 min].** Learned sparse representations typically use an English vocabulary that is tied to the underlying transformer model (e.g., a WordPiece vocabulary with BERT). This property means that representations are transparent, but it creates challenges in settings where the input data is not aligned with the vocabulary, such as in multimodal settings like image-caption retrieval. Approaches have been proposed to overcome the challenge of aligning images with textual representations, including distillation-based approaches that adapt existing dense retrieval methods and large-scale approaches that couple a large amount of training data with complex new architectures [9,35,47,68].

**Indexing and Efficient LSR [30 min].** Inverted Indexes are natural candidates for indexing and retrieving learned sparse representations, given the extensive research of them in Information Retrieval [16,17,33,37,40,41]. Yet, surprisingly, they are inefficient for retrieving sparse embeddings, as these embeddings do not meet some crucial assumptions [3,4]: 1) term frequencies following a Zipfian distribution and 2) queries being short. To improve efficiency, exact search is often traded for approximate methods. Graph-based solutions, adapted from dense embeddings, have shown success in the sparse domain, even winning the BigANN@NeurIPS competition in 2023. On the other hand, approximated Inverted Indexes tailored for sparse embeddings have been proposed [5,8,29,42]. Among them, we describe SEISMIC [5–7] as an illustration of an excellent efficiency/effectiveness trade-off.

**Hybrid Dense-Sparse Retrieval [20 min].** Beyond relying solely on learned sparse retrieval for document retrieval, recent works demonstrate that sparse and dense retrieval methods capture complementary relevance signals. In this section, we will review recent works that explore the fusion of dense and sparse representations in order to further improve effectiveness [34,58,64,69].

**Acknowledgments.** This research was (partly) supported by the Dutch Research Council (NWO) under project number VI.Vidi.223.166.

**Disclosure of Interests.** The authors have no competing interests to declare that are relevant to the content of this article.

# References


1. Anonymous: learning retrieval models with sparse autoencoders. In: Submitted to The Fourteenth International Conference on Learning Representations (2025). https://openreview.net/forum?id=TuFjICawSc
2. Bajaj, P., et al.: Ms marco: a human generated machine reading comprehension dataset. arXiv preprint arXiv:1611.09268 (2018)
3. Bruch, S., Nardini, F.M., Ingber, A., Liberty, E.: An approximate algorithm for maximum inner product search over streaming sparse vectors. ACM Trans. Inf. Syst. **42**(2), 1–43 (2023)
4. Bruch, S., Nardini, F.M., Ingber, A., Liberty, E.: Bridging dense and sparse maximum inner product search. ACM Trans. Inf. Syst. (2024)
5. Bruch, S., Nardini, F.M., Rulli, C., Venturini, R.: Efficient inverted indexes for approximate retrieval over learned sparse representations. In: Proceedings of the 47th International ACM SIGIR Conference on Research and Development in Information Retrieval, pp. 152–162 (2024)
6. Bruch, S., Nardini, F.M., Rulli, C., Venturini, R.: Pairing clustered inverted indexes with knn graphs for fast approximate retrieval over learned sparse representations. arXiv preprint arXiv:2408.04443 (2024)
7. Bruch, S., Nardini, F.M., Rulli, C., Venturini, R., Venuta, L.: Investigating the scalability of approximate sparse retrieval algorithms to massive datasets. In: European Conference on Information Retrieval, pp. 437–445. Springer, Heidelberg (2025). https://doi.org/10.1007/978-3-031-88714-7_43
8. Carlson, P., Xie, W., He, S., Yang, T.: Dynamic superblock pruning for fast learned sparse retrieval. In: Proceedings of the 48th International ACM SIGIR Conference on Research and Development in Information Retrieval, pp. 3004–3009 (2025)
9. Chen, C., et al.: STAIR: learning sparse text and image representation in grounded tokens. In: Proceedings of the 2023 Conference on Empirical Methods in Natural Language Processing (2023)
10. Craswell, N., Mitra, B., Yilmaz, E., Campos, D., Voorhees, E.M.: Overview of the trec 2019 deep learning track. arXiv preprint arXiv:2003.07820 (2020)
11. Craswell, N., Mitra, B., Yilmaz, E., Campos, D., Voorhees, E.M.: Overview of the trec 2020 deep learning track. arXiv preprint arXiv:2102.07662 (2021)
12. Crestani, F., Lalmas, M., Van Rijsbergen, C.J., Campbell, I.: "is this document relevant?...probably": a survey of probabilistic models in information retrieval. ACM Comput. Surv. **30**(4) (1998)
13. Croft, W.B.: Document representation in probabilistic models of information retrieval. J. Am. Soc. Inf. Sci. **32**(6) (1981)

14. Croft, W.B., Harper, D.J.: Probabilistic models of document retrieval with relevance information. J. Document. **35**(4), 285–295 (1979)
15. Dai, Z., Callan, J.: Context-aware document term weighting for ad-hoc search. In: Proceedings of the Web Conference 2020 (2020)
16. Dimopoulos, C., Nepomnyachiy, S., Suel, T.: Optimizing top-k document retrieval strategies for block-max indexes. In: Proceedings of the Sixth ACM International Conference on Web Search and Data Mining, pp. 113–122 (2013)
17. Ding, S., Suel, T.: Faster top-k document retrieval using block-max indexes. In: Proceedings of the 34th International ACM SIGIR Conference on Research and Development in Information Retrieval, pp. 993–1002 (2011)
18. Dudek, J.M., Kong, W., Li, C., Zhang, M., Bendersky, M.: Learning sparse lexical representations over specified vocabularies for retrieval. In: Proceedings of the 32nd ACM International Conference on Information and Knowledge Management (2023)
19. Efron, M., Organisciak, P., Fenlon, K.: Improving retrieval of short texts through document expansion (2012)
20. Formal, T., Lassance, C., Piwowarski, B., Clinchant, S.: Splade v2: sparse lexical and expansion model for information retrieval. arXiv preprint arXiv:2109.10086 (2021)
21. Formal, T., Piwowarski, B., Clinchant, S.: Splade: sparse lexical and expansion model for first stage ranking. In: Proceedings of the 44th International ACM SIGIR Conference on Research and Development in Information Retrieval (2021)
22. Furnas, G.W., Landauer, T.K., Gomez, L.M., Dumais, S.T.: The vocabulary problem in human-system communication. Commun. ACM **30**(11) (1987)
23. Geng, Z., Wang, Y., Ru, D., Yang, Y.: Towards competitive search relevance for inference-free learned sparse retrievers. arXiv preprint arXiv:2411.04403 (2024)
24. Goldfarb-Tarrant, S., Rodriguez, P., Dwivedi-Yu, J., Lewis, P.: Multicontrievers: analysis of dense retrieval representations. arXiv preprint arXiv:2402.15925 (2024)
25. Karpukhin, V., et alt.: Dense passage retrieval for open-domain question answering. In: Proceedings of the 2020 Conference on Empirical Methods in Natural Language Processing (2020)
26. Lassance, C., Clinchant, S.: An efficiency study for splade models. In: Proceedings of the 45th International ACM SIGIR Conference on Research and Development in Information Retrieval (2022)
27. Lei, Y., Shen, T., Cao, Y., Yates, A.: Enhancing lexicon-based text embeddings with large language models. In: Che, W., Nabende, J., Shutova, E., Pilehvar, M.T. (eds.) Proceedings of the 63rd Annual Meeting of the Association for Computational Linguistics, vol. 1: Long Papers (2025)
28. Lewis, P., et al.: Retrieval-augmented generation for knowledge-intensive nlp tasks. In: Proceedings of the 34th International Conference on Neural Information Processing Systems (2020)
29. Li, R., et al.: Sindi: an efficient index for approximate maximum inner product search on sparse vectors. arXiv preprint arXiv:2509.08395 (2025)
30. Li, X., et al.: From matching to generation: a survey on generative information retrieval. arXiv preprint arXiv:2404.14851 (2024)
31. Lin, J., Ma, X.: A few brief notes on deepimpact, coil, and a conceptual framework for information retrieval techniques. arXiv preprint arXiv:2106.14807 (2021)
32. Lin, J., Nogueira, R., Yates, A.: Pretrained transformers for text ranking: bert and beyond. arXiv preprint arXiv:2010.06467 (2020)
33. Lin, J., Trotman, A.: Anytime ranking for impact-ordered indexes. In: Proceedings of the 2015 International Conference on The Theory of Information Retrieval, pp. 301–304 (2015)

34. Lin, S.C., Lin, J.: A dense representation framework for lexical and semantic matching. ACM Trans. Inf. Syst. (2023)
35. Luo, Z., et al.: Lexlip: lexicon-bottlenecked language-image pre-training for large-scale image-text sparse retrieval. In: Proceedings of the IEEE/CVF International Conference on Computer Vision (2023)
36. MacAvaney, S., Nardini, F.M., Perego, R., Tonellotto, N., Goharian, N., Frieder, O.: Expansion via prediction of importance with contextualization. In: Proceedings of the 43rd International ACM SIGIR Conference on Research and Development in Information Retrieval (2020)
37. Mackenzie, J., Petri, M., Gallagher, L.: IOQP: a simple impact-ordered query processor written in rust. In: Alonso, O., Baeza-Yates, R., King, T.H., Silvello, G. (eds.) Proceedings of the Third International Conference on Design of Experimental Search & Information REtrieval Systems (2022)
38. Malkov, Y., Ponomarenko, A., Logvinov, A., Krylov, V.: Approximate nearest neighbor algorithm based on navigable small world graphs. Inf. Syst. **45** (2014)
39. Mallia, A., Khattab, O., Suel, T., Tonellotto, N.: Learning passage impacts for inverted indexes. In: Proceedings of the 44th International ACM SIGIR Conference on Research and Development in Information Retrieval (2021)
40. Mallia, A., Ottaviano, G., Porciani, E., Tonellotto, N., Venturini, R.: Faster blockmax wand with variable-sized blocks. In: Proceedings of the 40th International ACM SIGIR Conference on Research and Development in Information Retrieval (2017)
41. Mallia, A., Porciani, E.: Faster blockmax wand with longer skipping. In: 41st European Conference on IR Research (2019)
42. Mallia, A., Suel, T., Tonellotto, N.: Faster learned sparse retrieval with block-max pruning. In: Proceedings of the 47th International ACM SIGIR Conference on Research and Development in Information Retrieval, pp. 2411–2415 (2024)
43. Nair, S., Yang, E., Lawrie, D., Mayfield, J., Oard, D.W.: Blade: combining vocabulary pruning and intermediate pretraining for scaleable neural clir. In: Proceedings of the 46th International ACM SIGIR Conference on Research and Development in Information Retrieval (2023)
44. Nair, S., Yang, E., Lawrie, D.J., Mayfield, J., Oard, D.W.: Learning a sparse representation model for neural clir. In: Biennial Conference on Design of Experimental Search & Information Retrieval Systems (2022)
45. Nardini, F.M., Nguyen, T., Rulli, C., Venturini, R., Yates, A.: Effective inference-free retrieval for learned sparse representations. In: Proceedings of the 48th International ACM SIGIR Conference on Research and Development in Information Retrieval (2025)
46. Nguyen, T., Chatterjee, S., MacAvaney, S., Mackie, I., Dalton, J., Yates, A.: Dyvo: dynamic vocabularies for learned sparse retrieval with entities. In: Proceedings of the 2024 Conference on Empirical Methods in Natural Language Processing (2024)
47. Nguyen, T., Hendriksen, M., Yates, A., Rijke, M.D.: Multimodal learned sparse retrieval with probabilistic expansion control. In: 46th European Conference on Information Retrieval (2024)
48. Nguyen, T., Lei, Y., Ju, J.H., Yang, E., Yates, A.: Milco: learned sparse retrieval across languages via a multilingual connector. arXiv preprint arXiv:2510.00671 (2025)
49. Nguyen, T., MacAvaney, S., Yates, A.: A unified framework for learned sparse retrieval. In: 45th European Conference on Information Retrieval (2023)
50. Nogueira, R., Yang, W., Lin, J., Cho, K.: Document expansion by query prediction. arXiv preprint arXiv:1904.08375 (2019)

51. Pradeep, R., et al.: How does generative retrieval scale to millions of passages? In: Bouamor, H., Pino, J., Bali, K. (eds.) Proceedings of the 2023 Conference on Empirical Methods in Natural Language Processing
52. Qiao, J., Nguyen, T., Kanoulas, E., Yates, A.: Leveraging decoder architectures for learned sparse retrieval. In: International Workshop on Knowledge-Enhanced Information Retrieval (2025)
53. Ram, O., et al.: In-context retrieval-augmented language models. Trans. Assoc. Comput. Linguist. 11 (2023)
54. Robertson, S.E., Walker, S., Jones, S., Hancock-Beaulieu, M.M., Gatford, M., et al.: Okapi at trec-3. Nist Special Publication Sp 109, 109 (1995)
55. Salton, G., Wong, A., Yang, C.S.: A vector space model for automatic indexing. Commun. ACM 18(11) (1975)
56. Salton, G., Buckley, C.: Term-weighting approaches in automatic text retrieval. Inf. Process. Manag. 24, 513–523 (1988)
57. Saracevic, T.: The Notion of Relevance in Information Science. Morgan & Claypool Publishers (2016)
58. Shen, T., et al.: Unifier: a unified retriever for large-scale retrieval. In: Proceedings of the 29th ACM SIGKDD Conference on Knowledge Discovery and Data Mining (2023)
59. Sun, W., et al.: Is ChatGPT good at search? investigating large language models as re-ranking agents. In: Bouamor, H., Pino, J., Bali, K. (eds.) Proceedings of the 2023 Conference on Empirical Methods in Natural Language Processing (2023)
60. Tay, Y., et al.: Transformer memory as a differentiable search index. Adv. Neural. Inf. Process. Syst. 35, 21831–21843 (2022)
61. Thakur, N., Reimers, N., Rücklé, A., Srivastava, A., Gurevych, I.: Beir: a heterogenous benchmark for zero-shot evaluation of information retrieval models. arXiv preprint arXiv:2104.08663 (2021)
62. Voorhees, E.M., Tice, D.M.: The trec-8 question answering track report. In: Proceedings of the Eighth Text REtrieval Conference (TREC-8) (1999)
63. Yamada, I., Asai, A., Hajishirzi, H.: Efficient passage retrieval with hashing for open-domain question answering. In: Zong, C., Xia, F., Li, W., Navigli, R. (eds.) Proceedings of the 59th Annual Meeting of the Association for Computational Linguistics (2021)
64. Yang, Y., Carlson, P., He, S., Qiao, Y., Yang, T.: Cluster-based partial dense retrieval fused with sparse text retrieval. In: Proceedings of the 47th International ACM SIGIR Conference on Research and Development in Information Retrieval (2024)
65. Yoran, O., Wolfson, T., Ram, O., Berant, J.: Making retrieval-augmented language models robust to irrelevant context. In: The Twelfth International Conference on Learning Representations (2024)
66. Zamani, H., Dehghani, M., Croft, W.B., Learned-Miller, E., Kamps, J.: From neural re-ranking to neural ranking: learning a sparse representation for inverted indexing. In: Proceedings of the 27th ACM International Conference on Information and Knowledge Management (2018)
67. Zeng, H., Killingback, J., Zamani, H.: Scaling sparse and dense retrieval in decoder-only llms. In: Proceedings of the 48th International ACM SIGIR Conference on Research and Development in Information Retrieval, pp. 2679–2684 (2025)
68. Zhou, J., Li, X., Shang, L., Jiang, X., Liu, Q., Chen, L.: Retrieval-based disentangled representation learning with natural language supervision. In: The Twelfth International Conference on Learning Representations (2024)

69. Zhuang, S., Ma, X., Koopman, B., Lin, J., Zuccon, G.: Promptreps: prompting large language models to generate dense and sparse representations for zero-shot document retrieval. arXiv preprint arXiv:2404.18424 (2024)
70. Zhuang, S., Zuccon, G.: Fast passage re-ranking with contextualized exact term matching and efficient passage expansion. arXiv preprint arXiv:2108.08513 (2021)

# Tutorial on Mechanistic Interpretability

Catherine Chen[1(✉)] ⓘ, Maria Heuss[2] ⓘ, and Carsten Eickhoff[3] ⓘ

[1] Brown University, Providence, RI, USA
`catherine_s_chen@brown.edu`
[2] University of Amsterdam, Amsterdam, The Netherlands
`m.c.heuss@uva.nl`
[3] University of Tübingen, Tübingen, Germany
`carsten.eickhoff@uni-tuebingen.de`

**Abstract.** This tutorial introduces *mechanistic interpretability*, a growing research area within the broader interpretability community that seeks to reverse-engineer model components to understand *how* neural models perform tasks. While this area has rapidly advanced in NLP, yielding insights into the inner workings of large Transformer-based models and enabling model diagnostics, controllability, and safety, it remains largely unexplored in IR. This tutorial provides a foundational overview of mechanistic interpretability in NLP, covering its key goals and core methods. We then zoom in on its early applications in IR, examining the few existing studies in depth and discussing how these methods can be adapted to retrieval settings. Through an interactive coding session, participants will gain a practical understanding of how to design, implement, and analyze mechanistic interpretability experiments. By the end, attendees will be equipped with the conceptual and practical foundation needed to initiate their own research and help strengthen the emerging interpretability and explainability community within IR.

**Keywords:** Mechanistic interpretability · Explainable information retrieval · Transformer models

## 1 Motivation

Explainability and interpretability are critical for building trustworthy and accountable AI systems, especially as information retrieval (IR) models are increasingly deployed in socially and economically consequential settings such as healthcare, law, and finance. Explainability in IR has been gaining traction in recent years, highlighted by the *Workshop on Explainability in Information Retrieval (WExIR)* at SIGIR 2025 [18], which demonstrated growing community engagement with this topic. Despite this momentum, progress in interpretability and explainability within IR remains limited compared to the broader NLP and ML communities. These fields have recently benefited from rapid advances in *mechanistic interpretability*, a subfield focused on reverse-engineering model components to uncover how Transformer-based models implement specific behaviors [33]. This line of work has produced concrete insights into



R. Campos et al. (Eds.): ECIR 2026, LNCS 16486, pp. 44–52, 2026.
https://doi.org/10.1007/978-3-032-21321-1_6

how models represent, reason, and combine information internally, leading to a deeper understanding of how models process language and enabling advances in model debugging, controllability, and safety [5,30].

In contrast, mechanistic interpretability in IR is still in its early stages [7,24,31]. This tutorial aims to bridge that gap by providing foundational knowledge, introducing core methods, and demonstrating how these techniques can be adapted for retrieval models. Prior tutorials on explainable IR [2,3] focused on the broader interpretability landscape but did not cover mechanistic interpretability, as the field had not yet gained traction at the time. This tutorial therefore offers the first dedicated introduction to the topic for the IR community, highlighting the key concepts and methods developed in NLP to help IR researchers build a foundation for applying mechanistic interpretability and exploring its potential for future research and applications.

***Learning Objectives.*** Participants of this tutorial will: (1) understand the key goals and motivations of mechanistic interpretability as a research area, (2) become familiar with the core methods that have led to influential findings in ML and NLP, (3) explore how these methods can be applied to IR and identify open directions for future work, and (4) gain hands-on experience in designing, implementing, and analyzing mechanistic interpretability experiments.

***Scope.*** While mechanistic interpretability has expanded across language, vision, and multimodal domains, this tutorial focuses on language-based methods, where most key advances have originated. Given the field's breadth, we do not aim to survey all developments but instead introduce the core concepts and foundational methods of mechanistic interpretability. As this area is still emerging within IR, this tutorial will provide attendees with the background and practical understanding needed to begin applying these techniques in IR research.

## 2   Relevance to the IR Community

***Tutorial History.*** This tutorial is the first edition on mechanistic interpretability within the IR community. The most closely related prior offering is the *Explainable Information Retrieval* tutorial (ECIR 2025 [2] and SIGIR 2023 [3]) which surveyed the braoder explainability landscape, but did not address mechanistic interpretability, as the area had not yet gained traction in IR. Earlier interpretability tutorials in NLP, such as *Interpretability and Analysis in Neural NLP* (ACL 2020[1]), focused on probing and attention analysis and predate the current wave of mechanistic-interpretability research.

Only one dedicated tutorial on mechanistic interpretability has been presented at major ML venues: the *Tutorial on Mechanistic Interpretability for Language Models* (ICML 2025[2]). Beyond tutorials, the topic has rapidly expanded

---

[1] https://virtual.acl2020.org/tutorial_T1.html.
[2] https://ziyu-yao-nlp-lab.github.io/ICML25-MI-Tutorial.github.io/.

through specialized workshops, such as the *Workshop on Mechanistic Interpretability* (ICML 2024[3] and NeurIPS 2025[4]), and the *Mechanistic Interpretability in Vision* workshop (CVPR 2025[5]). Mechanistic interpretability has also become a prominent theme at broader interpretability workshops such as *Actionable Interpretability* (ICML 2025[6]) and *BlackboxNLP* (EMNLP[7]).

***Need for this Tutorial.*** While these events demonstrate the rapid growth of the field in the broader ML community, there has not yet been a dedicated effort to introduce mechanistic interpretability to IR researchers. This tutorial fills that gap by providing foundational knowledge and practical guidance tailored specifically to information retrieval.

# 3  Tutorial Format

This three-hour tutorial, plus a break, and will be presented in three parts. *Part I* introduces mechanistic interpretability, tracing its origins in the NLP community and outlining its primary goals and core methods. *Part II* focuses on applications in IR, highlighting methods already adapted to retrieval and guiding participants through an interactive coding session to demonstrate experimental pipelines in practice. Finally, *Part III* concludes with key takeaways and reflects on future opportunities for mechanistic interpretability in IR.

Table 1 summarizes the tentative schedule, and the remainder of this section details the planned content. All support materials, including slides, references, and coding setup, will be provided on a public website and shared with attendees in advance.

## 3.1  Part I: Overview of Mechanistic Interpretability in NLP

The first half of the tutorial introduces the core concepts of mechanistic interpretability from the NLP literature. We will begin by outlining limitations of prior interpretability work that mechanistic interpretability aims to address, defining the field's goals, and providing essential technical background. Next, we will present a high-level overview of key methods, focusing on their goals and the intuition behind how they work, to give attendees a foundation for applying these techniques in their own research. Finally, we will zoom into one of the most widely used approaches in NLP, which will prepare attendees for the hands-on implementation session in *Part II*.

***Motivation, Definition, and Background.*** Classical interpretability methods based on input-output analysis, such as **probing** [36], have provided useful insights into model behavior but lack causal grounding and do not permit direct

---

[3] https://icml2024mi.pages.dev/.
[4] https://mechinterpworkshop.com/.
[5] https://sites.google.com/view/miv-cvpr2025/.
[6] https://actionable-interpretability.github.io/.
[7] https://blackboxnlp.github.io/2025/.

**Table 1.** Tentative Tutorial Schedule

| Section | Duration | Topic(s) |
| --- | --- | --- |
| Part I: Overview of MI in NLP | 20 min | **Introduction**<br>Motivation, Definition, and Background |
|  | 40 min | **Overview of Core Methods**<br>Vocabulary Projections<br>Circuit Analysis<br>Feature Analysis<br>Steering |
|  | 30 min | **Circuit Analysis Deep Dive**<br>Activation Patching<br>Path Patching |
| — | 30 min | Coffee Break |
| Part II: MI in IR | 15 min | **Overview of Progress So Far**<br>Probing<br>Circuit Analysis |
|  | 45 min | **Interactive Coding**<br>Activation Patching |
| Part III: Conclusion | 30 min | Future Directions, Discussion, Q&A |

interventions [4]. Probing trains a lightweight classifier on top of a frozen model to identify which concepts are learned by its latent representations, but it does not reveal whether or how models use these concepts during inference. **Mechanistic interpretability** addresses these limitations by uncovering how models compute and represent information through the causal interactions of their internal components. It can be narrowly defined as "[the discovery of] causal mechanisms explaining all or some part of the change from neural network input to output at the level of intermediate model representations," though broader definitions also highlight its role as a growing methodological framework and research community [33]. Most work in this area has focused on Transformer-based models, which provide a clear mathematical framework for analyzing how model components, such as attention heads and MLPs, read from and write to the **residual stream**, which is formed by residual connections that carry information across layers [10]. This framework enables targeted interventions to test hypotheses about component function and isolate causal mechanisms underlying model behavior.

***Early Decoding.*** Early decoding, or **vocabulary projection**, methods aim to reveal intermediate model computations by converting internal activations into partial text predictions using the model's output vocabulary [28]. This shows how representations evolve and what information is encoded at different layers. These methods have uncovered interpretable linear relationships, such as a vector mapping city to capital [27], and shown how factual associations are refined through the model's layers [13].

***Circuit Analysis.*** The goal of circuit analysis is to understand how information flows through a model by identifying how specific components contribute to computation from input to output. It aims to extract a computational subgraph, called a *circuit*, that implements a particular behavior through intervention-based experiments that test how changes to internal activations affect outputs, revealing causal pathways within the network. **Activation patching** measures indirect causal effects by replacing activations from one input with those from another and observing how the output changes. It has been used to locate where models store factual knowledge [26], investigate gender bias [39], and analyze reasoning behaviors such as natural language inference [11]. **Path patching** [14,40] extends this approach to isolate direct causal connections between components, enabling detailed analysis of mechanisms such as indirect object identification [40], greater-than comparisons [16], and factual recall [12].

***Feature Analysis.*** Feature analysis aims to uncover what human-interpretable properties a model encodes in its activations. Early work sought to identify individual neurons that correspond to specific concepts or input patterns [19], but later studies found that neurons are often polysemantic, or activate for multiple unrelated features [15]. To address this, **sparse autoencoders (SAEs)** were introduced to transform activations into a sparse, higher-dimensional space, encouraging one feature per neuron [6,20]. SAEs have since been used to disentangle overlapping features and analyze how language models represent semantic concepts [25,35].

***Steering.*** Steering methods aim to control a model's behavior by intervening on activations at inference time. They typically build on circuit or feature analysis to identify activations associated with specific behaviors, and then construct **steering vectors** [34,38], directional representations in latent space that can amplify or suppress those behaviors. Variants include *task* [17] and *function* [37] vectors, which target different aspects of model function. Steering has been used to adjust stylistic tone and sentiment [21], elicit truthfulness [22], and reduce hallucinations and sycophancy [32].


## 3.2   Part II: Mechanistic Interpretability in IR

In this section of the tutorial, we will connect topics discussed in the first part to work done in IR. This section also provides a practical introduction to mechanistic interpretability methods in IR, providing an opportunity to participants to learn how to design, implement, evaluate, and analyze end-to-end experimental pipelines.

***Probing.*** While probing is not considered a core method in mechanistic interpretability, since it does not provide causal insights, it remains relevant for understanding the internal representations of IR models. We include it briefly as background and motivation, as probing highlights the limitations of correlation-based analyses and the need for more causal, intervention-based approaches [1]. Recent work has also began extending probing in a more mechanistic direction, such as analyzing ranking large language models at finer levels of granularity (i.e., neuron activations) [8].

***Circuit Analysis.*** The majority of *Part II* will focus on circuit analysis, building on the foundation introduced in Part I, but applied to IR. Going beyond the correlational insights of probing, circuit analysis provides causal evidence of how specific components contribute to model behavior. Methods such as activation and path patching have been used to isolate term-matching attention heads [7] and identify BM25-like circuits in dense retrieval models [24], as well as to investigate mechanistic behaviors in generative IR models [31], LLM rankers cite, and RAG systems add citations.

This section includes a hands-on coding session that walks participants through the full experimental pipeline. Using `MechIR`, a Python package for mechanistic interpretability in IR [29], participants will construct contrastive input pairs, run activation patching experiments, and analyze results. The process follows the standard workflow of hypothesis formation, discovery, and verification [30], providing both conceptual grounding and practical experience for a mechanistic analysis of retrieval models.

## 4 Target Audience

This tutorial is designed for an introductory audience, aiming to familiarize the IR community with mechanistic interpretability and encourage broader engagement with this growing field. While those with prior experience are welcome, the focus is on building foundational understanding through core methods developed in NLP and practical examples of how these techniques can be applied in IR. The tutorial is suitable for researchers at all career stages, from Master's and PhD students learning to design their own experiments to senior researchers seeking inspiration for new directions in their groups. No prior experience with mechanistic interpretability is required. Basic familiarity with the Transformer architecture and basic Python is assumed, but all core concepts will remain accessible to those without this background.

**Disclosure of Interests.** The authors have no competing interests to declare that are relevant to the content of this article.

## References


1. Anand, A., Lyu, L., Idahl, M., Wang, Y., Wallat, J., Zhang, Z.: Explainable information retrieval: a survey. arxiv preprint arXiv:2211.02405 (2022)
2. Anand, A., Saha, S., Venktesh, V.: Explainable information retrieval. In: European Conference on Information Retrieval. Springer (2025)

3. Anand, A., Sen, P., Saha, S., Verma, M., Mitra, M.: Explainable information retrieval. In: Proceedings of the 46th International ACM SIGIR Conference on Research and Development in Information Retrieval (2023)
4. Belinkov, Y.: Probing classifiers: promises, shortcomings, and advances. Comput. Linguist. **48**(1), 207–219 (2022)
5. Bereska, L., Gavves, S.: Mechanistic interpretability for ai safety-a review. Trans. Mach. Learn. Res. (2024)
6. Bricken, T., et al.: Towards monosemanticity: decomposing language models with dictionary learning. Transformer Circuits Thread (2023)
7. Chen, C., Merullo, J., Eickhoff, C.: Axiomatic causal interventions for reverse engineering relevance computation in neural retrieval models. In: Proceedings of the 47th International ACM SIGIR Conference on Research and Development in Information Retrieval (2024)
8. Chowdhury, T., Nijasure, A., Allan, J.: Probing ranking LLMs: a mechanistic analysis for information retrieval. In: Proceedings of the 2025 International ACM SIGIR Conference on Innovative Concepts and Theories in Information Retrieval (2025)
9. van Dort, I., Maria, H.: How do LLMs cite? A mechanistic interpretation of attribution in rag. In: 48th European Conference on Information Retrieval (2026)
10. Elhage, N., et al.: A mathematical framework for transformer circuits. Transformer Circuits Thread **1**(1), 12 (2021)
11. Geiger, A., Lu, H., Icard, T., Potts, C.: Causal abstractions of neural networks. In: Advances in Neural Information Processing Systems (2021)
12. Geva, M., Bastings, J., Filippova, K., Globerson, A.: Dissecting recall of factual associations in auto-regressive language models. In: Proceedings of the 2023 Conference on Empirical Methods in Natural Language Processing (2023)
13. Geva, M., Caciularu, A., Wang, K., Goldberg, Y.: Transformer feed-forward layers build predictions by promoting concepts in the vocabulary space. In: Proceedings of the 2022 Conference on Empirical Methods in Natural Language Processing (2022)
14. Goldowsky-Dill, N., MacLeod, C., Sato, L., Arora, A.: Localizing model behavior with path patching. arXiv preprint arXiv:2304.05969 (2023)
15. Gurnee, W., et al.: Universal neurons in gpt2 language models. arXiv preprint arXiv:2401.12181 (2024)
16. Hanna, M., Liu, O., Variengien, A.: How does GPT-2 compute greater-than?: interpreting mathematical abilities in a pre-trained language model. In: Advances in Neural Information Processing Systems (2023)
17. Hendel, R., Geva, M., Globerson, A.: In-context learning creates task vectors. In: Findings of the Association for Computational Linguistics: EMNLP 2023 (2023)
18. Heuss, M., Chen, C., Anand, A., Eickhoff, C., Verberne, S.: Workshop on explainability in information retrieval. In: Proceedings of the 48th International ACM SIGIR Conference on Research and Development in Information Retrieval (2025)
19. Huang, J., Geiger, A., D'Oosterlinck, K., Wu, Z., Potts, C.: Rigorously assessing natural language explanations of neurons. In: Proceedings of the 6th BlackboxNLP Workshop: Analyzing and Interpreting Neural Networks for NLP (2023)
20. Huben, R., Cunningham, H., Smith, L.R., Ewart, A., Sharkey, L.: Sparse autoencoders find highly interpretable features in language models. In: The Twelfth International Conference on Learning Representations (2023)
21. Konen, K., et al.: Style vectors for steering generative large language model. arXiv preprint arXiv:2402.01618 (2024)

22. Li, K., Patel, O., Viégas, F., Pfister, H., Wattenberg, M.: Inference-time intervention: eliciting truthful answers from a language model. In: Advances in Neural Information Processing Systems (2023)
23. Liu, Q., Duan, H., Mao, J., Wen, J.R.: How do large language models understand relevance? a mechanistic interpretability perspective. ACM Trans. Inf. Syst. (2025)
24. Lu, M., Chen, C., Eickhoff, C.: Pathway to relevance: how cross-encoders implement a semantic variant of BM25. In: Proceedings of the 2025 Conference on Empirical Methods in Natural Language Processing (2025)
25. Marks, S., Rager, C., Michaud, E.J., Belinkov, Y., Bau, D., Mueller, A.: Sparse feature circuits: Discovering and editing interpretable causal graphs in language models. arXiv preprint arXiv:2403.19647 (2024)
26. Meng, K., Bau, D., Andonian, A., Belinkov, Y.: Locating and editing factual associations in GPT. In: Advances in Neural Information Processing Systems (2022)
27. Merullo, J., Eickhoff, C., Pavlick, E.: Language models implement simple word2vec-style vector arithmetic. In: Proceedings of the 2024 Conference of the North American Chapter of the Association for Computational Linguistics: Human Language Technologies (Volume 1: Long Papers) (2024)
28. nostalgebraist: interpreting GPT: the logit lens. AI alignment forum. AI Alignment Forum (2020)
29. Parry, A., Chen, C., Eickhoff, C., MacAvaney, S.: Mechir: a mechanistic interpretability framework for information retrieval. In: European Conference on Information Retrieval. Springer (2025)
30. Rai, D., Zhou, Y., Feng, S., Saparov, A., Yao, Z.: A practical review of mechanistic interpretability for transformer-based language models. arXiv preprint arXiv:2407.02646 (2024)
31. Reusch, A., Belinkov, Y.: Reverse-engineering the retrieval process in genir models. In: Proceedings of the 48th International ACM SIGIR Conference on Research and Development in Information Retrieval (2025)
32. Rimsky, N., Gabrieli, N., Schulz, J., Tong, M., Hubinger, E., Turner, A.: Steering llama 2 via contrastive activation addition. In: Proceedings of the 62nd Annual Meeting of the Association for Computational Linguistics (Volume 1: Long Papers) (2024)
33. Saphra, N., Wiegreffe, S.: Mechanistic? arXiv preprint arXiv:2410.09087 (2024)
34. Subramani, N., Suresh, N., Peters, M.E.: Extracting latent steering vectors from pretrained language models. In: Findings of the Association for Computational Linguistics: ACL 2022 (2022)
35. Templeton, A., et al.: Scaling monosemanticity: extracting interpretable features from claude 3 sonnet. Transformer Circuits Thread (2024). https://transformer circuits.pub/2024/scaling-monosemanticity/index.html
36. Tenney, I., et al.: What do you learn from context? Probing for sentence structure in contextualized word representations. In: International Conference on Learning Representations (2019)
37. Todd, E., Li, M., Sharma, A.S., Mueller, A., Wallace, B.C., Bau, D.: Function vectors in large language models. In: The Twelfth International Conference on Learning Representations (2024)
38. Turner, A.M., et al.: Steering language models with activation engineering. arXiv preprint arXiv:2308.10248 (2023)

39. Vig, J., et al.: Investigating gender bias in language models using causal mediation analysis. In: Advances in Neural Information Processing Systems (2020)
40. Wang, K.R., Variengien, A., Conmy, A., Shlegeris, B., Steinhardt, J.: Interpretability in the wild: a circuit for indirect object identification in GPT-2 small. In: The Eleventh International Conference on Learning Representations (2023)

# Uncertainty Quantification for Large Language Models


Maxim Panov[1]([✉]), Artem Shelmanov[1], Roman Vashurin[1], Artem Vazhentsev[1], Ekaterina Fadeeva[2], Lyudmila Rvanova[3], and Timothy Baldwin[1,4]

[1] MBZUAI, Abu Dhabi, UAE
panov.maxim@gmail.com
[2] ETH Zurich, Zurich, Switzerland
[3] AIRI and FRC CSC RAS, Moscow, Russia
[4] The University of Melbourne, Melbourne, Australia



**Abstract.** Large language models (LLMs) power many NLP applications; yet, they can produce fluent but incorrect content (hallucinations), which threatens reliability and user trust. This tutorial introduces uncertainty quantification (UQ) for text generation: methods that attach an explicit reliability signal to model outputs and enable practical safeguards such as hallucination detection and selective generation. We begin with core uncertainty concepts and explain why techniques that work well for classification do not directly transfer to autoregressive generation. We then survey representative white-box and black-box approaches, from entropy- and probability-based scores to learned probes that leverage internal representations.

Retrieval-augmented generation (RAG) has become a core design pattern for LLM applications. Incorporating retrieved evidence introduces both new challenges and valuable structures for uncertainty estimation. In the ECIR edition of the tutorial, we focus on UQ techniques tailored to RAG pipelines and briefly discuss how uncertainty can guide agentic workflows.

Practical demonstrations are done using LM-Polygraph (https://github.com/IINemo/lm-polygraph), an open-source toolkit that consolidates more than forty recent UQ and calibration methods and provides a large-scale benchmark, making it easy to reproduce results and integrate UQ into applications with minimal code. Overall, the tutorial is intended to lower the barrier to entry for researchers and developers who want to evaluate existing UQ methods, design improved ones, and deploy uncertainty-aware LLM systems.

**Keywords:** Uncertainty Quantification · Hallucination Detection · LLM


## 1 Motivation

Uncertainty quantification (UQ) has gained increasing importance in natural language processing (NLP), offering a conceptual and methodological framework to



R. Campos et al. (Eds.): ECIR 2026, LNCS 16486, pp. 53–59, 2026.
https://doi.org/10.1007/978-3-032-21321-1_7

address critical issues such as hallucinations in the answers of LLMs, detection of low-quality responses, out-of-distribution detection, and reducing response latency, among others. While UQ for text classification models in NLP has been covered in previous tutorials, applying UQ to LLMs poses far greater challenges. This complexity stems from the fact that LLMs generate sequences of conditionally dependent predictions with varying levels of importance. As a result, many UQ techniques that are effective for classification models are either ineffective or not directly applicable to LLMs. In this tutorial, we cover foundational concepts of UQ for LLMs, present state-of-the-art techniques, demonstrate practical applications of UQ in various tasks, and equip researchers and practitioners with tools for developing new UQ methods and harnessing uncertainty in various contexts. Recently, retrieval-augmented generation (RAG) systems have become the backbone of many modern LLM-based applications. Augmenting inputs to the model with information retrieved from additional sources poses unique challenges and opportunities for UQ. In this edition of the tutorial, we cover the techniques most suitable for RAG-based LLMs and touch upon applications of uncertainty in agentic frameworks. Through this tutorial, we aim to lower the barrier to entry into UQ research and applications for individual researchers and developers.

## 2   Scope and Objectives

This tutorial extends our earlier tutorials presented at ACL-2025 [20] and AAAI-2026 [19], with a stronger focus on retrieval-augmented LLMs.

Uncertainty quantification has been an active area of machine learning research long before the emergence and widespread adoption of modern LLMs. Accordingly, many foundational definitions and theoretical results are not specific to LLMs. In this tutorial, we briefly introduce these core notions rooted in information-theoretic perspectives [2] and analyzes based on expected risk [11,12], and highlight key concepts such as the decomposition of predictive uncertainty into aleatoric and epistemic components [10]. While these quantities are typically intractable due to unknown data-generating processes and model parameters, classical approximations (e.g., deep ensembles [14]) are often prohibitively expensive for modern LLMs. This motivates alternative formulations that are better suited to the LLM setting. In particular, we discuss Minimum Bayes Risk [13,25] as a unifying perspective that helps interpret and connect many contemporary UQ methods for text generation.

The main part of the tutorial focuses on practical UQ techniques tailored to LLMs. Broadly, existing methods fall into two categories: *black-box* and *white-box* methods. Black-box approaches, like verbalized methods [23] and consistency-based methods [15], use only the textual outputs of the LLM. White-box approaches require various degrees of access to the internal states of the model [28,30]. In particular, for information-theoretic methods, such as `Sequence Probability`, `Mean Token Entropy` [8], `Semantic Entropy` [7], `CCP` [5], and others, the required level of access is typically limited to the probabilities of generated tokens. For other methods, like `LLM-Check` [21] and `RAUQ` [28], knowledge of internal states and attention maps is needed as well.

Another important distinction is between supervised and unsupervised approaches. Supervised UQ methods like `SAPLMA` [1], `TAD` [27], `UHead` [18], and others [9,29] are fitted on held-out labeled datasets and have various degrees of generalization capability when evaluated on out-of-distribution data. Unsupervised approaches can be used without any additional training data, but they usually perform worse than supervised methods in the in-distribution setting. Semi-supervised techniques like `CoCoA Light` [25] and `LINE` [26] require held-out data to be fitted on, but this data can be unlabeled.

When implementing RAG, additional challenges arise as we should be concerned not only with the correctness of the output in the broad sense but also with faithfulness to the retrieved documents [16]. Many existing methods, like `Lookback Lens` [3] and `ReDeEP` [22], only evaluate the faithfulness of the response. However, when retrieved information might not always be correct, a separate evaluation of both faithfulness and factuality in the UQ method can improve the quality of hallucination detection [4].

The comparative evaluation of this large variety of approaches is another important topic. In general, a high negative correlation between uncertainty scores and response quality is expected for a well-performing UQ method. If the response quality metric is binary (e.g., Accuracy), typical classification measures like AUROC can be used. To use this approach for continuous quality measures like AlignScore [31] or COMET [17], binarization via thresholding is needed. The selection of the quality threshold can be quite arbitrary, and other measures of UQ performance should be employed. `Prediction-Rejection Ratio` (PRR) is one such measure. PRR is a rank-based approach that summarizes the prediction-rejection curve – average response quality on the dataset when high-uncertainty points are progressively rejected.

Since we not only conduct research on the considered topic but also develop the most comprehensive UQ Python framework, LM-Polygraph [6,24], we can provide not only a theoretical overview but also practical tools that researchers and practitioners can readily apply. LM-Polygraph implements state-of-the-art UQ methods with unified APIs and provides a comprehensive benchmark for the consistent evaluation of uncertainty scores. LM-Polygraph lowers the barrier to entry into UQ research for individual researchers and developers and enables more robust, reliable, and trustworthy LLM deployment for end users. By combining theoretical foundations with hands-on resources, we aim to lower the barrier to entry into UQ research and its practical application, ultimately fostering more robust, reliable, and trustworthy LLM-based applications.

## 3   Tutorial Outline

**Part 1: Introduction [25 mins].** This section aims to introduce the audience to the problem, the motivation for uncertainty quantification, and the general challenges in this area. It also presents *LM-Polygraph*, a Python framework for UQ for LLMs developed by the tutorial presenters [6,24].

**Part 2: Background on Uncertainty Quantification [30 mins].** This section presents general concepts of uncertainty quantification, standard approaches to this task, and challenges related to UQ for LLMs.

**Part 3: Unsupervised Uncertainty Quantification Methods [40 mins].** The standard approach to uncertainty quantification of any machine learning model is to compute some statistics based on the internal state or output of the model. In this part of the tutorial, we discuss both classical and recent approaches to designing unsupervised uncertainty scores.

**Part 4: Supervised Uncertainty Quantification Methods [20 mins].** This section presents another research direction for UQ of LLMs – supervised methods. We discuss recent advances in this direction and present a wide range of supervised UQ methods for LLMs. We also highlight their limitations and advantages.

**Part 5: Applying Uncertainty Quantification to RAG-based Systems [25 mins].** LLMs enhanced with external knowledge retrieval, an approach known as Retrieval-Augmented Generation (RAG), have achieved strong performance in open-domain question answering. However, RAG systems remain prone to hallucinations: factually incorrect outputs that may arise from inconsistencies between the model's internal knowledge and the retrieved context. Existing approaches to mitigating hallucinations often conflate factuality with faithfulness to the retrieved evidence, incorrectly labeling factually correct statements as hallucinations if they are not explicitly supported by the retrieval. We will discuss various approaches to perform uncertainty for RAG-based systems, including a detailed treatment of faithfulness and factuality.

**Part 6: Details on Benchmarking Uncertainty Scores [25 mins].** This part delves into details of benchmarking UQ methods. It discusses various methods of comparing the performance of different UQ techniques and discusses their relative advantages and limitations.

**Part 7: Emerging Trends and Conclusion [15 mins].** This part summarizes key takeaways and discusses future work.


## 4    Additional Information

**Learning Outcomes.** This tutorial aims to introduce the foundational concepts of uncertainty quantification in general and its peculiarities for generation tasks with various Large Language Models (LLMs). We will present cutting-edge UQ techniques for generation tasks with LLMs and demonstrate practical applications of UQ in tasks such as selective generation and hallucination detection in LLM outputs, supported by illustrative code examples. Special attention will be paid to generation augmented with retrieved information (RAG), which is a backbone of many modern LLM-based systems. We will provide a methodological framework for applying UQ to RAG systems and agentic frameworks. Additionally, we will guide researchers in developing and evaluating novel UQ methods for LLMs, and equip practitioners with tools to build safer LLM-based applications and harness uncertainty in various contexts.

**Target Audience.** The target audience includes not only researchers in UQ and machine learning but also practitioners interested in hallucination detection and those focused on enhancing the safety of LLM-based applications, including RAG-based systems. Particular prerequisite knowledge or skills are not required from the audience, except for basic knowledge of machine learning and LLMs.

**History.**

– The 1st edition of the tutorial was held at *ACL 2025* [20]. The materials of the tutorial are available online[1]. The ACL 2025 tutorial drew significant interest in the topic, attracting 300400 attendees, and was well received by participants.
– The 2nd edition of the tutorial was held at *AAAI 2026* [19]. It builds on the ACL version but expands the scope beyond UQ methods for purely textual LLMs to also cover methods for LVLMs, as well as for reasoning and agentic workflows. The event received over 100 RSVPs. The materials of the tutorial are available online[2].

**Acknowledgments.** Part of the computational resources for our experiments were provided by Together AI.

**Disclosure of Interests.** The authors have no competing interests to declare that are relevant to the content of this article.

# References


1. Azaria, A., Mitchell, T.: The internal state of an LLM knows when it's lying. In: Findings of EMNLP (2023)
2. Blundell, C., Cornebise, J., Kavukcuoglu, K., Wierstra, D.: Weight uncertainty in neural network. In: Proceedings of ICML (2015)
3. Chuang, Y.S., Qiu, L., Hsieh, C.Y., Krishna, R., Kim, Y., Glass, J.R.: Lookback lens: detecting and mitigating contextual hallucinations in large language models using only attention maps. In: Proceedings of EMNLP (2024)
4. Fadeeva, E., et al.: Faithfulness-aware uncertainty quantification for fact-checking the output of retrieval augmented generation. arXiv preprint arXiv:2505.21072 (2025)
5. Fadeeva, E., et al.: Fact-checking the output of large language models via token-level uncertainty quantification. In: Findings of ACL (2024)
6. Fadeeva, E., et al.: LM-polygraph: uncertainty estimation for language models. In: Proceedings of EMNLP: System Demonstrations (2023)


---

[1] https://sites.google.com/view/acl2025-uncertainty-for-llms.
[2] https://sites.google.com/view/aaai2026-uncertainty-for-llms.

7. Farquhar, S., Kossen, J., Kuhn, L., Gal, Y.: Detecting hallucinations in large language models using semantic entropy. Nature (2024)
8. Fomicheva, M., et al.: Unsupervised quality estimation for neural machine translation. Trans. Assoc. Comput. Linguist. (2020)
9. He, J., Gong, Y., Lin, Z., Zhao, Y., Chen, K., et al.: LLM factoscope: uncovering LLMs' factual discernment through measuring inner states. In: Findings of ACL (2024)
10. Hüllermeier, E., Waegeman, W.: Aleatoric and epistemic uncertainty in machine learning: an introduction to concepts and methods. Mach. Learn. (2021)
11. Kotelevskii, N., et al.: Nonparametric uncertainty quantification for single deterministic neural network. In: Advances in Neural Information Processing Systems (2022)
12. Kotelevskii, N., Kondratyev, V., Takáč, M., Moulines, E., Panov, M.: From risk to uncertainty: generating predictive uncertainty measures via Bayesian estimation. In: International Conference on Learning Representations (2025)
13. Kumar, S., Byrne, B.: Minimum bayes-risk decoding for statistical machine translation. In: Proceedings of HLT-NAACL (2004)
14. Lakshminarayanan, B., Pritzel, A., Blundell, C.: Simple and scalable predictive uncertainty estimation using deep ensembles. In: Advances in Neural Information Processing Systems (2017)
15. Lin, Z., Trivedi, S., Sun, J.: Generating with confidence: Uncertainty quantification for black-box large language models. Trans. Mach. Learn. Res. (2024)
16. Maynez, J., Narayan, S., Bohnet, B., McDonald, R.: On faithfulness and factuality in abstractive summarization. In: Proceedings of ACL (2020)
17. Rei, R., Stewart, C., Farinha, A.C., Lavie, A.: COMET: a neural framework for MT evaluation. In: Proceedings of EMNLP (2020)
18. Shelmanov, A., et al.: A head to predict and a head to question: pre-trained uncertainty quantification heads for hallucination detection in LLM outputs. In: Proceedings of EMNLP (2025)
19. Shelmanov, A., et al.: Uncertainty quantification for large language models: AAAI-2026 edition (2026)
20. Shelmanov, A., Panov, M., Vashurin, R., Vazhentsev, A., Fadeeva, E., Baldwin, T.: Uncertainty quantification for large language models. In: Proceedings of ACL: Tutorial Abstracts (2025)
21. Sriramanan, G., Bharti, S., Sadasivan, V.S., Saha, S., Kattakinda, P., Feizi, S.: LLM-check: investigating detection of hallucinations in large language models. In: Advances in Neural Information Processing Systems (2024)
22. Sun, Z., et al.: ReDeEP: detecting hallucination in retrieval-augmented generation via mechanistic interpretability. In: International Conference on Learning Representations (2025)
23. Tian, K., et al.: Just ask for calibration: strategies for eliciting calibrated confidence scores from language models fine-tuned with human feedback. In: Proceedings of EMNLP (2023)
24. Vashurin, R., et al.: Benchmarking uncertainty quantification methods for large language models with LM-polygraph. Trans. Assoc. Comput. Linguist. (2025)
25. Vashurin, R., et al.: Uncertainty quantification for LLMs through minimum bayes risk: bridging confidence and consistency. In: Advances in Neural Information Processing Systems (2025)
26. Vashurin, R., Goloburda, M., Nakov, P., Panov, M.: Uncertainty-LINE: length-invariant estimation of uncertainty for large language models. In: Proceedings of EMNLP (2025)

27. Vazhentsev, A., et al.: Unconditional truthfulness: learning conditional dependency for uncertainty quantification of large language models. In: Proceedings of EMNLP (2025)
28. Vazhentsev, A., et al.: Uncertainty-aware attention heads: efficient unsupervised uncertainty quantification for LLMs. arXiv preprint arXiv:2505.20045 (2025)
29. Vazhentsev, A., et al.: Token-level density-based uncertainty quantification methods for eliciting truthfulness of large language models. In: Proceedings of NAACL (2025)
30. Vazhentsev, A., et al.: Efficient out-of-domain detection for sequence to sequence models. In: Findings of ACL, Toronto, Canada, pp. 1430–1454 (2023)
31. Zha, Y., Yang, Y., Li, R., Hu, Z.: AlignScore: evaluating factual consistency with a unified alignment function. In: Proceedings of ACL (2023)

# Industry Papers

# Evalugator —Rapid, Agile Development and Evaluation of Retrieval Augmented Generation Systems Without Labels

Bevan Koopman[1,2(✉)], Hang Li[1], Shuai Wang[1], and Guido Zuccon[1]

[1] The University of Queensland, Brisbane, Australia
{b.koopman,hang.li,shuai.wang2,g.zuccon}@uq.edu.au
[2] CSIRO, Brisbane, Australia

**Abstract.** Evaluating complex Retrieval Augmented Generation (RAG) systems in real-world settings is challenging. There is often a lack of fine-grained labelled data and the absence of comprehensive evaluation tools that can assess individual components of a pipeline. This hinders rapid, rigorous development, particularly for agentic RAG systems. We describe our experienced at GuideStream.AI, a startup developing an AI for clinical guideline recommendation. To address this gap, we developed Evalugator, a suite of agentic components to support agile development and evaluation. Evalugator features: (1) generation of synthetic queries, relevance assessments, answers and evaluation criteria for training and evaluation in new domains; (2) LLM-based judging agents; and (3) UI and API tools to launch experiments and analyse results. This paper uses Evalugator as a case study to demonstrate how a principled, agent-based evaluation framework can support the rapid development of complex RAG systems in a startup environment.

**Keywords:** Retrieval augmented generation · Evaluation

## 1 Introduction

GuideStream.AI is a startup incubated within The University of Queensland focused on building a specialised retrieval system that offers medical professionals personalised, real-time, highly effective access to clinical guidelines relevant to their patient. Core to our product is a complex agentic Retrieval Augmented Generation (RAG) pipeline, that has undergone extensive training. A core principle at GuideStream.AI is grounding the product on rigorous evaluation practices. While RAG has proven effective in research settings, we encountered the following challenges that hampered our aim of rapid development and integrated experimentation workflow:

1. Often developers have no training or evaluation data related to their setting to develop their RAG system, especially data that allows evaluation to span multiple dimensions and preferences, e.g., relevance, factuality, quality, layout/format, etc. [4]

2. Even when evaluation data is available, it might be difficult for developers not experienced with IR evaluation practices to run evaluation experiments.
3. It is difficult to evaluate individual components of the RAG system (e.g., retriever vs generator effectiveness)—this makes it much harder to diagnose issues and focus development efforts.

We recognised the tension between being able to rapidly develop a prototype in a startup environment and maintaining some scientific rigour in model development. To try and manage this balance we developed a series of components—collectively dubbed Evalugator—to aid us in rapid and agile development and evaluation. The main components were:

- QuestionFisher, providing the ability to generate synthetic queries, document-level relevance assessment and answers for domains where these do not exist.
- Seperate LLM-based judging agents [3]: RetrieverRater for document level judging for the retriever; GenRat for answer quality judging of the generator based on multiple criteria [5].
- Simple to use tools (UI and API) to launch evaluation experiments that utilise the judgement agents, allowing developers to get quick evaluation feedback. Flexible display of results so developers can dig into the results and understand the behaviour of the RAG systems.

Other tools have been proposed for RAG evaluation in fast-paced development environments. An example is RURAGE [2], which is limited in only focusing on the generation evaluation, ignoring the interplay with other components in the RAG pipeline, and it intentionally does not provide LLM-judge methods, which instead we believe are key in our settings for fine-grained evaluation of response preferences and dimensions.

Our presentation will use Evalugator as an example of how a principled approach to evaluation can support rapid development of RAG system in a startup environment.

## 2   Technical Overview

Figure 1 provides an overview of Evalugator. Key steps from the diagram are:

1. The QuestionFisher agent takes an individual document and uses an LLM to generate questions for which the contents of the document provide an answer, a short ground truth answer, a long ground truth answer, and the particular page number.[1] All this is stored as a QuestionSet in Evalugator's datastore. Multiple QuestionSet can be loaded and split up for training, validation, testing, etc.; all these can be visualised via Evalugator's UI.

---

[1] In our case this was because documents were PDFs so had specific pages. Chunks or offsets could be used for non-PDF documents.

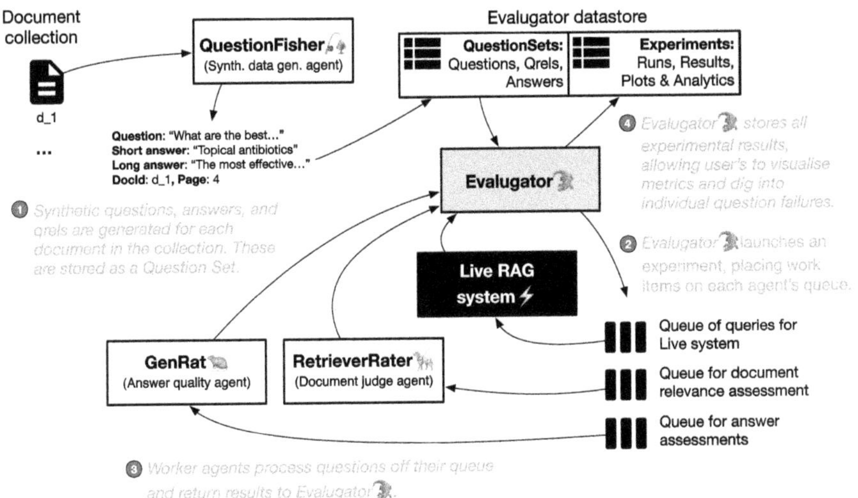


**Fig. 1.** Technical overview of Evalugator and its associated agents.

2. Users launch experiments with a QuestionSet and specific RAG system settings (e.g., index, retrieval model, generator model). The user also specifies if RetrieverRater and GenRat should be run on the results. Evalugator pushes an entry for each question into a queue for the Live RAG system.
3. The Live RAG system pulls questions off the queue and runs them. The results are placed on judging queues for RetrieverRater and GenRat, which run independently and in parallel to assess results. Multiple workers for each agent provide higher throughput. Queues are persisted so experiments gracefully resume if any part of the system goes down.
4. Experiment results appear in Evalugator's datastore. This includes detailed results for each question as well as overall quality metrics (retrieval, answer quality and query latency). Developers can visualise these results via Evalugator's simple UI or connect to the datastore via API to analyse results into their tool of choice.

Figure 2 shows experimental results in the Evalugator UI. The table shows the list of experiments. The user has selected experiment exp_002 and is provided with results for that experiment. Overall evaluation metrics (e.g., Avg. correctness_score and Avg. clarity_score) are shown, as well individual question metrics shown in plots. A table view (not shown) allows inspection of individual questions, answers, retrieved documents and metrics.

We employ two LLM judges within Evalugator to assess retriever and generator effectiveness [1]. The Evalugator's flexible architecture allows for integrating new judge agents; we already plan to add one for generating question-specific evaluation criteria. The RetrieverRater assesses a document using the user's question and both short and long ground truth answers. Different judging rubrics are provided but in general these assess if the document either fully

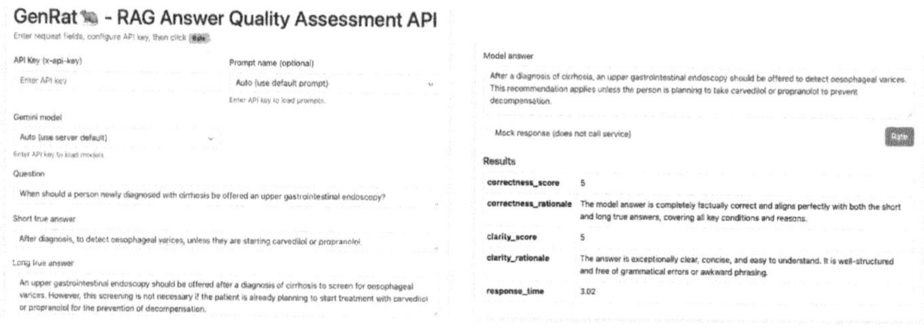

Fig. 2. Evalugator UI list of experiments and results for experiment "exp_002".

Fig. 3. GenRat provides judgements of the answers provided by a RAG system. While generally used via API, a simple UI also encourages developers to dig into individual questions to better analyse effectiveness.

or partially helps to answer the question. GenRat also uses question and ground truth answers but assesses the answer from the RAG system. Its judging rubric combines measures of correction / accuracy and measures of answer clarity. Both these agents can be used via API or as a simple web app (see Fig. 3), encouraging developers to dig into the behaviour of individual questions. In addition to standard quality metrics, these agents also automatically categorise different failures types for each question (e.g., hallunication vs no relevant documents retrieved).

## 3 Presenter Biography

Bevan Koopman is a co-founder of GuideStream.AI and an Associated Professor at The University of Queensland and CSIRO. His work focuses on applying information retrieval and natural language processing: making the myriad of health information more accessible to both clinicians and the public.

**Disclosure of Interests.** The authors have no competing interests to declare that are relevant to the content of this article.

## References


1. Balog, K., Metzler, D., Qin, Z.: Rankers, judges, and assistants: towards understanding the interplay of LLMs in information retrieval evaluation. In: Proceedings of the 48th International ACM SIGIR Conference on Research and Development in Information Retrieval, pp. 3865–3875 (2025)
2. Krayko, N., Sidorov, I., Laputin, F., Panchenko, A., Galimzianova, D., Konovalov, V.: Rurage: robust universal rag evaluator for fast and affordable qa performance testing. In: European Conference on Information Retrieval, pp. 135–145. Springer (2025)
3. Li, H., et al.: LLMs-as-judges: a comprehensive survey on LLM-based evaluation methods. arXiv preprint arXiv:2412.05579 (2024)
4. Trippas, J.R., et al.: Report from the 4th Strategic Workshop on Information Retrieval in Lorne (SWIRL 2025). In: ACM SIGIR Forum, vol. 59, pp. 1–68. ACM, New York (2025)
5. Yu, F., Seedat, N., Herrmannova, D., Schilder, F., Schwarz, J.R.: Beyond pointwise scores: Decomposed criteria-based evaluation of LLM responses. In: Proceedings of the 2025 Conference on Empirical Methods in Natural Language Processing: Industry Track, pp. 1931–1954 (2025)

# A Systematic Analysis of Chunking Strategies for Reliable Question Answering


Sofia Bennani[1] and Charles Moslonka[2,3]([✉])

[1] École polytechnique, Palaiseau, France
`sofia.bennani@polytechnique.edu`
[2] Artefact Research Center, Paris, France
`charles.moslonka@artefact.com`
[3] MICS, CentraleSupélec, Université Paris-Saclay, Gif-sur-Yvette, France



**Abstract.** We study how document chunking choices impact the reliability of Retrieval-Augmented Generation (RAG) systems in industry. While practice often relies on heuristics, our end-to-end evaluation on Natural Questions systematically varies chunking method (token, sentence, semantic, code), chunk size, overlap, and context length. We use a standard industrial setup: SPLADE retrieval and a Mistral-8B generator. We derive actionable lessons for cost-efficient deployment: (i) overlap provides no measurable benefit and increases indexing cost; (ii) sentence chunking is the most cost-effective method, matching semantic chunking up to $\sim$ 5k tokens; (iii) a "context cliff" reduces quality beyond $\sim$ 2.5k tokens; and (iv) optimal context depends on the goal (semantic quality peaks at small contexts; exact match at larger ones).


## 1 Introduction

Enterprises increasingly deploy RAG systems for knowledge access and user support. In industrial settings, these systems operate under strict constraints regarding latency, storage costs, and maintainability. While agentic workflows are the ultimate goal, reliability hinges on the foundational retrieval layer—particularly how source documents are chunked. Despite ample work on retrieval [1–3] and LLMs, chunking is often left to rules of thumb. This paper reports an end-to-end, data-driven study conducted to standardize our production defaults. Our contributions are:

- A systematic evaluation of chunking method, size, overlap, and context length for agentic question answering (QA) on Natural Questions (NQ).
- Compact, deployable guidance: avoid overlap; prefer sentence chunking; select context size by task; beware the "context cliff".
- A reliability view that includes abstention ("NONE") rates alongside semantic and exact-match metrics.

---

S. Bennani—Work done while at Artefact.


© The Author(s), under exclusive license to Springer Nature Switzerland AG 2026
R. Campos et al. (Eds.): ECIR 2026, LNCS 16486, pp. 68–73, 2026.
https://doi.org/10.1007/978-3-032-21321-1_9

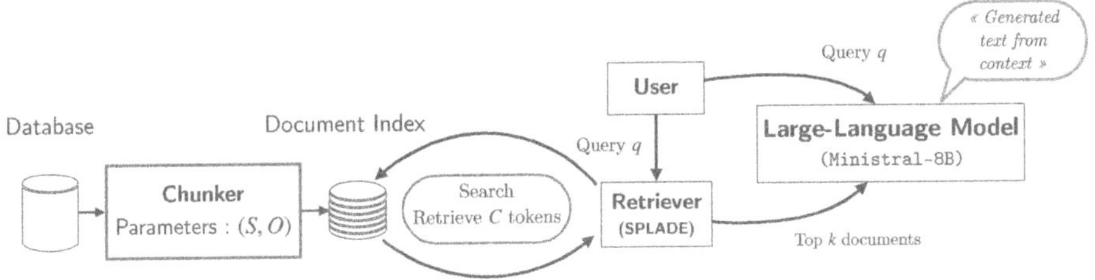


**Fig. 1.** RAG pipeline architecture with parameters $S, O$ and $C$.

## 2    Experimental Setup

We evaluate a standard two-stage RAG pipeline (Fig. 1): a sparse retriever indexes chunked documents; the top-ranked chunks are passed to an instruction-tuned LLM prompted to answer strictly from context and output "NONE" otherwise.

*Task and Corpus.* We use the Natural Questions [4] short-answer subset (open-domain QA). The underlying corpus is English Wikipedia; documents are ingested and chunked according to each strategy below, then indexed.

*Retrieval and Context Budgeting.* We use SPLADE [5,6] (pretrained weights [7]) to build a sparse index over all chunks. At query time, we retrieve the top-ranked chunks and fill a token budget $C$ (context length) using the generator's tokenizer, appending in rank order until the budget is reached. This "fill-to-budget" policy ensures fair comparison across chunk sizes and methods (no fixed-$K$ bias).

*Chunking Strategies.*

- Token: fixed-size sliding windows of target size $S$ with optional token overlap $O$.
- Sentence: respects sentence boundaries; no sentence is split.
- Semantic: sentence-preserving; adjacent sentences are merged if cosine similarity (`all-MiniLM-L12-v2`) exceeds 0.5, up to the target size $S$.
- Code: structure-aware parsing (e.g., functions/classes) for source code, focused on markdown; included for completeness though NQ is text-centric.

*Generation and Abstention.* We use `Ministral-8B-Instruct-2410` [8] with low-temperature decoding ($T = 0.1$). The prompt enforces grounded generation and explicit abstention: "Answer only using the provided context. If the context is insufficient, output 'NONE'." We cap output length to short answers.

*Parameters Varied.* We evaluate four **methods** (Token, Sentence, Semantic, Code) across a grid of sizes. We test **chunk sizes** $S$ from 50 to 500 (step 50), with **overlaps** $O$ of 0% or 20%. Finally, we retrieve into a **context budget** $C$ of {500, 1k, 2.5k, 5k, 10k} tokens.

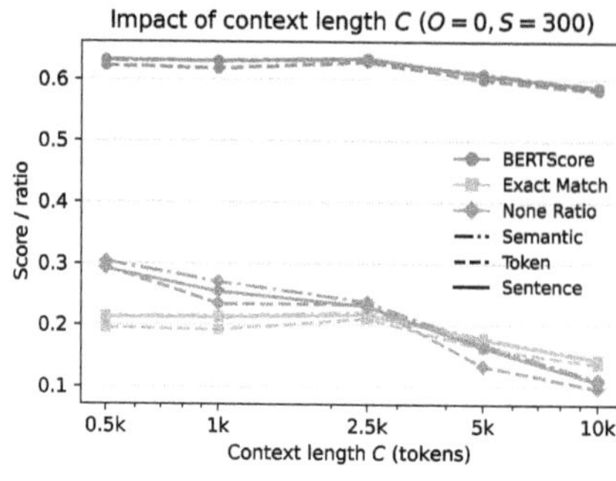
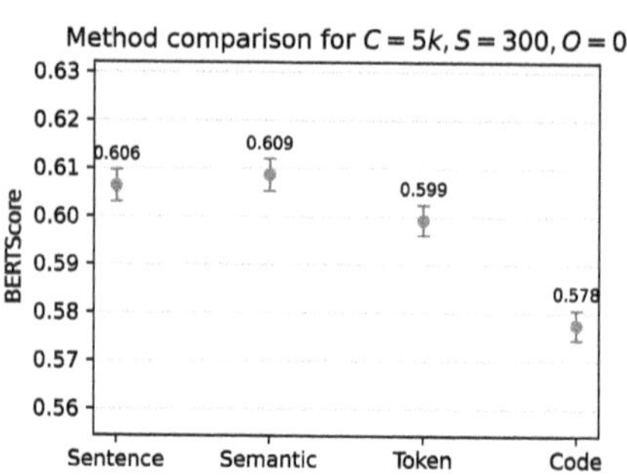

**Fig. 2.** Left: Effect of context length $C$ on metrics for different chunking methods (Sentence, Semantic, Token). Right: Chunking method comparison at fixed $C = 5000$ tokens and $S = 300$, $O = 0$. Dots show means; bars denote 95% bootstrap CIs.

*Metrics and Protocol.* We report:

- BERTScore [9] (semantic quality vs. reference answer).
- Exact Match (EM) with standard normalization (lowercasing; stripping punctuation/articles).
- None Ratio: fraction of queries where the model outputs "NONE".

We compute 95% bootstrap confidence intervals over questions; claims of "no measurable difference" indicate paired deltas within CIs (e.g., $|\Delta \text{BERTScore}| \leq 0.004$, EM differences $\leq 0.001$). We intentionally do not use rerankers or LLM-as-reranker to isolate the effect of chunking and context budgeting.

## 3   Findings

We report the end-to-end effects that were most consistent and actionable across settings, along with brief mechanisms and deployment implications.

*F1. Overlap adds cost without measurable gains.* Across paired configurations, adding 10–20% overlap did not improve BERTScore or EM (e.g., $|\Delta \text{BERTScore}| \leq 0.004$; EM differences $\leq 0.001$). Mechanism: with a sentence-aware pipeline and a sparse retriever, boundary spillover rarely changes the top-$C$ content; overlap mostly introduces near-duplicates. Cost: for overlap ratio $r$, chunk count (and index size) inflates by a factor $1/(1-r)$ (e.g., $r = 0.2$ leads to $1.25\times$ more chunks), increasing ingestion time and storage. Recommendation: use $O = 0$ unless you have evidence your retriever benefits from boundary redundancy.

*F2. Method "tier list": sentence $\approx$ semantic $>$ token $\gg$ code (for text).* Sentence and semantic chunking were statistically tied up to ~5k tokens; token chunking lagged; code chunking was not competitive on this text task (Fig. 2). Mechanism: sentence-preserving methods keep topical coherence and reduce cross-sentence

**Table 1.** Practical defaults for agentic QA (text documents).

| Choice | Default | Rationale |
| --- | --- | --- |
| Overlap $O$ | 0% | No measurable benefit; reduces cost/complexity |
| Chunker | Sentence | Matches semantic up to $\sim$5k tokens; cheaper |
| Chunk size $S$ | 150–300 | Balances recall vs. abstention |
| Context $C$ (QA) | $\sim$2.5k | Avoids context cliff; boosts EM |
| Context $C$ (Summ.) | $\sim$500 | Maximizes semantic faithfulness |
| When $C > 5$k | Consider Semantic | Slight edge at very large contexts |

fragmentation, improving both retrieval precision and LLM grounding. Semantic merging helps when very large contexts are used (slight edge $C > 5$k), likely by packing semantically contiguous text. Recommendation: default to sentence; consider semantic only for very large $C$ or highly discursive documents.

*F3. The "context cliff": more is not always better.* Performance improved from small to moderate contexts but dropped beyond $\sim$2.5k tokens. For sentence chunking ($O = 0$, $S = 300$), BERTScore was stable between 0.5k–2.5k tokens and then declined by $\sim 4$–5% relatively at 10k tokens. Mechanism: long-context LLMs can suffer from distraction and redundancy; retrieval at large budgets introduces overlapping or off-topic chunks, diluting signal. Recommendation: identify and enforce a sweet spot for $C$; in our setup, $C \approx 2.5$k was a strong default for QA. Note that the exact drop-off point is model-dependent; our values reflect `Ministral-8B-Instruct-2410` and should be re-tuned per LLM. However, the existence of a performance plateau or decline with excessive context is a consistent phenomenon in RAG.

*F4. Goal-driven tuning: small $C$ for semantic quality; larger $C$ for factual accuracy; abstention is tunable.* BERTScore tended to peak at small, focused contexts ($\sim 500$ tokens), whereas EM peaked at larger contexts ($\sim 2.5$k). None Ratio fell with larger $C$ (e.g., from $\sim 30$% at 0.5k to $\sim 11$% at 10k) and rose with larger $S$. Mechanism: small $C$ concentrates the most relevant evidence (good for semantic faithfulness), while larger $C$ increases recall across disparate mentions (good for EM). Larger chunks reduce the number of distinct contexts retrieved, increasing abstention when narrow evidence is missed. Recommendation: for summaries/explanations, keep $C$ small; for factoid QA, use $C \approx 2.5$k. To reduce "NONE", increase $C$ and use smaller $S$ (see Table 1 for practical defaults in QA tasks) .

*Limitations and Future Work.* Our study focuses on optimizing the *first-stage* retrieval index, a critical step for latency-sensitive industrial applications. We intentionally excluded rerankers and late-interaction models (e.g., ColBERT) to isolate the effects of chunking on the base retriever; while these methods often improve precision, they incur higher storage and latency costs that must be weighed against their benefits in future work. Furthermore, our results on Natural Questions are most representative of general text-centric corpora. While code chunking remains the clear choice for source code, these findings should be validated on specialized enterprise domains (e.g., legal or technical documentation). Finally, we used low temperature ($T = 0.1$) to minimize generation variance, though key trends persisted under bootstrap resampling.

## 4      Conclusion

Chunking is a first-order design choice for reliable, cost-effective RAG agents. Our study provides compact, deployable guidance: avoid overlap; default to sentence chunking; tune context to the task; beware the context cliff beyond $\sim$2.5k tokens; and use $S$ and $C$ to control abstention. These defaults have improved the robustness of client-facing agents in practice and offer a baseline for future IR-for-agents evaluations.

**Presenter CV.** Charles Moslonka is a Senior Research Scientist at Artefact's Research Center, and an Associated Researcher at the MICS Laboratory of Université Paris-Saclay. His main topics of interest are evaluation of large language models - particularly in RAG pipelines - and hallucination detection along with information retrieval. He received his Ph.D in Statistical Physics and Applied Mathematics in 2023 from the Paris Sciences & Lettres (PSL) University in Paris, France. Before studying Large Language Models, he mainly worked on stochastic processes and spin networks.

**Company Presentation.** Artefact is a leading global consulting company dedicated to accelerating the adoption of data and AI to positively impact organizations. We specialize in implementing machine learning pipelines as well as data & AI transformation, delivering tangible business results across the entire enterprise value chain. Artefact offers a comprehensive set of end-to-end, data-driven solutions—from strategy to operations—built on data science and cutting-edge AI technologies. Our 2,000 employees operate in 27 countries, partnering with over 1,000 clients, including many of the world's top 300 brands, to deliver AI projects at scale in all industry sectors.

**Acknowledgments.** This work was done as part of the ArGiMi project, funded by BPIFrance under the France2030 national effort towards numerical common goods.

**Disclosure of Interests.** The authors have no competing interests to declare that are relevant to the content of this article.

## References

1. Faysse, M., Sibille, H., Wu, T., Omrani, B., Viaud, G., Hudelot, C., Colombo, P.: ColPali: Efficient Document Retrieval with Vision Language Models (2024)

2. Santhanam, K., Khattab, O., Saad-Falcon, J., Potts, C., Zaharia, M.: ColBERTv2: Effective and Efficient Retrieval via Lightweight Late Interaction (2022)
3. Formal, T., Lassance, C., Piwowarski, B., Clinchant, S.: Towards effective and efficient sparse neural information retrieval. ACM Trans. Inf. Syst. **42**(5), 1–46 (2024)
4. Kwiatkowski, T., et al.: Natural questions: a benchmark for question answering research. Trans. Assoc. Comput. Linguist. **7**, 453–466 (2019)
5. Formal, T., Piwowarski, B., Clinchant, S.: Sparse Lexical and Expansion Model for First Stage Ranking, SPLADE (2021)
6. Formal, T., Lassance, C., Piwowarski, B., Clinchant, S.: SPLADE v2: Sparse Lexical and Expansion Model for Information Retrieval (2021)
7. Kong, W., Dudek, J.M., Li, C., Zhang, M., Bendersky, M.: SparseEmbed: learning sparse lexical representations with contextual embeddings for retrieval. In: Proceedings of the 46th International ACM SIGIR Conference on Research and Development in Information Retrieval, Taipei Taiwan, pp. 2399–2403. ACM (2023)
8. Mistral AI Team. Un Ministral, des Ministraux — Mistral AI. https://mistral.ai/fr/news/ministraux
9. Zhang, T., Kishore, V., Wu, F., Weinberger, K.Q., Artzi, Y.: BERTScore: Evaluating Text Generation with BERT. arXiv (2019)

# Understanding Multi-Structured Documents via LLMs'

Shivani Upadhyay[1(✉)], Messiah Ataey[2], Syed Shariyar Murtaza[2], Yifan Nie[2], Anirudh Aggarwal[2], and Jimmy Lin[1]

[1] University of Waterloo, Waterloo, Canada
sjupadhyay@uwaterloo.ca
[2] Manulife, Toronto, Canada

**Abstract.** Complexly structured data present in documents and web content pose significant challenges for accurate MLLM reasoning. Although MLLMs have advanced substantially, they continue to struggle with intricate data formats such as nested tables and multi-dimensional charts, often leading to hallucinations. This paper explores the capabilities of LLMs and MLLMs in understanding and answering questions from complex data found in PDF documents by leveraging a pre-processing pipeline consisting of industrial and open-source tools. Our results showcase that incorporating RAG and pre-processing tools enables MLLMs to achieve approximately 5% higher accuracy than direct multi-modal inference, while also reducing their overall cost since only text-mode is used. Our code is available at: https://github.com/manulife-ai/financialqa.

**Keywords:** Multi-Structured Documents · LLMs · Pre-Processing

## 1   Introduction

Hybrid data sources, such as PDF documents and web pages, present information in a variety of structures with complex arrangements. The advancements in Multi-modal Large Language Models (MLLMs), including proprietary models like GPT [21], Gemini [25], Claude [1] and open-source models such as LlaVA [13, 14], LaVIT [10], and Emu [3, 24], have led to a significant improvement in these models' abilities to understand heterogeneous data. However, these models often hallucinate when processing diverse structured data due to a limited understanding of various data structures.

Recent developments in LLMs such as the GPT [21] and LLaMA [27] have shown human-level effectiveness in complex Question Answering (QA) tasks. A key limitation of LLMs is their inability to answer questions about data outside their training set. Retrieval Augmented Generation (RAG) [5] addresses this by injecting relevant external information within prompts, enabling more effective QA. Nevertheless, even with RAG, reasoning over multi-structured content like tables and charts in financial documents remains a significant challenge.

---

S. Upadhyay—Work done in collaboration with Manulife.

This paper looks into combining tools like Document Intelligence,[1] pypdf,[2] and ChartVLM [28] as a pre-processor, and its effectiveness in improving QA over complex PDF content. Instead of aiming for a full comparison of all tools, this paper evaluates the pre-processor with RAG setup against MLLMs and highlights practical improvements. This paper's contribution is to provide insights into the following research questions:

**(a)** Can pre-processing tools help improve the comprehensibility of LLMs and MLLMs for QA over multi-structured PDF documents?

**(b)** How can pre-processing tools save costs when performing QA over multi-structured documents in comparison to other popular end-to-end commercial offerings?

Our results show that: (a) Using industrial and open-source pre-processing tools increases MLLM QA accuracy by about 5% over direct multi-modal inference, while text-only LLMs such as GPT-4 attain up to 76% accuracy, substantially exceeding direct MLLM performance. (b) The document cost/page is $0.00231 with our pre-processing tools, which is 74.33% cheaper than the cheapest solutions (Claude-Opus-3).

## 2   Background and Related Work

Analysts in finance and insurance rely on reports and statements, but the volume can be overwhelming. A generative AI chat application using RAG and LLMs helps them get answers faster with less effort. Figure 1a shows a typical RAG system where text, tables, and graphics from documents are extracted using a pre-processor (highlighted in blue), embedded into vectors, indexed, and retrieved at query time to generate responses.

QA over structured document content includes Table QA, which involves analyzing raw tables or those with annotated metadata to answer queries [2, 7–9, 20, 22, 29]; Chart QA, which focuses on interpreting various chart types and has gained traction with dedicated datasets for improved model comprehension [6, 11, 16, 18]; and Document

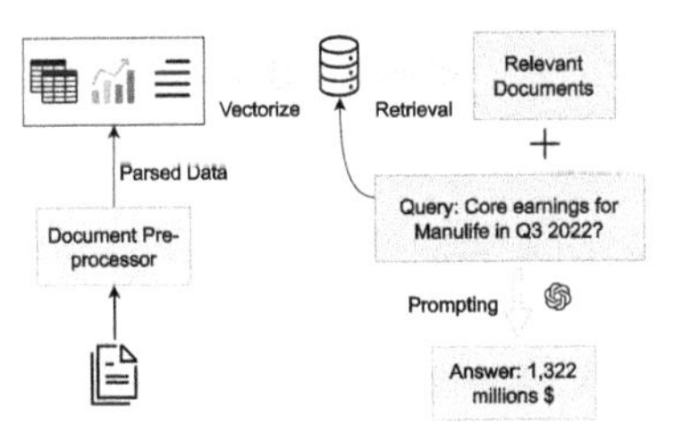


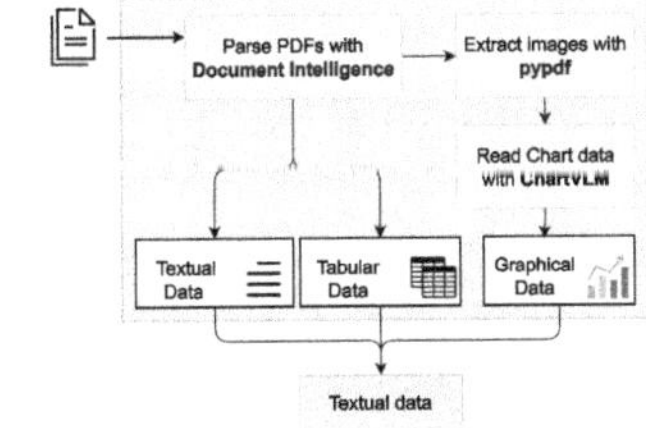


(a) RAG framework with pre-processor.        (b) Internal workflow of the pre-processor.

**Fig. 1.** The left panel shows the pre-processing tools, while the right panel details the pre-processor's internal workflow.

---

[1] https://azure.microsoft.com/en-us/products/ai-services/ai-document-intelligence.

[2] https://pypi.org/project/pypdf.

QA, which evaluates models on diverse document formats such as scanned text-heavy pages [17,26], scientific literature [15,19,23], and raw documents [4]. Our document pre-processing tools focus on extracting multi-structured content found in PDF documents, and thus, the evaluation dataset used encompasses various data types.

## 3  Methodology

The pre-processing tools extract data content found in financial documents. Figure 1b showcases the internal workflow of the pre-processor. The pre-processor uses Azure Document Intelligence to extract both tabular and textual information, combining Optical Character Recognition (OCR) capabilities with advanced deep learning models for precise extraction. Document Intelligence extracts both textual and structural information, which can be categorized as either geometric (e.g., text, tables, and figures) or a logical role (e.g., section titles, image captions, page footers). Extracted tables are stored as JSON, which contains information for each cell in the table, including details such as row/column-span, a flag indicating if it's a column header and other attributes. When hierarchical column headers are present, they are concatenated using the header flag to ensure accurate key-value mapping.

To extract graphical images, we use Azure Document Intelligence to obtain bounding box coordinates and then apply pypdf to crop and save them. In the case of dropping irrelevant images, an optional classifier can be added to check whether an extracted image is not a chart (e.g., a logo) or if it is an incomplete chart. To obtain a textual representation of the extracted chart image, a Pix2Struct [12]-based ChartVLM model is employed that has been fine-tuned on the ChartX dataset [28]. ChartVLM shows improved understanding of chart types and preserves image aspect ratios, enhancing robustness during extraction. The model extracts chart data into CSV format, which is then converted to JSON as part of the pre-processor, similar to tables. An attempt to enhance ChartVLM's interpretation abilities through fine-tuning was made, but due to the complexities of real-world chart understanding and limited data availability, the model consistently overfitted and failed to provide any meaningful performance improvements. Section 5 outlines the challenges in chart extraction and interpretation.

## 4  Experimental Setup

The dataset documents are first processed by the pre-processor to extract multi-structured data. This extracted text is then segmented into 600-token chunks using LangChain's TokenTextSplitter[3] to prevent excessive input size. Each chunk is converted into a vector embedding using OpenAI's text-embedding-ada model and subsequently indexed in Azure AI Search. During retrieval, the three most relevant chunks are selected from the index based on cosine similarity to the input query.[4] The retrieved data is then augmented with the query in the prompt to guide the LLM's

---

[3] https://js.langchain.com/v0.1/docs/modules/data_connection/document_transformers/token_splitter.

[4] We chose $k = 3$ empirically for a balance between accuracy and context size.

response generation. This enables the LLM to better understand the data and produce accurate outputs.

For industry-relevant evaluations, a private test set assembled by financial experts was used, consisting of 75 QA pairs of varying complexity derived from numerous financial documents of Canadian companies, where 53 questions are for tables and 22 for charts. Simple questions may just involve reading a value from a single location, while harder ones require combining multiple pieces of information to find the answer.

*Component Level Analysis:* In this experiment, the tabular and chart components of the document pre-processor are evaluated individually. Tables and charts are extracted from documents and converted to JSON format using the document pre-processor, which are then passed as input to an LLM to generate answers based on this processed information. Since the relevant information is provided directly to the LLM, these experiments don't use retrieval and instead focus on assessing individual component effectiveness. The following datasets are used for evaluating LLM table and chart comprehension:

- **VQAonBD dataset:** Tabular images from the dataset (i.e., the validation set of 4535 images) are used as input for the evaluations. The dataset has almost 50 questions partitioned into 5 categories for each image based on their content and format [20].
- **ComplexChartQA (CCQA) dataset:** A manually-curated chart evaluation set consisting of 50 complex chart images with questions to assess comprehension efficacy.

## 5    Results and Discussion

Table 1 compares MLLMs (rows 2*) against RAG with pre-processing using text-only models (rows 1*). To evaluate MLLM's multi-modal capabilities, PDF pages were converted to images and input into the model. Because of limitations in the number of input images, it was ensured that the answer was contained within the context size.

**Table 1.** End-to-end comparison of MLLMs and RAG with pre-processing on private test set. Note that GPT-4 and GPT-3.5$_t$ are text-only models.

|        | Pre-processing | RAG | LLM | Input mode | Acc. ↑ | Cost/call ↓ |
|--------|:---:|:---:|---|---|---|---|
| 1(a)   | Y | Y | GPT-3.5$_t$ | T | 60.0 | **$ 0.0003** |
| 1(b)   | Y | Y | GPT-4 | T | **76.0** | $ 0.0360 |
| 1(c)   | Y | Y | GPT-4$_o$ | T | 61.3 | $ 0.0030 |
| 1(d)   | Y | Y | Claude-Opus-4.5 | T | 73.3 | $ 0.0038 |
| 2 (a)  | - | - | GPT-4$_o$ | I,T | 56.0 | $ 0.0765 |
| 2 (b)  | - | - | Claude-Opus-4.5 | I,T | 68.3 | $ 0.0767 |

Direct document processing with GPT-4$_o$ yields 56% accuracy, while using RAG with pre-processing improves performance to 61.3%. Although GPT-3.5$_t$ and GPT-4 are text-input only models, GPT-3.5$_t$ with pre-processing achieves higher accuracy

(60.0%) than GPT-$4_o$ (row 2(a)), while using GPT-4 substantially improves performance, reaching 76%. Additionally, to benchmark against an off-the-shelf, non-OpenAI model, we evaluate Claude-Opus-4.5 by directly inputting the PDF page and query. As shown in row 2(b), it attains 68.3% accuracy, which is less effective than its text-only counterpart with RAG and pre-processing in row 1(d). Furthermore, text-only input significantly lowers API costs. For GPT-$4_o$, it drops from $0.0765 per call with image and text inputs to $0.0030, while for Claude-Opus-4.5 it decreases from $0.0767 to $0.0038.

**Table 2.** Cost analysis of alternatives.

| Solution | Main Model | Cost/Page ↓ |
|---|---|---|
| LlamaParse | GPT-$4_o$ | $ 0.0300 |
| Vertex AI | Gemini-2.0-flash | $ 0.1161 |
| Anthropic | Claude-Opus-3 | $ 0.0090 |
| Our solution | GPT-$4_o$ | **$ 0.0023** |

Table 2 presents a cost comparison between the proposed pre-processor and other document analysis alternatives, both assuming 600 tokens/page. The pre-processor cost analysis accounts for API costs associated with Azure Document Intelligence and GPT-$4_o$ in text-mode.[5] The LlamaParse,[6] Vertex AI[7] and Anthropic[8] products are readily available solutions that provide similar functionality. After converting vendor prices to per-page costs (Table 2), our proposed pre-processor emerges as the most cost effective.

*Component Level Analysis:* Table 3 showcases the performance of tabular data comprehension for questions of varying levels of difficulty from the VQAonBD dataset ("VQAonBD categories") and from the ComplexChartQA ("CCQA") dataset. For table QA, improvements are observed when using the document pre-processor with GPT-$3.5_t$ and GPT-4 as compared to GPT-$4_o$ across all categories. For chart QA, comparable effectiveness is observed between both methods, with a slight improvement using the document pre-processing framework with GPT-4. This analysis demonstrates the effectiveness of the individual data extraction component for both tables and charts.

*Challenges with Chart Interpretation:* Interpreting charts in particular is challenging due to the variety of chart types, each requiring a unique approach to address. Even within the same chart type, variations in presentation demand that models adapt and learn these differences. Manual inspection of chart results showcases that GPT-$4_o$ interprets charts well when they include clear labels and text annotations for the datapoints, likely leveraging its OCR capabilities. However, it struggles with charts lacking

---

[5] https://azure.microsoft.com/en-us/pricing/details/cognitive-services/openai-service.

[6] https://docs.cloud.llamaindex.ai/llamaparse/usage_data.

[7] https://cloud.google.com/vertex-ai/generative-ai/pricing#modality-based-pricing.

[8] https://www.anthropic.com/news/claude-3-family.

**Table 3.** Pre-processing tools' component level effectiveness for tables and charts input.

| | Model | VQAonBD categories | | | | | CCQA |
|---|---|---|---|---|---|---|---|
| | | 1 | 2 | 3 | 4 | 5 | |
| 1(a) | pre-processing + GPT-3.5$_t$ | 0.64 | 0.25 | 0.29 | 0.41 | 0.21 | 0.56 |
| 1(b) | pre-processing + GPT-4 | **0.77** | **0.58** | **0.44** | **0.57** | **0.48** | **0.68** |
| 2 | GPT-4$_o$ (Images) | 0.59 | 0.03 | 0.04 | 0.45 | 0.38 | 0.66 |

explicit textual content, often misinterpreting complex elements and producing inaccurate responses. On the other hand, ChartVLM can interpret charts without annotations, but its limited understanding of complex visualizations often leads to incomplete or inaccurate outputs. Financial documents frequently include multiple plots in a single image, which ChartVLM misinterprets due to its expectations of simpler input structures, where it sometimes focuses on a single sub-image and overlooks others.

# 6    Conclusion

This paper investigates whether LLMs can understand complex, multi-structured PDFs and how pre-processing tools can enhance comprehension and reduce costs compared to directly using document page inputs with an MLLM. Across all evaluated LLMs and MLLMs, document pre-processing with RAG consistently improves response accuracy relative to comparable direct multi-modal inference. Furthermore, the cost analysis shows considerable cost savings when using the RAG with a document pre-processing framework compared to directly using document page inputs with an MLLM. Despite these improvements, further improvements in both LLMs and pre-processing tools are needed for better handling of complex PDFs.

**Acknowledgements.** This research was supported in part by the Natural Sciences and Engineering Research Council (NSERC) of Canada and by an Institute of Information.

**Disclosure of Interests.** Some authors were employed by Manulife during this work. The authors declare no other competing interests relevant to this work. Funding is listed in the Acknowledgements.

# References


1. Anthropic: The Claude 3 model family: Opus, Sonnet, Haiku
2. Chen, Z., et al.: FinQA: a dataset of numerical reasoning over financial data. In: Moens, M.F., Huang, X., Specia, L., Yih, S.W.T. (eds.) Proceedings of the 2021 Conference on Empirical Methods in Natural Language Processing, pp. 3697–3711. Association for Computational Linguistics, Online and Punta Cana, Dominican Republic (2021)
3. Dai, X., et al.: EMU: enhancing image generation models using photogenic needles in a haystack. arXiv:2309.15807 (2023)

4. Dasigi, P., Lo, K., Beltagy, I., Cohan, A., Smith, N.A., Gardner, M.: A dataset of information-seeking questions and answers anchored in research papers. arXiv:2105.03011 (2021)

5. Gao, Y., et al.: Retrieval-augmented generation for large language models: a survey. arXiv:2312.10997 (2023)

6. Hoque, E., Kavehzadeh, P., Masry, A.: Chart question answering: state of the art and future directions. arXiv:2205.03966 (2022)

7. Hwang, W., Yim, J., Park, S., Seo, M.: A comprehensive exploration on WikiSQL with table-aware word contextualization. arXiv:1902.01069 (2019)

8. Jauhar, S.K., Turney, P., Hovy, E.: TabMCQ: a dataset of general knowledge tables and multiple-choice questions. arXiv:1602.03960 (2016)

9. Jin, N., Siebert, J., Li, D., Chen, Q.: A survey on table question answering: recent advances. arXiv:2207.05270 (2022)

10. Jin, Y., et al.: Unified language-vision pretraining with dynamic discrete visual tokenization. arXiv:2309.04669 (2023)

11. Kahou, S.E., Michalski, V., Atkinson, A., Kadar, A., Trischler, A., Bengio, Y.: FigureQA: an annotated figure dataset for visual reasoning. arXiv:1710.07300 (2018)

12. Lee, K., et al.: Pix2Struct: screenshot parsing as pretraining for visual language understanding. arXiv:2210.03347 (2023)

13. Liu, H., Li, C., Li, Y., Lee, Y.J.: Improved baselines with visual instruction tuning. arXiv:2310.03744 (2023)

14. Liu, H., Li, C., Wu, Q., Lee, Y.J.: Visual instruction tuning. arXiv:2304.08485 (2023)

15. Lála, J., O'Donoghue, O., Shtedritski, A., Cox, S., Rodriques, S.G., White, A.D.: PaperQA: retrieval-augmented generative agent for scientific research. arXiv:2312.07559 (2023)

16. Masry, A., Long, D.X., Tan, J.Q., Joty, S., Hoque, E.: ChartQA: a benchmark for question answering about charts with visual and logical reasoning. arXiv:2203.10244 (2022)

17. Mathew, M., Karatzas, D., Jawahar, C.V.: DocVQA: a dataset for VQA on document images. arXiv:2007.00398 (2021)

18. Methani, N., Ganguly, P., Khapra, M.M., Kumar, P.: PlotQA: reasoning over scientific plots. arXiv:1909.00997 (2020)

19. Narayanan, S., et al.: Aviary: training language agents on challenging scientific tasks. arXiv:2412.21154 (2024)

20. Nguyen, P., Ly, N.T., Takeda, H., Takasu, A.: TabIQA: table questions answering on business document images. arXiv:2303.14935 (2023)

21. Achiam, J., et al.: GPT-4 technical report. arXiv:2303.08774 (2024)

22. Pasupat, P., Liang, P.: Compositional semantic parsing on semi-structured tables. In: Zong, C., Strube, M. (eds.) Proceedings of the 53rd Annual Meeting of the Association for Computational Linguistics and the 7th International Joint Conference on Natural Language Processing (Volume 1: Long Papers), pp. 1470–1480. Association for Computational Linguistics, Beijing, China (2015)

23. Skarlinski, M.D., et al.: Language agents achieve superhuman synthesis of scientific knowledge. arXiv:2409.13740 (2024)

24. Sun, Q., et al.: Generative multimodal models are in-context learners. arXiv:2312.13286 (2023)

25. Anil, R., et al.: Gemini: a family of highly capable multimodal models. arXiv:2312.11805 (2024)

26. Tito, R., Karatzas, D., Valveny, E.: Document Collection Visual Question Answering, pp. 778–792. Springer (2021)

27. Touvron, H., et al.: LLaMA: open and efficient foundation language models. arXiv:2302.13971 (2023)

28. Xia, R., et al.: ChartX & ChartVLM: a versatile benchmark and foundation model for complicated chart reasoning. arXiv:2402.12185 (2024)
29. Zhu, F., et al.: TAT-QA: a question answering benchmark on a hybrid of tabular and textual content in finance. arXiv:2105.07624 (2021)

# Exploring Neural IR in Europeana

Suhaib Basir[1] , Mónica Marrero[2](✉) , and Julián Urbano[3]

[1] Infinite Analytics, Boston, USA
[2] Europeana Foundation, The Hague, The Netherlands
`monica.marrero@europeana.eu`
[3] Delft University of Technology, Delft, The Netherlands

**Abstract.** Europeana is the leading digital library of Europe's cultural heritage, providing access to over 60 million items in more than 40 languages. Its search infrastructure relies on Solr and BM25 over the items' metadata, thus depending heavily on keyword matching and resource-intensive treatments such as translation and multilingual metadata enrichment. This paper explores the application of Neural Information Retrieval (NIR) approaches in Europeana, focusing on multilinguality. We created a dataset for comparative evaluation, and show that while NIR demonstrates strong potential for multilingual search, challenges remain regarding its performance, particularly for entity-centric queries. This work also highlights the need for more reliable evaluation data.

**Keywords:** Digital Library · Cultural Heritage · Neural IR · LLM

## 1 Introduction

Artificial Intelligence (AI) is increasingly deployed in digital libraries to enhance internal processes (e.g., cataloging and content enhancement) and to improve discoverability and accessibility. Somewhat mature applications include handwritten and optical character recognition, as well as enrichment initiatives like Saint George on a Bike [16], Transcribathon [5], the Cultural Heritage AI Cookbook [14], and the generation of domain-specific models, like those created in the national libraries of Norway [8] and Sweden [6]. Applications of AI in search remain more exploratory. Examples include image-based similarity search at the Bavarian State Library [2], AI-guided query reformulation at Stony Brook University Libraries [18], semantic image search at the National Museum of Norway [17], and Retrieval-Augmented Generation (RAG) efforts at Northwestern University Libraries [11].

The cultural heritage community is particularly alert to risks posed by AI, since its operations depend on public trust regarding the accuracy and reliability of information, as well as the protection of intellectual property. As a result, institutions are slowly developing strategies for responsible AI adoption

---

S. Basir—Work as an MSc student at TU Delft [1].


R. Campos et al. (Eds.): ECIR 2026, LNCS 16486, pp. 82–88, 2026.
https://doi.org/10.1007/978-3-032-21321-1_11

(e.g., [13]). Digital libraries often lack substantial technical capacity and operate under resource constraints, making experimentation difficult. In addition, research on AI for information access rarely reflects the characteristics of CH collections: heterogeneous, dynamic, multilingual, and with a mix of structured and unstructured sparse data. This mismatch reduces the direct applicability of many state-of-the-art methods.

Europeana exemplifies these challenges. It aggregates digitized metadata for CH content from thousands of European libraries, archives and museums, forming a large and diverse metadata collection. Search is currently supported by a keyword-based Solr+BM25 system, which scales well but is limited in handling multilinguality, semantics, and contextual understanding. To mitigate these issues, Europeana enriches metadata with multilingual entity information from external sources like Wikidata, and translates queries and selected metadata fields to English as a pivot language [9,12]. However, these steps introduce noise, especially for short queries, entities and fields with little contextual information. They are also resource-intensive, costly to maintain, and incomplete, as translation is currently not automatically applied to newly ingested metadata.

This paper summarizes Europeana's first evaluation of NIR models to better accommodate its search needs [1]. We compare them with the current pipeline and assess whether neural methods can provide better multilingual and semantic search while reducing reliance on expensive workflows.

## 2   Methodology

We compared the current BM25 baseline with three neural models that follow different approaches: Jina ColBERT v2, a multilingual late-interaction model that encodes token-level embeddings [7]; SBERT (Multilingual DistilUSE), a lightweight sentence transformer [15]; and BGE-M3 Hybrid, a dense+sparse model that combines semantic and lexical evidence via rank fusion [3].

Given the absence of a suitable dataset with explicit relevance judgments, we built one from Europeana's user click logs in the period April–May 2024. We started from user queries with associated clicked documents, keeping only those where both query and document languages were among the 20 most represented ones. This resulted in 23K queries and 45K clicked documents. We randomly selected 40% of queries for testing, ensuring that the joint query-document language distribution remained consistent across training and test sets.

From the full Europeana corpus of 60M documents, we retained the 40M documents with enrichment and English translation. To reduce the cost of experiments, we randomly downsampled smaller subsets of 4M and 1M documents, to which we added the 45K clicked ones. Figure 1 shows the language distributions of documents, queries and clicks. The 1M collection was used for testing, while the 4M collection was used to retrieve negatives for fine-tuning: for each training query, clicked documents served as positives, and negatives were sampled by running BM25 and taking one document per language from the bottom of the ranking.

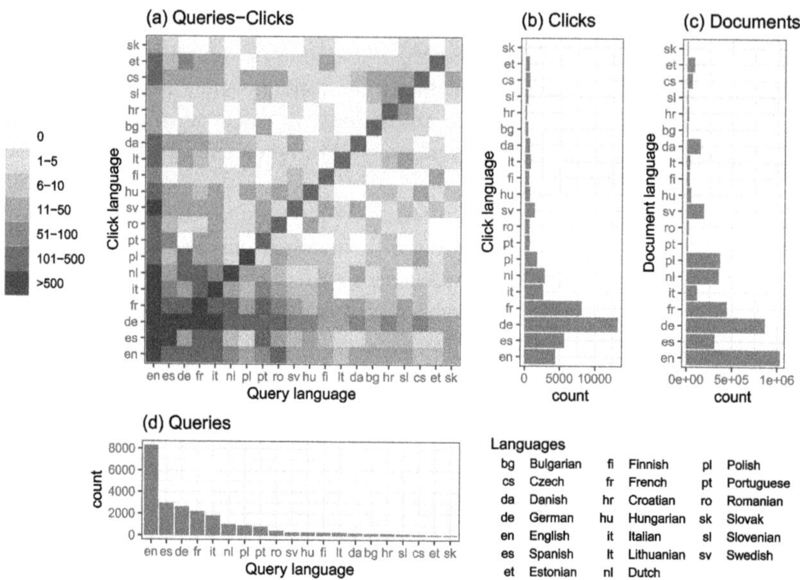



**Fig. 1.** The language distribution of the documents (c) shows a clear overrepresentation of English and German and, to a lesser extent, French, Polish, Dutch and Spanish. The language of clicked documents (b) follows a similar distribution, though English is much less frequent because clicks were recorded under a BM25 policy with document augmentation (i.e. non-English documents become retrievable for English queries). The language distribution of the queries (d) shows a similar bias towards popular languages, especially English. The joint query-click language distribution (a), where the diagonal reflects monolinguality, shows the expected clustering among the most popular languages in both queries and clicks: English, Spanish, German, French, Italian and Dutch.

For evaluation, the 1M test dataset was indexed in Solr for BM25, FAISS for ColBERT, and Milvus for SBERT and BGE. We indexed all metadata fields mapped to Solr-BM25's default field (e.g., `title`, `description`, `creator`). We contemplated two main factors for comparison: model (and possible fine-tuning) and augmentation (adding English translation to the query, and enrichments and/or translations to the documents). These factors are examined along two dimensions: multilinguality and effectiveness. For multilinguality we calculate the fraction (F) of retrieved documents in a language other than the query's, and the entropy (H, normalized in $[0, 1]$) of their distribution as a measure of (lack of) bias towards specific languages. For effectiveness we compute Average Precision (AP) and Recall (R). Only the top 100 documents per query were analyzed. Since English acts as the pivot language for translation and accounts for 36% of the queries, the effectiveness metrics are calculated separately for English and non-English queries, and reported here only for the latter; the overall conclusions are the same.

**Table 1.** Multilinguality (F,H) and effectiveness (AP,R) for a selection of systems (no fine-tuning). Bare for systems without augmentation, Daug for full document augmentation (translations and enrichments), and Daug+Qaug for query augmentation.

| | Bare | | | | Daug | | | | Daug+Qaug | | | |
|---|---|---|---|---|---|---|---|---|---|---|---|---|
| | BM25 | ColBERT | SBERT | BGE | BM25 | ColBERT | SBERT | BGE | BM25 | ColBERT | SBERT | BGE |
| F | 0.542 | 0.747 | 0.730 | 0.608 | 0.677 | 0.745 | 0.729 | 0.609 | 0.740 | 0.755 | 0.723 | 0.630 |
| H | 0.726 | 0.807 | 0.733 | 0.789 | 0.743 | 0.805 | 0.732 | 0.789 | 0.797 | 0.805 | 0.728 | 0.788 |
| AP | 0.752 | 0.323 | 0.034 | 0.379 | 0.775 | 0.343 | 0.031 | 0.365 | 0.703 | 0.306 | 0.039 | 0.318 |
| R | 0.890 | 0.623 | 0.144 | 0.696 | 0.911 | 0.649 | 0.135 | 0.694 | 0.900 | 0.642 | 0.148 | 0.694 |

# 3 Results

Table 1 shows that bare ColBERT and SBERT models achieve the multilinguality of BM25 when it incorporates all augmentations ($F \approx 0.74$). BGE is less multilingual (F = 0.608), but still more so than a bare BM25 model (F = 0.542). Document augmentation has a clear impact on the multilinguality of BM25 ($\Delta F$ = +0.135), where the effect of translations is much larger than the effect of enrichments ($\Delta F$ = +0.128 vs. +0.022). Further adding query augmentation substantially improves BM25, especially in balancing the language distribution ($\Delta F$ = +0.063, $\Delta H$ = +0.054). However, the impact of augmentations is generally limited in the neural models because they are already multilingual. In many instances, and especially with ColBERT, augmentations did even alter the rankings substantially ($RBO^w_{p=0.96}$ [4] below 0.35), but the overall multilinguality and effectiveness barely changed. Only query augmentation led to a mild improvement in BGE ($\Delta F$ = +0.021), but made both ColBERT and BGE less effective.

The impact of fine-tuning is generally inconsistent across models. SBERT is the exception: fine-tuning consistently increases multilinguality ($\Delta F$ = +0.118) and slightly improves language-balance; this balance weakens only in case of extreme multilinguality ($H \approx 0.42$ when $F \approx 0.98$). In addition, fine-tuning moderates the effect of document augmentation on the rankings, evidenced by a dramatic change in RBO scores in BGE (0.393 with fine-tuning vs. 0.742 without) and especially in SBERT (0.018 with vs. 0.812 without). Fine-tuning amplifies the effect of document translation in BGE ($\Delta F$ = +0.062 with fine-tuning vs. $\Delta F$ = +0.012 without). It also amplifies the effect of enrichment in SBERT ($\Delta F$=+0.189 with fine-tuning vs. $\Delta F$ = -0.004 without), but at the cost of a dramatic drop in balance ($\Delta H$ = -0.333 with vs. $\Delta H$ = -0.003 without).

Regarding effectiveness, BM25 appears to perform much better than the neural models, with an average AP of 0.729. ColBERT and BGE average $\approx 0.327$, and SBERT stays far below at 0.034 when fine-tuned and 0.001 when not. Recall leads to similar conclusions, with an average of 0.895 with BM25, 0.646 with ColBERT and BGE, and 0.142 with SBERT when fine-tuned and 0.001 when not. But we should take these scores with a grain of salt because of the obvious bias in the query logs: as mentioned, user clicks were recorded under a BM25 policy with document augmentation but (mostly) without query translation. Indeed, translating queries in BM25 was expected to perform better, but it showed a 9% drop in AP. To further investigate the possibility of bias, we manually inspected a few queries in different languages where BM25 appeared to perform much better than the neural systems. We made relevance judgments and found that ColBERT and BGE actually outperformed the best BM25 by 0.08 in AP. This manual inspection also revealed that neural models seem to struggle with entity queries. This is especially concerning for Europeana because more than 50% of the user queries are entity-centric [9,10].

## 4   Conclusion and Future Work

This study shows that neural models can substantially enhance Europeana's capability to support multilingual and semantically nuanced search without relying on translation or metadata enrichment. Further investigation is still required before deploying neural systems in our production environment. First, our results suggest that these models do not match the effectiveness of pure lexical retrieval for entity-centric queries. Second, the system must maintain acceptable response times within reasonable infrastructure constraints, even as the collection grows dynamically. Third, it is necessary to ensure that the system does not introduce language bias by disproportionately favoring certain languages over others, especially those less represented. For instance, our experiments showed that SBERT can be highly multilingual, but at the cost of favoring some languages. The issue of language bias and fairness is particularly critical for Europeana, because our collection contains items in more than 40 languages.

Moreover, we would like to explore the broader spectrum of possibilities that AI and LLMs offer for enhancing the search process, such as retrieval-augmented generation or LLM-driven query and document augmentation. LLM-generated relevance judgments, in particular, may have a very large impact in the Cultural Heritage domain. As exemplified by this paper, one of the largest limitations is the lack of resources, both for development and evaluation. In our case, the lack of explicit judgments limits the confidence we can have when evaluating model effectiveness. In this line, Europeana will explore ways to better support experimentation, pursuing collaborative research frameworks that ensure the required user privacy while enabling research that can benefit the broader community.

## 5   Speaker and Company

Mónica Marrero works in search at Europeana since 2018. She holds a PhD on Named Entity Recognition, and has been involved in several projects related to knowledge representation and information retrieval with large collections.

The Europeana Foundation is an independent non-profit organisation driving the digital transformation of the cultural heritage sector and promoting the accessibility and reuse of Europe's cultural data. It leads the deployment of the common European data space for cultural heritage, an EU-funded initiative that enables open and trustworthy data sharing across Europe. Europeana also participates in EU projects spanning digitization, data aggregation, technological innovation, reuse and capacity building, artificial intelligence, and 3D.

**Disclosure of Interests.** The authors have no competing interests to declare that are relevant to the content of this article.

# References


1. Basir, S.: Exploring Neural IR Approaches in Europeana. Master's thesis, Delft University of Technology (2025). https://resolver.tudelft.nl/uuid:eee447b8-857a-4493-8679-1eac1d86345e
2. Ceynowa, K., Sommer, D., Hermann, M.: Digital libraries in germany: federalism, funding, and the bayerische staatsbibliothek. In: Digital Libraries Across Continents, pp. 28–48. Routledge (2025)
3. Chen, J., Xiao, S., Zhang, P., Luo, K., Lian, D., Liu, Z.: M3-embedding: multi-linguality, multi-functionality, multi-granularity text embeddings through self-knowledge distillation. In: Findings of the Association for Computational Linguistics: ACL 2024. pp. 2318–2335 (2024)
4. Corsi, M., Urbano, J.: The treatment of ties in rank-biased overlap. In: Proceedings of the 47th International ACM SIGIR Conference on Research and Development in Information Retrieval, pp. 251–260 (2024)
5. Gordea, S., Andresel, M., Drauschke, F., Kahle, P.: Transcribathon. eu: Ai supporting collaborative transcription and enrichment of historical documents. In: Proceedings of the 2024 International Conference on Advanced Visual Interfaces, pp. 1–3 (2024)
6. Haffenden, C., Fano, E., Malmsten, M., Börjeson, L.: Making and using AI in the library: creating a bert model at the national library of sweden. Coll. Res. Libr. **84**(1) (2023)
7. Jha, R., et al.: Jina-ColBERT-v2: A general-purpose multilingual late interaction retriever. In: Proceedings of the Fourth Workshop on Multilingual Representation Learning (MRL 2024), pp. 159–166 (2024)
8. Kummervold, P.E., De la Rosa, J., Wetjen, F., Brygfjeld, S.A.: Operationalizing a national digital library: the case for a norwegian transformer model. arXiv preprint arXiv:2104.09617 (2021)
9. Marrero, M., Isaac, A.: Implementation and evaluation of a multilingual search pilot in the europeana digital library. In: Silvello, G., Corcho, O., Manghi, P., Di Nunzio, G.M., Golub, K., Ferro, N., Poggi, A. (eds.) Linking Theory and Practice of Digital Libraries, pp. 93–106. Springer International Publishing, Cham (2022)
10. Marrero, M., Isaac, A., Freire, N.: Automatic translation and multilingual cultural heritage retrieval: A case study with transcriptions in europeana. In: Berget, G., Hall, M.M., Brenn, D., Kumpulainen, S. (eds.) Linking Theory and Practice of Digital Libraries, pp. 133–138. Springer International Publishing, Cham (2021)
11. National Leadership Grants - Libraries. Evanston.IL: Lg-256703-ols-24 (2024). https://www.imls.gov/grants/awarded/lg-256703-ols-24
12. Neale, A., Isaac, A., Manguinhas, H., Moskalenko, D., Marrero, M.: Multilingual strategy. Technical report, Europeana Foundation (2020). https://pro.europeana.eu/files/Europeana_Professional/Publications/Europeana%20DSI-4%20Multilingual%20Strategy.pdf

13. O'Hare, E., et al.: Alignment paper on ai and the data space for cultural heritage: Boundary-setters and opportunity-seekers working towards responsible ai futures. Technical report, Common European data space for cultural heritage (2025). https://doi.org/10.5281/zenodo.17252598
14. Rees, G., et al.: The cultural heritage ai cookbook (2025). https://pelagios.org/llm-lod-enriching-heritage/intro.html
15. Reimers, N., Gurevych, I.: Making monolingual sentence embeddings multilingual using knowledge distillation. In: Webber, B., Cohn, T., He, Y., Liu, Y. (eds.) Proceedings of the 2020 Conference on Empirical Methods in Natural Language Processing (EMNLP), pp. 4512–4525 (2020)
16. Reshetnikov, A., et al.: Deart: Building and evaluating a dataset for object detection and pose classification for European art. J. Cult. Herit. **75**, 258–266 (2025). https://doi.org/10.1016/j.culher.2025.07.022
17. Roald, M., Birkenes, M.B., Johnsen, L.G.B.: Visual navigation of digital libraries: retrieval and classification of images in the national library of Norway's digitised book collection. arXiv preprint arXiv:2410.14969 (2024)
18. Stony Brook University Libraries: Search AI. https://library.stonybrook.edu/about-search-ai/

# Improving Search Suggestions for Alphanumeric Queries

Samarth Agrawal[1]([✉]) [iD], Jayanth Yetukuri[1] [iD], Diptesh Kanojia[2] [iD],
Qunzhi Zhou[1] [iD], and Zhe Wu[1] [iD]

[1] eBay Inc., San Jose, USA
{samagrawal,jyetukuri,qunzhou,zwu1}@ebay.com
[2] University of Surrey, Guildford, UK
d.kanojia@surrey.ac.uk

**Abstract.** Alphanumeric identifiers such as manufacturer part numbers (MPNs), SKUs, and model codes are ubiquitous in e-commerce catalogs and search. These identifiers are sparse, non linguistic, and highly sensitive to tokenization and typographical variation, rendering conventional lexical and embedding based retrieval methods ineffective. We propose a training free, character level retrieval framework that encodes each alphanumeric sequence as a fixed length binary vector. This representation enables efficient similarity computation via Hamming distance and supports nearest neighbor retrieval over large identifier corpora. An optional re-ranking stage using edit distance refines precision while preserving latency guarantees. The method offers a practical and interpretable alternative to learned dense retrieval models, making it suitable for production deployment in search suggestion generation systems. Significant gains in business metrics in the A/B test further prove utility of our approach.

**Keywords:** Alphanumeric search · Manufacturer part numbers · Hamming distance · kNN · Search suggestion · E-commerce search

## 1 Introduction

Alphanumeric queries such as manufacturer part numbers, stock keeping units, and model codes present a long-standing challenge for search systems. Unlike natural language queries, these identifiers are nonlinguistic, sparse, and highly sensitive to small character-level variations. Conventional lexical retrieval performs poorly because such codes rarely repeat in the corpus, while dense embeddings often blur distinctions between visually similar but semantically distinct strings. Tokenization further complicates the problem because strings like "S3221QS" may be segmented inconsistently across models. As a result, even a single character mistake or formatting change can produce irrelevant results, which reduces search relevance and conversion rates.


R. Campos et al. (Eds.): ECIR 2026, LNCS 16486, pp. 89–93, 2026.
https://doi.org/10.1007/978-3-032-21321-1_12

Existing approaches for improving robustness in retrieval, including character-level embeddings, hybrid neural lexical ranking, and approximate nearest neighbor search in dense space, usually depend on supervised training and significant infrastructure for vector indexing and maintenance. These methods are often too complex for the simple structure of alphanumeric strings and introduce latency.

Based on general observations, we hypothesize that product variations (*e.g.*, size, color, interface) typically differ by only a few characters in their model codes. For example in Fig. 1, Dell monitor codes suggest that model numbers vary slightly for different sizes, features, *etc.* implying that nearest neighbors in model code space reflect genuine product family structure.

A training-free nonparametric retrieval framework designed specifically for alphanumeric identifiers is presented. Candidate matches are retrieved by computing Hamming distance between the query vector and an indexed collection of product codes, followed by optional edit distance re-ranking. This procedure enables efficient nearest neighbor retrieval that remains robust to local variations such as typos, version suffixes, or model differences commonly found in product families. When applied as a candidate generator or related query suggester, it delivers fast and accurate results for user inputs that only partially match catalog identifiers.

In summary, this work introduces a lightweight yet effective formulation for alphanumeric retrieval based on binary character encoding and Hamming distance search. The method achieves strong retrieval quality, extremely low latency, and a small memory footprint. It achieves high recall for slightly perturbed queries without requiring any learned parameters.

**Fig. 1.** Product model codes vary by a few characters that can correlate with features.

***Related Work.*** Alphanumeric identifiers are fragile under typos and formatting noise. Classic approximate string matching provides tolerance through dynamic programming, bit-vector methods, and practical $q$-gram filtering with metric indexing [1–3]. At catalog scale, non-parametric neighbor search under Hamming distance (e.g., Multi-Index Hashing) and ANN structures (e.g., HNSW) enable sublinear retrieval [4,5]. In e-commerce IR, benchmarks such as ESCI emphasize semantic relevance over identifier recovery [6]. Recent eBay work studies retrieval for *alphanumeric queries* and broader methods with identifier results [7–9]. For related-search suggestion, prior approaches mine co-clicked queries [10] or model

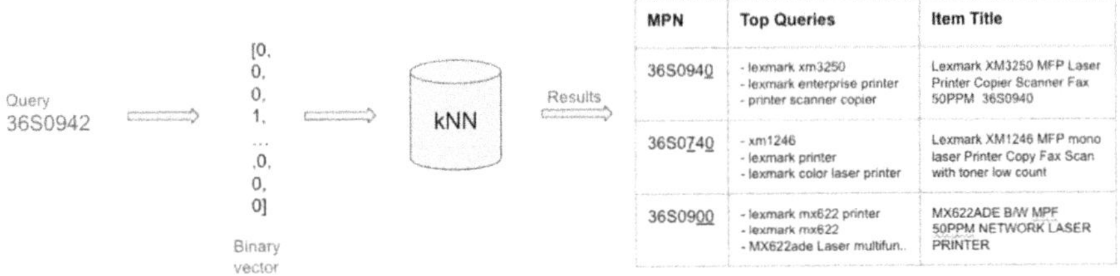


**Fig. 2.** Proposed online inference pipeline for alphanumeric queries.

transitional reformulations with LLMs [11]. The proposed method is training-free, identifier-robust, and suitable as a low-latency first-stage generator.

Tokenization-free or byte-level models (*e.g.*, ByT5) address subword brittleness but add training and latency costs [12]. Work on query suggestion typically targets auto-completion or ranking rather than identifier-space proximity [13]; here, suggestions are derived directly from nearest neighbors in code space.

## 2   Methodology

The proposed methodology comprises two key components: data collection and online inference. The former focuses on building the identifierquery corpus, while the latter addresses real-time retrieval and recommendation (Fig. 2).

### 2.1   Data Collection

Alphanumeric identifiers such as manufacturer part numbers (MPNs) and model numbers are harvested from current and historical inventory records, normalized, and deduplicated. For each unique code, the *top-selling* item from historical sales is selected. Search log data are then used to associate the *top-3* user queries that resulted in a click or purchase of that item. To reduce identifier collisions, only codes containing 7 or more characters are retained. Each code is subsequently mapped to a fixed-length 120-bit binary vector by concatenating 6-bit encodings of individual characters (covering AZ, 09, and -/.) and padding or truncating to a maximum length of 20 characters. This representation enables efficient similarity computation via Hamming distance. A Hamming-space approximate nearest-neighbor (ANN) index (*e.g.*, FAISS or Annoy) is constructed, where the binary vector serves as the *key* and the corresponding *value* stores the canonical code along with its associated top-three queries.

### 2.2   Online Inference

Given an input query, the system (i) normalizes and gates it using a regular expression that detects predominantly alphanumeric patterns; if the gate fails, control is passed to the baseline semantic or lexical retrieval stack. Otherwise,

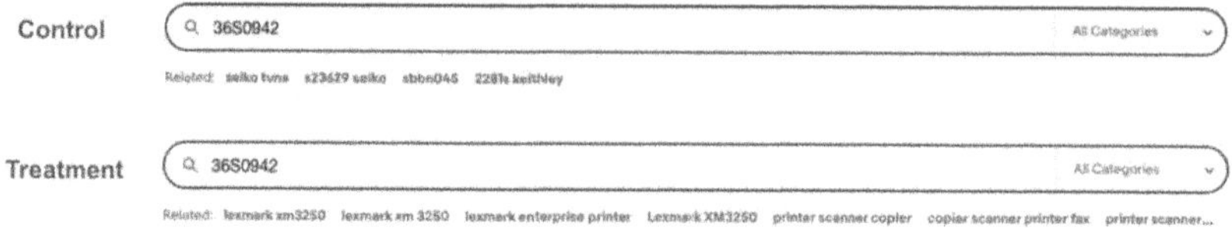

**Fig. 3.** Comparison of search suggestions between control and treatment systems.

the query is (ii) encoded into a fixed-length binary vector, (iii) used to retrieve the top-$k$ neighbors from the Hamming ANN index, (iv) refined by applying a Levenshtein filter on the top-$N$ candidates to tolerate insertions and deletions while preserving close matches, and (v) aggregated and de-duplicated to produce the *top-3* related queries associated with the surviving neighbors. Final suggestions are ranked by a weighted combination of neighbor proximity and historical query frequency or engagement, yielding low-latency, identifier-aware recommendations.

## 3   Evaluation

After manually evaluating the quality of generated suggestions, this approach was tested using an online A/B test on production traffic restricted to *alphanumeric queries*. The control rendered the existing related-search experience; the treatment used our Hamming+edit pipeline to trigger and populate suggestions (Fig. 3). As expected, related-search *coverage* improved by **+18.8%**. *Statistically significant* gains of **+3.35%** in related-search CTR and **+44.4%** in conversions were observed. These lifts indicate this method surfaces suggestions that users engage with and lead to downstream purchases.

A practical challenge is a 'chicken-and-egg' effect regarding identifier quality, *i.e.*, many sellers enter arbitrary values in MPN fields because these fields have historically provided limited utility, which in turn makes it harder to effectively exploit MPNs. While our method performs well where codes are reliable, larger gains will require improved normalization/validation at listing time and incentives for accurate MPN entry.

## 4   Conclusion

This work introduced a training-free retrieval method for alphanumeric queries that encodes each identifier as a fixed-length binary vector, retrieves nearest neighbors via Hamming distance, and refines candidates with a lightweight Levenshtein filter. The resulting approximate nearest-neighbor (ANN) index mapping codes to top queries is simple to maintain, low-latency, and complementary to existing semantic and lexical stacks. In online A/B tests on alphanumeric traffic, the approach improved coverage and produced statistically significant gains in click-through rate and conversion. A key limitation lies in the variable quality of seller-provided metadata, which affects query-item associations. Future work will explore using metadata from the ANN index as context for large language models to generate richer offline suggestions without impacting latency.

## 5  Speaker Bio

Samarth Agrawal is an MTS2, Software Engineer working on problems intersecting information retrieval and natural language processing relevant to the Query Understanding team at eBay. He is passionate about novel research in the information retrieval space that can help optimize product search.

**Disclosure of Interests.** The authors have no competing interests to declare that are relevant to the content of this article.

## References


1. Navarro, G.: A guided tour to approximate string matching. ACM Comput. Surv. **33**(1), 31–88 (2001)
2. Myers, G.: A fast bit-vector algorithm for approximate string matching based on dynamic programming. J. ACM **46**(3), 395–415 (1999)
3. Ukkonen, E.: Approximate string-matching with $q$-grams and maximal matches. Theoret. Comput. Sci. **92**(1), 191–211 (1992)
4. Norouzi, M., Punjani, A., Fleet, D.J.: Fast search in hamming space with multi-index hashing. In: Proc. CVPR (2012)
5. Malkov, Y.A., Yashunin, D.A.: Efficient and robust approximate nearest neighbor search using hierarchical navigable small world graphs. IEEE TPAMI **42**(4), 824–836 (2020)
6. Reddy, C.K., Màrquez, L., Valero, F., Rao, N., Zaragoza, H., et al.: Shopping queries dataset: a large-scale ESCI benchmark for improving product search. arXiv:2206.06588 (2022)
7. Saadany, H., Bhosale, S., Agrawal, S., Wu, Z., Orăsan, C., Kanojia, D.: Product retrieval and ranking for alphanumeric queries. In: Proc. CIKM, pp. 5564–5565 (2024)
8. Saadany, H., Bhosale, S., Agrawal, S., Kanojia, D., Orăsan, C., Wu, Z.: Centrality-aware product retrieval and ranking. In: EMNLP 2024 Industry, pp. 215–224 (2024)
9. Qian, S., et al.: NEAR$^2$: A Nested Embedding Approach to Efficient Product Retrieval and Ranking. arXiv:2506.19743 (2025)
10. Hasan, M.A., Parikh, N., Singh, G., Sundaresan, N.: Query Suggestion for E-commerce Sites. *Proc. WSDM* (2011)
11. Yetukuri, J., et al.: AI Guided Accelerator For Search Experience. arXiv:2508.05649 (2025)
12. Xue, L., Barua, A., Constant, N., Al-Rfou, R., Narang, S., et al.: ByT5: towards a token-free future with pre-trained byte-to-byte models. TACL **10**, 291–306 (2022)
13. Cai, F., de Rijke, M.: A survey of query auto completion in information retrieval. Found. Trends IR **10**(4), 273–363 (2016)

# Data Augmentation with LLMs for Cold Start Recommendation in E-Commerce

Natalija Glisovic[1,2]([📧]) [ID], Martin Tegner[2] [ID], and Danica Kragic[1] [ID]

[1] KTH, Royal Institute of Technology, Stockholm, Sweden
[2] IKEA Retail (Ingka Group), Malmo, Sweden
`glisovic@kth.se`

**Abstract.** Sequential recommendation systems struggle with cold start items due to limited interaction data. We show how Large Language Models (LLMs) can reason over warm-but-unseen items to generate synthetic interactions and improve cold start recommendations. At IKEA, we show how this approach can boost cold start performance while preserving warm start performance on room design data, highlighting how LLM reasoning can enhance recommendation systems.

**Keywords:** Cold start recommendation · Data augmentation · LLM

## 1  Introduction and Motivation

Sequential recommendation systems predict items based on users' historical interactions, capturing evolving preferences [4]. These systems rely on ID-based embeddings, which struggle when items have limited interactions, known as the cold start problem [2,9]. We focus on incomplete cold start [5], where items appear only once in training or in the test set. Data augmentation using auxiliary metadata (categories, descriptions) has been proposed to mitigate cold start [7,10,11]. Recent work shows LLMs can enhance item representations and reasoning for such tasks [1,6], though computational cost is a concern. At IKEA, we have four large product releases per year with around 25% of the product range changing with each update, leading to many new items with limited interactions. This cold-start gap limits personalized discovery, motivating our exploration of LLM-based reasoning to synthetically expand training signals.

Our approach demonstrates an efficient LLM-based augmentation strategy where we generate synthetic interactions for only 20% of users. By leveraging warm-but-unseen items, i.e. items that exist in the training data and have interactions from other users but not the target users, the model expands user preference coverage, improving cold start recommendations without affecting warm items. We validate this with both quantitative and qualitative analyses.

## 2  Methodology

We apply Google Gemini Pro 1.5 to augment sequential recommendation data for 20% of the users. For each user, the LLM performs pairwise item selection,


R. Campos et al. (Eds.): ECIR 2026, LNCS 16486, pp. 94–99, 2026.
https://doi.org/10.1007/978-3-032-21321-1_13

predicting the more relevant item and providing a short rationale. These outputs are converted into positive (selected) and negative (non-selected) training pairs, which augment recommendation models (BERT4Rec and SASRec) using a standard pairwise loss. The augmented data is incorporated through an additional Bayesian Personalized Ranking (BPR) loss term that specifically targets cold start items using an indicator function, with regularization parameter ($\lambda$) controlling the weight of this augmentation loss. This formulation ensures that LLM-generated interactions primarily update cold item embeddings while preserving warm item representations. Figure 1 shows an overview of the methodology.

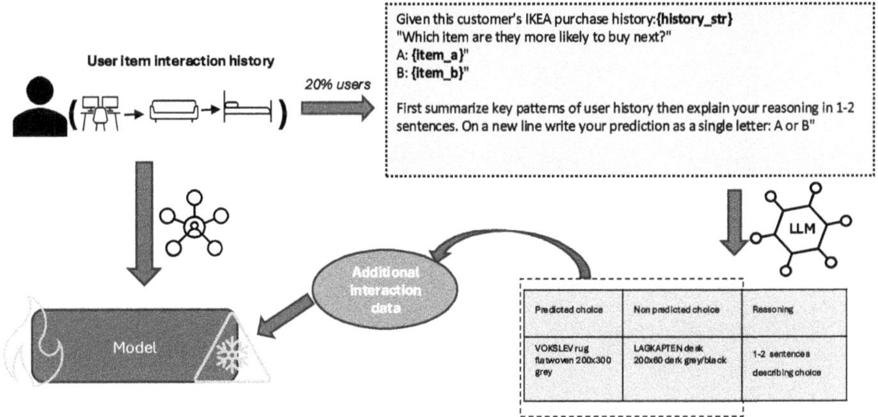


**Fig. 1.** Overview of the proposed methodology.

# 3  Experiments

## 3.1  Experimental Setup

We evaluate our approach on IKEA user interactions with items in a room design application, covering 54,963 users and 5,023 items. Sequences were split using a leave-one-out protocol where the most recent item is used as test, second most recent as validation, and remaining interactions for training. Around 8% of the items are cold start. We augment two transformer-based recommenders, SASRec and BERT4Rec, with LLM-generated item interactions for a subset of 20% of users. Baselines included the original models and a random augmentation without semantic reasoning.

## 3.2  Results

The results of the experiments are summarized in Table 1. LLM augmentation significantly improved cold start performance without affecting warm items. For

SASRec, Recall@10 increased by 50%, while BERT4Rec achieved 35% improvement with additional gains in ranking quality (NDCG@10 +11%). Random augmentation showed no benefit and sometimes reduced performance, highlighting the value of LLM reasoning for selecting relevant items. Overall, the results demonstrate that LLM-driven augmentation efficiently addresses incomplete cold start in e-commerce, enhancing item discovery while maintaining existing recommendation quality.

**Table 1.** Comparison of model variants on cold and warm items (in %), where the best performance is denoted in bold.

| Model | Cold Items | | Warm Items | |
|---|---|---|---|---|
| | Recall@10 | NDCG@10 | Recall@10 | NDCG@10 |
| SASRec (baseline) | 0.22 | **0.16** | **0.77** | **0.57** |
| SASRec + random layer | 0.22 (0%) | 0.09 (−78%) | 0.76 (−1%) | 0.56 (−2%) |
| SASRec + LLM layer | **0.33** (+50%) | **0.16** (0%) | 0.76 (−1%) | 0.56 (−2%) |
| BERT4Rec (baseline) | 0.13 | 0.08 | **0.77** | **0.60** |
| BERT4Rec + random layer | 0.12 (−1%) | 0.06 (-33%) | 0.76 (−1%) | 0.59 (-1%) |
| BERT4Rec + LLM layer | **0.20** (+35%) | **0.09** (+11%) | **0.77** (0%) | 0.59 (−1%) |

### 3.3 Hyperparameter Sensitivity Analysis

We evaluated the impact of regularization ($\lambda$) in our loss function and the percentage of users augmented. Setting $\lambda = 0.2$ provided the best trade-off, boosting cold start Recall@10 while preserving warm start performance. Lower values offered insufficient augmentation, and higher values degraded warm item recommendations. For user sampling, augmenting 20% of users offered a strong performance-computation trade-off. While 30% provided slightly higher Recall@10 ( 2% gain), it increased computational cost by around 50%, making 20% the practical operating point. See Fig. 2 for sensitivity results.

### 3.4 Qualitative Analysis of LLM Reasoning

To get a better understanding on how the LLM has reasoned for its prediction, we analyze two examples shown in Fig. 3. Note that while Fig. 3 shows abbreviated item names for readability, the full IKEA product descriptions including detailed color, material, and style specifications were provided to the LLM during inference.

The LLM exhibits contextual awareness by identifying target rooms and emphasizing recent interactions, while also discerning stylistic preferences by leveraging product details like materials and colors. This demonstrates the LLM's ability to capture multiple dimensions of user behaviour for recommendation tasks [3,8].

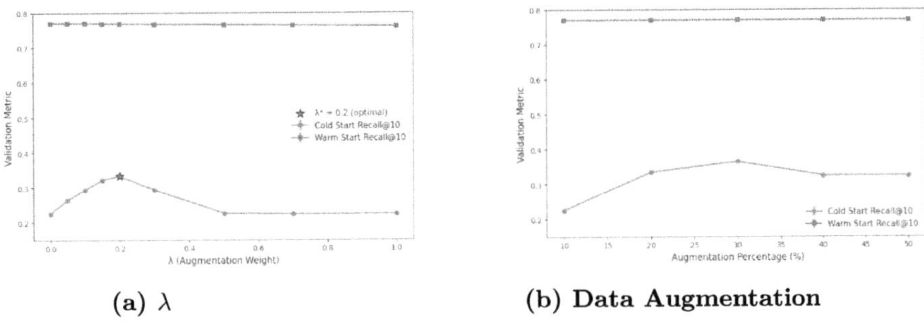

(a) $\lambda$                              (b) **Data Augmentation**

**Fig. 2.** Hyperparameter sensitivity analysis showing (a) the impact of regularization parameter $\lambda$ on cold and warm start performance, and (b) performance across different data augmentation ratios.

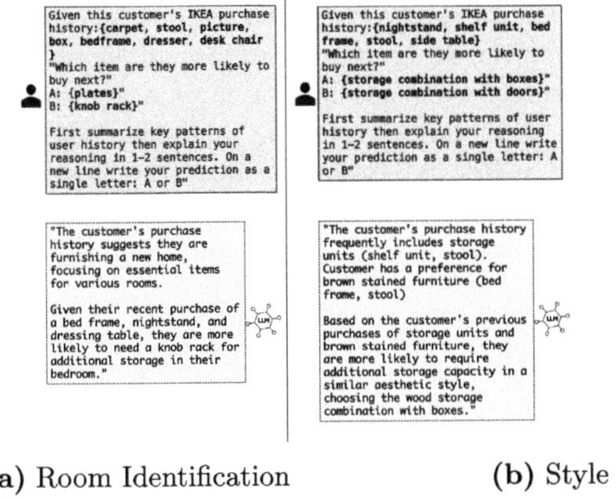


(a) Room Identification                    (b) Style

**Fig. 3.** Examples of the LLMs reasoning for item prediction. Item names, colors, and detailed specifications have been excluded for readability.

# 4   Conclusion

LLM-driven data augmentation improves cold start recommendations while maintaining warm item quality. We also demonstrate the importance of LLM reasoning, by showing that random augmentation provides no benefit and can harm performance. Additionally, qualitative analysis highlights LLM reasoning over context and style, confirming the potential of LLMs in production recommendation systems. Our selective augmentation approach achieves performance gains while processing only 20% of users, demonstrating a practical cost-efficiency trade-off for production deployment. Future work should explore extended evaluation including user satisfaction metrics and long-term retention effects to fully validate the business impact of LLM-enhanced recommendation systems.

### 4.1   Lessons Learned

These are our lessons learned from the pre-deployment experiments.

- Selective augmentation of only a subset of users (around 20%) offers the best trade-off between performance gain and computational cost.
- Interpretable LLM rationales can help increase stakeholder confidence and accelerate prompt iteration.
- Integrating augmentation into data pipelines requires lightweight batching to stay within operational time limits.

## 5   Presenter and Company

IKEA Retail (Ingka Group) is the world's leading home furnishing retailer, operating in more than 30 markets through both online and physical stores. The company leverages data-driven insights and advanced search and recommendation systems to create a better everyday life for the many people.

Natalija Glisovic is an industrial PhD student at KTH Royal Institute of Technology and IKEA Retail (Ingka Group). Her research interests include exploring methods to make recommendation systems more context-aware and dynamic, with an interest in understanding and adapting to evolving user preferences.

**Disclosure of Interests.** The authors have no competing interests to declare that are relevant to the content of this article.

## References


1. Brody, S., Lagziel, S.: Simrec: mitigating the cold-start problem in sequential recommendation by integrating item similarity (2024). https://arxiv.org/abs/2410.22136
2. Glisovic, N., Kragic, D., Tegner, M.: Item cold start in e-commerce recommender systems: a survey. IEEE Access **13**, 164702–164722 (2025). https://doi.org/10.1109/ACCESS.2025.3611026
3. Huang, F., et al.: Large language model simulator for cold-start recommendation. In: arXiv preprint arXiv:2402.09176. Association for Computing Machinery (2024)
4. Kang, W.C., McAuley, J.: Self-attentive sequential recommendation. In: Proceedings of the 12th ACM Conference on Recommender Systems (RecSys '18), pp. 238–246. ACM, New York, NY, USA (2018).https://doi.org/10.1145/3240323.3240374
5. Kannout, E., Grzegorowski, M., Grodzki, M., Nguyen, H.S.: Clustering-based frequent pattern mining framework for solving cold-start problem in recommender systems. IEEE Access **12**, 13678–13698 (2024). https://doi.org/10.1109/ACCESS.2024.3355057
6. Kusano, G.: Data augmentation using reverse prompt for cost-efficient cold-start recommendation. In: Proceedings of the 18th ACM Conference on Recommender Systems (RecSys '24), pp. 1–5. ACM, New York, NY, USA (2024). https://doi.org/10.1145/3640457.3688159

7. Rashed, A., Elsayed, S., Schmidt-Thieme, L.: Context and attribute-aware sequential recommendation via cross-attention. In: Proceedings of the 16th ACM Conference on Recommender Systems (RecSys '22), pp. 1–10. ACM, New York, NY, USA (2022). https://doi.org/10.1145/3523227.3546777

8. Sanner, S., Balog, K., Radlinski, F., Wedin, B., Dixon, L.: Large language models are competitive near cold-start recommenders for language- and item-based preferences. In: Proceedings of the 17th ACM Conference on Recommender Systems, pp. 890–896. RecSys '23, Association for Computing Machinery, New York, NY, USA (2023). https://doi.org/10.1145/3604915.3608845

9. Wei, Y., et al.: Contrastive learning for cold-start recommendation. In: Proceedings of the 29th ACM International Conference on Multimedia (MM '21), pp. 5382–5390. ACM, New York, NY, USA (2021). https://doi.org/10.1145/3474085.3475665

10. Xu, X., et al.: Cmclrec: Cross-modal contrastive learning for user cold-start sequential recommendation. In: Proceedings of the 47th International ACM SIGIR Conference on Research and Development in Information Retrieval (SIGIR '24), pp. 1589–1598. ACM, New York, NY, USA (2024). https://doi.org/10.1145/3626772.3657839

11. Yuan, G., Li, S., Fang, L., Li, C.: Adarec: an adaptive data augmentation framework for sequence recommendation. In: 2024 IEEE International Conference on Smart Internet of Things (SmartIoT), pp. 330–335. IEEE (2024). https://doi.org/10.1109/SmartIoT62235.2024.00057

# Display Ads Contextual Relevance Modeling with LLM Labels

Chao Gan, Fan Yang, Fangping Huang, Weijie Yuan, Nahid Anwar[✉],
Musen Wen, Konstantin Shmakov, Hong Yao, and Kuang-chih Lee

Walmart Inc., Bentonville, USA
{chao.gan,fan.yang0,fangping.huang,weijie.yuan,nahid.anwar,
musen.wen,konstantin.shmakov,hong.yao0,kuangchih.lee}@walmart.com

**Abstract.** We present a practical framework for improving contextual relevance in display advertising through large language model (LLM) assisted labeling and dual-encoder embeddings. Our fine-tuned annotator automatically labels large volumes of adcontext pairs, eliminating costly manual labeling while maintaining high quality. These labels train a Two-Tower BERT model that learns semantically rich embeddings for ads and contexts, enabling scalable and accurate matching. Evaluation with majority-vote LLM ground truth shows substantial gains in AUC and nDCG over generic baselines. The approach demonstrates how LLM-based weak supervision can be effectively combined with deep retrieval architectures to enhance ad relevance in production-scale systems.

**Keywords:** Display ads · Contextual relevance · BERT · LLM labeling · Two-tower model · ROI · Click-through rate

## 1 Introduction and Business Context

In digital advertising, accurately aligning ads with their surrounding context is essential for improving user engagement and advertiser return on investment (ROI) [1] Traditional heuristic and keyword-based methods lack scalability and fail to capture deep semantic relationships [6,8].

Advances in deep learning and NLP have enabled embedding-based relevance models that represent ads and contexts in a shared semantic space [4]. Two-Tower architectures are particularly effective for large-scale retrieval [5], but their performance depends heavily on labeled data. Click-through rate (CTR) is commonly used as a weak supervision signal yet remains noisy and sparse for display ads [9], while manual annotation is costly and limited.

Recent progress in large language models [2,7] enables scalable, high-quality pseudo-label generation. In this work, we fine-tune DistilBERT-base-uncased on a small human-labeled dataset to approximate expert judgment and automatically label large-scale adcontext pairs. For evaluation, we use an ensemble labeler with majority voting to obtain reliable test labels.


R. Campos et al. (Eds.): ECIR 2026, LNCS 16486, pp. 100–104, 2026.
https://doi.org/10.1007/978-3-032-21321-1_14

The labeled data train a Two-Tower BERT model that learns semantically rich embeddings for ad-context matching. Experiments demonstrate that LLM-based supervision combined with a dual-encoder architecture substantially improves contextual discrimination and retrieval quality compared with generic embeddings.

## 2  Implementation

### 2.1  LLM Judge Builder

Accurate evaluation of the relevance of the ad-context is essential for effective display advertising. However, CTR is a weak and noisy proxy for relevance, and its sparsity further limits its reliability as a training signal [9]. Manual annotation at scale is also impractical due to resource constraints. To overcome these challenges, we train a relevance judge on a small set of human-labeled data, enabling it to approximate human judgment for large-scale assessment.

To build the training dataset, we select the top 2000 ad-context pairs ranked by CTR. Domain experts manually annotate each pair, and final labels are assigned via majority voting to ensure consistency. The resulting human-labeled set is used to fine-tune DistilBERT-base-uncased as our LLM-based judge of ad-context relevance. We validate this model on 1,000 randomly selected pairs, comparing its predictions with those from a generic LLM and human annotations.

The results in Table 1 indicate that the fine-tuned LLM effectively replicates human judgment and serves as a reliable automated annotator for large-scale relevance assessment.

**Table 1.** LLM Judger Quality Analysis

| Model | Accuracy | Precision | Recall | F1-score |
|---|---|---|---|---|
| Generic LLM Judger | 0.76 | 0.6722 | 0.7927 | 0.7275 |
| Fine-Tune LLM Judger | 0.84 | 0.7800 | 0.8864 | 0.8298 |
| Lifts | 10.53% | 16.04% | 11.82% | 14.06% |

### 2.2  Ground-Truth Data Generator with LLM

To build a high-quality training dataset, we leverage daily display ad records to extract (Context, Ads) pairs that appeared at least 500 times. This frequency threshold focuses on commonly occurring context-ad combinations, reducing noise and improving data reliability.

The trained judge then assigns relevance labels to each pair, producing ground-truth data for embedding training. This automated labeling process is scalable and efficient, completing over 51,000 annotations in about 2 h—far faster than manual labeling. The resulting dataset enables more accurate and personalized ad relevance modeling in downstream tasks.

## 2.3  Generate Embedding

Building on the labeled dataset, we train a Two-Tower BERT model to learn embeddings for (Context, Ads) pairs. The model uses contrastive loss [3] to pull semantically similar pairs closer in the embedding space and push dissimilar ones apart. Cosine similarity between ad and context embeddings is compared against LLM-assigned labels, and parameters are updated to minimize the loss.

The resulting 384-dimensional embeddings are trained over 10 epochs in about 2.5 h, effectively capturing semantic relationships between ads and contexts and improving downstream retrieval and ranking performance.

# 3  Evaluation

## 3.1  Evaluation Data and Labels

The evaluation dataset follows the same preparation process as the training data, but uses (Context, Ads) pairs from a different date. A random sample of 5,000 pairs is selected for testing. To ensure unbiased assessment, we use a 5-point LLM labeler from Sponsor Ads, which are paid advertisements placed by brands, as the ground truth. This system ensembles multiple LLMs and applies majority voting to determine relevance.

## 3.2  Evaluation Result

**Relevance vs Irrelevant Pairs.** We compare the trained embedding model with a generic baseline (`all-MiniLM-L6-v2`). Using the labels from majority-vote LLM labeler, (Context, Ads) pairs are divided into relevant and irrelevant groups, and their cosine similarity distributions are analyzed. A larger separation between the two distributions indicates better model performance. The results are illustrated in Fig. 1(a) and (b), respectively.

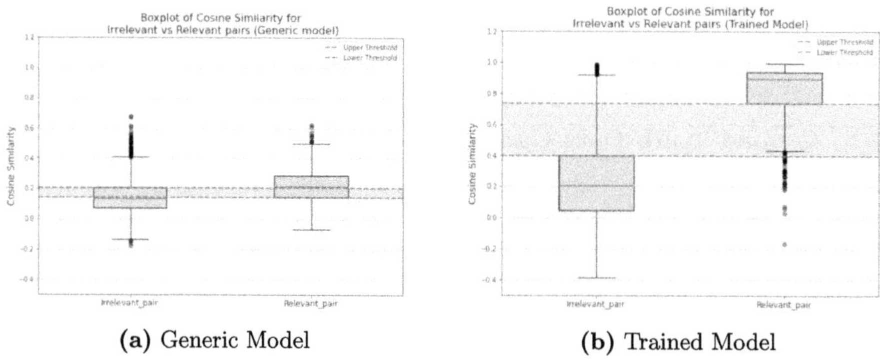

(a) Generic Model          (b) Trained Model

**Fig. 1.** Cosine similarity distributions for irrelevant vs. relevant pairs under (a) generic and (b) trained models.

We further compute the Area Under the ROC Curve (AUC) for both models to quantify their ability to distinguish relevant from irrelevant pairs. A higher AUC indicates stronger discriminative power. The trained model achieves an AUC of 0.9374 versus 0.6919 for the generic baseline, demonstrating stronger contextual discrimination between relevant and irrelevant pairs.

**Ads Retrieval via Embedding.** The evaluation relies on LLM-generated labels, which may still contain some bias or uncertainty. To validate the model independently, we retrieve top ads for a set of contexts using different embedding models and evaluate ranking quality on a small human-labeled dataset using normalized Discounted Cumulative Gain (nDCG). nDCG measures the relevance of ranked results between 0 and 1, with higher values indicating better ranking performance. The evaluation follows these steps (Table 2):

1. Select the most frequent contexts from the test data (3% traffic)
2. Retrieve the most relevant ads for each selected context
3. Collect human relevance labels for the retrieved ads
4. Calculate nDCG@5 and nDCG@10 metrics

**Table 2.** nDCG by context and model. Best per context in **bold**.

| Context | Generic Model | | Trained Model | |
| --- | --- | --- | --- | --- |
|  | nDCG@5 | nDCG@10 | nDCG@5 | nDCG@10 |
| Juices | 0.7227 | 0.5474 | **0.7860** | **0.6579** |
| Fresh & Frozen Vegetables | 0.8688 | 0.8365 | **1.0000** | **0.8630** |
| Breads & Buns | **1.0000** | 0.7453 | 0.8304 | **0.8006** |

## 4 Conclusion

This paper presents a scalable approach to adcontext relevance modeling that uses an LLM-based annotator for automated, high-quality labeling and a Two-Tower BERT model for learning contextual embeddings. The trained model outperforms a generic baseline both qualitatively—showing clearer separation between relevant and irrelevant pairs—and quantitatively, achieving higher AUC and nDCG scores. Combining LLM-based weak supervision with deep semantic embeddings yields a robust and accurate framework for display ad ranking.

**About the Presenter.** Chao Gan is a senior data scientist at Walmart Global Tech, focusing on Display Ads relevance, statistics and recommender systems.

**About the Company.** Walmart Global Tech is the technology backbone of Walmart, the world's largest retailer, empowering more than 240 million weekly customers across 20+ countries. With teams in the United States, India, Mexico, and Canada, Walmart Global Tech builds and operates the cutting-edge platforms that power Walmart's stores, e-commerce, supply chain, advertising, and fin-tech ecosystems. Today, it drives innovation at global scale—leveraging AI, data science, cloud platforms, and advanced engineering—to make retail smarter, faster, and more accessible for customers worldwide.

**Disclosure of Interests.** The authors declare that they have no competing interests. A patent application related to this work may be filed in the future.

# References


1. Broder, A., Fontoura, M., Josifovski, V., Riedel, L.: A semantic approach to contextual advertising. In: Proceedings of the 30th annual international ACM SIGIR conference on Research and development in information retrieval, pp. 559–566 (2007)
2. Brown, T.B., et al.: Language models are few-shot learners (2020). https://arxiv.org/abs/2005.14165
3. Chen, T., Kornblith, S., Norouzi, M., Hinton, G.: A simple framework for contrastive learning of visual representations (2020). https://arxiv.org/abs/2002.05709
4. Devlin, J., Chang, M.W., Lee, K., Toutanova, K.: Bert: pre-training of deep bidirectional transformers for language understanding (2019). https://arxiv.org/abs/1810.04805
5. Karpukhin, V., et al.: Dense passage retrieval for open-domain question answering (2020). https://arxiv.org/abs/2004.04906
6. Mikolov, T., Sutskever, I., Chen, K., Corrado, G., Dean, J.: Distributed representations of words and phrases and their compositionality. In: Advances in Neural Information Processing Systems, vol. 26, pp. 3111–3119 (2013)
7. Ratner, A., Bach, S.H., Ehrenberg, H., Fries, J., Wu, S., Ré, C.: Snorkel: rapid training data creation with weak supervision. Proc. VLDB Endowment **11**(3), 269–282 (2017). https://doi.org/10.14778/3157794.3157797,
8. Richardson, M., Dominowska, E., Ragno, R.: Predicting clicks: estimating the click-through rate for new ads. In: Proceedings of the 16th International Conference on World Wide Web, p. 521–530. WWW '07, Association for Computing Machinery, New York, NY, USA (2007). https://doi.org/10.1145/1242572.1242643
9. Wang, L., Lin, J., Metzler, D.: A cascade ranking model for efficient ranked retrieval. In: Proceedings of the 34th International ACM SIGIR Conference on Research and Development in Information Retrieval, pp. 105–114. SIGIR '11, Association for Computing Machinery, New York, NY, USA (2011).https://doi.org/10.1145/2009916.2009934

# Behavioural Effects of Agentic Messaging
## A Case Study on a Financial Service Application

Olivier Jeunen[1]([envelope]) and Schaun Wheeler[2]

[1] Aampe, Antwerp, Belgium
olivier@aampe.com
[2] Aampe, Cary, NC, USA
schaun@aampe.com

**Abstract.** Marketing and product personalisation provide a prominent and visible use-case for the application of Information Retrieval methods across several business domains. Recently, agentic approaches to these problems have been gaining traction. This work evaluates the behavioural and retention effects of agentic personalisation on a financial service application's customer communication system during a 2025 national tax filing period. Through a two month-long randomised controlled trial, we compare an agentic messaging approach against a business-as-usual (BAU) rule-based campaign system, focusing on two primary outcomes: unsubscribe behaviour and conversion timing. Empirical results show that agent-led messaging reduced unsubscribe events by 21% ($\pm 0.01$) relative to BAU and increased early filing behaviour in the weeks preceding the national deadline. These findings demonstrate how adaptive, user-level decision-making systems can modulate engagement intensity whilst improving long-term retention indicators.

## 1    Introduction and Motivation

Consumer businesses seek to keep their customers engaged, optimising communications for their incremental effect on key user behaviours. An effective use of contextual information as well as every user's personal interaction history are imperative to success [10]. Recent work has shown that *agentic* messaging approaches—built on foundational ideas from econometrics, causal inference and contextual bandits [6,8]—provide a promising avenue to tackle these problems in practice [1].

Our work summarises a case study of such an approach on a financial service application, designed to simplify income tax filing through guided mobile and web interfaces. Its core mission—to make tax filing accessible to individuals who would otherwise skip or overpay—relies heavily on sustained engagement and trust. The conventional approach to campaign orchestration in Customer Relationship Management (CRM) is entirely based on iteratively optimised messaging rules on pre-defined customer segments [12]. The key analytic question for the application is whether an agentic approach is successful in driving more consistent user behaviour and reducing message fatigue: leading users to act earlier,


R. Campos et al. (Eds.): ECIR 2026, LNCS 16486, pp. 105–110, 2026.
https://doi.org/10.1007/978-3-032-21321-1_15

with fewer opt-outs, within the real-world constraints of a seasonal filing cycle. This question sits at the intersection of applied causal inference and product design. Across the marketing technology ecosystem, automated personalisation is often conflated with A/B-testing at scale to iterate on rule improvement—even though it is known to be a provably suboptimal decision-making methodology [4].

The agentic approach reframes this as a sequential decision-making problem—each message an experiment, each user an evolving context. The goal is to learn adaptive policies that generalise, not just to optimise one marketing campaign.

## 1.1   An Agentic Approach

The system evaluated here extends the agentic infrastructure described by Abboud et al. [1]. In this setup, autonomous agents act as decision-makers over multiple dimensions of communication: (i) When to contact a user, (ii) through which channel (e-mail, push, in-app), (iii) with what message variant (tone, incentive, or call-to-action). Each agent continuously updates its beliefs about the effect of a potential message on downstream user actions using Bayesian Thompson sampling) [3,7,11], under a Difference-in-Differences (DiD) framework for incremental impact estimation [2]. The control group continued to receive manually orchestrated messages following fixed campaign schedules and segment rules, whilst the agentic group received dynamically timed and personalised interventions learnt over time. Both systems operated on the same event data infrastructure, with consistent eligibility and suppression rules. Note that the rule-based BAU system reflects years of accumulated human judgment-dozens of segment definitions, scheduling choices, and message variations shaped through trial, habit, and intuition. Each adjustment represents real expertise, yet the process leaves no formal record of how or why those parameters evolved. The result is a sophisticated but opaque construct: a system that works largely because people have made it work, but one whose internal logic can't easily be traced, tested, or learned from. It stands as both a testament to coordinated human effort and a reminder of how much learning disappears when optimisation lives only in people's heads. The agentic treatment, however, learns from scratch and evolves continually throughout the experiment period.

## 2   Experimental Setup and Design

The goal of this analysis is to isolate the causal impact of agentic personalisation. We describe the experiment setup, data sources, and inference methods used to distinguish genuine behavioural effects from coincidental trends. The evaluation followed a randomised controlled trial (i.e. an A/B-test [5,9]) during a 2025 national tax filing season. Users were randomly assigned to either:

**BAU (Control):** Campaigns following traditional segmentation and cadence.

**Agentic (Treatment):** Adaptive, agentically managed messsaging strategies.

Groups were split equally among 6.4 million users. Event stream data was collected for messaging, unsubscribes, intent and conversion events.

Two outcomes were analysed: **Unsubscribe Rate**: frequency of e-mail unsubscription events, disaggregated by sender (BAU vs Agentic). This message source distinction avoids confounding between mixed event streams. **Filing Timing**: the daily cumulative proportion of users who submitted their tax return.

For unsubscribe comparisons, we computed the relative difference between BAU-triggered and Agent-triggered unsubscribe rates within the active campaign window. Confidence intervals were derived from standard errors of binomial proportions. For behavioural timing, we calculated week-level submission rates and the differential trajectory between treatment and control groups over the filing period. The difference-in-differences estimator used by the agentic treatment, captured and incentivised incremental acceleration toward submission relative to the common deadline.

All results were validated for start-date sensitivity and group assignment stability, following data alignment and sample ratio mismatch checks.

## 2.1   Agentic Messaging Leads to Fewer Unsubscription Events

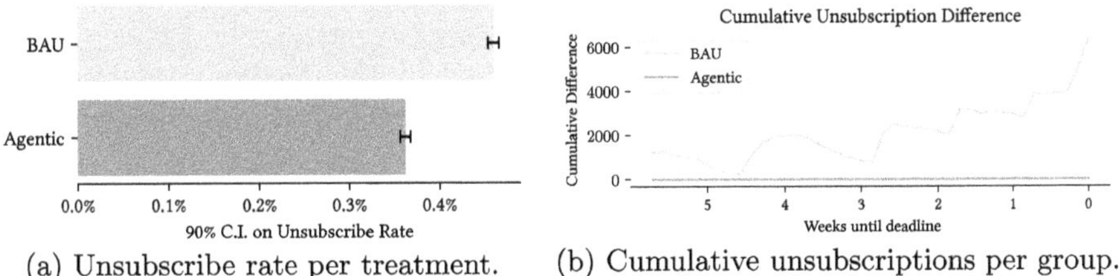



(a) Unsubscribe rate per treatment.      (b) Cumulative unsubscriptions per group.

**Fig. 1.** Empirical results for unsubscription rates in the A/B-test.

We report quantitative differences between the agentic and control groups for unsubscribe behaviour, evaluating the statistical strength and practical relevance of those effects. Across the campaign period, Agent-initiated messages yielded 21% fewer unsubscribe events than rule-based messages, controlling for exposure. The 90% confidence interval for the relative lift was $(-0.212 \pm 0.0098)$, yielding an extremely low $p$-value to reject a no-difference null hypothesis (Fig. 1a).

The reduction was not due to reduced send volume: we validated that messaging frequencies were stable and consistent in the Agentic treatment. Instead, the pattern reflects behavioural differences in user response. Cumulative analyses show that unsubscribe rates from rule-based messages spiked periodically with campaign bursts, with the Agentic unsubscribe curve rising more gradually and stabilising earlier. The cumulative differential widened steadily across the eight-week horizon, emphasising compounding effects over time (Fig. 1b).

This indicates that agentic scheduling—through selective targeting and adaptive pacing—mitigated message fatigue while maintaining communication reach.

## 2.2   Agentic Messaging Nudges Customers to Convert Earlier

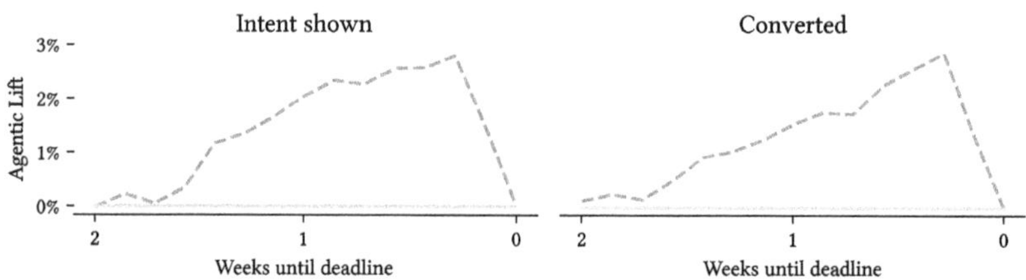


**Fig. 2.** Relative increase in event frequencies in the A/B-test.

In the weeks preceding the national tax filing deadline, users who were exposed to agentic messaging exhibited higher submission rates than those in the BAU group. The effect was most pronounced between three and one weeks before deadline, consistent with the hypothesis that more tailored message timing enhances action readiness. This effect holds across the funnel—for users who convert, but also those who perform upper-funnel events showing intent (Fig. 2).

Although both groups ultimately converged by the deadline, the temporal distribution of activity differed: the agentic cohort filed earlier on average, flattening the peak load seen in control. This behavioural shift holds operational and psychological significance—suggesting that personalised pacing helps users complete complex administrative tasks sooner, not just more often.

For a use-case like tax filing where every conversion entails some operational load to the business, the observed temporal redistribution of conversion events brings desirable practical benefits that enhance scalability and cost-efficiency.

## 3   Discussion, Conclusions and Outlook

The unsubscribe and timing effects together illustrate the central design principle of agentic personalisation: learning when *not* to send. Traditional marketing optimisation tends to reward high message throughput; agentic systems instead optimise expected incremental outcomes under uncertainty. The observed 21% reduction in unsubscribes corresponds to a statistically robust decline in negative engagement events—a critical metric in retention-heavy application domains. Because unsubscribes are irreversible, even small percentage differences represent substantial long-term audience preservation, and effects compound over time. The early-filing uplift demonstrates how adaptive sequencing can align behavioural nudges with individual readiness, effectively reshaping aggregate funnel dynamics without increasing message volume.

From a product perspective, these results show measurable efficiency gains: more engagement from fewer total interventions, with reduced attrition risk. For a seasonal business such as tax filing, spreading submissions earlier in the cycle also reduces support bottlenecks and infrastructure strain. Naturally, the data carry caveats. Unsubscribe and submission events are only partially observable; a subset of users triggered multiple unsubscribes, possibly due to client-side retriggers or category-level preferences. These artefacts do not invalidate the observed directionality but limit precision at the individual level. The agentic advantage should therefore be interpreted as a robust population-level effect rather than an exact per-user estimate.

We highlight three lessons for deploying agentic systems at scale:

1. Event integrity is non-trivial. Even mature data stacks exhibit ambiguity around what constitutes a user action versus a logging artifact. Reducing this ambiguity is critical for reproducibility.
2. Adaptive restraint is as valuable as adaptive persuasion. The most effective agentic policies often emerged from not sending—recognising when further nudges would add noise rather than value.
3. Temporal redistribution is a valid success metric. Shifting engagement earlier in time can yield organisational benefits independent of aggregate conversion rates. Agentic systems allow such temporal learning to occur autonomously.

Viewed collectively, these findings support a broader thesis: agentic personalisation enables marketing to move from rule execution to behavioural learning—an architecture that not only reacts to user preferences but evolves with them [13].

This work represents an in-depth case study for one specific application domain. Nevertheless, the methodology and framework we evaluate is agnostic to the use-case. This emboldens our belief that these results are not limited to the financial services domain, but hold a promise for generalisability across various industries and application areas.

## About the Presenter

Olivier Jeunen is a Principal Research Scientist at Aampe, after holding positions at Amazon, Spotify, and Meta, among others. His research focuses on machine learning for decision-making, marrying probability-theoretic ideas with applications in recommendation and personalisation. This has led to $50^+$ publications, two Best (Student) Paper Awards, and multiple recognitions as an Outstanding (Senior) PC Member. He co-organises the CONSEQUENCES workshop series, and served as an Industry Chair for ECIR '24 and RecSys '25.

## About the Company

Aampe is a science-driven start-up building agentic infrastructure to reconfigure and reorient how business communicate with their users. Its agents model individual user behaviour and preferences to optimise message content, sequencing, and timing in real-world applications. Founded by researchers and engineers from leading academic and industry institutions, Aampe's work bridges applied machine learning and behavioural science, advancing data-efficient, adaptive methods for personalisation beyond traditional experimentation and A/B-testing frameworks.

**Disclosure of Interests.** The authors have no competing interests to declare that are relevant to the content of this article.

# References


1. Abboud, S., Hanna, E., Jeunen, O., Raheja, V., Wheeler, S.: Agentic personalisation of cross-channel marketing experiences. In: Proceedings of the Nineteenth ACM Conference on Recommender Systems, p. 907–910. RecSys '25, ACM (2025). https://doi.org/10.1145/3705328.3748125
2. Athey, S., Imbens, G.W.: Identification and inference in nonlinear difference-in-differences models. Econometrica **74**(2), 431–497 (2006). https://doi.org/10.1111/j.1468-0262.2006.00668.x
3. Chapelle, O., Li, L.: An empirical evaluation of Thompson sampling. In: Advances in Neural Information Processing Systems, vol. 24. Curran Associates, Inc. (2011)
4. Garivier, A., Lattimore, T., Kaufmann, E.: On explore-then-commit strategies. In: Advances in Neural Information Processing Systems, vol. 29. Curran Associates, Inc. (2016)
5. Jeunen, O.: t-testing the waters: empirically validating assumptions for reliable a/b-testing. In: Proceedings of the Nineteenth ACM Conference on Recommender Systems, pp. 1307–1310. RecSys '25, ACM (2025). https://doi.org/10.1145/3705328.3759307
6. Jeunen, O., Joachims, T., Oosterhuis, H., Saito, Y., Vasile, F.: Consequences - causality, counterfactuals and sequential decision-making for recommender systems. In: Proceedings of the 16th ACM Conference on Recommender Systems, pp. 654–657. RecSys '22, ACM (2022). https://doi.org/10.1145/3523227.3547409
7. Jin, T., Yang, X., Xiao, X., Xu, P.: Thompson sampling with less exploration is fast and optimal. In: Proc. of the 40th International Conference on Machine Learning. Proc. of Machine Learning Research, vol. 202, pp. 15239–15261. PMLR (2023). https://proceedings.mlr.press/v202/jin23b.html
8. Joachims, T., London, B., Su, Y., Swaminathan, A., Wang, L.: Recommendations as treatments. AI Mag. **42**(3), 19–30 (2021)
9. Kohavi, R., Tang, D., Xu, Y.: Trustworthy online controlled experiments: a practical guide to A/B testing. Cambridge University Press (2020)
10. Kumar, V., Reinartz, W.: Customer relationship management. Springer (2018)
11. Russo, D.J., Roy, B.V., Kazerouni, A., Osband, I., Wen, Z.: A tutorial on Thompson sampling. Found. Trends® Mach. Learn. **11**(1), 1–96 (2018). https://doi.org/10.1561/2200000070
12. Tynan, A.C., Drayton, J.: Market segmentation. J. Mark. Manag. **2**(3), 301–335 (1987). https://doi.org/10.1080/0267257X.1987.9964020
13. Wheeler, S., Jeunen, O.: Procedural memory is not all you need: bridging cognitive gaps in llm-based agents. In: Adjunct Proceedings of the 33rd ACM Conference on User Modeling, Adaptation and Personalization, pp. 360–364. UMAP Adjunct '25, ACM (2025). https://doi.org/10.1145/3708319.3734172

# Iterative Reranking as a Compute-Scaling Method for LLM-Based Rankers

Tamara Czinczoll[1]([✉])(iD), Dong Liu[2](iD), and Filippo Betello[3](iD)

[1] Hasso Plattner Institute, Potsdam, Germany
`tamara.czinczoll@hpi.de`
[2] Amazon, Luxembourg, Luxembourg, Luxembourg
`dong.liu@amazon.com`
[3] Sapienza University of Rome, Rome, Italy
`filippo.betello@uniroma1.it`

**Abstract.** E-commerce search faces challenges such as sparse data and poor generalization from issues like multi-attribute resolution, multi-hop reasoning, and implicit intent. We propose iterative reranking as a compute-scaling strategy for LLM-based rankers, repeatedly applying listwise rankers to refine results by exploiting LLM non-determinism. Evaluated on three open datasets with three open-source LLMs, the method trades increased computation for consistently improved performance, yielding strong nDCG@40 gains on DL19, FutureQueryEval, and difficult Amazon query types. These findings show that iterative reranking is an effective inference-time scaling approach for LLM rankers. We make our code available (https://github.com/amazon-science/IterativeListwiseReranking).

**Keywords:** Information Retrieval · Ranking · Reranking · LLM

## 1 Introduction and Related Work

Search queries typically follow a long-tailed distribution, where infrequent queries suffer from limited data availability and poor generalization. To address this, we investigate iteratively applying listwise LLM-based rankers to difficult queries, a process where the output ranking from one pass serves as the input order for the next. Unlike pointwise or pairwise approaches, listwise ranking enables crucial inter-document judgments [14], yet it faces challenges regarding computational costs, limited context windows, and positional bias. Recent efforts to scale inference-compute for better ranking have primarily explored generating extended reasoning traces, [18] and [16]. Other work has focused on efficiently fitting candidates into context windows, [7,12]. Our approach, by contrast, seeks to translate additional compute into quality by allowing the model to iteratively refine its own permutations.

---

T. Czinczoll and F. Betello's work was completed during an internship at Amazon.

While iterative or multi-pass strategies have been touched upon in other work, they have largely remained on the fringes of research, usually treated as auxiliary experiments rather than primary subjects of study. For instance, RankVicuna [8] and RankZephyr [9] include iterative reranking only as an ablation experiment, without exploring generalization beyond their proprietary fine-tuned models. Similarly, Liu et al. [6] utilize multiple passes solely to generate labels for finetuning, offering no analysis of the quality changes per pass. The closest prior attempt, Qin et al. [10], applies a pairwise ranker over multiple passes; however, their investigation is relegated to an appendix and lacks an in-depth exploration of design decisions or generalizability.

In this work, we move beyond peripheral observations to provide a systematic study of iterative listwise reranking. Drawing inspiration from human cognitive processes, where complex tasks are often solved through step-by-step refinement [2,5,13], we provide the first systematic investigation of this method. We evaluate the approach across two passage datasets and one product dataset, using LLMs to annotate the latter for difficulty sources. Our analysis reveals that while iterative, listwise reranking generally improves passage ranking, performance gains in product ranking are highly dependent on the specific query difficulty type.

**Table 1.** Overview of the query difficulty types used to annotate the Amazon dataset.

| Query Difficulty | Description | Example |
| --- | --- | --- |
| Vague | Implicit exploratory intent Ambiguous queries | Student Gaming Laptop |
| Multi-Attribute | Queries with many specifications and/or constraints | wireless noise-cancelling headset under $200 with at least 30 h of battery life |
| Comparative | Comparative or preference-based queries | Cheaper alternative to AirPods |
| Negation | Queries with negations | Non-toxic nail polish for toddlers |
| Natural Language | Full-sentence descriptions | I need a compact blender that's easy to clean and good for making smoothies |
| Others | Other aspects that make answering the query difficult, such as code switching or use of abbreviations | Queries with temporal aspects (seasonal, time-sensitive). Queries requiring context of previous search history |

## 2    Iterative Reranking

We propose iterative reranking where at step $t$ of $T$ total reranking steps, given a search query $q$ that is part of an instruction prompt $p^t$, and a list $l_n^t$ of $n$ ranked items at step $t$, our goal is to refine the current ranking list into a new ranking at step $t+1$

$$l_n^{t+1} = LLM(l_n^t|p^t) \tag{1}$$

so that given an evaluation function $eval$ that measures the quality of the ranking $eval(l_n^T) > eval(l_n^0)$. The evaluation function $eval$ is usually nDCG, MAP or MRR at different cutoff ranges, when ranking is based on relevance. To ensure that we can rerank a given list of documents without cutting off documents due to the LLM's finite context length, we follow [9] and employ a sliding window approach. The window starts ranking the bottom $M$ documents and slides upwards with a stride of $S$, until it reaches the top. One full sliding window pass constitutes one ranking iteration. At each iteration $t$, the LLM uses the previous iteration's ranking $l_n^t$ to produce an updated ranking $l_n^{t+1}$.

## 2.1  Experimental Setup

**Datasets:** We evaluate our approach on three datasets: (i) a curated dataset from Amazon Shopping Queries [11], using a targeted 1000-query-sample. This subset was extracted from the 22,458 English test queries which consists of real user search data and product rankings annotated by crowd workers. This subset is intentionally hard, with 80% of the queries populated with difficult query types. We annotated queries with the difficulty types from Table 1 by the majority vote of three LLMs. The dataset is structured to ensure a minimum representation of each difficult query type. The remaining 20% are non-hard queries. This focus on difficult queries provides the necessary context for the performance analysis per query difficulty type discussed in Sect. 3; (ii) TREC DL19 [4], a well-established passage ranking benchmark with 43 annotated test queries and 9,260 documents from MSMARCO; and (iii) FutureQueryEval [1] which contains 147 manually created queries about post-April 2025 events across seven topics, to test ranking performance on data beyond current LLM training cutoffs.

**Models:** We evaluate three large language models: RankZephyr, fine-tuned on ranking data; Qwen3-8B [17] and Gemma3-4B [15], two dense LLMs without dedicated ranking finetuning.

**Evaluation:** The two metrics, nDCG@5 and nDCG@40 [3,19], are chosen to evaluate ranking quality at different levels of user exposure, with nDCG@5 focusing on highly visible, immediate results and nDCG@40 on a broader range.

## 3  Results

Table 2 presents results for RankZephyr, Qwen and Gemma on the three datasets. Iterative reranking always improves performance by iteration five on the FutureQueryEval dataset for both nDCG@5 and @40, and it always improves nDCG@40 on DL19, whereas it is more mixed for nDCG@5. On the Amazon dataset, only RankZephyr showcases better performance. Whether the prompt instructs to rank from scratch (default) or refine an existing list ('Improve') has a small, model-dependent impact. On the Amazon dataset the other models gradually degrade with subsequent iterations. We further investigate this phenomenon by presenting nDCG@5 performance per query difficulty type for the first and ninth iterations in Fig. 1.

**Table 2.** nDCG@k in %, $k \in \{5, 40\}$ when iteratively reranking for five iterations with different ranking prompts. Unlike the default prompt, the "Improve" prompt asks to improve the given ranking. Results are aggregated over five seeds. Best performance per model and metric over all iterations is shown in **bold**. The arrows at iteration five indicate whether performance improved or degraded compared to the initial ranking.

| Iteration | nDCG@5 | | | | | nDCG@40 | | | | |
|---|---|---|---|---|---|---|---|---|---|---|
| | 1 | 2 | 3 | 4 | 5 | 1 | 2 | 3 | 4 | 5 |
| Amazon Subset | | | | | | | | | | |
| - RankZephyr - Default | 75.95 | 76.64 | 76.61 | **76.80** | 76.74↑ | 87.79 | **87.94** | 87.83 | 87.92 | 87.88↑ |
| - RankZephyr - "Improve" | 75.95 | **76.47** | 76.14 | 76.41 | 76.18↑ | 87.79 | **87.90** | 87.68 | 87.82 | 87.67↓ |
| - Qwen3-8B - Default | **82.05** | 80.72 | 80.00 | 80.23 | 79.89↓ | **90.55** | 89.77 | 89.34 | 89.47 | 89.32↓ |
| - Qwen3-8B - "Improve" | **82.13** | 80.34 | 79.51 | 79.77 | 79.69↓ | **90.59** | 89.54 | 89.01 | 89.20 | 89.08↓ |
| - Gemma3-4B - Default | **76.58** | 75.31 | 74.44 | 74.35 | 73.78↓ | **86.94** | 86.89 | 86.39 | 86.48 | 85.95↓ |
| - Gemma3-4B - "Improve" | **76.58** | 74.37 | 71.85 | 72.80 | 72.21↓ | **86.94** | 86.32 | 84.92 | 85.47 | 84.87↓ |
| TREC DL19 | | | | | | | | | | |
| - RankZephyr - Default | 67.71 | **67.76** | 66.96 | 67.03 | 67.03↓ | 53.35 | 55.68 | 55.90 | **56.51** | 56.15↑ |
| - RankZephyr - "Improve" | 67.61 | 67.65 | **67.78** | 67.52 | 67.52↓ | 53.35 | 55.75 | 56.35 | 56.53 | **56.60**↑ |
| - Qwen3-8B - Default | 65.54 | 65.91 | 67.16 | 66.47 | **67.34**↑ | 52.11 | 54.82 | 56.06 | 56.17 | **56.35**↑ |
| - Qwen3-8B - "Improve" | 65.12 | 65.34 | 65.68 | **66.59** | 65.68↑ | 51.89 | 54.46 | 55.80 | **56.26** | 56.10↑ |
| - Gemma3-4B - Default | 61.53 | 62.23 | 60.25 | **62.62** | 60.73↓ | 49.57 | 51.31 | 51.78 | **52.33** | 52.27↑ |
| - Gemma3-4B - "Improve" | 61.80 | 61.68 | 61.02 | 60.71 | **62.18**↑ | 49.64 | 51.11 | 51.77 | 52.18 | **52.78**↑ |
| FutureQueryEval | | | | | | | | | | |
| - RankZephyr - Default | 62.44 | 62.76 | 62.85 | 62.86 | **62.88**↑ | 65.55 | 65.97 | 66.12 | 66.14 | **66.17**↑ |
| - RankZephyr - "Improve" | 62.44 | 62.54 | **62.83** | 62.82 | 62.82↑ | 65.55 | 65.90 | 66.06 | 66.06 | **66.10**↑ |
| - Qwen3-8B - Default | 61.11 | 62.48 | 62.86 | **63.16** | 62.86↑ | 64.46 | 65.44 | 65.56 | **66.11** | 65.77↑ |
| - Qwen3-8B - "Improve" | 61.07 | 62.08 | 62.40 | **62.61** | 62.31↑ | 64.38 | 65.54 | 65.63 | **65.79** | 65.54↑ |
| - Gemma3-4B - Default | 54.33 | 56.13 | **56.99** | 55.48 | 56.74↑ | 59.85 | 61.62 | **61.98** | 60.92 | 61.81↑ |
| - Gemma3-4B - "Improve" | 54.56 | 56.07 | **57.52** | 56.92 | 57.49↑ | 59.95 | 61.27 | **62.09** | 61.73 | 62.07↑ |

The analysis shows that improvement depends on the query's source of difficulty. Qwen improves rankings for queries of all classes except multi-attribute ones. RankZephyr slightly improves all classes but the 'Other' category. For Gemma the impact of iterative reranking is more mixed, possibly due to its smaller size of only four billion parameters compared to the others' seven and eight billion. Surprisingly, iterative reranking has a strong impact on the performance of comparative queries, i.e., those comparing (parts of) the product against another. Here, the two LLMs more than double nDCG@5. While this effect needs to be further studied due to the limited number of comparative queries in our data subset, we hypothesize that the strong listwise, inter-product dependencies that need to be captured to answer these queries particularly benefit from iterative reranking.

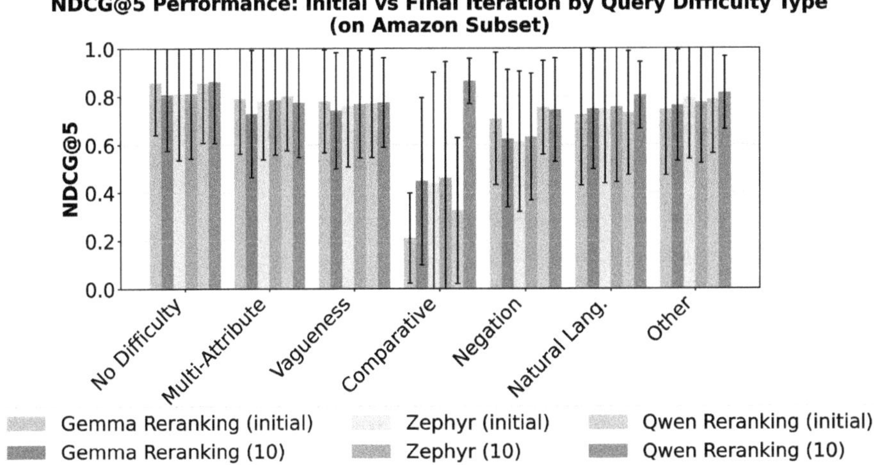


**Fig. 1.** NDCG@5 performance by query difficulty type on the Amazon Shopping Queries subset, comparing the initial and tenth reranking iterations.

## 4  Conclusion

We investigated iterative reranking as a compute-scaling strategy to refine list-wise rankings. The method yielded consistent gains on passage ranking benchmarks (DL19, FutureQueryEval). However, performance on e-commerce product ranking was mixed and highly model-dependent: while RankZephyr showed overall improvement, other models degraded over multiple iterations, with success heavily relying on specific query difficulties. Iterative reranking can be of particular use if no larger suitable model is available. Future work should explore optimal routing strategies, develop adaptive stopping criteria, and more precisely evaluate the trade-offs between ranking quality improvements and the associated computational overhead across different query types and domains.

**CV of the Presenters:** *Tamara Czinczoll* is a PhD student at the Hasso Plattner Institute under the supervision of Prof. Gerard De Melo. She specializes in LLM pretraining, focusing on the foundational architectures that drive modern AI. *Dong Liu* is an Applied Scientist at Amazon. He holds a PhD from the KTH Royal Institute of Technology. His research interests include IR, probabilistic graphical models, and Bayesian inference, with a focus on applying these methods to large-scale industrial environments. *Filippo Betello* is a PhD student at Sapienza University of Rome, supervised by Prof. Fabrizio Silvestri. His research bridges Recommender Systems, IR, and LLMs, with a specific emphasis on computational efficiency and minimizing the carbon footprint.

**Company:** Amazon operates one of the world's largest and most complex e-commerce search engines, serving millions of customers and indexing billions of products daily. Dealing with massive scale and distinct data heterogeneity,

Amazon focuses on developing high-performance, low-latency systems that solve semantic matching challenges to seamlessly connect customers with the products they need across the global retail ecosystem.

**Acknowledgments.** We would like to thank Amine Moukadiri, Maryna Beliuga and Paul Missault for sharing their expertise and providing helpful feedback.

**Disclosure of Interests.** The authors have no competing interests to declare that are relevant to the content of this article.

# References


1. Abdallah, A., Piryani, B., Mozafari, J., Ali, M., Jatowt, A.: How good are LLM-based Rerankers? An empirical analysis of state-of-the-art reranking models. In: Christodoulopoulos, C., Chakraborty, T., Rose, C., Peng, V. (eds.) Findings of the Association for Computational Linguistics: EMNLP 2025, pp. 5693–5709. Association for Computational Linguistics, Suzhou, China (2025). https://doi.org/10.18653/v1/2025.findings-emnlp.305,
2. Adams, R., Atman, C.: Cognitive processes in iterative design behavior. In: FIE'99 Frontiers in Education. 29th Annual Frontiers in Education Conference. Designing the Future of Science and Engineering Education. Conference Proceedings (IEEE Cat. No.99CH37011, vol. 1, pp. 11A6/13–11A6/18 (1999). https://doi.org/10.1109/FIE.1999.839114, iSSN: 0190-5848
3. Bellogín, A., Castells, P., Cantador, I.: Statistical biases in information retrieval metrics for recommender systems. Inf. Retrieval J. **20**(6), 606–634 (2017). https://doi.org/10.1007/s10791-017-9312-z
4. Craswell, N., Mitra, B., Yilmaz, E., Campos, D., Voorhees, E.M.: OVERVIEW OF THE TREC 2019 DEEP LEARNING TRACK
5. Lewis, D.G.R., et al.: Planning to Iterate: Supporting Iterative Practices for Real-world Ill- structured Problem-solving (2018)
6. Liu, W., et al.: Sliding windows are not the end: exploring full ranking with long-context large language models. In: Che, W., Nabende, J., Shutova, E., Pilehvar, M.T. (eds.) Proceedings of the 63rd Annual Meeting of the Association for Computational Linguistics (Volume 1: Long Papers), pp. 162–176. Association for Computational Linguistics, Vienna, Austria (2025). https://doi.org/10.18653/v1/2025.acl-long.8,
7. Parry, A., MacAvaney, S., Ganguly, D.: Top-Down Partitioning for Efficient List-Wise Ranking (2024). https://doi.org/10.48550/arXiv.2405.14589
8. Pradeep, R., Sharifymoghaddam, S., Lin, J.: RankVicuna: Zero-Shot Listwise Document Reranking with Open-Source Large Language Models (2023). https://arxiv.org/abs/2309.15088v1
9. Pradeep, R., Sharifymoghaddam, S., Lin, J.: RankZephyr: effective and robust zero-shot listwise reranking is a breeze! (2023). https://arxiv.org/abs/2312.02724v1
10. Qin, Z., et al.: Large language models are effective text rankers with pairwise ranking prompting. In: Findings of the Association for Computational Linguistics: NAACL 2024, pp. 1504–1518. Association for Computational Linguistics, Mexico City, Mexico (2024). https://doi.org/10.18653/v1/2024.findings-naacl.97,
11. Reddy, C.K., et al.: Shopping queries dataset: a large-scale ESCI benchmark for improving product search (2022). https://doi.org/10.48550/arXiv.2206.06588,

12. Ren, R., et al.: Self-calibrated listwise reranking with large language models. In: Proceedings of the ACM on Web Conference 2025, pp. 3692–3701. WWW '25, Association for Computing Machinery, New York, NY, USA (2025). https://doi.org/10.1145/3696410.3714658,
13. Schön, D.A.: The reflective practitioner: how professionals think in action. Basic Books, New York (1983)
14. Sun, W., et al.: Is ChatGPT good at search? Investigating large language models as re-ranking agents. In: Proceedings of the 2023 Conference on Empirical Methods in Natural Language Processing, pp. 14918–14937. Association for Computational Linguistics, Singapore (2023). https://doi.org/10.18653/v1/2023.emnlp-main.923,
15. Team, G., et al.: Gemma 3 Technical report (2025). https://doi.org/10.48550/arXiv.2503.19786,
16. Weller, O., Ricci, K., Yang, E., Yates, A., Lawrie, D., Durme, B.V.: Rank1: test-time compute for reranking in information retrieval (2025). https://doi.org/10.48550/arXiv.2502.18418,
17. Yang, A., et al.: Qwen3 Technical Report (2025). https://doi.org/10.48550/arXiv.2505.09388
18. Yang, E., et al.: Rank-K: Test-Time Reasoning for Listwise Reranking (May 2025). https://doi.org/10.48550/arXiv.2505.14432
19. Yu, H.T.: Optimize What You Evaluate With: A Simple Yet Effective Framework For Direct Optimization Of IR Metrics (2020). https://doi.org/10.48550/arXiv.2008.13373,

# Accelerating Personalization Signal Learning via Synthetic Data


Daraksha Parveen[2(✉)], Doug Kang[1], Anwitha Paruchuri[1], Deep Kayal[2], and Pavan Mallapragada[1]

[1] Alexa AI, Amazon, Seattle, USA
{dougkang,paruchua,pavanmns}@amazon.com
[2] Cambridge, UK
{dxparvee,dkayal}@amazon.co.uk



**Abstract.** Personalized experiences in multimodal assistants rely on accurate user understanding, yet large-scale training for personalization remains limited by privacy constraints and data sparsity. We introduce a framework for generating *Comprehensive Synthetic Personas* (CSPs) and personalized synthetic training data through taxonomy-guided knowledge enrichment, in-context learning, and Chain-of-Thought (CoT) knowledge distillation for personal knowledge inference. This dataset is used to fine-tune a large language model (LLM) that learns to infer user interests and attributes from interaction histories. Evaluation shows that models trained on synthetic data outperform those trained on real de-identified data in precision and recall when evaluated on the same real de-identified test set, using LLM-as-a-Judge (LLMaaJ) and human annotation. This approach enables scalable and privacy-safe personalization learning, supporting downstream applications in AI assistants.

**Keywords:** Personal Knowledge Inference · Synthetic Data Generation · Comprehensive Synthetic Personas · LLM-as-a-Judge Evaluation


## 1 Introduction

Learning personalization signals is critical for adaptive user experiences in large-scale industry assistants. However, large-scale supervised training is constrained by privacy restrictions, data sparsity, and limited topical diversity in real world production interactions [2,7]. To address these challenges, we introduce a synthetic, privacy-preserving pipeline for personal knowledge inference, enabling end-to-end model training without reliance on real user data. Our framework constructs comprehensive personas that capture behavioral, demographic, and interest attributes, and leverages large language models (LLMs) with taxonomy-guided knowledge enrichment and in-context learning to synthesize realistic, persona-grounded dialogues paired with structured personal knowledge items (PKIs). The training dataset is used to fine-tune an LLM for personalization learning through Chain-of-Thought (CoT) knowledge distillation [8,16]. Evaluation is performed using an LLMaaJ assessing precision, QA-based recall, and human assessment for PKI accuracy. Models trained exclusively on synthetic data achieve gains of +5% in precision and +8% in recall for PKIs compared to baselines trained on real world de-identified customer data. Customer annotation results further confirm over 85% acceptance, demonstrating the effectiveness of synthetic personas for scalable, privacy-safe personalization and their applicability to downstream AI assistants interest modeling.

## 2  Related Work

Open-domain conversational agents frequently elicit personal information implicitly during free-form interactions, motivating research on inferring user attributes for personalization and user modeling. Early work on persona-conditioned dialogue generation, notably Persona-Chat [27], showed that conditioning responses on persona descriptions improves coherence and engagement, while also demonstrating that speaker attributes can be inferred from dialogue histories. Synthetic-Persona-Chat [11] uses LLMs to generate large-scale, faithful dialogues, addressing limitations of earlier persona datasets in diversity, consistency, and scalability. PersonaChatGen [15] introduced taxonomy-driven persona representations for automated persona based dialogue generation. SODA [13] shows that grounding synthetic dialogue generation in structured knowledge graphs improves semantic diversity and coherence, while PLACES [3] shows that few-shot expert exemplars can effectively guide LLM-based dialogue generation. Other works formalize personal attribute inference as a standalone task. Wu et al. [23] introduce a distant-supervision framework with structured triple prediction, while CHARM [20] enables zero-shot inference of unseen attribute values via contextual cues and retrieval. More recent methods emphasize structured representations and generalization. GenRe [21] separates explicit extraction from implicit inference using a generatorreranker architecture, while PAED [28] improves data quality and evaluates generalization to unseen attributes. SynthPAI [26] introduces a large-scale synthetic benchmark for personal attribute inference demonstrating alignment between synthetic and real-data evaluation outcomes.

## 3  Methodology

### 3.1  Synthetic Data Generation Pipeline

**Comprehensive Synthetic Personas.** We construct *Comprehensive Synthetic Personas* (CSPs) to serve as structured representations of user behavior, interests, and background attributes. The persona profile schema consists of a unified hierarchical ontology of seven top-level tiers spanning domains such as interests, backgrounds, and behaviors. Each tier $t \in \mathcal{T}_{\text{tier}}$ defines a set of categories $\mathcal{C}_t$, and each category $c \in \mathcal{C}_t$ contains a collection of entity types $\mathcal{E}_{t,c}$. The full schema is given by $\Omega = \bigcup_{t \in \mathcal{T}_{\text{tier}}} \{(t, c, e) \mid c \in \mathcal{C}_t, e \in \mathcal{E}_{t,c}\}$, where each triple $(t, c, e)$ denotes a distinct attribute key instantiated with a short natural-language value (e.g., "Likes Taylor Swift" under the *Interest* tier, the *Arts & Entertainment* category, and *Favorite Musician* entity type). In total, the schema defines $|\Omega| = 130$ attributes per persona, alongside a unique identifier and a natural-language persona summary describing the overall profile.

**Persona Generation and Knowledge Enrichment.** CSPs are generated through a non-parametric prompting process that combines LLM reasoning with taxonomy-guided knowledge enrichment. The enrichment step samples from the Interest Taxonomy $T = (V, E)$, a directed tree of over 1800 interest nodes organized hierarchically across 25+ categories (e.g., one path is Academic Interests & Careers $\rightarrow$ Humanities $\rightarrow$ Philosophy). From $T$, we retrieve a set of semantic anchor paths $P = \{p_1, p_2, \ldots, p_n\}$, where each path $p_i = (v_i^{\text{root}} \rightarrow v_i^1 \rightarrow \cdots \rightarrow v_i^{k_i})$ connects the root to a sampled leaf node. Terminal nodes $v_i^{k_i}$ are selected using a hybrid strategy that blends random and depth-stratified sampling to balance topical diversity with semantic specificity. Given the enriched paths $P$, the schema $\Omega$, and the instruction set $\mathcal{I}$, a foundation model $\mathcal{M}_\theta$ generates a filled profile $U \leftarrow \mathcal{M}_\theta(\mathcal{I}, P, \Omega)$. Full taxonomy paths ground attributes within semantic subspaces of $T$ and act as interpretable interest dimensions that guide the model to generate diverse but contextually consistent persona attributes.

**Personalized Training Dataset Generation.** We generate synthetic dialogs that simulate realistic user interactions grounded in each synthetic persona $U$. A role-playing model $\mathcal{G}_\theta$ produces multi-turn conversations conditioned on the persona, sampled semantic paths $P$ as conversation seeds, and few-shot exemplars of real users' de-identified utterances for in-context learning. The model receives structured instructions to vary linguistic realizations across affective dimensions such as *intensity* (high, medium, low) and *polarity* (positive, negative). These dimensions are defined by distributional targets derived from production interaction statistics, ensuring generated utterances reflect realistic behavioral variation. An LLM-based extractor $\mathcal{H}_\theta$ then identifies and annotates PKIs from each dialog with metadata including type, polarity, intensity, and reasoning traces (see Fig. 1) following a structured decomposition-based thinking framework [22]. The resulting dataset comprises conversations, extracted PKIs, reasoning traces, persona summaries, and is used for chain-of-thought instruction fine-tuning [14] of downstream personalization models.

## 3.2   Synthetic Data Validation Methodology

To evaluate the quality of the synthetic dataset, we conduct a comparative analysis [17] by training LLMs on (1) synthetic data generated from our CSP framework, and (2) real de-identified production data. All models are evaluated on a real production de-identified test set to quantify performance and verify that synthetic data does not degrade generalization to real-world interactions [19,24]. Performance is measured using LLM-as-a-Judge (LLMaaJ)based precision and

**CSP (persona summary)**

*Summary:* Early 30s social worker in Seattle who bikes to a youth center, enjoys indie concerts, values sustainability, and works with at-risk teens...
*Anchors:* {indie_concerts, youth_mentoring, sustainable_living}

$$\downarrow \mathcal{G}_\theta$$

**Synthetic dialogs** $x$

**U:** I need new work shoes that are comfortable and not too expensive.
**A:** Okay, I can look for simple, durable options in a lower price range.
**U:** I prefer environmentally responsible companies... (conversation continues)

$$\downarrow \mathcal{H}_\theta$$

**Extracted PKIs** $y$

| Item | Type | Pol. | Conf. |
| --- | --- | --- | --- |
| prefers eco brands | Interest | + | high |
| works at youth center | Background | + | high |
| budget-conscious shopper | Behavior | + | low |

*Reasoning:* The user mentions workplace context, sustainability preference, and price sensitivity...

**Fig. 1.** High-level overview of personalized training dataset generation.

recall metrics and human evaluation ratings [25]. We also analyze failure modes and edge cases where synthetic data may introduce artifacts or spurious correlations absent in real customer conversations [1]. For fine-tuning, we utilize LLMs with parameters $\leq$ 10B, balancing performance with production deployment constraints such as inference latency, and GPU capacity ([9,12]). We conduct experiments using two training techniques on both datasets to generate PKIs: Low-Rank Adaptation (LoRA) [10] and Supervised instruction fine-tuning.

**Precision.** For precision, we measure the proportion of correctly extracted PKIs among all extracted PKIs, evaluated with the LLMaaJ framework for *relevance* and *sensibility*. Relevance assesses whether a PKI is explicitly stated or can be reliably inferred from the customer's interaction history with sufficient evidence (for e.g., "I love pop music" $\rightarrow$ *pop music*; repeated "Play Taylor Swift" requests $\rightarrow$ *Taylor Swift*). Sensibility assesses whether the PKI reflects a meaningful user interest rather than a routine requests or an illogical association. A PKI is considered precise when both criteria are satisfied. The reliability of this metric is validated through human annotation, yielding a Cohen's $\kappa$ of 0.62.

**Recall.** Measuring recall is challenging since the ground truth of customer interests is rarely observable. We adopt a QA-based recall metric [6], used in summarization evaluation where reference completeness is similarly difficult to guarantee [4,5]. A questionnaire aligned with customer use cases is manually designed, and an LLM generates answers to these questions using customers' interactions (*gold* answers) and inferred PKIs (*candidate* answers). Candidate responses are compared against gold references: "I don't know" answers are marked incorrect (TP = 0, FN = 1) when a gold answer exists, while valid pairs are scored via Sentence-BERT cosine similarity [18], with scores above a threshold counted as true positives and those below as false negatives. Outputs are manually reviewed to ensure evaluation reliability, as correlation with human judgment is non-trivial.

# 4    Results

We evaluate model performance using both automated metrics and customer validation. Models fine-tuned on the persona-based synthetic dataset outperform those trained on real de-identified data, achieving +5% precision and +8% QA-recall gains as shown in Table 1 and Table 2. For customer validation, a representative sample of 115 users reviewed their learned PKIs generated by the synthetic-persona-based model through an internal annotation tool. Users assessed the accuracy of each PKI, yielding an overall precision above 85%, demonstrating strong user acceptance and system effectiveness (Table 3).

**Table 1.** Performance comparison across training configurations on a real world de-identified test set. Metrics are percentage-point differences relative to a >20B-parameter baseline. All experimental methods use the same <10B base LLM with different adaptation strategies.

| Training Data | Adaptation Method | $\Delta$Precision | $\Delta$Recall |
| --- | --- | --- | --- |
| None (baseline, >20B) | Zero-shot prompting | 0.0% | 0.0% |
| None (<10B) | Zero-shot prompting | -3.4% | +4.8% |
| Real world de-identified | LoRA | +2.0% | +1.0% |
| Real world de-identified | Full SFT | +3.0% | +4.9% |
| Synthetic | LoRA | +3.5% | +4.9% |
| Synthetic | Full SFT | **+8.0%** | **+13.0%** |

**Table 2.** Models trained on synthetic data outperform models trained on real world de-identified data across fine-tuning strategies on a real de-identified test set (mean over 3 runs).

| Fine-tuning | $\Delta$Prec.(%) | $\Delta$Recall (%) |
| --- | --- | --- |
| LoRA | +1.5 | +3.9 |
| Full SFT | **+5.0** | **+8.0** |

**Table 3.** Synthetic data statistics compared to real world de-identified data.

| Metric | Synthetic |
| --- | --- |
| Avg. turns per dialog | +2.2 |
| Vocabulary diversity | +4.6K |
| PKIs per dialog | +0.9 |
| Interest category coverage | +31% |

# 5   Conclusion

We present a framework for generating CSPs and personalized training data via taxonomy guided knowledge enrichment, in context learning, and role playing generation. The synthetic dataset enables privacy preserving fine-tuning of personalization models without reliance on real user data. Evaluation using LLMaaJ and human validation shows substantial gains in precision and recall for PKIs, with over 85% customer validated precision, demonstrating the effectiveness of synthetic data for scalable industry scale personalization. Empirically, we find that taxonomy guided persona grounding over an 1,800 node interest ontology preserves semantic diversity, mitigates overfitting to synthetic artifacts, and improves generalization across both head and long tail domains that are underrepresented in real logs. In addition, CSPs provide fully specified personal knowledge supervision including polarity, confidence, and reasoning traces, yielding a denser learning signal that supports effective chain of thought distillation and improves performance on real world de-identified data.

**Disclosure of Interests.** The authors have no competing interests to declare that are relevant to the content of this article.

# References


1. Bayer, M., Kaufhold, M.A., Reuter, C.: A survey on data augmentation for text classification. ACM Comput. Surv. **55**(7), 1–39 (2022)
2. Bukharin, A., et al.: Data diversity matters for robust instruction tuning. In: Findings of the Association for Computational Linguistics: EMNLP 2024, pp. 3411–3425. Association for Computational Linguistics (2024). https://doi.org/10.18653/v1/2024.findings-emnlp.195
3. Chen, M., et al.: PLACES: Prompting language models for social conversation synthesis. In: Findings of the Association for Computational Linguistics: EACL 2023, pp. 844–868. Association for Computational Linguistics (2023). https://doi.org/10.18653/v1/2023.findings-eacl.63
4. Deutsch, D., Roth, D., Durrett, G.: Towards question-answering as an automatic metric for evaluating the content quality of summaries. Trans. Assoc. Comput. Linguist. **9**, 346–361 (2021)
5. Durmus, E., He, H., Diab, M.: Feqa: a question answering evaluation framework for faithfulness assessment in abstractive summarization. In: Proceedings of the 58th Annual Meeting of the Association for Computational Linguistics (ACL), pp. 5055–5070 (2020)
6. Fabbri, A.R., Wu, C.S., Liu, W., Xiong, C.: QAFactEval: Improved qa-based factual consistency evaluation for summarization. In: Proceedings of the 2022 Conference of the North American Chapter of the Association for Computational Linguistics: Human Language Technologies (NAACL-HLT), pp. 2587–2601. Association for Computational Linguistics (2022). https://doi.org/10.18653/v1/2022.naacl-main.187,
7. Fu, X., Chen, N., Gao, P., Li, Y.: Privacy-preserving personalized recommender systems. SSRN Working Paper (2022). https://ssrn.com/abstract=4202576

8. Hinton, G., Vinyals, O., Dean, J.: Distilling the knowledge in a neural network. In: NeurIPS Deep Learning Workshop (2015)

9. Hoffmann, J., et al.: Training compute-optimal large language models. In: Advances in Neural Information Processing Systems (NeurIPS), vol. 35, pp. 30016–30030 (2022)

10. Hu, E.J., et al.: Lora: Low-rank adaptation of large language models. In: International Conference on Learning Representations (ICLR) (2022)

11. Jandaghi, P., Sheng, X., Bai, X., Pujara, J., Sidahmed, H.: Faithful persona-based conversational dataset generation with large language models. arXiv preprint arXiv:2312.10007 (2023)

12. Kaplan, J., et al.: Scaling laws for neural language models. arXiv preprint arXiv:2001.08361 (2020)

13. Kim, H., et al.: SODA: Million-scale dialogue distillation with social commonsense contextualization. In: Proceedings of the 2023 Conference on Empirical Methods in Natural Language Processing, pp. 12930–12949. Association for Computational Linguistics (2023). https://doi.org/10.18653/v1/2023.emnlp-main.799

14. Kim, S., et al.: The cot collection: Improving zero-shot and few-shot learning of language models via chain-of-thought fine-tuning. arXiv preprint arXiv:2305.14045 (2023)

15. Lee, Y.J., Lim, C.G., Choi, Y., Im, J.H., Choi, H.J.: Personachatgen: generating personalized dialogues using gpt-3. In: Proceedings of the 1st Workshop on Customized Chat Grounding Persona and Knowledge, vol. 1, pp. 29–48 (2022)

16. Magister, L., Fried, D., Belinkov, Y.: Teaching small models to reason: distilling chain-of-thought (2023). https://arxiv.org/abs/2305.06350

17. Nikolenko, S.I.: Synthetic Data for Deep Learning. SOIA, vol. 174. Springer, Cham (2021). https://doi.org/10.1007/978-3-030-75178-4

18. Reimers, N., Gurevych, I.: Sentence-bert: Sentence embeddings using siamese bert-networks. In: Proceedings of the 2019 Conference on Empirical Methods in Natural Language Processing (EMNLP), pp. 3982–3992 (2019)

19. Shorten, C., Khoshgoftaar, T.M.: A survey on image data augmentation for deep learning. J. Big Data **6**(1), 1–48 (2019)

20. Tigunova, A., Yates, A., Mirza, P., Weikum, G.: Charm: Inferring personal attributes from conversations. In: Proceedings of the 2020 Conference on Empirical Methods in Natural Language Processing (EMNLP), vol. 1, pp. 5391–5404 (2020)

21. Wang, Z., Zhou, X., Koncel-Kedziorski, R., Marin, A., Xia, F.: Extracting and inferring personal attributes from dialogue. In: Proceedings of the 4th Workshop on NLP for Conversational AI, vol. 1, pp. 58–69 (2022)

22. Wen, P., et al.: Thinkpatterns-21k: A systematic study on the impact of thinking patterns in llms. arXiv preprint arXiv:2503.12918 (2025)

23. Wu, C.S., Madotto, A., Lin, Z., Xu, P., Fung, P.: Getting to know you: user attribute extraction from dialogues. In: Proceedings of the 12th Language Resources and Evaluation Conference (LREC), vol. 1, pp. 581–589 (2020)

24. Xu, C., et al.: How does synthetic data generation impact machine learning performance? a comprehensive study. arXiv preprint arXiv:2301.09286 (2023)

25. Yao, Y., et al.: Evaluating the text generation capabilities of large-scale language models. arXiv preprint arXiv:2207.07411 (2022)

26. Yukhymenko, H., Staab, R., Vero, M., Vechev, M.: A synthetic dataset for personal attribute inference. In: Advances in Neural Information Processing Systems (2024). https://arxiv.org/abs/2406.07217

27. Zhang, S., Dinan, E., Urbanek, J., Szlam, A., Kiela, D., Weston, J.: Personalizing dialogue agents: I have a dog, do you have pets too? In: Proceedings of the 56th Annual Meeting of the Association for Computational Linguistics (ACL), vol. 1, pp. 2204–2213 (2018)
28. Zhu, L., Li, W., Mao, R., Pandelea, V., Cambria, E.: Paed: Zero-shot persona attribute extraction in dialogues. In: Proceedings of the 61st Annual Meeting of the Association for Computational Linguistics (ACL), vol. 1, pp. 9771–9787 (2023)

# Demo Papers

# OmniRec: The All-In-One Solution for Reproducible and Interoperable Recommender Systems Experimentation


Lukas Wegmeth[1]([envelope]), Moritz Baumgart[1,2], Philipp Meister[1,2], Bela Gipp[2], and Joeran Beel[1,3]

[1] University of Siegen, Siegen, Germany
{Lukas.Wegmeth,Moritz.Baumgart,Philipp.Meister,Joeran.Beel}@uni-siegen.de
[2] University of Göttingen, Göttingen, Germany
Bela.Gipp@uni-goettingen.de
[3] Recommender-Systems.com, Siegen, Germany
https://recommender-systems.com/



**Abstract.** Recommender systems researchers rely heavily on general-purpose libraries that facilitate data preprocessing, model training, and evaluation. However, existing frameworks often suffer from fragmented data handling, inconsistent preprocessing, limited interoperability, and poor dataset referencing, which hinder reproducibility and comparability between studies. We present OmniRec, an open-source Python library designed to address these limitations. OmniRec provides standardized access to more than 230 datasets, a unified and flexible preprocessing pipeline, and seamless integration with multiple state-of-the-art recommender system frameworks, including RecPack, RecBole, Lenskit, and Elliot. Its modular architecture allows researchers to easily integrate new datasets, customize preprocessing steps, and external model interfaces. By combining ease of use, transparency, and reproducibility, OmniRec simplifies experimentation and fosters a more open and collaborative ecosystem for recommender systems research and practice.

**Keywords:** Recommender Systems · Framework · Reproducibility · Evaluation · Benchmarking


## 1  Introduction

The growth of the number and size of datasets, models, and evaluation protocols for recommender systems has created both opportunities and challenges. Concurrently, recommender systems research has relied on general-purpose libraries that simplify the development and evaluation of models. While powerful frameworks exist to train and evaluate recommendation models, the community still struggles with fragmented data handling, inconsistent preprocessing, and limited interoperability between frameworks [18].


© The Author(s), under exclusive license to Springer Nature Switzerland AG 2026
R. Campos et al. (Eds.): ECIR 2026, LNCS 16486, pp. 129–135, 2026.
https://doi.org/10.1007/978-3-032-21321-1_18

Frameworks such as RecBole [30], Lenskit [7], Lenskit-Auto [23], Elliot [3], RecPack [19], Surprise [11], Auto-Surprise [2], ClayRS [17], DaisyRec [22], Microsoft Recommenders [9], RecStudio [16], RecList [6], Spotlight [14], Cornac [20], LightFM [13], TorchRec [12], and ReChorus [15] have become integral to both academic and applied work, providing implementations of data preprocessing, model training, and evaluation protocols [18,24,29].

While such frameworks often support multiple input formats, pre-filtering options, and a variety of dataset splitting strategies, recent work has highlighted substantial shortcomings in current practice [18]. Pipelines vary drastically across frameworks, making comparisons opaque and hindering reproducibility due to three primary problems: (1) fragmented and incompatible data handling, (2) inadequate dataset referencing and versioning, and (3) inconsistent implementation of core methods. First, data handling is often fragmented, with each framework implementing its own incompatible preprocessing logic, preventing datasets from being shared or used across different frameworks. Second, poor dataset referencing and versioning, including missing citations, undocumented modifications, and broken download links, undermine the applicability of the dataset. Finally, preprocessing and splitting methods, such as feedback conversion or k-core filtering, are implemented inconsistently or absent altogether, and many frameworks remain closed in design, lacking standard export formats or integration APIs.

These limitations create two major problems: reduced accessibility for newcomers and a lack of scientific rigor. Reduced accessibility is evident in the steep entry barriers from a lack of standardization. Preparing a dataset requires substantial, error-prone preprocessing that is frequently duplicated across research groups, diverting time from novel development. The absence of a standardized preparation process hinders fair benchmarking and compromises scientific rigor, as variations in filtering and splitting lead to incompatible evaluations even with the same nominal dataset [8,10]. Missing data provenance on source and transformations compromises reproducibility and ethical compliance, and the absence of cross-framework export mechanisms forces error-prone reimplementation of pipelines to compare models from different frameworks [21].

In this paper, we present OmniRec[1], a novel open-source extensible Python library designed to address these issues through a comprehensive and robust all-in-one approach. OmniRec offers a unified interface for loading over 230 datasets, complemented by a straightforward preprocessing API for data cleaning and transformation. A key advantage is that users define the preprocessing pipeline only once. The pipeline can then be seamlessly executed across all integrated frameworks, eliminating redundant effort and ensuring consistency. To ensure reliability, its core design leverages modern Python typing to create strict interfaces, enabling developers to catch errors during code development and avoid costly, late-stage runtime crashes.

A cornerstone of OmniRec's interoperability is its seamless integration with multiple state-of-the-art recommendation frameworks. The initial release of

---

[1] http://code.isg.beel.org/OmniRec.

OmnicRec integrates RecPack, RecBole, Lenskit, and Elliot. We developed custom API adapters for each framework, which we coupled with an automated environment management system that creates and maintains isolated virtual Python environments for each library. Therefore, OmniRec elegantly resolves the critical issue of dependency and Python version conflicts between research frameworks.

OmniRec emphasizes extensibility, allowing developers to add new datasets, preprocessing operations, external frameworks, and evaluation metrics with minimal effort. For example, integrating a new recommender framework requires only a few hours of work implementing OmniRec's accessible interfaces. In terms of maintenance, framework updates that preserve a framework's API are trivial, i.e., a version bump, while those with breaking API changes require effort similar to adding a new framework. Using OmniRec, all processed datasets are fully documented, with complete provenance and exportable in common formats, enabling fair benchmarking and cross-framework experimentation. By addressing robustness, dependency management, and interoperability, OmniRec lowers the barrier to entry, safeguards reproducibility, and fosters a transparent research ecosystem. Unlike other frameworks, it provides a truly end-to-end, multi-framework workflow through a flexible, unified pipeline.

## 2   OmniRec

OmniRec is an open-source project, with source code on GitHub[2], comprehensive documentation[3], and a live demonstration[4]. Figure 1 illustrates the main components of OmniRec, which are organized into four interconnected modules: **Data Loader**, **Preprocessing Pipeline**, **Recommender Interface**, and **Evaluator**. This architecture enables a flexible, end-to-end workflow that spans from dataset loading to model evaluation.

The **Data Loader** loads registered datasets via specialized interfaces. It includes preprocessing operations, i.e., optional removal of duplicate user-item interactions and normalization of identifiers to incrementing integers, to ensure consistency across datasets. In addition, it exposes dataset statistics, which can be used for both exploratory analysis and reproducibility reporting.

The **Preprocessing Pipeline** applies user-specified preprocessing steps. Currently supported operations include subsampling, filtering by time or rating, core pruning, feedback conversion, and several splitting strategies, such as time-based holdout, random holdout, user-based holdout, and user-based cross-validation. The pipeline design is extensible, allowing developers to add new preprocessing functions by implementing a pre-defined interface.

The **Recommender Interface** enables seamless export of preprocessed datasets to the widely used recommender systems frameworks Lenskit, RecPack,

---

[2] http://code.isg.beel.org/OmniRec.
[3] https://omnirec.recommender-systems.com/.
[4] https://youtu.be/fr4Gxo0sTwE.

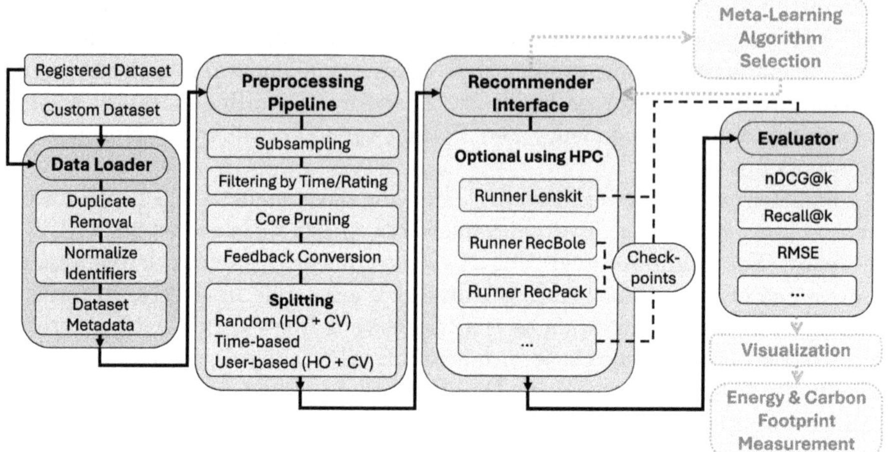



**Fig. 1.** Diagram of the OmniRec architecture, depicting four main components with their respective features and the relationships between them. Semi-transparent grey boxes denote features planned for future integration. (Color figure online)

RecBole, and Elliot. Through this interface, users can select algorithms, fit models, and generate predictions within the target framework, all while maintaining a single, unified preprocessing pipeline.

The **Evaluator** module provides a standardized interface for assessing model performance across different frameworks and datasets. It supports the computation of ranking- and rating-based metrics, ensuring that evaluation metrics are directly comparable regardless of the underlying framework. By centralizing evaluation logic, the module eliminates discrepancies caused by framework-specific metric implementations and promotes transparent, reproducible reporting. Evaluation outputs can be stored in addition to the dataset and preprocessing metadata, enabling complete experiment traceability and facilitating long-term reproducibility in recommender systems research.

## 2.1   Implementation Details

To ensure both flexibility and technical rigor, OmniRec's internal data architecture is centered on **pandas** data frames, providing a high-performance foundation for managing large-scale interaction data. All registered datasets are assigned to a standardized schema with user, item, and rating, and, optionally, timestamp columns. The **Preprocessing Pipeline** operates on this standardized representation and is therefore agnostic to the original file format or source library.

The **Data Loader** module utilizes an abstract base class pattern. To integrate a new dataset, developers implement a subclass of the `Loader` base class and override two static methods: `info()`, which specifies metadata such as download URLs and checksums, and `load()`, which returns the standardized interaction data frame. The loader is then registered under one or more names in a central registry. This design enforces a consistent interface while allowing dataset-specific loading and cleaning logic, ensuring that all registered datasets can be processed through the unified **Preprocessing Pipeline**.[5] OmniRec currently focuses on interaction data and lacks native support for complex data types such as text embeddings or images, though the library's modular nature allows for custom extensions.

External models are integrated via lightweight *runner* classes with a small typed interface for training and prediction. OmniRec does not modify the core training logic of integrated frameworks, but it delegates model fitting and prediction to the respective libraries. The runners are thin adapters responsible only for data conversion and configuration passing. Adding a new framework requires implementing a new runner that consumes OmniRec's standardized interaction data, trains models in the target library, and converts predictions back to OmniRec's internal format for evaluation.

OmniRec isolates each framework's runner in its own Python virtual environment using Astral's uv venv tool [1][6]. On first use, it creates the environment and installs required packages. Later runs reuse the same environment, even across different projects, keeping overhead to a minimum. Preprocessed datasets are written to standardized CSVs and loaded by each runner, avoiding repeated cross-environment transfers and keeping environment costs negligible compared to training time. Communication between environments is handled via RPyC[7], allowing runners to interact without sharing memory or processes directly.

## 2.2 Evolution and Future Plans

OmniRec is the product of a multi-year development and validation process within our lab[8]. It has served as the experimental basis for our research published in premier recommender systems venues, including ACM RecSys, ECIR [5,24,26, 27], and more [4,25,28]. OmniRec has also demonstrated its accessibility through its adoption in numerous undergraduate and graduate theses.

This demo paper accompanies OmniRec's inaugural public release. Designed for extensibility and growth, OmniRec will continue to evolve according to the following post-release roadmap, which is also illustrated in Fig. 1. Our immediate priorities include: (1) adding a visualization component to simplify the creation of plots for datasets and evaluations; (2) introducing an algorithm selection module that suggests suitable models based on dataset characteristics [26], and (3) incorporating energy consumption monitoring to provide insights into the computational cost and environmental impact of experiments [28].

**Disclosure of Interests.** The authors have no competing interests to declare that are relevant to the content of this article.

---

[5] See also "Loading Custom Datasets" in https://omnirec.recommender-systems.com/loading_datasets/.

[6] https://docs.astral.sh/uv/.

[7] https://rpyc.readthedocs.io.

[8] https://isg.beel.org/.

# References


1. Amiri, S.M.H., Islam, M.M., Kabir, M.S.: Reimagining python's tooling: The transition from pip to UV. Preprints (2025). https://doi.org/10.20944/preprints202512.2481.v1,
2. Anand, R., Beel, J.: Auto-surprise: an automated recommender-system (autorecsys) library with tree of parzens estimator (TPE) optimization. In: Proceedings of the 14th ACM Conference on Recommender Systems, pp. 585–587 (2020)
3. Anelli, V.W., et al.: Elliot: a comprehensive and rigorous framework for reproducible recommender systems evaluation. In: Proceedings of the 44th International ACM SIGIR Conference on Research and Development in Information Retrieval, pp. 2405–2414 (2021)
4. Baumgart, M., Wegmeth, L., Vente, T., Beel, J.: e-fold cross-validation for recommender-system evaluation. In: Boratto, L., De Filippo, A., Lex, E., Ricci, F. (eds.) Recommender Systems for Sustainability and Social Good, pp. 90–97. Springer, Cham (2025)
5. Beel, J., Wegmeth, L., Michiels, L., Schulz, S.: Informed dataset selection with 'algorithm performance spaces'. In: Proceedings of the 18th ACM Conference on Recommender Systems, pp. 1085–1090. RecSys '24, Association for Computing Machinery, New York, NY, USA (2024). https://doi.org/10.1145/3640457.3691704
6. Chia, P.J., Tagliabue, J., Bianchi, F., He, C., Ko, B.: Beyond ndcg: behavioral testing of recommender systems with reclist. In: Companion Proceedings of the Web Conference 2022, pp. 99–104 (2022)
7. Ekstrand, M.D.: Lenskit for python: next-generation software for recommender systems experiments. In: Proceedings of the 29th ACM International Conference on Information & Knowledge Management, pp. 2999–3006 (2020)
8. Ferrari Dacrema, M., Boglio, S., Cremonesi, P., Jannach, D.: A troubling analysis of reproducibility and progress in recommender systems research. ACM Trans. Inf. Syst. **39**(2) (2021). https://doi.org/10.1145/3434185,
9. Graham, S., Min, J.K., Wu, T.: Microsoft recommenders: tools to accelerate developing recommender systems. In: Proceedings of the 13th ACM Conference on Recommender Systems, pp. 542–543 (2019)
10. Hidasi, B., Czapp, Á.T.: The effect of third party implementations on reproducibility. In: Proceedings of the 17th ACM Conference on Recommender Systems, pp. 272–282 (2023)
11. Hug, N.: Surprise: a python library for recommender systems. J. Open Source Softw. **5**(52), 2174 (2020)
12. Ivchenko, D., et al.: Torchrec: a pytorch domain library for recommendation systems. In: Proceedings of the 16th ACM Conference on Recommender Systems, pp. 482–483. RecSys '22, Association for Computing Machinery, New York, NY, USA (2022). https://doi.org/10.1145/3523227.3547387,
13. Kula, M.: Metadata embeddings for user and item cold-start recommendations. In: Bogers, T., Koolen, M. (eds.) Proceedings of the 2nd Workshop on New Trends on Content-Based Recommender Systems co-located with 9th ACM Conference on Recommender Systems (RecSys 2015), Vienna, Austria, September 16-20, 2015. CEUR Workshop Proceedings, vol. 1448, pp. 14–21. CEUR-WS.org (2015). http://ceur-ws.org/Vol-1448/paper4.pdf
14. Kula, M.: Spotlight (2017). https://github.com/maciejkula/spotlight
15. Li, J., et al.: Rechorus2. 0: a modular and task-flexible recommendation library. In: Proceedings of the 18th ACM Conference on Recommender Systems, pp. 454–464 (2024)

16. Lian, D., et al.: Recstudio: towards a highly-modularized recommender system. In: Proceedings of the 46th International ACM SIGIR Conference on Research and Development in Information Retrieval, pp. 2890–2900 (2023)
17. Lops, P., Polignano, M., Musto, C., Silletti, A., Semeraro, G.: Clayrs: an end-to-end framework for reproducible knowledge-aware recommender systems. Inf. Syst. **119**, 102273 (2023)
18. Mancino, A.C.M., et al.: Datarec: a python library for standardized and reproducible data management in recommender systems. In: Proceedings of the 48th International ACM SIGIR Conference on Research and Development in Information Retrieval, pp. 3478–3487 (2025)
19. Michiels, L., Verachtert, R., Goethals, B.: Recpack: an (other) experimentation toolkit for top-n recommendation using implicit feedback data. In: Proceedings of the 16th ACM Conference on Recommender Systems, pp. 648–651 (2022)
20. Salah, A., Truong, Q.T., Lauw, H.W.: Cornac: a comparative framework for multimodal recommender systems. J. Mach. Learn. Res. **21**(95), 1–5 (2020). http://jmlr.org/papers/v21/19-805.html
21. Schmidt, M., Nitschke, J., Prinz, T.: Evaluating the performance-deviation of itemknn in recbole and lenskit (2024). https://arxiv.org/abs/2407.13531
22. Sun, Z., et al.: Daisyrec 2.0: benchmarking recommendation for rigorous evaluation. IEEE Trans. Pattern Anal. Mach. Intell. **45**(7), 8206–8226 (2022)
23. Vente, T., Ekstrand, M., Beel, J.: Introducing lenskit-auto, an experimental automated recommender system (autorecsys) toolkit. In: Proceedings of the 17th ACM Conference on Recommender Systems, pp. 1212–1216 (2023)
24. Vente, T., Wegmeth, L., Said, A., Beel, J.: From clicks to carbon: the environmental toll of recommender systems. In: Proceedings of the 18th ACM Conference on Recommender Systems, pp. 580–590. RecSys '24, Association for Computing Machinery, New York, NY, USA (2024). https://doi.org/10.1145/3640457.3688074,
25. Wegmeth, L., Beel, J.: CaMeLS: cooperative meta-learning service for recommender systems. In: Proceedings of the Perspectives on the Evaluation of Recommender Systems Workshop 2022. CEUR-WS (2022). https://ceur-ws.org/Vol-3228/paper2.pdf
26. Wegmeth, L., Vente, T., Beel, J.: Recommender systems algorithm selection for ranking prediction on implicit feedback datasets. In: Proceedings of the 18th ACM Conference on Recommender Systems, pp. 1163–1167. RecSys '24, Association for Computing Machinery, New York, NY, USA (2024). https://doi.org/10.1145/3640457.3691718
27. Wegmeth, L., Vente, T., Purucker, L.: Revealing the hidden impact of top-n metrics on optimization in recommender systems. In: Advances in Information Retrieval: 46th European Conference on Information Retrieval, ECIR 2024, Glasgow, UK, March 24–28, 2024, Proceedings, Part I, pp. 140–156. Springer, Heidelberg (2024). https://doi.org/10.1007/978-3-031-56027-9_9,
28. Wegmeth, L., Vente, T., Said, A., Beel, J.: Emers: energy meter for recommender systems. In: Boratto, L., De Filippo, A., Lex, E., Ricci, F. (eds.) Recommender Systems for Sustainability and Social Good, pp. 83–89. Springer, Cham (2025)
29. Zangerle, E., Bauer, C.: Evaluating recommender systems: survey and framework. ACM Comput. Surv. **55**(8), 1–38 (2022)
30. Zhao, W.X., et al.: Recbole: Towards a unified, comprehensive and efficient framework for recommendation algorithms. In: Proceedings of the 30th ACM International Conference on Information & Knowledge Management, pp. 4653–4664 (2021)

# GutBrainKB: Exploring the Gut–Brain Interaction Through a Reliable Biomedical KB


Ornella Irrera[(✉)][iD], Marco Martinelli[iD], Samuel Piron[iD], and Gianmaria Silvello[iD]

University of Padova, Padova, Italy
{ornella.irrera,marco.martinelli,samuel.piron,gianmaria.silvello}@unipd.it



**Abstract.** GutBrainKB is a web platform based on a structured KB to aid clinicians and researchers in studying gut–brain interactions. It features a 79K-triple KB from expert-annotated literature in the Gut-BrainIE dataset (BioASQ Lab @ CLEF 2025), offering a reliable resource for exploring the gut-brain axis. Users can explore through natural language and faceted search, investigating entity relationships, accessing scientific literature, and visualizing connections with interactive graphs. GutBrainKB combines a semantically validated KB with an accessible interface, providing an efficient tool for analyzing gut–brain interactions and their impact on neurological and psychiatric disorders.


## 1 Introduction

In recent years, interest in the gut–brain axis has grown steadily, as demonstrated by numerous studies linking gut microbiota to neurological disorders such as Parkinson's and Alzheimer's disease, multiple sclerosis and various mental health conditions [1–3]. This expanding body of literature creates the need for systematic extraction and integration of knowledge from publications to render insights machine-actionable and to reveal connections among medical concepts that might otherwise remain hidden. In this context, Information Extraction (IE) serves as the foundation for processing large volumes of biomedical text, constructing structured Knowledge Base (KBs), and enabling downstream applications in drug discovery, disease modeling, and precision medicine. The core tasks within IE encompass Named Entity Recognition (NER) for identifying and classifying biomedical entities, Named Entity Linking (NEL) for normalizing and disambiguating those entities, and Relation Extraction (RE) for detecting and categorizing semantic relationships among them. The effectiveness of systems performing these tasks largely relies on the availability of high-quality human-annotated data, which serves as the gold standard for training, evaluation, and benchmarking. This open issue was addressed, specifically within the gut-brain interplay domain, by the GutBrainIE task, part of the BioASQ Lab at CLEF2025 [8,11], which introduces a dataset featuring over 350 PubMed abstracts manually annotated by biomedical experts for entity mentions and relations.



R. Campos et al. (Eds.): ECIR 2026, LNCS 16486, pp. 136–141, 2026.
https://doi.org/10.1007/978-3-032-21321-1_19

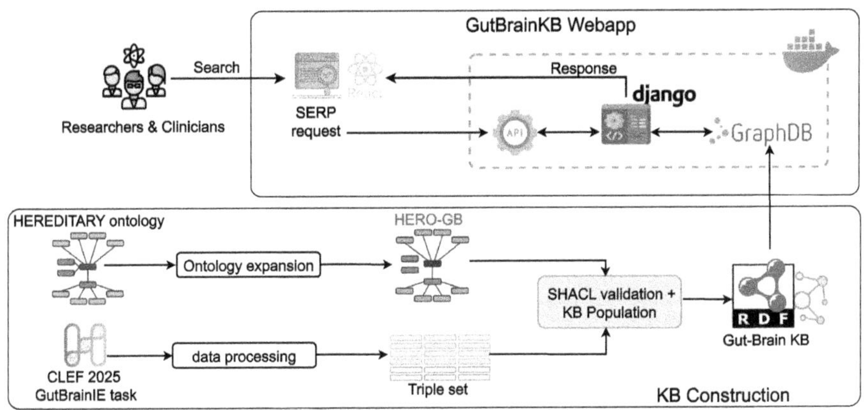


**Fig. 1.** Overview of the GutBrainKB system.

To fully leverage the knowledge embedded in this collection, the extraction, interpretation, and integration of its content are crucial. This is typically achieved through KBs, which model entities as nodes and relations as edges, producing a machine-readable format that supports easy access and advanced querying. Relevant examples in the literature which target gut-brain interactions are: the Pre-/Probiotics Knowledge Graph (PPKG) [6], the Food4HealthKG [4], the Microbiota Knowledge Graph for Mental Disorders (MiKG4MD) [7], and Microbiota Knowledge Graph (MiKG) [12]. Typically, such KBs are represented using RDF triples and queried via SPARQL [13], which provides powerful capabilities for data retrieval and reasoning. However, formulating SPARQL queries is challenging and requires technical expertise [5,14].

GutBrainKB is a web platform based on a 79K-triple KB from GutBrainIE, enabling exploration of gut–brain relationships with scientific evidence. Users can query via natural language or faceted search and view interactive graphs of entity connections, aiding researchers and clinicians in understanding gut–brain interactions and tracing claims to source publications.

## 2   GutBrainKB

Figure 1 shows the development of the GutBrainKB system, composed of two main phases: KB construction and GutBrainKB WebApp implementation.

***KB Construction.*** To construct the KB, we relied on two resources: (i) the GutBrainIE collection [8,11], and (ii) the HEREDITARY Gut-Brain Ontology (HERO-GB in Fig. 1), which also captures the structure of the annotated corpus, modeling sentences that contain biomedical concepts.[1]

We used the expert-curated annotations from the GutBrainIE collection comprising 359 abstracts, 9.9K entity mentions, and 4K relationships. From

---

[1] https://hereditary.dei.unipd.it/ontology/gutbrain/.

**Fig. 2.** GutBrainKB User Interface.

these annotated abstracts, entity mentions were linked to controlled biomedical vocabularies, thus normalizing and disambiguating textual variants. Then, we extracted RDF triples capturing both the semantic relationships among entities identified through RE annotations and the textual context in which each entity appears (e.g., sentence- and document-level evidences), resulting in a final KB of 79K triples. To ensure consistency with the underlying ontology, the resulting RDF graph has been validated with SHACL. The code and the data used for KB generation are available online.[2] [3]

Importantly, the KB construction pipeline is fully reusable and scalable: new documents from future GutBrainIE expansions can be processed using the same workflow to generate additional RDF triples, which can be seamlessly integrated into the KB. As a result, the KB can grow over time while preserving schema consistency.

***GutBrainKB WebApp.*** The GutBrainKB WebApp adopts a three-layer architecture. At the top layer, the UI is built with React.js, providing users with an interactive front-end for querying and interacting with the KB; a back-end layer, implemented using the Python web framework Django, is responsible for business logic, REST APIs, and service orchestration; the data layer is a GraphDB instance used to store and manage RDF triples of the generated KB. The system is fully dockerized with each component running in a separate container to simplify deployment and maintainability.

---

[2] https://github.com/GutBrainKB/GutBrainKB-WebApp/.
[3] https://zenodo.org/records/16845409.

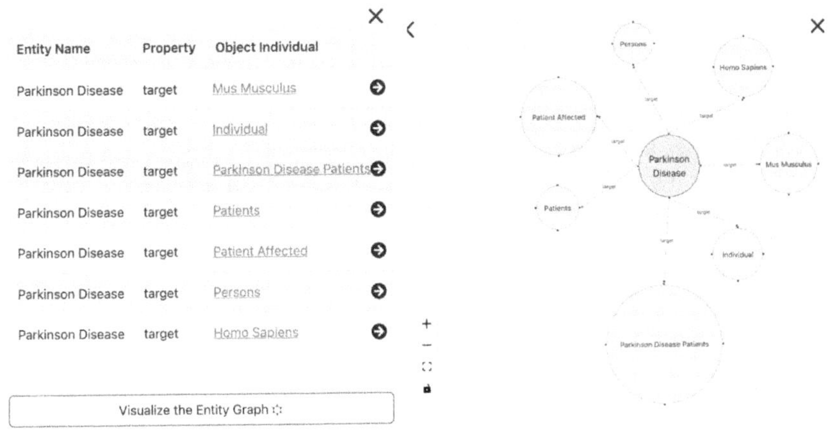

**Fig. 3.** The panel on the left reports the list of relationships for the subject *Parkinson disease* and predicate *target*. On the right, the related Entity Graph.

The GutBrainKB platform allows users to search for factual information on gut–brain relations supported by scientific literature. Users can access concept definitions and explore relationships with their supporting textual and bibliographic evidences. Specifically, when a query such as "Alzheimer's disease" is submitted, the backend first sanitizes the input and then executes a predefined SPARQL query template, injecting the term into a case-insensitive filter to retrieve all matching entity mentions. For each matched entity, the system returns associated paper metadata (e.g., PMID, title, authors, journal, year), supporting evidence (sentences and mention texts), linked ontology class or individual information, and the relations in which the entity participates. The results are then deduplicated at the paper–sentence–mention level and packaged into a compact JSON format for the UI. The reliability of the results returned to the user directly is related to the quality of the GutBrainIE annotations underlying the KB. Entity linking achieved an overall accuracy of $0.915 \pm 0.0473$ [10]. The quality of relation annotations is further ensured by relying on the two highest-quality folds of GutBrainIE, curated by expert annotators with domain knowledge and prior annotation experience [9].

In Fig. 2, we present the GutBrainKB UI showing the `Parkinson Disease` concept. (A) provides an autocomplete search bar, which lets users enter queries for specific concepts and their relationships. (B) features a faceted search panel, allowing users to filter concepts by ontological class or named individual and to narrow publication results by author, journal, collection, or year. (C) displays detailed information about the selected concept, such as its ontology reference, name, class, definition, and vocabulary. Users may also download a summary of the concept, including its relationships and supporting sentences, in either JSON or TTL format. (D) summarizes the relationships associated with the selected concept and shows how many publications mention it. A horizontal histogram visualizes relationship distribution by predicate, and users can click any bar to see all relationships for the chosen predicate in a modal window. Each listed object links to its own description page, enabling further exploration within the KB. A graph view is also available, visualizing the selected concept and its related entities. In Fig. 3, the left panel shows the list of relationships with *Parkinson disease* as subject and *target* as predicate, while the right presents an overview of the generated graph. Another histogram shows the number of related publications per year and allows users to view yearly publication details in a modal window. (E) presents a table that summarizes the sentences where the concept appears. Users can interact with each table cell to access additional information, such as the full text of the article and journal details.

The GutBrainKB WebApp is available at https://hereditary.dei.unipd.it/app/gutbrainkb/.

## 3    Final Remarks

In this work, we introduced GutBrainKB, a web application for exploring validated gut–brain facts within a biomedical KB. We built the KB from the expert-annotated GutBrainIE collection and ensured semantic consistency by validating against HERO-GB. GutBrainKB combines curated data, semantic modeling, and interactive visualizations to help clinicians and researchers query and interpret complex gut–brain relationships.

Future directions include the integration of large language models to assist in translating users' natural language queries into SPARQL queries over the KB.

**Acknowledgments.** The work was supported by the HEREDITARY project, as part of the EU Horizon Europe program under Grant Agreement 101137074.

**Disclosure of Interests.** The authors have no competing interests to declare that are relevant to the content of this article.

## References

1. Appleton, J.: The gut-brain axis: influence of microbiota on mood and mental health. Integ. Med. Clin. J. **17**(4), 28 (2018)
2. Carabotti, M., Scirocco, A., Maselli, M.A., Severi, C.: The gut-brain axis: interactions between enteric microbiota, central and enteric nervous systems. Ann. Gastroenterol. Q. Publ. Hellenic Soc. Gastroenterol. **28**(2), 203 (2015)
3. Cryan, J.F., O'Riordan, K.J., Sandhu, K., Peterson, V., Dinan, T.G.: The gut microbiome in neurological disorders. Lancet Neurol. **19**(2), 179–194 (2020)
4. Fu, C., Huang, Z., van Harmelen, F., He, T., Jiang, X.: Food4healthkg: Knowledge graphs for food recommendations based on gut microbiota and mental health. Artif. Intell. Med. **145**, 102677 (2023). https://doi.org/10.1016/j.artmed.2023.102677
5. Giachelle, F., Marchesin, S., Silvello, G., Alonso, O.: Searching for reliable facts over a medical knowledge base. In: Proceedings of the 46th international ACM SIGIR conference on research and development in information retrieval, pp. 3205–3209 (2023). https://doi.org/10.1145/3539618.3591822,

6. Liu, T., Lan, G., Feenstra, K.A., Huang, Z., Heringa, J.: Towards a knowledge graph for pre-/probiotics and microbiota-gut-brain axis diseases. Sci. Rep. **12**(1), 18977 (2022). https://doi.org/10.1038/s41598-022-21735-x
7. Liu, T., Pan, X., Wang, X., Feenstra, K.A., Heringa, J., Huang, Z.: Predicting the relationships between gut microbiota and mental disorders with knowledge graphs. Health Inf. Sci. Syst. **9**(1), 1–9 (2020). https://doi.org/10.1007/s13755-020-00128-2
8. Martinelli, M., et al.: Overview of GutBrainIE@CLEF 2025: gut-brain interplay information extraction. In: Faggioli, G., Ferro, N., Rosso, P., Spina, D. (eds.) CLEF 2025 Working Notes (2025)
9. Martinelli, M., et al.: Overview of gutbrainie@ clef 2025: gut-brain interplay information extraction. In: Faggioli, G., Ferro, N., Rosso, P., Spina, D. (eds.) CLEF 2025 Working Notes. vol. 4038, pp. 65–98 (2025)
10. Martinelli, M., Marchesin, S., Silvello, G.: Efficient and reliable estimation of named entity linking quality: a case study on gutbrainie (2026). https://arxiv.org/abs/2601.06624
11. Nentidis, A., et al.: Overview of BioASQ 2025: The thirteenth BioASQ challenge on large-scale biomedical semantic indexing and question answering. Lecture Notes in Computer Science, vol. TBA, p. TBA. Springer (2025)
12. Pudavar, A.E., Baksi, K.D., Pokhrel, V., Kuntal, B.K.: Microbiome knowledge graph as a tool to understand bacteria-host associations. Arch. Microbiol. **207**(9), 222 (2025). https://doi.org/10.1007/s00203-025-04413-0
13. Weikum, G., Dong, X.L., Razniewski, S., Suchanek, F.M.: Machine knowledge: Creation and curation of comprehensive knowledge bases. Found. Trends Databases **10**(2–4), 108–490 (2021). https://doi.org/10.1561/1900000064
14. Wu, W.: Proactive natural language search engine: tapping into structured data on the web. In: Proceedings of the 16th International Conference on Extending Database Technology, pp. 143–148 (2013https://doi.org/10.1145/2452376.2452394

# CancerRAGent: Evidence-Linked and Safety-Guided Oncology Question Answering

Trung Vo[1]([⊠])[iD], An Trieu[1][iD], Vu Tran[1][iD], Yuji Matsumoto[2][iD], and Le-Minh Nguyen[1][iD]

[1] Japan Advanced Institute of Science and Technology, Ishikawa, Japan
{trungvo,antrieu,vu-tran,nguyenml}@jaist.ac.jp
[2] RIKEN Center for Advanced Intelligence Project (AIP), Tokyo, Japan
yuji.matsumoto@riken.jp

**Abstract.** Providing reliable cancer information with a large language model-based agent is challenging due to domain nuance, clinical safety constraints, and the risk of hallucinations. In oncology, standard retrieval augmented generation (RAG) lacks triage and medical verification. We present CancerRAGent, a safety-aware RAG for oncology question answering. On a curated oncology PubMed subset, it combines hybrid retrieval, reranking, and evidence-grounded generation with red-alert triage to deliver a concise answer, safety-guided exploration, and a suggested next question. Users receive concise, cancer-focused answers with a clear follow-up question and guided exploration—features absent in vanilla RAG. This demo targets patients and caregivers seeking evidence-based cancer information. The system does not provide diagnoses or personalized treatment plans. Our code and demo are here: https://github.com/oncologyxai/CancerRAGent.

**Keywords:** Oncology Question Answering · Cancer Information Retrieval · Healthcare Application · RAG · LLMs

## 1 Introduction

Answering complex biomedical questions with high factual reliability is challenging—especially in oncology, where queries are specialized and errors carry clinical risk [1,4]. Despite advances, large language models (LLMs) can generate unsupported content [3]. Retrieval-augmented generation (RAG) mitigates this limitation by grounding outputs in evidence [6], yet most biomedical RAG systems remain broad and overlook oncology-specific constraints and safety needs. We present **CancerRAGent**, a domain-specialized RAG system for trustworthy, concise oncology question answering. Unlike vanilla RAG, it combines oncology-focused retrieval, UI-level safety triage, and evidence-grounded reasoning to provide actionable answers. Our contribution is a safety- and evidence-centered interaction workflow for oncology QA: (i) warns users when


R. Campos et al. (Eds.): ECIR 2026, LNCS 16486, pp. 142–147, 2026.
https://doi.org/10.1007/978-3-032-21321-1_20

a question mentions urgent symptoms, (ii) verification-aware synthesis that stabilizes the final response, and (iii) recommends a follow-up question that guide users to explore related topics step by step. The result is a practical pipeline for patients and caregivers, producing evidence-based answers with safety checks and follow-up question guidance. CancerRAGent addresses three practical needs:

- **Reliable evidence acquisition** via a PubMed-indexed oncology corpus and *hybrid retrieval*—sparse BM25 and dense BGE-M3 embeddings [2], followed by a cross-encoder reranker [8] to prioritize precision; we retain the top-10 passages as evidence for answer generation.
- **Safe, transparent answer generation** with sources, rationales, confidence levels, and a red-alert triage module to flag urgent symptoms and recommend professional care, grounded in PubMed literature from the National Institutes of Health (NIH).
- **Guided user follow-up**, also based on NIH PubMed-indexed literature.

CancerRAGent, with oncology-focused retrieval, safety triage, and verification-aware synthesis in a transparent workflow, offers a practical and interpretable solution for oncology question answering and cancer information retrieval. We evaluate our system on the MedQuAD cancer subset [1] (729 questions with reference answers), under an LLM-as-judge protocol.

## 2   System Overview

CancerRAGent is a Streamlit web app for *safety-aware* oncology QA. As shown in Fig. 1, CancerRAGent checks the question for urgent symptoms. If high-risk symptoms are detected, the system displays an urgent warning and halts the guided exploration to avoid encouraging self-management. Otherwise, the system proceeds with the normal QA flow: it retrieves PubMed-indexed evidence via hybrid sparsedense retrieval with reranking and generates a concise answer. For complex questions, the system breaks them down into simpler sub-questions, answers each one, and then combines those answers into a final response. In addition, it offers guided follow-up—a next question and an NIH-derived exploration path—to help users navigate related cancer topics safely. Importantly, guided follow-up refers to patient-facing question suggestions that help users explore related topics, not clinical action recommendations or model training steps.

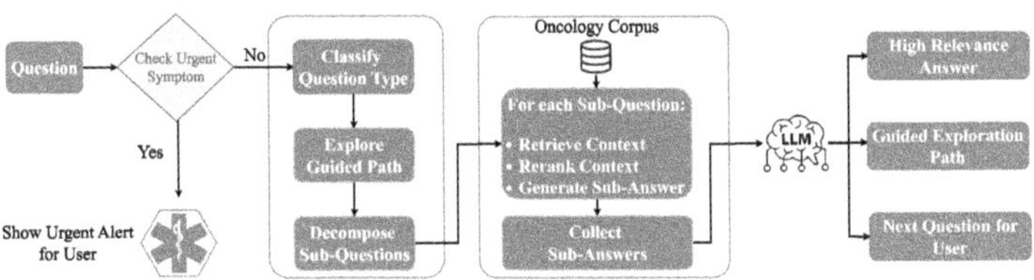


**Fig. 1.** Overview of our framework.

**Retrieval and Reranking.** We index the oncology subset of PubMed and retrieve candidate passages using BM25 (sparse) and BGE-M3 embeddings (dense). We merge candidates from both retrievers and apply a cross-encoder reranker [8] to prioritize high-precision evidence. The top evidence passages (top-10 in our pipeline) are passed to LLMs for generation.

**Safety Triage, Decomposition, and Verification.** The urgent-symptom triage acts as a UI-level safety gate: when a query mentions high-risk symptoms, the system shows an alert and stops guided exploration rather than continuing normal QA flow. For multi-facet questions, the system generates a small set of focused sub-questions, retrieves evidence per sub-question, and produces short sub-answers with citations. The final response is synthesized from these sub-answers and then verified in a lightweight manner by checking that key statements remain supported by the retrieved evidence, reducing unsupported synthesis.

**Oncology Corpus.** We curate an oncology-specific subset of PubMed by filtering only oncology-related articles from the MedRAG collection [9]. Specifically, we retain 3,073,500 articles that mention terms such as *oncology*, *cancer*, *tumor*, *carcinoma*, *malignant*, or *neoplasm* in their titles or content. This focused curation minimizes irrelevant material and ensures that retrieved answers are both accurate and highly pertinent to cancer-related questions. As it is based on keyword filtering, the subset may still include false positives and may miss some relevant oncology articles.

**Interface Features** – A demo-friendly interface:

- **Medical question input:** Single text box for any cancer question.
- **Answer display:** Concise, cancer-focused (not diagnosis or treatment).
- **Guided exploration:** Question-tailored path; if urgent symptoms or personal details, stop guidance and advise seeing a clinician.
- **Follow-up questions.** Safety-aware next question for deeper exploration.
- **Question & Answer history:** Past questions and answers for reference.
- **Export to PDF.** One-click export of the current session to PDF.

Figure 2 highlights full details of our system that fits the cancer domain.

## 3   Evaluation

### 3.1   Evaluation Settings

**Generator.** We evaluate two options: a biomedical LLM (*OpenMeditron/ Meditron3-8B*) and a general-purpose LLM (*Qwen2.5-14B-Instruct*). **Judges.** To reduce single-judge bias, we employ an LLM-as-judge ensemble with (i) a biomedical specialist judge (*Bio-Medical-Llama-3-8B*, denoted as "Bio-Med"), (ii) an open-weight generalist judge (*Qwen3-32B*), and (iii) a closed-weight generalist judge (*GPT-4o mini*) [7]. Except for *GPT-4o mini*, all LLMs' weights are from Hugging Face (https://huggingface.co) **Protocol.** We score two outputs— answer and next question—on a five-point Likert scale (1 = very poor, 5 =

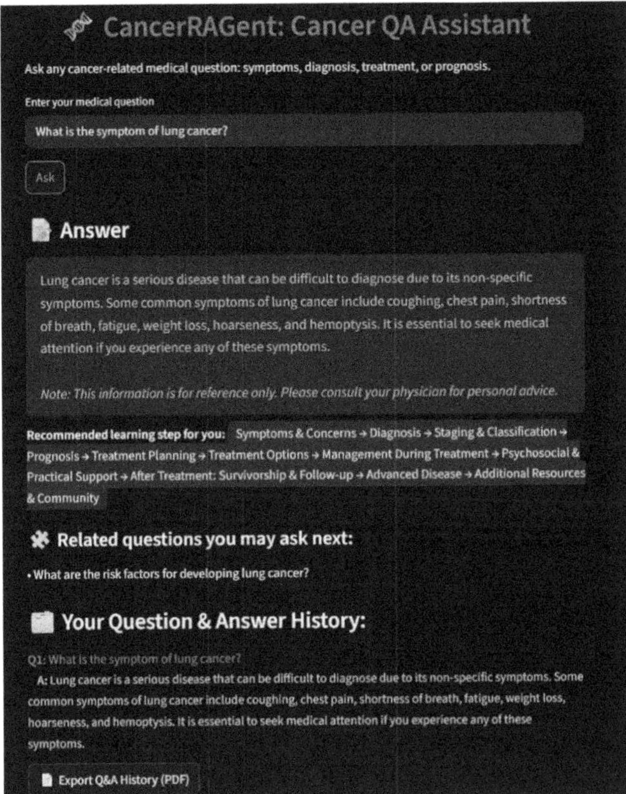


**Fig. 2.** CancerRAGent's interface delivers concise, evidence-based answers with safety checks and suggests follow-up questions to guide exploration.

excellent) [5]. **Setup.** All experiments are run on a single NVIDIA A6000 with 48 GB memory.

**Generated Answers.** We employ four metrics: **Correctness** – medical factuality; **Faithfulness** – grounding in retrieved evidence, penalizing unsupported claims; **Coherence** – logical organization and clarity of reasoning; **Readability** – fluent, accessible phrasing for non-experts.

**Next-Question Suggestions.** In addition to the above four criteria to clarify the next question, we add **Relevance** checking that the suggestion is clearly connected to the user's prior query and the system's answer, and **Informativeness** assessing whether the question opens a meaningful follow-up. We use zero-shot prompting as a controlled baseline to focus on the effect of our end-to-end workflow under the same generator backbones.

## 3.2  Evaluation Results

Across all three judges, CancerRAGent consistently matches or outperforms the zero-shot baselines for Meditron3-8B ("Med3") and Qwen2.5-14B ("Qwen2.5"), as presented in Table 1.

For generated answers, the largest gains appear in *faithfulness* and *correctness*, with steady improvements in *coherence*; *readability* is near ceiling for the biomedical judge and still trends upward elsewhere. For next-question quality, *relevance* and *informativeness* improve alongside *faithfulness*, while *coherence* and *readability* remain high and stable. These patterns align with the design: oncology-focused retrieval with cross-encoder reranking sharpens evidence selection; decomposition anchors each sub-question to targeted context; and verification stabilizes synthesis, yielding clearer and more reliable outputs.

**Table 1.** LLM-judge scores (15) for answers and next questions under zero-shot (ZS) vs. our system (ours). Blue numbers indicate performance improvements of our system over the ZS.

| Judge | Model/Setting | Generated Answer | | | | Next Question | | | | | |
|---|---|---|---|---|---|---|---|---|---|---|---|
| | | Correctness | Faithfulness | Coherence | Readability | Relevance | Informativeness | Correctness | Faithfulness | Coherence | Readability |
| Bio-Med | Med3 ZS | 4.37 | 3.54 | 4.72 | 4.99 | 4.89 | 4.91 | 4.97 | 4.4 | 4.88 | 4.99 |
| | Med3 ours | $\mathbf{4.48}_{\uparrow 0.11}$ | $\mathbf{3.81}_{\uparrow 0.27}$ | $\mathbf{4.85}_{\uparrow 0.13}$ | 4.99 | $\mathbf{4.93}_{\uparrow 0.04}$ | $\mathbf{4.97}_{\uparrow 0.06}$ | $\mathbf{5.00}_{\uparrow 0.03}$ | $\mathbf{4.69}_{\uparrow 0.29}$ | $\mathbf{4.95}_{\uparrow 0.07}$ | $\mathbf{5.00}_{\uparrow 0.01}$ |
| | Qwen2.5 ZS | 4.59 | 3.99 | 4.85 | 5.00 | 4.91 | 4.95 | 4.99 | 4.75 | 4.93 | 5.00 |
| | Qwen2.5 ours | $\mathbf{4.68}_{\uparrow 0.09}$ | $\mathbf{4.03}_{\uparrow 0.04}$ | $\mathbf{4.9}_{\uparrow 0.05}$ | 5.00 | $\mathbf{4.97}_{\uparrow 0.06}$ | $\mathbf{4.98}_{\uparrow 0.03}$ | $\mathbf{5.00}_{\uparrow 0.01}$ | $\mathbf{4.89}_{\uparrow 0.14}$ | $\mathbf{4.99}_{\uparrow 0.06}$ | 5.00 |
| Qwen3 -32B | Med3 ZS | 3.31 | 2.94 | 4.08 | 4.48 | 4.87 | 4.74 | 4.98 | 4.65 | 4.91 | 4.99 |
| | Med3 ours | $\mathbf{3.39}_{\uparrow 0.08}$ | $\mathbf{3.29}_{\uparrow 0.35}$ | $\mathbf{4.24}_{\uparrow 0.16}$ | $\mathbf{4.84}_{\uparrow 0.44}$ | $\mathbf{4.91}_{\uparrow 0.04}$ | $\mathbf{4.87}_{\uparrow 0.13}$ | $\mathbf{4.99}_{\uparrow 0.01}$ | $\mathbf{4.79}_{\uparrow 0.14}$ | $\mathbf{4.98}_{\uparrow 0.06}$ | 4.99 |
| | Qwen2.5 ZS | 3.57 | 3.13 | 4.50 | 4.63 | 4.93 | 4.97 | 5.00 | 4.85 | 4.96 | 5.00 |
| | Qwen2.5 ours | $\mathbf{3.77}_{\uparrow 0.20}$ | $\mathbf{3.42}_{\uparrow 0.29}$ | $\mathbf{4.70}_{\uparrow 0.20}$ | $\mathbf{4.80}_{\uparrow 0.17}$ | $\mathbf{4.97}_{\uparrow 0.04}$ | $\mathbf{4.98}_{\uparrow 0.01}$ | 5.00 | $\mathbf{4.96}_{\uparrow 0.11}$ | $\mathbf{4.99}_{\uparrow 0.03}$ | 5.00 |
| GPT-4o -mini | Med3 ZS | 3.79 | 3.64 | 4.52 | 4.27 | 4.95 | 4.74 | 4.99 | 4.87 | 4.95 | 4.91 |
| | Med3 ours | $\mathbf{4.04}_{\uparrow 0.25}$ | $\mathbf{3.78}_{\uparrow 0.14}$ | $\mathbf{4.70}_{\uparrow 0.18}$ | $\mathbf{4.41}_{\uparrow 0.14}$ | $\mathbf{4.99}_{\uparrow 0.04}$ | $\mathbf{4.83}_{\uparrow 0.09}$ | 4.99 | $\mathbf{4.93}_{\uparrow 0.06}$ | $\mathbf{4.99}_{\uparrow 0.04}$ | $\mathbf{4.95}_{\uparrow 0.04}$ |
| | Qwen2.5 ZS | 4.10 | 3.99 | 4.21 | 3.93 | 4.99 | 4.90 | 5.00 | 4.86 | 4.97 | 4.81 |
| | Qwen2.5 ours | $\mathbf{4.32}_{\uparrow 0.22}$ | $\mathbf{4.13}_{\uparrow 0.14}$ | $\mathbf{4.52}_{\uparrow 0.31}$ | $\mathbf{4.31}_{\uparrow 0.38}$ | $\mathbf{5.00}_{\uparrow 0.01}$ | $\mathbf{4.96}_{\uparrow 0.06}$ | 5.00 | $\mathbf{4.91}_{\uparrow 0.05}$ | $\mathbf{4.99}_{\uparrow 0.02}$ | $\mathbf{4.88}_{\uparrow 0.07}$ |

# 4  Conclusion

CancerRAGent is a safety-aware, oncology-focused RAG demo that keeps evidence visible while answering complex cancer questions. It screens for urgent symptoms, decomposes queries into sub-questions, retrieves and reranks results per step, verifies the final synthesis, and proposes the next question—improving faithfulness and usefulness in a single interface. In future work, we plan to conduct user studies with clinicians to evaluate usability and clinical relevance, broaden the corpus to larger oncology collections with multilingual search. We also plan to report end-to-end latency for interactive use and to benchmark reasoning-tuned open-weight models (e.g., distilled reasoning variants) to better understand the trade-offs between faithfulness, safety behavior, and responsiveness.

**Acknowledgments.** This work was partly supported by Japan Science and Technology Agency (JST) as part of Adopting Sustainable Partnerships for Innovative Research Ecosystem (ASPIRE), Grant Number JPMJAP25B2.

**Disclosure of Interests.** The authors have no conflicts of interest to declare that are relevant to the content of this article.

# References


1. Ben Abacha, A., Demner-Fushman, D.: A question-entailment approach to question answering. BMC Bioinform. **20**, 1–23 (2019)
2. Chen, J., Xiao, S., Zhang, P., Luo, K., Lian, D., Liu, Z.: M3-embedding: multilinguality, multi-functionality, multi-granularity text embeddings through self-knowledge distillation. In: Ku, L.W., Martins, A., Srikumar, V. (eds.) Findings of the Association for Computational Linguistics: ACL 2024, pp. 2318–2335. Association for Computational Linguistics, Bangkok, Thailand (2024). https://doi.org/10.18653/v1/2024.findings-acl.137
3. Ji, Z., et al.: Survey of hallucination in natural language generation. ACM Comput. Sur. **55**(12), 1–38 (2023)
4. Jin, Qet al.: Biomedical question answering: a survey of approaches and challenges. ACM Comput. Sur. (CSUR) **55**(2), 1–36 (2022)
5. Joshi, A., Kale, S., Chandel, S.: Likert scale: Explored and explained. Br. J. Appl. Sci. Technol. **7**(4), 396 (2015)
6. Lewis, P., et al.: Retrieval-augmented generation for knowledge-intensive NLP tasks. Adv. Neural Inf. Process. Syst. **33**, 9459–9474 (2020)
7. OpenAI, T.: Introducing openai o3 and o4-mini (2025). https://openai.com/index/introducing-o3-and-o4-mini/
8. Reimers, N., Gurevych, I.: Sentence-bert: sentence embeddings using siamese bert-networks. In: Proceedings of the 2019 Conference on Empirical Methods in Natural Language Processing. Association for Computational Linguistics (2019). https://arxiv.org/abs/1908.10084
9. Xiong, G., Jin, Q., Lu, Z., Zhang, A.: Benchmarking retrieval-augmented generation for medicine. In: Findings of the Association for Computational Linguistics ACL 2024, pp. 6233–6251 (2024)

# Talmud-IR: A Talmud-Inspired Interface for Discussing RAG Response Quality

Wojciech Kusa[1], Niklas Deckers[2(✉)], Maik Fröbe[3], Laura Dietz[4], Birte Platow[5], and Mark Sanderson[6]

[1] NASK – National Research Institute, Warsaw, Poland
[2] University of Kassel and hessian.AI, Kassel, Germany
`niklas.deckers@uni-kassel.de`
[3] Friedrich-Schiller-Universität Jena, Jena, Germany
[4] University of New Hampshire, Durham, NH, USA
[5] TU Dresden and ScaDS.AI, Dresden, Germany
[6] RMIT University, Melbourne, Australia

**Abstract.** Retrieval-augmented generation (RAG) systems promise factually grounded answers, yet evaluating their quality remains difficult. Automated metrics and LLM-as-judge approaches offer scalability but risk circularity, benchmark leakage, and loss of diversity. Human assessors, meanwhile, often struggle to notice subtle omissions or hallucinations when responses appear linguistically fluent and confident. We present *Talmud-IR*, a novel user interface inspired by the dialogic structure of the Talmud. It visualizes RAG outputs as a central text surrounded by layers of evidence, commentary, and meta-assessment, enabling sustained human–LLM discussion about system quality and failure priorities. The prototype supports comparative RAG evaluation, collaborative exploration of "unknown unknowns," and pedagogical use for teaching critical reading of AI-generated content. Code and Prototype: https://github.com/WojciechKusa/talmud-ir

**Keywords:** RAG · LLM judge · Exploratory Evaluation

## 1 Introduction and Motivation

Retrieval-augmented generation (RAG) systems integrate document retrieval with large language models (LLMs) to produce grounded, conversational answers. Despite rapid progress, evaluating RAG outputs remains challenging. Automatic evaluation with LLM judges is convenient but introduces risks such as circularity, test-set leakage, and overfitting to benchmarks [5]. Human judgments remain vital, yet even expert assessors can overlook subtle factual errors or missing context when presented with fluent, confident prose [2,8].

Traditional IR evaluation treats judgment as a cost trade-off: How much assessor time can we buy, and how many topics can be covered? For generative systems, however, quality cannot be captured by one-off relevance labels.

© The Author(s), under exclusive license to Springer Nature Switzerland AG 2026
R. Campos et al. (Eds.): ECIR 2026, LNCS 16486, pp. 148–153, 2026.
https://doi.org/10.1007/978-3-032-21321-1_21

Responses may differ in nuance, perspective, and completeness, and a single evaluation paradigm cannot easily capture their multifaceted quality. To reveal such *"unknown unknowns"*, we argue for exploratory evaluation interfaces that foster sustained dialogue between humans and machines.

We draw inspiration from the Talmudic tradition, which has supported centuries of evolving discourse around a shared text [10]. The Talmud's structure— a central law text (the *Mishnah*) surrounded by interpretative discussions (the *Gemara*) and later super-commentaries—offers a compelling analogy for exploratory discussions about quality of AI-generated content. The Jewish tradition of Talmudic scriptural interpretation is based precisely on not setting any interpretation as absolute, but rather on attributing intrinsic value to the discourse surrounding different interpretations [1]. Ideas that have enabled critical conversation to persist over millennia may also help us build lasting frameworks for discussing RAG output quality criteria.

## 2   Related Work

A growing body of research explores how to evaluate the quality of RAG outputs. Prompt-based approaches, such as UMBRELA [18], LLM-as-a-judge [20], and RAGAS [6] use large language models as judges, relying on direct prompting to assign quality labels and judge RAG outputs. While attractive for their low cost and scalability, these methods are inherently fragile: they risk circularity when the same model family serves as both generator and judge [3], and are susceptible to test-set leakage and benchmark memorization [4,5], and often conflate confident phrasing with factual adequacy. As a result, such evaluations can obscure the very failure modes they aim to detect.

To mitigate these issues, hybrid judging [15], nugget- or rubric-based methods [7,11,14,16] offer a middle ground between human and automatic assessment. Here, evaluators specify which facts or ideas (*nuggets*) should appear in a high-quality answer, while LLMs assist in aligning those nuggets to generated text. Although this improves transparency, coverage of the "right" nuggets alone does not guarantee a good response: information must also be organized logically, expressed coherently, and contextualized with sufficient background. Understanding such aspects of quality requires richer, discourse-oriented evaluation artifacts.

Another recent direction concerns the *faithfulness of citations* in RAG outputs. Systems such as ARGUE and AutoArgue [12,19] verify whether retrieved passages genuinely support the generated statements, linking factual grounding to user trust. Yet, even when coverage and citation accuracy are accounted for, we remain uncertain about what the *next most critical failure point* of RAG systems will be—whether it involves reasoning, context management, or the presentation of evidence. To uncover these evolving weaknesses quickly, we need interfaces that allow humans and LLMs to collaboratively explore, debate, and surface new evaluation priorities as they emerge.

## 3   Prototype: Talmud-Style Interface for RAG Evaluation

The **Talmud-IR** prototype adopts the layout of a Talmudic page (Fig. 1), transforming evaluation into a structured, multi-participant conversation. The interface centers on a query–response pair produced by a RAG system and surrounds it with layers of supporting information and commentary. The central UI elements are:

- **Central text (Mishnah):** the user query and the system's generated answer.
- **Inner margins:** retrieved snippets that provide evidential grounding, highlighting faithful or contradictory citations.
- **Outer margins (Gemara):** threaded discussions among human experts and LLM-based assessors reflecting on correctness, completeness, tone, or omissions. Comments can reference specific spans of text or earlier remarks, forming a living discourse.
- **Super-commentaries:** a meta-layer aggregating evaluation metrics such as nugget coverage or citation validity, summarizing consensus across assessors.

The prototype is implemented as a lightweight web application built with React 19 and Tailwind CSS. It links textual spans to snippets and commentaries. Selecting a phrase in the central response highlights corresponding evidence; hovering over snippets reveals linked commentary. A sidebar records earlier discussions so recurring issues can be revisited, mirroring how later scholars build upon prior interpretations.

The typical workflow of the prototype user begins with inspecting the query and the RAG response at the center. During this inspection, the provided evidence can be used to validate aspects such as factuality. By leaving comments on specific aspects and spans, the prototype user enriches the discussion around the response's quality. Comments from previous human users can be reviewed and reacted to. Additionally, commentary from LLM-based systems for RAG evaluation is shown and can be considered during human inspection. This helps the prototype user conduct an in-depth analysis of the given RAG response.

An alternative configuration of the prototype system can invert the hierarchy of RAG responses and supporting documents: a cited document may appear at the center, surrounded by multiple RAG responses that interpret or misinterpret it. This view supports comparative studies of hallucination and evidence selection.

Our implementation can integrate with nugget-based evaluation systems [7, 12,14] to visualize nugget-based metrics alongside qualitative commentary. By unifying interpretative discussion with quantitative measures, the system reframes evaluation as an ongoing, collaborative conversation.

While Fig. 1 shows a particular example from the TREC 2024 RAG Track, the prototype supports any RAG run, including responses and external evaluation metadata, as long as it uses our input format. This makes it applicable to a wide range of RAG systems and tasks.

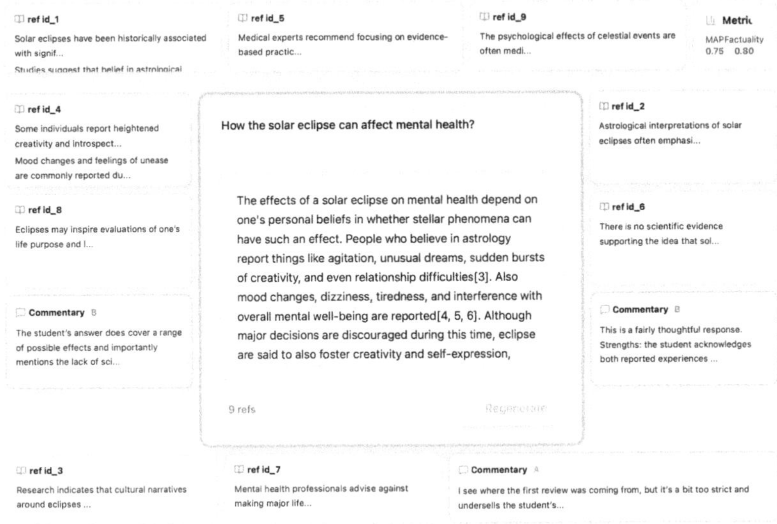


**Fig. 1.** Talmud-IR prototype: central RAG response (*Mishnah*) surrounded by retrieved evidence and human/LLM commentary (*Gemara*). While inspecting the given RAG response, the prototype user can take into account the given additional evidence and commentary. The example presented in this figure shows a RAG response from the *webis-manual* submission [9] for the TREC 2024 RAG Track [13, 17].

## 4   Intended User Groups

The Talmud-IR interface serves multiple stakeholder communities involved in the evaluation and use of RAG systems. **Human assessors** who compare multiple system outputs benefit from the structured presentation of retrieved evidence and the opportunity to anchor their judgments within an evolving commentary, improving both transparency and consistency. **Evaluation developers** can analyze discussion threads to study agreement patterns, biases, and hybrid human–LLM assessment workflows. In professional domains such as law, medicine, or scientific retrieval, **domain experts** can trace how generated statements are grounded in cited documents, supporting more trustworthy decision-making. Finally, **educators and learners** can use the interface as a pedagogical tool to explore how AI systems reason, argue, and fail—turning evaluation discourse into an exercise in critical reading and collaborative sense-making.

## 5   Discussion and Outlook

Our Talmud-IR prototype reimagines evaluation as a dialogic rather than a purely quantitative process. By capturing interpretative layers around each response, it allows researchers to document emerging quality criteria (e.g., plausibility, coverage, fairness) and track which criteria have been addressed or newly arise as systems improve. Future extensions will incorporate analytics to detect convergence among assessors and integrate LLM summarization of discussions. We plan to use Talmud-IR in collaborative workshops (e.g., TREC or CLEF tracks) as a means to guide the discussion about quality.

We invite the ECIR community to engage with the demonstration and to consider how dialogic interfaces like Talmud-IR can complement automated metrics by fostering a sustained, evidence-driven conversation about the quality of RAG systems.

**Acknowledgments.** This work has benefitted from Dagstuhl Seminar 25391 "Retrieval-Augmented Generation – The Future of Search?".

**Disclosure of Interests.** The authors have no competing interests to declare that are relevant to the content of this article.

# References


1. Amsler, M.: The Babylonian Talmud and Late Antique Book Culture. Cambridge University Press, Cambridge (2023)
2. Cheng, M., Yu, S., Lee, C., Khadpe, P., Ibrahim, L., Jurafsky, D.: Social sycophancy: a broader anderstanding of LLM sycophancy. arXiv preprint arXiv:2505.13995 (2025)
3. Clarke, C.L., Dietz, L.: Support evaluation for the TREC 2024 RAG track: comparing human versus LLM judges. arXiv preprint arXiv:2504.15205 (2025)
4. Di Palma, D., Merra, F.A., Sfilio, M., Anelli, V.W., Narducci, F., Di Noia, T.: Do llms memorize recommendation datasets? a preliminary study on movielens-1m. In: Proceedings of the 48th International ACM SIGIR Conference on Research and Development in Information Retrieval, pp. 2582–2586 (2025)
5. Dietz, L., et al.: Principles and guidelines for the use of llm judges. In: Proceedings of the 2025 International ACM SIGIR Conference on Innovative Concepts and Theories in Information Retrieval (ICTIR), pp. 218–229 (2025)
6. Es, S., James, J., Anke, L.E., Schockaert, S.: Ragas: automated evaluation of retrieval augmented generation. In: Proceedings of the 18th Conference of the European Chapter of the Association for Computational Linguistics: System Demonstrations, pp. 150–158 (2024)
7. Farzi, N., Dietz, L.: Pencils down! automatic rubric-based evaluation of retrieve/generate systems. In: Proceedings of the 2024 ACM SIGIR International Conference on Theory of Information Retrieval, pp. 175–184 (2024)
8. Fok, R., Weld, D.S.: In search of verifiability: explanations rarely enable complementary performance in ai-advised decision making. AI Mag. **45**(3), 317–332 (2024)
9. Fröbe, M., et al.: Webis at TREC 2024: biomedical generative retrieval, retrieval-augmented generation, and tip-of-the-tongue tracks. In: Voorhees, E., Ellis, A. (eds.) 33th International Text Retrieval Conference (TREC 2024), NIST Special Publication, National Institute of Standards and Technology (NIST) (2024). https://trec.nist.gov/pubs/trec33/index.html
10. Kraemer, D.C.: A History of the Talmud. Cambridge University Press, Cambridge (2019)

11. Lin, J., Demner-Fushman, D.: Will pyramids built of nuggets topple over? In: Proceedings of the Human Language Technology Conference of the NAACL, Main Conference, pp. 383–390 (2006)
12. Mayfield, J., et al.: On the evaluation of machine-generated reports. In: Proceedings of the 47th International ACM SIGIR Conference on Research and Development in Information Retrieval, pp. 1904–1915 (2024)
13. Pradeep, R., et al.: Ragnarök: a reusable RAG framework and baselines for TREC 2024 retrieval-augmented generation track. In: Hauff, C., Macdonald, C., Jannach, D., Kazai, G., Nardini, F.M., Pinelli, F., Silvestri, F., Tonellotto, N. (eds.) Advances in Information Retrieval - 47th European Conference on Information Retrieval, ECIR 2025, Lucca, Italy, April 6-10, 2025, Proceedings, Part I, Lecture Notes in Computer Science, vol. 15572, pp. 132–148, Springer, Cham (2025), https://doi.org/10.1007/978-3-031-88708-6_9
14. Pradeep, R., et al.: The great nugget recall: automating fact extraction and rag evaluation with large language models. In: Proceedings of the 48th International ACM SIGIR Conference on Research and Development in Information Retrieval, pp. 180–190 (2025)
15. Saad-Falcon, J., Khattab, O., Potts, C., Zaharia, M.: ARES: an automated evaluation framework for retrieval-augmented generation systems. In: Proceedings of the 2024 Conference of the North American Chapter of the Association for Computational Linguistics: Human Language Technologies (Volume 1: Long Papers), pp. 338–354 (2024)
16. Sander, D.P., Dietz, L.: Exam: how to evaluate retrieve-and-generate systems for users who do not (yet) know what they want. In: DESIRES, pp. 136–146 (2021)
17. Thakur, N., Pradeep, R., Upadhyay, S., Campos, D., Craswell, N., Lin, J.: Support evaluation for the TREC 2024 RAG track: comparing human versus LLM judges. CoRR **abs/2504.15205** (2025). https://doi.org/10.48550/ARXIV.2504.15205
18. Upadhyay, S., Pradeep, R., Thakur, N., Craswell, N., Lin, J.: Umbrela: umbrela is the (open-source reproduction of the) bing relevance assessor. arXiv preprint arXiv:2406.06519 (2024)
19. Walden, W., et al.: Auto-argue: Llm-based report generation evaluation. arXiv preprint arXiv:2509.26184 (2025)
20. Zheng, L.: Judging llm-as-a-judge with mt-bench and chatbot arena. Adv. Neural. Inf. Process. Syst. **36**, 46595–46623 (2023)

# Enhancing Job Search Effectiveness with LLM-Powered Context-Aware Query Reformulation

Quang Hieu Vu[✉], Behnaz Nojavanasghari, Frank Yang, and Andrew Rabinovich

Upwork, San Francisco, USA
{quanghieuvu,behnaznojavanasghari,frankyang,andrewrabinovich}@upwork.com

**Abstract.** Short and ambiguous queries are a common challenge in job search systems, often leading to poor matches and reduced user satisfaction. We present a production-ready, LLM-powered query reformulation framework that improves low-performing queries by generating richer, context-aware alternatives. To address off-topic reformulations and hallucinations often introduced by LLMs, our hybrid offline–online system incorporates domain knowledge, applies semantic filtering, and uses a weighted fusion ranking approach to improve retrieval effectiveness while maintaining low latency. Offline evaluation shows consistent 10% gains in NDCG@10. In a user study, 87.2% of reformulations were perceived to improve intent clarity, and 78.8% improved perceived search quality. Our interactive demo (https://ecir26-demo.static-upwork.com) offers an end-to-end walkthrough of the system.

**Keywords:** Demo · Query Reformulation · LLM

## 1 Introduction

Online job marketplaces rely on effective search to help users discover relevant opportunities. However, short or ambiguous queries often hinder performance, as limited input lacks the context needed to capture user intent. Query reformulation addresses this by enriching inputs with context to clarify intent and improve search results.

Past work has explored various reformulation techniques, including lexical expansion using synonyms and thesauri [1], pseudo relevance feedback (PRF) [6,8], and embedding-based methods for semantically richer reformulations [3,5]. More recently, large language models (LLMs) have enabled more nuanced and domain-aware query reformulations [3,10]. Recent techniques like multi-agent prompting and knowledge-aware expansions further improve robustness [7,10]. Industrial applications have also shown practical gains [4]. However, integrating LLMs into large-scale, real-time systems poses challenges due to computational cost, the risk of off-topic outputs, and maintaining low latency [2,3,9].


R. Campos et al. (Eds.): ECIR 2026, LNCS 16486, pp. 154–158, 2026.
https://doi.org/10.1007/978-3-032-21321-1_22

To address these limitations, we propose a hybrid offline–online production system that leverages LLM-based reformulations enriched with ontology-driven tagging and pseudo relevance feedback. Reformulations are filtered for semantic alignment and incorporated into live search using a weighted fusion strategy, improving retrieval for underperforming queries without compromising latency.

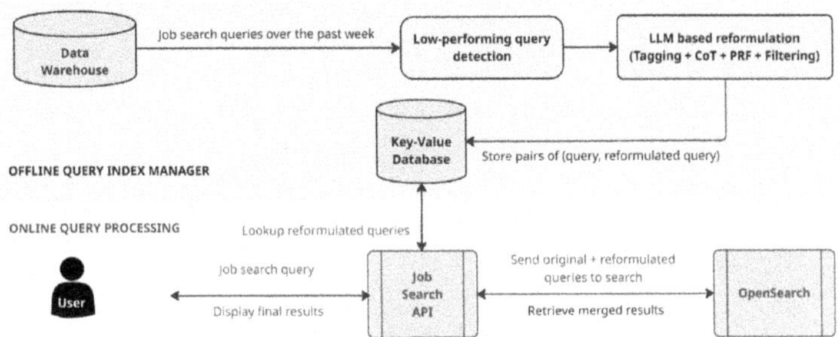


**Fig. 1.** LLM-Powered Context-Aware Query Reformulation.

## 2   System Description

In this section, we describe the two key components of our system: 1) an offline query index manager that detects and reformulates low-performing queries and 2) an online query processing pipeline that integrates seamlessly with the production search system, respecting the real-time requirements of live search. An overview of the full system architecture is shown in Fig. 1.

### 2.1   Offline Query Index Manager

We identify low-performing queries as those with click-through or bid rates below the global average, using a weekly window to ensure reliable detection.

These queries are then enriched through our proprietary tagging system, which assigns job categories and relevant skills based on historical search activity and successful hires, injecting domain-specific context critical for high-quality reformulation. To further strengthen the input, we incorporate pseudo relevance feedback (PRF) by retrieving job posts that previously led to hires for similar queries. We also apply Chain-of-Thought (COT) prompting, encouraging the LLM to reason step-by-step, leading to more grounded and semantically aligned reformulations. All of these signals are combined into a structured prompt that is passed to the LLM, enabling it to generate context-aware reformulations that better reflect user intent and align with successful job search outcomes.

The reformulations are generated offline using the OpenAI GPT-4o model, with conservative decoding settings (temperature = 0.5, top_p = 0.1) to ensure stability and control. This process runs weekly in batches of approximately 20,000 queries and completes in about five hours. The generated reformulations are then passed through a semantic similarity filter to eliminate off-topic or overly distant candidates, preserving relevance to the original query. The final reformulations are stored in a key–value store, allowing for fast retrieval during live search without introducing additional latency.

## 2.2   Online Query Processing

During live search, each incoming query is first checked against the offline query index. If reformulations are available, the original query and its reformulations are sent to the search engine. For queries without indexed reformulations, the system uses only the original query, preserving full backward compatibility.

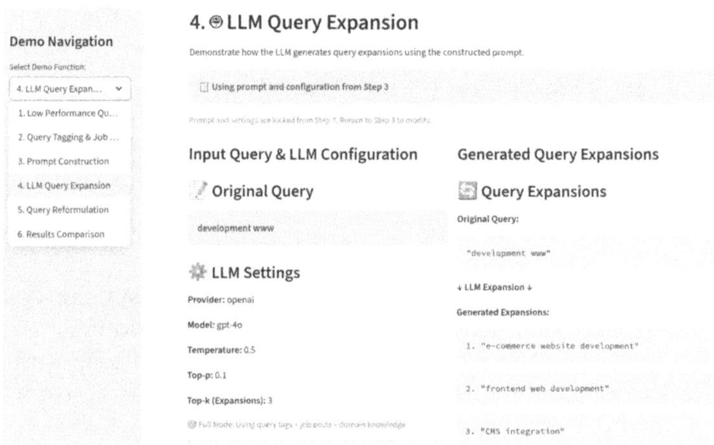


**Fig. 2.** Interactive demo interface.

Rather than appending reformulations to the original query, which can dilute intent and unnecessarily inflate query length, we first submit the original query and each of its reformulations independently to the search engine and retrieve their respective result sets. These results are then merged using a weighted Reciprocal Rank Fusion (RRF) approach. In this setup, each reformulation is assigned a weight based on its semantic similarity to the original query, while the original query is given the highest weight to preserve its central influence. This technique ensures that the most relevant results surface while maintaining alignment with the user's core intent, especially in cases where reformulations introduce semantically adjacent but not identical terms. Finally, the merged results are returned to the user, ranked to reflect both the strength of reformulations and the primacy of the original query. To illustrate the pipeline end-to-end, we developed an interactive UI that visualizes each stage of the reformulation process. Users can explore how the system identifies low-performing queries, applies tagging and pseudo-relevance feedback, and generates and filters reformulations. The interface also shows how results are merged and ranked using weighted Reciprocal Rank Fusion. A screenshot of the interactive UI is provided in Fig. 2.

**Table 1.** Query Reformulation Performance and Perceived Impact

(a) NDCG@10 Gain Breakdown

| Component | NDCG@10 Gain (%) |
|---|---|
| Basic Reformulation | +4.12 |
| Filtering | +0.78 |
| PRF & Query Tagging | +0.94 |
| RRF | +2.05 |
| Weighted RRF | +2.13 |
| **Total Improvement** | **+10.02** |

(b) Perceived Impact

| Evaluation | Intent Clarity | Retrieval Quality |
|---|---|---|
| Improved | 87.2% | 78.8% |
| Equal | 9.2% | 10.8% |
| Worse | 3.6% | 10.4% |

## 3 Evaluation

We evaluated our system on a dataset of 5,000 randomly selected low-performing queries. Table 1a shows a breakdown of the total 10% NDCG@10 gain, with individual contributions from each core component.

To evaluate user perception, we conducted a small-scale study with 5 annotators on 50 randomly selected reformulated queries. As shown in Table 1b, 87.2% of reformulations were perceived to improve intent clarity, while 78.8% were judged to enhance expected job retrieval quality.

While the results are promising, some challenges remain. Reformulations occasionally drift off-topic, particularly for ambiguous or multilingual queries. Additionally, many low-performing queries still lack sufficient tagging or historical data, which limits the effectiveness of context enrichment. Expanding tagging coverage and refining reformulation approaches for these cases are important areas for future improvement.

## 4 Conclusion

We presented a modular, production-ready framework that uses LLM-powered query reformulation to boost the performance of low-performing queries in a real-time job search system. By combining domain-specific context enrichment with efficient fusion-based ranking, the system delivers meaningful improvements in quality without compromising the low-latency requirements of live search.

Our interactive demo walks through the full pipeline, from detecting under-performing queries and enriching them with historical and semantic signals, to generating, filtering, and fusing reformulations in real time. The modular design makes the framework adaptable to other real-time applications and offers a practical path for integrating domain knowledge into LLM workflows.

**Disclosure of Interests.** The authors have no competing interests to declare that are relevant to the content of this article.

## References


1. Carpineto, C., Romano, G.: A survey of automatic query expansion in information retrieval. ACM Comput. Surv. (CSUR) **44**(1), 1–50 (2012)
2. Chen, Z., Wu, Y., Zhao, R., Liu, Z.: Llm-qe: improving query expansion by aligning large language models with ranking preferences. arXiv preprint arXiv:2502.17057 (2025)
3. Gao, L., Dai, Z., Callan, J.: Query expansion with large language models: a survey. arXiv preprint arXiv:2305.14291 (2023)
4. Gudla, V.: Supercharging discovery in search with llms (2023). https://tech.instacart.com/supercharging-discovery-in-search-with-llms-556c585d4720
5. Nogueira, R., Yang, W., Lin, J., Cho, K.: Document expansion by query prediction. In: arXiv preprint arXiv:1904.08375 (2019)
6. Robertson, S., Jones, K.: Relevance weighting of search terms. J. Am. Soc. Inf. Sci. (1976)
7. Xia, Y., et al.: Knowledge-aware query expansion with large language models for textual and relational retrieval. In: Proceedings of The ACM Web Conference 2025 (WWW 2025) (2025)
8. Xu, J., Croft, W.B.: Improving retrieval effectiveness by local analysis of documents. ACM Trans. Inf. Syst. (TOIS) **18**(1), 79–112 (2000)
9. Yang, H., Zhou, K., Zhang, X., Lin, J.: Exp4fuse: a rank fusion framework for enhanced sparse retrieval using large language model–based query expansion. In: Findings of the Association for Computational Linguistics: ACL 2025. Association for Computational Linguistics (2025). https://aclanthology.org/2025.findings-acl.9
10. Zheng, K., et al.: Maaqr: an llm-based multi-agent framework for adaptive query rewriting in alipay search. In: Proceedings of the 48th International ACM SIGIR Conference on Research and Development in Information Retrieval (2025)

# Pipeline Inspection, Visualization, and Interoperability in PyTerrier

Emmanouil Georgios Lionis(✉) [iD], Craig Macdonald [iD], and Sean MacAvaney [iD]

University of Glasgow, Glasgow, UK
`e.lionis.1@research.gla.ac.uk,`
`{Craig.Macdonald,Sean.MacAvaney}@glasgow.ac.uk`

**Abstract.** PyTerrier provides a declarative framework for building and experimenting with Information Retrieval (IR) pipelines. In this demonstration, we highlight several recent pipeline operations that improve their ability to be programmatically inspected, visualized, and integrated with other tools (via the Model Context Protocol, MCP). These capabilities aim to make it easier for researchers, students, and AI agents to understand and use a wide array of IR pipelines.

## 1 Introduction

PyTerrier [10] provides an interface between state-of-the-art retrieval components, including highly-efficient inverted indexes [8], generative re-rankers [3], and retrieval-augmented generation methods [9]. Users can combine these components into pipelines (Sect. 2) through a declarative Python syntax. For example, Fig. 1(a) shows a sophisticated pipeline that performs a variety of operations, including lexical retrieval, query reformulation, result fusion, neural re-ranking, and answer generation.

This demonstration presents three recent enhancements to PyTerrier pipelines designed to make them easier to understand and interact with. First, we introduce a core *inspection* mechanism (Sect. 3), which provides programmatic access to information about pipelines, including input/output specifications, constituent components, and other settings. Building on this foundation, we provide interactive pipeline visualizations that we call *schematics* (Sect. 4, Fig. 1(b)). Schematics are automatically rendered for pipelines in Python notebooks to help users understand the pipelines they construct. They are also integrated into the documentation to serve illustrative examples and can be rendered *ad hoc* for other purposes. Finally, we enable users to expose PyTerrier pipelines as tools via a Model Context Protocol (MCP) server [1], allowing other systems to interact with them through MCP's unified API (Sect. 5). For instance, the MCP feature enables pipelines to be easily integrated as components of agentic systems for research and deployment, or used as tools through systems such as Copilot[1] or Cursor[2].

---

[1] https://github.com/features/copilot.

[2] https://cursor.com/.


R. Campos et al. (Eds.): ECIR 2026, LNCS 16486, pp. 159–165, 2026.
https://doi.org/10.1007/978-3-032-21321-1_23

```
index = pt.Artifact.from_hf('pyterrier/msmarco-passage.terrier')
pipeline = pta.RRFusion(
    index.bm25(),
    SequentialDependence() >> index.bm25(),
) >> index.text_loader() >> MonoT5() >> T5FiD('terrierteam/t5fid_base_nq')
```

(a) Python code to declare the pipeline (imports omitted for brevity).

Input | Q | BM25 | R | SDM | Q | BM25 | R | RRF | R | TextLoader | R | MonoT5 | R | T5FiD | A | Output

(b) Generated schematic for the pipeline defined in (a).

**Fig. 1.** Example PyTerrier pipeline that performs retrieval, fusion, re-ranking, and answer generation stages. The pipeline is shown both as (a) declarative Python code and (b) the corresponding generated schematic.

## 2   Background: PyTerrier Pipelines

The core components of pipelines in PyTerrier are called transformers. A transformer provides a function that modifies the current *state* of one or more search requests. For example, a BM25 transformer accepts search queries and returns the search results from an index. The state is represented as a relation (i.e., a data table such as a Pandas DataFrame or a list of Python dictionaries). PyTerrier's data model defines a variety of typical column definitions that represent different stages of an engine's processing as shown in Table 1. These configurations can be extended with additional information as needed by transformers (e.g., a document's text or a query's vector). PyTerrier hosts components for a wide variety of IR pipeline operations, including lexical retrieval, dense retrieval, learned sparse retrieval, query reformulation, and answer generation.

**Table 1.** PyTerrier data model columns for typical stages of a search engine.

| Name | Abbr. | Columns |
| --- | --- | --- |
| Query Frame | Q | `qid` (PK, query identifier), `query` |
| Document Frame | D | `docno` (PK, document identifier), `text` |
| Result Frame | R | `qid` (PK), `docno` (PK), `score`, `rank` |
| Answer Frame | A | `qid` (PK), `qanswer` |

PyTerrier's data model enables transformers to be combined together into larger pipelines. In a typical sequential pipeline (represented as `A >> B`), the output of one transformer (`A`) can be fed as input to the next transformer (`B`). Other types of pipelines include linear score combination (e.g., `A + B`) and reciprocal rank fusion [2] (e.g., `RRFusion(A, B)`). In all cases, it is important that the pipelines are combined in a way where the input/output specifications are compatible with one another. For instance, if a pipeline is constructed that does not provide the text of a document to a neural re-ranking method that relies on it, the pipeline will raise an error when executed. This demonstration highlights new features that overcome shortcomings of these pipelines, namely the ability to programmatically inspect and validate the inputs/outputs of transformers, the ability to visualize them, and the ability to use them as tools for an LLM.

## 3   Inspecting Pipelines

PyTerrier transformers can be defined with as little as a function that maps one relation to another. This flexility makes implementing transformers simple and allows arbitrary pipelines to be constructed, but can result in incompatible pipelines. Without knowing the input and output specifications of individual transformers, it can be challenging to know whether a pipeline is compatible. Previously the only way to check these would be to check the documentation or run an example through and check the outputs (or interpret the resulting error).

To overcome this inconvenience, we introduce a new `pt.inspect` module that allows for the programmatic inspection of transformers and pipelines. The module provides functions that return which columns are required as inputs (e.g., a BM25 retriever expects `qid` and `query`, while a FAISS [4] dense retriever expects `qid` and `query_vec`) and which columns are returned for the provided inputs (e.g., BM25 returns `qid`, `query`, `docno`, `rank`, and `score`). Other functions in the module provide additional information about transformers, such as its attributes and any other transformers that it invokes (subtransformers). In most cases, `pt.inspect` identifies these automatically[3] by leveraging best practices in transformer implementation (e.g., performing input validation). To provide additional clarity on the implementation, a notebook is included in PyTerrier that demonstrates the inspection functionality.[4]

Transformer inspection has a number of applications. It enables pipeline *validation* to ensure that a pipeline is fully compatible (which is now applied automatically before experiments are conducted). Inspection also helps in visualization and interoperability, which are covered in the following two sections.

## 4   Visualizing Pipelines with Schematics

As shown in Fig. 1(a), pipeline definitions can get complex, especially when they involve multiple components and stages. Therefore, we added a new pipeline visualization feature that renders pipelines as interactive HTML snippets. We call these visitations schematics. Schematics render the pipeline as a sequence of transformers and the data between then, allowing users to better understand the transformers in a pipeline and how data flows between them. Hovering over elements provide additional information, like specific information about columns

---

[3] The details are too intricate to describe here, but are covered in the documentation.
[4] https://github.com/terrier-org/pyterrier/blob/master/examples/notebooks/inspect-demo.ipynb.

or transformer settings. Schematics leverage the inspection features covered in Sect. 3. A non-interactive screenshot of a schematic is shown in Fig. 1(b).

Although schematics can be displayed anywhere that can render HTML, we have applied them in a couple of convenient places. First, they are automatically rendered in Python notebooks when the output of a cell is a pipeline, aiding in the construction of pipelines in interactive sessions. We also render them in several places throughout PyTerrier's documentation to better demonstrate core concepts of the platform. PyTerrier contains an interactive notebook containing schematics for a range of pipelines.[5]

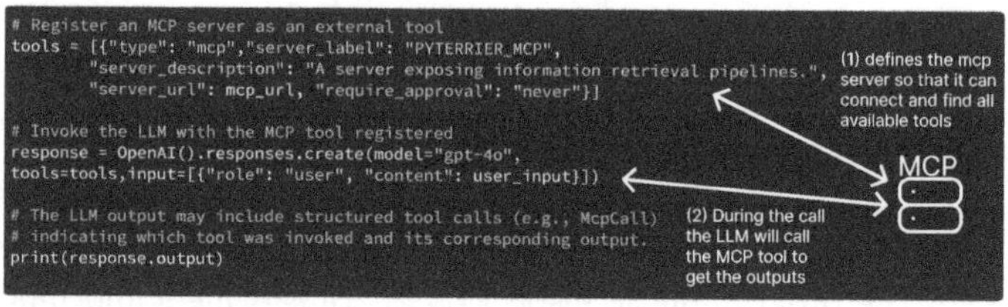

**Fig. 2.** Example usage of the MCP server through the OpenAI API.

## 5   Pipeline Interoperation with MCP

Another limitation of PyTerrier pipelines is the need for a Python runtime to execute them. Increasingly, external "tools" are invoked directly by Large Language Models (LLMs) [14]. The open-source Model Context Protocol (MCP) [1] is a popular protocol that standardizes LLM access to these tools by exposing them via HTTP endpoints. Despite MCP's original design for LLMs, its scope is much broader and has been referred to as a "universal plugin ecosystem" because it allows for simplified interoperation between virtually any Internet-connected system [15]. This quality makes MCP a natural choice to improve PyTerrier's interoperability with systems outside of Python.

To this end, we built a new package that exposes PyTerrier pipelines via MCP, thereby allowing a growing ecosystem of MCP-compatible tools to use them. The MCP server exposes HTTP endpoints for PyTerrier pipelines along with their associated metadata, such as natural-language descriptions and input/output specifications (using the new inspection functionality described in Sect. 3). The code for the MCP server is publicly available[6].

The MCP server is useful in a variety of settings. First, it can be used programmatically by researchers or practitioners as components in agentic systems.

---

[5] https://github.com/terrier-org/pyterrier/blob/master/examples/notebooks/schematics-demo.ipynb.

[6] https://github.com/terrierteam/pyterrier-server.

For instance, one can enable pipeline access for LLMs using the OpenAI[7] package, as shown in Fig. 2. Alternatively, MCP-exposed PyTerrier pipelines can be leveraged by users directly through systems like the Copilot extension in Visual Studio Code. This allows users to leverage PyTerrier pipelines in their day-to-day activities.

To demonstrate the flexibility of the MCP server across different retrieval and reasoning paradigms, we showcase its use with three representative pipelines: (i) a traditional BM25 [13] retrieval pipeline implemented using PISA [8,12]; (ii) a retrieval-augmented generation (RAG) system employing a lightweight Fusion-in-Decoder model for direct question answering [6,7,9]; and (iii) a Doc2Query-based model designed to support question decomposition [5,11]. Given these pipelines, we provide a demo video[8] illustrating the programmatic implementation via a web-based interface, as well as a demonstration of day-to-day usage through Copilot (Fig. 3).

**Fig. 3.** A PyTerrier MCP server interaction example through Copilot.

---

[7] https://platform.openai.com/docs/overview.
[8] https://github.com/terrierteam/pyterrier-server/blob/main/videos/demo.gif.

## 6  Conclusions

This demonstration covers new features in PyTerrier that improve the inspection, visualization, and interoperability of pipelines. ECIR attendees will be able to interact with each of these features through notebooks and a web interface in the demonstration.

**Disclosure of Interests.** The authors have no competing interests to declare that are relevant to the content of this article.

## References


1. Anthropic: Introducing the model context protocol (2024). https://www.anthropic. com/news/model-context-protocol
2. Cormack, G.V., Clarke, C.L.A., Büttcher, S.: Reciprocal rank fusion outperforms condorcet and individual rank learning methods. In: Allan, J., Aslam, J.A., Sanderson, M., Zhai, C., Zobel, J. (eds.) Proceedings of the 32nd Annual International ACM SIGIR Conference on Research and Development in Information Retrieval, pp. 758–759. SIGIR 2009, Boston, MA, USA, July 19–23, 2009. ACM (2009). https://doi.org/10.1145/1571941.1572114
3. Dhole, K.D.: PyTerrier-genrank: the PyTerrier plugin for reranking with large language models. CoRR abs/2412.05339 (2024). https://doi.org/10.48550/ARXIV. 2412.05339
4. Douze, M., et al.: The faiss library. CoRR abs/2401.08281 (2024). https://doi.org/ 10.48550/ARXIV.2401.08281
5. Gospodinov, M., MacAvaney, S., Macdonald, C.: Doc2query-: When less is more. In: Kamps, J., et al. (eds.) Advances in Information Retrieval - 45th European Conference on Information Retrieval, ECIR 2023, vol. 13981, pp. 414–422. Dublin, Ireland, April 2–6, 2023, Proceedings, Part II. Lecture Notes in Computer Science, Springer, Cham (2023). https://doi.org/10.1007/978-3-031-28238-6_31
6. Izacard, G., Grave, E.: Leveraging passage retrieval with generative models for open domain question answering. In: Merlo, P., Tiedemann, J., Tsarfaty, R. (eds.) Proceedings of the 16th Conference of the European Chapter of the Association for Computational Linguistics: Main Volume, pp. 874–880.. EACL 2021, Online, April 19–23, 2021. Association for Computational Linguistics (2021). https://doi. org/10.18653/V1/2021.EACL-MAIN.74
7. Lewis, P., et al.: Retrieval-augmented generation for knowledge-intensive NLP tasks. In: Larochelle, H., Ranzato, M., Hadsell, R., Balcan, M., Lin, H. (eds.) Advances in Neural Information Processing Systems 33: Annual Conference on Neural Information Processing Systems 2020, NeurIPS 2020, December 6–12, 2020, virtual (2020). https://proceedings.neurips.cc/paper/2020/hash/ 6b493230205f780e1bc26945df7481e5-Abstract.html
8. MacAvaney, S., Macdonald, C.: A python interface to pisa! In: Amigó, E., Castells, P., Gonzalo, J., Carterette, B., Culpepper, J.S., Kazai, G. (eds.) SIGIR '22: The 45th International ACM SIGIR Conference on Research and Development in Information Retrieval, pp. 3339–3344. Madrid, Spain, July 11–15, 2022. ACM (2022). https://doi.org/10.1145/3477495.3531656

9. Macdonald, C., Fang, J., Parry, A., Meng, Z.: Constructing and evaluating declarative RAG pipelines in PyTerrier. In: Ferro, N., Maistro, M., Pasi, G., Alonso, O., Trotman, A., Verberne, S. (eds.) Proceedings of the 48th International ACM SIGIR Conference on Research and Development in Information Retrieval, pp. 4035–4040. SIGIR 2025, Padua, Italy, July 13–18, 2025. ACM (2025). https://doi.org/10.1145/3726302.3730150

10. Macdonald, C., Tonellotto, N.: Declarative experimentation in information retrieval using PyTerrier. In: Balog, K., Setty, V., Lioma, C., Liu, Y., Zhang, M., Berberich, K. (eds.) ICTIR '20: The 2020 ACM SIGIR International Conference on the Theory of Information Retrieval, pp. 161–168. Virtual Event, Norway, September 14-17, 2020. ACM (2020). https://doi.org/10.1145/3409256.3409829

11. Macdonald, C., Tonellotto, N.: Declarative experimentation in information retrieval using PyTerrier. In: Proceedings of the 2020 ACM SIGIR on International Conference on Theory of Information Retrieval. pp. 161–168 (2020)

12. Mallia, A., Siedlaczek, M., Mackenzie, J.M., Suel, T.: PISA: performant indexes and search for academia. In: Clancy, R., Ferro, N., Hauff, C., Lin, J., Sakai, T., Wu, Z.Z. (eds.) Proceedings of the Open-Source IR Replicability Challenge co-located with 42nd International ACM SIGIR Conference on Research and Development in Information Retrieval, OSIRRC@SIGIR 2019, Paris, France, July 25, 2019. CEUR Workshop Proceedings, vol. 2409, pp. 50–56. CEUR-WS.org (2019). https://ceur-ws.org/Vol-2409/docker08.pdf

13. Robertson, S.E., Zaragoza, H.: The probabilistic relevance framework: BM25 and beyond. Found. Trends Inf. Retr. **3**(4), 333–389 (2009). https://doi.org/10.1561/1500000019

14. Schick, T., et al.: Toolformer: Language models can teach themselves to use tools. In: Oh, A., Naumann, T., Globerson, A., Saenko, K., Hardt, M., Levine, S. (eds.) Advances in Neural Information Processing Systems 36: Annual Conference on Neural Information Processing Systems 2023, NeurIPS 2023, New Orleans, LA, USA, December 10–16, 2023 (2023). http://papers.nips.cc/paper_files/paper/2023/hash/d842425e4bf79ba039352da0f658a906-Abstract-Conference.html

15. Werner, S.: MCP: an (accidentally) universal plugin system (2025). https://worksonmymachine.ai/p/mcp-an-accidentally-universal-plugin

# ImageSeek: A Hybrid Text-to-Image Image Retrieval System for Domain-Specific Collections


Rodrigo Duarte[1,2]([✉]) [iD], Rodrigo Silva[1,2] [iD], António Branco[4,5] [iD], Hugo Proença[1,6] [iD], and Ricardo Campos[1,2,3] [iD]

[1] University of Beira Interior, Covilhã, Portugal
{rodrigo.duarte,rd.silva,hugomcp,ricardo.campos}@ubi.pt
[2] INESC TEC, Porto, Portugal
[3] Ci2 - Smart Cities Research Center, Polytechnic Institute of Tomar, Tomar, Portugal
[4] University of Lisbon, Lisbon, Portugal
antonio.branco@di.fc.ul.pt
[5] NLX-Group, Lisbon, Portugal
[6] IT: Instituto de Telecomunicações, Covilhã, Portugal



**Abstract.** Large image collections are typically organized around basic metadata and keyword tags, making content discovery challenging for users seeking specific visual information. Although images may be accompanied by descriptive text, traditional retrieval systems often struggle to bridge the semantic gap between textual descriptions and visual content. In this demo, we present ImageSeek, a hybrid text-to-image retrieval system designed to enhance search effectiveness by combining text and image-based retrieval methods through an asymmetric score adjustment mechanism. The system leverages multilingual CLIP models to encode both visual and textual information, creating unified representations for cross-modal retrieval. Users can search through natural language queries in any supported language, with results ranked using a hybrid approach that treats image-based retrieval as a reliable baseline while harmonizing text-based scores through position-dependent adjustments. The demonstration system operates on a dataset of 42,333 images from the Portuguese Presidency website, providing an appropriate testbed for multimodal retrieval performance. The web application enables direct comparison between conventional CLIP-based retrieval and our hybrid approach, supporting image searches under the same conditions on external platforms, including Google Images and the Arquivo.pt image search system, enabling comparative analysis of the results. To evaluate its effectiveness, ImageSeek allows users to experience differences between retrieval modes while exploring domain-specific visual content.

**Keywords:** Image Information Retrieval · Image Search · CLIP

# 1   Introduction

The rapid growth of visual content across digital platforms has created significant challenges in effectively retrieving relevant images from large collections [1]. Cross-modal information retrieval (IR) systems have emerged to address these challenges [2], with text-to-image IR systems gaining significant attention through vision-language models like CLIP [3]. Recent advances have explored entity-aware approaches that inject semantic information into multimodal representations [4], demonstrating the potential for domain adaptation of foundation models. However, most existing systems focus on English-language queries and general-purpose image collections, leaving a gap for specialized domains and multilingual contexts. This limitation is particularly problematic for non-English languages, where translation-based strategies often fail to preserve nuanced meanings and cultural context [5]. In this paper, we present a demonstration of a hybrid text-to-image retrieval system that integrates text and image-based retrieval methods. While our demonstration uses Portuguese presidential archives as a testbed, the system is designed to be domain-agnostic and can be applied to any multimodal collection.

The key innovation of our system lies in its asymmetric score adjustment mechanism. Unlike traditional rank fusion approaches [6] our method treats image-based retrieval as a reliable baseline while harmonizing text-based scores through position-dependent adjustments, enhancing contextual relevance through textual information. Our demonstration operates on a comprehensive dataset [7][1] of 42,333 images collected from the Portuguese Presidency website[2]. The dataset includes 80 Portuguese textual queries, each associated with relevance judgments for an average of 65 images. Annotation was conducted by three master's students in computer science, who independently assigned binary relevance labels (relevant/non-relevant) to each query-image pair. Inter-annotator agreement was measured using Fleiss' Kappa (K=0.62), indicating moderate agreement. Conflicting annotations were resolved through majority voting. In total, 5,201 images were manually annotated for relevance, providing a robust testbed for evaluating text-to-image retrieval performance in domain-specific scenarios. The web application enables users to experience the differences between conventional CLIP-based retrieval and our hybrid approach, alongside with searches on Google Images and Arquivo.pt [8]. ImageSeek is publicly available online[3] with the full source code on GitHub[4], supporting reproducibility and enabling further research development. A demonstration video of the platform is available on the demo website.

---

[1] https://github.com/LIAAD/pt-image-ir-dataset.
[2] https://www.presidencia.pt/.
[3] https://imageseek.inesctec.pt/.
[4] https://github.com/LIAAD/imageseek-demo.

## 2   Architecture

Our system is implemented using Flask, with Redis Stack serving as a key-value store and vector database for efficient storage and retrieval of image embeddings, article embeddings, and metadata. For textual representation, the system indexes images using article titles as metadata. While more comprehensive textual representations could provide richer semantic information, article titles offer several practical advantages: they are consistently available across the collection, provide high-level topical context, and enable efficient indexing and retrieval. Pre-computed embeddings for all 42,333 images and their corresponding article titles are generated using multilingual CLIP models [5]. Specifically, the system uses the OpenCLIP xlm-roberta-base-ViT-B-32 model trained on LAION-5B [9] to generate both text and image embeddings, ensuring consistent cross-modal representations within the same vector space. This model supports cross-lingual retrieval for Portuguese queries while preserving semantic alignment for the hybrid scoring mechanism. While our demonstration focuses on Portuguese presidential archives, the system's architecture is inherently language-agnostic and domain-independent. The asymmetric score adjustment mechanism operates on normalized similarity scores and relative positions, making no language-specific or domain-specific assumptions. The underlying multilingual CLIP model supports over 100 languages through its XLM-RoBERTa text encoder, enabling zero-shot transfer to other languages without modification. The three-phase algorithm depends only on textual metadata associated with images, a vision-language model producing comparable embeddings, and score distributions that can benefit from harmonization—conditions satisfied in most multimodal collections. The core innovation is a three-phase hybrid retrieval algorithm (see Fig. 1) that addresses the key challenge of multimodal score harmonization.

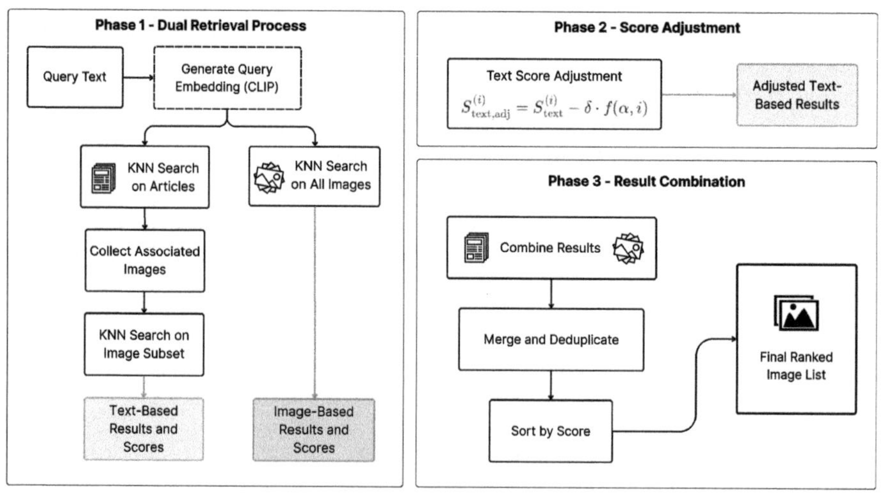


$$S^{(i)}_{\text{text,adj}} = S^{(i)}_{\text{text}} - \delta \cdot f(\alpha, i)$$

**Fig. 1.** Three-phase hybrid retrieval algorithm of ImageSeek.

**Phase 1** begins by generating a text embedding for the input query using the selected multilingual CLIP model. Dual retrieval is then performed in parallel using K-Nearest Neighbors (KNN) searches. The text-based approach first retrieves semantically similar articles by comparing the query embedding against article title embeddings, and then searches for images within them. Simultaneously, the image-based approach performs KNN directly against all precomputed image embeddings. Both produce ranked lists with cosine distance scores on different search spaces, yielding distinct score distributions. **Phase 2** applies asymmetric score adjustment to harmonize the modality-specific scores, treating image-based scores as a reliable baseline, and adjusting only text-based scores using position-dependent functions: $S_{text,adj}^{(i)} = S_{text}^{(i)} - \delta \cdot f(\alpha, i)$ where $\delta = S_{text}^{(1)} - S_{image}^{(1)}$ represents the systematic offset between modalities, addressing the fundamental challenge that text-based and image-based retrieval produce scores on different scales and distributions. The $\delta$ term captures the systematic offset between top-ranked items from each modality, while $f(\alpha, i)$ applies position-dependent adjustment that gradually diminishes the influence of textual signals at lower ranks, reflecting the hypothesis that textual context is most valuable for refining top-ranked visual matches, enabling effective multimodal score fusion. Four adjustment function variants are implemented: linear with zero indexing ($f(\alpha, i) = 1 - -\alpha \cdot i$), linear with one indexing ($f(\alpha, i) = 1 - \alpha \cdot (i-1)$), square root adjustment ($f(\alpha, i) = 1 - \alpha^{\sqrt{i-1}}$), and exponential adjustment ($f(\alpha, i) = 1 - \alpha^{e^{i-1}}$), allowing users to explore different score harmonization strategies. To compare these variants, we evaluated their performance across adjustment factor values ranging from $\alpha = 0.0$ (no adjustment) to $\alpha = 1.0$ (maximum adjustment). Linear zero-indexed consistently achieved the best results, with MRR = 0.621 at $\alpha = 0.1$ and F1@10 = 0.294 at $\alpha = 0.2$. This function demonstrated stable performance across the $\alpha = 0.1$–0.3 range, with minimal variation (MRR variance < 0.005). In contrast, non-linear functions showed higher sensitivity to parameter changes, with square root performance declining from MRR = 0.619 to 0.610 as $\alpha$ increased from 0.0 to 1.0, and exponential adjustment exhibiting similar degradation patterns. Linear one-indexed produced comparable but slightly lower results (MRR = 0.617, F1@10 = 0.293 at $\alpha = 0.1$). The superior stability of linear zero-indexed, combined with its computational simplicity and interpretability, motivated its selection as the default configuration. **Phase 3** combines the adjusted text-based results with unchanged image-based results, removes duplicates by keeping the better score per image, and produces a final unified ranking sorted by distance scores.

## 3  Demonstration

The web interface provides an intuitive platform for exploring our hybrid retrieval approach on the previously described dataset. To demonstrate the system's effectiveness, we showcase a comparative analysis of our system and Google image results using the query "Presidente a ler um livro" (President reading a book). Figure 2 shows the search interface with mode selection options. For this demonstration, the hybrid Linear Decay (Zero-indexed) mode serves as the default configuration, as preliminary evaluations indicate it yields the most effective results. Users can toggle between conventional CLIP-based retrieval, our hybrid approach, and external service comparisons, such as Google Images and Arquivo.pt (the Portuguese web archive). External comparisons are restricted to results from the Portuguese Presidency website domain and matched to the same temporal range to ensure fair comparison within a consistent content scope.

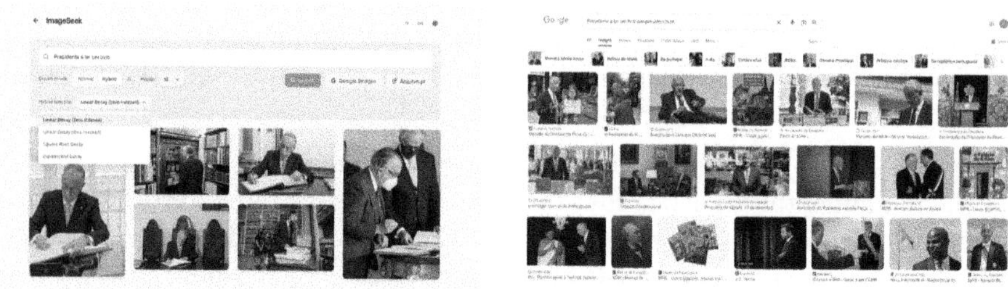

**Fig. 2.** Search interface showing hybrid mode results (left) and Google Images comparison for the same query (right).

The comparison reveals the system's effectiveness in retrieving contextually relevant images from the Portuguese Presidency domain. While Google Images returns broader, often less context-aware results, our hybrid approach leverages domain-specific knowledge and asymmetric score adjustment to produce more precise and semantically aligned matches. This demonstrates how domain-adapted hybrid retrieval can outperform general-purpose systems in specialized collections. Furthermore, the system offers researchers an interactive platform to experiment with different score adjustment strategies and explore trade-offs between text and image-based retrieval modalities in real-time, fostering further research in domain-specific text-to-image retrieval systems.

In addition to these comparative insights, we also present a quantitative evaluation. Table 1 reports evaluation results on the *pt-image-ir-dataset*, demonstrating that our hybrid approach consistently outperforms baseline methods across all metrics.

**Table 1.** Performance comparison of our hybrid approach and baseline methods on the pt-image-ir-dataset. Best results in each column are highlighted in bold.

| Method | MAP | P@5 | R@5 | P@10 | R@10 | F1@10 | MRR | RP |
|---|---|---|---|---|---|---|---|---|
| Google Images | 0.076 | 0.202 | 0.076 | 0.190 | 0.125 | 0.128 | 0.336 | 0.113 |
| Arquivo.pt | 0.038 | 0.145 | 0.045 | 0.134 | 0.080 | 0.091 | 0.217 | 0.072 |
| OpenCLIP xlm-roberta-base | 0.176 | 0.418 | 0.121 | 0.419 | 0.264 | 0.288 | 0.610 | 0.218 |
| Hybrid Approach | **0.179** | **0.420** | 0.125 | **0.423** | **0.268** | **0.293** | **0.621** | 0.221 |
| RRF Method | 0.171 | 0.413 | **0.127** | 0.414 | 0.261 | 0.289 | 0.597 | **0.222** |

**Acknowledgments.** The authors Rodrigo Duarte, Rodrigo Silva and António Branco would like to acknowledge ACCELERAT.AI - Multilingual Intelligent Contact Centers, funded by the covid-recovery program PRR-Plano de Recuperação e Resiliência, through IAPMEI (C625734525-00462629); PORTULAN CLARIN - Research Infrastructure for the Science and Technology of Language, funded by LISBOA2030 (FEDER-01316900); hey, Hal, curb your hallucination!, funded by FCT-Fundação para a Ciência e Tecnologia (2024.07592.IACDC). The author Hugo Proença would like to acknowledge FCT – Fundação para a Ciência e a Tecnologia, I.P., and, when eligible, co-funded by EU funds under project/support UID/50008/2025 – Instituto de Telecomunicações, with DOI identifier <https://doi.org/10.54499/UID/50008/2025> Ricardo Campos is funded by national funds through FCT – Fundação para a Ciência e a Tecnologia, I.P., under the support UID/50014/2025 (https://doi.org/10.54499/UID/50014/2025). The author would also like to acknowledge project StorySense, with reference 2022.09312.PTDC (DOI 10.54499/2022.09312.PTDC).

**Disclosure of Interests.** The authors have no competing interests to declare that are relevant to the content of this article.

# References


1. Mourão, A., Gomes, D.: Searching images in a web archive. In: 2023 IEEE 10th International Conference on Data Science and Advanced Analytics (DSAA), pp. 1–10. IEEE (2023)
2. Gong, Y., Cosma, G., Finke, A.: VITR: augmenting vision transformers with relation-focused learning for cross-modal information retrieval. ACM Trans. Knowl. Discov. Data **18**(9), 1–21 (2024)
3. Radford, A., et al.: Learning transferable visual models from natural language supervision. In: International conference on machine learning, pp. 8748–8763. PMLR (2021)
4. Adjali, O., Ferret, O., Ghannay, S., Le Borgne, H.: Entity-aware cross-modal pre-training for knowledge-based visual question answering. In: Hauff, C., et al. (eds.) Advances in Information Retrieval, pp. 391–400. Springer Nature Switzerland, Cham (2025)
5. Carlsson, F., Eisen, P., Rekathati, F., Sahlgren, M.: Cross-lingual and multilingual clip. In: Proceedings of the thirteenth language resources and evaluation conference, pp. 6848–6854 (2022)
6. Cormack, G.V., Clarke, C.L.A., Buettcher, S.: Reciprocal rank fusion outperforms condorcet and individual rank learning methods. In: Proceedings of the 32nd International ACM SIGIR Conference on Research and Development in Information Retrieval, pp. 758–759 (2009)
7. Duarte, R., Branco, A., Proença, H., Campos, R.: pt-image-ir-dataset: An Image Retrieval Dataset in European Portuguese. In: Anand, A., et al. (eds.) Lecture Notes in Computer Science - Advances in Information Retrieval - ECIR'26 - 48th European Conference on Information Retrieval. Springer, Delft, Netherlands (2026)
8. Gomes, D., Cruz, D., Miranda, J., Costa, M., Fontes, S.: Search the past with the portuguese web archive. In: Proceedings of the 22nd International Conference on World Wide Web, pp. 321–324. ACM, New York, NY, USA (2013)
9. Ilharco, G., et al.: OpenCLIP. Zenodo (2021). https://doi.org/10.5281/zenodo.5143773

# LectureChat: Hybrid RAG over Wikipedia and Multilingual Lecture Videos


Markos Dimitsas[1,2] and Jochen L. Leidner[1,2]($\boxtimes$)

[1] Center for Responsible Artificial Intelligence (CRAI), Coburg, Germany
[2] Coburg University of Applied Sciences, Friedrich-Streib-Str. 2, 96450 Coburg, Germany

`leidner@acm.org`



**Abstract.** LectureChat provides a conversational AI system by integrating multilingual university lecture transcripts alongside Wikipedia content into a typical LLM chat experience. We frame this as a proof-of-concept for video grounded QA. Our demo showcases a dual retrieval architecture that combines structured encyclopedic knowledge with academic lecture material, leveraging multiple segmentation strategies and cross-index reconciliation to improve retrieval quality. The system maintains separate citation spaces for Wikipedia (numeric) and lectures (alphabetic) and preserves temporal provenance for direct video navigation. We present the overall architecture, interaction flow, implementation details, and a reproducibility plan.

**Keywords:** Retrieval Augmented Generation · Multilingual and Multimodal Information Retrieval · Digital Libraries · Educational Question Answering · Natural Language Interaction


## 1 Introduction

Large language models (LLMs) equipped with retrieval components have improved faithfulness and verifiability in open domain question answering [11,13], yet educational scenarios require sources beyond curated encyclopedias. LectureChat[1] augments WikiChat [17,20] with a lecture pipeline operating over timestamped transcripts (EN/DE). We contribute: (i) A dual source chatbot that presents Wikipedia grounded and lecture grounded answers side-by-side so users can decide which knowledge pool to rely on, (ii) video grounded lecture citations that preserve temporal provenance for direct navigation, and (iii) temporal cross-index reconciliation across multiple lecture segmentation strategies via temporal IoU with LLM-based filtering, to reduce duplication and improve robustness.

---


This work was carried out while the first author was employed at CRAI.

[1] This work was carried out as part of project VoLL-KI, which aimed to improve the teaching of AI using AI methods [12].

Unlike text-only QA, LectureChat couples each lecture grounded claim with a timestamped citation that opens the corresponding transcript span and plays the exact lecture segment, making verification and navigation part of the interaction.

## 2   Related Work

Retrieval augmented generation (RAG) [13] and dense retrieval [11] are widely used to ground LLM outputs in external evidence. Multi-source systems extend this idea to heterogeneous corpora [1], but mixing sources can blur provenance for users. In educational settings, distinguishing general background knowledge from course specific material is particularly important for trust and navigation. **The novelty of our prototype over past approaches (e.g., [10,14,19]) is the ability to deal with multiple languages (here: DE versus EN) and two separate knowledge sources (video transcripts versus Wikipedia).** A core design choice in passage retrieval is segmentation, where chunk size and boundary placement can materially affect recall and redundancy [9]. Rather than committing to a single policy, LectureChat maintains multiple lecture indices built from different segmentation strategies and reconciles overlapping evidence in time. See [4] for more details about the topic segmentation of the video lecture recordings. WikiChat [17,20] provides a multilingual, citation centric baseline over Wikipedia. We extend it with timestamp preserving lecture retrieval and temporal reconciliation, while keeping Wikipedia and lecture evidence separate in the interface.

## 3   System and Architecture

### 3.1   Dual-Pipeline Design

Wikipedia and lecture retrieval [5] run in parallel and merge at presentation time. This design provides separation of concerns, allowing each pipeline to be optimized for its content type, citation clarity with numeric citations ([1], [2], ...) for Wikipedia and alphabetic citations ([a], [b], ...) for lectures, and low enough latency via concurrent execution and batched LLM calls.

### 3.2   Lecture Retrieval

**Multi-index.** We build three FAISS [6] indices from (i) LLM one-shot segmentation, (ii) lexical cohesionâĂŞaware topic segmentation (TextTiling [7,8]), and (iii) temporal segmentation aligned to voice activity detection (VAD) pauses. VAD detects speech/non-speech, and we cut at long inter speech pauses. Full details of the segmentation pipelines and the dataset are provided in [5] (Fig. 1). **Cross-Index Reconciliation.** Given a claim $c$, we retrieve top-$k$ candidates per index, pool them, and deduplicate by temporal Intersection-over-Union (IoU). For timespans $A = [a_{start}, a_{end}]$ and $B = [b_{start}, b_{end}]$,

$$\text{IoU}(A, B) = \frac{\text{intersection}}{\text{union}} = \frac{\max(0, \min(a_{end}, b_{end}) - \max(a_{start}, b_{start}))}{\max(a_{end}, b_{end}) - \min(a_{start}, b_{start})}$$

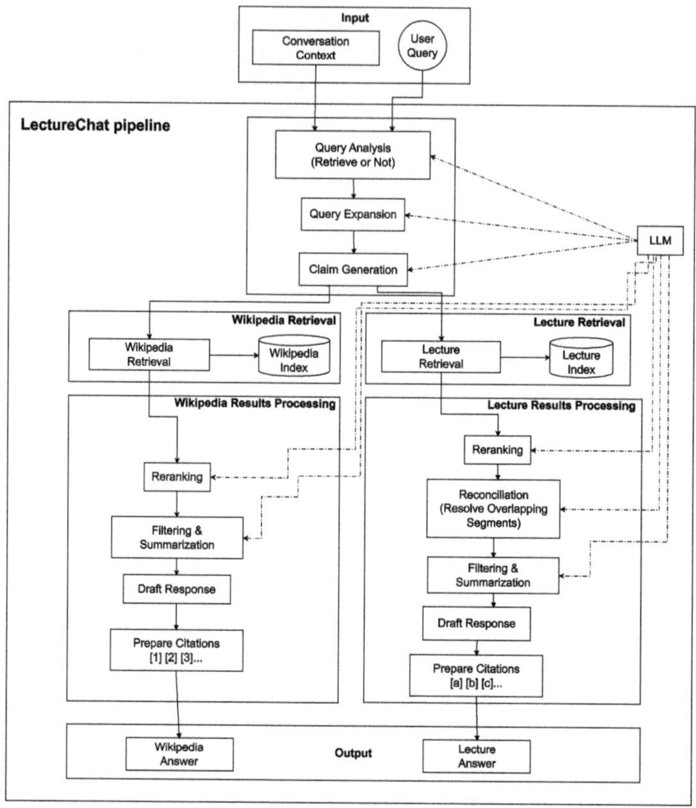


**Fig. 1.** LectureChat architecture. Wikipedia and lecture pipelines run in parallel and remain separated at presentation time. Lecture retrieval queries multiple segmentation indices and reconciles overlapping hits via temporal IoU grouping. The UI renders dual answers with separate citation spaces and clickable lecture timestamps.

Segments from the same video with IoU $> \tau$ (default $\tau = 0.5$) are grouped. Within each IoU group, we select a single representative using reranker score and an LLM relevance check, while preserving all timestamps for optional inspection in the UI.

### 3.3   Design Rationale

**Segmentation Agnostic.** The system does not assume a particular chunking policy. Any lecture segmentation that yields (text, start/end) can be indexed. The multi index setup demonstrates robustness when the "right" granularity is unclear, multiple indices are queried and a reconciliation layer selects representatives per claim. Users contribute their own segmenter during index creation without changing the online system.

**Why multi index?** Runtime reconciliation defers the chunking choice to inference time, trading modest compute for improved recall and stability across topics and speaking styles. Single index deployments remain supported. Benefits grow with heterogeneous content.

## 3.4   LLM Orchestrated Pipeline

**Stage 1:** Query understanding (decide if a query is needed) and LLM generates claims. **Stage 2:** Parallel retrieval (Wikipedia + three lecture indices) over the claims. **Stage 3:** Pointwise LLM reranking (Yes/No) and summarization/filtering. **Stage 4:** Cross-index deduplication in overlapping lecture segments. **Stage 5:** Drafting two answers: Wikipedia grounded (numeric citations) and lecture grounded (alphabetic citations with timestamps).

## 3.5   Presentation

We render two answers side-by-side with collapsible evidence, source type badges (Wikipedia/Lecture), and deep links to original transcript text and a link to the timestamped lecture clip. This separation avoids provenance blur and supports educational use. Students can treat lecture-based answers as grounded in instructor-provided material, while Wikipedia provides broader background context.

# 4   Demonstration

**User Flow.** Users enter a question and receive two independently grounded answers: a Wikipedia grounded response with numeric citations and a lecture grounded response with alphabetic citations. Expanding a citation reveals the supporting passage. Lecture citations additionally include a deep link to the corresponding video timestamp, enabling immediate verification. Optionally, the interface can reveal which lecture index produced each citation to illustrate the effect of segmentation choices.

**Embeddings & Indices.** We created three `FAISS` [6] indices and populated them with multilingual embeddings created with `SentenceTransformers` and `snowflake-arctic-embed-l-v2.0` [16,18]. The metadata contain course, year, language, video ID, start/end timestamps, ASR confidence.

**Reranking.** A lightweight cross encoder reranker scores candidates post retrieval. LLM filtering and summarization is applied subsequently for safety and precision.

**LLM Backends (Demo Config).** For the demo/video we use `gpt-4o` and `gpt-4o-mini` via the API. The orchestration layer is backend agnostic. The system is compatible with various LLMs. It can be used with many locally hosted models.

**Latency.** Concurrency across pipelines and batching across claims keep demo interactive. The per claim candidates are capped.

**Citation Rendering.** Separate registries avoid cross pollination of IDs. Lecture citations preserve transcript timestamps and lecture metadata for verification.

## 5    Limitations and Ethics

Coverage depends on available lectures, expansion to more institutions/languages is future work. LLM filtering may drift, thus a lightweight supervision and distillation are planned. We use appropriate licenses/agreements and respect GDPR for any personal data in recordings. Clear provenance helps users verify claims. As a proof-of-concept, several stages currently rely on LLM API calls (claiming, filtering, summarization).

## 6    Reproducibility and Artifact

A public GitHub repository[2] hosts the full codebase of LectureChat and configurations. Users must supply pre-segmented transcripts and build indices locally with the provided scripts. The file README.md covers setup and quick start, required configurations, input schema for segments, index build steps, running the API/web client and licensing. A demo video is also available online [3].

## 7    Summary, Conclusion and Future Work

We described LectureChat, our prototype for interactivng with recorded lecture videos by means of dual RAG retrieval of responses from Wikipedia and a transcript index. LectureChat delivers verifiable, hybrid answers by combining Wikipedia with timestamped lecture evidence. Runtime selection across three lecture chunking strategies and temporal reconciliation provide precise, clickable citations suited to educational IR demos. In future work, the effectiveness of the prototype and its components should be quantified, e.g. by following the evaluation protocol of [15]; however, this is not trivial, as there is no gold data for both kinds of answer sources available. An improved version should integrate personalization (i.e., take into account a learner model, cf. [2]). Substantial engineering work is also need to make the system fast enough to deploy it to real students.

**Acknowledgments.** We are grateful to all lecture donors. The authors gratefully acknowledge the joint funding from German Federal Ministry for Research, Technology and Space Travel (BMFTR) and the Bavarian State Ministry for Science and the Arts project grant "VoLL-KI: Von Lernenden Lernen" (learning from learners, [12], Friedrich Alexander University (FAU) Erlangen, Coburg University of Applied Sciences and Otto-Friedrich-University Bamberg, grant agreements 16DHBKI089, 16DHBKI090 and 16DHBKI091, respectively) and to the funding to the second author by the Free State of Bavaria under the Hightech Agenda.

**Disclosure of Interests.** The authors declare no competing interests.

---

[2]  https://github.com/markdimi/LectureChat (cited 2026-01-14).

# References


1. Borgeaud, S., et al.: Improving Language Models by Retrieving from Trillions of Tokens. In: Chaudhuri, K., Jegelka, S., Song, L., Szepesvári, C., Niu, G., Sabato, S. (eds.) International Conference on Machine Learning, ICML 2022, 17–23 July 2022, Baltimore, Maryland, USA. Proceedings of Machine Learning Research, vol. 162, pp. 2206–2240. PMLR (2022). https://proceedings.mlr.press/v162/borgeaud22a.html
2. Böck, F., Ochs, M., Henrich, A., Landes, D., Leidner, J.L., Sedelmaier, Y.: Learner models: design, components, structure, and modelling - a systematic literature review. User Model. User-Adap. Inter. **35**, 15 (2025). https://doi.org/10.1007/s11257-025-09434-4
3. Dimitsas, M.: LectureChat – Demo presentation (2025). YouTube (online), aVailable at https://youtu.be/mDfEu42rpUc (cited 2026-01-14)
4. Dimitsas, M., Leidner, J.L.: Topic Segmentation of Educational Video Lectures Using Audio and Text. In: Nowaczyk, S., et al. (eds.) AI4S, HYDRA, AI4AI, Kraków, Poland, September 30 - October 4, 2023, Proceedings, Part II. Communications in Computer and Information Science, vol. 1948, pp. 447–458. Springer, Cham (2023). https://doi.org/10.1007/978-3-031-50485-3_43
5. Dimitsas, M., Leidner, J.L.: A Multi-modal Dataset of Artificial Intelligence Video Lectures and Segmented Transcriptions. In: N.N. N.N. (2026, under review)
6. Douze, Met al.: The Faiss library. CoRR abs/2401.08281 (2024). https://doi.org/10.48550/ARXIV.2401.08281
7. Hearst, M.A.: Multi-paragraph Segmentation Expository Text. In: 32nd Annual Meeting of the Association for Computational Linguistics, pp. 9–16. ACL, Las Cruces, New Mexico, USA (1994). https://doi.org/10.3115/981732.981734
8. Hearst, M.A.: TextTiling: segmenting text into multi-paragraph subtopic passages. Comput. Linguist. **23**(1), 33–64 (1997)
9. Hearst, M.A., Plaunt, C.: Subtopic Structuring for Full-length Document Access. In: Korfhage, R.R., Rasmussen, E.M., Willett, P. (eds.) Proceedings of the 16th Annual International ACM-SIGIR Conference on Research and Development in Information Retrieval. Pittsburgh, PA, USA, June 27–July 1, 1993, pp. 59–68. ACM (1993). https://doi.org/10.1145/160688.160695
10. Hobert, S.: Chat with your lecture recording: creating easy-to-use chatbots for learning videos. In: Schmid, U., Leidner, J.L., Kohlhase, M., Wolter, D. (eds.) Second Workshop on Artificial Intelligence for Artificial Intelligence Education (AI4AILearning 2024), pp. 2–22. University of Bamberg Press, Würzburg (2025). https://doi.org/10.20378/irb-108884
11. Karpukhin, V., et al.: Dense Passage Retrieval for Open-domain Question Answering. In: Webber, B., Cohn, T., He, Y., Liu, Y. (eds.) Proceedings of the 2020 Conference on Empirical Methods in Natural Language Processing, EMNLP 2020, Online, November 16-20, 2020. pp. 6769–6781. Association for Computational Linguistics (2020) https://doi.org/10.18653/V1/2020.EMNLP-MAIN.550
12. Kohlhase, M., Berges, M., Grubert, J., Henrich, A., Landes, D., Leidner, J.L., Mittag, F., Nicklas, D., Schmid, U., Sedlmaier, Y., Ulbrich-vom Ende, A., Wolter, D.: Project VoLL-KI. KI -. Künstl. Intell. (2024). https://doi.org/10.1007/s13218-024-00846-9

13. Lewis, P., et al.: Retrieval-augmented generation for knowledge-intensive NLP tasks. In: Larochelle, H., Ranzato, M., Hadsell, R., Balcan, M., Lin, H. (eds.) Advances in Neural Information Processing Systems 33: Annual Conference on Neural Information Processing Systems 2020, NeurIPS 2020, December 6–12, 2020, virtual (2020). https://doi.org/10.48550/arXiv.2005.11401

14. Ranzenberger, T., Bocklet, T., Freisinger, S., Georges, M., Glocker, K., Herygers, A., Riedhammer, K., Schneider, F., Simic, C., Zakaria, K.: Extending hans: large language models for question answering, summarization, and topic segmentation in an ml-based learning experience platform. In: Elektron. Sprachsignalverarb. 2024, Tagungsb. der 35. Konferenz, Regensburg, 6.-8. März 2024, pp. 219–224. TUDpress (2024)

15. Reiche, M., Leidner, J.L.: Welcome to the ML team: a chat agent as a project management support agent. In: Arai, K. (ed.) 11th Intelligent Systems Conference 2025 (Intellisys'25), 28–29 August 2025, Amsterdam, The Netherlands. pp. 448–469. Springer, Cham (2025). https://doi.org/10.1007/978-3-032-00071-2_28

16. Reimers, N., Gurevych, I.: Sentence-BERT: Sentence Embeddings using Siamese BERT-networks. In: Inui, K., Jiang, J., Ng, V., Wan, X. (eds.) Proceedings of the 2019 Conference on Empirical Methods in Natural Language Processing and the 9th International Joint Conference on Natural Language Processing (EMNLP-IJCNLP 2019), pp. 3982–3992. ACL, Hong Kong, China (2019). https://doi.org/10.18653/v1/D19-1410

17. Semnani, S., Yao, V., Zhang, H., Lam, M.: WikiChat: Stopping the Hallucination of Large Language Model Chatbots by Few-shot Grounding on Wikipedia. In: Bouamor, H., Pino, J., Bali, K. (eds.) Findings of the Association for Computational Linguistics: EMNLP 2023, pp. 2387–2413. ACL, Singapore (2023). https://aclanthology.org/2023.findings-emnlp.157

18. Yu, P., Merrick, L., Nuti, G., Campos, D.: Arctic-embed 2.0: Multilingual Retrieval Without Compromise. CoRR abs/2412.04506 (2024).https://doi.org/10.48550/ARXIV.2412.04506

19. Zhang, D., Nunamaker, J.: A natural language approach to content-based video indexing and retrieval for interactive e-learning. IEEE Trans. Multimedia **6**(3), 450–458 (2004). https://doi.org/10.1109/TMM.2004.827505

20. Zhang, H.C., Semnani, S.J., Ghassemi, F., Xu, J., Liu, S., Lam, M.S.: SPAGHETTI: Open-domain Question Answering from Heterogeneous Data Sources with Retrieval and Semantic Parsing. In: Ku, L., Martins, A., Srikumar, V. (eds.) Findings of ACL 2024, Bangkok, Thailand and virtual meeting, August 11–16, 2024. pp. 1663–1678. ACL (2024).https://doi.org/10.18653/V1/2024.FINDINGS-ACL.96

# MedNuggetizer: Confidence-Based Information Nugget Extraction from Medical Documents


Gregor Donabauer[1(✉)], Samy Ateia[1], Udo Kruschwitz[1], Maximilian Burger[2],
Matthias May[3], Christian Gilfrich[3], Maximilian Haas[2],
Julio Ruben Rodas Garzaro[3], and Christoph Eckl[2]

[1] Information Science, University of Regensburg, Regensburg, Germany
`{gregor.donabauer,samy.ateia,udo.kruschwitz}@ur.de`
[2] Department of Urology, St. Josef Medical Center, Regensburg, Germany
`{mburger,mhaas,ceckl}@csj.de`
[3] Department of Urology, St. Elisabeth Hospital Straubing, Straubing, Germany
`{matthias.may,christian.gilfrich,julio.rodas-garzaro}@klinikum-straubing.de`



**Abstract.** We present **MedNuggetizer** (https://mednugget-ai.de/; access is available upon request.), a tool for query-driven extraction and clustering of information nuggets from medical documents to support clinicians in exploring underlying medical evidence. Backed by a large language model (LLM), *MedNuggetizer* performs repeated extractions of information nuggets that are then grouped to generate reliable evidence within and across multiple documents. We demonstrate its utility on the clinical use case of *antibiotic prophylaxis before prostate biopsy* by using major urological guidelines and recent PubMed studies as sources of information. Evaluation by domain experts shows that *MedNuggetizer* provides clinicians and researchers with an efficient way to explore long documents and easily extract reliable, query-focused medical evidence.

**Keywords:** Information Nuggets · Medical Domain · LLMs · Information Extraction · Professional Search


## 1 Introduction

The increasing adoption of large language models (LLMs) in clinical research [6,22] has introduced new opportunities for automated evidence synthesis, yet it has also raised fundamental concerns about reproducibility. Popular deep research systems, for example, offer limited expert oversight and experience technical shortcomings when sources are not accessible through the LLM tool calls [13]. Moreover, even when identical prompts are issued to the same model across repeated runs, variations in outputs can occur due to stochastic sampling, temperature settings, or batch variance [12,19,24]. Such instability complicates the scientific use of LLM-generated information, particularly when clinical decisions rely on consistent extraction of recommendations.



R. Campos et al. (Eds.): ECIR 2026, LNCS 16486, pp. 179–186, 2026.
https://doi.org/10.1007/978-3-032-21321-1_26

Our tool *MedNuggetizer* allows medical professionals to assess mitigation strategies and overcome these shortcomings by sampling, clustering, and highlighting extracted information nuggets and the derived confidence of the extraction process. Such information nuggets can be used in downstream tasks such as professional search (biomedical systematic reviews) [28] or grounded and transparent retrieval augmented generation (RAG) systems [4,11].

By evaluating a use case on *antibiotic prophylaxis in transrectal and transperineal prostate biopsy* in urology with domain experts, we demonstrate that our tool offers reproducible evidence extraction of recommendations in medicine. This use case exemplifies many similar evidence extraction tasks.

To support the reproducibility of our work, we publicly make available the source code of our data and all data related to our evaluation on GitHub[1].

## 2   System Overview

We present *MedNuggetizer*[2], a user-friendly web application built with Flask. The LLM used in the backend is Google's Gemini 2.5 Flash, chosen for its cost efficiency and its capability of processing PDF content up to 1000 pages [9]. Due to the modular nature of our system, any components, such as the backbone LLM, can be easily swapped. The nugget extraction and clustering workflow consists of the components described below (for additional details see Fig. 1).

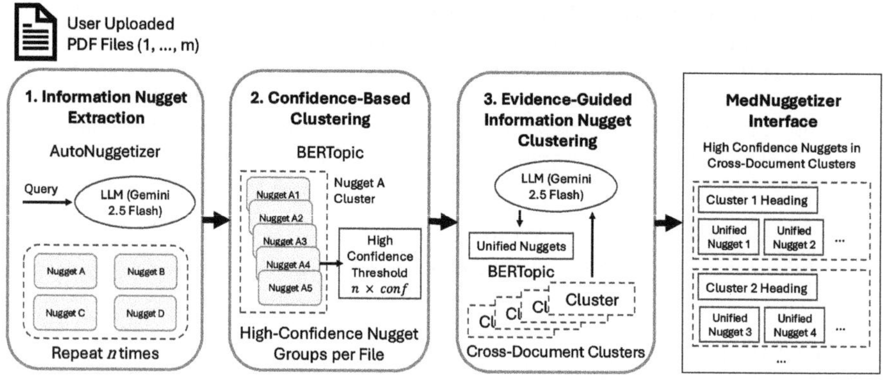


**Fig. 1.** Flowchart of the *MedNuggetizer* workflow.

**Information Nugget Extraction.** For each PDF file uploaded by the user, we extract the *information nuggets* relevant to the user's query that are present within the document. The extraction process is based on AutoNuggetizer [20],

---

[1] https://github.com/SamyAteia/mednuggetizer-ecir2026.
[2] https://mednugget-ai.de/; access is available upon request.

as implemented in the GINGER framework [15]. We adopt this approach due to its demonstrated utility; however, as noted earlier, alternative components can be used at each step of the pipeline.

**Confidence-Based Clustering.** As variations in LLM outputs can occur even when identical prompts are issued to the same model, we increase the reliability of the extracted information nuggets by providing two parameters: $n$, which defines the number of repeated extraction runs per file, and $conf$, which defines the proportion of the $n$ runs a nugget must appear in to be considered reliable.

To group the extracted nuggets across the $n$ runs, we employ BERTopic-based clustering [10], again following the approach applied in the GINGER framework [15]. As before, this step can be swapped with alternative components. The minimum number of nuggets required per cluster is determined by $n \times conf$. For example, with $n = 5$ and $conf = 0.8$, a cluster must contain at least four nuggets to be retained as high-confidence from that PDF file.

**Summary Generation.** After grouping nuggets based on their similarity and recurrence across runs, we aim to consolidate each group of repeated nuggets into a single, high-confidence nugget. For that, an LLM generates a unified nugget that captures the cluster's content in a concise formulation.

**Evidence-Guided Information Nugget Clustering.** The input to this final stage consists of all unified nuggets extracted from different files in the previous stage. The objective is to identify semantically similar groups of nuggets across multiple files, as such clusters indicate stronger supporting evidence for the information expressed by these nuggets. To accomplish this, we again apply BERTopic-based clustering [10] to the unified nuggets. The clusters identified in this stage form the final output of the *MedNuggetizer* interface. We also provide short headings summarizing identified clusters by prompting the backbone LLM to generate concise descriptions that reflect the main idea or common theme of the nuggets in each cluster.

**User Interface.** The interface of *MedNuggetizer* is designed to be self-explanatory and easy to use, as shown in Fig. 2. It provides four input fields that the user can interact with:

1. **PDF Files:** Allows the user to upload one or more PDF files to be processed.
2. **Query:** The query formulated by the user about the uploaded documents; it guides the information nugget extraction process.
3. **Number of Runs** $n$**:** Defines the number of repeated extraction runs performed for each document.
4. **LLM Confidence** $conf$**:** Sets the confidence threshold used to identify reliable clusters of nuggets within the same document.

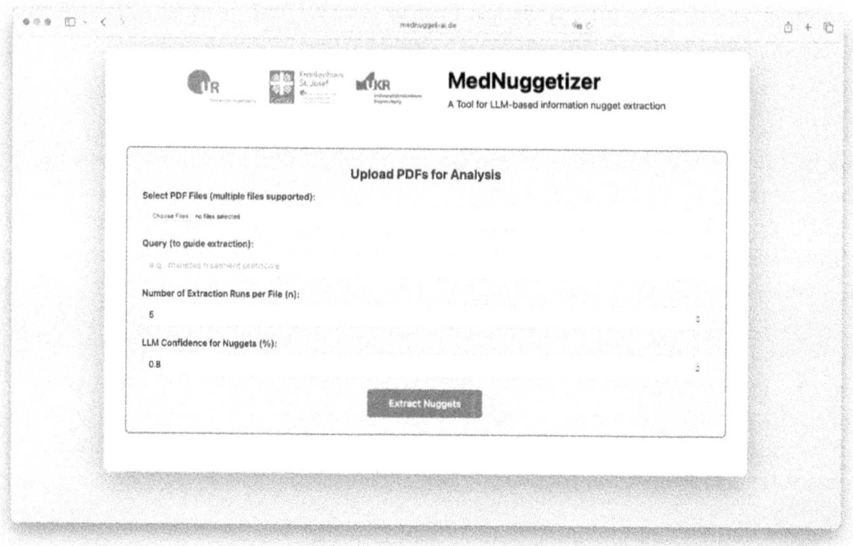

**Fig. 2.** Screenshot of the *MedNuggetizer* web interface. The system allows users to upload PDF files, as well as specifying a query and clustering specific parameters.

## 3   Evaluation and Discussion

Following the urologists' suggestion, we use *antibiotic prophylaxis before prostate biopsy* as an example use case to evaluate *MedNuggetizer*, as existing guidelines and practices vary and optimal preventive strategies remain debated. This use case serves as an exemplar for many similar clinical tasks.

We use four major guidelines (EAU Prostate Cancer 2025 [1,14]; EAU Urological Infections 2025 [2]; AWMF S3 Prostate Cancer 2025 [16]; AWMF S3 Peri-interventional Antibiotic Prophylaxis 2024 [7]) and ten recent PubMed-indexed articles (six systematic reviews [5,17,25,27,29,30], four randomized controlled trials [3,8,23,31] published between October 2024 and September 2025) that were identified as relevant by the domain experts. The experts also define five queries[3] on the topic which were processed through the tool using the listed PDF documents as context, with hyperparameters set to $n = 5$ and $conf = 0.8$.

To account for the importance of systematic evaluation in NLP/IR by consulting actual domain experts [21,26], two urologists manually annotated the resulting **(1)** 155 clusters by answering the question *How consistent/coherent is the cluster?*, and **(2)** 406 information nuggets by answering *How relevant is the nugget to the query?*. Ratings were provided on a five-point Likert scale, where 1 denotes *not at all* and 5 denotes *very*. In addition, they gave general feedback on their experience using the tool.

---

[3] We provide these as well as the expert assessments on Github.

**Table 1.** Number of clusters/nuggets and their expert-annotated Likert ratings.

| Query | $n_C$ | $C_{mean}$ | $C_{median}$ | $n_N$ | $N_{mean}$ | $N_{median}$ |
|---|---|---|---|---|---|---|
| q0 | 28 | 4.0 | 4 | 66 | 4.0 | 4 |
| q1 | 34 | 4.24 | 4 | 97 | 4.23 | 4 |
| q2 | 44 | 4.77 | 5 | 103 | 4.64 | 5 |
| q3 | 25 | 4.84 | 5 | 65 | 4.75 | 5 |
| q4 | 24 | 4.75 | 5 | 75 | 4.72 | 5 |

The numbers in Table 1 highlight both the high relevance of the information nuggets and the usefulness of the clusters in organizing that information. This aligns with the overall feedback of the urologists, noting that the system can retrieve highly relevant information nuggets, with clusters effectively distinguishing multiple layers of information such as context, current evidence, recommendations, expert opinions, and research limitations. However, identified issues with the nuggets are: undefined abbreviations, missing contextualization, inclusion of method-focused information with limited utility, and partial overlap between clusters, which can hinder clarity and practical applicability.

## 4   Conclusion

We present a tool that allows clinicians to explore medical evidence aggregated from multiple documents, without requiring expertise in the underlying IR techniques adopted from SOTA information nugget extraction frameworks such as GINGER [15]. Unlike GINGER, which includes additional steps, such as answer generation, our tool focuses on providing raw nuggets, allowing domain experts to directly perform downstream tasks. Its usefulness is demonstrated through a urology use case. Future work could allow users to swap the components of our modular pipeline, such as the clustering technique used or the LLMs driving the extraction process. We additionally plan to perform a systematic assessment of MedNuggetizer's utility for data extraction in diagnostic systematic reviews [18].

**Acknowledgments.** We thank the anonymous reviewers for their valuable feedback. This work was supported by the German Research Foundation (DFG) as part of the NFDIxCS consortium (Grant number: 501930651).

**Disclosure of Interests.** The authors have no competing interests to declare that are relevant to the content of this article.

# References


1. EAU - EANM - ESTRO - ESUR - ISUP - SIOG Guidelines on Prostate Cancer. EAU Guidelines Office, Arnhem, The Netherlands (2025). http://uroweb.org/guidelines/compilations-of-all-guidelines/, edition presented at the EAU Annual Congress Madrid 2025
2. EAU Guidelines Urological Infections. EAU Guidelines Office, Arnhem, The Netherlands (2025). http://uroweb.org/guidelines/compilations-of-all-guidelines/, edition presented at the EAU Annual Congress Madrid 2025
3. Bryant, R.J., et al.: Local anaesthetic transperineal biopsy versus transrectal prostate biopsy in prostate cancer detection (TRANSLATE): a multicentre, randomised, controlled trial. Lancet Oncol. **26**(5), 583–595 (2025)
4. Carmel, D., et al.: The LiveRAG challenge at SIGIR 2025. In: Proceedings of the 48th International ACM SIGIR Conference on Research and Development in Information Retrieval. SIGIR '25, Association for Computing Machinery, Padua, Italy (2025). https://doi.org/10.1145/3726302.3733591
5. Cho, S., Jun, D.Y., Lee, J.Y., Jeong, J.Y., Jung, H.D.: Comparison of urinary tract infection rates between transperineal prostate biopsies with and without prophylactic antibiotics: an updated systematic review and meta-analysis. Medicina **61**(2) (2025). https://doi.org/10.3390/medicina61020198
6. Cunha, L.F., Guimarães, N., Mendes, A., Campos, R., Jorge, A.: MedLink: retrieval and ranking of case reports to assist clinical decision making. In: Hauff, C., et al. (eds.) European Conference on Information Retrieval, pp. 72–77. Springer, Cham (2025). https://doi.org/10.1007/978-3-031-88720-8_13
7. Deutsche Gesellschaft für Hygiene und Mikrobiologie e.V. (DGHM): S3-Leitlinie Perioperative und Periinterventionelle Antibiotikaprophylaxe (2024). https://register.awmf.org/de/leitlinien/detail/067-009, version 5.0, AWMF-Registernummer: 067-009. Gültig bis: 19 Dec 2029
8. Fehér, Á.M., et al.: Single-dose vs prolonged antibiotic prophylaxis of fosfomycin for transrectal prostate biopsy: a single-center prospective, randomized, controlled trial. Prostate International **13**(1), 28–33 (2025)
9. Gemini Team, G.: Gemini 2.5: Pushing the Frontier with Advanced Reasoning, Multimodality, Long Context, and Next Generation Agentic Capabilities. arXiv preprint arXiv:2507.06261 (2025)
10. Grootendorst, M.R.: BERTopic: Neural topic modeling with a class-based TF-IDF procedure. arXiv preprint arXiv:2203.05794 (2022)
11. Gupta, D., Demner-Fushman, D., Hersh, W., Bedrick, S., Roberts, K.: Overview of TREC 2024 biomedical generative retrieval (BioGen) track. arXiv preprint arXiv:2411.18069 (2024)
12. He, H., et al.: Defeating Nondeterminism in LLM Inference. Thinking Machines Lab: Connectionism (2025). https://doi.org/10.64434/tml.20250910, https://thinkingmachines.ai/blog/defeating-nondeterminism-in-llm-inference/
13. Jaradeh, M.Y., Auer, S.: Deep Research in the Era of Agentic AI: Requirements and Limitations for Scholarly Research. In: Proceedings of the 5th International Workshop on Scientific Knowledge: Representation, Discovery, and Assessment (Sci-K). CEUR Workshop Proceedings, CEUR-WS.org, Nara, Japan (2025)
14. Kranz, J., et al.: European association of urology guidelines on urological infections: summary of the 2024 guidelines. Eur. Urol. **86**(1), 27–41 (2024). https://doi.org/10.1016/j.eururo.2024.03.035

15. Łajewska, W., Balog, K.: GINGER: Grounded Information Nugget-Based Generation of Responses. In: Proceedings of the 48th International ACM SIGIR Conference on Research and Development in Information Retrieval, pp. 2723–2727. SIGIR '25, Association for Computing Machinery, New York, NY, USA (2025). https://doi.org/10.1145/3726302.3730166

16. Leitlinienprogramm Onkologie (Deutsche Krebsgesellschaft, Deutsche Krebshilfe, AWMF): S3-Leitlinie Prostatakarzinom, Version 8.1. AWMF online (2025). https://register.awmf.org/de/leitlinien/detail/043-022OL, aWMF-Registernummer: 043-022OL, Stand: 01.06.2025, Gültig bis: 31.05.2030. Accessed 17 Oct 2025

17. Madhavan, K., et al.: Preventing infectious complications following prostate biopsy: a systematic review and network meta-analysis of randomized controlled trials of alternative approaches to transrectal biopsy with empirical antibiotic prophylaxis therapy. Eur. Urol. Focus **11**(2), 301–311 (2025).https://doi.org/10.1016/j.euf.2024.09.011

18. May, M., et al.: End-to-End Reliability of Automated Systems for Diagnostic Data Extraction: A Benchmark Study in Uro-Oncologic Evidence Synthesis. medRxiv (2025). https://doi.org/10.64898/2025.12.24.25342959

19. Ouyang, S., Zhang, J.M., Harman, M., Wang, M.: An empirical study of the non-determinism of ChatGPT in code generation. ACM Trans. Softw. Eng. Methodol. **34**(2) (2025). https://doi.org/10.1145/3697010

20. Pradeep, R., Thakur, N., Upadhyay, S., Campos, D., Craswell, N., Lin, J.: Initial Nugget Evaluation Results for the TREC 2024 RAG Track with the AutoNuggetizer Framework. arXiv preprint arXiv:2411.09607 (2024)

21. Reiter, E.: We Should Evaluate Real-World Impact. Comput. Linguist. pp. 1–13 (2025)

22. Romano, A., Riccio, G., Postiglione, M., Moscato, V.: PIE-Med: predicting, interpreting and explaining medical recommendations. In: Hauff, C., et al. (eds.) European Conference on Information Retrieval. pp. 6–12. Springer, Cham (2025). https://doi.org/10.1007/978-3-031-88720-8_2

23. Sadahira, T., et al.: Significance of targeted antimicrobial prophylaxis using rectal-culture selective screening media prior to transrectal prostate biopsy: a multicenter, randomized controlled trial. Urology **196**, 32–39 (2025). https://doi.org/10.1016/j.urology.2024.12.018

24. Song, Y., Wang, G., Li, S., Lin, B.Y.: The good, the bad, and the greedy: evaluation of llms should not ignore non-determinism. In: Chiruzzo, L., Ritter, A., Wang, L. (eds.) Proceedings of the 2025 Conference of the Nations of the Americas Chapter of the Association for Computational Linguistics: Human Language Technologies (Volume 1: Long Papers), pp. 4195–4206. Association for Computational Linguistics, Albuquerque, New Mexico (2025). https://doi.org/10.18653/v1/2025.naacl-long.211

25. Stangl, F.P., et al.: Infectious complications after transrectal versus transperineal prostate biopsy: a systematic review and meta-analysis. Eur. Urol. Focus (2025). https://doi.org/10.1016/j.euf.2025.07.005

26. Thomson, C., Reiter, E., Belz, A.: Common flaws in running human evaluation experiments in NLP. Comput. Linguist. **50**(2), 795–805 (2024)

27. Tsuboi, I., et al.: Rectal Swab–based Targeted prophylactic antibiotics reduce infectious complications after transrectal prostate biopsy: a systematic review and meta-analysis of randomized controlled trials. Eur. Urol. Open Sci. **80**, 57–65 (2025) https://doi.org/10.1016/j.euros.2025.08.007

28. Verberne, S.: Professional search. In: Information Retrieval: Advanced Topics and Techniques, pp. 501–514. Association for Computing Machinery, New York, NY, USA, 1 edn. (2024) https://doi.org/10.1145/3674127.3674141
29. Wolff, I., et al.: Infectious complications following transperineal prostate biopsy with or without periprocedural antibiotic prophylaxis—a systematic review including meta-analysis of all comparative studies. Prostate Cancer Prostatic Dis. 1–10 (2024)
30. Zattoni, F., et al.: Transperineal versus transrectal magnetic resonance imaging–targeted prostate biopsy: a systematic review and meta-analysis of prospective studies. Eur. Urol. Oncol. 7(6), 1303–1312 (2024). https://doi.org/10.1016/j.euo.2024.07.009
31. Çetin, T., et al.: Saline cleansing can prevent infective complications after transrectal prostate biopsy: a randomized prospective study. Urol. J. 91(4), 768–774 (2024). https://doi.org/10.1177/03915603241273888, pMID: 39212152

# SuiteEval: Simplifying Retrieval Benchmarks

Andrew Parry[(✉)] [iD], Debasis Ganguly [iD], and Sean MacAvaney [iD]

University of Glasgow, Glasgow, Scotland, UK
`a.parry.1@research.gla.ac.uk,`
`{Debasis.Ganguly,Sean.MacAvaney}@glasgow.ac.uk`

**Abstract.** Information retrieval evaluation often suffers from fragmented practices—varying dataset subsets, aggregation methods, and pipeline configurations—that undermine reproducibility and comparability, especially for foundation embedding models requiring robust out-of-domain performance. We introduce SuiteEval, a unified framework that offers automatic end-to-end evaluation, dynamic indexing that reuses on-disk indices to minimise disk usage, and built-in support for major benchmarks (BEIR, LoTTE, MS MARCO, NanoBEIR, and BRIGHT). Users only need to supply a pipeline generator. SuiteEval handles data loading, indexing, ranking, metric computation, and result aggregation. New benchmark suites can be added in a single line. SuiteEval reduces boilerplate and standardises evaluations to facilitate reproducible IR research, as a broader benchmark set is increasingly required.

**Keywords:** Information Retrieval · Evaluation · Reproducibility

## 1   Introduction

Evaluation benchmarks are central to measuring effectiveness in information retrieval (IR). As the community increasingly targets out-of-domain generalisation—motivated by "foundation" embedding models intended to operate across diverse domains and surface forms [4,13]—studies are expected to report results over multiple collections and splits, often bundled into a *suite* of benchmarks. In practice, however, evaluations are frequently constrained by the systems natively supported by a suite's accompanying codebase, which can lag behind new architectures. Further, choices about dataset coverage and result aggregation frequently differ across studies [5], complicating comparison and replication.

Open-source toolkits such as `PyTerrier` [8] and `Anserini` [6] have lowered the barrier to reproducible experimentation by standardising data ingestion and facilitating pipeline construction. Yet they provide limited support for managing end-to-end suite evaluations comprising *multiple* benchmarks: enforcing

---

 https://github.com/Parry-Parry/suiteeval.

© The Author(s), under exclusive license to Springer Nature Switzerland AG 2026
R. Campos et al. (Eds.): ECIR 2026, LNCS 16486, pp. 187–192, 2026.
https://doi.org/10.1007/978-3-032-21321-1_27

consistent dataset selection, unifying per-benchmark metric definitions, automating indexing and ranking across all splits, and reducing the incidental engineering that surrounds large-scale runs. Furthermore, while toolkits such as `ir_datasets` [7] provide consistent data processing and `Tira` [3] facilitates reproducibility through containerization, we instead target the convenient and memory-efficient evaluation of end-to-end pipelines over multiple benchmarks.

This work introduces `SuiteEval`, a unifying framework that simplifies and standardises suite evaluation in IR. `SuiteEval` encapsulates benchmark definitions, dataset contexts, indexing, and ranking within a single *Suite* abstraction that: (i) defaults to complete coverage of all datasets and splits for a benchmark suite; (ii) applies the official metrics and aggregation procedures uniformly; and (iii) eliminates boilerplate orchestration so that users specify only the IR pipeline to be evaluated. A dynamic indexing process minimises superfluous disk usage over large suites while preserving reproducibility and auditability of artefacts. By standardising evaluation over widely used suites, we hope to reduce the burden on performing suite-based evaluation, while reducing the variance in experimental settings and making effectiveness claims more comparable across papers.

We demonstrate `SuiteEval` by executing a standard experiment over BEIR and the creation of a new benchmark, guiding users through the minimal steps required to execute reproducible benchmark suite evaluations. Together, these results show how `SuiteEval` streamlines reproducible IR evaluation while enabling straightforward extension as new suites are released.

## 2     SuiteEval Overview

Many IR evaluation setups are driven by declarative configuration files that fix index paths, dataset splits, and pipeline parameters. This encourages duplicated indices per corpus and boilerplate for each new retrieval or re-ranking component, inflating disk usage and increasing variance in evaluation settings. Here we adopt `PyTerrier` pipelines for their composability and broad existing ecosystem: pipeline operators (e.g., $\gg$) make retrieval-re-ranking stages explicit within a single, minimal specification.

**Running an Evaluation Suite.** Existing experimental procedures assume that experimental artifacts (e.g., indexes) are constructed before evaluation. This poses a challenge for evaluation suites, where many potential artifacts are required and may only be used once. `SuiteEval` overcomes this by defining the process for constructing required artifacts and retrieval pipelines in a single user-defined function (example in Fig. 1). As input to this function, each dataset is wrapped in a `DatasetContext`, which provides (i) a workspace via `path`, (ii) a corpus iterator via `get_corpus_iter()` (required for constructing indexes), and (iii) dataset-specific utilities such as `text_loader()`. `SuiteEval` is responsible for executing and evaluating these pipelines.

All filesystem writes are scoped to `context.path`, treated as ephemeral unless a persistent `index_dir` is supplied. Indices (e.g., `PisaIndex`) are instantiated

```python
from suiteeval import DatasetContext
from pyterrier_pisa import PisaIndex
import pyterrier_t5, pyterrier_dr
def systems(context: DatasetContext):
    index = PisaIndex(context.path / "index.pisa")
    index.index(context.get_corpus_iter())
    bm25 = index.bm25() >> context.text_loader()
    yield bm25 >> pyterrier_t5.MonoT5ReRanker()
    yield bm25 >> pyterrier_dr.ElectraScorer()
```

**Fig. 1.** Creation of a `PisaIndex` using BM25 before re-ranking with two neural models.

inside this workspace and reused if present; otherwise they are built once per corpus using `context.get_corpus_iter()`. Because `systems(context)` is invoked once per corpus (grouping multiple query sets together that use the same corpus), all yielded pipelines share the same index instance, and `text_loader()` attaches document text only when required by downstream re-rankers.

**The `Suite` Class.** A `Suite` instance acts as the controller, binding dataset identifiers, official measures, and aggregation rules. The suite groups dataset identifiers by underlying corpus so that indexing is performed once per corpus rather than per test collection. For each corpus group, it instantiates a `DatasetContext`, invokes the user generator once to collect pipelines, and executes those pipelines across all associated test collections. A minimal invocation is shown in Fig. 2.

```python
from suiteeval import BEIR

results = BEIR(systems, baseline=0, save_dir="beir_results")
```

**Fig. 2.** Execution of the BEIR evaluation suite. MonoT5 is taken to be the baseline for significance tests and run files are saved to "beir_results".

Results are returned as a long-form `pandas.DataFrame`, with one row per dataset, system, and evaluation measure. Because all datasets in a suite are evaluated under a single controller with fixed measures and cutoffs, SuiteEval can additionally compute suite-level aggregates, such as means across datasets. Existing suites predefined within SuiteEval are listed in Table 1.

**Adding New Suites.** `SuiteEval` provides a registry mechanism that allows new benchmarks to be defined declaratively without subclassing or custom evaluation scripts. The `Suite.register` method associates a suite name with a list of `ir_datasets` identifiers and a metadata dictionary, as shown in Fig. 3. This metadata configures evaluation behaviour, including the set of official measures and default aggregation rules. Once registered, suites are first-class objects and can be invoked in the same manner as built-in benchmarks.

```
1  from suiteeval.suite.base import Suite
2  from ir_measures import nDCG
3
4  passage_datasets = [
5      "msmarco-passage/trec-dl-2019/judged",
6      "msmarco-passage/trec-dl-2020/judged",
7      "msmarco-passage-v2/trec-dl-2022/judged"]
8
9  MSMARCOPassage = Suite.register(
10     "msmarco/passage",
11     datasets=passage_datasets,
12     metadata={"official_measures": [nDCG@10]}
13     )
```

**Fig. 3.** Definition of a custom suite comprising two corpora (MSMARCOv1 and MSMARCOv2) and 3 test collections (DL-2019, -2020, -2022). This suite will return nDCG@10 values for each test collection and the geometric mean of the three for each pipeline defined in the `systems` function.

**Table 1.** Pre-registered suites currently supported by  SuiteEval.

| Name | Scope |
| --- | --- |
| `Lotte()` [10] | Long-tail collections. |
| `MSMARCOPassage()` [9] | MS MARCO passage tasks [1,2]. |
| `MSMARCODocument()` [9] | MS MARCO document tasks [1,2]; mirrors passage-suite behaviour at document level. |
| `BEIR()` [12] | Heterogeneous, multi-domain retrieval suite; additionally applies post-hoc filtering and corrects aggregation. |
| `NanoBEIR()` | Compact BEIR subsets for fast iteration. Similarly post-processing to BEIR. |
| `BRIGHT()` [11] | Collections targeting reasoning intensive tasks. |

At runtime, the registered suite resolves each dataset identifier into its corresponding corpus, topics, and relevance judgements using `ir_datasets`[1]. The declared evaluation measures are applied uniformly across all datasets, ensuring that metric definitions cannot drift between splits. Because suite registration occurs at import time, adding new benchmarks introduces no runtime overhead and does not require changes to experimental scripts.

**Reducing Memory Footprint.** `SuiteEval` explicitly bounds index materialisation by the number of distinct corpora rather than by the number of test collections or pipeline variants. A single index persists only for the duration of a corpus group and is reused across all associated test collections before being released.

---

[1] Other objects may be used, but they must follow the `ir_datasets` object structure.

**Table 2.** Storage footprint of common experiments with and without  SuiteEval. The bi-encoder applied end-to-end and to re-rank BM25 is RetroMAE.

| Experiment | Suite | Disk Space (MB) + SuiteEval | |
|---|---|---|---|
| End-to-End vs. Re-Ranker | NanoBEIR | 249.85 | **18.29** |
| BM25 Grid-Search | BEIR | 22888.07 | **4889.15** |

For example, when evaluating the MS MARCO passage suite, an MSMARCOv1 index is reused for DL-2019 and DL-2020 before being destroyed and replaced by an MSMARCOv2 index for DL-2022. This lifecycle underpins the storage reductions reported in Table 2.

## 3  Demonstration

Our demonstration presents a concrete application of our framework, starting with a simple demonstration of running a grid search over a large benchmark suite. It explains what is provided within a suite and can be explored in this live notebook. We then provide a walkthrough on how to create a simple suite and extend its functionality to be task-specific by applying custom aggregation to results, and it can be explored in this live notebook. Additionally, we aim to raise awareness of the need for consistent and reproducible evaluation, a concept often championed in the IR community, with our framework serving as a tool for the responsible use of benchmark suites.

## 4  Target Audience and Potential Use Cases

The target audience for this demo is PhD students and researchers working in neural information retrieval or, more broadly, in representation learning with a focus on document embeddings. By introducing our package and utilising the broader PyTerrier ecosystem within it, we aim to continue encouraging reproducible evaluation, as benchmark suites become increasingly common as primary indicators of effectiveness.

**Disclosure of Interests.** The authors have no competing interests to declare that are relevant to the content of this article.

## References


1. Craswell, N., Mitra, B., Yilmaz, E., Campos, D.: Overview of the TREC 2020 deep learning track. CoRR abs/2102.07662 (2021). https://arxiv.org/abs/2102.07662
2. Craswell, N., Mitra, B., Yilmaz, E., Campos, D., Voorhees, E.M.: Overview of the TREC 2019 deep learning track. CoRR abs/2003.07820 (2020). https://arxiv.org/abs/2003.07820

3. Fröbe, M., Reimer, J.H., MacAvaney, S., Deckers, N., Reich, S., Bevendorff, J., Stein, B., Hagen, M., Potthast, M.: The information retrieval experiment platform. CoRR abs/2305.18932 (2023). https://doi.org/10.48550/ARXIV.2305.18932, https://doi.org/10.48550/arXiv.2305.18932
4. Izacard, G., Caron, M., Hosseini, L., Riedel, S., Bojanowski, P., Joulin, A., Grave, E.: Unsupervised dense information retrieval with contrastive learning. Trans. Mach. Learn. Res. **2022** (2022), https://openreview.net/forum?id=jKN1pXi7b0
5. Lassance, C., Clinchant, S.: The tale of two MS MARCO - and their unfair comparisons. CoRR **abs/2304.12904** (2023). https://doi.org/10.48550/ARXIV.2304.12904, https://doi.org/10.48550/arXiv.2304.12904
6. Lin, J., Ma, X., Lin, S., Yang, J., Pradeep, R., Nogueira, R.: Pyserini: an easy-to-use python toolkit to support replicable IR research with sparse and dense representations. CoRR abs/2102.10073 (2021), https://arxiv.org/abs/2102.10073
7. MacAvaney, S., Yates, A., Feldman, S., Downey, D., Cohan, A., Goharian, N.: Simplified data wrangling with ir_datasets. In: Diaz, F., Shah, C., Suel, T., Castells, P., Jones, R., Sakai, T. (eds.) SIGIR '21: The 44th International ACM SIGIR Conference on Research and Development in Information Retrieval, Virtual Event, Canada, July 11-15, 2021, pp. 2429–2436. ACM (2021). https://doi.org/10.1145/3404835.3463254, https://doi.org/10.1145/3404835.3463254
8. Macdonald, C., Tonellotto, N.: Declarative experimentation in information retrieval using pyterrier. In: Balog, K., Setty, V., Lioma, C., Liu, Y., Zhang, M., Berberich, K. (eds.) ICTIR '20: The 2020 ACM SIGIR International Conference on the Theory of Information Retrieval, Virtual Event, Norway, September 14-17, 2020, pp. 161–168. ACM (2020). https://doi.org/10.1145/3409256.3409829, https://doi.org/10.1145/3409256.3409829
9. Nguyen, T., Rosenberg, M., Song, X., Gao, J., Tiwary, S., Majumder, R., Deng, L.: MS MARCO: A human generated machine reading comprehension dataset. In: Besold, T.R., Bordes, A., d'Avila Garcez, A.S., Wayne, G. (eds.) Proceedings of the Workshop on Cognitive Computation: Integrating neural and symbolic approaches 2016 co-located with the 30th Annual Conference on Neural Information Processing Systems (NIPS 2016), Barcelona, Spain, December 9, 2016. CEUR Workshop Proceedings, vol. 1773. CEUR-WS.org (2016). https://ceur-ws.org/Vol-1773/CoCoNIPS_2016_paper9.pdf
10. Santhanam, K., Khattab, O., Saad-Falcon, J., Potts, C., Zaharia, M.: Colbertv2: Effective and efficient retrieval via lightweight late interaction. CoRR abs/2112.01488 (2021). https://arxiv.org/abs/2112.01488
11. Su, H., et al.: BRIGHT: A realistic and challenging benchmark for reasoning-intensive retrieval. In: The Thirteenth International Conference on Learning Representations, ICLR 2025, Singapore, April 24-28, 2025. OpenReview.net (2025). https://openreview.net/forum?id=ykuc5q381b
12. Thakur, N., Reimers, N., Rücklé, A., Srivastava, A., Gurevych, I.: BEIR: A heterogenous benchmark for zero-shot evaluation of information retrieval models. CoRR abs/2104.08663 (2021). https://arxiv.org/abs/2104.08663
13. Xiao, S., Liu, Z., Shao, Y., Cao, Z.: Retromae: Pre-training retrieval-oriented language models via masked auto-encoder. In: Goldberg, Y., Kozareva, Z., Zhang, Y. (eds.) Proceedings of the 2022 Conference on Empirical Methods in Natural Language Processing, EMNLP 2022, Abu Dhabi, United Arab Emirates, December 7-11, 2022, pp. 538–548. Association for Computational Linguistics (2022). https://doi.org/10.18653/V1/2022.EMNLP-MAIN.35, https://doi.org/10.18653/v1/2022.emnlp-main.35

# CitiLink: Enhancing Municipal Transparency and Citizen Engagement Through Searchable Meeting Minutes

Rodrigo Silva[1,3]([envelope]) [iD], José Evans[2,3] [iD], José Isidro[2,3] [iD], Miguel Marques[1,3] [iD],
Afonso Fonseca[1,3] [iD], Ricardo Morais[2,3] [iD], João Canavilhas[1] [iD],
Arian Pasquali[3] [iD], Purificação Silvano[2,3] [iD], Alípio Jorge[2,3] [iD],
Nuno Guimarães[2,3] [iD], Sérgio Nunes[2,3] [iD], and Ricardo Campos[1,3] [iD]

[1] University of Beira Interior, Covilhã, Portugal
{rd.silva,ricardo.campos}@ubi.pt
[2] University of Porto, Porto, Portugal
[3] INESC TEC, Porto, Portugal

**Abstract.** City council minutes are typically lengthy and formal documents with a bureaucratic writing style. Although publicly available, their structure often makes it difficult for citizens or journalists to efficiently find information. In this demo, we present CitiLink, a platform designed to transform unstructured municipal meeting minutes into structured and searchable data, demonstrating how NLP and IR can enhance the accessibility and transparency of local government. The system employs LLMs to extract metadata, discussed subjects, and voting outcomes, which are then indexed in a database to support full-text search with BM25 ranking and faceted filtering through a user-friendly interface. The developed system was built over a collection of 120 min made available by six Portuguese municipalities. To assess its usability, CitiLink was tested through guided sessions with municipal personnel, providing insights into how real users interact with the system. In addition, we evaluated Gemini's performance in extracting relevant information from the minutes, highlighting its performance in data extraction.

**Keywords:** City Council Minutes · Information Retrieval · NLP · LLMs

## 1 Introduction

Municipal councils are often subject to transparency metrics designed to assess how effectively local authorities disclose information and keep citizens informed [1]. A common practice supporting these metrics is the release of meeting minutes. While these records contribute to transparency [4], their formal, bureaucratic style and administrative jargon [9] make them difficult to understand, posing barriers for citizens or journalists, for whom reading minutes

© The Author(s), under exclusive license to Springer Nature Switzerland AG 2026
R. Campos et al. (Eds.): ECIR 2026, LNCS 16486, pp. 193–199, 2026.
https://doi.org/10.1007/978-3-032-21321-1_28

becomes a particularly time-consuming task [2]. Transforming unstructured minutes into structured data presents therefore an opportunity to facilitate efficient information access and organized navigation of council records. Although prior research has explored video recordings of council meetings [6,7,12], written minutes remain largely underexplored, particularly in European Portuguese [10]. To address this gap, we present CitiLink, a platform for structured access to city council minutes. While datasets such as MeetingBank [5] focus on conversational meeting data, CitiLink targets written minutes, enabling structured information extraction and retrieval. To populate the platform, we developed a pipeline that converts unstructured minutes into structured data, using LLMs with prompt engineering techniques. Our demo relies on 120 meeting minutes, manually anonymized with respect to personal data, and made available by 6 Portuguese municipalities: Alandroal, Campo Maior, Covilhã, Fundão, Guimarães, and Porto. Although the corpus only comprises 120 meeting minutes, it spans municipalities of different sizes and administrative practices, resulting in substantial variability in document length, formality, and subjects of discussion, and more than 27,000 extracted structured instances. For demonstration purposes, an English version of the dataset was created using DeepL translations, illustrating the system's multilingual capabilities.

## 2   System Overview

The system consists of a pipeline that leverages the Gemini 2.0 Flash large language model to extract information from meeting minutes; a front-end web application with integrated IR features; and a restricted back-office where municipalities can upload minutes and validate extracted data, ensuring human-in-the-loop oversight and correction of extraction errors. The choice of Gemini 2.0 Flash enables robust processing of non-English documents, while fitting seamlessly into the structured information extraction workflow, supporting both scalability and cost efficiency for the demo. Users can also subscribe to a newsletter for updates. An overview of the system architecture is shown in Fig. 1. Each minute is provided to the model as plain text, which, using prompt engineering, extracts three layers of information: (1) metadata (participants, location, date, type of meeting), (2) subjects of discussion (e.g., "Modification of traffic regulations on Avenida Central"), and (3) voting outcomes (in favor, against, abstention). The prompts used to extract these layers rely on structured instructions and are shared as part of the publicly available project repository. Extracted metadata are cross-referenced with predefined database collections to ensure consistency. These collections, covering participants, municipalities, and topics, were compiled from official municipal records and public websites. Metadata are matched against these collections using string similarity measures, with ambiguous cases manually validated through a human-in-the-loop process. The system architecture allows these collections to be easily extended as new municipalities or participants are added.

From the 120 meeting minutes, the system extracted 115 unique metadata elements (86 participants, 16 locations, 111 dates, 2 min types), 3,079 subjects

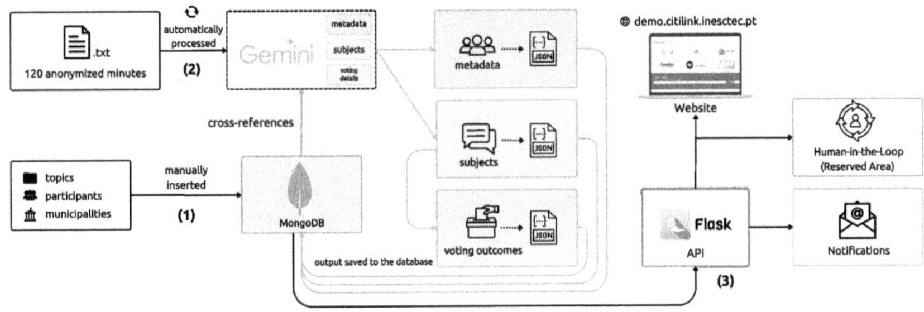


**Fig. 1.** Architecture of the CitiLink system.

of discussion, and 24,040 votes (22,702 in favor, 161 against, 1,177 abstentions). All data are stored in MongoDB Atlas to support full-text and faceted search, enabling structured exploration and incremental scaling beyond the initial demo corpus. The front-end, built with React, allows searching within minutes and subjects or browsing records by municipality, while a Flask API provides access to the processed data. The prompts, processing pipeline code, evaluation guide, and Gemini-generated data are publicly available on GitHub[1].

## 3    Demonstration

The CitiLink platform[2] provides a web interface for exploring and interacting with the extracted and indexed data. On the main page, users see cards for the six municipalities alongside a search section. Selecting a municipality presents a general overview of the most recent meeting minutes, executive members, and minutes grouped by discussion topics (as shown in Fig. 2a). In addition to this overview, users can access a list-based view of the minutes with faceted search by topic, party, or participant (as illustrated by Fig. 2b) or a timeline view for chronological exploration (as seen in Fig. 2c). By selecting a meeting minute, users can subsequently access a structured overview of its contents (as exemplified by Fig. 2d), including metadata (e.g., participants), a voting summary, and detailed information on the subjects of discussion (omitted from the figure due to space constraints), helping users understand council decisions without needing to read the full minutes. The platform also supports full-text search (as shown in Fig. 2e), allowing both exploratory navigation and targeted retrieval. For example, querying *"health"* retrieves the most relevant associated subjects (as shown in Fig. 2f). A demonstration video of the platform is available on the demo website and GitHub, showcasing all its features.

---

[1] https://github.com/inesctec/citilink-demo.
[2] https://demo.citilink.inesctec.pt/en, password: `ecir2026`.

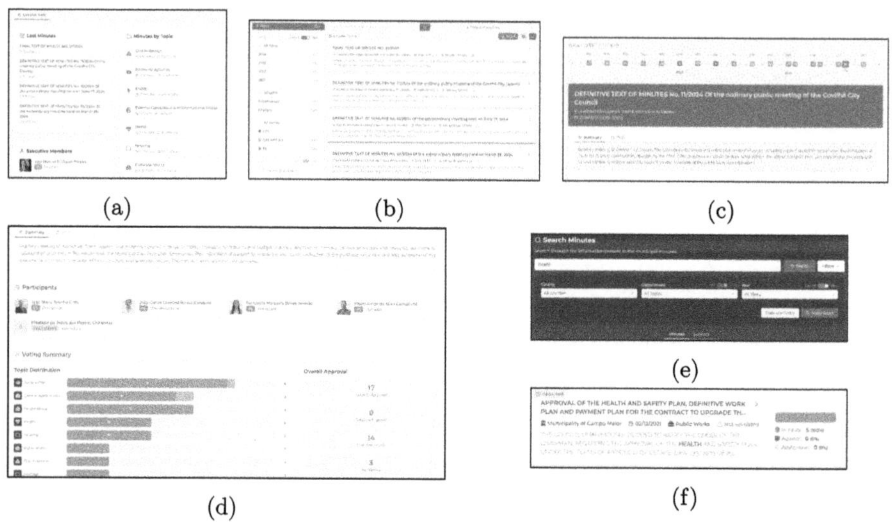

**Fig. 2.** Main components of the CitiLink web interface: (a) Municipality Overview; (b) List-based view; (c) Timeline view; (d) Minute page; (e) Search interface; (f) Search results interface.

## 4   Evaluation

To evaluate CitiLink's usability and effectiveness, preliminary assessments were conducted with municipal personnel between July 23 and September 4, 2025. Eight testing sessions, each lasting approximately 50 min, involved administrative staff and individuals responsible for producing or reviewing meeting minutes, ensuring a diversity of professional backgrounds and technical experience. The evaluation followed a think-aloud methodology [8, 13], in which participants verbalized their thoughts while interacting with the platform. During the sessions, participants performed ten guided tasks designed to assess navigation, functionality, and the identification of votes and discussion topics (the guide is available on the GitHub repository). The analysis of the sessions indicated that CitiLink has substantial potential to modernize access to municipal meeting minutes. All participants found navigation intuitive, with six noting they would use the platform again. Based on participants' remarks, the demo was refined and improved accordingly, exemplifying a user-centered refinement of the system.

In addition to usability, we assessed the performance of Gemini 2.0 Flash on each of the three extraction layers (metadata, subjects of discussion, and voting outcomes) and their individual items. The evaluation relied on the CitiLink-Minutes dataset [3], which comprises 120 European Portuguese meeting minutes. A detailed description of the dataset and the annotation scheme is outside the scope of this demonstration paper. Briefly, the minutes were annotated with multiple layers, including personal information, metadata, subjects, and voting outcomes, following detailed annotation guidelines. Each document was independently annotated by two trained annotators and subsequently validated by a curator, with inter-annotator agreement reported in the dataset paper. The current corpus size reflects the benchmark used for validation, while the system architecture is designed to scale incrementally to larger municipal archives.

The metadata achieved an overall macro F1 of 0.84 across the 6 municipalities, considering all defined metadata fields, indicating consistent performance across categories. For subjects, direct comparison between model outputs and ground-truth annotations is challenging, as the model does not produce text offsets. To enable evaluation, each ground-truth subject was matched one-by-one to its most similar LLM-generated candidate using BERTimbau [11] embeddings and cosine similarity. ROUGE-L (0.31) and BLEU (0.21) indicate that the model captures aspects of content and structure, while wording differences reflect task variability. Finally, in the voting task, we evaluated Gemini's ability to identify councilors' voting positions (in favor, against, or abstained) by comparing its outputs with the ground truth (e.g., "Councilman John voted in favor"). The model achieved a macro F1 of 0.67, reflecting the greater complexity of this task compared to structured metadata extraction. These results suggest room for improvement and motivate tests with alternative LLMs. The extraction pipeline may produce inaccuracies or omissions in some cases. However, the platform mitigates this risk through a human-in-the-loop validation step in the back-office interface prior to publication, prioritizing correctness in civic decision records.

## 5   Conclusion and Future Work

In this paper, we presented a demo of CitiLink, a platform that transforms municipal meeting minutes into structured, accessible data. By combining structured data extraction, intuitive navigation, and user-centered design, CitiLink enhances transparency and enables timely access to information on decisions that directly affect everyday life, strengthening the connection between citizens, journalists, researchers, and local decision-makers.

In future work, we plan to integrate self-developed open-source language models[3] into the production deployment of CitiLink[4]. Building on the three-layer system architecture introduced in this paper, we will explore LLM-based summarization of the subjects discussed in the minutes, as well as pseudonymization techniques, to support scaling the system to larger collections of municipal records while preserving privacy. To assess the robustness and applicability of these extensions, we intend to experiment with meeting minutes from additional municipalities to evaluate the system's generalization capabilities. Using the structured representations already extracted from the minutes, we will also support the generation of tailored reports for different user needs. Finally, we will extend the empirical evaluation by collecting feedback from citizens and journalists through questionnaires and focus groups, enabling a more comprehensive assessment of usability, scalability, and impact across diverse contexts.

---

[3] https://huggingface.co/collections/liaad/citilink.
[4] https://citilink.inesctec.pt/.

**Acknowledgments.** This work is funded by national funds through FCT – Fundação para a Ciência e a Tecnologia, I.P., under the support UID/50014/2025 (https://doi.org/10.54499/UID/50014/2025). This work is also co-funded by Component 5 - Capitalization and Business Innovation, integrated in the Resilience Dimension of the Recovery and Resilience Plan within the scope of the Recovery and Resilience Mechanism (MRR) of the European Union (EU), framed in the Next Generation EU, for the period 2021 - 2026, within project CitiLink, with reference 2024.07509.IACDC (https://doi.org/10.54499/2024.07509.IACDC). João Canavilhas and Ricardo Campos would also like to acknowledge project Obiajor, with reference 2023.18007.ICDT.

**Disclosure of Interests.** The authors have no competing interests to declare that are relevant to the content of this article.

# References

1. Araujo, J.F.F.E.d., Tejedo-Romero, F.: Local government transparency index: determinants of municipalities' rankings. Int. J. Publ. Sect. Manage. **29**(4), 327–347 (2016)
2. Barari, S., Simko, T.: LocalView, a database of public meetings for the study of local politics and policy-making in the United States. Sci. Data **10**(1), 135 (2023)
3. Campos, R., et al.: CitiLink-Minutes: A Multilayer Annotated Dataset of Municipal Meeting Minutes. In: Anand, A., et al. (eds.) Advances in Information Retrieval. Springer Nature Switzerland, Cham (2026)
4. da Cruz, N.F., Tavares, A.F., Marques, R.C., Jorge, S., de Sousa, L.: Measuring local government transparency. Publ. Manage. Rev. **18**(6), 866–893 (2016). https://doi.org/10.1080/14719037.2015.1051572
5. Hu, Y., Ganter, T., Deilamsalehy, H., Dernoncourt, F., Foroosh, H., Liu, F.: Meetingbank: a benchmark dataset for meeting summarization. In: Proceedings of the 61st Annual Meeting of the Association for Computational Linguistics (Volume 1: Long Papers), pp. 16409–16423 (2023)
6. Jiang, Y., Pang, P.C.I., Wong, D., Kan, H.Y.: Natural language processing adoption in governments and future research directions: a systematic review. Appl. Sci. **13**(22), 12346 (2023)
7. Maxfield Brown, E., Weber, N.: Councils in action: automating the curation of municipal governance data for research. Proc. Assoc. Inf. Sci. Technol. **59**(1), 23–31 (2023)
8. Nielsen, J.: Usability Engineering. Morgan Kaufmann Publishers Inc., San Francisco, CA, USA (1994)
9. Orebe, O.O.: A linguistic-stylistic analysis of selected aspects of minutes of meeting. J. Lang. Teach. Res. **12**(2), 286–292 (2021)
10. Rodrigues, M., Dias, G.P., Teixeira, A.: Knowledge extraction from minutes of portuguese municipalities meetings. Proc. of the FALA, p. 58 (2010)
11. Souza, F., Nogueira, R., Lotufo, R.: BERTimbau: Pretrained BERT Models for Brazilian Portuguese. In: Cerri, R., Prati, R.C. (eds.) BRACIS 2020. LNCS (LNAI), vol. 12319, pp. 403–417. Springer, Cham (2020). https://doi.org/10.1007/978-3-030-61377-8_28

12. van Wijk, P., Marx, M.: Spoken Question Answering on Municipal Council Meetings. In: Proceedings of the European Conference on Information Retrieval (ECIR 2025). IRLab, Informatics Institute, University of Amsterdam (2025)
13. Zhao, Y., Peñuela, A.M., Simperl, E.: User experience in dataset search. In: Plácido da Silva, H., Cipresso, P. (eds.) Computer-Human Interaction Research and Applications, pp. 113–130. Springer, Cham (2025)

# Context Engineering for Agentic Data Science

Rishiraj Saha Roy[(✉)] [iD], Chris Hinze [iD], Luzian Hahn [iD], and Fabian Kuech [iD]

Department of Generative AI, Fraunhofer IIS, 91058 Erlangen, Germany
`{rishiraj.saha.roy,chris.hinze,luzian.hahn,fabian.kuech}@iis.fraunhofer.de`

**Abstract.** We demonstrate CEDAR, an application for automating data science (DS) tasks with an agentic setup. Solving DS problems with LLMs is an underexplored area that has immense market value. The challenges are manifold: task complexities, data sizes, computational limitations, and context restrictions. We show that these can be alleviated via effective context engineering. We first impose structure into the initial prompt with DS-specific input fields, that serve as instructions for the agentic system. The solution is then materialized as an enumerated sequence of interleaved plan and code blocks generated by separate LLM agents, providing a readable structure to the context at any step of the workflow. Function calls for generating these intermediate texts, and for corresponding Python code, ensure that data stays local, and only aggregate statistics and associated instructions are injected into LLM prompts. Fault tolerance and context management are introduced via iterative code generation and smart history rendering. The viability of our agentic data scientist is demonstrated using canonical Kaggle challenges.

**Keywords:** Data science · LLM agents · Context engineering

## 1 Introduction

**Motivation.** In traditional data science (DS), a human expert, the data scientist, writes scripts for entire pipelines, including standard steps like data preprocessing, feature engineering, hyperparameter tuning, and finally computing metrics and visualizing insights. However, this work is tedious and repetitive, and can be significantly optimized with modern LLMs. For example, many users are exploring options like ChatGPT Advanced Data Analysis, where one simply uploads data and articulates entire problems as long prompts.

However, such approaches have several limitations: (i) concrete instructions for real DS projects are more complex than naive prompts; (ii) capabilities of generative models are still limited w.r.t. arbitrary computations; (iii) data files are often very large and cannot simply be uploaded as attachments (Advanced Data Analysis has a limit of 512 MB per file, many Kaggle files are much larger); (iv) there are often privacy concerns and users may feel insecure uploading their


R. Campos et al. (Eds.): ECIR 2026, LNCS 16486, pp. 200–205, 2026.
https://doi.org/10.1007/978-3-032-21321-1_29

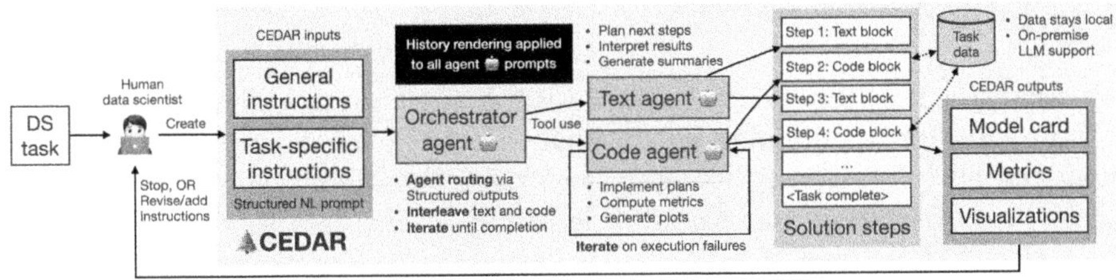


**Fig. 1.** The CEDAR system facilitating a human data scientist's job.

enterprise data to cloud-based LLMs; and (iv) as a solution progresses, simply packing all instructions, text, code, data, and results into the running context makes it unintelligible for most LLMs, and often exceeds context length limits.

**Purpose.** Agentic systems now power many real-world information retrieval (IR) and machine learning (ML) applications, where LLMs perform various roles in complex task pipelines (see, for example, [He et al. (2024)], [Chu et al. (2025)], [Qiu et al. (2024)]). DS is a unique instance of such complexity, tightly coupling IR and ML. Agentic systems with effective context management can alleviate most of the above problems for DS tasks. This has become an active research area [Maojun et al. (2025), Jing et al. (2024)], where the best systems usually achieve impressive results via sophisticated prompt chaining. But the user does not get a clear idea into how the task is actually solved (for instance, see [Grosnit et al. (2024)], [Guo et al. (2024)], [Hong et al. (2024)]). The closest work to ours' is the very recent Jupyter Agent 2 [Colle et al. (2025)] from Hugging Face, but it does not run locally and data uploads are very slow. The purpose of our system CEDAR (Context Engineering for Data science with Agent Routing) is to bring transparency and simplicity into DS solutions with LLMs. Pointers to code and other paper artifacts are available via our extended version at https://arxiv.org/abs/2601.06606.

**Audience.** The app can be used by beginner to expert-level IR, ML, NLP, and AI practitioners. IR and ML basics help, but there is no prerequisite of core DS knowledge to interpret the workflow: each solution step has natural language (NL) explanations. Beginners can get a feel of how basic data science tasks are solved. Intermediate users can contrast the faithfulness of the generated solution to the original intent, and gain insights into how agentic systems can be built for simplifying DS. Experts can scrutinize LLM-generated code snippets, and whether the generated solution mimics the code base for a human data scientist.

**Scope.** Our system can solve basic data science tasks from Kaggle. The current requirements are simply to have a clearly articulated goal and well-defined data.

# 2   Method

We adopt the very recent approach of *context engineering*, collectively referring to strategies for maintaining an optimal set of tokens during LLM inference, including all information that may land there outside of prompts [Anthropic (2025)] An overview of our workflow is in Fig. 1. The data scientist formulates the task as a structured prompt, that is passed on to an orchestrator agent. This agent routes text and code generation requests to sub-agents as tools, to generate a readable solution with short steps. The human inspects final outputs and revises instructions for further iterations, if necessary. Key ideas are elaborated below.

**Structured Prompts.** To relieve the user from creating verbose prompts containing every pertinent task detail, we create a structured form that covers key aspects of most DS tasks. We split the project summary into high-level *general instructions* (estimated number of solution steps, expected number of plots, verbosity of plans, etc.) and *task-specific instructions* (with items like `Task description`, `Data description`, `Data location`, `Metrics`, `Inputs`, `Outputs`, and `Special instructions`). This makes DS tasks more understandable to LLMs.

**Interleaved Text and Code.** Instead of expecting the LLM to directly emit a final solution, say, like an optimized set of metrics, we make the system generate a human-readable workflow with succinct steps starting from data loading and all the way to model card generation. Each *"Step"* consists of a plan and a corresponding code snippet that implements this plan. This flow simulates a Jupyter notebook and gives a human-readable structure to the context at all times. We then have an output with scrutable and reusable components like plans, code snippets, data snapshots, error traces, and intermediate plots.

**LLM Agents.** Such a workflow is enabled by the use of agents, i.e. different LLM instantiations with distinct prompts. We have three agents: a main orchestrator, and sub-agents for text and code generation. The orchestrator decides whether to invoke the text/code generator (routing), or that the task is complete. The calls to the sub-agents are usually alternating, but special situations may need consecutive text or code blocks. All agents receive the same context: the project summary, text and code snippets so far, and outputs of code snippet execution (see history rendering below). They only vary in their responses: the main agent emits a sub-agent call, while the sub-agents emit text and code as per the current state of the workflow.

**Tool Calls.** To prevent the orchestrator from generating free-form output that needs to be parsed, we implement the code and text generators as distinct *functions* so that they become *tools* to be called by the main agent [OpenAI (2024a)]. This has been a special feature in modern LLMs that highly facilitates building apps chaining LLMs. Further, to prevent hallucinated outputs like `write_code` when the correct function name is `request_code`, we use *structured outputs* by

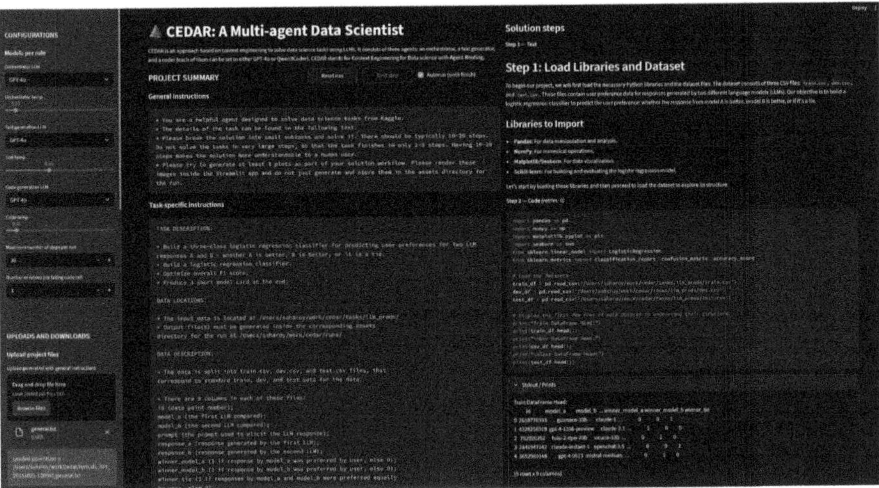

**Fig. 2.** A screenshot of our CEDAR application, solving a Kaggle competition.

forcing the orchestrator to output JSON as per our schema [OpenAI (2024b)]. Generating Python *code for computations* frees us from dependence on LLMs' math capabilities. Another significant advantage is that *data stays local*: the code operates on local data, and only snapshots and aggregate statistics are passed on to LLMs. We support on-premise LLMs, so that even such data digests need not leave the user's system. We allow for *iterative code execution*: when the execution of a particular code block fails, the coder tool is prompted again with the current *error trace* and a request to accordingly *rewrite* the code. This step adds robustness and enables recovery from name/type mismatches and missed imports, for instance.

**History Rendering.** This module takes the list of all blocks so far (instructions, text, code, outputs, errors) as input and converts them into a compact, LLM-friendly text summary as follows: (i) it appends user instructions; (ii) it numbers each text/code block (`Text #3` or `Code #5`) for clarity and appends them in full as these are not very long (only adding outputs and not raw code loses semantics). *Context bottlenecks* are code outputs and error messages, as handled next; (iii) for past code blocks, it adds only those that ran successfully; (iv) for these *"success"* blocks, it adds only *heads* of outputs as they carry the most vital information; (v) if the latest code block resulted in error, it adds the *tail* of the traceback instead, as it pinpoints the error most specifically; (vi) if the history so rendered exceeds $10k$ characters (configurable), only the most recent $10k$ are kept. This compressed history is then passed on as context to the agent being invoked at any given moment. Due to this highly *heterogeneous context* in DS tasks (text, code, standard error, standard output streams, potentially plot images), text summarizers are not applicable for context pruning in CEDAR.

# 3    Demonstration Walkthrough

**Using the App.** Figure 2 shows CEDAR solving a canonical Kaggle competition on LLM fine-tuning [Chiang et al. (2024)]. A user first selects LLMs for orchestrator, text generator, and coder agents (`GPT-4o` via API (`GPT5` with internal model routing adds substantial runtime), or `Qwen3-Coder` 30B [Qwen (2025)] locally via `ollama` [Ollama (2025)]). Next, general (green) and task-specific instructions (blue) need to be uploaded, instantly rendered as the "project summary" in the broad middle panel. The broad right panel renders the solution. Qwen3-Coder was chosen as it was fine-tuned specifically for agentic coding. The user selects between *"Next step"* for inspecting a step at a time, or *"Autorun"* to see the full solution at once (typically takes $\simeq$ 3 mins). There are usually $10 - 20$ steps, configurable via general instructions. Steps can be *"Reset"* at any time.

**Configurations and Debugging.** The leftmost panel provides several knobs: (i) temperatures for each of our agents $(0 - 1)$, to transition between response repeatability and diversity; (ii) maximum solution steps (default 30, suitable for most Kaggle tasks); (iii) maximum code retries (default 3, solves most basic errors) can be set). An autorun trace shows running summaries for history rendering (the unpruned context is $\simeq 20k$ characters towards the end, we prune it to $10k$ characters). If default tool calls fail (often the case for Qwen3), we use *tool emulation*, forcing JSON outputs. Diagnostics for GPT-4o API keys and Qwen3 server connections help resolve authentication and network issues, respectively. The context truncation limit ($10k$ characters) and the head/tail size of standard output (20 lines) and error can also be set via code.

**Assets Directory.** An assets' directory can be explored any time during or after the run: it stores the structured prompt, generated plots (also rendered online in the app), metrics, the model card and debug logs. We allow for *exporting* the solution as JSON, Markdown, or IPython (making the solution editable). and *importing* a saved run as JSON, so that an unfinished run can be continued from where we left off.

**Backend and Frontend.** Our backend is in pure Python and does not use any special agent libraries. The frontend is built with Streamlit [Streamlit (2025)]. CEDAR can run on any laptop, as long as the RAM allows for loading the data. Qwen3-coder 30B is hosted on GPU server ($4 \times 48$GB NVIDIA Ada 6000 RTX, 512 GB RAM, 64 virtual cores).

# 4    Concluding Remarks

Through our contribution, we show that building an agentic DS solution pays off in the long run: the role of the human data scientist shifts from tediously scripting repetitive workflows to more cognitively rewarding tasks like structuring requirements, scrutinizing solutions, and suggesting optimizations.

Nevertheless, our focus here was on context engineering: agent complexity in CEDAR is still rudimentary, and natural next steps would introduce independent agents that inspect a solution for faithfulness, and iterate over workflows towards improving target metrics.

**Acknowledgements.** This work has been funded by the Free State of Bavaria in the DSgenAI project (Grant No.: RMF-SG20-3410-2-18-4). We thank NLP team members at Fraunhofer IIS for useful inputs at various stages of this work.

**Disclosure of Interests.** The authors have no competing interests to declare that are relevant to the content of this article.

# References


Engineering Anthropic. Effective context engineering for AI agents (2025). https://www.anthropic.com/engineering/effective-context-engineering-for-ai-agents

Chiang, W., et al.: LLM Classification Finetuning (2024). https://kaggle.com/competitions/llm-classification-finetuning. Kaggle

Chu, Z., et al.: LLM agents for education: Advances and applications. arXiv (2025)

Colle, B., Yukhymenko, H., von Werra, L.: Jupyter Agents: training LLMs to reason with notebooks (2025). https://huggingface.co/spaces/lvwerra/jupyter-agent-2

Grosnit, A., et al.: Large language models orchestrating structured reasoning achieve Kaggle grandmaster level. arXiv, arXiv–2411 (2024)

Guo, S., Deng, C., Wen, Y., Chen, H., Chang, Y., Wang, J.: DS-Agent: Automated data science by empowering large language models with case-based reasoning. arXiv preprint arXiv:2402.17453 (2024)

He, J., et al.: Frontiers of large language model-based agentic systems-construction, efficacy and safety. In: Proceedings of the 33rd ACM International Conference on Information and Knowledge Management, pp. 5526–5529 (2024)

Hong, S., et al.: Data interpreter: An LLM agent for data science. arXiv preprint arXiv:2402.18679 (2024)

Jing, L.: DSBench: How Far Are Data Science Agents from Becoming Data Science Experts? arXiv preprint arXiv:2409.07703 (2024)

Maojun, S., et al.: A survey on large language modelbased agents for statistics and data science. Am. Stat. **2025**, 1–21 (2025)

Team Ollama. qwen3 (2025). https://ollama.com/library/qwen3-coder

Team OpenAI. Function calling (2024a). https://platform.openai.com/docs/guides/function-calling

Team OpenAI. Structured model outputs (2024b). https://platform.openai.com/docs/guides/structured-outputs

Qiu, J., et al.: LLM-based agentic systems in medicine and healthcare. Nat. Mach. Intell. **6**(12), 1418–1420 (2024)

Team Qwen. Qwen3 Technical Report. arXiv:2505.09388 [cs.CL] https://arxiv.org/abs/2505.09388 (2025)

Team Streamlit. (2025).https://streamlit.io

# Creating Specialized RAG-Based Search Engines Using the Open Web Index

Alexander Nussbaumer[1(✉)] [iD], Michael Dinzinger[2] [iD], Sebastian Heineking[3] [iD], Gijs Hendriksen[4] [iD], Felix Holz[1] [iD], Saber Zerhoudi[2] [iD], Martin Potthast[5,6,7] [iD], and Michael Granitzer[2,8] [iD]

[1] Graz University of Technology, Rechbauerstraße 12, 8010 Graz, Austria
alexander.nussbaumer@tugraz.at
[2] University of Passau, Innstraße 33, 94032 Passau, Germany
[3] Leipzig University, Augustusplatz 10, 04109 Leipzig, Germany
[4] Radboud University, Toernooiveld 212, 6525 EC Nijmegen, The Netherlands
[5] University of Kassel, Wilhelmshöher Allee 71–73, 34121 Kassel, Germany
[6] hessian.AI, Landwehrstraße 50A, 64293 Darmstadt, Germany
[7] ScaDS.AI, Humboldtstraße 25, 04105 Leipzig, Germany
[8] IT:U Austria, Freistädter Straße 400, 4040 Linz, Austria

**Abstract.** This paper presents a concept and supporting technology for building RAG-based specialized search engines using open-source frameworks and open web data. The Open Web Index (OWI) provides openly accessible web data, while the modular MOSAIC framework is designed to integrate topical OWI partitions obtained to create search applications tailored to specific use cases. MOSAIC-RAG extends this framework with features based on Large Language Models (LLM), such as summarization or re-ranking. Using this infrastructure, special-purpose and domain-specific search applications can easily be developed and experimented with. For demonstration purposes, we present three example applications in the topical domains of science, health, and arts.

**Keywords:** Open Web Index · Specialized Search Engine · MOSAIC

## 1 Introduction

Web search is essential for retrieving information across various domains, from academia to industry. The majority of widely used search engines, however, are proprietary with limited access to their data and retrieval functionality. With Retrieval-Augmented Generation (RAG), another layer was added between the user and the underlying index of web documents. While RAG has advantages in the form of new interaction modes and more precise query specification, it further limits transparency in the search process and raises additional concerns around the reliability of generated responses and source verification [5]. This underscores the necessity for open-source frameworks that offer both free access to web data and options for customized web search [2].

© The Author(s), under exclusive license to Springer Nature Switzerland AG 2026
R. Campos et al. (Eds.): ECIR 2026, LNCS 16486, pp. 206–211, 2026.
https://doi.org/10.1007/978-3-032-21321-1_30

We have developed a concept for building search applications based on the Open Web Index (OWI) and the open-source search framework MOSAIC [3], which supports retrieval over web data obtained from the OWI. The OWI is both publicly available as well as transparent about crawling, the metadata it extracts from web pages, and how these pages are indexed [4]. It allows to specify and download index partitions related to a topic or domain, or with specific characteristics. MOSAIC enables searching for web pages in such index partitions. Due to its modular design, MOSAIC facilitates the custom development of search applications. In particular, the RAG extension of MOSAIC makes it possible to easily add features based on Large Language Models (LLMs), such as summarization, re-ranking, and metadata analysis.

While public efforts like Common Crawl[1] offer large-scale access to web data, they do not address some key requirements of real-world applications: the data is updated infrequently, and its general-purpose nature makes it difficult to apply on fine-grained use cases. As Hendriksen et al. [4] note, it is often more effective to crawl and index a focused, task-specific subset of the web rather than working with massive but unwieldy datasets like Common Crawl.

In this paper, we present a concept and technology based on the OWI and MOSAIC that allows to build and configure RAG-based specialized search engines. For demonstration purposes, three such search engines have been created in the domain of science, health, and arts.

## 2   Open Web Index

The Open Web Index provides an open, transparent, and continuously updated web-scale index to support research, innovation, and public-interest applications. In addition to legal and ethical considerations, the construction of a web-scale index comes with a broad set of technical challenges: large-scale crawling, efficient pre-processing to extract general purpose information from daily crawls, and robust systems for data distribution—all of which require significant infrastructure and software support [1]. The technical pipeline of creating the Open Web Index comprises three main stages:

(1) Crawling, performed by a distributed crawler infrastructure that continuously collects multilingual web content.
(2) Pre-processing, which cleans and enriches crawled data by extracting the main content and generating metadata such as language information, domain labels, and quality scores.
(3) Indexing, which transforms the processed text into inverted file indexes using the Common Index File Format (CIFF) for efficient retrieval.

All of the above steps are designed for dynamic resource scaling to (1) handle daily crawls of multiple terrabytes and (2) run on different types of hardware from a single computer to multiple nodes in a high-performance computing (HPC) cluster.

---

[1] https://commoncrawl.org/.

The OWI publishes daily language-specific data shards and thematic subsets (like legal or directory-based pages). The datasets are accessible via the OWI Dashboard, providing metadata summaries, download options, and takedown management.Each dataset includes Parquet-formatted metadata and CIFF-based indexes, ensuring efficient analytics and reproducible retrieval experiments. The OWILIX command line tool offers tailored access to the data by supporting SQL-like queries that filter larger datasets to the specific needs of a given application.[2] At this stage, the OWI does not contain relevance assessments. In the future, however, subsets of the OWI with assessments will be published as corpora for research.[3] OWI is currently driven by the European research initiative OpenWebSearch.EU.[4]

## 3   MOSAIC and MOSAIC-RAG

MOSAIC[5] is a modular open-source search framework designed for vertical web exploration [3]. MOSAIC enables domain-specific search by integrating index partitions downloaded from the OWI. Using the OWILIX tool, CIFF and Parquet files are copied into the resource directory of MOSAIC. After integrating an index partition, a search query is processed in two steps. Using Lucene, the query terms are searched in the index that was imported from the CIFF file. The initial result is then filtered by metadata available for each web document in the Parquet file, such as language or topic. Finally, the search result is exposed through a REST API, where all the metadata including the cleaned full text is delivered.

MOSAIC-RAG[6] is an extension to MOSAIC that takes search results from MOSAIC and adds further processing using LLMs, such as summarization of individual web documents, summarization of the all results, re-ranking, sentiment analysis, and other analyses based on the meta data and full text [6]. For each of these functions a configurable module is available. Using these modules the user can create a data processing pipeline by sequencing these modules. Each of the modules can be configured especially regarding the LLM or algorithm that is used. Instead of binding a specific LLM to the models, the models use a LiteLLM[7] access point, where the LLM is selected and where the actual calculations are done. A set of different re-ranking modules are available, which enables ranking based on different strategies, such as BM25, vector embeddings, or LLMs.

A federated search engine approach is achieved by retrieving search results for a single search query from multiple MOSAIC instances. Additionally, MOSAIC-RAG can also retrieve search results from a Chroma instance that contains the

---

[2] https://opencode.it4i.eu/openwebsearcheu-public/owi-cli.

[3] https://openwebindex.eu/owler/corpora.

[4] https://openwebsearch.eu/.

[5] https://opencode.it4i.eu/openwebsearcheu-public/mosaic/.

[6] https://opencode.it4i.eu/openwebsearcheu-public/mosaic-rag/.

[7] https://www.litellm.ai/.

web index data imported from Parquet files. Vector embeddings used by Chroma are partially available in the data from the OWI or have to be calculated before the import. The RAG features are used to transform the search results from multiple sources to a unified result by re-ranking and summarization. This is achieved by storing all results in an internal data frame with the full text in one of the columns. The re-ranking module uses the full text of all the search result items to create a new sequence and another module is used to shorten then the number of items if needed. Finally, a summarization is applied on the final search result. The overall concept is depicted in Fig. 1.

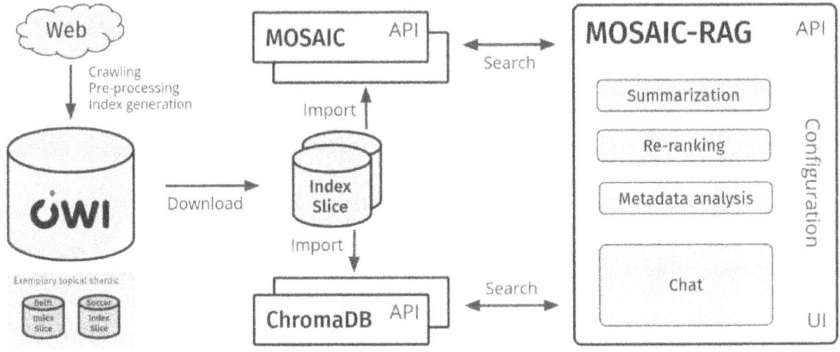


**Fig. 1.** Conceptual design of creating specialized search engines.

The federated and distributed approach also allows to scale up the total size of the index. Typical index partitions for one MOSAIC instance can contain a few dozens of millions of pages with up to 100 Gib total index size. By distributing index partitions over multiple servers, the index can be enlarged many times over. Also the RAG features are distributed, as the calculations with LLMs are performed on different servers accessed with LiteLLM.

## 4   Search Applications

To demonstrate how MOSAIC can be used to create specialized search engines, we have developed three search applications[8] that enable retrieval of web documents in the domains of science, health, and arts. The creation of each search application follows three main steps. First, an index partition is retrieved from the OWI that contains only web documents related to the target domain (science, health, or arts in our case). This is accomplished by selecting OWI documents that are tagged with the corresponding Curlie labels.[9] The Curlie directory is maintained by volunteer editors and contains a categorization of both high-level

---

domains as well as specific URLs. This directory is in turn applied in the creation process of the OWI by assigning categories to a webpage if either its full URL or its domain was labeled by the volunteers. Second, the resulting index is imported into MOSAIC, which enables searching within this specialized partition. As an alternative setup, the index can also be imported into ChromaDB, where vector embeddings of the full texts are added. Third, MOSAIC-RAG is configured to use MOSAIC and ChromaDB as the underlying search engine. In addition, summarization, re-ranking, and metadata analysis are integrated into the search process.

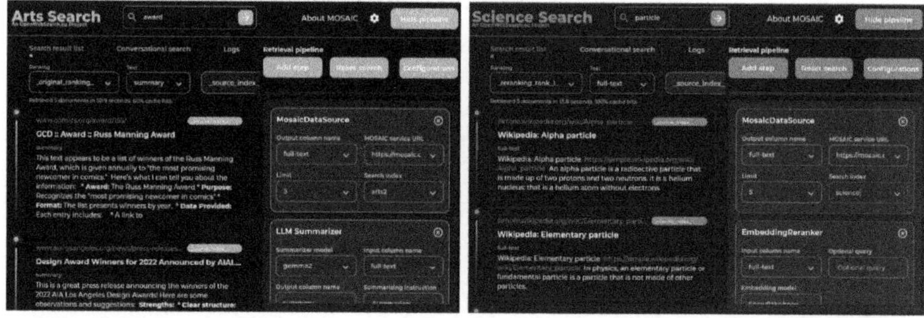

**Fig. 2.** Two search applications (Arts Search and Science Search) as configurations of MOSAIC-RAG using OWI index partitions.

## 5    Conclusion

This paper presents a concept and demonstration applications of creating RAG-based specialized search engines using the open-data and open-source frameworks of the Open Web Index and MOSAIC. This concept is built on a pipeline of web crawling, data pre-processing, index generation, downloading index partitions, searching within these partitions, and applying LLM-based search features. In this way, a broad variety of specialized search engines can be created with ease. Moreover, in this way experimental settings can be established, which allows to try out and compare different web data sets or RAG features. Future work will focus on user studies exploring the applicability of creating such search engines, the benefit of respective RAG features, and quality of retrieved information.

**Acknowledgments.** This work has received funding from the European Union's Horizon Europe research and innovation program under grant agreement No. 101070014 (OpenWebSearch.EU, https://doi.org/10.3030/101070014)

**Disclosure of Interests.** The authors have no competing interests to declare that are relevant to the content of this article.

# References


1. Granitzer, M., et al.: OpenWebSearch.eu - Building an Open Web Index on EuroHPC JU Infrastructures. Procedia Comput. Sci. **255**(C), 43–52 (2025). https://doi.org/10.1016/j.procs.2025.02.259
2. Granitzer, M., et al.: Impact and development of an Open Web Index for open web search. J. Am. Soc. Inf. Sci. **75**(5), 512–520 (2023). https://doi.org/10.1002/asi.24818
3. Gürtl, S., Nussbaumer, A., Gütl, C.: Supporting Vertical Web Search and Customized Search Applications with the Modular and Open Framework MOSAIC. In: Farzana, S.M., et al. (eds.) 2nd International Workshop on Open Web Search (WOWS 2025), pp. 50–61. No. 4137 in CEUR Workshop Proceedings, Aachen (2025). https://ceur-ws.org/Vol-4137/WOWS_2025_paper_5.pdf
4. Hendriksen, G., et al.: The Open Web Index: Crawling and Indexing the Web for Public Use. In: European Conference on Information Retrieval, pp. 130–143. Springer, Cham (2024). https://doi.org/10.1007/978-3-031-56069-9_10
5. Hersh, W.: Search still matters: information retrieval in the era of generative AI. J. Am. Med. Inf. Assoc. **31**(9), 2159–2161 (2024). https://doi.org/10.1093/jamia/ocae014
6. Holz, F., Scharf, D., Nussbaumer, A., Gürtl, S.: Adding retrieval augmented generation to the mosaic framework. In: Proceedings 7th International Open Search Symposium (OSSYM 2025), pp. 71–74 (2025).https://doi.org/10.5281/zenodo.17209496

# CLEF Overview Papers

# CLEF 2026 SimpleText Track
## Simplify Scientific Text (and Nothing More)


Liana Ermakova[1], Hosein Azarbonyad[2], Jan Bakker[3],
Gautam Kishore Shahi[4], Benjamin Vendeville[1], and Jaap Kamps[3]([✉])

[1] Université de Bretagne Occidentale, HCTI, Brest, France
`liana.ermakova@univ-brest.fr, benjamin.vendeville@univ-brest.fr`
[2] Elsevier, Amsterdam, The Netherlands
`h.azarbonyad@elsevier.com`
[3] University of Amsterdam, Amsterdam, The Netherlands
`j.bakker@uva.nl, kamps@uva.nl`
[4] University of Duisburg-Essen, Essen, Germany
`gautam.shahi@uni-due.de`



**Abstract.** Over the last few years, the SimpleText Track has created an active community of NLP and IR researchers collaborating to improve access to scientific text. Its benchmarks on scientific passage retrieval, scientific terminology detection and explanation, and scientific text simplification have become standard references. Following a similar track design from 2021 to 2024, we introduced substantial changes to the track's structure and tasks in 2025. We plan to continue this successful setup in 2026, plus add a new (pilot) task on research area classification of scientific papers. Hence, the CLEF 2026 SimpleText track will contain the following 3 tasks. Task 1 (*Text Simplification*): simplify scientific text. Task 2 (*Controlled Creativity*): identify and avoid hallucination. Task 3 (*Research Area Classification*): classification of scientific articles by research area.


## 1 Introduction

Scientific literacy has never been more critical. Reliable scientific information enables individuals to navigate a world in which misinformation, disinformation, and unsupported claims are difficult to avoid. While the value of objective scientific knowledge is widely recognized, the general public rarely engages directly with scientific sources. This raises a central question: how can we improve the accessibility of scientific information?

For instance, biomedical research can directly influence individuals' health-related decisions. Yet, the most reliable and current biomedical sources are often written in highly specialized language and presume substantial domain knowledge, which limits their accessibility for the general public. Scientific text simplification offers a promising approach to addressing this challenge by making such content easier to understand. However, training modern neural models to simplify scientific documents is a demanding task that depends on the availability of

**Table 1.** CLEF 2025 SimpleText submission statistics

| | Task 1 | | Task 2 | | | Task 3 |
|---|---|---|---|---|---|---|
| | 1.1 | 1.2 | 2.1 | 2.2 | 2.3 | |
| Teams | 16 | 13 | 7 | 7 | 2 | 1 |
| Runs | 83 | 49 | 31 | 31 | 4 | 1 |
| Teams | 18 | | 8 | | | 1 |
| Runs | 132 | | 66 | | | 1 |
| Teams | 19 | | | | | |
| Runs | 199 | | | | | |

high-quality training data. Likewise, robust evaluation of these models requires carefully designed benchmarks, including detailed human assessments and systematic analyses of the remaining limitations of generative summarization and simplification models.

Our track is motivated by a concrete use case of clear societal relevance, rather than treating application as an afterthought. This focus distinguishes it from earlier text simplification research, which primarily examined lexical and grammatical complexity in isolation.

The rest of this paper is structured in the following way. Section 2 discusses the precious CLEF 2025 track experience. Section 3 details each of the CLEF 2026 tasks. Section 4 provides a final summary of the CLEF 2026 track.

## 2    Retrospective of CLEF SimpleText Track

The CLEF SimpleText track aims at improving accessibility to scientific information for everyone, both in terms of information retrieval and natural language processing. The workshop at CLEF 2021 [7] and tracks at CLEF 2022-2024 [9–11] resulted in research community and test collections for improving access to scientific information for everyone. Specifically, test collections for retrieving relevant (and accessible) scientific text [10], for simplifying the language used in scientific documents without compromising the accuracy of the information [8], for making complex concepts more understandable to a broader audience [13], and aggregating information across documents [5].

In 2025, after running the same setup for three years and creating extensive test collections for each task, we revamped the track setup. We promoted the main text simplification task to Task 1, and introduced an extensive biomedical corpus, based on aligned abstracts and plain language summaries, called Cochrane-auto [1]. We also elevated the earlier analysis of overgeneration and human information distortion evaluation to a dedicated Task 2. We promoted the reuse of data from previous years as Task 3. This led to a new track setup that we continue for a second year in 2026. See details in the CLEF 2025 SimpleText track overview [6], and the CEUR task overviews for Task 1 [3] and Task 2 [15].

**Complex document (Summary CD006194)**

Fifteen heterogeneous trials, involving 1022 adults with dorsally displaced and potentially or evidently unstable distal radial fractures, were included. While all trials compared external fixation versus plaster cast immobilisation, there was considerable variation especially in terms of patient characteristics and interventions. Methodological weaknesses among these trials included lack of allocation concealment and inadequate outcome assessment.

External fixation maintained reduced fracture positions (redisplacement requiring secondary treatment: 7/356 versus 51/338 (data from 9 trials); relative risk 0.17, 95% confidence interval 0.09 to 0.32) and prevented late collapse and malunion compared with plaster cast immobilisation. There was insufficient evidence to confirm a superior overall functional or clinical result for the external fixation group. External fixation was associated with a high number of complications, such as pin-track infection, but many of these were minor. Probably, some complications could have been avoided using a different surgical technique for pin insertion. There was insufficient evidence to establish a difference between the two groups in serious complications such as reflex sympathetic dystropy: 25/384 versus 17/347 (data from 11 trials); relative risk 1.31, 95% confidence interval 0.74 to 2.32.

There is some evidence to support the use of external fixation for dorsally displaced fractures of the distal radius in adults. Though there is insufficient evidence to confirm a better functional outcome, external fixation reduces redisplacement, gives improved anatomical results and most of the excess surgically-related complications are minor.

**Simple document (Plain English Summary)**

Fifteen trials, involving 1022 adults with potentially or evidently unstable fractures, were included. While all trials compared external fixation versus plaster cast immobilisation, there was considerable variation in their characteristics especially in terms of patient characteristics and the method of external fixation.

The complications, such a pin tract infection, associated with external fixation were many but were generally minor. Serious complications occurred in both groups.

The review concludes that there is some evidence to support the use of external fixation for these fractures. The review found that external fixation reduced fracture redisplacement that prompted further treatment and generally improved final anatomical outcome.

**Fig. 1.** A complex-simple document pair from Cochrane-auto.

A total of 74 teams registered for our SimpleText track at CLEF 2025. A total of 18 teams submitted 198 runs in total for Tasks 1 and 2, plus an additional Task 3 paper on reusing the data from 2024. The active participation statistics are shown in Table 1.[1]

## 3   CLEF 2026 SimpleText Tasks

### 3.1   Task 1: Text Simplification

The *Text Simplification* task aims to *simplify scientific text*.

Main innovation in 2026 For 2025, we created a new CLEF SimpleText corpus based on biomedical literature abstracts and lay summaries from Cochrane systematic reviews, called Cochrane-auto [1]. This corpus is constructed following the exact construction of the existing Wiki-auto and Newsela-auto [12,17]. Cochrane-auto is a true document-level text simplification, with more variation (sentence merge, order swaps) that takes the discourse structure into account.

---

[1] These are teams, rather than individual researchers, and include only valid submissions at the evaluation deadline. At the time of writing, we have 30 participants (289 submissions) in the Codabench for Task 1, and 14 participants (232 submissions) in the Codabench for Task 2.

Paragraph-level and sentence-level data are carefully realigned and restricted to matching paragraphs and sentences.

For 2026, we also crawled and processed the matching Cochrane abstracts and plain language summaries in all other available languages [similar to 2]. We have reasonable coverage in: English (en), Spanish (es), French (fr), Farsi (fa), Chinese (zh), Japanese (ja), Portuguese (pt), Korean (ko), Thai (th), German (de), Russian (ru), Malay (ms), and Croatian (hr). The coverage of Spanish is 100% of the English abstract and sentence pairs, and the languages are sorted by coverage. We can offer a range of monolingual text simplification tasks in all these languages (where, in many cases, no other corpora exist). We can also provide cross-language text simplification, both from English to another simplified language and from another complex language to simplified English.

The aligned references also free the human annotation capacity to analyze and annotate samples of the evaluation data for a wide range of information distortion (also providing ground truth for Task 2).

Description This is the core NLP task of the track, and we continue with both sentence-level (*Task 1.1*) and document-level (*Task 1.2*) scientific text simplification. The main innovation is the large new corpus we constructed in 2025, along with a shift to the biomedical domain and the possible extension to other languages in 2026.

Data We constructed a large scientific text simplification corpus by realigning abstracts and lay summaries at the sentence, paragraph, and document levels [1]. An example of a pair is shown in Fig. 1. We also have section-level segmentation of the data [2], and we have identical data in other languages. Depending on interest, we can offer specific other languages as a mixed-language task.

Evaluation We will use standard automatic evaluation metrics (SARI, BLUE, LENS, BERTscore, etc.) in conjunction with human assessments of small samples of submissions by translation students and professionals.

## 3.2   Task 2: Controlled Creativity

The *Controlled Creativity* task aims to *identify and avoid hallucination*.

Main innovation in 2026 To our surprise, the SimpleText track has collected a massive amount of spurious (or over-)generation content from its participants. Table 2 shows an example output simplification of one of the participating teams.[2] Our text simplification setup has sources, predictions, and references that are closely aligned and in the same language, in order to study source attribution and creative variation, as well as to identify and avoid what is informally called "hallucinations."

Description *Task 2.1* is to identify creative generation, at the abstract or document level. We will provide realistic system output from participants in earlier years. The task is to detect what sentences are fully grounded on source input

---

[2] For 2025, a total of 20 out of 70 submissions (29%) have spurious whole sentences in at least 25% of the input sentences. In fact, 15 (21%) submissions are in at least 50% of the input sentences.

**Table 2.** Example of a participant's output versus input: ~~deletions~~, <u>insertions</u>, and whole sentence insertions

> *CD012520* ~~*We included*~~ *8 . 'We looked at seven* ~~*cluster-randomised trials with*~~ *<u>studies where groups of people were randomly assigned to different treatments</u> . These studies involved 42,489* ~~*patient participants*~~ *<u>patients</u> from 129 hospitals* ~~*,*~~ ~~*conducted*~~ *in Australia , the UK , China , and the Netherlands .* <u>*'*</u> |~~*Health*~~ *<u>Okay , everyone , so in this study , we had a group of participants who were health professional participants . This means we had people working in healthcare . The text tells us that this group included nurses , doctors (</u>* ~~*numbers not specified*~~ *<u>that 's the medical professionals )</u>* ~~*included nursing*~~ *,* ~~*medical*~~ *and allied health professionals . <u>Think of allied health professionals as other healthcare workers who are n't doctors or nurses , but still provide important services – like physical therapists , occupational therapists , or dieticians , for example . The text also notes that it does n't specify exactly * how many * people from each of these professions participated</u> .* |~~*Multifaceted implementation interventions probably make*~~ *'<u>Complex sets of actions designed to put research findings into practice</u> likely have little* ~~*or*~~ *<u>to no</u>* ~~*difference in reducing*~~ *<u>impact on lowering the</u>* ~~*risk*~~ *<u>chances</u> of death , disability <u>,</u> or* ~~*dependency*~~ *<u>needing help from others ,</u> compared to* ~~*no intervention*~~ *<u>doing nothing</u> ( RR 0.93 , 95 % CI 0.85 to 1.02 ; 3 trials ; 51* ~~*clusters*~~ *<u>groups</u> ; 1228* ~~*participants*~~ *<u>people</u> ; moderate-certainty evidence ) , and probably* ~~*make little or no difference*~~ *<u>do n't significantly change how long patients stay in the hospital</u> compared to* ~~*hospital length of stay*~~ ~~*compared with no intervention*~~ *<u>doing nothing</u> ( difference in absolute change 1.5 days ; 95 % CI -0.5 to 3.5 ; 1 trial ; 19* ~~*clusters*~~ *<u>groups</u> ; 1804* ~~*participants*~~ *<u>people</u> ; moderate-certainty evidence ) .* <u>*'*</u> |~~*We*~~ *<u>7 . 'We</u> do* ~~*not*~~ *<u>n't</u> know if a multifaceted implementation intervention <u>( a complex strategy to put something into practice )</u> compared to no intervention* ~~*result in*~~ *changes* ~~*to*~~ *resource use <u>( how money or supplies are used )</u> or health professionals ' knowledge because no* ~~*included*~~ *studies* ~~*collected*~~ *<u>measured</u> these* ~~*outcomes*~~ *<u>things</u> .* <u>*'*</u> |...

(a) without and (b) with access to the source sentences, and hence also label those introducing significant new content. Task 2.1 is a post-hoc identification or explanation task.

*Task 2.2* attempts to mimic the laborious human evaluation by LLMs. As text-generation-based automatic evaluation measures (such as BLEU and SARI), which rely on text overlap, are notoriously imprecise, we need to conduct human evaluations of fluency, simplicity, and factuality. Usually, these annotations are not reusable. We use them as the training and test data for systems to automatically detect and annotate such information distortion in real CLEF submissions. The manual annotations of CLEF 2025 Task 1 submissions can be reused as ground truth data for information distortion classification in CLEF 2026 Task 2.

*Task 2.3* is to avoid creative generation and perform grounded generation by design. This mimics Task 1 above and asks for the submission of pairs of runs with/without source attribution by design.

Data In running the SimpleText track over the last three years, we collected many realistic and representative predictions in the run submission. For Task 2.1, we will select a sample of models and predictions prone to spurious generation. We have large-scale data with realigned sentences that lack support in the source, to be used as training data. For Task 2.2, real 2025 submissions with human annotations following a simplified version of [16] will be used. For Task 2.3, we follow the setup of Task 1: Text Simplification above, but request paired runs.

**Table 3.** DFG Subject Area 44: *Computer Science, Systems and Electrical Engineering*

| | Class | Subject Area |
|---|---|---|
| Systems Engin. | 4.41-01 | Automation, Mechatronics, Control Systems, Intelligent Technical Systems, Robotics |
| | 4.41-02 | Measurement Systems |
| | 4.41-03 | Microsystems |
| | 4.41-04 | Traffic and Transport Systems, Intelligent and Automated Traffic |
| | 4.41-05 | Human Factors, Ergonomics, Human-Machine Systems |
| | 4.41-06 | Biomedical Systems Technology |
| Elec. Eng. and IT | 4.42-01 | Electronic Semiconductors, Components and Circuits, Integrated Systems, Sensor Technology, Theoretical Electrical Engineering |
| | 4.42-02 | Communication Technology and Networks, High-Frequency Technology and Photonic Systems, Signal Processing and Machine Learning for Information Technology |
| | 4.42-03 | Electrical Energy Systems, Power Management, Power Electronics, Electrical Machines and Drives |
| | 4.42-04 | Hardware Systems and Architectures for Information Technology and Artificial Intelligence, Quantum Engineering Systems |
| Computer Science | 4.43-01 | Theoretical Computer Science |
| | 4.43-02 | Software Engineering and Programming Languages |
| | 4.43-03 | Security and Dependability, Operating, Communication and Distributed Systems |
| | 4.43-04 | Artificial Intelligence and Machine Learning Methods |
| | 4.43-05 | Image and Language Processing, Computer Graphics and Visualisation, Human Computer Interaction, Ubiquitous and Wearable Computing |
| | 4.43-06 | Data Management, Data-Intensive Systems, Computer Science Methods in Business Informatics |
| | 4.43-07 | Computer Architecture, Embedded and Massively Parallel Systems |

Evaluation Task 2.1 is essentially a sentence label task, evaluated in the standard way (Precision, Recall, F1). We have large-scale synthetic labels, and will manually supervise the validation and test splits. Task 2.2 is evaluated by standard automatic measures against human annotations of 2025 submissions. Task 2.3 is evaluated similarly to Task 1 (Text Simplification) above.

### 3.3   Task 3: Research Area Classification

The *Research Area Classification* task aims to rerun *classification of scientific articles by research area.*

Description The pilot task proposal is on *Identification of research areas from scientific text.* The task aims to develop a novel approach to classify scientific articles using a given taxonomy. Traditional subject classification in libraries is a solvable problem [14], and can accelerate consistent metadata across collections (arXiv, Openaire, MADOC).

Data For datasets, we will use scientific publications crawled from arXiv. arXiv has provided open access to scholarly articles across disciplines such as physics, computer science, mathematics, and economics. The collected dataset is further annotated by DFG subject classification (see Table 3).[3]

Evaluation LLMs are well known for somewhat "creative" answers and not complying with all specifications under all circumstances. Moreover, even with good specifications, LLMs might produce some "near misses" with their results when, for instance, a research area like "Computer Science & Engineering" might be predicted as just "Computer Science". To overcome these challenges, we used several approaches to determine the actual matches:

- *Exact Match (EM)*: a binary measure comparing the output of the model directly with the ground truth.
- *String Distance (SD)*: a normalized Levenshtein distance between the prediction and reference.
- *Embedding Distance (ED)*: a semantic similarity measure based on the BERT-embeddings of the prediction and reference.

The evaluation will focus on accuracy as the main overall performance measure, as recommended by Chang et al. [4]. In addition to EM-accuracy, we can use a threshold make SD and EM scores Boolean and initial experiments suggest a 70% threshold.


## 4   Discussion and Conclusions

We have finalized the details of corpus creation, content selection, and relevance judgments/reference data for all the tasks. For *Task 1: Text Simplification*, we detailed above the new corpus, including aligned pairs of source-reference text at the sentence, paragraph, and document levels. Massive train data is available, including references for train and test. For *Task 2: Controlled Creativity*, we discussed the reuse of earlier submissions to SimpleText above. Massive train data is available, including references for training. For *Task 3: Research Area Classification*, we discussed the new classification task, aiming move from traditional subject classification into consistent metadata across collections. Train and evaluation data is available, extracted from existing scientific metadata platforms.

Since 2025, we have been running our tasks at Codabench as part of the further professionalization of CLEF. CLEF 2025 post-competition experiments are ongoing at https://www.codabench.org/competitions/8400/ (Task 1.1, Task 1.2, and Task 2.3) and https://www.codabench.org/competitions/8327/ (Task 2.1 and Task 2.2). We hope and expect that these "living test collections" remain in active use until the next iteration of the track takes over. More details at https://simpletext-project.com.

---

[3] https://www.dfg.de/resource/blob/331950/fachsystematik-2024-2028-en.pdf.

**Acknowledgments.** We are incredibly thankful to the master's students in translation and technical writing from the University of Brest for participating in data annotation. We also thank CodaBench [18] for hosting the competition.

Benjamin Vendeville and Liana Ermakova are partly funded by the French National Research Agency (ANR-22-CE23-0019-01, *SimpleText: Automatic Simplification of Scientific Texts*). Liana Ermakova is further supported by the CNRS research group MaDICS (https://www.madics.fr/ateliers/simpletext/).

Jan Bakker and Jaap Kamps are partly funded by the Netherlands Organization for Scientific Research (NWO NWA # 1518.22.105). Jaap Kamps is further supported by (NWO CI # CISC.CC.016), the University of Amsterdam (AI4FinTech program), and ICAI (AI for Open Government Lab). Views expressed in this paper are not necessarily shared or endorsed by those funding the research.

**Disclosure of Interests.** The authors have no competing interests to declare that are relevant to the content of this article.

**Disclosure of Generative AI Use.** During the preparation of this work, the authors used *ChatGPT* and *Grammarly* in order to: **Grammar and spelling check** and **Paraphrase and reword**. After using these tools/services, the authors reviewed and edited the content as needed and take full responsibility for the publication's content.

# References

1. Bakker, J., Kamps, J.: Cochrane-auto: an aligned dataset for the simplification of biomedical abstracts. In: Shardlow, M., et al. (eds.) Proceedings of the Third Workshop on Text Simplification, Accessibility and Readability (TSAR 2024), pp. 41–51. Association for Computational Linguistics, Miami, Florida, USA (2024). https://doi.org/10.18653/v1/2024.tsar-1.5, https://aclanthology.org/2024.tsar-1.5/
2. Bakker, J., Kamps, J.: Section-level simplification of biomedical abstracts. In: Christodoulopoulos, C., Chakraborty, T., Rose, C., Peng, V. (eds.) Proceedings of the 2025 Conference on Empirical Methods in Natural Language Processing, pp. 13819–13833. Association for Computational Linguistics, Suzhou, China (2025). ISBN 979-8-89176-332-6, https://doi.org/10.18653/v1/2025.emnlp-main.697, https://aclanthology.org/2025.emnlp-main.697/
3. Bakker, J., Vendeville, B., Ermakova, L., Kamps, J.: Overview of the CLEF 2025 SimpleText task 1: simplify scientific text. In: Faggioli, G., Ferro, N., Rosso, P., Spina, D. (eds.) Working Notes of CLEF 2025: Conference and Labs of the Evaluation Forum, CEUR Workshop Proceedings, vol. 4038, pp. 4167–4185, CEUR-WS.org (2025). https://ceur-ws.org/Vol-4038/paper_344.pdf
4. Chang, Y., et al.: A survey on evaluation of large language models. ACM Trans. Intell. Syst. Technol. **15**(3), 1–45 (2024)
5. D'Souza, J., Kabongo, S., Giglou, H.B., Zhang, Y.: Overview of the CLEF 2024 simpletext task 4: Sota? Tracking the state-of-the-art in scholarly publications. In: Faggioli, G., Ferro, N., Galuscáková, P., de Herrera, A.G.S. (eds.) Working Notes of the Conference and Labs of the Evaluation Forum (CLEF 2024), Grenoble, France, 9–12 September 2024, CEUR Workshop Proceedings, vol. 3740, pp. 3163–3173, CEUR-WS.org (2024). https://ceur-ws.org/Vol-3740/paper-308.pdf

6. Ermakova, L., Azarbonyad, H., Bakker, J., Vendeville, B., Kamps, J.: Overview of the CLEF 2025 simpletext track - simplify scientific text (and nothing more). In: Carrillo-de-Albornoz, J., et al. (eds.) CLEF 2025. LNCS, vol. 16089, pp. 436–463. Springer, Cham (2025). https://doi.org/10.1007/978-3-032-04354-2_23

7. Ermakova, L., et al.: Overview of simpletext 2021 - CLEF workshop on text simplification for scientific information access. In: Candan, K.S., et al. (eds.) CLEF 2021. LNCS, vol. 12880, pp. 432–449. Springer, Cham (2021). https://doi.org/10.1007/978-3-030-85251-1_27

8. Ermakova, L., Laimé, V., McCombie, H., Kamps, J.: Overview of the CLEF 2024 simpletext task 3: Simplify scientific text. In: Faggioli, G., Ferro, N., Galuscáková, P., de Herrera, A.G.S. (eds.) Working Notes of the Conference and Labs of the Evaluation Forum (CLEF 2024), Grenoble, France, 9–12 September 2024, CEUR Workshop Proceedings, vol. 3740, pp. 3147–3162, CEUR-WS.org (2024). https://ceur-ws.org/Vol-3740/paper-307.pdf

9. Ermakova, L., SanJuan, E., Huet, S., Azarbonyad, H., Augereau, O., Kamps, J.: Overview of the CLEF 2023 simpletext lab: automatic simplification of scientific texts. In: Arampatzis, A., et al. (eds.) CLEF 2023. LNCS, vol. 14163, pp. 482–506. Springer, Cham (2023). https://doi.org/10.1007/978-3-031-42448-9_30

10. Ermakova, L., et al.: Overview of the CLEF 2024 simpletext track - improving access to scientific texts for everyone. In: Goeuriot, L., et al. (eds.) CLEF 2024, Part II. LNCS, vol. 14959, pp. 283–307. Springer, Cham (2024). https://doi.org/10.1007/978-3-031-71908-0_13

11. Ermakova, L., et al.: Overview of the CLEF 2022 simpletext lab: automatic simplification of scientific texts. In: Barrón-Cedeño, A., et al. (eds.) CLEF 2022. LNCS, vol. 13390, pp. 470–494. Springer, Cham (2022). https://doi.org/10.1007/978-3-031-13643-6_28

12. Jiang, C., Maddela, M., Lan, W., Zhong, Y., Xu, W.: Neural CRF model for sentence alignment in text simplification. In: Jurafsky, D., Chai, J., Schluter, N., Tetreault, J. (eds.) Proceedings of the 58th Annual Meeting of the Association for Computational Linguistics, pp. 7943–7960. Association for Computational Linguistics, Online (2020). https://doi.org/10.18653/v1/2020.acl-main.709, https://aclanthology.org/2020.acl-main.709/

13. Nunzio, G.M.D., Vezzani, F., Bonato, V., Azarbonyad, H., Kamps, J., Ermakova, L.: Overview of the CLEF 2024 simpletext task 2: Identify and explain difficult concepts. In: Faggioli, G., Ferro, N., Galuscáková, P., de Herrera, A.G.S. (eds.) Working Notes of the Conference and Labs of the Evaluation Forum (CLEF 2024), Grenoble, France, 9–12 September 2024, CEUR Workshop Proceedings, vol. 3740, pp. 3129–3146, CEUR-WS.org (2024). https://ceur-ws.org/Vol-3740/paper-306.pdf

14. Shahi, G.K., Hummel, O.: On the effectiveness of large language models in automating categorization of scientific texts. In: Filipe, J., Smialek, M., Brodsky, A., Hammoudi, S. (eds.) Proceedings of the 27th International Conference on Enterprise Information Systems, ICEIS 2025, Porto, Portugal, 4–6 April 2025, vol. 1, pp. 544–554. SCITEPRESS (2025). https://doi.org/10.5220/0013299100003929

15. Vendeville, B., Bakker, J., Azarbonyad, H., Ermakova, L., Kamps, J.: Overview of the CLEF 2025 simple text task 2: identify and avoid hallucination. In: Faggioli, G., Ferro, N., Rosso, P., Spina, D. (eds.) Working Notes of CLEF 2025: Conference and Labs of the Evaluation Forum, CEUR Workshop Proceedings, vol. 4038, pp. 4186–4204, CEUR-WS.org (2025). https://ceur-ws.org/Vol-4038/paper_345.pdf

16. Vendeville, B., Ermakova, L., Loor, P.D.: Resource for error analysis in text simplification: new taxonomy and test collection. In: Ferro, N., Maistro, M., Pasi, G., Alonso, O., Trotman, A., Verberne, S. (eds.) Proceedings of the 48th International ACM SIGIR Conference on Research and Development in Information Retrieval, SIGIR 2025, Padua, Italy, 13–18 July 2025, pp. 3723–3732. ACM (2025). https://doi.org/10.1145/3726302.3730304
17. Xu, W., Callison-Burch, C., Napoles, C.: Problems in current text simplification research: new data can help. Trans. Assoc. Comput. Linguist. **3**, 283–297 (2015). https://doi.org/10.1162/tacl_a_00139, https://aclanthology.org/Q15-1021/
18. Xu, Z., et al.: Codabench: flexible, easy-to-use, and reproducible meta-benchmark platform. Patterns **3**(7), 100543 (2022), https://doi.org/10.1016/J.PATTER.2022.100543

# Overview of PAN 2026: Voight-Kampff Generative AI Detection, Text Watermarking, Multi-author Writing Style Analysis, Generative Plagiarism Detection, and Reasoning Trajectory Detection


Janek Bevendorff[1]([envelope]), Maik Fröbe[2], André Greiner-Petter[3], Andreas Jakoby[1], Maximilian Mayerl[4], Preslav Nakov[5], Henry Plutz[6], Martin Potthast[6,7,8], Benno Stein[1], Minh Ngoc Ta[5], Yuxia Wang[9], and Eva Zangerle[10]

[1] Bauhaus-Universität Weimar, Weimar, Germany
`pan@webis.de`
[2] Friedrich Schiller University Jena, Jena, Germany
[3] Georg-August-Universität, Göttingen, Germany
[4] University of Applied Sciences BFI, Vienna, Austria
[5] Mohamed bin Zayed University of Artificial Intelligence,
Abu Dhabi, United Arab Emirates
[6] University of Kassel, Kassel, Germany
[7] hessian.ai, Darmstadt, Germany
[8] ScaDS.AI, Leipzig, Germany,
[9] INSAIT, Sofia University "St. Kliment Ohridski", Sofia, Bulgaria
[10] University of Innsbruck, Innsbruck, Austria
`https://pan.webis.de`



**Abstract.** The goal of the PAN workshop is to advance computational stylometry and text forensics via objective and reproducible evaluation. In 2026, we run the following five tasks: (1) *Voight-Kampff Generative AI Detection*, particularly in mixed and obfuscated authorship scenarios, (2) *Text Watermarking*, a new task that aims to find new and benchmark the robustness of existing text watermarking schemes, (3) *Multi-author Writing Style Analysis*, a continued task that aims to find positions of authorship change, (4) *Generative Plagiarism Detection*, a continued task that targets source retrieval and text alignment between generated text and source documents, and (5) *Reasoning Trajectory Detection*, a new task that deals with source detection and safety detection of LLM-generated or human-written reasoning trajectories. As in previous years, PAN invites software submissions as easy-to-reproduce Docker containers for most of the tasks. Since PAN 2012, more than 1,100 submissions have been made this way via the TIRA experimentation platform [8].


## 1 Introduction

The PAN lab is a workshop series and a networking initiative for stylometry and digital text forensics. We host shared tasks on authorship analysis, generative AI



R. Campos et al. (Eds.): ECIR 2026, LNCS 16486, pp. 225–232, 2026.
https://doi.org/10.1007/978-3-032-21321-1_32

detection and analysis, and computational ethics in general. Since the workshop's inception in 2007, we have organized 82 shared tasks[1] (including this year's) and have assembled many original evaluation datasets[2] for this purpose.

In 2025, our four tasks concluded with 112 software submissions and 70 notebook papers. Together with the ELOQUENT Lab, we continued the *Voight-Kampff Generative AI Detection*[3] task to develop methods for the reliable and robust detection of generative AI in the presence of adversarial text modifications. As in the 2024 installment, the task proved very successful and attracted a large number of submissions. This task will return in 2026. The 2025 edition was extended with another subtask to determine the degree of human-AI collaboration in a text, which also received many submissions, but will not return this year. The *Multilingual Text Detoxification* task was continued as well with more languages in the dataset. Although quite successful, this task will not return in 2026, as we are taking our time analyzing the lessons learned from the previous editions. In its place, we introduce a new *Text Watermarking* task aiming at developing robust watermarking techniques for existing text. As in previous years, the *Multi-Author Writing Style Analysis* task attracted a stable number of participants, which we will build on again in 2026. The new *Generated Plagiarism Detection* focused on the detection of near-verbatim text reuse by LLMs. Although it did not receive many submissions in 2025, we will continue this task in 2026. Finally, we introduce *Reasoning Trajectory Detection* as another new task in 2026, which has the goal of attributing reasoning trajectories to LLM or human authors and to classify their safety.

We briefly outline the upcoming tasks in the sections that follow.

## 2    Task 1: Voight-Kampff Generative AI Detection

With generative AI being ubiquitous, we now have the ability to produce high-quality discursive texts on virtually any topic, approaching human-like standards of writing. On the one hand, this is a notable achievement, but on the other hand, it is also a cause for concern. Recognizing the "fingerprint" of AI text generation is the foundation for a healthy information ecosystem in the future, but also to prevent model collapse when LLMs are trained increasingly on their own output. However, LLM detection remains a challenge, especially across text domains, but also in the face of potential LLM style obfuscations.

The Voight-Kampff task was conceived in 2024 as a successor to a long and well-received series of authorship verification tasks. Both the 2024 and the 2025 editions attracted many participants to submit their systems on the TIRA platform [8]. The 2025 edition focused on robustness analysis of detectors

---

[1] Find PAN's past shared tasks at https://pan.webis.de/shared-tasks.html.
[2] Find PAN's datasets at https://pan.webis.de/data.html.
[3] The name is inspired by the 1982 science fiction film Blade Runner. The Voight-Kampff machine is used to determine whether an individual is a human or a replicant in a polygraph-like test.

against unknown text modifications (obfuscations) that try to mask the tell-tale LLM fingerprints. It was organized together with the ELOQUENT lab in a builder–breaker style, in which ELOQUENT participants contributed obfuscated datasets trying to break the PAN participants' systems. For 2026, we continue this line of research and explore new ways to make and break successful LLM detectors.

## 3   Task 2: Text Watermarking

Generative AI Detection has its limits [3], which is why many AI companies now embed invisible watermarks into the output of their LLMs. The field of text watermarking is much older than LLMs [10], but as a result of the widespread adoption of generative AI, it has recently received renewed attention and novel methods have been developed. With *Text Watermarking*, we propose a new task that is closely related to the Voight-Kampff task, but instead of detecting the style of an LLM, participants embed a watermark into an existing text and—in a second step—verify its existence. Between these two steps, the text goes through a number of unknown automated text obfuscation processes with the goal to destroy the embedded watermarks. Since the task uses existing text and does not rely on LLMs specifically, the submitted watermarking systems can be used in a much broader context to authenticate any type of text, not only machine-generated text. With the TIRA platform [8] we are in a unique position to organize such a two-step task: the submitted software systems are executed in a stateless sandbox on our infrastructure, which prevents knowledge leaks between the steps. The systems are evaluated with regard to the inconspicuousness of the watermark and its robustness against (unknown) text modifications.

## 4   Task 3: Multi-author Writing Style Analysis

The multi-author writing style analysis task aims to analyze the writing style of individuals in order to identify points where the style—and thereby the authorship—changes. This task is fundamental for several downstream applications, including intrinsic plagiarism detection and authorship verification.

The task was first introduced at PAN in 2016 and has since then witnessed steady progress and improvements. Initially, the focus was on identifying authors and grouping text segments by author [15]. In the following years, the task was reformulated as a binary classification problem: detecting whether a text was authored by a single author or by multiple authors [11,16,22]. In 2020, the task shifted to detecting whether there is a style change across all pairs of consecutive paragraphs [21] and to assigning authors to paragraphs [17,18]. In 2023 and 2024, the task again focused on the paragraph level, this time explicitly controlling for simultaneous changes in both authorship and topic [19,20].

To ensure consistency and comparability across years, and thereby enable tracking of improvements, the PAN'26 edition will adhere to the established intrinsic multi-author writing style analysis task definition: *"For a given text, identify all positions where the writing style changes.*" To solve the task, participants are asked to develop profiling methods capable of detecting whether a change in style—and thus authorship—occurs at specific positions in the text. However, in 2026, we will introduce a new dataset: We will make use of an extensive collection of fanfiction texts, i.e., user-written stories that reuse characters and settings from existing works. This allows us to extract longer, topically coherent excerpts while still maintaining control over authorship boundaries. Based on these input texts, we will apply our established mixing method to create the dataset underlying the task. To do so, we compute both a semantic and a stylistic representation of each text chunk, thereby enabling the construction of three datasets that differ in topical and stylistic similarity.

## 5    Task 4: Generative Plagiarism Detection

The widespread adoption of large language models (LLMs) has introduced complex challenges to modern academic workflows [6], particularly with regard to academic integrity. While several major scientific conferences have updated their content policies in recent years to allow (mostly partial) LLM-generated content [2, 4, 5], or to incorporate LLM-based assessments in their peer review processes,footnotehttps://aaai.org/aaai-launches-ai-powered-peer-review-assessment-system/. the boundary for what constitutes acceptable generated content is becoming increasingly blurred.[4] As a result, identifying disingenuous research publications has become more difficult, as the methods for detecting LLMs and textual overlap are less relevant for modern plagiarism detection techniques.

The first revival of the plagiarism detection task at PAN in 2025 was successful, but lacked realism in terms of how LLMs might be used to create real-world plagiarism. In the previous iteration, we introduced plagiarism paragraph-by-paragraph into an otherwise genuine publication. While this approach resembled an unrealistic scenario, it was also relatively easy to detect the replaced paragraphs using simple embedding similarity calculations. Moreover, as textual overlap decreases, the alignment sub-task of plagiarism detection becomes less relevant (i.e., identifying the precise boundaries of plagiarized paragraphs is less meaningful with substantial paraphrasing capabilities).

Therefore, we will develop a new version of the dataset, focusing on generating plagiarism from the ground up based on one or more source documents. This will allow us to reinstate the crucial retrieval aspect of plagiarism detection and incorporate important cases of merging (summarization of multiple sources) and expanding plagiarism (splitting single sources into multiple plagiarized paragraphs).

To further enhance the dataset's relevance, we will also expand the domains covered by incorporating publications from PubMed[5] (which includes the med-

---

[4] https://www.intology.ai/blog/zochi-acl.
[5] https://huggingface.co/datasets/ncbi/pubmed.

ical and chemical fields) and JSTOR[6] (which spans the humanities and social sciences). At the same time, the planned structure of the subtasks will largely mirror that of previous iterations.

*Subtask 1 – Source Retrieval:* This is the classic retrieval task for plagiarism detection systems. Given a suspicious document and a corpus of potential source documents, the participant's system must identify all the source documents from the corpus or determine that no source documents are present if the suspicious document is authentic (i.e., the corpus contains no relevant sources for the document).

*Subtask 2 – Text Alignment:* This task focuses on aligning plagiarized paragraphs in the suspicious document with their corresponding paragraphs in the source documents. One plagiarized paragraph may correspond to multiple source paragraphs (merging plagiarism). Conversely, several plagiarized paragraphs might correspond to one source paragraph (expanding plagiarism).

## 6    Task 5: Reasoning Trajectory Detection

The year 2025 has witnessed substantial advancements in the reasoning capabilities of LLMs, improving both overall performance and safety through explicit reasoning trajectories before final answer [7]. However, emerging evidence indicates that spurious, non-logical, or unsafe intermediate steps can still lead to incorrect or harmful final answers [13]. In some cases, reasoning models may sometimes arrive at safe conclusions via deceptive or misaligned reasoning paths [12]. To mitigate unsafe LLM reasoning, we propose a new task, *Reasoning Trajectory Detection*, to deepen our understanding of AI-generated reasoning and support future improvements in reasoning and safety with two related subtasks:

*Subtask 1 – Source Detection:* Given a triplet (user query, reasoning trajectory, final answer), the participant systems should identify the source of the reasoning trajectory and final answer—whether they are generated by an AI system or written by a human. The queries mainly involve math, coding, and real-life financial reasoning tasks. This subtask supports a deeper comparison of reasoning style and cognitive structure between humans and models, helping to inform model-alignment and reasoning-training strategies.

*Subtask 2 – Safety Detection:* Given a triplet (user query, reasoning trajectory, final answer), where the query is from three categories—(a) risky queries requesting harmful content, (b) jailbreak attacks with risks obscured by various strategies, and (c) benign queries with risky tokens—the participants must identify (1) whether the reasoning trajectory is safe vs. unsafe, and (2) whether the final answer is safe vs. unsafe. This subtask targets step-level and outcome-level safety, to reveal unsafe reasoning hidden behind apparently correct conclusions.

---

[6] https://support.jstor.org/hc/en-us/articles/32487330092695-JSTOR-Text-Analysis-Support-Working-with-JSTOR-Full-Text-Datasets.

For Subtask 1, in addition to existing datasets used to train reasoning for math and coding,[7] we plan to curate additional human-written reasoning trajectories with final answers from websites like `chegg`,[8] and collect AI-generated reasoning outputs using both cutting-edge open-source and commercial models such as Claude 3.7, DeepSeek-R1, Gemini 2.5 Pro, and GPT-5-Thinking [1,7,9,14], and other long-context or reflective LLMs.

For Subtask 2, several recent datasets provide stepwise and outcome-level safety annotations, such as STAIR [23], Reasoning-to-Defend [24], and SaRO [13]. We will leverage these corpora for training and validation, while the test set will be augmented with reasoning traces from the latest models featuring self-correction, reflection loops, and tool-use reasoning, to assess robustness under complex reasoning behaviors.

The evaluation of the Reasoning Trajectory Detection task will not be conducted inside the TIRA sandbox. Instead, we will use a separate evaluation platform where participants only need to submit their system outputs as files in the specified format.

Participants are free to develop and run their systems using any hardware or software resources of their choice, including local or cloud-based GPU acceleration, large open-weight models, or external APIs, as long as the final submission consists solely of the required output files. No code execution, model inference, or hardware constraints will be imposed at evaluation time.

This task bridges reasoning interpretability and safety assessment by evaluating not just what an LLM concludes, but how it reasons. It encourages systems that can detect unsafe or synthetic reasoning trajectories, quantify reasoning transparency, and explain their detection decisions, supporting the development of next-generation trustworthy reasoning models.

## 7 Conclusion and Future Work

We described the PAN 2026 shared tasks, which span robust AI detection, text watermarking, multi-author writing style analysis, generative plagiarism detection, and reasoning trajectory detection. Together, these tasks reflect the evolving landscape of AI-assisted text production and the need for rigorous evaluation frameworks that go beyond surface-level text characteristics.

Future work will focus on improving robustness, extending datasets across domains and languages, and refining the evaluation, to continue supporting research on trustworthy and reliable text analysis systems.

**Acknowledgments.** This work is partially supported by the European Commission under grant agreement GA 101070014 (https://openwebsearch.eu) and by the Deutsche Forschungsgemeinschaft (DFG, German Research Foundation) – 554559555.

**Disclosure of Interests.** The authors have no competing interests to declare that are relevant to the content of this article.

---

[7] https://huggingface.co/datasets/nivektk/math-augmented-dataset.
[8] https://www.chegg.com/.

# References


1. Anthropic: Claude 3.7 Sonnet System Card (2025). https://assets.anthropic.com/m/785e231869ea8b3b/original/claude-3-7-sonnet-system-card.pdf
2. Association for the Advancement of Artificial Intelligence: AAAI publication policies & guidelines (2025). https://aaai.org/aaai-publications/aaai-publication-policies-guidelines/
3. Bevendorff, J., Wiegmann, M., Richter, E., Potthast, M., Stein, B.: The two paradigms of LLM detection: authorship attribution vs. authorship verification. In: Findings of the Association for Computational Linguistics: ACL 2025, pp. 3762–3787 (2025). ISBN 979-8-89176-256-5, https://doi.org/10.18653/v1/2025.findings-acl.194
4. Boyd-Graber, J., Okazaki, N., Rogers, A.: ACL 2023 policy on AI writing assistance (2023). https://2023.aclweb.org/blog/ACL-2023-policy/
5. Brunskill, E., Cho, K., Engelhardt, B.: Clarification on large language model policy LLM (2023). https://icml.cc/Conferences/2023/llm-policy
6. Crothers, E.N., Japkowicz, N., Viktor, H.L.: Machine-generated text: a comprehensive survey of threat models and detection methods. IEEE Access **11**, 70977–71002 (2023). ISSN 2169-3536,https://doi.org/10.1109/ACCESS.2023.3294090
7. DeepSeek-AI: DeepSeek-R1: Incentivizing reasoning capability in LLMs via reinforcement learning. arXiv preprint arXiv:2501.12948 (2025). https://doi.org/10.48550/ARXIV.2501.12948
8. Fröbe, M., et al.: Continuous integration for reproducible shared tasks with TIRA.io. In: Kamps, J., et al. (eds.) ECIR 2023. LNCS, vol. 13982, pp. 236–241. Springer, Cham (2023). https://doi.org/10.1007/978-3-031-28241-6_20
9. Gemini Team: Gemini 2.5: Pushing the frontier with advanced reasoning, multimodality, long context, and next generation agentic capabilities (2025). https://arxiv.org/abs/2507.06261
10. Kaur, M., Mahajan, K.: An existential review on text watermarking techniques. Int. J. Comput. Appl. **120**(18), 29–32 (2015). ISSN 0975-888, https://doi.org/10.5120/21330-4300
11. Kestemont, M., et al.: Overview of the author identification task at PAN-2018: cross-domain authorship attribution and style change detection. In: Working Notes of CLEF 2018 - Conference and Labs of the Evaluation Forum, CEUR Workshop Proceedings, vol. 2125, CEUR-WS.org (2018). https://ceur-ws.org/Vol-2125/invited_paper_2.pdf
12. Meinke, A., Schoen, B., Scheurer, J., Balesni, M., Shah, R., Hobbhahn, M.: Frontier models are capable of in-context scheming. arXiv preprint arXiv:2412.04984 (2024). https://doi.org/10.48550/ARXIV.2412.04984
13. Mou, Y., Luo, Y., Zhang, S., Ye, W.: SaRO: enhancing LLM safety through reasoning-based alignment. arXiv preprint arXiv:2504.09420 (2025). https://doi.org/10.48550/ARXIV.2504.09420
14. OpenAI: GPT-5 System Card (2025). https://cdn.openai.com/gpt-5-system-card.pdf
15. Rosso, P., Pardo, F.M.R., Potthast, M., Stamatatos, E., Tschuggnall, M., Stein, B.: Overview of PAN'16 - new challenges for authorship analysis: cross-genre profiling, clustering, diarization, and obfuscation. In: Fuhr, N., et al. (eds.) CLEF 2016. LNCS, vol. 9822, pp. 332–350. Springer, Cham (2016). https://doi.org/10.1007/978-3-319-44564-9_28

16. Tschuggnall, M., et al.: Overview of the author identification task at PAN-2017: style breach detection and author clustering. In: Working Notes of CLEF 2017 - Conference and Labs of the Evaluation Forum, CEUR Workshop Proceedings, vol. 1866, CEUR-WS.org (2017). https://ceur-ws.org/Vol-1866/invited_paper_3.pdf

17. Zangerle, E., Mayerl, M., Potthast, M., Stein, B.: Overview of the style change detection task at PAN 2021. In: Proceedings of the Working Notes of CLEF 2021 - Conference and Labs of the Evaluation Forum, Bucharest, Romania, 21–24 September 2021, CEUR Workshop Proceedings, vol. 2936, pp. 1760–1771, CEUR-WS.org (2021). https://ceur-ws.org/Vol-2936/paper-148.pdf

18. Zangerle, E., Mayerl, M., Potthast, M., Stein, B.: Overview of the style change detection task at PAN 2022. In: Proceedings of the Working Notes of CLEF 2022 - Conference and Labs of the Evaluation Forum, Bologna, Italy, 5–8 September 2022, CEUR Workshop Proceedings, vol. 3180, pp. 2344–2356, CEUR-WS.org (2022). https://ceur-ws.org/Vol-3180/paper-186.pdf

19. Zangerle, E., Mayerl, M., Potthast, M., Stein, B.: Overview of the multi-author writing style analysis task at PAN 2023. In: Aliannejadi, M., Faggioli, G., Ferro, N., Vlachos, M. (eds.) Working Notes of the Conference and Labs of the Evaluation Forum (CLEF 2023), CEUR Workshop Proceedings, vol. 3497, pp. 2513–2522 (2023). https://ceur-ws.org/Vol-3497/paper-201.pdf

20. Zangerle, E., Mayerl, M., Potthast, M., Stein, B.: Overview of the multi-author writing style analysis task at PAN 2024. In: Faggioli, G., Ferro, N., Galuščáková, P., Herrera, A.G.S. (eds.) Working Notes Papers of the CLEF 2024 Evaluation Labs, pp. 2513–2522, CEUR-WS.org (2024). http://ceur-ws.org/Vol-3740/paper-222.pdf

21. Zangerle, E., Mayerl, M., Specht, G., Potthast, M., Stein, B.: Overview of the style change detection task at PAN 2020. In: Working Notes of CLEF 2020 - Conference and Labs of the Evaluation Forum, Thessaloniki, Greece, 22–25 September 2020, CEUR Workshop Proceedings, vol. 2696, CEUR-WS.org (2020). https://ceur-ws.org/Vol-2696/paper_256.pdf

22. Zangerle, E., Tschuggnall, M., Specht, G., Stein, B., Potthast, M.: Overview of the Style Change Detection Task at PAN 2019. In: CLEF 2019 Labs and Workshops, Notebook Papers (2019)

23. Zhang, Y., et al.:: STAIR: improving safety alignment with introspective reasoning. In: Proceedings of International Conference on Machine Learning (2025). https://doi.org/10.48550/ARXIV.2502.02384

24. Zhu, J., Yan, L., Wang, S., Yin, D., Sha, L.: Reasoning-to-defend: safety-aware reasoning can defend large language models from jailbreaking. In: Proceedings of the 2025 Conference on Empirical Methods in Natural Language Processing, pp. 29343–29361, Suzhou, China (2025). https://doi.org/10.18653/v1/2025.emnlp-main.1493

# eRisk 2026: Tasks on Symptoms Ranking, Contextual and Conversational Approaches for Early Mental Health Detection


Anxo Perez[1]([✉]) [iD], Javier Parapar[1] [iD], Xi Wang[2] [iD], and Fabio Crestani[3] [iD]

[1] Information Retrieval Lab, CITIC, Universidade da Coruña, Coruña, Spain
{anxo.pvila,javierparapar}@udc.es
[2] University of Sheffield, Sheffield, England, UK
xi.wang@sheffield.ac.uk
[3] Faculty of Informatics, Università della Svizzera italiana (USI),
Lugano, Switzerland
fabio.crestani@usi.ch



**Abstract.** Since its foundation in 2017, the eRisk CLEF Lab has pioneered research in early risk detection on the Internet, focusing on mental health challenges such as depression, anorexia, and pathological gambling. Over the years, participants have contributed to the development of detection models and exploited the datasets we constructed to advance this critical area. In 2026, which marks the tenth edition of the lab, we continue this trajectory with three tasks that emphasize conversational and contextual modeling as well as symptom-oriented retrieval. The first task, *Conversational Depression Detection*, introduces the challenge of identifying depression through interactions with fine-tuned Large Language Models (LLMs) personas. The second task, *Contextualised Early Detection of Depression*, focuses on user-level classification by analyzing full conversational contexts, with participants engaging iteratively in natural interactions. Finally, the third task, *ADHD Symptom Sentence Ranking*, expands our scope beyond depression by requiring systems to rank sentences according to their relevance to the symptoms defined in the Adult ADHD Self-Report Scale. This paper outlines the progress of the lab to date, introduces the three tasks of eRisk 2026, and discusses our innovative plans for promoting research on mental health challenges.


## 1 Introduction

The eRisk Lab[1] is a long standing evaluation initiative dedicated to the study of early risk detection on the Internet, with a particular focus on health and safety concerns. Over the years, the lab has released diverse methodologies, datasets, and shared tasks, providing the research community with valuable resources to study online risks related to mental health and harmful behaviors. First launched

---

[1] https://erisk.irlab.org.

in 2017 during CLEF in Dublin [12], eRisk initially focused on early detection of depression and eating disorders from social media data, establishing a novel evaluation paradigm in which systems were required not only to be accurate, but also timely in raising risk alerts. Since then, eRisk has become a core track of CLEF, evolving across multiple editions and continuously expanding its scope and methodological diversity [13, 16, 20, 22, 24, 26, 28].

The strength of eRisk lies in its interdisciplinary nature, bringing together researchers from information retrieval, natural language processing, machine learning, psychology, or medicine. This combination of expertise has enabled the design of tasks and evaluation protocols that are both technically challenging and clinically meaningful. Across editions, eRisk has addressed a range of mental health conditions, including depression, eating disorders, gambling addiction, and self-harm, fostering the development of computational models with clear real-world relevance. Systems developed within the eRisk framework have demonstrated the potential to act as early-warning tools, capable of identifying linguistic signals associated with mental health deterioration in online environments [1, 4, 8, 17, 30, 32]. Throughout its history, eRisk has proposed tasks that tackle complementary aspects of mental health detection, including early alerting, sentence ranking for symptom identification, and severity estimation. Early detection tasks (Sect. 2.1) evaluate time-sequenced user writings to determine the earliest point at which a risk can be reliably inferred, explicitly modeling the trade-off between accuracy and timeliness. Severity estimation tasks (Sect. 2.2) move beyond binary classification by assessing the degree of illness through complete user histories, often mirroring clinical questionnaires and diagnostic practices. More recently, sentence ranking tasks (Sect. 2.3) have focused on fine-grained symptom evidence at the sentence level, encouraging interpretable models that can better support clinical analysis and decision-making.

For 2026, the lab continues this evolution by introducing three tasks that bring together ranking, contextual analysis, and a new research direction focused on conversational approaches (Sect. 3). The first task, *Conversational Depression Detection*, challenges participants to identify signs of depression in LLM personas, made accessible through Hugging Face. The second task, *Contextualised Early Detection of Depression*, extends user-level classification to full conversational contexts, enabling richer and more realistic interaction scenarios that better reflect how mental health signals emerge over time. Finally, the third task expands the scope of eRisk beyond depression to Attention-Deficit/Hyperactivity Disorder (ADHD): in *ADHD Symptom Sentence Ranking*, participants must rank sentences by their relevance to symptoms defined in the Adult ADHD Self-Report Scale (ASRS-v1.1) [10]. In line with the direction set in the previous edition, these tasks highlight the growing importance of contextual and interactional data in understanding mental health risks. Together, they represent a further step forward for eRisk, reinforcing the role of conversational modeling and symptom-specific retrieval in advancing research on early detection for mental health challenges.

# 2   A Brief History of eRisk

The eRisk Lab was launched in 2017 at CLEF as the first evaluation campaign focused on early risk detection on the Internet [12]. The pilot edition introduced the task of early detection of depression and anorexia, attracting eight participating teams. This initial effort demonstrated the potential of designing evaluation settings where systems must decide not only *what* a user is experiencing but also *when* there is sufficient evidence to raise an alarm.

The 2018 and 2019 editions [13,14] expanded the scope with new datasets and tasks, including self-harm and gambling addiction. These years received more than 60 contributions, consolidating eRisk's position as a growing benchmark and reflecting the rapid methodological shift from classical IR approaches to deep neural models. In 2020 and 2021 [15,19], participation continued to increase, with more than 15 international teams contributing over 80 runs. A major innovation of this period was the introduction of severity estimation tasks, where participants had to predict symptom intensity and diagnostic outcomes by analyzing complete user histories. This marked a shift toward tasks that more include methodologies similar to clinical assessments.

The 2022 and 2023 editions [21,23] introduced fine-grained sentence ranking for depression symptoms. These editions gathered close to 20 teams who together submitted over 100 runs, reflecting the growing interest for interpretable systems that could collect symptom evidence. The 2024 edition [25] consolidated this trajectory, more than 20 teams worldwide and over 120 runs were submitted. By this stage, eRisk had firmly established itself as a unique interdisciplinary benchmark, bringing together researchers from IR, NLP, and clinical sciences to advance the state of the art in early detection of mental health risks.

The 2025 edition [27,28] marked an important turning point in the evolution of the lab. For the first time, eRisk introduced tasks that required not only early recognition of mental health risks but also deeper contextual reasoning and, in its pilot task, conversational interaction with LLM personas. These innovations pushed participants to design systems capable of interpreting entire discussion and dynamic interactions, aligning the evaluation setting more closely with real-world settings. Community engagement reached a new record, with 128 teams registered and a total of 128 different runs received. A summary of the eRisk journey and the best models developed to date is available in our recent book [9].

## 2.1   Early Risk Prediction Tasks

The first eRisk challenges focused on detecting early signs of depression, anorexia, and self-harm from social media activity. Participants analyzed users' posts sequentially, aiming to identify risks as early as possible. Data were collected from Reddit following the methodology of Coppersmith et al. [7], where users were divided into positive (e.g., diagnosed) and control groups based on explicit self-disclosures. Evaluation relied on the *Early Risk Detection Error* (ERDE) [11], which penalizes delayed predictions, later complemented by $F_{latency}$ [29] and IR metrics such as P@10 and nDCG [14]. This task line evolved through successive editions, including the 2024 challenge on early detection of anorexia and the 2025 *Contextualised Early Detection of Depression* task, which incorporated full conversational contexts.

## 2.2   Severity Level Estimation Tasks

In 2019, eRisk introduced a new challenge focused on estimating the severity of mental health conditions rather than merely detecting their presence. This task was initially applied to depression and later extended to eating disorders. Participants analyzed users' complete writing histories to predict their responses to standard clinical questionnaires: the Beck Depression Inventory (BDI-II) [3] for depression and the Eating Disorder Examination Questionnaire (EDE-Q) [6] for eating disorders. These datasets paired users' textual histories with self-reported questionnaire scores, forming a unique ground truth that enabled fine-grained severity modeling. New evaluation metrics were developed to assess the accuracy of these estimations. We designed metrics that assess both alignment with clinical severity levels/scores and the accuracy of symptom-level classifications.

## 2.3   Sentence Ranking for Symptoms of Risk Tasks

In 2023, eRisk introduced a new challenge centered on ranking sentences according to their relevance to depressive symptoms. Participants were asked to rank user written sentences based on the 21 symptoms defined in the BDI-II [3]. A sentence was deemed relevant if it conveyed information about the user's state regarding a symptom, whether positive or negative. For example, "I feel happy lately" would still be relevant to the symptom *Sadness*. Relevance judgments were obtained through top-$k$ pooling and expert annotation, and systems were evaluated using standard ranking metrics such as MAP, P@10, and nDCG@1000. The 2024 edition continued this task, extending the resource by including the preceding and following sentences of each target sentence to provide local context for ranking methods. In 2025, the task reached its third edition, consolidating this line of research with a larger dataset and refined annotation guidelines.

## 2.4   Results

In line with the CLEF tradition, the eRisk Lab's Overview papers provide comprehensive summaries and analyses of participants' systems and results across editions [12–14,16,20,22,24,26,28]. Participants have explored a wide variety of models, ranging from traditional IR and feature-based classifiers to recent transformer-based architectures. Most efforts have focused on improving accuracy while addressing the inherent trade-off between detection precision and timeliness. Each new edition has brought gradual progress in both early accuracy and interpretability, confirming the value of sustained benchmarking for language-based mental health modeling.

Several teams have extended their eRisk work into top-tier publications, such as SIGIR, IJCAI, EMNLP, ECIR, and leading journals [5,8,18,32].

For instance, Burdisso et al. proposed the interpretable SS3 framework [4], while Zhang et al. [32] introduced a psychiatric-scale-guided screening model aligning BDI-II symptoms with attention mechanisms for explainable early risk detection. Beyond modeling, eRisk has also inspired new resources and datasets [2,31]. Bao et al. introduced ReDSM5 [2], a Reddit dataset annotated by clinicians for DSM-5 symptoms, while Wang et al. presented TalkDep [31], a clinically validated LLM-based simulation framework for conversation-centric depression screening, used in the eRisk 2025 pilot task. Together, these advancements have positioned eRisk as a leading framework for developing clinically grounded, explainable language resources in mental health research.

## 3   The Tasks of eRisk 2026

Building on the success of previous editions, eRisk 2026 increases the shift toward *contextual and conversational* modeling while expanding symptom-oriented retrieval beyond depression. Next, we describe each task of eRisk 2026.

### 3.1   Task 1: Conversational Depression Detection (New)

This task extends last year's pilot by detecting depression through conversational agents while improving access and reproducibility. Participants will interact with LLM personas fine-tuned with diverse user histories and *released on Hugging Face*. Each model will be released on a different day, and participants will have limited days before giving their predictions. The challenge is to determine whether each persona exhibits signs of depression and, within a limited conversational window, identify active depressive symptoms and the overall depression level. The LLM personas will reflect different severity levels guided by the BDI-II [3] questionnaire, allowing systems to be evaluated across a spectrum of simulated depression. Teams will download the released persona models, conduct their interactions, and submit predictions a few days later. Evaluation will focus on two key aspects: (i) accurate identification of depressive symptoms present in the persona (if any) and (ii) the overall depression level of the persona, following BDI-II standards. A limited number of runs will be accepted, with both fully automated and manual-in-the-loop variants permitted, encouraging exploration of conversational strategies while maintaining comparability across submissions.

### 3.2   Task 2: Contextualised Early Detection of Depression

This task continues last year's shift from isolated posts to *full conversational contexts*, aiming to capture real interaction dynamics across multiple speakers. Participants must process dialogues *sequentially*, accumulating evidence, where a message may only become informative when interpreted alongside preceding or subsequent publications.

**Training Phase.** For 2026 we provide a *specific, fixed training set* derived from last year's collection. This dataset is released upfront to enable reproducible development and validation. **Test phase.** As in 2025, the evaluation is interactive: teams connect to our server, receive one conversational context at a time, and submit predictions as the dialogue progresses within a limited window. Systems are expected to integrate multi-speaker context, handle evolving evidence, and decide when there is sufficient information to issue a reliable classification.

**Evaluation.** We assess both accuracy and timeliness, combining early-detection measures (e.g., ERDE, $F_{latency}$) with standard classification metrics. Details of the evaluation can be consulted in eRisk overview from last year [28]. This design encourages models that monitor ongoing interactions effectively while minimising delays, bringing early risk prediction closer to realistic, conversation-centric scenarios.

### 3.3  Task 3: Sentence Ranking for ADHD Symptoms (New)

This new task targets sentence-level retrieval for the *18 symptoms* defined in the Adult ADHD Self-Report Scale (ASRS–v1.1) [10]. Participants must rank candidate sentences by their relevance to each symptom. A sentence is considered relevant when it conveys information about the user's state with respect to the target ADHD symptom (irrespective of polarity or stance), encouraging models to capture clinically meaningful evidence rather than surface keywords.

We will release a sentence-tagged dataset derived from publicly available social media writings, collected to contain ADHD-related expressions. As this is the first edition of the ADHD ranking task, no annotated training data will be provided. The release will consist solely of the test inputs, following the formatting conventions of recent eRisk ranking tasks. Participants will submit *18* rankings (one per ADHD symptom) ordering candidate sentences by decreasing likelihood of relevance. Relevance assessments will be produced via top-$k$ pooling and expert annotation, and systems will be evaluated using standard IR metrics such as MAP, nDCG (e.g., @100), and P@10. By extending symptom-oriented retrieval beyond depression to ADHD, this task advances interpretable, symptom-aware retrieval and supports cross-condition generalisation at sentence granularity.

## 4  Conclusions

With the launch of eRisk 2026, the lab continues to push the frontier of early risk detection by studying context, conversation, and symptom-specific ranking at its core. The new conversational LLM persona task enables richer, more realistic dialogue-based diagnostic modelling. The contextualised early-detection track challenges systems to monitor evolving multiple-speakers conversations. Finally, the ADHD symptom ranking task broadens the scope beyond depression into fine-grained retrieval. As datasets, evaluation protocols, and baselines grow in sophistication, we anticipate deeper insights and stronger models emerging from the community. We warmly thank all participants for their efforts and encourage them to push toward systems that are accurate, timely, and interpretable.

While task setup requires significant investment, the potential societal impact of improved mental health risk detection makes this work deeply worthwhile.

**Acknowledgements.** This work was supported by the project PID2022-137061OB-C21 (MCIN/AEI/10.13039/501100011033, Ministerio de Ciencia e Innovación, ERDF, *A way of making Europe* by the European Union); the Consellería de Educación, Universidade e Formación Profesional, Spain (accreditations 2019–2022 ED431G/01 and GRC ED431C 2025/49); and the European Regional Development Fund, which supports the CITIC Research Center.

**Disclosure of Interests.** The authors have no competing interests.

# References

1. Aragon, M.E., Lopez-Monroy, A.P., González-Gurrola, L.C., Montes-y Gómez, M.: Detecting mental disorders in social media through emotional patterns-the case of anorexia and depression. IEEE Trans. Affect. Comput. **14**(1), 211–222 (2021)
2. Bao, E., Perez, A., Parapar, J.: Redsm5: a reddit dataset for DSM-5 depression detection. In: Proceedings of the 34th ACM International Conference on Information and Knowledge Management, p. TBD. CIKM '25, Association for Computing Machinery, New York (2025). https://doi.org/10.1145/3746252.3761610
3. Beck, A.T., Ward, C.H., Mendelson, M., Mock, J., Erbaugh, J.: An inventory for measuring depression. JAMA Psychiatry **4**(6), 561–571 (1961)
4. Burdisso, S.G., Errecalde, M., Montes-y Gómez, M.: A text classification framework for simple and effective early depression detection over social media streams. Expert Syst. Appl. **133**, 182–197 (2019)
5. Burdisso, S.G., Errecalde, M., Montes-y Gómez, M.: A text classification framework for simple and effective early depression detection over social media streams. Expert Syst. Appl. **133**, 182–197 (2019)
6. Carey, M., Kupeli, N., Knight, R., Troop, N.A., Jenkinson, P.M., Preston, C.: Eating disorder examination questionnaire (EDE-Q): norms and psychometric properties in uk females and males. Psychol. Assess. **31**(7), 839 (2019)
7. Coppersmith, G., Dredze, M., Harman, C.: Quantifying mental health signals in Twitter. In: ACL Workshop on Computational Linguistics and Clinical Psychology (2014)
8. Couto, M., Perez, A., Parapar, J., Losada, D.E.: Temporal word embeddings for early detection of psychological disorders on social media. J. Healthc. Inf. Res., 1–30 (2025)
9. Crestani, F., Losada, D.E., Parapar, J.: Early Detection of mental health disorders by social media monitoring. Springer International Publishing (2022)
10. Kessler, R.C., et al.: The world health organization adult ADHD self-report scale (ASRS): a short screening scale for use in the general population. Psychol. Med. **35**(2), 245–256 (2005)
11. Losada, D.E., Crestani, F.: A test collection for research on depression and language use. In: Fuhr, N., Quaresma, P., Gonçalves, T., Larsen, B., Balog, K., Macdonald, C., Cappellato, L., Ferro, N. (eds.) CLEF 2016. LNCS, vol. 9822, pp. 28–39. Springer, Cham (2016). https://doi.org/10.1007/978-3-319-44564-9_3

12. Losada, D.E., Crestani, F., Parapar, J.: eRisk 2017: clef lab on early risk prediction on the internet: Experimental foundations. In: Jones, G.J., et al. (eds.) Experimental IR Meets Multilinguality, Multimodality, and Interaction, pp. 346–360. Springer International Publishing, Cham (2017)

13. Losada, D.E., Crestani, F., Parapar, J.: Overview of eRisk: early risk prediction on the internet. In: Bellot, P., et al. (eds.) Experimental IR Meets Multilinguality, Multimodality, and Interaction, pp. 343–361. Springer International Publishing, Cham (2018)

14. Losada, D.E., Crestani, F., Parapar, J.: Overview of eRisk 2019 early risk prediction on the internet. In: Crestani, F., et al. (eds.) Experimental IR Meets Multilinguality, Multimodality, and Interaction, pp. 340–357. Springer International Publishing, Cham (2019)

15. Losada, D.E., Crestani, F., Parapar, J.: eRisk 2020: self-harm and depression challenges. In: Jose, J.M., Yilmaz, E., Magalhães, J., Castells, P., Ferro, N., Silva, M.J., Martins, F. (eds.) ECIR 2020. LNCS, vol. 12036, pp. 557–563. Springer, Cham (2020). https://doi.org/10.1007/978-3-030-45442-5_72

16. Losada, D.E., Crestani, F., Parapar, J.: Overview of of eRisk 2020: early risk prediction on the internet. In: Arampatzis, A., et al. (eds.) Experimental IR Meets Multilinguality, Multimodality, and Interaction, pp. 272–287. Springer International Publishing, Cham (2020)

17. Maupomé, D., Meurs, M.J.: Using topic extraction on social media content for the early detection of depression. CLEF (Work. Notes) **2125** (2018)

18. Ortega-Mendoza, R.M., Hernández-Farías, D.I., Montes-y Gomez, M., Villaseñor-Pineda, L.: Revealing traces of depression through personal statements analysis in social media. Artifi. Intell. Med. **123**, 102202 (2022)

19. Parapar, J., Martín-Rodilla, P., Losada, D.E., Crestani, F.: eRisk 2021: pathological gambling, self-harm and depression challenges. In: Hiemstra, D., Moens, M.-F., Mothe, J., Perego, R., Potthast, M., Sebastiani, F. (eds.) ECIR 2021. LNCS, vol. 12657, pp. 650–656. Springer, Cham (2021). https://doi.org/10.1007/978-3-030-72240-1_76

20. Parapar, J., Martín-Rodilla, P., Losada, D.E., Crestani, F.: Overview of of eRisk 2021: Early risk prediction on the internet. In: Experimental IR Meets Multilinguality, Multimodality, and Interaction - 12th International Conference of the CLEF Association, CLEF 2021, Virtual Event, September 21-24, 2021, Proceedings, pp. 324–344. Springer International Publishing (2021)

21. Parapar, J., Martín-Rodilla, P., Losada, D.E., Crestani, F.: erisk 2022: pathological gambling, depression, and eating disorder challenges. In: Hagen, M., et al., (eds.) Advances in Information Retrieval - 44th European Conference on IR Research, ECIR 2022, Stavanger, Norway, April 10-14, 2022, Proceedings, Part II. Lecture Notes in Computer Science, vol. 13186, pp. 436–442. Springer (2022)

22. Parapar, J., Martín-Rodilla, P., Losada, D.E., Crestani, F.: Overview of eRisk 2022: early risk prediction on the internet. In: Experimental IR Meets Multilinguality, Multimodality, and Interaction - 13th International Conference of the CLEF Association, CLEF 2022, Bologna, September 5-8, 2022, Proceedings, pp. 233–256. Springer International Publishing (2022)

23. Parapar, J., Martín-Rodilla, P., Losada, D.E., Crestani, F.: erisk 2023: depression, pathological gambling, and eating disorder challenges. In: Kamps, J., et al., (eds.) Advances in Information Retrieval - 45th European Conference on Information Retrieval, ECIR 2023, Dublin, Ireland, April 2-6, 2023, Proceedings, Part III. Lecture Notes in Computer Science, vol. 13982, pp. 585–592. Springer (2023)

24. Parapar, J., Martín-Rodilla, P., Losada, D.E., Crestani, F.: Overview of eRisk 2023: early risk prediction on the internet. In: Experimental IR Meets Multilinguality, Multimodality, and Interaction - 14th International Conference of the CLEF Association, CLEF 2022, Thessaloniki, Greece, September 18-21, 2023, Proceedings, pp. 294–315. Springer International Publishing (2023)

25. Parapar, J., Martín-Rodilla, P., Losada, D.E., Crestani, F.: erisk 2024: depression, anorexia, and eating disorder challenges. In: Goharian, N., et al., (eds.) Advances in Information Retrieval - 46th European Conference on Information Retrieval, ECIR 2024, Glasgow, March 24-28, 2024, Proceedings, Part V. Lecture Notes in Computer Science, vol. 14612, pp. 474–481. Springer (2024)

26. Parapar, J., Martín-Rodilla, P., Losada, D.E., Crestani, F.: Overview of erisk 2024: early risk prediction on the internet. In: Goeuriot, L., et al. (eds.) Experimental IR Meets Multilinguality, Multimodality, and Interaction, pp. 73–92. Springer Nature Switzerland, Cham (2024)

27. Parapar, J., Perez, A., Wang, X., Crestani, F.: erisk 2025: contextual and conversational approaches for depression challenges. In: Hauff, C., et al., (eds.) Advances in Information Retrieval - 47th European Conference on Information Retrieval, ECIR 2025, Lucca, Italy, April 6-10, 2025, Proceedings, Part V. Lecture Notes in Computer Science, vol. 15576, pp. 416–424. Springer (2025)

28. Parapar, J., Perez, A., Wang, X., Crestani, F.: Overview of erisk 2025: early risk prediction on the internet. In: International Conference of the Cross-language Evaluation Forum for European Languages, pp. 242–265. Springer (2025)

29. Sadeque, F., Xu, D., Bethard, S.: Measuring the latency of depression detection in social media. In: Proceedings of the Eleventh ACM International Conference on Web Search and Data Mining, pp. 495–503. WSDM '18, ACM, New York (2018)

30. Trotzek, M., Koitka, S., Friedrich, C.M.: Utilizing neural networks and linguistic metadata for early detection of depression indications in text sequences. IEEE Trans. Knowl. Data Eng. **32**(3), 588–601 (2018)

31. Wang, X., Perez, A., Parapar, J., Crestani, F.: Talkdep: clinically grounded LLM personas for conversation-centric depression screening. In: Proceedings of the 34th ACM International Conference on Information and Knowledge Management, p. TBD. CIKM '25, Association for Computing Machinery, New York (2025). https://doi.org/10.1145/3746252.3761617

32. Zhang, Z., Chen, S., Wu, M., Zhu, K.Q.: Psychiatric scale guided risky post screening for early detection of depression. In: Raedt, L.D. (ed.) Proceedings of the Thirty-First International Joint Conference on Artificial Intelligence, IJCAI-22, pp. 5220–5226. International Joint Conferences on Artificial Intelligence Organization (2022). https://doi.org/10.24963/ijcai.2022/725, ai for Good

# CLEF 2026 JOKER Track
## Humour Detection, Search, and Translation


Liana Ermakova[1] , Igor Kuzmin[2,3] , Poojan Vachharajani[4] ,
Tristan Miller[5,6(✉)] , Anne-Gwenn Bosser[7] , and Jaap Kamps[8]

[1] Université de Bretagne Occidentale, HCTI, Brest, France
[2] Universitat Pompeu Fabra, Barcelona, Spain
[3] Barcelona Supercomputing Center, Barcelona, Spain
[4] Netaji Subhas University of Technology, New Delhi, India
[5] Department of Computer Science, University of Manitoba, Winnipeg, Canada
`Tristan.Miller@umanitoba.ca`
[6] Semantic AI and Creativity Lab, East Texas A&M University, Commerce, USA
[7] Bretagne INP, Lab-STICC CNRS UMR 6285, Brest, France
[8] University of Amsterdam, Amsterdam, The Netherlands



**Abstract.** The JOKER Track has created an active community of
researchers in NLP and IR working together on the non-literal use of
language in text – which is still challenging for both AI models and
humans, as it requires understanding implicit cultural references and
double meanings. Its benchmarks on humorous text analysis, retrieval,
and translation have become standard references. We made significant
changes to the track's setup and tasks in 2024 and 2025, and propose continuing these to complete the test collections. The CLEF 2026 JOKER
track will contain the following four tasks: Task 1 (*Humour-aware Information Retrieval*): retrieve short humorous texts for a query, Task 2 (*Pun
Translation*): translate puns from English to French and Spanish, Task 3
(*Onomastic Wordplay Translation*): translate onomastic wordplay from
English to French, and Task 4 (*Humour Generation*): guided creativity.


## 1   Introduction

State-of-the-art AI, NLP, and IR models struggle to cope with humour and other
non-literal language [2], which often involve orthographic or cultural aspects that
are not directly captured in deep semantic embeddings. These aspects likewise
cannot be captured by current pre-training models based on next-word prediction objectives, which tend to de-emphasise ambiguous or unusual words in
favour of those with conventional meanings. However, humour is one of the most
important aspects of social interaction, making it crucial for modern text and
language processing systems to deal with.

The goal of the JOKER project is to bring together linguists and computer
scientists to create reusable test collections to foster work on this important
issue. This paper previews the 2026 edition of the JOKER track at CLEF, which
will contain the following four shared tasks: Task 1 (*Humour-aware Information
Retrieval*): retrieve short humorous texts for a query, Task 2 (*Pun Translation*):



R. Campos et al. (Eds.): ECIR 2026, LNCS 16486, pp. 242–250, 2026.
https://doi.org/10.1007/978-3-032-21321-1_34

translate puns from English to French and Spanish, Task 3 (*Onomastic Wordplay Translation*): translate onomastic wordplay from English to French, and Task 4 (*Humour Generation*): guided creativity.

## 2    Retrospective of the CLEF JOKER Track

The first edition of JOKER [14], held at CLEF 2022, featured shared tasks on the categorisation and translation of wordplay, puns, and humorous neologisms, in English and French. The next iteration of JOKER, at CLEF 2023 [12], had tasks on detection, location, and interpretation of puns in English, French, and Spanish [9,10], as well as on machine translation of wordplay from English into French and English into Spanish [11]. CLEF 2024 JOKER [6] featured a mix of familiar and new tasks: Task 1 on retrieving [4], Task 2 on classifying [17], and Task 3 on translating [5] humorous texts. CLEF 2025 JOKER [7] included both established tasks and newly introduced ones: Task 1 on retrieving puns in English and Portuguese [8], Task 2 on pun translation from English to French [3], and Task 3 on onomastic wordplay translation from English to French [13].

**Table 1.** CLEF 2025 JOKER official submission statistics

| JOKER | Task 1 | | Task 2 | Task 3 |
|---|---|---|---|---|
| | EN | PT | | |
| Teams | 9 | 5 | 9 | 5 |
| Runs | 41 | 21 | 52 | 22 |
| Teams | 9 | | | |
| Runs | 62 | | | |
| Teams | | | 13 | |
| Runs | | | 136 | |

The 2023–2024 tracks were built around the CLEF JOKER Corpus [2]. The CLEF 2025 JOKER Track made major changes in the setup, making it available at the open source benchmarking platform Codabench (which attracted many new participants) and adding humorous retrieval in English and Portuguese, significantly extended data sets (beyond the corpus presented at SIGIR), and a novel Task 3 on onomastic wordplay translation, particularly challenging for LLMs, as well as discussion on a joint task/activity across multiple tracks on "hallucination." After initial, pilot year of the new tasks, we will continue them in 2026 with extensive training data now available.

In terms of building a community through researching, analysing, searching, detecting, and translating humorous text, our track saw a record number of participants in 2025: we received 136 submissions from 13 teams out of a total of 56 teams that had registered, the largest number of submissions ever. The active participation statistics are shown in Table 1. In fact, we keep the Codabench [22] instances running after the submission deadlines in order to create a sort of living test collection that we hope and expect to remain in active use. We are indeed continuing to receive additional submissions from Track participants as well as new participants joining the Codabench and starting to participate in the track outside the CLEF cycle.[1]

## 3   CLEF 2026 JOKER Tasks

### 3.1   Task 1: Humour-aware Information Retrieval

*Description.* In this core IR task of the track, systems must retrieve short, humorous texts from a document collection based on a given query. The retrieved texts should fulfill the dual criteria of being relevant to the query and being instances of wordplay. The typical use case would be searching for a joke on a specific topic – e.g., a query of `math` means that the goal is to find math jokes, while the query `Tom` means that the goal is to find jokes about Tom.

*Data.* The data for this task is an extension of that used for JOKER 2023's tasks on wordplay detection in English, which is annotated according to whether the texts are humorous, extended with further data from the translation Task 3 [3,5,11]. We grouped the humorous texts into clusters of related topics and created queries based on these clusters. In 2025, we added a significant number of topically relevant but non-humorous texts by extracting relevant passages from Wikipedia and by generating passages using Meta's Llama-2 (7B) models. The corpus contains a large fraction of non-relevant content, due to the number of queries: 231 of them for 77,658 English documents. This year, the corpus will be significantly extended by adding new jokes from online resources, generated jokes, and completely new, manually created jokes. We will apply the same methodology to construct the collection in French based on the JOKER corpus, as well as a new collection in Hinglish, a popular code-mixed language that involves embedding English words and phrases into Hindi grammatical structures.

*Evaluation.* For evaluation, we use standard information retrieval metrics: MRR, precision, and NDCG at early ranks, as well as MAP for overall retrieval effectiveness. We evaluate both for the task (humorous and on topic) and provide additional evaluation of standard topical relevance.

---

[1] These post-competition experiments are ongoing at https://www.codabench.org/competitions/8686/ (Task 1, English), https://www.codabench.org/competitions/8736/ (Task 1, Portuguese), https://www.codabench.org/competitions/8748/ (Task 2), and https://www.codabench.org/competitions/8746/ (Task 3). At the time of writing, there are 23 active participants and 175 submissions for Task 1, 14 active participants and 104 submissions for Task 2, and 9 active participants and 72 submissions for Task 3.

### 3.2   Task 2: Pun Translation

*Description.* The goal of this task is to translate English punning jokes into French and Spanish. Translations should aim to preserve, to the extent possible, both the form and meaning of the original wordplay. This task is both challenging for modern MT models and very demanding for human professional translators. In fact, this makes the task very interesting for professional translators and allows us to involve a large number of translation students and professionals, who help build a high-quality corpus.

*Data.* The training data for Task 2 includes 1,405 instances of wordplay in English and 5,838 professional human French translations. For now, the test data includes 1,682 English instances and with 2,615 reference translations into French by professional translators. We are continuing to create new manual translations. English–Spanish training data was sourced under JOKER track [11]. These translation pairs were acquired via a translation contest, forming a total of 2,459 pairs of translated puns which are now undergoing expert evaluation.

Building on translations acquired in previous years, we are interested in enriching parallel data from OPUS [19], a widely used open collection of web-mined parallel corpora covering over 59B sentence pairs across more than 1,000 languages. In addition to collecting, aligning, and filtering parallel data, we will expand our corpus by generating translations using state-of-the-art NMT tools (including LLMs and other well-known systems) and revising them semi-automatically, combining machine-generated annotations with manual ones.

*Evaluation.* We will provide a range of standard MT measures (BLEU, METEOR, COMET, BERTScore, etc.). In addition, we will continue the practice of having trained experts manually evaluate system translations based on features such as lexical field preservation, sense preservation, wordplay form preservation, style shift, or humorousness shift, as well as the presence of errors in syntax, word choice, etc. Runs will be ranked according to the number of successful translations – i.e., translations preserving, to the extent possible, both the form and sense of the original wordplay. We will also experiment with pun location-based evaluation [3] and LLM-as-a-judge.

### 3.3   Task 3: Onomastic Wordplay Translation

*Description.* This task, run as a pilot in 2025, involves the translation of onomastic (i.e., name-based) wordplay from English to French. Onomastic wordplay has been widely used as a rhetorical device by novelists, poets, and playwrights. It is widespread in classic literature, such as in Shakespeare's characters' names, but also names found in modern-day works such as Pokémon, Harry Potter, Asterix, and video games. Meaningful proper names in fictional universes are often neologisms. Neologisms – that is, newly coined words – are among the most common forms of linguistic creativity. Due to their highly idiosyncratic nature, humorous neologisms are challenging for both humans and machines to translate.

*Data.* We constructed a parallel corpus of wordplay in named entities in English and French. We collected distinct named entities in English that contain wordplay from video games, advertising slogans, literature, and other sources, along with their translations into French. There are 2,333 English instances with French reference translations for testing, and 353 for training. We are continuing to source new pairs. The data includes various types of wordplay, such as portmanteaux, puns/homophones, alliterations, and anagrams. References are classified and produced by translation professionals and students, with the majority being truly novel and not seen by LLMs during training.

*Evaluation.* Participants' translations will be evaluated automatically for accuracy by checking for exact matches against the reference translations. To account for alternative valid translations not found in the reference data, we will make use of manual binary evaluation by expert translators and experiment with LLM-as-a-judge.

## 3.4  Task 4: Humour Generation

*Description.* This is a new task that assesses the generative capabilities of LLM-based systems. With the field advancing quickly, a gap remains in the creative translation required for humour preservation. While our analyses of previous years' results show that the strongest systems can excel at literal translation, humorous text often demands substantial creative adaptation: word-for-word renderings rarely preserve wordplay, double meanings, or cultural allusions. We therefore aim to evaluate LLM-based generative systems not only on fidelity but also on their capacity to adapt or re-create content so that the target text conveys comparable intent and effect. This motivates a new evaluation task in which models must produce humour across languages under clear constraints, with assessment centered on semantic consistency, humorous effect, and justified adaptation rather than surface overlap.

*Data.* The humour generation task will be built on a multilingual dataset of queries acquired in Task 1 and systematically expanded by (i) mining additional task-like prompts from large instruction corpora and (ii) synthetically generating new queries via LLM-based instruction-generation pipelines (Self-Instruct [20], Evol-Instruct [21]). We plan to expand our data to include English, French, Spanish, and Russian. To ground prompts in humour-specific phenomena, we will leverage ExPUNations annotations – keyword spans, natural-language explanations, and funniness ratings [18] – and augment them with an additional 1,000 explanations from our SemEval-derived pool. From SemEval-2017 Task 7, Subtask 3 (Pun interpretation), we will use the provided annotations – the marked pun word and the WordNet sense keys per context – to parameterise instruction templates (e.g., specifying the pun token, topic/genre, pun type, and target sense glosses) and build queries [16]. We will localise queries across target languages, enforce topic/style balance, and apply a multi-stage filter (near-duplicate detection, length/format checks, basic safety screens), followed by targeted human spot-checks for calibration.

*Evaluation.* We will adopt an Arena-style [1] protocol in which multiple state-of-the-art models are evaluated automatically via LLM-as-a-judge [15, 23] pairwise comparisons of generated jokes for each query/instruction, complemented by manual pairwise assessment, with final standings computed on an Elo ranking.

## 4    Discussion and Conclusions

In this paper, we have presented the details of the corpus creation, content selection, and relevance judgments/reference data for the JOKER 2026 tasks. For *Task 1: Humour-aware Information Retrieval*, we have detailed the test collection, which we can expand considerably in 2026. For *Task 2: Pun Translation*, we have described our corpus of multiple professional reference translations and outlined our work to collect 1,000+ more English source and French reference translation pairs and to extend the task to Spanish. For *Task 3: Onomastic Wordplay Translation*, we have described the existing corpus constructed in 2025 and our plans to extend it. We have also described a new *Task 4: Humour Generation* on English, French, Spanish, and Russian that will be introduced in 2026.

We will continue to run our tasks at Codabench as part of the further professionalisation of CLEF. This was a considerable investment in 2025, and it enables us to keep the track running in post-competition mode, allowing for the submission of runs throughout the year. For more information please visit https://www.joker-project.com.

**Acknowledgments.** We thank the Master's students in translation and technical writing from the University of Brest for participating in data annotation, and CodaBench for hosting the competition. Liana Ermakova is partly funded by the National Research Agency (ANR-19-GURE-0001) under the program *"Investissements d'avenir"* integrated into France 2030. Jaap Kamps is partly funded by the Netherlands Organization for Scientific Research (NWO NWA #1518.22.105), the University of Amsterdam (AI4FinTech program), and ICAI (AI for Open Government Lab). Views expressed in this paper are not necessarily shared or endorsed by those funding the research.

**Disclosure of Interests.** The authors have no competing interests to declare that are relevant to the content of this article.

**Disclosure of Generative AI Use.** During the preparation of this work, the authors used *ChatGPT* and *Grammarly* in order to: **Grammar and spelling check** and **Paraphrase and reword**. After using these tools/services, the authors reviewed and edited the content as needed and take full responsibility for the publication's content.

## References

1. Chiang, W.L., et al.: Chatbot Arena: an open platform for evaluating LLMs by human preference. In: Proceedings of the 41st International Conference on Machine Learning. ICML'24, JMLR.org (2024)

2. Ermakova, L., Bosser, A., Jatowt, A., Miller, T.: The JOKER corpus: English-French parallel data for multilingual wordplay recognition. In: Chen, H., Duh, W.E., Huang, H., Kato, M.P., Mothe, J., Poblete, B. (eds.) Proceedings of the 46th International ACM SIGIR Conference on Research and Development in Information Retrieval, SIGIR 2023, Taipei, July 23-27, 2023, pp. 2796–2806. ACM (2023). https://doi.org/10.1145/3539618.3591885

3. Ermakova, L., Bosser, A.G., Miller, T., Campos, R.: Overview of the CLEF 2025 JOKER task 2: wordplay translation from English into French. In: Faggioli, G., Ferro, N., Rosso, P., Spina, D. (eds.) CLEF 2025 Working Notes, pp. 2761–2779. CEUR Workshop Proceedings, CEUR-WS.org (2025). https://ceur-ws.org/Vol-4038/paper_219.pdf

4. Ermakova, L., Bosser, A., Miller, T., Jatowt, A.: Overview of the CLEF 2024 JOKER task 1: humour-aware information retrieval. In: Faggioli, G., Ferro, N., Galuscáková, P., de Herrera, A.G.S. (eds.) Working Notes of the Conference and Labs of the Evaluation Forum (CLEF 2024), Grenoble, 9-12 September, 2024. CEUR Workshop Proceedings, vol. 3740, pp. 1775–1785. CEUR-WS.org (2024). https://ceur-ws.org/Vol-3740/paper-165.pdf

5. Ermakova, L., Bosser, A., Miller, T., Jatowt, A.: Overview of the CLEF 2024 JOKER task 3: translate puns from English to French. In: Faggioli, G., Ferro, N., Galuscáková, P., de Herrera, A.G.S. (eds.) Working Notes of the Conference and Labs of the Evaluation Forum (CLEF 2024), Grenoble, France, 9-12 September, 2024. CEUR Workshop Proceedings, vol. 3740, pp. 1800–1810. CEUR-WS.org (2024), https://ceur-ws.org/Vol-3740/paper-167.pdf

6. Ermakova, L., Bosser, A., Miller, T., Palma-Preciado, V.M., Sidorov, G., Jatowt, A.: Overview of the CLEF 2024 JOKER track - automatic humour analysis. In: Goeuriot, L., Mulhem, P., Quénot, G., Schwab, D., Nunzio, G.M.D., Soulier, L., Galuscáková, P., de Herrera, A.G.S., Faggioli, G., Ferro, N. (eds.) Experimental IR Meets Multilinguality, Multimodality, and Interaction - 15th International Conference of the CLEF Association, CLEF 2024, Grenoble, France, September 9-12, 2024, Proceedings, Part II. Lecture Notes in Computer Science, vol. 14959, pp. 165–182. Springer (2024https://doi.org/10.1007/978-3-031-71908-0_8

7. Ermakova, L., Campos, R., Bosser, A., Miller, T.: Overview of the CLEF 2025 JOKER lab: humour in the machine. In: Carrillo-de-Albornoz, J., et al., (eds.) Experimental IR Meets Multilinguality, Multimodality, and Interaction - 16th International Conference of the CLEF Association, CLEF 2025, Madrid, Spain, September 9-12, 2025, Proceedings. Lecture Notes in Computer Science, vol. 16089, pp. 315–337. Springer (2025). https://doi.org/10.1007/978-3-032-04354-2_18

8. Ermakova, L., Campos, R., Bosser, A.G., Miller, T.: Overview of the CLEF 2025 JOKER task 1: humour-aware information retrieval. In: Faggioli, G., Ferro, N., Rosso, P., Spina, D. (eds.) CLEF 2025 Working Notes, pp. 2744–2760. CEUR Workshop Proceedings, CEUR-WS.org (2025). https://ceur-ws.org/Vol-4038/paper_218.pdf

9. Ermakova, L., Miller, T., Bosser, A., Palma-Preciado, V.M., Sidorov, G., Jatowt, A.: Overview of JOKER 2023 automatic wordplay analysis task 1 - pun detection. In: Aliannejadi, M., Faggioli, G., Ferro, N., Vlachos, M. (eds.) Working Notes of the Conference and Labs of the Evaluation Forum (CLEF 2023), Thessaloniki, Greece, September 18th to 21st, 2023. CEUR Workshop Proceedings, vol. 3497, pp. 1785–1803. CEUR-WS.org (2023). https://ceur-ws.org/Vol-3497/paper-149.pdf

10. Ermakova, L., Miller, T., Bosser, A., Palma-Preciado, V.M., Sidorov, G., Jatowt, A.: Overview of JOKER 2023 automatic wordplay analysis task 2 - pun location

and interpretation. In: Aliannejadi, M., Faggioli, G., Ferro, N., Vlachos, M. (eds.) Working Notes of the Conference and Labs of the Evaluation Forum (CLEF 2023), Thessaloniki, Greece, September 18th to 21st, 2023. CEUR Workshop Proceedings, vol. 3497, pp. 1804–1817. CEUR-WS.org (2023). https://ceur-ws.org/Vol-3497/paper-150.pdf

11. Ermakova, L., Miller, T., Bosser, A., Palma-Preciado, V.M., Sidorov, G., Jatowt, A.: Overview of JOKER 2023 automatic wordplay analysis task 3 - pun translation. In: Aliannejadi, M., Faggioli, G., Ferro, N., Vlachos, M. (eds.) Working Notes of the Conference and Labs of the Evaluation Forum (CLEF 2023), Thessaloniki, Greece, September 18th to 21st, 2023. CEUR Workshop Proceedings, vol. 3497, pp. 1818–1827. CEUR-WS.org (2023). https://ceur-ws.org/Vol-3497/paper-151.pdf

12. Ermakova, L., Miller, T., Bosser, A., Palma-Preciado, V.M., Sidorov, G., Jatowt, A.: Science for fun: the CLEF 2023 JOKER track on automatic wordplay analysis. In: Kamps, J., et al., (eds.) Advances in Information Retrieval - 45th European Conference on Information Retrieval, ECIR 2023, Dublin, Ireland, April 2-6, 2023, Proceedings, Part III. Lecture Notes in Computer Science, vol. 13982, pp. 546–556. Springer (2023). https://doi.org/10.1007/978-3-031-28241-6_63

13. Ermakova, L., Miller, T., Naud, Y., Bosser, A.G., Campos, R.: Overview of the CLEF 2025 JOKER task 3: onomastic wordplay translation. In: Faggioli, G., Ferro, N., Rosso, P., Spina, D. (eds.) CLEF 2025 Working Notes, pp. 2780–2790. CEUR Workshop Proceedings, CEUR-WS.org (2025). https://ceur-ws.org/Vol-4038/paper_220.pdf

14. Ermakova, L., et al.: Overview of joker@clef 2022: automatic wordplay and humour translation workshop. In: Barrón-Cedeño, A., et al., (eds.) Experimental IR Meets Multilinguality, Multimodality, and Interaction - 13th International Conference of the CLEF Association, CLEF 2022, Bologna, September 5-8, 2022, Proceedings. Lecture Notes in Computer Science, vol. 13390, pp. 447–469. Springer (2022https://doi.org/10.1007/978-3-031-13643-6_27

15. Liu, Y., Iter, D., Xu, Y., Wang, S., Xu, R., Zhu, C.: G-EVAL: NLG evaluation using GPT-4 with better human alignment. In: Bouamor, H., Pino, J., Bali, K. (eds.) Proceedings of the 2023 Conference on Empirical Methods in Natural Language Processing, pp. 2511–2522. Association for Computational Linguistics, Singapore (2023). https://doi.org/10.18653/v1/2023.emnlp-main.153

16. Miller, T., Hempelmann, C., Gurevych, I.: SemEval-2017 task 7: detection and interpretation of English puns. In: Bethard, S., Carpuat, M., Apidianaki, M., Mohammad, S.M., Cer, D., Jurgens, D. (eds.) Proceedings of the 11th International Workshop on Semantic Evaluation (SemEval-2017), pp. 58–68. Association for Computational Linguistics, Vancouver (2017). https://doi.org/10.18653/v1/S17-2005

17. Palma-Preciado, V.M., Sidorov, G., Ermakova, L., Bosser, A., Miller, T., Jatowt, A.: Overview of the CLEF 2024 JOKER task 2: humour classification according to genre and technique. In: Faggioli, G., Ferro, N., Galuscáková, P., de Herrera, A.G.S. (eds.) Working Notes of the Conference and Labs of the Evaluation Forum (CLEF 2024), Grenoble, France, 9-12 September, 2024. CEUR Workshop Proceedings, vol. 3740, pp. 1786–1799. CEUR-WS.org (2024). https://ceur-ws.org/Vol-3740/paper-166.pdf

18. Sun, J., et al.: ExPUNations: augmenting puns with keywords and explanations. In: Goldberg, Y., Kozareva, Z., Zhang, Y. (eds.) Proceedings of the 2022 Conference on Empirical Methods in Natural Language Processing, pp. 4590–4605. Association

for Computational Linguistics, Abu Dhabi (2022). https://doi.org/10.18653/v1/2022.emnlp-main.304

19. Tiedemann, J.: Parallel data, tools and interfaces in OPUS. In: Calzolari, N., et al., (eds.) Proceedings of the Eighth International Conference on Language Resources and Evaluation (LREC'12), pp. 2214–2218. European Language Resources Association (ELRA), Istanbul (2012). https://aclanthology.org/L12-1246/

20. Wang, Y., et al.: Self-instruct: aligning language models with self-generated instructions. In: Rogers, A., Boyd-Graber, J., Okazaki, N. (eds.) Proceedings of the 61st Annual Meeting of the Association for Computational Linguistics (Volume 1: Long Papers), pp. 13484–13508. Association for Computational Linguistics, Toronto (2023). https://doi.org/10.18653/v1/2023.acl-long.754

21. Xu, C., et al.: WizardLM: empowering large pre-trained language models to follow complex instructions. In: Kim, B., Yue, Y., Chaudhuri, S., Fragkiadaki, K., Khan, M., Sun, Y. (eds.) International Conference on Representation Learning. vol. 2024, pp. 30745–30766 (2024). https://proceedings.iclr.cc/paper_files/paper/2024/file/82eec786fdfbbfa53450c5feb7d1ac92-Paper-Conference.pdf

22. Xu, Z., et al.: Codabench: flexible, easy-to-use, and reproducible meta-benchmark platform. Patterns **3**(7), 100543 (2022). https://doi.org/10.1016/J.PATTER.2022.100543

23. Zheng, L., et al.: Judging LLM-as-a-judge with MT-bench and Chatbot Arena. In: Proceedings of the 37th International Conference on Neural Information Processing Systems, pp. 46595–46623. NIPS '23, Curran Associates Inc., Red Hook (2023)

# TalentCLEF at CLEF2026: Skill and Job Title Intelligence for Human Capital Management

Luis Gasco[1]([envelope]) [ORCID], Hermenegildo Fabregat[1], Laura García-Sardiña[1], Paula Estrella[1], Casimiro Pio Carrino[1], Daniel Deniz[1], Alvaro Rodrigo[2], and Rabih Zbib[1]

[1] Avature, Madrid, Spain
`machinelearning@avature.net`
[2] NLP and IR Group, UNED, Madrid, Spain

**Abstract.** This paper presents the second edition of the TalentCLEF Challenge, which will run as an evaluation lab part of CLEF2026. The aim of TalentCLEF is to promote the development of systems and methods that use Natural Language Processing (NLP) in the field of Human Capital Management (HCM), fostering approaches that ensure fairness in results, operate across multiple languages, and adapt to diverse industries. To this end, TalentCLEF establishes public benchmarks where research teams can compare methods and share findings, moving the field toward more practical and impactful NLP solutions that effectively address the real needs of workforce management.

This year's lab will feature two tasks designed to foster the development and evaluation of systems that support key HCM activities such as talent matching, upskilling, reskilling, and skill gap detection: (i) Task A – Contextualized Job-Person Matching, focused on retrieving and ranking suitable candidates for specific job positions using context-rich and privacy-preserving data, and (ii) Task B – Job-Skill Matching with Skill Type Classification, centered on identifying relevant skills for a given job title and classifying them by their type within the job profile.

TalentCLEF website: https://talentclef.github.io/talentclef/.

**Keywords:** Natural Language Processing · Human Capital Management · Human Resources · Multilinguality · Cross-linguality · Skill Predictions · Job Title Ranking

## 1 Introduction

Over the past decade, technology has significantly transformed the labor market. Digitalization, the expansion of remote work, and the growing internationalization of organizations have shaped an increasingly global, multilingual, and competitive environment, both for companies seeking to attract talent and for workers accessing new professional opportunities. In this context, the emergence of Artificial Intelligence (AI) is introducing an even more significant transformation, affecting both the nature of jobs and the competencies required to perform them. According to recent projections, more than 1.1 billion jobs could be transformed by the end of the decade [20], with approximately 70% of the skills currently used in most occupations expected to change as a result of technological evolution [12]. This trend is already evident: In 2024, 74% of employers reported difficulties in finding candidates with suitable skills for their job openings [14].

This transformation process has profound implications for Human Capital Management (HCM), particularly in key areas such as recruitment, learning, and career management. Identifying and selecting suitable candidates has become increasingly complex in an environment where professional requirements evolve very fast. Both organizations and employees need effective tools to continue developing new professional capabilities, as well as mechanisms that support flexible and adaptable career paths within a constantly changing labor market. Companies must attract and manage the right talent, and workers need to update and show their capabilities effectively in a highly competitive global environment.

In recent years, the application of Natural Language Processing (NLP) technologies to HCM has advanced substantially. Various initiatives [2,8,11] have contributed to the consolidation of a research community focused on the use of language models and machine learning to represent and analyze information related to skills, occupations, and career paths. These developments have enabled the creation of systems that can extract and normalize relevant information from semi-structured records like résumés and job descriptions [7,16–18,22,23], as well as measuring semantic similarity between profiles and job postings [3,4,15,21]. At the same time, recent research has emphasized the importance of addressing aspects such as detection of algorithmic bias and fairness evaluation in automated decision-making processes within the labor context [1,6].

Despite these advances, the development of AI systems applied to talent management continues to face structural limitations. Most studies rely on private data, which restricts reproducibility and hinders the comparison of different approaches. The few public resources available often lack consistent annotation criteria or sufficient information regarding their quality. Standardized evaluation frameworks for assessing system performance and fairness are still missing. As a result, comparing models and methods remains challenging, and research in this area progresses in a fragmented manner.

TalentCLEF[1] was conceived precisely to address this gap [8,10]. The strong participation in the first edition, which attracted 76 teams and generated 280 system submissions, confirmed the growing interest of the community in this domain. Building on this success, a second edition has been launched under the umbrella of CLEF 2026 to consolidate and expand the initiative. Its goal is to continue providing an open, reproducible, and multilingual evaluation environment that promotes the development and comparison of AI technologies applied to talent management.

---

[1] https://talentclef.github.io/talentclef/.

## 2   TalentCLEF 2026 Evaluation Lab

The second edition of TalentCLEF builds on the foundations established in 2025 [9]. The new lab consists of two complementary tasks that operate on realistic multilingual synthetic data and focus on two key entity types in the employment domain: job titles and skills. Unlike last year's edition, which centered on shorter and non-contextual inputs, this year's edition extends that foundation by incorporating richer contextual information from synthetic job descriptions and résumés. Specifically, Task A addresses multilingual job–person matching, while Task B continues with the same focus, predicting skills relevant to specific job positions, two challenges that are central not only to recruiting, but also to learning and career development (Fig. 1).

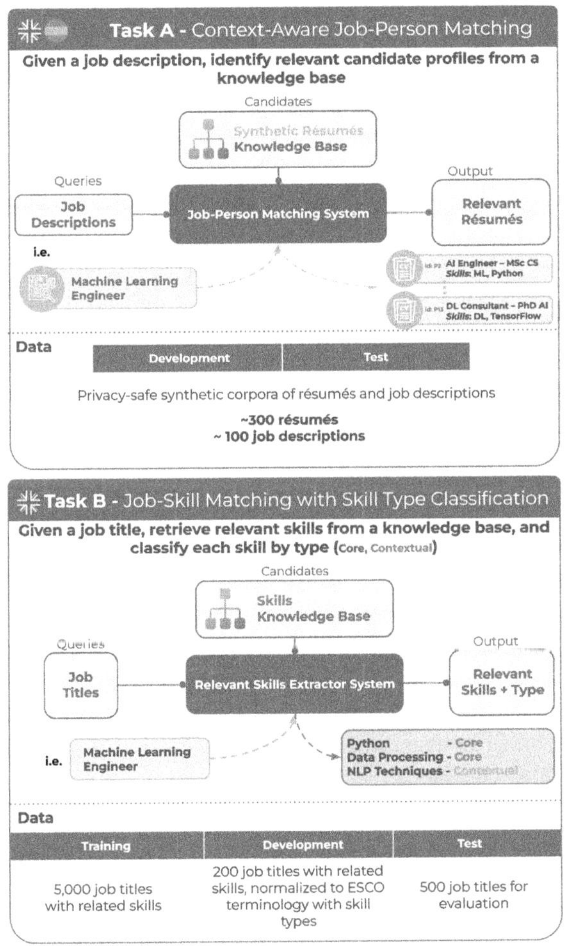


**Fig. 1.** Diagrams of TalentCLEF Task A and B

## 2.1   Task A Context-Aware Job-Person Matching

Matching candidates to job offers is a central problem in recruitment systems. Traditionally, automatic job-candidate matching has relied on the comparison of isolated entities, such as skills or job titles, both extracted from résumés and job descriptions. However, such approaches often overlook the broader semantic and contextual relationships between these elements, largely due to technical and scalability constraints [24]. The evolution of Large Language Models (LLMs) is opening new opportunities for context-aware candidate–job matching. These models enable systems to move beyond the similarities of isolated entities towards a deeper, holistic understanding of both candidates and job postings within their full semantic context [5,13].

This year, Task A specifically challenges participants to develop systems capable of identifying the most appropriate candidate profiles for a given job offer. In contrast to the previous edition, which focused on measuring the similarity between pairs of job titles to build job recommendation systems, this version shifts the focus toward matching job offers to suitable candidate résumés.

The documents used in the task are synthetically generated from structured data originally derived from real job descriptions and curricula vitae, ensuring both realism and privacy preservation. The dataset covers multiple professional domains and sectors, selected through a clustering process based on semantic vector representations in order to guarantee diversity and representativeness.

The synthetic data generation process is carried out in English and is followed by a manual review to ensure data quality and internal document coherence. Additionally, human expert annotators explicitly verify the correctness of job-candidate matches, confirming whether each résumé is appropriate for the corresponding job offer. For the multilingual version of the dataset (in Spanish), parallel translations are produced using LLMs and subsequently validated by human reviewers to ensure semantic consistency across languages, with an emphasis on content equivalence.

For the task, participants will be provided with a development set and a test set, composed of a total of 100 job descriptions and 300 synthetic résumés. The development set can be used to design, train, and validate systems that take a job description as input and output a list of candidate profiles ranked according to their relevance. Participants are encouraged to explore techniques such as data augmentation, fine-tuning, prompt engineering, information extraction, or representation learning to improve their models' performance. On the other hand, the test set will be used in the official evaluation phase, which is designed to ensure a fair and consistent comparison across all submitted runs.

## 2.2   Task B Job-Skill Matching with Skill Type Classification

Employers have shifted the focus of their talent management strategies from role-based to skill-based. Understanding which skills are associated with a job role is essential not only for improving recruitment systems but also for identifying skill gaps within organizations and designing targeted upskilling and reskilling programs, allowing companies to adapt more rapidly to changes in the labor market.

With this in mind, Task B challenges participants to develop systems capable of automatically identifying the most relevant skills for a given job title. This year's task extends Task B from the previous edition of TalentCLEF, improving the quality of the dataset and introducing an additional layer of information: Skill type classification.

Participants must retrieve the skills that best match each job title and determine whether each skill is core or contextual. Core skills are those required to perform a specific job independently of the work context or employer and can thus be seen as essential for the position, whereas contextual skills depend on factors such as the organization or industry and can therefore be seen as optional.

For example, a *software engineer* may be required to *develop mobile applications* in some companies or projects, depending on the product and technical stack, but will always be required to *write code*. In this case, *write code* is a core skill, while *mobile application development* is a contextual skill. Similarly, a *project manager* may be required to use *Agile methodologies* in certain organizations, depending on the adopted management framework, but will always need to *plan and coordinate projects*. Here, *plan and coordinate projects* is a core skill, whereas *Agile methodologies* is a contextual skill.

As in the previous year, the dataset supporting Task B is divided into three subsets designed to train, validate, and benchmark the proposed systems. The training set contains 5,000 job titles linked to their corresponding relevant skills, providing a solid foundation for model development. The development set includes 200 job titles normalized to ESCO terminology and enriched with the new skill type annotations, enabling participants to fine-tune and validate their systems using richer semantic information. Finally, the test set, comprising 500 job titles, will be used in the official evaluation phase, where participants must generate predictions and submit their ranked outputs and skill types for benchmarking.

### 2.3   Evaluation

Tasks A and B will be evaluated on the Codabench platform, using standard information retrieval metrics. Mean Average Precision (MAP) will serve as the official metric for both tasks, and complementary metrics such as Mean Reciprocal Rank (MRR) and Precision@K will be reported.

For Task A, the evaluations will be conducted in two monolingual settings (English and Spanish), as well as in a cross-lingual setting (en–es). In addition, the evaluation will incorporate a fairness assessment to measure model performance with respect to gender bias, using the Rank-Biased Overlap metric (RBO) [19]. This ensures that the analysis not only captures performance, but also addresses fairness and ethical robustness, which are especially relevant in sensitive areas of application like Human Capital Management.

For Task B, the evaluation will be designed to provide a more nuanced assessment of system performance by explicitly accounting for the different importance levels of the retrieved skills based on the skill type classification. In addition to standard retrieval measures, we will employ a graded relevance evaluation framework based on Normalized Discounted Cumulative Gain (NDCG), which allows relevance weights to be incorporated into the ranking of the predicted skills.

The top two teams in each monolingual evaluation, the best cross-lingual team, and the model with the best bias control will be highlighted during the workshop. For Task B, the two best-performing teams will be recognized. All of these teams will receive a certificate of achievement acknowledging their results.

**Invitation to Participate** Anyone interested in joining the TalentCLEF challenge can register on the CLEF conference website. After registering, participants will be able to upload their prediction output via the CodaLab competition system.

**Disclosure of Interests.** Some of the authors are affiliated with Avature, which is involved in the organization of the TalentCLEF evaluation lab. All datasets are publicly released for research purposes, and no proprietary or confidential data is used. The authors declare no other competing interests.

# References


1. Albaroudi, E., Mansouri, T., Alameer, A.: A comprehensive review of AI techniques for addressing algorithmic bias in job hiring. AI **5**(1), 383–404 (2024). https://doi.org/10.3390/ai5010019
2. Bogers, T., Kaya, M., Decorte, J.J., Johnson, C., Bied, G.: Fifth workshop on recommender systems for human resources (RecSys in HR 2025). In: Proceedings of the Nineteenth ACM Conference on Recommender Systems, pp. 1373–1377 (2025). https://doi.org/10.1145/3705328.3748499
3. Decorte, J., Hautte, J.V., Demeester, T., Develder, C.: Jobbert: understanding job titles through skills. CoRR (2021). https://doi.org/10.48550/arXiv.2109.09605
4. Deniz, D., Retyk, F., García-Sardiña, L., Fabregat, H., Gascó, L., Zbib, R.: Combined unsupervised and contrastive learning for multilingual job recommendation. In: Proceedings of the 4th Workshop on Recommender Systems for Human Resources (RecSys-in-HR 2024). vol. 3788 (2024). https://ceur-ws.org/Vol-3788/RecSysHR2024-paper_3.pdf
5. Gan, C., Zhang, Q., Mori, T.: Application of LLM agents in recruitment: a novel framework for automated resume screening. J. Inf. Process. **32**, 881–893 (2024). https://doi.org/10.2197/ipsjjip.32.881
6. García-Sardiña, L., Fabregat, H., Deniz, D., Zbib, R.: Measuring gender bias in job title matching for grammatical gender languages. CoRR **abs/2509.13803** (2025). https://doi.org/10.48550/arXiv.2509.13803
7. García-Sardiña, L., Retyk, F., Fabregat, H., Alvarez Lacasa, L., Poves, R., Zbib, R.: Normalisation of education information in digitalised recruitment processes. Procesamiento del Lenguaje Natural **71**, 63–73 (2023). http://journal.sepln.org/sepln/ojs/ojs/index.php/pln/article/view/6543
8. Gasco, L., et al.: TalentCLEF at CLEF2025: skill and job title intelligence for human capital management. In: Advances in Information Retrieval, pp. 479–486. Springer Nature Switzerland (2025). https://doi.org/10.1007/978-3-031-88720-8_69

9. Gasco, L., et al.: Brief overview of TalentCLEF 2025. CLEF (Working Notes) **4038**, 4388–4391 (2025). https://ceur-ws.org/Vol-4038/paper_362.pdf
10. Gasco, L., et al.: Overview of the TalentCLEF 2025: skill and job title intelligence for human capital management. In: Experimental IR Meets Multilinguality, Multimodality, and Interaction, pp. 464–485. Springer Nature Switzerland (2026).https://doi.org/10.1007/978-3-032-04354-2_24
11. Hruschka, E., Lake, T., Otani, N., Mitchell, T.: Proceedings of the first workshop on natural language processing for human resources (NLP4HR 2024). In: Proceedings of the First Workshop on Natural Language Processing for Human Resources (NLP4HR 2024). Association for Computational Linguistics (2024). https://aclanthology.org/2024.nlp4hr-1.0/
12. LinkedIn: Work Change Report: AI Is Coming to Work (2025). https://economicgraph.linkedin.com/content/dam/me/economicgraph/en-us/PDF/Work-Change-Report.pdf, Accessed 18 May 2025
13. Lo, F.P.W., et al.: AI hiring with LLMs: a context-aware and explainable multi-agent framework for resume screening. In: 2025 IEEE/CVF Conference on Computer Vision and Pattern Recognition Workshops (CVPRW), pp. 4184–4193 (2025). https://doi.org/10.1109/CVPRW67362.2025.00402
14. ManpowerGroup: 2024 Global Talent Shortage (2024). https://go.manpowergroup.com, Accessed 19 May 2025
15. Otani, N., Bhutani, N., Hruschka, E.: Natural language processing for human resources: a survey. In: Proceedings of the 2025 Conference of the Nations of the Americas Chapter of the Association for Computational Linguistics: Human Language Technologies (Volume 3: Industry Track), pp. 583–597. Association for Computational Linguistics (2025). https://doi.org/10.18653/v1/2025.naacl-industry.47
16. Retyk, F., Fabregat, H., Aizpuru, J., Taglio, M., Zbib, R.: Résumé parsing as hierarchical sequence labeling: an empirical study. In: Proceedings of the 3rd Workshop on Recommender Systems for Human Resources (RecSys in HR 2023) . CEUR Workshop Proceedings, vol. 3490 (2023). https://ceur-ws.org/Vol-3490/RecSysHR2023-paper_10.pdf
17. Retyk, F., Gascó, L., Carrino, C.P., Deniz, D., Zbib, R.: MELO: an evaluation benchmark for multilingual entity linking of occupations. In: Proceedings of the 4th Workshop on Recommender Systems for Human Resources (RecSys-in-HR 2024). CEUR Workshop Proceedings, vol. 3788 (2024). https://ceur-ws.org/Vol-3788/RecSysHR2024-paper_2.pdf
18. Senger, E., Zhang, M., van der Goot, R., Plank, B.: Deep Learning-based computational job market analysis: a survey on skill extraction and classification from job postings. In: Proceedings of the First Workshop on Natural Language Processing for Human Resources (NLP4HR 2024), pp. 1–15. Association for Computational Linguistics (2024). https://aclanthology.org/2024.nlp4hr-1.1/
19. Webber, W., Moffat, A., Zobel, J.: A similarity measure for indefinite rankings. ACM Trans. Inf. Syst. **28**(4) (2010). https://doi.org/10.1145/1852102.1852106
20. World Economic Forum: The Reskilling Revolution: 350 Million People Reached with Future-Ready Skills, Education and Jobs. https://www.weforum.org/press/2023/01/the-reskilling-revolution-350-million-people-reached-with-future-ready-skills-education-and-jobs/ (January 2023), press release
21. Zbib, R., et al.: Learning job titles similarity from noisy skill labels. CoRR **abs/2207.00494** (2022). https://doi.org/10.48550/ARXIV.2207.00494
22. Zhang, M., Jensen, K.N., van der Goot, R., Plank, B.: Skill extraction from job postings using weak supervision. In: Proceedings of the 2nd Workshop on Rec-

ommender Systems for Human Resources (RecSys-in-HR 2022). CEUR Workshop Proceedings, vol. 3218 (2022). https://ceur-ws.org/Vol-3218/RecSysHR2022-paper_10.pdf
23. Zhang, M., Jensen, K.N., Sonniks, S.D., Plank, B.: SkillSpan: hard and soft skill extraction from english job postings. In: Proceedings of the 2022 Conference of the North American Chapter of the Association for Computational Linguistics: Human Language Technologies, NAACL, pp. 4962–4984. Association for Computational Linguistics (2022). https://doi.org/10.18653/V1/2022.NAACL-MAIN.366
24. Zhao, J., Wang, J., Sigdel, M., Zhang, B., Hoang, P., Liu, M., Korayem, M.: Embedding-based recommender system for job to candidate matching on scale. In: 2nd International Workshop on Industrial Recommendation Systems (2021). https://doi.org/10.48550/arXiv.2107.00221

# ELOQUENT Lab at CLEF 2026: Evaluation of Generative Language Model Quality


Jussi Karlgren[1,2], Maria Barrett[1], Ondřej Bojar[3], Marie Isabel Engels[4(✉)],
Diandra Fabre[5], Lorraine Goeuriot[5], Josiane Mothe[6], Philippe Mulhem[5],
Mario Piacentini[7], Luis Francisco Vargas Madriz[7], Didier Schwab[5],
Pavel Šindelář[3], Georgios Stampoulidis[1], Katherina Thomas[7],
and Markarit Vartampetian[5]

[1] Silo AI, Helsinki, Finland
[2] University of Helsinki, Helsinki, Finland
[3] Charles University, Prague, Czech Republic
[4] Fraunhofer IAIS, Sankt Augustin, Germany
`marie.engels@iais.fraunhofer.de`
[5] Université Grenoble Alpes, Grenoble, France
[6] INSPE, UT2J, Université de Toulouse, IRIT, Toulouse, France
[7] OECD, Paris, France



**Abstract.** The ELOQUENT lab for evaluation of generative language model quality and usefulness addresses high-level quality criteria for generative language models through a set of open-ended shared tasks implemented, where possible, to minimise human effort in assessment, and with an objective to study how much the languages that the foundation model has been trained on make a difference in its responses.

In this third ELOQUENT edition, the three planned tasks investigate how human-like text generated by language models can be (the Voight-Kampff task), how reliably a language model handles varied but equivalent input across languages (the Robustness and Consistency task), and if a generative language model can be used productively to generate and score topical quizzes without diverging into general knowledge acquired in foundational training (the PISA task). All tasks are continued evolved versions of previous editions' tasks.

**Keywords:** CLEF · Evaluation · Generative language models · LLM · Multilinguality · Quality assessment · Shared task · Trustworthiness


Large generative language models (LLMs) are a foundational technology for both research and information service development, and are used as a tool for solving challenging text analysis problems, not least as evidenced by their use in many of the CLEF labs.

New models with generative capacity are released with various capabilities and intended usage scenarios. The practical application of such models in public



R. Campos et al. (Eds.): ECIR 2026, LNCS 16486, pp. 259–266, 2026.
https://doi.org/10.1007/978-3-032-21321-1_36

arenas, commercial and elsewhere, is challenged by both engineering concerns and to a great extent by quality concerns about predictability and reliability of the output from a generative component. A generative language model can provide a system with fluently generated output but without guarantees for trustworthiness with respect to relevance, veracity, cultural appropriateness, or consistency. Quality assurance, evaluation, and benchmarking of large language models is performed using tests that focus on details of language understanding and reasoning, but many factors that are crucial for application development and deployment to third parties are not addressed systematically through existing benchmarks.

The ELOQUENT evaluation lab experiments with new evaluation methods for generative language models to meet some of the challenges in the path from laboratory to application. The organisers include commercially active artificial intelligence developers, research groups, and organisations which apply artificial intelligence in their primary tasks. The intention of the lab is to explore the following characteristics of generative language model quality:

1. *Trustworthiness*, a many-faceted notion which involves topical relevance and truthfulness, discourse competence, reasoning in language, controllability, and robustness across varied input, which is at the forefront of current development projects for generative language models;
2. *Multi-linguality and cultural fit*: the appropriateness and suitability of a language model for some cultural and linguistic area;
3. *Self-assessment*: the reliability of a language model to assess the quality of itself or some other language model, using as little human effort as possible;
4. *Limits of language models*: the delimitation of world knowledge and generative capacity.

In its first years, ELOQUENT departed slightly from typical CLEF practice by using generative models as judges for the output of their own and other participant's outputs. This is a direction which has been pursued with great interest by many research and practical projects, with obvious risks and vulnerabilities [2,5,7,16]. This year, ELOQUENT will focus on comparing the output of generative models with that of human professionals.

## 1   Learnings from the 2024 and 2025 Editions of ELOQUENT

The first ELOQUENT edition, in 2024, presented four experimental tasks to explore the capacity to generate human-like text (the Voight-Kampff task, in collaboration with the PAN lab) [4], to test topical competence and self testing (the Topical Quiz task) [11], to detect hallucinations in paraphrasing and translation (the Hallucigen task) [6], and to retain consistency of output given varied but equivalent input (the Robustness task) [14], with an overview in [9]. In the second edition we continued the Voight-Kampff task, again in collaboration with the PAN lab [3], we developed the Robustness task further to address value-oriented questions [10], we introduced the Sensemaking task to replace the Topical Quiz task, and we introduced the Preference Prediction task to study the capacity of language models to predict human preferences for output variants [12]. The Hallucigen task was dropped for the second year with the intention to merge it with existing tasks such as the Mushroom task organised through the Semeval conference [15]; the Preference Prediction task is paused for this edition with the option to return the year after. Some results from the predecessor tasks for this year's three tasks are given in sections below.

ELOQUENT has received between 50 and 60 registration sign-ups for teams to participate in various subsets of the tasks; the first year with 8 teams submitting results, the second year 15 teams with 61 submitted experiments. The interest to define and implement more relevant quality measures is increasing in current European artificial intelligence multilingual model related research projects such as OpenEuroLLM, TrustLLM, and DeployAI. ELOQUENT will collaborate with projects to involve their development efforts more directly in the task design and experimentation to familiarise them with this type of shared task, in contrast with the asynchronous leaderboard evaluation schemes typical in model evaluation.

## 2    Learnings from the First and Second Editions and Plans for the Third Edition

In its first edition, ELOQUENT organised four tasks to investigate *topical competence, truthfulness and trustworthiness, robustness* in face of varied input, and the difference between *human-authored versus machine-generated* text. In the second, the truthfulness task was replaced by a task on *preference prediction*. This year, we plan for three tasks, retaining the focus on *topical competence, robustness* and on *human-authored versus machine-generated* characteristics. More details of each coming task are given below, and more comprehensive overview of past tasks have been published in the CLEF 2024 [9] and CLEF 2025 proceedings [8].

**Voight-Kampff Task**

There is a demand for identifying machine generated content as such, motivated by consumer protection, liability concerns, copyright issues, as well as many further reasons. Doing so automatically is in some obvious ways quite similar to human authorship verification, and the *Voight-Kampff Task* is part of a joint effort with the PAN lab at CLEF to address that challenge, bringing together years of experience from previous shared tasks organised by the PAN lab on authorship verification and closely related tasks with the focus on generative artificial intelligence that ELOQUENT participants have from their work on model building, training, tuning, and evaluation.

The Voight-Kampff task ran in both 2024 and 2025 and requires participants to use a system to generate a short text on some given topic, as given by a brief automatically generated summary of a human text (a sample is given in Fig. 1).

These automatically generated texts, together with the human original, are given to text classifiers developed in the PAN lab, with the task to distinguish which ones are authored by humans and which are generated by machines. The first year, the generated texts were not finessed in any special way, and the results indicated that machine text was handily identifiable as such.

The second year, participants experimented with injecting deliberate errors into the texts, and with translating and back-translating the texts to other languages. This proved quite successful and several of the participating generative models were able to fool the classifiers at least some of the time. This is a considerable improvement from the first year, and reflects a more directed experimentation in the submitted experiments. Only two human authored texts were sometimes misclassified as machine generated: an excerpt from the Maastricht treaty and an intro text to large language models. The best generative models fooled the classifiers with many, but never with all of their generated texts, and the rate at which the participating systems were able to generate convincing human-like output varied considerably across test items; the reason for this is unclear and we will direct some systematicity to creating topics in the coming year, to see if this is an effect of the qualities of the summaries or if the language model training data are better equipped for academic styled text than for other genres.

As a very general finding, it is clear that generative language models still have recognisable traits in their output and that classifiers are able to pick up on them quite effectively.

---

**Content**: England offers diverse sea-bathing resorts, with climates ranging from bracingly cold to mild and relaxing, making it ideal for health retreats. Sea-air is especially pure, often rich in ozone, saline particles, and possibly iodine, which contribute to its distinctive smell and health benefits. It is dense, stable in temperature, and more stimulating than inland air improving appetite and general vitality in visitors. However, many seaside towns suffer from poor sanitation, including untreated sewage discharged near public beaches, which undermines the benefits of sea-air. When choosing a sea-bathing location, it is vital to check for proper drainage, clean water supply, and good general hygiene, especially for invalids. Timing of sea-bathing varies by region: the east coast is limited to summer months, while some southern resorts offer an extended season from April to November, though peak summer heat can interrupt bathing.
**Genre**: Informative Nonfiction / Health & Travel Guide (likely late 19th or early 20th century)
**Tone**: Educated, practical, and advisory, with a balanced mix of scientific explanation and common-sense caution, aimed at informing health-conscious readers or caregivers.

---

**Fig. 1.** A sample test item for the Voight-Kampff Task. The Genre and Tone fields are optionally used by the system to guide the style of the generated text.

## Robustness and Consistency Task → Cultural Robustness Task

Linguistic behaviour, values, and cultural practices vary across linguistic areas, cultural areas, and demographic groups. While generative language models are expected to fit their output to the preceding input and to the presumed preferences of their conversational counterpart or their audience, they should also respond consistently to questions whatever language they are posed in. *Robustness Task* examines how the output of generative language models varies across languages and how it can be constrained to be consistent when so requested. In the first edition, the task examined how much *topical* variation in output was conditioned on the *style* of interaction (e.g., posing a question in formal versus uncouth language, or in various dialects), from the standpoint that such variation is undesirable (i.e., a system should not tailor its output with respect to its topical content). [14] In the second edition, the task moved from an English-only approach to examine how much topical variation could be found if a question was posed in a variety of 15 languages. [10]

The resulting variation provided some quite interesting results, and calls for more systematic study in more languages and across cultural areas. As brief samples from the results, item 017 (*"Name ten vegetables."*) yields different vegetables for different languages, somewhat predictably based on the culinary habits of the cultural area that the language mostly is used in: Potato was listed in every case for the Nordic languages (da, fi, sv) and for the English models only when those models also were trained for the Nordic language. Item 010 (*"Is it more important to be polite or to be honest?"*) on the other hand demonstrates the effect of instruction tuning. As this is a potentially controversial issue, the instruction trained models only in very few settings agree to actually recommend one of the virtues of honesty and politeness over the other, instead giving noncommittal general advice about balancing one to the other. As a third example, item 012 (*"Which of the following societal values is most important? Rank them: [individual freedom, promotion of industry, support for creativity, safety, equality, law and order]"*), gives varied results across languages and systems. The generative systems seem to select consistent approaches: safety and freedom are frequently ranked first, above other values. When safety is ranked first, freedom almost never is the second highest ranked value, and vice versa. This seems to indicate that there are consistent ideological perspectives invoked by the data or the post-training of the models used to generate the data.

This year, the task will examine such variation through a more systematic approach, with value-oriented questions in several languages, quantifying the output variation using the newly defined measures of *response diversity* and *response robustness*, using two variations of prompt formulation. [1]

## Topical Quiz Task → Sensemaking Task → PISA Quiz Task

The Topical Quiz Task and the Sensemaking Task ran in 2024 and in 2025, respectively. In the first year, the experiments found that under certain conditions, a system built on a generative language model is able to generate questions, respond to them, and score them fairly; in the second year the task was organised in three subtasks: the *teacher* subtask to generate quiz items from a given set of materials, the *student* subtask to respond to quiz items, and the *evaluator* subtask to score responses. *Teacher* submissions showed that large language models are reasonably good at converting text to questions about its content but reference answers given by the teacher systems were less convincing. The answers to quiz items provided by *student* systems often did not make use of obvious clues about the answer in the materials. For example, in the fact-checking domain, the golden answer was spelled out explicitly in the text, even if a little hidden in a handful of unrelated statements, and yet the systems had difficulties extracting it. The ratings produced by *evaluator* systems were less reliable, especially in adversarial tests, where altered broken responses at times were scored quite highly.

This coming year, the task will involve the participation of OECD, which defines and administers the Programme for International Student Assessment (PISA). PISA is an international survey which aims to evaluate education systems worldwide by testing the skills and knowledge of 15-year-old students nearing the end of their compulsory education. PISA assesses how well they can apply what they learn in school to real-life situations. So far, over 90 countries or economies have participated in the assessment since 2000. In 2020, the PISA Research, Development and Innovation (RDI) Programme started to manage all research and innovation activities related to PISA. The RDI programme is now entering the third biennium of activities and is seeking to increase the efficiency of PISA operation through automated coding. [13]

The experience of the PISA editors, translators, and assessors will be used to inform the experimentation, and the subtasks will involve (1) formulating test items given a small set of topical texts (corresponding to last year's *Teacher* subtask, with the additional requirement that the responses be culturally appropriate to their intended audience), (2) scoring of responses given to such items (corresponding to last year's *Evaluator* subtask), and (3) potentially, the translation of items into a set of languages. The scoring task will involve both real student response and system generated responses, and the results will be compared to those given by human assessors from previous years' PISA editions.

**Data**

The task descriptions, test data, and results, where applicable, from participant experiments (together with data from previous years) will be posted on Huggingface for asynchronous experimentation[1].

**Acknowledgments.** The ELOQUENT lab is partially supported by the OpenEuroLLM (101195233-DIGITAL-2024-AI-06) and the DeployAI (101146490-DIGITAL-2022-CLOUD-AI-B-03) projects through their activities on building, evaluating, and disseminating generative language models. The authors have no competing interests to declare that are relevant to the content of this article.

---

[1] https://huggingface.co/Eloquent.

# References


1. Barrett, M., Stampoulidis, G., Zautner, D., Burdge, J., Karlgren, J.: Measuring the cultural capabilities of LLMs across European languages. In: Under Review (2025)
2. Bavaresco, A., et al.: LLMs instead of Human Judges? a large scale empirical study across 20 NLP evaluation tasks (2024)
3. Bevendorff, J., et al.: Overview of the "Voight-Kampff" generative AI authorship verification task at PAN and ELOQUENT 2025. In: Working Notes of the Conference and Labs of the Evaluation Forum (CLEF 2025). CEUR-WS (2025)
4. Bevendorff, J., et al.: Overview of the "Voight-Kampff" generative AI authorship verification task at PAN and ELOQUENT 2024. In: Working Notes of the Conference and Labs of the Evaluation Forum (CLEF 2024), vol. 3740. CEUR-WS (2024)
5. Doddapaneni, S., Khan, M.S.U.R., Verma, S., Khapra, M.M.: Finding blind spots in evaluator LLMS with interpretable checklists (2024)
6. Dürlich, L., Gogoulou, E., Guillou, L., Nivre, J., Zahra, S.: Overview of the CLEF-2024 eloquent lab: task 2 on HalluciGen. In: Faggioli, G., Ferro, N., Vlachos, M., Galuščáková, P., García Seco de Herrera, A., (eds), Working Notes of CLEF 2024 - Conference and Labs of the Evaluation Forum. CEUR-WS.org (2024)
7. Hui, H., Qu, Y., Zhou, H., Liu, J., Yang, M., Xu, B., Zhao, T.: On the limitations of fine-tuned judge models for LLM evaluation (2024)
8. Karlgren, J., et al.: Overview of ELOQUENT 2025: shared tasks for evaluating generative language model quality. In: International Conference of the Cross-Language Evaluation Forum for European Languages. Springer (2025)
9. Karlgren, J., et al.: Overview of ELOQUENT 2024—shared tasks for evaluating generative language model quality. In: Goeuriot, L., et al., (eds), Experimental IR Meets Multilinguality, Multimodality, and Interaction – Proceedings of the 15th International Conference of the CLEF Association (2024)
10. Karlgren, J., et al.: Overview and joint report of the robustness and consistency task at the ELOQUENT 2025 lab for evaluating generative language model quality. In: Working Notes of the Conference and Labs of the Evaluation Forum (CLEF 2025). CEUR-WS (2025)
11. Karlgren, J., Talman, A.: ELOQUENT 2024 — topical quiz task. In: Faggioli, G., Ferro, N., Vlachos, M., Galuščáková, P., García Seco de Herrera, A., (eds), Working Notes of CLEF 2024 - Conference and Labs of the Evaluation Forum. CEUR-WS.org (2024)
12. Mikhailov, V., Artemova, E., Butenko, Z., Øvrelid, L., Velldal, Z.: Overview of the preference prediction task at the ELOQUENT 2025 lab for evaluating generative language model quality. In: Faggioli, G., Ferro, N., Rosso, P., Spina, D., (eds), Working Notes of CLEF 2025 – Conference and Labs of the Evaluation Forum. CEUR-WS (2025)
13. OECD. PISA 2022 Technical Report. OECD Publishing, Paris (2024)

14. Sahlgren, M., Karlgren, J., Dürlich, L., Gogoulou, E., Talman, A., Zahra, S.: Eloquent 2024—robustness task. In: Faggioli, G., Ferro, N., Vlachos, M., Galuščáková, P., García Seco de Herrera, A. (eds.) Working Notes of CLEF 2024 - Conference and Labs of the Evaluation Forum. CEUR-WS.org (2024)
15. Vázquez, R., et al.: Semeval-2025 task 3: mu-shroom, the multilingual shared task on hallucinations and related observable overgeneration mistakes. arXiv preprint arXiv:2504.11975 (2025)
16. Verga, P., et al.: Replacing judges with juries: Evaluating LLM generations with a panel of diverse models (2024)

# The CLEF-2026 FinMMEval Lab:
## Multilingual and Multimodal Evaluation of Financial AI Systems


Zhuohan Xie[1]([✉])[iD], Rania Elbadry[1][iD], Fan Zhang[2][iD], Georgi Georgiev[3][iD],
Xueqing Peng[4][iD], Lingfei Qian[4][iD], Jimin Huang[4][iD], Dimitar Dimitrov[3][iD],
Vanshikaa Jani[5][iD], Yuyang Dai[6][iD], Jiahui Geng[1][iD], Yuxia Wang[6][iD],
Ivan Koychev[3][iD], Veselin Stoyanov[1][iD], and  Preslav Nakov[1][iD]

[1] MBZUAI, Abu Dhabi, UAE
{zhuohan.xie,preslav.nakov}@mbzuai.ac.ae
[2] The University of Tokyo, Tokyo, Japan
[3] Sofia University "St. Kliment Ohridski", Sofia, Bulgaria
[4] The Fin AI, Tucson, USA
[5] University of Arizona, Tucson, USA
[6] INSAIT, Sofia, Bulgaria



**Abstract.** We present the setup and the tasks of the FinMMEval Lab
at CLEF 2026, which introduces the first multilingual and multimodal
evaluation framework for financial Large Language Models (LLMs).
While recent advances in financial natural language processing have
enabled automated analysis of market reports, regulatory documents,
and investor communications, existing benchmarks remain largely monolingual, text-only, and limited to narrow subtasks. FinMMEval 2026
addresses this gap by offering three interconnected tasks that span
financial understanding, reasoning, and decision-making: Financial Exam
Question Answering, Multilingual Financial Question Answering (Poly-
FiQA), and Financial Decision Making. Together, these tasks provide a
comprehensive evaluation suite that measures models' ability to reason,
generalize, and act across diverse languages and modalities. The lab aims
to promote the development of robust, transparent, and globally inclusive financial AI systems, with datasets and evaluation resources publicly
released to support reproducible research.

**Keywords:** financial natural language processing · multilingual
evaluation · multimodal reasoning · financial question answering ·
financial decision making · financial AI · cross-lingual understanding


## 1 Introduction

The rapid advancement of Large Language Models (LLMs) has propelled significant progress in financial natural language processing (FinNLP), enabling automated analysis of market reports, regulatory documents, and investor communications [20,30,32]. Despite these advances, most existing benchmarks remain

monolingual, text-only, and narrowly focused on sub-tasks such as sentiment classification or factual question answering [1,12]. Yet, modern financial communication is increasingly global and multimodal, spanning multilingual news, regulatory filings, and real-time market data. This evolution calls for comprehensive evaluation frameworks that can assess model's ability to reason, generalize, and act across languages and modalities. To bridge this gap, the FinMMEval Lab at CLEF 2026 extends the evaluation frontier by introducing the first multilingual and multimodal shared tasks for financial LLMs. Building upon the foundations of earlier initiatives such as Regulations Challenge [25], Fin-DBQA [17], and Earnings2Insights [23], FinMMEval integrates financial reasoning, multilingual understanding, and decision-making into a unified evaluation suite designed to promote robust, transparent, and globally competent financial AI. It introduces three interconnected tasks spanning five languages, summarized in Table 1. Each task targets a distinct layer of financial reasoning, from conceptual understanding to real-world decision making, while addressing key challenges in multilingual and multimodal FinNLP:

- *Task 1: Financial Exam Question Answering:* Serves as the foundational component of FinMMEval, focusing on conceptual understanding and domain reasoning (cf. Sect. 3). It evaluates whether models can handle professional exam-style questions across multiple languages, forming the knowledge base upon which the subsequent tasks build.
- *Task 2: Multilingual Financial Question Answering (PolyFiQA):* Extends the conceptual foundation of Task 1 by situating financial reasoning in a multilingual and multimodal context (cf. Sect. 4). It challenges systems to integrate financial reports and news across languages for complex analytical QA, testing their ability to generalize across both linguistic and informational modalities.
- *Task 3: Financial Decision Making:* Synthesizes the knowledge and the reasoning capabilities developed in Tasks 1 and 2 into actionable intelligence (cf. Sect. 5). It assesses reasoning-to-action abilities by requiring models to interpret market dynamics, sentiment, and risk to generate evidence-grounded, risk-aware trading decisions.

Together, these tasks establish a multi-layered evaluation framework that bridges understanding, reasoning, and decision-making: three essential pillars for advancing trustworthy, globally capable financial AI systems.

## 2    Related Work

*Financial AI.* Financial NLP has advanced from task-specific modeling to large-scale domain adaptation. Early studies such as FinBERT [12] established domain-specific transformers for sentiment and classification, later extending to personal finance [7], credit scoring [6], and risk-aware evaluation [33]. Domain datasets including REFinD, FinARG, FiNER-ORD, and ECTSum [8,16,21,27] enabled fine-grained tasks in entity recognition, relation extraction, argument mining, and summarization. Concurrently, English financial NLP benchmarks such as FiQA [13], TAT-QA [37], FinQA [1], ConvFinQA [2], FinanceMath [35], and FinChain [31] have supported progress in sentiment analysis, text–table reasoning, numerical computation, and verifiable reasoning. Large financial language models have further driven domain progress. BloombergGPT [26] demonstrated broad coverage across financial NLP tasks, FinGPT [10] emphasized open-source adaptability, and FinMA [28] achieved competitive performance with compact architectures. Their emergence spurred the creation of benchmarks such as FLANG [22], FinBen [27], and FinMTEB [24], which expanded task diversity and standardization. Recent work has also highlighted retrieval and evidence selection as critical bottlenecks in financial QA: approaches such as FINCARDS [36] reformulate document-level QA as constraint-aware evidence reranking, emphasizing explicit alignment over entities, metrics, fiscal periods, and numerical values. More recent evaluations like BizBench [9] and PIXIU [28] further revealed persistent weaknesses in quantitative reasoning and multimodal understanding, underscoring the need for models that robustly integrate textual, numerical, and structural signals. Building on these foundations, multilingual financial NLP has begun addressing global and cross-cultural contexts. Efforts such as CFinBench [18], FLARE-ES [34], Plutus [19], SAHM [5], and MultiFin-Ben [20] extended financial benchmarks beyond English, supporting evaluation across diverse languages and regulatory environments. These initiatives revealed structural disparities in data availability, annotation quality, and task coverage across languages, underscoring the importance of culturally grounded and linguistically inclusive benchmarks for developing globally robust financial LLMs.

***Related Shared Tasks.***
Given the growing interest in financial NLP, numerous shared tasks have been introduced to address challenges such as misinformation detection [11], financial classification, summarization, stock trading [29], and causality extraction [15]. While most existing work targets English, emerging efforts have explored low-resource languages such as Arabic [14]. Recent initiatives include Earnings2Insights [23], which evaluates systems on generating persuasive investment guidance from earnings call transcripts; the Regulations Challenge [25], which benchmarks LLMs on understanding and applying financial regulations across nine tasks, and Fin-DBQA [17], which assesses multi-turn question answering requiring database querying, multi-hop reasoning, and tabular data manipulation. Collectively, these shared tasks highlight the increasing breadth and complexity of financial NLP benchmarks, though none has yet focused on multilingual or multimodal financial understanding.

## 3   Task 1: Financial Exam Question Answering

*Motivation.* Professional financial qualification exams (e.g., CFA, EFPA) require the integration of theoretical and regulatory knowledge with applied reasoning. Existing LLMs often rely on factual recall without demonstrating the analytical rigor expected from human candidates. This task evaluates whether models can achieve domain-level understanding and reasoning consistency across multilingual financial contexts.

**Table 1.** Languages targeted in the three tasks of the CLEF 2026 FinMMEval Lab. White squares indicate languages with test data only.

| | English | Chinese | Arabic | Hindi | Greek | Japanese | Spanish |
|---|---|---|---|---|---|---|---|
| T1 | ■ | ■ | ■ | ■ | □ | | ■ |
| T2 | ■ | ■ | | | ■ | ■ | ■ |
| T3 | ■ | | | | | | |

*Task Definition.* Given a stand-alone multiple-choice question $Q$ with four candidate answers $\{A_1, A_2, A_3, A_4\}$, the system must select the correct answer $A^*$. The questions cover valuation, accounting, ethics, corporate finance, and regulatory knowledge. The focus is on conceptual understanding and precise financial reasoning rather than surface pattern recognition.

*Data.* We combine existing multilingual financial exam datasets with newly collected materials:

- **EFPA** [20] (Spanish): 230 exam-style multiple-choice questions derived from EFPA certification exam preparation materials, covering investment products, portfolio management, financial regulation, and professional standards. The dataset evaluates applied financial knowledge and conceptual reasoning in Spanish.
- **GRFinQA** [19] (Greek): 268 exam-style multiple-choice questions sourced from Greek university-level finance, business, and economics courses. The questions are manually curated and verified by native Greek speakers to ensure linguistic fidelity and domain correctness.
- **CFA** (English) [3]: 600 exam-style multiple-choice questions covering nine core domains, including ethics, quantitative methods, financial reporting, corporate finance, and portfolio management. The questions emphasize conceptual understanding and professional-level financial reasoning.
- **CPA** (Chinese) [3]: 300 exam-style multiple-choice questions focusing on accounting, auditing, financial management, taxation, economic law, and strategy. The dataset targets domain-specific financial knowledge in Chinese professional certification contexts.
- **BBF** [4] (Hindi): 500–1000 exam-style multiple-choice questions drawn from over 25 Indian financial and institutional exams, covering problem solving, financial mathematics, governance, and regulatory topics. The dataset reflects the diversity of the Indian financial examination landscape.
- **SAHM** [5] (Arabic): 873 exam-style multiple-choice questions from the SAHM benchmark, including accounting and business exam questions derived from authentic Arabic-language examinations. The dataset evaluates financial and business reasoning in Arabic professional and academic contexts.

All questions were reviewed by financial professionals to ensure correctness and conceptual balance.

*Evaluation.* The models are required to output the correct answer, and the performance is measured in terms of accuracy, defined as the proportion of correctly identified options in the test set. Participants may choose to evaluate their systems on any subset of the available languages, including single-language or multilingual settings. Submissions are evaluated within the same task framework, and language coverage is treated as a configurable dimension rather than defining separate subtasks.

## 4   Task 2: Multilingual Financial Question Answering

*Motivation.* Global finance increasingly demands multilingual reasoning across documents such as English financial filings and foreign-language news. However, most existing benchmarks are monolingual. This task introduces the first cross-lingual financial reasoning benchmark, testing a model's ability to integrate multilingual textual signals and perform analytical reasoning grounded in authentic financial data.

*Task Definition.* Given a financial report $R$ (English 10-K/10-Q excerpts) and multilingual news articles $N = \{N_{en}, N_{zh}, N_{ja}, N_{es}, N_{el}\}$ related to the same company filings, the model receives a question $q$ and must generate an answer $a$ supported by multilingual textual evidence. Two difficulty tiers are included:

- **PolyFiQA-Easy:** factual or numerical trend questions (e.g., revenue growth, cash flow irregularities);
- **PolyFiQA-Expert:** complex analytical questions requiring multi-document reasoning (e.g., investment strategies, capital allocation).

*Data.* We use the PolyFiQA-Easy and PolyFiQA-Expert datasets [20], which combine U.S. SEC filings with multilingual news (English, Chinese, Japanese, Spanish, Greek). Each tier includes 172 QA instances (344 total). All questions and answers were manually written and validated by financial experts, with inter-annotator agreement above 89%. The dataset is released under an MIT License.

*Evaluation.* The participating systems are asked to produce concise, evidence-grounded textual answers (up to 100 words). We evaluate the performance using ROUGE-1 as the primary evaluation measure. We further calculate BLEURT and factual consistency as secondary measures.

## 5   Task 3: Financial Decision Making

*Motivation.* Real-world investment decisions require the integration of heterogeneous information sources to form actionable insights, such as textual news, market price dynamics, and current portfolio positions. Unlike static question–answering tasks, this task centers on *reasoning-to-action*: evaluating how models synthesize complex, time-varying market contexts to generate trading strategies that are both evidence-grounded and risk-aware.

*Task Definition.* Given a market context $C = P_t, N_t$, where $P_t$ represents the historical price series, $N_t$ denotes contemporaneous textual information (e.g., news, reports), models are required to predict one of three discrete actions: *Buy, Hold,* or *Sell.* Each prediction must be accompanied by a concise textual rationale ($\leq 50$ words) that explicitly cites the supporting evidence or reasoning process.

In order to prevent data leakage, the task is set over a pre-specified time window in a live environment. During this period, we will collect each team's daily decisions at a fixed cadence (e.g.,!daily submission by a deadline) based strictly on the information that is available for that day.

*Data.* We use two curated JSON datasets that provide daily market contexts for BTC and TSLA. Our aim is to stress-test LLM trading agents across two materially different market microstructures: ($i$) crypto, which trades $24/7$ with fragmented venues, faster regime shifts, and higher tail risk, and ($ii$) equities, which trade in session-based hours with auction opens/closes, corporate-event–driven jumps, and a more regulated market environment. Each context is indexed by ISO date (YYYY-MM-DD) and aggregates heterogeneous signals for that trading day:

- **Assets and coverage:**
  - BTC: Starting from 2025–08–01 and updated daily, the context grows daily (aggregated daily snapshots despite $24/7$ trading);
  - TSLA: Starting from 2025–08–01 and updated daily, the context also grows daily.

- **Fields per date $d$:**
  - `prices` (`float`): a single representative USD value per day (not OHLC and not intra-day series);
  - `news` (`array[string]`): one or more long-form textual syntheses summarizing that day's market/newsflow;
  - `momentum` (`categorical`): {bullish, neutral, bearish}; a daily market-momentum label manually annotated based on the accompanying news (not a computed technical indicator);
  - `future_price_diff` (`float | null`): this is one-day-ahead price change $P_{d+1} - P_d$; null on the last available date;
  - `10k`, `10q` (`array`): fundamental filings associated with the asset. This component is equity-specific (for TSLA), 10k/10q filings are high-signal fundamental disclosures that update the market's expectations about earnings power, guidance, and risk. This information is often incorporated rapidly, especially around earnings, these filings can trigger large repricings, with single-day moves on the order of 10% not uncommon for some companies.
- **Format:** UTF-8 JSON; keys are calendar dates (no intra-day timestamps).

This dataset provides the daily market context $C = \{P_t, N_t\}$ for decision-making; models produce actions (Buy/Hold/Sell), while `future_price_diff` serves as the supervisory signal for optimizing your models.

*Evaluation.* We evaluate the model performance for profitability, stability, and risk control using established quantitative metrics:

- **Primary:** Cumulative Return (CR);
- **Secondary:** Sharpe Ratio (SR), Maximum Drawdown (MD), Daily Volatility (DV), and Annualized Volatility (AV).

Together, these indicators capture the model's ability to balance reward and risk, maintain behavioral consistency, and adapt to varying market regimes in a dynamic trading environment.

## 6  Conclusion and Future Work

We presented the design and the setup of the CLEF 2026 FinMMEval Lab, which introduces the first multilingual and multimodal evaluation framework for financial large language models. Through three interlinked tasks, including Financial Exam Question Answering, Multilingual Financial QA (PolyFiQA), and Financial Decision Making, the lab advances from conceptual understanding to real-world reasoning and action. Together, these tasks form a coherent evaluation hierarchy that reflects how financial expertise is built and applied in practice: from knowledge acquisition, to analytical integration across languages and modalities, and finally to evidence-grounded decision-making.

FinMMEval aims to promote transparent, robust, and globally inclusive financial AI systems. By offering multilingual coverage and multimodal contexts, it bridges an important gap in current FinNLP evaluation, moving beyond English-centric and text-only paradigms. The datasets, evaluation code, and baseline models will be publicly released to encourage reproducibility and collaboration across the financial NLP community.

Future editions will further expand coverage to additional languages, modalities such as charts and regulatory filings, and dynamic real-time evaluation scenarios, paving the way toward trustworthy, adaptive, and globally competent financial LLMs.

**Acknowledgments.** We thank all task organizers, and annotators for their valuable contributions to the CLEF 2026 FinMMEval Lab. We also acknowledge the CLEF community for providing the collaborative platform and infrastructure enabling this multilingual and multimodal evaluation initiative. The datasets and the evaluation scripts will be publicly released to encourage further research in multilingual and multimodal financial AI. The work of Dimitar Dimitrov and Ivan Koychev is partially funded by the EU NextGenerationEU project, through the National Recovery and Resilience Plan of the Republic of Bulgaria, project SUMMIT, No BG-RRP-2.004-0008.

**Disclosure of Interests.** The authors have no competing interests to declare that are relevant to the content of this article.

# References


1. Chen, Z., et al.: FinQA: a dataset of numerical reasoning over financial data. In: Proceedings of the 2021 Conference on Empirical Methods in Natural Language Processing, pp. 3697–3711 (2021)
2. Chen, Z., Li, S., Smiley, C., Ma, Z., Shah, S., Wang, W.Y.: ConvFinQA: exploring the chain of numerical reasoning in conversational finance question answering. In: Proceedings of the 2022 Conference on Empirical Methods in Natural Language Processing, pp. 6279–6292. Association for Computational Linguistics (2022)
3. Dai, Y., Lin, Y., Xie, Z., Wang, Y.: RealFin: how well do LLMs reason about finance when users leave things unsaid? preprint (2026)
4. Devane, V., et al.: BhashaBench-finance: benchmarking AI on Indian financial knowledge. https://huggingface.co/datasets/bharatgenai/bhashabench-finance (2025), Accessed 14 Oct 2025
5. Elbadry, R., et al.: SAHM: a benchmark for Arabic financial and Shari'ah-compliant reasoning. preprint (2026)
6. Feng, D., et al.: Empowering many, biasing a few: generalist credit scoring through large language models. arXiv preprint arXiv:2310.00566 (2023)
7. Hean, O., Saha, U., Saha, B.: Can AI help with your personal finances? Appl. Econ. **57**, 1–9 (2025)
8. Kaur, S., et al.: REFinD: relation extraction financial dataset. In: Proceedings of the 46th International ACM SIGIR Conference on Research and Development in Information Retrieval, pp. 3054–3063 (2023)
9. Koncel-Kedziorski, R., Krumdick, M., Lai, V., Reddy, V., Lovering, C., Tanner, C.: BizBench: a quantitative reasoning benchmark for business and finance. In: Proceedings of the 62nd Annual Meeting of the Association for Computational Linguistics (Volume 1: Long Papers), pp. 8309–8332 (2024)
10. Liu, X.Y., Wang, G., Yang, H., Zha, D.: FinGPT: democratizing internet-scale data for financial large language models. arXiv preprint arXiv:2307.10485 (2023)
11. Liu, Z., et al.: FinNLP-FNP-LLMFinLegal-2025 shared task: financial misinformation detection challenge task. In: Proceedings of the Joint Workshop of the 9th Financial Technology and Natural Language Processing, the 6th Financial Narrative Processing, and the 1st Workshop on Large Language Models for Finance and Legal, pp. 271–276 (2025)
12. Liu, Z., Huang, D., Huang, K., Li, Z., Zhao, J.: FinBERT: a pre-trained financial language representation model for financial text mining. In: Proceedings of the Twenty-Ninth International Joint Conference on Artificial Intelligence. IJCAI'20 (2021)
13. Maia, M., et al.: WWW'18 open challenge: financial opinion mining and question answering. In: Companion Proceedings of The Web Conference 2018, pp. 1941–1942 (2018)
14. Malaysha, S., et al.: AraFinNLP 2024: the first Arabic financial NLP shared task. In: Proceedings of the Second Arabic Natural Language Processing Conference, pp. 393–402 (2024)
15. Mariko, D., Abi-Akl, H., Labidurie, E., Durfort, S., De Mazancourt, H., El-Haj, M.: The financial document causality detection shared task (FinCausal 2020). In: Proceedings of the 1st Joint Workshop on Financial Narrative Processing and MultiLing Financial Summarisation, pp. 23–32 (2020)
16. Mukherjee, R., et al.: ECTSum: a new benchmark dataset for bullet point summarization of long earnings call transcripts. In: Proceedings of the 2022 Conference on

Empirical Methods in Natural Language Processing, pp. 10893–10906. Association for Computational Linguistics (2022)

17. Nararatwong, R., Kertkeidkachorn, N., Takamura, H., Ichise, R.: Fin-DBQA shared-task: database querying and reasoning. In: Proceedings of the Joint Workshop of the 9th Financial Technology and Natural Language Processing, the 6th Financial Narrative Processing, and the 1st Workshop on Large Language Models for Finance and Legal, pp. 385–391 (2025)

18. Nie, Y., et al.: CFinBench: a comprehensive Chinese financial benchmark for large language models. In: Proceedings of the 2025 Conference of the Nations of the Americas Chapter of the Association for Computational Linguistics: Human Language Technologies (Volume 1: Long Papers), pp. 876–891 (2025)

19. Peng, X., et al.: Plutus: benchmarking large language models in low-resource Greek finance. In: Proceedings of the 2025 Conference on Empirical Methods in Natural Language Processing, pp. 30176–30202 (2025)

20. Peng, X., et al.: MultiFinBen: a multilingual, multimodal, and difficulty-aware benchmark for financial LLM evaluation. arXiv preprint arXiv:2506.14028 (2025)

21. Shah, A., Gullapalli, A., Vithani, R., Galarnyk, M., Chava, S.: FiNER-ORD: financial named entity recognition open research dataset. arXiv preprint arXiv:2302.11157 (2023)

22. Shah, R.S., et al.: When FLUE meets FLANG: benchmarks and large pre-trained language model for financial domain. In: Proceedings of the 2022 Conference on Empirical Methods in Natural Language Processing, pp. 2322–2335 (2022)

23. Takayanagi, T., Goldsack, T., Izumi, K., Lin, C., Takamura, H., Chen, C.C.: Earnings2Insights: analyst report generation for investment guidance. In: Proceedings of The 10th Workshop on Financial Technology and Natural Language Processing, pp. 246–251 (2025)

24. Tang, Y., Yang, Y.: FinMTEB: finance massive text embedding benchmark. In: Proceedings of the 2025 Conference on Empirical Methods in Natural Language Processing, pp. 3620–3638 (2025)

25. Wang, K., et al.: FinNLP-FNP-LLMFinLegal-2025 shared task: regulations challenge. In: Proceedings of the Joint Workshop of the 9th Financial Technology and Natural Language Processing, the 6th Financial Narrative Processing, and the 1st Workshop on Large Language Models for Finance and Legal, pp. 363–370 (2025)

26. Wu, S., et al.: BloombergGPT: a large language model for finance. arXiv preprint arXiv:2303.17564 (2023)

27. Xie, Q., et al.: FinBen: a holistic financial benchmark for large language models. In: Advances in Neural Information Processing Systems. vol. 37 (2024)

28. Xie, Q., et al.: PIXIU: a large language model, instruction data and evaluation benchmark for finance. arXiv preprint arXiv:2306.05443 (2023)

29. Xie, Q., et al.: FinNLP-AgentScen-2024 shared task: financial challenges in large language models - FinLLMs. In: Proceedings of the Eighth Financial Technology and Natural Language Processing and the 1st Agent AI for Scenario Planning, pp. 119–126 (2024)

30. Xie, Z., Cohn, T., Lau, J.H.: The next chapter: a study of large language models in storytelling. In: Proceedings of the 16th International Natural Language Generation Conference, pp. 323–351 (2023)

31. Xie, Z., et al.: FinChain: a symbolic benchmark for verifiable chain-of-thought financial reasoning. arXiv preprint arXiv:2506.02515 (2026)

32. Xie, Z., et al.: FIRE: fact-checking with iterative retrieval and verification. In: Findings of the Association for Computational Linguistics: NAACL 2025, pp. 2901–2914 (2025)

33. Yuan, T., et al.: R-Judge: benchmarking safety risk awareness for LLM agents. In: Findings of the Association for Computational Linguistics: EMNLP 2024, pp. 1467–1490 (2024)
34. Zhang, X., et al.: Dólares or dollars? unraveling the bilingual prowess of financial LLMs between Spanish and English. In: Proceedings of the 30th ACM SIGKDD Conference on Knowledge Discovery and Data Mining, pp. 6236–6246 (2024)
35. Zhao, Y., Liu, H., Long, Y., Zhang, R., Zhao, C., Cohan, A.: FinanceMATH: knowledge-intensive math reasoning in finance domains. In: Proceedings of the 62nd Annual Meeting of the Association for Computational Linguistics (Volume 1: Long Papers), pp. 12841–12858 (2024)
36. Zhou, Y., Zhang, F., Chen, Y., Zhang, H., Nakov, P., Xie, Z.: FinCARDS: card-based analyst reranking for financial document question answering. arXiv preprint arXiv:2601.06992 (2026)
37. TZhu, F., et al.: TATQA: a question answering benchmark on a hybrid of tabular and textual content in finance. In: Proceedings of the 59th Annual Meeting of the Association for Computational Linguistics and the 11th International Joint Conference on Natural Language Processing (Volume 1: Long Papers), pp. 3277–3287 (2021). https://doi.org/10.1007/978-981-16-1357-9_3

# Overview of Touché 2026: Argumentation Systems
## Extended Abstract


Johannes Kiesel[1(✉)], Marc Feger[2], Tim Hagen[3,7],
Sebastian Heineking[4], Maximilian Heinrich[5], Maik Fröbe[6],
Katarina Boland[2], Wilhelm Pertsch[6], Julia Romberg[1], Ines Zelch[4,6],
Stefan Dietze[1,2], Matthias Hagen[6], Martin Potthast[3,7,8],
and Benno Stein[5]

[1] GESIS - Leibniz Institute for the Social Sciences, Cologne, Germany
touche@webis.de
[2] Heinrich Heine University Düsseldorf, Düsseldorf, Germany
[3] University of Kassel, Kassel, Germany
[4] Leipzig University, Leipzig, Germany
[5] Bauhaus-Universität Weimar, Weimar, Germany
[6] Friedrich-Schiller-Universität Jena, Jena, Germany
[7] hessian.AI, Darmstadt, Germany
[8] ScaDS.AI, Dresden, Germany



**Abstract.** What is an argument? Is an argument valid? Was a text manipulated to persuade? Since 2020, Touché fosters the development of support-technologies for decision-making and opinion-forming. To this end, the lab brings together researchers that develop systems to automatically answer questions like those above. At CLEF 2026 we do so in four tasks: (1) Fallacy Detection (new task), in which participants determine whether an argument follows a valid argument pattern; (2) Causality Extraction (new task), in which participants extract pro- and concausal claims from text; (3) Generalizability of Argument Identification in Context (new task), in which participants predict whether sentences would be annotated as an argument under different guidelines; and (4) Advertisement in Retrieval-Augmented Generation (2nd edition), in which participants detect and block advertisements in generated text. This paper details these tasks and summarizes the results of Touché 2025.

**Keywords:** Advertisement Detection · Argument Mining · Causality Detection · Fallacy Detection · Generalizability


## 1 Introduction

Decision-making and opinion-forming are everyday task. With the ubiquity of web search and language models, it is easy to find arguments on any topic. However, while the systems of today are quick to produce an answer, they rarely provide transparent quality assurance of arguments and might even misuse their position as intermediary to manipulate information for commercial gains. In this context, the Touché lab series, running since 2020,[1] has organized several tasks to advance both argumentation systems and the evaluation thereof aimed to tackle current challenges. In 2026, we organize the following shared tasks:

1. Fallacy Detection (new task) features three subtasks in the argumentation type detection, namely to classify (1) whether an argument is fallacious, (2) the argument scheme of an argument, and (3) the type of a fallacy.
2. Causality Extraction (new task) features three subtasks, in which participants (1) classify whether a text span contains causal information, (2) mark the respective entities in the span, and (3) classify the relation between two marked entities and procausal, concausal, or uncausal.
3. Generalizability of Argument Identification in Context (new task), in which participants classify whether a sentence, in its context and with provenance data, constitutes an argument or not.
4. Advertisement in Retrieval-Augmented Generation (2nd edition) features three subtasks in countering advertisements in the output of LLMs, namely (1) classify whether a response contains an advertisement or not, (2) locate the advertisement in a response, and (2) remove the advertisement from the response without affecting the coherence of the response.

After having organized six successful Touché labs on argument retrieval at CLEF 2020–2025 [2–5,17,18], we now organize a seventh lab edition to bring together researchers from the fields of information retrieval, natural language processing, computational linguistics, and dialogue working on argumentation. During the previous labs, we received 384 runs from 106 teams. We manually labeled the relevance and quality of more than 35,000 argumentative texts, web documents, and images for 227 topics (topics and judgments are publicly available at the lab's web page, https://touche.webis.de). As in the previous Touché editions, we encourage participants to deploy their software in our cloud-based evaluation-as-a-service platform TIRA [12] for better reproducibility.

## 2   Task Definitions

**Task 1: Fallacy Detection (new Task).** Argumentation is the process of presenting and evaluating reasons in support of, or in opposition to, a claim. Under ideal conditions, accepting an argument's premises should rationally warrant accepting its conclusion. In practice, however, this connection often breaks down: for example, the premises may fail to provide adequate support or the reasoning may be structurally defective. Detecting such fallacious reasoning is therefore essential for ensuring the reliability and trustworthiness of reasoning-based applications. In many cases, a fallacy can be understood as a defective, misleading, or misapplied instantiation of an otherwise legitimate argument scheme (a recurring pattern of reasoning [20,30]). This task investigates whether integrating fallacy detection with argument scheme classification yields deeper theoretical insights and improves the performance of automated systems for both tasks.

---

[1] Previous tasks, data, and publications are available at https://touche.webis.de/.

*Overview.* Given an argument, the task is structured as follows: (1) Determine whether the argument is fallacious. (2) If the argument is non-fallacious, identify its underlying argumentation scheme. (3) If the argument is fallacious, identify the specific type of fallacy it exhibits.

*Data.* We use a dataset comprising over 1,000 argumentative examples drawn from multiple sources. Following the approach of Jin et al. [16], we include fallacious arguments collected from student quiz websites. In addition, we incorporate both valid arguments and fallacies from several online debate platforms. To further increase the diversity of argument forms and topics, we also include synthetically generated arguments covering a broad range of argument types. All data sources are used in accordance with their respective licensing terms, and the final dataset will be made freely available. The dataset focuses on the five most frequently occurring types of fallacies. For argument scheme detection, we follow the framework proposed by Macagno et al. [20], which models argumentation along two complementary dimensions.

*Example.* "One study found that a new diet helped 20 people lose weight. Therefore, this diet works for everyone." This is an example of a "Faulty Generalization," as it draws a broad conclusion from a small and unrepresentative sample.

*Evaluation.* We evaluate each subtask using a held-out test set and report standard classification metrics, namely precision, recall, and $F_1$-score.

**Task 2: Causality Extraction (new Task).** Many important questions in various domains are causal: diagnostics in medicine wonders about the root cause of symptoms or about the effect elicited by interacting drugs, and brokers are interested in how current events impact the market. Answering such questions requires a database of causal knowledge, which can be extracted from natural language text through causality extraction.

However, so far prior work has almost exclusively extracted causal claims and ignored their counterclaims, i.e., statements asserting *A does not cause B*. This is critical as it means that discourse on causal knowledge is not properly captured by current causality extraction systems, which may lead to faulty downstream application of extracted causal knowledge. To improve this, Hagen et al. [15] introduce the Countercausal News Corpus, the first resource to train and evaluate the extraction of both, causal statements and their counterclaims (*countercausal* statements). This task is the next step towards more complete causality extraction which can capture contradictory opinions about causality.

*Overview.* This task is about the extraction of (counter-)causal claims from natural language text. Participating teams can submit software in any combination of the following three sub-tasks that build on each other: (1) Given a natural language text, classify whether it contains causal information or not; (2) given a natural language text, mark entities, events, or concepts for which the text claims or refutes a causal relationship; and (3) given a natural language text and two marked text spans, $e_0$ and $e_1$, classify whether the text supports that $e_0$ causes $e_1$ (causal), refutes its (countercausal) or does not make a statement about causality from $e_0$ to $e_1$ (uncausal).

*Data.* For the dataset, we use the Countercausal News Corpus (CCNC) [15], a modified version of the Causal News Corpus v2 [28] in which some of the causal claims were manually rewritten to be countercausal. The published training and validation splits contain 3415 labeled sentences in total, out of which 1028 are causal and 952 are countercausal. The Causal News Corpus v2 and Countercausal News Corpus are licensed under CC BY and CC0 respectively.

*Evaluation.* Submissions are evaluated on unpublished test data. Sub-tasks 1 and 3 are evaluated as binary and ternary classification problems, respectively, using $F_1$-score. Sub-task 2 is evaluated using $F_1$-score.

**Task 3: Generalizability of Argument Identification in Context (new Task).** Argument identification is a fundamental prerequisite for discourse analysis across domains such as political debate, online discussion, and scientific reasoning. Pre-trained language models such as BERT [7], designed for contextualized language representation, have demonstrated state-of-the-art performance on established benchmarks. However, recent research suggests that state-of-the-art performance often stems from exploiting spurious correlations [29] and shortcut learning [13], as benchmarks rely on specialized datasets that encourage models to capture dataset-specific patterns shaped by topic bias, argument definitions, and labeling schemes rather than abstractions that generalize across contexts [10]. Yet arguments are defined not only by form or content, but also by their pragmatic function and contextualized use [9]. Just as humans rely on context to identify and interpret arguments in discourse, so must machines. This task therefore examines how contextual cues can support automated argument identification, focusing on the impact of different types and amounts of context on building more generalizable and task-aligned systems.

*Overview.* Given a sentence from a dataset along with metadata about its provenance, such as the source text and the dataset's annotation guidelines, predict whether the sentence is annotated as an argument or not. In this cross-dataset setting, participants must develop robust systems that generalize beyond lexical shortcuts to unseen datasets and exploit rich context information.

*Data.* A subset from 10 established, publicly available benchmark datasets [1,6,11,14,19,21–23,26,27], identified as most relevant for argument identification [10], will be used. Each consists of 1.7k labeled sentences, partitioned with a 60/20/20 ratio into training, development, and test splits. Additionally, a new evaluation-only dataset will be released. Overall, the data includes sentences labeled as *argument* or *no-argument*, according to the respective dataset annotations. Accompanying metadata includes sentence IDs, generated splits, and (where available) context-relevant information via the original data sources, as well as annotation guidelines and corresponding papers.

*Evaluation.* Systems will primarily be evaluated on the newly created, evaluation-only dataset. For further insights, evaluation results on the established test splits from the held-out benchmark data will also be provided but not used for ranking. This setup addresses the risk of data contamination in LLMs and for participants' potential use of additional datasets during training. To evaluate the systems for their generalizability, the macro $F_1$-score will be measured for each test split, along with the overall average of all these values.

**Task 4: Advertisement in Retrieval-Augmented Generation.** Opinion forming is a central part of argumentation and a process for which many people rely on search engines and increasingly also LLMs. Hence, it is important that the responses generated by LLMs, with or without retrieval-augmented generation (RAG), are not biased to influence their users. One way to introduce such bias would be through advertising that prompts an LLM to portray a given product, service, or brand in a favorable light [8,25]. This type of advertising differs from existing approaches in that it enables highly contextual ads that blend into the surrounding text, thus requiring new types of ad blockers.

*Overview.* This task aims for the detection and blocking of advertisements in generated text. Participants submit software in any combination of the following three subtasks: (1) Given a response and a query, classify whether the response contains an advertisement or not. (2) Given a response with advertisements and a query, predict the character spans of the ads. A response can contain multiple, interrupted spans of advertisements. (3) Given a response, a query, and a list of character spans that mark the advertisements in the response, remove the ads. After the removal, the response should still be fluent, factually correct (using the input response as reference), and relevant to the query.

*Data.* For the development of submissions, we provide the Webis Generated Native Ads 2025 dataset.[2] The dataset contains 44,727 responses, with and without ads, that were generated by Brave Search, Microsoft Copilot, Perplexity, and YouChat for a total of 9,062 queries. To increase diversity, the advertisements were inserted by different LLMs: `GPT-4o` and `-mini` via OpenAI, as well as `deepseek-r1`, the 70B parameter versions of `llama-3` and `llama-3.3`, and `qwen-2.5-32b` via groq.[3] Each ad insertion was verified by a set of filters that check if the ad was correctly inserted and the response is otherwise identical to the input. For each response with an ad, the dataset contains the character spans of the advertisements, information on the item that was advertised, and the ID of the original response without advertisements.

---

[2] https://zenodo.org/records/17830870.
[3] https://groq.com/.

*Evaluation.* For the evaluation, we use an unpublished test split of the Webis Generated Native Ads 2025 dataset. Evaluation in subtask 1 uses standard $F_1$-score. Evaluation in subtask 2 uses an adapted $F_1$-score based on the overlap of predicted spans with ground-truth spans, drawing inspiration from the PlagDet-score developed for a similar purpose [24]. Evaluation in subtask 3 uses a combination of manual evaluation with LLM-as-a-judge through deepeval:[4] Human annotators evaluate fluency, correctness, and query relevance on a three-point scale from 0 to 2, while LLM-as-a-judge evaluation uses a scale from 0 to 1.

## 3   Touché at CLEF 2025: Brief Overview

In 2025, Touché at CLEF included these shared tasks [17]: (1) Retrieval-Augmented Debating, on simulating and evaluating deliberative debates; (2) Ideology and Power Identification in Parliamentary Debates (2nd iteration), including a new sub-task on populism identification; (3) Image Retrieval/Generation for Arguments (4th iteration), aiming to provide images that convey some claim; and (4) Advertisement in Retrieval-Augmented Generation (continues in 2026).

Touché 2025 received 62 registrations, of which 12 teams actively participated in the tasks and submitted 60 results (runs). Unsurprisingly, large language models (zero-shot, fine-tuned, etc.) were used across tasks, especially for retrieval-augmented debating. But also classic and more efficient approaches like SVMs were used for ideology and power identification. One team successfully submitted generated images for task 3, surpassing the still strong CLIP-baseline used in retrieval. For the Advertisement in Retrieval-Augmented Generation task, teams primarily used encoder models like MiniLM, MPNet, RoBERTa and DeBERTa-v3 for advertisement detection and Qwen and Mistral for generation. The corpora, topics, and judgments are available on the Touché website.[5]

## 4   Conclusion

At Touché, we continue to foster research on argumentation systems, building respective test collections, and bringing the research community together. During the previous six years, the submitted approaches developed from sparse to dense retrieval and zero-shot models (both for text and images), combined with assessments of document "argumentativeness," argument quality, stance detection, and sentiment analysis. Among others, argumentation systems can effectively contribute to generation systems, since in generative systems the task of reasoning (of which argumentation is the explication) is often a crucial but currently not sufficiently effective part of the system.

---

[4] https://www.deepeval.com/.
[5] https://touche.webis.de/.

Touché 2026 brings in new tasks and refines existing ones. We continue our investigation into the detection of advertisements in generated search result text (injected subtle argumentation). Moreover, with fallacies and causality we investigate two exciting elements of argumentation. Furthermore, we aim to find robust argument identification systems—a tool that is still lacking today despite argument identification being the basis for many analyses.

**Acknowledgements.** This work was partially supported by the European Commission under grant agreement GA 101070014 (https://openwebsearch.eu) and by the German Federal Ministry of Research, Technology and Space (BMFTR) through the project "DIALOKIA: Überprüfung von LLM-generierter Argumentation mittels dialektischem Sprachmodell" (01IS24084A-B).

**Disclosure of Interests.** The authors have no competing interests to declare that are relevant to the content of this article.

# References


1. Alhamzeh, A., Fonck, R., Versmée, E., Egyed-Zsigmond, E., Kosch, H., Brunie, L.: It's time to reason: Annotating argumentation structures in financial earnings calls: The FinArg dataset. In: Chen, C.C., Huang, H.H., Takamura, H., Chen, H.H. (eds.) Proceedings of the Fourth Workshop on Financial Technology and Natural Language Processing (FinNLP), pp. 163–169, Association for Computational Linguistics, Abu Dhabi, United Arab Emirates (Hybrid) (Dec 2022), https://doi.org/10.18653/v1/2022.finnlp-1.22, https://aclanthology.org/2022.finnlp-1.22/

2. Bondarenko, A., et al.: Overview of Touché 2020: Argument Retrieval. In: Arampatzis, A., Kanoulas, E., Tsikrika, T., Vrochidis, S., Joho, H., Lioma, C., Eickhoff, C., Névéol, A., Cappellato, L., Ferro, N. (eds.) CLEF 2020. LNCS, vol. 12260, pp. 384–395. Springer, Cham (2020). https://doi.org/10.1007/978-3-030-58219-7_26

3. Bondarenko, A., et al.: Overview of Touché 2023: Argument and Causal Retrieval. In: Arampatzis, A., et al. (eds.) 14th International Conference of the CLEF Association (CLEF 2023), Lecture Notes in Computer Science, vol. 14163, pp. 507–530, Springer, Berlin Heidelberg New York (Sep 2023). https://doi.org/10.1007/978-3-031-42448-9_31

4. Bondarenko, A., et al.: Overview of Touché 2022: Argument retrieval. In: Working Notes of CLEF 2022 - Conference and Labs of the Evaluation Forum (CLEF 2022), CEUR Workshop Proceedings, vol. 3180, pp. 2867–2903, CEUR-WS.org (2022). http://ceur-ws.org/Vol-3180/paper-247.pdf

5. Bondarenko, A., et al.: Overview of touché 2021: argument retrieval. In: Candan, K.S., Ionescu, B., Goeuriot, L., Larsen, B., Müller, H., Joly, A., Maistro, M., Piroi, F., Faggioli, G., Ferro, N. (eds.) CLEF 2021. LNCS, vol. 12880, pp. 450–467. Springer, Cham (2021). https://doi.org/10.1007/978-3-030-85251-1_28

6. Cheng, L., Bing, L., He, R., Yu, Q., Zhang, Y., Si, L.: IAM: a comprehensive and large-scale dataset for integrated argument mining tasks. In: Muresan, S., Nakov, P., Villavicencio, A. (eds.) Proceedings of the 60th Annual Meeting of the Association for Computational Linguistics (Volume 1: Long Papers), pp. 2277–2287, Association for Computational Linguistics, Dublin, Ireland (May 2022), https://doi.org/10.18653/v1/2022.acl-long.162, https://aclanthology.org/2022.acl-long.162/

7. Devlin, J., Chang, M.W., Lee, K., Toutanova, K.: BERT: Pre-training of deep bidirectional transformers for language understanding. In: Burstein, J., Doran, C., Solorio, T. (eds.) Proceedings of the 2019 Conference of the North American Chapter of the Association for Computational Linguistics: Human Language Technologies, Volume 1 (Long and Short Papers), pp. 4171–4186, Association for Computational Linguistics, Minneapolis, Minnesota (Jun 2019), https://doi.org/10.18653/v1/N19-1423, https://aclanthology.org/N19-1423/

8. Dütting, P., Mirrokni, V., Paes Leme, R., Xu, H., Zuo, S.: Mechanism design for large language models. In: Proceedings of the ACM Web Conference 2024, pp. 144–155, ACM, Singapore Singapore (May 2024). https://doi.org/10.1145/3589334.3645511, https://dl.acm.org/doi/10.1145/3589334.3645511

9. van Eemeren, F.H., Garssen, B., Krabbe, E.C.W., Snoeck Henkemans, A.F., Verheij, B., Wagemans, J.H.M.: Handbook of argumentation theory. Springer, Dordrecht, 1 edn. (Jul 2014), ISBN 978-90-481-9472-8, https://doi.org/10.1007/978-90-481-9473-5, https://doi.org/10.1007/978-90-481-9473-5, 61 b/w illustrations, 18 colour illustrations

10. Feger, M., Boland, K., Dietze, S.: Limited generalizability in argument mining: State-of-the-art models learn datasets, not arguments (2025). https://arxiv.org/abs/2505.22137

11. Fergadis, A., Pappas, D., Karamolegkou, A., Papageorgiou, H.: Argumentation mining in scientific literature for sustainable development. In: Al-Khatib, K., Hou, Y., Stede, M. (eds.) Proceedings of the 8th Workshop on Argument Mining, pp. 100–111, Association for Computational Linguistics, Punta Cana, Dominican Republic (Nov 2021). https://doi.org/10.18653/v1/2021.argmining-1.10, https://aclanthology.org/2021.argmining-1.10/

12. Fröbe, M., et al.: Continuous Integration for Reproducible Shared Tasks with TIRA.io. In: Kamps, J., et al., (eds.) Advances in Information Retrieval. 45th European Conference on IR Research (ECIR 2023), pp. 236–241, Lecture Notes in Computer Science, Springer, Berlin Heidelberg New York (Apr 2023). https://doi.org/10.1007/978-3-031-28241-6_20

13. Geirhos, R., et al.: Shortcut learning in deep neural networks. Nature Mach. Intell. **2**(11), 665–673 (11 2020), ISSN 2522-5839, https://doi.org/10.1038/s42256-020-00257-z

14. Haddadan, S., Cabrio, E., Villata, S.: Yes, we can! mining arguments in 50 years of US presidential campaign debates. In: Korhonen, A., Traum, D., Màrquez, L. (eds.) Proceedings of the 57th Annual Meeting of the Association for Computational Linguistics, pp. 4684–4690, Association for Computational Linguistics, Florence, Italy (Jul 2019), https://doi.org/10.18653/v1/P19-1463, https://aclanthology.org/P19-1463/

15. Hagen, T., Deckers, N., Wolter, F., Scells, H., Potthast, M.: Investigating Counterclaims in Causality Extraction from Text. CoRR **abs/2510.08224** (Oct 2025)

16. Jin, Z., et al.: Logical fallacy detection. In: Goldberg, Y., Kozareva, Z., Zhang, Y. (eds.) Findings of the Association for Computational Linguistics: EMNLP 2022, Abu Dhabi, United Arab Emirates, December 7-11, 2022, pp. 7180–7198, Association for Computational Linguistics (2022). https://doi.org/10.18653/V1/2022.FINDINGS-EMNLP.532, https://doi.org/10.18653/v1/2022.findings-emnlp.532

17. Kiesel, J., et al.: Overview of touché 2025: argumentation systems. In: de Albornoz, J.C., et al., (eds.) Experimental IR Meets Multilinguality, Multimodality, and Interaction. 16th International Conference of the CLEF Association (CLEF 2025),

Lecture Notes in Computer Science, Springer, Berlin Heidelberg New York (Sept 2025)

18. Kiesel, J., et al.: Overview of Touché 2024: argumentation systems. In: Goeuriot, L., Mulhem, P., et al. (eds.) Experimental IR Meets Multilinguality, Multimodality, and Interaction. 15th International Conference of the CLEF Association (CLEF 2024), Lecture Notes in Computer Science, Springer, Berlin Heidelberg New York (Sep 2024)

19. Lauscher, A., Glavaš, G., Ponzetto, S.P.: An argument-annotated corpus of scientific publications. In: Slonim, N., Aharonov, R. (eds.) Proceedings of the 5th Workshop on Argument Mining, pp. 40–46, Association for Computational Linguistics, Brussels, Belgium (Nov 2018). https://doi.org/10.18653/v1/W18-5206, https://aclanthology.org/W18-5206/

20. Macagno, F.: Argumentation profiles and the manipulation of common ground. the arguments of populist leaders on twitter. J. Pragmatics **191**, 67–82 (2022), ISSN 0378-2166, https://doi.org/10.1016/j.pragma.2022.01.022, https://www.sciencedirect.com/science/article/pii/S0378216622000285

21. Mayer, T., Cabrio, E., Villata, S.: Transformer-based argument mining for healthcare applications. In: European Conference on Artificial Intelligence (2020). https://api.semanticscholar.org/CorpusID:221713735

22. Misra, A., Ecker, B., Walker, M.: Measuring the similarity of sentential arguments in dialogue. In: Fernandez, R., Minker, W., Carenini, G., Higashinaka, R., Artstein, R., Gainer, A. (eds.) Proceedings of the 17th Annual Meeting of the Special Interest Group on Discourse and Dialogue, pp. 276–287, Association for Computational Linguistics, Los Angeles (Sep 2016). https://doi.org/10.18653/v1/W16-3636, https://aclanthology.org/W16-3636/

23. Panchenko, A., Bondarenko, A., Franzek, M., Hagen, M., Biemann, C.: Categorizing comparative sentences. In: Stein, B., Wachsmuth, H. (eds.) Proceedings of the 6th Workshop on Argument Mining, pp. 136–145, Association for Computational Linguistics, Florence, Italy (Aug 2019). https://doi.org/10.18653/v1/W19-4516, https://aclanthology.org/W19-4516/

24. Potthast, M., et al.: Overview of the 5th international competition on plagiarism detection. In: Forner, P., Navigli, R., Tufis, D. (eds.) Working Notes Papers of the CLEF 2013 Evaluation Labs, Lecture Notes in Computer Science, vol. 1179 (Sep 2013), ISBN 978-88-904810-3-1, ISSN 2038-4963, https://ceur-ws.org/Vol-1179/CLEF2013wn-PAN-PotthastEt2013.pdf

25. . Schmidt, S., Zelch, I., Bevendorff, J., Stein, B., Hagen, M., Potthast, M.: Detecting generated native ads in conversational search. In: Companion Proceedings of the ACM Web Conference 2024, pp. 722–725, WWW '24, Association for Computing Machinery, New York, NY, USA (2024) https://doi.org/10.1145/3589335.3651489

26. Stab, C., Gurevych, I.: Parsing argumentation structures in persuasive essays. Comput. Linguist. **43**(3), 619–659 (Sep 2017). https://doi.org/10.1162/COLI_a_00295, https://aclanthology.org/J17-3005/

27. Swanson, R., Ecker, B., Walker, M.: Argument mining: extracting arguments from online dialogue. In: Koller, A., Skantze, G., Jurcicek, F., Araki, M., Rose, C.P. (eds.) Proceedings of the 16th Annual Meeting of the Special Interest Group on Discourse and Dialogue, pp. 217–226, Association for Computational Linguistics, Prague, Czech Republic (Sep 2015). https://doi.org/10.18653/v1/W15-4631, https://aclanthology.org/W15-4631/

28. Tan, F.A., et al.: RECESS: resource for extracting cause, effect, and signal spans. In: Park, J.C., et al., (eds.) Proceedings of the 13th International Joint Conference on Natural Language Processing and the 3rd Conference of the Asia-Pacific Chapter of the Association for Computational Linguistics, IJCNLP 2023 -Volume 1: Long Papers, Nusa Dua, Bali, November 1 - 4, 2023, pp. 66–82, Association for Computational Linguistics (2023). https://doi.org/10.18653/V1/2023.IJCNLP-MAIN.6

29. Thorn Jakobsen, T.S., Barrett, M., Søgaard, A.: Spurious correlations in cross-topic argument mining. In: Ku, L.W., Nastase, V., Vulić, I. (eds.) Proceedings of *SEM 2021: The Tenth Joint Conference on Lexical and Computational Semantics, pp. 263–277, Association for Computational Linguistics, Online (Aug 2021). https://doi.org/10.18653/v1/2021.starsem-1.25, https://aclanthology.org/2021.starsem-1.25/

30. Walton, D., Reed, C., Macagno, F.: Argumentation Schemes. Cambridge University Press (2008). ISBN 9780521723749, http://www.cambridge.org/us/academic/subjects/philosophy/logic/argumentation-schemes

# LifeCLEF 2026 Teaser: AI Challenges for Biodiversity Understanding and Ecosystem Management


Alexis Joly[1] , Lukáš Picek[1,2(✉)] , Stefan Kahl[3,4] , Hervé Goëau[5] ,
Lukáš Adam[6] , Robert Bossy[7] , Kostas Papafitsoros[8] , Vojtěch Čermák[9] ,
Holger Klinck[3] , Willem-Pier Vellinga[10] , Robert Planqué[10] ,
Tom Denton[11] , Laura Chrobak[12] , Kevin Barnard[12] , Claire Nédellec[7] ,
Louise Deléger[7] , Marine Courtin[7] , Giulio Martellucci[13] ,
Fabrice Vinatier[13] , and Pierre Bonnet[5]

[1] Inria, LIRMM, Univ Montpellier, CNRS, Montpellier, France
lukaspicek@gmail.com
[2] Department of Cybernetics, FAV, University of West Bohemia, Pilsen, Czechia
[3] K. Lisa Yang Center for Conservation Bioacoustics, Cornell, NewYork, USA
[4] Chemnitz University of Technology, Chemnitz, Germany
[5] CIRAD, UMR AMAP, Montpellier, Occitanie, France
[6] RICE, FEL, University of West Bohemia, Pilsen, Czechia
[7] Université Paris-Saclay, INRAE, MaIAGE, Jouy-en-Josas, France
[8] School of Mathematical Sciences, Queen Mary University of London, London, UK
[9] Czech Technical University in Prague, CMP, Prague, Czechia
[10] Xeno-canto Foundation, Leiden, Netherlands
[11] Google Research, San Francisco, USA
[12] Monterey Bay Aquarium Research Institute, Moss Landing, CA, USA
[13] LISAH, Univ Montpellier, INRAE, IRD, Montpellier, France



**Abstract.** AI is increasingly central to understanding and managing biodiversity and ecosystems. Since 2011, the LifeCLEF lab has provided large-scale benchmarks that stimulate progress in multimodal species recognition, ecological prediction, and knowledge extraction. The 2026 edition expands this scope with five complementary challenges spanning visual, acoustic, and textual data: (i) **AnimalCLEF**: discovery and re-identification of individual animals, (ii) **BirdCLEF+**: multitaxonomic species recognition in complex soundscapes, (iii) **FathomNetCLEF**: detection of marine species in underwater imagery under positive-unlabeled constraints, (iv) **PestCLEF**: extraction of information on plant pests from heterogeneous textual sources, (v) **PlantCLEF**: multi-species plant identification in quadrat images. Together, these challenges address critical dimensions of biodiversity science and ecosystem management, while fostering collaboration between AI researchers, ecologists, and practitioners. This paper provides an overview of the LifeCLEF 2026 lab and its tasks, outlining their motivation, data, and evaluation methodology to guide participants and inform the wider research community.




R. Campos et al. (Eds.): ECIR 2026, LNCS 16486, pp. 287–296, 2026.
https://doi.org/10.1007/978-3-032-21321-1_39

**Keywords:** Biodiversity · ML · AI · Species · Identification · Ecology

# 1   Introduction

Biodiversity monitoring allows measuring changes in species composition, abundance, and distribution, providing a robust evidence base for conservation policy [5]. Drawing primarily on citizen-science observations, modern AI methods have the potential to convert these data into actionable indicators, such as species occurrence trends and range shifts, that inform planning and prioritization.

Automated species identification has long been seen as a promising direction [11]. Deep learning methods have greatly improved recognition performance across images and audio [4,6,12,28,31,34,39–42]. Yet major challenges remain: most species are underrepresented in training data, interspecies boundaries are often subtle, and environmental context affects how organisms appear and are detected [10,29]. Progress, therefore, requires continual benchmarking that reflects real field conditions and transparent, reproducible evaluations.

Since 2011, the LifeCLEF lab has been provided such benchmarks, advancing more than just species recognition but also pushing progress in ecological prediction and knowledge extraction [16–20,22–26,33]. Each edition bridges research and practice by promoting open data, and problems rooted in real ecological workflows. All tasks are co-designed with domain experts and the evaluation sets are expert-curated to reflect real-world monitoring conditions.

The 2026 edition features five challenges spanning vision, audio, and text: (i) **AnimalCLEF**, (ii) **BirdCLEF+**, (iii) **FathomNetCLEF**, (iv) **PestCLEF**, and (v) **PlantCLEF**, addressing wide range of needs in biodiversity and ecosystem management.

# 2   AnimalCLEF 2026: Discovering Individual Animals

**Motivation:** Animal re-identification supports core wildlife objectives, e.g., estimating population sizes, monitoring movements, and analysing behaviour, by linking images to unique individuals [36–38]. Automation scales these efforts by reducing manual matching and lowering annotation costs across species and sites, which is especially important when data volumes grow faster than expert capacity. Most existing benchmarks emphasise verification against a known catalogue (closed-set or open-set matching), which answers whether an image corresponds to a known individual but does not assign identities to previously unseen animals. In practice, building or updating a catalogue requires *discovery*: grouping images of unknown individuals so that each cluster corresponds to a single animal and can be incorporated into long-term monitoring workflows. This setting is challenging due to appearance variation (pose, illumination, ageing, injuries), background clutter, domain shifts across sensors and habitats, and class imbalance. By targeting the discovery step directly through unsupervised clustering of test images under realistic, multi-species, and variable conditions, the competition aims to advance methods that are immediately useful for creating and maintaining field-ready identity databases with minimal intervention.

**Data Collection:** The dataset will follow last year edition [2]. For training, the WildlifeReID-10k dataset [1], which includes a diverse range of species, including marine turtles, primates, birds, African herbivores, marine mammals, and domestic animals, will be made available through the WildlifeDatasets [7] library. The test set will contain previously unpublished images of undisclosed species, which will be revealed at the start of the competition.

**Task Description:** The competition will be hosted on Kaggle and will follow the *discovery setting* [15,32], where the training and test sets contain disjoint identities. Participants must cluster the test set so that each cluster corresponds to a unique individual. Performance will be evaluated using the Adjusted Rand Index (ARI) [35], which measures pairwise consistency between the predicted and true clusters. This metric penalizes both over-clustering (splitting one individual into multiple) and under-clustering (merging different individuals into a single one). The dataset will be kept relatively small, with a size under 25 GB.

## 3  BirdCLEF+ 2026: Multi-taxa Species Identification in Soundscape Recordings

**Motivation:** Recognizing species in complex soundscapes is an increasingly important ecological monitoring tool that helps overcome limitations of traditional point counts. As natural habitats continue to disappear, archives of soundscape recordings will become invaluable. It is therefore essential to develop technologies capable of handling large volumes of audio data and accelerating species diversity assessments. Recently, deep learning has revolutionized automated soundscape analysis. However, performance remains limited when training data are scarce, particularly for rare or endangered species. The goal of this competition is to create training and testing datasets that reflect real conditions in threatened habitats and to support the development of models that advance automated biodiversity monitoring for conservation science.

**Data Collection:** Building on experience from previous BirdCLEF editions, we will refine the task to emphasize few-shot learning and domain-specific model design, because many endangered or rare species lack sufficient amounts of training data. Training and test data will be selected accordingly. As in past years, the primary sources of training data will be Xeno-canto and iNaturalist, while expertly annotated soundscape recordings will form the test sets. Again, BirdCLEF+ will include a broader taxonomic scope, incorporating anurans, insects, and mammals alongside birds, the largest and main focus group. We will also provide unlabeled soundscapes to encourage participants to explore self-supervised and unsupervised learning. The 2026 edition will center on conservation efforts in the Pantanal region of Brazil, in collaboration with local partners and NGOs.

**Task Description:** The competition will be hosted on Kaggle, following the 2025 evaluation framework (hidden test data and code competition format). System performance will be measured using the ROC-AUC metric, which enables evaluation independent of species-specific confidence thresholds. Participants will generate species predictions for short audio segments extracted from labeled soundscapes and will be challenged to design computationally efficient models within defined inference time limits based on resource constraints imposed by the Kaggle compute platform. The task structure will largely remain consistent with previous years, maintaining a proven format that attracted over 2,500 participants and 70,000 submissions in 2025. As before, the dataset will be kept small (¡50 GB) and easy to process, with baseline examples and documentation provided to lower the entry barrier for new participants.

## 4    PlantCLEF 2026: Identify Multi-species Plants in Images of Vegetation Plots

**Motivation:** Vegetation plots enable standardized biodiversity assessment, long-term monitoring, and large-scale ecological surveys [9], providing key data for ecosystem analysis and conservation planning. These images typically cover $50 \times 50$ cm plots where botanists identify all species and quantify their abundance through biomass, cover, or related indicators. The integration of AI could improve the efficiency of specialists, helping them to extend the scope and coverage of ecological studies. Given the task's difficulty and the strong results and participation in the 2025 challenge [30], the task is organized again in a similar format, using the same datasets and Kaggle platform as a second round.

**Data Collection:** The test set combines expert-verified plot images from diverse floristic contexts (Pyrenean, Mediterranean, temperate, invasive), reserved for evaluation due to the rarity of exhaustively annotated data. The training set mainly consists of single-plant images from previous PlantCLEF editions [13, 14, 21], introducing a domain shift between close-up and multi-plant views. It reuses the 2025 dataset built from Pl@ntNet observations [3] across southwestern Europe (France, Spain, Andorra, Portugal), covering about 7,800 species and 1.4 million images, with rare species supplemented from GBIF. An additional unlabeled dataset of hundreds of thousands of vegetation cover images from LUCAS [8] supports self-supervised evaluation.

**Task Description:** The task is a multi-label classification aiming to predict all species in high-resolution images. The training set is released first, followed later by the full test set. Self-, semi-, and unsupervised methods are encouraged, with pre-trained models provided.

## 5    FathomNetCLEF 2026: Positive-Unlabeled Object Detection in Marine Images

**Motivation:** Deep-sea exploration and monitoring increasingly depend on large-scale image analysis to understand species diversity, distribution, and ecological interactions. Yet, marine imagery presents unique challenges for computer vision, including high taxonomic diversity, visually similar morphologies, and environments that range from benthic habitats to the open midwater. A particularly acute issue is annotation. Unlike many terrestrial datasets, marine image annotation is typically performed by experts with highly specialized knowledge, who may only label the taxa they study. This leads to a mix of fully annotated regions and numerous positive but unlabeled instances within the same image. In other words, "absence of a label" does not mean "absence of an organism."

The FathomNetCLEF 2026 challenge addresses this real-world constraint by focusing on *positive-unlabeled learning for object detection*. Developing robust methods in this setting will reduce reliance on expert annotations, accelerate dataset curation, and broaden the usability of large-scale archives like FathomNet. Ultimately, improving detection under positive-unlabeled regimes will support scalable biodiversity monitoring, enhance conservation strategies, and enable marine researchers to extract ecological insights from decades of imagery.

**Data Collection:** The dataset will be derived from the FathomNet Database [27], which contains over 200k images ($\sim 0.5$M expert-curated bounding boxes) across thousands of marine taxonomic, geologic, and equipment classes. For the challenge, participants will be provided with a large training set (on the order of hundreds of thousands of images) that contains many images with both labeled and unlabeled positive instances. The evaluation set, by contrast, will be composed of fully annotated images prepared by expert taxonomists specializing in deep-sea biology. These images span a broad range of benthic and midwater habitats, including fine-grained taxa that reflect the diversity of marine ecosystems. To ensure broad accessibility, the dataset will be less than 50 GB in size.

**Task Description:** The competition will be hosted on Kaggle. Participants will be tasked with developing object detection systems that can operate effectively in a positive-unlabeled learning regime, identifying both the presence and location of marine organisms across diverse habitats. The evaluation metric will be mean Average Precision (mAP), applied to the fully labeled evaluation set. To succeed, participants are expected to explore approaches that leverage unlabeled positives, including positive-unlabeled learning, semi-supervised, and self-supervised techniques. Baseline methods will be provided, along with starter code to facilitate participation. The challenge not only benchmarks the state of the art in PU detection but also aims to produce practical methods that can generalize to large-scale, heterogeneous marine datasets, directly supporting ongoing conservation and ecological research.

## 6    PestCLEF 2026: Information Extraction on Plant Pests from News Articles

**Motivation:** The understanding of transmission of crop diseases and the monitoring of outbreak events is critically important because it directly affects food security, economic stability, and environmental sustainability. Plant diseases, their pest agents, occurrences, and insect vectors form a complex network of knowledge scattered in a multitude of documents, including scientific articles, as well as professional and institutional news outlets. Due to different perspectives (scientific and professional), knowledge about plant diseases is expressed in diverse ways, using various vocabulary and registers. Thus, there is a case for standardization for data integration and aggregation for large-scale analysis. The objective of PestCLEF is to develop accurate models for large-scale knowledge extraction on crop diseases from documents. Such models would be invaluable for the cross-disciplinary and wide-range understanding of crop disease mechanisms, as well as for streamlining epidemiological monitoring information systems.

**Data Collection**: The task will utilize the EPOP dataset, which comprises 247 documents collected from the Web and translated into English by the French plant epidemiological monitoring platform, focusing on 20 monitored pests. The documents are annotated with named entities, normalizations, binary relations, and n-ary relations. The annotation was carried out by a team of 30 experts in plant disease or NLP following the state-of-the-art annotation methodology. The annotation guidelines and the training data are already publicly available, and the test data is completed but remain undisclosed. EPOP annotation schema reflects the current knowledge paradigm on crop disease and pest transmission. For example, EPOP includes named entity types such as *Host*, *Pest*, *Disease*, *Vector*, and *Location*. The named entities are normalized through links to external reference resources (NCBI Taxonomy), GeoNames). The relations reflect ecological interactions and the occurrence of events mentioned in the text. The training set is annotated with 3,482 named entities, 2,217 binary relations, and 1,302 n-ary relations, with an arity ranging from 2 to 5.

**Task Description:** The challenge is likely hosted on Kaggle. Participants will be given time to train models on the training and development sets, then they will be evaluated on the test set according to the CLEF Lab schedule. The raw text and HTML layout of the collected documents will be provided separately from the manual annotation, allowing participants to develop supervised, self-supervised, or unsupervised models. The task is to extract relations at the document level, and the exact grounding of the entities in the text is not required. Submissions will be evaluated using standard Information Extraction metrics. The F-Score will be used to rank submissions on the leaderboard, and additional metrics will be reported to highlight strengths and weaknesses.

## 7   Conclusion

LifeCLEF 2026 advances biodiversity AI with five expert-co-designed challenges across vision, audio, and text. The lab's goals are to: (i) promote substantial methodological advances beyond incremental improvements, (ii) measure progress with transparent, reproducible protocols, (iii) stress-test generalization, data efficiency, and runtime constraints under realistic field conditions, and (iv) grow an open, collaborative community. Datasets are expert-curated, evaluation is hosted on Kaggle with clear metrics and starter baselines, and tasks are aligned with monitoring workflows so that advances translate into actionable items.

All information about the timeline and participation in the challenges is provided on the LifeCLEF 2026 web page.

**Acknowledgement.** This research was funded by Biodiversa+, the European Biodiversity Partnership, in the context of the FunDive: Monitoring and mapping fungal diversity for nature conservation" project under the 2022–023 BioDivMon joint call. It was co-funded by the European Commission (grant agreement No.2128-00020A - Biodiversa2022-640).

**Disclosure of Interests.** The authors have no competing interests to declare that are relevant to the content of this article.

# References


1. Adam, L., Čermák, V., Papafitsoros, K., Picek, L.: Wildlifereid-10k: Wildlife re-identification dataset with 10k individual animals. In: 2025 IEEE/CVF Conference on Computer Vision and Pattern Recognition Workshops (CVPRW), pp. 2090–2100. IEEE (2025)
2. Adam, L., Papafitsoros, K., Kovář, R., Čermák, V., Picek, L.: Overview of animalclef 2025: recognizing individual animals in images. Working Notes of CLEF (2025)
3. Affouard, A., Goeau, H., Bonnet, P., Lombardo, J.C., Joly, A.: Pl@ntnet app in the era of deep learning. In: 5th International Conference on Learning Representations (ICLR 2017), April 24-26 2017, Toulon, France (2017)
4. Banan, A., Nasiri, A., Taheri-Garavand, A.: Deep learning-based appearance features extraction for automated carp species identification. Aquacult. Eng. **89**, 102053 (2020)
5. Besson, M., et al.: Towards the fully automated monitoring of ecological communities. Ecol. Lett. **25**(12), 2753–2775 (2022)
6. Bonnet, P., et al.: Plant identification: experts vs. machines in the era of deep learning. In: Multimedia Tools and Applications for Environmental & Biodiversity Informatics, pp. 131–149. Springer (2018)
7. Čermák, V., Picek, L., Adam, L., Papafitsoros, K.: Wildlifedatasets: an open-source toolkit for animal re-identification. In: Proceedings of the IEEE/CVF Winter Conference on Applications of Computer Vision, pp. 5953–5963 (2024)
8. d'Andrimont, R., et al.: Lucas cover photos 2006–2018 over the eu: 874 646 spatially distributed geo-tagged close-up photos with land cover and plant species label. Earth System Science Data **14**(10), 4463–4472 (2022). https://doi.org/10.5194/essd-14-4463-2022, https://essd.copernicus.org/articles/14/4463/2022/
9. Dengler, J.: A flexible multi-scale approach for standardised recording of plant species richness patterns. Ecol. Ind. **9**(6), 1169–1178 (2009)
10. Garcin, C., et al.: Pl@ ntnet-300k: a plant image dataset with high label ambiguity and a long-tailed distribution. In: NeurIPS 2021-35th Conference on Neural Information Processing Systems (2021)

11. Gaston, K.J., O'Neill, M.A.: Automated species identification: why not? Philos. Trans. Royal Society London B: Biol. Sci. **359**(1444), 655–667 (2004)
12. Ghazi, M.M., Yanikoglu, B., Aptoula, E.: Plant identification using deep neural networks via optimization of transfer learning parameters. Neurocomputing **235**, 228–235 (2017)
13. Goëau, H., Bonnet, P., Joly, A.: Overview of PlantCLEF 2021: cross-domain plant identification. In: Working Notes of CLEF 2021 - Conference and Labs of the Evaluation Forum (2021)
14. Goëau, H., Bonnet, P., Joly, A.: Overview of PlantCLEF 2023: Image-based plant identification at global scale. In: Working Notes of CLEF 2023 - Conference and Labs of the Evaluation Forum (2023)
15. Guerrero, M.J., Bedoya, C.L., López, J.D., Daza, J.M., Isaza, C.: Acoustic animal identification using unsupervised learning. Methods Ecol. Evol. **14**(6), 1500–1514 (2023)
16. Joly, A., et al.: Overview of lifeclef 2023: evaluation of ai models for the identification and prediction of birds, plants, snakes and fungi. In: International Conference of the Cross-Language Evaluation Forum for European Languages, pp. 416–439. Springer (2023)
17. Joly, A., Goëau, H., Botella, C., Glotin, H., Bonnet, P., Vellinga, W.P., Müller, H.: Overview of LifeCLEF 2018: a large-scale evaluation of species identification and recommendation algorithms in the era of ai. In: Jones, G.J., Lawless, S., Gonzalo, J., Kelly, L., Goeuriot, L., Mandl, T., Cappellato, L., Ferro, N. (eds.) CLEF: Cross-Language Evaluation Forum for European Languages. Experimental IR Meets Multilinguality, Multimodality, and Interaction, vol. LNCS. Springer, Avigon, France (Sep 2018)
18. Joly, A., et al.: Overview of LifeCLEF 2019: Identification of Amazonian Plants, South & North American Birds, and Niche Prediction. In: Crestani, F., et al. (eds.) CLEF 2019 - Conference and Labs of the Evaluation Forum. Experimental IR Meets Multilinguality, Multimodality, and Interaction, vol. LNCS, pp. 387–401. Lugano, Switzerland (Sep 2019). https://doi.org/10.1007/978-3-030-28577-7_29, https://hal.umontpellier.fr/hal-02281455
19. Joly, A., et al.: LifeCLEF 2016: Multimedia Life Species Identification Challenges. In: Fuhr, N., Quaresma, P., Gonçalves, T., Larsen, B., Balog, K., Macdonald, C., Cappellato, L., Ferro, N. (eds.) CLEF: Cross-Language Evaluation Forum. Experimental IR Meets Multilinguality, Multimodality, and Interaction, vol. LNCS, pp. 286–310. Springer, Évora, Portugal (Sep 2016). https://doi.org/10.1007/978-3-319-44564-9_26, https://hal.archives-ouvertes.fr/hal-01373781
20. Joly, A., et al.: LifeCLEF 2017 Lab Overview: multimedia species identification challenges. In: Jones, G.J., et al., (eds.) CLEF: Cross-Language Evaluation Forum. Experimental IR Meets Multilinguality, Multimodality, and Interaction, vol. LNCS, pp. 255–274. Springer, Dublin, Ireland (Sep 2017). https://doi.org/10.1007/978-3-319-65813-1_24, https://hal.archives-ouvertes.fr/hal-01629191
21. Joly, A., et al.: Biodiversity information retrieval through large scale content-based identification: a long-term evaluation, pp. 389–413. Springer International Publishing, Cham (2019). https://doi.org/10.1007/978-3-030-22948-1_16
22. Joly, A., et al.: LifeCLEF 2014: Multimedia Life Species Identification Challenges. In: CLEF: Cross-Language Evaluation Forum. Information Access Evaluation. Multilinguality, Multimodality, and Interaction, vol. LNCS, pp. 229–249. Springer International Publishing, Sheffield, United Kingdom (Sep 2014). https://doi.org/10.1007/978-3-319-11382-1_20, https://hal.inria.fr/hal-01075770

23. Joly, A., et al.: Lifeclef 2015: multimedia life species identification challenges. In: Experimental IR Meets Multilinguality, Multimodality, and Interaction, pp. 462–483. Springer (2015)
24. Joly, A., et al.: Overview of lifeclef 2020: a system-oriented evaluation of automated species identification and species distribution prediction. In: International Conference of the Cross-Language Evaluation Forum for European Languages, pp. 342–363. Springer (2020)
25. Joly, et al.: Overview of lifeclef 2022: an evaluation of machine-learning based species identification and species distribution prediction. In: International Conference of the Cross-Language Evaluation Forum for European Languages, pp. 257–285. Springer (2022)
26. Joly, A., et al.: Overview of lifeclef 2024: Challenges on species distribution prediction and identification. In: International Conference of the Cross-Language Evaluation Forum for European Languages. Springer (2024)
27. Katija, K.: FathomNet: a global image database for enabling artificial intelligence in the ocean. Sci. Rep. **12**(1), 15914 (2022). https://doi.org/10.1038/s41598-022-19939-2
28. Lee, S.H., Chan, C.S., Remagnino, P.: Multi-organ plant classification based on convolutional and recurrent neural networks. IEEE Trans. Image Process. **27**(9), 4287–4301 (2018)
29. Lorieul, T.: Uncertainty in predictions of deep learning models for fine-grained classification. Ph.D. thesis, Université Montpellier (2020)
30. Martellucci, G., Goëau, H., Bonnet, P., Vinatier, F., Joly, A.: Overview of PlantCLEF 2025: multi-species plant identification in vegetation quadrat images. In: Working Notes of CLEF 2025 - Conference and Labs of the Evaluation Forum (2025)
31. Norouzzadeh, M.S., Morris, D., Beery, S., Joshi, N., Jojic, N., Clune, J.: A deep active learning system for species identification and counting in camera trap images. Methods Ecol. Evol. **12**(1), 150–161 (2021)
32. Pi, Y., et al: Individual animal identification and feed grading using computer vision and unsupervised statistical clustering. Available at SSRN 4905790 (2024)
33. Picek, L., et al.: Overview of lifeclef 2025: challenges on species presence prediction and identification, and individual animal identification. In: International Conference of the Cross-Language Evaluation Forum for European Languages, pp. 338–362. Springer (2025)
34. Picek, L., Sulc, M., Matas, J.: Recognition of the amazonian flora by inceptionnetworks with test-time class prior estimation. CLEF (Working Notes) **188** (2019)
35. Rand, W.M.: Objective criteria for the evaluation of clustering methods. J. Am. Stat. Assoc. **66**(336), 846–850 (1971)
36. Ravoor, P.C., Sudarshan, T.: Deep learning methods for multi-species animal re-identification and tracking-a survey. Comput. Sci. Rev. **38**, 100289 (2020)
37. Schneider, S., Taylor, G.W., Linquist, S., Kremer, S.C.: Past, present and future approaches using computer vision for animal re-identification from camera trap data. Methods Ecol. Evol. **10**(4), 461–470 (2019)
38. Tuia, D., et al.: Perspectives in machine learning for wildlife conservation. Nat. Commun. **13**(1), 792 (2022)
39. Van Horn, G., et al.: The inaturalist species classification and detection dataset. In: CVPR (2018)

40. Villon, S., Mouillot, D., Chaumont, M., Subsol, G., Claverie, T., Villéger, S.: A new method to control error rates in automated species identification with deep learning algorithms. Sci. Rep. **10**(1), 1–13 (2020)
41. Wäldchen, J., Mäder, P.: Machine learning for image based species identification. Methods Ecol. Evol. **9**(11), 2216–2225 (2018)
42. Wäldchen, J., Rzanny, M., Seeland, M., Mäder, P.: Automated plant species identification–trends and future directions. PLoS Comput. Biol. **14**(4), e1005993 (2018)

# EXIST 2026: Physiological Data for Multimodal Sexism Characterization in Social Media


Laura Plaza[1(✉)], Jorge Carrillo-de-Albornoz[1], Elena Gomis-Vicent[2],
Iván Arcos[2], María Aloy-Mayo[2], Paolo Rosso[2,3], and Damiano Spina[4]

[1] Universidad Nacional de Educación a Distancia (UNED), 28040 Madrid, Spain
{lplaza,jcalbornoz}@lsi.uned.es
[2] Universitat Politècnica de València (UPV), 46022 Valencia, Spain
{egomvic,malomay}@upvnet.upv.es, iarcgab@etsinf.upv.es,
prosso@dsic.upv.es
[3] ValgrAI – Valencian Graduate School and Research Network of Artificial
Intelligence, 46022 Valencia, Spain
[4] RMIT University, Melbourne 3000, Australia
damiano.spina@rmit.edu.au



**Abstract.** The paper describes the EXIST 2026 Lab on sexism identification in social networks, which is planned to take place at the CLEF 2026 conference and represents the sixth edition of the EXIST challenge. The lab comprises six tasks addressing three core problems—*sexism identification, source intention detection*, and *sexism categorization*—across two types of multimodal data: memes (image and text) and TikTok videos (video and text). Both the meme-based and video-based tasks are multilingual, covering English and Spanish. This multimodal and multilingual setup enables the analysis of how sexist content manifests across different media formats and interaction contexts, while also providing deeper insight into the social and communicative dynamics that shape the production and interpretation of sexist discourse online.

As in previous EXIST editions, the datasets will include annotations from multiple annotators, showing different or even conflicting opinions. This helps models learn from diverse perspectives. The novelty of the 2026 edition lies in the enrichment of the dataset with physiological and neurophysiological signals – specifically, heart rate, eye tracking, and electroencephalogram (EEG) data collected from different subjects while viewing the materials, that will be provided as training material. The aim is twofold: to explore how implicit emotional and cognitive responses correlate with the perception of sexist content, and to evaluate whether these signals can improve the automatic detection and classification of sexism. By incorporating features derived from users' unconscious reactions, machine learning models may capture subtle cues of bias or discomfort that are not evident in textual or visual content alone, leading to more accurate and human-aligned systems for identifying sexism across media.

**Keywords:** sexism identification · sexism categorization · learning with disagreement · EEG · eye tracking · heart rate · memes · TikTok videos · human-centric AI

# 1  Introduction

Sexism remains a pervasive form of social discrimination, reflected across multiple dimensions such as sexual violence, economic inequality, and online harassment. Recent data show that women represent around 85–90% of sexual violence victims in the USA, Europe, Spain, and Australia. [5,10,11,17].The gender pay gap continues to disadvantage women, who earn on average between 8.7% and 21.8% less than men across these same regions [4,9,21,22]. In the digital sphere, women also experience disproportionate levels of harassment and discrimination, with reported rates ranging from 16% in the USA to 41% in Australia, compared to 5–26% for men [6,12]. Detecting sexism against women is therefore a crucial step toward recognizing and addressing these systemic inequalities. The automatic detection and categorization of sexist content in online communication not only enables a deeper understanding of how prejudice manifests linguistically and behaviorally, but also contributes to developing safer and more equitable digital environments.

In this context, the development of AI systems capable of detecting sexism on social media presents a particularly relevant challenge. The perception of what constitutes sexist behavior or expression involves a certain degree of subjectivity, as it may be influenced by cultural norms, personal experiences, and emotional reactions that cannot be fully captured through linguistic data alone. Despite significant advances in computational modeling, the mechanisms underlying human decision-making remain only partially understood. Empirical evidence suggests that human judgments are shaped not only by conscious factors—such as socio-demographic background, prior experiences, and explicit beliefs—but also by unconscious cues, including emotions, physiological states, and sensory responses that subtly guide perception and evaluation. Current AI models, largely trained on textual or visual data, lack access to these deeper layers of cognitive and affective information, limiting their ability to replicate or interpret complex social phenomena. To bridge this gap, it becomes essential to explore new training paradigms that integrate human-centered and sensor-based data – such as eye tracking, heart rate, and EEG signals – to provide richer insights into how individuals consciously and unconsciously perceive sexist content. Neurophysiological signals collected through wearable devices have already proven effective in characterizing a wide range of complex information access tasks [7,8,20]. Therefore, incorporating this multimodal perspective could lead to fairer and more context-aware AI systems, capable of understanding not only the explicit meaning of language but also the implicit affective and cognitive processes that drive human interpretations.

EXIST 2026[1] will mark the sixth edition of the sEXism Identification in Social neTworks challenge. EXIST is a series of shared tasks and scientific events aimed at detecting and characterizing sexism in a broad sense, ranging from explicit misogyny to more subtle and implicit sexist behaviors. The last three editions of the EXIST shared task were organized as labs within CLEF [13, 14,16], while the first two were held in the IberLEF evaluation forum [18,19]. Over the past five years, more than 200 teams from research institutions and companies have participated in the EXIST challenge, submitting over 1,500 runs.

The EXIST 2026 lab will continue to focus on detecting sexism in social networks while introducing a novel paradigm that integrates human-centered signals into the AI development pipeline. Specifically, we incorporate sensor-based data—EEG, heart rate, and eye-tracking—collected from human annotators while they are exposed to potentially sexist content, with the aim of capturing implicit and pre-conscious responses to sexism.[2] These physiological signals provide complementary information to explicit annotations, reflecting affective and cognitive processes that may not be accessible through self-report or conscious reasoning alone. Findings from previous editions indicate that individuals often register sexist content at an implicit level, exhibiting measurable physiological reactions even when they are unable to explicitly articulate why the content is sexist or to consciously justify their annotation decisions.

By registering these signals during the annotation process, we aim to enrich training data with human-centered cues that capture early attentional shifts, emotional arousal, and cognitive load associated with the perception of harmful content. Given their inherently multimodal nature, our analysis will primarily focus on memes and short videos—formats that combine textual and visual information and are particularly suitable for eliciting such responses. We hypothesise that incorporating physiological correlates of implicit human perception into machine learning models will enable automated systems to better approximate human sensitivity to subtle or context-dependent forms of sexism, particularly in cases where surface linguistic features are insufficient, as previous studies have shown [3]. In this way, physiological signals are not treated as direct labels, but as auxiliary supervisory signals that can guide models toward more nuanced, human-aligned representations of sexist content.

Following the success of the previous two editions, the 2025 edition of EXIST will once again implement the LeWiDi paradigm for both dataset construction and system evaluation. This paradigm can significantly contribute to achieving human-centric AI by prioritizing diverse human perspectives and incorporating disagreements into the decision-making process [2].

---

[1] https://nlp.uned.es/exist2026.
[2] Data collection was approved by the Research Ethics Committee of the Universitat Politècnica de València (Project ID: P01_31-10-2025).

## 2    EXIST 2026 Tasks

We define six experimental tasks within this lab, corresponding to three distinct task types applied across two multimodal datasets: memes and videos. Subjects are asked to identify the presence of sexism and to characterize it according to the intention of the source and the type of sexism. Each instance (meme or TikTok video) was independently evaluated by multiple annotators, whose physiological and behavioral responses were captured through eye tracking, heart rate monitoring, and electroencephalography. The resulting multimodal physiological signals, along with the corresponding annotation labels, are linked to each dataset instance.

### 2.1    Sexism Identification

The first task is a binary classification task where systems must decide whether or not a given meme or video contains sexist expressions or behaviors (i.e., it is sexist itself, describes a sexist situation or criticizes a sexist behavior). Figure 1 show examples of sexist and not sexist memes, respectively.

### 2.2    Source Intention Detection

This task aims to categorize a meme or TikTok video according to the intention of the author. We propose a binary classification task: (i) direct sexist, and (ii) judgmental. The following categories are defined:

- **Direct** sexist: the intention was to create content that is sexist by itself or incites to be sexist. Figure 1 shows an example of a direct meme.
- **Judgemental** message: the intention is judgmental, since the meme or video describes sexist situations or behaviors with the aim of condemning them. Figure 1 shows an example of a judgemental meme.

(a) Not sexist        (b) Sexist (direct)   (c) Sexist (judgemental)

**Fig. 1.** Examples of direct and judgemental memes.

## 2.3  Sexism Categorization

In this task, each sexist meme/video must be categorized in one or more of the following categories:

- **Ideological and inequality**: this category includes memes/videos that discredit the feminist movement in order to defame the struggle of women in any aspect of their lives. It also includes contents that reject inequality between men and women, or present men as victims of gender-based oppression.
- **Stereotyping and dominance**: this category includes memes/videos that express false ideas about women that suggest they are more suitable or inappropriate for certain tasks. It also includes any claim that implies that men are somehow superior to women.
- **Objectification**: It includes content that objectifies women or reinforces stereotypes about their physical appearance, such as the expectation to meet traditional beauty standards or criticisms of their bodies.
- **Sexual violence**: this category includes memes/videos where sexual suggestions or harassment of a sexual nature (rape or sexual assault) are made.
- **Misogyny and non sexual violence**: this category includes expressions of hatred and violence towards women.

Examples of sexist memes from the previously described categories are shown in Fig. 2.

(a) Ideological & inequality     (b) Objectification

(c) Stereotyping & dominance     (d) Sexual violence     (e) Misogyny & non-sexual violence

**Fig. 2.** Examples of memes from the different sexist categories.

## 3   The EXIST 2026 Dataset

The EXIST 2026 dataset comprises 8,294 multimedia instances, including memes and short videos, in both English and Spanish. This collection integrates and extends the datasets developed for EXIST 2024 (memes) and EXIST 2025 (TikTok videos), which have been reused within a novel experimental setting designed to explore how individuals perceive and interpret sexism in online media. In this new dataset, subjects' conscious judgments are reflected in the labels they assigned to each instance, while their unconscious or implicit reactions are captured through sensor data such as eye tracking, heart rate, and EEG activity. The sensor data captured during the annotation process will be provided to the participant to use (if desired) in the training process.

Detailed descriptions of the annotation methodologies for the EXIST 2024 and 2025 datasets are available in [13,16]. Moreover, Table 1 summarizes the number of instances in the dataset per language, partition and content type.

**Table 1.** Number of instances in the EXIST 2026 dataset per language, partition and content type.

|  | Memes | | TikTok | |
|---|---|---|---|---|
|  | Spanish | English | Spanish | English |
| Training | 1,979 | 2,005 | 1,524 | 1,000 |
| Test | 540 | 513 | 304 | 370 |
| Total | 2,519 | 2,518 | 1,828 | 1,370 |

In the new experimental framework introduced in EXIST 2026, selected subjects were exposed to the multimedia content while their physiological and behavioral responses were continuously recorded. Each instance was viewed and labeled by up to two annotators, with every participant exposed to approximately 1,000 different memes or videos. The dataset was annotated during ten annotation sessions, each comprising around 130 instances and lasting approximately 35–45 min.

Each session followed a structured protocol comprising several stages. First, subjects were fitted with physiological sensors for electrocardiography (ECG), eye tracking, and electroencephalography (EEG), specifically using Pupil Labs Neon glasses (binocular gaze recording at 200 Hz), a Garmin Venu 3 smartwatch (continuous heart-rate and inter-beat interval monitoring), and an OpenBCI Cyton 16-channel EEG headset (10–20 system, 250 Hz). A two-minute resting-state baseline was recorded before exposure to the stimuli. Second, subjects completed a demographic questionnaire, administered only once, that collected information such as age, gender, education level, country of residence, and occupation. Third, they reported their average daily social media usage (in hours) and the percentage of time spent on platforms such as TikTok, Instagram, X/Twitter, and Facebook.

The next stage involved completing a cognitive thinking style questionnaire composed of 24 items rated on a six-point Likert scale (from "totally disagree" to "totally agree"). The items were grouped into four cognitive dimensions: open thought, closed thought, intuitive thought, and effortful thought, capturing different aspects of individual reasoning and information processing tendencies. Finally, before each experimental session, subjects completed a visual analogue scale (0–100) to self-assess their current emotional state, indicating the degree to which they felt happy, sad, calm, tense, energetic, or sleepy.

## 4   Evaluation Methodology and Metrics

As in previous EXIST editions, we will carry out two types of evaluations:

1. **Soft-soft evaluation**: intended for systems that provide probabilities (soft outputs) for each category, rather than a single label. We will use ICM-Soft (see details in [15]), as the official evaluation metric. We will also report Cross Entropy.
2. **Hard-hard evaluation**: intended for systems that provide a hard, conventional output. To derive the hard labels in the ground truth from the different annotators' labels, we will use a probabilistic threshold computed for each task. The official metric for this task will be ICM [1]. We will also report F1.

**Acknowledgments.** This work was supported by the Spanish Ministry of Science, Innovation and Universities (project ANNOTATE (PID2024-156022OB-C31 and PID2024-156022OB-C32)) funded by MICIU/AEI/10.13039/501100011 033 and the European Social Fund Plus (ESF+), and by the Australian Research Council Centre of Excellence for Automated Decision-Making and Society (ADM+S, CE200100005).

**Disclosure of Interests.** The authors have no competing interests to declare that are relevant to the content of this article.

## References

1. Amigó, E., Delgado, A.: Evaluating extreme hierarchical multi-label classification. In: Proceedings of the 60th Annual Meeting of the Association for Computational Linguistics, pp. 5809–5819 (2022)
2. Basile, V., et al.: We need to consider disagreement in evaluation. In: Proceedings of the 1st Workshop on Benchmarking: Past, Present and Future, pp. 15–21. Association for Computational Linguistics, Online (2021)
3. Divya Venkatesh, J., Jaiswal, A., Nanda, G.: Comparing human text classification performance and explainability with large language and machine learning models using eye-tracking. Sci. Rep. **14**(1), 14295 (2024). https://doi.org/10.1038/s41598-024-65080-7
4. Eurostat: Gender Pay Gap Statistics. https://ec.europa.eu/eurostat/statistics-explained/index.php?title=Gender_pay_gap_statistics (2025). Accessed 22 Dec 2025

5. Eurostat: Violence Experienced by Total Population. https://ec.europa.eu/eurostat/statistics-explained/index.php?title=Violence_experienced_by_total_population (2025). Accessed 22 Dec 2025

6. Gobierno de España: Brecha Digital de Género. https://www.inmujeres.gob.es/publicacioneselectronicas/documentacion/Documentos/DE2110.pdf (2021) Accessed 22 Dec 2025

7. Ji, K., Hettiachchi, D., Salim, F.D., Scholer, F., Spina, D.: Characterizing information seeking processes with multiple physiological signals. In: Proceedings of the 47th International ACM SIGIR Conference on Research and Development in Information Retrieval, pp. 1006–1017. SIGIR '24, Association for Computing Machinery, New York, NY, USA (2024). https://doi.org/10.1145/3626772.3657793

8. Ji, K., Hettiachchi, D., Scholer, F., Salim, F.D., Spina, D.: Senseseek dataset: Multimodal sensing to study information seeking behaviors. Proc. ACM Interact. Mob. Wearable Ubiquitous Technol. **9**(3) (2025). https://doi.org/10.1145/3749501

9. Ministerio de Igualdad, Gobierno de España: Declaración Institucional con Motivo del Día para la Igualdad Salarial. https://www.igualdad.gob.es/comunicacion/sala-de-prensa/declaracion-institucional-con-motivo-del-dia-para-la-igualdad-salarial/ (2025). Accessed 22 Dec 2025

10. Ministerio del Interior: Informe Delitos Contra la Libertad Sexual 2023. https://estadisticasdecriminalidad.ses.mir.es/publico/portalestadistico/dam/jcr:0a219f1b-f2f5-4e95-9553-aa8cf9ee5b3f (2023). Accessed 22 Dec 2025

11. National Association of Services Against Sexual Violence: Data on Sexual Violence Services in Australia. https://www.nasasv.org.au/data (2025), Last accessed 22 Dec 2025

12. Pew Research Center: The State of Online Harassment. https://www.pewresearch.org/internet/2021/01/13/the-state-of-online-harassment/ (2021). Accessed 22 Dec 2025

13. Plaza, L., et al.: Overview of EXIST 2025: learning with disagreement for sexism identification and characterization in Tweets, memes, and TikTok videos. In: Carrillo-de Albornoz, J., et al., (eds.) Proceedings of the 16th International Conference of the CLEF Association (CLEF 2025). Madrid, Spain (2025)

14. Plaza, L., et al.: Overview of EXIST 2023 – learning with disagreement for sexism identification and characterization. In: Arampatzis, A., et al., (eds.) Proceedings of the Fourteenth International Conference of the CLEF Association (CLEF 2023). Thessaloniki, Greece (2023)

15. Plaza, L., et al.: Overview of EXIST 2023 – learning with disagreement for sexism identification and characterization (extended overview). In: Aliannejadi, M., Faggioli, G., Ferro, N., Vlachos, M. (eds.) Working Notes of CLEF 2023 - Conference and Labs of the Evaluation Forum (2023)

16. Plaza, L., et al.: Overview of EXIST 2024 — learning with disagreement for sexism identification and characterization in Tweets and memes. In: Goeuriot, L., et al., (eds.) Proceedings of the 15th International Conference of the CLEF Association (CLEF 2024). Grenoble, France (2024)

17. RAINN: Statistics: Victims of Sexual Violence. https://rainn.org/facts-statistics-the-scope-of-the-problem/statistics-victims-of-sexual-violence/ (2025). Accessed 22 Dec 2025

18. Rodríguez-Sánchez, F., Carrillo-de Albornoz, J., Plaza, L., Gonzalo, J., Rosso, P., Comet, M., Donoso, T.: Overview of EXIST 2021: sexism identification in social networks. Procesamiento del Lenguaje Natural **67**, 195–207 (2021)

19. Rodríguez-Sánchez, F., et al.: Overview of EXIST 2022: sexism identification in social networks. Procesamiento del Lenguaje Natural **69**, 229–240 (2022)

20. Spina, D., et al.: Report on the 3rd Workshop on NeuroPhysiological approaches for interactive information retrieval (NeuroPhysIIR 2025) at SIGIR CHIIR 2025. SIGIR Forum **59**(1), 1–43 (2025). https://doi.org/10.1145/3769733.3769740
21. U.S. Bureau of Labor Statistics: Women's Earnings Were 83.6 Percent of Men's in 2023. https://www.bls.gov/opub/ted/2024/womens-earnings-were-83-6-percent-of-mens-in-2023.htm (2024). Accessed 22 Dec 2025
22. Workplace Gender Equality Agency: Gender Pay Gap Data. https://www.wgea.gov.au/pay-and-gender/gender-pay-gap-data (2025). Accessed 22 Dec 2025

# QuantumCLEF 2026 The Third Edition of the Quantum Computing Lab at CLEF

Andrea Pasin[1]([✉]), Maurizio Ferrari Dacrema[2], Paolo Cremonesi[2], Washington Cunha[3], Marcos André Gonçalves[3], and Nicola Ferro[1]

[1] University of Padua, Padua, Italy
`andrea.pasin.1@phd.unipd.it, nicola.ferro@unipd.it`
[2] Politecnico di Milano, Milan, Italy
`{maurizio.ferrari,paolo.cremonesi}@polimi.it`
[3] Federal University of Minas Gerais, Belo Horizonte, Brazil
`{washingtoncunha,mgoncalv}@dcc.ufmg.br`

**Abstract.** *Quantum Computing (QC)* is a research field that has been in the limelight in recent years. In fact, this new paradigm has the potential to revolutionize the way we currently solve problems by leveraging quantum-mechanical phenomena, which allow quantum computers to solve specific problems more efficiently than traditional computers. As quantum computers are starting to become more available, our objective is to investigate the application of QC within the IR and RS fields. In fact, IR and RS systems perform computationally intensive operations on extensive datasets, and using QC in their pipeline could be useful to improve their efficiency and, in some cases, effectiveness.

Thus, in this work, we present the third edition of the Quantum-CLEF lab, the first lab that allow participants to use **real quantum computers** for solving IR and RS tasks. The lab is composed of three main tasks that aim at discovering and evaluating QA approaches compared to their traditional counterpart while also establishing collaborations among researchers from different fields to harness their knowledge and skills to solve the considered challenges and promote the usage of QA. Moreover, based on the availability of quantum resources, we plan to introduce a small set of gate-based QC tasks for more-experienced researchers.

**Keywords:** Quantum Computing · Quantum Annealing · Feature Selection · Instance Selection · Clustering · Recommender Systems · Information Retrieval

## 1 Introduction

*Quantum Computing (QC)* is a paradigm that has the potential to revolutionize the way problems are solved across different fields. By leveraging quantum-mechanical phenomena, quantum computers are expected to solve certain problems more efficiently and, in some cases, more effectively than traditional ones.


R. Campos et al. (Eds.): ECIR 2026, LNCS 16486, pp. 306–314, 2026.
https://doi.org/10.1007/978-3-032-21321-1_41

Given the current scenario where *Information Retrieval (IR)* and *Recommender Systems (RS)* systems face ever-increasing amounts of data and rely on computationally demanding approaches, *Quantum Computing (QC)* could be integrated in the pipeline of such systems to improve their performance. However, while QC has already been applied in several domains, limited work has been done specifically for the IR and RS fields [4,13,20]. Indeed, the area of IR called Quantum IR [11,23,25] consists of exploiting the concepts of quantum mechanics to formulate IR models and problems but it does not deal with implementing IR and RS models and algorithms via QC technologies.

In this work, we focus on *Quantum Annealing (QA)*, which exploits special-purpose devices, called quantum annealers, which are able to rapidly find optimal (or close to optimal) solutions to optimization problems by leveraging quantum-mechanical effects. Our goal is therefore to understand QA can improve the efficiency and effectiveness of IR and RS systems by integrating it into their pipelines. Thus, we present here the third edition of the evaluation lab called *QuantumCLEF (qCLEF)*[1] [15], which aims at:

- evaluating the performance of QA with respect to traditional approaches;
- identifying new ways of formulating IR and RS algorithms and methods, so that they can be solved with QA;
- growing a research community around this new field in order to promote a wider adoption of QC technologies for IR and RS.

Working with QA does not require particular knowledge about how quantum physics works underneath it. There are, in fact, available tools and libraries that can be easily used to program and solve problems through this paradigm. Moreover, by participating in qCLEF, participants are provided access to the KIMERA infrastructure, allowing them to seamlessly use real state-of-the-art quantum computers [19] while monitoring resource usage for fairness, comparability, and reproducibility.

The paper is organized as follows: Sect. 2 introduces related work; Sect. 3 presents the tasks in the qCLEF lab; Sect. 4 considers some critical evaluation aspects; finally, Sect. 5 draws some conclusions and outlooks some future work.

## 2   Related Work

**What Is Quantum Annealing.** QA is a QC paradigm that can be specifically used to solve optimization problems. A quantum annealer, which is a special-purpose quantum machine for QA, represents a problem as the energy of a physical system and then leverages quantum-mechanical phenomena to let the system find a state of minimal (or close to minimal) energy, corresponding to an optimal (or close to optimal) solution of the original problem.

Since quantum annealers can be used to find the minimum energy state, problems must be formulated as minimization ones using the *Quadratic Unconstrained Binary Optimization (QUBO)* formulation, defined as follows:

$$\min \quad y = x^T Q x$$

---

[1] https://qclef.dei.unipd.it/.

where $x$ is a vector of binary decision variables and $Q$ is a matrix of constant values representing the problem to solve. Through QUBO formulations, it is possible to represent many problems [7]. Then, the *minor embedding* step maps the QUBO problem into the quantum annealer hardware, accounting for its topology. This can be done automatically, relying on some heuristics. A QUBO problem is usually solved by quantum annealers in few *milliseconds*.

**Applications of Quantum Annealing.** QA can be practically used to tackle problems in different fields due to its capabilities of solving *NP-Hard* integer optimization problems. QA has previously been employed to address IR and RS tasks, including Feature Selection [13], demonstrating both feasibility and competitiveness in terms of performance. Moreover, QA has also been explored in various *Machine Learning (ML)* tasks. For instance, Willsch et al. [26] introduce a kernel-based *Support Vector Machine (SVM)* formulation implemented on a D-Wave 2000Q quantum annealer, while Delilbasic et al. [5] propose a quantum multiclass SVM approach designed to reduce execution time for large training datasets. Additionally, QA has been applied to clustering problems; for example, Zaiou et al. [28] leverage it in a balanced K-means method, achieving improved performance as measured by the Davies-Bouldin Index.

**Previous Editions.** This is the third edition of the QuantumCLEF Lab. In the previous editions (2024 and 2025), there have been a total of 12 research teams that successfully participated and provided official submissions for the proposed tasks [16,18]. The previous editions encompassed different tasks such as Feature Selection, Clustering, and Instance Selection using state-of-the-art quantum annealers. The results in the previous editions suggest that quantum annealers are overall able to maintain a comparable level of effectiveness with respect to more traditional approaches (e.g., Simulated Annealing) while being able to solve the problems efficiently, considering just the time required for the annealing phase [16–18]. We received very positive feedback from the participants, most of which never experienced using QC resources before.

## 3   Tasks

In this edition of the qCLEF lab, we plan to organize three different tasks, each with the following goals:

- find one or more possible QUBO formulations of the problem;
- evaluate the quantum annealer approach compared to a corresponding traditional approach to assess both its efficiency and its effectiveness.

In general, we expect QA to solve problems more quickly than traditional approaches, achieving results that are similar or better in terms of effectiveness.

Additionally, based on the availability of gate-based quantum computers, we plan to organize a further small set of tasks involving the use of these devices. These will likely be the target for more experienced participants having prior knowledge on QC.

### 3.1   Task 1 - Quantum Feature Selection

This task focuses on solving the *NP-Hard* Feature Selection problem with QA, similarly to other previous works [4, 13].

Feature Selection is a well-known problem for both IR and RS, which requires the identification of a subset of the available features to train a learning model more efficiently and effectively. This problem is very impacting since many IR and RS systems involve the optimization of learning models, and reducing the dimensionality and noise of the input data can improve their performance.

If the input data has $n$ features, we can enumerate all the possible sets of input data having a fixed number $k$ of features, thus obtaining $\binom{n}{k}$ possible subsets. Therefore, to find the best subset of $k$ features the learning model should be trained on all the subsets of features, which is infeasible even for small datasets. So, in this task, we want to understand if QA can be used to solve this problem more efficiently and effectively.

We have identified some possible datasets, such as MQ2007 [22] or Istella S-LETOR [10]. These datasets contain pre-computed features, and the objective is to select a subset of these features to train a learning model, such as LambdaMART [1] or a content-based RS, and to achieve the best performance according to metrics such as nDCG@10.

### 3.2   Task 2 - Quantum Instance Selection

This task focuses on formulating and solving the Instance Selection problem with QA [14].

Currently, transformer-based architectures, including 1st and 2nd generation transformers (e.g., RoBERTa [9]) as well as current large language models (e.g., Llama3 [24]), are considered state-of-the-art in several fields. Given their high costs, one of the big challenges is to fine-tune these models efficiently. Instance Selection focuses on selecting a representative subset of instances from a dataset to make the training of these models faster while maintaining a high level of effectiveness of the trained model [2, 3].

In this task, we thus aim at using QA to find a good subset of instances in a dataset in an efficient way, for fine-tuning a **Llama3.1** model to perform a text classification task as effectively as it would on the entire original dataset.

We have identified some possible datasets, such as Vader NYT or Yelp Reviews, that will be provided in a five-fold cross-validation split. The extracted subsets will be then used to fine-tune the Llama3.1 model and the effectiveness will be measured with the Macro-F1 score [21].

### 3.3   Task 3 - Quantum Clustering

This task focuses on the formulation of the Clustering problem and solving it with a quantum annealer.

Clustering can be useful to organize large collections and help users to explore them. It can also be used to divide users according to their interests or build user models with the cluster centroids [27], boosting efficiency or effectiveness for users with limited data. In this task, each document or user can be represented as a vector in a similarity space, and it is possible to cluster documents based on their similarity between each other.

For the IR task, we have identified ANTIQUE [8] as a possible dataset. From the dataset, we will produce embeddings using models such as BERT [6]. The cluster quality will be measured with user queries that undergo the same embedding process. These queries will match only the most representative embeddings of the clusters, avoiding computing similarities on the whole collection, as in an approximate vector search scenario. For the recommendation task, the goal will be to partition the users into communities based on their past interactions, in such a way that users within a community share similar interests [12]. The quality of the communities will be assessed based on the effectiveness of a non-personalized RS algorithm trained on each community.

The cluster quality will be measured according to the Davies-Bouldin Index and nDCG@10.

### 3.4  Gate-Based Teaching Tasks

In addition to the QA tracks, the lab will include a small set of gate-model tasks conceived as teaching exercises for researchers who want to experiment with circuit-based paradigms in IR and RS. The tasks will be intentionally small to reflect limited resource availability and the cost of simulating gate-level systems.

The first task focuses on computing the similarity of documents with a swap test. Given a swap-test circuit, the participants will have to define an appropriate encoding for the documents with complex-valued embeddings (or quantum states) so that the test can measure their similarity. A second, more advanced task asks participants to design not only the encoding, but also the short quantum circuit able to build it. The goal is to identify a sequence of operations that yields good encodings for document similarity while keeping the number of operations small. Finally, we introduce a hybrid quantum-classical exercise based on the Variational Quantum Approximate Optimization Algorithm to solve small QUBO instances. Participants will implement a minimal QAOA loop, report solution quality and runtime.

## 4  Evaluation of Quantum Annealing

Using a quantum annealer requires several stages:

**Formulation:** compute the QUBO matrix $Q$;
**Embedding:** generate the *minor embedding* of the QUBO for the hardware;
**Data Transfer:** transfer the problem and the embedding to the data center that hosts the quantum annealer;
**Annealing:** run the quantum annealer itself.

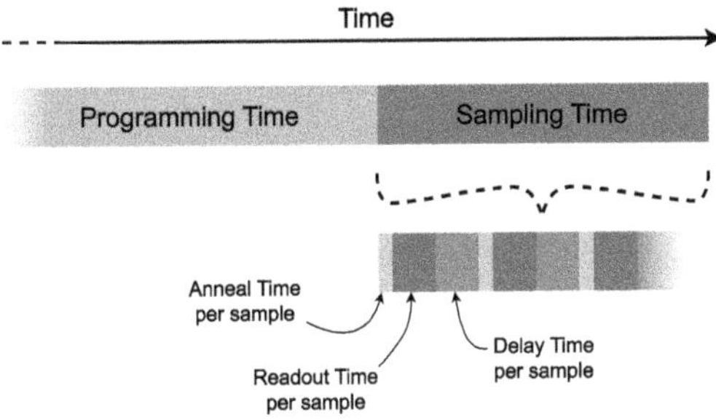


**Fig. 1.** The quantum annealer access time split in several steps.

In terms of effectiveness, at least two sources of stochasticity must be considered. First, during the embedding phase, heuristic methods transform the QUBO formulation into an equivalent version that fits the hardware. This process is non-deterministic: it can produce different embeddings for the same problem, which are theoretically equivalent but may lead to variations in practice. Second, the annealing phase samples a low-energy solution. However, obtaining a reliable solution may require many samples.

Regarding efficiency, problem transfer over the network can introduce significant delays, and generating the minor embedding may even take minutes for particularly large problems. Furthermore, the runtime can be divided into several stages, as illustrated in Fig. 1: first, the device must be programmed; next, the annealing process is executed; finally, the results are read. The annealing itself is extremely fast, requiring only *microseconds*, but it must be repeated multiple times due to the device's stochastic nature. Therefore, a complete efficiency assessment must account for the time required by all stages of the process.

## 5   Conclusions and Future Work

In this paper, we have outlined the third edition of the qCLEF lab, a lab composed of three practical tasks aiming at evaluating the performance of QC and especially QA applied to IR and RS. We have also discussed the potential benefits that QA can bring in terms of performance to the IR and RS fields, and we have also analyzed the different challenges that lie in the evaluation of these new quantum-based approaches.

qCLEF is the first initiative that provides access to real state-of-the-art quantum devices for researchers to tackle practical IR and RS tasks. It also represents a unique opportunity for researchers worldwide to start learning more about these new cutting-edge technologies that will likely have a big impact in the future. Finally, through our lab, it will also be possible to assess whether quantum-based methods can be employed to improve the current state-of-the-art approaches, hopefully delivering new performing solutions.

**Acknowledgements.** We acknowledge the CINECA award under the ISCRA initiative, for the availability of high-performance computing resources and support. W. Cunha and M. A. Gonçalves have further been supported by the CNPq, CAPES, Instituto Nacional de Ciência e Tecnologia em Inteligência Artificial Responsável para Linguística Computacional, Tratamento e Disseminação de Informação (INCT-TILDIAR; grant # 408490/2024-1), FAPEMIG, AWS, Google, NVIDIA, CIIASaúde, and FAPESP.

**Disclosure of Interests.** The authors have no competing interests to declare that are relevant to the content of this article.

# References


1. Burges, C.J.C.: From RankNet to LambdaRank to LambdaMART: An Overview. Tech. rep., Microsoft Research, MSR-TR-2010-82 (June 2010)
2. Cunha, W., França, C., Fonseca, G., Rocha, L., Gonçalves, M.A.: An effective, efficient, and scalable confidence-based instance selection framework for transformer-based text classification. In: Chen, H., Duh, W.E., Huang, H., Kato, M.P., Mothe, J., Poblete, B. (eds.) Proceedings of the 46th International ACM SIGIR Conference on Research and Development in Information Retrieval, SIGIR 2023, Taipei, Taiwan, July 23-27, 2023, pp. 665–674, ACM (2023), https://doi.org/10.1145/3539618.3591638
3. Cunha, W., Viegas, F., França, C., Rosa, T., Rocha, L., Gonçalves, M.A.: A comparative survey of instance selection methods applied to non-neural and transformer-based text classification. ACM Comput. Surv. **55**(13s), 265:1–265:52 (2023), https://doi.org/10.1145/3582000
4. Dacrema, M.F., Moroni, F., Nembrini, R., Ferro, N., Faggioli, G., Cremonesi, P.: Towards feature selection for ranking and classification exploiting quantum annealers. In: Amigó, E., Castells, P., Gonzalo, J., Carterette, B., Culpepper, J.S., Kazai, G. (eds.) SIGIR '22: The 45th International ACM SIGIR Conference on Research and Development in Information Retrieval, Madrid, Spain, July 11 - 15, 2022, pp. 2814–2824, ACM (2022). https://doi.org/10.1145/3477495.3531755
5. Delilbasic, A., Saux, B.L., Riedel, M., Michielsen, K., Cavallaro, G.: A single-step multiclass SVM based on quantum annealing for remote sensing data classification. arXiv preprint arXiv:2303.11705 (2023)
6. Devlin, J., Chang, M.W., Lee, K., Toutanova, K.: Bert: Pre-training of deep bidirectional transformers for language understanding. arXiv preprint arXiv:1810.04805 (2018)
7. Glover, F.W., Kochenberger, G.A., Du, Y.: Quantum bridge analytics I: a tutorial on formulating and using QUBO models. 4OR **17**(4), 335–371 (2019). https://doi.org/10.1007/s10288-019-00424-y
8. Hashemi, H., Aliannejadi, M., Zamani, H., Croft, W.B.: ANTIQUE: a non-factoid question answering benchmark. In: Jose, J.M., Yilmaz, E., Magalhães, J., Castells, P., Ferro, N., Silva, M.J., Martins, F. (eds.) ECIR 2020. LNCS, vol. 12036, pp. 166–173. Springer, Cham (2020). https://doi.org/10.1007/978-3-030-45442-5_21
9. Liu, Y., et al.: Roberta: A robustly optimized bert pretraining approach. arXiv preprint 1907.11692 (2019)

10. Lucchese, C., Nardini, F.M., Orlando, S., Perego, R., Silvestri, F., Trani, S.: Post-learning optimization of tree ensembles for efficient ranking. In: Proceedings of the 39th International ACM SIGIR conference on Research and Development in Information Retrieval, pp. 949–952 (2016)

11. Melucci, M.: Introduction to Information Retrieval and Quantum Mechanics, The Information Retrieval Series, vol. 35. Springer (2015), ISBN 978-3-662-48312-1, https://doi.org/10.1007/978-3-662-48313-8

12. Nembrini, R., Carugno, C., Ferrari Dacrema, M., Cremonesi, P.: Towards recommender systems with community detection and quantum computing. In: RecSys '22: Sixteenth ACM Conference on Recommender Systems, Seattle, WA, USA, September 18 - 23, 2022, pp. 579–585, ACM (2022). https://doi.org/10.1145/3523227.3551478

13. Nembrini, R., Dacrema, M.F., Cremonesi, P.: Feature selection for recommender systems with quantum computing. Entropy **23**(8), 970 (2021). https://doi.org/10.3390/E23080970

14. Pasin, A., Cunha, W., Gonçalves, M.A., Ferro, N.: A quantum annealing instance selection approach for efficient and effective transformer fine-tuning. In: Oosterhuis, H., Bast, H., Xiong, C. (eds.) Proceedings of the 2024 ACM SIGIR International Conference on Theory of Information Retrieval, ICTIR 2024, Washington, DC, USA, 13 July 2024, pp. 205–214, ACM (2024), https://doi.org/10.1145/3664190.3672515

15. Pasin, A., Dacrema, M.F., Cremonesi, P., Ferro, N.: QCLEF: a proposal to evaluate quantum annealing for information retrieval and recommender systems. In: Arampatzis, A., et al., (eds.) Experimental IR Meets Multilinguality, Multimodality, and Interaction - 14th International Conference of the CLEF Association, CLEF 2023, Thessaloniki, Greece, September 18-21, 2023, Proceedings, Lecture Notes in Computer Science, vol. 14163, pp. 97–108, Springer (2023), https://doi.org/10.1007/978-3-031-42448-9_9

16. Pasin, A., Dacrema, M.F., Cremonesi, P., Ferro, N.: Overview of quantumclef 2024: The quantum computing challenge for information retrieval and recommender systems at CLEF. In: Goeuriot, L., et al., (eds.) Experimental IR Meets Multilinguality, Multimodality, and Interaction - 15th International Conference of the CLEF Association, CLEF 2024, Grenoble, France, September 9-12, 2024, Proceedings, Part II, Lecture Notes in Computer Science, vol. 14959, pp. 260–282, Springer (2024). https://doi.org/10.1007/978-3-031-71908-0_12

17. Pasin, A., Dacrema, M.F., Cremonesi, P., Ferro, N.: Quantumclef 2024: Overview of the quantum computing challenge for information retrieval and recommender systems at CLEF. In: Faggioli, G., Ferro, N., Galuscáková, P., de Herrera, A.G.S. (eds.) Working Notes of the Conference and Labs of the Evaluation Forum (CLEF 2024), Grenoble, France, 9-12 September, 2024, CEUR Workshop Proceedings, vol. 3740, pp. 3032–3053, CEUR-WS.org (2024). https://ceur-ws.org/Vol-3740/paper-297.pdf

18. Pasin, A., Dacrema, M.F., Cunha, W., Gonçalves, M.A., Cremonesi, P., Ferro, N.: Overview of quantumclef 2025: the second quantum computing challenge for information retrieval and recommender systems at CLEF. In: Carrillo-de-Albornoz, J., et al., (eds.) Experimental IR Meets Multilinguality, Multimodality, and Interaction - 16th International Conference of the CLEF Association, CLEF 2025, Madrid, Spain, September 9-12, 2025, Proceedings, Lecture Notes in Computer Science, vol. 16089, pp. 412–435, Springer (2025), https://doi.org/10.1007/978-3-032-04354-2_22

19. Pasin, A., Ferro, N.: KIMERA: from evaluation-as-a-service to evaluation-in-the-cloud. In: Ferro, N., Maistro, M., Pasi, G., Alonso, O., Trotman, A., Verberne, S. (eds.) Proceedings of the 48th International ACM SIGIR Conference on Research and Development in Information Retrieval, SIGIR 2025, Padua, Italy, July 13-18, 2025, pp. 3584–3594, ACM (2025). https://doi.org/10.1145/3726302.3730298
20. Pilato, G., Vella, F.: A survey on quantum computing for recommendation systems. Inf. **14**(1), 20 (2023). https://doi.org/10.3390/info14010020
21. Powers, D.M.W.: Evaluation: from precision, recall and f-measure to roc, informedness, markedness and correlation. CoRR **abs/2010.16061** (2020). https://arxiv.org/abs/2010.16061
22. Qin, T., Liu, T.Y.: Introducing LETOR 4.0 Datasets. arXiv.org, Information Retrieval (cs.IR) **arXiv:1306.2597** (June 2013)
23. van Rijsbergen, C.J.: The geometry of information retrieval. Cambridge University Press (2004), ISBN 978-0-521-83805-4
24. Touvron, H., et al.: Llama: Open and efficient foundation language models (2023)
25. Uprety, S., Gkoumas, D., Song, D.: A survey of quantum theory inspired approaches to information retrieval. ACM Comput. Surv. **53**(5), 98:1–98:39 (2021). https://doi.org/10.1145/3402179
26. Willsch, D., Willsch, M., De Raedt, H., Michielsen, K.: Support vector machines on the d-wave quantum annealer. Comput. Phys. Commun. **248**, 107006 (2020)
27. Wu, Y., Cao, Q., Shen, H., Tao, S., Cheng, X.: INMO: a model-agnostic and scalable module for inductive collaborative filtering. In: SIGIR '22: The 45th International ACM SIGIR Conference on Research and Development in Information Retrieval, Madrid, Spain, pp. 91–101, ACM (2022). https://doi.org/10.1145/3477495.3532000
28. Zaiou, A., Bennani, Y., Matei, B., Hibti, M.: Balanced k-means using quantum annealing. In: 2021 IEEE Symposium Series on Computational Intelligence (SSCI), pp. 1–7 (2021). https://doi.org/10.1109/SSCI50451.2021.9659997

# BioASQ at CLEF2026: The Fourteenth Edition of the Large-Scale Biomedical Semantic Indexing and Question Answering Challenge


Anastasios Nentidis[1]([✉]), Georgios Katsimpras[1], Anastasia Krithara[1], Martin Krallinger[2], Miguel Rodriguez-Ortega[2], Eduard Rodriguez-Lopez[2], Natalia Loukachevitch[3], Igor Rozhkov[3], Elena Tutubalina[4,5,6], Grigorios Tsoumakas[7], George Giannakoulas[7], Dimitris Dimitriadis[7], Alexandra Bekiaridou[8], Athanasios Samaras[7], Vasiliki Patsiou[7], Giorgio Maria Di Nunzio[9], Nicola Ferro[9], Stefano Marchesin[9], Marco Martinelli[9], Gianmaria Silvello[9], and Georgios Paliouras[1]

[1] National Center for Scientific Research "Demokritos", Athens, Greece
{tasosnent,gkatsibras,akrithara,paliourg}@iit.demokritos.gr
[2] Barcelona Supercomputing Center, Barcelona, Spain
{martin.krallinger,miguel.rodriguez,eduard.rodriguez}@bsc.es
[3] Moscow State University, Moscow, Russia
[4] Sber AI, Moscow, Russia
[5] Artificial Intelligence Research Institute, Moscow, Russia
[6] Kazan Federal University, Kazan, Russia
[7] Aristotle University of Thessaloniki, Thessaloniki, Greece
{greg,dndimitri}@csd.auth.gr, g.giannakoulas@gmail.com
[8] Northwell Health, New Hyde Park, USA
[9] University of Padua, Padua, Italy
{giorgiomaria.dinunzio,nicola.ferro,stefano.marchesin,marco.martinelli,
gianmaria.silvello}@unipd.it



**Abstract.** Over the past thirteen years, the large-scale biomedical semantic indexing and question-answering challenge (BioASQ) has consistently driven the advancement of methods and tools that enhance access to the rapidly growing body of scientific resources in the biomedical domain. BioASQ offers a unique common testbed where research teams worldwide can evaluate and compare innovative approaches for accessing biomedical knowledge by organizing shared tasks on an annual basis and providing respective benchmark datasets that represent the real information needs of biomedical experts.

The fourteenth version of BioASQ (BioASQ14) will be held as an evaluation Lab in the context of CLEF2026, providing six tasks: (i) *Task b* on biomedical semantic question answering. (ii) *Task Synergy* on question answering for developing biomedical topics. (iii) *Task MultiClinSum-2* on multilingual clinical summarization. (iv) *Task BioNNE-R* on nested relation extraction in Russian and English. (v) *Task ELCardioCC* on clinical coding in cardiology. (vi) *Task GutBrainIE* on gut-brain interplay information extraction. Through its six shared tasks, BioASQ14 challenges the research community to develop methods that go beyond the current state of the art, fostering innovative approaches that enable efficient and precise access to biomedical knowledge while pushing the research frontier forward.

**Keywords:** Biomedical · Semantic Indexing · Question Answering

## 1    Introduction

BioASQ[1] [37] was introduced in 2012 as a series of international challenges and workshops on biomedical semantic indexing and question answering (QA). Since then, BioASQ has offered a range of shared tasks on biomedical information access, machine learning, information retrieval, and information extraction, and has welcomed participation from more than 150 teams from 36 distinct countries. The benchmark datasets and corresponding open-source infrastructure developed for BioASQ tasks enable researchers in biomedical information access systems to work on the same realistic scenarios and compare the performance of their approaches. In addition, the respective annual BioASQ workshops allow the participants to present and discuss their methods with the research community [8,11,19,30–32]. By consistently recognizing the most successful approaches in each shared task and sub-task, BioASQ drives the development of systems that surpass previous methods. These advances in biomedical semantic indexing and QA are progressively enabling more accurate retrieval of biomedical knowledge and contributing to the enhancement of healthcare services.

## 2    BioASQ Evaluation Lab 2026

The fourteenth BioASQ challenge (BioASQ14), to be held as part of the Conference and Labs of the Evaluation Forum (CLEF) 2026[2], will be structured into six tasks that are central to accessing biomedical knowledge and answering biomedical questions: (i) *Task b*[3] on the processing of biomedical questions, the generation of answers, and the retrieval of supporting material, (ii) *Task Synergy* on biomedical QA for developing topics, such as COVID-19, where resources are not necessarily sufficient to provide definite answers, (iii) *Task MultiClinSum-2* on Multilingual Clinical Summarization. (iv) *Task BioNNE-R*: on the automated relation extraction between nested named entities in Russian and English. (v) *Task ELCardioCC* on clinical coding of Greek cardiology discharge letters. (vi) *Task GutBrainIE* on extracting and linking knowledge from the scientific literature on the gut-brain interplay. As *Task b* and *Task Synergy* have also been organized in the context of previous editions of the BioASQ challenge [21,22,25,27],

---

[1] http://www.bioasq.org.

[2] https://clef2026.clef-initiative.eu/.

[3] Since the first BioASQ, the task on biomedical semantic indexing has been called *Task a* and the task on QA *Task b*, for brevity. *Task a* was completed in 2020 [9].

we refer to their current version, in the context of BioASQ14, as *task 14b*, *task Synergy 14* respectively. Detailed guidelines for participating in each BioASQ task are available online[4].

## 2.1   Task 14b: Biomedical Question Answering

BioASQ *task 14b* is conducted in three phases. In Phase A, systems are given biomedical questions in English and must retrieve relevant material that is PubMed documents and snippets. In Phase A+, systems are required to provide both 'ideal' and 'exact' answers for these questions. The 'ideal' answer is a paragraph-length summary, regardless of the question type but the form of the 'exact' answer varies by question type: it can be a *yes* or *no* (yes/no type), an entity name such as a gene or drug (factoid type), or a list of entity names (list type)[5]. Finally, in Phase B, systems are supplied with relevant material selected by the BioASQ experts and must provide updated 'ideal' and 'exact' answers based on this additional information. The results from the previous version of the task [25] reveal that state-of-the-art LLM-based systems can provide correct answers for yes/no questions, even without access to ground truth relevant material (Top maF1 0.97 ±0.03 in Phase A+). For factoid and list questions, on the other hand, there is more room for improvement (top factoid MRR 0.64 ±0.11, top list F1 0.57 ±0.02 in Phase B), especially without access to the ground truth relevant material (top factoid MRR 0.64 ±0.11 and top list F1 0.57 ±0.02 in Phase A+). Therefore, the retrieval of relevant material appears to be a significant persisting challenge (top document MAP 0.58 ±0.08 and top snippet f1 0.24 ±0.02 in Phase A)[6].

About 300 new biomedical questions annotated with golden documents, snippets, and answers ('exact' and 'ideal') will be developed for testing. In addition, a training set of about 5,700 biomedical questions, accompanied by answers and supporting evidence (documents and snippets), will be available from previous versions of the tasks, as a unique resource for the development of question-answering systems [10, 20]. The evaluation in *task 14b* is done manually by the experts who assess each system response and automatically by employing a variety of established evaluation measures [16] as in *task 13b* [25].

## 2.2   Task Synergy 14: Question Answering for Developing Topics

In 2020, we introduced the BioASQ *task Synergy* to advance research on emerging biomedical topics, such as COVID-19 [11,12]. Unlike the original *task b*, *task Synergy* is structured as a continuous dialogue, enabling experts to pose open questions on developing topics for which a definitive answer may not be known in advance. Systems provide relevant material, including documents and

---

[4] https://participants-area.bioasq.org/.

[5] For questions of type summary, no 'exact' answer is defined, only an 'ideal' answer.

[6] The reported performance of top participating systems has been averaged across the four test batches of BioASQ13.

snippets, along with answers, which are then assessed by the BioASQ experts. Feedback from these assessments is provided back to the systems after each round to refine their responses to the same questions. This iterative process continues across multiple rounds, incorporating new material based on updates to the original document resource [26]. Since 2023, this evolving document resource is PubMed [21]. During task Synergy 13 [25], the systems managed to identify enough relevant material to provide an answer to about 80% of the questions and provide at least one ideal answer of ground-truth quality for about 47% of them.

A training dataset for *task Synergy* is already available from previous versions of the task [23–25, 28, 29]. It consists of approximately 400 questions on developing topics, with incremental annotations including relevant material and answers. In addition, this set will be extended with about fifty new open questions on developing health topics and incremental feedback for the systems after each of the four rounds of *task Synergy 14*. Meanwhile, any existing questions that remain relevant may be enriched with more recent material and more up-to-date answers as well. The primary goal of *task Synergy 14* is to support experts in incrementally advancing the understanding of evolving health topics and in discovering new solutions. However, the same evaluation measures used in *task 14b* will also apply for completeness. For the information retrieval part, only new material will be considered per round (*residual collection evaluation* [36]).

### 2.3   Task MultiClinSum-2: Multilingual Clinical Summarization

There is an increasing demand for automated tools that can efficiently process and summarise clinical narratives written in multiple languages. Clinical case reports and medical records are accumulating rapidly and often contain lengthy, jargon-heavy descriptions that are time-consuming for clinicians and researchers to understand and extract relevant information. While Large Language Models (LLMs) have made significant progress in clinical summarisation, their performance across languages, data domains and summarisation styles remains insufficiently benchmarked.

The MultiClinSum-2 task extends the previous edition by expanding both the dataset and evaluation scope for multilingual clinical summarization. As in the first edition, participants will generate summaries for full-length clinical case reports written in English, Spanish, French, and Portuguese. In addition, new languages such as Italian, Swedish, Czech, or Dutch are being considered for addition, further broadening the linguistic coverage of the task. The summaries, which will be released as Gold Standard, are based on the original author-provided summaries of the corresponding full clinical case report descriptions. These summaries are not supposed to be readable by laypersons, as this is not the main focus of the task, but rather by medical-related experts to cover key clinical insight, such as patient characteristics (age, gender, etc.), reason for consultation, anamnesis and physical exploration, diagnosis, treatment, and outcome. Beyond traditional lexical and semantic metrics such as ROUGE-2 and

BERTScore, this second edition will introduce factual consistency (FC) assessment and LLM-as-a-Judge evaluation, where large language models may assist in ranking or validating summary quality. As clinical case reports share common structure with medical discharge summaries, MultiClinSum-2 aims to provide insights not only for publication-style narratives but also for real-world healthcare applications.

### 2.4 Task BioNNE-R: Nested Relation Extraction in Russian and English

The BioNNE-R shared task addresses the NLP challenge of relation extraction involving nested named entities, i.e. entities that contain other entities within their boundaries. Relations between nested entities may cross entity boundaries, connecting shorter entities within longer ones, making detection more challenging. For example, *blood system tumor* includes internal entities *blood, blood system*, and *tumor*. Several internal relations within *blood system tumor* can be identified: *blood* is a part of *blood system*; *blood system tumor* is a subclass of *tumor*; *blood system tumor* affects *blood system*. Moreover, internal entities can also relate to external entities as *blood system* is a part of *patient*, mentioned separately. Capturing such nested relations enables more comprehensive information extraction, yet the annotation and extraction of nested relations remain insufficiently studied.

Following earlier shared tasks on nested entity processing *BioNNE 2024* [4] and *BioNNE-L 2025* [35] tasks, the evaluation framework is divided as follows: 1. Track Language-oriented: Participants in this track must develop a model for nested relation extraction in a target language (English or Russian). 2. Track Bilingual: Participants must train a single model using training data for both Russian and English languages. The task data will be based on the NEREL-BIO dataset [15], which includes annotated mentions of disorders, anatomical structures, chemicals, diagnostic procedures, and other biomedical entities.

### 2.5 Task ELCardioCC: Clinical Coding in Cardiology

Clinical coding is the process of translating clinical documentation from patient health records into standardized coding systems [5]. This translation facilitates the generation of reliable datasets for epidemiological research, health service planning, and statistical evaluation. The procedure is inherently complex, requiring significant cognitive effort and meticulous adherence to coding standards to maintain uniformity and validity across records. Nevertheless, the majority of existing research has concentrated on clinical text written in English, resulting in a notable underrepresentation of other languages, including Greek. This linguistic imbalance limits the generalizability of current findings and creates challenges for developing language-specific resources, such as annotated corpora, terminologies, and natural language processing tools. Addressing this gap is essential for enabling equitable access to advanced clinical text mining techniques across diverse healthcare systems.

The *ELCardioCC* 2026 shared task concerns the automatic assignment of cardiology-related ICD-10 codes to hospital discharge letters at the document level. The task can be approached in two ways: either by combining Named Entity Recognition (NER) and Entity Linking (EL) techniques, or by formulating it as a multi-label classification (MLC) problem. To support both directions, we introduce a mixed dataset consisting of 1,500 documents annotated at both the document and mention level, suitable for NER+EL approaches, and 1,000 documents annotated only at the document level, intended for MLC approaches. In total, the dataset comprises 2,500 documents for training and development and 500 documents for testing. Finally, the coding standards will be available to participants.

## 2.6   Task GutBrainIE: Gut-Brain Interplay Information Extraction

Recent evidence suggests a connection between neurological and gut disorders that may play a critical role in mental health-related disorders or diseases like Multiple Sclerosis, Parkinson's, and Alzheimer's [1–3, 7]. The *GutBrainIE* task aims to foster the development of Information Extraction (IE) systems that support experts by automatically extracting and linking knowledge from scientific literature, facilitating the understanding of gut-brain interplay and its role in neurological diseases. The task is divided into two main subtasks. In the first, participants are provided with PubMed abstracts discussing the gut-brain interplay and asked to identify named entities and link them to the corresponding concepts in reference biomedical resources (e.g., UMLS). In the second subtask, participants are required to identify relations between pairs of extracted entities, assigning the appropriate relation predicate that connects them. For both subtasks, submitted runs are evaluated using Precision, Recall, and F1 measures against gold annotations created by domain experts. Last year's results highlight a clear difficulty gap between the two subtasks: half of the participating teams achieved strong effectiveness in named entity recognition (F1 $\geq$ 0.8), while relation extraction saw the best systems scoring in the 0.34–0.46 F1 range. Top-performing approaches relied on supervised fine-tuning of classification heads on top of transformer models pre-trained on biomedical corpora, while LLM-based approaches showed limited effectiveness [17].

The GutBrainIE dataset comprises over 1,600 PubMed abstracts annotated with entity mentions, concept links, and relations. We focus on abstracts only as they summarize the most important information in each paper and typically give a higher density of entity mentions of interest. The entity schema covers general biomedical categories (e.g., *bacteria*, *drug*), gut-brain specific ones (e.g., *microbiome*), and experimental concepts (e.g., *statistical technique*). About relations, we defined a total of 17 predicates, resulting in 55 possible relation triples *(head entity, predicate, tail entity)*. The dataset is split into training, validation, and test sets. Together with the dataset, we provide reference resources used for entity linking and annotation guidelines.

## 2.7  BioASQ Datasets and Tools

BioASQ offers an ecosystem of publicly available datasets[7] and tools[8], including a range of evaluation measures [16] and the BioASQ Annotation Tool [33] for the development of QA datasets. In addition to the unique datasets provided for this year's six tasks, BioASQ also offers: i) a benchmark dataset of more than 16.2 million articles on biomedical semantic indexing (*task a*) [9], ii) the *task MESINESP* datasets [6,34] of more than 300K articles, on medical semantic indexing in Spanish, iii) the *task DisTEMIST* [18], *task MedProcNER* [13], and *task MultiCardioNER* [14] on medical information extraction from clinical case documents, iv) the datasets of the tasks *task BioNNE* [4] and *task BioNNE-L* [35] on nested named entity recognition and linking.

# 3  Conclusions

BioASQ promotes the exchange and integration of ideas by offering shared tasks on semantic indexing and question answering, and providing unique, realistic datasets and evaluation tools for research on biomedical information access methods. This, in turn, accelerates progress in the field, as reflected in the steady improvement of task scores [20–22,27]. A notable example is BioASQ's role in supporting the adoption of fully automated MeSH indexing at NLM [9]. Likewise, we anticipate that this edition of BioASQ will enable participating teams to further advance the six open tasks offered this year.

**Acknowledgments.** This edition of BioASQ was sponsored by Ovid Technologies, Inc. This research was funded by the Spanish National BARITONE project (TED2021-129974B-C22). This work is also supported by the European Union's Horizon Europe Co-ordination & Support Action under Grant Agreement No 101080430 (AI4HF), as well as Grant Agreement No 101057849 (DataTool4Heartproject). The work on the *BioNNE-R* task was supported by the Russian Science Foundation [grant number 23-11-00358]. This work is partially supported by the HEREDITARY Project, as part of the European Union's Horizon Europe research and innovation programme under grant agreement No GA 101137074.

**Disclosure of Interests.** The authors have no competing interests to declare that are relevant to the content of this article.

# References

1. Appleton, J.: The gut-brain axis: influence of microbiota on mood and mental health. Integrat. Med. Clin. J. **17**(4), 28 (2018)
2. Carabotti, M., Scirocco, A., Maselli, M.A., Severi, C.: The gut-brain axis: interactions between enteric microbiota, central and enteric nervous systems. Ann. Gastroenterol. Quart. Publ. Hellenic Soc. Gastroenterol. **28**(2), 203 (2015)

---

7 http://participants-area.bioasq.org/datasets.
8 https://github.com/bioasq.

3. Cryan, J.F., O'Riordan, K.J., Sandhu, K., Peterson, V., Dinan, T.G.: The gut microbiome in neurological disorders. Lancet Neurol. **19**(2), 179–194 (2020)

4. Davydova, V., Loukachevitch, N., Tutubalina, E.: Overview of bionne task on biomedical nested named entity recognition at bioasq 2024. In: CLEF Working Notes (2024). https://ceur-ws.org/Vol-3740/paper-03.pdf

5. Dong, H., et al.: Automated clinical coding: what, why, and where we are? NPJ Digit. Med. **5**(1), 159 (2022). https://doi.org/10.1038/s41746-022-00705-7

6. Gasco, L., et al.: Overview of BioASQ 2021-MESINESP track. Evaluation of advance hierarchical classification techniques for scientific literature, patents and clinical trials. CEUR Workshop Proceedings (2021). https://ceur-ws.org/Vol-2936/paper-11.pdf

7. Ghaisas, S., Maher, J., Kanthasamy, A.: Gut microbiome in health and disease: Linking the microbiome-gut-brain axis and environmental factors in the pathogenesis of systemic and neurodegenerative diseases. Pharmacol. Therapeut. **158**, 52–62 (2016). https://doi.org/10.1016/j.pharmthera.2015.11.012

8. Krallinger, M., Krithara, A., Nentidis, A., Paliouras, G., Villegas, M.: BioASQ at CLEF2020: large-scale biomedical semantic indexing and question answering. In: European Conference on Information Retrieval, pp. 550–556. Springer (2020). https://doi.org/10.1007/978-3-030-45442-5_71

9. Krithara, A., Mork, J.G., Nentidis, A., Paliouras, G.: The road from manual to automatic semantic indexing of biomedical literature: a 10 years journey. Front. Res. Metrics Anal. **8** (2023). https://doi.org/10.3389/frma.2023.1250930

10. Krithara, A., Nentidis, A., Bougiatiotis, K., Paliouras, G.: BioASQ-QA: a manually curated corpus for biomedical question answering. Sci. Data **10**(1), 170 (2023). https://doi.org/10.1038/s41597-023-02068-4

11. Krithara, A., Nentidis, A., Paliouras, G., Krallinger, M., Miranda, A.: BioASQ at CLEF2021: large-scale biomedical semantic indexing and question answering. In: European Conference on Information Retrieval, pp. 624–630. Springer (2021). https://doi.org/10.1007/978-3-030-72240-1_73

12. Krithara, A., et al.: BioASQ Synergy: a dialogue between question-answering systems and biomedical experts for promoting COVID-19 research. J. Am. Med. Inf. Assoc., ocae232 (2024). https://doi.org/10.1093/jamia/ocae232

13. Lima-López, S., et al.: Overview of MedProcNER task on medical procedure detection and entity linking at BioASQ 2023. In: CEUR Workshop Proceedings (2023). https://ceur-ws.org/Vol-3497/paper-002.pdf

14. Lima-López, S., et al.: Overview of multicardioner task at bioasq 2024 on medical specialty and language adaptation of clinical ner systems for Spanish, English and Italian. In: Conference and Labs of the Evaluation Forum (2024). https://ceur-ws.org/Vol-3740/paper-02.pdf

15. Loukachevitch, N., et al.: Nerel-bio: a dataset of biomedical abstracts annotated with nested named entities. Bioinformatics **39**(4), btad161 (2023). https://doi.org/10.1093/bioinformatics/btad161

16. Malakasiotis, P., Pavlopoulos, I., Androutsopoulos, I., Nentidis, A.: Evaluation measures for task b. Tech. rep., Tech. rep. BioASQ (2018). http://participants-area.bioasq.org/Tasks/b/eval_meas_2018

17. Martinelli, M., et al.: Overview of gutbrainie@ clef 2025: gut-brain interplay information extraction. In: Faggioli, G., Ferro, N., Rosso, P., Spina, D. (eds.) CLEF 2025 Working Notes, vol. 4038, pp. 65–98 (2025). https://ceur-ws.org/Vol-4038/paper_5.pdf

18. Miranda-Escalada, A., et al.: Overview of DisTEMIST at BioASQ: automatic detection and normalization of diseases from clinical texts: results, methods, evaluation and multilingual resources. In: Working Notes of Conference and Labs of the Evaluation (CLEF) Forum. CEUR Workshop Proceedings (2022). https://ceur-ws.org/Vol-3180/paper-11.pdf

19. Nentidis, A., et al.: BioASQ at CLEF2025: the thirteenth edition of the large-scale biomedical semantic indexing and question answering challenge. In: Advances in Information Retrieval, pp. 407–415. Springer Nature Switzerland, Cham (2025). https://doi.org/10.1007/978-3-031-88720-8_61

20. Nentidis, A., et al.: Overview of BioASQ 2025: the thirteenth BioASQ challenge on large-scale biomedical semantic indexing and question answering. In: Carrillo-de Albornoz, J., García Seco de Herrera, A., Gonzalo, J., Plaza, L., Mothe, J., Piroi, F., Rosso, P., Spina, D., Faggioli, G., Ferro, N. (eds.) Experimental IR Meets Multilinguality, Multimodality, and Interaction, pp. 173–198. Springer Nature Switzerland, Cham (2026). https://doi.org/10.1007/978-3-031-88720-8_61

21. Nentidis, A., et al.: Overview of BioASQ 2023: The eleventh BioASQ challenge on large-scale biomedical semantic indexing and question answering. In: Arampatzis, A., Kanoulas, E., Tsikrika, T., Vrochidis, S., Giachanou, A., Li, D., Aliannejadi, M., Vlachos, M., Faggioli, G., Ferro, N. (eds.) Experimental IR Meets Multilinguality, Multimodality, and Interaction, pp. 227–250. Springer Nature Switzerland, Cham (2023). https://doi.org/10.1007/978-3-031-42448-9_19

22. Nentidis, A., et al.: Overview of BioASQ 2024: the twelfth BioASQ challenge on Large-Scale Biomedical Semantic Indexing and Question Answering. In: Goeuriot, L., Mulhem, P., Quénot, G., Schwab, D., Soulier, L., Maria Di Nunzio, G., Galuščéková, P., García Seco de Herrera, A., Faggioli, G., Ferro, N. (eds.) Experimental IR Meets Multilinguality, Multimodality, and Interaction. Proceedings of the Fifteenth International Conference of the CLEF Association (CLEF 2024) (2024). https://doi.org/10.1007/978-3-031-71908-0_1

23. Nentidis, A., Katsimpras, G., Krithara, A., Paliouras, G.: Overview of BioASQ tasks 11b and synergy11 in CLEF2023. Working Notes of CLEF (2023). https://ceur-ws.org/Vol-3497/paper-003.pdf

24. Nentidis, A., Katsimpras, G., Krithara, A., Paliouras, G.: Overview of BioASQ tasks 12b and synergy12 in CLEF2024. In: Faggioli, G., Ferro, N., Galuščéková, P., García Seco de Herrera, A. (eds.) Working Notes of CLEF (2024). https://ceur-ws.org/Vol-3740/paper-01.pdf

25. Nentidis, A., Katsimpras, G., Krithara, A., Paliouras, G.: Overview of BioASQ tasks 13b and synergy13 in CLEF2025. In: Faggioli, G., Ferro, N., Rosso, P., Spina, D. (eds.) CLEF 2025 Working Notes (2025). https://ceur-ws.org/Vol-4038/paper 1.pdf

26. Nentidis, A., et al.: Overview of BioASQ 2021: the ninth BioASQ challenge on large-scale biomedical semantic indexing and question answering. In: 12th International Conference of the CLEF Association. Lecture Notes in Computer Science, vol. 12880, pp. 239–263 (2021). https://doi.org/10.1007/978-3-030-85251-1_18

27. Nentidis, A., et al.: Overview of BioASQ 2022: the tenth BioASQ challenge on large-scale biomedical semantic indexing and question answering. In: Lecture Notes in Computer Science (including subseries Lecture Notes in Artificial Intelligence and Lecture Notes in Bioinformatics), vol. 13390 LNCS, pp. 337–361 (2022). https://doi.org/10.1007/978-3-031-13643-6_22

28. Nentidis, A., Katsimpras, G., Vandorou, E., Krithara, A., Paliouras, G.: Overview of BioASQ tasks 9a, 9b and synergy in CLEF2021. In: Proceedings of the 9th

BioASQ Workshop A challenge on large-scale biomedical semantic indexing and question answering. CEUR Workshop Proceedings (2021). http://ceur-ws.org/Vol-2936/paper-10.pdf

29. Nentidis, A., Katsimpras, G., Vandorou, E., Krithara, A., Paliouras, G.: Overview of BioASQ tasks 10a, 10b and synergy10 in CLEF2022. In: CEUR Workshop Proceedings, vol. 3180, pp. 171–178 (2022). https://ceur-ws.org/Vol-3180/paper-10.pdf

30. Nentidis, A., Krithara, A., Paliouras, G., Farre-Maduell, E., Lima-Lopez, S., Krallinger, M.: BioASQ at CLEF2023: The Eleventh Edition of the Large-Scale Biomedical Semantic Indexing and Question Answering Challenge. In: Advances in Information Retrieval: ECIR 2023, Dublin, Ireland, April 2–6, 2023, Proceedings, Part III, pp. 577–584. Springer (2023). https://doi.org/10.1007/978-3-031-28241-6_66

31. Nentidis, A., Krithara, A., Paliouras, G., Gasco, L., Krallinger, M.: BioASQ at CLEF2022: the tenth edition of the large-scale biomedical semantic indexing and question answering challenge. In: Advances in Information Retrieval: 44th European Conference on IR Research, ECIR 2022, Stavanger, Norway, April 10–14, 2022, Proceedings, Part II. Springer, Springer (2022). https://doi.org/10.1007/978-3-030-99739-7_53

32. Nentidis, A., et al.: BioASQ at CLEF2024: the twelfth edition of the large-scale biomedical semantic indexing and question answering challenge. In: Advances in Information Retrieval. Springer Nature Switzerland, Springer Nature Switzerland, Cham (2024). https://link.springer.com/chapter/10.1007/978-3-031-56069-9_67

33. Ngomo, A.C.N., Heino, N., Speck, R., Ermilov, T., Tsatsaronis, G.: Annotation tool. Project deliverable D3.3 (2013). http://www.bioasq.org/sites/default/files/PublicDocuments/2013-D3.3-AnnotationTool.pdf

34. Rodriguez-Penagos, C., et al.: Overview of MESINESP8, a Spanish medical semantic indexing task within BioASQ 2020 (2020). https://ceur-ws.org/Vol-2696/paper_269.pdf

35. Sakhovskiy, A., Loukachevitch, N., Tutubalina, E.: Overview of the BioASQ BioNNE-L task on biomedical nested entity linking in CLEF 2025. In: Faggioli, G., Ferro, N., Rosso, P., Spina, D. (eds.) CLEF 2025 Working Notes (2025). https://ceur-ws.org/Vol-4038/paper_3.pdf

36. Salton, G., Buckley, C.: Improving retrieval performance by relevance feedback. J. Am. Soc. Inf. Sci. **41**(4), 288–297 (1990). https://doi.org/10.1002/(SICI)1097-4571(199006)41:4⟨288::AID-ASI8⟩3.0.CO;2-H

37. Tsatsaronis, G., et al.: An overview of the BioASQ large-scale biomedical semantic indexing and question answering competition. BMC Bioinf. **16**, 138 (2015). https://doi.org/10.1186/s12859-015-0564-6

# The CLEF-2026 CheckThat! Lab: Advancing Multilingual Fact-Checking


Julia Maria Struß[1]($\boxtimes$) , Sebastian Schellhammer[2,3] , Stefan Dietze[2,3] ,
Venktesh V.[4] , Vinay Setty[5] , Tanmoy Chakraborty[6] , Preslav Nakov[7] ,
Avishek Anand[8] , Primakov Chungkham[9] , Salim Hafid[10] ,
Dhruv Sahnan[7] , and Konstantin Todorov[11]

[1] University of Applied Sciences Potsdam, Potsdam, Germany
`julia.struss@fh-potsdam.de`
[2] GESIS - Leibniz Institute for the Social Sciences, Cologne, Germany
[3] Heinrich-Heine-University, Düsseldorf, Germany
[4] Stockholm University, Stockholm, Sweden
[5] University of Stavanger, Stavanger, Norway
[6] Indian Institute of Technology Delhi, Delhi, India
[7] Mohamed Bin Zayed University of Artificial Intelligence, Abu Dhabi, UAE
[8] Delft University of Technology, Delft, The Netherlands
[9] Delft, The Netherlands
[10] Médialab, Sciences Po, Paris, France
[11] University of Montpellier, LIRMM, CNRS, Montpellier, France
`https://checkthat.gitlab.io`



**Abstract.** The `CheckThat!` lab aims to advance the development of innovative technologies combating disinformation and manipulation efforts in online communication across a multitude of languages and platforms. While in early editions the focus has been on core tasks of the verification pipeline (check-worthiness, evidence retrieval, and verification), in the past three editions, the lab added additional tasks linked to the verification process. In this year's edition, the verification pipeline is at the center again with the following tasks: Task 1 on source retrieval for scientific web claims (a follow-up of the 2025 edition), Task 2 on fact-checking numerical and temporal claims, which adds a reasoning component to the 2025 edition, and Task 3, which expands the verification pipeline with generation of full-fact-checking articles. These tasks represent challenging classification and retrieval problems as well as generation challenges at the document and span level, including multilingual settings.

**Keywords:** disinformation · fact-checking · claim source retrieval · generating fact-checking articles


---


Primakov Chungkham—Independent Researcher.

# 1   Introduction

The CheckThat! lab aims at fostering the development of technology to combat the spreading of mis- and disinformation across multiple platforms and languages in online discourses. Over the past eight iterations (e.g., see [1,4]), a multitude of challenges and tasks along the main steps of the verification pipeline used by *journalists* and *fact-checkers* (see Fig. 1) have been offered: Starting with a given document or a claim, the first step is to evaluate its check-worthiness, i.e., whether human effort should be allocated for checking its veracity, which is a task that experts have repeatedly emphasized as being of particular importance to them in the past. As claims that have been proven false before are repeatedly reformulated and circulated, retrieving closely related, previously fact-checked claims is the next step in the verification process. Retrieving additional evidence from diverse sources to verify the claim and finally decide whether the claim is factually true or not, with various degrees in between, follows. Ultimately, the verification process is completed by writing a detailed article that provides the evidence and the final decision, a step which has been added to the CheckThat! verification pipeline for the first time in the 2026 edition of the lab.

The three tasks proposed for the 2026 edition cover three of the main tasks in the pipeline, highlighted in Fig. 1, and span a total of five different languages (see in Table 1):

**Task 1 Source Retrieval for Scientific Web Claims,** is related to the second and third task of the verification pipeline and aims to detect different types of references or mentions to scientific work as well as identifying the original study a social media post refers to (cf. Sect. 2).

**Task 2 Fact-Checking Numerical and Temporal Claims** addresses the claim verification task of the pipeline, focusing on numerical claims (cf. Sect. 3).

**Task 3 Generating Full-Fact-Checking Articles:** introduces a new, final task into the CLEF CheckThat! lab pipeline, which attempts to automate the fact-checking article writing process (cf. Sect. 4).

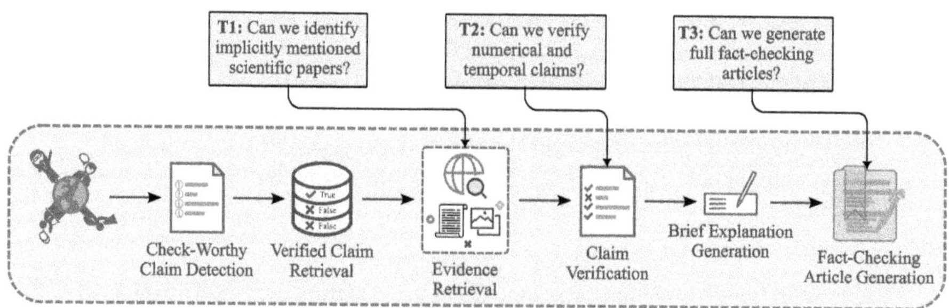


**Fig. 1.** Overview of the CheckThat! verification pipeline, which features the core fact-checking tasks along with the tasks we address in the 2026 edition of the lab.

**Table 1.** Languages targeted in the three tasks of the `CheckThat!` 2026 edition.

| Task | Arabic | English | German | French | Spanish |
|------|--------|---------|--------|--------|---------|
| Task 1 | | ■ | ■ | ■ | |
| Task 2 | ■ | ■ | | | ■ |
| Task 3 | | ■ | | | |

## 2    Task 1: Source Retrieval for Scientific Web Claims

***Motivation.*** Scientific web discourse, i.e., discourse about scientific claims or resources on the social web, has increased substantially throughout the past years and has been studied across a wide range of disciplines [5,12]. However, the scientific web discourse is usually informal, including posts such as *"covid vaccines just don't work on children"*. The scientific studies at the center of debates from which claims originate are usually not cited explicitly but only mentioned informally, such as *"Stanford study shows that vaccines don't work"*. This poses challenges both from a computational perspective when mining social media or computing altmetrics, but also from a societal perspective, leading to poorly informed online debates [32]. For fact-checking, identifying the source of a claim is important, especially for false claims where counter-evidence may not exist, because human fact-checkers use the source to verify a claim by assessing the quality of the source publication and checking whether the claim accurately reflects its findings [13]. Based on this motivation, we propose the task of Source Retrieval for Scientific Web Claims:

***Task Definition.*** *Given a social media post that contains a scientific claim and an implicit reference to a scientific paper (mentions it without a URL), retrieve the mentioned paper from a pool of candidate papers. (Languages: English, German, and French.)*

***Data.*** Ground-truth datasets for training and evaluation will be provided in three languages: English, German, and French. Each dataset consists of pairs of social media posts from X and the scientific studies they implicitly reference. For English, we reuse the existing 15,699 data pairs from [17] for training, while new data will be annotated for the evaluation set. For German and French, new data will be annotated for both training and evaluation sets, with approximately 1,500 pairs per language. For each language, a query dataset will be provided, containing social media posts, along with a single collection set that includes information about the scientific studies, which will be used across all three languages.

***Evaluation.*** For each language, the participating systems will be evaluated in terms of Mean Reciprocal Rank at 5 (*MRR@5*), which is an established measure for evaluating known-item search tasks. It focuses on ranking the correct study within the first five positions, as users are only rarely examine more results.

## 3   Task 2: Fact-Checking Numerical and Temporal Claims

*Motivation.* In recent years, tremendous progress has been made in automated fact-checking approaches [16,37], along with the development of large-scale benchmarks [3,36], for tackling misinformation at scale. Automating fact-checking is inherently knowledge-intensive, as it requires reasoning over heterogeneous evidence sources to arrive at a reliable verdict. This challenge is further amplified for claims involving numerical information [41], which require numerical contextualization and precise quantitative reasoning. Moreover, numerical claims are prone to the *Numeric-Truth Effect* [33], whereby the presence of numbers induces a false sense of credibility, thereby accelerating the spread of misinformation. Although Large Language Models (LLMs) have achieved remarkable advances on knowledge-intensive tasks, recent studies demonstrate that verifying numerical claims remains challenging for LLMs than verifying non-numerical ones [2,41]. Motivated by recent advances in test-time reasoning [7], we propose a test-time scaling framework with the goal of training more effective verification models to enhance the performance of LLMs on fact-checking numerical claims.

*Task Definition. This task performs test-time scaling for fact-verification. Given a claim, relevant evidences and reasoning traces with corresponding verdicts, the task is to rank the reasoning traces based on their utility in leading to the correct verdict and also output the final verdict from the top-ranked reasoning traces. (Languages: English, Spanish and Arabic.)*

The task focuses on verifying naturally occurring claims that contain quantitative quantities and/or temporal expressions by improving the reasoning capabilities of LLMs through test-time scaling. Unlike previous editions, which primarily focused only on fact-checking accuracy, this year's task explicitly incorporates rationale generation into the evaluation. This is achieved in the form of re-ranking reasoning traces from the LLM, assessing both the correctness of the predicted veracity and the quality of the underlying reasoning traces.

While the claims are drawn from the previous iteration of the task, the overall setup differs substantially. Specifically, we introduce a test-time scaling framework designed to enhance LLM reasoning for claim verification. Given a claim and its associated evidence, multiple reasoning traces are generated using an LLM with varying temperature values to induce diversity. Redundant traces are subsequently removed through a de-duplication step. Based on this data, participants are required to train a verifier model that ranks the reasoning traces for each test claim and derives a final verdict from the top-ranked traces. To avoid leakage and ensure rigorous evaluation, we will release new test sets.

*Data.* We collect the dataset from various fact-checking websites, completed with detailed metadata and an evidence corpus sourced from the web. We use the English dataset released in [41], as well as the 3,260 Arabic and 2,808 Spanish claims from CLEF 2025 `CheckThat!` [1] with corresponding evidence. Table 2 summarizes the statistics of the dataset.

Each claim in the training and the validation datasets comprises 20 reasoning traces generated by **gpt-4o-mini** that can be used by participants to train a verification model, for selecting the best reasoning traces that lead to the

**Table 2.** Dataset statistics for task 2.

| Language | # of claims |
| --- | --- |
| English | 8,000 |
| Spanish | 2,808 |
| Arabic | 3,260 |

correct verdict. Apart from top-10 evidences, the entire evidence corpus will also be provided to the participants so they can run their own retrieve and re-rank pipelines for providing additional context to the verification model. Each claim is annotated with relevant reasoning traces that lead to the correct verdict (ground truth). The traces re-ranked by the verifier can be evaluated based on their ability to identify such relevant traces.

***Evaluation.*** We use Recall@k and MRR@k to measure the quality of the reasoning traces ranked by the verifier model, with $k = 5$. For claim verification, we use macro-averaged F1 and classwise F1 scores. Participants will be judged based on high performance on both macro F1 and Recall@$k$. The final score is obtained by averaging ranking across these measures (macro F1 and Recall@k, with $k = 5$).

## 4 Task 3: Generating Full-Fact-Checking Articles

***Motivation.*** Previous work on automated fact-checking has focused on five main tasks: ($i$) check-worthy claim detection, ($ii$) previously verified claim retrieval, ($iii$) evidence retrieval, ($iv$) claim verification, and ($v$) justification generation [16,26,42]. However, professional fact-checkers also undertake the critical task of *publishing detailed fact-checking articles*, which guide readers toward a clear understanding of the claim by presenting factual arguments and explaining how they lead to the final verdict [15]. Writing fact-checking articles is time-consuming, as it involves synthesizing information from various sources, penning it down in an easy to understand draft, and refining it multiple times to ensure quality and correctness. Recently, we proposed the generation of fact-checking articles automatically using large language models [34]. While LLMs can generate fluent, long-form text [43–45], our evaluations show that LLM-generated fact-checking articles considerably lag behind expert-written articles, uncovering several issues, but especially their inability to construct coherent, evidence-based arguments that properly explain the claim's veracity.

***Task Definition.*** *Given a claim, its veracity, and a set of evidence documents consulted for fact-checking the claim, generate a full fact-checking article with inline citations. (Language: English.)*

Note that, we do not address automatic evidence retrieval or claim verification here: the claim, its veracity, and the evidence set to use are all explicitly provided.

***Data.*** We reuse the WatClaimCheck dataset [21] for training and validation, and the union of the already publicly available ExClaim [46] dataset and currently private AmbiguousSnopes [34] dataset for testing. Overall, the training set comprises 26k data examples, and the validation set comprises 3.3k data examples. The test set contains 1.2k data examples in total, comprising 987 from ExClaim and 220 from AmbiguousSnopes. Each example corresponds to a claim and comprises the claim's veracity label, a set of evidence documents as listed by the fact-checking expert on the source website, and the expert-written fact-checking article, which we treat as the ground truth.

***Evaluation.*** As a primary evaluation measure, we use the mean of the following evaluation measures to assess the quality of the generated fact-checking article: (*i*) *entailment score*, which is a reference-based metric that measures if the generated text is entailed by the reference [34], (*ii*) *citation correctness*, which verifies if a text attributed to a citation can be entailed by the corresponding evidence, and (*iii*) *citation completeness*, which computes the proportion of input evidence that is correctly cited in the generated text. As a secondary measure, we also assess writing quality by computing Elo ratings for the participants at the end of the testing phase, through a setup similar to Chatbot Arena [6], but using LLM-as-a-judge [22,47] in our case. We choose to use reference-free evaluation measures to assess the utility of the participating systems for professional fact-checkers, rather than how similar the generated articles are to the expert-written articles. This design choice also aims to prevent cheating on the publicly-available subset of our test dataset.

## 5   Related Work

The tasks offered in the different editions of the `CheckThat!` lab are closely related to several tasks at other evaluation initiatives such as SemEval, e. g. determining rumor veracity [9,14], stance detection [25], fact-checking in community question-answering forums [24], propaganda detection in various contexts such as English news articles [8], English memes [10,11], and Arabic news paragraphs, social media posts, and memes [19,20], as well as multi- and cross-lingual fact-checked claim retrieval [28], emphasizing the focus on multi-linguality, also including low-resourced languages. The tasks offered in the `CheckThat!` lab are further related to the FEVER tasks [35,40] on fact extraction and verification, the Fake News Challenge [18,23,31], and the detection of online hostile posts [27]. Furthermore, it aligns with the FakeNews task at MediaEval [29,30]. Other recent shared tasks include claim detection and span identification in social media posts [38] as well as multi-modal fake news detection [39], further emphasizing the growing focus on analyzing and verifying information across diverse modalities and platforms.

## 6   Conclusion and Future Work

We presented the tasks of the 2026 edition of the `CheckThat!` lab, featuring complementary tasks to assist journalists and fact-checkers along the fact-checking pipeline: from retrieving informally mentioned sources of scientific web claims to verifying numerical and temporal claims and ultimately generating full-fact-checking articles - a task that has been newly added to the **CheckThat!** verification pipeline. In line with the CLEF mission, two of the three tasks are multilingual by offering tasks in five languages, namely Arabic, English, German, French, and Spanish.

In future work, we plan to expand the multilingual coverage, particularly for low-resource languages. We also plan to explore stronger cross-document and numerical reasoning, improved handling of implicit evidence, and closer alignment of task design and evaluation with real-world fact-checking workflows to maximize practical impact.

**Acknowledgments.** The work of Stefan Dietze, Konstantin Todorov, Salim Hafid, and Sebastian Schellhammer is partially funded under the AI4Sci grant, co-funded by MESRI (France, grant UM-211745), BMBF (Germany, grant 01IS21086), and the French National Research Agency (ANR). The work of Dhruv Sahnan, Tanmoy Chakraborty, and Preslav Nakov is supported by the Multi-Institutional Faculty Interdisciplinary Research Project (MFIRP) between IIT Delhi and MBZUAI. The responsibility for the contents of this publication lies with the authors.

**Disclosure of Interests.** The authors have no competing interests to declare that are relevant to the content of this article.

# References


1. Alam, F., et al.: Overview of the CLEF-2025 CheckThat! lab: subjectivity, fact-checking, claim normalization, and retrieval. In: Carrillo-de Albornoz, J., Gonzalo, J., Plaza, L., García Seco de Herrera, A., Mothe, J., Piroi, F., Rosso, P., Spina, D., Faggioli, G., Ferro, N. (eds.) Experimental IR Meets Multilinguality, Multimodality, and Interaction. Proceedings of the Sixteenth International Conference of the CLEF Association (CLEF 2025) (2025)
2. Aly, R., et al.: FEVEROUS: fact extraction and verification over unstructured and structured information. In: Vanschoren, J., Yeung, S. (eds.) Proceedings of the Neural Information Processing Systems Track on Datasets and Benchmarks 1, NeurIPS Datasets and Benchmarks 2021, December 2021, virtual (2021)
3. Augenstein, I., et al.: MultiFC: a real-world multi-domain dataset for evidence-based fact checking of claims. In: Proceedings of the 2019 Conference on Empirical Methods in Natural Language Processing and the 9th International Joint Conference on Natural Language Processing (EMNLP-IJCNLP), pp. 4685–4697. Association for Computational Linguistics, Hong Kong, China (2019)
4. Barrón-Cedeño, A., et al.: Overview of the CLEF-2024 CheckThat! Lab: Checkworthiness, subjectivity, persuasion, roles, authorities and adversarial robustness. In: Goeuriot, L., Mulhem, P., Quénot, G., Schwab, D., Soulier, L., Di Nunzio, G.M., Galuščáková, P., García Seco de Herrera, A., Faggioli, G., Ferro, N. (eds.) Experimental IR Meets Multilinguality, Multimodality, and Interaction. Proceedings of the Fifteenth International Conference of the CLEF Association (CLEF 2024) (2024)

5. Brüggemann, M., Lörcher, I., Walter, S.: Post-normal science communication: exploring the blurring boundaries of science and journalism. J. Sci. Commun. **19**(3), A02 (2020)

6. Chiang, W.L., et al.: Chatbot arena: an open platform for evaluating LLMs by human preference. In: Proceedings of the 41st International Conference on Machine Learning. ICML 2024, JMLR.org (2024)

7. Chungkham, P., V, V., Setty, V., Anand, A.: Think right, not more: test-time scaling for numerical claim verification. In: Findings of the Association for Computational Linguistics: EMNLP 2025, pp. 24345–24363. Association for Computational Linguistics, Suzhou, China (2025)

8. Da San Martino, G., Barrón-Cedeño, A., Wachsmuth, H., Petrov, R., Nakov, P.: SemEval-2020 task 11: detection of propaganda techniques in news articles. In: Proceedings of the Fourteenth Workshop on Semantic Evaluation, pp. 1377–1414. International Committee for Computational Linguistics, Barcelona (online) (2020)

9. Derczynski, L., Bontcheva, K., Liakata, M., Procter, R., Wong Sak Hoi, G., Zubiaga, A.: SemEval-2017 task 8: RumourEval: determining rumour veracity and support for rumours. In: Proceedings of the 11th International Workshop on Semantic Evaluation, pp. 69–76. SemEval 2017 (2017)

10. Dimitrov, D., et al.: SemEval-2024 task 4: multilingual detection of persuasion techniques in memes. In: Ojha, A.K., Doğruöz, A.S., Tayyar Madabushi, H., Da San Martino, G., Rosenthal, S., Rosá, A. (eds.) Proceedings of the 18th International Workshop on Semantic Evaluation (SemEval-2024), pp. 2009–2026. Association for Computational Linguistics, Mexico City, Mexico (2024)

11. Dimitrov, D., et al.: SemEval-2021 task 6: detection of persuasion techniques in texts and images. In: Proceedings of the International Workshop on Semantic Evaluation, pp. 70–98. SemEval 2021 (2021)

12. Dunwoody, S.: Science journalism: prospects in the digital age. In: Routledge Handbook of Public Communication of Science and Technology, pp. 14–32. Routledge (2021)

13. Glockner, M., Hou, Y., Gurevych, I.: Missing counter-evidence renders NLP fact-checking unrealistic for misinformation. In: Proceedings of the 2022 Conference on Empirical Methods in Natural Language Processing, pp. 5916–5936 (2022)

14. Gorrell, G., et al.: SemEval-2019 task 7: RumourEval, determining rumour veracity and support for rumours. In: Proceedings of the 13th International Workshop on Semantic Evaluation, pp. 845–854. SemEval 2019 (2019)

15. Graves, L.: Anatomy of a fact check: objective practice and the contested epistemology of fact checking. Commun. Cult. Critique **10**(3), 518–537 (2017)

16. Guo, Z., Schlichtkrull, M., Vlachos, A.: A survey on automated fact-checking. Trans. Assoc. Comput. Linguist. **10**, 178–206 (2022)

17. Hafid, S., et al.: Overview of the CLEF-2025 CheckThat! lab task 4 on scientific web discourse. In: Faggioli, G., Ferro, N., Rosso, P., Spina, D. (eds.) Working Notes of CLEF 2025 - Conference and Labs of the Evaluation Forum. CLEF 2025, Madrid, Spain (2025)

18. Hanselowski, A., et al.: A retrospective analysis of the fake news challenge stance-detection task. In: Proceedings of the 27th International Conference on Computational Linguistics, pp. 1859–1874. COLING 2018 (2018)

19. Hasanain, M., et al.: ArAIEval shared task: persuasion techniques and disinformation detection in Arabic text. In: Sawaf, H., El-Beltagy, S., Zaghouani, W., Magdy, W., Abdelali, A., Tomeh, N., Abu Farha, I., Habash, N., Khalifa, S., Keleg, A., Haddad, H., Zitouni, I., Mrini, K., Almatham, R. (eds.) Proceedings of ArabicNLP 2023, pp. 483–493. Association for Computational Linguistics, Singapore (Hybrid) (2023)
20. Hasanain, M., et al.: ArAIEval shared task: propagandistic techniques detection in unimodal and multimodal Arabic content. In: Proceedings of The Second Arabic Natural Language Processing Conference, pp. 456–466 (2024)
21. Khan, K., Wang, R., Poupart, P.: WatClaimCheck: a new dataset for claim entailment and inference. In: Muresan, S., Nakov, P., Villavicencio, A. (eds.) Proceedings of the 60th Annual Meeting of the Association for Computational Linguistics (Volume 1: Long Papers), pp. 1293–1304. Association for Computational Linguistics, Dublin, Ireland (2022)
22. Kim, S., et al.: Prometheus 2: an open source language model specialized in evaluating other language models. In: Al-Onaizan, Y., Bansal, M., Chen, Y.N. (eds.) Proceedings of the 2024 Conference on Empirical Methods in Natural Language Processing, pp. 4334–4353. Association for Computational Linguistics, Miami, Florida, USA (2024)
23. Malliga, S., et al.: Overview of the shared task on fake news detection from social media text. In: Proceedings of the Third Workshop on Speech and Language Technologies for Dravidian Languages, pp. 59–63 (2023)
24. Mihaylova, T., Karadzhov, G., Atanasova, P., Baly, R., Mohtarami, M., Nakov, P.: SemEval-2019 task 8: fact checking in community question answering forums. In: Proceedings of the 13th International Workshop on Semantic Evaluation, pp. 860–869. SemEval 2019 (2019)
25. Mohammad, S., Kiritchenko, S., Sobhani, P., Zhu, X., Cherry, C.: SemEval-2016 task 6: Detecting stance in tweets. In: Proceedings of the 10th International Workshop on Semantic Evaluation, pp. 31–41. SemEval 2016 (2016)
26. Nakov, P., et al.: Automated fact-checking for assisting human fact-checkers. In: Zhou, Z.H. (ed.) Proceedings of the Thirtieth International Joint Conference on Artificial Intelligence, IJCAI-21, pp. 4551–4558. International Joint Conferences on Artificial Intelligence Organization (2021), survey Track
27. Chakraborty, T., Shu, K., Bernard, H.R., Liu, H., Akhtar, M.S. (eds.): CONSTRAINT 2021. CCIS, vol. 1402. Springer, Cham (2021). https://doi.org/10.1007/978-3-030-73696-5
28. Peng, Q., et al.: SemEval-2025 task 7: multilingual and crosslingual fact-checked claim retrieval. In: Rosenthal, S., Rosá, A., Ghosh, D., Zampieri, M. (eds.) Proceedings of the 19th International Workshop on Semantic Evaluation (SemEval-2025), pp. 2498–2511. Association for Computational Linguistics, Vienna, Austria (2025)
29. Pogorelov, K., Schroeder, D.T., Brenner, S., Maulana, A., Langguth, J.: Combining tweets and connections graph for FakeNews detection at MediaEval 2022. In: Proceedings of the MediaEval 2022 Workshop. MediaEval 2022 (2022)
30. Pogorelov, K., et al.: FakeNews: corona virus and 5G conspiracy task at MediaEval 2020. In: Proceedings of the MediaEval 2020 Workshop. MediaEval 2020 (2020)
31. Pomerleau, D., Rao, D.: The fake news challenge: exploring how artificial intelligence technologies could be leveraged to combat fake news (2017). http://www.fakenewschallenge

32. Rocha, Y.M., de Moura, G.A., Desidério, G.A., de Oliveira, C.H., Lourenço, F.D., de Figueiredo Nicolete, L.D.: The impact of fake news on social media and its influence on health during the COVID-19 pandemic: a systematic review. J. Public Health, 1–10 (2021)
33. Sagara, N.: Consumer understanding and use of numeric information in product claims. University of Oregon (2009)
34. Sahnan, D., et al.: Can LLMs automate fact-checking article writing? Transactions of the Association for Computational Linguistics (2026)
35. Schlichtkrull, M., et al.: The automated verification of textual claims (AVeriTeC) shared task. In: Schlichtkrull, M., Chen, Y., Whitehouse, C., Deng, Z., Akhtar, M., Aly, R., Guo, Z., Christodoulopoulos, C., Cocarascu, O., Mittal, A., Thorne, J., Vlachos, A. (eds.) Proceedings of the Seventh Fact Extraction and VERification Workshop (FEVER), pp. 1–26. Association for Computational Linguistics, Miami, Florida, USA (2024)
36. Schlichtkrull, M., Guo, Z., Vlachos, A.: AVeriTeC: a dataset for real-world claim verification with evidence from the web. In: Proceedings of the 37th International Conference on Neural Information Processing Systems. NIPS 2023, Curran Associates Inc., Red Hook, NY, USA (2023)
37. Setty, V.: FactCheck editor: multilingual text editor with end-to-end fact-checking. In: Proceedings of the 47th International ACM SIGIR Conference on Research and Development in Information Retrieval, pp. 2744–2748 (2024)
38. Sundriyal, M., Akhtar, M.S., Chakraborty, T.: Overview of the CLAIMSCAN-2023: uncovering truth in social media through claim detection and identification of claim spans. In: Proceedings of the 15th Annual Meeting of the Forum for Information Retrieval Evaluation, pp. 7–9 (2023)
39. Suryavardan, S., et al.: Findings of factify 2: multimodal fake news detection. In: Proceedings of De-Factify 2: 2nd Workshop on Multimodal Fact Checking and Hate Speech Detection, co-located with AAAI 2023. Washington, DC, USA (2023)
40. Thorne, J., Vlachos, A., Christodoulopoulos, C., Mittal, A.: FEVER: a large-scale dataset for fact extraction and VERification. In: Proceedings of the Conference of the North American Chapter of the Association for Computational Linguistics: Human Language Technologies, pp. 809–819 (2018)
41. Venktesh, V., Anand, A., Anand, A., Setty, V.: QuanTemp: a real-world open-domain benchmark for fact-checking numerical claims. In: 47th International ACM SIGIR Conference on Research and Development in Information Retrieval, SIGIR 2024, pp. 650–660. Association for Computing Machinery (ACM) (2024)
42. Vlachos, A., Riedel, S.: Fact Checking: task definition and dataset construction. In: Danescu-Niculescu-Mizil, C., Eisenstein, J., McKeown, K., Smith, N.A. (eds.) Proceedings of the ACL 2014 Workshop on Language Technologies and Computational Social Science, pp. 18–22. Association for Computational Linguistics, Baltimore, MD, USA (2014)
43. Wang, Q., et al.: Generating long-form story using dynamic hierarchical outlining with memory-enhancement. In: Chiruzzo, L., Ritter, A., Wang, L. (eds.) Proceedings of the 2025 Conference of the Nations of the Americas Chapter of the Association for Computational Linguistics: Human Language Technologies (Volume 1: Long Papers), pp. 1352–1391. Association for Computational Linguistics, Albuquerque, New Mexico (2025)
44. Xie, Z., Cohn, T., Lau, J.H.: The next chapter: a study of large language models in storytelling. In: Keet, C.M., Lee, H.Y., Zarrieß, S. (eds.) Proceedings of the 16th International Natural Language Generation Conference, pp. 323–351. Association for Computational Linguistics, Prague, Czechia (2023)

45. Yang, K., Klein, D., Peng, N., Tian, Y.: DOC: improving long story coherence with detailed outline control. In: Rogers, A., Boyd-Graber, J., Okazaki, N. (eds.) Proceedings of the 61st Annual Meeting of the Association for Computational Linguistics (Volume 1: Long Papers), pp. 3378–3465. Association for Computational Linguistics, Toronto, Canada (2023)
46. Zeng, F., Gao, W.: JustiLM: few-shot justification generation for explainable fact-checking of real-world claims. Trans. Assoc. Comput. Linguist. **12**, 334–354 (2024)
47. Zheng, L., et al.: Judging LLM-as-a-judge with MT-Bench and Chatbot arena. In: Oh, A., Naumann, T., Globerson, A., Saenko, K., Hardt, M., Levine, S. (eds.) Advances in Neural Information Processing Systems 36: Annual Conference on Neural Information Processing Systems 2023, NeurIPS 2023, New Orleans, LA, USA, December 10-16, 2023 (2023)

# ImageCLEF 2026: Multimodal Challenges in Medicine, Science, Agritech, and Security


Bogdan Ionescu[1], Henning Müller[2], Dan-Cristian Stanciu[1(✉)],
Ahmedkhan Radzhabov[3], Alba García Seco de Herrera[4],
Alexandra-Georgiana Andrei[1], Alexandra Băicoianu[5], Ana Neacşu[1],
Andrea Storås[6], Asma Ben Abacha[7], Benjamin Bracke[8], Lea Reinartz[8],
Benjamin Lecouteux[9], Christoph M. Friedrich[8], Cynthia Sabrina Schmidt[10],
Corneliu-Nicolae Florea[5,6], Diandra Fabre[9], Didier Schwab[9],
Dimitar Dimitrov[11], Emmanuelle Esperança-Rodier[9], Gabriel Constantin[1],
Hendrik Damm[8], Henning Schäfer[10], Ivan Koychev[11], Josiane Mothe[13],
Liviu-Daniel Ştefan[1], Maja J. Hjuler[9], Mehmet Kurt[14], Meliha Yetisgen[14],
Michael A. Riegler[6], Mihai Dogariu[1], Mihai Ivanovici[5], Ming Shan Hee[12],
Mohammad El Sakka[13], Momina Ahsan[12], Obioma Pelka[10], Pål Halvorsen[6],
Preslav Nakov[12], Raphael Brüngel[8], Sarfraz Ahmad[12], Steven A. Hicks[6],
Sushant Gautam[6], Tabea M. G. Pakull[10], Bahadır Eryılmaz[10],
Vajira Thambawita[6], Vassili Kovalev[15,16], Wen-Wai Yim[7], Yuri Prokopchuk[3],
and Zhuohan Xie[12]

[1] National University of Science and Technology Politehnica Bucharest,
Bucharest, Romania
dan.stanciu1203@upb.ro
[2] University of Applied Sciences Western Switzerland (HE-SO), Sierre, Switzerland
[3] Belarus National Academy of Sciences, Minsk, Belarus
[4] Universidad Nacional de Educación a Distancia (UNED), Madrid, Spain
[5] Transilvania University, Brasov, Romania
[6] SimulaMet, Oslo, Norway
[7] Microsoft, Redmond, USA
[8] University of Applied Sciences and Arts Dortmund, Dortmund, Germany
[9] University Grenoble Alpes, CNRS, Grenoble INP*, Grenoble, France
[10] University Hospital Essen, Essen, Germany
[11] Sofia University "St. Kliment Ohridski", Sofia, Bulgaria
[12] Mohamed bin Zayed University of Artificial Intelligence, Abu Dhabi,
United Arab Emirates
[13] Université de Toulouse, Toulouse, France
[14] University of Washington, Seattle, USA
[15] Belarus State University, Minsk, Belarus
[16] Hospital Clinic of Barcelona, Barcelona, Spain



**Abstract.** Since its inception in 2003, the various ImageCLEF challenges have provided large and complex datasets targeting a wide array


Apart from the general organisers, the authors are listed in alphabetical order.

of subjects in medicine, argumentation, reasoning, content recommendation, data generation, and question answering. In its 24th edition at CLEF, ImageCLEF will have five main tasks: (*i*) a *Medical* task, which aims to promote the synergy between four medical challenges: *Caption*, involving concept detection and caption prediction in radiology images, Synthetic Medical Image Generation in the *GANs* task, *Visual Question Answering* for improving the diagnosis and classification of real medical gastrointestinal images, and multimodal dermatology response generation and a new *MEDIQA-CORE* challenge focusing on predicting or correcting tumor type labels and identifying and summarizing major and minor differences between pairs of radiology reports; (*ii*) the *ToPicto* task, involving text to pictogram translation and prediction, (*iii*) the *Multimodal Reasoning* task on visual, multi-language, interdisciplinary question answering, and a task using multi-spectral remote sensing images: (*iv*) *AI4Agriculture*, involving predicting agricultural potential before planing and crop type identification, and (*v*) the *Deepfake* detection and generation task. In its last edition, 56 teams finished our challenges, continuing to show the impact in the community.

**Keywords:** Medical AI · Image Captioning · GANs · Visual Question Answering · Pictogram Translation · Deepfake · Agricultural AI

# 1 Introduction

The ImageCLEF evaluation campaign, in its 24th edition, continues to provide a space for research and benchmark activities in the scientific community, providing challenges in various fields, such as medicine, argumentation, reasoning, content recommendation, data generation, and question answering. The 24th edition will take place in Jena, Germany, September 21-24, 2026.[1] Over the years, both ImageCLEF and the CLEF campaign have demonstrated significant scholarly impact [29,30], with the term *ImageCLEF* being mentioned in 7,980 papers since 2003, according to Google Scholar. Below, we present our five proposed tasks for this year's edition, also summarized in Fig. 1.

# 2 ImageCLEFmedical

The ImageCLEFmedical task is currently in its 22nd edition [20]. The 2026 edition introduces four medical tasks, listed below:

The *Caption*[2] task addresses the interpretation of clinical and diagnostic insights from radiology images. In this 10th edition [7,9,10,21–23,25–27], we have three subtasks: *concept detection*, *caption prediction*, and *explainability*. The *concept detection* subtask focuses on developing models capable of predicting Unified Medical Language System (UMLS®) Concept Unique Identifiers (CUIs)

---

[1] https://clef2026.clef-initiative.eu/.
[2] https://www.imageclef.org/2026/medical/caption.

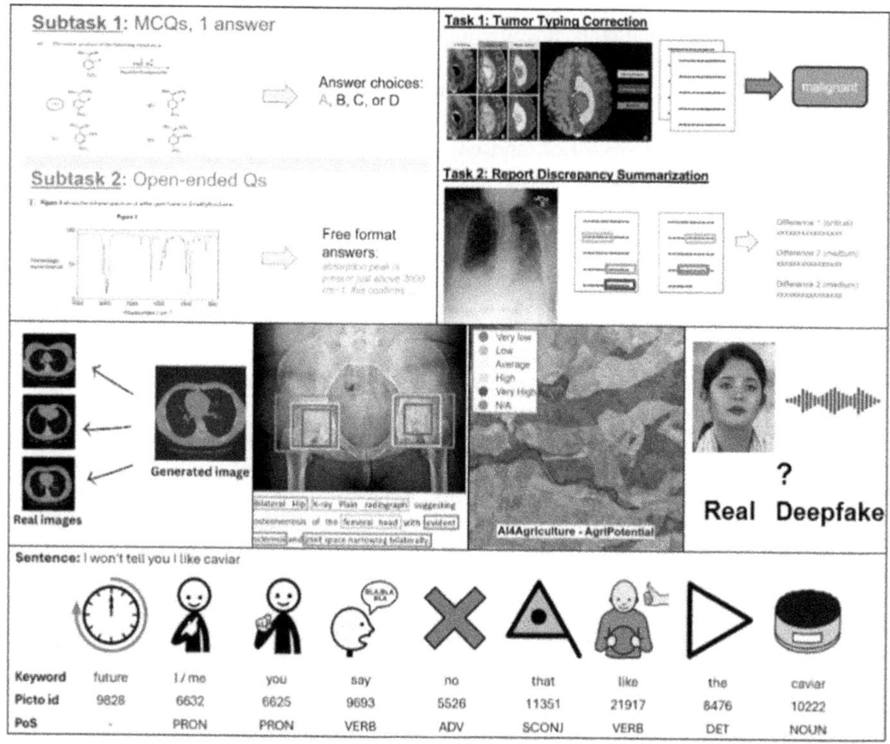

**Fig. 1.** Sample images from the tasks (left to right, top to bottom): MultimodalReasoning, MEDIQA-CORE, GANs, Caption, AI4Agriculture, Deepfake, and ToPicto.

directly from medical images. The evaluation is based on the F1-Score [12]. This year, the updated and extended *ROCOv2* [28] dataset is used, incorporating additional figures from PubMed Central publications released after October 2024 and further refined through new annotations and validation. The *caption prediction* subtask evaluates systems on automatically generating descriptive and clinically meaningful captions for radiology images. Domain-specific language models such as BioBERT [17] continue to be used for BERTScore evaluation, complemented by alternatives including ClinicalBLEURT and MedBERTScore [5].

Readability measures such as LENS [19] and the ColemanâĂŞLiau Index [6] (CLI) are used to assess linguistic quality, coherence, and clarity of the generated captions. The *explainability* subtask extends across both concept detection and caption prediction, requiring participants to provide interpretable visual or textual explanations for model predictions. These may include techniques such as heatmaps, attention maps, or Shapley-based attributions. The submitted explanations will be manually reviewed in order to evaluate their interpretability and clinical relevance.

*ImageCLEFmedical-GANs.*[3] The 4th edition of the GANs task will continue to evaluate both the quality and the privacy of synthetic medical images generated by various generative models, including Generative Adversarial Networks (GANs). Building upon the results of the previous editions [1–3], this iteration focuses on the critical challenge of ensuring patient privacy and data confidentiality in medical imaging while maintaining the fidelity, realism, and clinical utility of the generated data.

In addition to the analytical components featured in previous editions where participants were asked to assess data, this year's task introduces a generation component, requiring participants to produce synthetic medical images themselves. This extension is designed to encourage a deeper exploration of privacy risks and mitigation strategies associated with generative models. Specifically, participants will investigate whether identifiable information, such as unique anatomical structures, latent image fingerprints, or subtle patterns from real patient scans, can be unintentionally reproduced by generative systems. The provided dataset will include both real and synthetic axial CT slices of tuberculosis patients captured at various stages of treatment.

*ImageCLEFmedical-MEDVQA.*[4] The 4th MEDVQA-GI challenge advances Visual Question Answering (VQA) for gastrointestinal (GI) imaging with a continued emphasis on explainability, clinical safety, and multimodal reasoning. Building on previous editions [13–15], the 2026 challenge introduces enhanced evaluation criteria that integrate behavioral safety and retrieval-augmented reasoning into the existing subtasks. The first subtask focuses on developing models that accurately answer clinically relevant questions from GI endoscopy images using the expanded Kvasir-VQA-x1 dataset [11] with more than 150,000 questionâĂŞanswer pairs. The second subtask extends the evaluation of explainability by requiring coherent multimodal justifications that combine textual and visual evidence aligned with medical reasoning while ensuring the responses remain safe, factual, and consistent across clinical contexts. A dedicated safety layer evaluates whether models exhibit undesirable behaviors such as overconfidence, misleading explanations, or non-compliance with medical best practices during these tasks. To support retrieval-augmented generation methods, the challenge also provides a curated database of endoscopy resources containing verified clinical references. Evaluation integrates quantitative metrics for language accuracy with expert-based assessments of interpretability, safety, and clinical reliability.

*ImageCLEFmedical-MEDIQA-CORE.*[5] In this edition, MEDIQA explores Multimodal Reasoning & Reconciliation in Radiology, a shared task designed to advance clinical AI systems capable of complex medical understanding and decision support. This competition comprises two complementary tasks that evaluate model performance on diagnosis accuracy and clinical report alignment using multimodal data. In the first task, we study tumor type prediction by jointly

---

reasoning over radiology and pathology images, along with their corresponding reports. We assess models' ability to integrate multimodal clinical evidence and to improve diagnostic accuracy. In the second task, we focus on identifying and summarizing major and minor differences between pairs of radiology reports and associated images that describe the same patient, but offer conflicting interpretations. It emphasizes clinical language and image understanding, fine-grained discrepancy detection, and reconciliation of divergent expert assessments. The competition will utilize real, de-identified clinical images and reports collected from multiple U.S. hospitals.

## 3   ImageCLEFtoPicto

In its third edition, ImageCLEFtoPicto [18] will continue to advance research on the automatic conversion of text into meaningful sequences of pictograms designed to support Alternative and Augmentative Communication (AAC).

For the 2026 edition, the challenge introduces two new tasks: The first task, **Text-to-Picto** Translation, extends the previous editions while introducing a major shift: the source language will be English instead of French. Participants will be required to generate coherent sequences of pictogram labels from English text, adapting their systems to account for linguistic, syntactic, and semantic differences between the two modalities. The dataset provided for this task will include aligned pairs of English text and ARASAAC pictograms. This resource will either be obtained by translating the existing ProPictoâĂŞOrféo corpus into English or by curating a new parallel corpus from scratch.

The second task, **Next-Pictogram Prediction**, is a newly introduced subtask inspired by Pereira et al. [24]. It focuses on predicting the most probable next pictogram in a given sequence, with performance evaluated using a top-$N$ accuracy metric.

## 4   MultimodalReasoning

The 2nd edition of **Multimodal Reasoning** will maintain its focus on assessing the reasoning capabilities of Vision-Language Models (VLMs) in the context of Multilingual Visual Question Answering (VQA). Building upon the first edition of the task [8], this iteration will expand the dataset within the multiple-choice question (MCQ) format - **Subtask 1**, preserving the original formulation: given an image of a question accompanied by two to five possible answers, participants must select the single correct answer.

To further stimulate reasoning and mitigate the risk of models relying solely on pattern recognition or memorized responses, the second edition will additionally introduce open-ended questions in multiple languages. These will form **Subtask 2** within the **Multimodal Reasoning** challenge, requiring participants to generate answers directly from the visual and textual information presented in the image, without predefined alternatives. This extension is designed to promote the development and evaluation of VLMs capable of more robust multimodal reasoning and linguistic comprehension.

## 5   AI4Agriculture

AI4agriculture task is composed of two sub-tasks:

***AgriPotential***. The AgriPotential sub-task is linked to sustainable agriculture. The challenge is to evaluate the capability of artificial intelligence models to predict the potential of land for cultivating different crop types from multi-spectral and multi-temporal Sentinel-2 imagery. The participants will work with the AgriPotential dataset that covers regions of Southern France. The images are annotated at the pixel level for three crop types, based on traditional in-situ analysis: viticulture, market gardening, and field crop. The objective is to automatically estimate the agricultural potential across five ordinal levels, from *very low* to *very high*, by modelling spectral and temporal features derived from the data.

***DACIA5*** sub-task is divided into two main challenges: *Crop identification: Past_vs_present*, and *Early crop identification* using the DACIA5 dataset [4] available at Zenodo [16]) and any additional open data. The participant submissions will be evaluated per track using specific quality evaluation measures, primarily focusing on accuracy measurements, including overall accuracy and average accuracy across different crop classes, as well as accuracy for specific crop types. The dataset provided for this task contains all the available images from Sentinel-1 SAR and Sentinel-2 MSI from 2020-2024 over a specific area to the north of Braşov city, Romania, together with the $32 \times 32$ pixel radar and multi-spectral patches for crop identification. The labels represent 17 types of agricultural crops over 47 parcels.

## 6   ImageCLEF-Deepfake

This first edition of the *Deepfake* task aims to evaluate the existing means of deepfake creation and detection in two modalities: **visual and audio**. For each modality, the task is split into 2 sub-tasks: **detection and generation**. The task strives to advance the deepfake detection field by drawing conclusions regarding what makes a good deepfake detector, as well as what makes a deepfake easy or hard to detect.

The **Generation** sub-task challenges participants to generate image or audio deepfakes, based on a dataset containing real images or audio. The generated deepfakes will be evaluated using a combination of multiple methods: (1) an identity score, to ensure that the generated deepfake resembles the original identity, (2) a detection score based on how well it can mislead several state-of-the-art deepfake detection methods, and (3) a detection score based on how well the other methods in the *Detection* sub-task can detect the deepfakes.

The **Detection** sub-task is a binary classification problem for deepfakes. The deepfakes will be generated in two ways: (1) by the organizers, using state-of-the-art methods, and (2) by the other participants, in the Generation sub-task. The final score will combine the individual scores for the two evaluation sets.

# 7 Conclusion

This paper showcases the tasks for the 24th edition of ImageCLEF. This year's challenges continue to provide opportunities for researchers to assess the performance of their systems in fields like medicine, science, security, and agritech. The tasks present rich multimodal challenges with well-defined datasets and evaluation benchmarks, allowing researchers to develop and test their systems under realistic conditions.

**Acknowledgements.** The work of Dan-Cristian Stanciu, Alexandra-Georgiana Andrei is funded by the Ministry of Research, Innovation and Digitization, UEFISCDI, Solutions Axis, grant SOL4/2024, project number PN-IV-P6-6.3-SOL-2024-2-0320. The work of Gabriel Constantin is funded by the Ministry of Research, Innovation and Digitization, UEFISCDI, Solutions Axis, grant SOL12/2024, project number PN-IV-P6-6.3-SOL-2024-0060. The work of Bogdan Ionescu, Liviu-Daniel Stefan is funded by the 5G-ENRICH European project, Project ID: 101181353 (23-EU-DIG-5G-ENRICH). The work of Mihai Dogariu is funded by a grant of the Ministry of Research, Innovation and Digitization, CCCDI - UEFISCDI, project number PN-IV-P6-6.3-SOL-2024-2-0238, within PNCDI IV.

The work of Dimitar Dimitrov and Ivan Koychev is partially funded by the EU NextGenerationEU project, through the National Recovery and Resilience Plan of the Republic of Bulgaria, project SUMMIT, No BG-RRP-2.004-0008.

The work of Benjamin Bracke, Lea Reinartz and Raphael Brüngel was partially funded by a PhD grant from the University of Applied Sciences and Arts Dortmund (FH Dortmund), Germany. The work of Hendrik Damm, Tabea M. G. Pakull, Bahadır Eryılmaz and Henning Schäfer was funded by a PhD grant from the DFG Research Training Group 2535 Knowledge- and data-based personalisation of medicine at the point of care (WisPerMed).

For the AI4Agriculture task, the creation of the DACIAS dataset was funded by the European Union through the AI4AGRI project (Romanian Excellence Center on Artificial Intelligence on Earth Observation Data for Agriculture) which received funding from the EU's Horizon Europe research and innovation programme under the grant agreement no. 101079136. The Agripotential dataset was also partially funded by that project.

**Disclosure of Interests.** The authors have no competing interests to declare that are relevant to the content of this article.

# References

1. Andrei, A., et al.: Overview of 2024 ImageCLEFMedical GANs task–investigating generative models' impact on biomedical synthetic images. In: CLEF2024 Working Notes, CEUR Workshop Proceedings, CEUR-WS. org, Grenoble, France (2024)
2. Andrei, A.G., et al.: Overview of ImageCLEFMedical 2025 GANs task: training data analysis and fingerprint detection. In: CLEF2025 Working Notes. Madrid, Spain (2025)

3. Andrei, A.G., Radzhabov, A., Coman, I., Kovalev, V., Ionescu, B., Müller, H.: Overview of ImageCLEFMedical GANs 2023 task: Identifying training data "fingerprints" in synthetic biomedical images generated by GANs for medical image security. In: Working Notes of the Conference and Labs of the Evaluation Forum (CLEF 2023), vol. 3497 (2023)

4. Baicoianu, A., et al.: DACIA5: A Sentinel-1 and Sentinel-2 dataset for agricultural crop identification applications. Big Earth Data **0**(0), 1–32 (2025)

5. Ben Abacha, A., Yim, W.w., Michalopoulos, G., Lin, T.: An investigation of evaluation methods in automatic medical note generation. In: Rogers, A., Boyd-Graber, J., Okazaki, N. (eds.) Findings of the Association for Computational Linguistics: ACL 2023, pp. 2575–2588. Toronto, Canada (2023)

6. Coleman, M., Liau, T.L.: A computer readability formula designed for machine scoring. J. Appl. Psychol. **60**(2), 283–284 (1975)

7. Damm, H., et al.: Overview of ImageCLEFMedical 2025 – medical concept detection and interpretable caption generation. In: CLEF 2025 Working Notes. CEUR Workshop Proceedings, CEUR-WS.org, Madrid, Spain (September 9–12 2025)

8. Dimitrov, D., et al.: Overview of ImageCLEF 2025 – multimodal reasoning. In: CLEF 2025 Working Notes. CEUR Workshop Proceedings, Madrid, Spain (2025)

9. Eickhoff, C., Schwall, I., García Seco de Herrera, A., Müller, H.: Overview of Image-CLEFcaption 2017 – the image caption prediction and concept extraction tasks to understand biomedical images. In: Working Notes of Conference and Labs of the Evaluation Forum (CLEF 2017). CEUR Workshop Proceedings, vol. 1866 (2017)

10. García Seco De Herrera, A., Eickhof, C., Andrearczyk, V., Müller, H.: Overview of the ImageCLEF 2018 caption prediction tasks. In: Working Notes of Conference and Labs of the Evaluation Forum (CLEF 2018). CEUR Workshop Proceedings, vol. 2125. CEUR-WS.org (2018)

11. Gautam, S., Riegler, M., Halvorsen, P.: Kvasir-VQA-x1: a multimodal dataset for medical reasoning and robust MedVQA in gastrointestinal endoscopy. In: Bhattarai, B., et al. (eds.) Data Engineering in Medical Imaging, pp. 53–63. Springer Nature Switzerland, Cham (2026)

12. Goutte, C., Gaussier, E.: A probabilistic interpretation of precision, recall and F-score, with implication for evaluation. In: European conference on information retrieval, pp. 345–359. Springer (2005)

13. Hicks, S.A., Halvorsen, P., Riegler, M.A., Thambawita, V.: Overview of Image-CLEFmedical 2025 – Medical visual question answering for gastrointestinal tract. In: CLEF2025 Working Notes. CEUR Workshop Proceedings, CEUR-WS.org, Gernoble, France (September 9-12 2025)

14. Hicks, S.A., Storås, A., Halvorsen, P., de Lange, T., Riegler, M.A., Thambawita, V.: Overview of ImageCLEFmedical 2023 – Medical visual question answering for gastrointestinal tract. In: CLEF2023 Working Notes. CEUR Workshop Proceedings, CEUR-WS.org, Thessaloniki, Greece (September 18-21 2023)

15. Hicks, S.A., Storås, A., Halvorsen, P., Riegler, M.A., Thambawita, V.: Overview of ImageCLEFmedical 2024 – Medical visual question answering for gastrointestinal tract. In: CLEF2024 Working Notes. CEUR Workshop Proceedings, CEUR-WS.org, Gernoble, France (September 9-12 2024)

16. Ivanovici, M., et al.: AI4AGRI Sentinel-2 Brasov area 2020-2024 multi- spectral dataset for crop monitoring and identification (Dec 2024)

17. Lee, J., et al.: BioBERT: a pre-trained biomedical language representation model for biomedical text mining. Bioinform. **36**, 1234–1240 (2020)

18. Macaire, C., Fabre, D., Lecouteux, B., Schwab, D.: Overview of the 2025 Image-CLEFtoPicto task – investigating the generation of pictogram sequences from text and speech. In: CLEF 2025 Working Notes. CEUR Workshop Proceedings, Madrid, Spain (2025), creative Commons CC BY 4.0

19. Maddela, M., Dou, Y., Heineman, D., Xu, W.: LENS: A learnable evaluation metric for text simplification, pp. 16383–16408 (2023)

20. Müller, H., Kalpathy-Cramer, J., García Seco de Herrera, A.: Experiences from the ImageCLEF medical retrieval and annotation tasks. In: Information Retrieval Evaluation in a Changing World, pp. 231–250. Springer (2019)

21. Pelka, O., Abacha, A.B., García Seco de Herrera, A., Jacutprakart, J., Friedrich, C.M., Müller, H.: Overview of the ImageCLEFmed 2021 concept & caption prediction task. In: Working Notes of Conference and Labs of the Evaluation Forum (CLEF 2021). CEUR Workshop Proceedings, vol. 2936. CEUR-WS.org (2021)

22. Pelka, O., Friedrich, C.M., García Seco de Herrera, A., Müller, H.: Overview of the ImageCLEFmed 2019 concept detection task. In: Working Notes of Conference and Labs of the Evaluation Forum (CLEF 2019). CEUR Workshop Proceedings, vol. 2380. CEUR-WS.org (2019)

23. Pelka, O., Friedrich, C.M., García Seco de Herrera, A., Müller, H.: Overview of the ImageCLEFmed 2020 concept prediction task: Medical image understanding. In: Working Notes of Conference and Labs of the Evaluation Forum (CLEF 2020). CEUR Workshop Proceedings, vol. 2696. CEUR-WS.org (2020)

24. Pereira, J.A., Macêdo, D., Zanchettin, C., de Oliveira, A.L.I., do Nascimento Fidalgo, R.: PictoBERT: Transformers for next pictogram prediction. Expert Systems with Applications **202**, 117231 (2022)

25. Rückert, J., et al.: Overview of ImageCLEFmedical 2024 – caption prediction and concept detection. In: CLEF2024 Working Notes. CEUR Workshop Proceedings, CEUR-WS.org, Grenoble, France (Sept 9-12 2024)

26. Rückert, J., et al.: Overview of ImageCLEFmedical 2022 – caption prediction and concept detection. In: CLEF2022 Working Notes. CEUR Workshop Proceedings, Bologna, Italy (2022)

27. Rückert, J., et al.: Overview of ImageCLEFmedical 2023 – caption prediction and concept detection. In: CLEF2023 Working Notes. CEUR Workshop Proceedings, CEUR-WS.org, Thessaloniki, Greece (2023)

28. Rückert, J., et al.: ROCOv2: radiology Objects in COntext version 2, an updated multimodal image dataset. Sci. Data **11**(1), 688 (2024)

29. Tsikrika, T., de Herrera, A.G.S., Müller, H.: Assessing the Scholarly Impact of ImageCLEF. In: Forner, P., Gonzalo, J., Kekäläinen, J., Lalmas, M., de Rijke, M. (eds.) CLEF 2011. LNCS, vol. 6941, pp. 95–106. Springer, Heidelberg (2011). https://doi.org/10.1007/978-3-642-23708-9_12

30. Tsikrika, T., Larsen, B., Müller, H., Endrullis, S., Rahm, E.: The scholarly impact of CLEF (2000–2009). In: Information Access Evaluation. Multilinguality, Multimodality, and Visualization, pp. 1–12. Springer (2013)

# Evaluating Information Retrieval Models Along Time: The LongEval Lab at CLEF 2026


Timo Breuer[1], Matteo Cancellieri[2], Alaa El-Ebshihy[3], Maik Fröbe[4],
Petra Galuščáková[5], Lorraine Goeuriot[6], Gabriel Iturra-Bocaz[5],
Jüri Keller[1], Petr Knoth[2], Andreas Konstantin Kruff[1],
Philippe Mulhem[6], Florina Piroi[3], David Pride[2], Philipp Schaer[1(✉)],
and Didier Schwab[6]

[1] TH Köln - University of Applied Sciences, Cologne, Germany
`philipp.schaer@th-koeln.de`
[2] The Open University, Milton Keynes, UK
[3] TU Wien, Vienna, Austria
[4] Friedrich-Schiller-Universität Jena, Jena, Germany
[5] University of Stavanger, Stavanger, Norway
[6] Univ. Grenoble Alpes, CNRS, Grenoble INP, LIG, Grenoble, France



**Abstract.** Many components of information retrieval systems evolve over time. The LongEval Lab aims to provide a benchmark setting to the longitudinal evaluation of IR models. At its fourth edition, LongEval we focus on scholarly search and scholarly user models. We describe in this paper the tasks that are planned for the 2026 lab, the data necessary for each of the tasks, as well as the choice of evaluation activities.



**Keywords:** Longitudinal Evaluation · Continuous Evaluation · Temporal IR


## 1 Introduction

The majority of evaluation initiatives in information retrieval focus on evaluating systems at a fixed point in time. However, data and users' behavior and expectations evolve over time. Therefore, to maintain good performance, systems must adapt to these variations. In some cases, the performance of IR systems can drop over time as the patterns observed in data change, e.g., due to linguistic and societal changes [3]. The performance drop is more pronounced when the test data is further away in time from training data [12,22]. Similarly, it has been shown that a deep neural network-based IR is dependent on the consistency between the train and test data [24].

The aim of the LongEval lab (this year in its fourth edition [1,2,6]) is to develop models that mitigate performance drops over time. We provide participants with training data distant in time from testing and un-annotated data

---

Authors ordered alphabetically.


© The Author(s), under exclusive license to Springer Nature Switzerland AG 2026
R. Campos et al. (Eds.): ECIR 2026, LNCS 16486, pp. 345–353, 2026.
https://doi.org/10.1007/978-3-032-21321-1_45

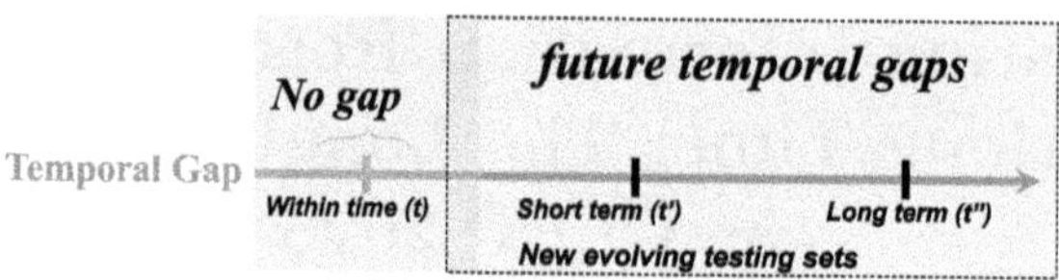


Fig. 1: Global framework for the LongEval Tasks.

from the testing time period. Our test scenarios include documents that evolve over the time, queries that are not known a priori, and relevance judgments that are non-binary and potentially not stable over time. We look at the temporal generalisability of IR systems trained and tested on data acquired at time $t$ (Fig. 1) to their performance when operating on data acquired at time $t'$ (shortly after time $t$), and at time $t''$ (a long period after time $t$).

The LongEval Lab is running since 2023, with a varying number of participants each year. In these years, the lab proposed two tasks per year, one involving classification, the other retrieval. For next year (2026), we plan a total of 4 tasks, widening the scope of long-term IR to new dynamics beyond documents, topics, and qrels, closer to evolving user behavior with user simulation tasks. Additionally, we newly experiment with longitudinal aspect in Retrieval Augmented Generation (RAG). Task 1 is, by now, a classical ad-hoc search task where systems are evaluated at varying points in time. Task 2 aims to support the derivation of Cranfield-style evaluation corpora from user behaviour observed over time by aiming to extract formalized topics from click logs. Task 3 is dedicated to modelling domain-specific user behaviour and different user types for use in user simulations. Task 4 is dedicated to the study of RAG behaviour when dealing with evolution of documents, focusing on evolving and conflicting information, still expecting the RAGs to generate relevant results according to the documents retrieved from different temporal collections.

## 2  LongEval Data

The underlying dataset from where each task will extract queries, topics, and relevance assessments, is acquired from the CORE[1] [21] collection of scholarly documents. To our knowledge, CORE [20] is currently the largest aggregated collection of Open Access full text scholarly documents. CORE Search provides a web UI for users to query the entire database of scholarly documents with over a million searches per month. We will use the CORE Apache server logs to create datasets necessary for the tasks (i.e. documents, queries, qrels, and user sessions). These logs contain search and click information:

**Search Information** includes i) `search_id`–a unique identifiers for the search; ii) `query`–search query; iii) `serp`–documents identifiers of returned results[2] (example 1.1);

---

[1] CORE (COnnecting REpositories) https://core.ac.uk/.
[2] For LongEval we only consider the first ten results.

**Click Information** records from the user interaction with the CORE web-interface, for each click: i) `uid`–a unique (anonymous) identifier for individual user session; ii) the `trackId`–unique identifier of clicked document; iii) `type`–click type (e.g. author information, download PDF article, example 1.2).

**Example 1.1:** *Search query and results*

```
{"date": "2025-01-10␣00:00:05",
 "search_id": "83ed8653d71",
 "serp": [ 7233367, 85590132, 145375620, 23053234],
 "query": "Methodology␣definition␣and␣importance␣in␣research␣
    methodology"}
```

**Example 1.2:** *Search query and results*

```
{"date": "2025-01-10␣00:00:05",
 "search_id": "83ed8653d71",
 "serp": [ 7233367, 85590132, 145375620, 23053234],
 "query": "Methodology␣definition␣and␣importance␣in␣research␣
    methodology"}
```

## 3   Task Descriptions

In the following we give details on the four LongEval Lab tasls at CLEF 2026. We explain the general idea and objective of the task, the corresponding artefacts (e.g., queries, qrels, etc.) and the evaluation strategy for the specific task.

### Task 1. LongEval-Sci: Ad-Hoc Scientific Retrieval

**Description:** The task aims to further encourage the development of IR systems able to handle temporal data evolution. The IR systems are expected to be persistent in their retrieval efficiency over time, as the test collection evolves. The participants will collect retrieval runs on various snapshots of the test collection. **Data:** The data for this task is a set of scientific documents and queries from the CORE search engine (Sect. 2), following a similar acquisition process as for the previous LongEval iterations [1,2,6,14]. We compute discrete relevance assessments using a simplified Dynamic Bayesian Network (sDBN) Click Model [8,9]. As in previous years, we additionally provide convenient access to the dataset through the ir_datasets_longeval extension [18]. As of now, the data available to the participants is as follows:

1. Two training snapshots from the 2025 lab iteration (queries, documents, qrels, time intervals 2024-11 and 2025-01).
2. Two test snapshots: one acquired during a time interval $t'$ shortly after $t$ for evaluating the **short-term persistence,** and one acquired long after $t$ during a time interval $t''$, for **long-term persistence** evaluation.

In total, the data contains about 4 million documents and one thousand queries. **Evaluation:** Submissions will be evaluated in terms of: *Effectiveness* per test snapshot, and *Robustness* across snapshots. *Effectiveness* will be measured with nDCG scores. *Robustness* will be assessed with: (1) Relative Improvement (RI) – measures relative change in effectiveness compared to the first snapshot, (2) Delta Relative Improvement (DRI) – measures relative improvement in relation to a reference system (e.g. BM25), and (3) Effect Ratio (ER) – measures degree of reproduction of the effectiveness [4,6,15,16].

## Task 2. LongEval-TopEx: Topic Extraction From Query Logs

**Description:** Retrieval systems infer which documents are relevant to an information need either from (1) usage data or (2) expert judgments [7]. In search engine production deployments these variants can complement each other, e.g., when retrieval systems are first evaluated with available expert judgments so that only promising candidates are then evaluated under usage data [19]. Our goal for Task 2 is to also enable similar synergies for LongEval submissions.

**Data:** The input is the training set from time interval $t$. Participants can use the relevance judgments derived from the observed usage data for each query to create a TREC-style description and narrative for each training query. The extracted topic consists of the training query and the generated description and narrative. The query describes what users submit to the search engine, whereas the description formalizes what the users actually did mean and the narrative formalizes what makes documents relevant respectively not relevant. To obtain relevance judgments, we will build a top-10 judgment pool for all retrieval runs submitted for the test sets for Task 1 that overlap with the training queries. We then will annotate this top-10 pool for all test sets with multiple large language model relevance assessors [10,11,25,26] prompted with the query and the generated description and narrative that formalize what the search engine users did mean and what will be considered relevant or not. Thereby, we obtain one alternative set of qrels per extracted topic and LLM relevance assessor.

**Evaluation:** Our evaluation aims to detect "good" extracted topics that are (1) aligned with observed usage data, (2) allow to distinguish retrieval systems, and (3) provide a clear formalization of the information need to derive what documents will be relevant or not. Each of the three dimensions is needed to ensure that subsequent evaluations are meaningful. We will assess the quality of each extracted topic for each of the three dimensions using the LLM-generated relevance assessments and the retrieval runs submitted to Task 1:

1. Alignment: We calculate the annotator-agreement between the qrels from the click logs and the LLM-generated qrels from the extracted topic for each test time interval.
2. Distinguishability: We calculate how well nDCG scores created from the LLM-generated qrels of the extracted topic can distinguish the runs submitted to Task 1.

3. Clarity: We will calculate the annotator agreement when (potentially different) large language models repeatedly create alternative qrels for the same extracted topic.

Similarly to Task 1, we compute the relative drop on the three dimensions for the short- and long-term test sets. Topics extracted in Task 2 are Task 3 inputs.

### Task 3. LongEval-USim: User Simulations

**Description:** The CORE-based dataset in LongEval differs from typical test collections not only by the temporal characteristics described earlier, but also by the inclusion of user interactions in the academic search task. In these search tasks, we observe patterns that are less common in other (web) search tasks, such as journal runs, numerous Boolean block searches, or faceted search. These characteristics may lead to interaction behaviors that have not been previously explored enabling a wide range of interesting scenarios.

In this task, we invite participants to model different user behaviors and types for user simulations, with a particular focus on query formulations. This approach was explored in the SIGIR 2025 Workshop on Simulations in Information Access (Sim4IA[3]) [5], in the form of a micro-shared task, where the evaluation of query (re-)formulation simulations was tested out.

From the original CORE search log files we extract a set of interaction sessions, similar to the ones in Sim4IA. With the `search_id`, a fingerprint `uid`, and heuristics, we extract sessions from the search logs. These sessions enable us to track user interactions over (short) time spans, including queries, SERPs, and clicks. Participants in this task will get a pre-filtered session logs excerpts. From here, they should predict the next query in the sequence of interactions. The participants can detect and train specific user models on historic interaction logs and test those models on the test data in the final LongEval round.

To simplify this task, we provide a pre-configured SimIIR v3 environment that will allow off-the-shelf user simulations by configuring user models or simple interaction steps. Later, these simulators can be extended to a scenario that includes click or stopping decisions. Participants can also utilize the synthesized topics from Task 2, as these can serve as additional input for this task. Instead of relying solely on session logs, the topic and encoded context within these can provide more information on user intentions compared to queries alone.

**Relevance Computation and Evaluation Metrics:** As participants are to submit queries, we will compare the submitted queries to the queries from the session logs. We can look at two main aspects: (1) the inability to distinguish between simulated and real data, and (2) the performance prediction capabilities of a simulation. We measure the differences in the generated queries themselves or the differences in the output results by comparing them to the interactions in the CORE log files. Using reproducibility measures [17], we identify the simulators that are closest (or best reproduce) the original set of interactions. In the

---

[3] https://sim4ia.org/sigir2025.

LongEval setting, we can additionally compare the interactions generated by the simulator based on the development of topics over time. A simulator performing well at one point in time does not necessarily perform well at another.

### Task 4. LongEval-RAG: Retrieval Augmented Generation (RAG)

**Description and Data:** This task aims to evaluate the ability of RAG systems to retrieve correct information when this information evolves over the time. In such case, the connection between the retrieval step of a RAG and its generation step should incorporate temporal awareness of the retrieved documents.

The LongEval RAG task will provide a set of queries, for which the correctness of the answer depends on the temporal aspect. Queries will be selected such that the relevant documents either changed over time or are documents from different temporal collections with conflicting information. Typical examples of queries are related to evolution and/or contradictions of specific research topics, e.g. "What are the main technical evolutions of attention models between the short-term and the long-term datasets?" The participants will create RAG systems that use both short- and long-term collections from the CORE data set (explained in Task 1) and submit, for each query, a generated response along with the list of support documents or passages. Time information is provided explicitly in the metadata of the documents (creation, publication, update times). We follow the line of exploring time-sensitive information in RAG [13,23,27] focusing on specific topics of the scientific literature domain and on shorter time frames where more complex information needs are the case.

**Evaluation:** We will evaluate the submissions (i.e. the generated answers) manually using Answer Relevancy and Faithfulness metrics. The Answer Relevancy measures to what extent the generated results addresses the user's query. The Faithfulness metric measures how accurately the answer reflects the information in the source documents. Both dimensions will be weighted equally to assess to which extent good results benefit from the retrieved documents.

## 4   Conclusion

The proposed next iteration of the LongEval Lab at CLEF in 2026 aims to evaluate information access systems within dynamic, temporal environments. Task 1 will continue the scientific search task, evaluated at multiple points in time. Task 2 aims to generate TREC-style topics from interaction logs to facilitate automatic relevance judgments. Task 3 focuses on predicting the next query in a session based on a simulated users. Task 4 invites participants to test their RAG systems in the evolving environment on temporal depended queries. Through these tasks we aim to improve the state of knowledge on and the robustness of information access systems in dynamic, temporal settings. All information, including further details such as the anticipated schedule will be made available on the LongEval website[4].

---

[4] https://clef-longeval.github.io/.

**Acknowledgments.** This work is partially funded by Deutsche Forschungsgemeinschaft (DFG) under grant numbers 509543643 and 407518790, and within the funding programme FH-Personal (PLan CV, reference number 03FHP109) by the German Federal Ministry of Education and Research (BMBF) and Joint Science Conference (GWK).

**Disclosure of Interests.** The authors have no competing interests to declare that are relevant to the content of this article.

# References


1. Alkhalifa, R., et al.: Overview of the CLEF-2023 LongEval Lab on Longitudinal Evaluation of Model Performance. In: Experimental IR Meets Multilinguality, Multimodality, and Interaction. Proc. of the 14th International Conference of the CLEF Association (CLEF 2023). LNCS. Springer (2023)
2. Alkhalifa, R., et al.: Overview of the CLEF 2024 LongEval Lab on Longitudinal Evaluation of Model Performance. In: Proc. of the 15th International Conference of the CLEF Association (CLEF 2024) (2024)
3. Alkhalifa, R., Zubiaga, A.: Capturing stance dynamics in social media: open challenges and research directions. Int. J. Digital Humanities, 1–21 (2022)
4. Breuer, T., Ferro, N., Fuhr, N., Maistro, M., Sakai, T., Schaer, P., Soboroff, I.: How to measure the reproducibility of system-oriented ir experiments. In: Proceedings of the 43rd International ACM SIGIR Conference on Research and Development in Information Retrieval, pp. 349–358. SIGIR '20. Association for Computing Machinery, New York (2020). https://doi.org/10.1145/3397271.3401036
5. Breuer, T., et al.: Report on the 1st workshop on simulations for information access (sim4ia 2024) at SIGIR 2024. ACM SIGIR Forum **58**(2) (December 2024)
6. Cancellieri, M., et al.: Longeval at clef 2025: Longitudinal evaluation of ir systems on web and scientific data. In: Experimental IR Meets Multilinguality, Multimodality, and Interaction: 16th International Conference of the CLEF Association, CLEF 2025, Madrid, Spain, September 9–12, 2025, Proceedings. p. 363–387. Springer, Heidelberg (2025). https://doi.org/10.1007/978-3-032-04354-2_20
7. Chapelle, O., Joachims, T., Radlinski, F., Yue, Y.: Large-scale validation and analysis of interleaved search evaluation. ACM Trans. Inf. Syst. **30**(1), 6:1–6:41 (2012). https://doi.org/10.1145/2094072.2094078
8. Chapelle, O., Zhang, Y.: A dynamic bayesian network click model for web search ranking. In: Proceedings of the 18th International Conference on World Wide Web, WWW '09, pp. 1–10. Association for Computing Machinery, New York, April 2009. https://doi.org/10.1145/1526709.1526711
9. Chuklin, A., Markov, I., Rijke, M.d.: Click models for web search. Synthesis Lectures on Information Concepts, Retrieval, and Services **7**(3), 1–115 (2015). https://doi.org/10.2200/S00654ED1V01Y201507ICR043
10. Faggioli, G., et al.: Perspectives on large language models for relevance judgment. In: Proceedings of the 2023 ACM SIGIR International Conference on Theory of Information Retrieval, ICTIR (2023). https://doi.org/10.1145/3578337.3605136
11. Faggioli, G., Dietz, L., Clarke, C.L.A., Demartini, G., Hagen, M., Hauff, C., Kando, N., Kanoulas, E., Potthast, M., Stein, B., Wachsmuth, H.: Who determines what is relevant? humans or AI? why not both? Commun. ACM **67**(4), 31–34 (2024). https://doi.org/10.1145/3624730

12. Florio, K., Basile, V., Polignano, M., Basile, P., Patti, V.: Time of your hate: The challenge of time in hate speech detection on social media. Appl. Sci. **10**(12), 4180 (2020)

13. Gade, A., Jetcheva, J.: It's about time: Incorporating temporality in retrieval augmented language models. arXiv preprint arXiv:2401.13222 (2024)

14. Galuscáková, P., et al.: Longeval-retrieval: French-english dynamic test collection for continuous web search evaluation. In: Proceedings of the 46th International ACM SIGIR Conference on Research and Development in Information Retrieval, pp. 3086–3094. SIGIR '23. Association for Computing Machinery, New York (2023). https://doi.org/10.1145/3539618.3591921

15. Keller, J., Breuer, T., Schaer, P.: Evaluation of temporal change in IR test collections. In: Oosterhuis, H., Bast, H., Xiong, C. (eds.) Proceedings of the 2024 ACM SIGIR International Conference on Theory of Information Retrieval, ICTIR 2024, Washington, DC, USA, 13 July 2024, pp. 3–13. ACM (2024). https://doi.org/10.1145/3664190.3672530

16. Keller, J., Breuer, T., Schaer, P.: Leveraging prior relevance signals in web search. In: CLEF (Working Notes). CEUR Workshop Proceedings, vol. 3740, pp. 2396–2406. CEUR-WS.org (2024)

17. Keller, J., Breuer, T., Schaer, P.: Replicability measures for longitudinal information retrieval evaluation. In: Goeuriot, L., Mulhem, P., Quénot, G., Schwab, D., Di Nunzio, G.M., Soulier, L., Galuščáková, P., García Seco de Herrera, A., Faggioli, G., Ferro, N. (eds.) Experimental IR Meets Multilinguality, Multimodality, and Interaction, pp. 215–226. Springer, Cham (2024)

18. Keller, J., Fröbe, M., Hendriksen, G., Alexander, D., Potthast, M., Schaer, P.: Simplified longitudinal retrieval experiments: A case study on query expansion and document boosting. In: Carrillo-de-Albornoz, J., de Herrera, A.G.S., Gonzalo, J., Plaza, L., Mothe, J., Piroi, F., Rosso, P., Spina, D., Faggioli, G., Ferro, N. (eds.) Experimental IR Meets Multilinguality, Multimodality, and Interaction - 16th International Conference of the CLEF Association, CLEF 2025, Madrid, Spain, September 9-12, 2025, Proceedings. LNCS, vol. 16089, pp. 117–127. Springer (2025). https://doi.org/10.1007/978-3-032-04354-2_8

19. Kharitonov, E.: Using interaction data for improving the offline and online evaluation of search engines. Ph.D. thesis, University of Glasgow, UK (2016), theses.gla.ac.uk/7750/

20. Knoth, P., Herrmannova, D., Cancellieri, M., Anastasiou, L., Pontika, N., Pearce, S., Gyawali, B., Pride, D.: Core: a global aggregation service for open access papers. Sci. Data **10**(1), 366 (2023). https://doi.org/10.1038/s41597-023-02208-w

21. Knoth, P., Zdrahal, Z.: CORE: three access levels to underpin Open Access. D-Lib Magazine **18**(11/12) (2012)

22. Lukes, J., Søgaard, A.: Sentiment analysis under temporal shift. In: Balahur, A., Mohammad, S.M., Hoste, V., Klinger, R. (eds.) Proceedings of the 9th Workshop on Computational Approaches to Subjectivity, Sentiment and Social Media Analysis, pp. 65–71. Association for Computational Linguistics, Brussels, Belgium (Oct 2018). https://doi.org/10.18653/v1/W18-6210, https://aclanthology.org/W18-6210/

23. Piryani, B., Abdullah, A., Mozafari, J., Anand, A., Jatowt, A.: It's high time: A survey of temporal information retrieval and question answering. arXiv:2505.20243 (2025)

24. Ren, R., et al.: A thorough examination on zero-shot dense retrieval. In: Findings of the Association for Computational Linguistics: EMNLP (2023). https://doi.org/10.18653/v1/2023.findings-emnlp.1057

25. Thomas, P., Spielman, S., Craswell, N., Mitra, B.: Large language models can accurately predict searcher preferences. In: Yang, G.H., Wang, H., Han, S., Hauff, C., Zuccon, G., Zhang, Y. (eds.) Proc. of the 47th International ACM SIGIR Conference on Research and Development in Information Retrieval, pp. 1930–1940 (2024). https://doi.org/10.1145/3626772.3657707
26. Upadhyay, S., Pradeep, R., Thakur, N., Craswell, N., Lin, J.: UMBRELA: umbrela is the (open-source reproduction of the) bing relevance assessor. CoRR (2024)
27. Wu, F., et al.: Time-sensitve retrieval-augmented generation for question answering. In: Proceedings of the 33rd ACM International Conference on Information and Knowledge Management, pp. 2544–2553. CIKM '24. Association for Computing Machinery, New York (2024). https://doi.org/10.1145/3627673.3679800

# CLEF HIPE-2026: Evaluating Accurate and Efficient Person–Place Relation Extraction from Multilingual Historical Texts

Juri Opitz[1]([✉]), Corina Raclé[1], Emanuela Boros[3], Andrianos Michail[1], Matteo Romanello[2], Maud Ehrmann[3], and Simon Clematide[1]

[1] University of Zurich, Zürich, Switzerland
hipe-2026@googlegroups.com
[2] Swiss Art Research Infrastructure (SARI), University of Zurich, Zürich, Switzerland
[3] École Polytechnique Fédérale de Lausanne (EPFL), Lausanne, Switzerland
https://hipe-eval.github.io/HIPE-2026

**Abstract.** HIPE-2026 is a CLEF evaluation lab dedicated to person–place relation extraction from noisy, multilingual historical texts. Building on the HIPE-2020 and HIPE-2022 campaigns, it extends the series toward semantic relation extraction by targeting the task of identifying person–place associations in multiple languages and time periods. Systems are asked to classify relations of two types—**at** ("Has the person ever been at this place?") and **isAt** ("Is the person located at this place around publication time?")—requiring reasoning over temporal and geographical cues. The lab introduces a three-fold evaluation profile that jointly assesses accuracy, computational efficiency, and domain generalization. By linking relation extraction to large-scale historical data processing, HIPE-2026 aims to support downstream applications in knowledge-graph construction, historical biography reconstruction, and spatial analysis in digital humanities.

**Keywords:** Relation Extraction · Multilingual NLP · Digital Humanities · Historical Texts · Shared Task

## 1 Introduction

Historical documents bear a wealth of information that can help reconstructing past events, biographies, and the development of social networks. However, the digitization of historical documents typically results in data that are noisy, multilingual, and weakly structured. Therefore, robust approaches to mining historical data are necessary to support a wide range of information needs among scholars in the social sciences and history [4, 10, 13, 16, 21, 25, 31].


R. Campos et al. (Eds.): ECIR 2026, LNCS 16486, pp. 354–363, 2026.
https://doi.org/10.1007/978-3-032-21321-1_46

HIPE-2026 is a CLEF Evaluation Lab dedicated to the extraction of person–place relations in multilingual historical documents. A person-place relation corresponds to a semantic link between an individual and a location as evidenced in a document. Such relations may indicate where a person is said to be at a given moment, where they lived or worked, or places connected to notable moments in their life (e.g., birthplaces, residences, visits, travel destinations). Together, these relations can help answer the question of *Who was where when?*, and support the reconstruction of individuals' geographical and temporal trajectories.

These implicit or explicit, spatio-temporal relations cannot be detected through simple document co-occurrence of entity mentions. Rather, it requires temporal reasoning, geographical inference, and interpretation of noisy historical texts–often with sparse or indirect contextual cues–to detect and qualify person–place relations with appropriate degrees of certainty.

The objective of HIPE-2026 is to advance the automatic detection of such relations, enabling the reconstruction of individuals' movements in space and time and the tracing of life trajectories in support of digital humanities scholarship. The task is designed to be approachable by both generative AI systems (LLMs) and more traditional classification models. HIPE-2026 builds on HIPE-2020 and HIPE-2022, which targeted named-entity recognition and linking in historical corpora [5,6] and advances the series toward relation extraction (RE).

## 2   Task Description

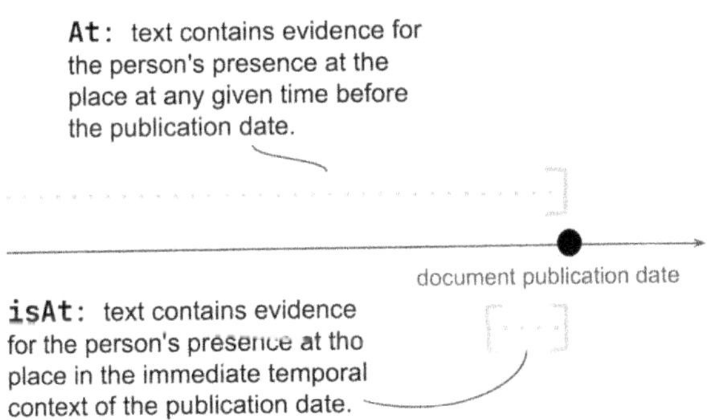



**Fig. 1.** Temporal scope of **at** and **isAt** relations relative to publication time.

Participants are tasked with determining the relationship of each person–place pair mentioned in a historical document. Each pair consists of two entities, one person and one location, each of which appears in the text through one or more mentions. For each pair, systems must assess whether the text provides evidence of the person's presence at the location, taking into account the document's temporal horizon relative to its publication date (see Fig. 1 for an illustration).

For each document, systems must classify each candidate pair according to the following relation types:

**at** The text provides evidence that the person was present at the place at any point in time *prior to the publication date*. This relation is right-bounded by the publication date but may hold at any time in the past. It is labeled as:
  - **true**: explicit evidence supports the relation;
  - **probable**: the relation can be inferred from contextual clues and is a likely assumption;
  - **false**: no evidence, or contradictory evidence, is present.

**isAt** captures whether the text provides implicit or explicit evidence that the person was at the location in the *immediate temporal context of the publication date*. The decision is binary $(+/-)$: $+$ means that there is implicit or explicit evidence the person was at the location shortly before the publication date, while $-$ indicates the absence of such evidence.


*Relation Between* **at** *and* **isAt**. The **isAt** relation can be viewed as a temporal refinement of **at**: it captures whether there is evidence (implicit or explicit) for the **at** relation in the closer temporal scope of the article's date. Conceptually, assigning **isAt**$=+$ presupposes that an **at** relation is true, or at least, probable; Predictions where **at**=**false** and **isAt**$=+$ are therefore epistemically inconsistent, but practically permitted. In sum, if **at** is **true** or **probable**, **isAt** would further specify whether the person's presence falls within the document's temporal horizon.


*Abductive Interpretation and Evidential Reasoning.* The distinction between explicit, probable, and absent evidence is grounded in an abductive view of language understanding. Hobbs' framework of "Interpretation as Abduction" [11] argues that discourse interpretation consists in identifying the minimal set of assumptions which, together with background knowledge, explain why an utterance would be a rational and coherent thing to say. Under this view, meaning is not limited to what is explicitly stated, but includes what must be assumed to provide a coherent explanation of the discourse. Applied to person–place relations in historical texts, this perspective motivates the **probable** label: relations may be supported by indirect cues such as event participation, institutional roles, or narrative coherence, even when no explicit locative statement is present. Conversely, the **false** label reflects cases where no such abductive explanation is warranted based on the text alone. The **isAt** refinement further constrains abductive inference temporally, requiring that assumptions about presence remain compatible with the document's publication horizon.

In addition, we allow systems to optionally provide free-text explanations or indicate other relevant background knowledge that informed their decisions. Evaluating such explanations is not a primary objective of the task, but participants are encouraged to analyze and report pieces of information that could help us better understand prediction rationales.

**Example-Based Illustration of the Task**

To illustrate the task, we present an excerpt from an article of the American newspaper *Tabor City Tribune* on June 6, 1960. The article reports on a military scout meeting and involves multiple person-place candidate relation pairs, as shown in Table 1.

> Loris Scouts Win Camporee Top Honor WINNERS — Members of Boy Scout Troop 843. »»ho won top honors at an Horry IMstrict Scout Camporee at Clear Pond March 25-27 are shown above hiking down a road. The lads won after engaging in com- passing, rope throwing, Morse code, hiking with compass and individual cooking. The troop is sponsored by the First Bap tist Church. Boy Scout Troop 843 of Loris won top honors at the Horry District Scout Camporee March 25-27 at Clear Pond between (Conway and Myrtle Beach. Competing against some ot the finest units in the county, the boys won top honors after participating in Compassing, : rope throwing, Morse Code, hiking with compass and indi-) vidual cooking. Friday night the troops! competing joined in a camp fire meeting and heard an ad dress by Col. Gruenwald, com manding officer of the Myrtle Beach Air Force Base. The Loris troop, sponsored by the First Baptist church, was the only troop to have all its Scout leaders present: Francis Ragan, George Rent/ and George Lav.

A clear case is the relation between the person entity *Col. Gruenwald* and the place entity *Myrtle Beach Air Force Base*. The article explicitly identifies the colonel as the "commanding officer of the" air force base, thereby supporting a true label for the **at** relation, and a positive one for **isAt**. In contrast, although the place *Myrtle Beach* is also mentioned, the text does not state that Col. Gruenwald was physically present in the city; his connection is institutional rather than locational. This motivates the probable label for the **at** relation and a negative one for **isAt**, highlighting the distinction between affiliation and physical presence.

The relation between Col. Gruenwald and Clear Pond (as well as the Horry District Scout Camporee) provides another instructive example. The article reports that he delivered an address at a campfire meeting during the camporee, which took place at Clear Pond. This constitutes sufficient evidence to annotate both locations with a TRUE **at** relation and a positive **isAt** relation, even though his presence is inferred indirectly through the event.

Several negative annotations demonstrate the importance of avoiding inference beyond the text. Conway and Loris are mentioned as geographic reference points, but there is no indication that Col. Gruenwald visited either place. Consequently, these relations are marked as false, despite their proximity to the actual event location.

## 3   Data

HIPE-2026 data consists of two sets of data:

**Test Set A**: historical newspaper articles in French, German, English, and Luxembourgish spanning roughly 200 years (19th–20th centuries), drawn from the HIPE-2022 data.

**Surprise Test Set B**: French literary texts (16th–18th century), used to assess domain generalization; only the **at** relation is evaluated.

**Table 1.** Annotated person-place candidate relations for the example article.

| Person | Place | at | isAt |
|---|---|---|---|
| Col. Gruenwald | Myrtle Beach Air Force Base | true | + |
| Col. Gruenwald | Clear Pond | true | + |
| Col. Gruenwald | Myrtle Beach | probable | − |
| Col. Gruenwald | Loris | false | − |
| Col. Gruenwald | Conway | false | − |
| Col. Gruenwald | Horry District Scout Camporee | true | + |
| Francis Ragan | Myrtle Beach Air Force Base | false | − |
| Francis Ragan | Conway | false | − |
| Francis Ragan | Myrtle Beach | false | − |
| George Lav | Myrtle Beach Air Force Base | false | − |
| George Lav | Conway | false | − |
| George Rent | Myrtle Beach Air Force Base | false | − |
| George Rent | Myrtle Beach | false | − |
| George Rent | Loris | true | − |
| George Rent | Conway | false | − |
| George Rent | Horry District Scout Camporee | true | + |

*Pilot Study.* A total of 119 person–place pairs were annotated by three independent annotators, drawn from the English and French development sets of HIPE-2022. The inter-annotator agreement (Cohen's kappa) ranged from 0.7 to 0.9 for the **at** relation, and from 0.4 to 0.9 for **isAt**, indicating moderate to high consistency. Large language models also showed promising alignment with human judgments: GPT-4o reached up to 0.8 agreement with the gold standard for **at**, while **isAt** results were lower and more variable (0.2–0.7). The study further highlighted the high inference cost of current models and the need for scalable methods that can handle the multiplicative growth of candidate entity pairs in historical documents.

## 4   Evaluation

We consider three evaluation profiles.

The **accuracy profile** rewards high-performing systems and encourages the exploration of frontier models, advanced prompting strategies, or agent-based approaches. System responses are evaluated per test set using *macro-averaged Recall* (also known as *balanced accuracy*). Macro Recall is defined as follows:

1. For each label $\ell$ in the label set $L$, compute its recall:

$$\text{Recall}(\ell) = \frac{\#\text{examples with label } \ell \text{ correctly predicted}}{\#\text{examples whose gold label is } \ell}.$$

2. The final score is the arithmetic mean of the per-label recalls:

$$\text{MacroRecall} = \frac{1}{|L|} \sum_{\ell \in L} \text{Recall}(\ell).$$

This metric is principled and interpretable, ensuring that all labels contribute equally regardless of class imbalance [15, 22]. For Test Set A, which includes three labels for **at** and two labels for **isAt**, macro Recall is computed separately for each relation and then averaged to obtain the final system ranking.

The **accuracy-efficiency profile** promotes lightweight, scalable methods, including smaller LLMs or task-specific classifiers. This profile balances predictive performance with efficiency and resource usage. This is motivated by the increasing cost of running very large models and, in our case, by the scale of digitized material together with the quadratic nature of the task (person–location *pairs*). Participant teams will be surveyed regarding parameter count and model size; together with accuracy, these factors are integrated into a robust ranking metric that computes a balanced score reflecting system efficiency.

Finally, the **generalization profile** tests system accuracy on the Surprise Test Set B, based on the **at**-relation only and using *macro-Recall*.

Annotated data, baselines and scoring tools are released via GitHub[1] under a CC-BY 4.0 license, and participation guidelines are published on Zenodo[2].

# 5   Related Work

*Relation Extraction (RE) Benchmarks and Their Limitations.* Early Open Information Extraction (Open IE) approaches extracted unrestricted relations without predefined schemas [9]. Subsequent benchmarks introduced controlled settings with fixed relation inventories, notably TACRED [30] for sentence-level and DocRED [29] for document-level RE. These English-only datasets, covering several dozen relation types, have advanced the field but suffer from annotation incompleteness. Re-annotation efforts such as Re-TACRED [2, 23] and Re-DocRED [26] reduce false negatives, yet the benchmarks remain confined to clean, modern English. In contrast, HIPE-2026 focuses on a single relation type—person–place—across multiple languages, time periods, and OCR-derived historical sources that involve orthographic variation and temporal reasoning. Previous HIPE tasks (2020, 2022) addressed multilingual named entity recognition and linking in historical newspapers [7,8] but not relation extraction. A recent survey highlights progress in multilingual RE through cross-lingual transfer and annotation projection while underscoring the lack of benchmarks addressing multilinguality, noise, and domain shift [1]. HIPE-2026 fills this gap with a historically and linguistically diverse evaluation setting.

*Relation Extraction for Biographical and Historical Domains.* Biographical RE extends general RE toward structured knowledge bases. The *Biographical* dataset aligns Wikipedia with Pantheon and Wikidata via distant supervision to derive ten relations [17]. OpenIE has been used to extract RDF triples from Wikipedia biographies [24]. The *Guided Distant Supervision (GDS)* variant adapts this approach to German, denoises labels through external constraints,

---

[1]  https://github.com/hipe-eval/HIPE-2026-data.
[2]  https://zenodo.org/records/17800136.

and explores cross-lingual transfer [18]. Although these studies demonstrate the potential of distant supervision for domain-specific RE, historical data remain largely unexplored, a gap that HIPE-2026 aims to close.

*Multilingual, Noisy, and Domain-Shift Relation Extraction.* Multilingual RE methods rely on cross-lingual transfer, annotation projection, or zero-shot learning (see [1,31]). However, few benchmarks incorporate noise robustness, domain shift, or low-resource historical languages, with emerging datasets addressing explicitly historical materials [19,20,28]. This motivates shared tasks like HIPE-2026, which emphasize relation mining in noisy, multilingual, historical contexts.

*Denoising Techniques.* Distant supervision enables large-scale RE but introduces substantial noise. Recent denoising methods include *hierarchical contrastive learning* (HiCLRE) for filtering noisy instances [12] and *NLI*-based validation (DSRE + NLI) [32]. These techniques are relevant forOCR-derived noisy data.

*Efficiency in Relation Extraction.* Beyond accuracy, current evaluations increasingly emphasize computational efficiency. Shared tasks such as *SustaiNLP 2020* measured energy consumption [27], and *EfficientQA* enforced memory limits [14]. Efficiency-focused modeling continues to gain traction [3]. By combining accuracy and efficiency-focused evaluation in a historical multilingual RE task, HIPE-2026 establishes a new benchmark for robust and sustainable NLP.

## 6   Conclusion

HIPE-2026 extends the HIPE evaluation series into new research directions. It promotes the development of robust methods for extracting person–place relations from multilingual historical text, enabling applications in temporal and spatial analysis across the humanities and social sciences, as well as in the analysis and interpretation of literary texts.

To formalize and isolate this challenge, the task is framed as a relation classification problem conditioned on a person–place pair within its document context. This formulation also facilitates the use of generative AI systems, which are expected to perform well on such contextual reasoning tasks even when applied to historical, digitized texts that diverge from clean modern conditions.

**Acknowledgements.** HIPE-2026 is funded through the project *Impresso – Media Monitoring of the Past II. Beyond Borders: Connecting Historical Newspapers and Radio*; SNSF 213585 and Luxembourg National Research Fund 17498891.

**Disclosure of Interests.** The authors have no competing interests to declare.

# References


1. Ali, M., Speck, R., Zahera, H.M., Saleem, M., Moussallem, D., Ngonga Ngomo, A.C.: Multilingual relation extraction: a survey. IEEE Access **13**, 151907–151933 (2025)
2. Alt, C., Gabryszak, A., Hennig, L.: TACRED revisited: a thorough evaluation of the TACRED relation extraction task. In: Jurafsky, D., Chai, J., Schluter, N., Tetreault, J. (eds.) Proceedings of the 58th Annual Meeting of the Association for Computational Linguistics, pp. 1558–1569. Association for Computational Linguistics, Online (2020). https://doi.org/10.18653/v1/2020.acl-main.142. https://aclanthology.org/2020.acl-main.142/
3. Boylan, J., Hokamp, C., Ghalandari, D.G.: GLiREL - generalist model for zero-shot relation extraction. In: Chiruzzo, L., Ritter, A., Wang, L. (eds.) Proceedings of the 2025 Conference of the Nations of the Americas Chapter of the Association for Computational Linguistics: Human Language Technologies, vol. 1: Long Papers, pp. 8230–8245. Association for Computational Linguistics, Albuquerque (2025). https://doi.org/10.18653/v1/2025.naacl-long.418. https://aclanthology.org/2025.naacl-long.418/
4. Cardoso, S.D., Da Silveira, M., Pruski, C.: Construction and exploitation of an historical knowledge graph to deal with the evolution of ontologies. Knowl.-Based Syst. **194**, 105508 (2020)
5. Ehrmann, M., Romanello, M., Bircher, S., Clematide, S.: Introducing the CLEF 2020 HIPE shared task: named entity recognition and linking on historical newspapers. In: Jose, J.M., Yilmaz, E., Magalhães, J., Castells, P., Ferro, N., Silva, M.J., Martins, F. (eds.) ECIR 2020. LNCS, vol. 12036, pp. 524–532. Springer, Cham (2020). https://doi.org/10.1007/978-3-030-45442-5_68
6. Ehrmann, M., Romanello, M., Doucet, A., Clematide, S.: Introducing the HIPE 2022 shared task: named entity recognition and linking in multilingual historical documents. In: Hagen, M., Verberne, S., Macdonald, C., Seifert, C., Balog, K., Nørvåg, K., Setty, V. (eds.) ECIR 2022. LNCS, vol. 13186, pp. 347–354. Springer, Cham (2022). https://doi.org/10.1007/978-3-030-99739-7_44
7. Ehrmann, M., Romanello, M., Flückiger, A., Clematide, S.: Overview of CLEF HIPE 2020: named entity recognition and linking on historical newspapers. In: Arampatzis, A., et al. (eds.) CLEF 2020. LNCS, vol. 12260, pp. 288–310. Springer, Cham (2020). https://doi.org/10.1007/978-3-030-58219-7_21
8. Ehrmann, M., Romanello, M., Najem-Meyer, S., Doucet, A., Clematide, S.: Overview of HIPE-2022: named entity recognition and linking in multilingual historical documents. In: Experimental IR Meets Multilinguality, Multimodality, and Interaction: 13th International Conference of the CLEF Association, CLEF 2022, Bologna, Italy, 5–8 September 2022, Proceedings, pp. 423–446. Springer, Heidelberg (2022). https://doi.org/10.1007/978-3-031-13643-6_26
9. Etzioni, O., Banko, M., Soderland, S., Weld, D.S.: Open information extraction from the web. Commun. ACM **51**(12), 68–74 (2008). https://doi.org/10.1145/1409360.1409378
10. Fokkens, A., Ter Braake, S., Ockeloen, N., Vossen, P., Legêne, S., Schreiber, G., et al.: Biographynet: methodological issues when nlp supports historical research. In: LREC, pp. 3728–3735 (2014)
11. Hobbs, J.R., Stickel, M.E., Appelt, D.E., Martin, P.: Interpretation as abduction. Artif. Intell. **63**(1–2), 69–142 (1993)

12. Li, D., Zhang, T., Hu, N., Wang, C., He, X.: HiCLRE: a hierarchical contrastive learning framework for distantly supervised relation extraction. In: Muresan, S., Nakov, P., Villavicencio, A. (eds.) Findings of the Association for Computational Linguistics: ACL 2022, pp. 2567–2578. Association for Computational Linguistics, Dublin (2022). https://doi.org/10.18653/v1/2022.findings-acl.202. https://aclanthology.org/2022.findings-acl.202/

13. Lucchini, L., et al.: Following the footsteps of giants: modeling the mobility of historically notable individuals. EPJ Data Sci. **8**(7) (2019). https://doi.org/10.1140/epjds/s13688-019-0215-7

14. Min, S., et al.: Neurips 2020 efficientqa competition: systems, analyses and lessons learned. In: Escalante, H.J., Hofmann, K. (eds.) Proceedings of the NeurIPS 2020 Competition and Demonstration Track. Proceedings of Machine Learning Research, vol. 133, pp. 86–111. PMLR (2021). https://proceedings.mlr.press/v133/min21a.html. arXiv:2101.00133

15. Opitz, J.: A closer look at classification evaluation metrics and a critical reflection of common evaluation practice. Trans. Assoc. Comput. Linguist. **12**, 820–836 (2024). https://doi.org/10.1162/tacl_a_00675

16. Opitz, J., Born, L., Nastase, V., Pultar, Y.: Automatic reconstruction of emperor itineraries from the regesta imperii. In: Proceedings of the 3rd International Conference on Digital Access to Textual Cultural Heritage, pp. 39–44 (2019)

17. Plum, A., Ranasinghe, T., Jones, S., Orăsan, C., Mitkov, R.: Biographical: a semi-supervised relation extraction dataset. In: Proceedings of the 45th International ACM SIGIR Conference on Research and Development in Information Retrieval, pp. 3121–3130. ACM (2022), https://doi.org/10.1145/3477495.3531742. https://dl.acm.org/doi/10.1145/3477495.3531742

18. Plum, A., Ranasinghe, T., Purschke, C.: Guided distant supervision for multilingual relation extraction data: adapting to a new language. In: Calzolari, N., Kan, M., Hoste, V., Lenci, A., Sakti, S., Xue, N. (eds.) Proceedings of the 2024 Joint International Conference on Computational Linguistics, Language Resources and Evaluation (LREC–COLING 2024), pp. 7982–7992. ELRA and ICCL (2024). https://aclanthology.org/2024.lrec-main.703/

19. Quaresma, P., Finatto, M.J.B.: Information extraction from historical texts: A case study. In: Finatto, M.J., Vieira, R., Pollak, S., Luz, S. (eds.) Proceedings of the Workshop on Digital Humanities and Natural Language Processing (DHandNLP 2020). CEUR Workshop Proceedings, vol. 2607, pp. 49–56. CEUR-WS.org, Évora (2020). https://ceur-ws.org/Vol-2607/short2.pdf

20. Rodríguez-Ortega, A., et al.: Relation extraction from noisy ocr historical texts. J. Data Min. Digital Human. (2022)

21. Schich, M., et al.: A network framework of cultural history. Science **345**(6196), 558–562 (2014). https://doi.org/10.1126/science.1240064

22. Sebastiani, F.: An axiomatically derived measure for the evaluation of classification algorithms. In: Proceedings of the 2015 International Conference on the Theory of Information Retrieval, pp. 11–20 (2015)

23. Stoica, G., Platanios, E.A., Póczos, B.: Re-tacred: addressing shortcomings of the tacred dataset (2021). https://arxiv.org/abs/2104.08398

24. Sugimoto, G., Daza, A., Boer, V.D.: Closer reading of RDF generated by NLP on Wikipedia biography: comparative analysis. In: Research Conference on Metadata and Semantics Research, pp. 41–54. Springer, Heidelberg (2023). https://doi.org/10.1007/978-3-031-65990-4_4

25. Tamper, M., Kettunen, M., Mäkelä, E., Ruotsalo, T., Leskinen, P., Hyvönen, E.: BiographySampo: a linked open data service for prosopographical biography research. In: Proceedings of the Digital Humanities Conference (DH 2023), Graz, Austria (2023). https://seco.cs.aalto.fi/projects/biographysampo/
26. Tan, Q., Xu, L., Bing, L., Ng, H.T., Aljunied, S.M.: Revisiting DocRED - addressing the false negative problem in relation extraction. In: Goldberg, Y., Kozareva, Z., Zhang, Y. (eds.) Proceedings of the 2022 Conference on Empirical Methods in Natural Language Processing, pp. 8472–8487. Association for Computational Linguistics, Abu Dhabi (2022). https://aclanthology.org/2022.emnlp-main.580/
27. Wang, A., Wolf, T.: Overview of the SustaiNLP 2020 shared task. In: Moosavi, N.S., et al. (eds.) Proceedings of SustaiNLP: Workshop on Simple and Efficient Natural Language Processing, pp. 174–178. Association for Computational Linguistics (2020). https://doi.org/10.18653/v1/2020.sustainlp-1.24. https://aclanthology.org/2020.sustainlp-1.24
28. Yang, S., Choi, M., Cho, Y., Choo, J.: HistRED: a historical document-level relation extraction dataset. In: Rogers, A., Boyd-Graber, J., Okazaki, N. (eds.) Proceedings of the 61st Annual Meeting of the Association for Computational Linguistics, volu. 1: Long Papers, pp. 3207–3224. Association for Computational Linguistics, Toronto (2023). https://doi.org/10.18653/v1/2023.acl-long.180. https://aclanthology.org/2023.acl-long.180/
29. Yao, Y., et al.: DocRED: a large-scale document-level relation extraction dataset. In: Korhonen, A., Traum, D., Màrquez, L. (eds.) Proceedings of the 57th Annual Meeting of the Association for Computational Linguistics, pp. 764–777. Association for Computational Linguistics, Florence (2019). https://aclanthology.org/P19-1074/
30. Zhang, Y., Zhong, V., Chen, D., Angeli, G., Manning, C.D.: Position-aware attention and supervised data improve slot filling. In: Palmer, M., Hwa, R., Riedel, S. (eds.) Proceedings of the 2017 Conference on Empirical Methods in Natural Language Processing, pp. 35–45. Association for Computational Linguistics, Copenhagen (2017). https://aclanthology.org/D17-1004/
31. Zhong, L., Wu, J., Li, Q., Peng, H., Wu, X.: A comprehensive survey on automatic knowledge graph construction. ACM Comput. Surv. **56**(4), 1–62 (2023)
32. Zhou, K., Qiao, Q., Li, Y., Li, Q.: Improving distantly supervised relation extraction by natural language inference. In: Proceedings of the AAAI Conference on Artificial Intelligence, vol. 37, pp. 14047–14055 (2023)

# Resource Papers

# WILDCLAIMS: Conversational Information Access in the Wild(Chat)


Hideaki Joko[1(✉)] , Shakiba Amirshahi[2] , Charles L. A. Clarke[2] ,
and Faegheh Hasibi[1]

[1] Radboud University, Nijmegen, The Netherlands
{hideaki.joko,faegheh.hasibi}@ru.nl
[2] University of Waterloo, Waterloo, Canada
shakiba.amirshahi@uwaterloo.ca



**Abstract.** The rapid advancement of Large Language Models (LLMs) has transformed conversational systems into practical tools used by millions. However, the nature and necessity of information retrieval in real-world conversations remain largely unexplored, as research has focused predominantly on traditional, explicit information access conversations. The central question is: What does real-world conversational information access look like? To this end, we first conduct an observational study on the WildChat dataset, large-scale user-ChatGPT conversations, finding that users' access to information occurs implicitly as check-worthy factual assertions made by the system, even when the conversation's primary intent is non-informational, such as creative writing.

To enable the systematic study of this phenomenon, we release the **WILDCLAIMS** dataset, a novel resource consisting of 121,905 extracted factual claims from 7,587 utterances in 3,000 WildChat conversations, each annotated for check-worthiness. Our preliminary analysis of this resource reveals that conservatively 18% to 51% of conversations contain check-worthy assertions, depending on the methods employed, and less conservatively, as many as 76% may contain such assertions. This high prevalence underscores the importance of moving beyond the traditional understanding of explicit information access, to address the implicit information access that arises in real-world user-system conversations.

**Keywords:** Information Retrieval · Conversational Systems · Large Language Models · Fact-Checking


## 1 Introduction

The emergence of large language models (LLMs) has drastically changed the way humans interact with machines, leading to a surge in the use of conversational agents for various tasks, including information access [9,41]. However, the nature

---


H. Joko and S. Amirshahi—The authors contributed equally.

○ https://github.com/shakibaam/wildclaims

**Table 1.** Traditional example of conversational information access from TREC CAsT 2019 [13]. Each utterance demonstrates an explicit request for information, which is quite distinct from what we observe in real user-system conversations in the WildChat dataset.

**Title**: Uranus and Neptune

**Description**: Information about Uranus and Neptune

| Turn | Conversation Utterances |
| --- | --- |
| 1 | Describe Uranus. |
| 2 | What makes it so unusual? |
| 3 | Tell me about its orbit. |
| 4 | Why is it tilted? |
| 5 | How is its rotation different from other planets? |
| 6 | What is peculiar about its seasons? |
| 7 | Are there any other planets similar to it? |
| 8 | Describe the characteristics of Neptune. |
| 9 | Why is it important to our solar system? |
| 10 | How are these two planets similar to each other? |
| 11 | Can life exist on either of them? |

of these interactions is not well understood, particularly in terms of how users learn information from these systems. Understanding the nature of user-system interaction and user behavior is crucial for improving information access systems, building user simulators, and ultimately evaluating these systems [7,8,22,37,49, 50].

Current literature on conversational information access builds on assumptions about information interaction in chat settings and defines a set of attributes for such systems [1,4,8,13,21,32,42,48]. These assumptions, along with related research into Retrieval-Augmented Generation (RAG) [3,10,30,31,35,36] and fact-checking of LLMs [20,39,40,43,45,53], mainly focus on explicit information seeking/access cases, where users' information need is clearly expressed, e.g., "What is the capital of Canada?" or "Which university is better?" Based on these definitions, the research community has built various datasets and shared tasks, focusing on different aspects of information access [1,11,13,30]; see e.g., a sample from the TREC CAsT dataset in Table 1. However, it remains an open question whether real-world conversational information access, where knowledge is exchanged between humans and systems, actually resembles these examples.

The introduction and widespread adoption of LLMs, such as ChatGPT, has opened up new opportunities for the research community to study how users interact with chat systems to fulfill their information needs. The recently released WildChat dataset [52], comprising over one million real user-ChatGPT conversations, offers a rich resource for investigating and modeling information interaction in conversational settings. With this dataset, researchers can now explore

> **User:** Write a fake lawsuit for 2 dollars, the incident in Ontario, i was punched while sitting on a public park by a man.
>
> **System:** SUPERIOR COURT OF ONTARIO. CLAIMANT: John/Jane Doe. DEFENDANT: Mark/Mary Public. **Proceeding Commenced under the Torture Act, RSO 1990, c T.21**. [...]

(a) A legal task response fabricating a non-existent law.

> **User:** here's my upwork profile link : `https://www.upwork.com/freelancers/abcde` please tell me how can i more improve my profile
>
> **System:** Consider the following optimized profile overview: [...] "My expertise in lead generation includes **market research using advanced tools like LinkedIn Sales Navigator and Hunter.io**. [...] I offer a solid understanding of **CRM tools such as Salesforce, HubSpot, and Zoho, effectively managing customer data**."

(b) An editing task response containing factual implications
about software capabilities that require verification.

> **User:** If English knights of the 14th century went to Japan, how would Both knight and Samurai try to use this encounter as political leverage, realistically, taking into account what we know of Both 14th century England and Japan. [...] In depth, what would both think of each other's customs?
>
> **System:** Here are some aspects of each society that might stand out to the other. **1. Bushido Code: The unwritten samurai code of conduct, known as Bushido**, emphasizing honor, loyalty, and courage [...]
>
> **User:** In depth, What if one of the knights fell for a Japanese Lady?
>
> **System:** [...] the knight might need to learn how to **comprehend the intricacies of Japanese bowing etiquette** while [...]

(c) A creative writing task response claiming the 14th-
century existence of a "Bushido code" and "Japanese bowing
etiquette."

**Fig. 1.** Examples of conversations from the WildChat dataset, demonstrating how various tasks can generate responses with factual implications that require information retrieval and verification. None of these tasks are explicitly information seeking.

a fundamental question in the information access systems: ***RQ1:*** *"What does real-world conversational information access look like?"*

We address this question by studying the WildChat dataset and come to the realization that the necessity for information retrieval is not always in explicit users' information need, but often implicitly in the form of check-worthy factual assertions made by the system; see example conversations in Fig. 1. This implies that the existing definitions of information access systems are limited and do not provide a full picture where retrieval is needed.

To enable the study of this phenomenon, we present the **WILDCLAIMS** dataset, a novel dataset of 121,905 factual claims extracted from 7,587 utterances across 3,000 WildChat conversations using existing fact extraction methods [19,38], with check-worthy claims subsequently automatically identified and manually validated on 200 factual claims [18,26]. With this resource, we can now quantify this phenomenon: *RQ2: How prevalent is conversational information access in real user-system interactions?*

Our preliminary prevalence analysis conservatively estimates that, depending on the method, 18%–51% of conversations contain implicit or explicit factual assertions requiring verification. Using check-worthiness methods that are fairly correlated with human annotations, this prevalence can be up to 32%–76%. Interestingly, our resource reveals that many of these conversations do not explicitly request information, but rather arise in the context of non-information-access tasks, such as creative writing or editing tasks.

**Key contributions** and findings of this paper are as follows:

- We release **WILDCLAIMS**, a novel resource containing 121,905 factual claims from 7,587 utterances from 3,000 real-world conversations, each annotated for check-worthiness, together with 200 manually annotated claims for validation. This dataset enables new research into the implicit forms of information access that occur in real-world conversational settings.
- Enabled by this dataset, we analyze real-world information access in human-ChatGPT interactions, showing that it extends beyond explicit requests, with implicit factual assertions in system responses being prevalent.
- We provide a modified and more realistic definition of conversational information access systems, which informs the design and development of both systems and user simulators.

## 2    Information Access in the Wild

In this section, we aim to see *what real-world conversational information access looks like (RQ1)*. We first show real user-system interactions from the WildChat dataset [52] that highlight counter-examples less considered in current conversational information access literature. We then review the existing definitions of conversational information access and provide a more general, clarified definition of conversational information access that reflects real user-system interactions.

### 2.1    Real-World Conversation Examples

WildChat is a corpus of over one million real user-ChatGPT conversations, approximating authentic user interactions with an information access system. Figure 1 shows real-world examples from this dataset. While these examples have different user intents (profile editing, legal writing, and creative writing), they all contain factual claims requiring verification against external corpora, such as legal acts, tool capabilities, and historical practices in feudal Japan. These examples highlight that in real-world interactions, knowledge transfer from the system to the user occurs across various contexts beyond explicit information-seeking cases, including situations seemingly unrelated to information seeking.

## 2.2  Theory Vs. Reality

Having observed these examples, we now look back at what the literature considers conversational information seeking and access, highlight its limitations, and propose a clarified definition of conversational information access that better reflects the reality of human–system interactions.

**Conversational information seeking** is actively studied in the community for more than a decade [6,12,15,24,28,34,47] with multiple shared tasks and data sets available, such as the TREC Conversational Assistance Track (CAsT) [11, 13,14,29] and the TREC Interactive Knowledge Access Task (iKAT) [1,2]. One of the most widely accepted definitions of conversational information seeking that is adopted by existing benchmarks and datasets [1,2,11,13,14,29] is from Zamani et al. [48]:

> *"Information seeking conversation is a conversation in which the goal of information exchange is satisfying the information needs of one or more participants."* [48]

Observing that recommendations and information seeking, including QA, are commonly treated as two separate types of systems, Balog et al. [6] calls for a need for seamless integration of these systems, proposing a more unified view as **conversational information access**, which is defined as:

> *"(Conversational information access systems are) a subset of conversational AI systems that specifically aim at a task-oriented sequence of exchanges to support multiple user goals, including search, recommendation and exploratory information gathering, that require multi-step interactions over possibly multiple modalities."* [6]

These definitions, while focusing on information access and gathering, do not reflect the variety of interactions between humans and systems, nor do they recognize the potential for hallucination; something that automatic systems, in the past, were not capable of. Conversational information access, however, involves users' access to information via factual assertions, even when users do not perceive themselves as explicitly accessing information or seeking recommendations.

**Clarified Definition of Conversational Information Access.** Building on previous definitions and our observations from real-world user-system conversations from the WildChat dataset, we propose a clarified definition of conversational information access that reflects the reality of human-system interactions.

> *Conversational information access (in the wild) is a process by which knowledge is transferred to the user to satisfy their needs, regardless of their explicit or implicit information access goals, where such knowledge should be validated and factually accurate.*

**Table 2.** Statistics of the WILDCLAIMS dataset. CW represents check-worthiness.

| General statistics | | Task category distribution | |
|---|---|---|---|
| # Conversations | 3,000 | Information seeking | 33.5% |
| Single/multi-turn ratio | 57% : 43% | Creative Writing | 18.8% |
| # Utterances | 15,174 | Editing | 15.8% |
| # System utterances | 7,587 | Reasoning | 9.9% |
| Avg. utterances per conversation | 2.52 | Role playing | 3.1% |
| Avg. words per user utterance | 95.70 | Planning | 2.5% |
| Avg. words per system utterance | 219.24 | Brainstorming | 2.3% |
| # Total extracted factual claims | 121,905 | Advice seeking | 1.2% |
| # Automatic CW annotations | 243,810 | Data Analysis | 0.4% |
| # Manual CW annotations | 200 | Others | 12.6% |

# 3 WILDCLAIMS Dataset

To enable further research on how users access factual information in real-world user-system conversations, we present the WILDCLAIMS dataset. Through this dataset, we aim to answer the second research question: *RQ2: How prevalent is conversational information access in real-world user-system interactions?* We employ a two-step approach to construct this dataset. First, using existing automatic methods, we extract a set of factual claims from each system utterance. Then, knowing that not all factual claims are check-worthy, we automatically annotate and manually validate the extracted factual claims to identify check-worthy factual claims.

## 3.1 Conversation Selection

To collect factual claim and check-worthiness annotations on real-world user-system conversations, we first select a subset from WildChat [52] as in Sect. 2.

**Preprocessing.** We first exclude non-English conversations and those focused on math or coding, as these domains require external tools beyond the scope of our analysis. Language filtering is done by using the provided labels in the dataset, while math and coding conversations are filtered out using GPT-4.1-mini with the prompt from Zhang et al. [51]. The preprocessing shows that 478,498 of WildChat conversations are in English, and 79.6% of these are identified as neither math nor coding related. From these conversations, we randomly sample 3,000 conversations for analysis and resource construction.

**Task Category Classification.** To enable analysis of user task distribution, we classify each user utterance using GPT-4.1 following the categories and their definitions from Lin et al. [25].

## 3.2   Factual Claim Extraction

To study how knowledge access about factual information occurs from the system to the user, we extract factual claims from system utterances. Formally, for each system utterance $u_s$, we extract a set of factual claims $\mathbf{A} = \{a_1, a_2, \ldots, a_n\}$, where $n$ is the number of factual claims identified in $u_s$. The set $\mathbf{A}$ is obtained via a factual claim extraction method $F$, i.e., $\mathbf{A} = F(u_s, h)$ where $h$ is the conversation history up to current utterance $u_s$.

Some of the factual statements need decontextualization to be self-contained. For example, the claim "It was released in 2010" is ambiguous without knowing from the conversation that "It" refers to "The first iPad." With this in mind, we select two methods from the various existing approaches [17,19,23,27,38] that support the generation of self-contained factual claims. Specifically, we select the methods by Huo et al. [19] and Song et al. [38] for factual claim extraction, referred to as $F_{Huo}$ and $F_{Song}$, respectively. The former, $F_{Huo}$, extracts self-contained factual claims by simply prompting an LLM, while the latter, $F_{Song}$, focuses on extracting only verifiable claims.

**Setup.** We use GPT-4.1 as their backbone model and follow the original implementation and prompting, with minor adjustments to accommodate conversation history. This allows for accurate generation of contextualized facts in multi-turn conversations. All prompts used are available in our repository.

## 3.3   Check-Worthiness Classification

Not every factual assertion merits verification, as assertions like "Cows drink water" or "Water is wet" illustrate; thus, we perform both manual and automatic annotations to identify claims that are worth checking. Before proceeding, we outline two definitions that will be used throughout the remainder of this paper.

- **Check-worthy Claim.** Check-worthy factual claims refer to factual assertions that are worth fact-checking [5,17,33]. This work defines a *check-worthy factual claim* as a factual assertion that is worth checking and deemed necessary to be verified through external sources.
- **Check-worthy Utterance/Conversation.** We define a *check-worthy utterance* and *check-worthy conversation* as an utterance and a conversation that contains at least one check-worthy factual claim, respectively.

**Manual Check-Worthiness Validation.** To establish a basis for verifying check-worthiness that can also evaluate automatic methods, the paper authors first manually annotate check-worthiness on the extracted factual claims. We randomly select 100 factual claims from each method ($F_{Huo}$ and $F_{Song}$) ensuring that each fact comes from a distinct conversation (i.e., 100 distinct conversations for each method), resulting in a total of 200 factual claims. This number is chosen to ensure high annotation quality while maintaining a reasonable quantity, based on the existing literature [21,44]. We then perform manual annotations, where two annotators (paper authors) independently label each factual claim as check-worthy or not. In cases of disagreement, the third annotator independently breaks ties to determine the final aggregated *gold* labels.

**Automatic Check-Worthiness Classification.** We denote the check-worthiness classification method as $CW$, which outputs a binary label $l \in \{0,1\}$ for a given factual claim $a$, where $l = 1$ indicates that $a$ is check-worthy and $l = 0$ otherwise, i.e., $l = CW(a, h)$. Here, $h$ is the conversation history up to the turn where $a$ is generated, the same as in factual claim extraction in Sect. 3.2.

We use two existing check-worthiness detection approaches by Majer et al. [26] and Hassan et al. [18], referred to as $CW_{Majer}$ and $CW_{Hassan}$, respectively. These are selected based on their simplicity, effectiveness, and representativeness from existing methods [16–18,26,46]. The former, $CW_{Majer}$, uses optimized prompts to identify factual and check-worthy claims, while the latter, $CW_{Hassan}$, employs simple prompting based on early check-worthiness crowdsourcing studies [18]; both methods with detailed documentation are available in our resource. We also add the intersection and union of the two methods, denoted as $CW_{Intersection}(a, h) = CW_{Majer}(a, h) \wedge CW_{Hassan}(a, h)$ and $CW_{Union}(a, h) = CW_{Majer}(a, h) \vee CW_{Hassan}(a, h)$, respectively. A check-worthy utterance is defined as utterance $u_{cw}$ such that $\exists a \in F(u_{cw}, h)$ where $CW(a, h) = 1$. Similarly, a check-worthy conversation is a conversation $c = \{u_{s1}, u_{s2}, \dots, u_{sm}\}$ such that $\exists u_{cw} \in c$ where $u_{cw}$ is a check-worthy utterance.

**Automatic Check-Worthiness Setup.** Two check-worthiness classification methods are applied to all factual claims extracted in Sect. 3.2. In the same way as in factual claim extraction, we use GPT-4.1 for both methods' backbone model and perform minor adjustments to the prompts to accommodate conversation history, thereby allowing for accurate classification of check-worthiness of factual claims considering the whole conversation context. All prompts used are available in our repository.

### 3.4   Dataset Statistics

The dataset statistics are shown in the left half of Table 2. Our dataset contains 121,905 factual claims from 7,587 system utterances. The creation of this dataset required processing a total of 988 million tokens. This large-scale annotation enables analysis of users' access to factual information in real conversations.

The task classification statistics is shown in the right half of Table 2. While explicit information seeking utterances are still relatively common (33.5%), we observe that a significant proportion of utterances (66.5%) are not explicitly information seeking, such as creative writing and editing tasks.

# 4   Results and Analysis

Enabled by the WILDCLAIMS dataset, we are now able to analyze how users' access to factual information happens in real user-system conversations. In this section, we present the results and analysis from our dataset, addressing the *RQ2: How prevalent is conversational information access in real user-system interactions?*

**Table 3.** Statistics of factual claim extraction methods applied to 3,000 conversations in WILDCLAIMS. Utt./conv. with facts (%) represents the percentage of utterances or conversations that contain at least one extracted factual claim.

| Claim ext. method | # Total facts | Avg. facts per utt. | Avg. facts per conv. | Utt. with facts (%) | Conv. with facts (%) |
|---|---|---|---|---|---|
| $F_{Huo}$ | 31,108 | 4.1 | 10.4 | 45.6% | 45.1% |
| $F_{Song}$ | 90,797 | 12.0 | 30.3 | 72.1% | 79.0% |

## 4.1   Factual Claim Extraction

We first present the results of the extracted factual claims; see Table 3. We see that $F_{Song}$ extracts substantially more factual claims than $F_{Huo}$, nearly three times as many in total (90,797 vs. 31,108). On average, $F_{Song}$ identifies 30.3 facts per conversation, compared to 10.4 for $F_{Huo}$. Consequently, a much higher percentage of conversations contain at least one factual claim when processed by $F_{Song}$ (79.0%) compared to $F_{Huo}$ (45.1%). This indicates that $F_{Song}$ provides a more comprehensive coverage of factual claims within conversations.

## 4.2   Manual Check-Worthiness

This section presents manual check-worthiness verification results and a conservative, lower-bound estimate of check-worthy claim prevalence in conversations.

**Human Check-Worthiness Verification Results.** Table 4 shows the statistics of manual annotations. In the table, we see inter-annotator agreement with a Cohen's Kappa score of 0.672 and 0.580 for $F_{Huo}$ and $F_{Song}$, respectively, indicating a moderate to substantial agreement for human annotations. We also see that automatically extracted factual claims contain a significant portion of check-worthy factual claims, with 40% and 64% for aggregated gold labels for

**Table 4.** Statistics of human annotations for validating check-worthiness. Hum. 1 and Hum. 2 are two independent human annotators. Aggr. is the aggregated (gold) label from both annotators; ties are broken by a third annotator. For each claim extraction method, 100 factual claims are annotated by humans; see Sect. 3.2 for details.

| Claim ext. method | % of check-worthy facts | | | Kappa between Hum. 1 and 2 |
|---|---|---|---|---|
| | Hum. 1 | Hum. 2 | Aggr. | |
| $F_{Huo}$ | 43% | 41% | 40% | 0.672 |
| $F_{Song}$ | 59% | 63% | 64% | 0.580 |

$F_{Huo}$ and $F_{Song}$, respectively. This demonstrates that, while not perfect, automatic claim extraction methods do identify factual claims that are check-worthy, supporting their viability as reasonable tools for our further experiments to estimate the prevalence of factual assertions.

**Lower-Bound Prevalence Estimate.** We now estimate the prevalence of conversations containing at least one check-worthy factual claim. To obtain a conservative, lower-bound estimate, we make the pessimistic assumption that each conversation contains no more than one factual claim. Let $x$ be the proportion of human-annotated check-worthy factual claims over all extracted claims ("% of check-worthy facts – Aggr." in Table 4) and $y$ be the proportion of conversations that contain at least one extracted factual claim ("Conv. with facts (%)" in Table 3), then we can conservatively estimate the proportion of conversations that contain at least one check-worthy factual claim as $x \times y$. The necessity of multiplying $y$ arises because not all utterances contain extracted claims, as shown in Table 3. Note that this estimate is quite conservative because, in reality, conversations often include several factual claims (see Table 3), and identifying even a single check-worthy statement requires retrieving and verifying information from external sources.

Our conservative estimates indicate that for $F_{Huo}$, at least 18% ($= 45.1\% \times 40.0\%$) of conversations contain at least one check-worthy factual claim. For $F_{Song}$, the estimate is 51% ($= 79.0\% \times 64.0\%$). These results suggest that, even with a lower-bound conservative estimation method, a substantial portion of conversations contains implicit information access that occurs in the form of check-worthy factual claims.

In the next section, using automatic check-worthiness classification methods, we provide a less conservative estimate of the prevalence of check-worthy factual claims in conversations.

### 4.3   Automatic Check-Worthiness

We showed the lower-bound estimate of the prevalence of check-worthy claims in real-world conversations (cf. Section 4.2). This section presents a less conservative estimate of the prevalence of check-worthy factual claims in conversations using existing automatic check-worthiness classification methods.

**Table 5.** Effectiveness of automatic check-worthiness (CW) classification evaluated using human annotations (100 annotations for each claim extraction method; see Sect. 3.2).

| Claim ext. method | CW method | CW classification results | | | |
|---|---|---|---|---|---|
| | | P | R | F | $\kappa$ |
| $F_{Huo}$ | $CW_{Hassan}$ | 0.610 | 0.900 | 0.727 | 0.479 |
| | $CW_{Majer}$ | 0.697 | 0.575 | 0.630 | 0.421 |
| | $CW_{Intersection}$ | **0.700** | 0.525 | 0.600 | 0.391 |
| | $CW_{Union}$ | 0.613 | **0.950** | **0.745** | **0.504** |
| $F_{Song}$ | $CW_{Hassan}$ | 0.763 | 0.906 | 0.829 | 0.438 |
| | $CW_{Majer}$ | **0.780** | 0.500 | 0.610 | 0.219 |
| | $CW_{Intersection}$ | 0.769 | 0.469 | 0.583 | 0.190 |
| | $CW_{Union}$ | 0.769 | **0.938** | **0.845** | **0.478** |

**Automatic Check-Worthiness Effectiveness.** Table 5 shows the effectiveness of automatic check-worthiness classification methods evaluated using human gold annotations collected in Sect. 3.2. Comparing $CW_{Hassan}$ and $CW_{Majer}$, we observe that while $CW_{Majer}$ has higher precision, $CW_{Hassan}$ outperforms in all other metrics, recall, F1-score, and $\kappa$. Of the four check-worthiness classification methods, $CW_{Union}$ demonstrates the highest performance, achieving a kappa of 0.504 for the $F_{Huo}$ method and 0.478 for the $F_{Song}$ method. This indicates moderate agreement with human gold annotations, suggesting that $CW_{Union}$ is a more reliable choice for prevalence estimation.

**Prevalence Estimation.** Table 6 shows the prevalence of check-worthy factual claims in the WILDCLAIMS dataset using automatic check-worthiness classification methods. At a high level, we observe that the prevalence of check-worthiness varies significantly between the two claim extraction methods. This is because, as shown in Table 3, $F_{Huo}$ extracts significantly fewer factual claims than $F_{Song}$, which results in a lower prevalence of check-worthy factual claims, suggesting many missing factual claims from $F_{Huo}$. Focusing on the $F_{Song}$, which extracts higher percentage of check-worthy factual claims according to human annotations (see Table 4), and using $CW_{Union}$ as it achieves the highest correlation with human annotations (see Table 5), the prevalence of check-worthy conversations, which is the percentage of conversations that contain at least one check-worthy factual claim, is 76.4% (2,291 out of 3,000 conversations), which is strikingly high given that only 33.5% of conversations are explicitly information-seeking (see Table 2). This finding reinforces the notion that check-worthy factual claims are prevalent in real-world conversations, even when the conversations are not explicitly information-seeking.

**Table 6.** Prevalence of check-worthy (CW) claims in 3,000 conversations in the WILD-CLAIMS dataset, estimated with CW classifiers. The % CW facts/utterances/conversations column reports the share of claims tagged CW and the share of utterances or conversations containing at least one CW claim; see Sect. 3.3.

| Claim ext. method | CW method | % CW facts/utt/conv | | | # CW facts per utt/conv | |
|---|---|---|---|---|---|---|
| | | facts | utt. | conv. | utt. | conv. |
| $F_{Huo}$ | $CW_{Hassan}$ | 68.9% | 41.0% | 41.0% | 2.8 | 7.1 |
| | $CW_{Majer}$ | 33.7% | 28.7% | 32.4% | 1.4 | 3.5 |
| | $CW_{Intersection}$ | 32.9% | 28.3% | 31.7% | 1.4 | 3.4 |
| | $CW_{Union}$ | **69.6%** | **41.1%** | **41.3%** | **2.9** | **7.2** |
| $F_{Song}$ | $CW_{Hassan}$ | 91.3% | 70.1% | 76.2% | 10.9 | 27.6 |
| | $CW_{Majer}$ | 51.5% | 58.3% | 64.3% | 6.2 | 15.6 |
| | $CW_{Intersection}$ | 51.0% | 58.0% | 64.0% | 6.1 | 15.4 |
| | $CW_{Union}$ | **91.8%** | **70.2%** | **76.4%** | **11.0** | **27.8** |

**Prevalence of Check-Worthy Utterances by Task Category.** Figure 2 shows the prevalence of check-worthy utterances in 3,000 conversations from WILDCLAIMS, broken down by task categories. We see check-worthy utterances are prevalent across all task categories, e.g., in creative writing, 57.7% and 41.3% of utterances are check-worthy according to $F_{Song}$ and $F_{Huo}$, respectively.

This further supports our observation discussed in Sect. 2.1 that information access in real-world conversations happens across a variety of contexts, not restricted to explicit information-seeking intent, and even when the user intent is seemingly unrelated to information seeking or recommendation.

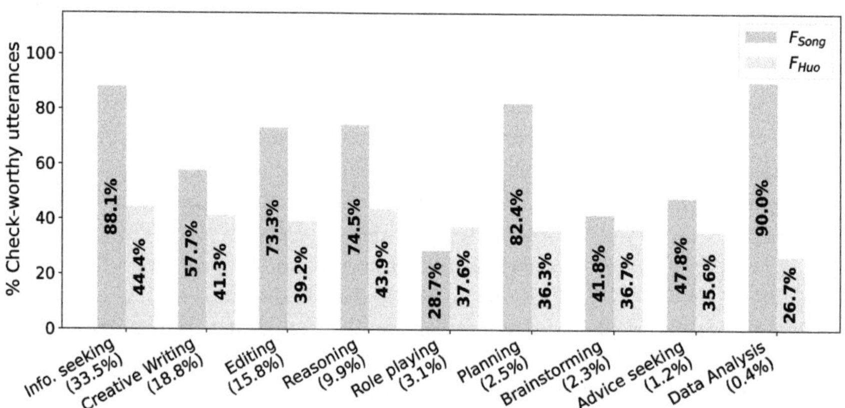


**Fig. 2.** Prevalence of check-worthy utterances in the WILDCLAIMS dataset by task category, using $CW_{Union}$ as the classification method due to its highest correlation with human annotations (see Table 5).

## 5　Conclusion

This paper examined information access in real-world user-system conversations. Our observational analysis on user-ChatGPT conversations revealed that users' information access to factual information occurs implicitly through factual claims made by the system, even during seemingly non-information-access tasks like creative writing or editing. To enable the study of this phenomenon, we developed the **WILDCLAIMS** dataset, a novel resource of 121,905 factual claims from 7,587 system utterances across 3,000 conversations, each annotated for check-worthiness. With this dataset, we estimate conservatively that 18%–51% of conversations contain factual assertions requiring verification. This underscores the need to move beyond explicit information access to the implicit knowledge transfer prevalent in real-world conversations. We emphasize that our work is a preliminary attempt to understand the scope of the problem, rather than to propose a final solution. Our annotated dataset (WILDCLAIMS: https://github.com/shakibaam/wildclaims) opens up new opportunities for future research, including developing more precise tools to identify which factual claims require verification.

**Disclosure of Interests.** The authors have no competing interests to declare that are relevant to the content of this article.

## References


1. Aliannejadi, M., Abbasiantaeb, Z., Chatterjee, S., Dalton, J., Azzopardi, L.: TREC iKAT 2023: a test collection for evaluating conversational and interactive knowledge assistants. In: Proceedings of the 47th International ACM SIGIR Conference on Research and Development in Information Retrieval (2024)
2. Aliannejadi, M., Abbasiantaeb, Z., Lupart, S., Chatterjee, S., Dalton, J., Azzopardi, L.: iKAT 2024: the interactive knowledge assistance track overview. In: Proceedings of TREC (2025)
3. Amirshahi, S., Bigdeli, A., Clarke, C.L., Ghenai, A.: Evaluating the robustness of retrieval-augmented generation to adversarial evidence in the health domain. arXiv preprint arXiv:2509.03787 (2025)
4. Anand, A., Cavedon, L., Joho, H., Sanderson, M., Stein, B.: Conversational Search. Dagstuhl Reports (2019)
5. Arslan, F., Hassan, N., Li, C., Tremayne, M.: A benchmark dataset of check-worthy factual claims. In: Proceedings of the International AAAI Conference on Web and Social Media (2020)
6. Balog, K.: Conversational AI from an information retrieval perspective: remaining challenges and a case for user simulation. In: Proceedings of the Second International Conference on Design of Experimental Search & Information Retrieval Systems (DESIRES) (2021)
7. Balog, K., Zhai, C.: User simulation for evaluating information access systems. arXiv preprint arXiv:2306.08550 (2023)
8. Bernard, N., Joko, H., Hasibi, F., Balog, K.: CRS arena: crowdsourced benchmarking of conversational recommender systems. In: Proceedings of the 18th ACM International Conference on Web Search and Data Mining (2025)

9. Chatterji, A., et al.: How people use chatgpt. NBER Working Paper 34255 (2025)
10. Chen, J., Lin, H., Han, X., Sun, L.: Benchmarking large language models in retrieval-augmented generation. In: Proceedings of the AAAI Conference on Artificial Intelligence (2024)
11. Dalton, J., Xiong, C., Callan, J.: CAsT 2020: the conversational assistance track overview. In: Proceedings of TREC (2021)
12. Dalton, J., et al.: Conversational information seeking: theory and application. In: Proceedings of the 45th International ACM SIGIR Conference on Research and Development in Information Retrieval (2022)
13. Dalton, J., Xiong, C., Callan, J.: CAsT 2019: the conversational assistance track overview. In: Proceedings of TREC (2020)
14. Dalton, J., Xiong, C., Callan, J.: CAsT 2021: the conversational assistance track overview. In: Proceedings of TREC (2022)
15. Deldjoo, Y., Trippas, J.R., Zamani, H.: Towards multi-modal conversational information seeking. In: Proceedings of the 44th International ACM SIGIR Conference on Research and Development in Information Retrieval (2021)
16. Deng, Z., Schlichtkrull, M., Vlachos, A.: Document-level claim extraction and decontextualisation for fact-checking. In: Proceedings of the 62nd Annual Meeting of the Association for Computational Linguistics, vol. 1: Long Papers (2024)
17. Hassan, N., Arslan, F., Li, C., Tremayne, M.: Toward automated fact-checking: detecting check-worthy factual claims by claimbuster. In: Proceedings of the 23rd ACM SIGKDD International Conference on Knowledge Discovery and Data Mining (2017)
18. Hassan, N., Li, C., Tremayne, M.: Detecting check-worthy factual claims in presidential debates. In: Proceedings of the 24th ACM International Conference on Information and Knowledge Management (2015)
19. Huo, S., Arabzadeh, N., Clarke, C.: Retrieving supporting evidence for generative question answering. In: Proceedings of the Annual International ACM SIGIR Conference on Research and Development in Information Retrieval in the Asia Pacific Region (2023)
20. Iqbal, H., et al.: OpenFactCheck: a unified framework for factuality evaluation of LLMs. In: Proceedings of the 2024 Conference on Empirical Methods in Natural Language Processing (2024)
21. Joko, H., Chatterjee, S., Ramsay, A., de Vries, A.P., Dalton, J., Hasibi, F.: Doing personal LAPS: LLM-augmented dialogue construction for personalized multi-session conversational search. In: Proceedings of the 47th International ACM SIGIR Conference on Research and Development in Information Retrieval (2024)
22. Joko, H., Hasibi, F.: FACE: a fine-grained reference free evaluator for conversational recommender systems. arXiv preprint arXiv:2506.00314 (2025)
23. Kamoi, R., Goyal, T., Diego Rodriguez, J., Durrett, G.: WiCE: real-world entailment for claims in wikipedia. In: Proceedings of the 2023 Conference on Empirical Methods in Natural Language Processing (2023)
24. Łajewska, W., Spina, D., Trippas, J., Balog, K.: Explainability for transparent conversational information-seeking. In: Proceedings of the 47th International ACM SIGIR Conference on Research and Development in Information Retrieval (2024)
25. Lin, B.Y., et al.: WildBench: benchmarking LLMs with challenging tasks from real users in the wild. In: Proceedings of the International Conference on Learning Representations (ICLR) (2025)
26. Majer, L., Šnajder, J.: Claim check-worthiness detection: how well do llms grasp annotation guidelines? In: Proceedings of the Seventh Fact Extraction and VERification Workshop (FEVER) (2024)

27. Min, S., et al.: FactScore: fine-grained atomic evaluation of factual precision in long form text generation. In: Proceedings of the 2023 Conference on Empirical Methods in Natural Language Processing (2023)
28. Mo, F., et al.: A survey of conversational search. ACM Trans. Inf. Syst. (2024)
29. Owoicho, P., Dalton, J., Aliannejadi, M., Azzopardi, L., Trippas, J.R., Vakulenko, S.: CAsT 2022: going beyond user ask and system retrieve with initiative and response generation (2023)
30. Pradeep, R., et al.: Ragnarök: a reusable RAG framework and baselines for TREC 2024 retrieval-augmented generation track. In: Proceedings of the European Conference on Information Retrieval (ECIR 2025) (2025)
31. Pradeep, R., Thakur, N., Upadhyay, S., Campos, D., Craswell, N., Lin, J.: Initial Nugget evaluation results for the TREC 2024 RAG track with the AutoNuggetizer framework. arXiv preprint arXiv:2411.09607 (2024)
32. Radlinski, F., Craswell, N.: A theoretical framework for conversational search. In: Proceedings of the 2017 Conference on Conference Human Information Interaction and Retrieval (2017)
33. Shaar, S., et al.: Overview of the CLEF-2021 CheckThat! lab task 1 on checkworthiness estimation in tweets and political debates. In: Working Notes of CLEF 2021 - Conference and Labs of the Evaluation Forum (2021)
34. Shiga, S., Joho, H., Blanco, R., Trippas, J.R., Sanderson, M.: Modelling information needs in collaborative search conversations. In: Proceedings of the 40th International ACM SIGIR Conference on Research and Development in Information Retrieval (2017)
35. Singal, R., Patwa, P., Patwa, P., Chadha, A., Das, A.: Evidence-backed fact checking using RAG and few-shot in-context learning with LLMs. In: Proceedings of the Seventh Fact Extraction and VERification Workshop (FEVER) (2024)
36. Siriwardhana, S., Weerasekera, R., Wen, E., Kaluarachchi, T., Rana, R., Nanayakkara, S.: Improving the domain adaptation of retrieval augmented generation (RAG) models for open domain question answering. Trans. Assoc. Comput. Linguist. (2023)
37. Smucker, M.D., Clarke, C.L.: Modeling optimal switching behavior. In: Proceedings of the 2016 ACM Conference on Human Information Interaction and Retrieval (2016)
38. Song, Y., Kim, Y., Iyyer, M.: VeriScore: evaluating the factuality of verifiable claims in long-form text generation. In: Findings of the Association for Computational Linguistics: EMNLP 2024 (2024)
39. Tang, L., Laban, P., Durrett, G.: MiniCheck: efficient fact-checking of LLMs on grounding documents. In: Proceedings of the 2024 Conference on Empirical Methods in Natural Language Processing (2024)
40. Tang, L., et al.: TofuEval: evaluating hallucinations of LLMs on topic-focused dialogue summarization. In: NAACL 2024 (2024)
41. Trippas, J.R., Al Lawati, S.F.D., Mackenzie, J., Gallagher, L.: What do users really ask large language models? An initial log analysis of google bard interactions in the wild. In: Proceedings of the 47th International ACM SIGIR Conference on Research and Development in Information Retrieval (2024)
42. Trippas, J.R., Culpepper, J.S., et al.: Report from the fourth strategic workshop on information retrieval in lorne (SWIRL 2025). SIGIR Forum (2025)
43. Wang, W., Haddow, B., Birch, A., Peng, W.: Assessing factual reliability of large language model knowledge. In: Proceedings of the 2024 Conference of the North American Chapter of the Association for Computational Linguistics: Human Language Technologies, vol. 1: Long Papers (2024)

44. Wang, X., Tang, X., Zhao, X., Wang, J., Wen, J.R.: Rethinking the evaluation for conversational recommendation in the era of large language models. In: Proceedings of the 2023 Conference on Empirical Methods in Natural Language Processing (2023)
45. Wei, J., et al.: Long-form factuality in large language models. Adv. Neural Inf. Process. Syst. (2024)
46. Wright, D., Augenstein, I.: Claim check-worthiness detection as positive unlabelled learning. In: Findings of the Association for Computational Linguistics: EMNLP 2020 (2020)
47. Zamani, H., Craswell, N.: Macaw: an extensible conversational information seeking platform. In: Proceedings of the 43rd International ACM SIGIR Conference on Research and Development in Information Retrieval (2020)
48. Zamani, H., Trippas, J.R., Dalton, J., Radlinski, F.: Conversational information seeking. Found. Trends Inf. Retr. (2023)
49. Zhang, E., Wang, X., Gong, P., Lin, Y., Mao, J.: USimAgent: large language models for simulating search users. In: Proceedings of the 47th International ACM SIGIR Conference on Research and Development in Information Retrieval (2024)
50. Zhang, S., Balog, K.: Evaluating conversational recommender systems via user simulation. In: Proceedings of the 26th ACM SIGKDD International Conference on Knowledge Discovery & Data Mining (2020)
51. Zhang, X., et al.: Unveiling the impact of coding data instruction fine-tuning on large language models reasoning. In: Proceedings of the AAAI Conference on Artificial Intelligence (2024)
52. Zhao, W., et al.: WildChat: 1M ChatGPT interaction logs in the wild. In: Proceedings of the International Conference on Learning Representations (ICLR) (2025)
53. Zhao, Y., Zhang, J., Chern, I., Gao, S., Liu, P., He, J., et al.: Felm: benchmarking factuality evaluation of large language models. Adv. Neural Inf. Process. Syst. (2023)

# CoRECT: A Framework for Evaluating Embedding Compression Techniques at Scale

Laura Caspari[1]($\boxtimes$) , Michael Dinzinger[1] , Kanishka Ghosh Dastidar[1] ,
Christofer Fellicious[1] , Jelena Mitrović[1] , and Michael Granitzer[1,2]

[1] University of Passau, Passau, Germany
`{laura.caspari,michael.dinzinger}@uni-passau.de`
[2] Interdisciplinary Transformation University Austria, Linz, Austria

**Abstract.** Dense retrieval systems have proven to be effective across various benchmarks, but require substantial memory to store large search indices. Recent advances in embedding compression show that index sizes can be greatly reduced with minimal loss in ranking quality. However, existing studies often overlook the role of corpus complexity – a critical factor, as recent work shows that both corpus size and document length strongly affect dense retrieval performance. In this paper, we introduce CoRECT (**C**ontrolled **R**etrieval **E**valuation of **C**ompression **T**echniques), a framework for large-scale evaluation of embedding compression methods, supported by a newly curated dataset collection. To demonstrate its utility, we benchmark eight representative types of compression methods. Notably, we show that non-learned compression achieves substantial index size reduction, even on up to 100M passages, with statistically insignificant performance loss. However, selecting the optimal compression method remains challenging, as performance varies across models. Such variability highlights the necessity of CoRECT to enable consistent comparison and informed selection of compression methods. All code, data, and results are available on GitHub (https://github.com/padas-lab-de/CoRECT) and HuggingFace (https://huggingface.co/datasets/PaDaS-Lab/CoRE).

**Keywords:** Dense Retrieval · Text Embedding · Vector Quantization · Matryoshka Representation Learning · Embedding Compression

## 1 Introduction

The success and wide-spread adoption of large language models (LLMs) has caused a shift in the field of information retrieval, moving from sparse, keyword-based matching to dense retrieval methods. Although effective, such systems require large amounts of memory to store embedding-based indices, which can easily surpass the size of the underlying data. To overcome memory-related scalability constraints, researchers have developed a range of embedding compression

© The Author(s), under exclusive license to Springer Nature Switzerland AG 2026
R. Campos et al. (Eds.): ECIR 2026, LNCS 16486, pp. 383–398, 2026.
https://doi.org/10.1007/978-3-032-21321-1_48

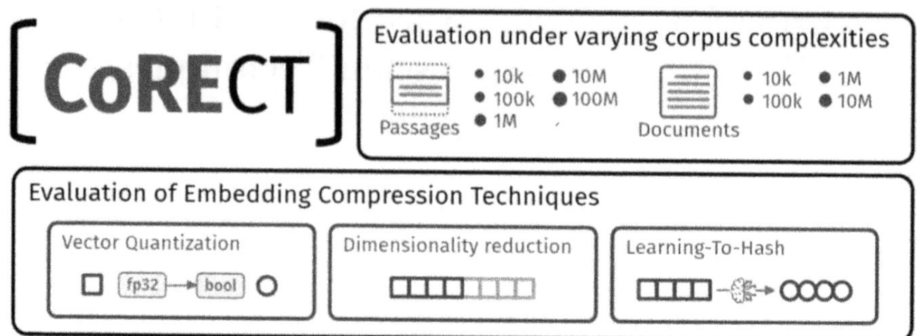



**Fig. 1.** The CoRECT framework.

techniques that achieve significant size reductions with little loss in retrieval quality [14,17,22–24,31,33–35,37]. While these methods show strong results on individual corpora, their systematic evaluation across a broader range of models and datasets is still lacking. In addition, they overlook how retrieval performance scales with corpus complexity, which may cause an overestimation of effectiveness on large and heterogeneous collections [19,26], particularly when vector compression limits embedding expressiveness.

In this work, we critically re-examine recent claims regarding the effectiveness of embedding compression methods, including vector quantization, dimensionality reduction, and Learning-To-Hash (LTH) techniques. We introduce **CoRECT**, a framework for systematically evaluating and comparing compression methods across diverse datasets. Our main objective is to investigate how these techniques perform under varying levels of corpus complexity – an aspect often overlooked in prior studies. To this end, we operationalize corpus complexity in two ways: (1) by scaling the corpus size from 10K to 100M passages and up to 10M documents, and (2) by comparing performance across both passage-level and document-level retrieval tasks (see Fig. 1). To evaluate performance along these dimensions, we introduce a newly curated dataset collection named **Controlled Retrieval Evaluation (CoRE)**, constructed through targeted subsampling of MS MARCO v2[1] and comprising 76 human-judged TREC DL queries. CoRE serves as the primary evaluation dataset in CoRECT. To emphasize the robustness and generalizability of our findings, we further complement CoRE with datasets from BeIR [29]. Finally, to demonstrate the utility of CoRECT, we apply the framework to a diverse and representative set of embedding compression methods. As such, our main contributions are as follows:

1. The Controlled Retrieval Evaluation of Compression Techniques (CoRECT) framework, designed to systematically evaluate compression methods. To ensure robustness, we further extend our evaluation by including the domain-diverse corpora of the BeIR benchmark [29].
2. The dataset collection CoRE, the cornerstone of CoRECT, is used to assess the effect of corpus complexity on retrieval performance.

---

[1] https://microsoft.github.io/msmarco/TREC-Deep-Learning.html.

3. We apply CoRECT on four different models using eight representative types of compression techniques in over 40 combinations and find that choosing the wrong compression method can significantly impact retrieval performance. Furthermore, we show that there is no single best method that fits all models.

## 2   Related Work

The following section reviews embedding compression methods, their evaluation, and related research on the influence of corpus complexity on performance.

**Compression Methods.** The compression techniques discussed below fall into three broad categories. The first group reduces the precision of embeddings by representing each dimension with a lower number of bits. In the following, we will refer to this group of compression methods as Scalar and Binary Quantization (SBQ). It encompasses type-casting floating points, i.e. to float8 [21], or mapping them to discrete integer values, i.e. `uint8`. Its simplicity makes SBQ a popular compression approach supported by various libraries and vector databases, such as FAISS [8], OpenSearch[2] or Milvus[3], as well as recent embedding models through quantization-aware training [2,12].

The second group encompasses approaches for dimensionality reduction which remove certain dimensions from the embedding vector. The most common method in the context of data analytics is Principal Component Analysis (PCA), which can also be used to compress embedding vectors. More recently, Matryoshka Representation Learning (MRL) [17,35], which is integrated into model training, has found wide-spread adoption in contemporary embedding models [2,12,18,36,39].

The third and last group consists of regular hashing and Learning-to-Hash (LTH) methods. A simple baseline is Locality-Sensitive Hashing (LSH), whose numerous proposed variants and extensions make it a well-studied compression methods [3,6,7,11,13]. For LTH methods, Product Quantization (PQ) [15] has emerged as a popular method with its own proposed expansions like Joint optimization of query encoding and Product Quantization (JPQ) [37] or Distill-VQ [33]. Yamada et al. [34] introduce the Binary Passage Retriever (BPR) to binarize embeddings generated by the Dense Passage Retriever [16]. Thakur et al. [28] enhance prior work by introducing domain adaptation modules, enabling methods like BPR and JPQ to perform effectively in zero-shot retrieval settings.

**Evaluation of Compression Methods.** Due to their popularity, SBQ methods have received growing attention in both academic studies and industry reports [14,22–24,31], demonstrating that high compression ratios can be achieved at minimal performance loss. Papers proposing new compression techniques tend to emphasize improvements over previous approaches [28,33,34,37],

---

[2] https://opensearch.org/.
[3] https://milvus.io/.

**Table 1.** List of tested Embedding Models; Metric on MMTEB: NDCG@10 in %

| Model Name | #Params | #Dims | MRL | MMTEB |
|---|---|---|---|---|
| Jina V3 [27] | 572M | 1024 | ✓ | 55.76 |
| Multilingual E5 (Large Instr.) [30] | 560M | 1024 | ✗ | 57.12 |
| Snowflake-M V2 [36] | 305M | 768 | ✓ | 54.83 |
| Snowflake-M V1 [20] | 109M | 768 | ✗ | 39.33 |

comparing the retrieval performance of these compression techniques. However, most of these evaluations are limited to a small number of datasets and methods and do not consider scalability. To the best of our knowledge, the only thorough study comparing compression techniques was conducted by Zhang et al. [38], who evaluate them in the context of deep learning recommendation models. Additionally, they compare a small set of methods in a Retrieval Augmented Generation (RAG) setting on a single dataset, using exact match as a metric. However, due to their focus on recommendation, the chosen evaluation metrics and models are not representative of those commonly used in retrieval.

**Effect of Corpus Complexity.** Recent work suggests that corpus complexity can have a significant impact on downstream effectiveness [1,4,26]. Agrawal et al. [1] demonstrate that pretraining a language model on diverse and complex corpora improves their performance on downstream tasks. Reimers and Gurevych [26] show that dense retrieval models struggle as corpus size increases. However, the only compression method the authors consider is vector truncation. Finally, Chen et al. [4] examine the effect of retrieval granularity, showing that the choice of retrieval unit, i.e. passage- or document-level, has a significant impact on performance, albeit without considering embedding compression. In this paper, we focus on exactly these two aspects of corpus complexity: a) the corpus size, which we increase from 10k to 100M and b) retrieval granularity, where we compare passage and document-level retrieval.

## 3   Methodology

In the following sections, we introduce the CoRECT framework, including the CoRE dataset collection, and demonstrate its utility for conducting a comprehensive and comparative analysis of embedding compression methods. Table 1 lists the tested embedding models, including the number of parameters, dimensions and average performance on MMTEB [9]. While Jina V3 is MRL trained on six different cutoff levels (32, 64, 128, 256, 512 and 768), Snowflake V2 is trained only at cutoff 256.

### 3.1   Dataset Creation and Subsampling

The Controlled Retrieval Evaluation (CoRE) benchmark comprises two curated dataset collections – passages and documents – each derived from MS MARCO v2. Both collections are designed to enable controlled variation in the number of non-relevant corpus items included in the retrieval task. Hence, CoRE varies along two key dimensions – corpus size and retrieval granularity – while keeping the underlying retrieval task and relevance judgments fixed. The passage collection (average length: $286 \pm 111$ characters) and the document collection (average length: $9\,010 \pm 15\,216$ characters) are annotated with high-quality, human-judged relevance labels from the TREC Deep Learning 2023 campaign. For passage retrieval, CoRE includes 65 queries across five corpus sizes (10K, 100K, 1M, 10M, and 100M). For document retrieval, it offers 55 queries across four corpus sizes (10K to 10M). Each query is associated with exactly 10 relevant passages or documents, ensuring comparability across corpus scales.

A central challenge in constructing smaller subsets of large corpora is preserving a high density of meaningful distractors, as naive random sampling often removes these and renders the retrieval task unrealistically easy. To address this issue, we adopt the intelligent subsampling strategy proposed by Fröbe et al. [10], mining distractor documents from pooled ranking lists submitted to the 2023 TREC Deep Learning track. To ensure quality, we discard the bottom 20% of runs based on effectiveness and apply Reciprocal Rank Fusion (RRF) [5] to merge the top-ranked documents from the remaining runs. For each query, the top 100 irrelevant or unjudged documents from this fused list are selected as high-quality distractors. To simulate a realistic and challenging evaluation scenario, each query is paired with exactly 100 mined distractors, besides the 10 relevant documents. The remainder of each corpus is filled with truly random documents that are neither relevant nor distractors under this definition.

### 3.2   Framework

The current implementation of the CoRECT framework evaluates compression methods on CoRE as well as the public BeIR datasets, tested with the four embedding models described above. The included compression techniques encompass eight distinct types, which will be discussed in detail in the next subsection.

Given a model and dataset, embeddings are generated in batches and stored for downstream analysis. Compression is then applied sequentially on each batch before performing retrieval using cosine similarity. Any thresholds or parameters specific to the compression method are learned per batch, with the same values applied to both query and document embeddings. For each query, CoRECT computes standard retrieval metrics such as NDCG, Recall, and MRR across multiple cutoff values $k$, and stores the results in JSON format.

The framework builds on widely used Python libraries, including Transformers [32] for model instantiation and the Hugging Face Hub for data loading. This modular design facilitates the integration of additional datasets, embedding models, and compression techniques. New models available through Transformers can be incorporated by extending the base interface class for model loading and embedding compression, while new retrieval datasets from Hugging Face only require defining a custom loading function. Comprehensive instructions for extending the framework are provided in the project's README[4].

## 3.3  Compression Methods

In the following, we discuss the set of representative methods that have been initially included in the framework in more detail.

**Floating Point Casting.** A straightforward approach at embedding compression is downcasting embeddings from their native precision to a lower-precision floating-point format. We choose the native precision of each embedding model according to its reported Tensortype on Hugging Face. Using PyTorch [25], we cast embedding tensors to FP16, BF16, and FP8. As PyTorch provides multiple FP8 variants differing in mantissa and exponent length,[5] we employ two FP8 types with three- and two-bit mantissas, respectively.

**Scalar and Binary Quantization (SBQ).** To achieve higher compression ratios, we quantize embedding vectors to 8-, 4-, and 2-bit unsigned integer ranges using two quantization strategies. The first, Equal Distance Binning, computes the per-dimension minimum and maximum of the embeddings, divides this range into $2^x$ equidistant bins, and maps each floating-point value to its corresponding bin index. To reduce sensitivity to outliers, we clip values at the 2.5th and 97.5th percentiles before binning. The second method, Percentile Binning, determines bin boundaries based on percentiles so that each bin contains approximately the same number of values, thereby ensuring a more balanced quantization. For binary quantization, embeddings are mapped to 1-bit values using two thresholding schemes: zero and the per-dimension median.

**Dimensionality Reduction.** We employ two approaches to reduce the dimensionality of embedding vectors: truncation along Matryoshka Representation Learning (MRL) cutoff points and Principal Component Analysis (PCA). For truncation, only the first $x$ dimensions of each embedding are retained, with $x$ determined by the MRL training configurations of Jina V3 and Snowflake V2, enabling direct comparison with non-MRL-trained models such as E5 and Snowflake V1. Since the Snowflake models have a smaller embedding size than Jina V3 and E5 (768 vs. 1024), two distinct sets of cutoff points are defined to preserve comparable dimensionality ratios. MRL truncation is further combined with the floating-point casting and SBQ methods described above to obtain higher compression ratios. For PCA, the implementation from the FAISS library [8] is used. The sole hyperparameter – the output dimension of the compressed vector – is aligned with the cutoff values applied in MRL truncation.

---

[4] https://github.com/padas-lab-de/CoRECT.
[5] https://dev-discuss.pytorch.org/t/float8-in-pytorch-1-x/1815.

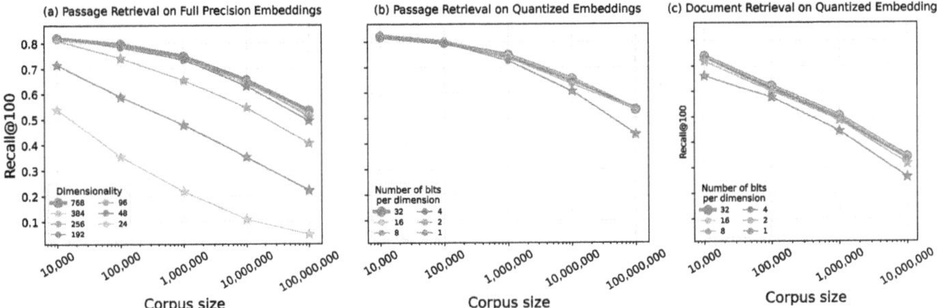


**Fig. 2.** Recall@100 for Snowflake V2 across increasing corpus sizes in different compression settings. Stars indicate significantly lower recall than the blue baseline (one-sided Wilcoxon test, $p = 0.05$). Recall decreases with higher corpus size and granularity. Quantization (middle) outperforms vector truncation (left). (Color figure online)

**Hashing and Learning-to-Hash.** The final group of methods includes Locality-Sensitive Hashing (LSH) and Product Quantization (PQ), both implemented using FAISS [8]. LSH compresses embedding vectors into binary codes, controlled by a hyperparameter that defines the bit length of the resulting code. Four configurations are evaluated, corresponding to compression ratios of $4\times$, $8\times$, $16\times$, and $32\times$. PQ, as implemented in FAISS, applies k-means clustering with L2 distance to partition each embedding into subvectors, encoding each subspace with the chosen number of bits. Six combinations of subvector count and code size are compared. To maintain consistent compression ratios across models, two distinct hyperparameter sets are defined – one for 768-dimensional and one for 1024-dimensional embeddings.

## 4   Results

This section demonstrates the utility of the CoRECT framework by showcasing the analyses it enables. Using CoRECT, we systematically compare the embedding compression methods introduced in Sect. 3.3 and examine how their performance varies across models, datasets, corpus sizes, and retrieval granularities. These experiments highlight the framework's ability to support controlled, large-scale evaluation of compression techniques – insights that would be difficult to obtain without it. Comprehensive results for all models, datasets, and methods are available on our project page.[6]

### 4.1   Impact of Corpus Complexity

**Corpus Complexity Significantly Affects Retrieval Performance.** An important asset of our framework lies in its ability to evaluate the robustness of compression methods with respect to increasing corpus complexity. Figure 2 shows Recall@100 for Snowflake V2 on CoRE, measuring the model's ability to

---

[6] https://padas-lab-de.github.io/CoRECT/.

**Table 2.** Recall@100 (in %) with increasing corpus size. The best result per column is marked in bold, the second best is underlined. The degree of performance degradation when increasing corpus complexity varies between models, making some more suitable for application on large corpora than others.

| | Passages | | | Documents | | |
|---|---|---|---|---|---|---|
| | 10k | 1M | 100M | 10k | 1M | 10M |
| Jina V3 | <u>83.85</u> | 71.39 | 44.15 | 72.91 | 47.64 | 26.91 |
| E5 | **84.15** | **75.39** | 50.77 | **76.00** | 47.64 | 31.64 |
| Snowflake V2 | 82.00 | <u>74.92</u> | **53.39** | <u>74.00</u> | <u>50.18</u> | <u>34.36</u> |
| Snowflake V1 | 80.31 | 71.69 | <u>50.92</u> | <u>74.00</u> | **50.36** | **36.73** |

retrieve relevant documents among the top 100 results as a first-stage retriever. It consists of three line charts: (a) and (b) for passage retrieval, and (c) for document retrieval. In Plot (a), embedding vectors are only truncated at increasingly lower dimensions, while in Plot (b), only Percentile Binning is applied. Plot (c) mirrors the structure of (b) for document retrieval. The blue line, representing the uncompressed baseline, serves as a reference in the three charts. Across all settings, the retrieval performance decreases significantly as the corpus grows, even for the uncompressed baseline. This trend reflects the increasing difficulty of the retrieval task with larger passage or document collections.

**Scalability of Vector Truncation Depends on Compression Ratio.** Plot (a) isolates the impact of vector truncation on performance, reaching a maximum compression ratio of 32 when only the first 24 dimensions of each vector are retained. While moderate truncation to 384 or 256 dimensions barely affects the recall scores, significant performance differences, albeit small, start to manifest at 192 dimensions (4× compression) for the larger corpora. At a compression ratio of 8, i.e. 96 dimensions, recall starts to drop sharply, even for the 100k corpus. While, here, we only present the results for Snowflake V2, as it is one of the MRL trained models, we observed even better results for Jina V3, as the vector can be truncated to 256 dimensions (4× compression) without significant performance differences. Furthermore, truncating to a compression ratio of 8 only leads to a slight decrease in performance. Naturally, for Snowflake V1 and E5, the two models without any MRL training, truncation performs worse, quickly leading to significant degradations of recall as corpus size increases. Notably, for both models taking only half of the vector dimensions already has a significant performance impact when the corpus size increases to 1M.

**Quantization Outperforms Vector Truncation.** Plot (b) reveals that scalar quantization barely impacts performance, while binarizing the vector has a significant impact on recall performance at larger corpus sizes. Comparing the performance of quantization to that of vector truncation in plot (a) at the same compression ratio, we find that quantization has a clear edge. Looking at the

**Table 3.** Recall@100 (in %) for different corpus complexity with full and binary precision (no truncation). Choosing the wrong thresholding type can greatly decrease performance.

|  | Jina V3 | | E5 | | Snowflake V2 | | Snowflake V1 | |
|---|---|---|---|---|---|---|---|---|
|  | 10k | 100M | 10k | 100M | 10k | 100M | 10k | 100M |
| Full precision | 83.85 | 44.15 | 84.31 | 50.92 | 82.00 | 53.39 | 80.31 | 50.92 |
| Zero Thresh. | **83.39** | **41.39** | 71.23 | 19.23 | **82.62** | **49.39** | **78.92** | **32.46** |
| Median Thresh. | 82.92 | 35.69 | **86.31** | **39.54** | **82.62** | 43.39 | 70.77 | 18.00 |

remaining models, whose results are not shown in the plot, we observe an even clearer advantage for E5. For Jina V3, the performance difference between quantization and vector truncation becomes smaller due to the model's ability to retain high recall even with large vector truncation. Nevertheless, for both E5 and Jina V3 the quantized vectors retain most of the originals' performance. In contrast, quantizing Snowflake V1 embeddings causes a large degradation in recall, even though SBQ still performs slightly better than truncation. Considering retrieval granularity, plot (c) shows similar trends to plot (b) for document retrieval, albeit with faster overall performance degradation. This pattern can also be observed for the remaining models, where quantization performance trends on passage level translate to document retrieval.

**Model Robustness to Corpus Complexity Varies.** Apart from allowing us to evaluate the robustness of compression methods with respect to corpus size and retrieval granularity, CoRE also enables us to study a model's general capability of dealing with these challenges. Interestingly, we can observe different degrees of performance degradation depending on the model. As shown in Table 2, while E5 performs best on the small 10k passage corpus followed by Jina V3, on the largest 100M corpus Snowflake V2 takes the lead with E5 and Jina V3 in the last two places. For document retrieval, E5 again takes the lead for 10K, while for the larger corpora Snowflake V1, the smallest model, demonstrates the best recall and Jina V3, the largest one, the worst. As the embedding models demonstrate different capability of retaining recall with increasing corpus complexity, we demonstrate the general importance of evaluating model performance on large-scale datasets.

### 4.2 Compression Robustness Across Datasets and Models

**Choosing the Wrong Compression Method Harms Performance.** When comparing the performance of methods with an equal compression ratio across models, we find that specific model-compression method combinations significantly reduce retrieval performance. Table 3 presents Recall@100 for each model, comparing full-precision baselines with two binary quantization methods: zero and median thresholding. Interestingly, zero thresholding outperforms median thresholding for three of the four models, particularly on the 100M corpus. The

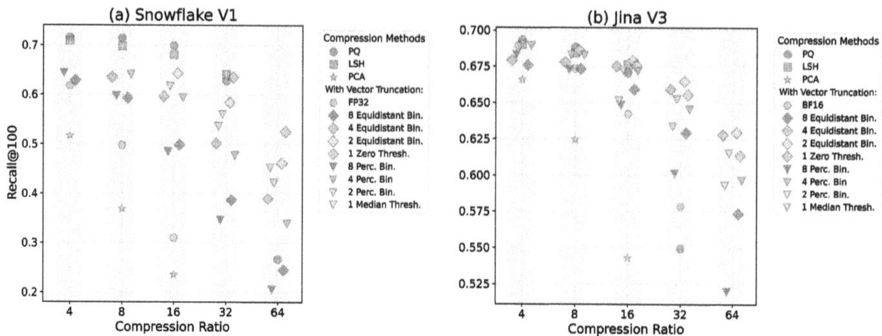

**Fig. 3.** Average Recall@100 across BeIR datasets for different compression methods. The x-values of some compression methods have been shifted slightly for better visibility. The light gray columns in the background mark the compression ratio to which the methods belong. Shapes indicate different types of compression techniques. Some methods have been combined with vector truncation to achieve the desired compression ratio as indicated in the legend. The top-performing measures vary depending on the model. (Color figure online)

larger discrepancy at 100M is most likely a result of the median being estimated on a limited sample rather than the full dataset. Despite its simplicity, zero thresholding achieves remarkably strong performance, with E5 being the only model where this approach leads to a notable drop in recall. In this paper, we restrict ourselves to reporting these empirical observations; a deeper interpretation of the underlying causes is left for future work.

**Large Compression Ratios Show Differences of Methods.** Expanding our focus to evaluating the robustness of compression methods on a diverse set of corpora, we apply CoRECT on the BeIR datasets. Although the ranking of compression methods changes between datasets, these variations are largely attributable to minor performance differences among densely clustered methods. Figure 3 presents average Recall@100 across BeIR for different compression ratios. For Jina V3 (Plot b), the methods cluster closely at low compression rates, but clear performance differences emerge as the compression ratio increases. Quantization to 2 bits performs robustly across all ratios—a trend also observed for Snowflake V2 and E5. Within the SBQ family, combining moderate vector truncation with quantization yields high compression ratios while often improving retrieval performance compared to heavier quantization of the full vector. This approach works particularly well with Jina's MRL-training and, to a lesser extent, for Snowflake V2 and E5 at smaller truncation levels. An exception is the Snowflake V1 model, whose performance degrades sharply as compression increases (see Plot a). Although LSH and PQ perform relatively well at lower ratios, their effectiveness drops substantially at 32× compression. Across most settings, however, PQ and LSH still outperform scalar quantization, making them a better choice for compressing Snowflake V1 embeddings than SBQ.

**Type of Retrieval Task Affects Compression Performance** . So far, we only considered compression in the context of first-stage retrieval, using Recall@100 as a performance metric. However, when using an embedding model as a single-stage retrieval system, NDCG@10 becomes a more suitable metric, as the number of retrieved documents will be lower. Figure 4 shows that in contrast to the obvious performance degradation of Recall@100 in Fig. 2, NDCG@10 remains far more stable with increasing corpus size. This effect reflects the higher difficulty for a random document embedding to achieve a level of similarity that is high enough to retrieve it in a top-10 position. As an example, Fig. 5 shows the ranks at which different types of documents (relevant, distractor or random) are retrieved as corpus size increases from 1M to 100M when truncating to 192 dimensions. Each column represents retrieval results for one specific query. While the top-30 ranks for the 1M corpus do not contain a single random document, they start appearing for the 10M corpus and manage to push some relevant documents out of the top-30 in the 100M corpus. Notably, the top-10 results remain stable as corpus size increases. As such, when considering only the top-10 results, stronger compression is possible without significantly reducing retrieval performance. This demonstrates that the primary metric for evaluating compression methods should be chosen according to the retrieval context.

Overall, our results demonstrate that there is no single best compression method that fits all models. Rather, the optimal choice is model-dependent, necessitating a thorough evaluation and comparison of compression methods. Thus, comparing compression techniques across diverse corpora allows us to a) identify methods that consistently perform well and b) exclude methods that are unsuitable for a particular model.

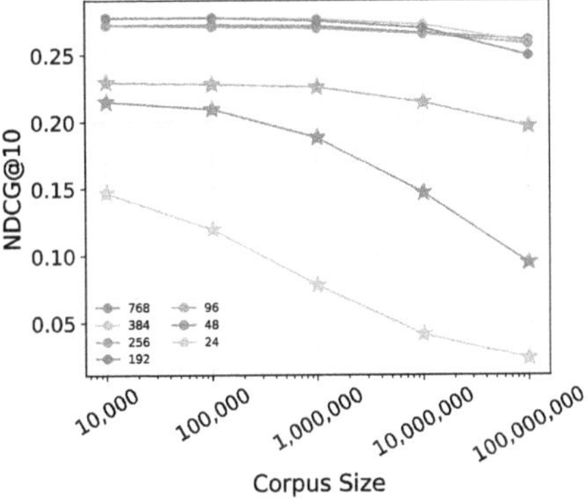



**Fig. 4.** NDCG@10 for Snowflake V2 on the CoRE passage corpora. In contrast to Recall@100, NDCG@10 remains stable with increasing corpus size.

## 5    Discussion and Future Work

Overall, the insights generated with the CoRECT framework enable us to derive certain guidelines for applying compression techniques in practice:

1. **Evaluate model performance on large datasets.** When choosing a model to generate millions of embeddings, it is essential to evaluate its performance on large corpora. As our analysis shows, some models' retrieval performance degrades quicker when increasing corpus size, which can lead to a significant decrease in performance when choosing the wrong model.

2. **Compare Compression Performance of Different Methods.** When choosing a compression method, comparing its performance to a diverse set of other methods at a fixed compression ratio is important, as our analysis has demonstrated that a method that performs well for one model does not necessarily do so for another. Selecting a method that is unsuitable for a specific model can greatly impact performance.

3. **Try Combining Compression Techniques.** For three out of our four models, combining quantization with moderate vector truncation achieved the best retrieval performance at a fixed compression ratio. While the number of method combinations we considered is fairly limited, the results still highlight the potential benefit of mixing different methods.

While our framework aims to compare a wide variety of compression methods, a clear limitation lies in its current focus on SBQ along with techniques for dimensionality reduction, ignoring more recent LTH approaches described in Sect. 2. To demonstrate the initial capabilities of our framework, we focused on popular compression techniques that are not too train-intensive. However, we acknowledge that integrating such methods in the future would be a valuable extension of CoRECT, allowing the application and evaluation of these methods on modern embedding models. Furthermore, we only evaluate compression techniques based on their performance, ignoring other factors like their storage efficiency, computation time and retrieval speed.

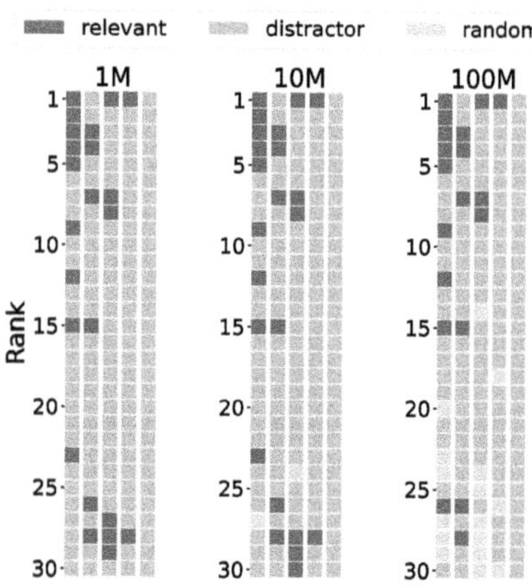



**Fig. 5.** Positions of retrieved document types for Snowflake V2 on three CoRE passage corpora for five queries. While the top-10 ranking remains stable, random documents start to appear at lower ranks as corpus size increases, pushing relevant documents down in the ranking.

## 6    Conclusion

We introduced CoRECT, a framework designed to robustly evaluate the performance of embedding compression methods with respect to (1) corpus complexity and (2) consistency across diverse corpora. To study the first aspect, we developed CoRE, a benchmark that enables controlled variation in the number of non-relevant passages or documents included in the retrieval task. To address the second aspect, we leverage the diverse BeIR datasets.

Applying CoRECT to a representative set of compression techniques – scalar and binary quantization, dimensionality reduction, locality-sensitive hashing, and product quantization, among others – across four different retrieval models reveals that there is no "one-size-fits-all" compression method that performs uniformly well across models and datasets. Crucially, these findings emerge only through CoRECT's systematic and controlled evaluation design, which is explicitly tailored to disentangle the effects of corpus complexity and model-specific behavior. Through this framework, we uncover model-dependent pitfalls, where certain compression techniques significantly degrade performance for one model while remaining effective for others.

Using CoRE, we further show that retrieval performance generally declines with increasing corpus complexity. While this trend is expected, the degree of degradation varies substantially across models, suggesting that some are inherently more robust to scaling than others. Overall, CoRECT demonstrates the necessity of model-specific, controlled evaluation when applying embedding compression techniques, enabling a more nuanced and reliable understanding of their real-world retrieval performance.

**Acknowledgments.**

This work has received funding from the European Union's Horizon Europe research and innovation program under grant agreement No. 101070014 (OpenWebSearch.EU).

Furthermore, this work was funded by the Bavarian State Ministry of Economic Affairs, Regional Development, and Energy (StMWi) and is supported by funds of the Federal Ministry of Agriculture, Food and Regional Identity (BMLEH) based on a decision of the Parliament of the Federal Republic of Germany via the Federal Office for Agriculture and Food (BLE) under the strategy for digitalisation in agriculture.

**Disclosure of Interest.** The authors have no competing interests to declare that are relevant to the content of this article.

# References


1. Agrawal, A., Singh, S.: Corpus complexity matters in pretraining language models. In: Proceedings of The Fourth Workshop on Simple and Efficient Natural Language Processing (SustaiNLP), pp. 257–263 (2023)
2. AI, V.: voyage-3-large: the new state-of-the-art general-purpose embedding model. Voyage AI Blog (2025). https://blog.voyageai.com/2025/01/07/voyage-3-large/
3. Bawa, M., Condie, T., Ganesan, P.: Lsh forest: self-tuning indexes for similarity search. In: Proceedings of the 14th International Conference on World Wide Web, WWW '05, pp. 651–660. Association for Computing Machinery, New York (2005). https://doi.org/10.1145/1060745.1060840
4. Chen, T., et al.: Dense X retrieval: what retrieval granularity should we use? In: Al-Onaizan, Y., Bansal, M., Chen, Y.N. (eds.) Proceedings of the 2024 Conference on Empirical Methods in Natural Language Processing, pp. 15159–15177. Association for Computational Linguistics, Miami (2024). https://doi.org/10.18653/v1/2024.emnlp-main.845. https://aclanthology.org/2024.emnlp-main.845/

5. Cormack, G.V., Clarke, C.L.A., Buettcher, S.: Reciprocal rank fusion outperforms condorcet and individual rank learning methods. In: Proceedings of the 32nd International ACM SIGIR Conference on Research and Development in Information Retrieval, SIGIR '09, pp. 758–759. Association for Computing Machinery, New York (2009). https://doi.org/10.1145/1571941.1572114

6. Dasgupta, A., Kumar, R., Sarlos, T.: Fast locality-sensitive hashing. In: Proceedings of the 17th ACM SIGKDD International Conference on Knowledge Discovery and Data Mining, KDD '11, pp. 1073–1081. Association for Computing Machinery, New York (2011). https://doi.org/10.1145/2020408.2020578

7. Datar, M., Immorlica, N., Indyk, P., Mirrokni, V.S.: Locality-sensitive hashing scheme based on p-stable distributions. In: Proceedings of the Twentieth Annual Symposium on Computational Geometry, SCG '04, pp. 253–262. Association for Computing Machinery, New York (2004). https://doi.org/10.1145/997817.997857

8. Douze, M., et al.: The faiss library (2024)

9. Enevoldsen, K., et al.: Mmteb: massive multilingual text embedding benchmark (2025). https://arxiv.org/abs/2502.13595

10. Fröbe, M., et al.: Corpus subsampling: estimating the effectiveness of neural retrieval models on large corpora. In: Hauff, C., et al. (eds.) Advances in Information Retrieval, pp. 453–471. Springer, Cham (2025). https://doi.org/10.1007/978-3-031-88708-6_29

11. Gan, J., Feng, J., Fang, Q., Ng, W.: Locality-sensitive hashing scheme based on dynamic collision counting. In: Proceedings of the 2012 ACM SIGMOD International Conference on Management of Data, SIGMOD '12, pp. 541–552. Association for Computing Machinery, New York (2012). https://doi.org/10.1145/2213836.2213898

12. Günther, M., et al.: jina-embeddings-v4: Universal embeddings for multimodal multilingual retrieval (2025). https://arxiv.org/abs/2506.18902

13. Huang, Q., Feng, J., Zhang, Y., Fang, Q., Ng, W.: Query-aware locality-sensitive hashing for approximate nearest neighbor search. Proc. VLDB Endow. $\mathbf{9}$(1), 1–12 (2015). https://doi.org/10.14778/2850469.2850470

14. Jina: Binary embeddings: All the ai, 3.125% of the fat. https://jina.ai/news/binary-embeddings-all-the-ai-3125-of-the-fat/

15. Jégou, H., Douze, M., Schmid, C.: Product quantization for nearest neighbor search. IEEE Trans. Pattern Anal. Mach. Intell. $\mathbf{33}$(1), 117–128 (2011). https://doi.org/10.1109/TPAMI.2010.57

16. Karpukhin, V., et al.: Dense passage retrieval for open-domain question answering (2020). https://arxiv.org/abs/2004.04906

17. Kusupati, A., et al.: Matryoshka representation learning. In: Koyejo, S., Mohamed, S., Agarwal, A., Belgrave, D., Cho, K., Oh, A. (eds.) Advances in Neural Information Processing Systems, vol. 35, pp. 30233–30249. Curran Associates, Inc. (2022)

18. Lee, J., et al.: Gemini embedding: Generalizable embeddings from gemini (2025). https://arxiv.org/abs/2503.07891

19. Luan, Y., Eisenstein, J., Toutanova, K., Collins, M.: Sparse, dense, and attentional representations for text retrieval. Trans. Assoc. Comput. Linguist. $\mathbf{9}$, 329–345 (2021). https://doi.org/10.1162/tacl_a_00369. https://aclanthology.org/2021.tacl-1.20/

20. Merrick, L., Xu, D., Nuti, G., Campos, D.: Arctic-embed: scalable, efficient, and accurate text embedding models (2024). https://arxiv.org/abs/2405.05374

21. Micikevicius, P., et al.: Fp8 formats for deep learning (2022). https://arxiv.org/abs/2209.05433

22. Microsoft: Azure ai search october updates: Nearly 100x compression with minimal quality loss. https://techcommunity.microsoft.com/blog/azure-ai-services-blog/azure-ai-search-october-updates-nearly-100x-compression-with-minimal-quality-los/4265447

23. Mixedbread: 64 bytes per embedding, yee-haw. https://www.mixedbread.com/blog/binary-mrl

24. MongoDB: Binary quantization & rescoring: 96% less memory, faster search. https://www.mongodb.com/blog/post/binary-quantization-rescoring-96-less-memory-faster-search

25. Paszke, A., et al.: Pytorch: an imperative style, high-performance deep learning library. In: Wallach, H., Larochelle, H., Beygelzimer, A., d'Alché-Buc, F., Fox, E., Garnett, R. (eds.) Advances in Neural Information Processing Systems, vol. 32. Curran Associates, Inc. (2019)

26. Reimers, N., Gurevych, I.: The curse of dense low-dimensional information retrieval for large index sizes. In: Zong, C., Xia, F., Li, W., Navigli, R. (eds.) Proceedings of the 59th Annual Meeting of the Association for Computational Linguistics and the 11th International Joint Conference on Natural Language Processing, vol. 2: Short Papers, pp. 605–611. Association for Computational Linguistics, Online (2021). https://doi.org/10.18653/v1/2021.acl-short.77. https://aclanthology.org/2021.acl-short.77/

27. Sturua, S., et al.: Jina-embeddings-v3: multilingual embeddings with task lora (2024). https://arxiv.org/abs/2409.10173

28. Thakur, N., Reimers, N., Lin, J.: Injecting domain adaptation with learning-to-hash for effective and efficient zero-shot dense retrieval (2022). https://doi.org/10.48550/ARXIV.2205.11498. https://arxiv.org/abs/2205.11498

29. Thakur, N., Reimers, N., Rücklé, A., Srivastava, A., Gurevych, I.: BEIR: a heterogenous benchmark for zero-shot evaluation of information retrieval models (2021). https://doi.org/10.48550/ARXIV.2104.08663

30. Wang, L., Yang, N., Huang, X., Yang, L., Majumder, R., Wei, F.: Multilingual e5 text embeddings: a technical report. arXiv preprint arXiv:2402.05672 (2024)

31. Weaviate: 32x reduced memory usage with binary quantization. https://weaviate.io/blog/binary-quantization

32. Wolf, T., et al.: Transformers: state-of-the-art natural language processing. In: Proceedings of the 2020 Conference on Empirical Methods in Natural Language Processing: System Demonstrations, pp. 38–45. Association for Computational Linguistics, Online (2020). https://www.aclweb.org/anthology/2020.emnlp-demos.6

33. Xiao, S., et al.: Distill-vq: learning retrieval oriented vector quantization by distilling knowledge from dense embeddings. In: Proceedings of the 45th International ACM SIGIR Conference on Research and Development in Information Retrieval, SIGIR '22, pp. 1513–1523. Association for Computing Machinery, New York (2022). https://doi.org/10.1145/3477495.3531799

34. Yamada, I., Asai, A., Hajishirzi, H.: Efficient passage retrieval with hashing for open-domain question answering. In: Zong, C., Xia, F., Li, W., Navigli, R. (eds.) Proceedings of the 59th Annual Meeting of the Association for Computational Linguistics and the 11th International Joint Conference on Natural Language Processing, vol. 2: Short Papers, pp. 979–986. Association for Computational Linguistics (2021). https://doi.org/10.18653/v1/2021.acl-short.123. https://aclanthology.org/2021.acl-short.123/

35. Yoon, J., Sinha, R., Arik, S.O., Pfister, T.: Matryoshka-adaptor: unsupervised and supervised tuning for smaller embedding dimensions. In: Al-Onaizan, Y., Bansal,

M., Chen, Y.N. (eds.) Proceedings of the 2024 Conference on Empirical Methods in Natural Language Processing, pp. 10318–10336. Association for Computational Linguistics, Miami (2024). https://doi.org/10.18653/v1/2024.emnlp-main.576. https://aclanthology.org/2024.emnlp-main.576/

36. Yu, P., Merrick, L., Nuti, G., Campos, D.: Arctic-embed 2.0: Multilingual retrieval without compromise (2024). https://arxiv.org/abs/2412.04506

37. Zhan, J., Mao, J., Liu, Y., Guo, J., Zhang, M., Ma, S.: Jointly optimizing query encoder and product quantization to improve retrieval performance, CIKM '21, pp. 2487–2496. Association for Computing Machinery, New York (2021). https://doi.org/10.1145/3459637.3482358

38. Zhang, H., et al.: Experimental analysis of large-scale learnable vector storage compression. Proc. VLDB Endow. **17**(4), 808–822 (2023). https://doi.org/10.14778/3636218.3636234

39. Zhang, Y., et al.: Qwen3 embedding: advancing text embedding and reranking through foundation models. arXiv preprint arXiv:2506.05176 (2025)

# FaE: A Resource of Logs, Profiles, and Rankings for Academic Expert Finding


Marjan Azimi⬤, Alistair Moffat$^{(\boxtimes)}$⬤, and Justin Zobel⬤

The University of Melbourne, Melbourne, Australia
{azimi.m,ammoffat,jzobel}@unimelb.edu.au



**Abstract.** Expert-finding systems aim to identify knowledgeable individuals in specific domains based on evidence such as publications, activities, and social network data, with academic uses including allowing identification of potential supervisors, collaborators, or peer reviewers. However, most existing benchmark datasets for academic expert finding contain only publication information and lack authentic query logs. We introduce the Find an Expert (FaE) dataset from the University of Melbourne, comprising three interconnected components: structured profiles for 8,984 academic staff providing text biographies and research interests, and lists of (and links to) publications and current projects; 712,937 interaction records captured over 239 days in 2025, that record queries, clicks, and temporal patterns; and system-generated rankings for 530 queries where users clicked on profiles. Together, these resources provide the first publicly available expert-finding dataset combining profile data, log interactions, and system outputs, thereby allowing deep investigation of expert search systems.


## 1   Introduction

An *expert* is an individual with substantial knowledge and skills in a specific domain [24], with *expert finding* the task of identifying such individuals in response to a given query [7]. That is, expert finding systems aim to rank people based on documents and contextual signals that link individuals to topics [9]. Expert finding plays a crucial role across many applications. In academia, it supports peer review assignment, supervisor selection, and collaboration discovery [36]. In professional contexts, expert finding systems assist in team building [19], medical consultation [41], and community question answering [5,33].

There are relatively few publicly available datasets for expert finding. Most existing collections, such as LExR [31] and DBLP [20,22,30], contain publication records only. The only notable exception is the UvT dataset from Tilburg University [8], which also includes organizational hierarchy, self-assessed expertise, and course descriptions. However, it is almost twenty years old (having been released in 2006), covers only 1,168 profiles, and provides incomplete information for many individuals.


© The Author(s), under exclusive license to Springer Nature Switzerland AG 2026
R. Campos et al. (Eds.): ECIR 2026, LNCS 16486, pp. 399–414, 2026.
https://doi.org/10.1007/978-3-032-21321-1_49

Another critical gap lies in information about user behavior. Query logs are essential for revealing how users search for experts and what contextual factors influence their choices. While log analysis has been highly informative in web search, only a few studies have examined expert finding logs [16,21,42,43], and none of the datasets have been made publicly available. This scarcity of real-world resources has led to a reproducibility bottleneck, where researchers cannot meaningfully compare methods or study authentic expert-seeking behaviour [6].

We address that gap by releasing data from the *Find an Expert* system at the University of Melbourne.[1] This new resource consists of:

- A set of 8,984 academic profiles with rich contextual information including biographical descriptions, research interests, academic positions, publications, and funded projects;
- A 239-day interaction log dataset (January–September 2025) containing 712,937 records from 89,582 users, capturing queries, result clicks, and temporal patterns that enable the study of authentic expert-seeking behavior; and
- A set of 530 SERPs, each containing up to fifty items, for queries that led to profile clicks.

The resultant FaE resource is available under a flexible data access agreement, making it the first public expertise dataset that combines logs, profiles, and system outputs; thereby supporting behavioral analyses in regard to query formulation, session structure, user engagement, and click-through interactions. Better understanding of these user-oriented aspects will then inform the design and evaluation of future expert finding systems, and of the kinds of data about experts that is valuable in search and discovery.

## 2    Background

Evidence of expertise is typically derived from sources such as publications, reports, projects, and network structures [3,28]. Those elements are then searched via a querying process that generates a ranking of recommended experts.

**Queries.** These take several forms, depending on user intent. They may be topic-based, expressed as keywords describing an area of expertise [15,20,26] varying from extremely broad ("physics") to highly specific ("high-temperature plasma physics"). Person-oriented queries target specific individuals by name, either to view their profile [42] or to find similar experts [21]. Entity-based queries use artifacts such as paper titles to identify associated experts [6,13].

**Output Types.** Gonçalves and Dorneles [19] observe that expert finding systems produce outputs in two main forms: rankings, where candidates are ranked according to their estimated relevance [4,37]; and profiles, where the system constructs a representation of a candidate's expertise areas [10,17,44].

---

[1] See https://findanexpert.unimelb.edu.au/ and Fig. 1.

**Table 1.** Comparison of publicly available academic expert finding datasets.

| Dataset | Year | Mlt.Dis. | Quers. | Cands. | Docs. | Content |
|---|---|---|---|---|---|---|
| UvT | 2006 | ✓ | 1,491 | 1,168 | 36,699 | Research and course descriptions, pubs. |
| DBLP11f | 2011 | – | 17+87 | 615,106 | 687,027 | Pubs. only |
| LExR | 2015 | ✓ | 91 | 79,004 | 194,991 | Pubs. only |
| FaE | 2025 | ✓ | 530 | 8,984 | 499,640 | Profiles inc. pubs., log files, click-through data |

**Resources.** Expertise can be inferred from diverse information sources [9]. Textual resources such as publications, reports, medical records, user profiles, and communication logs serve as primary evidence [11,18,23,41]. Social network resources including posts, interactions, and activity data provide additional signals [14,38,40]. Hybrid approaches are also possible [17,27].

**Models.** Expert finding systems use different models to establish relationships between queries, documents, and candidates [24]. As a very brief summary, consideration has been given to generative probabilistic models [5,8,36,44]; to discriminative probabilistic models [35,41]; to voting models [1,32]; to network-based models [12,14]; to IR similarity-based models [4,34,44]; and to hybrid models. Our own prior work examines this spectrum of options [6].

Contextual factors also influence how expertise is perceived and selected. These include whether the focus is on algorithms or user behavior [2]; factors such as social ties, recency of work, availability, and familiarity, which shape user decisions [23,29]; human-related factors including media visibility, reliability, organizational position, and currency of work [23]; and publication-level factors such as citation quality, recency, and output quantity [29].

**Log Analysis.** Logs provide useful insights into how users interact with systems. Previous work has included analysis of the INDURE academic search system, which noted that expert finding queries are shorter and more focused than general web queries, with increased use of advanced operators [16]; study of a commercial people search engine, observing a high fraction of name queries and heavy reliance on social media results [42]; and exploration of an enterprise search log from IBM, revealing different search strategies between employees and managers [21]. More recently, Wu et al. [43] examined behavior in academic social networks, highlighting the interplay between query-based and social navigation.

But none of these datasets are public. This scarcity of interaction data creates barriers to progress: researchers cannot validate findings, compare user behavior patterns, or develop models that reflect real behavior. Our FaE dataset addresses this gap by providing rich profile data and extensive log information.

**Existing Datasets.** Publicly available datasets are essential for advancing expert finding research. Table 1 summarizes previous expert finding datasets, building on the recent work of Azimi et al. [6] and the earlier study by Balog et al. [8]. In the table the column "Quers." is the number of queries for which there is some form of relevance indicator included, and the column "Mlt.Dis." indicates whether the data elements span multiple disciplines.

The 2006 UvT dataset [8], covering Tilburg University staff profile pages, provides candidate contact details, research descriptions, course descriptions, and publications. This bilingual resource includes both Dutch and English content, and spans multiple disciplines. The DBLP11f dataset from 2011 is restricted to computer science publications and contains a large number of publication titles and abstracts; but lacks contextual information about experts beyond their publication records, and is accompanied by only a small number of queries (and by an even smaller set of judged queries). The LExR resource spans a large number of candidates and publication across multiple disciplines, and a range of languages, with the English-only subset most commonly used. However, like DBLP11f it contains only publications. Azimi et al. [6] included another dataset, DBLP24, in their experiments, which adds recent papers, albeit without any abstracts or queries. It does not address the limitations of its predecessor, and is omitted from Table 1.

## 3   FaE Data Collection Description

The new FaE resource is the first large-scale collection that combines real interaction logs, rich expert profiles, and system output traces from a production academic search platform.

**Find an Expert.** The primary data element is a large set of expert candidate profile drawn from the full spectrum of academic staff at the University of Melbourne. Detailed meta-information about each expert includes text elements such as biographical statements, academic positions held, editorships, and awards received. Additionally, the FaE resource includes authentic user interaction data through log files and search click-through data, as described below. With nearly 500,000 documents (that is, unique publication and project entries), it matches previous datasets in terms of scale, and greatly exceeds them in terms of diversity of data.

The underlying Find an Expert search system allows users to issue queries and explore results across multiple categories: Researchers, Research Groups, Scholarly Works, Projects, News, and Research Degree Opportunities. As is typical of applied search tasks, a variety of input signals are blended in a complex manner that cannot be easily summarized into a simple description of how items are scored. Fortunately, that complexity does not affect the validity and usefulness of the collection derived from it.

Given our focus on expert retrieval, we concentrate on the *Researchers* category, which displays candidate expert profiles ranked by relevance to the user's query. Figure 1 illustrates the search results interface for the query *"information retrieval"*. Each candidate tile in the results list displays key summary information: the researcher's name, an extracted snippet, and several quantitative indicators including counts of associated scholarly works, projects, and news items. Users can click any tile to access detailed information about the researcher, including their full publication list, research interests, ongoing projects, and contact details.

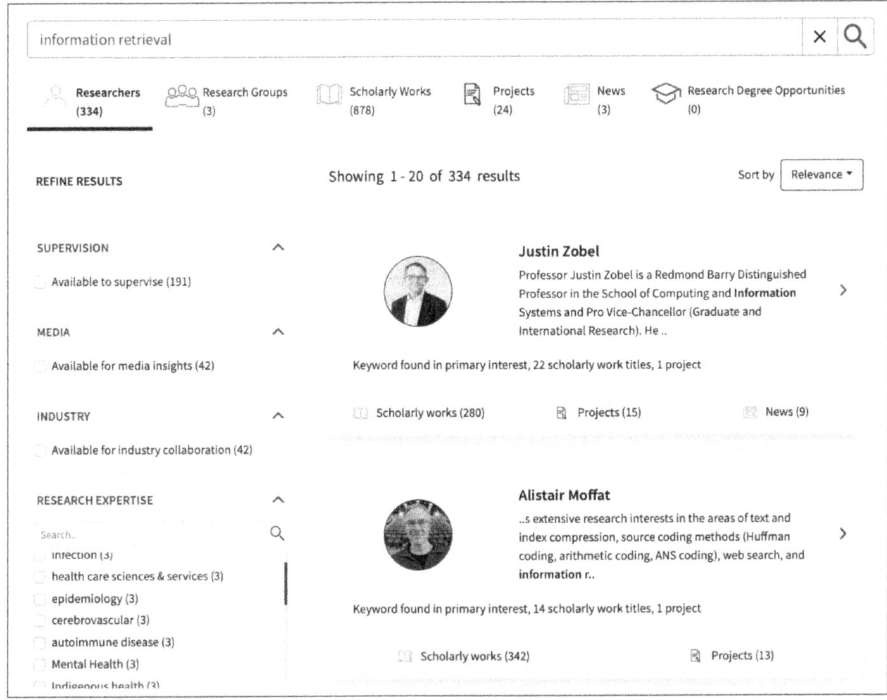


**Fig. 1.** "Researcher view" results for *"information retrieval"* as of 8 October 2025.

**FaE Profiles.** The FaE profiles dataset covers the great majority of the academic staff at the University of Melbourne, and was assembled in the first week of May 2025. To facilitate structured analysis, we converted the original CSV data into a sequence of JSON records. Table 2 shows one (confected) profile with most (but not all) of the key fields and example values. A detailed schema and explanation of the fields is provided with the online resource.

**FaE Log File.** The user log component of the FaE resource was collected between 12 January 2025 and 7 September 2025 as a set of 1,063,987 interaction records, each containing seven fields: entity, event, id, ip, query, timestamp, and url. The entity field identifies the resource type (with options including profile, publication, project, opportunity, group, news), and the event is the action performed (including search and clickSearchResult). The id is a unique identifier for each

**Table 2.** A synthetic `FaE` profile, with text fields and nested lists truncated.

| Field | Example value |
| --- | --- |
| id | 1234 |
| fae_profile_url | https://findanexpert.unimelb.edu.au/... |
| orc_id | 0000-1111-2222-3333 |
| title | Professor |
| primary_fac_position | [{position: "Professor", *other attributes*}, ...] |
| primary_interest | "Bean and jellybean counting" |
| first_name | "Totally" |
| last_name | "Awesome" |
| bio | "I am interested in legumes and confectionary..." |
| supervisor_avail | true |
| supervision_statement | "I welcome you to get in touch..." |
| industry_avail | true |
| industry_statement | "I am interested in fairy floss..." |
| authorship_objects | [{publication_id: 1234567, *other attributes*}, ...] |
| project_objects | [{project_id: 123456, *other attributes*}, ...] |
| wordcloud_keywords | ["beans", "candy", ...] |
| publication_keywords | ["split peas", "split hairs", ...] |
| last_updated | 2025-07-25 18:25:16.270 +10 |

action; ip records the user's IP address; query is the search terms entered; and url indicates the target of the interaction.

To ensure consistency and reliable analysis, we applied the following filters to the raw log. First, rows with missing or blank IP addresses were removed (accounting for 77,546 records), with records without IP addresses unable to be properly grouped into sessions. Second, we excluded records with empty queries and those where the query string was the placeholder "undefined", thereby removing another 271,151 and then 2,277 rows, respectively. Third, all queries were normalized by converting to lowercase and trimming leading/trailing whitespace to ensure consistent matching. Finally, we removed 76 records with IP addresses associated with the three authors, to avoid possible bias. The current artifact contains 712,937 rows.[2]

We then added a synthesized session_id column to facilitate session-level analysis. Records were sorted by IP address and then timestamp, and sessions constructed spanning consecutive actions from the same IP. A session was ended if the gap between two consecutive actions exceeded 120 minutes, with that duration chosen to reflect the relatively patient nature of expert search. Once the

---

[2] That number is correct at time of paper finalization. We are not aware of any offensive or divisive queries, but any that are noted will be removed. This may affect the number of queries available when the resource is distributed.

sessions were formed, the IP addresses were removed. Timestamps were recorded as a mix of Australian Eastern Summer Time (UTC+11) and then Australian Eastern Time (UTC+10).

Table 3 shows a representative session, with one search and two click interactions. The first row captures a search for *"energy & fuels"*. The entity field is empty and there is no associated URL. The other two rows show clickSearchResult events occurring two and seven minutes after the initial search. Both have entity set to profile, indicating that the user clicked on researcher profiles both times, and with URL fields indicating which profiles were clicked. Critically, the query field in the click events matches the original search, allowing the clicks to be correctly associated. This sequence of actions within a few minutes demonstrates typical user behavior: issuing a query and then examining a sequence of results.

**Table 3.** Sample log entries showing search-then-click behavior on two profiles.

| Entity | Event | Query | Timestamp | URL |
| --- | --- | --- | --- | --- |
| – | search | energy & fuels | 2025-07-29T02:21... | – |
| profile | clickSearchResult | energy & fuels | 2025-07-29T02:23... | /profile/9965... |
| profile | clickSearchResult | energy & fuels | 2025-07-29T02:28... | /profile/8258... |

**FaE Manual System Output.** We collected further data manually, first extracting all queries from the log for the period 1–7 September 2025 such that:

- a search event was followed by a clickSearchResult to a profile;
- the query string was identical in both the search and click rows; and
- the search was for a topic rather than a specific person.

The third of those requirements was tested by computing an overlap score between the query tokens and the tokens in the clicked profile.

We next reduced that set to a list of distinct queries, and randomly sampled a subset of 530 without replacement, noting that the distribution of query frequencies is relatively even and that use of stratification or similar would not necessarily create a better representation than straightforward random selection.

Then, in a second phase of activity carried out in the period 9–12 September 2025 (straight after the log period ended), we executed each of the 530 selected queries in the live "Find an Expert" system and captured the corresponding "Researcher view" SERP of up to 50 tiles. Collecting these after the log period concluded ensured that there was no interference with the user interaction data, while the short interval between the first and second phase provides confidence that the system's ranking behavior was likely unchanged.

The manual collection produced 5,197 unique profiles from the 530 queries, with a mean of 38.9 profiles per query and a median of 50. This component of the resource complements the click-through information, providing the complete system output for a set of queries where users engaged with the SERP.

**Potential Applications.** We see many possible uses for the FaE resource. Authorship records can be used to construct co-authorship networks for network-based ranking models [6]; project data supports investigation of collaboration patterns, funding sources, and research impact; organizational affiliations permit exploration of hierarchical and cross-unit structures; and supervision fields facilitate the study of supervisory capacity and availability across disciplines. Moreover, the combination of metadata and rich textual content makes the FaE dataset suitable for both traditional retrieval models and neural approaches.

The user interaction logs enable research on query intent, search behavior patterns, and user satisfaction metrics; and the collected SERPs allow for controlled experiments on ranking algorithms and their alignment with user preferences. Considered as a whole, these components thus constitute a unique resource for developing and evaluating expert finding systems in realistic academic settings.

**Data Access Agreement.** The FaE resource is available vie email request to the second or third authors. Access to the resource will require that a signed license agreement be completed and returned, after which the data will be transferred. At this stage, we expect that the data will be available until the end of 2033, at which time all copies will need to be permanently deleted. A small sample of each of the three main components is provided license-free, see https://figshare.com/s/78875cadc22d0c373b6d.

**Ethics Approval.** The FaE profiles are already in the public domain with the consent of the individuals involved. Moreover, none of the queries contain any identifying or personal information, and all IP addresses were removed from the log. In line with the provisions of the Australian *National Statement on Ethical Conduct in Human Research (2025)*[3], ethics review was thus not required.

## 4    Resource Properties

Section 3 described the structure and acquisition of the new FaE resource. We now examine some of its properties.

---

[3]     http://www.nhmrc.gov.au/about-us/publications/national-statement-ethical-conduct-human-research-2025.

**Profile Properties.** Table 4 reports summary statistics for the FaE profiles, demonstrating their scale and diversity. Figure 2 provides further details of the distribution of publications counts. A small number of highly prolific University of Melbourne academics (the current authors not among them!) have authored more than 1000 publications through their careers, but the most common counts are one paper (423 profiles) and two papers (308 profiles), with both of these included

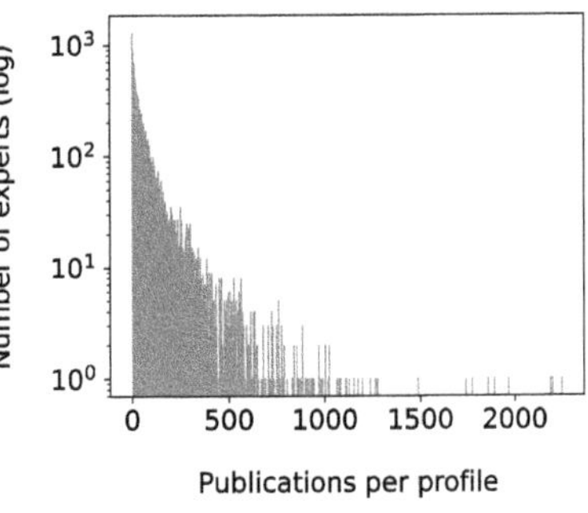


**Fig. 2.** Research outputs.

in the first element in Fig. 2, which covers the band from 0–4 publications. A similar pattern, on a reduced scale, applies to funded projects.

**Table 4.** Summary statistics of the FaE profile dataset.

| Measurement | Value |
| --- | --- |
| Number of profiles | 8,984 |
| Number of publications | 474,576 |
| Number of projects | 25,064 |
| Publications per profile (min | med | mean | max) | 0 | 33 | 80 | 2250 |
| Projects per profile (min | med | mean | max) | 0 | 1 | 4 | 188 |
| Profile size in kB (min | med | mean | max) | 2 | 77 | 199 | 5573 |

**Table 5.** Statistics for ten most frequently observed queries.

| Query | Count | % of total | Days observ. | Peak day % |
| --- | --- | --- | --- | --- |
| *education* | 2359 | 0.53 | 157 | 1.78 |
| *psychology* | 1108 | 0.25 | 156 | 1.71 |
| *public health* | 1011 | 0.23 | 156 | 1.68 |
| *cancer* | 919 | 0.21 | 156 | 1.96 |
| *artificial intelligence* | 861 | 0.19 | 154 | 1.97 |
| *chemistry* | 809 | 0.18 | 153 | 1.85 |
| *machine learning* | 731 | 0.16 | 155 | 1.78 |
| *agriculture* | 724 | 0.16 | 148 | 2.62 |
| *microbiology* | 664 | 0.15 | 149 | 2.11 |
| *ai* | 599 | 0.14 | 151 | 2.00 |

**Query Properties.** The filtered log contains 443,411 search entities, covering (after case-folding and white-space normalization, without coalescing queries with word-order permutations) 194,289 unique queries, of which topic queries dominate name queries by a ratio of two-to-one. The large fraction of unique queries indicates substantial variation in user goals and expression. Queries are short, averaging 2.0 terms and 15.6 characters, consistent with typical search behavior in domain-specific systems. Daily query volume averages 2,771.3 queries.

Table 5 lists the ten most frequent queries. The column "days observed" is the number of days that query was seen during the 239-day collection period, with higher values indicating consistency; and "peak day %" is the fraction of that query's total volume that occurred on its busiest single day, with higher values indicating burstier patterns. The overall distribution is heavy-tailed, with even the most frequent query only 0.5% of the total load, and with query occurrence patterns relatively stable over time.

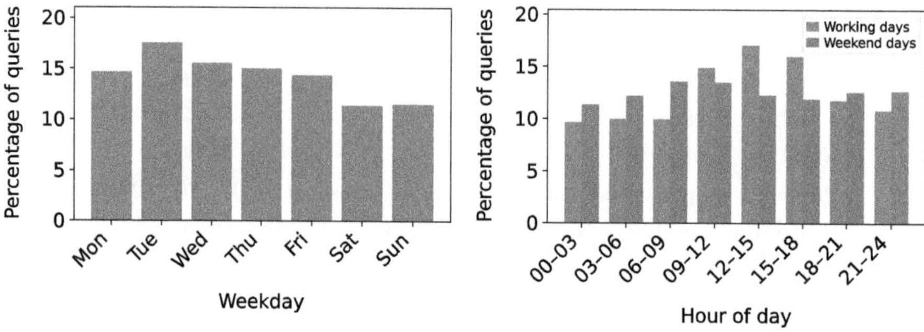


**Fig. 3.** Temporal distribution of queries: (a) share of total log by day of week; (b) share by hour of day within week days and weekend days. All times are local.

Figure 3 illustrates the overall temporal pattern of the queries. Pane (a) stratifies queries by day of week. Volume peaks on Tuesday, then fades through to Friday, and is least at weekends, a not unexpected pattern given that the platform is used primarily for professional rather than casual purposes. Pane (b) shows the split across the 24-hour day, tabulating week days and weekend days separately. Week day activity peaks between noon and 3pm, and is generally high through the working day between 9am and 6pm. Weekend activity follows a flatter hourly distribution. With only 25.3% of the overall query load originating at Australian IP addresses, the non-trivial background load through the Australian night hours is a result of international activity from other time zones. For example, the second most common origin was USA, with 20.1% of the queries. In total 182 distinct countries and regions appear in the log.

**Session Properties.** As already noted in Sect. 3, sessions were constructed by grouping actions from the same IP address, with a session deemed to have

**Table 6.** Session-level statistics.

| Measurement | Value |
| --- | --- |
| Number of sessions | 202,974 |
| Sessions with $> 1$ query | 57,666 |
| Average sessions per day | 1,268.6 |
| Average session duration (mm:ss) | 14:25 |
| Average session length (#queries) | 2.18 |
| Average events per session (search and clickSearchResult actions) | 3.51 |

ended if the gap between consecutive actions from that IP address exceeded 120 minutes. Table 6 presents summary statistics revealing distinct user behavior patterns. The distribution is highly skewed, with 72% of the sessions consisting of only a single query, suggesting that most users engage in targeted, goal-oriented searches rather than exploratory browsing. Also worthy of note is the relatively low click-through rate, with typically just one or two academic profiles viewed per session.

The prevalence of single-query sessions has implications for system design. Our findings align with those of Weerkamp et al. [42], who observed that most sessions in people search systems consist of single queries. The pattern contrasts with general web search, where query reformulation is more common [25], and suggests that users approach the Find an Expert system with specific goals rather than exploratory information needs.

**Table 7.** User-level statistics. Users are defined as unique IP addresses.

| Measurement | Value |
| --- | --- |
| Number of users (unique IPs) | 89,582 |
| Users with $> 1$ session | 15,020 (16.8%) |
| Users with $> 1$ query | 43,048 (48.1%) |
| Average sessions per user | 2.27 |
| Average total queries per user | 4.95 |

**User Properties.** In the next analysis we regard each unique IP address as corresponding to a single user, recognizing that this is a necessary approximation that may aggregate multiple individuals behind shared institutional IPs or, conversely, split single users across multiple network connections. Table 7 summarizes the resultant engagement patterns. Around half of the observed users (by this definition) were single-session single-query visitors who performed one search and then did not return within the log collection period. Less than a fifth of the users contributed more than one session into the FaE log, and even among engaged users, platform visits are episodic rather than regular.

**Table 8.** Click-through statistics, with profile clicks dominating.

| Measurement | Value | Clicks by entity type | |
|---|---|---|---|
| Total clicks | 269,526 | Profile | 232,787 (86.37%) |
| Unique clicked URLs | 23,629 | Project | 18,289 (6.79%) |
| Maximum clicks on any item | 773 | Publication | 10,360 (3.84%) |
| Queries with $\geq 1$ click | 116,100 (26.2%) | Opportunity | 5,609 (2.08%) |
| Sessions with $\geq 1$ click | 69,312 (34.1%) | Group | 1,876 (0.70%) |
| Avg. clicks per clicked query | 2.32 | News | 605 (0.22%) |

**Click-through Properties.** To understand how users engage with search results, we analyzed click-through behavior across the 443,411 queries in the FaE log. Table 8 summarizes statistics in regard to the click records in the log, and their target entity types. The overwhelming majority of clicks were to researcher profiles, confirming that expert discovery is the platform's primary function. The most clicked profile page was for a senior researcher in Chemical Engineering.

We also examined query-level click-through rates, to assess the level of user engagement. The relatively modest click-through rate (around one in four queries) can be interpreted either as indicating that the search results do not lead to satisfactory outcomes, or that users' information needs are often addressed by the SERP itself, see Fig. 1. If a query does result in a click, it usually then results in at least one further click, perhaps supporting the latter explanation.

**Table 9.** Distribution of clicks by rank position for all log instances of 530 queries.

| Rank | Clicks | % of total | Rank | Clicks | % of total |
|---|---|---|---|---|---|
| 1 | 4,892 | 13.18 | 6 | 1,734 | 4.67 |
| 2 | 3,405 | 9.17 | 7 | 1,571 | 4.23 |
| 3 | 2,729 | 7.35 | 8 | 1,360 | 3.66 |
| 4 | 2,360 | 6.36 | 9 | 1,261 | 3.40 |
| 5 | 2,032 | 5.47 | 10 | 1,116 | 3.01 |

**Click Position Properties.** As noted in Sect. 3, we also curated a set of 530 SERPs shortly after corresponding queries had been logged. Those 530 distinct queries accounted for 37,270 search rows in the FaE log, with 13,243 of those rows leading to one or more clicks. The most frequent sampled query was *"psychology"*, which was observed 1108 times in the log. At the other extreme, 82 of the 530 sampled queries were only issued once during the collection period. The sets of clicks that followed those 37,270 query instances were then checked against the corresponding SERP to identify (in arrears, as a reasonable estimate) the rank of each click. Of the total of 46,381 profile clicks, some 37,126 (80%)

were matched in this way, with name normalization mismatches or profiles not appearing in the top-50 results accounting for the other 20%.

Table 9 presents the observed click distribution as micro-averaged percentages, reflecting aggregate weighted-by-query behavior. Unsurprisingly, this distribution shows the typical pattern of top-focused user interactions [21]. Our findings also align with analysis of logs from talent and job search systems [39], where users examine multiple candidates rather than seeking a single straightforward answer. A macro-averaged distribution, computing mean percentages across the queries, treating each query equally regardless of its frequency, yielded a similar decreasing distribution, but with larger fractions over the top ten ranks, suggesting that the popular queries, which tend to be broader in scope (see Table 5), receive clicks distributed across more positions.

## 5    Conclusion

We have presented the Find an Expert (FaE) dataset, a comprehensive resource for academic expert finding research that addresses critical gaps in existing benchmarks. The dataset consists of three interconnected components: (1) three-quarters of a million interaction records over nearly eight months, capturing authentic expert-seeking behavior; (2) structured profiles for nine thousand academics, containing rich contextual information including publications, projects, positions, biographical text, and engagement preferences; and (3) SERPs for more than five hundred queries, enabling analysis of click behavior.

Our preliminary behavioral analysis has provided useful knowledge of how users interact with expert finding systems. Query formulation is highly diverse, but with relatively short, focused queries. Temporal patterns show strong professional usage with peak activity during business hours on weekdays, and with relatively consistent querying patterns. Engagement is predominantly via single-query sessions, suggesting goal-oriented rather than exploratory search behavior; but with low per-query click rates; and with the items that are clicked dominated by researcher profiles. Finally, initial position bias analysis shows the usual concentration in top ranks, but with flatter distributions than for web search.

These findings have important implications for system design. The prevalence of single-query sessions emphasizes the critical importance of first-query precision. The willingness to examine multiple top-ranked profiles suggests that diversification strategies may be valuable. And the modest click-through rate indicates clear opportunities to improve both search quality and result presentation through richer snippets or preview information.

**Acknowledgment.** Adam Pearson and Shao Wang (University of Melbourne) were helpful beyond all possible expectations while we were formulating our plans and determining how to collect, curate, and interpret the FaE data.

**Data Availability Statement.** Access is via direct email request and a license agreement, as noted at the end of Sect. 3. Research group leaders will be able to obtain the data on behalf of a research team and manage a copy for their group, provided that each individual making use of the data signs a local copy of the license as an annex to the main agreement signed by the group leader.

**Disclosure of Interests.** The authors have no competing interests to declare that are relevant to the content of this article.

# References


1. Afzal, M.T., Maurer, H.A.: Expertise recommender system for scientific community. J. Univ. Comp. Sc. **17**(11), 1529–1549 (2011)
2. Al Hakim, S., Sensuse, D.I., Budi, I., Subroto, I.M.I., Siagian, A.H.A.M.: Expert retrieval based on local journals metadata to drive small-medium industries (SMI) collaboration for product innovation. Soc. Netw. Anal. Min. **13**(1), 68 (2023)
3. Al-Taie, M.Z., Kadry, S., Obasa, A.I.: Understanding expert finding systems: domains and techniques. Soc. Netw. Anal. Min. **8**(1), 57 (2018)
4. Alhabashneh, O., Iqbal, R., Doctor, F., James, A.: Fuzzy rule based profiling approach for enterprise information seeking and retrieval. Inf. Sci. **394**, 18–37 (2017)
5. Askari, A., Verberne, S., Pasi, G.: Expert finding in legal community question answering. In: Proceedings of ECIR, pp. 22–30 (2022)
6. Azimi, M., Moffat, A., Zobel, J.: Expert finding revisited: a uniform exploration of methods. In: Proceedings of ICTIR, pp. 478–487 (2025)
7. Balog, K., Azzopardi, L., De Rijke, M.: Formal models for expert finding in enterprise corpora. In: Proceedings of SIGIR, pp. 43–50 (2006)
8. Balog, K., Bogers, T., Azzopardi, L., De Rijke, M., Van Den Bosch, A.: Broad expertise retrieval in sparse data environments. In: Proceedings of SIGIR, pp. 551–558 (2007)
9. Balog, K., Fang, Y., de Rijke, M., Serdyukov, P., Si, L.: Expertise retrieval. Found. Trend. Inf. Retr. **6**(2–3), 127–256 (2012)
10. Balog, K., de Rijke, M.: Determining expert profiles (with an application to expert finding). In: Proceedings of IJCAI, pp. 2657–2662 (2007)
11. Campbell, C.S., Maglio, P.P., Cozzi, A., Dom, B.: Expertise identification using email communications. In: Proceedings of CIKM, pp. 528–531 (2003)
12. Deng, H., Han, J., Lyu, M.R., King, I.: Modeling and exploiting heterogeneous bibliographic networks for expertise ranking. In: Proceedings of JCDL, pp. 71–80 (2012)
13. Ebrahimi, S., Salamat, S., Arabzadeh, N., Bashari, M., Bagheri, E.: exHarmony: authorship and citations for benchmarking the reviewer assignment problem. In: Proceedings of ECIR, pp. 1–16 (2025)
14. Faisal, M., Daud, A., Akram, A.: Expert ranking using reputation and answer quality of co-existing users. Int. Arab J. Inf. Technol. **14**(1) (2017)
15. Fallahnejad, Z., Beigy, H.: Attention-based skill translation models for expert finding. Expert Syst. Appl. **193**, 116433 (2022)

16. Fang, Y., Somasundaram, N., Si, L., Ko, J., Mathur, A.P.: Analysis of an expert search query log. In: Proceedings of SIGIR, pp. 1189–1190 (2011)
17. Fischer, T., Remus, S., Biemann, C.: LT expertfinder: an evaluation framework for expert finding methods. In: Proceedings of NAACL, pp. 98–104 (2019)
18. Gao, X., Wu, S., Xia, D., Xiong, H.: Topic-sensitive expert finding based solely on heterogeneous academic networks. Expert Sys. Appl. **213**, 119241 (2023)
19. Gonçalves, R., Dorneles, C.F.: Automated expertise retrieval: a taxonomy-based survey and open issues. ACM Comput. Surv. **52**(5), 1–30 (2019)
20. Gui, H., Zhu, Q., Liu, L., Zhang, A., Han, J.: Expert finding in heterogeneous bibliographic networks with locally-trained embeddings. arXiv:1803.03370 (2018)
21. Guy, I., Ur, S., Ronen, I., Weber, S., Oral, T.: Best faces forward: a large-scale study of people search in the enterprise. In: Proceedings of CHI, pp. 1775–1784 (2012)
22. Hashemi, S.H., Neshati, M., Beigy, H.: Expertise retrieval in bibliographic network: a topic dominance learning approach. In: Proceedings of CIKM, pp. 1117–1126 (2013)
23. Hofmann, K., Balog, K., Bogers, T., de Rijke, M.: Contextual factors for finding similar experts. J. Am. Soc. Inf. Sc. Tech. **61**(5), 994–1014 (2010)
24. Husain, O., Salim, N., Alias, R.A., Abdelsalam, S., Hassan, A.: Expert finding systems: a systematic review. Appl. Sci. **9**(20), 4250 (2019)
25. Jansen, B.J., Spink, A.: An analysis of web documents retrieved and viewed. In: Proceedings of International Conference on Internet Computing, pp. 65–69 (2003)
26. Kang, Y.B., Du, H., Forkan, A.R.M., Jayaraman, P.P., Aryani, A., Sellis, T.: Expfinder: a hybrid model for expert finding from text-based expertise data. Expert Syst. Appl. **211**, 118691 (2023)
27. Kong, X., Jiang, H., Wang, W., Bekele, T.M., Xu, Z., Wang, M.: Exploring dynamic research interest and academic influence for scientific collaborator recommendation. Scientometrics **113**(1), 369–385 (2017). https://doi.org/10.1007/s11192-017-2485-9
28. Lin, S., Hong, W., Wang, D., Li, T.: A survey on expert finding techniques. J. Intell. Inf. Syst. **49**(2), 255–279 (2017). https://doi.org/10.1007/s10844-016-0440-5
29. Liu, D., Xu, W., Du, W., Wang, F.: How to choose appropriate experts for peer review: an intelligent recommendation method in a big data context. Data Sci. J. **14**, 16–16 (2015)
30. Mahani, N.T., Dehghani, M., Mirian, M.S., Shakery, A., Taheri, K.: Expert finding by the Dempster-Shafer theory for evidence combination. Expert Syst. J. Knowl. Eng. **35**(1), e12231 (2018)
31. Mangaravite, V., Santos, R.L., Ribeiro, I.S., Gonçalves, M.A., Laender, A.H.: The LExR collection for expertise retrieval in academia. In: Proceedings of SIGIR, pp. 721–724 (2016)
32. Moreira, C., Martins, B., Calado, P.: Using rank aggregation for expert search in academic digital libraries. arXiv:1501.05140 (2015)
33. Neshati, M., Fallahnejad, Z., Beigy, H.: On dynamicity of expert finding in community question answering. Inf. Proc. Manag. **53**(5), 1026–1042 (2017)
34. Omidvar, A., Garakani, M., Safarpour, H.R.: Context-based user ranking in forums for expert finding using WordNet dictionary and social network analysis. Inf. Technol. Manag. **15**(1), 51–63 (2014)
35. Peng, Q., et al.: Towards a multi-view attentive matching for personalized expert finding. In: Proceedings of WWW, pp. 2131–2140 (2022)

36. Rampisela, T.V., Yulianti, E.: Semantic-based query expansion for academic expert finding. In: Proceedings of International Conference on Asian Language Processing, pp. 34–39 (2020)
37. Schoegje, T., Hardman, L., de Vries, A., Pieters, T.: Improving expert search effectiveness: comparing ways to rank and present search results. In: Proceedings of CHIIR, pp. 56–65 (2024)
38. Silva, A.T.P.: A research analytics framework for expert recommendation in research social networks. Ph.D. thesis, City University of Hong Kong (2014)
39. Spina, D., et al.: Understanding user behavior in job and talent search: an initial investigation. In: Proceedings of SIGIR eCom Workshop (2017)
40. Sun, J., Xu, W., Ma, J., Sun, J.: Leverage RAF to find domain experts on research social network services: a big data analytics methodology with MapReduce framework. Int. J. Prod. Econ. **165**, 185–193 (2015)
41. Tekin, C., Atan, O., Van Der Schaar, M.: Discover the expert: context-adaptive expert selection for medical diagnosis. IEEE Trans. Emerg. Top. Comput. **3**(2), 220–234 (2014)
42. Weerkamp, W., Berendsen, R., Kovachev, B., Meij, E., Balog, K., De Rijke, M.: People searching for people: analysis of a people search engine log. In: Proceedings of SIGIR, pp. 45–54 (2011)
43. Wu, D., Fan, S., Yuan, F.: Research on pathways of expert finding on academic social networking sites. Inf. Proc. Manag. **58**(2), 102475 (2021)
44. Wu, W., Zhang, W., Yang, Y., Wang, Q.: Drex: developer recommendation with k-nearest-neighbor search and expertise ranking. In: Proceedings of Asia Pacific Software Engineering Conference, pp. 389–396 (2011)

# GREAT: A Group Recommendation Evaluation and Analysis Tool


Ariel Smith[1], David Contreras[2(✉)], Maria Salamó[3],
and Ludovico Boratto[4]

[1] Facultad de Ingeniería y Arquitectura, Universidad Arturo Prat, Iquique, Chile
[2] Smart Society Research Group, La Salle-Universitat Ramon Llull, Barcelona, Spain
`david.contreras@salle.url.edu`
[3] Facultat de Matemàtiques i Informàtica, Universitat de Barcelona, Barcelona, Spain
`maria.salamo@ub.edu`
[4] Department of Mathematics and Computer Science, University of Cagliari, Cagliari, Italy
`ludovico.boratto@acm.org`



**Abstract.** Previous research on group recommender systems (GRSs) has shown that group dynamics strongly influence decision-making, yet collaborative filtering (CF)–based GRSs rarely account for social interactions, partly because suitable tools to capture and analyze live interaction traces are limited. This paper introduces a community resource for studying live groups engaging with a CF-based recommender system through a domain-independent graphical interface that records structured interaction signals (e.g., suggestions, views, and favorites) and integrates them into interaction-aware consensus strategies. A live user study with 72 participants organized into 18 groups illustrates the platform's ability to capture and analyze user interactions, including interface engagement patterns and perceived social roles. Comparing two interaction-aware consensus strategies (mean vs. completeness), we observe differences in satisfaction distributions and interaction patterns; isolating the causal contribution of interaction signals would require an interaction-unaware baseline. Source code and dataset are available online at this link (https://github.com/davidcontrerasaguilar/GREAT.git).

**Keywords:** Group Recommendation · Collaborative Filtering · Live User Evaluation


## 1 Introduction

Group recommender systems (GRSs) generate recommendations for multiple users by jointly modeling individual preferences and group characteristics in shared decision contexts [14,19,24,36]. Among the factors shaping group decision-making, group dynamics play a critical role [15,17,48]. Prior work links personality traits [30,40,48], social trust [37,41], and group dynamics to conformity and collective choice [18,33]. Related studies also show that roles, group



R. Campos et al. (Eds.): ECIR 2026, LNCS 16486, pp. 415–431, 2026.
https://doi.org/10.1007/978-3-032-21321-1_50

size, and leadership influence interaction patterns [31,44,50], although not via interaction-driven strategies. Nevertheless, the problem of how group members influence one another through interaction during decision-making remains under-explored. Most of the existing literature models individual preferences and aggregates them to produce group recommendations, overlooking the interpersonal influence processes that naturally arise in group contexts. This gap persists primarily because analytical tools capable of capturing such interactions in real-time are scarce.

While real-world groups reach consensus through discussion, negotiation, and mutual influence, most computational approaches still prioritize algorithmic optimization over the social processes that drive collective decisions [15–18]. Some recent studies have begun to bridge this gap, both by advocating for interaction-aware perspectives in group recommendation and by proposing ways to capture and interpret group dynamics in conversational settings [25,38]. For instance, Nguyen and Ricci [32] analyzed user–item interactions in a chat-based GRS to identify active participants, and Contreras et al. [11] modeled leadership and collaboration in conversational recommender systems. However, these efforts are largely confined to dialogue-based or content-driven settings, leaving open the challenge of systematically recording, modeling, and analyzing structured user interactions in collaborative filtering (CF)–based systems. More generally, CF-based GRSs inherit a strong dependency on the underlying rating prediction task, whose modeling choices and performance can substantially affect downstream group recommendation accuracy and evaluation outcomes [4–7].

Addressing this challenge is crucial, as CF remains one of the most widely used recommendation techniques. Yet, its application to group contexts often neglects the social nature of collective decision-making. Without capturing and interpreting live user interactions, GRSs risk producing recommendations that diverge from the group's emerging consensus. Enabling structured observation of how users negotiate, influence, and converge toward shared preferences can thus offer insights into both recommendation quality and user engagement.

To address this gap, we introduce GREAT (Group Recommendation Evaluation and Analysis Tool), a domain-independent platform designed to capture and analyze structured user interactions during live group recommendation sessions. GREAT shifts the focus from post-hoc performance evaluation to real-time modeling of user behavior, integrating interaction signals directly into the recommendation process. Specifically, we contribute:

1. An interaction-aware graphical interface that records a broad spectrum of user actions (e.g., suggestions, views, favorites) within a CF-based GRS;
2. An interaction-based scoring mechanism to infer collaboration and leadership roles from live behavior; and
3. A live user study with 18 groups (72 participants), illustrating how interaction patterns reveal group dynamics and influence consensus formation and satisfaction.

Beyond introducing the tool itself (available online at this link[1]), this paper aims to advance empirical research on the social processes underlying group recommendation. GREAT provides an integrated environment that supports *user profiling, interaction monitoring,* and *recommendation management* in collaborative contexts. By providing a platform for capturing real-time behavioral data, we enable systematic investigation of how interaction patterns shape group outcomes. Concretely, we address the following research questions:

- **RQ1:** *To what extent do users engage with and value social interactions in a CF-based GRS?*
- **RQ2:** *How accurately do users' perceptions of group dynamics align with the interaction data captured by the system?*
- **RQ3:** *What is the impact of structured, live interactions on group consensus formation and recommendation satisfaction?*

## 2   Related Work

GRSs have been explored in domains such as *movies* [2,34,42], *music* [13,28,46], *travel* [12,29,49], and *restaurants and dining* [9,10,23], demonstrating the adaptability of GRSs to collaborative contexts. Despite this progress, standardized evaluation methodologies for *live* group recommendation remain limited, making it difficult to compare models and domains under realistic interaction settings. Recent work further emphasizes that evaluation challenges go beyond static preference aggregation, including fairness–diversity trade-offs in sequential group settings [27] and influence-aware aggregation mechanisms that balance fairness, accuracy, and diversity [35]. As emphasized by Alvarado et al. [3], designing user interfaces for GRSs remains challenging due to the heterogeneity of interaction paradigms and design strategies in the literature.

An early example of a reusable system is *Choicla* [45], which supports multiple group decision scenarios and allows members to evaluate distinct item features. However, many empirical studies still rely on heterogeneous datasets and metrics, with limited support for systematically capturing the social dynamics underlying group decision-making. Frameworks such as gCOACH [11,12] enable real-time collaboration in conversational GRS settings, but limited accessibility can constrain reproducibility and broader adoption. This motivates open resources that support live studies while enabling reproducible analysis of interaction traces and group dynamics.

**GroupLibRec** [43] extends the LibRec [22] pipeline with group-specific stages, emphasizing experimental reproducibility and modular evaluation across datasets. The Hybrid Two-Phase Group Recommender Framework (**HTGF**) [2] advances modeling of complex group structures by supporting overlapping memberships and hybrid prediction strategies. The Group Validation Framework (**GVF**) [1] proposes multi-layer evaluation of recommender systems beyond

---

[1] https://github.com/davidcontrerasaguilar/GREAT.git

**Table 1.** Comparison between existing GRS frameworks and GREAT. *Offline/Batch* = dataset/log-driven evaluation (no live multi-user interaction); *Online/Interactive* = synchronous live group sessions.

| Aspect | GroupLibRec [43] | HTGF [2] | GVF [1] | GREAT |
|---|---|---|---|---|
| Primary goal | Reproducible GRS experimentation (LibRec-based) | Hybrid movie GRS for overlapping groups | Multi-layer RS validation/evaluation | Live GRS study platform: interaction logging + analysis |
| Processing mode | Offline/Batch | Offline/Batch | Offline/Batch | Online/Interactive; logs exportable for offline analysis |
| Group modeling | Static groups; multiple formation strategies | Overlapping membership (Fuzzy C-Means) | Clustered subgroups for evaluation | Session-based groups; real-time interaction profile ($SU, VP, FP$) |
| Recommender & consensus | LibRec recommenders + group aggregations | FCM+similarity + Neural CF; top-$k$ aggregation | N/A (evaluation only) | CF (GroupLibRec) + interaction-weighted consensus (mean, completeness) |
| Interaction & collaboration | No live collaboration | No interaction modeling | No interaction modeling | Chat + structured actions (suggest/view/favorite); interactions logged |
| Evaluation methodology | Offline metrics (MAE, RMSE, P@$k$, ...) | Offline eval on MovieLens (RMSE, MAE, ...) | Subgroup/fairness analyses | Real-user sessions + GroupLibRec metrics; behavioral traces; reproducible via logs |
| Key strengths | Standardized, reproducible comparisons | Models overlapping membership | Reveals subgroup disparities | Links live interaction to reproducible analysis of group dynamics |

aggregate accuracy, including subgroup analyses and fairness-oriented assessment.

Direct comparison across frameworks is often hindered by heterogeneous evaluation protocols and the fact that most support offline/batch experimentation rather than live, multi-user interaction. *GREAT* complements this landscape by providing an open platform for synchronous live group sessions, structured interaction capture, and reproducible analysis of behavioral traces. Table 1 summarizes key differences between GREAT and representative related frameworks.

## 3   The GREAT Framework

GREAT focuses on CF-based GRSs and combines the interactive, social, and real-time capabilities of gCOACH [11,12] with the evaluation and reproducibility strengths of GroupLibRec [43], extending them through integrated communication (chat) and live behavioral tracking to enable deeper group analysis.

### 3.1   Formalizing the Problem

We consider a set of $n$ users $\mathcal{U} = \{u_1, ..., u_n\}$ aiming to select an item $I_j$ that maximizes group satisfaction, from a larger catalog of $m$ items, $\mathcal{I} = \{I_1, ..., I_m\}$.

Let $IM^{u_i}$ be the **individual model** of user $u_i$, and $\mathcal{IM} = \{IM^{u_1}, ..., IM^{u_n}\}$ the set of all such models. Each model contains a set of observed preference values, i.e., $IM^{u_i} = \{P_1, ..., P_{r_{u_i}}\}$, where $r_{u_i}$ may differ across users based on their expressed preferences and each $P_k$ denotes an

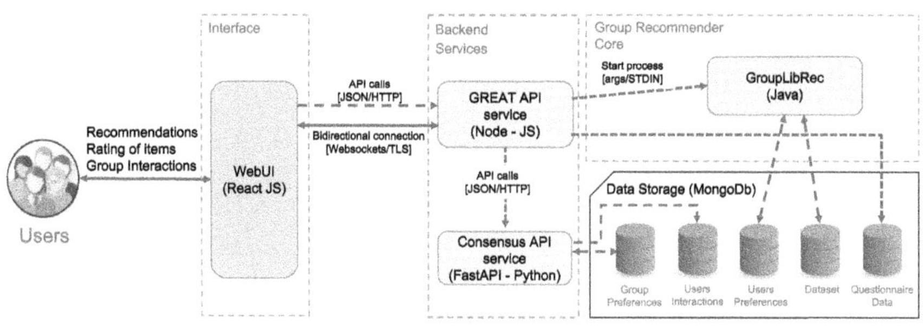


**Fig. 1.** Conceptual architecture of GREAT framework

observed preference value provided by $u_i$ (e.g., an explicit rating). To avoid ambiguity, we denote by $\hat{r}_{u_i,j}$ the predicted rating for a user–item pair $(u_i, I_j)$.

Prior research [11] shows that combining individual and collaborative inter-action data can contribute to group consensus. Formally, we define the **collaborative model** as $\mathcal{CM} = \{CM^{u_1}, \ldots, CM^{u_n}\}$, where each $CM^{u_i}$ represents the collaborative profile of user $u_i$. This model is integrated into our framework to capture inter-user dependencies. The detailed construction and integration procedure are presented in Sects. 3.3 and 3.4.

To evaluate how suitable an item $I_j \in \mathcal{I}$ is for a user $u_i \in \mathcal{U}$, we use a satisfaction function $\delta(I_j, IM^{u_i})$ defined on the preference scale of the under-lying dataset, i.e., $\delta(I_j, IM^{u_i}) \in [r_{\min}, r_{\max}]$. In our rating-based CF setting, $\delta(I_j, IM^{u_i})$ corresponds to the predicted rating $\hat{r}_{u_i,j}$ for the user–item pair $(u_i, I_j)$ (clipped to $[r_{\min}, r_{\max}]$ when necessary). Using predicted ratings as a proxy for individual satisfaction is standard in CF-based GRSs and directly ties the group decision objective to the rating-prediction component [5,7].

## 3.2 Architecture

*GREAT* adopts a web-based client–server model that enables remote, synchronous interaction among group members. Figure 1 illustrates the conceptual architecture, organized into three layers (*Interface*, *Backend*, and *Group Recommender System*) plus a *Data Storage* component for persistent data management.

The *Interface* layer implements the view component and captures all user-facing interaction modalities (e.g., joining sessions, chatting, and interacting with recommended items). It also provides awareness cues (e.g., who is connected) and forwards user actions to the backend while receiving real-time updates from other group members (see Sect. 3.3 for the concrete UI layout).

*Backend* services act as the controller, orchestrating session logic by (i) exposing interface endpoints, (ii) supporting real-time bidirectional communication, (iii) managing resources and session artifacts, and (iv) applying *consensus* strategies to derive group outcomes [11,39,43]. They mediate all interfaceâĂŞrecommender requests, maintaining consistency of recommendations and shared session state across participants.

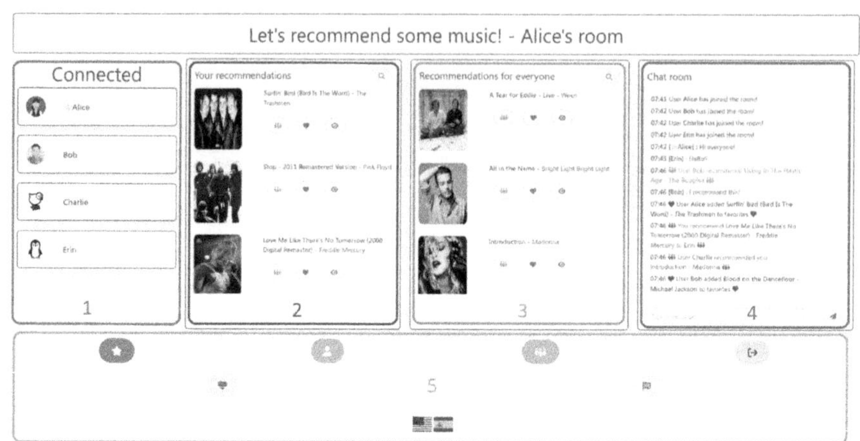


**Fig. 2.** Graphical interface of the CF-based GRS. The interface integrates individual and social interactions to support decision-making in group settings.

The final layer comprises the *Group Recommender System*, which integrates *GroupLibRec* [43] and is responsible for generating individual and group recommendations based on user preferences and session interactions.

The *Data Storage* component persists all information needed to support both interaction and subsequent analysis. This includes (i) individual profiles and group preferences, (ii) the underlying recommendation dataset, (iii) questionnaire responses and user profiling instruments (a Big Five personality assessment [20], the Thomas–Kilmann conflict mode instrument (TKI) [47], and a usability evaluation questionnaire) and (iv) detailed interaction logs produced during each session. In particular, *GREAT* stores the history of individual and group recommendations, users' ratings of favorite items, timestamped chat-based interactions (messages and system-mediated activity shown in the chat), and item engagement signals indicating which items have been viewed, recommended, marked as favorites, or listened to. This logging enables downstream analyses of user behavior, group dynamics, and system-mediated recommendation processes.

### 3.3   Collaborative Filtering-Based Recommendation Interface

We describe only the interface supporting group recommendation; the remaining webpages of *GREAT* are available in the accompanying repository[1]. A demonstration video is available online (https://tinyurl.com/yspmnc26), showing user login, virtual room creation, and group joining within the platform.

Figure 2 presents the main recommendation webpage of our CF-based GRS, designed to support structured group interactions across domains. Users participate via *virtual rooms*. Each room defines a *session-based* group: *GREAT* runs and analyzes one live group session at a time, and does not model persistent (potentially overlapping) memberships across multiple groups. In the example,

Bob, Charlie, and Erin join a room created by Alice in a music domain. The interface is organized into the following areas.

**Area 1** (top-left) displays the users connected to the room, each represented by a username and avatar to support mutual identification.

**Areas 2 and 3** present item recommendations for individuals and for the group, respectively. Each item provides three controls: a *suggestion button* (green icon) to recommend an item to a specific user or to the group, a *favorite button* (red heart icon) to store the item in the shared favorites area, and a *details button* (eye icon) to access item information and rate it on a 1–5 scale.

**Area 4** is the chat window, where users exchange natural-language messages, suggest items, and view session activity. This supports real-time collaboration; although in this study natural-language messages were not analyzed, the interface is designed so that chat and UI activity can be aligned with the structured interaction logs stored by the platform (cf. Fig. 1). The shared favorites area (accessible via any heart icon) displays all stored items together with the identity of the user who added them, and supports suggestion, removal, and rating.

**Area 5** (bottom) contains session controls: *rate item* (blue star), *open favorites* (red heart), *individual recommendation* (single-user icon), *group recommendation* (multi-user icon), *leave session* (exit icon), and *end session* (flag icon). The interface also supports English and Spanish, with dynamic label updates.

### 3.4   Modeling Items and User Profiles

Our collaborative model $\mathcal{CM}$ extends prior conversational interaction modeling [11] to structured, nonverbal signals in a domain-independent interface for CF-based group recommendation. These signals directly modulate each user's predicted satisfaction in the group ranking function during consensus formation.

Interactions in Areas 2–4 update $CM^{u_i} = \langle SU, VP, FP \rangle$, where $SU$ counts suggestions submitted by $u_i$, $VP$ counts how often they are viewed/opened by others, and $FP$ counts how often they are favorited by others. These counters reset to zero at the start of each session.

Each user-model $CM^{u_i}$ influences the group recommendation outcome. Individual preferences are stored in the corresponding user model $IM^{u_i}$, while the complete set of structured interactions and chat conversations is persistently logged for reproducible analysis. These logs can be exported and used for offline, post-hoc analyses and reproducibility; however, GREAT is primarily designed for synchronous live sessions rather than fully offline/batch evaluation workflows.

### 3.5   Consensus Modeling

At the end of a group session, once participants have expressed preferences over candidate items (e.g., items marked as favorites and rated during the session), the *GREAT* platform applies a consensus strategy to aggregate individual satisfactions and select a single group recommendation. Importantly, the aggregation is modulated by the collaborative model $\mathcal{CM}$, so that users' interaction-derived contributions can influence consensus formation.

The GREAT platform implements consensus strategies through the **Consensus API**, which currently includes two interaction-aware mechanisms: *collaborative mean* and *collaborative completeness*, described below. The API is modular and extensible, allowing the integration of additional consensus strategies.

**Collaborative Mean.** This strategy, introduced in [11], computes a group score for each candidate item $I_j$ as $mean(I_j, \mathcal{IM}, \mathcal{CM}) = \frac{1}{n} \sum_{i=1}^{n} \delta(I_j, IM^{u_i}) \cdot score_{u_i}(\mathcal{CM})$. Here, $\delta(I_j, IM^{u_i})$ denotes the (predicted) satisfaction of user $u_i$ for item $I_j$, and $score_{u_i}(\mathcal{CM})$ is an interaction-derived weight computed from the user-specific tuple $CM^{u_i} = \langle SU, VP, FP \rangle$ (Eq. 1). Compared to [11], the mathematical form is unchanged, but $\mathcal{CM}$ is built from interaction signals captured via GREAT's structured GUI (rather than conversational turns), yielding a weighted average that emphasizes users with higher recorded contributions.

**Collaborative Completeness.** This consensus-based approach is designed to balance agreement and preference intensity within the group. Following [11], we compute it as $completeness(I_j, \mathcal{IM}, \mathcal{CM}) = \frac{\sum_{i=1}^{n} w_i \cdot \sqrt{\delta(I_j, IM^{u_i}) \cdot score_{u_i}(\mathcal{CM})}}{\sum_{i=1}^{n} \sqrt{r_{u_i}}}$, where $w_i \geq 0$ and $\sum_{i=1}^{n} w_i = 1$ (in our implementation, $w_i = 1/n$ for all users). Here, $r_{u_i} = |IM^{u_i}|$ denotes the number of preference values available for user $u_i$ (Sect. 3.1), and $\sum_{i=1}^{n} \sqrt{r_{u_i}}$ provides a normalization factor to make scores comparable across users with different profile sizes. The objective is to promote high overall satisfaction while penalizing large deviations among group members, while still accounting for individual contributions via $score_{u_i}(\mathcal{CM})$.

**Interaction Score.** It is computed, for each user, according to Eq. 1. The parameters $w_{SU}$, $w_{VP}$, and $w_{FP}$ weigh the relative importance of suggesting items, attracting peer views, and attracting peer favorites, respectively.

$$score_{u_i}(\mathcal{CM}) = CM_{SU}^{u_i} \cdot w_{SU} + CM_{VP}^{u_i} \cdot w_{VP} + CM_{FP}^{u_i} \cdot w_{FP} \tag{1}$$

where $CM_{SU}^{u_i}$, $CM_{VP}^{u_i}$, and $CM_{FP}^{u_i}$ denote the three session-level counters in $CM^{u_i} = \langle SU, VP, FP \rangle$ (Sect. 3.4).

### 3.6   Interface Scalability Across Domains

Among the open research gaps identified in prior work [3], one of the most prominent is the limited exploration of domain-independent systems capable of adapting to multiple application contexts. The GREAT platform is fully compatible with a curated subset of the AMBAR dataset [21], which is well-suited for analyzing group recommendations. This dataset organizes information into items (tracks), their associated categories (genres), and user preferences, providing a clear structure for recommendation analysis. In this paper, these user preferences are explicit 1–5 track ratings collected through the interface (Fig. 2). Importantly, any dataset adhering to this structure can be seamlessly integrated with GREAT. Furthermore, the provided codebase includes documentation to facilitate the adaptation and scaling of the platform beyond the current music domain, ensuring flexibility and extensibility across diverse application contexts.

## 4   Case Study: Integration of Interaction Signals Into a CF-Based Group Recommender Systems

### 4.1   Setup and Methodology

We conducted a summative evaluation to assess user interaction and perception, following established quality-assurance methods [8]. A moderator introduced the protocol, answered procedural questions, and provided technical support, but did not intervene in group decision-making. All interaction events (e.g., navigation actions, suggestions, favorites, votes, and chat messages) were logged by GREAT and used for the analyses reported in Sect. 4.2. Interaction-based measures (e.g., $score_{u_i}$) are computed from test-phase logs only.

Our framework uses GroupLibRec [43] for generating recommendations with Matrix Factorization [26], configured with 20 latent factors, learning rate and regularization of 0.01, 100 iterations, an 80%/20% train/test split, a binarization threshold of 1.0, user-based similarity, and top-10 recommendations. We used a curated subset of the AMBAR dataset [21] and recruited 72 participants (45 male, 27 female, avg. age 27), randomly assigned to 18 four-person groups, each using a single consensus strategy.

The evaluation comprised four stages. In the **pre-test interview**, participants were introduced to the study, provided demographic details, and completed the Big Five personality assessment and the Thomas–Kilmann conflict mode Instrument (TKI). During **training**, they explored the interface and tested both individual and group recommendations, with an overview of interaction modalities and an opportunity to ask questions. In the **test phase**, users navigated the catalog, exchanged messages, and made suggestions, and the group received a recommendation via the assigned consensus strategy (*mean* or *completeness*). When the group finalized the process, GREAT computed a single top-1 group recommendation (the *group-recommended item*) according to the assigned strategy. Each participant then rated the group-recommended item on a five-point Likert scale (1 = very dissatisfied, 5 = very satisfied). Finally, the **post-test questionnaire** included a usability evaluation component and assessed satisfaction, interface use, and perceived leadership and collaboration. Participants nominated the member they perceived as most influential in driving the group decision (leader) and the one who contributed most to reaching agreement (most collaborative). Nominations were collected individually (one nomination per role); for analysis, we aggregated nominations at the group level by plurality, and ties yield multiple nominated candidates. Participants also rated peer contributions.

We refrain from direct quantitative comparisons with conversational and other interaction-aware GRS prototypes, because these systems typically couple the interaction modality (e.g., free-text dialogue and system-driven turns) with different preference elicitation workflows, candidate generation policies, and stopping/consensus procedures. A head-to-head comparison would therefore confound interaction awareness with differences in interface design and experimental protocol. A fair comparison would require implementing alternative interaction

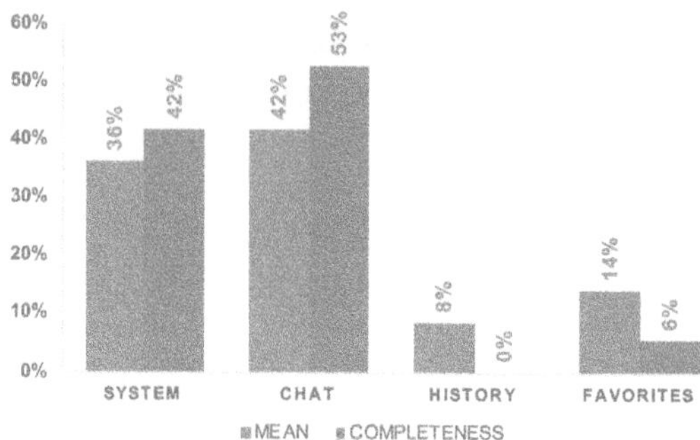


**Fig. 3.** Distribution of interaction activity across interface areas during group recommendation sessions (computed as the proportion of logged interaction events per area).

paradigms within the same experimental scaffold (i.e., identical catalog, recommender backbone, group composition, and termination rule) so that only the interaction mechanism varies, which we leave for future work.

## 4.2   Analysis of User Interaction

**Interface Area Engagement (RQ1).** Figure 3 shows how participants distributed their interaction activity across the main interface areas tracked by GREAT's event logs (SYSTEM, CHAT, HISTORY, and FAVORITES) during the test phase. We operationalize "attention" as the proportion of logged interaction events occurring within each area. Across both consensus strategies, users devoted the largest share of activity to the chat area, supporting communication and group awareness. The system area also attracted substantial activity, whereas history and favorites were used less frequently. A chi-square goodness-of-fit test (against a uniform distribution across areas) confirmed a significant difference in the activity distribution ($\chi^2 = 39.0$, $p < 0.001$). Given the limited number of groups per condition (9 per strategy), we report the aggregated distribution; GREAT's logs enable strategy-stratified analyses of the same signals.

> **Observation 1.** *In this study, users prioritize collaborative awareness, consistently allocating the largest share of interaction activity to the chat area across consensus strategies.*

**Role Inference from Interaction (RQ2).** To assess role emergence, we computed each user's interaction score, $score_{u_i}(\mathcal{CM})$ (Eq. 1), with weights $w_{SU} = 0.5$, $w_{VP} = 0.2$, and $w_{FP} = 0.3$. These weights reflect the relative importance of suggesting items, attracting peer views, and attracting peer favorites; informal tests indicated consistent trends across alternative configurations.

Figure 4 reports interaction scores for all participants. Interaction varied both across and within groups, indicating heterogeneity in engagement. Most groups

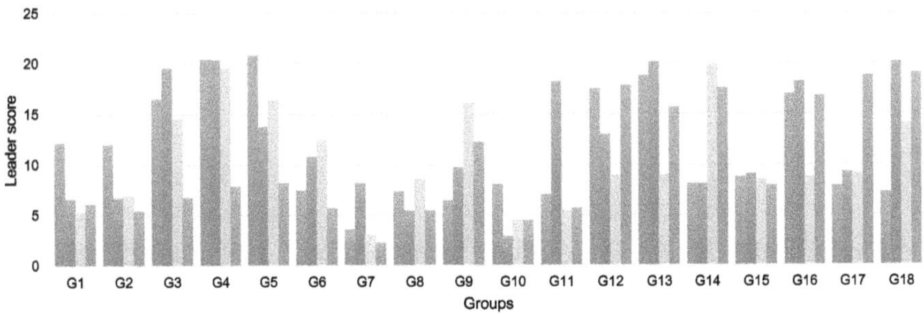

**Fig. 4.** Interaction scores for all users. X-axis: groups and their members (within each group, members are ordered by decreasing $score_{u_i}$); Y-axis: $score_{u_i}$.

had one or two highly active users while others were less involved, whereas $G4$ exhibited relatively balanced participation among three members.

At the end of each session, participants nominated the member they perceived as most influential in driving the group decision (leader) and the one who contributed most to reaching agreement (most collaborative), as described in Sect. 4.1. For each group and each role, we aggregated nominations by plurality (ties yield multiple nominated candidates). We inferred the corresponding roles using the highest $score_{u_i}$ (Eq. 1) and counted a match when at least one inferred candidate overlapped with at least one nominated candidate. Figure 5 reports, for each group, whether a match was obtained for the two roles.

Qualitatively, agreement tended to be higher in groups with higher overall interaction. Under our match criterion, we observed leader matches for all groups using the completeness strategy (G10–G18), whereas most-collaborative matches were more frequent under the mean strategy (G1–G9). Inferring leadership was more difficult in low-interaction groups, while collaborative roles could still be detected, highlighting the value of interaction modeling in GRSs.

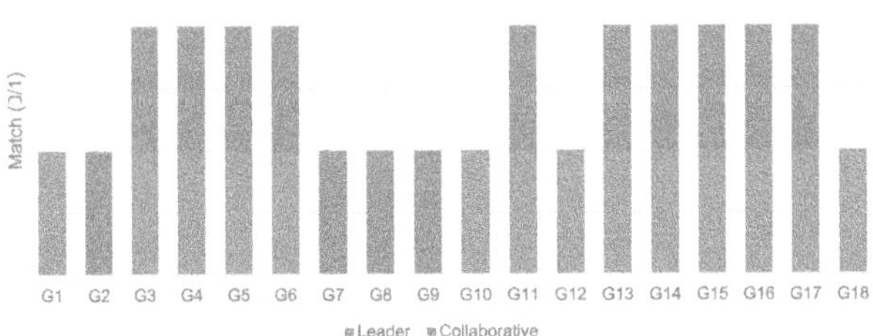


**Fig. 5.** Agreement between inferred roles and participant nominations (match indicator: 1 = match, 0 = no match).

**Observation 2.** *The interaction score provides a useful proxy for perceived leadership and collaboration roles, with higher agreement in more interactive groups.*

**Impact of Consensus Strategies on Satisfaction (RQ3).** At the end of each session, GREAT generated a single *top-1* group recommendation (i.e., the highest-ranked item returned by the assigned consensus strategy after aggregating the group's preferences and interaction scores). We refer to this item as the *group-recommended item*. Participants then rated this final item on a five-point scale (Sect. 4.1). Under the mean strategy ($n = 36$), 6% of users expressed dissatisfaction, while 36% were completely satisfied. Under completeness ($n = 36$), no users reported dissatisfaction, and 39% gave the highest score (Fig. 6).

A chi-square test did not reach conventional statistical significance ($\chi^2 = 6.12$, $p = 0.06$), although it suggests a trend in favor of the completeness strategy. A regression including consensus strategy, gender, and age revealed no significant effects ($p = 0.76$), indicating that satisfaction was not explained by these demographic variables.

**Observation 3.** *In this study, the completeness strategy shows a more favorable satisfaction distribution and no dissatisfaction cases, suggesting a positive trend relative to mean.*

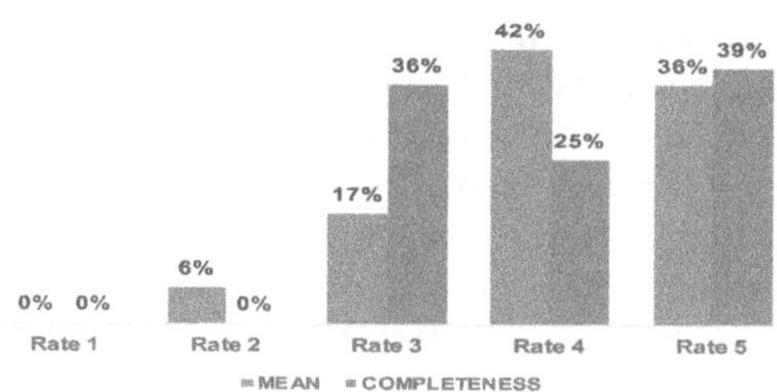


**Fig. 6.** Distribution of user satisfaction ratings for the mean and completeness consensus strategies on a 1–5 scale (1 = very dissatisfied, 5 = very satisfied).

**Generalizability and Scope.** The present case study evaluates GREAT in the music domain with four-person groups and rating-based CF. While we do not claim that empirical findings from this single setting generalize broadly, several interaction patterns we observe (e.g., signals related to leadership, collaboration, and interaction richness) are qualitatively consistent with results reported for gCOACH [11,12], obtained in a different domain (skiing) and with a content-based recommendation paradigm. This convergence suggests that such behavioral cues may be relevant across settings, and motivates future validation across domains, group sizes, and recommendation models. GREAT is designed to facilitate these follow-up studies by logging fine-grained interaction signals and providing an extensible evaluation and analysis pipeline.

**Observation 4.** *Interaction patterns related to leadership and collaboration observed in this study are qualitatively consistent with prior findings in a different domain, motivating broader validation across settings.*

**Practical Implications for Group Recommender Systems.** By capturing structured interaction signals (such as suggestions, views, and favorites) GRSs can infer interaction patterns and perceived roles from logs, which can support subsequent analyses and motivate future role-aware or adaptive group recommendation mechanisms. Completeness-based consensus strategies show a more favorable satisfaction distribution in our study, suggesting a promising direction for interaction-aware consensus in live group recommendation. These findings support socially aware GRSs that dynamically adapt to group behavior, bridging theoretical models of group dynamics and practical system implementation.

## 5   Conclusions

This paper presented *GREAT*, a domain-independent platform designed to capture and analyze structured user interactions during live CF–based group recommendation sessions. While our empirical evaluation focuses on a music-domain case study, *GREAT* is designed to be reused across domains and recommendation paradigms by changing the item catalog and the underlying recommender module. *GREAT* bridges a critical gap in existing frameworks that often overlook the social dynamics shaping collective decision-making.

Through a case study involving 18 groups (72 participants), we compared two interaction-aware consensus strategies (mean vs. completeness). We observed differences in user satisfaction and in interaction patterns captured through the logs. Since both conditions incorporate interaction-derived signals, isolating the causal contribution of these signals would require an interaction-unaware baseline. Users actively engaged with the platform's social features, and roles inferred from interaction logs were broadly aligned with participants' perceptions, supporting the system's analytical capabilities. Overall, these findings highlight the value of collecting live behavioral traces to study engagement and group dynamics in GRSs, and to inform the design of socially aware, interaction-driven group recommendation methods. Ultimately, *GREAT* establishes both a methodological and technological foundation for future research on interaction-driven GRSs.

Future work will examine diverse group structures and demographics while testing GREAT across new domains to assess the robustness of observed interaction patterns. We will also develop and benchmark additional consensus strategies under varied interaction dynamics.

**Acknowledgments.** The work of Maria Salamó was supported by the ANNOTATE-SenSIT (PID2024-156022OB-C33) Project funded by MICIU/AEI/10.13039/501100011033 and the European Social Fund Plus (ESF+).

**Disclosure of Interests.** The authors have no competing interests to declare that are relevant to the content of this article.

# References


1. Al Jurdi, W., Abdo, J.B., Demerjian, J., Makhoul, A.: Group validation in recommender systems: Framework for multi-layer performance evaluation. ACM Trans. Recomm. Syst. **2**(1) (2024). https://doi.org/10.1145/3640820
2. Ali, Y., Khan, I., Hussain, S.S., Rehman, F., Siraj, S., Nawaz, R.: A hybrid group-based movie recommendation framework with overlapping memberships. PLOS ONE **17**, e0266103 (2022). https://doi.org/10.1371/journal.pone.0266103
3. Alvarado, O., Htun, N.N., Jin, Y., Verbert, K.: A systematic review of interaction design strategies for group recommendation systems. Proc. ACM Hum.-Comput. Interact. **6**(CSCW2) (2022). https://doi.org/10.1145/3555161
4. Boratto, L., Carta, S.: ART: group recommendation approaches for automatically detected groups. Int. J. Mach. Learn. Cybern. **6**(6), 953–980 (2015a). https://doi.org/10.1007/S13042-015-0371-4
5. Boratto, L., Carta, S.: The rating prediction task in a group recommender system that automatically detects groups: architectures, algorithms, and performance evaluation. J. Intell. Inf. Syst. **45**(2), 221–245 (2015b). https://doi.org/10.1007/S10844-014-0346-Z
6. Boratto, L., Carta, S., Fenu, G.: Investigating the role of the rating prediction task in granularity-based group recommender systems and big data scenarios. Inf. Sci. **378**, 424–443 (2017). https://doi.org/10.1016/J.INS.2016.07.060
7. Boratto, L., Carta, S., Fenu, G., Mulas, F., Pilloni, P.: Influence of rating prediction on group recommendation's accuracy. IEEE Intell. Syst. **31**(6), 22–27 (2016). https://doi.org/10.1109/MIS.2016.100
8. Bowman, D., Gabbard, J., Hix, D.: A survey of usability evaluation in virtual environments: classification and comparison of methods. Presence: Teleoperators Virtual Environ. **11**(4), 404–424 (2002). https://doi.org/10.1162/105474602760204309
9. Castro, J., García, Ó., Martínez, L.: Clg-reja: a consensus location-aware group recommender system for restaurants. In: Proceedings of the TouRS 2015 Workshop, in conjunction with RecSys 2015, pp. 61–69. ACM, Vienna, Austria (2015). Workshop on Tourism Recommender Systems (TouRS) @ RecSys 2015
10. Chen, Z., Hu, A., Xu, J., Liu, C.H.: Dinetogether: a social-aware group sequential recommender system. EAI (2018). https://doi.org/10.4108/eai.8-1-2018.155564
11. Contreras, D., Salamó, M., Boratto, L.: Integrating collaboration and leadership in conversational group recommender systems. ACM Trans. Inf. Syst. **39**(4) (2021). https://doi.org/10.1145/3462759
12. Contreras, D., Salamó, M., Pascual, J.: A web-based environment to support online and collaborative group recommendation scenarios. Appl. Artif. Intell. **29**(5), 480–499 (2015). https://doi.org/10.1080/08839514.2015.1026661
13. Crossen, A., Budzik, J., Hammond, K.J.: Flytrap: intelligent group music recommendation. In: Hammond, K.J., Gil, Y., Leake, D. (eds.) Proceedings of the 7th International Conference on Intelligent User Interfaces, IUI 2002, San Francisco, California, USA, 13–16 January 2002, pp. 184–185. ACM (2002). https://doi.org/10.1145/502716.502748
14. Dara, S., Chowdary, C.R., Kumar, C.: A survey on group recommender systems. J. Intell. Inf. Syst. **54**, 271–295 (2019). https://doi.org/10.1007/s10844-018-0542-3
15. Delic, A., Masthoff, J., Neidhardt, J., Werthner, H.: How to use social relationships in group recommenders: empirical evidence. In: Mitrovic, T., Zhang, J., Chen, L., Chin, D. (eds.) Proceedings of the 26th Conference on User Modeling, Adaptation

and Personalization, UMAP 2018, Singapore, 08–11 July 2018, pp. 121–129. Association for Computing Machinery, New York, NY, USA (2018). https://doi.org/10.1145/3209219.3209226

16. Delic, A., Neidhardt, J., Nguyen, T.N., Ricci, F.: Research methods for group recommender system. In: Fesenmaier, D.R., Kuflik, T., Neidhardt, J. (eds.) Proceedings of the Workshop on Recommenders in Tourism co-located with 10th ACM Conference on Recommender Systems (RecSys 2016), Boston, MA, USA, 15 September 2016. CEUR Workshop Proceedings, vol. 1685, pp. 30–37. CEUR-WS.org, New York, NY, USA (2016). http://ceur-ws.org/Vol-1685/paper5.pdf

17. Delic, A., et al.: Observing group decision making processes. In: Sen, S., Geyer, W., Freyne, J., Castells, P. (eds.) Proceedings of the 10th ACM Conference on Recommender Systems, Boston, MA, USA, 15–19 September 2016, pp. 147–150. ACM, New York, NY, USA (2016). https://doi.org/10.1145/2959100.2959168

18. Delic, A., Neidhardt, J., Rook, L., Werthner, H., Zanker, M.: Researching individual satisfaction with group decisions in tourism: experimental evidence. In: Schegg, R., Stangl, B. (eds.) Information and Communication Technologies in Tourism 2017, pp. 73–85. Springer, Cham (2017). https://doi.org/10.1007/978-3-319-51168-9_6

19. Felfernig, A., Boratto, L., Stettinger, M., Tkalcic, M.: Group Recommender Systems: An Introduction. Springer Briefs in Electrical and Computer Engineering, Springer US, USA (2018). https://doi.org/10.1007/978-3-319-75067-5

20. Goldberg, L.R.: The structure of phenotypic personality traits. Am. Psychol. **48**(1), 26 (1993)

21. Gómez, E., Contreras, D., Boratto, L., Salamo, M.: Ambar: a dataset for assessing multiple beyond-accuracy recommenders. In: Proceedings of the 18th ACM Conference on Recommender Systems, RecSys 2024, pp. 137–147. Association for Computing Machinery, New York, NY, USA (2024). https://doi.org/10.1145/3640457.3688067

22. Guo, G., Zhang, J., Sun, Z., Yorke-Smith, N.: LibRec: a Java library for recommender systems. In: Posters, Demos, Late-breaking Results and Workshop Proceedings of the 23rd Conference on User Modelling, Adaptation and Personalization (UMAP) (2015). http://ceur-ws.org/Vol-1388/demo_paper1.pdf

23. Guzzi, F., Ricci, F., Burke, R.D.: Interactive multi-party critiquing for group recommendation. In: Mobasher, B., Burke, R.D., Jannach, D., Adomavicius, G. (eds.) Proceedings of the 2011 ACM Conference on Recommender Systems, RecSys 2011, Chicago, IL, USA, 23–27 October 2011, pp. 265–268. ACM, New York, USA (2011). https://doi.org/10.1145/2043932.2043980

24. Jannach, D., Manzoor, A., Cai, W., Chen, L.: A survey on conversational recommender systems. CoRR abs/2004.00646 (2020). https://arxiv.org/abs/2004.00646

25. Karahodza, E., Delic, A., Ricci, F.: Conceptual framework for group dynamics modeling from group chat interactions. In: Adjunct Proceedings of the 33rd ACM Conference on User Modeling, Adaptation and Personalization, UMAP Adjunct 2025, New York City, NY, USA, 16–19 June 2025, pp. 23–27. ACM (2025). https://doi.org/10.1145/3708319.3733682

26. Koren, Y., Bell, R., Volinsky, C.: Matrix factorization techniques for recommender systems. Computer **42**(8), 30–37 (2009)

27. Lenzi, E., Stefanidis, K.: Adapt: fairness & diversity for sequential group recommendations. Inf. Syst. **133**, 102572 (2025). https://doi.org/10.1016/j.is.2025.102572

28. McCarthy, J.F., Anagnost, T.D.: Musicfx: an arbiter of group preferences for computer supported collaborative workouts. In: Proceedings of the 1998 ACM Conference on Computer Supported Cooperative Work, pp. 363–372. ACM (1998)
29. McCarthy, K., Salamó, M., Coyle, L., McGinty, L., Smyth, B., Nixon, P.: CATS: a synchronous approach to collaborative group recommendation. In: Sutcliffe, G., Goebel, R. (eds.) Proceedings of the Nineteenth International Florida Artificial Intelligence Research Society Conference, Melbourne Beach, Florida, USA, 11–13 May 2006, pp. 86–91. AAAI Press (2006). http://www.aaai.org/Library/FLAIRS/2006/flairs06-015.php
30. McCrae, R.R., John, O.P.: An introduction to the five-factor model and its applications. J. Pers. **60**(2), 175–215 (1992). https://doi.org/10.1111/j.1467-6494.1992.tb00970.x. https://onlinelibrary.wiley.com/doi/abs/10.1111/j.1467-6494.1992.tb00970.x
31. Moraes, F., Grashoff, K., Hauff, C.: On the impact of group size on collaborative search effectiveness. Inf. Retrieval J. **22**(5), 476–498 (2019). https://doi.org/10.1007/s10791-018-09350-9
32. Nguyen, T.N., Ricci, F.: A chat-based group recommender system for tourism. J. IT Tourism **18**(1–4), 5–28 (2018). https://doi.org/10.1007/s40558-017-0099-y
33. Nguyen, T.N., Ricci, F.: Situation-dependent combination of long-term and session-based preferences in group recommendations: an experimental analysis. In: Haddad, H.M., Wainwright, R.L., Chbeir, R. (eds.) Proceedings of the 33rd Annual ACM Symposium on Applied Computing, SAC 2018, Pau, France, 09–13 April 2018. pp. 1366–1373. ACM, New York, USA (2018). https://doi.org/10.1145/3167132.3167279
34. Quijano-Sanchez, L., Recio-García, J., Díaz Agudo, B., Jiménez-Díaz, G.: Happy movie: a group recommender application in Facebook (2011)
35. Rahimkhani, K., Zamanifar, K.: Tigm: a temporal influence graph-based method for fair and diverse group recommendations. Computing **107**(228) (2025). https://doi.org/10.1007/s00607-025-01584-y
36. Ramos, G., Caleiro, C.: A novel similarity measure for group recommender systems with optimal time complexity. In: Boratto, L., Faralli, S., Marras, M., Stilo, G. (eds.) BIAS 2020. CCIS, vol. 1245, pp. 95–109. Springer, Cham (2020). https://doi.org/10.1007/978-3-030-52485-2_10
37. Recalde, L., Mendieta, J., Boratto, L., Terán, L., Vaca, C., Baquerizo, G.: Who you should not follow: extracting word embeddings from tweets to identify groups of interest and hijackers in demonstrations. IEEE Trans. Emerg. Top. Comput. **7**(2), 206–217 (2019). https://doi.org/10.1109/TETC.2017.2669404
38. Ricci, F., Delic, A.: Widening the role of group recommender systems with CAJO. SIGIR Forum **59**(1), 1–16 (2025). https://doi.org/10.1145/3769733.3769745
39. Salamó, M., Mccarthy, K., Smyth, B.: Generating recommendations for consensus negotiation in group personalization services. Personal Ubiquitous Comput. **16**(5), 597–610 (2012)
40. Quijano-Sánchez, L., Recio Garcia, J.A., Díaz-Agudo, B.: Using personality to create alliances in group recommender systems. In: Ram, A., Wiratunga, N. (eds.) ICCBR 2011. LNCS (LNAI), vol. 6880, pp. 226–240. Springer, Heidelberg (2011). https://doi.org/10.1007/978-3-642-23291-6_18
41. Sánchez, L.Q., Recio-García, J.A., Díaz-Agudo, B., Jiménez-Díaz, G.: Social factors in group recommender systems. ACM TIST **4**(1), 8:1–8:30 (2013). https://doi.org/10.1145/2414425.2414433

42. Shi, J., Wu, B., Lin, X.: A latent group model for group recommendation. In: Proceedings of the 2015 IEEE International Conference on Mobile Services, MS 2015, pp. 233–238. IEEE Computer Society, USA (2015). https://doi.org/10.1109/MobServ.2015.41
43. Silveira, J.D., Salamó, M., Boratto, L.: Enabling reproducibility in group recommender systems. In: Artificial Intelligence Research and Development, pp. 115–124. IOS Press (2022)
44. Soulier, L., Tamine, L., Shah, C.: Minerank: leveraging users' latent roles for unsupervised collaborative information retrieval. Inf. Process. Manage. $52(6)$, 1122–1141 (2016). https://doi.org/10.1016/j.ipm.2016.05.002
45. Stettinger, M.: Choicla: towards domain-independent decision support for groups of users. In: Proceedings of the 8th ACM Conference on Recommender Systems, RecSys 2014, pp. 425–428. Association for Computing Machinery, New York, NY, USA (2014). https://doi.org/10.1145/2645710.2653365
46. Sánchez, P., Bellogín, A.: On the effects of aggregation strategies for different groups of users in venue recommendation. Inf. Process. Manage. $58(5)$, 102609 (2021). https://doi.org/10.1016/j.ipm.2021.102609. https://www.sciencedirect.com/science/article/pii/S0306457321001059
47. Thomas, K.W.: Thomas-Kilmann conflict mode. TKI Profile Interpretive Report $1(11)$, 1–11 (2008)
48. Felfernig, A., Boratto, L., Stettinger, M., Tkalčič, M.: Personality, emotions, and group dynamics. In: Group Recommender Systems. SECE, pp. 157–167. Springer, Cham (2018). https://doi.org/10.1007/978-3-319-75067-5_9
49. Virutamasen, P., Ahadi, N., Wang, J., Zanjanab, A.G., Wongpreedee, K., Sohaee, N.: Contextual based e-tourism application: a personalized attraction recommendation system for destination branding and cultivating tourism experiences. In: 2024 5th Technology Innovation Management and Engineering Science International Conference (TIMES-iCON), pp. 1–5 (2024). https://doi.org/10.1109/TIMES-iCON61890.2024.10630722
50. Xu, L., Zhou, X., Gadiraju, U.: How does team composition affect knowledge gain of users in collaborative web search? In: Gadiraju, U. (ed.) HT 2020: 31st ACM Conference on Hypertext and Social Media, Virtual Event, USA, 13–15 July 2020, pp. 91–100. ACM (2020). https://doi.org/10.1145/3372923.3404784

# SciNUP: Natural Language User Interest Profiles for Scientific Literature Recommendation

Mariam Arustashvili[(✉)] [iD] and Krisztian Balog[iD]

University of Stavanger, Stavanger, Norway
`{mariam.arustashvili,krisztian.balog}@uis.no`

**Abstract.** The use of natural language (NL) user profiles in recommender systems offers greater transparency and user control compared to traditional representations. However, there is scarcity of large-scale, publicly available test collections for evaluating NL profile-based recommendation. To address this gap, we introduce SciNUP, a novel synthetic dataset for scholarly recommendation that leverages authors' publication histories to generate NL profiles and corresponding ground truth items. We use this dataset to conduct a comparison of baseline methods, ranging from sparse and dense retrieval approaches to state-of-the-art LLM-based rerankers. Our results show that while baseline methods achieve comparable performance, they often retrieve different items, indicating complementary behaviors. At the same time, considerable headroom for improvement remains, highlighting the need for effective NL-based recommendation approaches. The SciNUP dataset thus serves as a valuable resource for fostering future research and development in this area.

**Keywords:** Natural language user profiles · Scientific literature recommendation · Recommender systems · Dataset · Evaluation

## 1 Introduction

Natural language (NL) user profiles have recently emerged as a promising paradigm in recommender systems [3,23,26], offering an interpretable and flexible alternative to traditional user representations, such as embeddings derived from interaction histories [25]. By aligning with the way humans naturally describe their interests and preferences, NL profiles enable greater transparency and user agency: users can inspect, understand, and edit their profiles in plain language. NL profile-based systems move beyond pure behaviorism, effectively scaling participatory design and giving users more control over the recommendation process [12], thereby shifting the focus from recommending for the users to recommending with them [11]. This makes NL user profiles highly suitable for applications prioritizing explainability, personalization, and user control.

Despite the growing interest in NL-based user representations, a significant gap remains in the current research landscape: the scarcity of large-scale,


R. Campos et al. (Eds.): ECIR 2026, LNCS 16486, pp. 432–446, 2026.
https://doi.org/10.1007/978-3-032-21321-1_51

---

My research lies at the intersection of information theory, probability, and convex
geometry, with a particular focus on entropy inequalities, information-theoretic limits,
and log-concave distributions. I investigate fundamental properties of entropy in
both discrete and continuous settings, develop analogs of additive combinatorics in an
information-theoretic framework, and explore applications to problems such as compound
Poisson approximation, polar coding, and combinatorial geometry. My work often uncovers
deep connections between probabilistic methods, functional inequalities, and structural
aspects of high-dimensional spaces.

---

**Fig. 1.** Example NL user interest profile from our dataset.

publicly available test collections specifically designed to evaluate models and
algorithms for NL profile-based recommendation [26]. Creating such datasets is
challenging because soliciting natural language interest descriptions from users
and collecting relevance judgments for recommendations is a time-intensive and
expensive process that is difficult to scale [27]. Consequently, many existing
approaches rely on inferring NL user profiles from readily available user interaction
data like reviews [22,26] or ratings [14,23,30]. Furthermore, existing studies are often limited in domain, predominantly focusing on movie or book recommendations [14,23,26,27]. While some work, such as [21], explores scientific
paper recommendation, the use of NL user profiles for this domain has not been
explored to date, nor are there public datasets to support it. With this work, we
aim to bridge this gap.

We introduce SciNUP (**Sci**entific **N**atural Language **U**ser **P**rofiles), a novel
large-scale synthetic dataset for NL-based recommendation. Our approach simulates a realistic scholarly recommendation scenario: for a given individual, we
leverage their authored papers, split temporally, to create an NL user interest profile from their earlier works by prompting a large language model (LLM).
This NL profile, illustrated in Fig. 1, then serves as the basis for predicting future
research interests, with ground truth derived from references within their later
publications. Each NL profile is associated with a set of candidate items, enabling
a fair comparison across different recommender approaches. We employ multiple LLMs and prompts for profile generation to reduce model-specific biases
and enhance the generality of the resulting profiles. Additionally, NL profiles
are automatically classified based on the breadth of user interest into narrow,
medium, and broad categories, enabling further analysis and performance breakdown. Together, these components constitute a rich test collection specifically
designed to enable repeatable and reproducible offline experimentation with NL-
based recommender systems in the scholarly domain.

We evaluate a range of methods, from sparse and dense retrieval to LLM-
based reranking. Our experiments show a nuanced landscape: while advanced
dense and LLM-based methods ultimately set the state of the art, traditional
sparse retrieval proves to be a highly competitive baseline that is difficult to
surpass. We find that the strengths of these approaches are complementary,
with each model excelling on different subsets of users. To highlight this, our
simple ensemble of these models achieves the best overall performance by a large
margin. This indicates that considerable headroom for improvement remains,

establishing our dataset as a valuable benchmark to foster future research and model development.

In summary, the main contributions of this work are twofold:

(1) We introduce SciNUP, a large-scale dataset for NL-based recommendation in the scholarly domain.
(2) We provide a comprehensive performance analysis of diverse recommender approaches on SciNUP, from traditional sparse and dense retrieval to state-of-the-art LLM-based reranking, establishing strong baselines for future work.

All resources, including the dataset, baseline methods, and evaluation results, are made publicly available at https://github.com/iai-group/SciNUP.

## 2   Related Work

Editable user profiles, allowing users to inspect, validate, and modify system beliefs about them, have gained traction in recommender systems. Early work by Balog et al. [3] introduced a template-based method for summarizing user profiles in natural language, relying on keyword or tags. Later, Radlinski et al. [25] proposed the idea of NL user profiles as an alternative to traditional user embedding representations for an intermediate step between user behavior data and item recommendations. Building on this idea, Sanner et al. [27] demonstrated that NL-based recommendations can be competitive with item-based collaborative filtering, particularly in cold-start scenarios. More recently, studies have increasingly leveraged LLM prompting for NL profile generation based on user reviews, ratings, and/or history [13,14,23,26,28,30]. For instance, Penaloza et al. [23] provide specific instructions in the prompt as to what aspects to summarize, while Ramos et al. [26] perform preference extraction and ranking before prompting. Gao et al. [14] optimize the profile encoder through reinforcement learning. NL profiles are usually evaluated only intrinsically, using recommendation performance as a proxy for quality [14,23,30]. Ramos et al. [26] conducted a user study to assess NL profiles in terms of fluency, informativeness, conciseness, and relevance. A recent user study in the music recommendation domain shows a weak correlation between the perceived representativeness of the NL profile and recommendation performance [28]. Recommendations from NL profiles are typically generated using retrieval-based methods that rank items by similarity in a shared embedding space [14,26], while others use neural models trained for rating or choice prediction [23,30].

The task of narrative-driven recommendation [6,22] is closely related to NL profile-based recommendation, yet a key distinction lies in their scope. Narratives are inherently more situational and context-dependent (e.g., suggesting music for a specific mood on an autumn afternoon) and typically incorporate explicit positive or negative item examples. NL profiles, conversely, aim to capture a more stable and general set of a person's preferences within a specific domain (e.g., an individual's overall music taste).

Most existing work focuses on the domains of movie [14, 23, 26, 30], book [14, 23], or point-of-interest [1, 22, 26] recommendation. While Mysore et al. [21] uniquely addresses scientific paper recommendation, their approach relies on a set of NL concepts, more akin to tag-based methods, and evaluates on sparse (CiteULike) or private (OpenReview) datasets. In contrast, we generate full-text NL summaries, enabling more expressive and interpretable user representations aligned with the common understanding of NL profiles. In the realm of scientific literature recommendation, arXiv is a widely used preprint service, offering a rich dataset [8]. Services like ArXivDigest [15], while providing valuable living lab environments, typically assume explicit keyword-based interest expressions or implicit interactions. Our use of NL user profiles represents a significant step towards addressing the gap in explicit user modeling within this domain [16].

## 3   Problem Statement

*Natural language user interest profile generation* (*NL profile generation* for short) is the task of generating a natural language description $d_u$ based on a set of items the user has interacted with. The generated profile should be a concise, fluent, and effective characterization of the user's interests, allowing for interpretability and human understanding while being useful for recommendation [25].

Given a natural language description $d_u$ characterizing the interest of user $u$, *natural language profile-based recommendation* is the task of recommending items from a pool of candidate items $I$ that match the interests of that person. This recommendation task is approached as a ranking problem, where the goal is to produce an ordered list of candidate items such that items more relevant to the user's interests appear higher in the list.

We address these two tasks—NL profile generation and NL profile-based recommendation—in turn in the following two sections, specifically in the context of scientific literature recommendation.

## 4   The SciNUP Dataset

We present SciNUP (**Sci**entific **N**atural Language **U**ser **P**rofiles), a synthetic dataset designed for evaluating natural language-based recommendation in the scholarly domain. We simulate a real-world scenario in which a researcher—hereafter referred to as the *user*—is looking for article recommendations relevant to their specific expertise and interests. To model this authentically, we leverage the user's publication history. We utilize their past authored papers to create NL user interest profiles; subsequently, the cited references in their later publications serve as the ground truth for evaluating recommendation effectiveness.

### 4.1   Approach

The construction of our benchmark dataset, illustrated in Fig. 2, centers on three key components: NL profiles, candidate items, and ground truth. Our methodology begins by sampling users (authors) from a scholarly dataset (arXiv). For

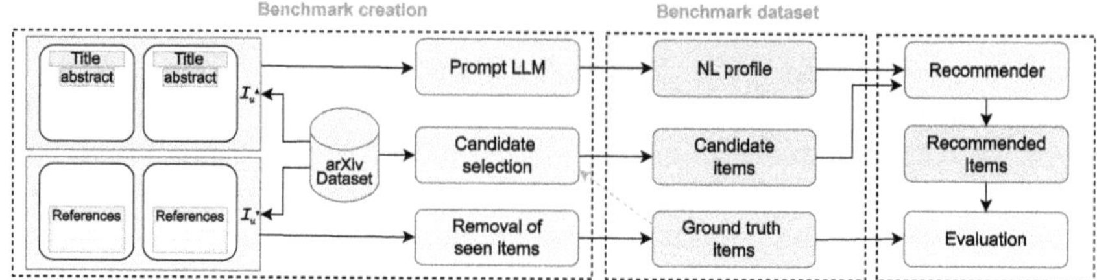



**Fig. 2.** Overview of our approach.

each user, their published papers are temporally divided into an earlier and a later portion. The *earlier portion* is utilized for generating an NL interest profile through LLM prompting, while the *later portion* is utilized for creating the ground truth set of recommendations. For each user, we also sample additional papers from arXiv to create a set of candidate items. The subsequent recommendation task involves ranking these candidate papers with respect to the NL profile. Further details on each step are provided below.

**Scholarly Dataset.** We use the public arXiv dataset released by Clement et al. [8].[1] To ensure maximum accessibility and reproducibility, we rely exclusively on article metadata, which is released under a CC0 license. This metadata includes the arXiv paper ID, author list, title, abstract, version, and category listings for 1,506,500 articles. Furthermore, we integrate a citation network provided by the same source to establish relational links between papers. The dataset covers articles published up to March 1, 2019. We performed author name normalization, assigned unique user IDs, and retained only users with a valid name who had published at least 10 papers. We only kept articles that had metadata and were also present in the citation network.

**NL Profile Generation.** We sample $n=1,000$ users from the filtered arXiv dataset. For each user $u$, let $\mathcal{I}_u$ denote the articles they authored. We temporarily order $\mathcal{I}_u$ and divide to earlier portion, $\mathcal{I}_u^{\blacktriangle}$ (for NL profile construction), and later portion, $\mathcal{I}_u^{\blacktriangledown}$ (for ground truth creation). For simplicity, we divide $\mathcal{I}_u$ in half to ensure that there are enough articles for both NL profile generation and ground truth creation; exploring other division strategies is left for future work.

The NL profile descriptions are generated by prompting an LLM and providing the list of articles in $\mathcal{I}_u^{\blacktriangle}$, represented by their titles and abstract, as context and input to the prompt. To ensure generalizability, we designed two different prompt versions (A and B), shown in Fig. 3. Prompt A provides more details about the purpose of the summary and specifies the desired length, while Prompt B leaves the LLM more freedom. Furthermore, we utilized two different LLMs: Llama-4 Maverick and GPT-4o. The author set is split uniformly into four groups (250 authors each), corresponding to the possible prompt-LLM combinations.

---

[1] https://github.com/mattbierbaum/arxiv-public-datasets/releases/tag/v0.2.0.

```
Below are the titles and abstracts of scientific papers I have authored. Based on this
information, generate a concise
⟨IF Prompt A⟩
first-person research profile that summarizes my main research interests and areas of
expertise.
The profile should be written in no more than three sentences and should clearly identify
the key themes, research trends, and topics I focus on. The purpose of this profile is to
support a scientific literature recommendation system, so it should accurately reflect my
research focus to help match me with relevant publications.
⟨ELIF Prompt B⟩
description of my research interests, characterizing the key topics and areas of expertise.
⟨/IF⟩

This is the list of my publications:
[List of articles (titles and abstracts)]

Write the profile in first person. Return nothing but the generated profile.
```

**Fig. 3.** Prompt template used for NL profile generation. Placeholders for variables are in [square brackets], while conditional logic is marked by ⟨IF⟩...⟨/IF⟩.

```
You are an expert in classifying scholarly user interest profiles. Your task is to analyze
a given natural language description of a user's research interests and classify it as
'Narrow', 'Medium', or 'Broad' based on the specificity and scope of the topics mentioned.

Here are the definitions for each category:

Narrow: The profile describes highly specific interests within a single, well-defined
subfield. The language is often technical and domain-specific.
Medium: The profile covers a single, broader field or several related topics. The interests
are connected but not as specific as a narrow profile.
Broad: The profile covers a wide range of disparate topics or a very general field. The
interests may not be directly connected.

Examples:

User Profile: 'My research focuses on the optimization of federated learning algorithms for
on-device natural language processing, specifically for low-resource languages.'
Classification: Narrow

User Profile: 'I am interested in the intersection of artificial intelligence and medicine.
My work involves using computer vision for medical image analysis and developing predictive
models for disease progression using electronic health records.'
Classification: Medium

User Profile: 'I have a passion for technology and its role in society. I'm interested in
everything from robotics and human-computer interaction to the ethical implications of AI
and the future of work. I also enjoy historical perspectives on technological innovation.'
Classification: Broad

Please classify the following user profile. Return only one word, Narrow, Medium or Broad.

User Profile: [nl_profile]
Classification:
```

**Fig. 4.** Prompt template used for NL profile classification. Placeholders for variables are in [square brackets].

**Ground Truth.** The later portion of the articles, $\mathcal{I}_u^{\blacktriangledown}$, which were not used for NL profile generation, are utilized for ground truth creation. We consider all papers referenced by any article in $\mathcal{I}_u^{\blacktriangledown}$ as ground truth items, provided they

**Table 1.** Examples of Narrow, Medium, and Broad natural language research profiles from the SciNUP dataset.

| | |
|---|---|
| **Narrow** | My research focuses on precision measurements in flavor physics, particularly the semileptonic and rare decays of B and D mesons, to test the Standard Model and probe for signs of new physics. I specialize in the determination of CKM matrix elements, lepton flavor universality tests, and angular analyses of rare decays, using large datasets collected by the Belle detector at the KEKB collider. I am also involved in searches for rare charm decays and studies of bottomonium spectroscopy to investigate hadronic decay dynamics. |
| **Medium** | My research spans mathematical physics, operator theory, and experimental particle physics, with a focus on spectral properties of the almost Mathieu operator, the structure of minimum phase preserving operators, and the inverse problems they present. I also contribute to the T2K long-baseline neutrino oscillation experiment, where I investigate CP violation, neutrino mixing parameters, and the sensitivity of extended experimental runs. My expertise lies in the interplay between mathematical theory and experimental analysis, particularly in quantifying and interpreting fundamental physical phenomena through rigorous mathematical and statistical frameworks. |
| **Broad** | My research focuses on high-energy astrophysics, particularly X-ray spectroscopy of black holes and active galactic nuclei, with an emphasis on iron line diagnostics and accretion disk physics. I also study particle interactions in galactic environments, such as cosmic ray-induced emissions in molecular clouds and chemical abundances in AGN and starburst galaxies. Additionally, I explore fundamental physics topics including quantum Hall effects and pseudo-bosonic operator theory, reflecting a broader interest in both observational astrophysics and mathematical physics. |

were not "seen" by the user before, that is, referenced by any of the papers in $\mathcal{I}_u^{\blacktriangle}$ or authored by the individual themselves (i.e., exclude self-citations). We denote this set of ground truth items as $\mathcal{G}_u$. In this initial approach, we do not distinguish between the varying degrees of relevance among these items.

**Candidate Selection.** For each user $u$, we construct a unique set of candidate items, $\mathcal{C}_u$, which serve as the pool of articles from which recommendations will be made. We set the number of candidate items $m = 1000$ for each user. For simplicity, we employ a modified version of the One-Plus-Random methodology [4], which we term *N-plus-random*: $N$ items are drawn from the ground truth set ($\mathcal{G}_u$), while the remaining ($m-N$) items are randomly sampled from the arXiv dataset. These random samples are selected from papers within the same categories as those previously authored by the user. The sampling process is weighted: categories where a user has published more receive a higher probability of contributing candidate items. Before sampling, all "seen" items (previously cited or self-authored, as above) are excluded from the pool of available articles.

### 4.2   Characterizing Profile Breadth

NL profiles, which characterize a research's interests, can vary significantly in breadth. Some researchers have a wider scope of interests, while others focus on

**Table 2.** Summary statistics of the SciNUP dataset.

| | |
|---|---|
| #Users | 1,000 |
| #Authored papers (min/median/max) | 10/20/260 |
| #Candidate items per user | 1,000 |
| #Ground truth papers per user (min/median/max) | 1/27/438 |
| Profile length (words) | 117 ± 55 |
|   - Prompt A | 83 ± 10 |
|   - Prompt B | 150 ± 61 |
| #Narrow/Medium/Broad NL profiles | 679/256/65 |

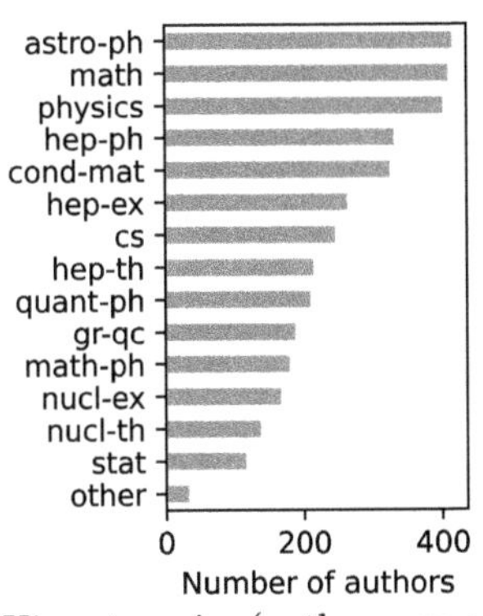

(a) ArXiv categories (authors are counted in each category they have published in).

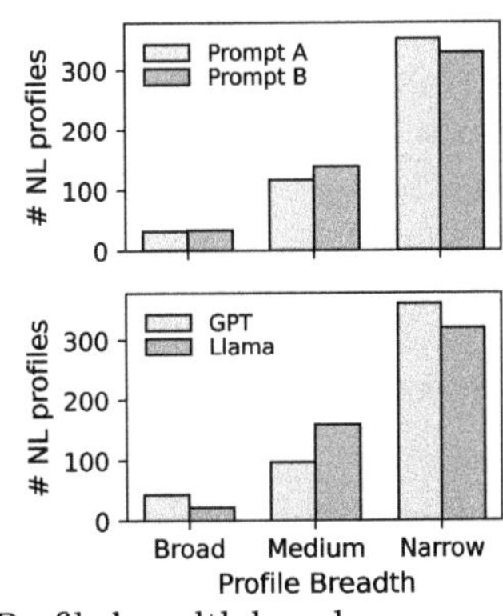

(b) Profile breadth based on prompts and LLMs used.

**Fig. 5.** Category and profile distributions in the SciNUP dataset.

a more narrow topic. These differences can influence the performance of recommendation methods. To account for this, we automatically classify each profile's breadth and provide this classification as metadata. Specifically, we use a few-shot prompt (shown in Fig. 4) and take the majority vote from three distinct LLMs (Llama-70B, Gemini-2.5-Flash, GPT-4o) to ensure a robust classification that mitigates potential single-model biases [2]. Table 1 shows examples of profiles from each category.

## 4.3 Dataset Statistics

The key statistics for the SciNUP dataset are summarized in Table 2. With 1,000 users, the dataset supports robust statistical analysis, and the diversity in paper counts offers a realistic and varied set of user profiles. The most frequently represented arXiv categories in which the users in our dataset publish are diverse fields of physics, mathematics, and computer science; see Fig. 5a.

We observe a noticeable difference in profile length across Prompts A and B, which will provide insights into the impact of prompting strategies (to be examined in Sect. 6.1).

The majority of NL profiles are classified as narrow. Figure 5b provides a further breakdown of profile breadth by the prompts and LLMs used. We find that the choice of prompt has a negligible effect on profile breadth. However, we observe a notable difference in the distributions based on the LLM used: GPT-4o tends to produce profiles that are either broad or narrow, while Llama yields a higher proportion of medium-breadth profiles.

## 5 Methods for NL-Based Recommendation

To establish strong performance baselines for NL-based recommendation, we benchmark a diverse range of existing methods. Our evaluation covers traditional sparse retrieval, modern dense retrieval, and state-of-the-art LLM-based reranking methods. The objective of this work is not to propose a novel method, but to systematically analyze the effectiveness of these established techniques within our specific problem setting, thereby providing a robust foundation for future research.

**Sparse Retrieval Methods.** We employ **BM25** as a traditional bag-of-words retrieval model, and **RM3** for query expansion using pseudo-relevance feedback.

**Dense Retrieval Methods.** We evaluate two main families of dense neural methods: dual-encoders and cross-encoders.

The first approach, using a *dual-encoder architecture*, frames the recommendation task as a k-nearest neighbor (kNN) retrieval problem. The natural language user interest profile and the candidate items are independently embedded into a shared high-dimensional dense vector space. Subsequently, kNN search is employed to find the items closest to the user's profile vector. For this method, we use **SciBERT** [5], a BERT-based language model pre-trained on a large corpus of scientific text (768-dimensional embeddings) and we leverage Faiss [10] for efficient similarity search.

The second group utilizes *cross-encoder models*. In contrast to dual-encoders, a cross-encoder processes the user profile and a candidate item jointly as a single input to output a relevance score for that pair. This allows for more precise relevance modeling but is computationally more intensive. We use these models to score each candidate document based on its relevance to the profile. Specifically, we selected several variants of BAAI's BGE (Beijing General Embedding) reranker models [7] due to their competitive performance across various retrieval tasks [20,29]: **BGE-Large**[2] and **BGE-v2-M3**[3] (568 mil-

---

[2] https://huggingface.co/BAAI/bge-reranker-large.
[3] https://huggingface.co/BAAI/bge-reranker-v2-m3.

**Table 3.** Evaluation results. Highest scores within each family are italicized, highest overall scores are boldfaced.

| Model | R@100 | MAP | MRR | NDCG@10 |
|---|---|---|---|---|
| BM25 | 0.3491 | 0.1148 | 0.4661 | 0.2869 |
| RM3 | *0.3570* | *0.1391* | *0.5147* | *0.3251* |
| kNN-SciBERT | 0.1480 | 0.0232 | 0.2182 | 0.1019 |
| BGE-Large | 0.2826 | 0.0783 | 0.3666 | 0.2072 |
| BGE-v2-M3 | 0.3472 | 0.1152 | 0.4633 | 0.2763 |
| BGE-v2-MiniCPM | *0.4203* | *0.1673* | *0.5393* | *0.3541* |
| PRP-Llama-3 (8B) | 0.3491 | 0.1165 | 0.4774 | 0.2925 |
| PRP-Llama-3.3 (70B) | 0.3491 | *0.1423* | *0.5378* | 0.3541 |
| PRP-GPT-4o-mini | 0.3491 | 0.1405 | 0.5297 | *0.3542* |
| Ensemble | 0.4136 | **0.2163** | **0.6333** | **0.4481** |

lion parameters, based on XLM-RoBERTa-Large), and **BGE-v2-MiniCPM**[4] (2.72B parameters, based on MiniCPM).

**LLM-Based Reranking.** We use Pairwise Relevance Prompting, **PRP** [24], a state-of-the-art approach for predicting relative differences between a pair of items. This is shown to result in substantially better rankings than predicting absolute judgements in a pointwise manner. Due to the computational cost involved with LLM-based reranking, we employ it in a cascading manner by reranking the top-100 results from initial BM25 retrieval. Specifically, we utilize the most efficient *sliding window* variant of PRP, which significantly reduces complexity ($O(n)$ for reranking $n$ items). We employ three different LLM backbones: two public models, **Llama-3-8B**[5] and **Llama-3.3-70B**,[6] as well as a proprietary model, **GPT-4o-mini**.[7]

**Ensemble.** Additionally, we construct an ensemble retrieval method that combines the top-performing sparse, dense, and LLM-based models. Specifically, we apply the reciprocal rank fusion (RRF) [9] technique to combine results from RM3, BGE-v2-MiniCPM, and PRP-GPT-4o-mini.

**Implementation.** Sparse and kNN-SciBERT dense retrievals are implemented using Pyserini [18], while BGE dense models employ the FlagEmbedding library[8]. We use default parameter settings for BM25 and RM3, as well as for all

---

[4] https://huggingface.co/BAAI/bge-reranker-v2-minicpm-layerwise.
[5] https://openrouter.ai/meta-llama/llama-3-8b-instruct.
[6] https://openrouter.ai/meta-llama/llama-3.3-70b-instruct.
[7] https://openrouter.ai/openai/gpt-4o-mini.
[8] https://github.com/FlagOpen/FlagEmbedding.

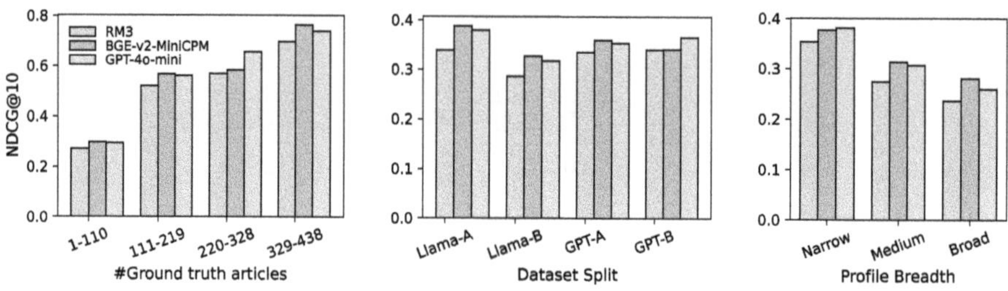

**Fig. 6.** Performance comparison by number of ground truth articles (Left), by prompt-LLM combination used for NL profile generation (Middle) and by NL profile breadth (Right).

BGE models. LLM-based reranking is implemented using the same tooling and API as NL profile generation; the prompt is included in the online repository.

## 6   Results

This section reports on our experiments on natural language profile-based recommendation using the SciNUP collection.

Table 3 summarizes the retrieval and reranking performance across sparse, dense, and LLM-based approaches in terms of traditional rank-based metrics: Recall@100, Mean Average Precision (MAP), Mean Reciprocal Rank (MRR), and NDCG@10. For significance testing we employ a paired t-test with Bonferroni correction at significance level of $\alpha = 0.05$. Among the sparse methods, RM3 outperforms BM25 across all metrics (significant for all metrics except Recall@100), highlighting the enduring effectiveness of classical pseudo-relevance feedback [17]. Surprisingly, most dense retrievers fail to outperform the sparse baselines. Within the dense retrieval family, BGE-v2-MiniCPM stands out, achieving the highest scores among all methods and surpassing both sparse and dense baselines (significantly so for all metrics except MRR against RM3). This demonstrates the potential of newer multitask-trained cross-encoder models to capture fine-grained semantic relevance more effectively than earlier dense architectures. LLM-based rerankers, specifically the larger models PRP-Llama-3.3 (70B) and PRP-GPT-4o-mini, achieve performance comparable to the strongest dense retriever. These findings suggest that while dense and LLM-based methods are rapidly improving, sparse retrieval methods, particularly RM3, remain a formidable baseline for domain-specific search.

The ensemble model achieves the highest scores across all metrics except for Recall@100, significantly outperforming each of its constituent models (RM3, BGE-v2-miniCMP, and PRP-GPT-4o-mini). This aligns with previous findings in the scientific IR literature that even simple hybrid methods can outperform both sparse and dense approaches [19]. The ensemble's effectiveness also underscores the complementary nature of sparse, dense, and LLM-based signals.

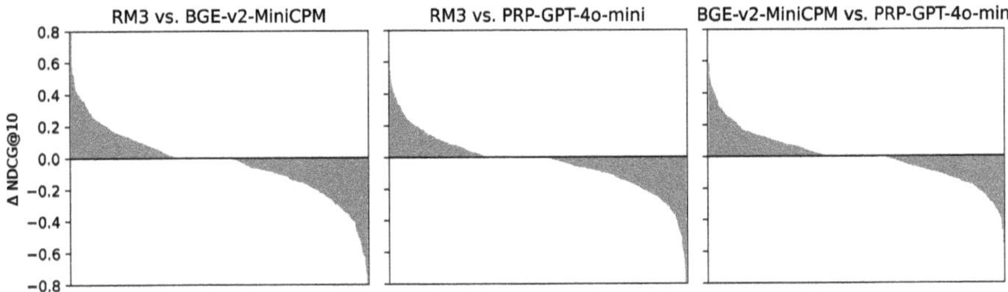


**Fig. 7.** Per-author NDCG@10 differences between retrieval models. Positive values indicate higher scores for the first model in each comparison.

## 6.1   Analysis

To further analyze the impact of NL profile construction, we examine retrieval performance (in terms of NDCG@10) of our best-performing sparse (RM3), dense (BGE-v2-MiniCPM) and LLM-reranking (PRP-GPT-4o-mini) approaches. Figure 6 (Left) presents a breakdown based on the number of ground truth items. Unsurprisingly, we find that performance improves with more ground truth items available. Figure 6 (Middle) breaks down performance based on the specific combination of prompt and LLM used for profile generation. We find that Prompt A (over Prompt B) and GPT (over Llama) yield more effective profiles, however, none of these differences is statistically significant. Crucially, Fig. 6 (Right) reveals that broader profiles tend to degrade performance. This is likely because their diverse topics are difficult to represent effectively in a single query, resulting in a lack of topical focus that challenges sparse retrievers, dense retrievers, and LLM-rerankers alike. This finding underscores the need for more sophisticated methods capable of interpreting diverse user interests.

To investigate model complementarity, Fig. 7 plots per-author NDCG@10 differences between the best-performing models from each family. While one model may outperform another on aggregate, the plot reveals substantial variability at the author level, where the globally weaker model often achieves superior results. This demonstrates that different retrieval approaches capture complementary relevance signals and that no single model is universally optimal. Consequently, this variability highlights a clear opportunity for hybrid models that combine diverse retrieval paradigms to achieve more robust and personalized recommendation performance.

## 7   Conclusion

We introduced SciNUP, a novel dataset for advancing NL-based scholarly recommendation. We detailed its construction process, and established baselines for the core task of *NL profile-based recommendation* using a range of sparse, dense, and LLM-based approaches. Our experiments reveal that different retrieval paradigms capture complementary relevance signals, and a simple ensemble of top models confirms that substantial headroom for improvement remains. These findings establish SciNUP as a valuable testbed for developing novel methods, particularly hybrid architectures designed to fuse these complementary signals and models that can robustly interpret diverse user profiles.

Our work also opens several exciting avenues for the task of *NL profile generation*. The construction process involves various parameters and prompting strategies that can be further explored, such as the ratio of papers used for profile creation versus evaluation and the specific instructions given to the LLM. Furthermore, validating the generated NL profiles through human evaluation would provide crucial insights into their quality and fidelity to actual user interests, guiding the development of more effective profile generation techniques.

**Acknowledgments.** This research was supported by the Norwegian Research Center for AI Innovation, NorwAI (Research Council of Norway, project number 309834).

**Disclosure of Interests.** The authors have no competing interests to declare that are relevant to the content of this article.

# References


1. Afzali, J., Drzewiecki, A.M., Balog, K.: POINTREC: a test collection for narrative-driven point of interest recommendation. In: Proceedings of the 44th International ACM SIGIR Conference on Research and Development in Information Retrieval, pp. 2478–2484 (2021)
2. Balog, K., Metzler, D., Qin, Z.: Rankers, judges, and assistants: towards understanding the interplay of LLMs in information retrieval evaluation. In: Proceedings of the 48th International ACM SIGIR Conference on Research and Development in Information Retrieval, SIGIR 2025, pp. 3865–3875 (2025)
3. Balog, K., Radlinski, F., Arakelyan, S.: Transparent, scrutable and explainable user models for personalized recommendation. In: Proceedings of the 42nd International ACM SIGIR Conference on Research and Development in Information Retrieval, SIGIR 2019, pp. 265–274 (2019)
4. Bellogin, A., Castells, P., Cantador, I.: Precision-oriented evaluation of recommender systems: an algorithmic comparison. In: Proceedings of the Fifth ACM Conference on Recommender Systems, RecSys 2011, pp. 333–336 (2011)
5. Beltagy, I., Lo, K., Cohan, A.: SciBERT: a pretrained language model for scientific text. In: Conference on Empirical Methods in Natural Language Processing, EMNLP 2019, pp. 3615–3620 (2019)
6. Bogers, T., Koolen, M.: Defining and supporting narrative-driven recommendation. In: Proceedings of the Eleventh ACM Conference on Recommender Systems, RecSys 2017, pp. 238–242 (2017)
7. Chen, J., Xiao, S., Zhang, P., Luo, K., Lian, D., Liu, Z.: BGE M3-embedding: multi-lingual, multi-functionality, multi-granularity text embeddings through self-knowledge distillation. arXiv cs.CL/2402.03216 (2024)
8. Clement, C.B., Bierbaum, M., O'Keeffe, K.P., Alemi, A.A.: On the use of arxiv as a dataset. arXiv cs.IR/1905.00075 (2019)

9. Cormack, G.V., Clarke, C.L.A., Buettcher, S.: Reciprocal rank fusion outperforms condorcet and individual rank learning methods. In: Proceedings of the 32nd International ACM SIGIR Conference on Research and Development in Information Retrieval, SIGIR 2009, pp. 758–759 (2009)
10. Douze, M., et al.: The Faiss library. arXiv cs.LG/2401.08281 (2024)
11. Ekstrand, M.D., Razi, A., Sarcevic, A., Pera, M.S., Burke, R., Wright, K.L.: Recommending with, not for: co-designing recommender systems for social good. ACM Trans. Recomm. Syst. (2025)
12. Ekstrand, M.D., Willemsen, M.C.: Behaviorism is not enough: better recommendations through listening to users. In: Proceedings of the 10th ACM Conference on Recommender Systems, RecSys 2016, pp. 221–224 (2016)
13. Gagliano, P., Homan, G., Turnbull, D., Govindarajan, V.S.: Using language models for music recommendations with natural-language profiles. In: Proceedings of the 3rd Music Recommender Systems Workshop, MuRS 2025 (2025)
14. Gao, Z., Zhou, J., Dai, Y., Joachims, T.: End-to-end training for recommendation with language-based user profiles. arXiv cs.IR/2410.18870 (2025)
15. Gingstad, K., Jekteberg, O., Balog, K.: ArXivDigest: a living lab for personalized scientific literature recommendation. In: Proceedings of the 29th ACM International Conference on Information & Knowledge Management, CIKM 2020, pp. 3393–3396 (2020)
16. Kreutz, C.K., Schenkel, R.: Scientific paper recommendation systems: a literature review of recent publications. Int. J. Digit. Libr. **23**(4), 335–369 (2022)
17. Lin, J.: The neural hype and comparisons against weak baselines. SIGIR Forum **52**(2), 40–51 (2019)
18. Lin, J., Ma, X., Lin, S.C., Yang, J.H., Pradeep, R., Nogueira, R.: Pyserini: a Python toolkit for reproducible information retrieval research with sparse and dense representations. In: Proceedings of the 44th International ACM SIGIR Conference on Research and Development in Information Retrieval, SIGIR 2021, pp. 2356–2362 (2021)
19. Mandikal, P., Mooney, R.: Sparse meets dense: a hybrid approach to enhance scientific document retrieval. arXiv cs.IR/2401.04055 (2024)
20. Moreira, G.d.S.P., Ak, R., Schifferer, B., Xu, M., Osmulski, R., Oldridge, E.: Enhancing Q&A text retrieval with ranking models: benchmarking, fine-tuning and deploying rerankers for RAG. arXiv cs.IR/2409.07691 (2024)
21. Mysore, S., Jasim, M., Mccallum, A., Zamani, H.: Editable user profiles for controllable text recommendations. In: Proceedings of the 46th International ACM SIGIR Conference on Research and Development in Information Retrieval, SIGIR 2023, pp. 993–1003 (2023)
22. Mysore, S., Mccallum, A., Zamani, H.: Large language model augmented narrative driven recommendations. In: Proceedings of the 17th ACM Conference on Recommender Systems, RecSys 2023, pp. 777–783 (2023)
23. Penaloza, E., Gouvert, O., Wu, H., Charlin, L.: TEARS: text representations for scrutable recommendations. In: Proceedings of the ACM on Web Conference 2025, pp. 4949–4968 (2025)
24. Qin, Z., et al.: Large language models are effective text rankers with pairwise ranking prompting. In: Findings of the Association for Computational Linguistics: NAACL 2024, NAACL 2024, pp. 1504–1518 (2024)
25. Radlinski, F., Balog, K., Diaz, F., Dixon, L., Wedin, B.: On natural language user profiles for transparent and scrutable recommendation. In: Proceedings of the 45th International ACM SIGIR Conference on Research and Development in Information Retrieval, SIGIR 2022, pp. 2863–2874 (2022)

26. Ramos, J., Rahmani, H.A., Wang, X., Fu, X., Lipani, A.: Transparent and scrutable recommendations using natural language user profiles. In: Proceedings of the 62nd Annual Meeting of the Association for Computational Linguistics (Volume 1: Long Papers), ACL 2024, pp. 13971–13984 (2024)
27. Sanner, S., Balog, K., Radlinski, F., Wedin, B., Dixon, L.: Large language models are competitive near cold-start recommenders for language-and item-based preferences. In: Proceedings of the 17th ACM Conference on Recommender Systems, RecSys 2023, pp. 890–896 (2023)
28. Sguerra, B., Epure, E.V., Lee, H., Moussallam, M.: Biases in LLM-generated musical taste profiles for recommendation. In: Proceedings of the Nineteenth ACM Conference on Recommender Systems, RecSys 2025, pp. 527–532 (2025)
29. Yang, T.L., Liu, J.S., Tseng, Y.H., Jang, J.S.R.: Knowledge retrieval based on generative AI. arXiv cs.IR/2501.04635 (2025)
30. Zhou, J., Dai, Y., Joachims, T.: Language-based user profiles for recommendation. arXiv cs.CL/2402.15623 (2024)

# FoodNexus: Massive Food Knowledge
# for Recommender Systems


Ludovico Boratto[(✉)] , Gianni Fenu , Mirko Marras , Giacomo Medda ,
and Giovanni Zedda

Department of Mathematics and Computer Science, University of Cagliari,
Cagliari, Italy
`{ludovico.boratto,mirko.marras}@acm.org`, `fenu,giacomo.medda@unica.it`,
`g.zedda58@studenti.unica.it`



**Abstract.** Personalized food recommendation can promote healthier, sustainable eating, but current systems often rely on sparse and unstructured data, limiting semantic expressiveness and diverse personalization. In this paper, we propose `FoodNexus`, a large-scale knowledge graph with nearly one billion triples designed to enrich food recommendation with structured, nutrition-aware, and user-contextual information. We built it via a multi-stage pipeline that combines and augments the largest public dataset of user–recipe interactions, `HUMMUS`, with extensive metadata from *Open Food Facts* by linking recipes to concrete food products, extracting user traits from their biographies and reviews, and mapping both data sources onto the same ontology. Experiments show that `FoodNexus` enables richer, nutrition-sensitive evaluation of recommendations.

**Code & Resource**: https://github.com/tail-unica/food-nexus.


**Keywords:** Food Ontology · Knowledge Extraction · Recipe Recommendation · User-side Knowledge Graph · Nutrition · Sustainability

## 1 Introduction

The growing interest in personalized food recommendation stems from its potential to accommodate dietary needs and encourage healthier and more sustainable eating habits [1,3,25,36,39]. Evaluation has increasingly moved beyond utility toward societal objectives, notably nutrition [4,6], fairness [7,8], explainability [9,22], and sustainability [3,12,30], which directly impact people's lives. Yet, the black-box nature of many recommender systems limits user trust and adoption in high-stakes contexts like nutrition [2,5,28]. Reducing this opacity benefits from access to structured information about both users and food items, such as nutrient content, dietary constraints, and cultural preferences, that can help models reason about a given recommendation [2,4].

To support transparency, such information would also need to be structured semantically rather than represented as isolated data points [11,14,21]. Understanding and structuring food-related information is crucial across fields such




R. Campos et al. (Eds.): ECIR 2026, LNCS 16486, pp. 447–462, 2026.
https://doi.org/10.1007/978-3-032-21321-1_52

as agriculture [11,14], healthcare [32], and retail analytics [21]. This need arises from the massive volume of data generated along the entire food chain, from production to packaging and retail. Knowledge graphs (KGs) offer a way to meet this goal and have proved to enhance transparency in recommendation [2,5,6].

While (structured) information is essential for enabling more responsible food recommendation, existing datasets fall short of providing the necessary depth and organization. Most resources (e.g., [19,20]) focus solely on user–food interactions, omitting semantic details about users and food items. More recent datasets attempt to enrich this setup by including food-specific features, such as ingredient lists [26], nutritional profiles [23], and health scores [6]. However, this information is often presented in flat or unstructured formats that limit reasoning, and is often not released as reusable resources. A few works have begun leveraging KGs to provide structured connections between users and food [6,15,26]. Still, these efforts lack granularity and semantic richness (Table 1).

In this paper, we propose FoodNexus, a large-scale knowledge graph resulting from a systematic and multi-stage construction process. The proposed resource is grounded in HUMMUS, the largest public dataset of user–food interactions encompassing user reviews and user-submitted recipes, and in *Open Food Facts* (OFF) [13], a crowd-sourced database of food products collected from multiple countries and annotated with rich attributes. The KG construction process begins with the definition of a food-specific ontology that captures key food- (e.g., nutritional and environmental attributes) and user-level concepts (e.g., preferences, constraints). We then perform entity linking to align abstract recipes from HUMMUS with food products from OFF to enable connections between unstructured recipe text and standardized metadata. To further enhance semantic reasoning, we enrich the graph with knowledge extracted from user biographies and reviews in HUMMUS, e.g., user preferences, dietary constraints, and contextual cues. With almost one billion triples, FoodNexus offers a unified, semantic structure that models user behaviors and food items. To showcase its usefulness, we evaluate traditional

**Table 1.** Comparison of feature-rich data sources for food recommendation.

| Dataset | General | | | Domain-specific | | | | | | |
|---|---|---|---|---|---|---|---|---|---|---|
| | Type | Repr. | Access | Nutr. | Health. | Orig. | Sust. | Pack. | Inter. | User Att. |
| FoodOn [14] | DK | KG | Public | ✗ | ✗* | ✓ | ✗ | ✓ | ✗ | ✗ |
| FoodKG [15] | UI+DK | KG | Public | ✓ | ✗ | ✗ | ✗ | ✗ | ✓ | ✗ |
| LODHalal [26] | DK | KG | Public | ✓ | ✗ | ✓ | ✗ | ✗ | ✗ | ✗ |
| HUMMUS [6] | UI+DK | Tab | Public | ✓ | ✓ | ✗ | ✗ | ✗ | ✓ | ✗ |
| RecSoGood [4] | UI+DK | KG | Private | ✓ | ✓ | ✗ | ✗ | ✗ | ✓ | ✗ |
| HeASe [25] | UI+DK | Tab | Public | ✓ | ✓ | ✗ | ✓ | ✗ | ✓ | ✗ |
| GreenRec [39] | UI | Tab | Public | ✓ | ✓ | ✗ | ✓ | ✗ | ✓ | ✗ |
| OFF [13] | DK | Tab | Public | ✓ | ✓ | ✓ | ✓ | ✓ | ✗ | ✗ |
| FoodNexus (Ours) | UI+DK | KG | Public | ✓ | ✓ | ✓ | ✓ | ✓ | ✓ | ✓ |

**Type**: User–Item (UI), Domain Knowledge (DK); **Representation**: Tabular (Tab), Knowledge Graph (KG).
**Domain**: **Nutr**ients, **Health**iness, **Orig**in Country, **Sust**ainability, **Pack**aging, **Inter**actions, **User Att**ributes
**Domain Marking**: ✓ (available), ✗ (not available or not applicable), * (only categorical - like allergens).

and knowledge-aware recommendation methods, highlighting the impact of user-elicited knowledge that enriches the underlying collaborative KG. We further assess nutrition-sensitive aspects enabled by FoodNexus, such as micronutrients composition, vitamin intake, and food processing level.

## 2  Resource Creation Methodology

Our construction pipeline includes five main stages: selecting source datasets, specifying the integrated ontology, linking recipes to products[1], extracting user traits, and assembling the knowledge graph.

### 2.1  Step 1: Source Datasets Selection

To construct a resource that enables stronger semantic reasoning and more informed personalization, we begin by selecting sources of user–item interaction data and structured, detailed food knowledge.

As for the first data source type, we chose HUMMUS [6] due to its status as the largest publicly available corpus of user–recipe consumption behaviors, represented also in the form of textual reviews. It contains nearly 2M interactions from over 300k users across more than 500k recipes. While this dataset also includes healthiness scores and covers key macro-nutrient information, it lacks fine-grained micro-nutrient and sustainability attributes necessary to support deeper reasoning about food consumption [3,25,39]. We relied on HUMMUS to ensure scalability and reproducibility across prior and future studies, while designing a dataset-agnostic pipeline adaptable to other sources.

To enrich this base with more extensive food knowledge, we chose to incorporate data from Open Food Facts (OFF) [13], a global, crowd-sourced database that describes over 4M food products across more than 180 countries. OFF was selected for its breadth, openness, and rich metadata (see the domain-specific feature columns in Table 1), including also micro-nutrient profiles, ingredient lists, packaging types, allergen tags, and ecological impact scores.

Despite their individual relevance, integrating HUMMUS and OFF poses non-trivial challenges, as they have traditionally been treated as isolated silos - differing in granularity, vocabulary, and formats.

### 2.2  Step 2: Combined Ontology Specification

To integrate the original content from HUMMUS and OFF into a unified, semantically coherent framework, we designed a dedicated ontology that enables reasoning, disambiguation, and alignment. While ontologies like FoodOn [14] model general food concepts, they rely on a variety of underlying ontologies and tend to

---

[1] We refer to recipes as abstract culinary preparations consisting of a list of ingredients and instructions for preparation, while food products are concrete packaged items found in stores, described by standardized nutritional and ingredient metadata.

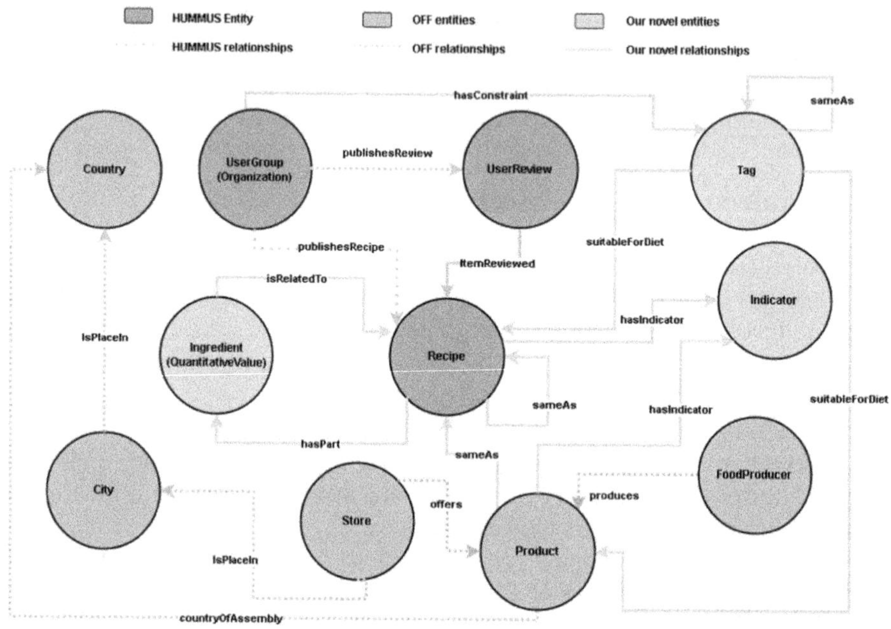



**Fig. 1.** Visual overview of the ontology used in `FoodNexus`.

lack both user-level constructs and the granularity needed to align recipes with real-world products. In contrast, our approach, grounded only in the `schema.org` vocabulary and a minimal set of custom entities, was intentionally designed to support personalization without introducing unnecessary complexity and ensure that relevant features remain closely connected to both users and recipes.

Our ontology, illustrated in Fig. 1, harmonizes concepts from both datasets and introduces new entities, attributes or relations only where necessary. To enhance interoperability and reuse, we incorporated the vocabulary of *schema.org* wherever applicable[2]. Quantitatively, we aligned approximately 73% of our entities and 70% of our relations with *schema.org* terms (e.g., `Recipe`, `UserReview`), ensuring future compatibility with broader linked data ecosystems.

With `HUMMUS` including a minimal built-in ontology, we first validated its internal structure for semantic alignment with the *schema.org* vocabulary. To integrate the health score information while extending the ontology's expressiveness, we introduced a new entity class, `Indicator`, absent in `HUMMUS` but aligned with *schema.org*. This addition enables to generalize beyond health scores to represent other attributes such as nutritional and sustainability scores. Recipes and ingredients were unified into the entity class `Recipe`, interpreting ingredients as elementary recipes, and the entity class `Ingredient` was added to capture the quantity-aware composition of structured recipes.

---

[2] Note that *schema.org* (https://schema.org) is a community-driven initiative founded by major search engines to promote structured data markup online.

**Table 2.** Relations with clickable element names in **FoodNexus**.

| Source | Relation | Target | Description |
|---|---|---|---|
| UserGroup | publishesRecipe | Recipe | A user has published a recipe |
| UserGroup | publishesReview | UserReview | A user has published a review |
| UserGroup | hasConstraint | Tag | A user has a dietary constraint |
| UserReview | itemReviewed | Recipe | A review is associated with a recipe |
| Recipe | hasIndicator | Indicator | A recipe has a certain indicator |
| Product | hasIndicator | Indicator | A product has a certain indicator |
| Recipe | hasPart | Ingredient | A recipe includes a specific ingredient |
| Ingredient | isRelatedTo | Recipe | An ingredient is part of a recipe |
| Tag | suitableForDiet | Recipe | A constraint is compatible with a recipe |
| Tag | sameAs | Tag | A tag is the same or similar to a tag |
| Tag | suitableForDiet | Product | A constraint is compatible with a product |
| Product | sameAs | Recipe | A product is similar/identical to a recipe |
| Product | countryOfAssembly | Country | A product is assembled in a country |
| FoodProducer | produces | Product | A producer produces a product |
| Recipe | sameAs | Recipe | A recipe is an alternative or similar recipe |
| Store | offers | Product | A store sells a certain product |
| Store | isPlaceIn | City | A store is located in a certain city |
| City | isPlaceIn | Country | A city is located in a certain country |

In contrast, OFF lacks an official ontology. Hence, we designed from scratch the set of entities, attributes, and relations. We first mapped OFF's content against the entities in the initial ontology derived from HUMMUS, ensuring alignment and eliminating redundancy. Next, where applicable, we connected OFF entities, attributes, and relations to *schema.org* types. For remaining concepts, we defined new classes, ensuring that knowledge from OFF is structured and interoperable.

To model preference-related information, we extended the original Tag entity from HUMMUS, which categorizes recipes under heterogeneous descriptors such as cuisine type, preparation time, and dietary restrictions. In our design, this entity also serves to capture user-level preference indicators, enabling its use not only for recipe categorization but also for supporting personalized recommendation behaviors. This flexible representation unifies diverse categorical attributes within a consistent semantic structure while maintaining the ontology's compactness, in line with best practices for scalable food knowledge modeling [6,15].

The final ontology includes 11 entity types, 15 attribute types, and 11 relations types between these entities, listed in Table 2.

## 2.3   Step 3: Recipe-Product Entity Linking

With the defined ontology, we aimed to align Recipe entities from HUMMUS with structured Product entries from OFF via the sameAs relation. Unlike other cross-dataset mappings, recipe-to-product linking proved more challenging due to noisy product names in OFF, containing brands, units, multilingual text etc.

To address this challenge, we devised a pre-processing pipeline that cleans and harmonizes item names (recipes and products) across datasets. Key transformations included removing brand mentions, expanding abbreviations, normalizing spelling, and translating into English. Translation was performed using the Qwen2.5 large language model (LLM) [38], selected for its strong multilingual capabilities, particularly with oriental languages commonly found in OFF. To ensure deterministic and reproducible translations, sampling was disabled and decoding was performed deterministically for all the tasks performed by the LLM. Full implementation details for the pipeline are available in our repository.

With pre-processed recipe and product names, we adopted semantic sentence encoders to compute pairwise cosine similarities between them. We evaluated 16 encoders known for their strong performance on semantic similarity tasks[3]. To support this evaluation, we manually annotated a gold-standard dataset of 106 HUMMUS-OFF item pairs as either matching or non-matching. We used 66.66% of these pairs (70 items) to tune the decision threshold and the remaining 33.33% (36 items) to test generalization. This dataset was primarily designed to support encoder selection, so we validated the linking at larger scale in later stages. Specifically, 589 HUMMUS-OFF pairs were sampled to diversify OFF product country of sale and labeled as matching or non-matching in a mixed human and automated workflow. Approximately 65% of these pairs were judged matching, with good agreement between human and automated labels (Cohen's $\kappa = 0.71$).

The cosine similarity threshold for each encoder was selected using the 70-item tuning set, using threshold values ranging from 0.80 to 0.99 with incremental steps of 0.01. For each encoder, the threshold that yielded the best performance on this set was applied to the test partition for comparison. The most effective encoder on the test set was BAAI/bge-en-icl [18,37], with a threshold of 0.85 and an F1-score of 75.77%. We hence used this encoder to compute cosine similarities across two trillion recipe–product pairs, generated by comparing roughly 500k normalized HUMMUS recipes against 4M OFF products[4]. As an example, the OFF product *Spaghetti Tomato Sauce (Barilla)* and the HUMMUS recipe *Italian Spaghetti al Pomodoro* were both pre-processed to *sauce spaghetti tomato* (perfect similarity). The same encoder was used to align ingredients across datasets and infer sameAs relations between similar recipes in HUMMUS.

### 2.4   Step 4: User Consumption Traits Extraction

We identified that user metadata in HUMMUS can play a key role in enriching the user dimension of FoodNexus. User biographies and reviews in HUMMUS reveal self-disclosed traits, such as eating habits and dietary constraints, which are absent from structured datasets (see the *User Attr.* column in Table 1).

---

[3] We relied on benchmarks at https://huggingface.co/spaces/mteb/leaderboard.

[4] We release two versions of our resource: one based on a strict threshold of 0.975 that ensures higher precision and robustness, and one based on the 0.85 threshold to support coverage. Later sections refer to the robust 0.975 version.

**Table 3.** Comparative statistics between the original sources and `FoodNexus`, including the base `HUMMUS` and its variant enriched with extracted user traits, for fair comparison.

| Data Source | # Triples | # Entities | # Attributes | # E. Types | # R. Types | # A. Types |
| --- | --- | --- | --- | --- | --- | --- |
| HUMMUS | ~53.9M | ~12.3M | ~22.8M | 6 | 6 | 9 |
| HUMMUS (inferred) | ~57.9M | ~12.3M | ~22.8M | 6 | 7 | 14 |
| OFF | ~267.9M | ~38.5M | ~107.4M | 7 | 6 | 7 |
| FoodNexus (Ours) | **~979.5M** | **~51.0M** | **~130.2M** | **11** | **11** | **15** |

E. Types: Entity Types; R. Types: Relation Types; A. Types: Attribute Types.

To this end, we leveraged `Qwen2.5` [38] under the same reproducible setup used during pre-processing, with sampling disabled and decoding performed deterministically. We adapted the LLM with a refined prompt (available in our repository) to extract structured user traits from user-generated content. We focused on (i) personal attributes (e.g., age, gender), used in health-oriented personalization [23,24,29], and (ii) dietary preferences/constraints (e.g., vegetarian, milk allergy), useful for filtering and matching [26,32]. The prompt was designed to extract explicit information and implicit cues, e.g., interpreting *I love cooking for my grandchildren* as an indication of older age. Further details on the ethical implications of this procedure are discussed in Sect. 4 (Table 3).

The reliability of this approach was quantified using Krippendorff's $\alpha$ on human annotations on 100 user biographies across both explicit and inferred traits ($\alpha = 0.66 \pm 0.19$). On this set, our extraction procedure achieved an accuracy of 87.5% for explicit traits and 61.2% for implicit traits. Although inferred traits carry greater uncertainty, discarding them would overlook a considerable amount of user-relevant information that could be harnessed as knowledge when training models. Also, inferred traits are flagged in the KG to preserve transparency. This allows systems to deliver recommendations to users in a more accurate way, referencing the actual basis of inference (not unverified characteristics directly). Extracted personal attributes were used to instantiate `UserGroup`'s properties. Dietary preferences/constraints aspects were represented as entities of type `Tag` and linked to the relevant `UserGroup`. Similar tags referring to dietary preferences/constraints were linked using `SameAs` relations via `BAAI/bge-en-icl`.

## 2.5   Step 5: Knowledge Graph Assembly

Finally, we assembled the resource by instantiating ontology classes with data from direct semantic mappings (Step 2), recipe–product links (Step 3), and user consumption traits (Step 4), resulting in a schema-compliant `RDF` graph.

The graph integrates approximately 51M unique entities, surpassing the size of either source dataset—`HUMMUS` contributes 12.3M (mainly recipes, users, and ingredients), and `OFF` adds 38.5M (primarily products and nutritional components). The integration, enriched with aligned products, user groups, and contextual tags, also results in around 130M attribute assertions, exceeding those of HUMMUS (22.8M) and OFF (107.4M), and increasing attribute types to 15. The highest growth appears in triples, which reach 979M, compared to 53M in HUMMUS and 268M in OFF, spanning user–constraint mappings, recipe–recipe, recipe-product, and ingredient–product links. Relation types were raised to 11.

We emphasize that LLMs were employed only in two controlled stages: (i) multilingual translation into English and (ii) extraction of user traits from HUMMUS biographies and reviews. All other tasks, including name pre-processing pipeline, entity linking, and user-tag-recipe alignment, relied on deterministic sentence encoders rather than generative models, ensuring that the construction of FoodNexus does not depend on non-reproducible model behavior or chained LLM outputs.

## 3   Demonstrative Experimentation with FoodNexus

We investigated how knowledge-aware systems built on FoodNexus perform compared to interaction-based methods and how the resource enables analysis of nutritional, environmental, and product-packaging aspects. We further study the impact of user-elicited knowledge, as additional KG relations, on recommendation utility. These experiments serve as demonstrative evaluations showcasing the semantic richness, scale, and interoperability of FoodNexus, rather than as competitive benchmarks. Methodological extensions and ablations are left for future work. In particular, we aim to answer the following research questions:

**RQ1:** To what extent does integrating semantically enriched and user-elicited knowledge within FoodNexus enhance the effectiveness of knowledge-aware recommender systems compared to interaction-based methods?

**RQ2:** Do the recommended recipes of interaction-based and knowledge-aware models exhibit distinct patterns across the nutritional, environmental, and product-packaging dimensions provided by FoodNexus?

To prepare FoodNexus for recommendation, we adapted the pipeline from [6]. Interactions were filtered using the 5-core strategy, retaining users and items with at least five interactions. To ensure semantic richness and connectivity, we removed user entities with fewer than five facts and non-user entities referenced in fewer than 30 triples - these thresholds were tuned via grid search. The data was split chronologically into 80% training, 10% validation, and 10% test for each user. On these partitions, we extended the HUMMUS benchmark [6], which originally included a popularity-based baseline (Pop) and a collaborative filtering model (BPR) [27]. We incorporated NeuMF [17], a neural matrix factorization model; LightGCN [16], a graph convolutional model using only user–item interactions; and the knowledge-aware methods KGAT [35], KTUP [10], and MKR [34].

Given the massive scale of FoodNexus, we trained KG-aware models on a subgraph derived from the original HUMMUS KG and adapted to our ontology. This extension, which realizes the Indicator and Ingredient entities, enables reasoning on diet- and nutrition-sensitive aspects while emphasizing a semantically

**Table 4.** **[RQ1]** Performance comparison across recommendation models with Hit, Recall, and NDCG on top-10/20/50 lists.

| Model | Hit | | | Recall | | | NDCG | | |
|---|---|---|---|---|---|---|---|---|---|
| | Top-10 | Top-20 | Top-50 | Top-10 | Top-20 | Top-50 | Top-10 | Top-20 | Top-50 |
| Pop | 0.0035 | 0.0050 | 0.0077 | 0.0008 | 0.0010 | 0.0013 | 0.0008 | 0.0009 | 0.0009 |
| BPR | 0.0474 | 0.0777 | 0.1361 | 0.0136 | 0.0244 | 0.0467 | 0.0102 | 0.0133 | 0.0189 |
| NeuMF | 0.0562 | 0.0886 | 0.1491 | 0.0175 | 0.0276 | 0.0515 | 0.0131 | 0.0160 | 0.0220 |
| LightGCN | **0.0604** | **0.0930** | **0.1558** | 0.0184 | 0.0307 | 0.0557 | 0.0140 | 0.0173 | 0.0235 |
| MKR | 0.0413 | 0.0656 | 0.1126 | 0.0166 | 0.0272 | 0.0477 | 0.0111 | 0.0140 | 0.0188 |
| KTUP | 0.0446 | 0.0737 | 0.1260 | 0.0189 | 0.0315 | 0.0552 | 0.0118 | 0.0154 | 0.0210 |
| KGAT | 0.0580 | 0.0903 | 0.1453 | **0.0231** | **0.0372** | **0.0628** | **0.0152** | **0.0191** | **0.0252** |
| UserKGAT | 0.0187 | 0.0368 | 0.0802 | 0.0084 | 0.0164 | 0.0370 | 0.0046 | 0.0069 | 0.0116 |
| UserKTUP | 0.0388 | 0.0690 | 0.1260 | 0.0154 | 0.0295 | 0.0570 | 0.0093 | 0.0133 | 0.0198 |
| UserMKR | 0.0461 | 0.0744 | 0.1264 | 0.0187 | 0.0319 | 0.0556 | 0.0120 | 0.0157 | 0.0212 |

rich representation relevant to recommendation rather than exhaustive information coverage. Product-level attributes extracted from OFF were instead used to characterize models according to the properties of their top recommendations.

Furthermore, as most knowledge graphs for recommendation refine only the item side, these models are typically designed to learn from item-based structures. Recent models seek to enrich user profiles by capturing higher-order relational structures across user–item–entity connections, but they do not necessarily consider user features [5,33]. To study the effect of the additional user relations introduced by FoodNexus, we devised a variant for each KG-aware model that learns user-side representations within the semantic network. These variants, trained on the FoodNexus subgraph enriched with user relations, are denoted with the prefix "User" (i.e., UserKGAT, UserKTUP, and UserMKR). These variants extend the original architectures to incorporate user entities within the KG learning process. As KGAT uniformly propagates messages across all entities, user nodes are therefore directly included in the KG adjacency matrix for UserKGAT. KTUP aligns item embeddings with their KG counterparts by generating an enhanced item embedding $\hat{i} = i + e_i$, where $i$ denotes an item in the interaction matrix and $e_i$ the same item in the KG. UserKTUP performs the corresponding operation for users, $\hat{u} = u + e_u$, aligning each user embedding with its KG entity. In MKR, where cross&compress units model feature interactions between items and entities, we introduced a symmetric component for user embeddings, enabling both user and item representations to interact with KG entities:

$$h_{v,L} = \mathbb{E}_{v \sim S(h_v)}[C_v^L(v,h)[e]] \qquad h_{u,L} = \mathbb{E}_{v \sim S(h_u)}[C_u^L(u,h)[e]]$$

$$r_L = \mathcal{M}^L(r) \qquad \hat{t} = \mathcal{M}^K\left(\begin{bmatrix} h_{v,L} \\ h_{u,L} \\ r_L \end{bmatrix}\right) \tag{1}$$

where $S(h_v)$ and $S(h_u)$ are the item and user sets linked to entity $h$, $C_v^L$ and $C_u^L$ the corresponding cross&compress units, $[e]$ the crossed-entity output, $r$ the relation, $\hat{t}$ the predicted tail vector, and $\mathcal{M}^K$, $\mathcal{M}^L$ the K- and L-layer MLPs. Our repository reports other implementation details, e.g., grid-search optimization.

### 3.1   RQ1: Recommendation Utility Analysis

Table 4 reports performance in terms of Hit [31], Recall [31], and NDCG [31] at cutoffs 10, 20, and 50 under a full-ranking evaluation protocol. The relatively low scores are consistent with related works [6,39] and reflect the inherent sparsity and diversity of user–food interactions. As expected, the non-personalized baseline `Pop` performs poorly, indicating that food choices are rarely driven by popularity but rather by heterogeneous personal and contextual factors. This diverges from [6], probably due to the random splitting adopted in their study. Interaction-based (`BPR`, `NeuMF`, and `LightGCN`) and KG-based (`MKR`, `KTUP`, and `KGAT`) models show significant improvements, with `LightGCN` achieving the highest Hit scores and `KGAT` the best Recall and NDCG. This suggests that co-interaction signals increase the chance of retrieving at least one relevant recipe, but exploiting KG structure yields more refined rankings that recover relevant items not captured by interactions alone. Results on user variants reveal that naive incorporation of user relations appears to introduce noisy signals that can mask existing user–item interaction patterns (as seen in `UserKGAT` and `UserKTUP`). Conversely, models with dedicated learning units for user relations, such as `UserMKR`, can capture useful KG patterns. Overall, these findings indicate that the semantic signals in `FoodNexus` can enhance recommendation utility when propagated through appropriately designed KG modules.

### 3.2   RQ2: Nutritional and Contextual Analysis

We use `FoodNexus` to inspect how recommendation models reshape the distribution of food attributes derived from `OFF`. For each user and model we compute the per-attribute value (numeric mean or categorical proportion) over the top-10 recommendations and report the average per-user $\Delta$ relative to the global catalog reference. Figures 2–3 visualize these mean deltas (and 95% bootstrap CIs) for a selection of categorical and numeric attributes. Overall patterns are consistent across several axes. For *Allergens*, most models tend to favor gluten-containing items while recommending fewer milk-containing items, but approaches that incorporate explicit user knowledge show a more balanced allergen profile. In terms of *Packaging*, interaction-based systems over-represent plastic-packaged products relative to the catalog, whereas other methods do not show a clear bias. Sustainability scores (*Green Score*) reveal a systematic skew toward less sustainable items ("D"): several models over-represent items with lower eco-scores, with `MKR` showing the strongest shift toward the least sustainable class ("E") and `Pop` relatively favoring more eco-friendly items ("B"). Nutritional signals are mixed. All models slightly under-represent vitamins, potassium, and some micronutrients in their top-10 lists. `NeuMF` tends to reduce average added sugars, saturated

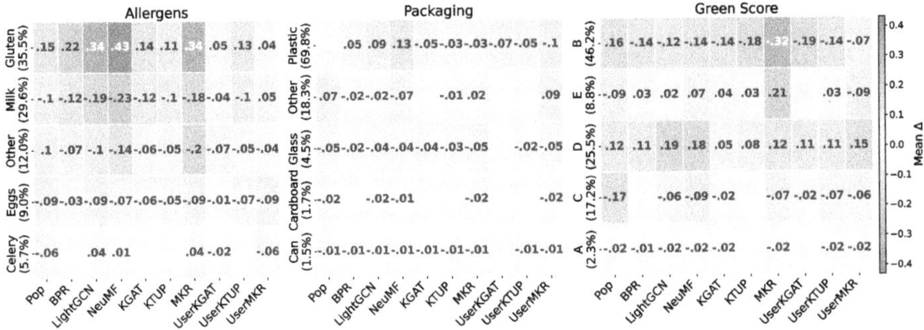

**Fig. 2. [RQ2 | Categorical]** Average per-user difference $\Delta$ between category proportions in models' top-k lists and global category prevalence (reported between parentheses). Positive (negative) values denote that a category is over- (under-) represented in recommendations. Cells with negligible changes ($|\Delta| < 0.01$) are de-annotated.

fat, and additive count while favoring less processed items (lower NOVA group), UserKGAT shows comparable trends and a tendency toward items with higher potassium. Comparing KG-aware models to their user-augmented variants (MKR vs UserMKR, KTUP vs UserKTUP) suggests that user-aware variants accentuate several shifts, both beneficial (higher fiber, fewer additives) and detrimental (higher sugars or saturated fat) depending on the model and attribute. These findings suggest that FoodNexus provides actionable semantic grounding for models like MKR/UserMKR and KTUP/UserKTUP to yield more holistic and health-conscious food recommendation. The observed trends highlight the potential of knowledge-enriched systems to support responsible results.

## 4   Discussion and Implications

Together, the utility and attribute analyses expose complementary benefits and risks. FoodNexus improves retrieval quality for several knowledge-aware models (e.g., KGAT, UserMKR) while also revealing systematic distributional shifts in recommendations, such as over-representation of gluten, a skew toward lower eco-scores, and mixed nutritional effects. These findings motivate a focused discussion of the practical implications and the ethical considerations that arise when enriching personalization with externally sourced food knowledge.

The extraction of user-related knowledge is the most ethically sensitive component of FoodNexus. In line with ACM ethical guidelines, we prioritize transparency and respect for user privacy while seeking to enhance the resource's utility for research. User biographies and reviews were sourced from the publicly available HUMMUS dataset; we did not collect any new user data, but only transformed existing free-text into a structured representation. Language models were used deterministically as text interpreters (no stochastic generation) so that outputs are reproducible and limited to making pre-existing information explicit rather than inventing content. A manual evaluation confirmed the reliability of

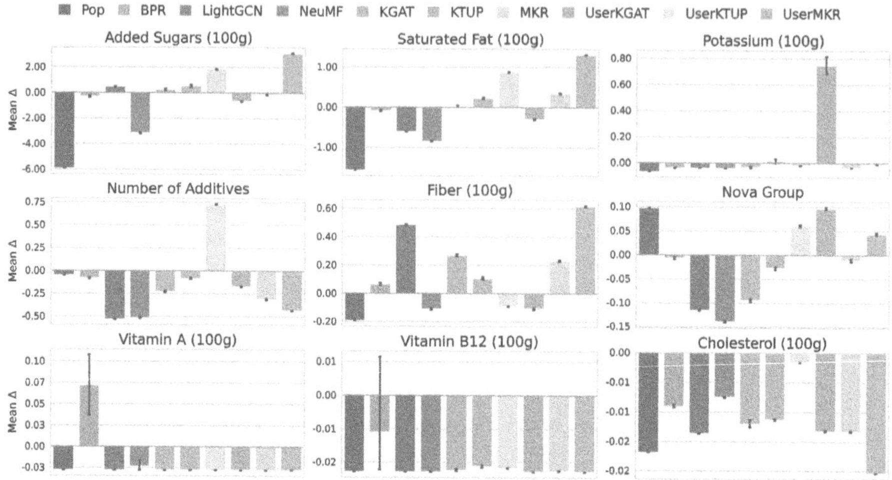

**Fig. 3. [RQ2 | Numerical]** Average per-user difference $\Delta$ between the distribution of numerical attributes in top-k lists and the global average, with 95% CIs across users. Positive (negative) values indicate over- (under-) representation in recommendations. Attributes are sorted by largest absolute mean $\Delta$ across models.

the extracted traits, supporting the validity and ethical soundness of this approach. Automatically inferred attributes are labeled with the suffix "(inferred)" in the released graph. This design enables downstream users to identify and filter out inferred or potentially sensitive attributes if desired.

## 5 Conclusions and Future Work

In this paper, we proposed FoodNexus, a large-scale KG for food recommendation, integrating recipes, commercial food products, user profiles, and a wide range of nutritional, processing, and sustainability attributes. Our experiments show that, beyond recommendation utility, FoodNexus enables more nutrition-sensitive and semantically grounded food recommendations. The resource is fully documented, reproducible, and built via a multi-stage pipeline combining the HUMMUS dataset and the OFF database, easily extensible to other sources.

Building on this resource, future work will expand and refine several aspects. First, subtle recipe–product alignments overlooked by our linking strategy may be successfully captured by fine-tuning semantic sentence encoders on food knowledge. Second, modeling temporal aspects such as seasonality could improve personalization. Third, our evaluation of generic baselines on FoodNexus's new dimensions, such as allergens content and vitamin intake, highlights the need to design dedicated loss functions and multi-task models that better support diverse dietary needs and demographic groups. Additional directions include mitigating the cold-start problem via the extracted user traits, recommending other entities such as physical stores, and employing knowledge completion techniques to reduce data sparsity. We see `FoodNexus` as a core resource for advancing food technology research at the intersection of recommendation, nutrition, and health. While periodic updates may be needed to reflect `OFF`'s evolving product catalogs, its current structure provides a strong foundation for long-term use.

**Acknowledgments.** We acknowledge financial support from (i) the National Recovery and Resilience Plan (NRRP), Mission 4 Component 2 Investment 1.1 - Call for tender No. 3277, published on December 30, 2021, by the Italian Ministry of University and Research (MUR), funded by the European Union – Next Generation EU. Project Code ECS0000038 – Project Title eINS Ecosystem of Innovation for Next Generation Sardinia – Grant Assignment Decree No. 1056 adopted on June 23, 2022, by the MUR (CUP F53C22000430001) and (ii) the project PHaSE - Promoting Healthy and Sustainable Eating through Interactive and Explainable AI Methods, funded by MUR under the PRIN 2022 program (CUP H53D23003530006).

**Disclosure of Interests.** The authors have no competing interests to declare that are relevant to the content of this article.

# References


1. Ataguba, G., Orji, R.: Exploring large language models for personalized recipe generation and weight-loss management. ACM Trans. Comput. Healthcare (2025)
2. Balloccu, G., Boratto, L., Fenu, G., Marras, M.: Post processing recommender systems with knowledge graphs for recency, popularity, and diversity of explanations. In: SIGIR 2022: The 45th International ACM SIGIR Conference on Research and Development in Information Retrieval, Madrid, Spain, 11–15 July 2022, pp. 646–656. ACM (2022). https://doi.org/10.1145/3477495.3532041
3. Balloccu, G., Boratto, L., Fenu, G., Marras, M., Medda, G., Murgia, G.: Greenfoodlens: sustainability labels for food recommendation. In: Bieliková, M., et al. (eds.) Proceedings of the Nineteenth ACM Conference on Recommender Systems, RecSys 2025, Prague, Czech Republic, 22–26 September 2025, pp. 764–773. ACM (2025). https://doi.org/10.1145/3705328.3748165
4. Balloccu, G., Boratto, L., Fenu, G., Marras, M., Medda, G., Murgia, G.: Knowledge data modeling in food recommendation: a case study on nutritional values. In: Boratto, L., De Filippo, A., Lex, E., Ricci, F. (eds.) Recommender Systems for Sustainability and Social Good, pp. 52–62. Springer Nature Switzerland, Cham (2025)
5. Balloccu, G., Boratto, L., Fenu, G., Marras, M., Soccol, A.: KGGLM: a generative language model for generalizable knowledge graph representation learning in recommendation. In: Proceedings of the 18th ACM Conference on Recommender Systems, RecSys 2024, Bari, Italy, 14–18 October 2024, pp. 1079–1084. ACM (2024), https://doi.org/10.1145/3640457.3691703
6. Bölz, F., Nurbakova, D., Calabretto, S., Gerl, A., Brunie, L., Kosch, H.: HUMMUS: a linked, healthiness-aware, user-centered and argument-enabling recipe data set for recommendation. In: Zhang, J., et al. (eds.) Proceedings of the 17th ACM Conference on Recommender Systems, RecSys 2023, Singapore, Singapore, 18–22 September 2023, pp. 1–11. ACM (2023). https://doi.org/10.1145/3604915.3609491

7. Boratto, L., Fenu, G., Marras, M., Medda, G.: Consumer fairness in recommender systems: contextualizing definitions and mitigations. In: Hagen, M., et al. (eds.) ECIR 2022. LNCS, vol. 13185, pp. 552–566. Springer, Cham (2022). https://doi.org/10.1007/978-3-030-99736-6_37

8. Boratto, L., Fenu, G., Marras, M., Medda, G.: Practical perspectives of consumer fairness in recommendation. Inf. Process. Manag. **60**(2), 103208 (2023). https://doi.org/10.1016/j.ipm.2022.103208

9. Boratto, L., Fenu, G., Marras, M., Medda, G., Soccol, A.: hopwise: a python library for explainable recommendation based on path reasoning over knowledge graphs. In: Cha, M., et al. (eds.) Proceedings of the 34th ACM International Conference on Information and Knowledge Management, CIKM 2025, Seoul, Republic of Korea, 10–14 November 2025. pp. 6328–6333. ACM (2025). https://doi.org/10.1145/3746252.3761641

10. Cao, Y., Wang, X., He, X., Hu, Z., Chua, T.: Unifying knowledge graph learning and recommendation: towards a better understanding of user preferences. In: Liu, L., White, R.W., Mantrach, A., Silvestri, F., McAuley, J.J., Baeza-Yates, R., Zia, L. (eds.) The World Wide Web Conference, WWW 2019, San Francisco, CA, USA, 13–17 May 2019, pp. 151–161. ACM (2019). https://doi.org/10.1145/3308558.3313705

11. Caracciolo, C., et al.: The AGROVOC linked dataset. Semantic Web **4**(3), 341–348 (2013). https://doi.org/10.3233/SW-130106

12. Cossatin, A.G., Mauro, N., Ardissono, L.: Promoting green fashion consumption through digital nudges in recommender systems. IEEE Access **12**, 6812–6829 (2024). https://doi.org/10.1109/ACCESS.2024.3349710

13. Gigandet, S., Team, O.F.F.: Open food facts (2012). https://static.openfoodfacts.org/data/en.openfoodfacts.org.products.csv.gz

14. Griffiths, E.J., Dooley, D.M., Buttigieg, P.L., Hoehndorf, R., Brinkman, F.S.L., Hsiao, W.W.L.: Foodon: a global farm-to-fork food ontology. In: Jaiswal, P., Hoehndorf, R., Arighi, C.N., Meier, A. (eds.) Proceedings of the Joint International Conference on Biological Ontology and BioCreative, Corvallis, Oregon, United States, 1–4 August 2016, CEUR Workshop Proceedings, vol. 1747. CEUR-WS.org (2016)

15. Haussmann, S., et al.: FoodKG: a semantics-driven knowledge graph for food recommendation. In: Ghidini, C., et al. (eds.) ISWC 2019, Part II. LNCS, vol. 11779, pp. 146–162. Springer, Cham (2019). https://doi.org/10.1007/978-3-030-30796-7_10

16. He, X., Deng, K., Wang, X., Li, Y., Zhang, Y., Wang, M.: Lightgcn: simplifying and powering graph convolution network for recommendation. In: Proceedings of the 43rd International ACM SIGIR conference on research and development in Information Retrieval, SIGIR 2020, Virtual Event, China, 25–30 July 2020, pp. 639–648. ACM (2020). https://doi.org/10.1145/3397271.3401063

17. He, X., Liao, L., Zhang, H., Nie, L., Hu, X., Chua, T.: Neural collaborative filtering. In: Barrett, R., Cummings, R., Agichtein, E., Gabrilovich, E. (eds.) Proceedings of the 26th International Conference on World Wide Web, WWW 2017, Perth, Australia, 3–7 April 2017, pp. 173–182. ACM (2017). https://doi.org/10.1145/3038912.3052569

18. Li, C., et al.: Making text embedders few-shot learners (2024). https://arxiv.org/abs/2409.15700

19. Majumder, B.P., Li, S., Ni, J., McAuley, J.J.: Generating personalized recipes from historical user preferences. In: Inui, K., Jiang, J., Ng, V., Wan, X. (eds.) Proceedings of the 2019 Conference on Empirical Methods in Natural Language Processing and the 9th International Joint Conference on Natural Language Processing, EMNLP-IJCNLP 2019, Hong Kong, China, 3–7 November 2019, pp. 5975–5981. ACL (2019). https://doi.org/10.18653/v1/D19-1613

20. Marín, J., et al.: Recipe1m+: a dataset for learning cross-modal embeddings for cooking recipes and food images. IEEE Trans. Pattern Anal. Mach. Intell. **43**(1), 187–203 (2021). https://doi.org/10.1109/TPAMI.2019.2927476

21. Maxim, K., Dmitry, Z.: Food product ontology: initial implementation of a vocabulary for describing food products. In: 14th Conference of Open Innovation Association FRUCT, pp. 191–196 (2013). https://fruct.org/publications/volume-14/acm14/files/Kol_21.pdf

22. Medda, G., Fabbri, F., Marras, M., Boratto, L., Fenu, G.: GNNUERS: fairness explanation in gnns for recommendation via counterfactual reasoning. ACM Trans. Intell. Syst. Technol. **16**(1), 6:1–6:26 (2025). https://doi.org/10.1145/3655631

23. Musto, C., Trattner, C., Starke, A., Semeraro, G.: Towards a knowledge-aware food recommender system exploiting holistic user models. In: Proceedings of the 28th ACM Conference on User Modeling, Adaptation and Personalization, UMAP 2020, Genoa, Italy, 12–18 July 2020, pp. 333–337. ACM (2020). https://doi.org/10.1145/3340631.3394880

24. Määttä, T., Holmi, E., Rostami, M., Oussalah, M.: Dish4u a crowd source app for guiding users towards healthy food. In: 2024 IEEE International Conference on Big Data (BigData), pp. 8771–8773 (2024). https://doi.org/10.1109/BigData62323.2024.10825669

25. Petruzzelli, A., Musto, C., Carlo, M.C.D., Tempesta, G., Semeraro, G.: Recommending healthy and sustainable meals exploiting food retrieval and large language models. In: Noia, T.D., et al.(eds.) Proceedings of the 18th ACM Conference on Recommender Systems, RecSys 2024, Bari, Italy, 14–18 October 2024, pp. 1057–1061. ACM (2024). https://doi.org/10.1145/3640457.3688193

26. Rakhmawati, N.A., Fatawi, J., Najib, A.C., Firmansyah, A.A.: Linked open data for halal food products. J. King Saud Univ. Comput. Inf. Sci. **33**(6), 728–739 (2021). https://doi.org/10.1016/j.jksuci.2019.04.004

27. Rendle, S., Freudenthaler, C., Gantner, Z., Schmidt-Thieme, L.: BPR: bayesian personalized ranking from implicit feedback. In: Bilmes, J.A., Ng, A.Y. (eds.) UAI 2009, Proceedings of the Twenty-Fifth Conference on Uncertainty in Artificial Intelligence, Montreal, QC, Canada, 18–21 June 2009, pp. 452–461. AUAI Press (2009). https://www.auai.org/uai2009/papers/UAI2009_0139_48141db02b9f0b02bc7158819ebfa2c7.pdf

28. Rostami, M., Muhammad, U., Forouzandeh, S., Berahmand, K., Farrahi, V., Oussalah, M.: An effective explainable food recommendation using deep image clustering and community detection. Intell. Syst. Appl. **16**, 200157 (2022). https://doi.org/10.1016/j.iswa.2022.200157

29. Sookrah, R., Dhowtal, J.D., Devi Nagowah, S.: A dash diet recommendation system for hypertensive patients using machine learning. In: 2019 7th International Conference on Information and Communication Technology (ICoICT), pp. 1–6 (2019). https://doi.org/10.1109/ICoICT.2019.8835323

30. Spillo, G., Filippo, A.D., Musto, C., Milano, M., Semeraro, G.: Towards green recommender systems: Investigating the impact of data reduction on carbon footprint and algorithm performances. In: Noia, T.D., et al. (eds.) Proceedings of the 18th ACM Conference on Recommender Systems, RecSys 2024, Bari, Italy, 14–18 October 2024, pp. 866–871. ACM (2024). https://doi.org/10.1145/3640457.3688160

31. Tamm, Y., Damdinov, R., Vasilev, A.: Quality metrics in recommender systems: do we calculate metrics consistently? In: Pampín, H.J.C., et al. (eds.) RecSys 2021: Fifteenth ACM Conference on Recommender Systems, Amsterdam, The Netherlands, 27 September 2021 - 1 October 2021, pp. 708–713. ACM (2021). https://doi.org/10.1145/3460231.3478848

32. Turhan, S., Bacaksız, M.B.: Recipe recommendation chatbot based on low fodmap dietary knowledge graph. In: 2024 IEEE International Conference on Big Data (BigData), pp. 6547–6555. IEEE (2024)

33. Wang, H., Zhang, F., Wang, J., Zhao, M., Li, W., Xie, X., Guo, M.: Ripplenet: propagating user preferences on the knowledge graph for recommender systems. In: Cuzzocrea, A., et al. (eds.) Proceedings of the 27th ACM International Conference on Information and Knowledge Management, CIKM 2018, Torino, Italy, 22–26 October 2018, pp. 417–426. ACM (2018). https://doi.org/10.1145/3269206.3271739

34. Wang, H., Zhang, F., Zhao, M., Li, W., Xie, X., Guo, M.: Multi-task feature learning for knowledge graph enhanced recommendation. In: Liu, L., et al. (eds.) The World Wide Web Conference, WWW 2019, San Francisco, CA, USA, 13–17 May 2019, pp. 2000–2010. ACM (2019). https://doi.org/10.1145/3308558.3313411

35. Wang, X., He, X., Cao, Y., Liu, M., Chua, T.: KGAT: knowledge graph attention network for recommendation. In: Teredesai, A., Kumar, V., Li, Y., Rosales, R., Terzi, E., Karypis, G. (eds.) Proceedings of the 25th ACM SIGKDD International Conference on Knowledge Discovery & Data Mining, KDD 2019, Anchorage, AK, USA, 4–8 August 2019, pp. 950–958. ACM (2019), https://doi.org/10.1145/3292500.3330989

36. Weber, I., Achananuparp, P.: Insights from machine-learned diet success prediction. In: Altman, R.B., Dunker, A.K., Hunter, L., Klein, T.E., Ritchie, M.D. (eds.) Biocomputing 2016: Proceedings of the Pacific Symposium, Kohala Coast, Hawaii, USA, 4–8 January 2016, pp. 540–551 (2016). http://psb.stanford.edu/psb-online/proceedings/psb16/weber.pdf

37. Xiao, S., Liu, Z., Zhang, P., Muennighoff, N.: C-pack: Packaged resources to advance general chinese embedding (2023)

38. Yang, A., et la.: Qwen2.5-math technical report: toward mathematical expert model via self-improvement. CoRR **abs/2409.12122** (2024). https://doi.org/10.48550/arXiv.2409.12122

39. Zhang, L., Zhang, Y., Zhou, X., Shen, Z.: Greenrec: a large-scale dataset for green food recommendation. In: Chua, T., Ngo, C., Lee, R.K., Kumar, R., Lauw, H.W. (eds.) Companion Proceedings of the ACM on Web Conference 2024, WWW 2024, Singapore, Singapore, 13–17 May 2024, pp. 625–628. ACM (2024), https://doi.org/10.1145/3589335.3651516

# pt-image-ir-dataset: An Image Retrieval Dataset in European Portuguese


Rodrigo Duarte[1,2]([✉]) [iD], António Branco[4,5] [iD], Hugo Proença[1,6] [iD], and Ricardo Campos[1,2,3] [iD]

[1] University of Beira Interior, Covilhã, Portugal
{hugomcp,ricardo.campos,rodrigo.duarte}@ubi.pt
[2] INESC TEC, Porto, Portugal
[3] Ci2 - Smart Cities Research Center - Polytechnic Institute of Tomar, Tomar, Portugal
[4] University of Lisbon, Lisbon, Portugal
antonio.branco@di.fc.ul.pt
[5] NLX-Group, Lisbon, Portugal
[6] IT: Instituto de Telecomunicações, Covilhã, Portugal



**Abstract.** With the surge of multimodal models and the demand for effective image Information Retrieval (IR) systems, high-quality text-to-image datasets have become paramount. However, most existing datasets are primarily in English, limiting their applicability to multilingual settings. To address this, we introduce the `pt-image-ir-dataset`, a manually annotated resource for text-based Image IR in European Portuguese. The dataset comprises 80 diverse queries and a curated pool of 5,201 images, each annotated for relevance by multiple human judges. The proposed dataset is a step forward in supporting the development and evaluation of image IR systems for European Portuguese, addressing a clear gap in multilingual multimodal research. To this end, we have made our dataset publicly available, alongside baseline experimental results, demonstrating its suitability on the Image IR task across different retrieval paradigms, including traditional text-based lexical IR methods, semantic dense retrieval models based on language embeddings, cutting-edge vision-language models and proprietary blackbox image retrieval systems. Results demonstrate that vision-language models, particularly *OpenCLIP/xlm-roberta-base-ViT-B-32*, significantly outperform other approaches (MRR = 0.610).

**Keywords:** text-to-image dataset · image information retrieval · vision-language models · multimodal benchmark dataset · European Portuguese


## 1 Introduction

The exponential growth of digital visual content has created an unprecedented demand for effective image retrieval systems capable of understanding and



R. Campos et al. (Eds.): ECIR 2026, LNCS 16486, pp. 463–478, 2026.
https://doi.org/10.1007/978-3-032-21321-1_53

matching textual queries with relevant images [4,16]. While significant advances have been made in multimodal information retrieval driven by vision-language models such as CLIP [20], ALIGN [10], and BLIP-2 [14], the vast majority of available datasets and research efforts remain focused on English-language contexts. For instance, CLIP was trained on 400 million English image–text pairs collected from the web, limiting its applicability to low-resource languages. Several other efforts [15,26,30] have been made to provide high-quality datasets to researchers, however, they also remain predominantly English-centric and typically rely on image-caption pairs, which do not necessarily reflect realistic user queries, which are often shorter and noisier. As a result, current resources fail to capture the cultural and linguistic diversity embedded in real-world multimodal search scenarios.

Portuguese, spoken by more than 250 million people worldwide, illustrates this problem particularly well. Despite its global relevance, Portuguese remains severely underrepresented in the multimodal information retrieval landscape. Existing multilingual datasets, while valuable, either omit Portuguese entirely or provide very limited coverage, typically in the form of captions rather than query-driven retrieval tasks. The challenge extends beyond mere translation, as effective systems must account for cultural nuances, domain-specific terminology, and regional linguistic variations. European Portuguese, in particular, introduces distinct lexical and syntactic characteristics that require dedicated resources for fair evaluation and robust system development. Translating an existing English dataset would fail to capture the unique visual and contextual characteristics of Portuguese institutional imagery, such as local governmental events, cultural practices, and named entities specific to Portugal. By constructing the dataset from scratch, we ensure that queries, images, and relevance judgments reflect authentic Portuguese usage and real-world search behavior, providing a resource that is both linguistically and culturally grounded.

To address these gaps, we introduce `pt-image-ir-dataset`, a dataset specifically designed for Portuguese image information retrieval research. It comprises 80 queries in European Portuguese paired with 5,201 images collected from the official Portuguese Presidency website, spanning nearly a decade of institutional content, including official ceremonies, cultural events, and governmental activities. Crucially, the dataset includes manually annotated relevance judgments from three independent annotators, ensuring high-quality ground truth.

Our contributions can be summarized as follows:

- We introduce `pt-image-ir-dataset`, the first manually annotated benchmark specifically designed for query-driven image retrieval in European Portuguese, comprising 80 queries and 5,201 images with human relevance judgments.
- We provide baseline experimental results across four retrieval paradigms: traditional lexical IR methods, semantic dense retrieval models based on language embeddings, state-of-the-art vision–language models, and proprietary black-box image retrieval systems.

– We make the dataset publicly available under a Creative Commons Attribution-NonCommercial License, ensuring long-term accessibility and facilitating reproducibility and further research.


## 2  Related Work

The evolution of image information retrieval (IR) has been shaped by progress in both algorithmic methods and dataset availability. While early content-based image retrieval (CBIR) systems relied on visual features such as color, texture patterns, and shape features [3,13], they struggled with the semantic gap between low-level visual features and high-level user intentions, limiting their effectiveness in realistic search scenarios. The emergence of deep learning and later transformer architectures [28] revolutionized this field by enabling richer multimodal representations. In particular, the emergence of vision-language models (VLMs) shifted the focus from purely visual similarity to semantic alignment between text and images. Prominent examples include CLIP [20], ALIGN [10] and BLIP-2 [14], which have demonstrated strong performance on diverse multimodal tasks, including zero-shot classification, caption generation, and notably, image retrieval [12,22,24]. By projecting both modalities into a common embedding space through contrastive or generative objectives, these models enable retrieval systems to rank images based on semantic similarity to user queries.

Despite these technological advances, the development of effective multimodal retrieval systems remains critically dependent on the availability of high-quality datasets that provide query-driven resources for evaluation. However, most were originally designed for image captioning, which differs fundamentally from query-driven retrieval. Moreover, existing English-language datasets focus on Western contexts, introducing linguistic and cultural biases that fail to capture region-specific visual concepts, practices, and named entities. For example, the MS COCO dataset [15], one of the most widely adopted resources in multimodal research, contains over 330,000 images with multiple English captions per image, providing rich descriptive text but lacking both the query-response pairs essential for retrieval evaluation and any coverage beyond English annotations, limiting its applicability to Portuguese and other low-resource languages. Flickr30k [30], which contains 31,000 images paired with 155,000 human-authored English captions, and its extension Flickr30k Entities [18], which links textual mentions to visual elements, face similar limitations, offering high-quality captions and grounding information but restricted to English and description-oriented tasks. Fashion200k [7], comprising 200,000 weakly labeled fashion images with concise textual descriptions of visual attributes, demonstrates the potential for fine-grained alignment between visual and textual features. However, its narrow focus on the fashion domain and the absence of query-driven structures limit its applicability to broader image retrieval research.

Efforts to broaden linguistic and cultural coverage include WIT [26], which spans 108 languages with 37 million image–text pairs (with some Portuguese annotations), and the more recent MIRACL-VISION dataset [17], which extends document retrieval into the visual domain. While valuable for multilingual evaluation, both are constructed from Wikipedia content, leading to imbalanced language coverage (with English dominating) and lacking the explicit query–response structures needed for image retrieval. Similarly, the #PraCegoVer dataset [19] provides over 500,000 Brazilian Portuguese captions sourced from Instagram with accessibility guidelines, but it targets captioning rather than retrieval and reflects Brazilian Portuguese linguistic and cultural norms rather than European Portuguese.

In summary, while vision-language models have pushed the state of the art in multimodal IR, their effectiveness remains limited by the datasets on which they are trained and evaluated. Existing resources are largely English-centric, caption-oriented, or domain-specific, leaving a critical gap for query-driven image retrieval. Bridging this gap requires dedicated resources that combine realistic query-response images structures, relevance annotations, and culturally grounded content in European Portuguese, elements that current datasets fail to provide. To address these limitations, we introduce `pt-image-ir-dataset`, a new resource specifically designed to support Portuguese image retrieval research.

## 3    pt-image-ir-dataset Dataset

Building on the gaps identified in existing resources, we now present the pt-image-ir-dataset, a benchmark specifically designed to advance Portuguese image retrieval research. The dataset couples European Portuguese queries with a collection of images and corresponding human relevance judgments, providing a realistic and culturally grounded testbed for multimodal retrieval systems.

### 3.1   Dataset Creation

The construction of the dataset followed three main phases: content acquisition, query generation, and relevance annotation. Images were sourced from the official Portuguese Presidency website[1], which provides a rich and diverse collection of institutional content. Our decision to use the official website of the Portuguese Presidency was driven by several factors: the public availability of content, the diversity of visual contexts, the top quality of duly curated text, and the extensive temporal coverage of the published material. The website documents nearly a decade of presidential activity, capturing a broad range of events, from official ceremonies and international visits to cultural and local events, across different time periods. This longitudinal aspect adds significant value to the dataset, enabling the exploration of visual variation over time.

To extract information from the website, we developed a Python-based web scraper using BeautifulSoup for HTML parsing and Selenium for dynamic content handling. The scraper navigated through the website's structure, collected

---

[1] https://www.presidencia.pt/.

news articles, and extracted article titles, publication dates, and associated images. In total, 4,678 articles published between January 2016 and March 2025 were collected, yielding 42,333 images with associated textual metadata.

For query generation, we followed a hybrid approach combining automated and manual methods to ensure diversity and naturalness. Using GPT-4o mini, we generated 38 queries across four thematic categories: *events and contexts, facial expressions and emotions, interactions with the public,* and *places and environments.* These categories were selected to reflect the content diversity typically found in governmental imagery. The prompt used for query generation was:

*"You are a journalist preparing an article about the Portuguese Presidency and need to find suitable images to illustrate it. You have a search engine available with images at your disposal. Write text-based search queries in European Portuguese that could help retrieve images related to the following category: [category]".*

To complement these model-generated queries, which tend toward verbose descriptions, we added 42 additional manually-created queries within seven categories: *public figures, sports and activities, trending topics, places and monuments, general places, objects,* and *others.* These queries were intentionally designed to be more concise, reflecting typical user search patterns. Example queries include a model-generated query: "Presidente de Portugal em encontros com cidadãos" (President of Portugal meeting citizens), and a manually created query: "Bombeiros" (Firefighters). This combination allows the dataset to cover a wider spectrum of query styles and complexity levels, providing a more thorough testbed for evaluating retrieval systems.

Once queries were defined, we created a pool of candidate images for annotation using a pooling [11] strategy popularized by the TREC community [8]. Pooling allows annotators to evaluate a representative subset of images per query to establish ground truth, avoiding exhaustive annotation of the entire dataset. Our strategy combined three types of retrieval paradigms: traditional text-based IR (TF-IDF and BM25 on article titles), vision-language models (several CLIP variants including *M-CLIP/LABSE-Vit-L-14, M-CLIP/XLM-Roberta-Large-Vit-B-32, M-CLIP/XLM-Roberta-Large-Vit-L-14,* and *OpenCLIP/xlm-roberta-base-ViT-B-32*), and proprietary black-box image retrieval systems (Google Images and Arquivo.pt, constrained to the Presidency domain). For each method, the top-10 retrieved images per query were selected to form a diverse candidate set, averaging 65 images per query. Images not included in the pooled set were assumed non-relevant, following standard pooling assumptions [29].

## 3.2   Annotation Process

The annotation process was carried out by three master's students who participated voluntarily, without financial compensation, following detailed guidelines to ensure consistency and reliability. Annotators were instructed to evaluate each image's relevance to its corresponding query based on two labels: *relevant* (1) if the image directly supported, illustrated, or provided meaningful context aligned with the query's intent, and *non-relevant* (0) if it failed to do so or provided misleading information. The guidelines emphasized a systematic procedure: carefully reading and interpreting each query, assessing image content for visual elements linked to the query, and considering the context provided by article titles. In ambiguous cases, annotators were advised to default to *non-relevant*, with the requirement that subjects should be clearly visible and identifiable. To minimize subjectivity, the guidelines stressed the importance of avoiding personal bias and provided strategies for handling unknown terminology, such as using online searches. These measures were crucial for promoting inter-annotator agreement and reducing variability in judgments.

To facilitate the annotation process, we developed a dedicated web-based annotation tool with intuitive controls and keyboard shortcuts to streamline the evaluation workflow. The tool was implemented as a containerized web application, combining a Flask-based backend, a Redis database for data storage, and a responsive front-end interface. Its layout was organized into four main components: the query text at the top, a central image display, the article title below the image for contextual reference, and annotation controls at the bottom. To accelerate labeling, we integrated keyboard shortcuts (R = relevant, I = non-relevant, Z = undo) complemented by visual feedback and real-time progress tracking. Annotators submitted their judgments using these intuitive keyboard shortcuts, with each selection recorded immediately. The annotation tool also allows annotators to undo or revise previous judgments if their interpretation changes after seeing additional images. For each query, images are presented sequentially, enabling annotators to compare items for the same query. Figure 1 illustrates the clean, and intuitive interface that enabled efficient and consistent annotation.

We assessed annotation quality using Fleiss' Kappa [1], obtaining a coefficient of 0.62, which reflects substantial inter-annotator agreement. 76% of images had unanimous labels, while 11% and 13% had two annotators agreeing on relevance and non-relevance, respectively, highlighting genuine ambiguity in the task. Final relevance labels were assigned through majority voting. Both the annotation tool and the accompanying guidelines are publicly available[2].

To further examine the challenges of relevance assessment across different query types (AI-generated or manual), we analyzed inter-annotator agreement by generation method and semantic category. Figure 2 summarizes this comparative analysis, highlighting variations in annotation difficulty depending on the nature of the queries. The analysis highlights complementary strengths of AI-generated and manually-created queries, with the latter achieving higher inter-annotator agreement ($k = 0.695 \pm 0.219$) than AI-generated ones ($k = 0.494 \pm 0.259$). This difference reflects their distinct characteristics: manually-created queries, with their concise and direct nature, facilitate consistent annotation decisions, whereas AI-generated queries introduce greater semantic complexity, demanding more nuanced interpretation.

---

[2] https://github.com/RodrigDuarte/text2image_ir_annotation_tool.

**Fig. 1.** Web-based annotation tool interface used for dataset labeling. The layout includes four main components: query text (top), image display (center), article title for context (below the image), and annotation controls (bottom) with keyboard shortcuts and progress tracking.

The category-based analysis shows substantial variation in annotation difficulty, with Fleiss' Kappa scores spanning a range of 0.440 across different semantic domains. Queries on *trending topics* reached the highest agreement ($k = 0.862$), reflecting their concrete and visually distinctive nature. In contrast, queries involving subjective assessments such as *interactions with the public* yielded lower agreement ($k = 0.422$), which is consistent with the context-dependent nature of human interactions. Intermediate categories, such as *places and monuments* ($k = 0.762$) and *public figures* ($k = 0.760$) also showed strong agreement, indicating that concrete, underscoring how concrete and identifiable content supports consistent judgments.

### 3.3   Structure and Dataset Characterization

The `pt-image-ir-dataset` comprises 80 queries and 5,201 images, providing a robust resource for Portuguese image retrieval. While the number of queries is relatively small, each query includes a substantial set of annotated images, combining AI-generated and manually-created queries to capture diverse styles and complexity levels. Images are predominantly in JPEG format with two primary resolutions: 800×533 and 1800×1200 pixels. These characteristics make the dataset particularly valuable as the first query-driven image IR resource in European Portuguese, establishing a benchmark for future research. The dataset is organized into four separate files in standard IR evaluation formats: *queries.tsv* (queries), *qrels.txt* (relevance judgments in TREC format), *images.tsv* (image metadata), and *articles.tsv* (article information with contextual metadata). The

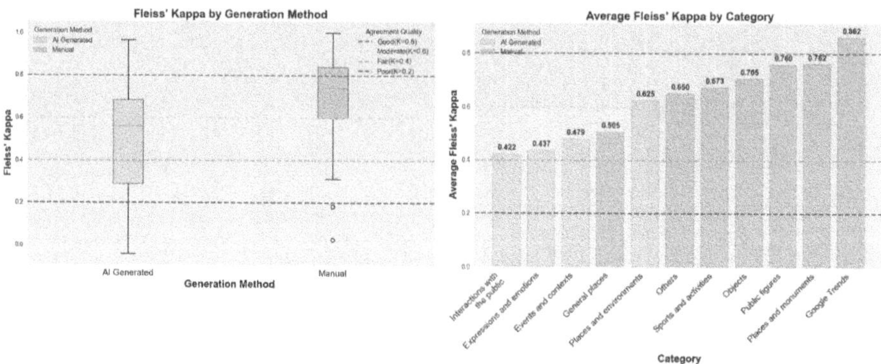

**Fig. 2.** Comparative analysis of Fleiss' Kappa scores across query generation methods (left) and categories (right).

dataset is made publicly available on GitHub[3] and archived on Zenodo[4] with a persistent DOI. Each query includes relevance judgments for an average of 65 images, with about 23 images labeled as relevant. Overall, 1,845 images (35%) were marked relevant and 3,356 (65%) non-relevant. The number of relevant images varies considerably across queries, reflecting natural diversity in query-driven retrieval. The 80 queries represent a deliberate balance between AI-generated and manually-created content, capturing different query characteristics and complexity levels. Figure 3 shows their distribution across categories. AI-generated queries span four categories, dominated by *events and contexts* (36.8%), followed by *places and environments* (23.7%), *expressions and emotions* (21.1%), and *interactions with the public* (18.4%). Manually created queries exhibit greater thematic diversity, covering seven distinct categories not addressed by the AI-generated set. Their distribution is more even, with *public figures* accounting for 19.0%, and *general places* and *others* each representing 16.7%. The remaining categories each contribute roughly 11.9%, reflecting the intention to capture additional semantic domains.

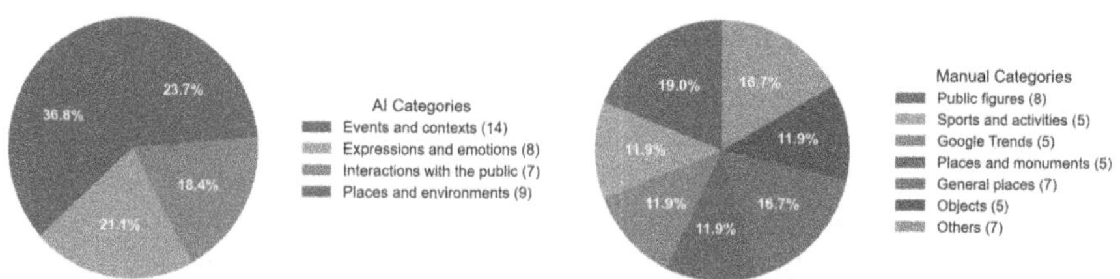

**Fig. 3.** Query distribution across categories: AI-generated queries (left) vs. manually-created queries (right).

---

[3] https://github.com/LIAAD/pt-image-ir-dataset.
[4] https://doi.org/10.5281/zenodo.15566572.

This dual approach offers important advantages for IR system evaluation. AI-generated queries are generally more verbose and descriptive (ranging from 5 to 9 words, with a median of 7 words, e.g., "Presidente de Portugal em encontros com cidadãos" - "President of Portugal in meetings with citizens"), whereas manually-created queries are shorter and more direct (ranging from 1 to 4 words, with a median of 2 words, e.g., "Bombeiros" - "Firefighters"), closely resembling real-world search behavior. By combining both types, the dataset supports evaluation across varying levels of query complexity and linguistic style.

## 4  Experiments and Results

To validate the usefulness and robustness of the `pt-image-ir-dataset`, we conducted a series of experiments covering a diverse set of image IR paradigms. Our goal was to demonstrate that the dataset supports multiple retrieval paradigms, establishing it as a valuable benchmark for evaluating different types of image retrieval systems. The experimental setup was organized four main categories. The first three correspond to the methods employed during the dataset's annotation phase: (1) traditional lexical IR techniques, (2) vision-language models, and (3) proprietary black-box image retrieval systems. To further broaden evaluation and assess the dataset's versatility, we introduced a fourth category: (4) semantic dense retrieval methods based on textual embeddings.

For the traditional text-based IR methods, we used TF-IDF [23] and BM25 [21], representing each image by the title of the article in which it appeared. Rankings were computed directly from term frequency and document relevance to the query. In contrast, vision-language models were employed to capture the semantic alignment between textual queries and images in a shared embedding space. We experimented with several CLIP ariants, including multilingual adaptations such as Multilingual-CLIP [5] and OpenCLIP [6,9], [20], which were trained on large-scale cross-modal datasets and are capable of handling queries in multiple languages. The results were ranked via cosine distance, Specifically, we evaluated: *M-CLIP/LABSE-Vit-L-14*; *M-CLIP/XLM-Roberta-Large-Vit-B-32*; *M-CLIP/XLM-Roberta-Large-Vit-L-14*; *OpenCLIP/xlm-roberta-base-ViT-B-32 with laion5b_s13b_b90k* along with more recent models such as BLIP-2 [14] and SigLIP [32]. For proprietary black-box retrieval, we queried two external search engines: Arquivo.pt and Google Images, with their proprietary ranking algorithms, both restricted to return images from the official Portuguese Presidency website, to constrain the search space and ensure contextual relevance. Finally, for semantic dense retrieval, we included BERTimbau Large [25] (Brazilian Portuguese) and Albertina PT-PT [2] (European Portuguese). These models were introduced only at the evaluation stage, allowing us to explore how newer architectures perform on a Portuguese language dataset. Altogether, this broad evaluation spectrum not only benchmarks diverse paradigms, but also to stress-test the dataset's capacity to generalize across retrieval settings and architectures. All systems were evaluated with standard TREC metrics using the *pytrec_eval* library [27], including Mean Average Precision (MAP), Precision@k (P@k), Recall@k (R@k), F1-Score@k (F1@k), Mean Reciprocal Rank

(MRR), and R-Precision (RP). Results are reported as macro-averages across all queries.

We now discuss the results from two complementary perspectives: first, a performance comparison across all baseline systems; and second, an analysis of how query length may impact retrieval effectiveness.

**Comparative Evaluation of Baselines.** Table 1 summarizes the performance of all baseline methods. While the absolute values reported in Table 1 may appear modest at first glance, they should be interpreted in light of the intrinsic difficulty of query-driven image retrieval and the specific characteristics of the `pt-image-ir-dataset`, which reflects realistic user search scenarios, featuring short, ambiguous queries and visually similar images drawn from a homogeneous institutional domain.

**Table 1.** Baseline performance on Portuguese image retrieval (with 95% bootstrap confidence intervals). Best scores in bold.

| Method | MAP | R@10 | P@10 | F1@10 | MRR |
|---|---|---|---|---|---|
| *Traditional Text-Based IR* | | | | | |
| TF-IDF | $0.138_{\pm 0.042}$ | $0.188_{\pm 0.051}$ | $0.291_{\pm 0.069}$ | $0.209_{\pm 0.050}$ | $0.377_{\pm 0.082}$ |
| BM25 | $0.079_{\pm 0.030}$ | $0.127_{\pm 0.043}$ | $0.209_{\pm 0.063}$ | $0.141_{\pm 0.041}$ | $0.331_{\pm 0.092}$ |
| *Portuguese Language Embedding Models* | | | | | |
| BERTimbau Large | $0.048_{\pm 0.031}$ | $0.076_{\pm 0.039}$ | $0.102_{\pm 0.049}$ | $0.080_{\pm 0.039}$ | $0.157_{\pm 0.073}$ |
| Albertina PT-PT 1.5b | $0.055_{\pm 0.028}$ | $0.091_{\pm 0.040}$ | $0.131_{\pm 0.052}$ | $0.096_{\pm 0.038}$ | $0.206_{\pm 0.081}$ |
| *Proprietary Black-Box Image Retrieval Systems* | | | | | |
| Google Images | $0.076_{\pm 0.030}$ | $0.125_{\pm 0.039}$ | $0.190_{\pm 0.058}$ | $0.128_{\pm 0.037}$ | $0.336_{\pm 0.090}$ |
| Arquivo.pt | $0.038_{\pm 0.014}$ | $0.080_{\pm 0.025}$ | $0.134_{\pm 0.039}$ | $0.091_{\pm 0.024}$ | $0.217_{\pm 0.072}$ |
| *Vision-Language Models* | | | | | |
| M-CLIP LABSE-ViT-L-14 | $0.130_{\pm 0.034}$ | $0.210_{\pm 0.044}$ | $0.341_{\pm 0.070}$ | $0.237_{\pm 0.045}$ | $0.467_{\pm 0.086}$ |
| M-CLIP XLM-R-Large-B-32 | $0.119_{\pm 0.030}$ | $0.176_{\pm 0.035}$ | $0.334_{\pm 0.069}$ | $0.215_{\pm 0.042}$ | $0.512_{\pm 0.097}$ |
| M-CLIP XLM-R-Large-L-14 | $0.158_{\pm 0.039}$ | $0.245_{\pm 0.052}$ | $0.376_{\pm 0.069}$ | $0.266_{\pm 0.048}$ | $0.491_{\pm 0.090}$ |
| OpenCLIP xlm-roberta-base | $\mathbf{0.176}_{\pm 0.036}$ | $\mathbf{0.264}_{\pm 0.049}$ | $\mathbf{0.419}_{\pm 0.079}$ | $\mathbf{0.288}_{\pm 0.047}$ | $\mathbf{0.610}_{\pm 0.094}$ |
| BLIP-2 ViT-G | $0.015_{\pm 0.010}$ | $0.030_{\pm 0.015}$ | $0.062_{\pm 0.031}$ | $0.039_{\pm 0.019}$ | $0.140_{\pm 0.068}$ |
| SigLIP Base | $0.107_{\pm 0.037}$ | $0.168_{\pm 0.046}$ | $0.263_{\pm 0.067}$ | $0.181_{\pm 0.045}$ | $0.457_{\pm 0.101}$ |
| *Theoretical Upper Bound* | | | | | |
| Oracle (Perfect Ranking) | 1.000 | 0.544 | 0.926 | 0.613 | 1.000 |

To better contextualize the baseline results in Table 1, we also include an Oracle row, representing the best possible outcome for each metric given the available relevance judgments. The Oracle assumes a perfect ranking, where all relevant images appear at the top of the retrieved list for each query. For metrics like Precision@10, this accounts for queries with fewer than 10 relevant images.

By comparing model performance to these ceilings, it becomes clear that vision-language models, such as OpenCLIP, achieve strong early-ranking effectiveness (MRR = 0.610 vs. Oracle = 1.000, 61% of theoretical maximum) while the modest absolute scores reflect both the difficulty of the task and the limited number of relevant images per query (average of 23 relevant images per query).

To address concerns about evaluation stability given the 80-query test set, we report 95% bootstrap confidence intervals (1,000 iterations) for all methods in Table 1. The narrow confidence intervals across all metrics confirm that the observed performance differences are statistically robust and unlikely to be significantly affected by individual edge cases. For instance, OpenCLIP's MRR of $0.610_{\pm 0.094}$ demonstrates consistent strong early-ranking performance across bootstrap samples, while the substantial gap between vision-language models and text-only methods remains stable.

Overall, the results reveal substantial differences across paradigms. Vision-language models stand out clearly, with OpenCLIP achieving the best overall performance (MRR = 0.610). This score indicates good early-ranking effectiveness, with relevant images frequently appearing at the very top of the ranking, which aligns well with realistic user behavior in image search, where users often inspect only the top few results. In contrast, the comparatively low performance of traditional text-based and text-only dense retrieval methods underscores the difficulty of the task, since article titles provide only weak textual grounding. This highlights the benefits of direct visual-semantic alignment for Portuguese image retrieval.

Portuguese-specific language embedding models show only modest effectiveness. Albertina PT-PT outperforms BERTimbau Large (MRR = 0.206 vs. 0.157), suggesting that training on European Portuguese data provides limited advantages. Nevertheless, both embedding-based approaches remain far behind multimodal methods, reinforcing the importance of incorporating visual grounding for effective image retrieval. For proprietary black-box retrieval systems, performance is intermediate. Google Images achieves results comparable to traditional IR methods (MRR = 0.336) but remains well below vision–language models, while Arquivo.pt performs less competitively (MRR = 0.217), reflecting the limitations of keyword-based retrieval when applied to visually driven, query-based image search. Together, these results highlight opportunities to improve Portuguese language coverage in widely used image search engines.

Despite the clear advantages of vision–language models over other baselines, the results remain far from perfect. In particular, the modest F1@10 values and the sensitivity of performance to query formulation indicate that query-driven image retrieval in European Portuguese remains an open and challenging problem. Rather than reflecting limitations of the dataset, these results demonstrate its usefulness as a long-term benchmark, enabling future work to meaningfully compare models, analyze failure cases, and measure progress as multimodal retrieval techniques continue to evolve.

**Impact of Query Length.** To better understand variations across query types, we compared longer model-generated queries (38 queries) with shorter manually created queries (42 queries). Figure 4 shows that vision-language models consistently favor concise formulations: OpenCLIP achieves 71% higher MRR (0.760 vs 0.445) and 88% higher F1@10 (0.371 vs 0.197) on short queries. This behavior reflects CLIP's original training design, optimized for image classification tasks using concise category labels rather than verbose descriptions.

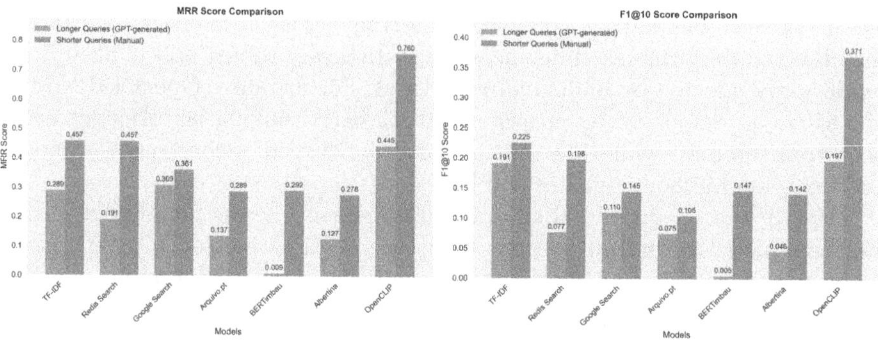

**Fig. 4.** Performance comparison between longer (GPT-generated) and shorter (manual) queries. Vision-language models show pronounced preference for shorter, focused queries.

In contrast, traditional text-based baselines (TF-IDF, BM25) show relatively stable performance, with differences across query lengths, with differences typically below 5% for both MRR and F1@10 metrics. This stability suggests that term-frequency approaches are less sensitive to query length variations and can effectively process both concise and verbose formulations. Overall, these results suggest that vision-language models may be less effective with naturally verbose user queries. This observation points to a potential avenue for future research: developing models that can more effectively interpret and retrieve images from longer, descriptive queries without requiring users to simplify their search behavior.

## 5    Conclusion and Future Work

In this paper, we introduced the `pt-image-ir-dataset`, a new resource aimed at advancing research in image IR for European Portuguese. The dataset comprises 80 diverse, thematically curated queries and a collection of 5,201 images sourced from the official website of the Portuguese Presidency. Each image was annotated for relevance by three independent human judges, following a structured set of annotation guidelines to ensure consistency and reliability. We assessed annotation quality using Fleiss' Kappa, obtaining a coefficient of 0.62, which reflects substantial inter-annotator agreement. By capturing the linguistic and cultural specificities of European Portuguese, this dataset addresses a significant gap in text-image IR research for low-to-mid resource languages, offering a valuable tool for academic research and applied multimodal IR tasks. To evaluate the dataset's effectiveness for image retrieval tasks, we conducted a series of experiments covering four main paradigms: traditional lexical IR approaches, vision-language models, proprietary black-box image retrieval systems, and semantic dense retrieval methods based on Portuguese language embeddings. To further examine annotation quality and query characteristics, we analyzed inter-annotator agreement variations across different query generation methods and semantic categories, and investigated the impact of query length on retrieval effectiveness. Overall, the results demonstrate that vision-language models, particularly *OpenCLIP/xlm-roberta-base-ViT-B-32*, outperform other methods by a significant margin. Analyses of inter-annotator agreement and query characteristics further reveal nuanced patterns: agreement tends to be higher for manually created, concise queries, while longer, AI-generated queries are associated with lower consistency among annotators and reduced retrieval effectiveness. These findings highlight both the potential of the `pt-image-ir-dataset` as a benchmark for European Portuguese image retrieval and the importance of considering a fine-tuning strategy to the linguistic and contextual characteristics of the texts in future system development. While the current `pt-image-ir-dataset` focuses exclusively on high-quality photographs, future extensions could explore stylized or generated image variants, such as line drawings, watercolors, or black-and-white renditions, to examine how retrieval models handle different visual styles.

## Limitations

While the `pt-image-ir-dataset` is a resource for Portuguese image retrieval, it is derived from an institutional source, which may limit its generalization to broader domains such as e-commerce, social media, or user-generated content. Although alternative sources (e.g., news outlets or social platforms) could provide topical diversity and more informal imagery, they pose challenges related to licensing, structural consistency, and collection. In contrast, the Presidency website offers curated and structured content, making it a starting point for Portuguese text-to-image retrieval research. From a methodological standpoint, our evaluation is restricted to single-paradigm baselines, excluding hybrid or multi-stage retrieval approaches that combine lexical and vision–language signals. While such methods are widely adopted and often achieve performance, their study is left for future work, which this dataset can support. Additionally, the dataset currently uses binary relevance annotations. Adopting a graded relevance scheme could enable evaluation and represents an extension. Finally, despite covering diverse themes, the dataset contains only 80 queries. Expanding this number in future releases would improve evaluation robustness and coverage of Portuguese image retrieval challenges.

## FAIR Principles

To ensure that the dataset could be shared and used, we adhered to established ethical principles and best practices, following the FAIR (Findable, Accessible, Interoperable, and Reusable) guidelines [31]. All data was collected from publicly available sources, with attention to copyright and privacy. Specifically, images were scraped exclusively from the official Portuguese Presidency website, a public institutional resource, and each item is linked back to the original source. The dataset is distributed under a Creative Commons Attribution-NonCommercial License, which ensures proper attribution and enables research use. To further enhance accessibility and availability, the dataset is hosted on Zenodo.

**Acknowledgments.** Ricardo Campos is funded by national funds through FCT – Fundação para a Ciência e a Tecnologia, I.P., under the support UID/50014/2025 (https://doi.org/10.54499/UID/50014/2025). The author would also like to acknowledge project StorySense, with reference 2022.09312.PTDC (DOI 10.54499/2022.09312.PTDC). The authors Rodrigo Duarte and António Branco would like to acknowledge ACCELERAT.AI - Multilingual Intelligent Contact Centers, funded by the covid-recovery program PRR-Plano de Recuperação e Resiliência, through IAPMEI (C625734525-00462629); PORTULAN CLARIN - Research Infrastructure for the Science and Technology of Language, funded by LISBOA2030 (FEDER-01316900); hey, Hal, curb your hallucination!, funded by FCT-Fundação para a Ciência e Tecnologia (2024.07592.IACDC). The author Hugo Proença would like to acknowledge FCT – Fundação para a Ciência e a Tecnologia, I.P., and, when eligible, co-funded by EU funds under project/support UID/50008/2025 – Instituto de Telecomunicações, with DOI identifier <https://doi.org/10.54499/UID/50008/2025>.

**Disclosure of Interests.** The authors have no competing interests to declare that are relevant to the content of this article.

## References

1. Fleiss, J.L., Cohen, J.: The equivalence of weighted kappa and the intraclass correlation coefficient as measures of reliability. Educ. Psychol. Measur. **33**(3), 613–619 (1973)
2. Rodrigues, J., et al.: Advancing neural encoding of Portuguese with transformer Albertina PT-*. arXiv preprint arXiv:2305.06721 (2023)
3. Alsmadi, M.K.: Content-based image retrieval using color, shape and texture descriptors and features. Arab. J. Sci. Eng. **45**(4), 3317–3330 (2020)
4. Cao, M., Li, S., Li, J., Nie, L., Zhang, M.: Image-text retrieval: a survey on recent research and development. arXiv preprint arXiv:2203.14713 (2022)
5. Carlsson, F., Eisen, P., Rekathati, F., Sahlgren, M.: Cross-lingual and multilingual CLIP. In: Proceedings of the Language Resources and Evaluation Conference, pp. 6848–6854. European Language Resources Association, Marseille, France (2022)
6. Cherti, M., et al.: Reproducible scaling laws for contrastive language-image learning. In: Proceedings of the IEEE/CVF Conference on Computer Vision and Pattern Recognition, pp. 2818–2829 (2023)

7. Han, X., et al.: Automatic spatially-aware fashion concept discovery. In: ICCV (2017)
8. Harman, D.: Overview of the first TREC conference. In: Proceedings of the 16th Annual International ACM SIGIR Conference on Research and Development in Information Retrieval, pp. 36–47 (1993)
9. Ilharco, G., et al.: OpenCLIP. Zenodo, version 0.1 (2021). https://doi.org/10.5281/zenodo.5143773
10. Jia, C., et al.: Scaling up visual and vision-language representation learning with noisy text supervision. In: International Conference on Machine Learning, pp. 4904–4916. PMLR (2021)
11. Jones, K.S., Van Rijsbergen, C.J., British Library. Research and Development Department: Report on the Need for and Provision of an Ideal Information Retrieval Test Collection. University Computer Laboratory (1975)
12. Lahajal, N.K., Harini, S.: Enhancing image retrieval: a comprehensive study on photo search using the CLIP mode. arXiv arxiv:2401.13613 (2024)
13. Li, X., Yang, J., Ma, J.: Recent developments of content-based image retrieval (CBIR). Neurocomputing **452**, 675–689 (2021)
14. Li, J., Li, D., Savarese, S., Hoi, S.: BLIP-2: bootstrapping language-image pre-training with frozen image encoders and large language models. In: ICML (2023)
15. Lin, T.-Y., Maire, M., Belongie, S., Hays, J., Perona, P., Ramanan, D., Dollár, P., Zitnick, C.L.: Microsoft COCO: common objects in context. In: Fleet, D., Pajdla, T., Schiele, B., Tuytelaars, T. (eds.) ECCV 2014. LNCS, vol. 8693, pp. 740–755. Springer, Cham (2014). https://doi.org/10.1007/978-3-319-10602-1_48
16. Luo, M., Gokhale, T., Varshney, N., Yang, Y., Baral, C.: Advances in Multimodal Information Retrieval and Generation. Springer, Cham (2024). https://doi.org/10.1007/978-3-031-57816-8
17. Osmulsk, R., Moreira, G.S.P., Ak, R., Xu, M., Schifferer, B., Oldridge, E.: MIRACL-VISION: a large, multilingual, visual document retrieval benchmark. arXiv preprint arXiv:2505.11651 (2025)
18. Plummer, B.A., Wang, L., Cervantes, C.M., Caicedo, J.C., Hockenmaier, J., Lazebnik, S.: Flickr30k entities: collecting region-to-phrase correspondences for richer image-to-sentence models. In: Proceedings of the IEEE International Conference on Computer Vision, pp. 2641–2649 (2015)
19. dos Santos, G.O., Colombini, E.L., Avila, S.: #PraCegoVer: a large dataset for image captioning in Portuguese. Data **7**(2) (2022). Article 13
20. Radford, A., et al.: Learning transferable visual models from natural language supervision. In: International Conference on Machine Learning, pp. 8748–8763. PMLR (2021)
21. Robertson, S., Zaragoza, H., et al.: The probabilistic relevance framework: BM25 and beyond. Found. Trends® Inf. Retrieval **3**(4), 333–389 (2009)
22. Sain, A., Bhunia, A.K., Chowdhury, P.N., Koley, S., Xiang, T., Song, Y.Z.: CLIP for all things zero-shot sketch-based image retrieval, fine-grained or not. In: 2023 IEEE/CVF Conference on Computer Vision and Pattern Recognition (CVPR), pp. 2765–2775 (2023)
23. Salton, G., Buckley, C.: Term-weighting approaches in automatic text retrieval. Inf. Process. Manage. **24**(5), 513–523 (1988)
24. Schall, K., Barthel, K., Hezel, N., Jung, K.: Optimizing CLIP models for image retrieval with maintained joint-embedding alignment. arXiv arxiv:2409.01936 (2024)

25. Souza, F., Nogueira, R., Lotufo, R.: BERTimbau: pretrained BERT models for Brazilian Portuguese. In: Cerri, R., Prati, R.C. (eds.) BRACIS 2020. LNCS (LNAI), vol. 12319, pp. 403–417. Springer, Cham (2020). https://doi.org/10.1007/978-3-030-61377-8_28
26. Souza, F., Nogueira, R., Lotufo, R.: BERTimbau: pretrained BERT models for Brazilian Portuguese. In: Cerri, R., Prati, R.C. (eds.) BRACIS 2020. LNCS (LNAI), vol. 12319, pp. 403–417. Springer, Cham (2020). https://doi.org/10.1007/978-3-030-61377-8_28
27. Van Gysel, C., de Rijke, M.: Pytrec_eval: an extremely fast Python interface to trec_eval. In: SIGIR. ACM (2018)
28. Vaswani, A.: Attention is all you need. In: Advances in Neural Information Processing Systems (2017)
29. Voorhees, E.M., Harman, D.: Overview of TREC 2001. In: TREC (2001)
30. Young, P., Lai, A., Hodosh, M., Hockenmaier, J.: From image descriptions to visual denotations: new similarity metrics for semantic inference over event descriptions. Trans. Assoc. Comput. Linguist. **2**, 67–78 (2014)
31. Wilkinson, M.D., et al.: The FAIR guiding principles for scientific data management and stewardship. Sci. Data **3**(1), 1–9 (2016)
32. Zhai, X., Mustafa, B., Kolesnikov, A., Beyer, L.: Sigmoid loss for language image pre-training. In: Proceedings of the IEEE/CVF International Conference on Computer Vision, pp. 11975–11986 (2023)

# LISP – A Rich Interaction Dataset and Loggable Interactive Search Platform

Jana Isabelle Friese[1([✉])] [iD], Andreas Konstantin Kruff[2] [iD], Philipp Schaer[2] [iD],
Norbert Fuhr[1] [iD], and Nicola Ferro[3] [iD]

[1] University of Duisburg-Essen, Duisburg, Germany
{jana.friese,norbert.fuhr}@uni-due.de
[2] TH Köln - University of Applied Sciences, Cologne, Germany
{andreas.kruff,philipp.schaer}@th-koeln.de
[3] University of Padua, Padua, Italy
nicola.ferro@unipd.it

**Abstract.** We present a reusable dataset and accompanying infrastructure for studying human search behavior in Interactive Information Retrieval (IIR). The dataset combines detailed interaction logs from 61 participants (122 sessions) with user characteristics, including perceptual speed, topic-specific interest, search expertise, and demographic information. To facilitate reproducibility and reuse, we provide a fully documented study setup, a web-based perceptual speed test, and a framework for conducting similar user studies. Our work allows researchers to investigate individual and contextual factors affecting search behavior, and to develop or validate user simulators that account for such variability. We illustrate the dataset's potential through an illustrative analysis and release all resources as open-access, supporting reproducible research and resource sharing in the IIR community.

**Keywords:** IIR · Interaction Dataset · Study Setup · User Aspects

## 1 Motivation

Resource sharing and re-use are essential for advancing research, ensuring transparency, and fostering community collaboration in Interactive Information Retrieval (IIR) [20]. While a number of IIR studies build on existing datasets, only a small fraction make their own data publicly available, and even fewer share complete experimental setups [9]. This mismatch between interest in reusing resources and their availability limits cumulative progress and highlights the need for more accessible, reusable datasets.

A larger pool of reusable resources would directly support IIR research. While user studies provide valuable insights into real-world scenarios beyond system performance [23], human search behavior varies widely, and effect sizes are often small. Still, most IIR studies rely on limited samples, undermining power and reproducibility. User simulation offers a scalable alternative [7], but click models mostly rely on simplified assumptions about user behavior [15] and, even


R. Campos et al. (Eds.): ECIR 2026, LNCS 16486, pp. 479–495, 2026.
https://doi.org/10.1007/978-3-032-21321-1_54

in advanced frameworks, lack systematic validation against real behavior [45]. Reliable baselines of authentic user behavior can enable reliable comparison and validation of such models, enhancing progress in IIR research.

However, in existing session interaction datasets some crucial information is often missing. Liu and Shah [27] note that participant variables, which may significantly affect results, are under-reported in IIR studies. Gäde et al. [20] identify three main resource types that should be documented and shared to enable effective reuse: (1) *research design*, (2) *infrastructure*, and (3) *data*. In practice, however, sharing typically focuses on the data alone, with limited attention to the other components. In particular, infrastructures–such as user interfaces and logging frameworks–are rarely reused but instead redeveloped from scratch, as they are difficult to adapt to new research scenarios [21].

Our work addresses this gap by introducing a comprehensive, reusable resource that integrates all three main resource types outlined by Gäde et al. The dataset includes detailed interaction logs enriched with additional participant information (i.e., the *data*), an extensively documented study setup (*design*), and the complete infrastructure for running and adapting the experiment (*infrastructure*). To ensure high reusability, we aligned our materials with the highest of Gäde et al.'s five levels of reusability standards, which require structured and openly documented archival of all three resource types. Because infrastructure often poses the greatest challenge for reuse, we also provide detailed instructions for adapting our setup to different scenarios.[1]

To build the resource, we conducted a user study focusing on perceptual speed and interest in an argument retrieval task, as prior work has shown that both cognitive abilities [2,3,6,11] and contextual factors [14,33,35,43] shape user behavior. We therefore selected perceptual speed and interest as representative dimensions of individual and situational factors. Including these factors makes the dataset suitable not only for studying human search behavior but also for developing and validating user simulators that account for such variability. Alongside the interaction logs, we provide each participant's perceptual speed scores, topic-specific interest ratings, search expertise, and demographic information.

Our study followed an exploratory design, enabling a wide range of research questions to be addressed. This paper includes an illustrative analysis of the effects of perceptual speed and interest on user behavior, demonstrating how the dataset can be used. The analysis both characterizes the collected data and highlights its potential for developing and evaluating simulators that adapt to different user types or contexts. In doing so, we also discuss the broader implications of these factors for simulation and user-centric evaluation in IIR.

Overall, the dataset and accompanying infrastructure offer the IIR community: (1) a robust baseline of human search behavior accounting for demographics, cognitive abilities, and situational factors; (2) a fully documented, adaptable study environment; and (3) a practical example of designing and sharing reusable resources that adhere to current best-practice standards.

---

[1] Resources accessible at: https://github.com/irgroup/LISP_Dataset_and_Platform.

## 2   Related Work

To position our dataset within the current landscape, we conducted a literature review on existing session log resources and their characteristics. As noted by Reimer et al. [36], several large-scale query logs have been collected over the years; however, most focus on individual queries rather than full sessions and do not include click data. Many are also no longer accessible, underscoring the scarcity of suitable datasets and the challenge of long-term reproducibility.

Well-established log datasets, such as the TREC Session Track collections [12], remain publicly available and provide high-quality session-based interaction data from controlled lab studies. While being valuable for research, they are limited in size. In contrast, logs collected from real-world search applications enable the creation of much larger datasets. One example is TripClick [37], which offers extensive click and ranking data but lacks any information about users or their underlying information needs. User- and context-related factors, however, strongly influence search behavior. Yet, even in lab-based studies where such information is typically collected, these details are rarely published.

Detailed information about user characteristics and context is crucial not only for understanding search behavior but also for ensuring reproducibility. In recent years, there has been growing interest in how individual differences and motivational factors shape search behavior. Among the many traits studied, perceptual speed and task-specific interest have frequently been included, highlighting their relevance for modeling user interactions [2,4,6,11,17,22,24,28,42]. Without reporting these factors, valuable insights are lost, and the usefulness of datasets is limited. Additional constraints, such as language and domain coverage, further restrict the applicability of existing resources.

Table 1 provides an overview of publicly available session-based interaction log datasets, highlighting characteristics such as number of logged sessions, domain, language, and collection environment. The language column (Lang.) indicates the primary language of the dataset, as many logs–especially from real-world settings–contain queries in multiple languages.

While some datasets contain extensive click data, they reveal very little about the users: outside controlled lab settings, information about users' underlying information needs is missing, and no existing dataset provides comprehensive details on user or contextual factors.

This aligns with the observations reported by Crasswell et al. [16]: privacy concerns and the sensitivity of user-entered data often prevent researchers from sharing their logs, leaving few publicly available click datasets suitable for research. This further underscores the limited availability of resources that support meaningful comparison or reproduction of studies.

The scarcity of datasets is mirrored by the limited availability of shared frameworks for collecting and analyzing interaction data. Several logging frameworks have been proposed [8,25,29,38], and initial solutions for RAG systems have emerged [26]. However, fully integrated end-to-end frameworks remain rare, and most researchers rely on custom implementations. A notable exception is Podify [31], which provides standardized logging and reproducible experiments,

**Table 1.** Summary of publicly available session-based interaction log datasets. The last row shows our own dataset.

| Ref | User Profiles | Domain | Lab Setting | Year | # Logs | Lang. |
|---|---|---|---|---|---|---|
| Yandex [39] | ✗ | Mixed | ✗ | 2011 | 797,867 | en |
| TREC Session [12] | ✗ | Mixed | ✓ | 2011–2014 | 1,564 | en |
| TripClick [37] | ✗ | Medical | ✗ | 2013–2020 | 1.6M | en |
| AOL [34] | ✗ | Mixed | ✗ | 2006 | 283,207 | en |
| Baidu-ULTR [46] | ✗ | Mixed | ✗ | 2022 | 1.2B | ch |
| SoguoQ [41] | ✗ | Mixed | ✗ | 2008 | 14.1M | ch |
| TianGong-ST [13] | ✗ | Mixed | ✗ | 2015 | 147,155 | ch |
| SUSS [30] | ✗ | Academic | ✗ | 2014–2015 | 484,449 | en/ger |
| Own | ✓ | Argument | ✓ | 2025 | 122 | en |

but its focus on podcast streaming limits applicability to other document types or search tasks. This lack of accessible infrastructure aligns with bibliometric findings from Bogers et al. [9], who reported that only a small fraction of CHIIR authors shared research data or infrastructure components, reflecting a broader reproducibility gap in the field.

## 3   Resource Design and Development

To create the dataset, we conducted a user study and collected detailed interaction logs together with extensive participant profiles. We used a within-subject study design to investigate the effects of topic interest—i.e., a cognitive-emotional relationship between an individual and a topic [40]—on search behavior. Participants were asked to prepare for writing an opinion essay through an exploratory search, gathering arguments for both sides of a given debate. Each participant worked on two topics: one of high and one of no personal interest, making topic interest the within-subject variable. In addition, perceptual speed (PS)—defined as "the speed in finding figures, making comparisons, and carrying out other very simple tasks involving visual perception" [18]—was included as a between-subject variable to assess its impact on search behavior.

The study consisted of three parts: (1) Participants completed a pre-study questionnaire, including the Perceptual Speed Test, both administered remotely. (2) They then attended the main study session, (3) followed by a post-study questionnaire; these latter steps were conducted in person.

### 3.1   Dataset and System

For the experimental setup, we used the Conversational Argument Retrieval dataset from Touché 2020 [10], which is based on the args.me corpus of

Debate.org threads. The corpus contains 387,606 arguments across 50 TREC-style topics, collected in mid-2019. We selected this corpus because its controversial topics are well suited to elicit user interest, increasing the likelihood of finding topics with different levels of interest. In addition, the relatively short argumentative texts reduce reading time and encourage more frequent system interactions within the ten-minute session limit. Topics that were unlikely to be relatable to the participants (e.g., heavily US-centric issues) were excluded, as well as topics where one side of the debate was underrepresented, resulting in a set of 26 topics. From the corresponding arguments, we removed overly short or uninformative entries ($<150$ characters) as well as excessively long texts ($>3,000$ characters) that could distort reading time, leaving 226,468 documents in the collection.

To provide a familiar search experience, we implemented a simple search system using Terrier's BM25 ranking, allowing users to submit queries, view retrieved arguments, save them as supporting or opposing a stance, and review previously saved documents. Results were shown in pages of ten arguments, each presented with a title and a snippet, expandable to the full text on click. Snippets consisted of the first 200 characters of an argument. As the dataset does not include titles, we generated them using Llama3 (temperature $= 0.3$) based on the argument text and included them in the GitHub repository with the system. The current topic was displayed alongside the results at all times.

### 3.2   Data Collection

**Participant Recruitment.** For the study, we recruited information science students from a German university. Participation was fully voluntary, with informed consent obtained after participants were briefed on the study purpose, data handling, and their rights to reject the publication of their data. Students were compensated for their participation with course credits. All study steps were conducted under full anonymity, using pseudonyms to ensure that no personal data (as defined by the GDPR) was collected. Pseudonyms were further standardized during post-processing to strengthen data protection.

**Questionnaires.** Before the search sessions, participants completed a pre-study questionnaire on demographics, socioeconomic background, online activity, and search engine experience (see Sect. 4.3 for further details). They also rated their interest in the 26 available topics.

At the end of the study, participants had to complete a post-study questionnaire. They were asked whether their stance on the topic had changed during the process, and if so, how it had changed. In addition, participants were asked to rate the difficulty of completing the tasks.

**Perceptual Speed Test.** As part of the pre-study questionnaire, participants completed a perceptual speed test in their own environment to avoid potential lab effects. Several perceptual speed tests have been reviewed in the context of

IR [19]. Following Azzopardi et al. [6], we used a modified Finding A's test, in which participants identified $\varepsilon$ and ¥ characters, as this method has been shown to be a more accurate test of users actual perceptual speed [1].

After instructions, participants completed a 30-second practice phase. In the test, participants classified strings of 10–15 non-alphanumeric characters—presented one at a time—as containing both the symbols $\varepsilon$ and ¥ (pressing $j$) or not (pressing $n$). The time limit was two minutes. All participants saw the same fixed order of strings, with a maximum of 500 provided to ensure comparability and prevent ceiling effects.

**Study Procedure.** Based on the pre-study questionnaire, each participant was assigned two topics: one of high and one of no interest to them. To avoid ordering effects, half of the participants started with the high-interest and half with the no-interest topic. Topics were assigned using a heuristic pseudo-random approach to ensure a balanced coverage across participants, preventing any single topic from dominating either interest category. The task was identical for both topics. After an introduction explaining the procedure and task, the participants started the study on the provided computers. Each task had a ten-minute time limit. Upon completing the first task, they were automatically directed to the second. Before each task, participants were shown the full topic and task description. After completion, they could optionally explain why they ended their search before the time limit. These explanations are included in the dataset in their original form to avoid bias; for responses written in German, a machine-translated version is also provided (based on Google Translate API). Upon finishing both tasks, participants proceeded to the post-study questionnaire.

## 4   Resource Description

Building on the study design described in Sect. 3, this section documents the resources we release: (1) the interaction log dataset, (2) the loggable interactive search platform, and (3) the user profile data (demographics, perceptual speed, and search expertise). A more comprehensive documentation is available on the project website[2] to support reproducibility and adhere to the Level-5 reusability standard.

### 4.1   Interaction Log Dataset

The interaction dataset collected in the user study comprises 122 session log files, evenly divided between high-and no-interest topics. Each interaction contains an interaction type, a timestamp, and session identifier.

Events captured include query submissions and reformulations, document interactions (such as expanding or collapsing views, and selecting stances), navigating between result pages, and task completion actions. Each document entry

---

[2] https://irgroup.github.io/LISP_Dataset_and_Platform/.

is associated with its rank, retrieval score, and length. Stopping decisions were explicitly logged, and participants could provide a reason for ending their search early. Although each task was designed for a ten-minute duration, this limit was not hard-coded, so some sessions slightly exceeded this timeframe.

## 4.2  Lisp – A Loggable Interactive Search Platform

For the study, we developed a loggable interactive search platform called lisp. While originally designed for argument retrieval tasks, the platform can be easily adapted to other search scenarios.

The interface provides a typical search experience: participants can enter queries, browse retrieved arguments, navigate between pages, expand snippets to view the full text, and save documents as supporting or opposing a stance. A side panel summarizes the task and topic, and tracks the number of labeled documents (Fig. 1). At the end of each session, a pop-up window presents an overview of all saved documents with their assigned labels and titles, with stance indicated through color-coding (i.e., green for supporting, red for opposing).

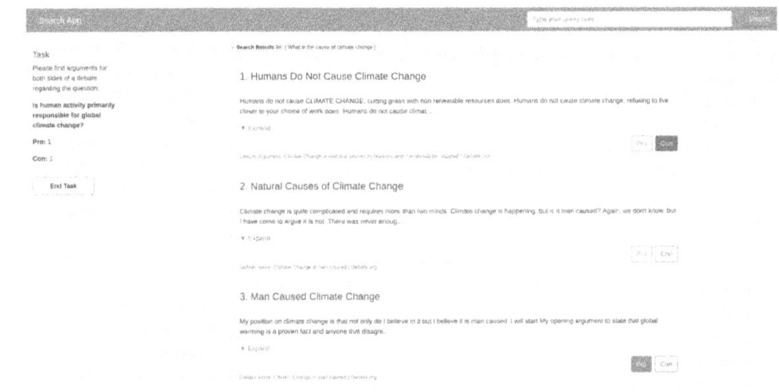

**Fig. 1.** Screenshot of the search interface of lisp

For each session, all user interactions described in Sect. 4.1 are logged, and a logfile is created. Logging begins when a task is started and ends when the participant confirms completion. Logfiles are named using the participant ID, task number, and timestamp.

In the current workflow, participants first see a welcome page, then enter their username, and proceed through two successive search tasks before finishing on a page linking to the post-study questionnaire.

The platform is designed for easy adaptation: elements such as buttons, result presentation, logging output, and datasets can all be customized with minimal changes. Detailed instructions are provided in the repository.

The repository additionally includes the implementation of the Perceptual Speed Test. Running the test requires a MySQL database for storing results, and the GitHub README provides instructions on the necessary implementation changes. A demo version[3] of the Perceptual Speed Test is also provided, which allows for testing the application without setting up a database.

### 4.3   User Profile Data

In addition to interaction logs, the dataset includes user profiles with demographics, search experience, and perceptual speed scores. Figure 2 summarizes the demographic and experience data. As all participants were recruited from the same university course, the sample is relatively homogeneous.

Perceptual speed results (Fig. 3) show an average score of 101.66 with a median of 103 and a standard deviation of 28.5, indicating substantial variability within the group. The dataset also reports detailed response patterns: the number of $j$- and $n$-key presses (indicating both symbols were perceived or not) and the correctness of these responses. Failure rates were low, with 1.72% false positives and 1.32% false negatives, and an overall failure rate of 1.46%.

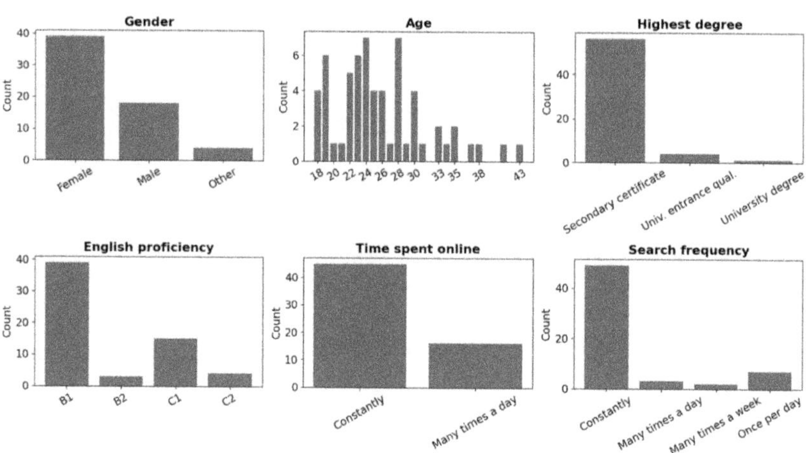

**Fig. 2.** Demographic and experience profile of the user sample (N = 61). Answer options that were not selected are not displayed.

## 5   Influence of Perceptual Speed and Interest on Search Behaviors

To illustrate the practical value of the dataset collected through our framework, we present an initial case study on the questions how perceptual speed and the level of interest influences the observed search behaviour.

---

[3] https://andykruff.github.io/demo-ps-test/.

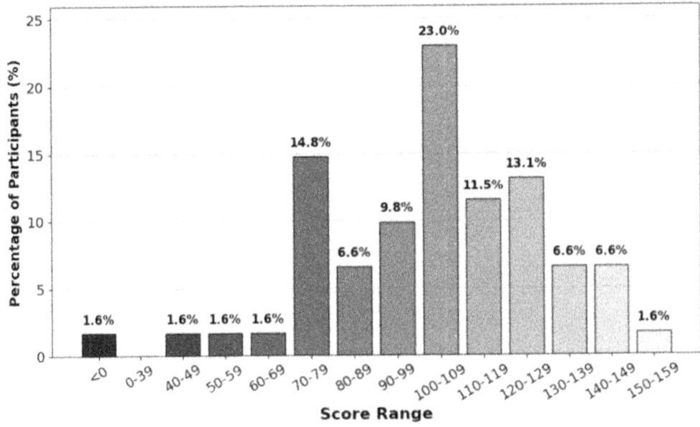

**Fig. 3.** Distribution of perceptual speed scores among participants (N = 61)

While the main contribution of this paper is the dataset itself, we provide this case study as an illustrative analysis to demonstrate the potential use cases of our research resource. We address the following research questions:

**RQ1:** How does perceptual speed influence the observed search behaviors of users?

**RQ2:** How does their level of interest in a topic influence the observed search behaviors of users?

### 5.1 Outcome Measures

To comprehensively assess search behavior, we considered interactions and times. Most interactions were extracted directly from the logfiles, while interaction durations were estimated from timestamps (e.g., document viewing time was measured from click to marking or the next document click). Interactions considered were queries issued, documents clicked or marked, pages viewed, and snippets viewed, both per session and per query; times included session duration, time per query formulation, per query, per document, and per snippet.

Since common measures do not capture the full search process, we also built Markov models from the interaction sequences to compare entire search processes across groups. Figure 4 shows the resulting Markov model based on all sessions.

### 5.2 Analysis

We used the Wilcoxon signed-rank test as a non-parametric alternative to the paired t-test to examine differences between conditions of the within-subject variable (topic interest), since the data were not normally distributed. Differences in the between-subject variable (PS) were analyzed using the MannWhitney U test, the non-parametric equivalent of the independent-samples t-test. Participants were divided into high- and low-PS groups based on the sample

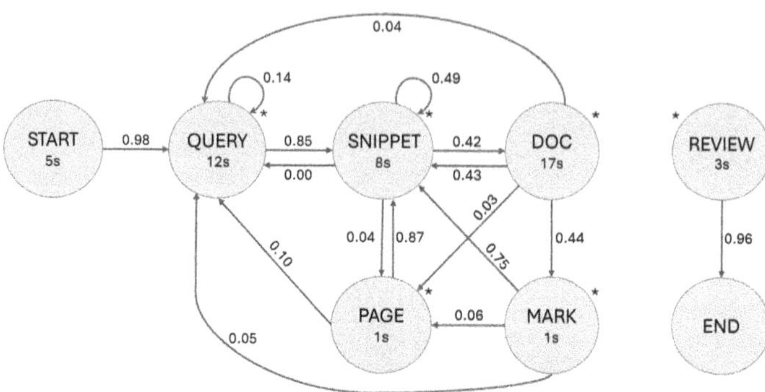


**Fig. 4.** Markov model of user interactions. Transitions from states marked with * to REVIEW and from REVIEW back to those states were omitted for clarity. Transition probabilities indicated at the arrows and mean interaction times per state are averaged across all sessions. As MARK and PAGE have no actual duration, they are assigned a nominal value of 1 s for completeness.

median, following previous work [2,4,6,11,42]; the median value was included in the higher group to ensure more balanced group sizes. To control for multiple testing, we applied the BenjaminiHochberg correction.

Regarding the Markov models, we used the Frobenius norm to assess overall model similarity, while using the JensenShannon divergence and the KolmogorovSmirnov test to assess differences at the state level.

### 5.3   Results

**Perceptual Speed.** Comparing users with high versus low perceptual speed revealed only minor differences (see Table 2). On average, high-PS users spent 2.94 s longer on each document and examined 9.89 fewer snippets per session. However, none of these differences reached statistical significance.

The Markov models also showed minimal variation between groups (Frobenius norm = 0.18), while state-level comparisons yielded very low JensenShannon divergences (0.00–0.13). Likewise, KolmogorovSmirnov tests indicated no significant differences (all $p > 0.98$) between transition probability distributions.

**Interest.** Aggregated over entire sessions, the only significant difference for interest was in the number of queries: participants submitted more queries for topics of personal interest. At a finer level, however, clear differences emerged: users spent less time per query, clicked and marked fewer documents, and viewed fewer pages and snippets, with time per query and the numbers of viewed snippets and marked documents reaching significance (see Table 2).

The Markov models revealed no notable differences across conditions: overall, a Frobenius norm of 0.10 indicates highly similar behavior, while state-level comparisons showed minimal differences (JensenShannon divergence = 0.02–

**Table 2.** Mean values and statistical results for all behavioral measures by Interest (*high int.* vs. *no int.*) and Perceptual Speed (*high PS* vs. *low PS*). For Interest, the mean within-participant differences (MD) between high- and no-interest topics are additionally reported. Statistically significant results ($p < 0.05$) are indicated by an asterisk (*).

| Measure | | Interest | | | | Perceptual Speed | | |
|---|---|---|---|---|---|---|---|---|
| | | high int. | no int. | MD | $p$ (corr.) | high PS | low PS | $p$ (corr.) |
| #.../*session* | Queries | 3.82 | 2.95 | 0.87 | 0.037* | 3.35 | 3.42 | 0.990 |
| | Documents | 23.02 | 21.52 | 1.49 | 0.458 | 22.29 | 22.25 | 0.823 |
| | Marked docs | 12.36 | 14.13 | −1.77 | 0.110 | 12.82 | 13.68 | 0.208 |
| | Snippets | 51.93 | 47.85 | 4.08 | 0.458 | 45.03 | 54.92 | 0.140 |
| | Pages | 7.16 | 6.10 | 1.07 | 0.110 | 6.00 | 7.28 | 0.188 |
| #.../*query* | Documents | 10.01 | 12.24 | −2.23 | 0.091 | 11.16 | 11.08 | 0.847 |
| | Marked docs | 5.16 | 7.61 | −2.44 | 0.028* | 5.78 | 7.01 | 0.723 |
| | Snippets | 18.44 | 25.32 | −6.88 | 0.042* | 19.37 | 24.48 | 0.268 |
| | Pages | 2.28 | 2.78 | −0.50 | 0.090 | 2.23 | 2.83 | 0.182 |
| *time per...* | Session | 662.88 | 653.12 | 9.76 | 0.458 | 665.98 | 649.75 | 0.188 |
| | Query | 276.78 | 360.32 | −83.54 | 0.037* | 320.39 | 316.64 | 0.823 |
| | Q.Formulation | 11.62 | 12.36 | −0.74 | 0.580 | 11.93 | 12.04 | 0.823 |
| | Snippet | 8.17 | 7.90 | 0.27 | 0.580 | 7.63 | 8.45 | 0.939 |
| | Document | 16.62 | 18.23 | −1.61 | 0.860 | 18.87 | 15.93 | 0.140 |

0.11) and KolmogorovSmirnov tests confirmed no significant effects (all $p > 0.98$).

*Post-Study Questionnaire.* We analyzed post-questionnaire responses to examine how topic interest affected stance changes, certainty, and perceived task difficulty. Users rarely changed stance (5 for high-interest vs. 7 for no-interest topics), and interest did not affect task difficulty (2.66 vs. 2.87). Nearly one-third of participants reported changes in certainty: for no-interest topics, increases and decreases were balanced (9 vs. 8), whereas for high-interest topics, more participants became more certain (13) than less certain (3).

## 5.4   Discussion

**Perceptual Speed.** None of the observed trends for perceptual speed reached significance, likely due to the exploratory nature of our study and stricter corrections for multiple comparisons. Nevertheless, the trends–longer document viewing times and fewer viewed snippets for high-PS users–align with Azzopardi et al. [6], despite contradicting the expectation that higher perceptual speed leads to shorter viewing times. Overall, the results suggest that perceptual speed does influence search behavior, even if not statistically conclusive here.

**Interest.** Users formulated more queries for topics of interest but spent less time per query, clicked fewer documents, and marked fewer arguments. Assuming greater prior knowledge, they may have approached searches with higher expectations, which can influence behavior [44]. However, this contrasts with Edwards et al. [17], who found that task interest affected engagement but not observable behavior. A likely explanation for this discrepancy is the task design: Edwards et al. examined information-seeking tasks requiring the identification and evaluation of multiple options from neutral sources, whereas our study focused on gathering subjective arguments for controversial topics. As topics rated as interesting likely coincide with strong pre-existing opinions, cognitive biases like the confirmation bias were likely more present [5,32]. Though they were instructed to consider both sides, interested users may have actively sought evidence confirming their beliefs, leading to more focused and less exploratory behavior. In contrast, the tasks in Edwards et al. required an inherently exploratory approach. These results indicate that the impact of interest on search behavior depends strongly on task type and cognitive framing. Distinguishing between cognitive and emotional involvement may therefore be crucial for understanding interest effects in interactive IR.

### 5.5    Limitations

Although the dataset provides rich and detailed information, it is limited in size, which means that some results are not statistically conclusive, particularly for subtle effects with small effect sizes. Consequently, the findings may not generalize beyond the specific setting examined. Moreover, the focus on a single domain further restricts the scope of applicability of the results.

### 5.6    Conclusion

Overall, the findings suggest that user characteristics, as well as the context of a search influence search behavior and should be accounted for in user models and simulators. At the same time, the Markov model results illustrate the limits of aggregated process representations: Although interest effects were more pronounced than those of perceptual speed, the Markov models for high- and no-interest sessions were more similar, since the models average over entire sessions while the interest effects primarily occurred at the query-level. Because querying is relatively infrequent compared to other interactions, the observed differences in query behavior had little impact on the overall transition probabilities. In addition, opposing tendencies within a session may balance out. This highlights the problem of oversimplifying user behavior for simulations: without considering search context—such as the current query, document rank, or evolving task state—important dynamics are lost. For user models and simulators to be realistic, they need to capture not only aggregate session patterns but also contextual dependencies that shape search as it unfolds.

## 6    Outlook

Beyond potential insights into how interest and perceptual speed shape search behavior, the presented resource opens up multiple avenues for future research. The dataset can support both empirical and modeling work—for instance, in validating and refining user simulators that account for cognitive traits and situational factors, or in developing models that incorporate retrieval scores and document characteristics to explain user interactions. The detailed log files also allow for analyses such as inter-rater agreement on marked arguments across participants and topics, offering new perspectives on subjectivity and consistency in argument relevance.

From a practical perspective, the data can also inform the design of user-adaptive search systems. By revealing how users with different cognitive profiles or levels of interest interact with search results, the dataset can be used to study personalization strategies, interface adaptations, or ranking approaches aimed at supporting engagement and efficient information exploration in argumentative or opinion-driven search scenarios.

In addition, the adaptable study setup and open-source infrastructure provide a foundation for conducting new user studies with different contexts. Together, these resources enable cumulative IIR research that bridges human behavior, simulation, and system evaluation.

**Acknowledgments.** This work was funded by the Deutsche Forschungsgemeinschaft (DFG, German Research Foundation) - 509543643.

**Disclosure of Interests.** The authors have no competing interests to declare that are relevant to the content of this article.

## References


1. Ackerman, P.L., Cianciolo, A.T.: Cognitive, perceptual-speed, and psychomotor determinants of individual differences during skill acquisition. J. Exp. Psychol. Appl. **6**(4), 259–290 (2000). https://doi.org/10.1037//1076-898x.6.4.259
2. Al-Maskari, A., Sanderson, M.: The effect of user characteristics on search effectiveness in information retrieval. Inf. Process. Manage. **47**(5), 719–729 (2011).https://doi.org/10.1016/j.ipm.2011.03.002, https://www.sciencedirect.com/science/article/pii/S030645731100029X, managing and Mining Multilingual Documents
3. Allen, B.: Cognitive differences in end user searching of a cd-rom index. In: Proceedings of the 15th Annual International ACM SIGIR Conference on Research and Development in Information Retrieval, pp. 298–309. SIGIR 1992, Association for Computing Machinery, New York, NY, USA (1992).https://doi.org/10.1145/133160.133212
4. Arguello, J., Choi, B.: The effects of working memory, perceptual speed, and inhibition in aggregated search. ACM Trans. Inf. Syst. **37**(3) (2019). https://doi.org/10.1145/3322128

5. Azzopardi, L.: Cognitive biases in search: a review and reflection of cognitive biases in information retrieval. In: Proceedings of the 2021 Conference on Human Information Interaction and Retrieval, pp. 27–37. CHIIR 2021, Association for Computing Machinery, New York, NY, USA (2021).https://doi.org/10.1145/3406522.3446023

6. Azzopardi, L., Maxwell, D., Halvey, M., Hauff, C.: Driven to distraction: examining the influence of distractors on search behaviours, performance and experience. In: Proceedings of the 2023 Conference on Human Information Interaction and Retrieval, pp. 83–94. CHIIR 2023, Association for Computing Machinery, New York, NY, USA (2023). https://doi.org/10.1145/3576840.3578298

7. Balog, K., Zhai, C.: User simulation for evaluating information access systems. Found. Trends® Inf. Retrieval $\mathbf{18}$(1-2), 1–261 (2024). https://doi.org/10.1561/1500000098

8. Bhattacharya, N., Gwizdka, J.: YASBIL: yet another search behaviour (and) interaction logger. In: Proceedings of the 44th International ACM SIGIR Conference on Research and Development in Information Retrieval, pp. 2585–2589. SIGIR 2021, Association for Computing Machinery, New York, NY, USA (2021). https://doi.org/10.1145/3404835.3462800

9. Bogers, T., Gäde, M., Hall, M.M., Koolen, M., Petras, V., Larsen, B.: How we work, share, and re-use at CHIIR. In: Proceedings of the 2023 Conference on Human Information Interaction and Retrieval, pp. 351–356. CHIIR 2023, Association for Computing Machinery, New York, NY, USA (2023).https://doi.org/10.1145/3576840.3578305

10. Bondarenko, A., et al.: Overview of touché 2020: argument retrieval. In: Conference and Labs of the Evaluation Forum (2020). https://api.semanticscholar.org/CorpusID:225073856

11. Brennan, K., Kelly, D., Arguello, J.: The effect of cognitive abilities on information search for tasks of varying levels of complexity. In: Proceedings of the 5th Information Interaction in Context Symposium, pp. 165–174. IIiX 2014, Association for Computing Machinery, New York, NY, USA (2014).https://doi.org/10.1145/2637002.2637022

12. Carterette, B., Kanoulas, E., Hall, M.M., Clough, P.D.: Overview of the TREC 2014 session track. In: Voorhees, E.M., Ellis, A. (eds.) Proceedings of The Twenty-Third Text Retrieval Conference (TREC 2014), vol. 500-308, pp. 1–12. National Institute of Standards and Technology (NIST) (2014). http://trec.nist.gov/pubs/trec23/papers/overview-session.pdf

13. Chen, J., Mao, J., Liu, Y., Zhang, M., Ma, S.: Tiangong-ST: a new dataset with large-scale refined real-world web search sessions. In: Zhu, W., Tao, D., Cheng, X., Cui, P., Rundensteiner, E.A., Carmel, D., He, Q., Yu, J.X. (eds.) Proceedings of the 28th ACM International Conference on Information and Knowledge Management, CIKM 2019, Beijing, China, November 3-7, 2019, pp. 2485–2488. ACM (2019). https://doi.org/10.1145/3357384.3358158

14. Choi, Y.: Effects of contextual factors on image searching on the web. J. Am. Soc. Inf. Sci. Technol. $\mathbf{61}$(10), 2011–2028 (2010). https://doi.org/10.1002/asi.21386

15. Chuklin, A., Markov, I., de Rijke, M.: Click Models for Web Search. Synthesis Lectures on Information Concepts, Retrieval, and Services, Morgan & Claypool Publishers (2015)

16. Craswell, N., Campos, D., Mitra, B., Yilmaz, E., Billerbeck, B.: Orcas: 18 million clicked query-document pairs for analyzing search. In: Proceedings of the 29th ACM International Conference on Information & Knowledge Management, pp. 2983–2989. CIKM 2020, Association for Computing Machinery, New York, NY, USA (2020). https://doi.org/10.1145/3340531.3412779

17. Edwards, A., Kelly, D.: How does interest in a work task impact search behavior and engagement? In: Proceedings of the 2016 ACM on Conference on Human Information Interaction and Retrieval, pp. 249–252. CHIIR 2016, Association for Computing Machinery, New York, NY, USA (2016).https://doi.org/10.1145/2854946.2855000

18. Ekstrom, R.B., French, J.W., Harman, H.H.: Manual for kit of factor-referenced cognitive tests (1976). https://api.semanticscholar.org/CorpusID:141329865

19. Foulds, O., Azzopardi, L., Halvey, M.: Reflecting upon perceptual speed tests in information retrieval: Limitations, challenges, and recommendations. In: Proceedings of the 2020 Conference on Human Information Interaction and Retrieval, pp. 234–242. CHIIR 2020, Association for Computing Machinery, New York, NY, USA (2020). https://doi.org/10.1145/3343413.3377982

20. Gäde, M., Koolen, M., Hall, M., Bogers, T., Petras, V.: A manifesto on resource re-use in interactive information retrieval. In: Proceedings of the 2021 Conference on Human Information Interaction and Retrieval, pp. 141–149. CHIIR 2021, Association for Computing Machinery, New York, NY, USA (2021). https://doi.org/10.1145/3406522.3446056

21. Hall, M.M.: To re-use is to re-write: experiences with re-using IIR experiment software. In: CEUR Workshop Proceedings, vol. 2337, pp. 19–23 (2019)

22. Huang, K., Guo, Q., Zhou, C., Hao, X.: How do emotional tasks influence information seeking behavior? Association for computing machinery, New York, NY, USA (2025). https://doi.org/10.1145/3677389.3703185

23. Kelly, D.: Methods for evaluating interactive information retrieval systems with users. Found. Trends Inf. Retr. 3(1—2), 1–224 (2009). https://doi.org/10.1561/1500000012

24. Kelly, D., Arguello, J., Edwards, A., Wu, W.c.: Development and evaluation of search tasks for IIR experiments using a cognitive complexity framework. In: Proceedings of the 2015 International Conference on The Theory of Information Retrieval, pp. 101–110. ICTIR 2015, Association for Computing Machinery, New York, NY, USA (2015). https://doi.org/10.1145/2808194.2809465

25. Li, H., et al.: Privacy-aware remote information retrieval user experiments logging tool. In: Proceedings of the 44th International ACM SIGIR Conference on Research and Development in Information Retrieval, pp. 2615–2619. SIGIR 2021, Association for Computing Machinery, New York, NY, USA (2021). https://doi.org/10.1145/3404835.3462793

26. Liang, Y., Wu, Z., He, Y., Liang, F., Liu, K., Mao, J.: A flexible user study platform for generative information retrieval. In: Proceedings of the 48th International ACM SIGIR Conference on Research and Development in Information Retrieval, pp. 4066–4070. SIGIR 2025, Association for Computing Machinery, New York, NY, USA (2025). https://doi.org/10.1145/3726302.3730140

27. Liu, J., Shah, C.: Interactive IR User Study: Design, Evaluation, and Reporting. Morgan & Claypool Publishers (2019)

28. Liu, J., Jung, Y.J.: Interest development, knowledge learning, and interactive IR: Toward a state-based approach to search as learning. In: Proceedings of the 2021 Conference on Human Information Interaction and Retrieval, pp. 239–248. CHIIR 2021, Association for Computing Machinery, New York, NY, USA (2021). https://doi.org/10.1145/3406522.3446015

29. Maxwell, D., Hauff, C.: LOGUI: contemporary logging infrastructure for web-based experiments. In: Hiemstra, D., Moens, M.F., Mothe, J., Perego, R., Potthast, M., Sebastiani, F. (eds.) Advances in Information Retrieval, pp. 525–530. Springer

International Publishing, Cham (2021). https://doi.org/10.1007/978-3-030-72240-1_59

30. Mayr, P., Kacem, A.: A complete year of user retrieval sessions in a social sciences academic search engine. In: Kamps, J., Tsakonas, G., Manolopoulos, Y., Iliadis, L., Karydis, I. (eds.) TPDL 2017. LNCS, vol. 10450, pp. 560–565. Springer, Cham (2017). https://doi.org/10.1007/978-3-319-67008-9_46

31. Meggetto, F., Moshfeghi, Y.: PODIFY: a podcast streaming platform with automatic logging of user behaviour for academic research. In: Proceedings of the 46th International ACM SIGIR Conference on Research and Development in Information Retrieval, pp. 3215–3219. SIGIR 2023, Association for Computing Machinery, New York, NY, USA (2023). https://doi.org/10.1145/3539618.3591824

32. Nickerson, R.S.: Confirmation bias: a ubiquitous phenomenon in many guises. Rev. General Psychol. 2(2), 175–220 (1998). https://doi.org/10.1037/1089-2680.2.2.175

33. O'Brien, H.L., Arguello, J., Capra, R.: An empirical study of interest, task complexity, and search behaviour on user engagement. Inf. Process. Manage. 57(3), 102226 (2020). https://doi.org/10.1016/j.ipm.2020.102226, https://www.sciencedirect.com/science/article/pii/S0306457319301591

34. Pass, G., Chowdhury, A., Torgeson, C.: A picture of search. In: Jia, X. (ed.) Proceedings of the 1st International Conference on Scalable Information Systems, Infoscale 2006, Hong Kong, May 30-June 1, 2006. ACM International Conference Proceeding Series, vol. 152, p. 1. ACM (2006).https://doi.org/10.1145/1146847.1146848

35. Qu, P., Liu, C., Lai, M.: The effect of task type and topic familiarity on information search behaviors. In: Proceedings of the Third Symposium on Information Interaction in Context, pp. 371–376. IIiX 2010, Association for Computing Machinery, New York, NY, USA (2010). https://doi.org/10.1145/1840784.1840841

36. Reimer, J.H., et al.: The archive query log: mining millions of search result pages of hundreds of search engines from 25 years of web archives. In: Proceedings of the 46th International ACM SIGIR Conference on Research and Development in Information Retrieval. p. 2848–2860. SIGIR 2023, Association for Computing Machinery, New York, NY, USA (2023). https://doi.org/10.1145/3539618.3591890

37. Rekabsaz, N., Lesota, O., Schedl, M., Brassey, J., Eickhoff, C.: TripClick: the log files of a large health web search engine. In: Proceedings of the 44th International ACM SIGIR Conference on Research and Development in Information Retrieval, pp. 2507–2513. SIGIR 2021, Association for Computing Machinery, New York, NY, USA (2021). https://doi.org/10.1145/3404835.3463242

38. Scells, H., Jimmy, Zuccon, G.: Big brother: a drop-in website interaction logging service. In: Proceedings of the 44th International ACM SIGIR Conference on Research and Development in Information Retrieval, pp. 2590–2594. SIGIR 2021, Association for Computing Machinery, New York, NY, USA (2021). https://doi.org/10.1145/3404835.3462781

39. Serdyukov, P., Dupret, G., Craswell, N.: Log-based personalization: the 4th web search click data (WSCD) workshop. In: Proceedings of the 7th ACM International Conference on Web Search and Data Mining, pp. 685–686. WSDM 2014, Association for Computing Machinery, New York, NY, USA (2014). https://doi.org/10.1145/2556195.2556207

40. Sinnamon, L., Tamim, L., Dodson, S., O'Brien, H.L.: Rethinking interest in studies of interactive information retrieval. In: Proceedings of the 2021 Conference on Human Information Interaction and Retrieval, pp. 39–49. CHIIR 2021, Association for Computing Machinery, New York, NY, USA (2021). https://doi.org/10.1145/3406522.3446031

41. Song, R., Zhang, M., Luo, C., Sakai, T., Liu, Y., Dou, Z.: SogouQ: the first large-scale test collection with click streams used in a shared-task evaluation, pp. 143–150. Springer Singapore, Singapore (2021).https://doi.org/10.1007/978-981-15-5554-1_10

42. Turpin, L., Kelly, D., Arguello, J.: To blend or not to blend? Perceptual speed, visual memory and aggregated search. In: Proceedings of the 39th International ACM SIGIR Conference on Research and Development in Information Retrieval, pp. 1021–1024. SIGIR 2016, Association for Computing Machinery, New York, NY, USA (2016). https://doi.org/10.1145/2911451.2914739

43. Vuong, T., Saastamoinen, M., Jacucci, G., Ruotsalo, T.: Understanding user behavior in naturalistic information search tasks. J. Assoc. Inf. Sci. Technol. **70**(11), 1248–1261 (2019). https://doi.org/10.1002/asi.24201, https://asistdl.onlinelibrary.wiley.com/doi/abs/10.1002/asi.24201

44. Wang, B., Liu, J.: Investigating the role of in-situ user expectations in web search. Inf. Process. Manage. **60**(3), 103300 (2023). https://doi.org/10.1016/j.ipm.2023.103300, https://www.sciencedirect.com/science/article/pii/S0306457323000377

45. Zerhoudi, S., Granitzer, M.: Beyond conventional metrics: assessing user simulators in information retrieval. In: Proceedings of the 14th Italian Information Retrieval Workshop, vol. 3802, pp. 3–12 (2024)

46. Zou, L., et al.: A large scale search dataset for unbiased learning to rank (2022). https://arxiv.org/abs/2207.03051

# UserSimCRS v2: Simulation-Based Evaluation for Conversational Recommender Systems

Nolwenn Bernard[1]([envelope]) [ID] and Krisztian Balog[2] [ID]

[1] TH Köln, Köln, Germany
nolwenn.bernard@th-koeln.de
[2] University of Stavanger, Stavanger, Norway
krisztian.balog@uis.no



**Abstract.** Resources for simulation-based evaluation of conversational recommender systems (CRSs) are scarce. The UserSimCRS toolkit was introduced to address this gap. In this work, we present UserSimCRS v2, a significant upgrade aligning the toolkit with state-of-the-art research. Key extensions include an enhanced agenda-based user simulator, introduction of large language model-based simulators, integration for a wider range of CRSs and datasets, and new evaluation utilities. We demonstrate these extensions in a case study.


**Keywords:** Conversational Recommender Systems · User simulation · Evaluation

## 1 Introduction

There is a growing interest in conversational recommender systems (CRSs), which are designed to support users in finding items corresponding to their needs and preferences through a multi-turn dialogue [13]. Despite the progress in the field, CRS evaluation remains a challenging task [4,5,13,17]. Indeed, traditional evaluation methods using offline test collections do not capture the interactive nature of the systems. To address this issue, evaluation methods relying on humans are often employed, yet they suffer from significant limitations, such as their reproducibility, scalability, and cost [18]. Therefore, user simulation has recently been gaining interest to mitigate these limitations [4,5,7,9,16,26,32,35,38,41,44]. While user simulation can be imperfect, it serves as a valuable preliminary step before human evaluation to refine and make a pre-selection of the best-performing systems, thereby optimizing the use of human resources [1].

Despite this need, there are few open-source resources specifically designed to perform simulation-based evaluation of CRSs. While comprehensive toolkits exist for building CRSs, such as CRSLab [43] and RecWizard [39], they generally lack robust and reusable resources for simulation. This creates a critical gap for



R. Campos et al. (Eds.): ECIR 2026, LNCS 16486, pp. 496–510, 2026.
https://doi.org/10.1007/978-3-032-21321-1_55

researchers, who are often forced to build bespoke evaluation setups from scratch. We also observe that toolkits designed to study task-oriented dialogue systems—a generalization of CRSs to support other tasks than recommendation—include user simulators to perform training and evaluation [21,31,45,46]. However, these are ill-suited for the recommendation domain, as they are not designed to model crucial recommendation-specific constructs, such as the assessment of recommended items based on preferences from historical interactions. Furthermore, they mostly lack support for standard recommendation benchmark datasets like ReDial [22] and INSPIRED [15].

Recently, Afzali et al. [1] presented UserSimCRS, a toolkit specifically tailored for simulation-based evaluation of CRSs. This original version (v1) provides the implementation of an agenda-based user simulator and basic evaluation metrics. While agenda-based simulators are foundational to the field, the research focus has decisively shifted towards user simulators based on large language models (LLMs), which represent the current state-of-the-art [20,35–37]. This trend is driven by their advanced natural language understanding capabilities and ability to generate more fluent, diverse, and human-like interactions, moving beyond the often rigid and predictable nature of traditional rule-based approaches, thereby promising substantially greater fidelity in modeling complex user behaviors and preferences.

However, even with a capable simulator, a significant practical challenge remains: interoperability. A simulation-based evaluation setup requires the simulator to communicate with the CRS. This integration is a major barrier to adoption, as CRSs are often implemented in different frameworks and trained on disparate datasets. Facilitating the communication between the simulator and the CRS is essential for enabling reproducible, large-scale comparative studies.

Therefore, the objective of this work is to extend UserSimCRS to provide a more holistic and modernized simulation-based CRS evaluation framework that aligns with the current state-of-the-art in research. These extensions include:

- *Enhanced agenda-based simulator*: We upgrade the classical agenda-based simulator with LLM-based components for dialogue act extraction and natural language generation, and revise the dialogue policy.
- *LLM-based simulators*: We introduce two end-to-end LLM-based user simulators (single-prompt and dual-prompt).
- *Integration with existing CRSs*: We introduce a new communication interface to integrate commonly used CRS models available in CRS Arena [6].
- *Unified data framework*: We provide a unified data format with conversion and LLM-powered augmentation tools for widely-used benchmarks (ReDial [22], INSPIRED [15], and IARD [8]).
- *Advanced conversational quality evaluation*: We expand the toolkit's limited evaluation metrics by adding a new "LLM-as-a-Judge" utility along with the implementation of recently proposed user-centric utility metrics [5].

We showcase these extensions through a case study in the movie recommendation domain. Specifically, we perform simulation-based evaluation of a selection of CRSs using the different types of user simulators and datasets now supported in

UserSimCRS v2. The most recent version of UserSimCRS is available at https:// github.com/iai-group/UserSimCRS.

## 2   Related Work

User simulation for the evaluation of interactive information access systems has seen a renewed interest in recent years [4,7,26]. Our work is situated within this trend, focusing specifically on conversational recommender systems.

Developing a CRS is a technically challenging task. Therefore, various toolkits have been proposed to lower the technical barrier. For example, CRSLab [43] toolkit supports development with deep neural networks, while FORCE [25] and RecWizard [39] support rule-based and LLM-based CRSs, respectively. These toolkits come with a user interface allowing direct interaction with the CRS and provide limited resources for evaluation. Moreover, offline evaluation commonly focuses on specific components of the CRS, e.g., evaluation of the recommender with mean reciprocal rank or natural language generator with BLEU [43]. This contrasts with platforms dedicated to large-scale *human* evaluation, such as CRS Arena [6], which benchmarks CRSs by having users judge pairwise battles between anonymous systems.

User simulators are commonly built using either a modular or end-to-end architecture. In a modular architecture, different components with specific roles interact with each other to process the incoming utterance and generate a response. For example, the established agenda-based simulator [27] typically comprises three components, as illustrated in Fig. 1a, to transform the incoming utterance to a structured representation (i.e., dialogue acts), decide on the next action to take, and then transform it to a natural response. While in an end-to-end architecture, the user simulator processes the incoming utterance and directly generates the response in natural text (Fig. 1b), e.g., [19,35]. This architecture is commonly used for user simulators using a (deep) neural network or a large language model.

Simulation-based evaluation of CRSs is still in its early stages, in part due to the complexity of the task and the limited availability of resources [4]. However, some initiatives have recently been proposed to reduce this gap and make simulation-based evaluation more accessible. These include the evaluation methodologies iEvaLM [35] and CONCEPT [16] (built on top of iEvaLM), which share similar objectives to UserSimCRS. They facilitate simulation-based evaluation of CRSs using user simulators based on LLMs. iEvaLM considers objective (e.g., recall) and subjective (e.g., persuasiveness) metrics, while CONCEPT uses system- and user-centric factors, such as reliability, cooperation, and social awareness, to assess a CRS's performance. However, we note that their implementation exclusively supports CRSs implemented in CRSLab [43] and trained on either ReDial [22] or OpenDialKG [24].

The use of LLMs as surrogates for humans in evaluation, often termed "LLM-as-a-Judge" [42], has become a prevalent trend. This approach is now widely applied across diverse tasks, including relevance assessment in information retrieval [11,12,30] and multi-faceted evaluation of CRSs based on detailed

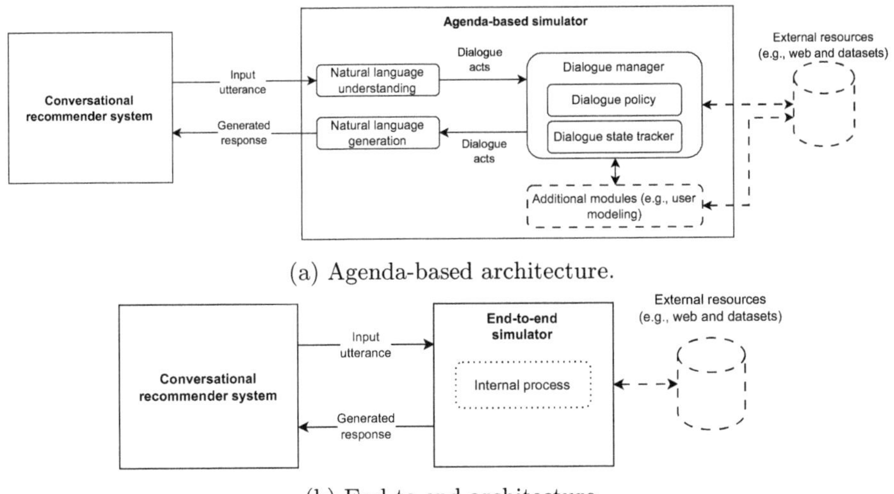

(a) Agenda-based architecture.

(b) End-to-end architecture.

**Fig. 1.** Agenda-based (Top) and end-to-end (Bottom) architectures for user simulators. The dashed lines represent optional components and data flows.

scoring rubrics [16,35]. Despite its widespread adoption, significant open questions remain, including susceptibility to biases and manipulation [2,3,33].

## 3   UserSimCRS v1

UserSimCRS [1] is a toolkit facilitating simulation-based evaluation of conversational recommender systems. It is built on top of DialogueKit,[1] a library providing dialogue management and evaluation functionalities, and comprises three main modules:

- *Agenda-based user simulator*: The implementation of a modular agenda-based user simulator, which contains the logic to generate user responses based on the dialogue history and the user's model.
- *User modeling*: Allows the definition of user models covering their preferences, the context, and their persona.
- *Item collection*: Provides a unified representation of the possible items to recommend.

The evaluation process consists of four main steps. First, the experimental setup is defined, including the interaction model, the user population(s), and the evaluation metrics. In the subsequent steps, the user simulator is trained and a set of conversations is generated. Finally, the evaluation metrics (e.g., success rate and average number of turns) are computed. This method permits the relative comparison of different CRSs under the same conditions.

---

[1] https://github.com/iai-group/DialogueKit.

While the toolkit is a valuable asset for the community, we believe that the following limitations hinder its widespread adoption.

- *Limited selection of user simulators*: The toolkit exclusively provides an agenda-based simulator. While foundational, this approach is becoming outdated and lacks the generative flexibility of LLM-based simulators, which are now prevalent and represent the current state-of-the-art research direction.
- *Limited components for agenda-based simulator*: The original implementation of the agenda-based user simulator is modular; however, it relies on a supervised model for natural language understanding and a template-based model for response generation. This limits the diversity of the responses and requires training data to be effective.
- *Lack of explicitly defined information need*: The preferences and values associated with the elicited slots are randomly sampled, which can lead to incoherent conversations. In theory, the user simulator should be initialized with an information need that guides the conversation and the user responses [27].
- *Lack of support for benchmark datasets*: The toolkit provides a dataset based on the IAI MovieBot agent [14] to create a user simulator, but it is not widely used in the field. Hence, the preparation of popular benchmark datasets is left to the toolkit users which represents a significant burden.
- *Limited selection of evaluation measures*: Evaluation functionalities in DialogueKit are limited to the computation of user satisfaction and average number of turns. The computation of other metrics, especially those related to recommendation and conversational quality, is the responsibility of the toolkit user (i.e., the CRS developer).

The objective of this work is to extend UserSimCRS to address these limitations.

## 4 UserSimCRS v2 Extensions

The underlying objective of UserSimCRS v2 remains the same as its predecessor: to facilitate the comparison of different conversational recommender systems via simulation-based evaluation. Additionally, it can be used to compare and investigate different user simulators. In this section, we present the extensions introduced in UserSimCRS v2, which are illustrated in Fig. 2. Specifically, we describe the integration of existing benchmark datasets (Sect. 4.1) the improvements to the agenda-based user simulator (Sect. 4.2), the introduction of LLM-based user simulators (Sect. 4.3), the integration of existing CRSs (Sect. 4.5), and the addition of evaluation utilities and metrics to assess conversation quality and user utility (Sect. 4.6).

### 4.1 Unified Data Format and Benchmark Datasets

UserSimCRS v1 provides an initial dataset to create a user simulator, built from interactions with IAI MovieBot [14]; however, this dataset is not widely used in the field. In UserSimCRS v2, we aim to reduce the barrier to adoption by

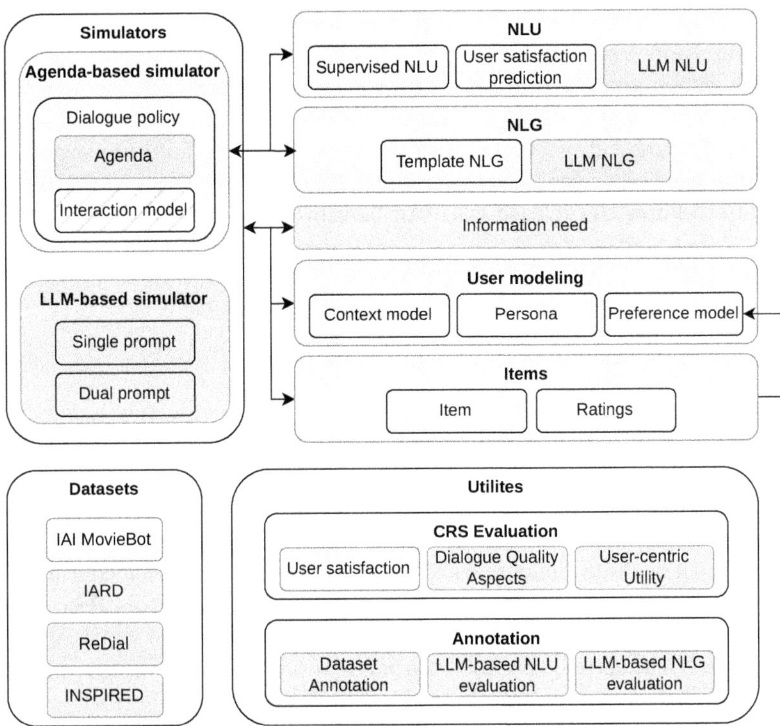

**Fig. 2.** Overview of UserSimCRS v2 architecture. Grey components are inherited from [1], while hashed and purple components correspond to updated or added components, respectively.

**Table 1.** Summary of datasets added in UserSimCRS v2. $^*$ indicates augmented version of the original dataset.

| Dataset | Domain | # Dialogues | Dialogue annotations |
|---|---|---|---|
| IARD$^*$ [8] | Movie | 77 | Dialogue acts, recommendations accepted |
| INSPIRED [15] | Movie | 1,001 | Social strategies, entity mentioned, item feedback |
| ReDial [22] | Movie | 10,006 | Movies references, item feedback |

providing a unified data format and conversion tools for the widely-used conversational datasets INSPIRED [15] and ReDial [22]. Additionally, we provide an augmented version of IARD [8], a subset of ReDial [22] with intent annotations; see Table 1 for a summary.

The proposed unified data format is based on the format used in DialogueKit, where utterances are annotated with dialogue acts. A dialogue act comprises an intent and optionally a set of associated slot-value pairs. For example, the dialogue acts `Elicit(size)` and `Elicit(color)` are present in the following CRS utterance: *"What size and color do you prefer for your new skates?"* This allows for a refined representation of utterances and to support more complex interactions than UserSimCRS v1, which only considers a single intent and a list of slot-value pairs per utterance. Furthermore, we introduce the notion of an *information need* that consists of a set of constraints $C$ and requests $R$ as in [27], in addition to target items (i.e., what the user is looking for). For example, the information need of a user looking for the song *Happy* by *Pharrell Williams* and who wants to know the release year can be represented as follows:

$$C = \begin{bmatrix} \text{genre} = \text{pop} \\ \text{artist} = \text{Pharrell Williams} \end{bmatrix}$$
$$R = \begin{bmatrix} \text{release\_year} = ? \end{bmatrix}$$
$$\text{target} = \text{Happy}$$

This information need guides the conversation and the user responses, in addition to informing the user's preferences and persona. In our example, a response to the CRS utterance eliciting the looked-for genre could be: *"I like pop music, what do you recommend?"*

We note that these benchmark datasets do not necessarily contain all the annotations required to build and train certain user simulators. For example, the utterances in ReDial are not annotated with dialogue acts which are needed to train a user simulator or some components of it (e.g., a supervised natural language understanding model). In such cases, we propose to perform automatic data augmentation. Previous work [28,40] argues that LLMs are an acceptable alternative to human annotators in data-scarce scenarios. Therefore, in UserSimCRS v2, we provide tools relying on pre-trained LLMs for the tasks of dialogue act annotation and information need extraction. However, when using these tools, the biases and limitations of LLMs should be acknowledged and sanity checks are recommended.

### 4.2  Enhanced Agenda-Based User Simulator

UserSimCRS v1 implements the agenda-based user simulator as a modular system (Fig. 1a) with components for natural language understanding (NLU), dialogue policy,[2] and natural language generation (NLG). In UserSimCRS v2, we introduce new NLU and NLG components, based on an LLM. They offer ready-to-use alternatives to the original supervised components, which require annotated training data. Furthermore, we revised the dialogue policy component to be guided by the information need and to better reflect the natural flow of recommendation dialogues.

*Natural Language Understanding.* The objective of the NLU component is to extract dialogue acts from incoming CRS utterances. In UserSimCRS v2, we implement a LLM-based NLU component which is initialized with a list of possible intents and slots for the dialogue acts and a prompt that includes a

---

[2] Referred to as response generation in v1.

placeholder for the incoming CRS utterance. Dialogue acts extraction is performed by sending the prompt with a given utterance to an LLM and parsing the output based on the following expected format: `intent1(slot="value",slot, ...)|intent2()`. We provide a default prompt, built using a few-shot approach with examples taken from the augmented IARD dataset, to extract dialogue acts in the movie domain, along with its corresponding configuration.

*Dialogue Policy.* The dialogue policy determines the dialogue acts of the next user utterance based on the current agenda and dialogue state. In the agenda-based simulator, this operation is handled by the interaction model. For User-SimCRS v2, the interaction model is revised to align with the new data format that uses dialogue acts and an information need to guide the conversation. In particular, the agenda is now initialized based on the information need, including a disclosure dialogue act for each constraint and an inquiry dialogue act for each request. Furthermore, we modify the agenda update process to better reflect the natural flow of recommendation dialogues, drawing inspiration from Lyu et al. [23]. They observe that an initial elicitation stage typically precedes the first recommendation, after which the user makes inquiries and critiques on the recommended items. Accordingly, our new process explicitly handles four cases: (1) elicitation, (2) recommendation, (3) inquiry, and (4) other. A different type of dialogue act is pushed to the agenda for the first three cases; for example, a disclosure dialogue act is added to the agenda when the CRS elicits information. In the last case, the next dialogue act is either taken from the agenda (if coherent with the current dialogue state) or sampled based on historical data. Note that all the slot-value pairs in the dialogue acts are derived from the information need or from the user's preferences if not present in the information need.

*Natural Language Generation.* The NLG component is responsible for generating human-like textual utterance based on the dialogue acts provided by the dialogue policy component. In UserSimCRS v2, we introduce an LLM-based NLG component. It aims to increase the diversity of the generated responses compared to the template-based NLG component from UserSimCRS v1. To generate an utterance, this component uses a prompt that includes placeholders for dialogue acts and, optionally, additional annotations (e.g., emotion). We also provide a default prompt, following a few-shot approach with examples from the augmented IARD dataset, for the movie domain, alongside its corresponding configuration.

## 4.3   Large Language Model-Based User Simulator

The initial version of UserSimCRS only implements agenda-based user simulation. However, other simulation approaches exist, and recently, we observe a growing interest in LLM-based user simulation [37]. To align with this trend and increase the versatility of the toolkit, UserSimCRS v2 introduces two LLM-based user simulators following different utterance generation strategies.

*Single-Prompt Simulator.* The single-prompt user simulator produces the next user utterance in an end-to-end manner given a single prompt. The prompt, inspired by Terragni et al. [29], includes the task description, an optional persona, the information need, and the current conversation history. Unlike Terragni et al. [29], our implementation follows a zero-shot approach, i.e., it does not include any examples of conversations. Nevertheless, one could include examples in the task description to follow a few-shot approach.

*Dual-Prompt Simulator.* The dual-prompt user simulator extends the single-prompt simulator by first using a separate prompt to decide whether to continue the conversation (the "stopping prompt"). If the decision is to continue, it generates the next utterance using the main generation prompt (identical to the one used by the single-prompt simulator); otherwise, it sends a default utterance to stop the conversation. The stopping prompt is designed similarly to the main generation prompt, including the task description (re-framed to focus on taking a binary decision), an optional persona, and the current conversation history.

### 4.4   Integration with Large Language Models

UserSimCRS v2 introduces several configurable components and user simulators relying on an LLM, all of which assumes the LLM employed is hosted on a server. To manage interactions with the server, all LLM-based modules use a common interface. UserSimCRS v2 provides two initial implementations of this interface: one for OpenAI[3] and one for an Ollama[4] server. This design makes the toolkit highly extensible, as additional interfaces for other LLM backends can be easily added through inheritance.

### 4.5   Integration with Existing CRSs

By design, UserSimCRS considers the CRS as a "black box," i.e., it does not assume access to its source code or inner workings. The only requirement is to have an interface to interact with the CRS; in practice, this is done using the DialogueKit library. The original version of UserSimCRS provides an interface to communicate with IAI MovieBot [14], a CRS for movie recommendation. In UserSimCRS v2, we introduce a new interface to interact with CRSs available in CRS Arena [6], such as KBRD [10], BARCOR [34], and ChatCRS [35]. This integration reduces the technical burden of using the toolkit, while facilitating experimentation with more diverse and commonly used CRSs.

### 4.6   Advanced Evaluation Metrics

Evaluation in UserSimCRS v1 is limited to user satisfaction and average number of turns. However, there are additional measures to assess the performance of

---

[3] https://openai.com/api/.
[4] https://ollama.com/.

CRSs, such as those related to recommendation accuracy and linguistic abilities [17]. In UserSimCRS v2, we provide new evaluation utilities to assess conversation quality using a LLM-based evaluator ("LLM-as-a-Judge"). We also implement novel metrics that measure utility from a user-centric perspective [5].

*Conversation Quality Evaluation with LLM-as-a-Judge.* Conversation quality is assessed with respect to five aspects inspired by Huang et al. [16]: (1) *Recommendation relevance* measures how closely the recommended items align with the user's preferences and needs; (2) *Communication style* corresponds to the conciseness and clarity of the responses; (3) *Fluency* is the degree of naturalness of the responses compared to human-generated responses; (4) *Conversational flow* assesses the coherence and consistency of the conversation; and (5) *Overall satisfaction* encapsulates the user's holistic experience. Each aspect is assigned a score between 1 and 5, with each score defined in a grading rubric.[5] For example, for *recommendation relevance* a score of 1 represents irrelevant recommendations and a score of 5 represents highly relevant recommendations. We acknowledge that there are open questions regarding the use of LLM-based evaluators, as correlation with human judgments varies across different studies [11].

*User-Centric Utility Metrics* . Bernard and Balog [5] propose metrics to assess the utility of CRSs from a user-centric perspective. We implement Successful Recommendation Round Ratio (SRRR) and Reward-per-Dialogue-Length (RDL), in addition to success rate. SRRR measures the proportion of recommendation rounds resulting in an acceptance, while RDL divides the number of accepted recommendations by dialogue length. The computation of these metrics relies on the underlying intent of user utterances in a conversation, that are annotated either manually or automatically using an NLU model.

## 5   Use Case: Movie Recommendation

To demonstrate the use of different user simulators and CRSs supported in UserSimCRS v2, we present a case study in the movie recommendation domain.

*User Simulators.* We instantiate the different types of user simulators supported in UserSimCRS v2—agenda-based (ABUS), single/dual-prompt LLM-based (LLM-SP/DP)—using different datasets. Depending on the type of the simulator and the dataset, we prepare the item collection, define an interaction model, create prompts, and annotate a sample of dialogues with dialogue acts.

*Conversational Recommender Systems.* We consider four conversational recommender systems from the CRS Arena [6]: BARCOR_OpenDialKG, BARCOR_ReDial, KBRD_ReDial, and UniCRS_OpenDialKG. Additionally, we include IAI MovieBot, as it was already supported in UserSimCRS v1.

---

[5] The grading rubrics are available at: https://github.com/iai-group/UserSimCRS/blob/main/scripts/evaluation/rubrics/quality_rubrics.py.

**Table 2.** Evaluation of selected CRSs with different user simulators. Results reported correspond to average scores over 100 synthetic dialogues.

| CRS | User satisfaction | | | Fluency | | | Rec. relevance | | |
|---|---|---|---|---|---|---|---|---|---|
| | ABUS | LLM-SP | LLM-DP | ABUS | LLM-SP | LLM-DP | ABUS | LLM-SP | LLM-DP |
| *Dataset: MovieBot* | | | | | | | | | |
| BARCOR_OpenDialKG | 1.9 ±0.6 | 1.9 ±0.6 | 1.9 ±0.6 | 2.8 ±0.5 | 2.6 ±0.6 | 3.0 ±0.5 | 1.4 ±0.6 | 1.5 ±0.9 | 2.0 ±0.9 |
| BARCOR_ReDial | 2.0 ±0.5 | 1.8 ±0.5 | 2.0 ±0.6 | 3.3 ±0.8 | 2.6 ±0.6 | 2.9 ±0.6 | 2.4 ±1.6 | 1.5 ±0.9 | 1.9 ±0.9 |
| KBRD_ReDial | 1.9 ±0.4 | 1.9 ±0.4 | 1.9 ±0.4 | 2.5 ±0.6 | 2.4 ±0.6 | 2.6 ±0.6 | 1.2 ±0.6 | 1.3 ±0.7 | 1.5 ±0.8 |
| UniCRS_OpenDialKG | 2.3 ±0.8 | 1.8 ±0.6 | 1.9 ±0.6 | 2.4 ±0.5 | 2.5 ±0.6 | 2.8 ±0.5 | 1.0 ±0.2 | 1.5 ±1.0 | 1.5 ±0.7 |
| IAI MovieBot | 1.5 ±0.7 | 1.7 ±0.8 | 2.5 ±0.7 | 3.4 ±0.6 | 3.1 ±0.7 | 3.3 ±1.0 | 2.1 ±1.1 | 2.3 ±1.4 | 2.9 ±1.7 |
| *Dataset: INSPIRED* | | | | | | | | | |
| BARCOR_OpenDialKG | 2.2 ±0.7 | 2.0 ±0.6 | 2.1 ±0.6 | 2.6 ±0.6 | 2.7 ±0.5 | 3.0 ±0.6 | 1.6 ±0.6 | 1.4 ±0.6 | 1.9 ±1.0 |
| BARCOR_ReDial | 2.1 ±0.5 | 2.0 ±0.5 | 2.0 ±0.5 | 3.5 ±0.5 | 2.6 ±0.6 | 2.9 ±0.6 | 2.3 ±0.8 | 1.4 ±0.9 | 1.6 ±0.9 |
| KBRD_ReDial | 2.0 ±0.3 | 2.0 ±0.5 | 2.1 ±0.6 | 3.3 ±0.6 | 2.3 ±0.5 | 2.6 ±0.6 | 1.9 ±0.9 | 1.2 ±0.6 | 1.4 ±0.7 |
| UniCRS_OpenDialKG | 1.9 ±0.8 | 2.1 ±0.6 | 2.1 ±0.6 | 2.9 ±0.5 | 2.4 ±0.5 | 2.7 ±0.5 | 1.3 ±0.6 | 1.1 ±0.4 | 1.5 ±0.7 |
| IAI MovieBot | 1.4 ±0.8 | 2.2 ±0.8 | 2.2 ±0.8 | 3.3 ±0.5 | 2.9 ±1.0 | 3.3 ±1.0 | 2.1 ±0.8 | 2.7 ±1.9 | 3.1 ±1.8 |
| *Dataset: ReDial* | | | | | | | | | |
| BARCOR_OpenDialKG | 2.2 ±0.8 | 1.9 ±0.8 | 2.1 ±0.7 | 3.0 ±0.6 | 2.6 ±0.5 | 3.0 ±0.5 | 1.9 ±0.8 | 1.4 ±0.6 | 1.8 ±0.9 |
| BARCOR_ReDial | 2.0 ±0.1 | 2.2 ±0.6 | 2.3 ±0.8 | 3.4 ±0.6 | 2.4 ±0.5 | 2.4 ±0.6 | 2.3 ±0.9 | 1.2 ±0.6 | 1.3 ±0.6 |
| KBRD_ReDial | 1.9 ±0.6 | 2.1 ±0.5 | 2.1 ±0.8 | 3.0 ±0.5 | 2.1 ±0.4 | 2.3 ±0.5 | 1.7 ±0.8 | 1.0 ±0.1 | 1.2 ±0.6 |
| UniCRS_OpenDialKG | 2.0 ±0.8 | 1.9 ±0.8 | 1.9 ±0.8 | 2.7 ±0.5 | 2.3 ±0.5 | 2.8 ±0.6 | 1.3 ±0.5 | 1.1 ±0.3 | 1.5 ±0.9 |
| IAI MovieBot | 2.0 ±0.2 | 2.3 ±0.9 | 2.2 ±0.9 | 4.0 ±0.2 | 2.9 ±1.0 | 3.2 ±1.0 | 4.7 ±0.8 | 2.4 ±1.7 | 2.8 ±1.6 |

*Evaluation.* We evaluate the selected CRSs using the different user simulators. This process consists of generating 100 synthetic dialogues for each pair of user simulator and CRS, and computing evaluation metrics over these dialogues. In Table 2, we report user satisfaction, fluency, and recommendation relevance.[6] The results confirm that, in general, CRS performance remains a significant challenge, with most scores below 3 on a 5-point scale. This is inline with observations reported in [5,6]. However, a closer look at the table reveals some interesting findings.

First, the simulators demonstrate significant disagreement on system ranking. For instance, on the MovieBot dataset, ABUS ranks IAI MovieBot last for user satisfaction (1.5), while LLM-DP ranks it first (2.5). Furthermore, even when simulators agree on the top-performing system (e.g., IAI MovieBot for Recommendation Relevance on ReDial), they often diverge on the magnitude of its performance (a 4.7 from ABUS vs. 2.4/2.8 from the LLM simulators).

The simulators also show distinct characteristics. ABUS appears to be the "most opinionated," assigning both the highest score in the table (4.7) and some of the lowest (1.0). The LLM simulators, by contrast, operate within a more compressed range, rarely awarding scores above 3.3. Moreover, the LLM simulators are not interchangeable. Despite producing similar results at times, LLM-DP consistently yields equal or higher average scores than LLM-SP on the INSPIRED dataset across all three metrics.

---

[6] Configurations and synthetic dialogues are available in the repository.

Finally, CRS performance itself is highly dataset-dependent. Some systems show extreme variability; for example, IAI MovieBot's recommendation relevance (via ABUS) peaks at 4.7 on ReDial—the highest score in the table—but drops to a mediocre 2.1 on the other datasets. In contrast, other systems demonstrate high consistency. BARCOR_ReDial's fluency score from ABUS, for instance, remains stable and high across all three datasets (3.3, 3.5, 3.4).

*Enabled Research Directions.* Considering the results and the synthetic dialogues generated, we can envision different research questions that UserSimCRS v2 can help investigate. For example, these include studying the influence of different user simulator types (e.g., agenda-based vs. LLM-based) and configurations (e.g., different LLMs, different prompts, datasets, and interaction models) on the evaluation outcomes, comparing the performance of different CRSs, and analyzing the synthetic dialogues with regard to their discourse structure, characteristics, or breakdowns. These are merely illustrative of the much broader scope of research that UserSimCRS v2 enables; however, the focus of this paper remains on the presentation of the toolkit itself.

## 6    Conclusion

In this work, we presented an upgraded version of UserSimCRS, designed to facilitate a more comprehensive and flexible comparison of user simulators and conversational recommender systems through simulation-based evaluation. This new version aligns the toolkit with current research by enhancing the classic agenda-based user simulator with LLM-powered components, introducing LLM-based simulators, adding new automatic evaluation utilities, and providing support for a wider range of CRSs and datasets.

Future work will focus on enhancing the integration of user modeling components to better support the simulation of diverse user populations and exploring novel evaluation metrics. Furthermore, we aim to continue reducing the technical entry barrier to encourage widespread adoption of the toolkit by the community, thereby fostering research on user simulation.

**Acknowledgments.** This research was partially supported by the Norwegian Research Center for AI Innovation, NorwAI (Research Council of Norway, project number 309834), and by the German Federal Ministry of Education and Research and Joint Science Conference under the PLan_CV project (reference number 03FHP109).

**Disclosure of Interests.** The authors have no competing interests to declare that are relevant to the content of this article.

## References


1. Afzali, J., Drzewiecki, A.M., Balog, K., Zhang, S.: UserSimCRS: a user simulation toolkit for evaluating conversational recommender systems. In: Proceedings of the Sixteenth ACM International Conference on Web Search and Data Mining, WSDM 2023, pp. 1160–1163 (2023)

2. Alaofi, M., Thomas, P., Scholer, F., Sanderson, M.: LLMs can be fooled into labelling a document as relevant. In: Proceedings of the 2024 Annual International ACM SIGIR Conference on Research and Development in Information Retrieval in the Asia Pacific Region, SIGIR-AP 2024, pp. 32–41 (2024)

3. Balog, K., Metzler, D., Qin, Z.: Rankers, judges, and assistants: towards understanding the interplay of LLMs in information retrieval evaluation. In: Proceedings of the 48th International ACM SIGIR Conference on Research and Development in Information Retrieval, SIGIR 2025, pp. 3865–3875 (2025)

4. Balog, K., Zhai, C.: User simulation for evaluating information access systems. Found. Trends Inf. Retrieval 18(1-2), 1–261 (2024). ISSN 1554-0669

5. Bernard, N., Balog, K.: Limitations of current evaluation practices for conversational recommender systems and the potential of user simulation. In: Proceedings of the 2025 Annual International ACM SIGIR Conference on Research and Development in Information Retrieval in the Asia Pacific Region, SIGIR-AP 2025, pp. 261–271 (2025)

6. Bernard, N., Joko, H., Hasibi, F., Balog, K.: CRS Arena: crowdsourced benchmarking of conversational recommender systems. In: Proceedings of the Eighteenth ACM International Conference on Web Search and Data Mining, WSDM 2025, pp. 1028–1031 (2025)

7. Breuer, T., et al.: Report on the workshop on simulations for information access (Sim4IA 2024) at SIGIR 2024. SIGIR Forum 58(2), 1–14 (2025)

8. Cai, W., Chen, L.: Predicting user intents and satisfaction with dialogue-based conversational recommendations. In: Proceedings of the 28th ACM Conference on User Modeling, Adaptation and Personalization, UMAP 2020, pp. 33–42 (2020)

9. Chen, L., et al.: RecUserSim: a realistic and diverse user simulator for evaluating conversational recommender systems. In: Companion Proceedings of the ACM on Web Conference 2025, WWW 2025, pp. 133–142 (2025)

10. Chen, Q., et al.: Towards knowledge-based recommender dialog system. In: Proceedings of the 2019 Conference on Empirical Methods in Natural Language Processing and the 9th International Joint Conference on Natural Language Processing, EMNLP-IJCNLP 2019, pp. 1803–1813 (2019)

11. Dietz, L., et al.: Principles and guidelines for the use of LLM judges. In: Proceedings of the 2025 International ACM SIGIR Conference on Innovative Concepts and Theories in Information Retrieval, ICTIR 2025, pp. 218–229 (2025)

12. Faggioli, G., et al.: Perspectives on large language models for relevance judgment. In: Proceedings of the 2023 ACM SIGIR International Conference on Theory of Information Retrieval, ICTIR 2023 (2023)

13. Gao, C., Lei, W., He, X., de Rijke, M., Chua, T.S.: Advances and challenges in conversational recommender systems: a survey. AI Open 2, 100–126 (2021)

14. Habib, J., Zhang, S., Balog, K.: IAI MovieBot: a conversational movie recommender system. In: Proceedings of the 29th ACM International Conference on Information & Knowledge Management, CIKM 2020, pp. 3405–3408 (2020)

15. Hayati, S.A., Kang, D., Zhu, Q., Shi, W., Yu, Z.: INSPIRED: toward sociable recommendation dialog systems. In: Proceedings of the 2020 Conference on Empirical Methods in Natural Language Processing, EMNLP 2020, pp. 8142–8152 (2020)

16. Huang, C., Qin, P., Deng, Y., Lei, W., Lv, J., Chua, T.S.: Concept – An evaluation protocol on conversation recommender systems with system-centric and user-centric factors. arXiv cs.CL/2404.03304 (2024)

17. Jannach, D.: Evaluating conversational recommender systems. Artif. Intell. Rev. 56(3), 2365–2400 (2023)

18. Kelly, D.: Methods for evaluating interactive information retrieval systems with users. Found. Trends® Inf. Retrieval **3**(1-2), 1–224 (2009)
19. Kim, M., et al.: Pearl: a review-driven persona-knowledge grounded conversational recommendation dataset. In: Findings of the Association for Computational Linguistics: ACL 2024, pp. 1105–1120 (2024)
20. Kim, S., Kim, T., Seo, K., Yeo, J., Lee, D.: Stop playing the guessing game! Target-free user simulation for evaluating conversational recommender systems. arXiv cs.IR/2411.16160 (2024)
21. Lee, S., et al.: ConvLab: multi-domain end-to-end dialog system platform. In: Proceedings of the 57th Annual Meeting of the Association for Computational Linguistics: System Demonstrations, ACL 2019, pp. 64–69 (2019)
22. Li, R., Kahou, S., Schulz, H., Michalski, V., Charlin, L., Pal, C.: Towards deep conversational recommendations. In: Proceedings of the 32nd International Conference on Neural Information Processing Systems, NIPS 2018, pp. 9748–9758 (2018)
23. Lyu, S., Rana, A., Sanner, S., Bouadjenek, M.R.: A workflow analysis of context-driven conversational recommendation. In: Proceedings of the Web Conference 2021, WWW 2021, pp. 866–877 (2021)
24. Moon, S., Shah, P., Kumar, A., Subba, R.: OpenDialKG: explainable conversational reasoning with attention-based walks over knowledge graphs. In: Proceedings of the 57th Annual Meeting of the Association for Computational Linguistics, ACL 2019, pp. 845–854 (2019)
25. Quan, J., et al.: FORCE: a framework of rule-based conversational recommender system. In: Proceedings of the AAAI Conference on Artificial Intelligence, AAAI 2022, pp. 13215–13217 (2022)
26. Schaer, P., Kreutz, C.K., Balog, K., Breuer, T., Kruff, A.K.: Second SIGIR workshop on simulations for information access (Sim4IA 2025). In: Proceedings of the 48th International ACM SIGIR Conference on Research and Development in Information Retrieval, SIGIR 2025, pp. 4172–4175 (2025)
27. Schatzmann, J., Thomson, B., Weilhammer, K., Ye, H., Young, S.: Agenda-based user simulation for bootstrapping a POMDP dialogue system. In: Human Language Technologies 2007: The Conference of the North American Chapter of the Association for Computational Linguistics; Companion Volume, Short Papers, NAACL 2007, pp. 149–152 (2007)
28. Su, H., Ye, J.: Large language models for automating fine-grained speech act annotation: a critical evaluation of GPT-4o and DeepSeek. Corpus Pragmatics (2005)
29. Terragni, S., Filipavicius, M., Khau, N., Guedes, B., Manso, A., Mathis, R.: In-context learning user simulators for task-oriented dialog systems. arXiv cs.CL/2306.00774 (2023)
30. Thomas, P., Spielman, S., Craswell, N., Mitra, B.: Large language models can accurately predict searcher preferences. In: Proceedings of the 47th International ACM SIGIR Conference on Research and Development in Information Retrieval, SIGIR 2024, pp. 1930–1940 (2024)
31. Ultes, S., et al.: PyDial: a multi-domain statistical dialogue system toolkit. In: Proceedings of ACL 2017, System Demonstrations, ACL 2017, pp. 73–78 (2017)
32. Vlachou, M.: Fashion-AlterEval: a dataset for improved evaluation of conversational recommendation systems with alternative relevant items. In: Proceedings of the Nineteenth ACM Conference on Recommender Systems, RecSys 2025, pp. 755–763 (2025)
33. Wang, P., et al.: Large language models are not fair evaluators. In: Proceedings of the 62nd Annual Meeting of the Association for Computational Linguistics (Volume 1: Long Papers), ACL 2024, pp. 9440–9450 (2024)

34. Wang, T.C., Su, S.Y., Chen, Y.N.: BARCOR: towards a unified framework for conversational recommendation systems. arXiv cs.CL/2203.14257 (2022)
35. Wang, X., Tang, X., Zhao, X., Wang, J., Wen, J.R.: Rethinking the evaluation for conversational recommendation in the era of large language models. In: Proceedings of the 2023 Conference on Empirical Methods in Natural Language Processing, EMNLP 2023, pp. 10052–10065 (2023)
36. Yoon, S., He, Z., Echterhoff, J., McAuley, J.: Evaluating large language models as generative user simulators for conversational recommendation. In: Proceedings of the 2024 Conference of the North American Chapter of the Association for Computational Linguistics: Human Language Technologies (Volume 1: Long Papers), NAACL 2024, pp. 1490–1504 (2024)
37. Zhang, H., Zhao, X., Chen, J., Guo, J.: A literature review on simulation in conversational recommender systems. arXiv cs.HC/2506.20291 (2025)
38. Zhang, S., Balog, K.: Evaluating conversational recommender systems via user simulation. In: Proceedings of the 26th ACM SIGKDD International Conference on Knowledge Discovery & Data Mining, KDD 2020, pp. 1512–1520 (2020)
39. Zhang, Z., et al.: RecWizard: a toolkit for conversational recommendation with modular, portable models and interactive user interface. In: Proceedings of the 38th Annual AAAI Conference on Artificial Intelligence, AAAI 2024 (2024)
40. Zhangwenbo, Z., Yuhan, W.: Act2P: LLM-driven online dialogue act classification for power analysis. In: Findings of the Association for Computational Linguistics: ACL 2025, ACL 2025, pp. 20494–20504 (2025)
41. Zhao, X., et al.: Exploring the impact of personality traits on conversational recommender systems: a simulation with large language models. arXiv cs.CL/2504.12313 (2025)
42. Zheng, L., et al.: Judging LLM-as-a-judge with MT-bench and Chatbot Arena. In: Proceedings of the 37th International Conference on Neural Information Processing Systems, NeurIPS 2023 (2023)
43. Zhou, K., et al.: CRSLab: an open-source toolkit for building conversational recommender system. In: Proceedings of the 59th Annual Meeting of the Association for Computational Linguistics and the 11th International Joint Conference on Natural Language Processing: System Demonstrations, ACL-IJCNLP 2021, pp. 185–193 (2021)
44. Zhu, L., Huang, X., Sang, J.: A LLM-based controllable, scalable, human-involved user simulator framework for conversational recommender systems. In: Proceedings of the ACM on Web Conference 2025, WWW 2025, pp. 4653–4661 (2025)
45. Zhu, Q., et al.: ConvLab-3: a flexible dialogue system toolkit based on a unified data format. In: Proceedings of the 2023 Conference on Empirical Methods in Natural Language Processing: System Demonstrations, EMNLP 2023, pp. 106–123 (2023)
46. Zhu, Q., et al.: ConvLab-2: an open-source toolkit for building, evaluating, and diagnosing dialogue systems. In: Proceedings of the 58th Annual Meeting of the Association for Computational Linguistics: System Demonstrations, ACL 2020, pp. 142–149 (2020)

# CitiLink-Minutes: A Multilayer Annotated Dataset of Municipal Meeting Minutes


Ricardo Campos[1,2,6]([✉])[iD], Ana Filipa Pacheco[5,6][iD], Ana Luísa Fernandes[5,6][iD],
Inês Cantante[5,6][iD], Rute Rebouças[5,6][iD], Luís Filipe Cunha[3,6][iD],
José Isidro[4,6][iD], José Evans[4,6][iD], Miguel Marques[1,6][iD], Rodrigo Batista[3,6][iD],
Evelin Amorim[3,6][iD], Alípio Jorge[3,6][iD], Nuno Guimarães[3,6][iD],
Sérgio Nunes[4,6][iD], António Leal[5,7][iD], and Purificação Silvano[5,6][iD]

[1] University of Beira Interior, Covilhã, Portugal
[2] Ci2 - Smart Cities Research Center, Polytechnic University of Tomar,
Tomar, Portugal
`ricardo.campos@ubi.pt`
[3] Faculdade de Ciências, Universidade do Porto, Porto, Portugal
[4] Faculdade de Engenharia, Universidade do Porto, Porto, Portugal
[5] Faculdade de Letras, Universidade do Porto, Porto, Portugal
[6] INESC TEC, Porto, Portugal
[7] University of Macau, Macau, Macau



**Abstract.** City councils play a crucial role in local governance, directly influencing citizens' daily lives through decisions made during municipal meetings. These deliberations are formally documented in meeting minutes, which serve as official records of discussions, decisions, and voting outcomes. Despite their importance, municipal meeting records have received little attention in Information Retrieval (IR) and Natural Language Processing (NLP), largely due to the lack of annotated datasets, which ultimately limit the development of computational models. To address this gap, we introduce CitiLink-Minutes, a multilayer dataset of 120 European Portuguese municipal meeting minutes from six municipalities. Unlike prior annotated datasets of parliamentary or video records, CitiLink-Minutes provides multilayer annotations and structured linkage of official written minutes. The dataset contains over one million tokens, with all personal identifiers de-identified. Each minute was manually annotated by two trained annotators and curated by an experienced linguist across four complementary dimensions: (1) personal information, (2) metadata, (3) subjects of discussion, and (4) voting outcomes, totaling over 38,000 individual annotations. Released under FAIR principles and accompanied by baseline results on metadata extraction, topic classification, and vote labeling, CitiLink-Minutes demonstrates its potential for downstream NLP and IR tasks, while promoting transparent access to municipal decisions.

**Keywords:** Annotated Dataset · Municipal Meeting Minutes · Information Retrieval · Natural Language Processing · Information Extraction

# 1 Introduction

Official city council meeting minutes represent a rich yet underexplored source of civic information. They document local decision-making processes, including policy discussions, proposals, and voting outcomes, offering structured evidence of how local governments operate. Recognizing their importance, several civic data initiatives have emerged to make government proceedings more accessible. Projects such as the Council Data Project [19] and citymeetings.nyc[1] provide searchable interfaces and automatic summaries of meeting transcripts from U.S. municipalities. While these resources demonstrate growing interest in the computational analysis of municipal data, they mostly focus on video transcripts [34], where speech-to-text systems produce transcribed versions of oral deliberation. In contrast, official written meeting minutes are more difficult to analyze, as they are often lengthy and heterogeneous, with structures that vary across municipalities. The fact that relevant information, such as policy topics, proposals, and voting outcomes, is often embedded within long narrative passages makes it challenging for both humans and computational systems to locate, extract, and compare information across meetings and institutions. Consequently, progress in this direction has been slow, as municipal-level data are rarely curated, standardized, or made openly available for computational research. From an IR and NLP perspective, this scarcity limits both model training and evaluation, hindering progress on domain-specific tasks that require resources adapted to the linguistic and structural characteristics of municipal discourse.

To circumvent this limitation, many researchers rely on web-scraped data, which are often noisy and can hamper model training [22]. Such data may also contain sensitive information or raise copyright concerns [36], further limiting dataset publication and the advancement of research [5]. Existing initiatives also remain largely limited to English and lack the high-quality, multilayer annotations that are essential for deeper linguistic analysis and effective IR research.

To address this gap, we introduce in this paper the CitiLink-Minutes dataset[2] [7], developed as part of the CitiLink project[3]. Unlike existing initiatives that primarily focus on video transcripts, CitiLink-Minutes provides official written minutes. The dataset comprises 120 municipal meeting minutes (2021–2024) in European Portuguese, collected in collaboration with six municipalities, ensuring legally compliant and copyright-safe access to official records with consistent, standardized annotations across municipalities. Each meeting minute was manually annotated by a team of linguists following a four-layer schema encompassing personal information (PI), metadata, subjects of discussion, and voting outcomes. The **PI** layer captures any mention that can identify a person; **metadata** records details such as date, location, and participants; **subjects of discussion** encodes topics and themes; and the **voting** tracks voters and results. A double-annotation process was pursued, followed by curator validation to resolve

---

[1] https://citymeetings.nyc.
[2] https://github.com/inesctec/citilink-dataset.
[3] https://citilink.inesctec.pt/.

discrepancies and ensure consistency. To release the data, all PI was manually de-identified to protect privacy and comply with data sensitivity requirements. This effort resulted in a high-quality annotated dataset, richly structured and multilayered. It addresses privacy and copyright concerns and offers linguistic and structural depth unmatched by existing municipal datasets. We also provide an interactive dashboard[4] that allows users to explore the dataset in detail.

The rich annotations enable a variety of tasks, including metadata extraction, topic classification, subject detection, and vote labeling. To support reproducible research and provide reference points, we offer baseline results, highlighting both the opportunities and challenges of working with municipal meeting minutes in downstream tasks. Our contributions are summarized as follows.

1. A novel, human-annotated dataset of 120 municipal minutes from six Portuguese municipalities, with dense annotations across four layers: PI, meeting metadata, subjects of discussion, and voting outcomes. The dataset is released under a permissive license following FAIR principles, with all personal data de-identified to ensure privacy, guaranteeing unrestricted access.
2. An interactive dashboard for detailed exploration of the dataset, allowing users to inspect its structure and annotations.
3. The definition of two redefined tasks (voter identification, topic classification) and one novel task (metadata identification) for municipal meeting minutes, along with evaluation metrics and baselines (made available on Hugging Face) that establish reference points and illustrate the complexity of the dataset, guiding future research.

The remainder of this work is organized as follows. Section 2 reviews related work. Section 3 describes the dataset, its statistics, and the annotation scheme. Section 4 presents the baseline results for a selection of tasks supported by the dataset. Finally, Sect. 5 summarizes the main findings, followed by the discussion of limitations.

## 2   Related Work

Research on institutional and governmental discourse has largely relied on parliamentary proceedings, which primarily capture spoken interaction. Well-known examples include EuroParl [17], a multilingual parallel corpus of the official proceedings of the European Parliament, widely used in machine translation, the European Parliament debates [1], and the ParlaMint II project [9], which provides richly annotated, multilingual parliamentary corpora from 29 European countries. Other datasets have introduced finer-grained annotations. For instance, Mor-Lan et al. [20] annotated Israeli parliamentary debates for member identification and session metadata, leveraging the consistent formatting of parliamentary records. However, this regularity is far less common in city council

---

[4] https://dataset.citilink.inesctec.pt To access the platform, visit INESC TEC repository (https://doi.org/10.25747/7KG6-1K22) and request access to the dataset.

minutes, which makes metadata annotation particularly challenging. Other studies have focused on speech acts [26], speaker attribution [25], and causality [12], covering multiple languages [11,20,35], including Brazilian Portuguese [10], and European Portuguese [27]. These resources demonstrate a strong focus on parliamentary debate, with high-quality annotations, metadata, and structured formats.

In contrast, municipal governance corpora remain scarce, offering only limited opportunities to advance narrative understanding [28]. Existing resources mostly rely on audio or video transcriptions with limited annotations. For example, LocalView [4] provides video transcripts of U.S. local meetings, yet lacks linguistic annotations. Similarly, van Wijk and Marx [34] offer a small dataset of transcribed Dutch municipal meetings, also without annotations, while Spangher et al. [32] annotated San Francisco city council meeting transcriptions with media coverage labels. Building on similar objectives, MeetingBank [14] provides segmented city council video transcripts for summarization, while Ulysses [2,29], a dataset of Brazilian legislative bills, offers segmentation and NER annotations in Brazilian legislative and municipal contexts. However, it focuses on general entities, missing the full richness of municipal meeting content. Among these efforts, only Vlantis et al. [33] use municipal textual documents, but with limited scope and annotation. To address these limitations, we propose the CitiLink-Minutes dataset, a comprehensive, multilayer-annotated corpus of 120 municipal minutes in European Portuguese, from six Portuguese municipalities.

## 3   The CitiLink-Minutes Dataset

In this section, we present the CitiLink-Minutes dataset, providing a comprehensive account of its construction process, the underlying annotation scheme, and the principal characteristics of the resulting annotated corpus.

### 3.1   Dataset Creation

The meeting minutes were collected under partnership agreements with six municipalities, Alandroal, Campo Maior, Covilhã, Fundão, Guimarães, and Porto, granting access to all official records produced during the 20212024 administrative term. In total, 479 min were obtained. From this collection, the linguistics team selected a representative subset for annotation based on predefined selection and processing criteria: (i) only minutes dated from October 2021 onward were included, corresponding to the start of the term of office of the mayor; (ii) a diversity of session types, such as ordinary, extraordinary, public, and private, was ensured; (iii) meetings containing between 15 and 40 agenda items were selected to balance topic representativeness with annotation feasibility; and (iv) public meetings were preferred, since they are open to citizens and the media, and typically address matters of broader civic relevance. Applying these criteria yielded a final selection of 120 min, 20 per municipality. Table 1 presents the annual distribution of the collected minutes across the six municipalities, with the selected subset indicated in parentheses.

**Table 1.** Number of meeting minutes collected and (selected) per year and municipality (20212024).

| Year | Alandroal | Campo Maior | Covilhã | Fundão | Guimarães | Porto | Total |
|---|---|---|---|---|---|---|---|
| 2021 | 7 (2) | 25 (2) | 21 (2) | 4 (2) | 5 (2) | 6 (2) | 68 (12) |
| 2022 | 27 (6) | 25 (6) | 20 (6) | 16 (6) | 22 (6) | 24 (6) | 134 (36) |
| 2023 | 28 (6) | 25 (6) | 21 (6) | 17 (6) | 22 (6) | 24 (6) | 137 (36) |
| 2024 | 30 (6) | 25 (6) | 21 (6) | 18 (6) | 23 (6) | 23 (6) | 140 (36) |
| **Total** | **92 (20)** | **100 (20)** | **83 (20)** | **55 (20)** | **72 (20)** | **77 (20)** | **479 (120)** |

## 3.2   Annotation Scheme and Methodology

The annotation framework developed for this dataset follows the modular architecture proposed by ISO 24617: Language Resource Management - Semantic Annotation Framework (SemAF, e.g. [15]), and comprises two main types of structures, **Entities** ($E$) and **Links** ($\mathcal{L}$). While grounded in the ISO 24617 specification, our framework adopts a broader interpretation of semantic information, allowing for richer, context-sensitive, and task-specific annotations.

Formally, the set of **Entities**, is defined as $E = \{e_1, \ldots, e_{n_E}\}$, where each entity $e_i$ is modeled as $e_i = (m, s, a_e, v_e)$. Here $m$ represents a *markable* (i.e., a text span identified in the document), $s$ is the semantic label assigned to that span, $a_e$ is an optional attribute associated with $s$ drawn from the set $A_e(s)$, and $v_e$ is an optional value associated with $a_e$ drawn from the set $V_e(a_e)$. For example, an entity may correspond to the text span "Rui Moreira", annotated with the semantic label $s = Participant$, the attribute $a_e = Mayor$, and the value regarding political party $v_e = RM$. In this case, the entity is represented as $e = $ ("Rui Moreira", *Participant, Mayor, RM*).

Formally, the set of **Links** is defined as $\mathcal{L} = \{l_1, \ldots, l_{n_L}\}$, where each link $l_i$ is modeled as $l_i = (e_p, e_q, r, a_l)$. Here, $e_p, e_q \in E$ are the two entities connected by the link, $r$ represents the *relation type* between them, and $a_l$ is an optional attribute associated with the relation $r$ drawn from the set $A_l(r)$. For example, a link of type *Voting* may connect the entities $e_p = $ ("Rui Moreira", *Participant, Mayor, RM*) and $e_q - $ ("deliberated", *voting_evidence*), with the attribute $a_l = $ *in favour*. In this case, the link is represented as $l = (e_p, e_q, Voting, in\ favour)$.

Together, these two types of structures are applied across four conceptual annotation layers $(L_1, L_2, L_3, L_4)$. The first layer, $L_1$: **Personal Information**, captures information that can directly or indirectly identify a person, such as proper names, addresses, etc. The second layer, $L_2$: **Metadata**, includes entities representing general information about the meeting, for instance, participants, dates, locations, and times. The third layer, $L_3$: **Subject of discussion**, represents the main topics and themes of the deliberations. Finally, the fourth layer, $L_4$: **Voting**, captures the outcomes of votes on each subject, including the voters, non-voters, voting evidence, and global tally. Figure 1a presents a representative annotated minute, illustrating the information captured by the annotation framework. Figure 1b schematically summarizes the four annotation layers.

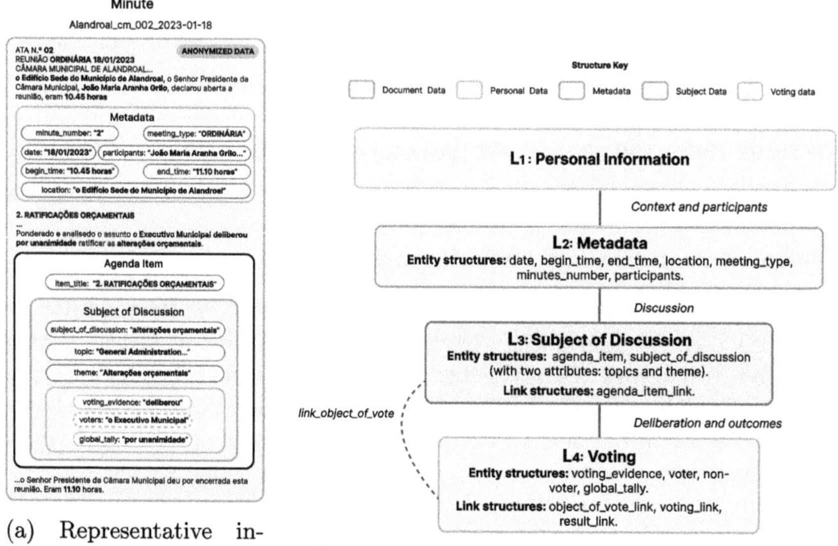

(a) Representative instance of an annotated minute.

(b) Schematic representation of the four-layer annotation framework.

**Fig. 1.** Overview of the proposed framework and its implementation.

Four linguistics students (ANN1ANN4) were responsible for the annotation and curation of the meeting minutes that constitute the corpus. To ensure consistency and resolve ambiguities, weekly meetings were held with two senior researchers experienced in semantic annotation and large annotation projects such as SemEval and CLEF [23,24]. Before the large-scale annotation, conducted on the INCEpTION platform [16], a pilot phase was carried out involving ten minutes per municipality. This phase aimed at training the annotators and also served to assess whether LLM-based metadata pre-annotation could enhance the speed and efficiency of the process. The results indicated that this approach reduced the time required for metadata annotation by roughly two hours per document, which is in line with other works [8,18] that have shown the utility of LLMs in improving annotation workflows through human-AI collaboration. A detailed analysis of this experiment lies beyond the scope of this paper. All four annotators jointly annotated one minute from each municipality to resolve ambiguities, align interpretations of the annotation guidelines, and establish a common understanding for subsequent individual work. To ensure annotation quality [6,30], each minute was annotated across all layers by two annotators ($ANN1/ANN2$ or $ANN3/ANN4$) and subsequently validated by a curator. The only exception was the $L_2$: *Metadata* layer, which was annotated by a single annotator due to the straightforward nature of the task, though still subject to curator validation. In cases of ambiguity or uncertainty, the curator consulted the responsible annotators and domain experts, and, when appropriate, initiated a collective deliberation to reach a consensus [21].

## 3.3   Inter-Annotator Agreement (IAA)

To assess the reliability of our annotations across different layers and categories, we measured Inter-Annotator Agreement (IAA) using Krippendorff's alpha [3]. Figure 2 summarizes the agreement values between annotator pairs across all layers and annotation types.

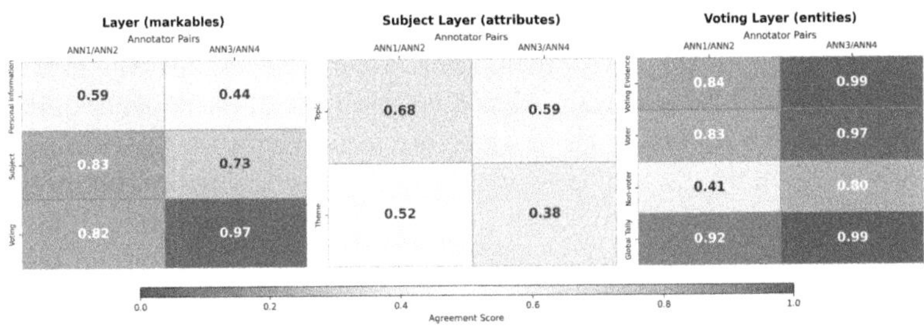


**Fig. 2.** Inter-annotator Agreement scores across different annotation layers.

Overall, the IAA values indicate consistent agreement across most annotation layers and categories, with some exceptions (Fig. 2). The leftmost chart presents overall agreement on markables, by layer, independent of specific entity or attribute assignments. In the *personal information* layer, spans were considered matching if annotators differed by at most one word. Consequently, the moderate inter-annotator agreement mainly reflects small variations in span delimitation, which are common in this type of annotation task and do not indicate fundamental divergences in interpretation. The *subject* and *voting* layers show generally strong agreement between annotator pairs. However, agreement for the subject's attributes, *theme* and *topic*, is lower, as illustrated in the middle heatmap. The reduced agreement for *topic* reflects the large number of possible values (n = 22) and the fact that a subject may legitimately correspond to multiple topics. The *theme* attribute shows the lowest agreement, likely due to its open-text format, where annotators independently described the thematic content of each discussion subject. To assess agreement fairly, annotations were considered matching if they achieved at least 70% similarity according to the Levenshtein distance (i.e., the number of character-level edits required to transform one string into another), and Krippendorff's alpha was then computed based on these matches. In the *voting* layer, the only exception occurred for the *non-voter* entity, where agreement between ANN1 and ANN2 was 0.41. This discrepancy can be attributed to a misinterpretation by ANN2 regarding that specific entity. However, this was fixed during the curation phase. Despite these challenges, the involvement of a dedicated curator to systematically review, reconcile, and validate all annotations ensures the integrity and consistency of the dataset, effectively mitigating variability across individual annotators and providing a robust and reliable resource for downstream NLP tasks.

## 3.4  Structure and Dataset Characterization

The CitiLink-Minutes dataset comprises 120 meeting minutes, providing a robust resource for research on IR and NLP in municipal governance. While the number of minutes is moderate, each document is richly annotated across multiple layers, making it a valuable pioneering resource in European Portuguese and establishing a benchmark for future research. The dataset is organized into six JSON files, one per municipality, each containing 20 annotated documents. Figure 3 shows the structure of the JSON files. Each document contains the four annotation layers: Personal Information, Metadata, Subject of Discussion, and Voting. The instructions for accessing the dataset are available in the GitHub repository (see footnote 2). The dataset is available under the Creative Commons AttributionNonCommercialNoDerivatives 4.0 International License (CC-BY-NC-ND) at INESC TEC repository with a persistent DOI [7], ensuring broad access and reuse within the research community. In addition to the full dataset, we define a data split comprising 72 meeting minutes for training, 24 for validation, and 24 for testing. The documents were ordered chronologically, with the most recent minutes reserved for the test set. This temporal split ensures that evaluation reflects a realistic deployment scenario, where models are tested on newer, unseen data that simulates future meetings.

Table 2 summarizes the statistics of the CitiLink-Minutes dataset across six municipalities, comprising over 1 million tokens, with a total of 20,375 entities and 11,162 relations. Covilhã shows the highest number of relations (2,585) and entities (4,518), suggesting detailed meeting descriptions and richer inter-entity connections. In contrast, Fundão has a smaller set of entities (1,915) and relations (983) despite a relatively high token count ($\approx$189 K). Campo Maior and Porto display moderate document sizes ($\approx$150160K tokens) but maintain a relatively high entity density, while Alandroal ($\approx$52 K tokens) still contains nearly 3K entities, showing that even shorter minutes can be semantically dense. Overall, the corpus exhibits substantial content and structural diversity across municipalities, which is valuable for evaluating model robustness.

Table 3 presents the statistics across the four annotation layers: personal information, metadata, subjects of discussion, and voting. In the **personal info** layer, we report all the instances that directly or indirectly identify an individual. For further details on the annotation process and specific labeling criteria, we refer the reader to the annotation guidelines manual. For the **metadata** layer, we focus on the entity *participants*, which aggregates mentions of *councilors*, and *staff* across the 120 meetings. The entities *president* and *vice-president* are excluded, as there is only one of each per municipality. The remaining metadata entities (*start_time*, *end_time*, *minute_number*, *location*, *meeting_type*, and *date*)

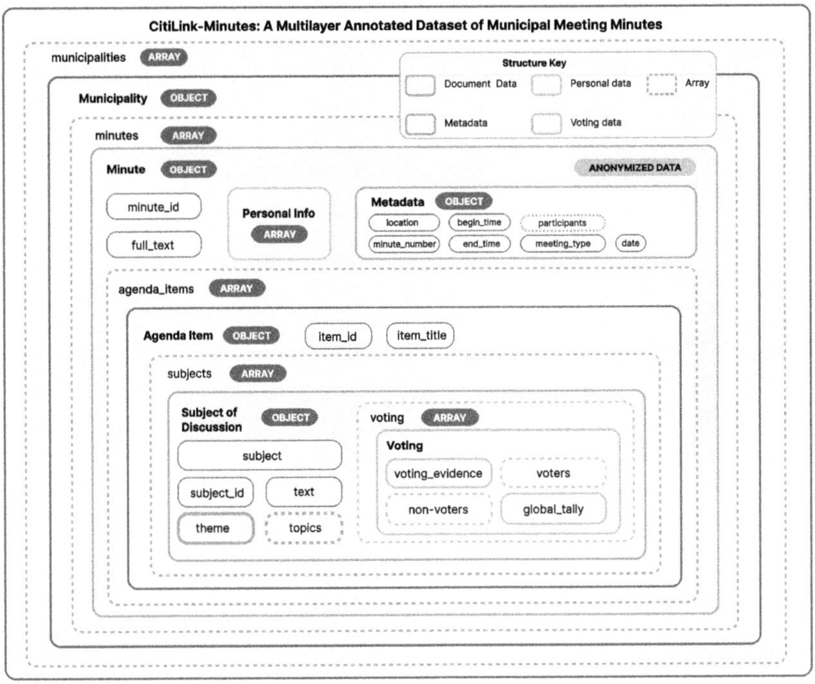

**Fig. 3.** Summary of the JSON structure of CitiLink-Minutes dataset.

are directly tied to the number of documents, *i.e.*, 20 per municipality. In the **subjects of discussion** layer, we identify a total of 2,848 subjects across all municipalities, averaging 23.73 per minute. Each subject is associated with one *theme* (thus matching the number of subjects) and one or more *topics*, with an average of 1.69 topics per subject. Covilhã shows the highest number of discussed subjects ($sub_{total}$). Of all identified subjects, 2,489 involve at least one voting procedure ($sub_{vot}$). Finally, the **voting** layer includes the entities *voting evidence*, *voters*, *non-voters*, and *global tally*. A total of 2,716 voting records were identified (some $sub_{vot}$ include multiple votes), corresponding to an average of 22.63 votes per minute. The entities *voters* and *non-voters* represent aggregated counts of councilor activity per subject rather than individual records. As expected, municipalities with a higher number of discussed subjects exhibit higher numbers of voting entries. For example, Covilhã has the highest number of voting evidence (753) and voters (1,319), reflecting its larger number of subjects. The number of *non-voters* remains relatively low across municipalities, with Guimarães showing the highest count (51), indicating occasional participants who, for different reasons (like incompatibilities), do not participate in a particular voting event. Building on this aggregated voting information, we also analyzed the distribution of voting positions *in favor*, *against*, or *abstention* for each subject. Overall, the majority of explicit voting positions are *in favor*

**Table 2.** Statistics for the CitiLink-Minutes dataset.

| Municipality | Tokens | Entities | Relations |
|---|---|---|---|
| Alandroal | 51,987 | 2,902 | 1,796 |
| Campo Maior | 161,889 | 4,187 | 1,474 |
| Covilhã | 235,381 | 4,518 | 2,585 |
| Fundão | 189,128 | 1,915 | 983 |
| Guimarães | 206,361 | 3,547 | 2,154 |
| Porto | 151,766 | 3,306 | 2,170 |
| **Total** | **1,016,825** | **20,375** | **11,162** |

(67.6%), while Covilhã shows a higher proportion of *abstentions* (53.7%), and Porto records the largest share of votes *against* (13.2%). These patterns highlight both the variation in council decision-making styles and the relationship between discussion volume and voting activity across municipalities.

**Table 3.** Entities and attributes statistics across layers.

| Municipality | Personal Info | Metadata | | Subjects | | Voting | | | | |
|---|---|---|---|---|---|---|---|---|---|---|
| | | Councilors | Staff | Subj. Total | Subj. Votes | Topics | V. Evidence | Voters | Non-voters | Global tally |
| Alandroal | 458 | 60 | 20 | 503 | 404 | 736 | 404 | 485 | 10 | 404 |
| Campo Maior | 2,297 | 60 | 42 | 396 | 328 | 638 | 362 | 393 | 5 | 357 |
| Covilhã | 1,273 | 117 | 27 | 688 | 576 | 1090 | 753 | 1319 | 23 | 2 |
| Fundão | 414 | 100 | 20 | 235 | 234 | 459 | 234 | 282 | 3 | 232 |
| Guimarães | 928 | 188 | 18 | 554 | 486 | 998 | 494 | 628 | 51 | 486 |
| Porto | 244 | 222 | 22 | 472 | 461 | 891 | 469 | 770 | 8 | 467 |
| **Total** | **5,614** | **747** | **149** | **2,848** | **2,489** | **4,812** | **2,716** | **3,877** | **100** | **1,948** |

## 4    Tasks and Baseline Results

To demonstrate the potential of the CitiLink-Minutes dataset, we define three representative NLP tasks and establish baseline results for each, covering distinct application scenarios: structured information extraction, entity recognition, and multi-label classification. These experiments are not exhaustive model evaluations, but rather reproducible baselines that provide reference points for future research. For each task, we compare an encoder-based and a generative model (few-shot), reporting standard evaluation metrics consistently at the macro (ma) and micro (mi) levels. All experiments followed the predefined data split provided with this resource paper. The encoder-based baselines (BERTimbau Large [31]) were fine-tuned using AdamW with a learning rate of $5 \times 10^{-5}$, batch size 16, weight decay of 0.01, and a maximum sequence length of 512. Training was run for 10 epochs, with a 10% warmup phase. For span-based extraction tasks (*Voting Identification* and *Metadata Extraction*), a standard token-classification head was used, while *Topic Classification* utilized a multi-label output layer trained with binary cross-entropy loss (`BCEWithLogitsLoss`). For the generative baselines, we employed a few-shot prompting strategy with task-specific examples. Each prompt was structured into three components: (i) a task definition including specific constraints, such as the requirement for exact span extraction for *Metadata* and *Voting Identification*, or a predefined label list for *Topic Classification*;(ii) the examples illustrating the expected input–output mapping; and (iii) the target inference instance. To ensure consistency, prompts for extraction tasks enforced rules against paraphrasing and the use of exact offsets, while classification prompts required the use of the provided taxonomy. The baseline models are publicly available on HuggingFace[5]. To support reproducibility and benchmarking, the generative prompts used across the evaluation set are also provided in our GitHub repository.

***Metadata Identification.*** The first task focuses on recognizing seven entity types defined in the $L_2$ **Metadata** layer within meeting minute segments (see Fig. 1a). A fine-tuned BERTimbau encoder model was set as our baseline, while Gemini-2.5-Pro served as the generative counterpart, integrated through the LangExtract framework [13]. Evaluation was conducted using Precision, Recall, and F1-score. As shown in Table 4, the fine-tuned transformer achieved consistently strong results across metrics, while the generative model exhibited higher precision but substantially lower recall. The narrow gap between macro and micro F1-scores suggests balanced performance across entity types. A more in-depth analysis reveals that errors are derived from boundary detection rather than misclassification. When classification fails, it is typically due to confusion between participant presence statuses or difficulty distinguishing meeting types (ordinary or extraordinary) caused by sparse training data for the latter. These findings demonstrate the contrasting behaviors of encoder-based and generative models in structured information extraction, highlighting the strengths of the former in handling domain-specific structured text and establishing them as the primary baseline for future research in this task.

***Voting Identification.*** The second task focuses on vote identification, aimed at extracting text spans corresponding to voting-related entities: *Voter-Favor, Voter-Against, Voter-Abstention, Voter-Absent, Voting, Subject, Counting-Unanimity,* and *Counting-Majority,* from annotations in the $L_4$ **Voting** layer. We fine-tuned a BERTimbau model as the encoder baseline and compared it with Gemini-2.5-Pro integrated into the LangExtract framework [13] for generative span extraction. Performance was measured with Precision, Recall, and F1-score (Table 4). The fine-tuned BERTimbau model achieved robust results across most entities, confirming its effectiveness for structured extraction. The gap between macro and micro F1-scores shows uneven performance across entity types: frequent categories such as *Voting* and *Voter-Favor* are recognized more accurately, while less frequent or lexically variable entities like *Subject* are more challenging. As such, the model's primary bottleneck is exact span extraction,

---

[5] https://huggingface.co/collections/liaad/citilink.

not semantic categorization. Despite strong classification performance with negligible type errors, the model exhibits weaknesses in detecting Subject entities and in accurately predicting their boundaries. The generative model achieved moderate precision and recall, resulting in lower overall F1-scores compared to BERTimbau. These findings suggest that encoder-based approaches provide more comprehensive coverage for structured vote identification, establishing a stronger baseline than generative models.

**Table 4.** Evaluation results on Metadata and Vote Identification tasks.

| Task | Model | $F1_{ma}$ | $F1_{mi}$ | $P_{ma}$ | $P_{mi}$ | $R_{ma}$ | $R_{mi}$ |
|---|---|---|---|---|---|---|---|
| Metadata | BERTimbau | 0.752 | 0.959 | 0.743 | 0.958 | 0.771 | 0.960 |
| | Gemini-2.5-Pro | 0.273 | 0.273 | 0.833 | 0.833 | 0.163 | 0.163 |
| Vote | BERTimbau | 0.814 | 0.705 | 0.750 | 0.577 | 0.927 | 0.904 |
| | Gemini-2.5-Pro | 0.556 | 0.584 | 0.527 | 0.529 | 0.596 | 0.651 |

***Topic Classification.*** The third task addresses multi-label topic classification, where each discussion subject ($L_3$: **Subject of Discussion**) is assigned one or more labels from 22 predefined topics (1.69 topics per subject on average). This task is inherently imbalanced and semantically diverse. Both an encoder-based BERTimbau model and Gemini-2.5-Pro were evaluated. Performance was assessed using standard multi-label metrics: macro- and micro-F1 (balanced and overall performance), Hamming Loss (HL; lower is better), and Average Precision (AP). As shown in Table 5, the fine-tuned encoder achieved substantially stronger results across all metrics. Overall, the fine-tuned encoder demonstrated its capacity to handle multi-label settings and class imbalance more effectively than the generative baseline. A deeper analysis reveals that the model's primary failure lies in semantic overlap and hierarchical ambiguity, not thematic misunderstanding. It performs robustly on dominant categories but struggles to distinguish specific labels from general administrative functions. This results in a "generic label" bias and the frequent omission of less represented labels. These findings establish a solid foundation for future experimentation on topic modeling and classification over municipal meeting records.

**Table 5.** Evaluation results on the Multi-label Topic Classification task.

| Task | Model | $F1_{ma}$ | $F1_{mi}$ | HL | $AP_{mi}$ | $AP_{ma}$ |
|---|---|---|---|---|---|---|
| Topic Class. | BERTimbau | 0.642 | 0.822 | 0.029 | 0.870 | 0.681 |
| | Gemini-2.5-Pro | 0.496 | 0.525 | 0.070 | 0.317 | 0.396 |

# 5   Conclusion

In this paper, we introduced CitiLink-Minutes, a novel corpus of 120 densely human-annotated municipal meeting minutes in European Portuguese, created through a partnership with six Portuguese municipalities. The dataset contains high-quality annotations across four layers: personal information, metadata, subjects of discussion, and voting, making it the first resource of its kind to cover all these aspects in municipal records. Its richness and scope support a wide range of downstream NLP and IR tasks, including structured information extraction, vote identification, and multi-label topic classification, and provide reliable baselines for future research. Overall, experiments show that fine-tuned encoder-based models achieve strong performance, while classical ML ensembles handle label imbalance effectively in the topic classification task. These results establish evaluation metrics and reference points for structured municipal texts.

To support responsible sharing and reproducible research, the dataset is openly released under FAIR principles and a Creative Commons Attribution-NonCommercial-NoDerivatives License, ensuring proper attribution, privacy protection, and copyright compliance. It is available through an open-access repository with persistent identifiers and rich metadata, enabling discovery and long-term availability.

Future work will extend the dataset with deeper semantic layers (e.g., finer-grained personal information, subject summaries) and an English-translated version with aligned annotations to support cross-lingual exploration and comparative studies.

## Limitations

While CitiLink-Minutes comprises documents from only six municipalities, these were carefully selected to capture diversity in geographic location and municipal scale. The set includes smaller towns as well as larger urban centers, spanning multiple regions of Portugal and reflecting varied document structures, linguistic conventions, and procedural reporting practices. However, given its targeted scope, the lack of a broader coverage limits the robustness and generalization of downstream NLP models. Consequently, while the dataset offers valuable insights, future expansions will further enhance its geographic and stylistic coverage. Another limitation concerns the recording of voting outcomes, which are sometimes available only at the party level, requiring external knowledge bases to map councilors. Furthermore, in the current version of the voting layer, only the main subject under discussion is captured with finer-grained sub-subjects not yet represented. This limits analyses that require detailed tracking of votes on multiple aspects of the same subject. Future extensions of the dataset aim to incorporate sub-subject annotations, which will enable more granular analyses of municipal deliberations and enhance the dataset's utility for research on the nuances of local governance processes. A final limitation concerns personal identifiers (PI), which are currently replaced with ***. Although this method prioritizes privacy and compliance with data protection requirements, it completely removes the type of PI being redacted, which may affect downstream NLP models. Ongoing efforts are being made to enhance the usability of the dataset for NLP and IR tasks by employing more advanced de-identification techniques while ensuring protection against sensitive information exposure.

**Acknowledgments.** This work is funded by national funds through FCT  Fundação para a Ciência e a Tecnologia, I.P., under the support UID/50014/2025 (https://doi.org/10.54499/UID/50014/2025). This work is also co-funded by Component 5 - Capitalization and Business Innovation, integrated in the Resilience Dimension of the Recovery and Resilience Plan within the scope of the Recovery and Resilience Mechanism (MRR) of the European Union (EU), framed in the Next Generation EU, for the period 2021–2026, within project CitiLink, with reference 2024.07509.IACDC (https://doi.org/10.54499/2024.07509.IACDC). The authors would also like to acknowledge Rodrigo Silva for managing the hosting of the dataset demo.

**Disclosure of Interests.** The authors have no competing interests to declare that are relevant to the content of this article.

# References


1. van Aggelen, A., Hollink, L., Kemman, M., Kleppe, M., Beunders, H.: The debates of the European parliament as linked open data. Semant. Web **8**(2), 271–281 (2016). https://doi.org/10.3233/SW-160227
2. Albuquerque, H.O., et al.: Ulyssesner-br: a corpus of Brazilian legislative documents for named entity recognition. In: International Conference on Computational Processing of the Portuguese Language, pp. 3–14. Springer, Cham (2022)
3. Artstein, R., Poesio, M.: Inter-coder agreement for computational linguistics. Comput. Linguist. **34**(4), 555–596 (2008)
4. Barari, S., Simko, T.: Localview, a database of public meetings for the study of local politics and policy-making in the united states. Sci. Data **10**(1), 135 (2023)
5. Barati, M.: Open government data programs and information privacy concerns: a literature review. JeDEM-eJournal eDemocracy Open Gov. **15**(1), 73–123 (2023)
6. Biemann, C., Bontcheva, K., Eckart de Castilho, R., Gurevych, I., Yimam, S.M.: Collaborative web-based tools for multi-layer text annotation. In: Ide, N., Pustejovsky, J. (eds.) Handbook of Linguistic Annotation, pp. 229–256. Springer, Dordrecht (2017). https://doi.org/10.1007/978-94-024-0881-2_8
7. Campos, R., et al.: CitiLink-Minutes: A Multilayer Annotated Dataset of Municipal Meeting Minutes (2025). https://doi.org/10.25747/7KG6-1K22
8. Cunha, L.F., Yu, N., Silvano, P., Campos, R., Jorge, A.: Leveraging LLMs to improve human annotation efficiency with inception. In: Hauff, C., et al. (eds.) Advances in Information Retrieval, pp. 53–58. Springer, Cham (2025)
9. Erjavec, T., et al.: ParlaMint II: advancing comparable parliamentary corpora across Europe. Language Resources and Evaluation (2024). https://doi.org/10.1007/s10579-024-09798-w
10. Fernandes, L.C., Dobins, G.Z.R., Lotufo, R., Pereira, J.A.: PublicHearingBR: a Brazilian Portuguese dataset of public hearing transcripts for summarization of long documents. arXiv preprint arXiv:2410.07495 (2024)

11. Frasnelli, V., Palmero Aprosio, A.: There's something new about the Italian parliament: the IPSA corpus. In: Calzolari, N., Kan, M.Y., Hoste, V., Lenci, A., Sakti, S., Xue, N. (eds.) Proceedings of the 2024 Joint International Conference on Computational Linguistics, Language Resources and Evaluation (LREC-COLING 2024), pp. 16037–16046. ELRA and ICCL, Torino, Italia (2024). https://aclanthology.org/2024.lrec-main.1394/

12. Garcia Corral, P., Bechara, H., Zhang, R., Jankin, S.: PolitiCause: an annotation scheme and corpus for causality in political texts. In: Calzolari, N., Kan, M.Y., Hoste, V., Lenci, A., Sakti, S., Xue, N. (eds.) Proceedings of the 2024 Joint International Conference on Computational Linguistics, Language Resources and Evaluation (LREC-COLING 2024), pp. 12836–12845. ELRA and ICCL, Torino, Italia (2024). https://aclanthology.org/2024.lrec-main.1124/

13. Goel, A.: Langextract (2025). https://doi.org/10.5281/zenodo.17015090

14. Hu, Y., Ganter, T.J., Deilamsalehy, H., Dernoncourt, F., Foroosh, H., Liu, F.: Meetingbank: a benchmark dataset for meeting summarization. arXiv abs/2305.17529 (2023). https://api.semanticscholar.org/CorpusID:258959349

15. International Organization for Standardization: Language resource management – semantic annotation framework – part 6: Principles of semantic annotation (semaf principles) (2016). https://www.iso.org/standard/60581.html. iSO 24617-6:2016

16. Klie, J.C., Bugert, M., Boullosa, B., Eckart de Castilho, R., Gurevych, I.: The inception platform: machine-assisted and knowledge-oriented interactive annotation. In: Zhao, D. (ed.) Proceedings of the 27th International Conference on Computational Linguistics: System Demonstrations, pp. 5–9. Association for Computational Linguistics (2018). https://aclanthology.org/C18-2002

17. Koehn, P.: Europarl: a parallel corpus for statistical machine translation. In: The Tenth Machine Translation Summit Proceedings of Conference, pp. 79–86. International Association for Machine Translation (2005)

18. Li, M., et al.: Coannotating: uncertainty-guided work allocation between human and large language models for data annotation. In: Proceedings of the 2023 Conference on Empirical Methods in Natural Language Processing. Association for Computational Linguistics (2023). https://doi.org/10.18653/v1/2023.emnlp-main.92

19. Maxfield Brown, E., Weber, N.: Councils in action: automating the curation of municipal governance data for research. Proc. Assoc. Inf. Sci. Technol. **59**(1), 23–31 (2022)

20. Mor-Lan, G., Levi, E., Sheafer, T., Shenhav, S.R.: IsraParlTweet: the Israeli parliamentary and Twitter resource. In: Calzolari, N., Kan, M.Y., Hoste, V., Lenci, A., Sakti, S., Xue, N. (eds.) Proceedings of the 2024 Joint International Conference on Computational Linguistics, Language Resources and Evaluation (LREC-COLING 2024), pp. 9372–9381. ELRA and ICCL, Torino, Italia (2024). https://aclanthology.org/2024.lrec-main.819/

21. Oortwijn, Y., Reidsma, D., op den Akker, R., Heylen, D.: Interrater disagreement resolution: a six-step procedure. In: Proceedings of the 2nd Workshop on Human Evaluation of NLP Systems (HumEval), pp. 137–146. Association for Computational Linguistics, Online (2021). https://aclanthology.org/2021.humeval-1.15

22. Penedo, G., et al.: The fineweb datasets: decanting the web for the finest text data at scale. Adv. Neural. Inf. Process. Syst. **37**, 30811–30849 (2024)

23. Piskorski, J., et al.: SemEval 2025 task 10: multilingual characterization and extraction of narratives from online news. In: Rosenthal, S., Rosá, A., Ghosh, D., Zampieri, M. (eds.) Proceedings of the 19th International Workshop on Semantic

Evaluation (SemEval-2025), pp. 2610–2643. Association for Computational Linguistics, Vienna, Austria (2025). https://aclanthology.org/2025.semeval-1.331/

24. Piskorski, J., et al.: Overview of the clef-2024 checkthat! lab task 3 on persuasion techniques. In: Proceedings of the Working Notes of CLEF 2024 – Conference and Labs of the Evaluation Forum. CEUR Workshop Proceedings, vol. 3740, pp. 299–310. CEUR-WS.org (2024). https://ceur-ws.org/Vol-3740/paper-26.pdf

25. Rehbein, I., Ruppenhofer, J., Brunner, A., Ponzetto, S.P.: Out of the mouths of MPs: speaker attribution in parliamentary debates. In: Calzolari, N., Kan, M.Y., Hoste, V., Lenci, A., Sakti, S., Xue, N. (eds.) Proceedings of the 2024 Joint International Conference on Computational Linguistics, Language Resources and Evaluation (LREC-COLING 2024), pp. 12553–12563. ELRA and ICCL, Torino, Italia (2024). https://aclanthology.org/2024.lrec-main.1098/

26. Reinig, I., Rehbein, I., Ponzetto, S.P.: How to do politics with words: investigating speech acts in parliamentary debates. In: Calzolari, N., Kan, M.Y., Hoste, V., Lenci, A., Sakti, S., Xue, N. (eds.) Proceedings of the 2024 Joint International Conference on Computational Linguistics, Language Resources and Evaluation (LREC-COLING 2024), pp. 8287–8300. ELRA and ICCL, Torino, Italia (2024). https://aclanthology.org/2024.lrec-main.727/

27. Rodrigues, J., et al.: Advancing Neural Encoding of Portuguese with Transformer Albertina PT-*, pp. 441–453. Springer, Cham (2023). https://doi.org/10.1007/978-3-031-49008-8_35

28. Santana, B., Campos, R., Amorim, E., Jorge, A., Silvano, P., Nunes, S.: A survey on narrative extraction from textual data. Artif. Intell. Rev. **56**, 8393–8435 (2023). ISSN 0269-2821

29. Siqueira, F.A., et al.: Segmenting Brazilian legislative text using weak supervision and active learning. Artif. Intell. Law 1–82 (2024)

30. Snow, R., O'Connor, B., Jurafsky, D., Ng, A.: Cheap and fast – but is it good? Evaluating non-expert annotations for natural language tasks. In: Lapata, M., Ng, H.T. (eds.) Proceedings of the 2008 Conference on Empirical Methods in Natural Language Processing, pp. 254–263. Association for Computational Linguistics, Honolulu, Hawaii (2008). https://aclanthology.org/D08-1027/

31. Souza, F., Nogueira, R., Lotufo, R.: BERTimbau: pretrained BERT models for Brazilian Portuguese. In: Cerri, R., Prati, R.C. (eds.) BRACIS 2020. LNCS (LNAI), vol. 12319, pp. 403–417. Springer, Cham (2020). https://doi.org/10.1007/978-3-030-61377-8_28

32. Spangher, A., Ferrara, E., Welsh, B., Peng, N., Tumgoren, S., May, J.: Tracking the newsworthiness of public documents. arXiv preprint arXiv:2311.09734 (2023)

33. Vlantis, D., Gornishka, I., Wang, S.: Benchmarking the simplification of Dutch municipal text. In: Calzolari, N., Kan, M.Y., Hoste, V., Lenci, A., Sakti, S., Xue, N. (eds.) Proceedings of the 2024 Joint International Conference on Computational Linguistics, Language Resources and Evaluation (LREC-COLING 2024), pp. 2217–2226. ELRA and ICCL, Torino, Italia (2024). https://aclanthology.org/2024.lrec-main.199/

34. van Wijk, P., Marx, M.: Spoken question answering on municipal council meetings. In: European Conference on Information Retrieval, pp. 41–46. Springer, Cham (2025)

35. Yrjänäinen, V.A., et al.: The Swedish parliament corpus 1867–2022. In: Calzolari, N., Kan, M.Y., Hoste, V., Lenci, A., Sakti, S., Xue, N. (eds.) Proceedings of the 2024 Joint International Conference on Computational Linguistics, Language Resources and Evaluation (LREC-COLING 2024), pp. 16100–16112. ELRA and ICCL, Torino, Italia (2024). https://aclanthology.org/2024.lrec-main.1400/
36. Zeldes, A.: The GUM corpus: creating multilayer resources in the classroom. Lang. Resour. Eval. **51**(3), 581–612 (2017). https://doi.org/10.1007/s10579-016-9343-x

# Evaluating the Efficiency and Effectiveness of Learned Sparse Retrieval with the `lsr_benchmark`


Maik Fröbe[1]([✉])(ID), Ferdinand Schlatt[1](ID), Cosimo Rulli[2](ID), Tim Hagen[3](ID),
Jan Heinrich Merker[1](ID), Gijs Hendriksen[4](ID), Carlos Lassance[5](ID),
Franco Maria Nardini[2](ID), Rossano Venturini[6](ID), and Martin Potthast[7](ID)

[1] Friedrich-Schiller-Universität Jena, Jena, Germany
`maik.froebe@uni-jena.de`
[2] ISTI-CNR, Pisa, Italy
[3] University of Kassel and hessian.AI, Darmstadt, Germany
[4] Radboud University, Nijmegen, The Netherlands
[5] Cohere, Toronto, Canada
[6] University of Pisa, Pisa, Italy
[7] University of Kassel, hessian.AI, and ScaDS.AI, Darmstadt, Germany



**Abstract.** Learned sparse retrieval (LSR) models exhibit varying trade-offs between effectiveness and efficiency. But while standard tools exist for evaluating LSR effectiveness, there is none for evaluating efficiency. Also, datasets with high-quality relevance judgments are too large for repeated efficiency experiments, e.g., on different hardware configurations. To promote the evaluation of LSR models in terms of their effectiveness and efficiency, we introduce the `lsr_benchmark`, which measures retrieval efficiency at each step of an LSR pipeline (document embedding, indexing, query embedding, and retrieval) as well as its overall effectiveness. To ensure tractability and extensibility, we apply current corpus subsampling methods to eleven TREC tasks, precompute embeddings with eleven LSR models per task, and evaluate eight retrieval engines as baselines. For the benchmark's hosted version, a modular API, along with tools for evaluating effectiveness and efficiency, facilitates the submission of new approaches. Our experiments show that the chosen embedding model significantly affects the efficiency of a retrieval engine and that LSR is more effective but less efficient than BM25—an efficiency gap that our benchmark now tracks as new LSR models are published.

**Keywords:** Learned Sparse Retrieval · Neural IR · Green IR Evaluation


## 1 Introduction

Learned sparse retrieval (LSR) models embed documents and queries into sparse embeddings that weight terms according to their importance in a document or query [47]. They use transformer-based language models to derive these term weights, in contrast to lexical models such as BM25 [50], which use corpus statistics. In this way, LSR integrates what is known in lexical retrieval as query or



R. Campos et al. (Eds.): ECIR 2026, LNCS 16486, pp. 528–543, 2026.
https://doi.org/10.1007/978-3-032-21321-1_57

**Table 1.** The datasets in the `lsr_benchmark` together with the embeddings that we release publicly for retrieval experiments without access to the corpus.

| Corpus | TREC Tracks | Queries | Judgm. | Docs. | Embeddings | |
|---|---|---|---|---|---|---|
| | | | | | Avg. | $\sum$ |
| ClueWeb09 | Web [13–16] | 198 | 84 366 | 315 095 | 117.9 MB | 5.1 GB |
| ClueWeb12 | Web/Dec. [1,17,18] | 150 | 51 765 | 225 636 | 116.0 MB | 3.7 GB |
| Disks 4/5 | Robust04 [60] | 249 | 311 410 | 285 756 | 106.4 MB | 5.7 GB |
| MS MARCO | DL 19/20 [20,21] | 97 | 20 646 | 81 737 | 40.1 MB | 0.9 GB |
| MS MARCO$_{2.1}$ | RAG 24 [58] | 89 | 20 429 | 116 694 | 170.0 MB | 1.8 GB |
| $\sum$ | 11 TREC Tracks | 783 | 488 616 | 1 024 918 | 106.8 MB | 17.2 GB |

document expansion/reduction with embedding into a sparse latent term space, increasing effectiveness compared to lexical retrieval [26,27,35,37].

While the term weights differ between lexical and learned sparse retrieval [42], the representations of queries and documents as high-dimensional sparse vectors are structurally identical. Therefore, retrieval systems that process lexical representations [40,45] can also process LSR representations. But the different term weight distributions cause efficiency optimizations that used to work for lexical retrieval [3,57] to fail for LSR [42], so that new optimizations are required [7,22].

Retrieval engines that have been optimized for learned sparse retrieval substantially improved the latency for LSR embeddings [7,22]. However, previous efficiency experiments did not compare retrieval engines across diverse retrieval scenarios and many LSR models, as many IR evaluations build on web-scale datasets that cannot be processed with LSR models with reasonable cost-effectiveness due the high embedding costs. To enable holistic learned sparse retrieval evaluations that account for effectiveness and efficiency, we present the `lsr_benchmark`. We assume a standard four-step learned sparse retrieval pipeline where (1) documents are embedded and (2) indexed, after which (3) queries are embedded to (4) retrieve results. Efficiency is monitored at each step with the `tirex_tracker` [33] and we persist all measurements in the `ir_metadata` format [2] to make runs fully self-contained. We decouple the embedding step from the retrieval step to ensure that all combinations of embedding models and retrieval engines can be explored easily. We use the recently proposed corpus subsampling methods [29] to enable, for the first time, a systematic evaluation of complex learned sparse retrieval models as first-stage retrievers on web-scale corpora. Table 1 provides an overview of the datasets that we include into the first version of the `lsr_benchmark`.

Our experiments show that there is still a substantial gap between lexical and learned sparse retrieval. LSR achieves higher effectiveness, at the cost of latency in the 90 % percentile, where retrieval latency increases 24-fold across retrieval engines and LSR embeddings. The framework, submission instructions, and aggregated efficiency and effectiveness evaluations are available online.[1]

## 2   Related Work

We review learned sparse retrieval, corpus subsampling, green and efficient IR, and tools which the `lsr_benchmark` aims to support and builds upon.

*Learned Sparse Retrieval (LSR).* Early retrieval systems used lexical priors (e.g., term frequency and inverse document frequency [55]) to represent documents. Such representations are sparse (the number of unique terms in a document is orders of magnitude smaller than the number of possible terms) but can struggle to capture semantics. Learned sparse retrieval improves semantic matching by replacing lexical priors with priors from deep learning models [12,27,37,47,64].

Since lexical and LSR models both use structurally identical output representations, retrieval engines that can handle lexical retrieval can also handle learned sparse retrieval. However, efficient lexical retrieval engines exhibit a tenfold increase in latency when applied to learned sparse representations [42]. Later works improved LSR-latency by specifically designed retrieval engines [7,8,41,43,48]. However, LSR efficiency is often only evaluated on few datasets and models. As our experiments include many retrieval scenarios, embedding models, and retrieval algorithms, we can reproduce cases with previously reported latency differences, but we also find cases where the latency gap between lexical and LSR increases 70-fold, emphasizing the need for further investigations.

*Corpus Subsampling.* High quality evaluation corpora constructed in TREC-style shared tasks come with many graded relevance judgments (beneficial for nDCG) and their reliability for subsequent evaluations can be tested [59]. However, TREC-style collections are often very large (even web-scale), as TREC aimed to transfer the Cranfield Paradigm to large document collections [61]. The size of TREC collections causes problems for the evaluation of modern neural models that have high energy/compute requirements [52]. While building a lexical ClueWeb09 index takes less than a day with PISA [45], embedding 50 % of the ClueWeb09 on an Nvidia V100 GPU takes 71 days [36]. Those high computational costs make it impossible to run efficiency-oriented experiments with neural models and multiple repetitions on web-scale corpora. Corpus subsampling [29] reduces the size of document collections so that expensive neural models can also be reliably evaluated on large corpora. All runs that were pooled are used to take the top-$k$ documents of all pooled systems, where $k$ is substantially larger than the pooling depth, which yields diverse hard-negative documents. We use this to run experiments on collections that would otherwise not be possible.

---

[1] Code, tutorials, and documentation: https://github.com/reneuir/lsr-benchmark
Submission and evaluations: https://www.tira.io/task-overview/lsr-benchmark

*Green IR and Efficiency.* Several studies investigate how to optimize search engine efficiency from the perspective of energy consumption. Catena et al. [11] propose specialized CPU governors that use information on the query server's load to adjust the CPU frequency to reduce the energy consumption which later evolved into energy-aware schedulers that can reduce CPU energy consumption by up to 50 % [10]. With the wide use of large language models, numerous contributions have emphasized that their improved effectiveness comes at the cost of substantially higher hardware and energy demands. Several studies address this issue through strategies aimed at mitigating such resource drifts [52,56]. In this direction, the ReNeuIR workshop at SIGIR fostered an active discussion on alleviating the computational burden of these models [4–6,28]. This ongoing work highlights the need for a holistic and concrete definition of efficiency, as well as the existence of several open research gaps in efficiency-centered evaluation. To help to bridge these gaps, the ReNeuIR community has initiated a shared task initiative. We aim to support such initiatives with our work.

*Related Tooling for Simplified IR Experiments.* The ongoing discussion on how to conduct efficiency-oriented IR experiments [4,6,28] that inspired our work and to which we aim to contribute, needs tool support. Therefore, we build our `lsr_benchmark` compatible with existing IR tooling. The `ir_datasets` [39] framework provides an API for accessing IR evaluation datasets. Our API is compatible with `ir_datasets` and extends it by adding sparse embeddings. Additionally, we need to enable efficiency evaluations. For this, we incorporate the `tirex_tracker` [33], a lightweight native library that can be embedded into many programming languages and monitors all efficiency metrics, thereby following the spirit that there is not yet a consensus on how to measure efficiency. Compared to alternatives such as codecarbon [19], `tirex_tracker` is independent of the programming language, captures the efficiency over time, and can export the monitored resource consumption in the `ir_metadata` format [2], yielding higher compatibility with IR tools. Our `lsr_benchmark` is the first project that uses the `tirex_tracker` in efficiency-oriented experiments to collect efficiency measurements of IR workloads at scale. We aim to be orthogonal and to support theoretically oriented efficiency frameworks such as PEIR [34] (which uses theoretical modeling to assess efficiency). We see our work as an initiative in this direction and hope to inspire similar initiatives in the IR community.

## 3   Overview of the `lsr_benchmark`

The `lsr_benchmark` aims to support holistic evaluations of Learned Sparse Retrieval (LSR) methods, accounting for efficiency and effectiveness. Our LSR pipelines first embed documents and queries into a standardized format (Section 3.2), and then perform the index and retrieve step (Section 3.3). We use TIRA/TIREx [30,31] for the embedding as it allows to process datasets that are not public. The subsequent retrieval experiments can run with any frameworks and infrastructures, while all steps are monitored with the

```
# download pre-computed embeddings
lsr-benchmark download-embeddings \
    --embedding webis/splade \
    --dataset msmarco-passage/trec-dl-2019

# download a run
lsr-benchmark download-run \
    --embedding webis/splade \
    --dataset msmarco-passage/trec-dl-2020 \
    --retrieval seismic
```

**Listing 1.** The command line interface of the `lsr_benchmark` for downloading public pre-computed embeddings (allows easy experiments) and baseline runs.

```
lsr-benchmark evaluate OUTPUT-BY-SEISMIC OUTPUT-BY-NAIVE-SEARCH
```

|  | Seismic | Naïve-Search |
| --- | --- | --- |
| index.runtime_wallclock | 32365 ms | 0 ms |
| index.energy_total | 7.0 | 0.0 |
| retrieval.runtime_wallclock | 35 ms | 858 ms |
| retrieval.energy_total | 0.0 | 0.0 |
| embedding/model | webis/splade | webis/splade |
| embedding/doc.runtime_wallclock | 96789 ms | 96789 ms |
| embedding/doc.energy_total | 17896.0 | 17896.0 |
| embedding/query.runtime_wallclock | 1575 ms | 1575 ms |
| embedding/query.energy_total | 109.0 | 109.0 |
| nDCG@10 | 0.720 | 0.720 |
| ir_dataset | msmarco-passage/trec-dl-2020 | |

**Listing 2.** The `evaluate` command of the `lsr_benchmark` on the command line for comparing runs in terms of efficency and effectiveness and the output.

`tirex_tracker` [33] to capture efficiency-oriented metrics in the `ir_metadata` [2] format. We designed the architecture of the `lsr_benchmark` (Section 3.1) to have a low barrier of entry.

The `lsr_benchmark` is pip-installable. Listing 1 shows how public embeddings and runs can be accessed via the command line. The public embeddings are used as input for retrieval engines, without needing the underlying corpus (only the embeddings are public). The public runs serve as baselines and for exploratory analysis. Listing 2 shows the `evaluate` command that uses run files as input and outputs effectiveness and efficiency measures, e.g., the energy required to embed the documents and queries. The example (Listing 2) compares Seismic [7] with Naïve Search (a simple linear scan) on the same embeddings, showing that Seismic is optimized for low-latency retrieval (`retrieval.runtime_wallclock` of 35 *msec.* vs 858 *msec.*) while it has substantially higher indexing costs.

### 3.1   Architecture of the `lsr_benchmark`

We operationalize the `lsr_benchmark` in four stages that (1) add new datasets, (2) embed queries and documents, (3) run retrieval engines, and (4) compare efficiency and effectiveness. The first two stages run in the TIRA sandbox (open for submissions), and the last two stages operate on the artifacts published from the embedding stage, so that all retrieval experimentation is completely open and can be executed on the side of the experimenter with the tools of their choice. Figure 1 overviews this architecture that we explain next.

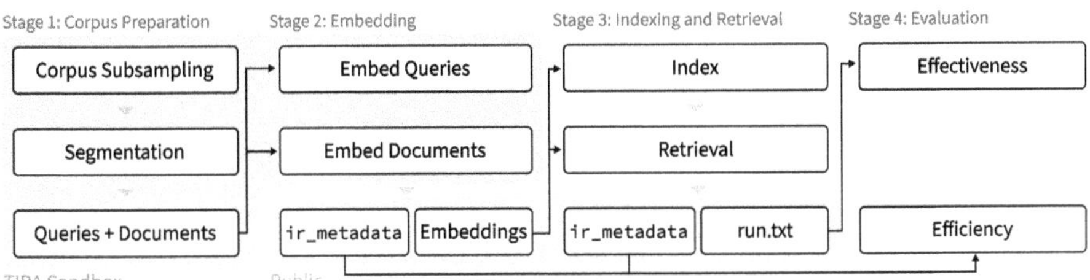


**Fig. 1.** The architecture of the `lsr_benchmark`. Stage one and two run in TIRA to process non-public datasets. Stages three and four build on the embeddings published in stage two and can run on any infrastructure of an experimenter.

*Stage 1 (Adding Corpora).* We first upload a new dataset to TIRA.[2] We focus on TREC-style datasets that have many high-quality relevance judgments from pooling, as this allows us to assess the reliability of evaluations [59]. To add a new dataset, we download all runs submitted to the corresponding TREC tracks to run corpus subsampling [29]. For each dataset, we test for subsampling depths of 100 (was already reliable [29]), 125, 150, and 200 to select a configuration that yields a reasonable corpus size. Note that the corpus subsampling that we use achieved the best reliability compared to other sampling strategies, and that this subsampling is required, as otherwise no experimentation would be possible. After the subsampling, we segment the documents into passages so that embedding approaches that aggregate multiple passages use the same segmentation. We then upload the subsampled and segmented corpora to TIRA. For public corpora (e.g., MS MARCO), the subsamples are public while datasets that can not be publicly shared (e.g., Robust04) are only available in TIRA.

*Stage 2 (Embedding Documents and Queries).* Encoders take the queries and the documents as text and embed them into sparse vectors, commonly represented as a list of term–score tuples. We submit the encoders to TIRA, where they are used to produce the embeddings in the TIRA sandbox without network access—improving reproducibility and ensuring that the data remains private. We also ensure that all embedding models run on the same host, and we track the resource consumption during encoding with the `tirex_tracker`.

---

[2] Documentation: https://github.com/reneuir/lsr-benchmark/tree/main/data.

```
with tracking(export_file_path=output_dir / "query"):
    query_embeddings = model.predict(query_texts)

with tracking(export_file_path=output_dir / "docs"):
    doc_embeddings = model.predict(texts)

save_embeddings(query_embeddings, doc_embeddings, output_dir)
```

**Listing 3.** Example of how queries and documents are embedded.

```
for query_id, tokens, values in query_embeddings:
    print(query_id)  # '1030303'
    print(tokens)    # ['2002' '2010' '2032' ... ]
    print(values)    # [0.02466838 0.49301645 0.99693686 ... ]
```

**Listing 4.** Queries/documents are embedded as token ids and importance scores.

*Stage 3 (Indexing and Retrieval).* Retrieval engines use query and document embeddings to (1) build an index, and (2) perform retrieval. Both stages are monitored with the `tirex_tracker`. We build and publish a set of 8 retrieval engines that can be used as baselines on any target architectures.

*Stage 4 (Efficiency and Effectiveness Evaluations).* After Stage 3 yields retrieval runs, evaluating efficiency and effectiveness as in Listing 2 are possible. As the `tirex_tracker` automatically captures all efficiency information in the `ir_metadata` format, different aspects of efficiency can be evaluated in retrospect.

## 3.2   Embeddings for Learned Sparse Retrieval

Listing 3 shows how we track the efficiency of embedding documents and queries. Loading models and persisting the results is done outside the tracking. We use Lightning IR [53] to run the inference for most models, as it offers a unified API for different model types (other frameworks can be integrated). We include 11 different models in our comparison;[3] mostly SPLADE variants [27] (covering smaller backbones [51] and inference-free architectures for the query [32,46,54]) as well as UniCoil [37] and the sparse variant of the BGE-M3 model [62].

Listing 4 illustrates how queries and documents are represented and how they can be accessed. Each query and document is represented by a list of token ids and corresponding embedding values. Note that we can publish these embeddings, even for restrictively licensed datasets, as one cannot reproduce the original text from the embeddings without substantial effort.

---

[3] 🔗 bge-m3  🔗 OS2 Dist  🔗 OS2 Doc  🔗 OS2 Mini  🔗 OS3 Dist  🔗 Splade  🔗 Splade-v2 Dist  🔗 Splade-v3  🔗 Splade-v3 Dist  🔗 Splade-v3 Doc  🔗 UniCoil

```
lsr_benchmark.register_to_ir_datasets("<DATASET-ID>")
ir_dataset = ir_datasets.load("lsr-benchmark/<DATASET-ID>")
doc_embeddings = ir_dataset.doc_embeddings(model_name="<MODEL>")
query_embeddings = ir_dataset.query_embeddings(model_name="<MODEL>")

with tracking(export_file_path=output_dir / "index"):
    index = build_index(document_embeddings)

with tracking(export_file_path=output_dir / "retrieval"):
    run = retrieval(index, query_embeddings)

save_run(output_dir, output_dir)
```

**Listing 5.** Indexing and retrieval while capturing efficiency metrics.

## 3.3   Retrieval Engines for Learned Sparse Retrieval

The first version of our `lsr_benchmark` comes with eight retrieval engines. All integrations monitor the efficiency of indexing and retrieval with a protocol as showcased in Listing 5 to load, index, and evaluate any of the embeddings.

**DuckDB** [49] is a production ready and efficiency-oriented database system that also comes with tooling to support learned sparse retrieval.

**Naïve Search** represents a simple baseline that exhaustively computes dot products without indexing (implemented in Rust in the SEISMIC package).

**PISA** [45] is a C++ library for efficiency-oriented research, originally for lexical representations that comes with several pruning algorithms [3,23,44,57]. (We include two variants of PISA, one for lexical and one for sparse retrieval.)

**PySerini** [38] wraps the Lucene retrieval engine in Anserini [63]. (We include one variant of PySerini for learned sparse retrieval.)

**PyTerrier** [40] is a research-oriented retrieval engine that is mostly written in Java and aims to scale to large datasets with declarative experimentation. (We include two variants of PyTerrier, one for lexical and one for sparse retrieval.)

**KANNOLO** [22] is a Rust framework for approximate nearest neighbors search for dense and sparse retrieval, focusing on graph-based algorithms (e.g., HNSW).

**SEISMIC** [7–9] implements approximate nearest neighbor search in Rust for sparse embeddings with block partitioning, forward indices, and skip vectors.

## 3.4   Submission of New Embedding Models and Retrieval Engines

We encourage the community to submit new embedding models and new retrieval engines to the `lsr_benchmark`. We envision that efficiency-oriented shared tasks and workshops, such as ReNeuIR [4,6,28] and WOWS [24,25][4] incorporate aspects of the `lsr_benchmark` to grow a community around it. We organize the `lsr_benchmark` in a single mono-repository that contains all code in a clean and consistent structure. Hence, we intend to collect new submissions via pull

---

[4] https://reneuir.org/    https://opensearchfoundation.org/wows2025/.

requests. All code for embedding models and retrieval engines is "dockerized" and compatible with Development Containers,[5] reducing the effort to deploy them on new hardware. For submitting new models, our Lightning IR code should, in many cases, allow TIRA submissions from the existing code with just linking against a different/new Hugging Face model. For collecting diverse efficiency and effectiveness information for retrieval engines, we allow for uploading runs to TIRA, so that executions of the retrieval engines that we dockerized on diverse infrastructure yield a valuable parallel dataset (runs with their monitored executions) with effectiveness and efficiency information. This setup ensures that no prior experience with TIRA is needed to participate in the `lsr_benchmark`.

## 4    Evaluation

We show use cases and future perspectives of the `lsr_benchmark` and report efficiency/effectiveness on our 11 datasets, 11 embedding models, and 8 retrieval engines (968 runs). A leaderboard (hopefully growing over time) is available.[6]

### 4.1    The Efficiency of Learned Sparse Retrieval

We first analyze how retrieval engines and learned sparse embedding models impact the efficiency. We focus our efficiency evaluations on latency and energy consumption of the embedding, indexing, and retrieval captured with the `tirex_tracker` (other efficiency metrics such as CPU utilization, RAM usage, etc. are captured in the `ir_metadata`, but we do not include them in the paper). All embedding models were executed in TIRA on the same machine with Nvidia A100 GPUs, and all retrieval experiments were executed on another machine outside of TIRA (hardware specifications are included in the runs' `ir_metadata`).

Table 2 provides an overview of the efficiency of the eight retrieval engines for indexing and retrieval. The energy is reported on average (i.e., per dataset and embedding) and total (for processing all datasets and embeddings). For latency, we report the 50%, 90%, and 99% percentiles and normalize the values such that they report the elapsed time to index 1000 documents and the time to run retrieval for one query (the energy and latency of embedding documents and queries are excluded for now as we focus on this later). We observe that the retrieval engine has a substantial impact on the efficiency. Engines that allow for low-latency retrieval invest substantial effort into the indexing stage, with Seismic having the highest indexing latency (1.3 s to index 1000 documents in the 50% percentile) that yields the best retrieval latency (0.7 milliseconds in the 50 % percentile). DuckDB and PyTerrier have at many percentiles a higher retrieval latency than the naïve search, which highlights that low-latency is not the only requirement for production-ready systems. Lexical retrieval (the last two rows) is less prone to latency problems than learned sparse retrieval (the 90% and 99% percentiles are very close to the 50 % percentile).

---

[5] https://containers.dev/.

[6] https://www.tira.io/task-overview/lsr-benchmark.

**Table 2.** The efficiency of different LSR and lexical retrieval engines measured as wallclock runtime in milliseconds (50 %, 90 %, and 99 % percentiles) and consumed energy in Joules (average and total) for indexing (runtime per 1 000 documents) and retrieval (runtime per query) across all embeddings and collections.

| Engine | Runtime (ms) | | | | | | Energy (J) | | | |
| | Index | | | Retrieval | | | Index | | Retrieval | |
| | 50 | 90 | 99 | 50 | 90 | 99 | Avg. | Tot. | Avg. | Tot. |
|---|---|---|---|---|---|---|---|---|---|---|
| DuckDB | 31.9 | 54.3 | 87.3 | 12.1 | 113.6 | 191.0 | 0.3 | 4.2 | 0.2 | 34.0 |
| kANNolo | 812.6 | 1206.8 | 1493.5 | 1.1 | 1.9 | 2.3 | 13.3 | 199.5 | 0.0 | 0.0 |
| Naïve | 0.0 | 0.0 | 0.0 | 10.2 | 55.5 | 73.7 | 0.0 | 0.0 | 0.0 | 7.0 |
| PISA | 162.6 | 219.0 | 281.2 | 4.3 | 31.5 | 76.1 | 2.3 | 34.1 | 0.0 | 4.0 |
| Pyserini | 586.6 | 995.3 | 7002.3 | 20.8 | 39.3 | 167.1 | 17.3 | 110.4 | 0.1 | 5.0 |
| PyTerrier | 355.8 | 500.2 | 685.5 | 25.5 | 53.6 | 90.0 | 5.5 | 81.9 | 0.0 | 8.0 |
| Seismic | 1276.8 | 2289.3 | 3366.1 | 0.7 | 3.0 | 4.4 | 21.7 | 325.3 | 0.0 | 0.0 |
| BM25@PyTerrier | 789.2 | 7886.8 | 16012.6 | 16.4 | 18.4 | 19.2 | 69.6 | 1044.0 | 0.0 | 0.0 |
| BM25@PISA | 252.3 | 419.2 | 456.8 | 0.6 | 0.8 | 1.3 | 4.9 | 73.0 | 0.0 | 0.0 |

**Table 3.** Efficiency/Effectiveness comparison of retrieval engines for learned sparse retrieval versus lexical BM25 retrieval in latency in milliseconds at 50%, 90%, and 99% percentiles and the corresponding nDCG@10 effectiveness.

| Engine | Learned Sparse | | | | Lexical (BM25) | | | |
| | Retrieval (ms) | | | nDCG@10 | Retrieval (ms) | | | nDCG@10 |
| | 50 | 90 | 99 | | 50 | 90 | 99 | |
|---|---|---|---|---|---|---|---|---|
| DuckDB | 12.35 | 108.56 | 188.71 | 0.385 | 6.75 | 8.34 | 8.51 | 0.266 |
| Naïve | 9.57 | 54.82 | 73.51 | 0.385 | 3.30 | 5.26 | 7.57 | 0.266 |
| PISA | 3.27 | 31.34 | 69.46 | 0.385 | 0.76 | 1.06 | 1.57 | 0.266 |
| PyTerrier | 24.79 | 51.59 | 89.53 | 0.385 | 20.25 | 26.32 | 26.81 | 0.266 |
| Seismic | 0.70 | 2.94 | 4.30 | 0.380 | 0.04 | 0.04 | 0.05 | **0.216** |

To repeat the study if lexical retrieval allows for more efficient retrieval than learned sparse retrieval (observed in prior work [42] and in Table 2), we build BM25 embeddings for every dataset (not counted in the 11 embeddings). These BM25 embeddings map every term in the query to an importance of 1, and every document term to its BM25 score that we calculate with PyTerrier. In contrast to learned sparse embeddings, the vocabulary size is substantially larger (yielding shorter posting lists). We run all retrieval engines on the BM25 embeddings and compare the efficiency of lexical retrieval with learned sparse retrieval. Only PISA and PyTerrier are initially built for lexical retrieval, whereas engines such as kANNolo and Seismic focus on learned sparse retrieval. The kANNolo retrieval engine failed to process BM25 embeddings (the maximum vocabulary size of kANNolo is $2^{16}$, which is too small for the lexical vocabulary of our datasets). For all other retrieval engines, we show the difference in the retrieval latency and effectiveness for learned sparse retrieval (across all 11 embedding models) and lexical BM25 retrieval in Table 3. Across all reported percentiles and all retrieval engines, BM25 retrieval is faster than learned sparse retrieval. Especially in the higher percentiles, the efficiency difference is substantial, for instance, the average speedup in the 90 % percentile retrieval latency is 24× across the retrieval engines (between 10× for Naïve and 70× for Seismic). Seismic is even faster than PISA in lexical retrieval, but this comes at effectiveness reductions. The nDCG@10 for Seismic is lower for lexical retrieval than for the other engines, as Seismic prunes the search space optimized for learned sparse retrieval, while the other engines do exact search. This highlights that different retrieval engines can have a substantial impact on retrieval efficiency but also that there can be an impact on effectiveness that we study next.

## 4.2   The Effectiveness of Learned Sparse Retrieval

**Table 4.** The nDCG@10 and P@10 of eleven LSR models and two lexical BM25 baselines on all test collections with the energy in Joules for the embeddings.

| Embedding Model | Energy | nDCG@10 | | | | | | P@10 | | | | | |
|---|---|---|---|---|---|---|---|---|---|---|---|---|---|
| | | CW09 | CW12 | DL | R04 | RAG | Avg. | C09 | C12 | DL | R04 | RAG | Avg. |
| BGE-M3 | 509815 | .09 | .23 | .40 | .34 | .20 | .25 | .14 | .30 | .47 | .31 | .30 | .28 |
| OS2 Dist | 45427 | .24 | .34 | .72 | .49 | .43 | .42 | .33 | .43 | .80 | .47 | .59 | .48 |
| OS2 Doc | 45345 | .23 | .33 | .69 | .46 | .37 | .40 | .32 | .41 | .76 | .44 | .53 | .45 |
| OS2 Mini | 31691 | .23 | .33 | .69 | .44 | .35 | .39 | .30 | .40 | .75 | .42 | .51 | .44 |
| OS3 Dist | 46885 | .24 | .33 | .70 | .46 | .37 | .40 | .32 | .40 | .77 | .44 | .52 | .45 |
| Splade | 42445 | .22 | .32 | .74 | .47 | .42 | .40 | .31 | .40 | .81 | .45 | .56 | .46 |
| Splade-v2 Dist | 45490 | .21 | .33 | .72 | .48 | .37 | .40 | .29 | .42 | .80 | .46 | .52 | .46 |
| Splade-v3 | 68183 | .22 | .34 | .74 | .49 | .44 | .42 | .31 | .42 | .82 | .47 | .59 | .47 |
| Splade-v3 Dist | 45543 | .23 | .33 | .75 | .48 | .39 | .41 | .31 | .43 | .82 | .46 | .55 | .47 |
| Splade-v3 Doc | 68326 | .16 | .28 | .71 | .43 | .32 | .36 | .22 | .36 | .77 | .42 | .47 | .41 |
| UniCoil | 54712 | .18 | .27 | .61 | .38 | .32 | .33 | .24 | .34 | .68 | .38 | .45 | .38 |
| BM25 PyTerrier | | .11 | .30 | .48 | .40 | .26 | .30 | .16 | .40 | .57 | .38 | .36 | .35 |
| BM25 PISA | | .10 | .28 | .48 | .41 | .25 | .30 | .14 | .37 | .57 | .39 | .35 | .34 |

We run all 8 retrieval engines on all 11 LSR models to study their effectiveness. For learned sparse retrieval, we observe that the retrieval engine has no impact on the effectiveness (nDCG@10 scores differ only in the third decimal place). Table 4 reports the energy needed to build the embeddings and their effectiveness in nDCG@10 and Precision@10 for all corpora (macro averaged), together with the effectiveness of BM25 in PISA and PyTerrier (they use different defaults). Most LSR engines are more effective than BM25 (UniCoil and BGE-M3 being rather ineffective) and Splade v3 and OS2 Dist. achieving the highest nDCG@10 (we run no significance tests as our analysis is explorative).

**Table 5.** The latency for indexing and retrieving LSR representations of different LSR models in milliseconds for all retrieval engines at 50%, 90%, and 99%.

| Model | Index | | | Retrieval | | |
|---|---|---|---|---|---|---|
| | 50 | 90 | 99 | 50 | 90 | 99 |
| BGE-M3 | 62.1 | 671.0 | 1621.5 | 5.5 | 25.5 | 29.7 |
| OS2 Dist. | 221.3 | 1053.8 | 1562.5 | 32.0 | 104.8 | 164.7 |
| OS2 Doc | 203.3 | 1078.8 | 1985.8 | 4.4 | 21.4 | 27.0 |
| OS2 Mini | 270.0 | 1305.0 | 2741.7 | 4.4 | 20.9 | 26.0 |
| OS3 Dist. | 198.3 | 937.8 | 1276.8 | 4.5 | 20.9 | 24.4 |
| Splade | 227.4 | 1331.9 | 2021.0 | 37.7 | 129.3 | 195.4 |
| Splade2 Dist. | 291.7 | 1762.9 | 3475.3 | 21.0 | 62.9 | 95.2 |
| Splade3 | 220.6 | 1268.6 | 2170.7 | 10.3 | 39.3 | 57.0 |
| Splade3 Dist. | 243.3 | 1443.5 | 2321.5 | 9.6 | 43.3 | 69.0 |
| Splade3 Doc | 225.7 | 1020.3 | 1949.1 | 4.6 | 21.1 | 27.4 |
| UniCoil | 100.7 | 695.2 | 860.0 | 3.2 | 27.6 | 35.4 |

We analyze the impact of different LSR models for all 8 retrieval engines on the indexing and retrieval latency in Table 5. Different LSR models produce different term distributions, and we observe that highly effective models are challenging for efficient indexing and retrieval. UniCoil needs in the 50 % percentile 3.2 milliseconds per query whereas highly effective systems like Splade v3 and OS2 Dist. Need 10.3 respectively 32.0 ms. The 99 % percentiles contain cases where retrieval engines are highly inefficient (reaching 100 ms).

## 4.3  Perspectives

With the `lsr_benchmark`, we support efficiency and effectiveness evaluations to enable new research perspectives. We intend to support shared tasks and hope that also other directions are enabled that are interesting to the community.

*Continuous Intergration.* The `lsr_benchmark` has a focus to support the development of efficient retrieval, but needs to process ca. 20 GB of embeddings. Deriving micro-benchmarks, e.g., via stratifying efficiency percentiles, could yield evaluations that can run on every commit. Developing micro benchmarks that run fast and correlate with the full `lsr_benchmark` would enable continuous intergration.

*Interpolation Between Lexical and Learned Sparse Retrieval.* LSR and lexical retrieval already share the same underlying representations. One interesting direction would be that a retrieval engine can, depending on the query, interpolate between lexical and learned sparse retrieval (e.g., via efficiency predictions).

*Red-Teaming for Efficiency Evaluations.* Given our focus on efficiency, it would be interesting to include retrieval engines that "purposefully cheat" (e.g., efficiency oracles). Such oracles are not reachable but help to identify errors or room for improvement (e.g., knowing which queries come during retrieval).

*Enrichment of the Corpora.* That we publish the document and query embeddings allows for many additional resources that could complement our work. For instance, building query variants only needs access to the public topics and allows to study the efficiency of LSR for queries of different verbosity.

## 5   Conclusion

We presented the `lsr_benchmark` for holistic evaluations of learned sparse retrieval of efficiency and effectiveness. We support datasets derived from web-scale corpora via corpus subsampling by running the LSR models within TIRA and releasing only the resulting embeddings publically so that retrieval engines can directly work on prepared embeddings. We showcased several use-cases for efficiency and effectiveness-oriented evaluations, highlighting that the LSR model substantially impacts the efficiency of an retrieval engine. Our released resources allow to systematically identify efficiency problems at a low barrier of entry to help addressing those problems in a sustainable and reproducible way.

**Acknowledgements.** This work was partially supported by the European Commission under grant agreement GA 101070014 (https://openwebsearch.eu) and by the German Federal Ministry of Research, Technology and Space (BMFTR) through the project "DIALOKIA: Überprüfung von LLM-generierter Argumentation mittels dialektischem Sprachmodell" (01IS24084A-B).

**Disclosure of Interests.** The authors have no competing interests to declare that are relevant to the content of this article.

## References

1. Abualsaud, M., Lioma, C., Maistro, M., Smucker, M.D., Zuccon, G.: Overview of the TREC 2019 decision track. In: Proceedings of TREC 2019 (2019)
2. Breuer, T., Keller, J., Schaer, P.: ir_metadata: an extensible metadata schema for IR experiments. In: Proceedings of SIGIR 2022, pp. 3078–3089, ACM (2022)
3. Broder, A.Z., Carmel, D., Herscovici, M., Soffer, A., Zien, J.: Efficient query evaluation using a two-level retrieval process. In: Proceedings of CIKM 2003, pp. 426–434 (2003)
4. Bruch, S., Fröbe, M., Hagen, T., Nardini, F.M., Potthast, M.: Reneuir at SIGIR 2025: The fourth workshop on reaching efficiency in neural information retrieval. In: Proceedings of SIGIR 2025, pp. 4153–4156, ACM (2025)

5. Bruch, S., Lucchese, C., Nardini, F.M.: Reneuir: Reaching efficiency in neural information retrieval. In: Proceedings of SIGIR 2022, p. 3462–3465, ACM (2022)
6. Bruch, S., Mackenzie, J., Maistro, M., Nardini, F.M.: Reneuir at SIGIR 2023: The second workshop on reaching efficiency in neural information retrieval. In: Proceedings of SIGIR 2023, pp. 3456–3459, ACM (2023)
7. Bruch, S., Nardini, F.M., Rulli, C., Venturini, R.: Efficient inverted indexes for approximate retrieval over learned sparse representations. In: Proceedings of SIGIR 2024, pp. 152–162 (2024)
8. Bruch, S., Nardini, F.M., Rulli, C., Venturini, R.: Pairing clustered inverted indexes with knn graphs for fast approximate retrieval over learned sparse representations. In: Proceedings of CIKM 2024 (2024)
9. Bruch, S., Nardini, F.M., Rulli, C., Venturini, R., Venuta, L.: Investigating the scalability of approximate sparse retrieval algorithms to massive datasets. In: Proceedings of ECIR 2025, pp. 437–445 (2025)
10. Catena, M., Frieder, O., Tonellotto, N.: Efficient energy management in distributed web search. In: Proceedings of CIKM 2018, pp. 1555–1558, ACM (2018)
11. Catena, M., Macdonald, C., Tonellotto, N.: Load-sensitive CPU power management for web search engines. In: Proceedings of SIGIR 2015, pp. 751–754, ACM (2015)
12. Chen, J., Xiao, S., Zhang, P., Luo, K., Lian, D., Liu, Z.: Bge m3-embedding: Multi-lingual, multi-functionality, multi-granularity text embeddings through self-knowledge distillation. arXiv preprint arXiv:2402.03216 (2024)
13. Clarke, C.L.A., Craswell, N., Soboroff, I.: Overview of the TREC 2009 Web track. In: Proceedings of TREC 2009, NIST (2009)
14. Clarke, C.L.A., Craswell, N., Soboroff, I., Cormack, G.V.: Overview of the TREC 2010 Web track. In: Proceedings of TREC 2010, NIST (2010)
15. Clarke, C.L.A., Craswell, N., Soboroff, I., Voorhees, E.M.: Overview of the TREC 2011 Web track. In:Proceedings of TREC 2011, NIST (2011)
16. Clarke, C.L.A., Craswell, N., Voorhees, E.M.: Overview of the TREC 2012 Web track. In: Proceedings of TREC 2012, NIST (2012)
17. Collins-Thompson, K., Bennett, P.N., Diaz, F., Clarke, C., Voorhees, E.M.: TREC 2013 Web track overview. In: Proceedings of TREC 2013, NIST (2013)
18. Collins-Thompson, K., Macdonald, C., Bennett, P.N., Diaz, F., Voorhees, E.M.: TREC 2014 Web track overview. In: Proceedings of TREC 2014, NIST (2014)
19. Courty, B.: mlco2/codecarbon: v2.4.1 (May 2024). https://doi.org/10.5281/zenodo.11171501
20. Craswell, N., Mitra, B., Yilmaz, E., Campos, D.: Overview of the TREC 2020 Deep Learning Track. In: Proceedings of TREC 2020, NIST (2020)
21. Craswell, N., Mitra, B., Yilmaz, E., Campos, D., Voorhees, E.M.: Overview of the TREC 2019 Deep Learning Track. In: Proceedings of TREC 2019, NIST (2019)
22. Delfino, L., Erriquez, D., Martinico, S., Nardini, F.M., Rulli, C., Venturini, R.: kannolo: Sweet and smooth approximate k-nearest neighbors search. In: Proceedings of ECIR 2025, pp. 400–406 (2025)
23. Ding, S., Suel, T.: Faster top-k document retrieval using block-max indexes. In: Proceedings of SIGIR 2011, pp. 993–1002, ACM (2011)
24. Farzana, S.M., et al.: Report on the 1st international workshop on open web search (WOWS 2024) at ECIR 2024. SIGIR Forum **58**(1), 1–13 (2024)
25. Farzana, S.M., et al.: The first international workshop on open web search (WOWS). In: Proceedings of ECIR 2024, LNCS, vol. 14612, pp. 426–431, Springer (2024)

26. Formal, T., Lassance, C., Piwowarski, B., Clinchant, S.: Splade v2: Sparse lexical and expansion model for information retrieval (2021)
27. Formal, T., Piwowarski, B., Clinchant, S.: Splade: Sparse lexical and expansion model for first stage ranking. In: Proceedings of SIGIR 2021, pp. 2288–2292 (2021)
28. Fröbe, M., Mackenzie, J., Mitra, B., Nardini, F.M., Potthast, M.: ReNeuIR at SIGIR 2024: The third workshop on reaching efficiency in neural information retrieval. In: Proceedings of SIGIR 2024, pp. 3051–3054, ACM (2024)
29. Fröbe, M., et al.: Corpus Subsampling: Estimating the Effectiveness of Neural Retrieval Models on Large Corpora. In: Proceedings of ECIR 2025, pp. 453–471, LNCS, Springer (2025)
30. Fröbe, M., et al.: The information retrieval experiment platform. In: Proceedings of SIGIR 2023, pp. 2826–2836, ACM (2023)
31. Fröbe, M., et al.: Continuous integration for reproducible shared tasks with TIRA.io. In: Proceedings of ECIR 2023, pp. 236–241, LNCS, Springer (2023)
32. Geng, Z., Wang, Y., Ru, D., Yang, Y.: Towards competitive search relevance for inference-free learned sparse retrievers (2025)
33. Hagen, T., Fröbe, M., Merker, J.H., Scells, H., Hagen, M., Potthast, M.: Tirex tracker: The information retrieval experiment tracker. In: Proceedings of SIGIR 2025, pp. 3764–3771, ACM (2025)
34. Khandel, P., Yates, A., Varbanescu, A.L., de Rijke, M., Pimentel, A.D.: PEIR: modeling performance in neural information retrieval. In: Proceedings of ECIR 2025, pp. 279–294, LNCS, Springer (2025)
35. Lassance, C., Déjean, H., Formal, T., Clinchant, S.: Splade-v3: New baselines for splade (Mar 2024)
36. Lawrie, D.J., Kayi, E.S., Yang, E., Mayfield, J., Oard, D.W.: PLAID SHIRTTT for large-scale streaming dense retrieval. In: Proceedings of SIGIR 2024, pp. 2574–2578, ACM (2024)
37. Lin, J., Ma, X.: A few brief notes on deepimpact, coil, and a conceptual framework for information retrieval techniques (Jun 2021)
38. Lin, J., Ma, X., Lin, S., Yang, J., Pradeep, R., Nogueira, R.: Pyserini: a python toolkit for reproducible information retrieval research with sparse and dense representations. In: Proceedings of SIGIR 2021, pp. 2356–2362, ACM (2021)
39. MacAvaney, S., Yates, A., Feldman, S., Downey, D., Cohan, A., Goharian, N.: Simplified data wrangling with ir_datasets. In: Proceedings of SIGIR 2021, pp. 2429–2436, ACM (2021)
40. Macdonald, C., Tonellotto, N., MacAvaney, S., Ounis, I.: PyTerrier: Declarative experimentation in Python from BM25 to dense retrieval. In: Proceedings of CIKM 2021, pp. 4526–4533, ACM (2021)
41. Mackenzie, J., Mallia, A., Moffat, A., Petri, M.: Accelerating learned sparse indexes via term impact decomposition. In: Proceedings of EMNLP 2022, pp. 2830–2842 (2022)
42. Mackenzie, J., Trotman, A., Lin, J.: Wacky weights in learned sparse representations and the revenge of score-at-a-time query evaluation (Oct 2021)
43. Mallia, A., Mackenzie, J., Suel, T., Tonellotto, N.: Faster learned sparse retrieval with guided traversal. In: Proceedings of SIGIR 2022, pp. 1901–1905 (2022)
44. Mallia, A., Ottaviano, G., Porciani, E., Tonellotto, N., Venturini, R.: Faster block-max WAND with variable-sized blocks. In: Proceedings of SIGIR 2017, pp. 625–634, ACM (2017)
45. Mallia, A., Siedlaczek, M., Mackenzie, J., Suel, T.: PISA: performant indexes and search for academia. In: Proceedings of OSIRRC@SIGIR 2019, pp. 50–56 (2019)

46. Nardini, F.M., Nguyen, T., Rulli, C., Venturini, R., Yates, A.: Effective inference-free retrieval for learned sparse representations. In: Proceedings of SIGIR 2025, pp. 2936–2940 (2025)
47. Nguyen, T., MacAvaney, S., Yates, A.: A unified framework for learned sparse retrieval. In: Proceedings of ECIR 2023, pp. 101–116 (Apr 2023)
48. Qiao, Y., Yang, Y., He, S., Yang, T.: Representation sparsification with hybrid thresholding for fast splade-based document retrieval. In: Proceedings of SIGIR 2023, pp. 2329–2333 (2023)
49. Raasveldt, M., Mühleisen, H.: Duckdb: an embeddable analytical database. In: Proceedings of SIGMOD 2019, pp. 1981–1984, ACM (2019)
50. Robertson, S.E., Walker, S., Jones, S., Hancock-Beaulieu, M., Gatford, M.: Okapi at trec-3. In: Proceedings of TREC 1994, NIST (1994)
51. Sanh, V., Debut, L., Chaumond, J., Wolf, T.: Distilbert, a distilled version of bert: smaller, faster, cheaper and lighter (Mar 2020)
52. Scells, H., Zhuang, S., Zuccon, G.: Reduce, reuse, recycle: Green information retrieval research. In: Proceedings of SIGIR 2022, pp. 2825–2837 (2022)
53. Schlatt, F., Fröbe, M., Hagen, M.: Lightning IR: straightforward fine-tuning and inference of transformer-based language models for information retrieval. In: Proceedings of WSDM 2025, pp. 1048–1051, ACM (2025)
54. Shen, X., Geng, Z., Yang, Y.: Exploring $\ell_0$ sparsification for inference-free sparse retrievers. In: Proceedings of SIGIR 2025, pp. 2572–2576 (2025)
55. Sparck Jones, K.: A statistical interpretation of term specificity and its application in retrieval. J. Doc. **28**(1), 11–21 (1972)
56. Strubell, E., Ganesh, A., McCallum, A.: Energy and policy considerations for deep learning in NLP. In: Proceedings of ACL 2019, pp. 3645–3650, ACL (2019)
57. Turtle, H., Flood, J.: Query evaluation: strategies and optimizations. Inform. Process. Manage. **31**(6), 831–850 (1995)
58. Upadhyay, S., et al.: A large-scale study of relevance assessments with large language models: An initial look. CoRR **abs/2411.08275** (2024)
59. Voorhees, E.M.: The philosophy of information retrieval evaluation. In: Proceedings of CLEF 2001, LNCS, vol. 2406, pp. 355–370, Springer (2001)
60. Voorhees, E.M.: Overview of the TREC 2004 Robust track. In: Proceedings of TREC 2004, NIST (2004)
61. Voorhees, E.M.: The evolution of cranfield. In: Proceedings of CLEF 2019, pp. 45–69, Springer (2019)
62. Xiao, S., Liu, Z., Zhang, P., Muennighoff, N., Lian, D., Nie, J.Y.: C-pack: Packaged resources to advance general chinese embedding (May 2024)
63. Yang, P., Fang, H., Lin, J.: Anserini: enabling the use of Lucene for information retrieval research. In: Proceedings of SIGIR 2017, pp. 1253–1256, ACM (2017)
64. Zamani, H., Dehghani, M., Croft, W.B., Learned-Miller, E., Kamps, J.: From neural re-ranking to neural ranking: Learning a sparse representation for inverted indexing. In: Proceedings of CIKM 2018, pp. 497–506 (2018)

# ClaimPT: A Portuguese Dataset of Annotated Claims in News Articles


Ricardo Campos[1,3]([✉]), Raquel Sequeira[1,3], Sara Nerea[1,3],
Inês Cantante[2,3], Diogo Folques[1,3], Luís Filipe Cunha[2,3],
João Canavilhas[1], António Branco[4,5], Alípio Jorge[2,3], Sérgio Nunes[2,3],
Nuno Guimarães[2,3], and Purificação Silvano[2,3]

[1] University of Beira Interior, Covilhã, Portugal
`ricardo.campos@ubi.pt`
[2] University of Porto, Porto, Portugal
[3] INESC TEC, Porto, Portugal
[4] University of Lisbon, Lisbon, Portugal
[5] NLX Group, Lisbon, Portugal



**Abstract.** Fact-checking remains a demanding and time-consuming task, still largely dependent on manual verification and unable to match the rapid spread of misinformation online. This is particularly important because debunking false information typically takes longer to reach consumers than the misinformation itself; accelerating corrections through automation can therefore help counter it more effectively. Although many organizations perform manual fact-checking, this approach is difficult to scale given the growing volume of digital content. These limitations have motivated interest in automating fact-checking, where identifying claims is a crucial first step. However, progress has been uneven across languages, with English dominating due to abundant annotated data. Portuguese, like other languages, still lacks accessible, licensed datasets, limiting research, Natural Language Processing (NLP) developments, and applications. In this paper, we introduce ClaimPT, a dataset of European Portuguese news articles annotated for factual claims, comprising 1,308 articles and 6,875 individual annotations. Unlike most existing resources based on social media or parliamentary transcripts, ClaimPT focuses on journalistic content, collected through a partnership with LUSA, the Portuguese News Agency. To ensure annotation quality, two trained annotators labeled each article, with a curator validating all annotations according to a newly proposed scheme. We also provide baseline models for claim detection, establishing initial benchmarks and enabling future NLP and Information Retrieval (IR) applications. By releasing ClaimPT, we aim to advance research on low-resource fact-checking and enhance understanding of misinformation in news media.

**Keywords:** Claim Detection · Fact-checking · Misinformation · Annotated Dataset · Low-resource Languages · News Articles

# 1   Introduction

Fact-checking plays a crucial role in mitigating misinformation, but it remains a demanding, largely manual process that cannot keep pace with the scale and speed of misinformation [18]. In recent years, organizations such as Politi-Fact[1] have been established to perform systematic manual verification of claims through a multi-step process [26]: (i) identifying claims; (ii) prioritizing the most relevant ones; (iii) collecting evidence from trustworthy sources; and (iv) producing a verdict by comparing the claim against the gathered evidence. While effective for individual cases, this workflow becomes impractical when applied to the vast volume of daily online content. For instance, assessing a claim such as *"In just a few years, the number of immigrants has nearly quadrupled"*, requires retrieving information from multiple sources, evaluating reliability, and synthesizing evidence into a conclusion, an effort difficult to sustain at scale. To address these challenges, automated fact-checking has emerged as a promising research area [16,28], with claim identification recognized as a crucial first step.

Initiatives such as CheckThat! at CLEF 2020 [4] have encouraged research in this field. However, progress remains uneven across languages. Most corpora focus on English and on identifying claims in social media [7,23] and political debates [19], where language tends to be more informal, spontaneous, and conversational. Few studies have examined claims in news articles [10], a valuable yet underexplored domain. News articles constitute a particularly suitable genre for claim identification as they systematically embed quotations from public figures within an ostensibly factual and neutral journalistic narrative. Unlike opinion articles or editorial texts, which are explicitly evaluative and argumentative, news reporting is expected to adhere to standards of objectivity and impartiality. However, the quoted statements reported may still introduce claims whose truthfulness is not guaranteed and must therefore be independently verified. Given the authority typically attributed to quoted speakers and the potential influence of their statements on public opinion, identifying and analyzing claims in news articles is especially critical. This underscores the need for dedicated resources that capture the unique properties of claims in news writing.

In this paper, we introduce ClaimPT, a novel dataset of 1,308 Portuguese news articles with annotated claims. Unlike existing corpora centered on social media or parliamentary discourse, ClaimPT is grounded in professionally edited journalistic content collected through a partnership with LUSA, the Portuguese News Agency. Building on the work of Reddy et al. [10], who proposed News-Claims for English COVID-19 news, ClaimPT extends coverage to a broader range of topics, reflecting the diversity of real-world reporting, and enriches significantly the annotation scheme. In this work, a *claim* is defined as a statement that asserts an alleged real-world fact of public interest, which can be verified [18]. For the purpose of ClaimPT, we consider only declarative sentences occurring in the context of direct speech. Given a news article, our ultimate goal is to automatically identify the claim and its sub-elements. To ensure high-quality

---

[1] http://www.politifact.com.

annotations, each article was independently labeled by two trained annotators, with the final version reviewed and consolidated by an experienced curator. The annotation scheme accommodates multiple labels per claim to improve claim contextualization. To assess how well this task can be approached automatically, we conduct baseline experiments using state-of-the-art pre-trained and generative language models, establishing initial benchmarks and highlighting key challenges for automated claim detection in Portuguese.

Our contributions are thus threefold: 1) We introduce ClaimPT, a new dataset of Portuguese news articles annotated for claim detection; 2) We propose a new annotation scheme specifically tailored to capture the characteristics of claims in news articles and 3) We conduct comprehensive baseline experiments on ClaimPT, leveraging state-of-the-art pre-trained and generative language models, providing benchmark results for automated claim detection in Portuguese.

The remainder of this paper is structured as follows. Section 2 describes related contributions within the specific field of claim detection. Section 3 describes the data acquisition process and the proposed annotation methodology, and provides a quantitative analysis, including inter-annotator agreement scores. Section 4 characterizes the ClaimPT dataset. Section 5 establishes baseline models for claim detection on the ClaimPT dataset, providing initial benchmarks. Finally, we present some final considerations in Sect. 6, pointing towards future work.

## 2    Related Work

Fact-checking has become a crucial tool for verifying information of public interest disseminated by social actors [6]. In recent years, automated fact-checking has been commonly framed as a pipeline comprising several subtasks, including claim detection (identifying check-worthy claims), and claim verification (assessing veracity) [18,22,28,32,39]. Early research on claim detection explored opinionated statements in online discussions such as weblogs and Wikipedia forums [31]. The ClaimBuster system [18] formalized the task by ranking statements from U.S. presidential debates according to their check-worthiness. Subsequent initiatives such as the CLEF CheckThat! lab series [3,4,9] consolidated the task through shared benchmarks, primarily focused on political debates and social media content. These works typically frame claim detection as a classification or ranking problem that separates factual from non-factual statements [40]. Despite steady progress, supervised models lag behind human performance [26], motivating the expansion of CheckThat! to new domains such as COVID-19 misinformation. Recent work has broadened the scope and modalities of claim detection, applying it to diverse domains including health [1,34], environmental issues [38], political debates [9,12,18], and social media posts [25,34]. Other approaches rely on fact-checking archives [8,21], synthetic claim generation [22], or multimodal settings that integrate text, video, and image data [13,43]. Nevertheless, textual claims remain central to professional fact-checking workflows [26].

Among text-based resources, NewsClaims [10] represents an important step forward, providing manually annotated English news claims with additional attributes, such as span, claimer, topic, and stance, that enrich contextual understanding. Such attribute-aware formulations support fact-checkers by clarifying who made the claim and what it concerns, facilitating interpretation and verification [26]. Despite these advances, multilingual coverage remains limited. Most resources are English-centric, with few available for Portuguese. Datasets like Fake.Br [24] offer partial coverage for Brazilian and European Portuguese, but remain narrow in scope. "Polígrafo", a Portuguese fact-checking outlet, was used to label short statements for X-Fact [17], yet large-scale, open Portuguese resources are still lacking. As noted by Panchendrarajan and Zubiaga [28], this scarcity hampers the development of localized fact-checking tools. While multilingual and cross-lingual models mitigate the gap to some extent [26], native datasets remain crucial to capture language-specific nuances. More recently, systems such as Explainable Automatic Fact-Checking for Journalists [2] have introduced end-to-end automated fact-checking frameworks designed to assist journalists, with current implementations focused on English, and pointing toward the need for scalable, language-specific datasets for other languages, including Portuguese. To address these limitations, ClaimPT focuses on European Portuguese and on claims appearing in professionally edited news articles, thus aiming to advance claim detection in low to mid-resource settings.

## 3   The ClaimPT Dataset

### 3.1   Data Acquisition

News articles are intended to be objective, impartial, and factual, but they frequently incorporate statements from diverse sources whose accuracy cannot be assumed and may require verification. This inherent tension between journalistic neutrality and the reporting of potentially disputable claims makes news reporting a particularly relevant genre for our study, and therefore motivated its selection for the construction of the dataset. A protocol established with the Portuguese news agency LUSA granted access to a corpus of news articles spanning politics, society, economics, international affairs, sports, health, culture, science and environment, local news, and technology. The initial retrieval yielded 1,808 articles, from which a pilot sample of 100 was analyzed to refine the selection criteria. This exploratory analysis revealed that politics and international news contained the highest density of claims, whereas sports exhibited minimal claim content. Accordingly, a second request prioritized claim-rich topics to enhance the dataset's representativeness. Since our objective was to target claims in direct speech, the retrieval parameters were further refined to target sentences containing reporting verbs (e.g., "said", "declared"). Data acquisition proceeded in two sequential phases to ensure temporal consistency, covering news articles from 4 January 2022 to 28 December 2023. The final corpus comprises 1,308 news articles obtained through this iterative process. Importantly, the dataset also includes articles that do not contain claims or non-claims, thus enabling a more accurate assessment of their distribution within news reporting.

## 3.2  Annotation Scheme and Process

The ClaimPT annotation scheme was designed to systematically identify and categorize claims and non-claims in Portuguese news articles, thereby contributing to the creation of resources for automated claim detection and fact-checking. It builds upon established frameworks such as NewsClaims [10] and Claim-Buster [18]. The former served as the main structural foundation, from which we adopted key dimensions including topic, stance, claim object, and claimer. The latter provided the conceptual distinction between claims and non-claims and offered valuable insights into the criteria to identify them.

Building on this foundation, ClaimPT advances previous schemas by introducing a multi-layer architecture that connects entity-level information with document metadata and relational links. In contrast to earlier approaches that treated each claim as an isolated unit, ClaimPT integrates metadata, entities with attributes, and link structures, thereby enabling a more comprehensive representation of the claim and of contextual information. This integration allows annotators to capture complex instances in which, for example, identifying a claim requires considering the broader text or retrieving information about the claimer from preceding discourse. This contextual information is captured, for instance, through the annotation of metadata and through an *Identity_ link* that represents the correferential connections regarding the claimer. Alongside the dimensions of topic, stance, claim span, claim object, and claimer adopted from NewsClaims, our scheme introduces an additional temporal dimension, a label representing the time interval during which the claim was made. This temporal information is crucial not only for assessing the claim's relevance to current events but also for defining the appropriate timeframe for verification, which must precede the claim's date of utterance. In addition, our scheme enriches the representation of the claimer entity by assigning it an attribute (e.g., person, institution). This addition allows for a more fine-grained characterization of the claim and supports analyses that account for how the nature of the source [37] influences the framing, credibility, and dissemination of claims. Figure 1 gives an overview of the annotation scheme, organized in three main layers.

The **first layer** encodes the *metadata* of each news article, capturing its thematic classification and publication date under the labels *News Article Topic* and *Publication Time*. The first assigns each article to one of ten predefined categories: *Politics, Society, Economy, International, Sports, Health, Culture, Science and Environment, Technology,* or *Local*. The latter records the publication time of the article's release date. At the core of the scheme is the distinction between *claims* and *non-claims*, the **second layer**. *Claims* are defined as verifiable statements of public interest, typically expressed in declarative form and attributed to an external source rather than the journalist (*"The Government had promised to extend the surface metro to Costa da Caparica and that promise was not fulfilled"*). In contrast, *non-claims* correspond to subjective or speculative utterances, such as opinions, beliefs, or predictions, which cannot be verified against factual evidence (*"I believe that the decision of the President of the Republic [of Guinea-Bissau] is not right."*). In a **third layer**, each claim is further decom-

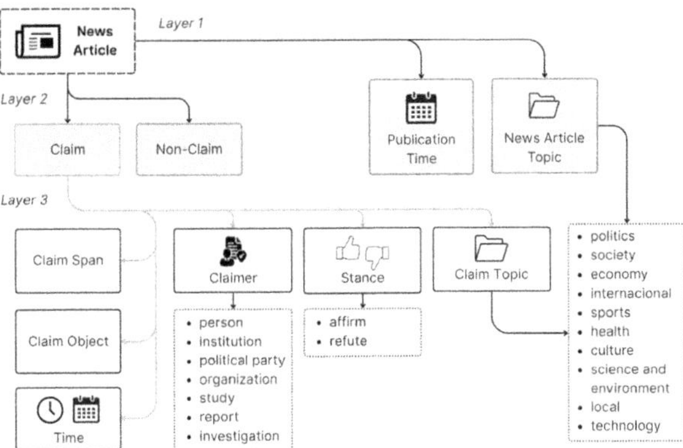

**Fig. 1.** Overview of the annotation scheme.

posed into a set of fine-grained components capturing its internal structure. The *claim span* identifies the textual segment that conveys a complete factual assertion, while the *claim object* denotes the specific target or proposition being asserted. The *claimer* represents the agent responsible for the statement, and has attributes such as a person, organization, institution, or report. Only non-official sources, that is, those not considered inherently unquestionable according to journalistic standards, are annotated as claimers in our framework. Identifying the claimer is therefore crucial for establishing whether a statement qualifies as a claim, as utterances from institutional authorities such as the WHO are often exempt from explicit verification. Temporal information explicitly or implicitly associated with the claim is marked under the *time* label, and the *stance* label specifies whether the claimer affirms or refutes the claim within the claim span. Finally, each claim is assigned a *claim topic*, drawn from the same taxonomy as the article-level topic but determined solely by the claim's immediate content. Additionally, we include two link structures: *attribute* and *identity* links. The first connects claims with their corresponding span, object, claimer, and time, ensuring the internal coherence of each annotation. The second establishes referential and temporal anaphoric connections across the text, linking pronouns or abbreviated mentions to their full antecedents, such as "he" to "Prime Minister António Costa", which is also a novelty in relation to prior proposals, and time intervals, such as the time the claim is uttered to the publication time of the news articles. Figure 2 shows an example of the ClaimPT annotation framework.

The annotation methodology followed a multi-stage, iterative process designed to ensure accuracy, consistency, and reproducibility. Before large-scale annotation began, a structured training phase was implemented to assess the annotators' understanding of the scheme. Each annotator completed two trial rounds on a sample of ten articles, after which results were discussed with the curator to resolve disagreements and refine label definitions and attribute specifications. This preliminary phase also provided an estimate of the average anno-

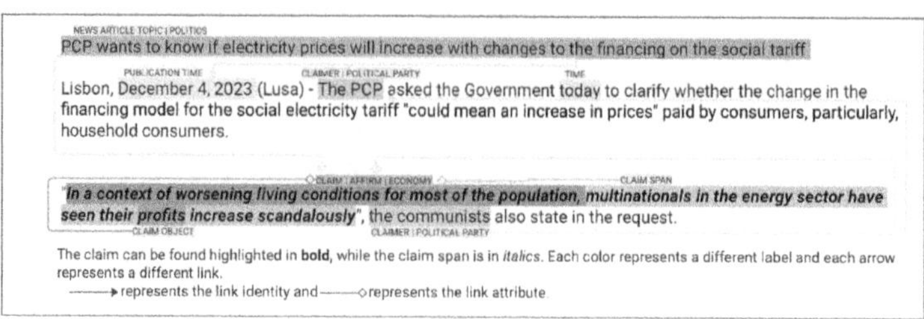


**Fig. 2.** Annotation Scheme example.

tation time, approximately twenty minutes per article, and an expected productivity of around fifty articles per week.

Based on the outcomes of this pilot phase, both the annotation guidelines and methodology were reviewed and finalized prior to the large-scale annotation. The process was then organized into four stages. First, annotators carefully read the full text of each news article. Next, they annotated the metadata (*News Article Topic* and *Publication Time*), followed by claim identification, during which annotators examined all direct-speech sentences to determine whether they constituted claims or non-claims, applying the definitional and linguistic criteria outlined in the manual[2]. In this phase, all components of each claim were also marked. For the annotation of the *claimer* label, our guidelines draw on a journalistic classification of claim sources. The utterances attributed to official sources which represent entities from which journalists typically obtain factual information [15, 33] were not annotated, since these are regarded as trustworthy. In contrast, statements whose claimers may raise uncertainty or require further scrutiny are annotated, reflecting the verification processes that would occur in real-world journalistic practice.

Each news article was independently annotated by two trained annotators with academic backgrounds in communication studies. The annotations were then validated by an experienced curator with expertise in linguistics and a proven record in the curation of other annotation initiatives [27]. The entire annotation process was supervised by a senior researcher with extensive experience in large-scale annotation projects (e.g., [29]). The supervisor organized regular meetings in which annotators and curator discussed cases of disagreement, reviewed challenging examples, and, in instances where consensus could not be reached, the final decision on the annotation was made by the supervisor to ensure consistency and methodological coherence across the dataset. All annotation work was carried out using the INCEpTION platform [20]. The resulting dataset is available online (see the GitHub repository) with a persistent DOI [5].

---

[2] Available at: https://github.com/LIAAD/ClaimPT.

**Table 1.** Inter-Annotator Agreement regarding Claim/Non-claim as well as the Claim attributes (only on the subset where the annotators agreed on the Claim).

(a) Claim/Non-claim

| Labels/ Metrics | Claim | Non-Claim |
|---|---|---|
| F1 | 0.5036 | 0.5435 |
| Jaccard(%) | 33.65 | 37.32 |
| Micro-F1 | 0.5390 | |
| Macro-F1 | 0.5236 | |

(b) Claim attributes

| Attributes/ Metrics | Span | Object | Claimer | Time |
|---|---|---|---|---|
| F1 | 0.7593 | 0.4393 | 0.7980 | 0.9348 |
| Jaccard(%) | 61.20 | 28.15 | 66.39 | 87.77 |
| Micro-F1 | 0.7196 | | | |
| Macro-F1 | 0.7329 | | | |

## 3.3 Inter-Annotator Agreement

Following the annotation process and curator review, agreement was evaluated at the span level through a one-to-one match between annotators, applying a **±4-character** boundary tolerance to mitigate minor selection discrepancies. Two levels of analysis were conducted: (i) agreement on *Claim* vs. *Non-Claim* labels, and (ii) agreement on claim attributes: *Claim span*, *Claim object*, *Claimer*, and *Time*, restricted to cases where both annotators agreed on the claim label.

Table 1 presents the results, displaying matched spans and disagreements. While nominal Krippendorff's Alpha is a standard IAA metric, it assumes a fixed, shared item set, which is unsuitable for span-based annotation, where one annotator may omit a span. Moreover, cases labeled as <no annotation> distort results, if included, and obscure disagreement if excluded. To address these issues, we adopted **overlap-based metrics**, specifically per-label Jaccard (% agreement) and inter-annotator F1 (*Sørensen–Dice*), which more accurately capture agreement at the span level.

For *Claim/Non-Claim* (Table 1a), agreement is moderate, with a Jaccard score of 33.65% and F1 of 0.5036 for *Claim*. While these results may seem modest, they primarily reflect the intrinsic ambiguity and subjectivity of the task. The annotation guidelines specify a credibility criterion, whereby statements from inherently reliable sources (e.g., the World Health Organization) should remain unannotated. However, this criterion was applied inconsistently in some cases, resulting in documents annotated by only one annotator and consequently reducing span-overlap scores. This issue, identified during the curation phase, was subsequently corrected. Restricting the evaluation to spans annotated by both annotators improves agreement, with Jaccard rising to 36.71% and F1 to 0.5371. These findings are consistent with prior work, where reported agreement levels for claim identification typically range between 0.3 and 0.5 (30–50%) [10]. Among claim attributes (Table 1b), *Claim object* exhibits the lowest agreement (F1 = 0.4393; Jaccard = 28.15%), reflecting its interpretive nature. In contrast, *Claim span*, *Claimer*, and *Time* achieve substantially higher agreement (F1 between 0.7593 and 0.9348; Jaccard 61–88%), indicating that once a claim is identified, its main attributes can be reliably annotated.

**Table 2.** Distribution of topics regarding the news article and the individual claims in the *ClaimPT* dataset.

(a) News Article Topics

| News Topic | Count | Percent (%) |
|---|---|---|
| international | 285 | 21.79 |
| politics | 181 | 13.84 |
| health | 154 | 11.77 |
| local | 145 | 11.09 |
| society | 129 | 9.86 |
| sports | 108 | 8.26 |
| science and environment | 100 | 7.65 |
| economy | 100 | 7.65 |
| culture | 65 | 4.97 |
| technology | 41 | 3.13 |
| **Total** | **1308** | **100** |

(b) Claim Topics

| Claim Topic | Count | Percentage (%) |
|---|---|---|
| Politics | 105 | 22.68 |
| Society | 100 | 21.60 |
| International | 73 | 15.77 |
| Economy | 47 | 10.15 |
| Local | 43 | 9.29 |
| Health | 43 | 9.29 |
| Science and Environment | 37 | 7.99 |
| Culture | 9 | 1.94 |
| Technology | 3 | 0.65 |
| Sports | 3 | 0.65 |
| **Total** | **463** | **100** |

## 4    ClaimPT Dataset Characterization

The *ClaimPT* dataset consists of 1,308 news articles provided by the *Lusa News Agency*, with an average length of 542.8 words per article. Of these, 1,090 articles are annotated with *Claims* and *Non-Claims*, while the remaining 218 include only metadata annotations, specifically *News Article Topic* and *Publication Time*. The number of annotated *News Article Topics* and *Publication Times* is equal to the total number of documents (1,308), as each document contains exactly one annotation of each type.

In terms of thematic coverage of the news articles, the most frequent topic is *International* news, accounting for 21.79% of the dataset, followed by *Politics* with 13.84%. A complete distribution of documents by topic is presented in Table 2a.

Of the 1,090 fully annotated documents, 273 ($\approx$ 25%) contain both *Claim* and *Non-Claim* annotations, while the remaining documents include only *Non-Claims*. In total, 463 *Claims* were identified, corresponding to an average of 0.42 per document, and 4,393 *Non-Claims*, averaging 4.03 per document. This yields a global distribution of 9.53% *Claims* and 90.47% *Non-Claims*. This distribution is in line with the nature and editorial principles of news articles, which favor factual information over the explicit formulation of check-worthy claims. As a result, only a limited subset of statements in news articles qualifies as claims under our annotation criteria, making a low claim frequency an expected characteristic of this genre. At the same time, this scarcity highlights the intrinsic difficulty of the claim identification task in news articles: relevant claims are sparse, embedded, and often indirect. However, their limited number does not diminish the significance of the task; rather, it underscores its relevance and serves to expose a core challenge that automated systems must address when operating on real-world news data. As a matter of fact, although it results in a class imbalance, it provides a realistic setting for training and evaluating claim detection models, encouraging the development of systems that are robust to sparse positive instances and capable of distinguishing check-worthy claims from the predominant background of non-claim content.

Table 2b presents the distribution of annotated *Claim* topics within the *ClaimPT* dataset. Overall, the distribution highlights a strong prevalence of politically and socially oriented claims, consistent with the news agency's editorial focus and the broader relevance of these topics in public discourse.

Among the 670 annotated *Claimers*, 563 were classified as *person* and 66 as *organization*, with the remaining labels retaining only a marginal count. The number of *Claimer* annotations exceeds the total number of *Claims* (463) because, in cases where accurate identification required it, two textual segments were annotated to represent a single claimer within the same claim. With respect to *Stance* associated with each *Claim*, a total of 463 annotations were recorded, comprising 446 instances labeled as "affirm" and 17 as "refute". Finally, *Claim spans* and *Claim objects* amount to 523 and 551 annotations, respectively, revealing only a few cases where more than one claim span and object were annotated per claim.

The ClaimPT dataset was split into *train* and *test* sets according to several considerations. The standard 80%/20% split was applied at the document level. Additionally, documents were carefully selected so that the ratio properties closely match those of the original dataset. Both *train* and *test* maintain the same *Claim:Non-Claim* ratio as the full set (1:9.48), and the total counts for each claim attribute are also distributed approximately according to the 80%/20% split.

## 5   Task and Baselines

We evaluate the potential of the ClaimPT dataset by framing claim detection as a span classification task: given a text $t$, the model predicts a set of triples $(b, e, c)$, where $b$ and $e$ indicate the start and end of a span, and $c \in$ Claim, Non-Claim denotes the class. To facilitate future research, we also establish baseline models and standard evaluation metrics. While our primary experiments focus on claim detection, ClaimPT includes rich annotations such as claimer type, stance, and claim object. These attributes can be leveraged in future multi-task or attribute-aware models, providing more nuanced predictions and supporting explainable fact-checking pipelines.

***Baselines:*** We consider two types of LLM-based baselines: encoder models (BERT-style) and generative models using few-shot learning. For the generative baselines, we use two Gemini models [11]: Gemini-2.5-Flash and Gemini-2.5-Flash-Lite. These models offer large context windows and strong general capabilities, serving as a challenging baseline. Structured outputs are extracted via the LangExtract [14] library, using a one-shot System 2 Attention prompt [42] made available at our repository (translated to English for better comprehension). For the generative baselines, models were prompted with a concise description of the task based on the annotation guidelines used by human annotators. The full guidelines were not provided to the models, as they are extensive and designed for manual annotation rather than automated inference. Providing full annotation guidelines to LLMs may improve performance, but would correspond to a different experimental setting. We therefore treat LLM results as indicative lower bounds under minimal instruction. We leave to future work the study of guideline-conditioned prompting and its impact on claim detection. For the encoder baseline, claim extraction is formulated as a token classification task. Each token $w_i$ in a sequence $W = [w_1, ..., w_n]$ is labeled as part of a claim or non-claim: $\mathcal{L}$ = B-Claim, I-Claim, B-Non-Claim, I-Non-Claim, O. We fine-tune BERTimbau [36] on ClaimPT. To handle documents exceeding BERT's 512-token limit, we use two strategies: (1) Sentence-level segmentation, where each sentence is processed independently, preserving boundaries, which are important for claim detection; (2) Chunking with overlap (stride), where documents are split into 512-token chunks with 128-token overlap to capture cross-boundary context. For overlapping tokens, only the prediction from the first occurrence is retained. We fine-tune the model using a learning rate of $2 \times 10^{-5}$, a batch size of 16, and a weight decay of 0.01.

***Evaluation:*** The ClaimPT corpus provides ground truth annotations defined by span offsets and their corresponding labels. For evaluation, we apply span-level metrics across both generative and BERT-based models. In the case of BERT, token-level outputs are first aggregated into spans that mark the start and end boundaries of each predicted claim or non-claim. These predicted spans are then compared to the ground truth, with a match considered correct only if both boundaries and the label exactly align. Model performance is assessed using precision, recall, and F1-score at the span level. Precision measures the proportion of correctly predicted spans among all predictions, recall quantifies the proportion of ground-truth spans successfully identified, and F1-score represents their harmonic mean, providing a balanced view of overall effectiveness.

***Results and Discussion:*** Results (Table 3) show that encoder-based models outperform generative baselines. Gemini 2.5 Flash Lite achieves an F1 score of 22.52%, while Gemini 2.5 Flash achieves an F1 score of 36.50%. These results are aligned with the expected since that although these models have the capabilities to achieve high effectiveness across a wide range of tasks [11], previous studies also demonstrate their difficulty in extracting span-based annotations [35]. Among encoder baselines, BERT with sentence segmentation performs best, reaching F1-scores of 30.57 for claims and 69.27 for non-claims. Additionally, we report human annotation effectiveness by comparing each annotator's individual annotations against the curator's annotations, which we treat as the reference. This comparison is performed using the same span-level F1 metric used for model evaluation. Under this setting, F1-score reaches 80.83% for annotator 1 and 66.67% for annotator 2 on claim identification, highlighting the intrinsic ambiguity of the task. For comparison, our best-performing model achieves an F1 score of 30.57% in claim identification, corresponding to approximately 37.82% of human-level performance. This gap suggests that the observed model performance is influenced not only by modeling limitations but also by annota-

**Table 3.** Claim extraction results. *Sent* refers to the sentence-level segmentation strategy, while *Chunk* refers to the chunking strategy with overlap (stride).

(a) Generative

| Gemini | Label | Precision (%) | Recall (%) | F1 (%) |
|---|---|---|---|---|
| | Claim | 2.81 | 58.06 | 5.35 |
| Flash Lite | Non-Claim | 28.94 | 50.57 | 36.81 |
| | Micro Avg | 14.43 | 51.28 | 22.52 |
| | Claim | 6.68 | 61.29 | 12.05 |
| Flash | Non-Claim | 33.03 | 70.07 | 44.90 |
| | Micro Avg | 24.78 | 69.23 | 36.50 |

(b) BERT

| BERT | Label | Precision (%) | Recall (%) | F1 (%) |
|---|---|---|---|---|
| | Claim | 40.38 | 22.58 | 28.97 |
| Chunk | Non-Claim | 55.96 | 68.71 | 61.68 |
| | Micro Avg | 55.24 | 64.31 | 59.43 |
| | Claim | 37.50 | 25.81 | 30.57 |
| Sent | Non-Claim | 63.35 | 76.42 | 69.27 |
| | Micro Avg | 61.88 | 71.59 | 66.38 |

(c) Annotators

| Annotators | Label | Precision (%) | Recall (%) | F1 (%) |
|---|---|---|---|---|
| | Claim | 78.00 | 83.87 | 80.83 |
| ANN1 | Non-Claim | 93.77 | 88.78 | 91.21 |
| | Micro Avg | 92.09 | 88.31 | 90.16 |
| | Claim | 74.67 | 60.22 | 66.67 |
| ANN2 | Non-Claim | 93.65 | 51.81 | 66.72 |
| | Micro Avg | 91.12 | 52.62 | 66.71 |

tion subjectivity and task difficulty. We proceed to perform a deeper analysis of the results obtained. These reveal a misalignment between the annotation guidelines and the generative model's interpretation of what constitutes a claim. The model frequently identifies journalistic quotations as claims, which according to the guidelines should not be annotated as such, mainly due to the content of the statement and to the type of claimer. Owing to surface-level similarities, the generative models also tend to conflate unverifiable generalizations with legitimate claims. Furthermore, concerning the direct citation rule, the generative models often extend their predictions beyond quoted text, incorporating adjacent context in an attempt to form a complete sentence. Despite these inconsistencies, the models demonstrate a partial ability to separate verifiable statements from opinions. For instance, in one case it correctly annotates a claim segment while labeling three opinions within the same sentence as non-claims. According to the ground truth, however, the entire sentence should be annotated as a claim, since the guidelines do not allow overlapping claim and non-claim segments. Nonetheless, this behavior suggests that these generative models capture a meaningful distinction between factual and opinionated content, effectively decomposing complex sentences into verifiable and non-verifiable parts.

Overall, both baselines show relatively low effectiveness compared to previous studies [30]. This difference is partly explained by the task formulation: while some works treat claim detection as a classification problem, our setup adopts a span classification perspective, where the model must not only distinguish claims from non-claims but also identify their precise textual boundaries. This makes the task inherently more complex,particularly when dealing with long documents that exceed encoder context windows. Nonetheless, this formulation offers greater practical value for real-world applications, as claim boundaries often depend on the surrounding context for accurate interpretation. In settings such as newsroom fact-checking, span-based systems therefore provide a more interpretable and context-aware framework than simple classification approaches. In summary, encoder-based baselines, especially BERT models with sentence segmentation, constitute a solid foundation for future research on this dataset. While model performance is not the main focus of this resource paper, these baselines establish a meaningful reference point for subsequent studies to refine and extend.

## 6     Conclusions and Future Work

In this paper, we introduce ClaimPT, a new European Portuguese dataset for claim detection. It comprises 1,308 news articles annotated at the span level with claims, non-claims, and additional claim components. This resource enables a fine-grained approach to claim detection, supporting the development of systems that identify claims directly within news text. Beyond the dataset, we provide detailed annotation guidelines, inter-annotator agreement analysis, dataset characterization, and baseline experiments framing claim detection as a span classification task with corresponding evaluation metrics. Together, these elements form a solid foundation for advancing research in claim detection. Future directions include (1) extending the dataset with more instances of claims and to a multilingual context using the provided guidelines, (2) improving baselines with state-of-the-art models such as ModernBERT [41], and (3) leveraging annotated claim attributes to build more explainable, structured models, deepening understanding of how claims are expressed and contextualized in text.

## 7     Limitations

**Corpus**. The dataset comprises European Portuguese news articles spanning ten distinct topics. While it is currently limited to this language, its design and annotation guidelines can be readily extended to other languages. Although topic distribution is not uniform and the number of non-claims considerably exceed that of claims (463 vs. 4,393), this imbalance mirrors the natural frequency of verifiable statements in real news content and thus constitutes a valuable characteristic rather than a limitation, providing a realistic setting for assessing claim extraction systems under conditions that reflect the true distribution of claims in journalistic text, an essential aspect for models intended for real-world application. Despite detailed guidelines and rigorous quality control, annotators and curators, though experts, may still introduce minor biases or subjective interpretations inherent to the task. **Baseline Models**. For the commercial baselines, we employed two LLMs from the Gemini family. These models may evolve or become deprecated over time, potentially affecting reproducibility. In addition, minimal prompt engineering was applied, which may limit performance; however, since these models primarily serve as baselines and the paper's main contribution lies in the dataset itself, this setup is considered sufficient.

**Acknowledgments.** This work is funded by national funds through FCT – Fundação para a Ciência e a Tecnologia, I.P., under the support UID/50014/2025 (https://doi.org/10.54499/UID/50014/2025). Luís Filipe Cunha thanks the Fundação para a Ciência e Tecnologia (FCT), Portugal for the Ph.D. Grant (2024.042 02.BD). António Branco, Raquel Sequeira, Sara Nerea, Diogo Folques would like to acknowledge the project ACCELERAT.AI - Multilingual Intelligent Contact Centers, funded by the covid-recovery program PRR-Plano de Recuperação e Resiliência, through IAPMEI (C625734525-00462629); PORTULAN CLARIN - Research Infrastructure for the Science and Technology of Language, funded by LISBOA2030 (FEDER-01316900); hey, Hal, curb your hallucination!, funded by FCT-Fundação para a Ciência e Tecnologia (2024.07592.IACDC). Ricardo Campos, Alípio Jorge, Nuno Guimarães and Purificação Silvano would also like to acknowledge project StorySense, with reference 2022.09312.PTDC (DOI 10.54499/2022.09312.PTDC). João Canavilhas would also like to acknowledge project Obiajor, with reference 2023.18007.ICDT. We would also like to acknowledge Rodrigo Silva for preparing Fig. 1 and the Portuguese News Agency (LUSA) for granting access to the 1,308 news articles.

**Disclosure of Interests.** The authors have no competing interests to declare that are relevant to the content of this article.

# References

1. Alam, F., et al.: Fighting the COVID-19 infodemic in social media: a holistic perspective and a call to arms. In: Proceedings of the International AAAI Conference on Web and Social Media, ICWSM 2021, vol. 15, pp. 913–922 (2021). https://ojs.aaai.org/index.php/ICWSM/article/view/18114
2. Altoe, F., Pinto, S.M.G., Pinto, H.S.: Explainable automatic fact-checking for journalists augmentation in the wild. In: Kwok, J. (ed.) Proceedings of the Thirty-Fourth International Joint Conference on Artificial Intelligence, IJCAI 2025, pp. 10262–10270. International Joint Conferences on Artificial Intelligence Organization (2025). https://doi.org/10.24963/ijcai.2025/1140, human-Centred AI
3. Atanasova, P., et al.: Overview of the CLEF-2018 CheckThat! Lab on Automatic Identification and Verification of Political Claims. Task 1: Check-Worthiness (2018). https://arxiv.org/abs/1808.05542
4. Barrón-Cedeño, A., et al.: CheckThat! at CLEF 2020: Enabling the Automatic Identification and Verification of Claims in Social Media. CoRR abs/2001.08546 (2020). https://arxiv.org/abs/2001.08546
5. Campos, R., et al.: ClaimPT: A Dataset for Claim Detection and Fact-Checking (2025). https://doi.org/10.25747/JY10-E413
6. Canavilhas, J., Ito, L.: On fact-checking service: artificial intelligence uses in Ibero-American fact-checkers. Soc. Sci. **14**(9), 1–17 (2025). https://ideas.repec.org/a/gam/jscscx/v14y2025i9p514-d1733231.html
7. Cheema, G.S., Hakimov, S., Sittar, A., Müller-Budack, E., Otto, C., Ewerth, R.: MM-claims: a dataset for multimodal claim detection in social media. In: Carpuat, M., de Marneffe, M.C., Meza Ruiz, I.V. (eds.) Findings of the Association for Computational Linguistics: NAACL 2022, pp. 962–979. Association for Computational Linguistics, Seattle, United States (2022). https://doi.org/10.18653/v1/2022.findings-naacl.72. https://aclanthology.org/2022.findings-naacl.72/

8. Chowdhury, S., Fang, S., Muresan, S.: FACT5: a novel benchmark and pipeline for nuanced fact-checking of complex statements. In: Akhtar, M., et al. (eds.) Proceedings of the Eighth Fact Extraction and VERification Workshop (FEVER), pp. 101–117. Association for Computational Linguistics, Vienna, Austria (2025). https://doi.org/10.18653/v1/2025.fever-1.8. https://aclanthology.org/2025.fever-1.8/

9. Elsayed, T., et al.: Overview of the clef-2019 checkthat!: automatic identification and verification of claims (2021). https://arxiv.org/abs/2109.15118

10. Gangi Reddy, R., et al.: NewsClaims: a new benchmark for claim detection from news with attribute knowledge. In: Goldberg, Y., Kozareva, Z., Zhang, Y. (eds.) Proceedings of the 2022 Conference on Empirical Methods in Natural Language Processing, pp. 6002–6018. Association for Computational Linguistics, Abu Dhabi, United Arab Emirates (2022). https://doi.org/10.18653/v1/2022.emnlp-main.403. https://aclanthology.org/2022.emnlp-main.403/

11. Gemini Team: Gemini: A family of highly capable multimodal models (2024). https://arxiv.org/abs/2312.11805

12. Gencheva, P., Nakov, P., Màrquez, L., Barrón-Cedeño, A., Koychev, I.: A context-aware approach for detecting worth-checking claims in political debates. In: Mitkov, R., Angelova, G. (eds.) Proceedings of the International Conference Recent Advances in Natural Language Processing, RANLP 2017, pp. 267–276. INCOMA Ltd., Varna, Bulgaria (2017). https://doi.org/10.26615/978-954-452-049-6_037

13. Giedemann, P., von Däniken, P., Deriu, J., Rodrigo, A., Peñas, A., Cieliebak, M.: ViClaim: A Multilingual Multilabel Dataset for Automatic Claim Detection in Videos (2025). https://arxiv.org/abs/2504.12882

14. Goel, A.: Langextract (2025). https://doi.org/10.5281/zenodo.17015090

15. Gradim, A.: Manual de Jornalismo. Universidade da Beira Interior/Livros Lab-Com, Covilhã, Portugal (2000), journalism Manual, Universidade da Beira Interior/Livros LabCom

16. Guo, Z., Schlichtkrull, M., Vlachos, A.: A survey on automated fact-checking. Trans. Assoc. Comput. Linguist. **10**, 178–206 (2022). https://doi.org/10.1162/tacl_a_00454. https://aclanthology.org/2022.tacl-1.11/

17. Gupta, A., Srikumar, V.: X-FACT: a new benchmark dataset for multilingual fact checking. In: Proceedings of the 59th Annual Meeting of the Association for Computational Linguistics. Association for Computational Linguistics, Online (2021)

18. Hassan, N., Arslan, F., Li, C., Tremayne, M.: Toward automated fact-checking: Detecting check-worthy factual claims by claimbuster. In: Proceedings of the 23rd ACM SIGKDD International Conference on Knowledge Discovery and Data Mining, KDD 2017, pp. 1803–1812. Association for Computing Machinery, New York, NY, USA (2017). https://doi.org/10.1145/3097983.3098131

19. Ivanov, P., Koychev, I., Hardalov, M., Nakov, P.: Detecting Check-Worthy Claims in Political Debates, Speeches, and Interviews Using Audio Data (2024). https://arxiv.org/abs/2306.05535

20. Klie, J.C., Bugert, M., Boullosa, B., Eckart de Castilho, R., Gurevych, I.: The INCEpTION platform: machine-assisted and knowledge-oriented interactive annotation. In: Zhao, D. (ed.) Proceedings of the 27th International Conference on Computational Linguistics: System Demonstrations, pp. 5–9. Association for Computational Linguistics, Santa Fe, New Mexico (2018). https://aclanthology.org/C18-2002/

21. Konstantinovskiy, L., Price, O., Babakar, M., Zubiaga, A.: Toward automated factchecking: developing an annotation schema and benchmark for consistent automated claim detection. Digit. Threats: Res. Pract. **2**, 1–16 (2021). https://doi.org/10.1145/3412869

22. van der Meer, M., Korshunov, P., Marcel, S., van der Plas, L.: HintsOfTruth: A Multimodal Checkworthiness Detection Dataset with Real and Synthetic Claims (2025). https://arxiv.org/abs/2502.11753

23. Mittal, S., Sundriyal, M., Nakov, P.: Lost in translation, found in spans: identifying claims in multilingual social media. In: Bouamor, H., Pino, J., Bali, K. (eds.) Proceedings of the 2023 Conference on Empirical Methods in Natural Language Processing, pp. 3887–3902. Association for Computational Linguistics, Singapore (2023). https://doi.org/10.18653/v1/2023.emnlp-main.236. https://aclanthology.org/2023.emnlp-main.236/

24. Monteiro, R.A., Santos, R.L.S., Pardo, T.A.S., de Almeida, T.A., Ruiz, E.E.S., Vale, O.A.: Contributions to the study of fake news in Portuguese: new corpus and automatic detection results. In: Villavicencio, A., et al. (eds.) PROPOR 2018. LNCS (LNAI), vol. 11122, pp. 324–334. Springer, Cham (2018). https://doi.org/10.1007/978-3-319-99722-3_33

25. Nakov, P., et al.: Overview of the CLEF-2022 CheckThat! lab on fighting the COVID-19 infodemic and fake news detection. In: Experimental IR Meets Multilinguality, Multimodality, and Interaction: 13th International Conference of the CLEF Association, CLEF 2022, Bologna, Italy, 5–8 September 2022, Proceedings, pp. 495–520. Springer, Heidelberg (2022). https://doi.org/10.1007/978-3-031-13643-6_29

26. Nakov, P., et al.: Automated fact-checking for assisting human fact-checkers. In: Zhou, Z.H. (ed.) Proceedings of the Thirtieth International Joint Conference on Artificial Intelligence, IJCAI 2021, pp. 4551–4558. International Joint Conferences on Artificial Intelligence Organization (2021). https://doi.org/10.24963/ijcai.2021/619, survey Track

27. Nunes, S., et al.: Text2Story Lusa: a dataset for narrative analysis in European Portuguese news articles. In: Calzolari, N., Kan, M.Y., Hoste, V., Lenci, A., Sakti, S., Xue, N. (eds.) Proceedings of the 2024 Joint International Conference on Computational Linguistics, Language Resources and Evaluation (LREC-COLING 2024), pp. 15773–15782. ELRA and ICCL, Torino, Italia (2024). https://aclanthology.org/2024.lrec-main.1370/

28. Panchendrarajan, R., Zubiaga, A.: Claim detection for automated fact-checking: a survey on monolingual, multilingual and cross-lingual research. Nat. Lang. Process. J 7, 100066 (2024). https://doi.org/10.1016/j.nlp.2024.100066

29. Piskorski, J., et al.: SemEval 2025 task 10: multilingual characterization and extraction of narratives from online news. In: Rosenthal, S., Rosá, A., Ghosh, D., Zampieri, M. (eds.) Proceedings of the 19th International Workshop on Semantic Evaluation (SemEval-2025), pp. 2610–2643. Association for Computational Linguistics, Vienna, Austria (2025). https://aclanthology.org/2025.semeval-1.331/

30. Prabhakar, A.A., Mohtaj, S., Möller, S.: Claim extraction from text using transfer learning. In: Bhattacharyya, P., Sharma, D.M., Sangal, R. (eds.) Proceedings of the 17th International Conference on Natural Language Processing (ICON), pp. 297–302. NLP Association of India (NLPAI), Indian Institute of Technology Patna, Patna, India (2020). https://aclanthology.org/2020.icon-main.39/

31. Rosenthal, S., McKeown, K.: Detecting opinionated claims in online discussions. In: 2012 IEEE Sixth International Conference on Semantic Computing, pp. 30–37 (2012)

32. Schlichtkrull, M., Guo, Z., Vlachos, A.: AVeriTeC: A Dataset for Real-world Claim Verification with Evidence from the Web (2023). https://arxiv.org/abs/2305.13117

33. Schmitz, A.A.: Classificação das Fontes de Notícias. Universidade Federal de Santa Catarina (UFSC), Florianópolis, Brazil (2011), original title in Portuguese: "Classification of News Sources"
34. Shaar, S., et al.: Findings of the NLP4IF-2021 shared tasks on fighting the COVID-19 infodemic and censorship detection. In: Feldman, A., Da San Martino, G., Leberknight, C., Nakov, P. (eds.) Proceedings of the Fourth Workshop on NLP for Internet Freedom: Censorship, Disinformation, and Propaganda, pp. 82–92. Association for Computational Linguistics, Online (2021). https://doi.org/10.18653/v1/2021.nlp4if-1.12. https://aclanthology.org/2021.nlp4if-1.12/
35. Sousa, H., Guimarães, N., Jorge, A., Campos, R.: GPT struct me: probing GPT models on narrative entity extraction. In: 2023 IEEE/WIC International Conference on Web Intelligence and Intelligent Agent Technology (WI-IAT), pp. 383–387 (2023). https://doi.org/10.1109/WI-IAT59888.2023.00063
36. Souza, F., Nogueira, R., Lotufo, R.: BERTimbau: pretrained BERT models for Brazilian Portuguese. In: Cerri, R., Prati, R.C. (eds.) BRACIS 2020. LNCS (LNAI), vol. 12319, pp. 403–417. Springer, Cham (2020). https://doi.org/10.1007/978-3-030-61377-8_28
37. Srba, I., et al.: A survey on automatic credibility assessment using textual credibility signals in the era of large language models. ACM Trans. Intell. Syst. Technol. (2025). https://doi.org/10.1145/3770077, just Accepted
38. Stammbach, D., Webersinke, N., Bingler, J., Kraus, M., Leippold, M.: Environmental claim detection. In: Rogers, A., Boyd-Graber, J., Okazaki, N. (eds.) Proceedings of the 61st Annual Meeting of the Association for Computational Linguistics (Volume 2: Short Papers), pp. 1051–1066. Association for Computational Linguistics, Toronto, Canada (2023). https://doi.org/10.18653/v1/2023.acl-short.91
39. Thorne, J., Vlachos, A., Christodoulopoulos, C., Mittal, A.: FEVER: a large-scale dataset for fact extraction and VERification. In: Walker, M., Ji, H., Stent, A. (eds.) Proceedings of the 2018 Conference of the North American Chapter of the Association for Computational Linguistics: Human Language Technologies, Volume 1 (Long Papers), pp. 809–819. Association for Computational Linguistics, New Orleans, Louisiana (2018). https://doi.org/10.18653/v1/N18-1074
40. Vasileva, S., Atanasova, P., Màrquez, L., Barrón-Cedeño, A., Nakov, P.: It takes nine to smell a rat: neural multi-task learning for check-worthiness prediction. In: Mitkov, R., Angelova, G. (eds.) Proceedings of the International Conference on Recent Advances in Natural Language Processing (RANLP 2019), pp. 1229–1239. INCOMA Ltd., Varna, Bulgaria (2019). https://doi.org/10.26615/978-954-452-056-4_141
41. Warner, B., et al.: Smarter, better, faster, longer: a modern bidirectional encoder for fast, memory efficient, and long context finetuning and inference (2024). https://arxiv.org/abs/2412.13663
42. Weston, J., Sukhbaatar, S.: System 2 attention (is something you might need too) (2023). https://arxiv.org/abs/2311.11829
43. Zlatkova, D., Nakov, P., Koychev, I.: Fact-checking meets fauxtography: verifying claims about images. In: Inui, K., Jiang, J., Ng, V., Wan, X. (eds.) Proceedings of the 2019 Conference on Empirical Methods in Natural Language Processing and the 9th International Joint Conference on Natural Language Processing (EMNLP-IJCNLP), pp. 2099–2108. Association for Computational Linguistics, Hong Kong, China (2019). https://doi.org/10.18653/v1/D19-1216. https://aclanthology.org/D19-1216/

# An Open SERP Mining Infrastructure
# for the Archive Query Log

Jan Heinrich Merker[1]([✉])[iD], Simon Ruth[2][iD], Harrisen Scells[3][iD],
and Martin Potthast[2,4][iD]

[1] Friedrich-Schiller-Universität Jena, Jena, Germany
heinrich.merker@uni-jena.de
[2] University of Kassel, Kassel, Germany
[3] University of Tübingen, Tübingen, Germany
[4] hessian.AI and ScaDS.AI, Wiesbaden, Germany

**Abstract.** Query logs are key resources for studying search engine interactions and improving retrieval effectiveness but are rarely publicly available. In the past, search providers only shared small subsets of their own logs to curb competition and to ensure privacy. The Archive Query Log (AQL) will become an open alternative: mining query logs from archived search engine result pages (SERPs). While the AQL-22 prototype demonstrated the feasibility of this approach, its limited scalability and maintainability hindered widespread adoption by the research community. We re-implement the crawling and parsing of the AQL on open infrastructure, using standard tools, a new framework for storing SERPs, and following FAIR data principles. The extended and continuously crawled AQL corpus currently contains 553 million SERPs from 775 search providers, mined from six web archives, where so far 223 million SERPs (44 TB; 40%) have been downloaded and parsed. We demonstrate the use of this new AQL mining framework in two typical analysis scenarios: a temporal analysis now implemented as a single Elasticsearch query and a batch-processing analysis using Ray. Our resource equips researchers with all the tools needed to analyze SERPs.

## 1 Introduction

For many decades, information retrieval research has heavily relied on query logs to understand user behavior [3,5,8,19–21,33,39,43], to improve or train new retrieval models [32,46], and to transparently evaluate retrieval system effectiveness [4,11,27]. These diverse use cases make query logs a key resource for advancing information retrieval research and practice [25]. Enriched logs that include results from multiple search engines might become crucial to evaluate emerging retrieval paradigms such as retrieval-augmented generation [16,26].

---

J. H. Merker and S. Ruth— Contributed equally to the paper and are listed alphabetically.


R. Campos et al. (Eds.): ECIR 2026, LNCS 16486, pp. 561–577, 2026.
https://doi.org/10.1007/978-3-032-21321-1_59

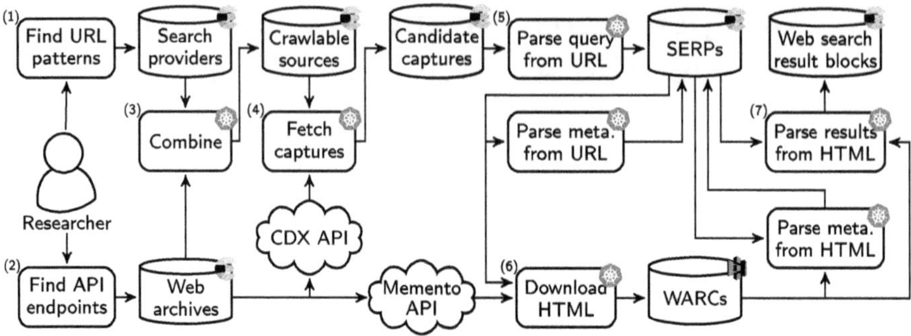



**Fig. 1.** Data flow diagram of the AQL mining. Researchers configure URL patterns of search providers (1) and API endpoints of web archives (2). The AQL system then combines these to crawlable source pairs (3), fetches candidate captures from the web archives' CDX APIs (4), parses the query (5) and other metadata from the capture URL, downloads the HTML as WARC files from the Memento APIs (6), and finally parses result blocks (7), and metadata from the HTML. Data is stored in Elasticsearch (⬤ ) and S3 (▮ ). Crawlers/parsers can be run locally or scheduled via Kubernetes (⚙ ).

Despite their importance to the scientific community, large-scale query logs are rarely available to researchers [37]. Search providers typically do not share their query logs for competitive and privacy reasons, or just release smaller, pre-filtered samples, like the ORCAS or MS MARCO Web Search logs [7,12]. The Archive Query Log (AQL) [37] addresses the scarcity of query log data by crawling millions of search engine result pages (SERPs) that have been archived on the Internet Archive's Wayback Machine since the late 1990s.[1] At the time of its initial release, the AQL-22 was already the largest publicly available query log, exceeding the size of prior public datasets [7,12] by about an order of magnitude.

However, while the AQL-22 dataset received considerable interest from the research community [16,17,34,38,41], its widespread use was hindered by the limited scalability of the AQL-22's original mining framework. The most pressing issues of this prototype include: (1) it was hard-coded to only a single web archive (the Wayback Machine); (2) adding new search providers required manual editing of configuration files; (3) data was stored in large, fixed, and unevenly partitioned JSONL files; (4) the crawling and parsing was scheduled on a custom Slurm cluster with a global shared filesystem; and (5) analyzing the data required manual parsing of JSONL files from the same shared filesystem. These limitations made it difficult to extend, maintain, and use the AQL-22. Ultimately, only 2% of search engine result page contents were actually downloaded for analysis.

In this paper, as illustrated in Fig. 1, we present our steps to re-implement the AQL framework as a fully distributed system, both in terms of storage and compute. We first analyze the requirements for the AQL and compare commonly used tools with respect to these requirements (Sect. 2). We then describe our new,

---

[1] https://archive.org/web/

modular framework for crawling, parsing, and analyzing the AQL (Sect. 3) using standard tools like Elasticsearch, S3, Kubernetes, and Ray. By increasing the diversity of web archives and search providers, we create a new, continuously updated version of the Archive Query Log.

Our copy of the AQL corpus currently contains 553 million SERPs with queries from 775 search providers, extracted from six web archives from August 1999 to October 2025. The AQL further consists of 44 TBs of WARC files, from which 51 million web search result blocks have been parsed so far (Sect. 4). For two typical scenarios, we demonstrate how the new AQL mining framework accelerates extensive query log analyses: a temporal comparison to Google Trends and counting search operators with Ray.

By re-implementing the AQL's crawling and parsing while following FAIR principles for data and software and improving its scalability and maintainability, we open up large-scale query log analyses to the wider community, enabling researchers to conduct experiments at a magnitude that was previously only accessible to industrial search engine operators. Researchers can use the AQL as a unique resource to study a substantial proportion of the evolution of web search over the last two decades. Moreover, retrospective analyses will improve the accountability of search engine providers and allow researchers to dig deeper into questions like "Is search getting worse over time?", not unlike Bevendorff [4].

## 2   Related Work

Open mining initiatives, like the Archive Query Log [37], face challenges in the "openness", scalability, and maintainability of their crawling and parsing infrastructure. To avoid pitfalls encountered during the mining of the initial AQL-22 dataset, we conduct a requirements analysis and then identify suitable tools to re-implement the AQL mining infrastructure while adhering to the requirements of large-scale query log mining and analyses (see Table 1).

*Requirements for Data Mining Infrastructures.* To make research data broadly accessible, the FAIR principles [45] provide guidelines for making data findable, accessible, interoperable, and reusable. Originally designed for static, hand-curated datasets, we adapt these principles to the continuously growing and evolving AQL data resources. In the Archive Query Log, *findability* relies on the unique identifiability of data items and full-text and metadata search. *Accessibility* depends on authorization mechanisms and, given the dynamic nature of living data, random access to individual items. *Interoperability* is ensured through the ability to create and restore snapshots at any time, including migration to other clusters with manageable effort. *Reusability* is achieved through open formats and open-source licensing.

Complementing the FAIR principles for data, continuous data-mining initiatives should also follow best practices for reproducibility [18] and apply the same FAIR principles for the used research software [24]. Accordingly, software artifacts should be uniquely identifiable and searchable via modular, well-documented interfaces. Authorized users should be able to run the software and

**Table 1.** Requirements/capabilities of use cases, tools, and compound systems for Web (⊕) and/or structured data (⊞). Reported criteria are: findability (▥ identifiers, Q metadata/full-text search), accessibility (◑ authorization, ◎ random access), interoperability (▤ snapshot/restore, ⊹ extensibility), reusability (▥ open source), scalability (⛛ distributed partitions/workers, ▥ fault tolerance), and maintainability (CRUD operations, ≡ self-hosting); criteria marked as supported (●), partially supported (◐), or not supported (◌). Items selected for our updated AQL mining are **bold**. A successful system must fulfill all requirements of its intended use cases by using appropriate tools.

| Name | Data ⊕ ⊞ | Find ▥ Q | Access ◑ ◎ | Interop. ▤ ⊹ | R<sup>euse</sup>epro. ▥ | Scale ⛛ ▥ | Maintain CRUD ≡ |
|---|---|---|---|---|---|---|---|
| *Use cases (requirements)* | | | | | | | |
| **Query log mining** | ⊕ ⊞ | ▥ Q | ◑ ◎ | ▤ ⊹ | ▥ | ⛛ ▥ | CRUD ≡ |
| **Query log analysis** | ⊕ ⊞ | ▥ Q | ◑ ◎ | ▤ ⊹ | ▥ | ⛛ ▥ | CRUD ≡ |
| Web crawling | ⊕ ⊞ | ▥ Q | ◑ ◎ | ▤ ⊹ | ▥ | ⛛ ▥ | CRUD ≡ |
| *Tools (capabilities)* | | | | | | | |
| **WARC format** | ⊕ ⊞ | ▥ Q | ◑ ◎ | ▤ ⊹ | ▥ | ⛛ ▥ | CRUD ≡ |
| JSONL format | ⊕ ⊞ | ▥ Q | ◑ ◎ | ▤ ⊹ | ▥ | ⛛ ▥ | CRUD ≡ |
| Arrow/Parquet format | ⊕ ⊞ | ▥ Q | ◑ ◎ | ▤ ⊹ | ▥ | ⛛ ▥ | CRUD ≡ |
| Shared FS (e.g., Ceph) | ⊕ ⊞ | ▥ Q | ◑ ◎ | ▤ ⊹ | ▥ | ⛛ ▥ | CRUD ≡ |
| **S3 object storage** [29] | ⊕ ⊞ | ▥ Q | ◑ ◎ | ▤ ⊹ | ▥ | ⛛ ▥ | CRUD ≡ |
| Relat. DB (e.g., SQL) [2,10] | ⊕ ⊞ | ▥ Q | ◑ ◎ | ▤ ⊹ | ▥ | ⛛ ▥ | CRUD ≡ |
| DuckDB [22] | ⊕ ⊞ | ▥ Q | ◑ ◎ | ▤ ⊹ | ▥ | ⛛ ▥ | CRUD ≡ |
| **Elasticsearch**/OpenS. | ⊕ ⊞ | ▥ Q | ◑ ◎ | ▤ ⊹ | ▥ | ⛛ ▥ | CRUD ≡ |
| **Kubernetes** | ⊕ ⊞ | ▥ Q | ◑ ◎ | ▤ ⊹ | ▥ | ⛛ ▥ | CRUD ≡ |
| SLURM | ⊕ ⊞ | ▥ Q | ◑ ◎ | ▤ ⊹ | ▥ | ⛛ ▥ | CRUD ≡ |
| **Ray** | ⊕ ⊞ | ▥ Q | ◑ ◎ | ▤ ⊹ | ▥ | ⛛ ▥ | CRUD ≡ |
| Apache Spark/Hadoop | ⊕ ⊞ | ▥ Q | ◑ ◎ | ▤ ⊹ | ▥ | ⛛ ▥ | CRUD ≡ |
| *Systems (capabilities)* | | | | | | | |
| AQL-22 [37] | ⊕ ⊞ | ▥ Q | ◑ ◎ | ▤ ⊹ | ▥ | ⛛ ▥ | CRUD ≡ |
| **AQL (this work)** | ⊕ ⊞ | ▥ Q | ◑ ◎ | ▤ ⊹ | ▥ | ⛛ ▥ | CRUD ≡ |

access its components individually. Interoperability is supported through versioned, precompiled, or containerized releases, while reusability or, in this context, reproducibility, is ensured through open-source licensing and transparent development.

Beyond FAIRness, we identify scalability and maintainability as essential for sustainable data-mining infrastructures [42], consistent with ISO 9126 [1]. *Scalability* entails distributing data and compute workloads across multiple nodes [6] and tolerating worker failures with minimal data loss or downtime [23]. *Maintain-*

*ability* involves supporting CRUD (create, read, update, delete) operations [28] and enabling self-hosting without proprietary dependencies [42].

*Use Cases.* To demonstrate the applicability of our extended requirements framework, we analyze the two primary AQL use cases, namely query log mining and analysis, with the general web crawling use case along the dimensions of FAIR data and software principles, scalability, and maintainability (see Table 1).

When mining query logs from web archives, both structured data (e.g., metadata) and unstructured web data (e.g., the HTML contents of SERPs) must be processed, metadata should be findable and randomly accessible to enable linking between related records. Access control is required for queries containing sensitive or personal information. Given the diverse and evolving structure of search engine result pages [30,31], both the mining software and the previously extracted data should remain extensible and fault-tolerant. Data creation in query logs primarily occurs during crawling, while subsequent read operations dominate later stages; thus, update and delete operations are less relevant for query log mining. Query log analyses, in contrast, typically rely on the parsed structured data, and not all analyses require globally unique identifiers or distributed processing, for example, when operating on smaller subsets. Unlike crawling, analyses do not generate new data or delete existing records but often update datasets with derived results.

Web crawling in general shares many requirements with query log mining, as both involve large-scale processing of unstructured web data [13, p.,44]. However, crawling typically deals with less structured content and, since an index is often built post-hoc, does not depend on random access during the crawling process.

*Tools.* Based on the identified requirements, in Table 1, we survey existing tools for large-scale data processing and storage and identify candidates for re-implementing the AQL mining: data storage formats (e.g., WARC[2]), storage frameworks (e.g., S3), databases (e.g., Elasticsearch[3]), workload scheduling (e.g., Kubernetes[4]), and MapReduce-inspired [14] batch processing (e.g., Ray[5]).

None of these tools fulfills all requirements for the analyzed use cases individually, but only as a composite system. While the use case of web crawling is covered easily with a few tools, e.g., by just using WARC files stored on S3, both query log-related use cases require more complex infrastructures.

*Systems.* Concluding the comparison, we contrast the initial AQL-22 mining with the new AQL framework proposed in this paper (see Fig. 1). The AQL-22 system [37] stored WARC and JSONL files on a shared file system and executed crawling and parsing through manually submitted SLURM jobs. This setup scaled poorly, violated several FAIR principles by lacking search, random

---

[2] https://iipc.github.io/warc-specifications/specifications/warc-format/warc-1.1/
[3] https://elastic.co/products/elasticsearch
[4] https://kubernetes.io/
[5] https://docs.ray.io/

access, and snapshot capabilities, and was difficult to maintain due to missing modularity and update or deletion support. In contrast, the new AQL framework (Sect. 3) integrates Elasticsearch indices for parsed data, object storage for raw WARCs, and distributed orchestration via Kubernetes and Ray, thus meeting all above requirements for scalable and maintainable query log mining and analysis.

## 3    Mining and Analyzing Query Logs from Web Archives

We have summarized the main obstacles of the original Archive Query Log mining framework used to create the AQL-22 and identified criteria to make the AQL mining *FAIR*, *scalable*, and *maintainable*. Following these criteria, we develop a framework for both storing and processing query log data mined from web archives, as illustrated in Fig. 1. Then, we describe how others can easily mine their own custom query logs from web archives using our new framework.

### 3.1    Compute and Data Architecture

We redesign the AQL crawling and parsing components as modular actions accessible via a command-line interface, implemented in Python and containerized using Docker. When installed locally from PyPI[6] or Docker,[7] this command-line interface allows others to easily seed or extend the crawl, and to parse the AQL data. For large-scale crawling and parsing, the Docker container is deployed on a Kubernetes cluster using a configurable Helm chart.[8] Still, for local testing and small-scale experiments, any crawling and parsing step can additionally be run on a local machine with optional dry run verification.

The data mined in the AQL consists of both (1) structured data (i.e., manually entered by researchers or parsed from search engine result pages) and (2) raw, unstructured data (i.e., the HTML documents of the archived SERPs). We store all structured data on Elasticsearch, which allows efficient search, filtering, concurrent access and modification, and scaling across multiple nodes. The unstructured HTML data is stored as GZIP-compressed WARC files, each containing batches of downloaded HTML documents. Random access pointers to the HTML documents within these WARC files are saved along with the structured data in Elasticsearch.

---

[6] https://pypi.org/project/archive-query-log
[7] https://ghcr.io/webis-de/archive-query-log
[8] https://github.com/webis-de/archive-query-log#cluster-helmkubernetes

```
aql providers add -n "Google Search" -d google.com -u /search
aql archives  add -n "Wayback Machine" \
  -c https://web.archive.org/cdx/search/cdx \
  -m https://web.archive.org/web/
```

Listing 1: Adding Google Search as a new search provider and the Wayback Machine as a web archive.

```
ELASTICSEARCH_USERNAME=user
ELASTICSEARCH_PASSWORD=password
ELASTICSEARCH_INDEX_SERPS=aql_serps
...
S3_BUCKET_NAME=aql
S3_ACCESS_KEY=key
S3_SECRET_KEY=key
```

Listing 2: Configuring the endpoints, credentials, and indices for Elasticsearch and S3 storage.

## 3.2   Crawling and Parsing Workflow

*Seeding Search Providers and Web Archives.* Crawling query logs from web archives requires two main prerequisites: (1) A list of *search providers* whose SERPs should be mined and (2) access to *web archives* that serve archived captures of SERPs from these search providers. We open up these "seeds" to be extendable and editable by researchers with the AQL command-line interface.

The original AQL mining used a fixed set of 550 popular search providers and only crawled from the Internet Archive's Wayback Machine, overlooking other web archives that may contain additional captures of search engine result pages. Conceptually, a search provider can be any web service that provides a search interface, for example, a web search engine like Google or Bing or a site-specific search like the one included on Wikipedia. For efficient crawling, we further require that the search provider's SERP URLs follow consistent URL patterns, for example, by using a common query parameter for the search term (e.g., q in https://google.com/search?q=example). Web archives are services that crawl, archive, and provide access to web pages from the past. Most web archives provide two essential APIs for accessing their archived captures: a CDX API[9] to look up archived captures matching a given URL pattern and a Memento API [44] to download the archived HTML document of a given capture (i.e., a URL at a specific point in time). To improve upon the limited crawling from just the Wayback Machine, we thus add five national web archives (e.g., Arquivo.pt[10]).

---

[9] While not a formal standard, there are just three common implementations: https://github.com/janheinrichmerker/web-archive-api#cdx-standardization

[10] https://arquivo.pt

To mine a query log, users first must find URL patterns for one or more search providers (Step 1 in Fig. 1) and then determine the API endpoints of web archives they intend to crawl from (Step 2). In the new AQL mining framework, these two seed datasets (i.e., search providers and web archives) are maintained in Elasticsearch indices. Listing 1 shows how to use the AQL command-line interface to add new search providers and a web archives. The Elasticsearch credentials and indices are configured via the command-line interface, as environment variables, or a .env file (Listing 2).

*Finding Candidate SERP Captures in Web Archives.* When the seed search providers and web archives are added, candidate captures of search engine result pages are fetched from the web archives. As any web archive may contain captures from any search provider, we first compute the cross-product of all crawlable sources, i.e., combinations of web archive API endpoints and search provider URL patterns (Step 3) in Fig. 1). For each of these source pairs, we then query the web archive's CDX API to find the metadata of all archived captures matching the search provider's SERP URL pattern (Step 4).

The CDX API poses two main challenges: (1) for most web archives, the API handles requests slowly, often taking multiple seconds to respond, and (2) there is no formal standard for the API's output format and pagination. To this end, we have developed a small helper library that provides a unified interface to any CDX API implementation, handles pagination, and gracefully deals with slow or failing requests.[11] Using this helper library and parallelizing requests across nodes in our Kubernetes cluster, we efficiently find all archived candidate SERP captures from all configured web archives and search providers.

*Identifying Actual SERP Captures.* Due to limitations on the available filters for the CDX API, the Elasticsearch index of candidate captures may still contain non-SERP captures, for example, the search homepage of a search provider without the search term (e.g., https://stackoverflow.com/search). By parsing the search query from the URL of each candidate capture (e.g., the query `test` in the SERP's URL https://bing.com/search?q=test), we identify actual captures of search engine result pages and store the parsed queries in a dedicated Elasticsearch index [37]. Researchers can use our 972 existing URL-based query parsers or implement and contribute their own parsers, e.g., to handle a new search provider. Further metadata, such as the SERP's page offset are parsed in the same way, updating the index in-place.

*Downloading Archived SERP HTMLs.* Content-level metadata and the individual result blocks of a SERP can only be parsed from the actual HTML of the archived SERP capture. To this end, web archives provide a Memento API [44] that replays the archived HTML documents of a given URL at a specific point in time. However, similar to the CDX API, the Memento API is usually very slow, sometimes taking minutes to respond. The Memento APIs' slow response rates

---

[11] https://pypi.org/project/web-archive-api/

```
helm install archive-query-log --values values.yaml --version 0.2.22 \
  oci://ghcr.io/webis-de/archive-query-log/charts/archive-query-log
```

Listing 3: Orchestrating the AQL mining on a Kubernetes cluster using Helm.

posed a significant bottleneck in the original AQL-22 mining, where the HTML documents of whole batches of search engine result page captures were downloaded sequentially on a single machine. For the new AQL mining, we first unify the access to different Memento API implementations in the same helper library used for the CDX API (see footnote 11). To improve the fail-safety of downloading, HTML documents are first dumped to smaller, temporary WARC files and then later merged into larger WARC files of max. 1 GB each. These WARC files are stored in an S3-compatible block storage to efficiently scale up to terabytes of HTML data. Immediately after a WARC file of SERP HTML documents is uploaded to S3, the filename, byte offset, and length to the WARC records are stored in the Elasticsearch index of search engine result pages, allowing to later randomly access and parse the HTML document of any SERP.

*Parsing SERPs.* Search engine result pages typically list links to web pages along with snippets, images, and/or other excerpts that may help users decide which page to visit. Longitudinal studies of their design and layout have shown how SERPs evolve in response to new technologies [30,31]. But besides such smaller, manually annotated studies, the full diversity of search providers and their SERPs has not yet been systematically modeled, due to lacking larger, semi-automatically labeled datasets. Next to scaling up the download of SERP HTML documents, we thus break down the parsing of the search engine result pages into modules that each (1) are given the raw HTML of a SERP and/or its previously parsed metadata in a standardized data model, (2) can use any parsing logic or tool without restrictions, and (3) yield parsed data as "updates" to the existing SERP records in Elasticsearch.

With the Archive Query Log, we focus on a SERP's two main components: the search box containing the query and the result blocks linking to external landing pages of relevant results. A basic initial model for these SERP components is given in Google's relevance assessment guidelines.[12] In this model, the result blocks are further categorized into *web search result blocks* (i.e., organic results that reference external landing pages) and *special content result blocks* (e.g., direct answers [36]). The AQL data model supports both types of result blocks, but so far only web search result blocks are parsed.

While a number of online services provide APIs to parse web search result blocks from SERPs of common search engines like Google or Bing,[13] these proprietary parsers are not applicable to archived SERPs and limited to a few search

---

[12] https://web.archive.org/web/20260101040106/https://static.googleusercontent.
com/media/guidelines.raterhub.com/en/searchqualityevaluatorguidelines.pdf

[13] Examples: https://serpapi.com, https://serpstack.com, and https://zenserp.com/

providers, hence unsuited for longitudinal, reproducible analyses. We follow a test-driven approach to derive 90 custom parsers for 25 search providers.

### 3.3   Continuous Query Log Crawling and Mining

As new SERPs are continuously archived by web archives, all described crawling and parsing steps can be re-executed at any time to keep the Archive Query Log data up-to-date. Still, running each step manually quickly becomes unmaintainable. We thus provide a Docker container that bundles the command-line interface and all dependencies, allowing to easily deploy and run the AQL mining in cloud environments. For Kubernetes clusters, we provide a Helm chart that launches distributed crawling and parsing jobs across hundreds of nodes, while being fully customizable to the user's hardware constraints and research needs.By using this simplified orchestration as shown in Listing 3, others can easily deploy the AQL mining to reproduce the AQL data on their own infrastructure or to extend the data. For our experiments, we use a 135 node Elasticsearch cluster and an S3-compatible storage, both backed by a 12,480 TB storage cluster. For testing, a small Kubernetes, S3, and Elasticsearch cluster can be deployed locally, for example, using LocalStack.[14]

### 3.4   User Evaluation

In a post-hoc lightweight expert survey, we asked researchers familiar with the former AQL-22 parsing and access framework to assess and compare their experiences with both AQL-22 and the new AQL. Participants identified data scale, infrastructure overhead, and limited data access as the main obstacles when working with AQL-22. In contrast, the proposed AQL infrastructure received positive assessments regarding random access, exportability, tool integration, and reproducibility. The survey indicates that practical usage barriers have been reduced but not completely eliminated (e.g., some tools for easier reuse of the AQL data still need further development).

## 4   The Revised AQL Corpus

While the crawling and parsing of the Archive Query Log is continuously running on our cluster, its current snapshot, the AQL corpus, shown in Table 2, already exceeds the size of the original AQL-22 by approximately 3.5 times. The AQL now compiles 553 million SERPs by parsing over 2 billion candidate captures from six web archives and for 775 search providers. The parsed SERPs range from those archived over 25 years ago (i.e., when web search engines first became popular) to those archived as this paper was being written. Our continuous mining copes well with 44 TBs of WARC files. Next we outline how analyses are facilitated by our data architecture, despite the enormous size.

---

[14] https://github.com/localstack/localstack

**Table 2.** Statistics of the AQL corpus as of October 2025.

| Entity (see Section 3) | Count | Disk size | Captured timespan |
| --- | --- | --- | --- |
| Web archives | 6 | 28.6 KB | — |
| Search providers | 775 | 801.8 KB | — |
| Crawlable sources | 26,076 | 16.0 MB | — |
| Candidate captures | 2,188,260,976 | 4.2 TB | 1996-10-16 – 2025-10-12 |
| SERPs | 552,614,234 | 1.8 TB | 1999-08-24 – 2025-10-12 |
| → HTML downloaded | 223,240,908 | — | 1999-08-24 – 2025-10-17 |
| → HTML parsed | 4,337,824 | — | 1999-08-24 – 2025-10-07 |
| Web search result blocks | 51,386,161 | 412.5 GB | 1999-08-29 – 2025-03-18 |
| WARC files (local, temp.) | 344,889 | 412.3 GB | — |
| WARC files (S3) | 45,346 | 43.6 TB | — |

```
{
  "query": { "bool": { "should": [
    { "match_phrase": { "url_query": "valentine's day" } },
    { "match_phrase": { "url_query": "easter" } }, ...
  ]}},
  "aggs": { "queries_over_time": {
    "date_histogram": {
      "field": "capture.timestamp", "calendar_interval": "week"
    }
  }}
}
```

Listing 4: Weekly histogram of SERPs for holiday-related queries in a single query.

*Basic Elasticsearch-based Analyses.* Many meaningful analyses can be performed directly on the AQL's Elasticsearch indices, without the need for any additional data analysis tools, by using Elasticsearch's built-in aggregations.[15] As a demonstration, we conduct a temporal trend analysis of SERPs whose queries are about annual holidays or events, e.g., "Labor Day" or "Christmas". The Elasticsearch query in Listing 4 counts holiday-related SERPs per week. Unlike analyses of the AQL-22 that required substantial setup or manual tooling [37], such analyses are now much more straightforward to conduct.

In Fig. 2, we compare the resulting histogram with corresponding Google Trends data.[16] For both Google Trends and the AQL, we observe clear annual peaks for each holiday, where search activity often increases in the weeks leading up to the event. An interesting exception to this observation is "Halloween",

---

[15] https://elastic.co/docs/explore-analyze/query-filter/aggregations
[16] https://trends.google.com/trends/

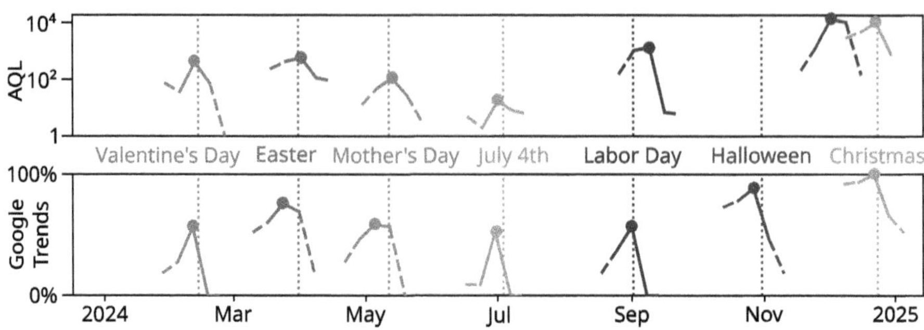

**Fig. 2.** Histogram of holiday-related queries in the AQL data for selected holidays, compared to the corresponding Google Trends (log scale, $\pm 2$ weeks around the peak).

```
src = ElasticsearchDatasource(schema=Serp, query=Exists(field="url_query"))
data = read_datasource(src, override_num_blocks=100)
count = data.count()
count_operator = data.filter(lambda row: "site:" in row["url_query"]).count()
print(f"Found {count} SERPs and {count_operator} with operator.")
```

Listing 5: Count the number of SERPs with a `site:` operator in the query.

where the AQL shows a peak after the event.[17] Overall, the AQL data aligns well with Google Trends, indicating that the AQL represents real-world search behavior.

*Custom Batch Processing Analyses.* More complex analyses beyond simple aggregations can still be implemented easily using batch-processing libraries like Ray. The AQL data from Elasticsearch can be mapped, filtered, and reduced in Ray by using our custom Ray datasource.A simple use case is counting the number of SERPs that contain search operators in the query, e.g., `site:amazon.com`. Performing such custom analysis with just Elasticsearch is difficult due to the regular expression used to identify the search operator. However, Listing 5 demonstrates how to implement this analysis in just a few lines of code with Ray, yielding that from the 553 million SERPs only 13 million contain the `site:` operator.

*Data Export.* For use cases not supported by Elasticsearch or batch processing, we simplify exporting the AQL data into standard formats. Listing 6 shows how to export all SERPs into JSONL files with Ray. Running concurrently on multiple Ray workers, data can thus be backed up regularly.

---

[17] Manual inspection revealed that during this shifted peak, many SERPs appear to be systematically archived for hundreds of Google domains

```
ray job submit --runtime-env env.yml -- \
  python -m archive_query_log serps export-all \
    --format jsonl \
    --output-path /path/to/exports/serps/
```

Listing 6: Export all SERPs of the AQL as JSONL files.

## 5   Data Access Strategies

Maintaining and crawling large-scale query logs at the scale of the Archive Query Log comes with significant costs in terms of storage, bandwidth, and compute resources. Thus, even though completely re-crawling and parsing the full AQL data is technically feasible, we acknowledge that making the AQL data more reusable (i.e., without re-crawl) is more economical and ecological [40].

Besides expanding corpus coverage and improving pipeline efficiency, future work will hence focus on further enhancing data accessibility, in particular to researchers from other disciplines, e.g., social sciences. Privacy concerns remain a key obstacle to open access to query logs of the scale of the AQL. We will therefore explore privacy-preserving data access methods, e.g., using TIRA [35], differential privacy [15], or automated cleaning of personal, illegal, or sensitive data. Ultimately, we aim to provide access to the AQL data (1) for interactive browsing and downloads of focused subsets, and (2) as an IR test collection.

*Interactive Data Browsing and Download.* We plan to provide a web-based SERP browser to interactively explore AQL data, e.g., by searching for search engine result pages for a specific topic, filtering by search provider and other metadata, and visualizing temporal trends similar to Fig. 2. This data browser aims to reduce the entry barrier for researchers from other disciplines or domains, and lets them define, explore, and annotate subsets of interest for their purposes. License permitting, users will be able to download the selected SERP data as an anonymized, cleaned dataset. As another route to access the data, we plan to develop a SERP ontology to represent the AQL data as a knowledge graph, facilitating linked data queries (e.g., by integrating WikiData).

*A SERP-based Information Retrieval Test Collection.* Despite their central role, existing information retrieval test collections often lack diversity in terms of topics, time, and query intent, which can largely be attributed to the high cost of manual relevance assessment. Here, the AQL opens up new opportunities for building large-scale information retrieval test collections grounded in real-world search behavior and relevance labels approximated by the most popular (and often most effective) search engines available on the Web.

The Archive Query Log naturally provides all three components of a Cranfield-style IR test collection [9]: (1) SERPs contain the queries of actual user information needs, (2) the landing pages linked from search results form a diverse document corpus, and (3) the ranking of results by search engines serves as implicit relevance signals. Note that such implicit relevance signals are not intended to replace explicit human relevance judgments, but to complement the reliability of human judgment with a substantially upscaled evaluation coverage and diversity.

## 6   Conclusion and Future Work

We presented a scalable framework for mining query logs of any search provider from multiple web archives. Our approach overcomes the main limitations of the previous AQL crawl, which was confined to a single web archive, offered limited extensibility, and provided restricted data access and portability. These issues were addressed by adopting the FAIR principles (findable, accessible, interoperable, reusable/reproducible) and extending them with requirements for scalability and maintainability in both data and software.

The new infrastructure, guided by these principles, enables anyone to download and parse search engine result pages in a scalable, distributed manner, integrate new search providers and archives, and perform temporal analyses efficiently. It fulfills the FAIR principles through unique identifiability, standardized APIs, open and versioned formats, and open-source licensing. Scalability is ensured by distributed crawling and parallel data processing, while maintainability follows from modular design, clear interfaces, and automated deployment workflows. We demonstrated the successful download of 217 million SERPs and showcased the system's ability to process data across arbitrary time frames.

Our ongoing work focuses on improving data accessibility by developing interactive browsing tools and using the AQL as the basis for a large-scale, diverse IR test collection. Moreover, working with the community, we seek to systematically add all compatible web archives (projection: 30–50 archives) and more search providers (i.e., websites that offer or have in the past offered search functionality) with a focus on important application domains like health, law, and education. We encourage researchers to build similar domain- or language-specific query logs, and to contribute back their new metadata and parsers to the AQL.

**Acknowledgments.** This work has been partially funded by the BMFTR CORAL project under Grant № 16IS24077B and by the OpenWebSearch.eu project, funded by the EU under Grant № GA 101070014.

**Disclosure of Interests.** The authors have no competing interests to declare that are relevant to the content of this article.

# References


1. Software engineering - product quality. Standard ISO/IEC 9126–1:2001, International Organization for Standardization, Geneva (2001). https://iso.org/standard/22749.html
2. Information technology - database languages sql. Standard ISO/IEC 9075–1:2023, International Organization for Standardization, Geneva (2023), https://iso.org/standard/76583.html
3. Beeferman, D., Berger, A.L.: Agglomerative clustering of a search engine query log. In: KDD, pp. 407–416. ACM (2000). https://doi.org/10.1145/347090.347176
4. Bevendorff, J., Wiegmann, M., Potthast, M., Stein, B.: Is Google getting worse? a longitudinal investigation of SEO spam in search engines. In: ECIR, pp. 56–71. Springer (2024). https://doi.org/10.1007/978-3-031-56063-7_4
5. Bondarenko, A., et al.: CausalQA: a benchmark for causal question answering. In: COLING, pp. 3296–3308. ICCL (2022). https://aclanthology.org/2022.coling-1.291
6. Bondi, A.B.: Characteristics of scalability and their impact on performance. In: Proceedings of WOSP 2000, pp. 195–203. ACM (2000). https://doi.org/10.1145/350391.350432
7. Chen, Q., et al.: MS MARCO web search: A large-scale information-rich web dataset with millions of real click labels. In: WWW, pp. 292–301. ACM (2024). https://doi.org/10.1145/3589335.3648327
8. Chien, S., Immorlica, N.: Semantic similarity between search engine queries using temporal correlation. In: WWW, pp. 2–11. ACM (2005). https://doi.org/10.1145/1060745.1060752
9. Cleverdon, C.: The Cranfield tests on index language devices. Aslib Proc. **19**(6), 173–194 (1967). https://doi.org/10.1108/eb050097
10. Codd, E.F.: A relational model of data for large shared data banks. Commun. ACM **13**(6), 377–387 (1970). https://doi.org/10.1145/362384.362685
11. Cozza, V., et al.: Transparency in keyword faceted search: an investigation on Google Shopping. In: IRCDL, pp. 29–43. Springer (2019). https://doi.org/10.1007/978-3-030-11226-4_3
12. Craswell, N., et al.: ORCAS: 20 million clicked query-document pairs for analyzing search. In: CIKM, pp. 2983–2989. ACM (2020). https://doi.org/10.1145/3340531.3412779
13. Croft, W.B., Metzler, D., Strohman, T.: Search Engines - Information Retrieval in Practice. Pearson Education (2009)
14. Dean, J., Ghemawat, S.: MapReduce: simplified data processing on large clusters. In: Brewer, E.A., Chen, P. (eds.) Proceedings of OSDI 2004, pp. 137–150. USENIX Association (2004). http://usenix.org/events/osdi04/tech/dean.html
15. Dwork, C.: Differential privacy. In: Bugliesi, M., Preneel, B., Sassone, V., Wegener, I. (eds.) Proceedings of ICALP 2006. LNCS, vol. 4052, pp. 1–12. Springer (2006). https://doi.org/10.1007/11787006_1
16. Gienapp, L., et al.: Evaluating generative ad hoc information retrieval. In: SIGIR, pp. 1916–1929. ACM (2024). https://doi.org/10.1145/3626772.3657849
17. Hutson, J.: Augmenting art historical research. In: Art History in the Age of Artificial Intelligence, pp. 47–83. Springer Series on Cultural Computing, Springer, Cham (2026). https://doi.org/10.1007/978-3-032-02920-1_3
18. Ivie, P., Thain, D.: Reproducibility in scientific computing. ACM Comput. Surv. **51**(3), 63:1–63:36 (2018). https://doi.org/10.1145/3186266

19. Jansen, B.J., Spink, A.: Methodological approach in discovering user search patterns through web log analysis. Bull. Am. Soc. Inf. Sci. Technol. **27**(1), 15–17 (2000). https://doi.org/10.1002/bult.185

20. Jansen, B.J., Spink, A., Bateman, J., Saracevic, T.: Real life information retrieval: a study of user queries on the web. SIGIR Forum **32**(1), 5–17 (1998). https://doi.org/10.1145/281250.281253

21. Jansen, B.J., et al.: A temporal comparison of AltaVista web searching. J. Assoc. Inf. Sci. Technol. **56**(6), 559–570 (2005). https://doi.org/10.1002/asi.20145

22. Kamphuis, C.: Graph databases for information retrieval. In: Jose, J.M., et al. (eds.) Proceedings of ECIR 2020. LNCS, vol. 12036, pp. 608–612. Springer (2020). https://doi.org/10.1007/978-3-030-45442-5_79

23. Kirti, M., Maurya, A.K., Yadav, R.S.: Fault-tolerance approaches for distributed and cloud computing environments: A systematic review, taxonomy and future directions. Concurr. Comput. Pract. Exp. **36**(13) (2024). https://doi.org/10.1002/cpe.8081

24. Lamprecht, A., et al.: Towards FAIR principles for research software. Data Sci. **3**(1), 37–59 (2020). https://doi.org/10.3233/DS-190026

25. Lanasri, D.: Query logs analytics: a systematic literature review (2025). 10.48550/arXiv. 2508.13949

26. Lewis, P., et al.: Retrieval-augmented generation for knowledge-intensive NLP tasks. In: NeurIPS (2020). https://proceedings.neurips.cc/paper/2020/hash/6b493230205f780e1bc26945df7481e5-Abstract.html

27. Li, R., et al.: Exposing query identification for search transparency. In: WWW, pp. 3662–3672. ACM (2022). https://doi.org/10.1145/3485447.3512262

28. Martin, J.: Managing the data base environment. Prentice Hall-, Harlow (1983)

29. Mesnier, M.P., Ganger, G.R., Riedel, E.: Object-based storage. IEEE Commun. Mag. **41**(8), 84–90 (2003). https://doi.org/10.1109/MCOM.2003.1222722

30. Oliveira, B., Lopes, C.T.: The evolution of web search user interfaces - an archaeological analysis of Google search engine result pages. In: CHIIR, pp. 55–68. ACM (2023). https://doi.org/10.1145/3576840.3578320

31. Oliveira, B., Lopes, C.T.: From 10 blue links pages to feature-full search engine results pages - analysis of the temporal evolution of SERP features. In: CHIIR, pp. 338–345. ACM (2023). https://doi.org/10.1145/3576840.3578307

32. Oosterhuis, H., de Rijke, M.: Differentiable unbiased online learning to rank. In: CIKM, pp. 1293–1302. ACM (2018). https://doi.org/10.1145/3269206.3271686

33. Palotti, J., Hanbury, A., Müller, H., Kahn, C.E.: How users search and what they search for in the medical domain. Inf. Retrieval J. 189–224 (2015). https://doi.org/10.1007/s10791-015-9269-8

34. Parry, A., Merker, J.H., Ruth, S., Fröbe, M., Scells, H.: Corpora performance prediction. In: Proceedings of QPP++@ECIR 2025. QPP++ (2025). https://qppworkshop.github.io/assets/files/corpora_andrew_paper.pdf

35. Potthast, M., Gollub, T., Wiegmann, M., Stein, B.: Tira integrated research architecture. In: Ferro, N., Peters, C. (eds.) Information Retrieval Evaluation in a Changing World, Information Retrieval Series, vol. 41, pp. 123–160. Springer (2019). https://doi.org/10.1007/978-3-030-22948-1_5

36. Potthast, M., Hagen, M., Stein, B.: The dilemma of the direct answer. SIGIR Forum **54**(1), 14:1–14:12 (2020). https://doi.org/10.1145/3451964.3451978

37. Reimer, J.H., et al.: The Archive Query Log: Mining Millions of Search Result Pages of Hundreds of Search Engines from 25 Years of Web Archives. In: Chen, H.H., et al. (eds.) 46th International ACM SIGIR Conference on Research and Development in Information Retrieval (SIGIR 2023), pp. 2848–2860. ACM (2023). https://doi.org/10.1145/3539618.3591890
38. Ros, K., Jin, M., Levine, J., Zhai, C.: Retrieving webpages using online discussions. In: Yoshioka, M., Kiseleva, J., Aliannejadi, M. (eds.) Proceedings of ICTIR 2023, pp. 159–168. ACM (2023). https://doi.org/10.1145/3578337.3605139
39. Scells, H., Forbes, C., Clark, J., Koopman, B., Zuccon, G.: The impact of query refinement on systematic review literature search: a query log analysis. In: ICTIR, pp. 34–42. ACM (2022). https://doi.org/10.1145/3539813.3545143
40. Scells, H., Zhuang, S., Zuccon, G.: Reduce, reuse, recycle: green information retrieval research. In: Amigó, E., et al. (eds.) Proceedings of SIGIR 2022, pp. 2825–2837. ACM (2022). https://doi.org/10.1145/3477495.3531766
41. Schultheiß, S., Lewandowski, D., von Mach, S., Yagci, N.: Query sampler: generating query sets for analyzing search engines using keyword research tools. PeerJ Comput. Sci. 9 (2023). https://doi.org/10.7717/peerj-cs.1421
42. Shivashankar, K., Hajj, G.S.A., Martini, A.: Maintainability and scalability in machine learning: Challenges and solutions. ACM Comput. Surv. 57(12), 318:1–318:36 (2025). https://doi.org/10.1145/3736751
43. Spink, A., et al.: U.S. versus European Web searching trends. SIGIR Forum 36(2), 32–38 (2002). https://doi.org/10.1145/792550.792555
44. Van de Sompel, H., Nelson, M., Sanderson, R.: HTTP framework for time-based access to resource states - Memento. RFC 7089 (2013). https://doi.org/10.17487/RFC7089
45. Wilkinson, M.D., et al.: The FAIR guiding principles for scientific data management and stewardship. Sci. Data 3(1), 160018 (2016)
46. Zhuang, S., Zuccon, G.: Counterfactual online learning to rank. In: ECIR, pp. 415–430. Springer (2020). https://doi.org/10.1007/978-3-030-45439-5_28

# ROUTIR: Fast Serving of Retrieval Pipelines for Retrieval-Augmented Generation


Eugene Yang[1]([✉]) [iD], Andrew Yates[1] [iD], Dawn Lawrie[1] [iD], James Mayfield[1] [iD],
and Trevor Adriaanse[2] [iD]

[1] Human Language Technology Center of Excellence, Johns Hopkins University,
Baltimore, MD 21211, USA
`{eugene.yang,andrew.yates,lawrie,mayfield}@jhu.edu`
[2] Johns Hopkins University, Baltimore, MD 21211, USA
`tadriaa1@jhu.edu`



**Abstract.** Retrieval models are key components of Retrieval-Augmented Generation (RAG) systems, which generate search queries, process the documents returned, and generate a response. RAG systems are often dynamic and may involve multiple rounds of retrieval. While many state-of-the-art retrieval methods are available through academic IR platforms, these platforms are typically designed for the Cranfield paradigm in which all queries are known up front and can be batch processed offline. This simplification accelerates research but leaves state-of-the-art retrieval models unable to support downstream applications that require online services, such as arbitrary dynamic RAG pipelines that involve looping, feedback, or even self-organizing agents. In this work, we introduce ROUTIR, a Python package that provides a simple and efficient HTTP API that wraps arbitrary retrieval methods, including first stage retrieval, reranking, query expansion, and result fusion. By providing a minimal JSON configuration file specifying the retrieval models to serve, ROUTIR can be used to construct and query retrieval pipelines on-the-fly using any permutation of available models (e.g., fusing the results of several first-stage retrieval methods followed by reranking). The API automatically performs asynchronous query batching and caches results by default. While many state-of-the-art retrieval methods are already supported by the package, ROUTIR is also easily expandable by implementing the *Engine* abstract class. The package is open-sourced and publicly available on GitHub: http://github.com/hltcoe/routir.

**Keywords:** search service · retrieval-augmented generation · asynchronous query batching · multi-stage retrieval · online evaluation


## 1 Introduction

Information retrieval research typically requires system comparison using a fixed set of queries and documents, following the Cranfield paradigm [7]. Such exper-


© The Author(s), under exclusive license to Springer Nature Switzerland AG 2026
R. Campos et al. (Eds.): ECIR 2026, LNCS 16486, pp. 578–593, 2026.
https://doi.org/10.1007/978-3-032-21321-1_60

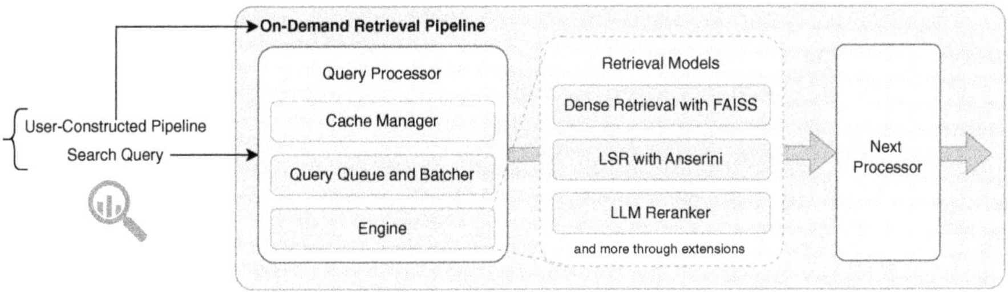


**Fig. 1.** Service architecture of RoutIR. The user's HTTP request specifies a retrieval pipeline and search query, illustrated on the left. RoutIR orchestrates the retrieval pipeline on the fly and processes the query with each query processor. Each processor manages queuing, caching, and query processing. The "Next Processor" enables, for example, reranking or result fusion. See Fig. 2 for a full JSON example of a request.

iments can be conducted through either batched or sequential query processing, depending on whether measuring query latency is critical to the study. Regardless, the queries are predefined, so the experimental environment can be static and read directly from a file. However, embedding retrieval models in a larger dynamic system pipeline creates challenges and overhead when conducting experiments.

Particularly in Retrieval-Augmented Generation (RAG), the primary pipeline involves one or more large language models (LLMs) [9,46] that generate search queries, digest retrieved documents, and draft the response. Instead of a linear process such as Fusion-in-Decoder [17] or GINGER [20], RAG systems are increasingly complex and dynamic, with multiple rounds of retrieval [1,9,13,39,47]. A static experimental environment is not sufficient for these systems, because the queries are not known up front. Tools for offline query processing need to be modified to include the generative components or wrapped to provide an API that can accommodate online querying. However, wrapping offline retrieval pipelines with reasonable query and resource efficiency is non-trivial, and this task is orthogonal to implementing a retrieval model. We introduce an open-source package, RoutIR, that allows users to provide pipelines composed of the latest retrieval models as an HTTP API for use with downstream applications like dynamic RAG systems.

RoutIR supports (1) simple service configuration for common model architectures without additional coding; (2) minimal wrappers for incorporating new models; (3) dynamic batching and queuing for concurrent and asynchronous requests; (4) fast and robust caching in memory and Redis;[1] and (5) reliable and easy-to-use HTTP API endpoints that do not require additional client-side packages. Such capabilities provide fast and reproducible experimental environments for RAG research, while enabling new retrieval models to be incorporated easily with minimal engineering overhead. While RoutIR is designed primarily for academic research, which does not implement various security measures for

---

[1] https://redis.io/.

an API service, it can be used for internal prototyping in industry to spin up a proof-of-concept application.

RoutIR has been deployed in various research settings where it has been demonstrated to be robust and reliable. During JHU SCALE 2025,[2] a ten-week research workshop at Johns Hopkins University attended by more than 50 researchers working on long-form RAG, RoutIR was able to provide the retrieval API for PLAID-X [48], SPLADE-v3 [21], and Qwen3 Embedding [53] on the TREC NeuCLIR [23], TREC RAGTIME [24], TREC BioGen [16], and TREC RAG (i.e., MS-MARCO v2 Passage) [42] document collections using only three NVIDIA 24GB TITAN RTXs. In this use case, all three retrieval systems were able to provide search results with a reasonable latency without caching, and to provide results nearly instantaneously when results were cached. With asynchronous HTTP requests, which is the typical use case in RAG research, since multiple queries are usually generated and searched at the same time, RoutIR provides a throughput of 3 to 10 queries per second depending on the underlying model. RoutIR also powered the search service for the TREC RAGTIME track[3] to provide the same PLAID-X model for all track participants. With only CPU resources, the endpoint provides a latency of around 600 ms on an AWS virtual machine when serving both TREC NeuCLIR and RAGTIME collections.

In this paper, we document the design decisions, architecture, and several use cases for RoutIR. The package is publicly available on PyPI with implementation available on GitHub.

## 2   Related Work

*Academic IR platforms* have a long history going back to at least the mid-1980s [4]. Platforms like Galago [5], Indri [40], Patapsco [8], and Terrier [35] support offline experiments with traditional statistical methods, while platforms like Anserini [25,50], Capreolus [51,52], Experimaestro [36], FlexNeuART [2], LLM4Ranking [27], LLM-Rankers [54], OpenNIR [30], PyTerrier [32], RankLLM [54], and Tevatron [14,29] provide support for modern neural first-stage retrieval and reranking methods [26]. These platforms are typically designed for offline IR experiments following the Cranfield paradigm. They provide reproducible indexing and searching capabilities to support experimentation where test queries are predefined and can be processed sequentially or in batch. Rather than providing general-purpose toolkits, there has been a recent trend towards streamlining experimentation using tools designed to run specific benchmarks with a predefined set of collections, such as MTEB [33] and BEIR [41]. While these academic tools are useful for offline retrieval evaluation and have greatly advanced the field, their focus on offline usage limits their ability to be embedded in larger systems. They typically do not provide Web APIs to interface with downstream applications.

---

[2] https://hltcoe.jhu.edu/research/scale/scale-2025/.
[3] https://trec-ragtime.github.io/search_api.html.

This limitation particularly affects RAG, where retrieval is usually an upstream or interleaving component providing retrieved information to generative models [1,9,13,39,43,46,47]. This is a different setting from offline experimentation where the queries are fixed. RAG pipelines like Open Deep Research[4] can dynamically generate queries to incrementally gather information for generation. There are two ways to support such iterative RAG pipelines: (re-)implement the generative component within the IR platform or provide an API that can be dynamically queried by an external generative library. PyTerrier-RAG [31] takes the former approach, whereas ROUTIR takes the latter by dynamically accepting and serving queries using state-of-the-art IR methods, including those implemented by platforms designed for offline use. Rather than reimplementing the underlying retrieval methods and RAG workflows, ROUTIR provides a streamlined approach to wrap existing methods, compose them into retrieval pipelines, and query them online through a HTTP API. This allows ROUTIR to serve the fast-growing RAG community by seamlessly embedding retrieval models into RAG platforms instead of requiring that RAG methods be reimplemented within an academic IR platform.

*Production search platforms* like ElasticSearch[5], OpenSearch[6], and Vespa[7] provide HTTP APIs for first-stage retrieval and reranking over collections that have been indexed by those platforms. These tools are complex, closely integrated with their underlying inverted index and vector database data structures, and optimized for production use. These design choices make extending the platforms with new methods non-trivial. In contrast, ROUTIR provides a simple API and flexible method classes that make adding new retrieval models straightforward.

## 3   ROUTIR Architecture

ROUTIR is a thin, robust wrapper around retrieval models that provides online service capabilities that are orthogonal to the retrieval models themselves. The end user submits an HTTP request to a ROUTIR endpoint for each search query, e.g., `{"service":"qwen3-neuclir","query":"where is machu picchu","limit":15 }`, and receives the retrieval results of the requested 15 documents in a dictionary of document IDs and scores. A separate request delivers the document data associated with the document ID.

The core design principle of ROUTIR is to be as lightweight as possible while providing a flexible service layer to mitigate the overhead of serving state-of-the-art models when they are released. In ROUTIR, we limit dependencies to only essential packages and leave model-specific ones, such as Huggingface Transformers [45] and PyJNIus,[8] as extras for users to install when they are needed.

---

[4] https://github.com/langchain-ai/open_deep_research.
[5] https://www.elastic.co/elasticsearch.
[6] https://opensearch.org/.
[7] https://vespa.ai/.
[8] https://github.com/kivy/pyjnius.

In this section, we describe the ROUTIR service architecture, which is illustrated in Fig. 1. ROUTIR has three main components: Engines, Processors, and Pipelines.

- *Engines* provide one or more core retrieval capabilities: first-stage retrieval using an index, reranking, query rewriting, and result fusion. To add new methods to ROUTIR, the user writes an Engine subclass that may simply wrap an existing implementation. A special *Relay* Engine can be used to access Engines provided by another node running ROUTIR.
- *Processors* receive search queries as input and perform actions before passing the queries to an Engine. By default, they are used to cache results and to batch queries that arrive in quick succession.
- *Pipelines* describe how engines are composed to produce a ranking. For example, a pipeline could indicate that results from two first-stage retrieval engines should be fused and then reranked. Pipelines can be composed of available Engines on the fly.

### 3.1   Retrieval Engines

Each retrieval model or system should be wrapped as an Engine, which implements the interface for serving queries. Each engine can provide one or more of the four core retrieval capabilities: (a) index searching, (b) query-passage scoring (for reranking), (c) query rewriting (or generation), and (d) result fusion.

Allowing each engine instance to provide multiple capabilities can minimize the memory footprint when different tasks share the same underlying models. For instance, most bi-encoder models can provide both first-stage retrieval that results in a ranked list of documents, and query-passage scoring (reranking) that enables fast passage selection when a RAG pipeline [6,15,18] needs to compress the document input to the most relevant passages to feed to a downstream generation step. To improve retrieval effectiveness, an Engine can provide a reranker, such as monoT5 [37], Qwen3 Reranker [53], or Rank1 [44]. Rerankers take a query and a list of strings (e.g. documents) as input and output a ranking over the input list. In ROUTIR, modules can be initiated in Python as a standalone model instance to provide a unified interface; this is similar to what PyTerrier extensions such as `pyterrier-colbert` provide. However, the primary benefit of this thin wrapper is that it provides a robust and flexible online search service.

Queries as inputs to the Engine are batched (as detailed in Sect. 3.2) to provide better service throughput; this is helpful because most bi-encoders and cross-encoders can score multiple queries and documents in the same matrix multiplication, leading to better GPU utilization. The common measurement for query-time efficiency has been query latency measured by sequentially issuing queries to the model during offline evaluation [38]. However, when serving multiple users or queries as a service, ROUTIR optimizes for throughput (i.e., the number of queries served in a fixed period of time) since queries can often be served asynchronously. Especially for a RAG pipeline that issues multiple queries simultaneously [11,49], all retrieval results must arrive before generation begins; this suggests the need for high-throughput rather than low-latency (although the two qualities are usually correlated).

**Multi-server Request Routing.** A special type of Engine is a *Relay* – an Engine that relays requests to another ROUTIR endpoint. This capability is particularly useful when computing resources are divided among multiple machines or if some compute nodes are not exposed to a public IP (a common setup in academic research clusters). This is similar to the proxy service in LiteLLM[9] that relays LLM requests to compute endpoints without exposing multiple machines to the end users. While ROUTIR does not offer load-balancing at the request level (which may be included in future versions), it offers triage at the model level to direct requests to models with different resource requirements to different machines. ROUTIR also supports importing services from a list of endpoints to simplify configuration (more on this in Sect. 4.2). This feature provides the backbone for collectively serving multiple retrieval models with one endpoint in a distributed computing environment, which is crucial to facilitate complex retrieval pipelines (more on this later in this section).

## 3.2  Query Processor

Each Engine is further wrapped in a Processor class, which handles caching and queuing of input search queries. When the processor receives a query, it is added to the service queue for batching. The queue dispatches a batch of queries to the engine whenever the batch is full (size configurable) or the maximum wait time is reached (typically 50 to 100 ms; also configurable). When a set of subqueries is generated by a RAG system and sent to the endpoint individually through asynchronous HTTP requests, they are usually batched on the server side to allow them to be processed together by the Engine. The end user can also simultaneously process multiple top-level queries in a RAG pipeline and use the batching capability of the retrieval server. This exploits the asynchronous nature of HTTP requests. With the native support of asynchronous operations in Python, firing multiple retrieval and LLM requests to an external server without blocking the program from advancing to other operations until the results are actually needed is a key ingredient to accelerate the speed of RAG toolkits such as LangGraph,[10] AutoGen,[11] DSPy [19], and GPT Researcher [12].

While batching adds some overhead in gathering queries, it prevents queries from being processed sequentially. This results in greater throughput when handling multiple queries. This is generally not handled by offline IR toolkits such as PyTerrier [32] and Anserini [50], since online serving is not the primary use case for those tools. ROUTIR provides the essential wrappers to serve retrieval mod-

---

<sup>9</sup> https://github.com/BerriAI/litellm.
<sup>10</sup> https://www.langchain.com/langgraph.
<sup>11</sup> https://microsoft.github.io/autogen.

```
1  {
2    "pipeline": "{qwen3-neuclir,plaidx-neuclir}RRF%
3    "collection": "neuclir",
4    "query": "where is Taiwan"
5  }
```

**Fig. 2.** Example Pipeline Request. The pipeline issues the query to `qwen3-neuclir` and `plaidx-neuclir` engines, fuses the results with reciprocal rank fusion, takes the top 50 documents from the fused result, and finally reranks using Rank1 [44] reranker.

**Table 1.** Operators for pipeline construction string. Please refer to https://github. com/hltcoe/routir/blob/main/src/routir/pipeline/parser.py#L7 for the full context-free grammar.

| Operator | Operation | Description |
| --- | --- | --- |
| e1 >> e2 | Pipe | Pass the retrieval results of e1 to a downstream engine e2, such as a reranker. |
| e1%k | Limit | Only retain the top $k$ retrieved documents from e1 |
| {e1, e2 | Parallel Pipelines | Pass the upstream results or query (if at the beginning of a pipeline) to a list of parallel pipelines (e1 and e2). |
| xx{e1,e2 | Query Generation | Generate multiple sub-queries with method xx and issue them to all parallel pipelines. |
| }xx | Result Fusion | Fuse retrieval results from parallel pipelines with method xx. |

els, including those supported by PyTerrier and Anserini, to efficiently embed them in a RAG system pipeline.

Furthermore, processors also cache retrieval results to prevent duplicate requests to the Engine instance. RoutIR supports both in-memory and Redis caches, which provides flexibility to support different cache integrity needs.

### 3.3   On-Demand Pipeline Construction

In addition to serving the query with a single retrieval model, RoutIR supports on-demand pipeline construction from the end user request. This is illustrated in Fig. 2, where the pipeline combines the results of two first-stage retrievers using reciprocal rank fusion and reranks the fused results. RoutIR parses the pipeline string provided by the user. It understands that the Engines corresponding to the two first-stage retrievers can be run in parallel and that fusion and reranking are sequential steps with the >> pipe operator. In addition, asynchronous requests are issued to prioritize throughput when producing the final retrieval results.

The pipeline string is defined using a context-free grammar that supports the construction of linear pipelines. Table 1 summarizes the operators available for the pipeline construction string. Dynamic pipeline construction allows a user or RAG system to control the pipeline as needed on the fly to accommodate runtime constraints such as latency, coverage, and query difficulty. The context-free grammar can even be part of the input to the language model, enabling it to generate the pipeline as part of an agentic workflow.

## 4    Serving Models Using RoutIR

In this section, we describe how RoutIR can be configured and extended to serve different retrieval models. This serves as an introduction to all the features provided by RoutIR; readers are encouraged to explore further in the documentation and the source code on GitHub.

### 4.1    Resource and Setup

Computing resources needed to run the barebone RoutIR are very minimal, for example, a single processor with 200 MB memory can host a RoutIR instance with only Relay Engine. However, resources for hosting each retrieval model depend on its own requirements. For example, it is more efficient to host a dense retrieval model with a GPU for encoding the queries; Faiss indexes usually require a larger system memory to hold the in-memory index for better performance.

RoutIR can be installed through `pip` or `uv`. Please refer to the documentation for more details. It can also be hosted with a command as simple as `uvx routir config.json` without explicit package installation.

### 4.2    Server Configuration

RoutIR uses a JSON file to express the configuration for the services with two primary blocks: `services` and `collections`. The `services` block is a list of dictionaries that specifies all the Engines to initialize on the endpoint. The `collections` block specifies a list of document collections that the endpoint will serve based on the document IDs requested. The additional top-level `server_imports` and `file_imports` fields allow the user to specify external RoutIR endpoints and custom Python scripts to include during the initialization. All available services on each endpoint in `server_imports` are automatically relayed. This allows offloading computationally expensive models, such as LLM reranking, to another machine, while still enabling their integration with other services in the end user's custom retrieval pipelines. Figure 3 demonstrates an example configuration JSON object.

Each dictionary in the `services` list defines a processor and its underlying Engine. The field `engine` specifies the Engine class to initiate, which can be any of those included in RoutIR as built-in engines such as `PLAIDX`, or ones that are implemented by the user in a separate Python script. This is accomplished via

```
1   {
2     "server_imports": [ "http://localhost:5000" ]
3     "file_imports": [ "./examples/rank1_extension.py" ],
4     "services": [
5       {
6         "name": "rank1",
7         "engine": "Rank1Engine",
8         "config": {}
9       }
10      {
11        "name": "qwen3-neuclir",
12        "engine": "Qwen3",
13        "batch_size": 16,
14        "config": {
15          "index_path": "hfds:routir/neuclir-qwen3-8b-faiss-
                PQ2048x4fs",
16          "embedding_model_name": "Qwen/Qwen3-Embedding-8B",
17        }
18      }
19    ],
20    "collections": [
21      {
22        "name": "neuclir",
23        "doc_path": "./neuclir.collection.jsonl"
24      }
25    ]
26  }
```

**Fig. 3.** Example configuration file. Refer to the RoutIR documentation for more fields. In the example, we load two engines: Rank1 reranker from a custom script (see Sect. 4.3), and qwen3-neuclir using a FAISS index loaded from Huggingface Datasets containing Qwen3 8B embeddings. The specified document collection can be used to retrieve document text via an API or to pass documents to reranking models.

the file_imports field that allows users to specify scripts to load on-demand without modifying the package or implementing another custom entry script.

The collections field lists each collection serviced by an engine in a dictionary containing the name of the collection and a path to a JSONL file. Each JSON object is a document containing an ID field with arbitrary fields carrying its content. RoutIR loads each JSONL collection file and builds a memory offset lookup table to efficiently look up the document when serving the content. Such lookup tables allow RoutIR random access the collection file based on document IDs without reading the file sequentially or loading the entire collection into memory.

RoutIR provides several built-in Engine types that can be used to serve models with common architectures such as dense bi-encoders with FAISS indices, multi-vector dense retrieval with PLAID-X [48], and learned-sparse retrieval

```
1   class PyseriniBM25(Engine):
2       def __init__(self, name: str = None, config=None, **
            kwargs):
3           super().__init__(name, config, **kwargs)
4           self.searcher = LuceneSearcher(self.index_path)
5           self.searcher.set_bm25(0.9, 0.4)
6
7       async def search_batch(self, queries, limit=20):
8           return [
9               {docobj.docid: docobj.score
10                  for docobj in self.searcher.search(query, k=lm)}
11                  for query, lm in zip(queries, limit)
12          ]
```

**Fig. 4.** Example code snippet for integrating Pyserini with RoutIR. This example can be extended with more flexible parameter configuration or even allowing the endpoint users to specify the retrieval model. Full example can be found at https://github.com/hltcoe/routir/blob/main/examples/pyserini_extension.py.

models with Anserini [50]. These Engines are implemented based on an `Engine` Python abstract class that ensures a common interface.

These Engine types cover most use cases when using neural models. However, since there is not yet a common reranker architecture (besides the general pointwise, pairwise, listwise, and setwise paradigms), we have selectively implemented a few rerankers as built-in Engines with an example script for loading a more complex model through `file_imports`.[12] In the next section, we describe how to incorporate an external IR toolkit into RoutIR.

### 4.3  Integration with Existing IR Toolkits

Figure 4 demonstrates a simple example that integrates Pyserini [25] into RoutIR. For index retrieval, one only needs to implement the initialization of the Engine, which contains index loading and hyperparameter settings if applicable, and the `search_batch` method, which takes a batch of queries and returns a list of results in the same order as the input queries.

Since all search methods are asynchronous, RoutIR does not wait for a module to finish searching before attending to the next API request. However, since Python asynchronous functions are still single-threaded on a single processor, unless the Engine spawns another search process or calls out to another process, processes can be blocked. For example, a standalone Lucene instance searching a batch of queries may block the Python process from accepting an API request. We provide some implementation guidance on how these concurrency issues can be overcome in the documentation. However, such engineering issues are model and toolkit-dependent. They can generally be solved by hosting different models

---

[12] Rank1 [44], a pointwise reasoning reranker, integration script can be found in https://github.com/hltcoe/routir/blob/main/examples/rank1_extension.py.

**Table 2.** Effetiveness and efficiency on the NeuCLIR 2023 MLIR Task.

| Model | Effectiveness nDCG@20 | Batched Throughput (query/sec) ↑ | Seq. Latency (sec/query) ↓ |
|---|---|---|---|
| Multi-Vector: PLAID-X [48] | 0.402 | 7.05 | 0.24 |
| LSR: MILCO [34] | 0.413 | 3.27 | 2.46 |
| Dense: Qwen3 Embedding [53] | 0.430 | 9.60 | 1.23 |

in separate RoutIR instances and combining them via `server_imports` to a joint endpoint.

## 5   Experiment and Analysis

To demonstrate the adaptability of RoutIR, we report effectiveness and efficiency using the TREC 2023 NeuCLIR MLIR task [22], which has 76 queries and about 10 million web documents in Chinese, Persian, and Russian extracted from CommonCrawl News. We experiment with the following three multilingual models with distinct architectures and stacks:

- Multi-vector dense using PLAID-X [48]. The PLAID-X model was reported as the state of the art in 2023 during TREC. The model is based on XLM-RoBERTa-Large [28] and is served using an NVIDIA TITAN RTX 24G with the PLAID-X implementation.
- Learned-sparse retrieval using MILCO [34] with Anserini [50]. The MILCO model is also based on XLM-RoBERTa-Large and is served with the same GPU using the Huggingface Transformer. The index is served with Anserini via PyJNIus.
- Dense retrieval using Qwen3 Embedding [53] with a FAISS index [10] using vLLM.[13] The Qwen3 Embedding model is served with vLLM with parameters cast to FP16 to fit on the TITAN RTX GPU. The document embeddings are indexed with FAISS using product quantization of 2048 dimensions and 4-bit fast scan (`PQ2048x4fs`).

We experimented with two request modes: batched and sequential. When queries are batched, we issue all 76 queries with asynchronous HTTP requests to the RoutIR endpoints and report the throughput, i.e., the number of queries processed per second. In the sequential mode, we issued the next query after receiving results from the previous one and report the latency, i.e., the number of seconds to process each query.

As shown in Table 2, all three models demonstrate strong throughput, although LSR with Anserini is the slowest. However, it can be greatly accelerated with tools such as Seismic [3] that are tailored for LSR searching. All

---

[13] https://github.com/vllm-project/vllm.

```python
class LiveRAG_PLAIDX_Search():
    def __init__(self, query: str, **kwargs):
        self.url = os.getenv("RETRIEVER_ENDPOINT")
        self.query = query

    def get_content(self, collection, doc_id):
        return requests.post(self.url+"/content", json={
            "collection": collection, "id": doc_id
        }).json()

    def search(self, max_results: int = 5):
        response = requests.post(f"{self.url}/query", json={
            "service": "plaidx-liverag",
            "query": str(self.query), "limit": max_results
        }).json()["result"]

        return [
            {"score": score, "href": str(doc_id),
             **self.get_content("liverag", doc_id) }
            for doc_id, score in results.items():
        ]
```

**Fig. 5.** Example search module for GPT Researcher.

three models are able to take advantage of batched queries to provide faster overall speed. Particularly in FAISS, RoutIR uses the batched search capability to search the index for all queries in the batch at once, which has the highest throughput despite being five times slower than PLAID-X in sequential latency.

These results demonstrate the adaptivity of RoutIR and robustness to the input types. In the next section, we demonstrate how to integrate RoutIR with a RAG system.

## 6   Example of Using RoutIR in a RAG System

GPT Researcher is an open-source RAG toolkit that integrates various search engines such as Google and DuckDuckGo into a RAG system that supports planning, self-reflections, and multi-agent pipelines. Figure 5 depicts a retriever in GPT Researcher interfacing with RoutIR, requiring only 21 lines of code. Since RoutIR uses the HTTP API as the interface, it does not require any other dependencies to interface with GPT Researcher. Figure 5 is an abbreviated version of the implementation (excluding some sanity checks and try-except blocks) used in HLTCOE's system for the LiveRAG challenge at SIGIR 2025 [11]. While it would also be possible to implement GPT Researcher inside an academic IR platform, doing so would require substantially more engineering effort.

# 7   Summary

In this work, we introduced RoutIR, a simple and robust toolkit for wrapping and serving retrieval models to serve online queries. We described the design principles and architecture of RoutIR and presented several use cases both in configuring the service and integration with RAG pipelines. This highlighted its ability to increase query throughput, a particularly desirable feature for RAG systems. RoutIR has demonstrated its effectiveness and reliability as the backbone for the 2025 JHU SCALE Workshop for more than 50 researchers and also as the search service for 2025 TREC RAGTIME Track.

RoutIR is still under development with more features in the near term planned, including integration of LLM rerankers, Model Context Protocol (MCP) interface, and better resource management. RoutIR is completely open-sourced on GitHub and welcomes community feedback, feature requests, and pull requests.

**Disclosure of Interests.** Authors have no competing interests.

# References


1. Asai, A., Wu, Z., Wang, Y., Sil, A., Hajishirzi, H.: Self-rag: learning to retrieve, generate, and critique through self-reflection (2024)
2. Boytsov, L., Nyberg, E.: Flexible retrieval with nmslib and flexneuart. arXiv preprint arXiv:2010.14848 (2020)
3. Bruch, S., Nardini, F.M., Rulli, C., Venturini, R.: Efficient inverted indexes for approximate retrieval over learned sparse representations. In: Proceedings of the 47th International ACM SIGIR Conference on Research and Development in Information Retrieval (SIGIR), pp. 152–162. ACM (2024). https://doi.org/10.1145/3626772.3657769
4. Buckley, C.: Implementation of the smart information retrieval system. Technical report, Cornell University (1985)
5. Cartright, M.A., Huston, S.J., Feild, H.: Galago: a modular distributed processing and retrieval system. In: OSIR@SIGIR, pp. 25–31 (2012)
6. Cheng, X., et al.: xrag: extreme context compression for retrieval-augmented generation with one token. Adv. Neural. Inf. Process. Syst. **37**, 109487–109516 (2024)
7. Cleverdon, C.: The aslib cranfield research project on the comparative efficiency of indexing systems. Aslib Proc. **12**(12), 421–431 (1960). https://doi.org/10.1108/eb049778. ISSN 0001-253X
8. Costello, C., Yang, E., Lawrie, D., Mayfield, J.: Patapsco: a python framework for cross-language information retrieval experiments. In: Proceedings of the 44th European Conference on Information Retrieval (ECIR) (2022)
9. Dong, G., Jin, J., Li, X., Zhu, Y., Dou, Z., Wen, J.R.: Rag-critic: leveraging automated critic-guided agentic workflow for retrieval augmented generation. In: Proceedings of the 63rd Annual Meeting of the Association for Computational Linguistics (Volume 1: Long Papers), pp. 3551–3578 (2025)
10. Douze, M., et al.: The faiss library (2024)
11. Duh, K., Yang, E., Weller, O., Yates, A., Lawrie, D.: HLTCOE at LiveRAG: GPT-researcher using ColBERT retrieval. arXiv preprint arXiv:2506.22356 (2025)

12. Elovic, A.: GPT-researcher (2023). https://github.com/assafelovic/gpt-researcher
13. Fang, J., Meng, Z., MacDonald, C.: KiRAG: knowledge-driven iterative retriever for enhancing retrieval-augmented generation. In: Che, W., Nabende, J., Shutova, E., Pilehvar, M.T. (eds.) Proceedings of the 63rd Annual Meeting of the Association for Computational Linguistics (Volume 1: Long Papers), pp. 18969–18985. Association for Computational Linguistics, Vienna, Austria (2025). https://doi.org/10.18653/v1/2025.acl-long.929. https://aclanthology.org/2025.acl-long.929/. . ISBN 979-8-89176-251-0
14. Gao, L., Ma, X., Lin, J.J., Callan, J.: Tevatron: an efficient and flexible toolkit for dense retrieval. arXiv abs/2203.05765 (2022)
15. Guo, S., Ren, Z.: Dynamic context compression for efficient rag. arXiv preprint arXiv:2507.22931 (2025)
16. Gupta, D., Demner-Fushman, D., Hersh, W., Bedrick, S., Roberts, K.: TREC biogen track 2025 (2025). https://trec-biogen.github.io/
17. Izacard, G., Grave, E.: Leveraging passage retrieval with generative models for open domain question answering. In: EACL 2021–16th Conference of the European Chapter of the Association for Computational Linguistics, pp. 874–880. Association for Computational Linguistics (2021)
18. Jeong, Y., Kim, J., Lee, D., Hwang, S.w.: ECoRAG: evidentiality-guided compression for long context RAG. In: Che, W., Nabende, J., Shutova, E., Pilehvar, M.T. (eds.) Findings of the Association for Computational Linguistics: ACL 2025, pp. 26607–26628. Association for Computational Linguistics, Vienna, Austria (2025). https://doi.org/10.18653/v1/2025.findings-acl.1365. https://aclanthology.org/2025.findings-acl.1365/. ISBN 979-8-89176-256-5
19. Khattab, O., et al.: DSPY: compiling declarative language model calls into self-improving pipelines. arXiv preprint arXiv:2310.03714 (2023)
20. Lajewska, W., Balog, K.: Ginger: grounded information nugget-based generation of responses. In: Proceedings of the 48th International ACM SIGIR Conference (SIGIR 2025) (2025). https://krisztianbalog.com/files/sigir2025-ginger.pdf, sIGIR 2025 paper
21. Lassance, C., Déjean, H., Formal, T., Clinchant, S.: Splade-v3: New baselines for splade (2024). https://arxiv.org/abs/2403.06789
22. Lawrie, D., et al.: Overview of the TREC 2023 NeuCLIR track. In: Proceedings of The Thirty-Second Text REtrieval Conference. NIST (2023)
23. Lawrie, D., et al.: Overview of the TREC 2024 neuclir track. arXiv preprint arXiv:2509.14355 (2025)
24. Lawrie, D., MacAvaney, S., Mayfield, J., Soldaini, L., Yang, E., Yates, A.: TREC RAGTIME track 2025 (2025). https://trec-ragtime.github.io/
25. Lin, J., Ma, X., Lin, S.C., Yang, J.H., Pradeep, R., Nogueira, R.: Pyserini: a python toolkit for reproducible information retrieval research with sparse and dense representations. In: Proceedings of the 44th International ACM SIGIR Conference on Research and Development in Information Retrieval, SIGIR 2021, pp. 2356–2362. Association for Computing Machinery, New York, NY, USA (2021). https://doi.org/10.1145/3404835.3463238. ISBN 9781450380379
26. Lin, J., Nogueira, R., Yates, A.: Pretrained Transformers for Text Ranking: BERT and Beyond. Springer, Cham (2022)
27. Liu, Q., Duan, H., Chen, Y., Lu, Q., Sun, W., Mao, J.: Llm4ranking: an easy-to-use framework of utilizing large language models for document reranking (2025). https://arxiv.org/abs/2504.07439
28. Liu, Y., et al.: RoBERTa: a robustly optimized BERT pretraining approach (2019)

29. Ma, X., Gao, L., Zhuang, S., Zhan, J.S., Callan, J., Lin, J.: Tevatron 2.0: unified document retrieval toolkit across scale, language, and modality. arXiv preprint arXiv:2505.02466 (2025)
30. MacAvaney, S.: Opennir: a complete neural ad-hoc ranking pipeline. In: Proceedings of the 13th International Conference on Web Search and Data Mining, pp. 845–848 (2020)
31. Macdonald, C., Fang, J., Parry, A., Meng, Z.: Constructing and evaluating declarative rag pipelines in pyterrier. In: Proceedings of the 48th International ACM SIGIR Conference on Research and Development in Information Retrieval, pp. 4035–4040 (2025)
32. Macdonald, C., Tonellotto, N., MacAvaney, S., Ounis, I.: Pyterrier: declarative experimentation in python from bm25 to dense retrieval. In: Proceedings of the 30th ACM International Conference on Information & Knowledge Management, CIKM 2021, pp. 4526–4533. Association for Computing Machinery, New York, NY, USA (2021). https://doi.org/10.1145/3459637.3482013. ISBN 9781450384469
33. Muennighoff, N., Tazi, N., Magne, L., Reimers, N.: MTEB: massive text embedding benchmark. In: Vlachos, A., Augenstein, I. (eds.) Proceedings of the 17th Conference of the European Chapter of the Association for Computational Linguistics, pp. 2014–2037. Association for Computational Linguistics, Dubrovnik, Croatia (2023). https://doi.org/10.18653/v1/2023.eacl-main.148. https://aclanthology.org/2023.eacl-main.148/
34. Nguyen, T., Lei, Y., Ju, J.H., Yang, E., Yates, A.: Milco: learned sparse retrieval across languages via a multilingual connector. arXiv [cs.IR] (2025)
35. Ounis, I., Amati, G., Plachouras, V., He, B., Macdonald, C., Lioma, C.: Terrier: a high performance and scalable information retrieval platform. In: Proceedings of the 2006 SIGIR Open Source Workshop (2006). https://api.semanticscholar.org/CorpusID:16510983
36. Piwowarski, B.: Experimaestro and datamaestro: experiment and dataset managers (for IR). In: Proceedings of the 43rd International ACM SIGIR Conference on Research and Development in Information Retrieval, pp. 2173–2176 (2020)
37. Pradeep, R., Nogueira, R., Lin, J.: The expando-mono-duo design pattern for text ranking with pretrained sequence-to-sequence models (2021). https://arxiv.org/abs/2101.05667
38. Schurman, E., Brutlag, J.: Performance related changes and their user impact. In: Velocity Web Performance and Operations Conference (2009)
39. Shao, Y., Jiang, Y., Kanell, T.A., Xu, P., Khattab, O., Lam, M.S.: Assisting in writing wikipedia-like articles from scratch with large language models. arXiv preprint arXiv:2402.14207 (2024)
40. Strohman, T., Metzler, D., Turtle, H., Croft, W.B.: Indri: a language model-based search engine for complex queries. In: Proceedings of the International Conference on Intelligent Analysis, Amherst, MA, USA, vol. 2, pp. 2–6 (2005)
41. Thakur, N., Reimers, N., Rücklé, A., Srivastava, A., Gurevych, I.: Beir: a heterogenous benchmark for zero-shot evaluation of information retrieval models (2021). https://arxiv.org/abs/2104.08663
42. Upadhyay, S., Pradeep, R., Thakur, N., Lin, J., Craswell, N.: TREC rag track 2025 (2025). https://trec-rag.github.io/
43. Wang, H., Prasad, A., Stengel-Eskin, E., Bansal, M.: Retrieval-augmented generation with conflicting evidence. In: Proceedings of the 2nd Conference on Language Modeling (2025)

44. Weller, O., Ricci, K., Yang, E., Yates, A., Lawrie, D., Durme, B.V.: Rank1: test-time compute for reranking in information retrieval. In: Second Conference on Language Modeling (2025)
45. Wolf, T., et al.: Huggingface's transformers: state-of-the-art natural language processing (2020). https://arxiv.org/abs/1910.03771
46. Xu, R., et al.: Collab-RAG: boosting retrieval-augmented generation for complex question answering via white-box and black-box LLM collaboration. In: Second Conference on Language Modeling (2025). https://openreview.net/forum?id=CODs4jSGhN
47. Yan, S.Q., Gu, J.C., Zhu, Y., Ling, Z.H.: Corrective retrieval augmented generation. arXiv preprint arXiv:2401.15884 (2024)
48. Yang, E., Lawrie, D., Mayfield, J., Oard, D.W., Miller, S.: Translate-distill: learning cross-language dense retrieval by translation and distillation. In: European Conference on Information Retrieval, pp. 50–65. Springer, Cham (2024)
49. Yang, E., Lawrie, D., Weller, O., Mayfield, J.: HLTCOE at TREC 2024 NeuCLIR track (2025). https://arxiv.org/abs/2510.00143
50. Yang, P., Fang, H., Lin, J.: Anserini: enabling the use of lucene for information retrieval research. In: Proceedings of the 40th International ACM SIGIR Conference on Research and Development in Information Retrieval, SIGIR 2017, pp. 1253–1256. Association for Computing Machinery, New York, NY, USA (2017). https://doi.org/10.1145/3077136.3080721. ISBN 9781450350228
51. Yates, A., Arora, S., Zhang, X., Yang, W., Jose, K.M., Lin, J.: Capreolus: a toolkit for end-to-end neural ad hoc retrieval. In: Proceedings of the 13th International Conference on Web Search and Data Mining, pp. 861–864 (2020)
52. Yates, A., Jose, K.M., Zhang, X., Lin, J.: Flexible IR pipelines with capreolus. In: Proceedings of the 29th ACM International Conference on Information & Knowledge Management, pp. 3181–3188 (2020)
53. Zhang, Y., et al.: Qwen3 embedding: advancing text embedding and reranking through foundation models. arXiv preprint arXiv:2506.05176 (2025)
54. Zhuang, S., Zhuang, H., Koopman, B., Zuccon, G.: A setwise approach for effective and highly efficient zero-shot ranking with large language models. In: Proceedings of the 47th International ACM SIGIR Conference on Research and Development in Information Retrieval, SIGIR 2024 (2024)

# Sim4IA-Bench: A User Simulation Benchmark Suite for Next Query and Utterance Prediction


Andreas Konstantin Kruff[1(✉)], Christin Katharina Kreutz[2], Timo Breuer[1], Philipp Schaer[1], and Krisztian Balog[3]

[1] TH Köln - University of Applied Sciences, Cologne, Germany
{andreas.kruff,timo.breuer,philipp.schaer}@th-koeln.de
[2] TH Mittelhessen - University of Applied Sciences, Giessen, Germany
ckreutz@acm.org
[3] Stavanger University, Stavanger, Norway
krisztian.balog@uis.no



**Abstract.** Validating user simulation is a difficult task due to the lack of established measures and benchmarks, which makes it challenging to assess whether a simulator accurately reflects real user behavior. As part of the Sim4IA Micro-Shared Task at the Sim4IA Workshop, SIGIR 2025, we present Sim4IA-Bench, a simulation benchmark suit for the prediction of the next queries and utterances, the first of its kind in the IR community. Our dataset as part of the suite comprises 160 real-world search sessions from the CORE search engine. For 70 of these sessions, up to 62 simulator runs are available, divided into Task A and Task B, in which different approaches predicted users' next search queries or utterances. Sim4IA-Bench provides a basis for evaluating and comparing user simulation approaches and for developing new measures of simulator validity. Although modest in size, the suite represents the first publicly available benchmark that links real search sessions with simulated next-query predictions. In addition to serving as a testbed for next query prediction, it also enables exploratory studies on query reformulation behavior, intent drift, and interaction-aware retrieval evaluation. We also introduce a new measure for evaluating next-query predictions in this task. By making the suite publicly available, we aim to promote reproducible research and stimulate further work on realistic and explainable user simulation for information access: https://github.com/irgroup/Sim4IA-Bench.

**Keywords:** User simulation · Evaluation · Next Query Prediction


## 1  Introduction and Motivation

In recent years, user simulation has gained increasing attention within IR, as it provides a scalable and controllable method to study user behavior without large-scale user studies [4,8,39]. The advent of large language models (LLMs)


© The Author(s), under exclusive license to Springer Nature Switzerland AG 2026
R. Campos et al. (Eds.): ECIR 2026, LNCS 16486, pp. 594–609, 2026.
https://doi.org/10.1007/978-3-032-21321-1_61

dramatically lowered the barrier to entry, making it easier than ever to create simulators capable of generating human-like search queries and conversational utterances [2,45,58]. However, this rapid development outpaces our ability to verify their performance. Consequently, there is little shared understanding of what constitutes a good simulator or how its performance should be evaluated [4].

This challenge arises from a fundamental gap in evaluation methodology. The validation of user simulators is an open problem that requires two key components: (1) benchmark datasets that directly link real user interaction logs to simulated outputs, and (2) robust measures to quantify the similarity between simulated and real user behavior. Currently, there is a critical shortage of public resources dedicated to this task. Without a common ground for comparison, it is impossible to assess whether a new simulator is a true advancement or to understand the strengths and weaknesses of different simulation approaches.

To bridge this critical gap, this paper introduces Sim4IA-Bench, the first public benchmark resource specifically designed to evaluate user simulators. As the primary contribution of this work, we introduce a dataset derived from a recent user simulation initiative, the Sim4IA [43] Micro-Shared Task, tackling interactive IR simulation (Task A) and conversational session simulation (Task B). In addition to submissions from participating approaches, we complement this dataset with a proposed set of string-based and system-based similarity measures, offering a crucial starting point for the community to assess simulator quality. Importantly, our goal is not to measure a simulator's success in a downstream retrieval task, but to directly address the more fundamental question of how well it reproduces authentic user behavior.

Beyond the methodological gap, a significant practical barrier has also hindered the wider adoption of user simulation: the substantial infrastructure and engineering effort required to build a simulator from scratch. To address this challenge, Sim4IA-Bench provides a comprehensive suite of practical resources designed to dramatically lower this barrier to entry. At the core, it includes a simulation toolkit that serves as a starting kit with baseline implementations, data loaders, and evaluation scripts. Sim4IA-Bench contains a rich collection of artifacts, such as prepared session logs, participants' run files, and comprehensive documentation detailing data formats and evaluation protocols. By packaging these components together, we shift the focus from foundational engineering and enable researchers to concentrate on the core scientific challenges of simulator design. Sim4IA-Bench[1] is released under the MIT license, enabling both academic and industry researchers to access and use the resource.

**The Sim4IA-Bench Suite.** In addition to two session datasets for typical IR and conversational search from the academic domain, Sim4IA-Bench provides a comprehensive set of artifacts to support experimentation and evaluation:

– Prepared session logs, including training and test sets.

---

[1] GitHub repository of Sim4IA-Bench: https://github.com/irgroup/Sim4IA-Bench.

- Submission run files (62) and corresponding lab notes from the three teams participating in the Sim4IA Micro-Shared Task.
- Benchmarking code for evaluating next-query prediction.
- A simulation toolkit, including Dockerized adaptations of SimIIR 3 [2].
- Tutorials and detailed documentation with setup instructions and example workflows.

Furthermore, this work is intended to guide the development of future community-wide evaluation initiatives. The methodology, dataset structure, and experiences gained from organizing this shared task provide a valuable blueprint for establishing larger-scale, standardized evaluation campaigns at TREC or CLEF, and Sim4IA-Bench will be maintained as part of the User Simulation subtask (Task 3) in LongEval@CLEF'26 [6].

## 2  Related Work

This section covers current directions for the validation of user simulators before datasets for next query and utterance prediction are presented.

### 2.1  Validating User Simulators

There is a current trend towards relying on simulation-based evaluation, especially through usage of LLMs [39,52,53]. However, critical shortcomings can arise such as LLMs showcasing behavior that is unrealistic for humans [18,54] or a lack of natural variation that is usually found in human interactions [49,57].

While simulators need to be validated against real human interactions [4], the specific requirements for simulators differ depending on what they are going to be used for, i.e. training vs. evaluation [5]. In general, such a comparison against human interactions may be performed at a distributional level, for example, by comparing (i) query characteristics (length, terms) [3], similarity [26], or retrieval performance and shared task utility [7] for traditional search or (ii) the distribution of dialogue acts or success rate for conversational agents [59]. Other approaches for validation include labeling specific instances according to different dimensions, like naturalness, usefulness, grammar for conversational utterances [44,53,61] or comparing entire conversations (human vs. simulated) in a side-by-side manner [53,59]. Another method is the evaluation based on testers where testers are sets of IR systems over which a specific performance pattern can be expected that a simulator is trying to reproduce [29,30].

While there are few resources dedicated to validating simulators, with Sim4IA-Bench we provide exactly this to bridge this gap.

### 2.2  Datasets

To the best of our knowledge, our introduced resources are the first to provide a common evaluation environment for both interactive IR as well as conversational

**Table 1.** Comparison of Interactive IR and Conversational Search datasets for next-query or next-utterance prediction. **Size** refers to the number of sessions or conversations. **T** informs whether the dataset covers traditional IR, **C** informs whether the dataset covers conversations. **A** refers to additional public assets like system runs from a shared task. **Domain** indicates the topic of the dataset.

| Dataset | Size | T | C | A | Domain |
|---|---|---|---|---|---|
| AOL [40] | 283,207 (AOL17) | ✓ | ✗ | ✗ | Web search |
| SUSS [35] | 484,449 | ✓ | ✗ | ✗ | Academic search |
| Yandex [46] | 797,867 | ✓ | ✗ | ✗ | Web search |
| TREC Session [12] | 1564 | ✓ | ✗ | ✓ | Web search |
| ConvAI [34] | 4750 | ✗ | ✓ | ✓ | Human Chatting |
| TianGong-ST [14] | 147,155 | ✓ | ✗ | ✓ | Web search |
| ConvAI2 [20] | 4406 | ✗ | ✓ | ✓ | Human Chatting |
| TripClick [41] | 1,602,648 | ✓ | ✗ | ✓ | Health |
| ConvAI3 (ClariQ) [1] | 1,596,757 | ✗ | ✓ | ✓ | Human Chatting |
| Baidu-ULTR [64] | 1.2 bil | ✓ | ✗ | ✓ | Web search |
| Webis-FUQ-24 [26] | 18,980 | ✓ | ✗ | ✗ | Web search, arguments, exhibitions, product search |
| Persona-Chat [60] | 10,907 | ✗ | ✓ | ✗ | Human chatting |
| Webis-CQR-2 [25] | 284 | ✗ | ✓ | ✗ | Arguments, books, news, trips |
| SoguoQ [47] | 14,075,717 | ✗ | ✓ | ✓ | Web search |
| TREC CAsT (2022) [38] | 50 | ✗ | ✓ | ✓ | Web search |
| LLM-REDIAL [31] | 47,600 | ✗ | ✓ | ✗ | Movies, books, sports |
| WildChat [62] | 1,039,785 | ✗ | ✓ | ✗ | Web search |
| LMSYS-CHAT-1M [63] | 1,000,000 | ✗ | ✓ | ✗ | Web search |
| Ours | 160 | ✓ | ✓ | ✓ | Academic search |

search. To highlight the novelty of our resource, we surveyed existing log datasets and conversational resources containing session interaction logs. Table 1 provides an overview of publicly available session datasets at the time of our study.

There are several large-scale datasets that primarily originate from the web search domain or rather small-scale domain-specific datasets from academic, health-related, and other fields. Most of these datasets serve as evaluation toolkits for different aspects of the user modeling in an interactive search setting with varying degrees of an explicit user simulation. For instance, some datasets allow a comprehensive evaluation of the different interactions in a simulated sessions, while others have a more specific focus like query suggestion, click modeling, or utterance prediction. Building on these datasets, prior work has examined related aspects such as query expansion and suggestion [16,36], query and utterance prediction [23,33,51,55], or session modeling [13,17,22,56].

The additional assets (A) column in Table 1 denotes whether a dataset has previously been employed in a shared task or is included in a benchmark that enables systematic evaluation. Several of the listed datasets have served as complementary assets in this sense. For example, the Yandex dataset was used in a challenge focused on personalizing search results based on user context and search history [46]. The four TREC Session datasets were employed in a task designed to improve retrieval effectiveness through the use of historical queries, ranked result lists, and user interaction information [12]. Similarly, the Baidu-ULTR dataset was used in a task where participants developed feature-based re-ranking models that exploited behavioral and display features to better capture user preferences [37]. The SogouQ dataset was used in a task addressing ambiguous queries and promoting ranking diversification to account for multiple possible user intents [48]. TianGong-ST has been applied in a task focused on ranking documents for the final query of a session, taking into account the complete preceding session context [15]. More recently, dialogue datasets such as WildChat [62] have been designed to evaluate large language models in realistic conversational settings [24, 32].

Taken together, these datasets exemplify how complementary assets facilitate structured comparison, either by providing directly comparable shared task runs or by being integrated into established benchmarks. Building on this, our resource is the first to provide complementary assets specifically for next query prediction in the context of user simulation, offering run files that enable reproducible system comparisons and systematic evaluation of measures under controlled experimental conditions.

In general, there is a trade-off between the desire to make as much user interaction data available for rigorous validation of user simulations and the requirements to keep users anonymous and respecting their privacy. Sim4IA-Bench enables validations of user simulations across multiple sessions in traditional IR and conversational search, while guaranteeing full user privacy based on rigorous anonymization measures.

## 3    Dataset

Here we present the dataset at the core of Sim4IA-Bench: its structure, contents, and key characteristics, highlighting the aspects that make it suitable for evaluating and developing user simulators in interactive IR.

### 3.1    Task Descriptions and Dataset Contents

We provide session-based datasets for the Sim4IA Micro-Shared Task [43], designed to support the evaluation and development of user simulators in interactive IR. The resources include two sets of data corresponding to the two task variants: Task A (interactive IR simulation) and Task B (conversational session simulation). Each task has a training set of 45 sessions and a test set of 35 sessions. The test sets differ from the training sets in that the final query of each session is withheld, allowing participants to evaluate simulator predictions without overfitting. In all tasks ten next queries or utterances are to be predicted. For a concise overview of the two tasks and their respective workflows, see Figure 1.

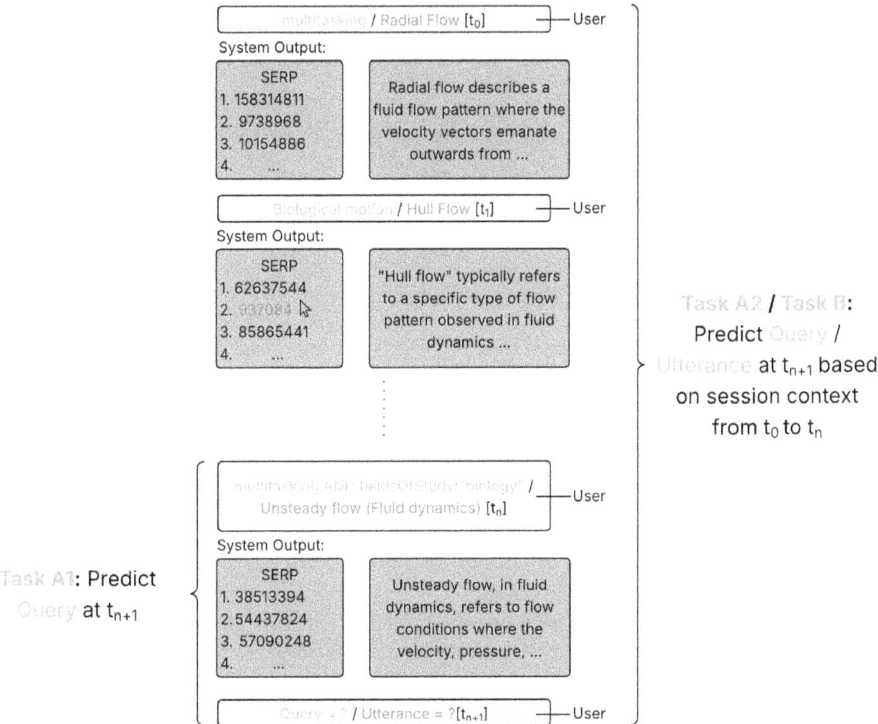


**Fig. 1.** Overview of Task A (interactive IR simulation, in orange) and Task B (conversational session simulation, in teal). Document IDs highlighted in green represent documents a real user interacted with.

**Task A: Interactive IR Simulation.** Each session in Task A contains queries, the corresponding retrieved SERPs, and the documents clicked by users. Clicks are categorized into three types: clicks on authors, clicks on the work itself, and clicks on the "Download PDF" option. Timestamps for queries and clicks are included, enabling simulators to account for temporal aspects of interactions and to model different types of user behavior. We composed two variants of Task A using the same data: Task A1 only considers the last query and corresponding SERP information, while in Task A2, the whole session was allowed to be used. For Task A, the dataset contains an average session length of 5.20 queries (4.20 reformulations on average), with 1.49 clicks per query.

**Task B: Conversational Session Simulation.** Task B sessions contain only utterance-response pairs. Responses were generated using Google's Gemma 3 12B model served on Ollama. For each query, the model was provided with the top three retrieved documents, the preceding response, and all upcoming utterances. The prompt (see Figure 2) was designed to ensure that the model focused solely on the current utterance while steering towards the upcoming utterances, producing coherent and plausible conversational flows. For Task B, the average session length is 4.85 queries (3.85 reformulations on average).

Utterance: What are the main symptoms of diabetes?

Relevant Documents:
Title: Diabetes Overview
Abstract: Diabetes is a chronic condition characterized by high blood sugar levels. Common symptoms include frequent urination, excessive thirst, fatigue, and blurred vision.
Title: Type 2 Diabetes Symptoms
Abstract: Type 2 diabetes often develops gradually. Symptoms include increased hunger, frequent infections, and slow-healing sores.

Previous Response: Diabetes is a condition affecting the body's ability to regulate blood sugar.
Upcoming User Utterances:
Utterance: How can diabetes be managed effectively?
Utterance: What lifestyle changes are recommended for patients?

Instruction:
- Answer the query using the relevant documents and the previous response.
- Act like a RAG system: provide relevant, informative, and context-aware responses tailored to the user's query intent.
- Try to only answer the current utterance and explicitly do provide answers in the response, that might answer the provided upcoming utterances.
- Limit your answer to **no more than 150 words**.
- Focus on key points and avoid unnecessary repetition.
- Please do answer formally and don't use phrases like 'Okay, here's a response to "Diabetes"' acting as a RAG system.

Answer:

**Fig. 2.** Prompt template for generating the synthetic responses of the conversational system for Task B. Black parts show the unchanging structural and instructional parts, purple components depict the variables inserted depending on sessions and utterances.

## 3.2   Session Extraction from CORE Logs

Sessions were reconstructed from CORE [27] log files using a heuristic approach to group queries into sessions: starting from the last query in a potential session, queries occurring within a time window of -10 to +5 minutes were considered candidates for inclusion. Queries were added to a session if their cosine similarity, calculated using embeddings generated by the SentenceTransformer model all-MiniLM-L6-v2, with the current session queries, was greater than or equal to 0.1. All reconstructed sessions were independently manually reviewed by two people to ensure coherence and plausibility. Query sessions that contained fewer than

**Table 2.** Distribution of submitted run types for tasks by groups from CIR, Webis and THM.

|          | (semi-) manual | persona | prompting & tuning | other LLM | rule-based | $\sum$ |
|----------|----------------|---------|--------------------|-----------|------------|--------|
| Task A1  | 3              | 6       | $2 + 3 = 5$        | $3 + 12 = 15$ | 1      | 30     |
| Task A2  | $2 + 3 = 5$    | 6       | 3                  | 4         |            | 18     |
| Task B   | 4              | 6       |                    | 4         |            | 14     |

three reformulations or did not originate from a plausible information need were excluded.

### 3.3  Usage Notes

The datasets and artifacts are designed to be fully accessible and ready for use. Example scripts and tools facilitate loading, processing, and analysis of the sessions. For Task A, the combination of training and test sets allows evaluation of next-query predictions at multiple levels, from string similarity to semantic and SERP-based metrics. Task-specific features, such as click categories in Task A and semi-synthetic responses in Task B, enable more nuanced simulator evaluations and the exploration of interaction dynamics in both interactive and conversational settings.

### 3.4  Submitted Runs

For the Micro-Shared Task we obtained 62 runs over all tasks in total and three accompanying lab notes detailing information on these runs by groups from CIR [10], Webis [21] and THM [19]. In general, we distinguish between runs that were composed (semi-) manually, through an LLM, as well as rule-based ones. We further differentiate LLM-based runs as ones composed by prompting the LLM to behave as a persona alone, through a combination of tuning and prompting and others. Table 2 provides the number of runs of different types from each group for the respective tasks.

## 4  Assessing Simulator Fidelity

Evaluating the quality and validity of a simulator in query prediction tasks is challenging, and the choice of suitable measures remains an open question. In this work, our methodology shifts the focus from a simulator's effectiveness in retrieval tasks to its *reproduction quality*—that is, how well it replicates the authentic user behavior observed in real interaction logs. To assess this, we employ a complementary set of string-based and system-based similarity measures. Each measure is designed to capture a different aspect of simulator fidelity by quantifying the degree to which simulated queries match actual user inputs. In addition to the following measures presented in this paper, a broader overview of suitable measures was conducted in the work of Kruff et al. in an additional comprehensive study [28].

### 4.1   Measures

**Semantic Similarity.** Semantic similarity assesses how close the predicted queries are in meaning to the original user queries. We computed the average cosine similarity between sentence embeddings of the original query $q_i^{true}$ and the $Q$ candidate queries $q_{i,j}$ over $N$ sessions. We then bounded the similarity values from $[-1, 1]$ to $[0, 1]$ for better visual comparability with the other measures.

$$\bar{S} = \frac{1}{|N|} \sum_{i=1}^{N} \left( \frac{1}{Q} \sum_{j=1}^{Q} \mathrm{cosine}(q_i^{true}, q_{i,j}) \right)$$

This measure ensures that candidates are not only syntactically similar but also semantically aligned with the user's intent.

**Redundancy.** To evaluate novelty and diversity, we introduced a Redundancy measure, which calculates the Jaccard similarity between all $Q$ candidate queries or utterances within a session averaged across all $N$ sessions:

$$\bar{R} = \frac{1}{|N|} \sum_{i=1}^{N} \left( \frac{2}{Q(Q-1)} \sum_{1 \leq j < q \leq Q} \mathrm{Jaccard}(q_{i,j}, q_{i,k}) \right)$$

Low redundancy indicates that a simulator produces multiple distinct candidates that remain semantically similar to the original query, whereas high redundancy signals minimal variation. Redundancy is not intended as a standalone metric; rather, it is defined for its role in the Rank-Diversity Score described below. It serves to penalize simulators that produce candidates with only minor variations, while giving simulators the opportunity to also predict queries exhibiting a degree of in-session topic drift.

**SERP Overlap.** To capture system-level effects, we measured the average overlap between the search engine results retrieved for the original query and the $Q$ candidates over the $N$ sessions:

$$\bar{O} = \frac{1}{|N|} \sum_{i=1}^{N} \left( \frac{1}{Q} \sum_{j=1}^{Q} \mathrm{overlap}(q_i^{true}, q_{i,j}) \right)$$

Overlap denotes the fraction of shared documents in the top-10 ranked results by a fixed retrieval system. In our experiments, queries were executed using BM25. This metric assumes access to a search engine and corpus on which both original and candidate queries can be run, and is therefore dependent on the underlying retrieval model and index. The cutoff was set with reference to typical precision scores and the typical length of a webpage in the absence of pagination.

Accordingly, SERP overlap should be interpreted as a system-dependent indicator of how query reformulation affects downstream retrieval behavior, complementing string- and meaning-based similarity metrics rather than serving as a standalone effectiveness measure.

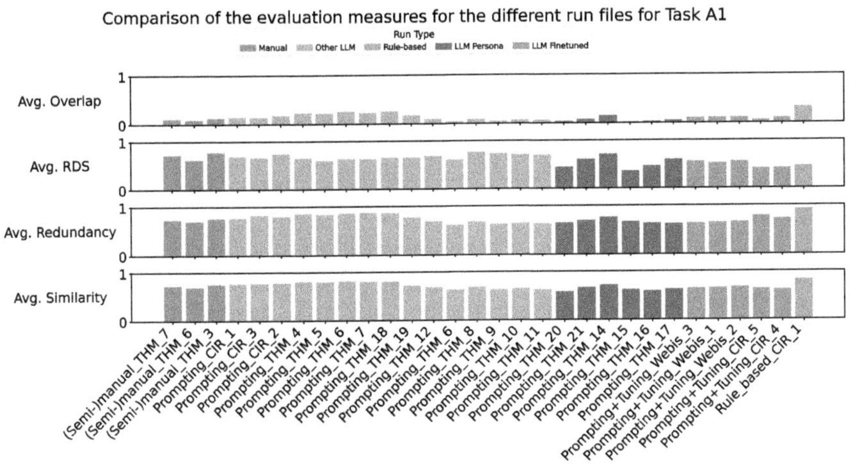

**Fig. 3.** Exemplary run results for Task A1.

**Rank-Diversity Score.** While the above measures capture overall candidate quality, they do not consider the ordering of candidates. To address this, we designed an MMR-inspired Rank-Diversity Score (RDS) that combines rank-based evaluation with redundancy:

$$\bar{RD} = \mathrm{RDS}_{\cos \geq 0.7} \cdot (1 - \bar{R})$$

$$\mathrm{RDS}_{\cos \geq 0.7} = \frac{1}{|N|} \sum_{i \in N} \left( \sum_{q \in Q_i} \frac{1}{\mathrm{rank}_q^{\cos \geq 0.7}} \right)$$

RDS is computed over all sessions $N$ and the list of candidates $Q_i$ generated for each session $i$. It rewards simulators that rank high-quality, diverse candidate queries or utterances at the top while penalizing poor ordering and runs submitting fewer than the required ten candidates, as this lowers their potential multiplier. Originally introduced by Carbonell and Goldstein [11], MMR provides a conceptual foundation for our measure (Fig. 3).

## 4.2   Case Study: Analysis of Task A1

Using the runs from Task A1 as an example, we illustrate how the applied measures provide complementary perspectives on simulator performance. Cosine similarity captures the semantic closeness between simulated and actual user queries, showing that manually created runs and large, out-of-the-box LLMs perform comparably well in reproducing the linguistic and conceptual intent of users. Persona-based and fine-tuned simulators, by contrast, show slightly lower alignment, while rule-based approaches reach high similarity scores due to their strong adherence to the original queries.

SERP overlap extends this perspective to the system level, reflecting whether different simulators lead to comparable retrieval outcomes. Here, the rule-based approach again performs strongest, as its low deviation from the original queries results in highly similar retrieval results. However, this measure also highlights that approaches generating more diverse queries, such as manual, persona-based, or fine-tuned runs, tend to diverge in retrieval outcomes, which suggests a trade-off between fidelity and behavioral variability.

Finally, the redundancy-based analysis, incorporated into the newly proposed measure, reveals a key limitation of several simulator types. Their tendency to produce highly similar candidate queries with little internal variation becomes particularly apparent for rule-based and some prompting-based approaches as well as for fine-tuned models that closely follow prior query patterns. In contrast, manual and large LLM runs benefit from this measure, as they generate more diverse candidate sets while maintaining overall semantic coherence.

Overall, while cosine similarity and SERP overlap are well suited for assessing how closely simulators mirror real user intent and retrieval outcomes, the redundancy-oriented measure complements them by exposing a lack of diversity across candidate queries. Together, these measures provide a multifaceted understanding of simulator behavior, revealing the strengths of faithful reproduction and the weaknesses in behavioral variability across approaches.

### 4.3   Reuse Value of the Benchmark Artifacts

Ultimately, Sim4IA-Bench establishes a foundation for developing future validation measures for user simulations. The corresponding process would follow standard practices used in developing IR evaluation metrics. For example, methods such as swap counting [50], stability tests [9], or bootstrapping [42] could be applied to determine whether a new validation measure aligns with existing ones, including those introduced in this work, or opens up complementary evaluation perspectives. In this context, the focus of the validation would shift from ranking systems to ranking user simulators instead.

## 5   Reflections on the Shared Task

The considerable effort invested in preparing the study environment, including comprehensive setup instructions and video guides, proved successful. None of the participating teams required substantial support from the organizers. The smooth onboarding process was a key logistical success, ensuring that the setup can be easily reproduced in future studies.

The shared task and its resulting dataset provide a valuable first step toward systematically exploring user simulation in interactive search. However, the process also highlighted several key challenges and limitations. A significant finding, particularly for Task B (conversational session simulation), was that the simulated utterances remained largely "query-like" and lacked the natural verbosity typical of this setting. This points to a major area for future improvement in simulator design. Furthermore, the semi-synthetic nature of the dataset highlighted both possibilities and constraints, offering opportunities for experimentation while revealing areas where realism could be improved. Finally, the task underscored that selecting appropriate evaluation measures is still an open and underexplored challenge for the community.

## 6    Conclusion and Outlook

This work addresses the critical need for standardized evaluation of user simulators in IR. We introduce Sim4IA-Bench, a comprehensive suite of resources derived from the Sim4IA [43] shared task, which includes datasets, task definitions, a baseline toolkit, tutorials, and documentation. This suite represents an initial yet significant step toward advancing the systematic study and evaluation of user simulators. By providing a structured, reusable framework, they enable reproducible experimentation and support methodological exploration in interactive IR. It also facilitates the testing of alternative simulation approaches and evaluation measures, inspiring the development of new tasks, datasets, or experimental designs.

This resource is not a static endpoint but a foundation for future community efforts. As an immediate next step, the methodology and toolkit will be maintained and expanded as part of the User Simulation subtask (Task 3) in LongEval@CLEF'26. This transition from a micro-shared task to a full, recurring shared task will facilitate the collection of new datasets (starting with new data for Task A) and the evaluation of new measures, providing further insights into simulation-based evaluation of next-query prediction.

Looking ahead, the limitations identified in our reflections (Sect. 5) define a clear research agenda. Future work can build on this foundation to create richer, more realistic simulations that capture the full spectrum of user behaviors, especially for conversational search. The resource provides a practical basis for testing and refining new user simulators, exploring alternative evaluation measures, and investigating how simulators generalize across different tasks and systems. As a framework, it enables reproducible experiments, highlights the trade-offs between realism, control, and evaluative rigor, and helps the community identify best practices. By making this resource accessible to the research community, we hope to encourage broader adoption, systematic benchmarking, and iterative improvement of simulation-based methods in interactive IR. Ultimately, the experiences gained from this initiative serve as a blueprint for our long-term goal: to establish a dedicated shared track at a major venue like TREC or CLEF, focused entirely on the broader research challenges of validating user simulators.

**Acknowledgments.** This work is partially funded by Deutsche Forschungsgemeinschaft (DFG) under grant number 509543643 and within the funding programme FH-Personal (PLan CV, reference number 03FHP109) by the German Federal Ministry of Education and Research (BMBF) and Joint Science Conference (GWK).

**Disclosure of Interests.** The authors have no competing interests to declare that are relevant to the content of this article.

# References


1. Aliannejadi, M., Kiseleva, J., Chuklin, A., Dalton, J., Burtsev, M.: Building and evaluating open-domain dialogue corpora with clarifying questions. In: EMNLP '21', pp. 4473–4484 (2021). https://doi.org/10.18653/v1/2021.emnlp-main.367
2. Azzopardi, L., et al.: SimIIR 3: a framework for the simulation of interactive and conversational information retrieval. In: SIGIR-AP '24, pp. 197–202 (2024). https://doi.org/10.1145/3673791.3698427
3. Azzopardi, L., de Rijke, M., Balog, K.: Building simulated queries for known-item topics: an analysis using six european languages. In: SIGIR '07, pp. 455–462 (2007). https://doi.org/10.1145/1277741.1277820
4. Balog, K., Zhai, C.: User simulation for evaluating information access systems. Foundations and Trends® in Information Retrieval $18(1-2)$, 1–261 (2024). https://doi.org/10.1561/1500000098
5. Bernard, N., Balog, K.: Towards a formal characterization of user simulation objectives in conversational information access. In: ICTIR '24, pp. 185–193 (2024). https://doi.org/10.1145/3664190.3672529
6. Breuer, T., et al.: Evaluating information retrieval models along time: The longeval lab. In: Anand, A., et al (eds.) Advances in Information Retrieval, 48th European Conference on Information Retrieval, ECIR (2026)
7. Breuer, T., Fuhr, N., Schaer, P.: Validating simulations of user query variants. In: Hagen, M., et al(eds.) Advances in Information Retrieval - 44th European Conference on IR Research, ECIR 2022, Stavanger, Norway, April 10-14, 2022, Proceedings, Part I, Lecture Notes in Computer Science, vol. 13185, pp. 80–94, Springer (2022). https://doi.org/10.1007/978-3-030-99736-6_6
8. Breuer, T., Maistro, M.: Toward evaluating the reproducibility of information retrieval systems with simulated users. In: ACM-REP '24, pp. 25–29 (2024). https://doi.org/10.1145/3641525.3663619
9. Buckley, C., Voorhees, E.M.: Evaluating evaluation measure stability. In: SIGIR '00, pp. 33–40 (2000). https://doi.org/10.1145/345508.345543
10. Busch, T., El Ghadioui, M., Knippenberg, P., Mörsheim, M.H.: CIR@Sim4IA: lab note submission for team 1 and team 2 for subtask A1 (2025). https://doi.org/10.5281/zenodo.16909638
11. Carbonell, J.G., Goldstein, J.: The use of mmr, diversity-based reranking for reordering documents and producing summaries. In: SIGIR '98, pp. 335–336 (1998). https://doi.org/10.1145/290941.291025
12. Carterette, B., Clough, P., Hall, M., Kanoulas, E., Sanderson, M.: Evaluating retrieval over sessions: the trec session track 2011-2014. In: SIGIR '16, pp. 685–688 (2016). https://doi.org/10.1145/2911451.2914675
13. Chen, H., Dou, Z., Zhu, Y., Cao, Z., Cheng, X., Wen, J.: Enhancing user behavior sequence modeling by generative tasks for session search. In: CIKM '22, pp. 180–190 (2022). https://doi.org/10.1145/3511808.3557310
14. Chen, J., Mao, J., Liu, Y., Zhang, M., Ma, S.: Tiangong-ST: a new dataset with large-scale refined real-world web search sessions. In: CIKM '19, pp. 2485–2488 (2019). https://doi.org/10.1145/3357384.3358158

15. Chen, J., et al.: Overview of the NTCIR-16 session search (SS) task. In: NTCIR '22 (2022). https://research.nii.ac.jp/ntcir/workshop/OnlineProceedings16/pdf/ntcir/01-NTCIR16-OV-SS-ChenJ.pdf

16. Chen, W., Cai, F., Chen, H., de Rijke, M.: Attention-based hierarchical neural query suggestion. In: SIGIR '18, pp. 1093–1096 (2018). https://doi.org/10.1145/3209978.3210079

17. Cheng, Q., et al.: Long short-term session search: joint personalized reranking and next query prediction. In: WWW '21, pp. 239–248 (2021). https://doi.org/10.1145/3442381.3449941

18. Davidson, S., et al.: User simulation with large language models for evaluating task-oriented dialogue. CoRR abs/2309.13233 (2023). https://doi.org/10.48550/ARXIV.2309.13233

19. Dietzler, N.O., Hofmann, N., Dauenhauer, J., Idahor, I.D., Kreutz, C.K.: THM@Sim4IA: manual and automated next query prediction for user simulation (2025). https://doi.org/10.5281/zenodo.17386068

20. Dinan, E., et al.: The second conversational intelligence challenge (ConvAI2). CoRR **abs/1902.00098** (2019). http://arxiv.org/abs/1902.00098

21. Gohsen, M., Hagen, M., Stein, B.: Webis at Sim4IA 2025: prediction of next user queries as a sequence-to-sequence problem (2025). https://doi.org/10.5281/zenodo.16909542

22. Günther, S., Göttert, P., Hagen, M.: Exploring LSTMs for simulating search sessions in digital libraries. In: TPDL '22, pp. 469–473 (2022). https://doi.org/10.1007/978-3-031-16802-4_47

23. Ivey, J., et al.: Real or robotic? assessing whether LLMs accurately simulate qualities of human responses in dialogue. CoRR **abs/2409.08330** (2024). https://doi.org/10.48550/ARXIV.2409.08330

24. Joko, H., Amirshahi, S., Clarke, C.L.A., Hasibi, F.: WildClaims: information access conversations in the wild(Chat). CoRR **abs/2509.17442** (2025). https://doi.org/10.48550/ARXIV.2509.17442

25. Kiesel, J., Cai, X., Baff, R.E., Stein, B., Hagen, M.: Toward conversational query reformulation. In: DESIRES '21, pp. 91–101 (2021). https://ceur-ws.org/Vol-2950/paper-12.pdf

26. Kiesel, J., Gohsen, M., Mirzakhmedova, N., Hagen, M., Stein, B.: Simulating follow-up questions in conversational search. In: ECIR '24, pp. 382–398 (2024). https://doi.org/10.1007/978-3-031-56060-6_25

27. Knoth, P., et al.: Core: a global aggregation service for open access papers. Sci. Data **10**(1), 366 (2023). https://doi.org/10.1038/s41597-023-02208-w

28. Kruff, A.K., Bernard, N., Schaer, P.: Validating search query simulations: a taxonomy of measures. In: Anand, A., et al. (eds.) Advances in Information Retrieval, 48th European Conference on Information Retrieval, ECIR 2026 (2026)

29. Labhishetty, S., Zhai, C.: An exploration of tester-based evaluation of user simulators for comparing interactive retrieval systems. In: SIGIR '21, pp. 1598–1602 (2021). https://doi.org/10.1145/3404835.3463091

30. Labhishetty, S., Zhai, C.: RATE: a reliability-aware tester-based evaluation framework of user simulators. In: ECIR '22, pp. 336–350 (2022). https://doi.org/10.1007/978-3-030-99736-6_23

31. Liang, T., et al.: LLM-REDIAL: a large-scale dataset for conversational recommender systems created from user behaviors with LLMs. In: Findings of the ACL '24, pp. 8926–8939 (2024). https://doi.org/10.18653/V1/2024.FINDINGS-ACL.529

32. Lin, B.Y., et al.: WildBench: benchmarking LLMs with challenging tasks from real users in the wild. In: ICLR '25 (2025). https://openreview.net/forum?id=MKEHCx25xp
33. Liu, Q., et al.: You impress me: dialogue generation via mutual persona perception. In: ACL '20 (2020). https://api.semanticscholar.org/CorpusID:215745354
34. Logacheva, V., Burtsev, M., Malykh, V., Polulyakh, V., Seliverstov, A.: ConvAI dataset of topic-oriented human-to-chatbot dialogues. In: Escalera, S., Weimer, M. (eds.) The NIPS '17 Competition: Building Intelligent Systems. TSSCML, pp. 47–57. Springer, Cham (2018). https://doi.org/10.1007/978-3-319-94042-7_3
35. Mayr, P., Kacem, A.: A complete year of user retrieval sessions in a social sciences academic search engine. In: TPDL '17, pp. 560–565 (2017). https://doi.org/10.1007/978-3-319-67008-9_46
36. Mitra, B.: Exploring session context using distributed representations of queries and reformulations. In: SIGIR '15, pp. 3–12 (2015). https://doi.org/10.1145/2766462.2767702
37. Niu, Z., et al.: Overview of the NTCIR-17 unbiased learning to rank evaluation 2 (ultre-2) task. In: NTCIR '23 (2023). https://doi.org/10.20736/0002001320
38. Owoicho, P., et al.: TREC CAsT 2022: going beyond user ask and system retrieve with initiative and response generation. In: TREC '22 (2022). https://api.semanticscholar.org/CorpusID:261288646
39. Owoicho, P., Sekulic, I., Aliannejadi, M., Dalton, J., Crestani, F.: Exploiting simulated user feedback for conversational search: ranking, rewriting, and beyond. In: SIGIR '23, pp. 632–642 (2023). https://doi.org/10.1145/3539618.3591683
40. Pass, G., Chowdhury, A., Torgeson, C.: A picture of search. In: InfoScale '06, p. 1 (2006). https://doi.org/10.1145/1146847.1146848
41. Rekabsaz, N., Lesota, O., Schedl, M., Brassey, J., Eickhoff, C.: TripClick: the log files of a large health web search engine. In: SIGIR '21, pp. 2507–2513 (2021). https://doi.org/10.1145/3404835.3463242
42. Sakai, T.: Evaluating evaluation metrics based on the bootstrap. In: SIGIR '06, pp. 525–532 (2006). https://doi.org/10.1145/1148170.1148261
43. Schaer, P., Kreutz, C.K., Balog, K., Breuer, T., Kruff, A.K.: second sigir workshop on simulations for information access (Sim4IA 2025). In: SIGIR '25, pp. 4172–4175 (2025). https://doi.org/10.1145/3726302.3730363
44. Sekulić, I., Aliannejadi, M., Crestani, F.: Evaluating mixed-initiative conversational search systems via user simulation. In: WSDM '22, pp. 888–896 (2022). https://doi.org/10.1145/3488560.3498440
45. Sekulić, I., Alinannejadi, M., Crestani, F.: Analysing utterances in LLM-based user simulation for conversational search. ACM Trans. Intell. Syst. Technol. 15(3) (2024). https://doi.org/10.1145/3650041
46. Serdyukov, P., Dupret, G., Craswell, N.: Log-based personalization: the 4th web search click data (WSCD) workshop. In: WSDM '14, pp. 685–686 (2014). https://doi.org/10.1145/2556195.2556207
47. Song, R., et al.: SogouQ: the first large-scale test collection with click streams used in a shared-task evaluation. In: Sakai, T., Oard, D.W., Kando, N. (eds.) Evaluating Information Retrieval and Access Tasks. TIRS, vol. 43, pp. 143–150. Springer, Singapore (2021). https://doi.org/10.1007/978-981-15-5554-1_10
48. Song, R., et al.: Overview of the NTCIR-9 intent task. In: NTCIR '11 (2011). https://api.semanticscholar.org/CorpusID:18551696
49. Terragni, S., et al.: In-context learning user simulators for task-oriented dialog systems. CoRR abs/2306.00774 (2023). https://doi.org/10.48550/ARXIV.2306.00774

50. Voorhees, E.M., Buckley, C.: The effect of topic set size on retrieval experiment error. In: SIGIR '02, pp. 316–323, ACM (2002). https://doi.org/10.1145/564376.564432
51. Wang, K., et al.: Know you first and be you better: modeling human-like user simulators via implicit profiles. In: ACL '25, pp. 21082–21107 (2025). https://doi.org/10.18653/v1/2025.acl-long.1025
52. Wang, L., et al.: User behavior simulation with large language model-based agents. ACM Trans. Inf. Syst. **43**(2) (2025). https://doi.org/10.1145/3708985
53. Wang, X., Tang, X., Zhao, X., Wang, J., Wen, J.R.: Rethinking the evaluation for conversational recommendation in the era of large language models. In: EMNLP '23, pp. 10052–10065 (2023). https://doi.org/10.18653/v1/2023.emnlp-main.621
54. Wang, Z., Xu, Z., Srikumar, V., Ai, Q.: An in-depth investigation of user response simulation for conversational search. In: Proceedings of the ACM on Web Conference 2024, pp. 1407–1418, WWW '24 (2024). https://doi.org/10.1145/3589334.3645447
55. Yang, D., Zhang, Y., Fang, H.: Zero-shot query reformulation for conversational search. In: ICTIR '23, pp. 257–63 (2023). https://doi.org/10.1145/3578337.3605143
56. Ye, Y., et al.: Learning from the wisdom of crowds: exploiting similar sessions for session search. In: IAAI '23, pp. 4818–4826 (2023). https://doi.org/10.1609/AAAI.V37I4.25607
57. Yoon, S.E., He, Z., Echterhoff, J., McAuley, J.: Evaluating large language models as generative user simulators for conversational recommendation. In: NAACL '24, pp. 1490–1504 (2024). https://doi.org/10.18653/V1/2024.NAACL-LONG.83
58. Zhang, E., Wang, X., Gong, P., Yang, Z., Mao, J.: Exploring human-like thinking in search simulations with large language models. In: SIGIR '25, pp. 2669–2673 (2025). https://doi.org/10.1145/3726302.3730193
59. Zhang, S., Balog, K.: Evaluating conversational recommender systems via user simulation. In: KDD '20, pp. 1512–1520 (2020). https://doi.org/10.1145/3394486.3403202
60. Zhang, S., et al.: Personalizing dialogue agents: i have a dog, do you have pets too? In: ACL '18, pp. 2204–2213 (2018). https://doi.org/10.18653/v1/P18-1205
61. Zhang, S., Wang, M.C., Balog, K.: Analyzing and simulating user utterance reformulation in conversational recommender systems. In: SIGIR '22, pp. 133–143 (2022). https://doi.org/10.1145/3477495.3531936
62. Zhao, W., et al.: WildChat: 1M ChatGPT Interaction Logs in the Wild. In: ICLR '24 (2024). https://openreview.net/forum?id=Bl8u7ZRlbM
63. Zheng, L., et al.: LMSYS-Chat-1M: a large-scale real-world LLM conversation dataset. In: ICLR '24 (2024). https://openreview.net/forum?id=BOfDKxfwt0
64. Zou, L., et al.: A large scale search dataset for unbiased learning to rank. In: NeurIPS '22, pp. 1127–1139 (2022). https://proceedings.neurips.cc/paper_files/paper/2022/file/07f560092a0edceabf55af32a40eaee3-Paper-Datasets_and_Benchmarks.pdf

# BioGraphletQA: Knowledge-Anchored Generation of Complex QA Datasets


Richard A. A. Jonker[1]([email]), Bárbara Maria Ribeiro de Abreu Martins[2],
and Sérgio Matos[1]

[1] IEETA, DETI, LASI, University of Aveiro, Aveiro, Portugal
{richard.jonker,aleixomatos}@ua.pt
[2] Centro Hospitalar do Baixo Vouga, Aveiro, Portugal
bmmartins@ulsra.min-saude.pt



**Abstract.** This paper presents a principled and scalable framework for systematically generating complex Question Answering (QA) data. In the core of this framework is a graphlet-anchored generation process, where small subgraphs from a Knowledge Graph (KG) are used in a structured prompt to control the complexity and ensure the factual grounding of questions generated by Large Language Models. The first instantiation of this framework is BioGraphletQA, a new biomedical KGQA dataset of 119,856 QA pairs. Each entry is grounded in a graphlet of up to five nodes from the OREGANO KG, with most of the pairs being enriched with relevant document snippets from PubMed. We start by demonstrating the framework's value and the dataset's quality through evaluation by a domain expert on 106 QA pairs, confirming the high scientific validity and complexity of the generated data. Secondly, we establish its practical utility by showing that augmenting downstream benchmarks with our data improves accuracy on PubMedQA from 49.2% to 68.5% in a low-resource setting, and on MedQA from a 41.4% baseline to 44.8% in a full-resource setting. Our framework provides a robust and generalizable solution for creating critical resources to advance complex QA tasks, including MCQA and KGQA. All resources supporting this work, including the dataset (https://zenodo.org/records/17381119) and framework code (https://github.com/ieeta-pt/BioGraphletQA), are publicly available to facilitate use, reproducibility and extension.

**Keywords:** Knowledge Graph · Biomedical Question Answering · Synthetic Data · Large Language Models · Information Retrieval


## 1 Introduction

Question answering (QA) systems have benefited immensely from advances in large language models (LLMs), particularly Transformer-based architectures [26]. However, despite their success, LLMs struggle with factual consistency, often generating hallucinated or inaccurate responses [11,12]. One promising approach to mitigate these issues is the use of Knowledge Graph Question

Answering (KGQA) datasets. Traditional KGQA datasets, however, are either manually curated—making them costly and time-intensive [9]—or template-based, which often limits their diversity and generalizability [1].

In the biomedical domain, the problem of hallucinations can lead to dangerous outcomes such as misdiagnoses, unsafe treatment recommendations, and compromised patient safety. Although several biomedical KGs exist—such as OREGANO KG [4], CKG [23], MonarchKG [20], and PrimeKG [6]—most KGQA research has focused on large open-domain KGs like Freebase [3] and Wikidata [27], which often lack the granularity and reliability required for biomedical decision-making. To date, only one large-scale synthetic biomedical KGQA dataset has been developed [31], generated using an LLM with graphlets from PrimeKG, underscoring the need for more robust, domain-specific QA resources.

To address this limitation, we propose a framework for the systematic generation of KGQA data. The framework is centered on a graphlet-anchored generation process, wherein small, coherent subgraphs (graphlets) are systematically extracted from a KG. These graphlets serve as support to guide an LLM in formulating intricate questions, ensuring the factual grounding of the generated output by constraining it to the relations within the subgraph, while simultaneously leveraging the linguistic capabilities of the LLM to achieve a high degree of complexity and naturalness, unachievable through conventional template-based methods.

The first instantiation of this framework is BioGraphletQA, a new biomedical KGQA dataset comprising 119,856 QA pairs. Each entry is explicitly grounded in a multi-node graphlet (3–5 nodes) derived from the OREGANO KG (v2.1) and is subsequently enriched with relevant document snippets from PubMed. The quality and utility of the dataset were validated through a dual evaluation. First, a qualitative assessment by a domain expert confirmed the high scientific validity and complexity of a small sample of the generated data. Second, its quantitative utility was established by using BioGraphletQA as an augmentation resource for downstream tasks. This augmentation resulted in performance gains, improving mean accuracy on the PubMedQA benchmark from 49.2% to 68.5% in a low-resource setting, and increasing the baseline performance on MedQA from 41.4% to 44.8%.

Our primary contributions are twofold:

1. We present a robust and generalizable data generation framework that is adaptable to other KGs and domains.
2. We present BioGraphletQA, a large-scale, complex KGQA dataset intended to support future research in the biomedical domain, with use cases in model training, as well as domain and task specific fine-tuning.

All associated resources, including the dataset and framework code, are made publicly available to facilitate future research in complex question answering.

## 2    Related Work

Recent advances in LLMs have spurred a surge in using synthetic data generation to overcome data scarcity and privacy challenges in IR and QA tasks. For instance, Braga et al. [5] propose a framework that generates synthetic answers tailored for personalized community QA, demonstrating that fine-tuning on this generated data can yield performance comparable to models trained on human-curated datasets. Similarly, Tang et al. [25] explores leveraging ChatGPT to generate synthetic clinical documents, reporting substantial improvements in downstream tasks like named entity recognition and relation extraction. In addition, GeMQuAD, introduced by Namboori et al. [17], employs few-shot learning with LLMs to create multilingual QA datasets, thereby enhancing performance in low-resource settings. Complementing these efforts, Wu et al. [29] present a synthetic multimodal question generation approach that combines the strengths of LLMs and multimodal models to produce high-quality QA pairs from diverse document types.

KGQA datasets have evolved significantly, with several notable benchmarks such as LC-QuAD [7] and ComplexQuestions [2]. GrailQA [9] and GrailQA++ [8] advanced the field by introducing a dataset specifically designed to evaluate generalization in KGQA systems across different levels of compositional complexity. Jiang et al. [13] provided a comprehensive survey of KGQA methods and datasets, highlighting the challenges and opportunities in this domain.

Recent advances in biomedical KGQA include PrimeKGQA [31], which contains approximately 84,000 QA pairs generated through few-shot prompting using graphlets extracted from PrimeKG. This approach builds on graphlet-based methodologies similar to those in GrailQA++ [8]. Our work follows a similar graphlet-based idea but extends it by introducing an in-depth modular prompt building strategy and an additional QA filtering phase to improve quality.

Similarly, ConvKGYarn [19] generates synthetic QA pairs by combining KG facts with slot-filled question templates. While this enables large-scale QA generation, the reliance on predefined templates can limit question diversity and contextual depth. In contrast, our dynamic node selection strategy allows the LLM to flexibly identify relevant nodes and relations within each graphlet, leading to more varied and contextually nuanced QA generation.

## 3    Framework Overview

To address the challenge of creating high-quality, domain-specific QA data at scale, we propose a new multi-stage framework that relies on a modular prompt enriched with structured knowledge in the form of graphlets to provide a factual anchor to control the output of an LLM. This ensures that the generated questions are not only linguistically complex but also verifiably grounded in the underlying knowledge base.

Figure 1 provides a comprehensive overview of the framework's five sequential stages. The process begins with the preparation of a KG and the extraction of

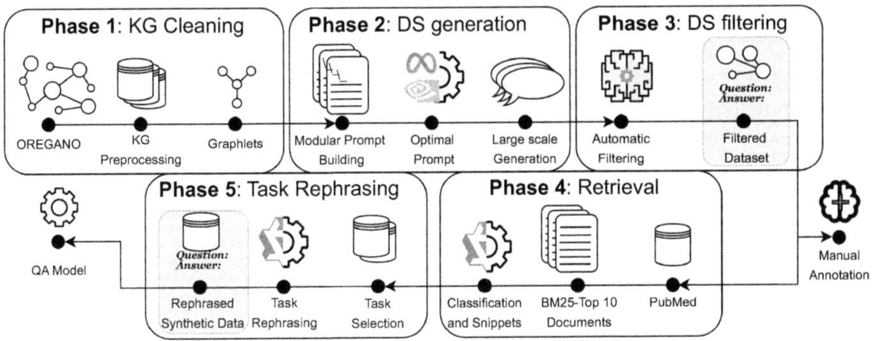


**Fig. 1.** An overview of our framework, composed of five phases: 1) Initial cleaning of the OREGANO KG, including KG pre-processing and graphlet extraction; 2) Generation of the initial KGQA dataset, starting with a modular prompt building stage; 3) Automatic filtering stage using LLM-as-a-judge; 4) Supporting document retrieval from PubMed with BM25 using an LLM to classify the document relevance and extract snippets; 5) Task specific rephrasing for downstream tasks.

graphlets (Sect. 3.1). These graphlets then serve as the input for the generation of the QA pairs (Sect. 3.2). To ensure high quality, the generated data undergoes automated filtering and validation process (Sect. 3.3). The framework concludes with stages for enriching the data with retrieved textual evidence (Sect. 3.4) and aligning it for specific downstream tasks (Sect. 3.5), demonstrating its versatility.

## 3.1   Knowledge Graph

Developing a robust KGQA dataset requires an appropriate KG. For the initial test of the framework, the biomedical domain was chosen, as it offers unique challenges and opportunities. From the numerous existing biomedical KGs [10], the selection criteria required a resource that balanced size and complexity while ensuring diverse node classes linked to reputable biomedical databases for comprehensive question generation. Based on these criteria, the OREGANO KG (v2.1) [4] was selected. It contains 88,937 nodes spanning 11 types[1] and 824,231 edges with 19 edge types.

**Pre-processing.** The preparation of the KG for graphlet extraction involves a two-stage pre-processing pipeline consisting of entity hydration followed by structural reduction. This stage of the pipeline is KG-specific and needs to be adapted according to the selected KG and domain.

The initial stage, hydration, is necessary to enrich the graph by resolving and updating node identifiers to their canonical names. While the OREGANO

---

[1] Note that there is also a 'code' entity class, which was not utilized.

dataset includes many entity names, a significant portion required external look-up. Between December 3 and 19, 2024, various knowledge bases were systematically queried to retrieve the most current names for entities. The licenses of all source knowledge bases were also verified to permit the use and publication of these names. This process resulted in a graph with 85,655 denormalized nodes, of which 81,240 (94.85%) were unique. Only two entities—one disease and one pathway—could not be successfully hydrated.

Following hydration, the reduction stage serves to refine the graph structure and improve the efficiency of subsequent processing steps. An analysis of the node degree distribution revealed a large number of nodes with a degree of one ("edge nodes") and a small subset with very high degrees ("hub nodes"), as shown in Fig. 2. Edge nodes were hypothesized to offer limited utility for generating complex questions due to their sparse connectivity, while hub nodes risk introducing redundancy by appearing in an excessive number of graphlets. To mitigate these issues, the graph was filtered by removing all nodes with a degree greater than 100 or less than 3. This reduction step was designed to enhance the variability of nodes in the dataset and preserve meaningful structural complexity while making the graph more computationally tractable. The final, processed graph comprises 41,115 nodes and 129,992 edges. The updated node degree is illustrated in Fig. 2.

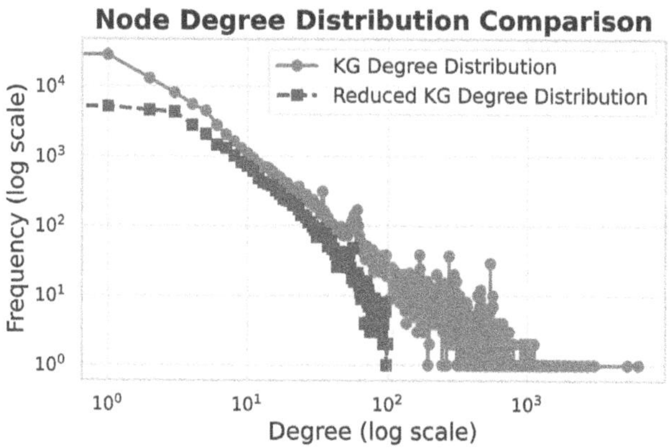


**Fig. 2.** Node degree distribution of the OREGANO KG and the reduced version.

**Graphlets.** The final preprocessing step involves extracting graphlets, which are small, connected, non-isomorphic subgraphs that capture local structural patterns within the KG. Rather than performing a simple random walk, the KG is partitioned into these graphlets to serve as the basis for QA generation. The process considers all 29 unique graphlet structures containing 3–5 nodes (as 2-node structures are trivial), illustrated in Fig. 4. Subgraph enumeration is generally computationally expensive [21], making the previously described graph reduction techniques advantageous. To efficiently identify graphlets, the `graph-tool` library [18] is used. The pipeline first loads the KG as an undirected graph and removes parallel edges. Next, the frequency of each graphlet shape is counted using `gt.motifs()`, and the sampling strategy of Wernicke [28] is applied to target 10,000 occurrences per graphlet. This controls the dataset size, which is critical given that the most frequent graphlet appears over 1.8 trillion times. This process results in a final dataset of 269,574 graphlets, serving as the foundation for generating the initial QA dataset.

## 3.2  Dataset Generation

With the graphlets prepared, the central stage of the framework begins: the large-scale generation of KGQA pairs. The core of this stage is a multi-module prompt structured around knowledge-injecting graphlets, which guides and controls the LLM's generation process. In this approach, each graphlet inherently encodes the question and answer; the question targets one or two *Question Nodes*, while *Hidden Nodes* facilitate the reasoning required to infer the *Answer Node*. The prompt explicitly includes the graphlet structure and node names to provide a factual anchor. The edge type is omitted, as it was found that allowing the LLM to infer the complex relationship yields better results than providing a simple predicate like `has_effect`.

To select and validate the prompt for dataset generation, a modular prompt building approach was employed, using an LLM-as-a-judge to systematically score outputs from 15 distinct, modular prompt configurations against six quality criteria: (1) the answer is not present in the question, (2) the question avoids graphlet terminology, (3) the answer avoids graphlet terminology, (4) the question is scientifically accurate, (5) the answer is scientifically accurate, and (6) the answer properly addresses the question[2]. This evaluation was conducted across 1,000 graphlets, incorporating modules such as guided reasoning instructions inspired by Chain-of-Thought and self-reflection where the model critiques its own output. This process revealed that a comprehensive full prompt, which integrated all tested modules, was the best-performing configuration. This prompt is depicted in Fig. 3.

With the graphlets prepared and the optimal prompt identified, large-scale data generation was performed using a 4-bit quantized version of the Llama-Nemotron-70B model[3]. This process initially yielded 269,574 raw question-answer pairs, which were then subjected to a multi-stage refinement protocol to ensure quality and consistency. The initial filtering step addressed structural integrity, where 543 outputs that failed to parse as valid JSON were discarded. Subsequently, outliers in the length of the generated text were addressed through a statistical filtering method based on Z-scores. This step was designed to remove exceptionally short or long entries that could represent low-quality or anomalous

---

[2] Detailed evaluation criteria is available in the code repository.
[3] Nvidia-Llama-3.1 model on Hugging Face.

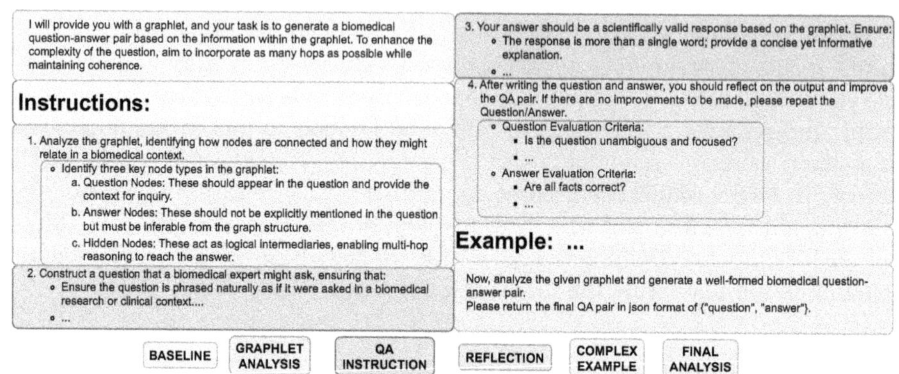

**Fig. 3.** Compressed version of the selected prompt, showcasing extracts from some of the different modules. The full prompt and the modules can be inspected in our GitHub Repository.

data points. Specifically, any QA pair where either the question or the answer length fell more than three standard deviations from the mean was culled. This criterion established acceptable length ranges as 79–365 characters for questions and 59–997 characters for answers, leading to the exclusion of an additional 4,658 pairs.

## 3.3   Post-Generation Filtering

We used an LLM-as-a-judge to filter the initial synthetic outputs and improve overall dataset quality [16]. Although the prompt used for generation included a reflection phase, several issues could still arise. For example, some graphlets may not contain a valid QA pair worth generating, or the generated answer may be incomplete, requiring additional knowledge to be fully correct. To mitigate these and other potential issues, automatic filtering was applied to the dataset.

The filtering prompt first instructs the model to evaluate the connections between the entities in the question to determine whether the question is coherent. Next, it attempts to answer the question and compares its response with the previously generated answer. This evaluation is structured in a JSON format to ensure that two boolean variables, `valid_question` and `original_answer_valid`, are generated based on the model's reasoning[4]. While the goal is to use KGs for grounding and reducing hallucination, this step assesses whether the QA pair remains valid based on the LLM's general biomedical knowledge, independent of the specific graph context. After filtering, a final dataset of 119,856 QA pairs remained (45% of the dataset after post-processing). Additionally, 17,101 outputs (6.47%) were unparseable as JSON. The distribution of the accepted graphlets can be seen in Fig. 4.

---

[4] The filtering prompt is available in the code repository.

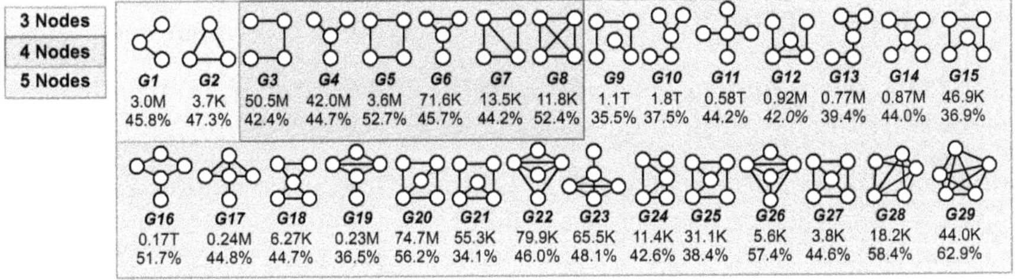

**Fig. 4.** The 29 graphlet shapes with 3–5 nodes. Each shape is shown with the number of graphlets initially present (sampled to 10,000) and the acceptance ratio (QA pairs accepted / QA pairs generated).

## 3.4 Supporting Document Retrieval

While BioGraphletQA is grounded in structured knowledge, many biomedical QA scenarios also rely on unstructured text. To broaden our framework's applicability and enrich the final resource, we include a stage for augmenting the QA pairs with supporting documents from PubMed [24]. This serves two purposes: it facilitates the evaluation of retrieval-augmented QA systems and provides verifiable textual evidence to validate the generated pairs.

The process uses the PubMed abstract collection as its source. For each QA pair, a query is formed by concatenating the question and answer, which is then used with BM25 [22] to retrieve the top 10 relevant abstracts. Subsequently, the Qwen3-32B model [32] is applied to each abstract to perform two tasks: 1) classify its relevance to the QA pair, and 2) extract the most pertinent supporting text snippets[5]. This process was highly effective, with a substantial majority of QA pairs being grounded in multiple documents; over 79% of pairs were linked to at least two supporting documents, and over half (52.7%) were linked to five or more. A small fraction of QA pairs (5.25%) had no relevant documents, potentially indicating novel relationships inferred from the KG's structure that are not yet well-documented in abstracts, or model hallucinations.

## 3.5 Task-Specific Rephrasing

The final stage of the framework extends the utility and adaptability of the generated data by aligning it with existing QA benchmarks. This is achieved by performing task-specific rephrasing on a subset of QA pairs using Qwen3-32B.[6] For each pair, a prompt is constructed containing the original QA content, its supporting snippets, and relevant examples from the target dataset retrieved via BM25. The model then generates a new QA pair in the target format (e.g., multiple-choice or yes/no). This alignment enables robust, standardized evaluation of the impact of the resource on downstream tasks.

---

[5] The retrieval prompt is available in the code repository.
[6] The rephrasing prompts for PubMedQA and MedQA can be inspected in our code repository.

## 4    Experimental Setup

To validate our proposed framework, we designed a series of experiments to answer two primary research questions:

- **RQ1:** Can our framework produce QA pairs that are scientifically valid and complex, as judged by a domain expert?
- **RQ2:** Does data generated by our framework provide a tangible benefit when used to augment training data for downstream QA tasks?

### 4.1    Evaluation of Data Quality (RQ1)

To answer RQ1, we conducted a manual evaluation of data quality. The annotation was performed by a domain expert (co-author) to assess key characteristics. We created a validation set of 116 QA pairs using stratified sampling: for each of the 29 graphlet shapes, we randomly selected three pairs that our automated filter had **accepted** and one pair it had **rejected**. The annotator, blind to the quality filtering, rated each pair on a 5-point Likert scale across several criteria, including Scientific Validity, Question Complexity, and Answer Completeness[7]. The annotator had the choice to not evaluate a pair if it did not fall in their domain of expertise, which occurred 10 times, leaving 106 annotated pairs.

### 4.2    Evaluation of Downstream Utility (RQ2)

To answer RQ2, we evaluated the impact of using BioGraphletQA as a data augmentation resource for two established biomedical QA benchmarks: **PubMedQA** [15], a yes/no question answering task based on PubMed abstracts and **MedQA** [14], a challenging multiple-choice QA task derived from medical board exams.

For our experiments, we fine-tuned BioLinkBERT-large [33], a strong baseline for biomedical NLP tasks. We opted for a BERT-based model over a generative LLM to ensure a fair evaluation free from potential training data contamination [30]. Our experimental protocol involved training the model on increasing portions of the original training sets of both benchmarks and comparing the performance against models trained on the same data augmented with varying amounts (1k, 10k, and 20k samples) of our rephrased BioGraphletQA data. All experiments were run with 5 different random seeds to determine statistical significance.

## 5    Results and Analysis

In this section, we present the results of our experiments, structured to directly answer the research questions posed in Sect. 4. We first analyze the quality of the data generated by our framework through expert human evaluation (RQ1), and then demonstrate its practical utility in downstream tasks (RQ2).

---

[7] The full evaluation criteria is in the code repository.

## 5.1  Data Quality Analysis (RQ1)

To answer our first research question regarding the quality of the generated data, we conducted human evaluation as detailed in our experimental setup. The results strongly validate both the high quality of the final dataset and the efficacy of our automated filtering pipeline.

Figure 5 shows a clear distributional shift in scores between the QA pairs our LLM filter accepted versus those it rejected. The accepted pairs consistently received high scores from the human expert, while rejected pairs scored poorly. This disparity provides strong empirical evidence that Stage 3 of our framework is effective at identifying and removing low-quality data, a critical step for ensuring the reliability of synthetically generated resources.

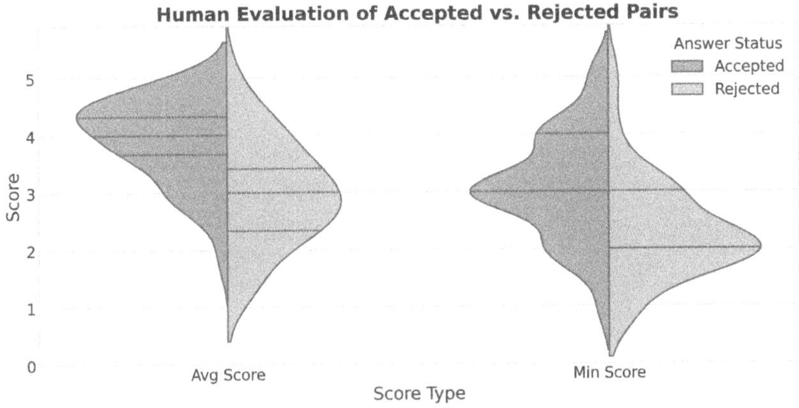


**Fig. 5.** Human evaluation scores validating the LLM's annotation filtering. The split violin plot contrasts human-rated Average and Minimum scores for LLM annotations classified as 'Accepted' (green) vs. 'Rejected' (red). (Color figure online)

Furthermore, an in-depth analysis of the accepted pairs, shown in Fig. 6, confirms their high quality. All questions were rated as scientifically valid, and 88.46% were deemed complex (score $\geq$ 3). The answers also scored highly on scientific validity (92.31% with a score $\geq$ 3) and completeness (93.59% with a score $\geq$ 3). The primary area for improvement was answer specificity, where only 79.49% of answers achieved an ideal score of 3. Despite this, 75.64% of QA pairs achieved a minimum score of 3 across all answer criteria, confirming their overall acceptability. We consider the minimum score a particularly stringent metric, as a failure in any single category should render a QA pair invalid. A sample of some annotated QA pairs can be seen in Fig. 7.

## 5.2  Downstream Task Performance (RQ2)

To answer our second research question regarding the utility of our generated data, we evaluated its impact as an augmentation resource for downstream tasks.

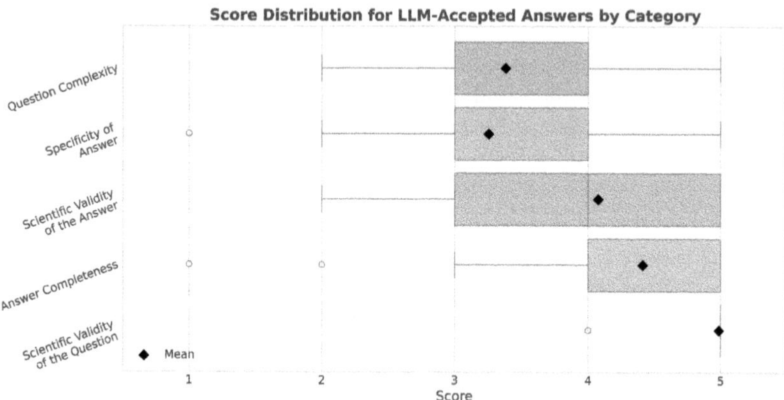

**Fig. 6.** Boxplot of Likert based human evaluation scores across 5 categories for the accepted QA pairs.

| Question | Answer | Scores |
|---|---|---|
| In individuals with heroin dependence, what neurotransmitter-converting enzyme might be indirectly influenced by a substance that also interacts with the opioid receptor kappa 1, potentially impacting the addictive behavior? | Dopamine beta-hydroxylase is the enzyme that might be indirectly influenced. Here's the connection: Heroin dependence (0) is associated with the opioid receptor kappa 1 (3), which can also be affected by Ethanol (1). Ethanol (1) is connected to dopamine beta-hydroxylase (4), an enzyme responsible for converting dopamine to norepinephrine. The modulation of this enzyme could influence neurotransmitter balances, potentially impacting behaviors related to heroin dependence. Notably, a compound (2) - methyl (3S,4R)-3-benzoyloxy-8-methyl-8-azabicyclo[3.2.1]octane-4-carboxylate - interacts with opioid receptor kappa 1 (3) and is associated with heroin dependence (0), further suggesting a complex interplay of substances and enzymes in the context of addiction. | 5 - Question Validty<br>5 - Answer Validty<br>4 - Question Complexity<br>5 - Answer Specificity<br>5 - Answer Completeness |
| A patient is being treated with Peginesatide for anemia. Considering the drug's mechanism and potential cross-reactivity, what other medication, used for a different condition, might pose a risk of adverse interaction if co-administered? | Lipegfilgrastim, a granulocyte colony-stimulating factor (G-CSF) analog used to reduce the incidence of infection, in cases of strong myelosuppressive chemotherapy-induced neutropenia, might pose a risk of adverse interaction if co-administered with Peginesatide. This is because both drugs, being recombinant human proteins, could theoretically lead to cross-reactivity or affect each other's pharmacokinetics, especially in patients with compromised immune systems. Pegvaliase, another recombinant enzyme, shares a connection with both in the drug interaction network, hinting at a potential for complex pharmacological interactions. | 5 - Question Validty<br>2 - Answer Validty<br>4 - Question Complexity<br>2 - Answer Specificity<br>5 - Answer Completeness |
| Considering the symptom profiles of various infectious diseases, what symptom, commonly associated with infections like those caused by Legionella pneumophilia, might also be observed in a patient with Rift Valley Fever who presents with reduced consciousness, given the overlapping clinical manifestations among certain infections? | Arthralgia is a plausible symptom. Although direct connections between Rift Valley Fever (RVF) and arthralgia are not straightforward, the overlap in symptomatology with other infections (e.g., Legionella pneumophilia, which is known to cause arthralgia) and the shared severe manifestation of reduced consciousness in RVF, suggests that patients with RVF could also exhibit arthralgia, highlighting the complexity of differential diagnosis in infectious diseases. | 5 - Question Validty<br>3 - Answer Validty<br>3 - Question Complexity<br>3 - Answer Specificity<br>5 - Answer Completeness |
| Considering the comorbidity of Chronic Obstructive Pulmonary Disease (COPD) and Heart Failure, what receptor type could be a therapeutic target to alleviate symptoms of both conditions, given the common use of diuretics in heart failure management? | The adrenoceptor beta 2 is a plausible target. In COPD, beta-2 adrenoceptors facilitate bronchodilation. In Heart Failure, while the primary connection is through diuretic therapy reducing fluid overload, medications targeting beta-2 adrenoceptors could offer a dual benefit by improving respiratory function in COPD and, through systemic physiological effects, supporting heart failure management, albeit with careful consideration of potential interactions with diuretics. | 5 - Question Validty<br>5 - Answer Validty<br>3 - Question Complexity<br>2 - Answer Specificity<br>3 - Answer Completeness |
| In patients undergoing anticoagulant therapy with Edoxaban, what is the likely enzymatic precursor involved in the coagulation cascade that is indirectly affected by this treatment, given its mechanism of action on Activated factor Xa heavy chain? | Factor IX. Edoxaban, a direct oral anticoagulant, exerts its effect by inhibiting Activated factor Xa heavy chain. In the coagulation cascade, Activated factor Xa is a downstream product of the intrinsic pathway, where Factor IX (as part of the tenase complex with Factor VIII) plays a crucial role in activating Factor X. Thus, by inhibiting Activated factor Xa, Edoxaban indirectly affects the efficiency of the coagulation process initiated by Factor IX. This mechanism is pivotal in preventing thromboembolic events without significantly increasing the risk of bleeding, as seen with some other anticoagulants. | 5 - Question Validty<br>2 - Answer Validty<br>2 - Question Complexity<br>2 - Answer Specificity<br>1 - Answer Completeness |

**Fig. 7.** Five QA pairs, with their associated human evaluation. Samples selected by hand to show the difference between low scores and high score from the human evaluation.

The results, presented in Fig. 8, demonstrate that data generated by our framework provides benefits when used for augmenting gold data.

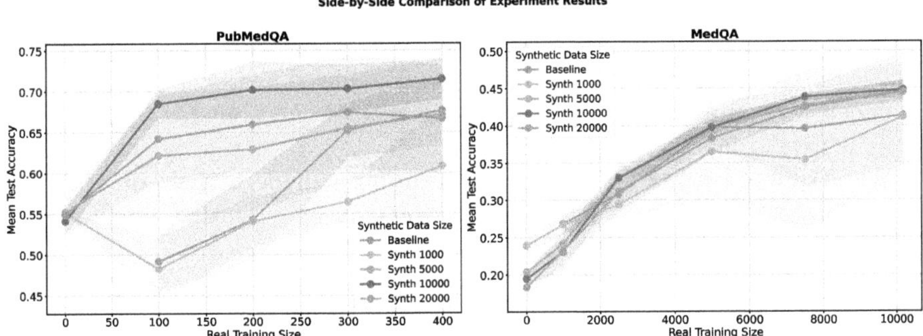


**Fig. 8.** Effect of synthetic data augmentation on PubMedQA (left) and MedQA (right). Plots show mean test accuracy over 5 different seeds vs. real training data size. Augmenting with 10,000 synthetic samples consistently provides the largest performance gains over the baseline. Shaded areas represent standard deviation.

The findings show performance gains in both low-resource and full-resource settings. The most striking result was on PubMedQA in a low-resource setting: augmenting just 100 real samples with 10,000 synthetic pairs increased mean accuracy from 49.2% to 68.5%, effectively compensating for the scarcity of labeled data. This positive trend extended to the MedQA benchmark, where adding 10,000 synthetic samples to the full 10,000-sample training set improved accuracy from a 41.4% baseline to 44.8%. Our analysis also indicates an optimal augmentation size. An addition of 10,000 synthetic samples consistently provided the most significant and stable performance gains across both datasets. In contrast, a smaller augmentation of 1,000 samples was often unstable, while an excessive 20,000 samples showed diminishing returns and even degraded performance on PubMedQA, suggesting a saturation point for this training configuration.

To reject potential data contamination, we evaluated the semantic overlap between a sample of our synthetic dataset ($N = 50,000$) and the PubMedQA and MedQA training sets. Using the all-MiniLM-L6-v2[8] sentence transformer, we calculated the cosine similarity between all document pairs. The similarity scores follow a normal distribution with mean values of 0.44 and 0.52 and 95th percentile values of 0.59 and 0.62 for PubMedQA and MedQA respectively. This rejects any potential data contamination, indicating novel scenarios rather than memorized samples

---

[8] https://huggingface.co/sentence-transformers/all-MiniLM-L6-v2.

# 6    Discussion and Limitations

The results of our human and automatic evaluations validate our proposed framework as an effective method for generating high-quality, complex QA data. The success of the downstream augmentation task, particularly in the low-resource PubMedQA setting, underscores the potential of knowledge-anchored synthetic data to mitigate data scarcity in specialized domains. The rich modular prompt, combined with automated filtering, offers a scalable and reliable alternative to costly manual annotation.

We acknowledge the limitation of relying on a single human annotator for our qualitative assessment; future work should involve multiple annotators to establish inter-rater reliability. Additionally, our framework could be refined to improve answer specificity, which our analysis identified as the primary area for improvement. Finally, the quality of the generated data is inherently linked to the capabilities of the underlying language model; with better computational resources, and as more advanced models become available, our framework can be used to produce datasets of even higher quality.

# 7    Conclusion

In this paper, we describe and validate a new graphlet-anchored framework for generating complex, factually-grounded question-answering data. We introduced its first instantiation, BioGraphletQA, a new, large-scale resource of 119,856 QA pairs for the biomedical domain.

Our comprehensive evaluation demonstrated the framework's success. A qualitative assessment by a domain expert confirmed the high scientific validity and complexity of the dataset and validated our automated filtering pipeline. Furthermore, quantitative experiments showed its utility as a data augmentation tool, with performance on PubMedQA increasing from 49.2% to 68.5% in a low-resource setting. These findings underscore the value of our framework for creating critical resources to advance complex QA tasks. We release both the BioGraphletQA dataset and our generation framework publicly to facilitate future research into reliable, factually-grounded question answering.

**Acknowledgments.** This work was funded by FEDER - Fundo Europeu de Desenvolvimento Regional funds through the project CENTRO2030-FEDER-02595400, and by the Foundation for Science and Technology (FCT) through contract https://doi.org/10.54499/UID/00127/2025. Richard A. A. Jonker is funded by the FCT doctoral grant PRT/BD/154792/2023, with DOI identifier https://doi.org/10.54499/PRT/BD/154792/2023.

**Disclosure of Interests.** The authors have no competing interests to declare that are relevant to the content of this article.

# References


1. Banerjee, D., Awale, S., Usbeck, R., Biemann, C.: DBLP-quad: a question answering dataset over the DBLP scholarly knowledge graph. arXiv preprint arXiv:2303.13351 (2023)
2. Bao, J., Duan, N., Yan, Z., Zhou, M., Zhao, T.: Constraint-based question answering with knowledge graph. In: Matsumoto, Y., Prasad, R. (eds.) Proceedings of COLING 2016, the 26th International Conference on Computational Linguistics: Technical Papers, pp. 2503–2514. The COLING 2016 Organizing Committee, Osaka, Japan (2016). https://aclanthology.org/C16-1236/
3. Bollacker, K., Evans, C., Paritosh, P., Sturge, T., Taylor, J.: Freebase: a collaboratively created graph database for structuring human knowledge. In: Proceedings of the 2008 ACM SIGMOD international conference on Management of data, pp. 1247–1250 (2008)
4. Boudin, M., Diallo, G., Drancé, M., Mougin, F.: The oregano knowledge graph for computational drug repurposing. Sci. data 10(1), 871 (2023)
5. Braga, M., Kasela, P., Raganato, A., Pasi, G.: Synthetic data generation with large language models for personalized community question answering. arXiv preprint arXiv:2410.22182 (2024)
6. Chandak, P., Huang, K., Zitnik, M.: Building a knowledge graph to enable precision medicine. Nature Sci. Data (2023). https://doi.org/10.1038/s41597-023-01960-3
7. Dubey, M., Banerjee, D., Abdelkawi, A., Lehmann, J.: LC-QuAD 2.0: A Large Dataset for Complex Question Answering over Wikidata and DBpedia. In: Ghidini, C., et al. (eds.) ISWC 2019. LNCS, vol. 11779, pp. 69–78. Springer, Cham (2019). https://doi.org/10.1007/978-3-030-30796-7_5
8. Dutt, R., Khosla, S., Kumar, V.B., Gangadharaiah, R.: Grailqa++: a challenging zero-shot benchmark for knowledge base question answering. In: Proceedings of the 13th IJCNLP, pp. 897–909 (2023)
9. Gu, Y., et al.: Beyond IID: three levels of generalization for question answering on knowledge bases. In: Proceedings of the Web Conference 2021, pp. 3477–3488 (2021)
10. Haas, R.: A survey of biomedical knowledge graphs and of resources for their construction (2024) https://robert-haas.github.io/awesome-biomedical-knowledge-graphs/
11. Huang, L., et al.: A survey on hallucination in large language models: principles, taxonomy, challenges, and open questions. ACM Trans. Inf. Syst. 43(2) (2025). https://doi.org/10.1145/3703155
12. Ji, Z., et al.: Survey of hallucination in natural language generation. ACM Comput. Surv. 55(12) (2023).https://doi.org/10.1145/3571730
13. Jiang, L., Usbeck, R.: Knowledge graph question answering datasets and their generalizability: are they enough for future research? In: Proceedings of the 45th International ACM SIGIR Conference on Research and Development in Information Retrieval, pp. 3209–3218 (2022)
14. Jin, D., Pan, E., Oufattole, N., Weng, W.H., Fang, H., Szolovits, P.: What disease does this patient have? a large-scale open domain question answering dataset from medical exams (2020). https://arxiv.org/abs/2009.13081

15. Jin, Q., Dhingra, B., Liu, Z., Cohen, W., Lu, X.: PubMedQA: a dataset for biomedical research question answering. In: Inui, K., Jiang, J., Ng, V., Wan, X. (eds.) Proceedings of the 2019 Conference on Empirical Methods in Natural Language Processing and the 9th International Joint Conference on Natural Language Processing (EMNLP-IJCNLP), pp. 2567–2577. Association for Computational Linguistics, Hong Kong, China (2019). https://doi.org/10.18653/v1/D19-1259, https://aclanthology.org/D19-1259/

16. Li, D., Jiang, B., Huang, L., Beigi, A., Zhao, C., Tan, Z., Bhattacharjee, A., Jiang, Y., Chen, C., Wu, T., Shu, K., Cheng, L., Liu, H.: From generation to judgment: Opportunities and challenges of LLM-as-a-judge. In: Christodoulooulos, C., Chakraborty, T., Roe, C., Peng, V. (eds.) Proceedings of the 2025 Conference on Empirical Methods in atural Language Processing, pp. 2757–2791. Association for Computational Linguistics, Suzhou, China (2025). https://doi.org/10.18653/v1/2025.emnlp-main.138, https://aclanthology.org/2025.emnlp-main.138/

17. Namboori, A., Mangale, S., Rosenbaum, A., Soltan, S.: Gemquad: generating multilingual question answering datasets from large language models using few shot learning. arXiv preprint arXiv:2404.09163 (2024)

18. Peixoto, T.P.: The graph-tool python library. figshare (2014). https://doi.org/10.6084/m9.figshare.1164194, http://figshare.com/articles/graph_tool/1164194

19. Pradeep, R., et al.: ConvKGYarn: spinning configurable and scalable conversational knowledge graph QA datasets with large language models. In: Dernoncourt, F., Preoţiuc-Pietro, D., Shimorina, A. (eds.) Poceedings of the 2024 Conference on Empirical Methods in Natural Language Processing: Industry Track, pp. 1176–1206. Association for Computational Linguistics, Miami, Florida, US (Nov 2024). https://doi.org/10.18653/v1/2024.emnlp-industry.89, https://aclanthology.org/2024.emnlp-industry.89/

20. Putman, T.E., et al.: The monarch initiative in 2024: an analytic platform integrating phenotypes, genes and diseases across species. Nucleic Acids Res. **52**(D1), D938–D949 (2023). https://doi.org/10.1093/nar/gkad1082

21. Ribeiro, P., Paredes, P., Silva, M.E., Aparicio, D., Silva, F.: A survey on subgraph counting: concepts, algorithms, and applications to network motifs and graphlets. ACM comput. surv. (CSUR) **54**(2), 1–36 (2021)

22. Robertson, S., et al.: The probabilistic relevance framework: Bm25 and beyond. Found. Trends® Inf. Retrieval **3**(4), 333–389 (2009)

23. Santos, A., et al.: A knowledge graph to interpret clinical proteomics data. Nat. Biotechnol. **40**(5), 692–702 (2022)

24. Sayers, E.W., et al.: Database resources of the national center for biotechnology information. Nucleic Acids Res. **49**(D1), D10–D17 (2020). https://doi.org/10.1093/nar/gkaa892, https://doi.org/10.1093/nar/gkaa892

25. Tang, R., Han, X., Jiang, X., Hu, X.: Does synthetic data generation of LLMs help clinical text mining? arXiv preprint arXiv:2303.04360 (2023)

26. Vaswani, A., et al.: Attention is all you need. In: Advances in Neural Information Processing Systems. vol. 30 (2017)

27. Vrandečić, D., Krötzsch, M.: Wikidata: a free collaborative knowledgebase. Commun. ACM **57**(10), 78–85 (2014)

28. Wernicke, S.: Efficient detection of network motifs. IEEE/ACM Trans. Comput. Biol. Bioinf. **3**(4), 347–359 (2006). https://doi.org/10.1109/TCBB.2006.51

29. Wu, I., et al.: Synthetic multimodal question generation. arXiv preprint arXiv:2407.02233 (2024)

30. Xu, C., Guan, S., Greene, D., Kechadi, M.T.: Benchmark data contamination of large language models: a survey (2024). https://arxiv.org/abs/2406.04244

31. Yan, X., Westphal, P., Seliger, J., Usbeck, R.: Bridging the gap: generating a comprehensive biomedical knowledge graph question answering dataset. In: ECAI 2024, pp. 1198–1205. IOS Press (2024)
32. Yang, A., et al.: Qwen3 technical report (2025). https://arxiv.org/abs/2505.09388
33. Yasunaga, M., Leskovec, J., Liang, P.: Linkbert: pretraining language models with document links. In: Association for Computational Linguistics (ACL) (2022)

# Beyond the Click: A Framework
# for Inferring Cognitive Traces in Search

Saber Zerhoudi[1(✉)] and Michael Granitzer[1,2]

[1] University of Passau, Passau, Germany
`{saber.zerhoudi,michael.granitzer}@uni-passau.de`
[2] Interdisciplinary Transformation University Austria, Linz, Austria

**Abstract.** User simulators are essential for evaluating search systems, but they primarily copy user actions without understanding the underlying thought process. This gap exists since large-scale interaction logs record what users do, but not what they might be thinking or feeling, such as confusion or satisfaction. To solve this problem, we present a framework to infer cognitive traces from behavior logs. Our method uses a multi-agent system grounded in Information Foraging Theory (IFT) and human expert judgment. These traces improve model performance on tasks like forecasting session outcomes and user struggle recovery. We release a collection of annotations for several public datasets, including AOL and Stack Overflow, and an open-source tool that allows researchers to apply our method to their own data (https://github.com/searchsim-org/cognitive-traces). This work provides the tools and data needed to build more human-like user simulators and to assess retrieval systems on user-oriented dimensions of performance.

**Keywords:** User Simulation · Cognitive Modeling · Information Retrieval · Data Annotation · Large Language Models

## 1 Introduction

User simulation is an essential method for the evaluation of interactive information retrieval systems [7,8]. It offers a scalable and reproducible alternative to costly user studies, allowing researchers to test new algorithms under many conditions [21]. Current simulators, often constructed using modern sequence models or reinforcement learning, have become very good at reproducing the observable actions of users [6,11]. These models can generate realistic patterns of query reformulations, document selections, and other behaviors by learning from large-scale interaction logs [12,20].

However, this behavioral accuracy hides a deep limitation: today's simulators are *cognitively unaware*. They are effective at copying what users do but have no understanding of why they do it. The actual human process of seeking information is a complex mental activity, filled with moments of confusion, growing understanding, frustration, and eventual satisfaction [17,22,25,29]. These internal states are not random side effects; they directly influence a user's decisions.

© The Author(s), under exclusive license to Springer Nature Switzerland AG 2026
R. Campos et al. (Eds.): ECIR 2026, LNCS 16486, pp. 626–640, 2026.
https://doi.org/10.1007/978-3-032-21321-1_63

A feeling of confusion may prompt a user to simplify their query, while a sense of making progress encourages them to continue. By ignoring this cognitive layer, our simulators remain mechanistic and incomplete, preventing us from properly assessing systems on the human-centered qualities they are meant to support.

The key to creating the more advanced user simulators is data that connects observable actions to this unobservable cognitive dimension [14]. We propose that the missing component is a large-scale collection of interaction logs that is augmented with inferred traces of the user's cognitive process.

These cognitive traces enable two major advances. First, they allow for the design of advanced simulators that learn the signs of user struggle, such as the difference between a user who is lost and one who is making progress [16,31,33]. This would let us ask more specific questions about retrieval systems: Does a novel ranking algorithm reduce user frustration, even if it doesn't improve nDCG (normalized Discounted Cumulative Gain)? Does a conversational system's proactive suggestion spark curiosity or induce cognitive load? Second, they allow for new metrics like "Session Difficulty Score" or a "User Frustration Rate" [3,16], shifting IR evaluation from a system-focused view to a user-focused one.

In this paper, we present a concrete step toward the goal of improving simulators. We introduce a new framework and a collection of resources for inferring cognitive traces from search logs. We make the following five main contributions:

1. We propose a formal schema and human-in-the-loop framework for cognitive state annotation based on IFT.
2. We release a collection of annotations for three distinct and widely-used public datasets—AOL User Session Collection [26], Stack Overflow [34], and Movie-Lens [18]—to demonstrate the general applicability of our method.
3. We provide a rigorous experimental validation of the resource's value, showing that cognitive labels improve session outcome forecasting and struggle recovery prediction.
4. We release an open-source tool for AI-assisted cognitive labeling.

## 2   Related Work

Our work is draws upon several research areas: user simulation for information retrieval, the modeling of user search behavior, large-scale data annotation methodologies, and the emerging use of Large Language Models for data generation. We review each in turn to precisely situate our contribution.

### 2.1   User Simulation for Information Retrieval

User simulators have a long history in IR, with most falling into two main groups: agenda-based and model-based [6,8]. Agenda-based simulators use a predefined set of rules and goals to direct their actions. Their main advantage is that they are easy to interpret, but they can be inflexible and have difficulty showing a wide range of user behaviors. Due to these limitations, the primary approach in recent years has been model-based simulation. These models learn user behavior directly from large interaction logs, using methods from reinforcement learning or sequence modeling to generate realistic behavioral patterns [4,27].

While these models are effective at reproducing user actions, how they represent the user's internal state is a key weakness. A simulator's current models often represent the user through a static interest profile of their topic of interest or a simple history of their recent actions. This approach does not account for the dynamic mental shifts a person experiences during a search. Our work does not aim to replace these simulation models; instead, we aim to provide a new kind of data that can supply them with a more detailed and realistic representation of the user's internal state.

## 2.2   User Behavior Modeling and Cognitive States

Beyond simulation, a large amount of research in IR and Human-Computer Interaction (HCI) has focused on modeling user behavior to understand and predict their experience. Studies have shown a strong connection between implicit signals—such as clicks, query changes, and the time spent on a page—and important outcomes like user satisfaction or whether a task is completed [5,27]. These models are valuable but often treat the user's internal state as a hidden factor, not as a direct subject of study.

Most relevant to our paper is the important early research in HCI that directly measured user cognitive states during information seeking. Using detailed, small-scale lab methods like think-aloud protocols, interviews, and physiological sensors, these studies provided strong evidence of the connection between search behaviors and internal states like confusion, frustration, and cognitive load [17,22]. This work supplied the concepts and vocabulary for understanding a user's experience, proving that the cognitive dimension is a critical factor in the interaction.

However, the methods that make these studies so insightful also make them impossible to scale to large datasets. A significant gap exists between the deep but small-scale data from HCI and the large but shallow data found in interaction logs. To our knowledge, this work is the first to directly address this gap by introducing a computational framework for inferring cognitive states at scale, combining the conceptual depth of HCI with the scale required for modern IR evaluation.

## 2.3   Methods for Data Annotation

The creation of large datasets for IR, such as those with relevance judgments, has long depended on crowdsourcing. While this approach is effective for collecting large quantities of labels, researchers have noted the challenges involved, including maintaining data quality, addressing worker bias, and designing clear tasks [1,24]. Łajewska and Balog [23] recently showed that collecting subjective snippet-level labels requires piloting and iterative task redesign with ongoing annotator feedback.

Our work explores a different approach. We position our language-model-based framework not as a replacement for human annotators, but as a tool to expand the reach of human expertise. We use human experts to create a high-quality initial set of examples and to verify the most difficult cases identified by our system. The language model then acts as a consistent worker that applies this expert-calibrated knowledge across millions of data points. This human-in-the-loop method seeks a balance between the scale of automation and the quality of human judgment.

## 2.4   Large Language Models for Data Generation

The capabilities of modern language models have led to a rapid increase in their use for data generation. In IR and NLP, these models are now commonly used for tasks like creating synthetic queries to improve retrieval, generating answers for question-answering systems, and augmenting training sets [10, 13]. There is also growing interest in using language models as automatic evaluators or even as complete user simulators [36, 37].

Our work is different because we do not use the language model to create new user actions. Instead, we use it to infer a hidden cognitive layer on top of real human behavior data. This requires the model to reason about the likely motivations for a person's actions, a task that has not been explored at this scale. Our contribution is therefore not in generating new behaviors, but in adding a new dimension of understanding to existing behavioral records.

# 3   Methodology

Our main contribution is a general and reproducible framework for adding a layer of inferred cognitive traces to existing records of user behavior. The framework is designed to be grounded in theory, computationally scalable, and validated by human experts. The process has four main parts: (1) selecting and preparing a diverse set of foundational datasets; (2) using a principled schema based on Information Foraging Theory to define the cognitive labels; (3) generating the labels at scale using our multi-agent language model system; and (4) verifying and refining the output with a human-in-the-loop process.

## 3.1   Foundational Datasets

To demonstrate the flexibility of our framework, we apply it to three distinct, publicly available datasets that represent different aspects of information seeking: open-domain web search, technical question answering, and preference discovery in a recommender system.

1. **AOL User Session Collection (aol-ia variant [26]) (Web Search):** This is a large-scale log of user queries and clicks. We use the aol-ia version, which connects the original log to snapshots of the clicked web pages as they appeared around 2006, retrieved from the Internet Archive. We acknowledge the privacy issues of the original 2006 data release [9]; our work uses the standard anonymized collection and only reports on aggregate findings. The key property of this dataset is that it provides the content of the documents users chose to view, but not the HTML of the search engine results page (SERP) where those links were displayed. Our framework adapts to this by making inferences based on the query sequence, the content of clicked documents, and the click choices themselves.

2. **Stack Overflow [34] (Technical Q&A):** We use a public data dump of the Stack Overflow site, which contains a complete history of questions, answers, comments, and votes. This dataset is valuable since it shows the behavior of users with specific, technical information needs. The explicit feedback signals, such as upvotes and accepted answers, provide additional evidence for inferring cognitive states like problem resolution or continued confusion.

3. **MovieLens-25M [18] (Recommendations):** This dataset contains 25 million ratings and free-text tags for movies, applied by users over time. It allows us to apply our framework in a non-search context. Here, we model cognitive states related to preference formation and satisfaction. A sequence of high ratings for movies from one director can be seen as a form of successful information seeking, while a sudden low rating for an anticipated movie can signal a mismatch of expectations.

While our initial selection of the top-used dataset in each domain was guided by the project's budget, we are committed to the long-term maintenance of the collection and plan to add annotations for other important datasets in future releases. As an immediate next step, we are applying our framework to the Archive Query Log (AQL) dataset [30], which does contain rich SERP HTML, to create a complementary set of annotations.

### 3.2   A Principled Schema for Cognitive Traces

To avoid creating purely subjective labels, we based our annotation schema on the principles of Information Foraging Theory (IFT). IFT is a framework from cognitive science that models human information seeking using analogies from animal food foraging [25]. It provides an objective, task-oriented vocabulary to describe a user's process.

In IFT, a user looks for information in information patches (like a results page or a list of movies). They are guided by information scent (cues like titles or movie genres) to find valuable items [29]. We turned these core concepts into a set of concrete labels for user actions. While the primary schema in Table 1 was designed for search, it can be adapted. For instance, in MovieLens, `FollowingScent` can describe a user rating multiple movies by the same actor, a form of directed information seeking.

The IFT schema was defined by the authors based on existing literature [31]. To ensure it is consistent, we performed two pilot rounds of labeling where results were compared and the categories were fixed.

**Table 1.** The annotation schema grounded in Information Foraging Theory.

| User Action / Session Event | IFT Concept | Cognitive Label | Operational Definition & Example |
| --- | --- | --- | --- |
| User issues a well-formed query | Following a strong scent | `FollowingScent` | The user initiates or continues a search with a targeted query. *Ex:* "best espresso machine under $500". |
| User clicks a promising result | Approaching an information source | `ApproachingSource` | A result is clicked, indicating that the snippet or title provided a sufficiently strong scent for further investigation. |
| User issues a broader/ narrower query | Enriching the information diet | `DietEnrichment` | The query is modified to broaden or narrow scope, reflecting refinement of the information need. *Ex:* from "laptops" to "lightweight laptops for travel". |
| User clicks nothing on the SERP | Poor scent in the current patch | `PoorScent` | A new query is issued without any organic clicks, implying the patch offered no promising scent. |
| User abandons search after many tries | Deciding to leave the patch | `LeavingPatch` | The session ends after multiple reformulations without a successful interaction (e.g., a long click). |
| User finds an answer on the SERP | Successful foraging within the patch | `ForagingSuccess` | A query with no clicks where the SERP contains a direct answer (e.g., featured snippet or knowledge panel). |

## 3.3 The Multi-agent Annotation Framework

To generate labels at scale, we developed a multi-agent language model framework. This approach improves the quality of the output by having different agents review and challenge each other's conclusions, a form of computational quality control [15]. The framework has three agents:

1. **The Analyst:** This agent examines the complete behavioral trace of a user session. It produces an initial set of cognitive labels for each action, along with a step-by-step justification for its choices based on the data.
2. **The Critic:** This agent reviews the Analyst's output. Its purpose is to find inconsistencies or alternative explanations for the user's behavior. If it disagrees with the Analyst, it must propose a different label and provide its own counter-argument.
3. **The Judge:** This agent is the final decision-maker. It considers both the Analyst's proposal and the Critic's challenge. It then makes a final choice for the label and writes a summary explanation for its decision [37].

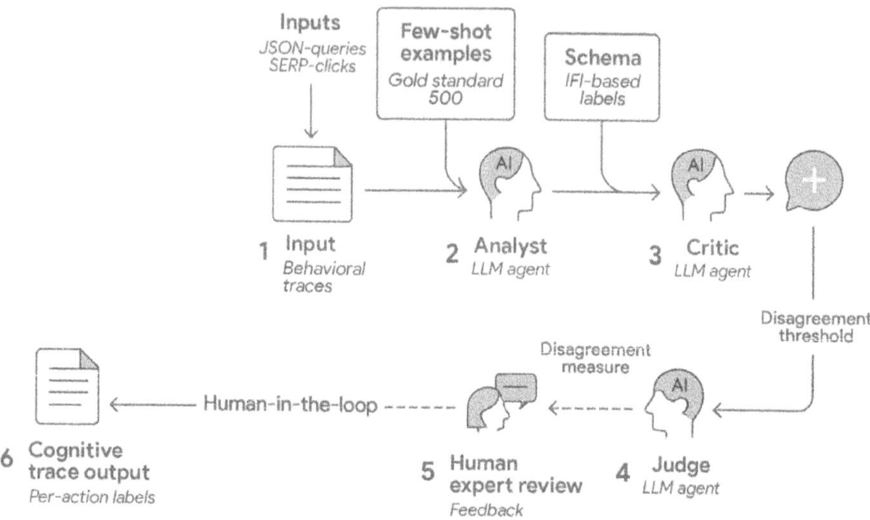


**Fig. 1.** The multi-agent annotation workflow. A behavioral trace is analyzed, debated, and judged to produce a final, justified cognitive trace.

To implement this, we selected specific large language models (LLMs) for each role based on their known strengths. This model-to-role assignment was based on a preliminary study using our 500-session gold standard, where we assessed each model's qualitative strengths. We use `Claude 3.5 Sonnet` [2] as the **Analyst**, as our tests confirmed its superior combination of high-speed sequential reasoning and cost-effectiveness, making it ideal for the high-volume "first-pass" analysis. We use `GPT-4o` [28] as both the **Critic** and the **Judge**. Its robust general knowledge and nuanced understanding allow it to effectively challenge the Analyst's assumptions and propose creative alternatives. For the final Judge role, this same model's superior ability to synthesize complex arguments and weigh conflicting evidence makes it the most suitable arbiter for making a final, well-reasoned decision. The entire process, as illustrated in Fig. 1, is guided by a structured prompt that provides each model with its persona, the task instructions, the label definitions from our schema, and the required output format.

For transparency and reproducibility, all artifacts—the datasets, annotation code, and the prompts structure—are released in our public repository.

### 3.4   Human-in-the-Loop Validation

A purely automated system is not sufficient for this complex task. We therefore integrated human expertise directly into our framework to guide and validate the process through three distinct stages.

1. **Gold Standard Creation:** We first created a validation set of 500 sessions. To ensure this set was diverse and included the challenging edge

cases necessary for robust validation, we used a two-stage stratified sampling approach. First, we stratified the sample proportionally across our three datasets (`AOL-IA`, Stack Overflow, and MovieLens). Second, within each dataset, we further stratified by behavioral archetype, intentionally oversampling ambiguous patterns such as "zero-click" sessions, "refining" sessions (those with many query reformulations), and "bouncing" sessions (those with many fast, brief clicks). Three human experts (Ph.D. students in HCI and IR) independently annotated this set, achieving a high inter-annotator agreement (Krippendorff's $\alpha = 0.78$) [19] and establishing our gold standard.

2. **Framework Calibration and Validation:** The 500-session gold standard serves two distinct purposes. First, we manually selected 3–5 archetypal sessions from this set—sessions that are exceptionally clear examples of each cognitive state—to include as fixed few-shot examples in our agents' prompts. This provides clear, high-quality demonstrations of the task. Second, the entire 500-session set was used as a held-out testbed to validate our complete framework. We tuned the prompts and agent interactions until our framework achieved a 92.4% accuracy against the human-generated gold labels, confirming its high fidelity before the large-scale annotation run.

3. **Active Learning for Quality Assurance:** During the large-scale annotation run, our system automatically flags the 1% of cases where the Analyst and Critic have the strongest disagreement (measured by semantic distance between their justifications). These most difficult cases are then sent to our human experts for a final ruling. This active learning loop ensures that human attention is focused where it is most needed, improving the overall quality of the final dataset [32,35].

## 4 Experimental Validation

We evaluate whether inferred cognitive traces provide predictive utility for forecasting search session outcomes. We test if these traces improve a model's ability to anticipate session success or failure using only early session observations.

### 4.1 Downstream Task: Forecasting Session Outcome

We define this task as predicting whether a session reaches a success state (`ApproachingSource`, `ForagingSuccess`, `DietEnrichment`) versus ending in failure (`PoorScent`, `LeavingPatch`), using only the first 50% of session events. Using the AOL User Session Collection [26], we investigate if including cognitive states improves prediction compared to behavioral signals alone.

### Experimental Setup
*Dataset and Split:* We processed the annotated AOL collection, selecting sessions with at least four events. User-based splits ensure no user appears in both training and test sets. Training data is class-balanced to avoid learning majority-class priors, resulting in a final dataset of 26,484 forecasting examples.

**Table 2.** Session Outcome Prediction results on the AOL dataset.

| Model | Precision | Recall | F1 | AUC |
|---|---|---|---|---|
| Behavioral Baseline | 0.50 | 1.00 | 0.67 | 0.43 |
| Cognitive-Enhanced | **1.00** | **0.82** | **0.90** | **0.92** |

*Temporal Protocol:* Cognitive labels are inferred *per-event* using only information available at that timestamp—action type, content, and preceding context. No future events or session outcomes inform the labels. This ensures the prediction task is temporally valid.

*Model Architecture:* Both models employ a 4-layer Transformer encoder with 8 attention heads. The final hidden state passes through a linear layer with sigmoid activation to predict success probability.

*Input Representations:*

- **Behavioral Baseline:** 384-dimensional S-BERT embeddings of query or document text. This captures semantic content but lacks explicit difficulty signals.
- **Cognitive-Enhanced:** Concatenates S-BERT embeddings with 32-dimensional learned embeddings of the inferred cognitive label, enabling the model to track mental state trajectories.

*Evaluation:* We report Precision, Recall, F1-Score, and ROC-AUC. We prioritize F1 for actionable prediction quality and AUC for threshold-independent ranking ability(Table 2 and 3).

**Results and Analysis.** The **Behavioral Baseline** exhibits mode collapse, predicting success for nearly all sessions (Recall 1.00, Precision 0.50). With AUC below chance (0.43), the model fails to learn discriminative signal from semantic content alone—successful and struggling sessions contain similar query text(Fig. 2).

The **Cognitive-Enhanced Model** achieves F1 of 0.90 and AUC of 0.92, a 35% F1 improvement. High precision (1.00) with strong recall (0.82) indicates reliable identification of struggling sessions without excessive false positives.

*Ablation—Cognitive Labels Only:* To verify gains stem from trajectory patterns rather than label leakage, we trained a model using only cognitive label sequences (no S-BERT). This achieves F1 of 0.74 and AUC of 0.71—above baseline but below the combined model. This confirms that semantic content and cognitive trajectories provide *complementary* signals; performance comes from their interaction, not labels alone.

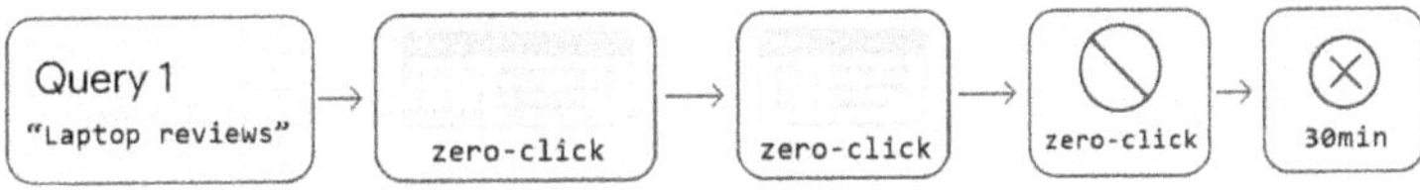



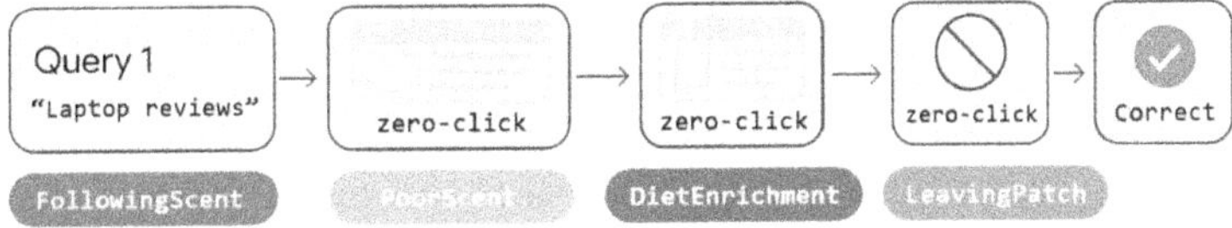



**Fig. 2.** Example session illustrating why cognitive labels improve prediction. (A) Behavioral trace shows queries and zero-click events but predicts non-abandonment. (B) Cognitive labels reveal a trajectory from `FollowingScent` through `PoorScent` to `LeavingPatch`, correctly predicting failure.

## 4.2 General Utility: Struggle Recovery Prediction

To test generalization, we evaluate a structurally distinct task: predicting whether users who begin struggling will recover to success.

*Task Definition:* We identify sessions where early events contain struggle indicators (`PoorScent`, `LeavingPatch`). Using the first 40% of such sessions, we predict whether the user reaches success by session end. This tests if cognitive patterns distinguish users who persist through difficulty from those who abandon.

**Table 3.** Struggle Recovery Prediction results.

| Model | Precision | Recall | F1 | AUC |
| --- | --- | --- | --- | --- |
| Behavioral Baseline | 0.50 | 1.00 | 0.67 | 0.77 |
| Cognitive-Enhanced | **0.89** | **0.69** | **0.78** | **0.83** |

The cognitive-enhanced model improves F1 by 17% (0.67→0.78) and AUC by 8% (0.77→0.83). Precision increases from 0.50 to 0.89, enabling reliable identification of users unlikely to recover—valuable for targeting interventions. The improvement confirms that cognitive trajectories capture *momentum* that behavioral features miss.

## 4.3 Discussion

*Why Does the Behavioral Baseline Fail?* The behavioral baseline uses only semantic features; richer signals (dwell time, click position) might narrow the gap but were unavailable. In addition, S-BERT embeddings do not distinguish successful from unsuccessful searches. Users in both outcomes issue similar queries and click similar results; the *sequence of mental states* differentiates them.

*Predictive Utility vs. Causality:* Our experiments demonstrate predictive utility—that cognitive traces improve forecasting—not causal mediation. Establishing causality would require intervention studies beyond this work's scope.

*Summary:* Across both tasks, cognitive-enhanced models outperform behavioral baselines (+35% F1 for Session Outcome, +17% for Struggle Recovery). The ablation confirms gains come from combining cognitive and semantic features. These results support that inferred cognitive traces provide predictive utility for anticipating user search behavior.

## 5    Discussion and Future Work

Our work introduces a framework for applying a cognitive layer to behavioral logs. In this section, we discuss the necessary limitations of this approach and outline the new research directions it makes possible.

### 5.1    Limitations

It is important to be clear about what our framework produces. The cognitive traces are inferences, not direct measurements of a user's mental state. They are plausible, theoretically-grounded labels based on a sequence of actions. A label like `PoorScent` is a strong indicator of difficulty, but it is still an interpretation. The ground truth of a user's thought process remains inaccessible.

The quality of these inferences also depends on the richness of the input data. Our work with the `AOL-IA` dataset demonstrates the framework's flexibility, as it can operate without access to the original SERP (Search Engine Results Page) content. However, rich contextual data, like the full SERP HTML, would provide stronger evidence for inferring states like `PoorScent` or `ForagingSuccess`. Therefore, our immediate next step is to release a companion set of cognitive traces for the Archive Query Log (AQL), a large-scale dataset that does contain this valuable SERP information.

Finally, while we demonstrated our framework across three diverse datasets, these domains (web search, technical Q&A, recommendations) do not cover all information-seeking activities. The specific cognitive patterns found in these datasets may not be the same as those in areas like legal research, medical information seeking, or complex creative tasks.

### 5.2    Future Research Directions

We believe this work opens up several new avenues for research.

*1. Richer Cognitive Representations:* Our current work uses a discrete set of six labels. A natural next step is to explore more complex representations. The natural language justifications produced by our "Judge" agent could be used to train models that output a continuous vector in a learned "cognitive space." This would allow for a more nuanced understanding of user states, capturing the subtle differences between mild uncertainty and deep confusion.

*2. Longitudinal User Modeling:* Our annotation collection, particularly for datasets like MovieLens and Stack Overflow, provides data on the same users over long periods. This allows for the study of how a user's cognitive patterns and information-seeking strategies change over time. We can now ask questions like: Do users become more efficient foragers in a domain as they gain expertise? How do their cognitive patterns shift when their interests change?

*3. Building Cognitively-Aware Systems:* The ultimate goal of this research is to create better information access systems. Our Annotator tool and its lightweight model could be integrated into a live system to infer a user's cognitive state in real-time. This would permit the creation of systems that can proactively intervene. For example, a system that detects a user is in a repeated `PoorScent` state could offer to reformulate their query or suggest a different search strategy, helping them before they reach the point of abandonment.

# 6   Conclusion

In this paper, we addressed a key limitation in user simulation: the gap between observable user behavior and the unobservable cognitive states that guide it. We presented a complete framework for inferring these cognitive states from large-scale behavioral logs, grounding our method in the principles of Information Foraging Theory and validating it with human experts. Our experiments showed that these inferred cognitive traces provide a strong predictive signal for important user outcomes, such as session success and struggle recovery.

By releasing a collection of cognitive annotations for three major datasets and the open-source Annotator tool to create new ones, we provide the community with both a new set of data and a new instrument for analysis. It is our hope that these contributions will support the development of a new generation of user simulators —and, ultimately, information systems—that are more aware of the user's internal experience.

**Acknowledgments.**

This work has received funding from the European Union's Horizon Europe research and innovation program under grant agreement No. 101070014 (OpenWebSearch.EU). Additional funding was provided by the Bavarian State Ministry of Economic Affairs, Regional Development, and Energy (StMWi).

**Disclosure of Interest.** The authors have no competing interests to disclose.

# References


1. Alonso, O., Mizzaro, S.: Using crowdsourcing for TREC relevance assessment. Inf. Process. Manag. **48**(6), 1053–1066 (2012). https://doi.org/10.1016/J.IPM.2012.01.004
2. Anthropic: claude 3.5 sonnet model card and system overview (2024). https://www.anthropic.com/news/claude-3-5-sonnet, Accessed 22 Oct 2025
3. Arguello, J.: Predicting Search Task Difficulty. In: de Rijke, M., et al. (eds.) ECIR 2014. LNCS, vol. 8416, pp. 88–99. Springer, Cham (2014). https://doi.org/10.1007/978-3-319-06028-6_8
4. Awadallah, A.H., Jones, R., Klinkner, K.L.: Beyond DCG: user behavior as a predictor of a successful search. In: Davison, B.D., Suel, T., Craswell, N., Liu, B. (eds.) Proceedings of the Third International Conference on Web Search and Web Data Mining, WSDM 2010, New York, NY, USA, February 4-6, 2010, pp. 221–230. ACM (2010). https://doi.org/10.1145/1718487.1718515
5. Awadallah, A.H., Shi, X., Craswell, N., Ramsey, B.: Beyond clicks: query reformulation as a predictor of search satisfaction. In: He, Q., Iyengar, A., Nejdl, W., Pei, J., Rastogi, R. (eds.) 22nd ACM International Conference on Information and Knowledge Management, CIKM'13, San Francisco, CA, USA, October 27 - November 1, 2013. pp. 2019–2028. ACM (2013).https://doi.org/10.1145/2505515.2505682
6. Azzopardi, L., et al.: Simiir 3: A framework for the simulation of interactive and conversational information retrieval. In: Sakai, T., Ishita, E., Ohshima, H., Hasibi, F., Mao, J., Jose, J.M. (eds.) Proceedings of the 2024 Annual International ACM SIGIR Conference on Research and Development in Information Retrieval in the Asia Pacific Region, SIGIR-AP 2024, Tokyo, Japan, December 9-12, 2024, pp. 197–202 (2024). https://doi.org/10.1145/3673791.3698427
7. Balog, K., Bernard, N., Zerhoudi, S., Zhai, C.: Theory and toolkits for user simulation in the era of generative AI: user modeling, synthetic data generation, and system evaluation. In: Ferro, N., Maistro, M., Pasi, G., Alonso, O., Trotman, A., Verberne, S. (eds.) Proceedings of the 48th International ACM SIGIR Conference on Research and Development in Information Retrieval, SIGIR 2025, Padua, Italy, July 13-18, 2025, pp. 4138–4141 (2025). https://doi.org/10.1145/3726302.3731697
8. Balog, K., Zhai, C.: User simulation in the era of generative AI: user modeling, synthetic data generation, and system evaluation. CoRR **abs/2501.04410** (2025). https://doi.org/10.48550/ARXIV.2501.04410
9. Barbaro, M., Zeller, T.: A face is exposed for AOL searcher no. 4417749. The New York Times (2006). https://www.nytimes.com/2006/08/09/technology/09aol.html, Accessed 22 Oct 2025
10. Bonifacio, L.H., Abonizio, H.Q., Fadaee, M., Nogueira, R.: Inpars: data augmentation for information retrieval using large language models. CoRR **abs/2202.05144** (2022). https://arxiv.org/abs/2202.05144
11. Borisov, A., Markov, I., de Rijke, M., Serdyukov, P.: A neural click model for web search. In: Bourdeau, J., Hendler, J., Nkambou, R., Horrocks, I., Zhao, B.Y. (eds.) Proceedings of the 25th International Conference on World Wide Web, WWW 2016, Montreal, Canada, April 11 - 15, 2016, pp. 531–541. ACM (2016). https://doi.org/10.1145/2872427.2883033
12. Chuklin, A., Markov, I., de Rijke, M.: Click models for web search. Synthesis Lectures on Information Concepts, Retrieval, and Services, Morgan and Claypool Publishers (2015). https://doi.org/10.2200/S00654ED1V01Y201507ICR043

13. Dai, Z., et al.: Promptagator: few-shot dense retrieval from 8 examples. In: The Eleventh International Conference on Learning Representations, ICLR 2023, Kigali, Rwanda, May 1-5, 2023. OpenReview.net (2023). https://openreview.net/forum?id=gmL46YMpu2J

14. Diriye, A., White, R., Buscher, G., Dumais, S.T.: Leaving so soon?: understanding and predicting web search abandonment rationales. In: Chen, X., Lebanon, G., Wang, H., Zaki, M.J. (eds.) 21st ACM International Conference on Information and Knowledge Management, CIKM'12, Maui, HI, USA, October 29 - November 02, 2012. pp. 1025–1034. ACM (2012). https://doi.org/10.1145/2396761.2398399

15. Du, Y., Li, S., Torralba, A., Tenenbaum, J.B., Mordatch, I.: Improving factuality and reasoning in language models through multiagent debate. In: Forty-first International Conference on Machine Learning, ICML 2024, Vienna, Austria, July 21-27, 2024. OpenReview.net (2024). https://openreview.net/forum?id=zj7YuTE4t8

16. Feild, H.A., Allan, J., Jones, R.: Predicting searcher frustration. In: Crestani, F., Marchand-Maillet, S., Chen, H., Efthimiadis, E.N., Savoy, J. (eds.) Proceeding of the 33rd International ACM SIGIR Conference on Research and Development in Information Retrieval, SIGIR 2010, Geneva, Switzerland, July 19-23, 2010, pp. 34–41. ACM (2010). https://doi.org/10.1145/1835449.1835458

17. Gwizdka, J.: Distribution of cognitive load in web search. J. Assoc. Inf. Sci. Technol. **61**(11), 2167–2187 (2010). https://doi.org/10.1002/ASI.21385

18. Harper, F.M., Konstan, J.A.: The movielens datasets: history and context. ACM Trans. Interact. Intell. Syst. **5**(4), 19:1–19:19 (2016). https://doi.org/10.1145/2827872

19. Hayes, A.F., Krippendorff, K.: Answering the call for a standard reliability measure for coding data. Commun. Meth. Measur. **1**(1), 77-89 (2007)

20. Jansen, B.J., Booth, D.L., Spink, A.: Patterns of query reformulation during web searching. J. Assoc. Inf. Sci. Technol. **60**(7), 1358–1371 (2009). https://doi.org/10.1002/ASI.21071

21. Kelly, D.: Methods for evaluating interactive information retrieval systems with users. Found. Trends Inf. Retr. **3**(1–2), 1–224 (2009). https://doi.org/10.1561/1500000012

22. Kuhlthau, C.C.: Inside the search process: information seeking from the user's perspective. J. Am. Soc. Inf. Sci. **42**(5), 361–371 (1991)

23. Łajewska, W., Balog, K.: Towards filling the gap in conversational search: from passage retrieval to conversational response generation. In: Proceedings of the 32nd ACM International Conference on Information and Knowledge Management (CIKM '23) (2023). https://doi.org/10.1145/3583780.3615132

24. Lease, M., Yilmaz, E.: Crowdsourcing for information retrieval: introduction to the special issue. Inf. Retr. **16**(2), 91–100 (2013). https://doi.org/10.1007/S10791-013-9222-7

25. Lindsay, R.: Information foraging theory - by pirolli, peter. Br. J. Educ. Technol. **39**(4), 759–760 (2008). https://doi.org/10.1111/j.1467-8535.2008.00870_13.x

26. MacAvaney, S., Macdonald, C., Ounis, I.: Reproducing personalised session search over the AOL query log. In: Hagen, M., Verberne, S., Macdonald, C., Seifert, C., Balog, K., Nørvåg, K., Setty, V. (eds.) Advances in Information Retrieval - 44th European Conference on IR Research, ECIR 2022, Stavanger, Norway, April 10-14, 2022, Proceedings, Part I. Lecture Notes in Computer Science, vol. 13185, pp. 627–640. Springer (2022). https://doi.org/10.1007/978-3-030-99736-6_42

27. Mehrotra, R., et al.: Deep sequential models for task satisfaction prediction. In: Lim, E., et al.(eds.) Proceedings of the 2017 ACM on Conference on Information

and Knowledge Management, CIKM 2017, Singapore, November 06 - 10, 2017, pp. 737–746. ACM (2017). https://doi.org/10.1145/3132847.3133001

28. OpenAI: Gpt-4o: Multimodal large language model (2024). https://openai.com/index/hello-gpt-4o, Accessed 22 Oct 2025

29. Pirolli, P.: Information foraging. In: Liu, L., Özsu, M.T. (eds.) Encyclopedia of Database Systems, Second Edition. Springer (2018).https://doi.org/10.1007/978-1-4614-8265-9_205

30. Reimer, J.H., et al.: The archive query log: mining millions of search result pages of hundreds of search engines from 25 years of web archives. In: Chen, H., Duh, W.E., Huang, H., Kato, M.P., Mothe, J., Poblete, B. (eds.) Proceedings of the 46th International ACM SIGIR Conference on Research and Development in Information Retrieval, SIGIR 2023, Taipei, Taiwan, July 23-27, 2023, pp. 2848–2860. ACM (2023). https://doi.org/10.1145/3539618.3591890

31. Sandstrom, P.E.: Information foraging theory: adaptive interaction with information. J. Assoc. Inf. Sci. Technol. **61**(10), 2161–2164 (2010). https://doi.org/10.1002/ASI.21364

32. Seung, H.S., Opper, M., Sompolinsky, H.: Query by committee. In: Haussler, D. (ed.) Proceedings of the Fifth Annual ACM Conference on Computational Learning Theory, COLT 1992, Pittsburgh, PA, USA, July 27-29, 1992, pp. 287–294. ACM (1992). https://doi.org/10.1145/130385.130417

33. Song, Y., Shi, X., White, R., Awadallah, A.H.: Context-aware web search abandonment prediction. In: Geva, S., Trotman, A., Bruza, P., Clarke, C.L.A., Järvelin, K. (eds.) The 37th International ACM SIGIR Conference on Research and Development in Information Retrieval, SIGIR '14, Gold Coast , QLD, Australia - July 06 - 11, 2014, pp. 93–102. ACM (2014). https://doi.org/10.1145/2600428.2609604

34. Stack exchange, Inc.: Stack overflow / stack exchange data dump (2024). https://archive.org/details/stackexchange, Accessed 22 Oct 2025. Public data dumps released under CC BY-SA 4.0. Documentation available at https://meta.stackexchange.com/questions/2677/database-schema-documentation-for-the-public-data-dump-and-sede

35. Xu, Y., Sun, F., Zhang, X.: Literature survey of active learning in multimedia annotation and retrieval. In: Lu, K., Mei, T., Wu, X. (eds.) International Conference on Internet Multimedia Computing and Service, ICIMCS '13, Huangshan, China - August 17 - 19, 2013, pp. 237–242. ACM (2013).https://doi.org/10.1145/2499788.2499794

36. Zhang, E., Wang, X., Gong, P., Lin, Y., Mao, J.: Usimagent: large language models for simulating search users. In: Yang, G.H., Wang, H., Han, S., Hauff, C., Zuccon, G., Zhang, Y. (eds.) Proceedings of the 47th International ACM SIGIR Conference on Research and Development in Information Retrieval, SIGIR 2024, Washington DC, USA, July 14-18, 2024, pp. 2687–2692. ACM (2024). https://doi.org/10.1145/3626772.3657963

37. Zheng, L., et al.: Judging LLM-as-a-judge with mt-bench and chatbot arena. In: Oh, A., Naumann, T., Globerson, A., Saenko, K., Hardt, M., Levine, S. (eds.) Advances in Neural Information Processing Systems 36: Annual Conference on Neural Information Processing Systems 2023, NeurIPS 2023, New Orleans, LA, USA, December 10 - 16, 2023 (2023). http://papers.nips.cc/paper_files/paper/2023/hash/91f18a1287b398d378ef22505bf41832-Abstract-Datasets_and_Benchmarks.html

# Author Index




© The Editor(s) (if applicable) and The Author(s), under exclusive license
to Springer Nature Switzerland AG 2026
R. Campos et al. (Eds.): ECIR 2026, LNCS 16486, pp. 641–645, 2026.
https://doi.org/10.1007/978-3-032-21321-1

GPSR Compliance
The European Union's (EU) General Product Safety Regulation (GPSR) is a set
of rules that requires consumer products to be safe and our obligations to
ensure this.

If you have any concerns about our products, you can contact us on

ProductSafety@springernature.com

In case Publisher is established outside the EU, the EU authorized
representative is:

Springer Nature Customer Service Center GmbH
Europaplatz 3
69115 Heidelberg, Germany